T0261165

Praise for *The Handbook of Computational Linguistics and Natural Language Processing*

"All in all, this is very well compiled book, which effectively balances the width and depth of theories and applications in two very diverse yet closely related elds of language research."

Machine Translation

"This *Handbook* is exceptionally broad and exceptionally deep in its coverage. The contributions, by noted experts, cover all aspects of the eld, from fundamental theory to concrete applications. Clark, Fox and Lappin have performed a great service by compiling this volume."

Richard Sproat, Oregon Health & Science University

Blackwell Handbooks in Linguistics

This outstanding multi-volume series covers all the major subdisciplines within linguistics today and, when complete, will offer a comprehensive survey of linguistics as a whole.

Already published:

This paperback edition rst published 2013
© 2013 Blackwell Publishing Ltd except for editorial material and organization
© 2013 Alexander Clark, Chris Fox, and Shalom Lappin

Edition History: Blackwell Publishing Ltd (hardback, 2010)

Blackwell Publishing was acquired by John Wiley & Sons in February 2007. Blackwell's publishing
program has been merged with Wiley's global Scienti c, Technical, and Medical business to form
Wiley-Blackwell.

Registered Office
John Wiley & Sons Ltd, The Atrium, Southern Gate, Chichester, West Sussex, PO19 8SQ, UK

Editorial Offices
350 Main Street, Malden, MA 02148-5020, USA
9600 Garsington Road, Oxford, OX4 2DQ, UK
The Atrium, Southern Gate, Chichester, West Sussex, PO19 8SQ, UK

For details of our global editorial of ces, for customer services, and for information about how
to apply for permission to reuse the copyright material in this book please see our website at
www.wiley.com/wiley-blackwell.

The right of Alexander Clark, Chris Fox, and Shalom Lappin to be identi ed as the authors of the
editorial material in this work has been asserted in accordance with the UK Copyright, Designs and
Patents Act 1988.

All rights reserved. No part of this publication may be reproduced, stored in a retrieval system,
or transmitted, in any form or by any means, electronic, mechanical, photocopying, recording
or otherwise, except as permitted by the UK Copyright, Designs and Patents Act 1988, without the
prior permission of the publisher.

Wiley also publishes its books in a variety of electronic formats. Some content that appears in print
may not be available in electronic books.

Designations used by companies to distinguish their products are often claimed as trademarks.
All brand names and product names used in this book are trade names, service marks, trademarks
or registered trademarks of their respective owners. The publisher is not associated with any product
or vendor mentioned in this book. This publication is designed to provide accurate and authoritative
information in regard to the subject matter covered. It is sold on the understanding that the publisher
is not engaged in rendering professional services. If professional advice or other expert assistance is
required, the services of a competent professional should be sought.

Library of Congress Cataloging-in-Publication Data

The handbook of computational linguistics and natural language processing / edited by
Alexander Clark, Chris Fox, and Shalom Lappin.
     p.   cm. – (Blackwell handbooks in linguistics)
  Includes bibliographical references and index.
  ISBN 978-1-4051-5581-6 (hardcover : alk. paper) ISBN 978-1-118-34718-8 (paperback : alk. paper)
1. Computational linguistics.   2. Natural language processing (Computer science).
I. Clark, Alexander (Alexander Simon)   II. Fox, Chris, 1965–   III. Lappin, Shalom.
  P98.H346 2010
  410_.285–dc22
                                                    2010003116

A catalogue record for this book is available from the British Library.

Cover image: Theo van Doesburg, Composition IX, opus 18, 1917. Haags Gemeentemuseum,
The Hague, Netherlands / The Bridgeman Art Library.
Cover design by Workhaus.

Set in 10/12pt Palatino by SPi Publisher Services, Pondicherry, India

1   2013

MIX
Paper from
responsible sources
FSC   FSC® C013604
www.fsc.org

The Handbook of Computational Linguistics and Natur Language Processing

Edited by

Alexander Clark, Chris Fox, and Shalom Lappin

WILEY-BLACKWELL

A John Wiley & Sons, Ltd., Publication

For Camilla
לאחיי דוד ודניאל, ולאחותי נעמי באהבה ובהומור

Contents

List of Figures

List of Tables

Notes on Contributors

Ciprian Chelba is a Research Scientist with Google. Between 2000 and 2006 he worked as a Researcher in the Speech Technology Group at Microsoft Research.

He received his Diploma Engineer degree in 1993 from the Faculty of Electronics and Telecommunications at "Politehnica" University, Bucuresti, Romania, M.S. in 1996 and PhD in 2000 from the Electrical and Computer Engineering Department at the Johns Hopkins University.

His research interests are in statistical modeling of natural language and speech, as well as related areas such as machine learning and information theory as applied to natural language problems.

Recent projects include language modeling for large-vocabulary speech recognition (discriminative model estimation, compact storage for large models), search in spoken document collections (spoken content indexing, ranking and snipeting), as well as speech and text classi cation.

Alexander Clark is an Honorary Research Fellow in the Department of Computer Science at Royal Holloway, University of London. His rst degree was in Mathematics from the University of Cambridge, and his PhD is from the University of Sussex. He did postdoctoral research at the University of Geneva. In 2007 he was a *Professeur invité* at the University of Marseille. He is on the editorial board of the journal *Research on Language and Computation,* and a member of the steering committee of the International Colloquium on Grammatical Inference. His research is on unsupervised learning in computational linguistics, and in grammatical inference; he has won several prizes and competitions for his research. He has co-authored with Shalom Lappin a book entitled *Linguistic Nativism and the Poverty of the Stimulus,* which is being published by Wiley-Blackwell in 2010.

Stephen Clark is a Senior Lecturer at the University of Cambridge Computer Laboratory where he is a member of the Natural Language and Information Processing Research Group. From 2004 to 2008 he was a University Lecturer at the Oxford University Computing Laboratory, and before that spent four years as a postdoctoral researcher at the University of Edinburgh's School of Informatics, working with Prof. Mark Steedman. He has a PhD in Arti cial Intelligence from the University of Sussex and a rst degree in Philosophy from the University of Cambridge. His main research interest is statistical parsing, with a focus on the grammar formalism combinatory categorial grammar. In 2009 he led a team at the Johns Hopkins University Summer Workshop working on "Large Scale Syntactic Processing: Parsing the Web." He is on the editorial boards of *Computational Linguistics* and the *Journal of Natural Language Engineering*, and is a Program Co-Chair for the 2010 Annual Meeting of the Association for Computational Linguistics.

Matthew W. Crocker obtained his PhD in Arti cial Intelligence from the University of Edinburgh in 1992, where he subsequently held appointments as Lecturer in Arti cial Intelligence and Cognitive Science and as an ESRC Research Fellow. In January 2000, Dr Crocker was appointed to a newly established Chair in Psycholinguistics, in the Department of Computational Linguistics at Saarland University, Germany. His current research brings together the experimental investigation of real-time human language processing and situated cognition in the development of computational cognitive models.

Matthew Crocker co-founded the annual conference on Architectures and Mechanisms for Language Processing (AMLaP) in 1995. He is currently an associate editor for *Cognition*, on the editorial board of Springer's *Studies in Theoretical Psycholinguistics*, and has been a member of the editorial board for *Computational Linguistics*.

Walter Daelemans (MA, University of Leuven, Belgium, 1982; PhD, Computational Linguistics, University of Leuven, 1987) held research and teaching positions at the Radboud University Nijmegen, the AI-LAB at the University of Brussels, and Tilburg University, where he founded the ILK (Induction of Linguistic Knowledge) research group, and where he remained part-time Full Professor until 2006. Since 1999, he has been a Full Professor at the University of Antwerp (UA), teaching Computational Linguistics and Arti cial Intelligence courses and co-directing the CLiPS research center. His current research interests are in machine learning of natural language, computational psycholinguistics, and text mining. He was elected fellow of ECCAI in 2003 and graduated 11 PhD students as supervisor.

Raquel Fernández is a Postdoctoral Researcher at the Institute for Logic, Language and Computation, University of Amsterdam. She holds a PhD in Computer Science from King's College London for work on formal and computational modeling of dialogue and has published numerous peer-review articles on dialogue research. She has worked as Research Fellow in the Center for the Study of Language and Information (CSLI) at Stanford University and in the Linguistics Department at the University of Potsdam.

Dr **Chris Fox** is a Reader in the School of Computer Science and Electronic Engineering at the University of Essex. He started his research career as a Senior Research Of cer in the Department of Language and Linguistics at the University of Essex. He subsequently worked in the Computer Science Department where he obtained his PhD in 1993. After that he spent a brief period as a Visiting Researcher at Saarbruecken before becoming a Lecturer at Goldsmiths College, University of London, and then King's College London. He returned to Essex in 2003. At the time of writing, he is serving as Deputy Mayor of Wivenhoe.

Much of his research is in the area of logic and formal semantics, with a particular emphasis on issues of formal expressiveness, and proof-theoretic approaches to characterizing intuitions about natural language semantic phenomena.

Jonathan Ginzburg is a Senior Lecturer in the Department of Computer Science at King's College London. He has previously held posts in Edinburgh and Jerusalem. He is one of the managing editors of the journal *Dialogue and Discourse*. He has published widely on formal semantics and dialogue. His monograph *The Interactive Stance: Meaning for Conversation* was published in 2009.

John A. Goldsmith is Edward Carson Waller Distinguished Service Professor in the Departments of Linguistics and Computer Science at the University of Chicago, where he has been since 1984. He received his PhD in Linguistics in 1976 from MIT, and taught from 1976 to 1984 at Indiana University. His primary interests are computational learning of natural language, phonological theory, and the history of linguistics.

Ralph Grishman is Professor of Computer Science at New York University. He has been involved in research in natural language processing since 1969, and since 1985 has directed the Proteus Project, with funding from DARPA, NSF, and other government agencies. The Proteus Project has conducted research in natural language text analysis, with a focus on information extraction, and has been involved in the creation of a number of major lexical and syntactic resources, including Comlex, Nomlex, and NomBank. He is a past President of the Association for Computational Linguistics and the author of the text *Computational Linguistics: An Introduction*.

Thomas Hain holds the degree Dipl.-Ing. with honors from the University of Technology, Vienna and a PhD from Cambridge University. In 1994 he joined Philips Speech Processing, which he left as Senior Technologist in 1997. He took up a position as Research Associate at the Speech, Vision and Robotics Group and Machine Intelligence Lab at the Cambridge University Engineering Department where he also received an appointment as Lecturer in 2001. In 2004 he joined the Department of Computer Science at the University of Shef eld where he is now a Senior Lecturer. Thomas Hain has a well established track record in automatic speech recognition, in particular involvement in best-performing ASR systems for participation in NIST evaluations. His main research interests are in speech recognition, speech and audio processing, machine learning, optimisation of large-scale statistical systems, and modeling of machine/machine interfaces. He is a member of the IEEE Speech and Language Technical Committee.

James B. Henderson is an MER (Research Professor) in the Department of Computer Science of the University of Geneva, where he is co-head of the interdisciplinary research group Computational Learning and Computational

Linguistics. His research bridges the topics of machine learning methods for structure-prediction tasks and the modeling and exploitation of such tasks in NLP, particularly syntactic and semantic parsing. In machine learning his current interests focus on latent variable models inspired by neural networks. Previously, Dr Henderson was a Research Fellow in ICCS at the University of Edinburgh, and a Lecturer in CS at the University of Exeter, UK. Dr Henderson received his PhD and MSc from the University of Pennsylvania, and his BSc from the Massachusetts Institute of Technology, USA.

Shalom Lappin is Professor of Computational Linguistics at King's College London. He does research in computational semantics, and in the application of machine learning to issues in natural language processing and the cognitive basis of language acquisition. He has taught at SOAS, Tel Aviv University, the University of Haifa, the University of Ottawa, and Ben Gurion University of the Negev. He was also a Research Staff member in the Natural Language group of the Computer Science Department at IBM T.J. Watson Research Center. He edited the *Handbook of Contemporary Semantic Theory* (1996, Blackwell), and, with Chris Fox, he co-authored *Foundations of Intensional Semantics* (2005, Blackwell). His most recent book, *Linguistic Nativism and the Poverty of the Stimulus*, co-authored with Alexander Clark, is being published by Wiley-Blackwell in 2010.

Jimmy Lin is an Associate Professor in the iSchool at the University of Maryland, af liated with the Department of Computer Science and the Institute for Advanced Computer Studies. He graduated with a PhD in Computer Science from MIT in 2004. Lin's research lies at the intersection of information retrieval and natural language processing, and he has done work in a variety of areas, including question answering, medical informatics, bioinformatics, evaluation metrics, and knowledge-based retrieval techniques. Lin's current research focuses on "cloud computing," in particular, massively distributed text processing in cluster-based environments.

Robert Malouf is an Associate Professor in the Department of Linguistics and Asian/Middle Eastern Languages at San Diego State University. Before coming to SDSU, Robert held a postdoctoral fellowship in the Humanities Computing Department, University of Groningen (1999–2002). He received a PhD in Linguistics from Stanford University (1998) and BA in linguistics and computer science from SUNY Buffalo (1992). His research focuses on the application of computational techniques to understanding how language works, particularly in the domains of morphology and syntax. He is currently investigating the use of evolutionary simulation for explaining linguistic universals.

Prof. **Ruslan Mitkov** has been working in (applied) natural language processing, computational linguistics, corpus linguistics, machine translation, translation technology, and related areas since the early 1980s. His extensively cited research covers areas such as anaphora resolution, automatic generation of multiple-choice tests, machine translation, natural language generation, automatic summarization, computer-aided language processing, centering, translation memory, evaluation, corpus annotation, bilingual term extraction, question answering, automatic identi cation of cognates and false friends, and an NLP-driven corpus-based study of translation universals.

Mitkov is author of the monograph *Anaphora Resolution* (2002, Longman) and sole editor of *The Oxford Handbook of Computational Linguistics* (2005, Oxford University Press). Current prestigious projects include his role as Executive Editor of the *Journal of Natural Language Engineering* (Cambridge University Press) and Editor-in-Chief of the *Natural Language Processing* book series (John Benjamins Publishing). Ruslan Mitkov received his MSc from the Humboldt University in Berlin, his PhD from the Technical University in Dresden and he worked as a Research Professor at the Institute of Mathematics, Bulgarian Academy of Sciences, So a. Prof. Mitkov is Professor of Computational Linguistics and Language Engineering at the School of Humanities, Languages and Social Sciences at the University of Wolverhampton which he joined in 1995, where he set up the Research Group in Computational Linguistics. In addition to being Head of the Research Group in Computational Linguistics, Prof. Mitkov is also Director of the Research Institute in Information and Language Processing.

Dr **Mark-Jan Nederhof** is a Lecturer in the School of Computer Science at the University of St Andrews. He holds a PhD (1994) and MSc (1990) in computer science from the University of Nijmegen. Before coming to St Andrews in 2006, he was Senior Researcher at DFKI in Saarbrücken and Lecturer in the Faculty of Arts at the University of Groningen. He has served on the editorial board of *Computational Linguistics* and has been a member of the programme committees of EACL, HLT/EMNLP, and COLING-ACL.

His research covers areas of computational linguistics and computer languages, with an emphasis on formal language theory and computational complexity. He is also developing tools for use in philological research, and especially the study of Ancient Egyptian.

Martha Palmer is an Associate Professor in the Linguistics Department and the Computer Science Department of the University of Colorado at Boulder, as well as a Faculty Fellow of the Institute of Cognitive Science. She was formerly an Associate Professor in Computer and Information Sciences at the University of Pennsylvania. She has been actively involved in research in natural language processing and knowledge representation for 30 years and did her PhD in Arti cial Intelligence at the University of Edinburgh in Scotland. She has a life-long interest in the use of semantic representations in natural language processing and is dedicated to the development of community-wide resources. She was the leader of the English, Chinese, and Korean PropBanks and the Pilot Arabic PropBank. She is now the PI for the Hindi/Urdu Treebank Project and is leading the English, Chinese, and Arabic sense-tagging and PropBanking efforts for the DARPA-GALE OntoNotes project. In addition to building state-of-the-art word-sense taggers and semantic role labelers, she and her students have also developed VerbNet, a public-domain rich lexical resource that can be used in conjunction with WordNet, and SemLink, a mapping from the PropBank generic arguments to the more ne-grained VerbNet semantic roles as well as to FrameNet Frame Elements. She is a past President of the Association for Computational Linguistics, and a past Chair of SIGHAN and SIGLEX, where she was instrumental in getting the Senseval/Semeval evaluations under way.

Ian Pratt-Hartmann studied Mathematics and Philosophy at Brasenose College, Oxford, and Philosophy at Princeton and Stanford Universities, gaining his PhD from Princeton in 1987. He is currently Senior Lecturer in the Department of Computer Science at the University of Manchester.

Ehud Reiter is a Reader in Computer Science at the University of Aberdeen in Scotland. He completed a PhD in natural language generation at Harvard in 1990 and worked at the University of Edinburgh and at CoGenTex (a small US NLG company) before coming to Aberdeen in 1995. He has published over 100 papers, most of which deal with natural language generation, including the rst book ever written on applied NLG. In recent years he has focused on data-to-text systems and related "language and the world" research challenges.

Steve Renals received a BSc in Chemistry from the University of Shef eld in 1986, an MSc in Arti cial Intelligence in 1987, and a PhD in Speech Recognition and Neural Networks in 1990, both from the University of Edinburgh. He is a Profes-sor in the School of Informatics, University of Edinburgh, where he is the Director of the Centre for Speech Technology Research. From 1991 to 1992, he was a Post-doctoral Fellow at the International Computer Science Institute, Berkeley, CA, and was then an EPSRC Postdoctoral Fellow in Information Engineering at the Uni-versity of Cambridge (1992–4). From 1994 to 2003, he was a Lecturer then Reader at the University of Shef eld, moving to the University of Edinburgh in 2003. His research interests are in the area of signal-based approaches to human com-munication, in particular speech recognition and machine learning approaches to modeling multi-modal data. He has over 150 publications in these areas.

Philip Resnik is an Associate Professor at the University of Maryland, College Park, with joint appointments in the Department of Linguistics and the Institute for Advanced Computer Studies. He completed his PhD in Computer and Infor-mation Science at the University of Pennsylvania in 1993. His research focuses on the integration of linguistic knowledge with data-driven statistical modeling, and he has done work in a variety of areas, including computational psycholinguis-tics, word-sense disambiguation, cross-language information retrieval, machine translation, and sentiment analysis.

Giorgio Satta received a PhD in Computer Science in 1990 from the University of Padua, Italy. He is currently a Full Professor at the Department of Infor-mation Engineering, University of Padua. His main research interests are in computational linguistics, mathematics of language and formal language theory.

For the years 2009–10 he is serving as Chair of the European Chapter of the Association for Computational Linguistics (EACL). He has joined the standing committee of the Formal Grammar conference (FG) and the editorial boards of the journals *Computational Linguistics, Grammars* and *Research on Language and Computation*. He has also served as Program Committee Chair for the Annual Meeting of the Association for Computational Linguistics (ACL) and for the International Workshop on Parsing Technologies (IWPT).

Helmut Schmid works as a Senior Scientist at the Institute for Natural Language Processing in Stuttgart with a focus on statistical methods for NLP. He developed a range of tools for tokenization, POS tagging, parsing, computational morphology, and statistical clustering, and he frequently used decision trees in his work.

Antal van den Bosch (MA, Tilburg University, The Netherlands, 1992; PhD, Computer Science, Universiteit Maastricht, The Netherlands, 1997) held Research Assistant positions at the experimental psychology labs of Tilburg University and the Université Libre de Bruxelles (Belgium) in 1993 and 1994. After his PhD project at the Universiteit Maastricht (1994–7), he returned to Tilburg University in 1997 as a postdoc researcher. In 1999 he was awarded a Royal Dutch Academy of Arts and Sciences fellowship, followed in 2001 and 2006 by two consecutively awarded Innovational Research funds of the Netherlands Organisation for Scientific Research. Tilburg University appointed him as Assistant Professor (2001), Associate Professor (2006), and Full Professor in Computational Linguistics and AI (2008). He is also a Guest Professor at the University of Antwerp (Belgium). He currently supervises ve PhD students, and has graduated seven PhD students as co-supervisor. His research interests include memory-based natural language processing and modeling, machine translation, and proo ng tools.

Prof. Andy Way obtained his BSc (Hons) in 1986, MSc in 1989, and PhD in 2001 from the University of Essex, Colchester, UK. From 1988 to 1991 he worked at the University of Essex, UK, on the Eurotra Machine Translation project. He joined Dublin City University (DCU) as a Lecturer in 1991 and was promoted to Senior Lecturer in 2001 and Associate Professor in 2006. He was a DCU Senior Albert College Fellow from 2002 to 2003, and has been an IBM Centers for Advanced Studies Scientist since 2003, and a Science Foundation Ireland Fellow since 2005. He has published over 160 peer-reviewed papers. He has been awarded grants totaling over €6.15 million since 2000, and over €6.6 million in total. He is the Centre for Next Generation Localisation co-ordinator for Integrated Language Technologies (ILT). He currently supervises eight students on PhD programs of study, all of whom are externally funded, and has in addition graduated 10 PhD and 11 MSc students. He is currently the Editor of the journal *Machine Translation*, President of the European Association for Machine Translation, and President-Elect of the International Association for Machine Translation.

Nick Webb is a Senior Research Scientist in the Institute for Informatics, Logics and Security Studies, at the University at Albany, SUNY, USA. Previously he was a Research Fellow in the Natural Language Processing Group at the University of Shef eld, UK, and a Research Of cer at the University of Essex, UK, where he obtained a BSc in Computer Science (with a focus on Arti cial Intelligence) and an MSc (in Computational Linguistics). His PhD from Shef eld concerns the analysis of dialogue corpora to build computational models of dialogue-act classi cation, and his research interests concern intelligent information access, including interactive question answering and dialogue systems.

Bonnie Webber was a Researcher at Bolt Beranek and Newman while working on the PhD she received from Harvard University in 1978. She then taught in the Department of Computer and Information Science at the University of Pennsylvania for 20 years before joining the School of Informatics at the University of Edinburgh. Known for research on discourse and on question answering, she is a Past President of the Association for Computational Linguistics, co-developer (with Aravind Joshi, Rashmi Prasad, Alan Lee, and Eleni Miltsakaki) of the Penn Discourse TreeBank, and co-editor (with Annie Zaenen and Martha Palmer) of the new electronic journal, *Linguistic Issues in Language Technology*.

Shuly Wintner is a Senior Lecturer at the Department of Computer Science, University of Haifa, Israel. His research spans various areas in computational linguistics, including formal grammars, morphology, syntax, development of language resources and machine translation, with a focus on Semitic languages. He has published over 60 scienti c papers in computational linguistics. Dr Wintner is the Editor-in-Chief of the journal *Research in Language and Computation*.

Nianwen Xue is an Assistant Professor of Languages & Linguistics and Computer Science at Brandeis University. His research interests include syntactic and semantic parsing, machine translation, temporal representation and inference, Chinese-language processing, and linguistic annotation (Chinese Treebank, Chinese Proposition Bank, OntoNotes). He serves on the ACL SIGANN committee and co-organized the Linguistic Annotation Workshops (LAW II and LAW III) and the 2009 CoNLL Shared Task on Syntactic and Semantic Dependencies in Multiple Languages. He got his PhD in linguistics from the University of Delaware.

Preface

We started work on this handbook three years ago and, while bringing it to fruition has involved a great deal of work, we have enjoyed the process. We are grateful to our colleagues who have contributed chapters to the volume. Its quality is due to their labor and commitment. We appreciate the considerable time and effort that they have invested in making this venture a success. It has been a pleasure working with them.

We owe a debt of gratitude to our editors at Wiley-Blackwell, Danielle Descoteaux and Julia Kirk, for their unstinting support and encouragement throughout this project. We wish that all scienti c-publishing projects were blessed with publishers of their professionalism and good nature.

Finally, we must thank our families for enduring the long period of time that we have been engaged in working on this volume. Their patience and good will has been a necessary ingredient for its completion.

The best part of compiling this handbook has been the opportunity that it has given each of us to observe in detail and in perspective the wonderful burst of creativity that has taken hold of our eld in recent years.

Alexander Clark, Chris Fox, and Shalom Lappin
London and Wivenhoe
September 2009

Introduction

The eld of computational linguistics (CL), together with its engineering domain of natural language processing (NLP), has exploded in recent years. It has developed rapidly from a relatively obscure adjunct of both AI and formal linguistics into a thriving scienti c discipline. It has also become an important area of industrial development. The focus of research in CL and NLP has shifted over the past three decades from the study of small prototypes and theoretical models to robust learning and processing systems applied to large corpora. This handbook is intended to provide an introduction to the main areas of CL and NLP, and an overview of current work in these areas. It is designed as a reference and source text for graduate students and researchers from computer science, linguistics, psychology, philosophy, and mathematics who are interested in this area.

The volume is divided into four main parts. Part I contains chapters on the formal foundations of the discipline. Part II introduces the current methods that are employed in CL and NLP, and it divides into three subsections. The rst section describes several in uential approaches to Machine Learning (ML) and their application to NLP tasks. The second section presents work in the annotation of corpora. The last section addresses the problem of evaluating the performance of NLP systems. Part III of the handbook takes up the use of CL and NLP procedures within particular linguistic domains. Finally, Part IV discusses several leading engineering tasks to which these procedures are applied.

In Chapter 1 Shuly Wintner gives a detailed introductory account of the main concepts of formal language theory. This subdiscipline is one of the primary formal pillars of computational linguistics, and its results continue to shape theoretical and applied work. Wintner offers a remarkably clear guide through the classical language classes of the Chomsky hierarchy, and he exhibits the relations between these classes and the automata or grammars that generate (recognize) their members.

While formal language theory identi es classes of languages and their decidability (or lack of such), complexity theory studies the computational resources

The Handbook of Computational Linguistics and Natural Language Processing, First Edition.
Edited by Alexander Clark, Chris Fox and Shalom Lappin.
© 2013 Blackwell Publishing Ltd except for editorial material and organization
© 2013 Alexander Clark, Chris Fox, and Shalom Lappin. Published 2013 by Blackwell Publishing Ltd.

in time and space required to compute the elements of these classes. Ian Pratt-Hartmann introduces this central area of computer science in Chapter 2, and he takes up its signi cance for CL and NLP. He describes a series of important complexity results for several prominent language classes and NLP tasks. He also extends the treatment of complexity in CL/NLP from classical problems, like syntactic parsing, to the relatively unexplored area of computing sentence meaning and logical relations among sentences.

Statistical modeling has become one of the primary tools in CL and NLP for representing natural language properties and processes. In Chapter 3 Ciprian Chelba offers a clear and concise account of the basic concepts involved in the construction of statistical language models. He reviews probabilistic n-gram models and their relation to Markov systems. He de nes and clari es the notions of perplexity and entropy in terms of which the predictive power of a language model can be measured. Chelba compares n-gram models with structured language models generated by probabilistic context-free grammars, and he discusses their applications in several NLP tasks.

Part I concludes with Mark-Jan Nederhof and Giorgio Satta's discussion of the formal foundations of parsing in Chapter 4. They illustrate the problem of recognizing and representing syntactic structure with an examination of (non-lexicalized and lexicalized) context-free grammars (CFGs) and tabular (chart) parsing. They present several CFG parsing algorithms, and they consider probabilistic CFG parsing. They then extend their study to dependency grammar parsers and tree adjoining grammars (TAGs). The latter are mildly context sensitive, and so more formally powerful than CFGs. This chapter provides a solid introduction to the central theoretical concepts and results of a core CL domain.

Robert Malouf opens the rst section of Part II with an examination of maximum entropy models in Chapter 5. These constitute an in uential machine learning technique that involves minimizing the bias in a probability model for a set of events to the minimal set of constraints required to accommodate the data. Malouf gives a rigorous account of the formal properties of MaxEnt model selection, and exhibits its role in describing natural languages. He compares MaxEnt to support vector machines (SVMs), another ML technique, and he looks at its usefulness in part of speech tagging, parsing, and machine translation.

In Chapter 6 Walter Daelemans and Antal van den Bosch give a detailed overview of memory-based learning (MBL), an ML classi cation model that is widely used in NLP. MBL invokes a similarity measure to evaluate the distance between the feature vectors of stored training data and those of new events or entities in order to construct classi cation classes. It is a highly versatile and ef cient learning framework that constitutes an alternative to statistical language modeling methods. Daelemans and van den Bosch consider modi ed and extended versions of MBL, and they review its application to a wide variety of NLP tasks. These include phonological and morphological analysis, part of speech tagging, shallow parsing, word disambiguation, phrasal chunking, named entity recognition, generation, machine translation, and dialogue-act recognition.

Helmut Schmid surveys decision trees in Chapter 7. These provide an ef cient procedure for classifying data into descending binary branching subclasses, and they can be quickly induced from large data samples. Schmid points out that simple decision trees often exhibit instability because of their sensitivity to small changes in feature patterns of the data. He considers several modi cations of decision trees that overcome this limitation, speci cally bagging, boosting, and random forests. These methods combine sets of trees induced for a data set to achieve a more robust classi er. Schmid illustrates the application of decision trees to natural language tasks with discussions of grapheme conversion to phonemes, and POS tagging.

Alex Clark and Shalom Lappin characterize grammar induction as a problem in unsupervised learning in Chapter 8. They compare supervised and unsupervised grammar inference, from both engineering and cognitive perspectives. They consider the costs and bene ts of both learning approaches as a way of solving NLP tasks. They conclude that, while supervised systems are currently more accurate than unsupervised ones, the latter will become increasingly in uential because of the enormous investment in resources required to annotate corpora for training supervised classi ers. By contrast, large quantities of raw text are readily available online for unsupervised learning. In modeling human language acquisition, unsupervised grammar induction is a more appropriate framework, given that the primary linguistic data available to children is not annotated with sample classi cations to be learned. Clark and Lappin discuss recent work in unsupervised POS tagging and grammar inference, and they observe that the most successful of these procedures are beginning to approach the performance levels achieved by state-of-the-art supervised taggers and parsers.

Neural networks are one of the earliest and most in uential paradigms of machine learning. James B. Henderson concludes the rst section of Part II with an overview in Chapter 9 of neural networks and their application to NLP problems. He considers multi-layered perceptrons (MLPs), which contain hidden units between their inputs and outputs, and recurrent MLPs, which have cyclic links to hidden units. These cyclic links allow the system to process unbounded sequences by storing copies of hidden unit states and feeding them back as input to units when they are processing successive positions in the sequence. In effect, they provide the system with a memory for processing sequences of inputs. Henderson shows how a neural network can be used to calculate probability values for its outputs. He also illustrates the application of neural networks to the tasks of generating statistical language models for a set of data, learning different sorts of syntactic parsing, and identifying semantic roles. He compares them to other machine learning methods and indicates certain equivalence relations that hold between neural networks and these methods.

In the second section (Chapter 10), Martha Palmer and Nianwen Xue address the central issue of corpus annotation. They compare alternative systems for marking corpora and propose clear criteria for achieving adequate results across distinct annotation tasks. They look at a number of important types of linguistic information that annotation encodes including, *inter alia*, POS tagging, deep and shallow syntactic parsing, coreference and anaphora relations, lexical meanings, semantic roles, temporal connections among propositions, logical entailments among propositions, and discourse structure. Palmer and Xue discuss the problems of securing reasonable levels of annotator agreement. They show how a sound and well-motivated annotation scheme is crucial for the success of supervised machine learning procedures in NLP, as well as for the rigorous evaluation of their performance.

Philip Resnik and Jimmy Lin conclude Part II with a discussion in the last section (Chapter 11) of methods for evaluating NLP systems. They consider both intrinsic evaluation of a procedure's performance for a speci ed task, and external assessment of its contribution to the quality of a larger engineering system in which it is a component. They present several ways to formulate precise quantitative metrics for grading the output of an NLP device, and they review testing sequences through which these metrics can be applied. They illustrate the issues of evaluation by considering in some detail what is involved in assessing systems for word-sense disambiguation and for question answering. This chapter extends and develops some of the concerns raised in the previous chapter on annotation. It also factors out and addresses evaluation problems that emerged in earlier chapters on the application of machine learning methods to NLP tasks.

Part III opens with Steve Renals and Thomas Hain's comprehensive account in chapter 12 of current work in automatic speech recognition (ASR). They observe that ASR plays a central role in NLP applications involving spoken language, including speech-to-speech translation, dictation, and spoken dialogue systems. Renals and Hain focus on the general task of transcribing natural conversational speech to text, and present the problem in terms of a statistical framework in which the problem of the speech recogniser is to nd the most likely word sequence given the observed acoustics. The focus of the chapter is acoustic modeling based on hidden Markov models (HMMs) and Gaussian mixture models. In the rst part of the chapter they develop the basic acoustic modeling framework that underlies current speech recognition systems, including re nements to include discriminative training and the adaptation to particular speakers using only small amounts of data. These components are drawn together in the description of a state-of-the-art system for the automatic transcription of multiparty meetings. The nal part of the chapter discusses approaches that enable robustness for noisier or less constrained acoustic environments, the incorporation of multiple sources of knowledge, the development of sequence models that are richer than HMMs, and issues that arise when developing large-scale ASR systems.

In Chapter 13 Stephen Clark discusses statistical parsing as the probabilistic syntactic analysis of sentences in a corpus, through supervised learning. He traces the development of this area from generative parsing models to discriminative frameworks. Clark studies Collins' lexicalized probabilistic context-free grammars (PCFGs) as a particularly successful instance of these models. He examines the parsing algorithms, procedures for parse ranking, and methods for parse optimization that are commonly used in generative parse models like PCFG. Discriminative parsing does not model sentences, but provides a way of modeling parses directly. It discards some of the independence assumptions encoded in generative parsing, and it allows for complex dependencies among syntactic features. Clark examines log-linear (maximum entropy) models as instantiations of this approach. He applies them to parsers driven by combinatory categorial grammar (CCG). He gives a detailed description of recent work on statistical CCG parsing, focusing on the ef ciency with which such grammars can be learned, and the impressive accuracy which CCG parsing has recently achieved.

John A. Goldsmith offers a detailed overview in Chapter 14 of computational approaches to morphology. He looks at unsupervised learning of word segmentation for a corpus in which word boundaries have been eliminated, and he identi es two main problems in connection with this task. The rst involves identifying the correct word boundaries for a stripped corpus on the basis of prior knowledge of the lexicon of the language. The second, and signi cantly more dif - cult, problem is to devise a procedure for constructing the lexicon of the language from the stripped corpus. Goldsmith describes a variety of approaches to word segmentation, highlighting probabilistic modeling techniques, such as minimum description length and hierarchical Bayesian models. He reviews distributional methods for unsupervised morphological learning which have their origins in Zellig Harris' work, and gives a very clear account of nite state transducers and their central role in morphological induction.

In Chapter 15 Chris Fox discusses the major questions driving work in logic-based computational semantics. He focuses on formalized theories of meaning, and examines what properties a semantic representation language must possess in order to be suf ciently expressive while sustaining computational viability. Fox proposes that implementability and tractability be taken as conditions of adequacy on semantic theories. Speci cally, these theories must permit ef cient computation of the major semantic properties of sentences, phrases, and discourse sequences. He surveys work on type theory, intensionality, the relation between proof theory and model theory, and the dynamic representation of scope and anaphora in leading semantic frameworks. Fox also summarizes current research on corpus-based semantics, speci cally the use of latent semantic analysis to identify lexical semantic clusters, methods for word-sense disambiguation, and current work on textual entailment. He re ects on possible connections between the corpus-based approach to semantics and logic-based formal theories of meaning, and he concludes with several interesting suggestions for pursuing these connections.

Jonathan Ginzburg and Raquel Fernández present a comprehensive account in Chapter 16 of recent developments in the computational modeling of dialogue. They rst examine a range of central phenomena that an adequate formal theory of dialogue must handle. These include non-sentential fragments, which play an important role in conversation; meta-communicative expressions, which serve as crucial feedback and clari cation devices to speakers and hearers; procedures for updating shared information and common ground; and mechanisms for adapting a dialogue to a particular conversational domain. Ginzburg and Fernández propose a formal model of dialogue, KoS, which they formulate in the type theoretic framework of type theory with records. This type theory has the full power of functional application and abstraction, but it permits the speci cation of recursively dependent type structures that correspond to re-entrant typed feature structures. They compare their dialogue model to other approaches current in the literature. They conclude by examining some of the issues involved in constructing a robust, wide-coverage dialogue management system, and they consider the application of machine learning methods to facilitate certain aspects of this task.

In Chapter 17 Matthew W. Crocker characterizes the major questions and theoretical developments shaping contemporary work in computational psycholinguistics. He observes that this domain of inquiry shares important objectives with both theoretical linguistics and psycholinguistics. In common with the former, it seeks to explain the way in which humans recognize sentence structure and meaning. Together with the latter, it is concerned to describe the cognitive processing mechanisms through which they achieve these tasks. However, in contrast to both theoretical linguistics and psycholinguistics, computational psycholinguistics models language understanding by constructing systems that can be implemented and rigorously tested. Crocker focuses on syntactic processing, and he discusses the central problem of resolving structural ambiguity. He observes that a general consensus has emerged on the view that sentence processing is incremental, and a variety of constraints (syntactic, semantic, pragmatic, etc.) are available at each point in the processing sequence to resolve or reduce different sources of ambiguity. Crocker considers three main approaches. Symbolic methods use grammars to represent syntactic structure and parsing algorithms to exhibit the way in which humans apply a grammar to sentence recognition. Connectionists employ neural nets as non-symbolic systems of induction and processing. Probabilistic approaches model language interpretation as a stochastic procedure, where this involves generating a probability distribution for the strings produced by an automaton or a grammar of some formal class. Crocker concludes with the observation that computational psycholinguistics (like theoretical linguistics) still tends to view sentence processing in isolation from other cognitive activities. He makes the important suggestion that integrating language understanding into the wider range of human functions in which it gures is likely to yield more accurate accounts of processing and acquisition.

Ralph Grishman starts off Part IV of the handbook with a review, in Chapter 18, of information extraction (IE) from documents. He highlights name, entity, relation, and event extraction as primary IE tasks, and he addresses each in turn. Name extraction consists in identifying names in text and classifying them according to semantic (ontological) type. Entity extraction selects referring phrases, assigns them to semantic classes, and speci es coreference links among them. Relation extraction recognizes pairs of related entities and the semantic type of the relation that holds between them. Event extraction picks out cases of events described in a text, according to semantic type, and it locates the entities that appear in the event. For each of these tasks Grishman traces the development of IE approaches from manually crafted rule-based systems, through supervised machine learning, to semi- and unsupervised methods. He concludes the chapter with some re ections on the challenges and opportunities that the web, with its enormous resources of online text in a variety of languages and formats, poses for future research in IE.

In Chapter 19 Andy Way presents a systematic overview of the current state of machine translation (MT). He discusses the evolution of statistical machine translation (SMT) from word-based n-gram language models speci ed for aligned multi-lingual corpora (originally developed by the IBM speech and language group in the 1990s) to the phrase-based SMT (PB-SMT) language models that currently dominate the eld. He also looks at the use of both generative and dis-criminative language models in SMT, and he considers results achieved with both supervised and unsupervised learning methods. Way offers a systematic compar-ison of PB-SMT with other paradigms of MT, including hierarchical, tree-based, and example-based approaches, as well as traditional rule-based systems, that continue to gure prominently in commercial MT products. He concludes with a detailed discussion of the MT work that his research group is doing. This work applies a hybrid view in which syntactic, morphological, and lexical semantic information is combined with statistical language modeling techniques to maxi-mize the accuracy and ef ciency of the distinct components of an MT system. He also discusses the role of MT in contemporary online and spoken applications.

Ehud Reiter describes natural language generation (NLG) in Chapter 20. He characterizes the generation problem as mapping representations in one format (or language) into text in a given language. As he observes, NLG is distinguished from most other areas of NLP by the pervasive complexity of making choices from a large set of alternatives at each point in the generation process. The mapping of representations to text involves resolving numerous one-to-many selections. Reiter identi es three main subtasks for NLG. Document planning determines the content of the representation to be realized in NL text, and the general structure of the content. Microplanning speci es the organization and linguistic structure of the text. Realization produces the text itself. In the course of implementing this sequence of tasks, an NLG procedure must decide on the general format of the message to be realized, the nature of the syntactic units in which it will be encoded, the internal structure of these sentences, and a variety of lexical and stylistic choices. Reiter reviews a number of current NLG systems, and he dis-cusses the central role of NLG in a variety of NLP applications. He concludes with some thoughtful proposals for future research directions in this domain.

Ruslan Mitkov reviews computational analysis of discourse structure in Chapter 21. He begins with algorithms for segmenting text into discourse ele-ments. He then describes three major computational treatments of discourse coherence relations: Hobbs' coherence account, rhetorical structure theory, and centering. He follows this with an extended discussion of anaphora resolution. He points out that accurate anaphora resolution is a necessary condition for success in many tasks, such as MT, text summarization, NLG, and IE. He concludes by surveying some of the signi cant contributions that discourse modeling has made to a wide variety of NLP applications.

Bonnie Webber and Nick Webb conclude Part IV, and the volume, with a presentation of current work on question answering (QA) in Chapter 22. They trace the development of QA from early procedures that mapped NL questions into queries in a standard database language for a closed data set, to contemporary open systems that seek answers to questions across a large set of documents, often the entire web. As with other NLP applications, this development has also involved a move from manually crafted rules to machine learning classi ers, and hybrid systems combining rule-based and probabilistic methods. They discuss the relation between QA and text retrieval. While the latter provides documents in response to user queries, the former seeks information expressed as natural language replies. They survey the design and performance of current QA procedures, focusing on the challenges involved in improving their coverage and extending their functionality. An important method for achieving such extension is to incorporate methods for identifying text entailments in order to move beyond simple word pattern matching. These entailments enrich the domain of possible answers that a QA system can consider by adding a set of semantic implications to a question and its range of possible answers. Webber and Webb also take up alternative ways of evaluating QA systems, and they consider issues for future research.

While we have tried to provide as broad and comprehensive a view of CL and NLP as possible, this handbook is, inevitably, not exhaustive. Many more chapters could have been added on a host of important issues, and the eld would still not have been fully covered. Considerations of space and manageability have forced us to limit the volume to a subset of central research themes. One might take issue with our selection, or with the way that we have chosen to organize the chapters. We suspect that this would be true for any handbook of this size. In many cases, topics to which one might plausibly devote a separate chapter are treated from different perspectives in a number of chapters. So, for example, nite state methods are discussed in the chapters on formal language theory, complexity, morphology, and speech recognition. Therefore, we were able to forego a distinct chapter on this area. In other instances, important new research, like work on text entailment, is touched on lightly (see the brief discussions of text entailment in the chapters on semantics and QA), but pressures of space and timely production prevented us from including fuller treatments.

The survey of work provided here indicates that both symbolic and information theoretic methods continue to play a major role across a large variety of tasks and domains. Moreover, rather than these approaches being in con ict, there is a strong movement towards hybrid models that integrate different approaches. It seems likely that this trend will continue, as each method carries strengths and weaknesses that complement the other. Symbolic techniques offer compact representations of high level information that generally eludes statistical models, while information theoretic procedures achieve a level of robustness and wide coverage that symbolic systems rarely, if ever, achieve on their own.

Above all the chapters of this volume give a clear view of the remarkable diversity and vitality of research being done in CL and NLP, and the enormous progress that has been made in these areas over the past several decades. We hope that the handbook communicates some of the excitement and the satisfaction that we and our colleagues experience from our work in this amazing eld.

Part I Formal Foundations

1 Formal Language Theory

SHULY WINTNER

1 Introduction

This chapter provides a gentle introduction to formal language theory, aimed at
readers with little background in formal systems. The motivation is natural language processing (NLP), and the presentation is geared towards NLP applications,
with linguistically motivated examples, but without compromising mathematical
rigor.

The text covers elementary formal language theory, including: regular languages and regular expressions; languages vs. computational machinery; nite
state automata; regular relations and nite state transducers; context-free grammars and languages; the Chomsky hierarchy; weak and strong generative
capacity; and mildly context-sensitive languages.

2 Basic Notions

Formal languages are de ned with respect to a given *alphabet*, which is a nite
set of symbols, each of which is called a *letter*. This notation does not mean, however, that elements of the alphabet must be "ordinary" letters; they can be any
symbol, such as numbers, or digits, or words. It is customary to use 'Σ' to denote
the alphabet. A nite sequence of letters is called a *string*, or a *word*. For simplicity, we usually forsake the traditional sequence notation in favor of a more
straightforward representation of strings.

Example 1 (Strings). Let $\Sigma = \{0,1\}$ be an alphabet. Then all binary numbers
are strings over Σ. Instead of $\langle 0,1,1,0,1 \rangle$ we usually write 01101. If $\Sigma = \{a,b,c,d,\ldots,y,z\}$ is an alphabet, then *cat, incredulous,* and *supercalifragilisticexp-
ialidocious* are strings, as are *tac, qqq,* and *kjshd kwjehr.*

The *length* of a string w is the number of letters in the sequence, and is denoted
$|w|$. The unique string of length 0 is called the *empty string* and is usually denoted ϵ
(but sometimes λ).

The Handbook of Computational Linguistics and Natural Language Processing, First Edition.
Edited by Alexander Clark, Chris Fox and Shalom Lappin.
© 2013 Blackwell Publishing Ltd except for editorial material and organization
© 2013 Alexander Clark, Chris Fox, and Shalom Lappin. Published 2013 by Blackwell Publishing Ltd.

Let $w_1 = \langle x_1, \ldots, x_n \rangle$ and $w_2 = \langle y_1, \ldots, y_m \rangle$ be two strings over the same alphabet Σ. The *concatenation* of w_1 and w_2, denoted $w_1 \cdot w_2$, is the string $\langle x_1, \ldots, x_n, y_1, \ldots, y_m \rangle$. Note that the length of $w_1 \cdot w_2$ is the sum of the lengths of w_1 and w_2: $|w_1 \cdot w_2| = |w_1| + |w_2|$. When it is clear from the context, we sometimes omit the '·' symbol when depicting concatenation.

Example 2 (Concatenation). Let $\Sigma = \{a, b, c, d, \ldots, y, z\}$ be an alphabet. Then *master · mind = mastermind*, *mind · master = mindmaster*, and *master · master = mastermaster*. Similarly, *learn · s = learns*, *learn · ed = learned*, and *learn · ing = learning*.

Notice that when the empty string ϵ is concatenated with any string w, the resulting string is w. Formally, for every string w, $w \cdot \epsilon = \epsilon \cdot w = w$.

We de ne an *exponent* operator over strings in the following way: for every string w, w^0 (read: w raised to the power of zero) is de ned as ϵ. Then, for $n > 0$, w^n is de ned as $w^{n-1} \cdot w$. Informally, w^n is obtained by concatenating w with itself n times. In particular, $w^1 = w$.

Example 3 (Exponent). If $w = go$, then $w^0 = \epsilon$, $w^1 = w = go$, $w^2 = w^1 \cdot w = w \cdot w = gogo$, $w^3 = gogogo$, and so on.

A few other notions that will be useful in the sequel: the *reversal* of a string w is denoted w^R and is obtained by writing w in the reverse order. Thus, if $w = \langle x_1, x_2, \ldots, x_n \rangle$, $w^R = \langle x_n, x_{n-1}, \ldots, x_1 \rangle$.

Example 4 (Reversal). Let $\Sigma = \{a, b, c, d, \ldots, y, z\}$ be an alphabet. If w is the string *saw*, then w^R is the string *was*. If $w = madam$, then $w^R = madam = w$. In this case we say that w is a *palindrome*.

Given a string w, a *substring* of w is a sequence formed by taking contiguous symbols of w in the order in which they occur in w: w_c is a substring of w if and only if there exist (possibly empty) strings w_l and w_r such that $w = w_l \cdot w_c \cdot w_r$. Two special cases of substrings are *prefix* and *suffix*: if $w = w_l \cdot w_c \cdot w_r$ then w_l is a pre x of w and w_r is a suf x of w. Note that every pre x and every suf x is a substring, but not every substring is a pre x or a suf x.

Example 5 (Substrings). Let $\Sigma = \{a, b, c, d, \ldots, y, z\}$ be an alphabet and $w = indistinguishable$ a string over Σ. Then ϵ, *in*, *indis*, *indistinguish*, and *indistinguishable* are pre xes of w, while ϵ, *e*, *able*, *distinguishable* and *indistinguishable* are suf xes of w. Substrings that are neither pre xes nor suf xes include *distinguish*, *gui*, and *is*.

Given an alphabet Σ, the set of all strings over Σ is denoted by Σ^* (the reason for this notation will become clear presently). Notice that no matter what the Σ is, as long as it includes at least one symbol, Σ^* is always in nite. A *formal language* over an alphabet Σ is any subset of Σ^*. Since Σ^* is always in nite, the number of formal languages over Σ is also in nite.

As the following example demonstrates, formal languages are quite unlike what one usually means when one uses the term "language" informally. They are essentially sets of strings of characters. Still, all natural languages are, at least super cially, such string sets. Higher-level notions, relating the strings to objects and actions in the world, are completely ignored by this view. While this is a rather radical idealization, it is a useful one.

Example 6 (Languages). Let $\Sigma = \{a, b, c, \ldots, y, z\}$. Then Σ^* is the set of all strings over the Latin alphabet. Any subset of this set is a language. In particular, the following are formal languages:

- Σ^*;
- the set of strings consisting of consonants only;
- the set of strings consisting of vowels only;
- the set of strings each of which contains at least one vowel and at least one consonant;
- the set of palindromes: strings that read the same from right to left and from left to right;
- the set of strings whose length is less than 17 letters;
- the set of single-letter strings;
- the set {*i, you, he, she, it, we, they*};
- the set of words occurring in Joyce's Ulysses (ignoring punctuation etc.);
- the empty set.

Note that the rst ve languages are in nite while the last ve are nite.

We can now lift some of the string operations de ned above to languages. If L is a language then the *reversal* of L, denoted L^R, is the language $\{w \mid w^R \in L\}$, that is, the set of reversed L-strings. *Concatenation* can also be lifted to languages: if L_1 and L_2 are languages, then $L_1 \cdot L_2$ is the language de ned as $\{w_1 \cdot w_2 \mid w_1 \in L_1 \text{ and } w_2 \in L_2\}$: the concatenation of two languages is the set of strings obtained by concatenating some word of the rst language with some word of the second.

Example 7 (Language operations). Let $L_1 = \{i, you, he, she, it, we, they\}$ and $L_2 = \{smile, sleep\}$. Then $L_1^R = \{i, uoy, eh, ehs, ti, ew, yeht\}$ and $L_1 \cdot L_2 = \{ismile, yous-mile, hesmile, shesmile, itsmile, wesmile, theysmile, isleep, yousleep, hesleep, shesleep, itsleep, wesleep, theysleep\}$.

In the same way we can de ne the *exponent* of a language: if L is a language then L^0 is the language containing the empty string only, $\{\epsilon\}$. Then, for $i > 0$, $L^i = L \cdot L^{i-1}$, that is, L^i is obtained by concatenating L with itself i times.

Example 8 (Language exponentiation). Let L be the set of words {*bau, haus, hof, frau*}. Then $L^0 = \{\epsilon\}$, $L^1 = L$ and $L^2 = \{baubau, bauhaus, bauhof, baufrau, hausbau, haushaus, haushof, hausfrau, hofbau, hofhaus, hofhof, hoffrau, fraubau, frauhaus, frauhof, fraufrau\}$.

The language obtained by considering any number of concatenations of words from L is called the *Kleene closure* of L and is denoted L^*. Formally, $L^* = \bigcup_{i=0}^{\infty} L^i$, which is a terse notation for the union of L^0 with L^1, then with L^2, L^3 and so on ad in nitum. When one wants to leave L^0 out, one writes $L^+ = \bigcup_{i=1}^{\infty} L^i$.

Example 9 (Kleene closure). Let $L = \{dog, cat\}$. Observe that $L^0 = \{\epsilon\}$, $L^1 = \{dog, cat\}$, $L^2 = \{catcat, catdog, dogcat, dogdog\}$, etc. Thus L^* contains, among its in - nite set of strings, the strings ϵ, *cat, dog, catcat, catdog, dogcat, dogdog, catcatcat, catdogcat, dogcatcat, dogdogcat*, etc.

As another example, consider the alphabet $\Sigma = \{a, b\}$ and the language $L = \{a, b\}$ de ned over Σ. L^* is the set of all strings over a and b, which is exactly the de nition of Σ^*. The notation for Σ^* should now become clear: it is simply a special case of L^*, where $L = \Sigma$.

3   Language Classes and Linguistic Formalisms

Formal languages are sets of strings, subsets of Σ^*, and they can be speci ed using any of the speci cation methods for sets (of course, since languages may be in nite, stipulation of their members is in the general case infeasible). When languages are fairly simple (not arbitrarily complex), they can be characterized by means of *rules*. In the following sections we de ne several mechanisms for de n- ing languages, and focus on the *classes* of languages that can be de ned with these mechanisms. A formal mechanism with which formal languages can be de ned is a *linguistic formalism*. We use L (with or without subscripts) to denote languages, and $\mathcal{L}$ to denote classes of languages.

Example 10 (Language class). Let $\Sigma = \{a, b, c, \ldots, y, z\}$. Let $\mathcal{L}$ be the set of all the *finite* subsets of Σ^*. Then $\mathcal{L}$ is a language class.

When classes of languages are discussed, some of the interesting properties to be investigated are *closures* with respect to certain operators. The previous section de ned several operators, such as concatenation, union, Kleene closure, etc., on languages. Given a particular (binary) operation, say union, it is interesting to know whether a class of languages is *closed under* this operation. A class of lan- guages $\mathcal{L}$ is said to be closed under some operation '•' if and only if, whenever two languages L_1 and L_2 are in the class ($L_1, L_2 \in \mathcal{L}$), the result of performing the operation on the two languages is also in this class: $L_1 • L_2 \in \mathcal{L}$.

Closure properties have a theoretical interest in and by themselves, but they are especially important when one is interested in processing languages. Given an ef cient computational implementation for a class of languages (for example, an algorithm that determines *membership*: whether a given string indeed belongs to a given language), one can use the operators that the class is closed under, and still preserve computational ef ciency in processing. We will see such examples in the following sections.

The membership problem is one of the fundamental questions of interest con- cerned with language classes. As we shall see, the more expressive the class, the harder it is to determine membership in languages of this class. Algorithms that determine membership are called *recognition* algorithms; when a recognition algorithm additionally provides the structure that the formalism induces on the string in question, it is called a *parsing* algorithm.

4 Regular Languages

4.1 Regular expressions

The rst linguistic formalism we discuss is *regular expressions*. These are expressions over some alphabet Σ, augmented by some special characters. We de ne a mapping, called *denotation*, from regular expressions to sets of strings over Σ, such that every well-formed regular expression denotes a set of strings, or a language.

DEFINITION 1. *Given an alphabet Σ, the set of **regular expressions** over Σ is defined as follows:*

- *$\emptyset$ is a regular expression;*
- *ϵ is a regular expression;*
- *if $a \in \Sigma$ is a letter, then a is a regular expression;*
- *if r_1 and r_2 are regular expressions, then so are $(r_1 + r_2)$ and $(r_1 \cdot r_2)$;*
- *if r is a regular expression, then so is $(r)^*$;*
- *nothing else is a regular expression over Σ.*

Example 11 (Regular expressions). Let Σ be the alphabet $\{a, b, c, \ldots, y, z\}$. Some regular expressions over this alphabet are $\emptyset$, a, $((c \cdot a) \cdot t)$, $(((m \cdot e) \cdot (o)^*) \cdot w)$, $(a + (e + (i + (o + u))))$, $((a + (e + (i + (o + u)))))^*$, etc.

DEFINITION 2. *Given a regular expression r, its **denotation,** $[\![r]\!]$, is a set of strings defined as follows:*

- *$[\![\emptyset]\!] = \{\}$, the empty set;*
- *$[\![\epsilon]\!] = \{\epsilon\}$, the singleton set containing the empty string;*
- *if $a \in \Sigma$ is a letter, then $[\![a]\!] = \{a\}$, the singleton set containing a only;*
- *if r_1 and r_2 are two regular expressions whose denotations are $[\![r_1]\!]$ and $[\![r_2]\!]$, respectively, then $[\![(r_1 + r_2)]\!] = [\![r_1]\!] \cup [\![r_2]\!]$ and $[\![(r_1 \cdot r_2)]\!] = [\![r_1]\!] \cdot [\![r_2]\!]$;*
- *if r is a regular expression whose denotation is $[\![r]\!]$ then $[\![(r)^*]\!] = [\![r]\!]^*$.*

Example 12 (Regular expressions). Following are the denotations of the regular expressions of the previous example:

$\emptyset$	$\emptyset$
ϵ	$\{\epsilon\}$
a	$\{a\}$
$((c \cdot a) \cdot t)$	$\{c \cdot a \cdot t\}$
$(((m \cdot e) \cdot (o)^*) \cdot w)$	$\{mew, meow, meoow, meooow, meoooow, \ldots\}$
$(a + (e + (i + (o + u))))$	$\{a, e, i, o, u\}$
$((a + (e + (i + (o + u)))))^*$	*the set containing all strings of 0 or more vowels*

Regular expressions are useful because they facilitate specification of complex languages in a formal, concise way. Of course, finite languages can still be specified by enumerating their members; but infinite languages are much easier to specify with a regular expression, as the last instance of the above example shows.

For simplicity, we omit the parentheses around regular expressions when no confusion can be caused. Thus, the expression $((a + (e + (i + (o + u)))))^*$ is written as $(a + e + i + o + u)^*$. Also, if $\Sigma = \{a_1, a_2, \ldots, a_n\}$, we use Σ as a shorthand notation for $a_1 + a_2 + \cdots + a_n$. As in the case of string concatenation and language concatenation, we sometimes omit the '$\cdot$' operator in regular expressions, so that the expression $c \cdot a \cdot t$ can be written *cat*.

Example 13 (Regular expressions). Given the alphabet of all English letters, $\Sigma = \{a, b, c, \ldots, y, z\}$, the language Σ^* is denoted by the regular expression Σ^*. The set of all strings which contain a vowel is denoted by $\Sigma^* \cdot (a + e + i + o + u) \cdot \Sigma^*$. The set of all strings that begin in "*un*" is denoted by $(un)\Sigma^*$. The set of strings that end in either "*tion*" or "*sion*" is denoted by $\Sigma^* \cdot (s + t) \cdot (ion)$. Note that all these languages are infinite.

The class of languages which can be expressed as the denotation of regular expressions is called the class of *regular languages*.

DEFINITION 3.   *A language L is **regular** iff there exists a regular expression r such that* $L = [\![r]\!]$.

It is a mathematical fact that some languages, subsets of Σ^*, are not regular. We will encounter such languages in the sequel.

4.2   *Properties of regular languages*

The class of regular languages is interesting because of its "nice" properties, which we review here. It should be fairly easy to see that regular languages are closed under union, concatenation, and Kleene closure. Given two regular languages, L_1 and L_2, there must exist two regular expressions, r_1 and r_2, such that $[\![r_1]\!] = L_1$ and $[\![r_2]\!] = L_2$. It is therefore possible to form new regular expressions based on r_1 and r_2, such as $r_1 \cdot r_2$, $r_1 + r_2$ and r_1^*. Now, by the definition of regular expressions and their denotations, it follows that the denotation of $r_1 \cdot r_2$ is $L_1 \cdot L_2$: $[\![r_1 \cdot r_2]\!] = L_1 \cdot L_2$. Since $r_1 \cdot r_2$ is a regular expression, its denotation is a regular language, and hence $L_1 \cdot L_2$ is a regular language. Hence the regular languages are closed under concatenation. In exactly the same way we can prove that the class of regular languages is closed under union and Kleene closure.

One of the reasons for the attractiveness of regular languages is that they are known to be closed under a wealth of useful operations: intersection, complementation, exponentiation, substitution, homomorphism, etc. These properties come in handy both in practical applications that use regular languages and in mathematical proofs that concern them. For example, several formalisms extend regular expressions by allowing one to express regular languages using not only the three basic operations, but also a wealth of other operations (that the class of regular languages is closed under). It is worth noting that such "good behavior" is not exhibited by more complex classes of languages.

4.3 Finite state automata

Regular expressions are a declarative formalism for specifying (regular) languages. We now present languages as entities generated by a *computation*. This is a very common situation in formal language theory: many language classes are associated with computing machinery that generates them. The dual view of languages (as the denotation of some specifying formalism and as the output of a computational process) is central in formal language theory.

The computational device we de ne in this section is *finite state automata* (FSA). Informally, they consist of a nite set of *states* (sometimes called *nodes* or *vertices*), connected by a nite number of *transitions* (also called *edges* or *links*). Each of the transitions is labeled by a letter, taken from some nite alphabet Σ. A computation starts at a designated state, the *start* state or *initial* state, and it moves from one state to another along the labeled transitions. As it moves, it prints the letter which labels the transition. Thus, during a computation, a string of letters is printed out. Some of the states of the machine are designated *final* states, or *accepting* states. Whenever the computation reaches a nal state, the string that was printed so far is said to be *accepted* by the machine. Since each computation de nes a string, the set of all possible computations de nes a set of strings or, in other words, a language. We say that this language is *accepted* or *generated* by the machine.

DEFINITION 4. *A **finite state automaton** is a five-tuple $\langle Q, q_0, \Sigma, \delta, F \rangle$, where Σ is a finite set of **alphabet** symbols, Q is a finite set of **states**, $q_0 \in Q$ is the **initial state**, $F \subseteq Q$ is a set of **final** states, and $\delta : Q \times \Sigma \times Q$ is a relation from states and alphabet symbols to states.*

Example 14 (Finite state automata). Finite state automata are depicted graphically, with circles for states and arrows for the transitions. The initial state is shaded and the nal states are depicted by two concentric circles. The nite state automaton $A = \langle Q, \Sigma, q_0, \delta, F \rangle$, where $Q = \{q_0, q_1, q_2, q_3\}$, $\Sigma = \{c, a, t, r\}$, $F = \{q_3\}$, and $\delta = \{\langle q_0, c, q_1 \rangle, \langle q_1, a, q_2 \rangle, \langle q_2, t, q_3 \rangle, \langle q_2, r, q_3 \rangle\}$, is depicted graphically as follows:

To de ne the *language* generated by an FSA, we rst extend the transition relation from single edges to *paths* by extending the transition relation δ to its re exive transitive closure, $\hat{\delta}$. This relation assigns a string to each path (it also assumes that an empty path, decorated by ϵ, leads from each state to itself). We focus on paths that lead from the initial state to some nal state. The strings that decorate these paths are said to be *accepted* by the FSA, and the *language* of the FSA is the set of all these strings. In other words, in order for a string to be in the language of the FSA, there must be a path in the FSA which leads from the initial state to some nal state decorated by the string. Paths that lead to non- nal states do not de ne accepted strings.

DEFINITION 5. *Given an FSA $A = \langle Q, q_0, \Sigma, \delta, F \rangle$, the reflexive transitive closure of the transition relation δ is $\hat{\delta}$, defined as follows:*

- *for every state $q \in Q$, $(q, \epsilon, q) \in \hat{\delta}$;*
- *for every string $w \in \Sigma^*$ and letter $a \in \Sigma$, if $(q, w, q') \in \hat{\delta}$ and $(q', a, q'') \in \delta$, then $(q, w \cdot a, q'') \in \hat{\delta}$.*

*A string w is **accepted** by A if and only if there exists a state $q_f \in F$ such that $\hat{\delta}(q_0, w) = q_f$. The **language** of A is the set of all the strings accepted by it: $L(A) = \{w \mid$ there exists $q_f \in F$ such that $\hat{\delta}(q_0, w) = q_f\}$.*

Example 15 (Language accepted by an FSA). For the nite state automaton of Example 14, $\hat{\delta}$ is the following set of triples: $\langle q_0, \epsilon, q_0 \rangle$, $\langle q_1, \epsilon, q_1 \rangle$, $\langle q_2, \epsilon, q_2 \rangle$, $\langle q_3, \epsilon, q_3 \rangle$, $\langle q_0, c, q_1 \rangle$, $\langle q_1, a, q_2 \rangle$, $\langle q_2, t, q_3 \rangle$, $\langle q_2, r, q_3 \rangle$, $\langle q_0, ca, q_2 \rangle$, $\langle q_1, at, q_3 \rangle$, $\langle q_1, ar, q_3 \rangle$, $\langle q_0, cat, q_3 \rangle$, $\langle q_0, car, q_3 \rangle$. The language of the FSA is thus $\{cat, car\}$.

Example 16 (Finite state automata). Following are some simple FSA and the languages they generate.

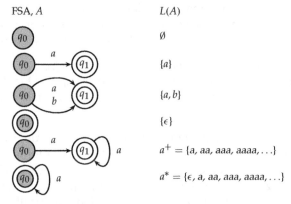

FSA, A   L(A)

$\emptyset$

$\{a\}$

$\{a, b\}$

$\{\epsilon\}$

$a^+ = \{a, aa, aaa, aaaa, \ldots\}$

$a^* = \{\epsilon, a, aa, aaa, aaaa, \ldots\}$

We now slightly amend the de nition of nite state automata to include what is called ϵ-*moves*. By our original de nition, the transition relation δ is a relation from states and alphabet symbols to states. We extend δ such that its second coordinate is now $\Sigma \cup \{\epsilon\}$, that is, any edge in an automaton can be labeled either by some alphabet symbol or by the special symbol ϵ, which as usual denotes the empty word. The implication is that a computation can move from one state to another over an ϵ-transition without printing out any symbol.

Example 17 (Automata with ϵ-moves). The language accepted by the following automaton is $\{do, undo, done, undone\}$:

Finite state automata, just like regular expressions, are devices for de ning formal languages. The major theorem of regular languages states that the class of languages which can be generated by FSA is exactly the class of regular languages. Furthermore, there are simple and ef cient algorithms for "translating" a regular expression to an equivalent automaton and vice versa.

THEOREM 1. *A language L is regular iff there exists an FSA A such that $L = L(A)$.*

Example 18 (Equivalence of finite state automata and regular expressions). For each of the regular expressions of Example 12 we depict an equivalent automaton below:

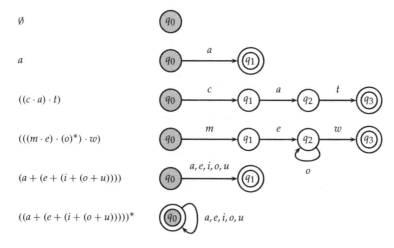

4.4 *Minimization and determinization*

The nite state automata presented above are non-deterministic. By this we mean that when the computation reaches a certain state, the next state is not uniquely determined by the next alphabet symbol to be printed. There might very well be more than one state that can be reached by a transition that is labeled by some symbol. This is because we de ned automata using a transition relation, δ, which is not required to be functional. For some state q and alphabet symbol a, δ might include the two pairs $\langle q, a, q_1 \rangle$ and $\langle q, a, q_2 \rangle$ with $q_1 \neq q_2$. Furthermore, when we extended δ to allow ϵ-transitions, we added yet another dimension of non-determinism: when the machine is in a certain state q and an ϵ-arc leaves q, the computation must "guess" whether to traverse this arc.

DEFINITION 6. *An FSA $A = \langle Q, q_0, \Sigma, \delta, F \rangle$ is **deterministic** iff it has no ϵ-transitions and δ is a function from $Q \times \Sigma$ to Q.*

Much of the appeal of nite state automata lies in their ef ciency; and their ef ciency is in great part due to the fact that, given some deterministic FSA A and a string w, it is possible to determine whether or not $w \in L(A)$ by "walking" the path labeled w, starting with the initial state of A, and checking whether the walk leads to a nal state. Such a walk takes time that is proportional to the length of w, and is completely independent of the number of states in A. We therefore say that the *membership* problem for FSA can be solved in *linear* time. But when automata are non-deterministic, an element of guessing is introduced, which may impair the ef ciency: no longer is there a single walk along a single path labeled w, and some control mechanism must be introduced to check that all possible paths are taken.

Non-determinism is important because it is sometimes much easier to construct a non-deterministic automaton for some language. Fortunately, we can rely on two very important results: every non-deterministic nite state automaton is equivalent to some deterministic one; and every nite state automaton is equivalent to one that has a minimum number of nodes, and the minimal automaton is unique. We now explain these results.

First, it is important to clarify what is meant by *equivalent*. We say that two nite state automata are equivalent if and only if they accept the same language.

DEFINITION 7. *Two FSA A_1 and A_2 are **equivalent** iff $L(A_1) = L(A_2)$.*

Example 19 (Equivalent automata). The following three nite state automata are equivalent: they all accept the set {go, gone, going}.

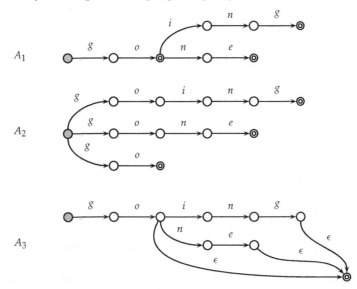

Note that A_1 is deterministic: for any state and alphabet symbol there is at most one possible transition. A_2 is not deterministic: the initial state has three outgoing arcs all labeled by g. The third automaton, A_3, has ϵ-arcs and hence is non-deterministic. While A_2 might be the most readable, A_1 is the most compact as it has the fewest nodes.

Given a non-deterministic FSA A, it is always possible to construct an equivalent deterministic automaton, one whose next state is fully determined by the current state and the alphabet symbol, and which contains no ϵ-moves. Sometimes this construction yields an automaton with more states than the original, non-deterministic one (in the worst case, the number of states in the deterministic automaton can be exponential in the size of the non-deterministic one). However, the deterministic automaton can then be minimized such that it is guaranteed that no deterministic nite state automaton generating the same language is smaller. Thus, it is always possible to determinize and then minimize a given automaton without affecting the language it generates.

THEOREM 2. *For every FSA A (with n states) there exists a deterministic FSA A' (with at most 2^n states) such that $L(A) = L(A')$.*

THEOREM 3. *For every regular language L there exists a minimal FSA A such that no other FSA A' such that $L(A) = L(A')$ has fewer states than A. A is unique (up to isomorphism).*

4.5 Operations on finite state automata

We know from Section 4.3 that nite state automata are equivalent to regular expressions; we also know from Section 4.2 that the regular languages are closed under several operations, including union, concatenation, and Kleene closure. So, for example, if L_1 and L_2 are two regular languages, there exist automata A_1 and A_2 which accept them, respectively. Since we know that $L_1 \cup L_2$ is also a regular language, there must be an automaton which accepts it as well. The question is, can this automaton be constructed using the automata A_1 and A_2? In this section we show how simple operations on nite state automata correspond to some operators on languages.

We start with concatenation. Suppose that A_1 is a nite state automaton such that $L(A_1) = L_1$, and similarly that A_2 is an automaton such that $L(A_2) = L_2$. We describe an automaton A such that $L(A) = L_1 \cdot L_2$. A word w is in $L_1 \cdot L_2$ if and only if it can be broken into two parts, w_1 and w_2, such that $w = w_1 \cdot w_2$, and $w_1 \in L_1$, $w_2 \in L_2$. In terms of automata, this means that there is an accepting path for w_1 in A_1 and an accepting path for w_2 in A_2; so if we allow an ϵ-transition from all the nal states of A_1 to the initial state of A_2, we will have accepting paths for words of $L_1 \cdot L_2$. The nite state automaton A is constructed by combining A_1 and A_2 in the following way: its set of states, Q, is the union of Q_1 and Q_2; its alphabet is the union of the two alphabets; its initial state is the initial state of A_1; its nal states are the nal states of A_2; and its transition relation is obtained by adding to $\delta_1 \cup \delta_2$ the set of ϵ-moves described above: $\{\langle q_f, \epsilon, q_{0_2}\rangle \mid q_f \in F_1\}$ where q_{0_2} is the initial state of A_2.

In a very similar way, an automaton A can be constructed whose languages is $L_1 \cup L_2$ by combining A_1 and A_2. Here, one should notice that for a word to be accepted by A it must be accepted either by A_1 or by A_2 (or by both). The combined automaton will have an accepting path for every accepting path in A_1 and in A_2. The idea is to add a new initial state to A, from which two ϵ-arcs lead to the initial states of A_1 and A_2. The states of A are the union of the states of A_1 and A_2, plus the new initial state. The transition relation is the union of δ_1 with δ_2, plus the new ϵ-arcs. The nal states are the union of F_1 and F_2.

An extension of the same technique to construct the Kleene closure of an automaton is rather straightforward. However, all these results are not surprising, as we have already seen in Section 4.2 that the regular languages are closed under these operations. Thinking of languages in terms of the automata that accept them comes in handy when one wants to show that the regular languages are closed under other operations, where the regular expression notation is not very sugges-tive of how to approach the problem. Consider the operation of *complementation*: if L is a regular language over an alphabet Σ, we say that the complement of L is the set of all the words (in Σ^*) that are not in L, and write $\overline{L}$ for this set. Formally, $\overline{L} = \Sigma^* \setminus L$. Given a regular expression r, it is not clear what regular expression r' is such that $[\![r']\!] = \overline{[\![r]\!]}$. However, with automata this becomes much easier.

Assume that a nite state automaton A is such that $L(A) = L$. Assume also that A is deterministic. To construct an automaton for the complemented language, all one has to do is change all nal states to non- nal, and all non- nal states to nal. In other words, if $A = \langle Q, \Sigma, q_0, \delta, F \rangle$, then $\overline{A} = \langle Q, \Sigma, q_0, \delta, Q \setminus F \rangle$ is such that $L(\overline{A}) = \overline{L}$. This is because every accepting path in A is not accepting in $\overline{A}$, and vice versa.

Now that we know that the regular languages are closed under complementa-tion, it is easy to show that they are closed under intersection: if L_1 and L_2 are regular languages, then $L_1 \cap L_2$ is also regular. This follows directly from funda-mental theorems of set theory, since $L_1 \cap L_2$ can actually be written as $\overline{\overline{L_1} \cup \overline{L_2}}$, and we already know that the regular languages are closed under union and comple-mentation. In fact, construction of an automaton for the intersection language is not very dif cult, although it is less straightforward than the previous examples.

4.6   Applications of finite state automata in natural language processing

Finite state automata are computational devices that generate regular languages, but they can also be viewed as *recognizing* devices: given some automaton A and a word w, it is easy to determine whether $w \in L(A)$. Observe that such a task can be performed in time linear in the length of w, hence the ef ciency of the represen-tation is optimal. This reversed view of automata motivates their use for a simple yet necessary application of natural language processing: dictionary lookup.

Example 20 (Dictionaries as finite state automata). Many NLP applications require the use of lexicons or dictionaries, sometimes storing hundreds of thousands of entries. Finite state automata provide an ef cient means for storing dictionar-ies, accessing them, and modifying their contents. Assume that an alphabet is xed (say, $\Sigma = \{a, b, \ldots, z\}$) and consider how a single word, say *go*, can be repre-sented. As we have seen above, a naïve representation would be to construct an automaton with a single path whose arcs are labeled by the letters of the word *go*:

To represent more than one word, add paths to the FSA, one path for each additional word. For example, after adding the words *gone* and *going*, we obtain:

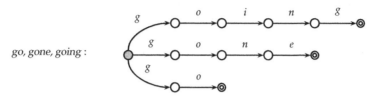

This automaton can then be determinized and minimized, yielding:

The organization of the lexicon as outlined above is extremely simplistic. A possible extension attaches to the nal states of the FSA additional information pertaining to the words that decorate the paths to those states. Such information can include de nitions, morphological information, translations, etc. FSA are thus suitable for representing various kinds of dictionaries, in addition to simple lexicons.

Regular languages are particularly appealing for natural language processing for two main reasons. First, it turns out that most phonological and morphological processes can be straightforwardly described using the operations that regular languages are closed under, in particular concatenation. With very few exceptions (such as the interdigitation word-formation processes of Semitic languages or the duplication phenomena of some Asian languages), the morphology of most natural languages is limited to simple concatenation of af xes, with some morphophonological alternations, usually on a morpheme boundary. Such phenomena are easy to model with regular languages, and hence are easy to implement with nite state automata. Second, many of the algorithms one would want to apply to nite state automata take time proportional to the length of the word being processed, independently of the size of the automaton. Finally, the various closure properties facilitate modular development of FSA for natural languages.

4.7 Regular relations

While nite state automata, which *define* (regular) languages, are suf cient for some natural language applications, it is often useful to have a mechanism for *relating* two (formal) languages. For example, a part-of-speech tagger can be viewed as an application that relates a set of natural language strings (the *source* language) to a set of part-of-speech tags (the *target* language). A morphological analyzer can be viewed as a relation between natural language strings (the surface forms of words) and their internal structure (say, as sequences of morphemes). In this section we discuss a computational device, very similar to nite state automata, which de nes a *relation* over two regular languages.

Example 21 (Relations over languages). Consider a simple part-of-speech tagger: an application which associates with every word in some natural language a tag, drawn from a nite set of tags. In terms of formal languages, such an application implements a relation over two languages. Assume that the natural language is de ned over $\Sigma_1 = \{a, b, \ldots, z\}$ and that the set of tags is $\Sigma_2 = \{PRON, V, DET, ADJ, N, P\}$. Then the part-of-speech relation might contain the following pairs (here, a string over Σ_1 is mapped to a single element of Σ_2):

I	PRON	*the*	DET
know	V	*Cat*	N
some	DET	*in*	P
new	ADJ	*the*	DET
tricks	N	*Hat*	N
said	V		

As another example, assume that Σ_1 is as above, and Σ_2 is a set of part-of-speech and morphological tags, including {*-PRON, -V, -DET, -ADJ, -N, -P, -1, -2, -3, -sg, -pl, -pres, -past, -def, -indef*}. A morphological analyzer is a relation between a language over Σ_1 and a language over Σ_2. Some of the pairs in such a relation are:

I	I-PRON-1-sg	*the*	the-DET-def
know	know-V-pres	*Cat*	cat-N-sg
some	some-DET-indef	*in*	in-P
new	new-ADJ	*the*	the-DET-def
tricks	trick-N-pl	*Hat*	hat-N-sg
said	say-V-past		

Finally, consider the relation that maps every English noun in singular to its plural form. While the relation is highly regular (namely, adding "*s*" to the singular form), some nouns are irregular. Some instances of this relation are:

cat	*cats*	*hat*	*hats*
ox	*oxen*	*child*	*children*
mouse	*mice*	*sheep*	*sheep*
goose	*geese*		

Summing up, a regular relation is de ned over *two* alphabets, Σ_1 and Σ_2. Of course, the two alphabets can be identical, but for many natural language applications they differ. If a relation in $\Sigma^* \times \Sigma^*$ is regular, its projections on both coordinates are regular languages (not all relations that satisfy this condition are regular; additional constraints must hold on the underlying mapping which we ignore here). Informally, a regular relation is a set of pairs, each of which consists of one string over Σ_1 and one string over Σ_2, such that both the set of strings over Σ_1 and that over Σ_2 constitute regular languages. We provide a precise characterization of regular relations via nite state transducers below.

4.8   Finite state transducers

Finite state automata are a computational device for de ning regular languages; in a very similar way, *finite state transducers (FSTs)* are a computational device for de ning regular relations. Transducers are similar to automata, the only difference being that the edges are not labeled by single letters, but rather by pairs of symbols: one symbol from Σ_1 and one symbol from Σ_2. The following is a preliminary de nition that we will revise presently:

DEFINITION 8.   *A **finite state transducer** is a six-tuple* $\langle Q, q_0, \Sigma_1, \Sigma_2, \delta, F \rangle$, *where Q is a finite set of states,* $q_0 \in Q$ *is the initial state,* $F \subseteq Q$ *is the set of final states,* Σ_1 *and* Σ_2 *are alphabets, and* δ *is a subset of* $Q \times \Sigma_1 \times \Sigma_2 \times Q$.

Example 22 (Finite state transducers). Following is a nite state transducer relating the singular forms of two English words with their plural form. In this case, both alphabets are identical: $\Sigma_1 = \Sigma_2 = \{a, b, \dots, z\}$. The set of nodes is $Q = \{q_1, q_2, \dots, q_{11}\}$, the initial state is q_6 and the set of nal states is $F = \{q_5, q_{11}\}$. The transitions from one state to another are depicted as labeled edges; each edge bears two symbols, one from Σ_1 and one from Σ_2, separated by a colon (:). So, for example, $\langle q_1, o, e, q_2 \rangle$ is an element of δ.

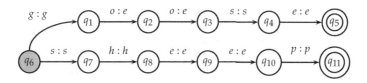

Observe that each path in this device de nes *two* strings: a concatenation of the left-hand-side labels of the arcs, and a concatenation of the right-hand-side labels. The upper path of the above transducer thus de nes the pair *goose:geese*, whereas the lower path de nes the pair *sheep:sheep*.

What constitutes a *computation* with a transducer? Similarly to the case of automata, a computation amounts to "walking" a path of the transducer, starting from the initial state and ending in some nal state. Along the path, edges bear bi-symbol labels: one can view the left-hand-side symbol as an "input" symbol and the right-hand-side symbol as an "output" symbol. Thus, each path of the transducer de nes a pair of strings, an input string (over Σ_1) and an output string (over Σ_2). This pair of strings is a member of the relation de ned by the transducer.

DEFINITION 9. *Let* $T = \langle Q, q_0, \Sigma_1, \Sigma_2, \delta, F \rangle$ *be a finite state transducer. Define* $\hat{\delta} \subseteq Q \times \Sigma_1^* \times \Sigma_2^* \times Q$ *as follows:*

- *for each* $q \in Q$, $\hat{\delta}(q, \epsilon, \epsilon, q)$;
- *if* $\hat{\delta}(q_1, w_1, w_2, q_2)$ *and* $\delta(q_2, a, b, q_3)$, *then* $\hat{\delta}(q_1, w_1 \cdot a, w_2 \cdot b, q_3)$.

Then a pair $\langle w_1, w_2 \rangle$ *is **accepted** (or **generated**) by T if and only if* $\hat{\delta}(q_0, w_1, w_2, w_f)$ *holds for some final state* $q_f \in F$. *The **relation defined by the transducer** is the set of all the pairs it accepts.*

As a shorthand notation, when an edge is labeled by two identical symbols, we depict only one of them and omit the colon.

The above de nition of nite state transducers is not very useful: since each arc is labeled by exactly one symbol of Σ_1 and exactly one symbol of Σ_2, any relation that is implemented by such a transducer must relate only strings of exactly the same length. This should not be the case, and to overcome this limitation we extend the de nition of δ to allow also ϵ-labels. In the extended de nition, δ is a relation over Q, $\Sigma_1 \cup \{\epsilon\}$, $\Sigma_2 \cup \{\epsilon\}$ and Q. Thus a transition from one state to another can involve "reading" a symbol of Σ_1 without "writing" any symbol of Σ_2, or the other way round.

Example 23 (Finite state transducer with ϵ-labels). With the extended de nition of transducers, we depict below an expanded transducer for singular–plural noun pairs in English.

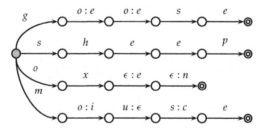

Note that ϵ-labels can occur on the left or on the right of the ':' separator. The pairs accepted by this transducer are *goose:geese, sheep:sheep, ox:oxen,* and *mouse:mice.*

4.9   Properties of regular relations

The extension of automata to transducers carries with it some interesting results. First and foremost, nite state transducers de ne exactly the set of regular relations. Many of the closure properties of automata are valid for transducers, but some are not. As these properties bear not only theoretical but also practical signi cance, we discuss them in more detail in this section.

Given some transducer T, consider what happens when the labels on the arcs of T are modi ed such that only the left-hand symbol remains. In other words, consider what is obtained when the transition relation δ is projected on three of its coordinates: Q, Σ_1, and Q only, ignoring the Σ_2 coordinate. It is easy to see that a finite state automaton is obtained. We call this automaton the *projection* of T to Σ_1. In the same way, we can define the projection of T to Σ_2 by ignoring Σ_1 in the transition relation. Since both projections yield finite state automata, they induce regular languages. Therefore the relation defined by T is a regular relation.

We can now consider certain operations on regular relations, inspired by similar operations on regular languages. For example, *union* is very easy to define. Recall that a regular relation is a subset of the Cartesian product of $\Sigma_1^* \times \Sigma_2^*$, that is, a set of pairs. If R_1 and R_2 are regular relations, then $R_1 \cup R_2$ is well defined, and it is straightforward to show that it is a regular relation. To define the union operation directly over transducers, extend the construction of FSA delineated in Section 4.5, namely add a new initial state with two edges labeled $\epsilon : \epsilon$ leading from it to the initial states of the given transducers. In a similar way, *concatenation* can be extended to regular relations: if R_1 and R_2 are regular relations then $R_1 \cdot R_2 = \{\langle w_1 \cdot w_2, w_3 \cdot w_4 \rangle \mid \langle w_1, w_3 \rangle \in R_1 \text{ and } \langle w_2, w_4 \rangle \in R_2\}$. Again, the construction for FSA can be straightforwardly extended to the case of transducers, and it is easy to show that $R_1 \cdot R_2$ is a regular relation.

Example 24 (Operations on finite state transducers). Let R_1 be the following relation, mapping some English words to their German counterparts: $R_1 = \{tomato:Tomate, cucumber:Gurke, grapefruit:Grapefruit, pineapple:Ananas, coconut:Koko\}$. Let R_2 be a similar relation: $R_2 = \{grapefruit:Pampelmuse, coconut:Kokusnuß\}$. Then: $R_1 \cup R_2 = \{tomato:Tomate, cucumber:Gurke, grapefruit:Grapefruit, grapefruit: Pampelmuse, pineapple:Ananas, coconut:Koko, coconut:Kokusnuß\}$.

A rather surprising fact is that regular relations are *not* closed under *intersection*. In other words, if R_1 and R_2 are two regular relations, then it very well might be the case that $R_1 \cap R_1$ is not a regular relation. It will take us beyond the scope of the material covered so far to explain this fact, but it is important to remember it when dealing with finite state transducers. For this reason exactly it follows that the class of regular relations is not closed under *complementation*: since intersection can be expressed in terms of union and complementation, if regular relations were closed under complementation they would have been closed also under intersection, which we know is not the case.

A very useful operation that is defined for transducers is *composition*. Intuitively, a transducer relates one word ("input") with another ("output"). When we have more than one transducer, we can view the output of the first transducer as the input to the second. The composition of T_1 and T_2 relates the input language of T_1 with the output language of T_2, bypassing the intermediate level (which is the output of T_1 and the input of T_2).

DEFINITION 10. *If R_1 is a relation from Σ_1^* to Σ_2^* and R_2 is a relation from Σ_2^* to Σ_3^* then the **composition** of R_1 and R_2, denoted $R_1 \circ R_2$, is a relation from Σ_1^* to Σ_3^* defined as $\{\langle w_1, w_3 \rangle \mid \text{there exists a string } w_2 \in \Sigma_2^* \text{ such that } w_1 R_1 w_2 \text{ and } w_2 R_2 w_3\}$.*

Example 25 (Composition of finite state transducers). Let R_1 be the following relation, mapping some English words to their German counterparts: $R_1 = \{tomato:$
*Tomate, cucumber:Gurke, grapefruit:Grapefruit, grapefruit:Pampelmuse, pine-
apple:Ananas, coconut:Koko, coconut:Kokusnuß}*. Let R_2 be a similar relation,
mapping French words to their English translations: $R_2 = \{tomate:tomato,$
*ananas: pineapple, pamplemousse:grapefruit, concombre:cucumber, cornichon:
cucumber, noix-de-coco:coconut}*. Then $R_2 \circ R_1$ is a relation mapping French
words to their German translations (the English translations are used to
compute the mapping, but are not part of the nal relation): $R_2 \circ R_1 =$
*{tomate:Tomate, ananas:Ananas, pamplemousse:Grapefruit, pamplemousse:
Pampelmuse, concombre:Gurke, cornichon:Gurke, noix-de-coco:Koko, noix-de-
coco:Kokusnuße}*.

5   Context-Free Languages

5.1   *Where regular languages fail*

Regular languages and relations are useful for various applications of natural language processing, but there is a limit to what can be achieved with such means.
We mentioned in passing that not *all* languages over some alphabet Σ are regular;
we now look at what kind of languages lie beyond the regular ones.

To exemplify a non-regular language, consider a simple language over the
alphabet $\Sigma = \{a, b\}$ whose members are strings that consist of some number, n,
of 'a's, followed by *the same* number of 'b's. Formally, this is the language $L =$
$\{a^n \cdot b^n \mid n > 0\}$. Assume towards a contradiction that this language is regular, and
therefore a deterministic nite state automaton A exists whose language is L. Consider the language $L_i = \{a^i \mid i > 0\}$. Since every string in this language is a pre x
of some string $(a^i \cdot b^i)$ of L, there must be a path in A starting from the initial state
for every string in L_i. Of course, there is an in nite number of strings in L_i, but by
its very nature, A has a nite number of states. Therefore there must be two different strings in L_i that lead the automaton to a single state. In other words, there
exist two strings, a^j and a^k, such that $j \neq k$ but $\hat{\delta}(q_0, a^j) = \hat{\delta}(q_0, a^k)$. Let us call this
state q. There must be a path labeled b^j leading from q to some nal state q_f, since
the string $a^j b^j$ is in L. This situation is schematically depicted below (the dashed
arrows represent paths):

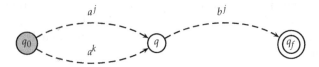

Therefore, there is also an accepting path $a^k b^j$ in A, and hence also $a^k b^j$ is in L, in
contradiction to our assumption. Hence no deterministic nite state automaton
exists whose language is L.

We have seen one language, namely $L = \{a^n \cdot b^n \mid n > 0\}$, which cannot be de ned by a nite state automaton and therefore is not regular. In fact, there are several other such languages, and there is a well-known technique, the so-called *pumping lemma*, for proving that certain languages are not regular. If a language is not regular, then it cannot be denoted by a regular expression. We must look for alternative means of speci cation for non-regular languages.

5.2   *Grammars*

In order to specify a class of more complex languages, we introduce the notion of a *grammar*. Intuitively, a grammar is a set of rules that manipulate symbols. We distinguish between two kinds of symbols: *terminal* ones, which should be thought of as elements of the target language, and *non-terminal* ones, which are auxiliary symbols that facilitate the speci cation. It might be instructive to think of the non-terminal symbols as *syntactic categories*, such as *Sentence, Noun Phrase,* or *Verb Phrase*. However, formally speaking, non-terminals have no "special," external interpretation where formal languages are concerned. Similarly, terminal symbols might correspond to letters of some natural language, or to words, or to something else: they are simply elements of some nite set.

Rules can express the internal structure of "phrases," which should not nec-essarily be viewed as natural language phrases. A rule is a non-empty sequence of symbols, a mixture of terminals and non-terminals, with the only requirement that the rst element in the sequence be a non-terminal one (alternatively, one can de ne a rule as an ordered pair whose rst element is a non-terminal symbol and whose second element is a sequence of symbols). We write such rules with a special symbol, '→,' separating the distinguished leftmost non-terminal from the rest of the sequence. The leftmost non-terminal is sometimes referred to as the *head* of the rule, while the rest of the symbols are called the *body* of the rule.

Example 26 (Rules). Assume that the set of terminals is {*the, cat, in, hat*} and the set of non-terminals is {*D, N, P, NP, PP*}. Then possible rules over these two sets include:

$D \rightarrow the$ $NP \rightarrow D\,N$
$N \rightarrow cat$ $PP \rightarrow P\,NP$
$N \rightarrow hat$ $NP \rightarrow NP\,PP$
$P \rightarrow in$

Note that the terminal symbols correspond to words of English, and not to letters as was the case above.

Consider the rule $NP \rightarrow D\,N$. If we interpret *NP* as the syntactic category *noun phrase, D* as *determiner,* and *N* as *noun,* then what the rule informally means is that one possible way to construct a noun phrase is by concatenating a determiner with a noun. More generally, a rule speci es one possible way to construct a "phrase" of the category indicated by its head: this way is by concatenating phrases of the categories indicated by the elements in the body of the rule. Of course, there might be more than one way to construct a phrase of some category. For example, there are two rules which de ne the structure of the category *NP* in Example 26: either by concatenating a phrase of category *D* with one of category *N*, or by concatenating an *NP* with a *PP*.

In Example 26, rules are of two kinds: the ones on the left have a single terminal symbol in their body, while the ones on the right have one or more non-terminal symbols, but no rule mixes both terminal and non-terminal symbols in its body. While this is a common practice where grammars for natural languages are concerned, nothing in the formalism requires such a format for rules. Indeed, rules can mix any combination of terminal and non-terminal symbols in their bodies.

Formal language theory de nes rules and grammars in a much broader way than that which was discussed above, and the de nition below is actually only a special case of rules and grammars. For various reasons that have to do with the format of the rules, this special case is known as *context-free* rules. This has nothing to do with the ability of grammars to refer to context; the term should not be taken mnemonically. In the next section we discuss other rule-based systems. In this section, however, we use the terms *rule* and *context-free rule* interchangeably, as we do for grammars, derivations, etc.

DEFINITION 11. *A **context-free grammar** is a four-tuple* $G = \langle V, \Sigma, P, S \rangle$, *where V is a finite set of **non-terminal symbols**, Σ is an alphabet of **terminal symbols**, $P \subseteq V \times (V \cup \Sigma)^*$ is a set of **rules** and $S \in V$ is the **start symbol**.*

Note that this de nition permits rules with empty bodies. Such rules, which consist of a left-hand-side only, are called ϵ-rules, and are useful both for formal and for natural languages. Example 33 below makes use of an ϵ-rule.

Example 27 (Grammar). The set of rules depicted in Example 26 can constitute the basis for a grammar $G = \langle V, \Sigma, P, S \rangle$, where $V = \{D, N, P, NP, PP\}$, $\Sigma = \{the, cat, in, hat\}$, P is the set of rules, and the start symbol S is *NP*.

In the sequel we depict grammars by listing their rules only, as we did in Example 26. We keep a convention of using uppercase letters for the non-terminals and lowercase letters for the terminals, and we assume that the set of terminals is the smallest that includes all the terminals mentioned in the rules, and the same for the non-terminals. Finally, we assume that the start symbol is the head of the rst rule, unless stated otherwise.

5.3   Derivation

In order to de ne the language denoted by a grammar we need to de ne the concept of *derivation*. Derivation is a relation that holds between two *forms*, each a sequence of grammar symbols (terminal and/or non-terminal).

DEFINITION 12. *Let $G = \langle V, \Sigma, P, S \rangle$ be a grammar. The set of **forms** induced by G is $(V \cup \Sigma)^*$. A form α **immediately derives** a form β, denoted by $\alpha \Rightarrow \beta$, if and only if there exist $\gamma_l, \gamma_r \in (V \cup \Sigma)^*$ such that $\alpha = \gamma_l A \gamma_r$ and $\beta = \gamma_l \gamma_c \gamma_r$, and $A \rightarrow \gamma_c$ is a rule in P. A is called the **selected symbol**.*

A form α immediately derives β if a single non-terminal symbol, A, occurs in α, such that whatever is to its left in α, the (possibly empty) sequence of terminal and non-terminal symbols γ_l, occurs at the leftmost edge of β; and whatever is to the right of A in α, namely the (possibly empty) sequence of symbols γ_r, occurs at the rightmost edge of β; and the remainder of β, namely γ_c, constitutes the body of some grammar rule of which A is the head.

Example 28 (Immediate derivation). Let G be the grammar of Example 27. The set of forms induced by G contains all the (in nitely many) sequences of elements from V and Σ, such as $\langle \rangle$, $\langle NP \rangle$, $\langle D \text{ cat } P \text{ } D \text{ hat} \rangle$, $\langle D \text{ } N \rangle$, $\langle$the cat in the hat$\rangle$, etc.

Let us start with a simple form, $\langle NP \rangle$. Observe that it can be written as $\gamma_l NP \gamma_r$, where both γ_l and γ_r are empty. Observe also that NP is the head of some grammar rule: the rule $NP \rightarrow D \text{ } N$. Therefore, the form is a good candidate for derivation: if we replace the selected symbol NP with the body of the rule, while preserving its environment, we obtain $\gamma_l D \text{ } N \gamma_r = D \text{ } N$. Therefore, $\langle N \rangle \Rightarrow \langle D \text{ } N \rangle$.

We now apply the same process to $\langle D \text{ } N \rangle$. This time the selected symbol is D (we could have selected N, of course). The left context is again empty, while the right context is $\gamma_r = N$. As there exists a grammar rule whose head is D, namely $D \rightarrow$ the, we can replace the rule's head by its body, preserving the context, and obtain the form $\langle$the $N \rangle$. Hence $\langle D \text{ } N \rangle \Rightarrow \langle$the $N \rangle$.

Given the form $\langle$the $N \rangle$, there is exactly one non-terminal that we can select, namely N. However, there are two rules that are headed by N: $N \rightarrow$ cat and $N \rightarrow$ hat. We can select either of these rules to show that both $\langle$the $N \rangle \Rightarrow \langle$the cat$\rangle$ and $\langle$the $N \rangle \Rightarrow \langle$the hat$\rangle$.

Since the form $\langle$the cat$\rangle$ consists of terminal symbols only, no non-terminal can be selected and hence it derives no form.

We now extend the immediate derivation relation from a single step to an arbitrary number of steps by considering the re exive transitive closure of the relation.

DEFINITION 13. *The **derivation** relation, denoted '$\overset{*}{\Rightarrow}$,' is defined recursively as follows: $\alpha \overset{*}{\Rightarrow} \beta$ if $\alpha = \beta$, or if $\alpha \Rightarrow \gamma$ and $\gamma \overset{*}{\Rightarrow} \beta$.*

Example 29 (Extended derivation). In Example 28 we showed that the following immediate derivations hold: $\langle NP \rangle \Rightarrow \langle D \text{ } N \rangle$; $\langle D \text{ } N \rangle \Rightarrow \langle$the $N \rangle$; $\langle$the $N \rangle \Rightarrow \langle$the cat$\rangle$. Therefore, $\langle NP \rangle \overset{*}{\Rightarrow} \langle$the cat$\rangle$.

The derivation relation is the basis for de ning the language denoted by a grammar. Consider the form obtained by taking a single grammar symbol, say $\langle A \rangle$; if this form derives a sequence of terminals, this string is a member of the language denoted by A. The language of a grammar G, $L(G)$, is the language denoted by its start symbol.

DEFINITION 14. *Let $G = \langle V, \Sigma, P, S \rangle$ be a grammar. The* **language of a non-terminal** *$A \in V$ is*

$$L_G(A) = \{a_1 \cdots a_n \mid a_i \in \Sigma \text{ for } 1 \leq i \leq n \text{ and } \langle A \rangle \overset{*}{\Rightarrow} \langle a_1, \ldots, a_n \rangle\}$$

The **language of the grammar** *G is $L(G) = L_G(S)$.*

Example 30 (Language of a grammar). Consider again the grammar G of Example 27. It is fairly easy to see that the language denoted by the non-terminal symbol D, $L_G(D)$, is the singleton set $\{the\}$. Similarly, $L_G(P)$ is $\{in\}$ and $L_G(N) = \{cat, hat\}$. It is more difficult to define the languages denoted by the non-terminals NP and PP, although it should be straightforward that the latter is obtained by concatenating $\{in\}$ with the former. We claim without providing a proof that $L_G(NP)$ is the denotation of the regular expression $(the \cdot (cat + hat) \cdot (in \cdot the \cdot (cat + hat))^*)$.

5.4   Derivation trees

Sometimes two derivations of the same string differ only in the order in which they were applied. Consider again the grammar of Example 27. Starting with the form $\langle NP \rangle$ it is possible to derive the string *the cat* in two ways:

(1) $\langle NP \rangle \Rightarrow \langle D\,N \rangle \Rightarrow \langle D\,cat \rangle \Rightarrow \langle the\ cat \rangle$
(2) $\langle NP \rangle \Rightarrow \langle D\,N \rangle \Rightarrow \langle the\ N \rangle \Rightarrow \langle the\ cat \rangle$

Derivation (1) applies first the rule $N \rightarrow cat$ and then the rule $D \rightarrow the$ whereas derivation (2) applies the same rules in the reverse order. But since both use the same rules to derive the same string, it is sometimes useful to collapse such "equivalent" derivations into one. To this end the notion of *derivation trees* is introduced.

A derivation tree (sometimes called *parse* tree, or simply tree) is a visual aid in depicting derivations, and a means for imposing structure on a grammatical string. Trees consist of vertices and branches; a designated vertex, the *root* of the tree, is depicted on the top. Branches are connections between pairs of vertices. Intuitively, trees are depicted "upside down," since their root is at the top and their leaves are at the bottom. An example of a derivation tree for the string *the cat in the hat* with the grammar of Example 27 is given in Example 31.

Example 31 (Derivation tree).

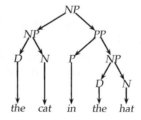

Formally, a tree consists of a nite set of vertices and a nite set of branches (or arcs), each of which is an ordered pair of vertices. In addition, a tree has a designated vertex, the *root*, which has two properties: it is not the target of any arc, and every other vertex is accessible from it (by following one or more branches). When talking about trees we sometimes use family notation: if a vertex v has a branch leaving it which leads to some vertex u, then we say that v is the *mother* of u and u is the *daughter*, or *child*, of v. If u has two daughters, we refer to them as *sisters*. Derivation trees are de ned with respect to some grammar G, and must obey the following conditions:

(1) every vertex has a *label*, which is either a terminal symbol, a non-terminal symbol, or ϵ;
(2) the label of the root is the start symbol;
(3) if a vertex v has an outgoing branch, its label must be a non-terminal symbol; furthermore, this symbol must be the head of some grammar rule; and the elements in the body of the same rule must be the labels of the children of v, in the same order;
(4) if a vertex is labeled ϵ, it is the only child of its mother.

A *leaf* is a vertex with no outgoing branches. A tree induces a natural "left-to-right" order on its leaves; when read from left to right, the sequence of leaves is called the *frontier*, or *yield*, of the tree.

Derivation trees correspond very closely to derivations. In fact, it is easy to show that a non-terminal symbol A derives a form α if and only if α is the yield of some parse tree whose root is A. In other words, whenever some string can be derived from a non-terminal, there exists a derivation tree for that string, with the same non-terminal as its root. However, sometimes there exist different derivations of the same string that correspond to a single tree. The tree representation collapses exactly those derivations that differ from each other only in the order in which rules are applied.

Sometimes, however, different derivations (of the same string!) correspond to different trees. This can happen only when the derivations differ in the rules which they apply. When more than one tree exists for some string, we say that the string is *ambiguous*. Ambiguity is a major problem when grammars are used for certain formal languages, in particular for programming languages. But for natural languages, ambiguity is unavoidable as it corresponds to properties of the natural language itself.

Example 32 (Ambiguity). Consider again the grammar of Example 27, and the string *the cat in the hat in the hat*. Intuitively, there can be (at least) two readings for this string: one in which a certain cat wears a hat-in-a-hat, and one in which a certain cat-in-a-hat is inside a hat. If we wanted to indicate the two readings with parentheses, we would distinguish between

((the cat in the hat) in the hat)

and

(the cat in (the hat in the hat))

This distinction in intuitive meaning is reflected in the grammar, and two different derivation trees, corresponding to the two readings, are available for this string:

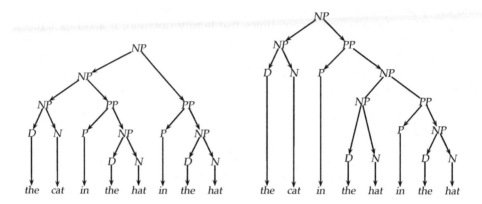

Using linguistic terminology, in the left tree the second occurrence of the prepositional phrase *in the hat* modifies the noun phrase *the cat in the hat*, whereas in the right tree it only modifies the (first occurrence of) the noun phrase *the hat*. This situation is known as *syntactic* or *structural* ambiguity.

5.5   *Expressiveness*

Context-free grammars are more expressive than regular expressions. In Section 5.1 we claimed that the language $L = \{a^n b^n \mid n > 0\}$ is not regular; we now show a context-free grammar for this language. The grammar, $G = \langle V, \Sigma, P, S \rangle$, has two terminal symbols, $\Sigma = \{a, b\}$, and one non-terminal symbol, $V = \{S\}$. The idea is that whenever S is used recursively in a derivation (rule 1), the current form is extended by exactly one a on the left and one b on the right, hence the number of 'a's and 'b's must be equal.

Example 33 (A context-free grammar for $L = \{a^n b^n \mid n \geq 0\}$).

(1) $S \rightarrow a\,S\,b$
(2) $S \rightarrow \epsilon$

DEFINITION 15. *The class of languages that can be generated by context-free grammars is the class of* **context-free languages**.

The class of context-free languages properly contains the regular languages: given some finite state automaton which generates some language L, it is always possible to construct a context-free grammar whose language is L. We conclude this section with a discussion of converting automata to context-free grammars.

Let $A = \langle Q, q_0, \delta, F \rangle$ be a deterministic finite state automaton with no ϵ-moves over the alphabet Σ. The grammar we define to simulate A is $G = \langle V, \Sigma, P, S \rangle$, where the alphabet Σ is that of the automaton, and where the set of non-terminals, V, is the set Q of the automaton states. The idea is that a single (immediate) derivation step with the grammar simulates a single arc traversal with the automaton. Since automata states are simulated by grammar non-terminals, it is reasonable to simulate the initial state by the start symbol, and hence the start symbol S is q_0. What is left, of course, are the grammar rules. These come in two varieties: rst, for every automaton arc $\delta(q, a) = q'$ we stipulate a rule $q \rightarrow a\, q'$. Then, for every nal state $q_f \in F$, we add the rule $q_f \rightarrow \epsilon$.

Example 34 (Simulating a finite state automaton by a grammar). Consider the automaton $\langle Q, q_0, \delta, F \rangle$ depicted below, where $Q = \{q_0, q_1, q_2, q_3\}$, $F = \{q_3\}$, and δ is $\{\langle q_0, m, q_1 \rangle, \langle q_1, e, q_2 \rangle, \langle q_2, o, q_2 \rangle, \langle q_2, w, q_3 \rangle, \langle q_0, w, q_2 \rangle\}$:

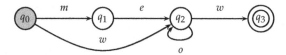

The grammar $G = \langle V, \Sigma, P, S \rangle$ which simulates this automaton has $V = \{q_0, q_1, q_2, q_3\}$, $S = q_0$, and the set of rules:

(1) $q_0 \rightarrow m\, q_1$
(2) $q_1 \rightarrow e\, q_2$
(3) $q_2 \rightarrow o\, q_2$
(4) $q_2 \rightarrow w\, q_3$
(5) $q_0 \rightarrow w\, q_2$
(6) $q_3 \rightarrow \epsilon$

The string *meoow*, for example, is generated by the automaton by walking along the path $q_0 - q_1 - q_2 - q_2 - q_2 - q_3$. The same string is generated by the grammar with the derivation

$$\langle q_0 \rangle \overset{1}{\Rightarrow} \langle mq_1 \rangle \overset{2}{\Rightarrow} \langle meq_2 \rangle \overset{3}{\Rightarrow} \langle meoq_2 \rangle \overset{3}{\Rightarrow} \langle meooq_2 \rangle \overset{4}{\Rightarrow} \langle meoowq_3 \rangle \overset{6}{\Rightarrow} \langle meoow \rangle$$

Since every regular language is also a context-free language, and since we have shown a context-free language that is not regular, we conclude that the class of regular languages is properly contained within the class of context-free languages.

Observing the grammar of Example 34, a certain property of the rules stands out: the body of each of the rules either consists of a terminal followed by a non-terminal or is empty. This is a special case of what are known as *right-linear* grammars. In a right-linear grammar, the body of each rule consists of a (possibly empty) sequence of terminal symbols, optionally followed by a single non-terminal symbol. Most importantly, no rule exists whose body contains more than one non-terminal; and if a non-terminal occurs in the body, it is in the nal position. Right-linear grammars are a restricted variant of context-free grammars, and it can be shown that they generate all and only the regular languages.

5.6 *Formal properties of context-free languages*

Context-free languages are more expressive than regular languages; this additional expressive power comes with a price: given an arbitrary context-free grammar G and some string w, determining whether $w \in L(G)$ takes time proportional to the cube of the length of w, $O(|w|^3)$ (in the worst case). In addition, context-free languages are not closed under some of the operations that the regular languages are closed under.

It should be fairly easy to see that context-free languages are closed under union. Given two context-free grammars $G_1 = \langle V_1, \Sigma_1, P_1, S_1 \rangle$ and $G_2 = \langle V_2, \Sigma_2, P_2, S_2 \rangle$, a grammar $G = \langle V, \Sigma, P, S \rangle$ whose language is $L(G_1) \cup L(G_2)$ can be constructed as follows: the alphabet Σ is the union of Σ_1 and Σ_2, the non-terminal set V is a union of V_1 and V_2, plus a new symbol S, which is the start symbol of G. Then, the rules of G are just the union of the rules of G_1 and G_2, with two additional rules: $S \rightarrow S_1$ and $S \rightarrow S_2$, where S_1 and S_2 are the start symbols of G_1 and G_2 respectively. Clearly, every derivation in G_1 can be simulated by a derivation in G using the same rules exactly, starting with the rule $S \rightarrow S_1$, and similarly for derivations in G_2. Also, since S is a new symbol, no other derivations in G are possible. Therefore $L(G) = L(G_1) \cup L(G_2)$.

A similar idea can be used to show that the context-free languages are closed under concatenation: here we only need one additional rule, namely $S \rightarrow S_1 \, S_2$, and the rest of the construction is identical. Any derivation in G will " rst" derive a string of G_1 (through S_1) and then a string of G_2 (through S_2). To show closure under the Kleene-closure operation, use a similar construction with the added rules $S \rightarrow \epsilon$ and $S \rightarrow S S_1$.

However, it is possible to show that the class of context-free languages is not closed under intersection. That is, if L_1 and L_2 are context-free languages, then it is not guaranteed that $L_1 \cap L_2$ is context-free as well. From this fact it follows that context-free languages are not closed under complementation either. While context-free languages are not closed under intersection, they *are* closed under intersection with regular languages: if L is a context-free language and R is a regular language, then it is guaranteed that $L \cap R$ is context-free.

In the previous section we have shown a correspondence between two speci cation formalisms for regular languages: regular expressions and nite state automata. For context-free languages, we focused on a declarative formalism, namely context-free grammars, but they, too, can be speci ed using a computational model. This model is called *push-down automata*, and it consists of nite state automata augmented with unbounded memory in the form of a *stack*. Computations can use the stack to store and retrieve information: each transition can either push a symbol (taken from a special alphabet) onto the top of the stack, or pop one element off the top of the stack. A computation is successful if it ends in a nal state with an empty stack. It can be shown that the class of languages de ned by push-down automata is exactly the class of context-free languages.

5.7   Normal forms

The general de nition of context-free grammars stipulates that the body of a rule may consist of any sequence of terminal and non-terminal symbols. However, it is possible to restrict the form of the rules without affecting the generative capacity of the formalism. Such restrictions are known as *normal forms* and are the topic of this section.

The best-known normal form is the Chomsky normal form (CNF): under this de nition, rules are restricted to be of either of two forms. The body of any rule in a grammar may consist either of a single terminal symbol, or of exactly two non-terminal symbols (as a special case, empty bodies are also allowed). For example, the rules $D \rightarrow the$ and $NP \rightarrow D N$ can be included in a CNF grammar, but the rule $S \rightarrow a S b$ cannot.

Unlike the right-linear grammars de ned in Section 5.5, which can only generate regular languages, CNF grammars are equivalent in their weak generative capacity to general context-free grammars: it can be proven that for every context-free language L there exists a CNF grammar G such that $L = L(G)$. In other words, CNF grammars can generate all the context-free languages.

The utility of normal forms is in their simplicity. When some property of context-free languages has to be proven, it is sometimes much simpler to prove it for the restricted version of the formalism (e.g., for CNF grammars only), because the result can then extend to the entire class of languages. Similarly, processing normal-form grammars may be simpler than processing the general class of grammars. Thus, the rst parsing algorithms for context-free grammars were limited to grammars in CNF. In natural language grammars, a normal form can embody the distinction between "real" grammar rules and the lexicon; a commonly used normal form de nes grammar rules to have either a single terminal symbol or any sequence of zero or more non-terminal symbols in their body (notice that this is a relaxation of CNF).

6   The Chomsky Hierarchy

6.1   A hierarchy of language classes

We focus in this section on grammars as formalisms which denote languages. We have seen two types of grammars: context-free grammars, which generate the class of context-free languages; and right-linear grammars, which generate the class of regular languages. Right-linear grammars are a special case of context-free grammars, where additional constraints are imposed on the form of the rules. More generally, constraining the form of the rules can constrain the expressive power of the formalism. Similarly, more freedom in the form of the rules can extend the expressiveness of the formalism.

One way to achieve this is to allow more than a single non-terminal symbol in the *head* of the rules or, in other words, restrict the application of rules to a speci ed *context*. In context-free grammars, a rule can be applied during a derivation whenever its head, A, is an element in a form. In the extended formalism such a derivation is allowed only if the context of A in the form, that is, A's neighbors to the right and left, are as speci ed in the rule. Due to this reference to context, this formalism is known as *context-sensitive* grammars. A rule in a context-sensitive grammar has the form $\alpha_1 \, A \, \alpha_2 \rightarrow \alpha_1 \beta \alpha_2$, where α_1, α_2, and β are all (possibly empty) sequences of terminal and non-terminal symbols. The other components of context-sensitive grammars are as in context-free grammars.

As usual, the class of languages that can be generated by context-sensitive grammars is called the *context-sensitive languages*. Considering that every context-free grammar is a special case of context-sensitive grammars (with an empty context), it should be clear that every context-free language is also context-sensitive or, in other words, that the context-free languages are contained in the set of the context-sensitive ones. As it turns out, this containment is proper, and there are context-sensitive languages that are not context-free.

This establishes a *hierarchy* of classes of languages: the regular languages are properly contained in the context-free languages, which are properly contained in the context-sensitive languages. These, in turn, are known to be properly contained in the set of languages generated by the so-called *unrestricted* or *general phrase-structure* grammars (this set is called the *recursively enumerable languages*). Each of the language classes in this hierarchy is associated with a computational model: FSA and push-down automata for the regular and context-free languages respectively; linear bounded Turing machines for the context-sensitive languages; and Turing machines for the recursively enumerable languages.

This hierarchy of language classes is called the *Chomsky hierarchy of languages*, and is schematically depicted in Figure 1.1.

6.2   The location of natural languages in the hierarchy

The Chomsky hierarchy of languages re ects a certain order of complexity: in some sense, the lower the language class is in the hierarchy, the simpler are its possible constructions. Furthermore, lower language classes allow for more ef - cient processing (in particular, the recognition problem is tractable for regular and context-free languages, but not for higher classes). If formal grammars are used to express the structure of *natural* languages, then we must know the location of these languages in the hierarchy.

Chomsky presents a theorem that says "English is not a regular language" (1957: 21); as for context-free languages, he says "I do not know whether or not English is itself literally outside the range of such analyses" (1957: 34). For many years, however, it was well accepted that natural languages were beyond the expressive power of context-free grammars. This was only proven in the 1980s, when two natural languages (Dutch and a dialect of Swiss German) were shown to be trans-context-free (that is, beyond the expressive power of context-free grammars). Still, the constructions in natural languages that necessitate more than

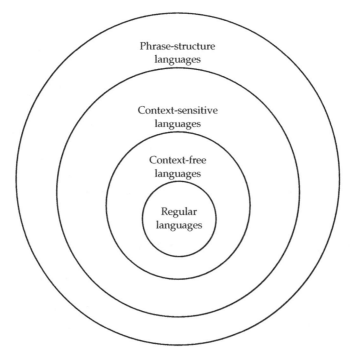

Figure 1.1   Chomsky's hierarchy of languages.

context-free power are few and very speci c. (Most of these constructions boil down to patterns of the form $a^n b^m c^n d^m$, known as *cross-serial dependencies*; with some mathematical machinery, based mostly on closure properties of the context-free languages, it can be proven that languages that include such patterns cannot be context-free.) This motivated the de nition of the class of *mildly context-sensitive languages*, which we discuss in Section 7.

6.3   *Weak and strong generative capacity*

So far we have only looked at grammars as generating sets of strings (i.e., languages), and ignored the structures that grammars impose on the strings in their languages. In other words, when we say that English is not a regular language we mean that no regular expression exists whose denotation is the set of all and only the sentences of English. Similarly, when a claim is made that some natural language, say Dutch, is not context-free, it should be read as saying that no context-free grammar exists whose language is Dutch. Such claims are propositions about the *weak generative capacity* of the formalisms involved: the weak generative capacity of regular expressions is insuf cient for generating English; the weak generative capacity of context-free languages is insuf cient for Dutch. Where natural languages are concerned, however, weak generative capacity might not correctly characterize the relationship between a formalism (such as regular expressions or context-free grammars) and a language (such as English or Dutch). This is because one expects the formalism not only to be able to generate the strings in a language, but also to assign them "correct" structures.

In the case of context-free grammars, the structure assigned to strings is a derivation tree. Other linguistic formalisms may assign other kinds of objects to their sentences. We say that the *strong generative capacity* of some formalism is suf cient to generate some language if the formalism can (weakly) generate all the strings in the language, and also to assign them the "correct" structures. Unlike weak generative capacity, which is a properly de ned mathematical notion, strong generative capacity is poorly de ned, because no accepted de nition of the "correct" structure for some string in some language exists.

7 Mildly Context-Sensitive Languages

When it was nally proven that context-free grammars are not even weakly adequate as models of natural languages, research focused on "mild" extensions of the class of context-free languages. In a seminal work, Joshi (1985) coined the term *mildly context-sensitive languages*, which is loosely de ned as a class of languages that:

(1) properly contains all the context-free languages;
(2) can be parsed in polynomial time;
(3) can properly account for the constructions in natural languages that context-free languages fail to account for, such as cross-serial dependencies; and
(4) has the linear-growth property (this is a formal property that we ignore here).

One formalism that complies with these speci cations (and which motivated their design) is *tree adjoining grammars* (TAGs). Motivated by linguistic considerations, TAGs extend the scope of locality in which linguistic constraints can be expressed. The elementary building blocks of the formalism are trees. Whereas context-free grammar rules enable one to express constraints among the mother in a local tree and its immediate daughters, the elementary trees of TAG facilitate the expression of constraints between arbitrarily distant nodes, as long as they are part of the same elementary tree. Two operations, *adjunction* and *substitution*, construct larger trees from smaller ones, so that the basic operations that take place during derivations are not limited to string concatenation. Crucially, these operations facilitate nesting of one tree within another, resulting in extended expressiveness.

The class of languages generated by tree adjoining grammars is naturally called the *tree adjoining languages*. It contains the context-free languages, and several trans-context-free ones, such as the language $\{a^n b^m c^n d^m \mid n, m \geq 0\}$. As usual, the added expressiveness comes with a price, and determining membership of a string w in a language generated by some TAG can only be done in time proportional to $|w|^6$.

Several linguistic formalisms were proposed as adequate for expressing the class of natural languages. Noteworthy among them are three formalisms: *head grammars*, *linear indexed grammars*, and *combinatory categorial grammars*. All three were developed independently with natural languages as their main motivation; and all three were proven to be (weakly) equivalent to TAG. The class of tree adjoining languages, therefore, may be just the correct formal class in which all natural languages reside.

8   Further Reading

Much of the material presented in this chapter can be found in introductory text-books on formal language theory. Hopcroft and Ullman (1979, chapter 1) provide a formal presentation of formal language theory; just as rigorous, but with an eye to linguistic uses and applications, is the presentation of Partee et al. (1990, chapters 1–3). For the ultimate reference, consult the *Handbook of Formal Languages* (Rozenberg & Salomaa 1997).

A very good formal exposition of regular languages and the computing machinery associated with them is given by Hopcroft and Ullman (1979, chapters 2–3). Another useful source is Partee et al. (1990, chapter 17). Theorem 1 is due to Kleene (1956); Theorem 2 is due to Rabbin and Scott (1959); Theorem 3 is a corollary of the Myhil–Nerode theorem (Nerode 1958). The pumping lemma for regular languages is due to Bar-Hillel et al. (1961).

For natural language applications of nite state technology refer to Roche and Schabes (1997a), which is a collection of papers ranging from mathematical properties of nite state machinery to linguistic modeling using them. The introduction (Roche & Schabes 1997b) can be particularly useful, as will be Karttunen (1991). Kaplan and Kay (1994) is a classic work that sets the very basics of nite state phonology, referring to automata, transducers, and two-level rules. As an example of an extended regular expression language, with an abundance of applications to natural language processing, see Beesley and Karttunen (2003). Finally, Karttunen et al. (1996) is a fairly easy paper that relates regular expressions and relations to nite automata and transducers, and exempli es their use in several language engineering applications.

Context-free grammars and languages are discussed by Hopcroft and Ullman (1979, chapters 4, 6) and Partee et al. (1990, chapter 18). The correspondence between regular languages and right-linear grammars is due to Chomsky and Miller (1958). A cubic-time parsing algorithm for context-free languages was rst proposed by Kasami (1965); see also Younger (1967). Push-down automata were introduced by Oettinger (1961); see also Schützenberger (1963). Chomsky (1962) proved that they were equivalent to context-free grammars.

A linguistic formalism that is based on the ability of context-free grammars to provide adequate analyses for natural languages is generalized phrase-structure grammars, or GPSGs (Gazdar et al., 1985).

The Chomsky hierarchy of languages is due to Chomsky (1956, 1959). The location of the natural languages in this hierarchy is discussed in several papers, of which the most readable, enlightening, and amusing is Pullum and Gazdar (1982). Several other works discussing the non-context-freeness of natural languages are collected in Part III of Savitch et al. (1987). Rounds et al. (1987) inquire into the relations between formal language theory and linguistic theory, in particular referring to the distinction between weak and strong generative capacity. Works showing that natural languages cannot be described by context-free grammars include Bresnan et al. (1982) (Dutch), Shieber (1985) (Swiss German), and Manaster-Ramer (1987) (Dutch). Miller (1999) is dedicated to generative capacity of linguistic formalisms, where strong generative capacity is de ned as the model theoretic semantics of a formalism.

Tree adjoining grammars were introduced by Joshi et al. (1975) and are discussed in several subsequent papers Joshi (1985; 1987; 2003). A polynomial-time parsing algorithm for TAG is given by Vijay-Shanker and Weir (1993) and Satta (1994). The three formalisms that are equivalent to TAG are head grammars (Pollard 1984), linear-indexed grammars (Gazdar 1988), and combinatory categorial grammars (Steedman 2000); they were proven equivalent by Vijay-Shanker and Weir (1994).

2 Computational Complexity in Natural Language

IAN PRATT-HARTMANN

We have become so used to viewing natural language in computational terms that we need occasionally to remind ourselves of the methodological commitment this view entails. That commitment is this: we assume that to understand linguistic tasks – tasks such as recognizing sentences, determining their structure, extracting their meaning, and manipulating the information they contain – is to discover the algorithms required to perform those tasks, and to investigate their computational properties. To be sure, the physical realization of the corresponding processes in humans is a legitimate study too, but one from which the computational investigation of language may be pursued in splendid isolation. Complexity theory is the mathematical study of the resources – both in time and space – required to perform computational tasks. What bounds can we place – from above or below – on the number of steps taken to compute such-and-such a function, or a function belonging to such-and-such a class? What bounds can we place on the amount of memory required? It is therefore not surprising that, in the study of natural language, complexity-theoretic issues abound.

Since *any* computational task can be the object of complexity-theoretic investigation, it would be hopeless even to attempt a complete survey of complexity theory in the study of natural language. We focus therefore on a selection of topics in natural language where there has been a particular accumulation of complexity-theoretic results. Section 2 discusses parsing and recognition; Section 3 discusses the computation of logical form; and Section 4 discusses the problem of determining logical relationships between sentences in natural language. But we begin with a brief review of complexity theory itself.

1 A Brief Review of Complexity Theory

Any account of complexity theory rests on some model of computation. The most widely used such model is the multi-tape Turing machine; and that is the model we use here. Throughout this chapter, we employ standard notation for strings: if

The Handbook of Computational Linguistics and Natural Language Processing, First Edition.
Edited by Alexander Clark, Chris Fox and Shalom Lappin.
© 2013 Blackwell Publishing Ltd except for editorial material and organization
© 2013 Alexander Clark, Chris Fox, and Shalom Lappin. Published 2013 by Blackwell Publishing Ltd.

Σ is an alphabet (a finite, non-empty set of symbols), Σ^* denotes the set of *strings* (finite sequences of elements) over Σ. The length of any string σ is denoted $|\sigma|$; the empty (zero-length) string is denoted ϵ; and the concatenation of strings σ and τ is denoted $\sigma\tau$. We follow standard practice in ignoring the difference between elements of Σ and the corresponding one-element strings.

1.1   Turing machines and models of computation

Informally, a *multi-tape Turing machine* comprises a finite number of *tapes*, a finite set of *states*, and an *instruction table*. The tapes may be thought of as the machine's memory, the states as the line numbers of its program, and the instruction table as the instructions of that program. The tapes are numbered consecutively from 1 to (say) $K \geq 2$; Tape 1 is referred to as the *input tape* and Tape K as the *output tape*; all other tapes are *work-tapes* (Figure 2.1). Each tape consists of a one-way infinite sequence of squares (i.e., there is a leftmost square, but no rightmost square), and is scanned by its own *tape-head*, which is always located over one of these squares. Every square contains a unique symbol, which is either a member of some non-empty, finite set Σ, called the *alphabet* of the Turing machine, or one of the special symbols $\sqcup$ (read: 'blank') or $\triangleright$ (read: 'start').

The set of states, Q, is assumed to contain a pair of distinguished states: the *initial state* q_0 and the *halting state* q_1; otherwise, states have no internal structure. The instruction table of the Turing machine is a finite set T of quintuples

(1) $\langle p, \bar{s}, q, \bar{t}, \bar{d} \rangle$,

where p and q are states (i.e., elements of Q), $\bar{s} = (s_1, \ldots, s_K)$ and $\bar{t} = (t_1, \ldots, t_K)$ are K-tuples of symbols (i.e., elements of $\Sigma \cup \{\sqcup, \triangleright\}$), and $\bar{d} = (d_1, \ldots, d_K)$ is a K-tuple whose elements are the special tags left, right, and stay. Informally, the Turing machine interprets the instruction (1) as follows:

(2)   If the current state is p, and, for each k $(1 \leq k \leq K)$, the square currently being scanned on Tape k contains the symbol s_k, then set the new state to be q, and, for each k $(1 \leq k \leq K)$ do the following: write t_k on the square currently being scanned on Tape k, and place Tape k's head either one square left, or one square right, or in its current location, as directed by d_k.

We can make Tape 1 a read-only tape by insisting that it is never altered (i.e., that $t_1 = s_1$); likewise, we can make Tape K a write-only tape by insisting that its head never moves to the left. The symbol $\triangleright$ is used to indicate the extreme left of a tape: we insist that, if any tape-head is over this symbol, it never receives an instruction to move left; moreover, $\triangleright$ is never written or overwritten. The halting state q_1 indicates that the computation is over, and we insist that no instruction can be executed in this state. (It is easy to specify these conditions formally.) Technically speaking, a Turing machine is simply a tuple $M = \langle K, \Sigma, Q, q_0, q_1, T \rangle$ conforming to the above specifications.

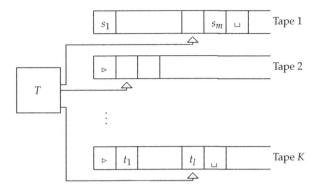

Figure 2.1   Architecture of a multi-tape Turing machine.

Turing machines perform *computations*, which proceed in discrete time-steps. At each time-step, the machine is in a speci c *configuration*, consisting of its current state q, the position of the tape-head for each of the tapes, and the contents of each of the tapes. The initial con guration is as follows: the current state is q_0 (the initial state), with each tape-head positioned over the leftmost square of the tape; Tape 0 has the symbol ▷ in the leftmost square, followed by a string $\sigma \in \Sigma^*$, called the *input* of the computation, and is otherwise   lled with ⊔; all other tapes have the symbol ▷ in the leftmost square, and are otherwise   lled with ⊔. At each time-step, an instruction from T of the form (1) is executed as speci ed in (2), resulting in the next con guration. The computation halts when (and only when) no instruction in T can be executed. Note that, if the halting state q_1 is reached, the computation necessarily halts at that point. A *run* is a (nite or in nite) sequence of con gura-tions obtained in this way; if the run is   nite, so that the Turing machine halts, we call it a *terminating* run. Given a terminating run, the *output* of the computation is the string of Σ^* which, in the   nal con guration, is written on the output tape (strictly) between the ▷ and the   rst ⊔. Notice that, in general, a Turing machine may be able to execute more than one instruction at any given time. In that case, we should think of the choice being made freely by the machine. We call a Turing machine *deterministic* just in case, for any state p and any K-tuple of symbols $\bar{s}$, T contains at most one instruction of the form (1) starting with the pair $\langle p, \bar{s} \rangle$ (i.e., the machine never has a choice as to which instruction to perform). A *non-deterministic Turing machine* is just another term for a Turing machine.

DEFINITION 1 (COMPUTABLE). *Let M be a deterministic Turing machine over alphabet Σ. For any string $\sigma \in \Sigma^*$, either M halts on input σ, or it does not. In the former case, M will output a definite string $\tau \in \Sigma^*$, and we can define the partial function $f_M : \Sigma^* \to \Sigma^*$ as follows.*

$$f_M(\sigma) = \begin{cases} \tau \text{ if M halts on input } \sigma \\ \text{undefined otherwise} \end{cases}$$

We say that M **computes** the function f_M. A partial function $f : \Sigma^* \to \Sigma^*$ is **Turing computable** (or just: **computable**) if it is computed by some deterministic Turing machine.

The instruction table of a Turing machine is xed. Thus, a Turing machine is not a model of a computing machine in the sense we normally imagine, but rather of a computer program: there is only one thing it computes. On the other hand, since Turing machines are, formally, just tuples of nite objects, any Turing machine M can easily be coded as a string σ'_M over a suitable alphabet Σ', and that string can be input to another Turing machine, say M'. It can be shown that there exists a *universal Turing machine* U, which is able to simulate *any* Turing machine M over an alphabet Σ in the following sense: for any string, $\sigma \in \Sigma^*$, M has a non-terminating run on input σ if and only if U has a terminating run on input $\sigma'_M\sigma$; moreover, in case of termination, the output of M' is the same as the output of M. Any such Turing machine U *is* a model of a computing machine in the sense we normally imagine: it is able to execute an arbitrary 'program' σ'_M on arbitrary 'data' σ. Given such a coding scheme, consider the *halting function,* $H : (\Sigma')^* \to \{\top, \bot\}$ de ned as

$$H(\sigma') = \begin{cases} \top \text{ if } \sigma' \text{ encodes a Turing machine } M \text{ that has a terminating run on input } \epsilon \\ \bot \text{ otherwise} \end{cases}$$

This function is clearly well de ned, and indeed total. Perhaps the most fundamental fact in computability theory is due to Turing (1936–7):

THEOREM 1 (TURING). *The halting function is not computable.*

De nition 1 applies to functions $f : \Sigma^* \to \Sigma^*$ for any alphabet Σ. However, this de nition can be extended to functions with other countable domains and ranges, relative to some coding of the relevant inputs and outputs as strings over an alphabet. Consider for instance the familiar coding of natural numbers as bit strings (elements of $\{0,1\}^*$). For $n \in \mathbb{N}$, denote by $\bar{n}$ the standard binary representation of n (without leading zeros); and for $s \in \{0,1\}^*$, denote by #s the natural number represented by s. If $f : \mathbb{N} \to \mathbb{N}$ is a function, we consider f computable if the function $g : \{0,1\}^* \to \{0,1\}^*$ de ned by

$$g(s) = \overline{(f(\#s))}$$

is computable in the sense of De nition 1. Computability of functions with other domains and ranges – e.g., rational numbers, lists, graphs, etc. – is understood similarly. Technically, this extended notion of computability is relative to the coding scheme employed. In practice, however, all reasonable coding schemes usually yield the same computability (and complexity) results; if so, it is legitimate to speak of such functions as being computable or non-computable, leaving the operative coding scheme implicit.

The architecture of Turing machines given above is, in all essential details, that set out in Turing (1936–7). We have followed more recent practice in distinguishing input, output and work-tapes (Turing's machine had a single tape) to make it a little easier to talk about space-bounded computations. But this makes no difference to any of the results reported here. The thesis that Turing computability captures our pre-theoretic notion of computability is generally referred to as the *Church–Turing thesis*. It is important to appreciate that this thesis does not rest on the existence of universal Turing machines, or indeed on any purely mathematical fact. Methodologically, the apparatus introduced above is an exercise in conceptual analysis: the proposed replacement of an informally understood notion with a rigorous de nition. Historically, several competing analyses of computability were proposed at more or less the same time, most notably Gödel's notion of *recursive function* and Church's λ-calculus. All three notions in effect coincide, however; so there is general consensus about the formal model presented here. For an accessible modern treatment, see Papadimitriou (1994, Chapter 2).

The fundamental goal of complexity theory is to analyze the resources, in either time or space, required to perform computational tasks. The rst step is to measure the computational resources required by particular algorithms.

DEFINITION 2. *Let M be a Turing machine with alphabet Σ, and let $g : \mathbb{N} \to \mathbb{N}$ be a function. We say M **runs in time** g if, for all but finitely many strings $\sigma \in \Sigma^*$, any run of M on input σ halts within at most $g(|\sigma|)$ steps. Similarly, M **runs in space** g if, for all but finitely many strings $\sigma \in \Sigma^*$, any run of M on input σ uses at most $g(|\sigma|)$ squares on any of its work-tapes.*

Allowing M to break the bound g in nitely many cases avoids problems caused by zero-length inputs and other trivial anomalies. Notice also the asymmetry in the de nitions of time and space complexity: because measures of space complexity include only the *work-tapes* (and so exclude the input and output tapes), they can be *sublinear*. For time complexity, sublinear bounds make little sense, because they do not give the machine the opportunity to read its input.

Unfortunately, De nition 2 is too fragile to provide a meaningful measure of algorithmic complexity. Suppose M is a deterministic Turing machine computing some function in time g, and let c be a positive number. Provided g is moderately fast-growing (say, faster than linear growth), it is routine to construct another deterministic Turing machine M' – perhaps with more tapes or more states or a larger alphabet – that computes the same function in time $cg(n)$. That is: we can always speed up M by a linear factor! Since M and M' do not represent interestingly different algorithms, the statement that a Turing machine runs in time – say – $3n^2 + n + 4$ as opposed to $14n^2 + 87n + 11$ is, from an algorithmic point of view, not signi cant. Similar remarks also apply to space bounds.

DEFINITION 3. *Let M be a Turing machine, and G a set of functions from $\mathbb{N}$ to $\mathbb{N}$. We say that M **runs in time** G if, for some $g \in G$, M runs in time g. Similarly, we say that M **runs in space** G if, for some $g \in G$, M runs in space g.*

In particular, the following classes of functions suggest themselves.

DEFINITION 4 (*O*-NOTATION). *Let $g : \mathbb{N}^k \to \mathbb{N}$ be a function. Denote by $O(g)$ the set of functions*

$$O(g) = \{g' : \mathbb{N}^k \to \mathbb{N} \mid \text{there exist } c \in \mathbb{N}, n'_1, \dots, n'_k \in \mathbb{N} \text{ s.t.}$$

$$\text{for all } n_1 > n'_1 \dots \text{for all } n_k > n'_k, g'(n_1, \dots, n_k) \leq cg(n_1, \dots, n_k)\}$$

Informally, $O(g)$ is the class of functions which are eventually dominated by some positive multiple of g. Combining Definitions 3 and 4, it makes sense to say, for example, that a given Turing machine runs in time (or space) $O(n^2)$, or $O(n^3)$, or $O(2^n)$. And this sort of complexity measure, it turns out, is *robust* under the expansions of computational resources considered above. For example, it can be shown that, for any $k > 0$, there is a function that can be computed by a deterministic Turing machine running in time $O(n^{k+1})$ which cannot be computed by any deterministic Turing machine running in time $O(n^k)$; and similarly for space bounds. (The precise statement of these theorems, known as *separation theorems*, is somewhat intricate; see Kozen, 2006, Lecture 3, or Papadimitriou, 1994: 143ff.) O-notation has the further advantage of permitting a useful degree of informality when analyzing the complexity of an algorithm, since a pseudo-code description of that algorithm, of the sort standardly found in computing texts, often suffices to show that it will run in time or space $O(g)$ (for some function g) without our having first to compile that description into a Turing machine. Finally, a word of caution. Knowing that a Turing machine (or algorithm) has time complexity $O(g)$ at best imposes a bound on how rapidly the cost of computation grows with the size of the input. That is, the complexity measures in question are *asymptotic*. In many cases, algorithms with suboptimal asymptotic complexity measures perform best in practice.

1.2   Decision problems

So far, we have discussed complexity measures for particular algorithms, understood as deterministic Turing machines. We now develop this idea in two crucial – though logically quite separate – ways.

The first development extends Definition 1 to *non-deterministic* computation. To do this, we first restrict attention to functions whose range contains just two elements – we conventionally employ $\top$ and $\bot$ – representing 'YES' and 'NO' respectively. A function $f : A \to \{\top, \bot\}$, where A is a countable set, is called a *decision problem*, or simply a *problem*. While decision problems may initially seem of limited practical interest, they play a central role in complexity theory. Moreover, the restriction to decision problems is less severe than might at first appear: the complexity of many functions can often be usefully characterized in terms of the complexity of closely related decision problems.

Now, any decision problem $f : A \to \{\top, \bot\}$ can alternatively be regarded as a *subset* of A – namely, the subset $\{a \in A \mid f(a) = \top\}$. In particular, if $A = \Sigma^*$ for some alphabet Σ (or if the encoding of A in Σ^* is obvious), a decision problem de ned on A is, in effect, a set of strings over Σ, or, in the parlance of formal language theory, a *language* over Σ. Conversely, of course, any language $L \subseteq \Sigma^*$ may be regarded as a decision problem $f : \Sigma^* \to \{\top, \bot\}$ given by:

$$f(\sigma) = \begin{cases} \top & \text{if } \sigma \in L \\ \bot & \text{otherwise} \end{cases}$$

The observation that decision problems and languages are essentially the same thing prompts the following de nition.

DEFINITION 5. *Let M be a Turing machine over the alphabet Σ, and suppose without loss of generality that Σ contains the symbol $\top$. We say that M **accepts** a string $\sigma \in \Sigma^*$ if there exists a terminating run of M with input σ and output $\top$. The language $L \subseteq \Sigma^*$ **recognized** by M, denoted $L(M)$, is the set of strings accepted by M.*

It is important to bear in mind that, in De nition 5, M can be *non-deterministic*. That is: $L(M)$ is the set of inputs for which M *may* yield the output $\top$. (It is sometimes convenient to imagine a benign helper guiding M to make the 'right' choice of instructions required to accept a string $\sigma \in L$.) Equally important is that, if $\sigma \notin L$, there is no requirement for M to produce any particular output (as long as it is not $\top$, of course), or indeed to halt at all.

The case where M halts on every input is of particular interest, however:

DEFINITION 6 (DECIDABLE). *Let L be a language. We call L **decidable** if it is recognized by a Turing machine guaranteed to halt on every input.*

It is routine to show that any decidable language is in fact recognized by a *deterministic* Turing machine that halts on every input. Furthermore, that machine can easily be modi ed so as always to produce one of the two outputs $\top$, $\bot$. Thus, a decision problem $f : \Sigma^* \to \{\top, \bot\}$ is a computable function, in the sense of De nition 1, just in case the corresponding language $L = \{\sigma | f(\sigma) = \top\}$ is decidable, in the sense of De nition 6. Henceforth, then, we shall identify decision problems and languages, employing whichever term is most appropriate in context.

We may think of De nition 5 as a generalization of De nition 1 to the case of *non-deterministic* computation. The signi cance of this generalization is that, while deterministic and non-deterministic Turing machines recognize the same class of languages, they may not in general do so within the same computational bounds, a possibility which plays a central role in complexity theory.

We can generalize the above observations on linear speedup to the case of non-deterministic computation for decision problems. We give a reasonably precise version here:

THEOREM 2. *Let L be a language over some alphabet, let $g : \mathbb{N} \to \mathbb{N}$ and $h : \mathbb{N} \to \mathbb{N}$ be functions, let $c \geq 1$, and suppose $g(n) \geq n + 1$, and $h(n) \geq \log n$. If L is recognized by some Turing machine running in time $cg(n)$, then it is recognized by some Turing machine running in time $g(n)$. If L is recognized by some Turing machine running in* *space ch(n), then it is recognized by some Turing machine running in space h(n). The previous statements continue to hold when "Turing machine" is replaced throughout by "deterministic Turing machine."*

Now for the second development in our analysis of complexity. So far, we have provided measures of the time and space requirements of particular *Turing machines* (or, by extension, and using *O*-notation, of particular *algorithms*). But what primarily interests us in complexity theory are the time and space requirements of a *maximally efficient* Turing machine for computing a particular *function* or, more speci cally, solving a particular *decision problem*. Recalling the equivalence between decision problems and languages discussed above, we de ne:

DEFINITION 7. *Let L be a language over some alphabet, and let G be a set of functions from* $\mathbb{N}$ *to* $\mathbb{N}$. *We say that L is in* TIME(G) (*or* SPACE(G)) *if there exists a deterministic Turing machine M recognizing L, such that M runs in time (respectively, space) G.*

Classes of languages of the form TIME(G) or SPACE(G) are referred to as (deterministic) complexity classes. To avoid notational clutter, if g is a function from $\mathbb{N}$ to $\mathbb{N}$, we write TIME(g) instead of TIME($\{g\}$); and similarly for other complexity classes.

So far, we have encountered classes of functions of the form $O(g)$ for various g. When analyzing the complexity of *languages* (rather than of speci c algorithms), however, larger classes of functions are typically more useful.

DEFINITION 8. *Let P, E, and* E_k (*for* $k > 1$) *be the sets of functions from* $\mathbb{N}$ *to* $\mathbb{N}$ *defined as follows:*

$$P = \left\{ n^c \mid c > 0 \right\}$$

$$E = \left\{ 2^{n^c} \mid c > 0 \right\}$$

$$E_2 = \left\{ 2^{2^{n^c}} \mid c > 0 \right\}$$

$$E_k = \left\{ \left. 2^{2^{\cdot^{\cdot^{2}}}} \right\}^{n^c}_{k \ times} \mid c > 0 \right\}$$

A function $g : \mathbb{N} \to \mathbb{N}$ *which is in* E_k *for some k is said to be* **elementary**.

Non-elementary functions grow rapidly. However, it is easy to de ne a computable function which is non-elementary:

$$f(n) = 2^{2^{\cdot^{\cdot^{2}}}} \}^{n \ times}$$

Combining De nitions 7 and 8, we obtain complexity classes which are often known under the following, more pronounceable names:

$$LOGSPACE = SPACE(\log n)$$

$$PTIME = TIME(P) \qquad PSPACE = SPACE(P)$$
$$EXPTIME = TIME(E) \qquad EXPSPACE = SPACE(E)$$
$$k\text{-}EXPTIME = TIME(E_k) \qquad k\text{-}EXPSPACE = SPACE(E_k)$$

Thus, PTIME is the class of languages recognizable by a deterministic Turing machine in polynomial time, EXPSPACE, the class of languages recognizable by a deterministic Turing machine in exponential space, and so on. In some texts, LOGSPACE is referred to as L, PTIME as P, and EXPTIME as EXP. Notice, incidentally, that there is no point in de ning, say, $G = \{\log(n^c) \mid c > 0\}$ and then setting LOGSPACE $=$ SPACE(G), since, by Theorem 2, linear factors may be ignored. Finally, if L is not recognizable by any Turing machine running in time bounded by an elementary function, then L is said to have *non-elementary complexity*. We shall encounter examples of decidable, but non-elementary, problems below.

De nition 7 may be adapted directly to deal with non-deterministic computation.

DEFINITION 9. *Let L be a language over some alphabet, and let G be a set of functions from $\mathbb{N}$ to $\mathbb{N}$. We say that L is in NTIME(G) (or NSPACE(G)) if there exists a Turing machine M recognizing L, such that M runs in time (respectively, space) G.*

Classes of languages of the form NTIME(G) or NSPACE(G) are referred to as (non-deterministic) complexity classes.

Combining De nitions 8 and 9, we obtain complexity classes which are often known under the following, more pronounceable names:

$$NLOGSPACE = NSPACE(\log n)$$

(3) $\qquad NPTIME = NTIME(P) \qquad NPSPACE = NSPACE(P)$
$$NEXPTIME = NTIME(E) \qquad NEXPSPACE = NSPACE(E)$$
$$Nk\text{-}EXPTIME = NTIME(E_k) \qquad Nk\text{-}EXPSPACE = NSPACE(E_k)$$

In some texts, NLOGSPACE is referred to as NL, NPTIME as NP, and NEXPTIME as NEXP.

Notice the asymmetry involved in the notion of non-deterministic computation: M recognizes $L \subseteq \Sigma^*$ just in case, for each string $\sigma \in \Sigma^*$, $\sigma \in L$ if and only if *there exists* a successfully terminating run of M (i.e., a terminating run with output $\top$) on input σ – that is to say, $\sigma \in \Sigma^* \setminus L$ if and only if *all* runs of M on input σ fail to halt successfully. This asymmetry prompts us to de ne the *complement* classes as follows.

DEFINITION 10. *If $\mathcal{C}$ is a class of languages, then Co-$\mathcal{C}$ is the class of languages L such that $\Sigma^* \setminus L$ is in $\mathcal{C}$, where Σ is the alphabet of L.*

It is easy to see that, for any interesting class of functions G, TIME(G) = Co-TIME(G) and SPACE(G) = Co-SPACE(G). For this reason, we never speak of

Co-PTIME, Co-PSPACE, etc. The situation with non-deterministic complexity classes is different, however. It is not known whether NPTIME = Co-NPTIME; and similarly for many other classes of the form Co-NTIME(G). Indeed, such complexity classes are regularly encountered. In particular, putting together Definition 10, and the NTIME-classes listed in (3), we obtain the complexity classes Co-NPTIME, Co-NEXPTIME, and Co-Nk-EXPTIME. (And similarly for the corresponding space-complexity classes; but see Theorem 4.)

1.3   Relations between complexity classes

It is obvious from the above definitions that any language in TIME(G) (or SPACE(G)) is non-deterministically recognizable within the same bounds. Formally,

$$\text{TIME}(G) \subseteq \text{NTIME}(G) \qquad \text{SPACE}(G) \subseteq \text{NSPACE}(G)$$

A little less obviously, we see that:

$$\text{NPTIME} \subseteq \text{EXPTIME} \qquad \text{NEXPTIME} \subseteq \text{2-EXPTIME} \qquad \cdots$$

Consider the first of these inclusions. If M non-deterministically recognizes L, and p is a polynomial such that M is guaranteed to halt within time $p(n)$ on input of size n, the number of possible runs of M on inputs of this size is easily seen to be bounded by $2^{q(n)}$ for some polynomial q. But then a deterministic Turing machine M', simulating M, can check all of these runs in exponential time, outputting $\top$ if any one of them halts successfully. Hence, NPTIME $\subseteq$ EXPTIME. The inclusion NEXPTIME $\subseteq$ 2-EXPTIME follows analogously; and so on up the complexity hierarchy. In fact, similar arguments establish the following more elaborate system of inclusions.

$$\begin{array}{c} \text{PTIME} \subseteq \text{NPTIME} \subseteq \text{PSPACE} \subseteq \\ \text{EXPTIME} \subseteq \text{NEXPTIME} \subseteq \text{EXPSPACE} \subseteq \\ \text{2-EXPTIME} \subseteq \text{2-NEXPTIME} \cdots \end{array}$$

(4)

The following result establishes that, for classes of sufficiently 'large' functions, non-determinism makes no difference to space complexity (Savitch 1970).

THEOREM 3 (SAVITCH). *If $g(n) \geq \log n$, then* NSPACE($g(n)$) $\subseteq$ SPACE($(g(n))^2$)

In some statements of this theorem, certain technical conditions are imposed on g; but see, e.g., Kozen (2006: 15–16). Since the classes of functions P, E, E_2, etc. are closed under squaring, we have NPSPACE = PSPACE, NEXPSPACE = EXPSPACE, and so on. As an instant corollary, since these deterministic classes are equal to their complements, we have NPSPACE = Co-NPSPACE, NEXPSPACE = Co-NEXPSPACE, and so on.

Care is required when applying the reasoning of the previous paragraph. Setting $g(n) = \log n$, Theorem 3 tells us that NLOGSPACE $\subseteq$ SPACE$((\log n)^2)$; however, this is not suf cient to imply that NLOGSPACE $\subseteq$ LOGPSPACE. Nevertheless, the following result establishes that equivalence under complementation continues to hold even in this case (Immerman 1988).

THEOREM 4 (IMMERMAN–SZELEPCSÉNYI). *If $g(n) \geq \log n$, then NSPACE$(g(n))$ = Co-NSPACE$(g(n))$*

In some statements of this theorem, certain technical conditions are imposed on g; but again, see Kozen (2006: 22–4). As a special case, we have NSPACE(n) = Co-NSPACE(n), which settled a long-standing conjecture in formal language theory (see Section 2.3 below). As an instant corollary of Theorem 4, NLOGSPACE = Co-NLOGSPACE.

Adding these 'small' complexity classes to the inclusions (4), we obtain

(5)
$$\begin{aligned}
\text{LOGSPACE} \subseteq \text{NLOGSPACE} \subseteq \text{PTIME} \subseteq \text{NPTIME} \subseteq \\
\text{PSPACE} \subseteq \text{EXPTIME} \subseteq \text{NEXPTIME} \subseteq \\
\text{EXPSPACE} \subseteq \text{2-EXPTIME} \subseteq \text{2-NEXPTIME} \cdots
\end{aligned}$$

1.4 Lower bounds

Notwithstanding the above caveats on the interpretation of asymptotic complexity measures, saying that a language is in a complexity class $\mathcal{C}$ places some kind of *upper bound* on the resources required to recognize it. But what of *lower bounds*? What if we want to say that a language *cannot* be recognized within certain time or space bounds? For the complexity classes introduced above, useful lower-bound characterizations are indeed possible.

The basic idea is that of a *reduction* of one language (or decision problem) to another. Let L_1 and L_2 be languages, perhaps over different alphabets Σ_1 and Σ_2. Suppose that there exists a function $g : \Sigma_1^* \to \Sigma_2^*$ such that, for any string $\sigma \in \Sigma_1^*$, $\sigma \in L_1$ if and only if $g(\sigma) \in L_2$. We may think of g as a means of 'translating' L_1 into L_2: in particular, any Turing machine recognizing L_2 can be modi ed to recognize L_1 by simply prepending the translation g. If the cost of this translation is small, then we may regard L_2 as being 'at least as hard to recognize as' L_1.

DEFINITION 11 (REDUCTION). *Let Σ_1 and Σ_2 be alphabets, and let L_i be a language over Σ_i ($i = 1, 2$). A **reduction** of L_1 to L_2 is a function $g : \Sigma_1^* \to \Sigma_2^*$, such that g can be computed by a (deterministic) Turing machine in space $O(\log n)$, and for all $\sigma \in \Sigma_1^*$, $\sigma \in L_1$ if and only if $g(\sigma) \in L_2$; in that case, we say that L_1 is **reducible to** L_2. If, instead, g can merely be computed in time $O(n^k)$ for some k, we call it a **polynomial reduction**, and we say that L_1 is **polynomially reducible to** L_2.*

Let C be any of the complexity classes mentioned in (5), or the complement of any of these classes. It can be shown that, if L_2 is in C, and L_1 is reducible to L_2, then L_1 is in C. We say that C is 'closed under reductions'. If C is any of the complexity classes mentioned in (4), then C is, similarly, 'closed under polynomial reductions.'

THEOREM 5. *The relation of reducibility is transitive: if L_1 is reducible to L_2, and L_2 to L_3, then L_1 is reducible to L_3.*

We remark that Theorem 5 is not obvious (though its analogue in the case of *polynomial* reducibility is) see, e.g., Papadimitriou (1994: 164).
    Now we can give our characterization of lower complexity bounds.

DEFINITION 12 (HARDNESS AND COMPLETENESS). *Let C be a complexity class. A language L is said to be **hard for** C, or C-**hard**, if any language in C is reducible to L; L is said to be **complete for** C, or C-**complete**, if L is C-hard and also in C. Additionally, L is said to be C-**hard under polynomial reduction** if any decision problem in C is polynomially reducible to L; similarly for C-**completeness under polynomial reduction**.*

It follows from Theorem 5 that, if L_1 is C-hard for some complexity class C, and L_1 is reducible to L_2, then L_2 is C-hard. Similarly, *mutatis mutandis*, for hardness under polynomial reductions. Notice that the notion of LOGSPACE-completeness is uninteresting: any problem in LOGSPACE is by de nition LOGSPACE-complete. Under polynomial reductions, the notion of PTIME-completeness is similarly uninteresting. De nition 12 re ects the fact that reducibility in logarithmic space is taken to be the default in complexity theory. However, for most higher complexity classes, it is generally easier and just as informative to work with reducibility in polynomial time; and this is what is often done in practice. Hardness results, in the sense of De nition 12, are sometimes referred to, for obvious reasons, as 'lower complexity bounds.' However, it is important not to be misled by this terminology: for example, it is easy to show that there are PTIME-hard problems in TIME(n); but TIME(n) is properly contained in PTIME!
    Many natural problems (it is easier here to speak of problems rather than languages) can be shown to be complete for the complexity classes introduced above. Here are three very well-known examples. In the context of propositional logic, a *literal* is a proposition letter or a negated proposition letter; proposition letters are said to be *positive* literals, their negations *negative* literals. A *clause* is a disjunction of literals; a clause is said to be *Horn* if it contains at most one positive literal. Theorems 6–9 are among the most fundamental in complexity theory. For an accessible treatment, see, e.g., Papadimitriou (1994: 171, 176, and 398 respectively). Theorem 6 is due to Cook (1971).

THEOREM 6 (COOK). *The problem of determining whether a given set of clauses is satisfiable is NPTIME-complete.*

THEOREM 7. *The problem of determining whether a given set of Horn clauses is satisfiable is PTIME-complete.*

THEOREM 8. *The problem of determining the satisfiability of a given set of clauses, all of which contain at most two literals, is NLOGSPACE-complete.*

Theorem 8 is very closely related to the following graph-theoretical problem. Given a finite directed graph, one node in that graph is said to be *reachable* from another if there is a finite sequence of directed edges in that graph leading from the first node to the second.

THEOREM 9. *The problem of determining whether, in a given directed graph, one node is reachable from another, is NLOGSPACE-complete.*

Note that, in each case, we assume that inputs (clauses, graphs, ...) are coded in some standard way as strings over some alphabet. All reasonable coding schemes yield the same complexity results.

Such completeness results are often less surprising than they at first appear. For example, Theorem 6 is established by showing that, given a non-deterministic Turing machine M that runs in polynomial time, the conditions for a sequence of configurations of M to be a run of M with input σ can be encoded, in a natural way, as a set of clauses whose size is bounded by a polynomial function of the length of σ. And once one language L is shown to be hard for a complexity class, other languages can be shown to be hard for that class by showing that L is reducible to them.

2 Parsing and Recognition

As already mentioned, in the context of formal language theory, a *language* is a set of strings over some alphabet Σ. Some languages are specified by *grammars*, which are themselves finite objects whose semantics is defined by a *grammar framework*. Familiar grammar frameworks are: context-sensitive grammars, definite clause grammars, tree adjoining grammars, context-free grammars, and non-deterministic finite state automata. Within a given grammar framework $\mathcal{F}$, any grammar G *recognizes* a unique language $L(G)$, namely, the set of strings *accepted* by G. Thus, the apparatus of the multi-tape Turing machine also constitutes a grammar framework in this sense. Each grammar in that framework – that is, each specific Turing machine M over signature Σ – recognizes the language $L(M)$ comprising the set of strings over Σ accepted by M, in the sense of Definition 5.

If $\mathcal{F}$ is a grammar framework, we understand the *universal recognition problem* for $\mathcal{F}$ to be the following problem: given a grammar G in $\mathcal{F}$ and a string σ over the alphabet of G, determine whether $\sigma \in L(G)$. This problem is to be distinguished from the *fixed-language recognition problem* for any G in $\mathcal{F}$: given a string σ over the alphabet of G, determine whether $\sigma \in L(G)$. The complexity of the universal recognition problem for a framework $\mathcal{F}$ is in general higher than that of the fixed-language recognition problem for any grammar in $\mathcal{F}$.

In this section, we survey the complexity of the universal recognition problem and the fixed-language recognition problem for various grammar frameworks. For the framework of Turing machines, we already know the answer: it is (essentially) a restatement of Theorem 1 that the universal recognition problem for Turing machines is undecidable; and it is an immediate consequence of the existence of a universal Turing machine that there exist Turing machines whose xed-language recognition problem is undecidable. For less expressive grammar frameworks, however, there is much more to be said, as we shall see.

2.1   Regular languages

Let us begin with one of the least expressive of the commonly encountered grammar frameworks. A *non-deterministic finite state automaton* (NFSA) is a tuple $\mathcal{A} = \langle \Sigma, Q, q_0, q_1, T \rangle$, where Σ is an alphabet, Q a set (the set of *states* of $\mathcal{A}$), q_0 and q_1 distinct elements of Q (the *initial state* and the *accepting state* respectively), and T a nite set of triples $\langle p, s, q \rangle$ (the *transitions* of $\mathcal{A}$), where $p, q \in Q$ and $s \in \Sigma$. Informally, the transition $\langle p, s, q \rangle$ has the interpretation

> If the current state is p, and the next symbol to be read is s, then set the new state to be q.

An NFSA $\mathcal{A}$ is said to *accept* the string $\sigma = s_1, \ldots, s_n$ if, starting in the state q_0, and reading the symbols $s_1, \ldots, s_n$ successively, there is a sequence of transitions in T leading to the state q_1. NFSAs may be pictured as labeled graphs in the obvious way: the nodes are labeled by elements of Q, and the edges by elements of Σ. A string is accepted if it is possible to step through the graph from the initial state to the nal state in such a way that the string is exactly consumed.

It is a standard result of formal language theory that the class of languages accepted by NFSAs coincides with the class of regular languages. A *regular expression* over an alphabet Σ is de ned recursively to be any expression of the forms $\emptyset$, ϵ, s, $e_1 \cup e_2$, $e_1 e_2$, or e^*, where $s \in \Sigma$ and e, e_1, and e_2 are regular expressions. Any regular expression e recognizes a language $L(e)$ over Σ, de ned (with harmless abuse of notation) as follows:

$$L(\emptyset) = \emptyset \qquad\qquad L(e_1 \cup e_2) = L(e_1) \cup L(e_2)$$
$$L(\epsilon) = \{\epsilon\} \qquad\qquad L(e_1 e_2) = \{\sigma\tau \mid \sigma \in L(e_1) \text{ and } \tau \in L(e_2)\}$$
$$L(s) = \{s\} \text{ for } s \in \Sigma \qquad L(e^*) = \{\sigma_1 \ldots \sigma_k \mid k \geq 0 \text{ and } \sigma_i \in L(e) \text{ for all } i \ (1 \leq i \leq k)\}$$

A *regular language* is any language $L(e)$, where e is a regular expression.

Deciding whether a given NFSA accepts a given string is easily reducible to the problem of reachability in directed graphs, and vice versa. By Theorem 9, therefore, we have:

THEOREM 10. *The universal recognition problem for NFSAs is NLOGSPACE-complete.*

What about the xed-language recognition problem? An NFSA can be thought of as a Turing machine with a nite memory – that is, a Turing machine which never uses more than a constant amount of space on any of its work-tapes. With a little care, this equivalence can be shown to be exact: a language is regular if and only if it can be recognized by a Turing machine with xed space bound. Hence:

THEOREM 11. *For any NFSA $\mathcal{A}$, $L(\mathcal{A})$ is in SPACE(c) for some constant c.*

Thus, the universal recognition problem for NFSAs has higher complexity than the recognition problem for any speci c regular language. A subtly different illustration of this phenomenon is provided by the grammar framework of extended regular expressions. An *extended regular expression* over an alphabet Σ is de ned exactly as for regular expressions, except that we have a complementation operator $\bar{e}$, with semantics given by:

$$L(\bar{e}) = \Sigma^* \setminus L(e)$$

A well-known theorem of formal language theory states that the class of regular languages is closed under complementation, and hence is equal to the class of languages recognized by extended regular expressions. Thus, the grammar frameworks of NFSAs and extended regular expressions are equal in expressive power. However, Stockmeyer and Meyer (1973: 3) show that:

THEOREM 12. *The universal recognition problem for extended regular expressions is in PTIME.*

Theorem 12 does not immediately follow from Theorem 10: extended regular expressions constitute a more compact way of specifying regular languages than do NFSAs. Of course, when it comes to the xed-language recognition problem for languages de ned by extended regular expressions, this must be the same as for NFSAs, because they are the same languages. For a useful list of complexity-theoretic results regarding regular languages, see Yu (1997: 96ff.).

2.2 Context-free languages

Probably the most familiar and useful grammar framework in linguistics is that of context-free grammars. Formally, a *context-free grammar* (CFG) is a quadruple $G = \langle N, \Sigma, S, P \rangle$, where N is a set of *non-terminals* (typically, category labels such as S, NP, VP, etc.), Σ an alphabet, S a distinguished *start symbol* in N (for example, the category S), and P a list of *productions* for rewriting non-terminals (such as S → NP VP, NP → Det N, etc.). Elements of Σ are usually referred to as *terminals* in this context. A CFG accepts the string of terminals σ if some sequence of productions can be found which rewrites the start symbol S to σ. A language recognized by a CFG is called a *context-free language*. For example, the language $\{a^n b^n \mid n \geq 0\}$ is context-free, but not regular. (For a detailed discussion, see Chapter 1, Section 6.)

A number of well-known algorithms exist to determine whether, given a CFG G and a string σ, G accepts σ. Perhaps the best known is the *CYK* algorithm, named after its simultaneous inventors, Cocke, Younger, and Kasami (see, e.g., Younger 1967). Under reasonable assumptions about what quali es as a constant-time operation, this algorithm runs in time $O(mn^3)$, where m is the number of productions in G, and n is the length of σ; however, it requires that the given grammar G be in Chomsky normal form. The slightly more sophisticated algorithm of Earley (1970) dispenses with this assumption. Thus, the universal recognition problem for context-free languages is in PTIME. Furthermore, it is easy to reduce this problem to the satis ability problem for Horn clauses in propositional logic, whence, by Theorem 7, it is also PTIME-hard (Jones & Laaser 1977). Hence:

THEOREM 13. *The universal recognition problem for CFGs is PTIME-complete.*

On the other hand, for the xed-language recognition problem, we can again do a little better (Lewis et al., 1965; Nepomnyashchii 1975):

THEOREM 14. *For any CFG G, $L(G)$ is in SPACE$((\log n)^2)$. Moreover, there exists a context-free language which is NLOGSPACE-hard.*

The proof in both cases is rather technical.

CFGs are not the only way of describing context-free languages: the framework of *Lambek grammars* (Lambek 1958) provides an alternative. We content ourselves with an informal explanation here, referring the reader to, e.g., Carpenter (1997). The *Lambek calculus (with product)* is a logical system allowing the derivation of *sequents* involving *category expressions*. A category expression is either a *basic category* or a *derived category* of the forms X/Y, $Y\backslash X$, or $X \cdot Y$. Examples of basic categories are S and NP. Examples of derived categories are NP$\backslash$S, NP $\cdot$ NP, and (NP$\backslash$S)/NP. Intuitively, a category expression X/Y describes a string which, when a string of category Y is placed to its *right*, will result in a string of category X; similarly, $Y\backslash X$ describes a string which, when a string of category Y is placed to its *left*, will result in a string of category X; and nally, $X \cdot Y$ describes a string which is the result of concatenating a string of category X and a string of category Y. Thus, an intransitive verb, and indeed any verb phrase, might be assigned category NP$\backslash$S, while a transitive verb might be assigned category (NP$\backslash$S)/NP.

A *sequent* in the Lambek calculus is an expression of the form

$$X_1 \cdots X_n \rightarrow X,$$

where $X_1, \ldots, X_n$ and X are category expressions. Intuitively, such a sequent has the meaning: "The result of concatenating any strings of categories $X_1, \ldots, X_n$, in that order, is a string of category X." An example of a sequent is

(6)   NP (NP$\backslash$S)/NP NP $\rightarrow$ S,

which thus has the informal interpretation

(7)   if σ_1, σ_2, and σ_3 are strings of categories NP, (NP$\backslash$S)/NP, and NP respectively, then $\sigma_1 \sigma_2 \sigma_3$ is of category S.

We remark that, under the advertised interpretations of the relevant derived categories, (7) is a true statement. Formally, however, it is the rules of the Lambek

$$\frac{\dfrac{S \to S \qquad NP \to NP}{NP \ (NP\backslash S) \to S} \ (\backslash I) \qquad NP \to NP}{NP \ (NP\backslash S)/NP \ NP \to S} \ (/I)$$

Figure 2.2   A derivation in the Lambek calculus.

calculus (rather than judgments such as (7)) that determine whether any given sequent is derivable. We do not give these rules here. As an example, however, Figure 2.2 shows the derivation of sequent (6). It can be shown that the rules of the Lambek calculus are correct and complete for the interpretation given above (Pentus 1994).

A *Lambek grammar (with product)* over a signature Σ is a ﬁnite list G of pairs of the form (s, C) where $s \in \Sigma$ and C is a category expression. We say that the grammar G *accepts* the string $\sigma = s_1 \ldots s_n$ just in case there exist category expressions $C_1, \ldots, C_n$ such that: (i) $(s_i, C_i) \in G$ for each i ($1 \le i \le n$), and (ii) the sequent $C_1 \cdots C_n \to S$ can be derived in the Lambek calculus. (Again, S is a distinguished start symbol.) For example, if G contains the pairs

$\quad$ (John, NP), $\qquad$ (Mary, NP), $\qquad$ (loves, (NP\S)/NP),

then, since (6) is a valid sequent, G accepts the sentence 'John loves Mary.' It is known (Pentus 1993, 1997) that the class of languages recognized by Lambek grammars is exactly the class of context-free languages.

A crucial result concerning the Lambek calculus is the so-called *cut-elimination theorem* (Lambek 1958), which allows us to show that the problem of determining the validity of a given sequent in the Lambek calculus is in NPTIME. More recently, Pentus (2006) has shown that the problem of determining the validity of a sequent in the Lambek calculus (with product) is NPTIME-complete. This immediately translates, in the present context, to the following result.

THEOREM 15 (PENTUS). *The universal recognition problem for Lambek grammars (with product) is NPTIME-complete.*

We remark in passing that the corresponding problem for the Lambek calculus without the product operation $\cdot$ (i.e., just the operations / and \) is, at the time of writing, open. This restriction does not decrease the class of languages which can be recognized by such grammars: these are still exactly the context-free languages.

2.3   *More expressive grammar frameworks*

As the preceding discussion illustrates, the complexity of the universal recognition problem for a grammar framework cannot be read off in any simple way from its expressive power. Nevertheless, commonly encountered grammar frameworks with higher expressive power do tend, by and large, to exhibit higher recognition complexity. A well-known example is provided by the class of *tree adjoining grammars* (TAGs). A more detailed explanation of TAGs can be found in Chapter 4, Section 7. Very roughly, a TAG is a nite set of 'local' trees which can be combined into larger trees to license sentences, much as CFGs combine productions (which can equally be thought of as local trees) into phrase structures. The essentially new element in TAGs is the operation of *adjunction*, in which a local tree may be 'spliced' into an existing tree. A language recognized by a TAG is called a *tree adjoining language*.

The more elaborate apparatus of TAGs leads to an increase in recognition capacity: the languages $\{a^n b^n c^n \mid n \geq 1\}$ and $\{a^n b^n c^n d^n \mid n \geq 1\}$ are tree adjoining languages, but not context-free languages. It also leads to an increase in recognition complexity. Various parsing algorithms have been developed which show that the recognition problem for a TAG can be solved in time $O(n^6)$, where n is the length of the input string (Schabes 1994). Interestingly, TAGs turn out to be expressively equivalent to several other natural grammar frameworks, including *head grammars*, *linear-indexed grammars*, and *combinatory categorial grammars* (Vijay-Shanker & Weir 1994). These equivalences can be used to establish that all these grammar frameworks have universal recognition problems with comparable complexity.

More expressive still is the framework of *definite clause grammars* (DCGs). Again, we give only an informal explanation here. Like a CFG, a DCG consists of a set of productions over xed sets of terminal and non-terminal symbols, together with a distinguished non-terminal S. The only difference is that the non-terminals now take *arguments* drawn from a *term-language* $\mathcal{T}$. The expressions of $\mathcal{T}$ are built up from a xed vocabulary of individual constants, variables, and function symbols. We assume that there is at least one individual constant in $\mathcal{T}$. Each non-terminal in a DCG is associated with a non-negative integer, called its *arity*, and, in any production, is supplied with a list of arguments according to that arity. A typical DCG production has the form

(8) $A(s_1, \ldots, s_n) \rightarrow B_1(t_{1,1}, \ldots, t_{1,\ell_1}) \cdots B_m(t_{m,1}, \ldots, t_{m,\ell_m}),$

where A is a non-terminal with arity n, and the B_i are non-terminals with arity ℓ_i for all i ($1 \leq i \leq m$). (In general, the right-hand side is also allowed to contain terminals.) The distinguished non-terminal S is assumed to have arity 0. A *ground instance* of a production is the result of consistently substituting, for the variables in that production, terms which contain no variables. The notion of *acceptance* is then de ned in the same way as for a CFG, by regarding each production as the set of its ground instances. (Of course, this set of productions may be in nite, and thus will not in general constitute an actual CFG.)

Figure 2.3 shows a set of productions for a DCG G with non-terminals $\{S, A, B, C, D, E\}$ and terminals $\{a, b, c, d, e\}$. Each of the non-terminals has arity 1, except for S, the distinguished non-terminal. Figure 2.4 shows a derivation of the string aabbccddee in G, where the variable x in the rst production takes the value f(1). This variable in effect counts the number of times the rules for the non-terminals A, …, E are invoked (with a value $f^{n-1}(1)$ encoding n

$$S \to A(x)\, B(x)\, C(x)\, D(x)\, E(x)$$

$A(1) \to a$	$A(f(x)) \to a\, A(x)$
$B(1) \to b$	$B(f(x)) \to b\, B(x)$
$C(1) \to c$	$C(f(x)) \to c\, C(x)$
$D(1) \to d$	$D(f(x)) \to d\, D(x)$
$E(1) \to e$	$E(f(x)) \to e\, E(x)$

Figure 2.3 Productions of a DCG recognizing the language $\{a^n b^n c^n d^n e^n \mid n \geq 0\}$.

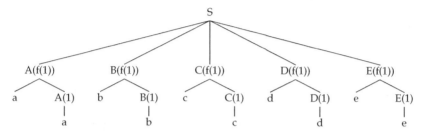

Figure 2.4 Derivation of the string aabbccddee in the DCG of Figure 2.3.

invocations), and ensures that this number is the same in each case. Thus, $L(G) = \{a^n b^n c^n d^n e^n \mid n \geq 0\}$; this language is not a tree adjoining language.

The DCG framework is of interest in part because it is so attractive to implement: indeed, DCGs are a built-in feature of the Prolog programming language (Pereira & Warren 1980). The basis for such implementations is the concept of *unification*. We say that any terms t_1 and t_2 of T *unify* if there is a simultaneous substitution of terms for variables in t_1 and t_2 which make these expressions identical. If two terms unify, then there is a 'most general' unifier, which is unique up to renaming of variables. In a DCG-parser, when a non-terminal $A(u_1, \ldots, u_n)$ is expanded by the production (8), the most general unifier of the terms $A(u_1, \ldots, u_n)$ and $A(s_1, \ldots, s_n)$ is first computed; if this unifier exists, all variable bindings thus created are carried through to all the non-terminals $B_1(\bar{t}_1), \ldots, B_m(\bar{t}_m)$, which are then subject to expansion as before. Computing an explicit representation of the most general unifier of two terms is computationally expensive, because that representation is in general exponentially large in the size of the terms. However, determining *whether* two terms unify is much easier (Paterson & Wegman 1978; de Champeaux 1986):

THEOREM 16. *The problem of determining whether two terms unify is in TIME$(n + 1)$.*

DCGs thus present an interesting object of study from a complexity-theoretic point of view. We have:

THEOREM 17. *The universal recognition problem for DCGs is undecidable. Indeed, there is a DCG G such that L(G) is undecidable.*

Theorem 17 follows almost directly from Theorem 1, because the operation of any Turing machine M can easily be simulated using a DCG in which the values of variables are used to store con gurations of M.

However, by imposing various reasonable constraints on DCGs, decidability can be restored. Let us say that a production is *consuming* if the right-hand side either consists of a single terminal or has a length of at least 2; and let us say that a DCG is *consuming* if all its productions are. For example, the production $a(f(x)) \rightarrow a(x)$ is not consuming, because its right-hand side consists of a single non-terminal; on the other hand, the DCG of Figure 2.3 is consuming. It is easy to show that, if a consuming DCG accepts a string σ of length n, the resulting parse-tree has at most $3n - 1$ nodes, so decidability in this case should not be a surprise. In fact, we have:

THEOREM 18. *The universal recognition problem for consuming DCGs is NPTIME-complete. Indeed, there exists a consuming DCG G such that L(G) is NPTIME-complete.*

The upper bound in Theorem 18 follows from the following observations. Given a consuming DCG G and a string σ of length n, we rst guess a parse-tree featuring at most $3n - 1$ nodes. Each non-leaf node is labeled with the (uninstantiated) production of G responsible for generating it, and each leaf node is labeled with a terminal, so as to form the string σ. (If the same production is used at more than one non-leaf node, new copies are made containing fresh variables.) We need only check that the terms in the copies of the productions at each node can be simultaneously uni ed in the obvious way. This check amounts to determining the uni ability of two (polynomially large) terms, and can be carried out in polynomial time by Theorem 16. The NPTIME-hardness of $L(G)$ for certain consuming DCGs G is easily shown by a simple reduction of the satis ability problem for propositional logic clauses; the result then follows by Theorem 6.

Alternatively, we might say that a DCG is *function-free* if there are no function symbols in its productions. (Thus, the DCG featured in Figure 2.4 is not function-free, because several of its productions feature the function symbol f.) We have:

THEOREM 19. *The universal recognition problem for function-free DCGs is EXPTIME-complete. However, for any fixed function-free DCG G, L(G) is in PTIME.*

Theorem 19 follows straightforwardly from the close connection between function-free DCGs and the logic programming language DATALOG (see, e.g., Libkin 2004, Chapter 10, or Dantsin et al., 2001). More generally, there is a close connection between DCGs on the one hand and so-called xed-point logics on the other, which allows standard results from complexity theory to be carried over to the study of DCGs. For example, Rounds (1988) describes two DCG-like grammar frameworks, one able to recognize all and only the languages in $\text{TIME}(2^n)$, the other able to recognize all and only the languages in PTIME. Rounds shows that the second of his two grammar frameworks is at least as expressive as that of TAG (and its equivalents), mentioned above.

A more traditional grammar framework generalizing CFGs is that of the context-sensitive grammars. A *context-sensitive grammar* (CSG) is like a CFG, except that the productions are now of the form $\alpha \to \beta$, where α and β are strings of symbols such that $|\alpha| \leq |\beta|$. These productions are interpreted as rewrite rules, in much the same way as productions of a CFG. For comparison, note that, in a CFG, all productions have the form $A \to \beta$, where A is a non-terminal. Indeed, if we assume (which we may without essential loss of generality) that productions in CFGs have non-empty right-hand sides, the condition $|\alpha| \leq |\beta|$ is then trivially satis ed, whence CFGs are a special case of CSGs. Recalling the equivalence of languages and decision problems, it is routine to show that the class of context-sensitive languages is exactly the complexity class NSPACE(n). In fact, we have the following result concerning recognition complexity for context-sensitive languages.

THEOREM 20. *The universal recognition problem for CSGs is PSPACE-complete. Indeed, there exists a CSG G such that L(G) is PSPACE-complete.*

For a formal de nition of context-sensitive grammars and a proof of Theorem 20, see Hopcroft and Ullman (1979b: 223 and 347ff.). It was long conjectured that the complement of a context-sensitive language is itself a context-sensitive language. This conjecture was settled, positively, by Theorem 4, using the fact that the context-sensitive languages coincide with NSPACE(n).

All the grammar frameworks examined so far have precise formal de nitions, which makes for a clear-cut complexity analysis. However, many mainstream grammar frameworks which aspire to describe natural languages are much less rigidly de ned (and indeed much more liable to periodic revision); consequently, it is harder to provide de nitive results about computational complexity. Transformational grammar is a case in point. Let us take a transformational grammar to consist of two components: a CFG generating a collection of phrase-structure trees – so-called *deep structures* – and a collection of *transformations* which map these deep structures to other phrase-structure trees – so-called *surface structures*. A string σ is *accepted* by G just in case σ can be read off the leaves of some surface structure obtained in this way. Absent a formal speci cation of the sorts of transformations allowed in transformational grammar, it is impossible to determine the complexity of its recognition problem. However, analyzing a version of Chomsky's *aspects* theory, Peters and Ritchie (1973) show the existence of transformational grammars which can recognize undecidable languages. Certainly, then, the universal recognition problem for transformational grammars (thus understood) is undecidable. Other analyses of grammar frameworks in the transformational tradition paint a picture of lower complexity, however. Thus, Berwick and Weinberg (1984: 125ff.) analyze the complexity of *government-binding grammars*, a formalization of the approach taken in Chomsky (1981), and show that recognition complexity for such grammars is in the class PSPACE.

2.4   Model-theoretic semantics

Recent trends in linguistics – particularly within the transformational tradition – have shown a preference for specifying grammars not in terms of generative mechanisms but, rather, in terms of constraints to which sentence structures are required to conform. On this view of grammar, a string σ is grammatical just in case it has a structure which satis es those constraints. How can we determine the complexity of the recognition problem when grammars are presented in this way? The answer is to employ a formal language: this formal language must be powerful enough to express the constraints constituting the grammar in question, and yet not so powerful that working with it leads to undecidable problems.

Monadic second-order logic (MSO) is a formal language containing two sorts of variables: those ranging over objects (as in ordinary rst-order logic), and those ranging over *sets* of objects. For the moment, let us suppose that the 'objects' in question are positions in a string σ over an alphabet Σ. We con ne ourselves to a language containing a unary atomic predicate s, for every $s \in \Sigma$, and binary predicates $\in$ and $\leq$. We now interpret these predicates over the set of positions in σ as follows (we adopt the convention of using lowercase letters for object variables and uppercase letters for set variables): $x \in X$ means 'x is a member of X'; $x \leq y$ means 'x is non-strictly to the left of y'; and $s(x)$ means 'position x is lled with symbol s,' for each $s \in \Sigma$. Formulas are built up from atomic formulas using Boolean connectives and quanti ers (over both sorts of variables) in the normal way. The standard semantics for these connectives then determines, for a given formula φ (with no free variables) and a given string σ, whether φ is true in σ. That is: any $\sigma \in \Sigma^*$ is a *structure* (in the logicians' sense) interpreting the above language.

On this view, we can think of an MSO-formula φ (with no free variables) as a *grammar*: a string σ is *accepted* by φ just in case φ is true in σ. The following result was proved by Büchi (1960).

THEOREM 21 (BÜCHI).   *A language is recognized by an MSO-formula if and only if it is regular.*

Now, this approach to de ning languages using formulas of MSO can be generalized in the following way. Suppose we take our variables to range, not over positions in strings, but over positions (nodes) in nite *trees*. (Think of the trees in question as phrase structures of sentences.) And suppose we take our language to feature the binary predicates $\in$, $\lhd_1$, and $\lhd_2$, as well as unary predicates drawn from a nite set of labels. These predicates are then interpreted as follows: $x \in X$ again means 'x is a member of X'; $x \lhd_1 y$ means 'x is the mother of y'; $x \lhd_2 y$ means 'x is a left sister of y'; and $s(x)$ means that x is labeled with s, for each label s. All other formulas are then interpreted according to the usual semantics of MSO. In this way, we can think of an MSO-formula φ (with no free variables) as licensing a set of labeled trees: namely, the trees in which φ is true. It was shown by Thatcher and Wright (1968) that the sets of trees (i.e., *tree languages*) recognized in this way are – to within some additional labeling – the sets of trees generated by CFGs.

Indeed, one can interpret MSO-formulas over 'trees' of higher dimensions, obtaining grammar frameworks of still greater expressive power. This approach to syntax is often referred to as *model-theoretic syntax* (Rogers 2003). Its appeal is partly due to the fact that MSO can express many relationships dear to linguists' hearts. For example, it is straightforward to write down a formula $\varphi_C(x, y)$ which is satis ed by nodes x and y in a tree just in case node x C-commands node y in that tree. Rogers (2003) notes that some principles of Rizzi's theory of *relativized minimality* (Rizzi 1990) can be expressed using formulas of the language sketched above. From a complexity-theoretic point of view, this approach is interesting because the problem of determining whether a formula of MSO is satis able over nite trees is decidable (see, e.g., Börger et al., 1997: 315ff.):

THEOREM 22. *The problem of determining the satisfiability of a formula of MSO over finite trees is decidable, but has non-elementary complexity.*

3 Complexity and Semantics

Most linguistic theories are more than a criterion for de ning a set of acceptable sentences: they also assign one or more levels of structure to those sentences which they do accept. The question then arises as to the computational complexity of recovering that structure.

Consider, for example, context-free grammars. Let G be a CFG. If $\sigma \in L(G)$, then G assigns to σ one or more phrase structures representing the derivation of σ by the productions of G. It is easy to construct a CFG G for which there exists a sequence $\{\sigma_n\}_{n \in \mathbb{N}}$ of strings accepted by G, such that the length of σ_n is bounded above by some polynomial function of n, while the number of phrase structures which G assigns to σ_n is bounded below by an exponential function of n. That is: the number of parses produced by a CFG G can grow exponentially. Nevertheless, the set of phrase structures assigned to any string σ by G may always be compactly represented in the form of an acyclic directed graph, which can be expanded into a complete list of the phrase structures in question; moreover, using a variant of the CYK or Earley algorithms, that compact representation may be computed in time $O(n^3 m)$. (Trivially, listing all the represented phrase structures will in general take exponential time.) For a general discussion on the relationship between the complexity of recognition and parsing, see Ruzzo (1979).

Arguably, determining the syntactic structure of a sentence is of little value unless we can use that structure to recover the sentence's meaning. The notion of meaning in general is too vague to admit of immediate formal analysis. However, we might sensibly begin with the more speci c problem of recovering, at least for certain fragments of natural languages, *logical form*, in the sense of producing translations such as:

(9)   Every boy loves some girl who admires him
       $\forall x(\text{boy}(x) \rightarrow \exists y(\text{girl}(y) \wedge \text{admire}(y, x) \wedge \text{love}(x, y)))$

$$\text{IP}/y_1(y_2) \to \text{NP}/y_1 \; \text{I}'/y_2 \qquad \text{Det}/\lambda p\lambda q[\exists x(p(x) \wedge q(x))] \to \texttt{some}$$
$$\text{I}'/y_1 \to \text{is a } \text{N}'/y_1 \qquad \text{Det}/\lambda p\lambda q[\forall x(p(x) \to q(x))] \to \texttt{every}$$
$$\text{I}'/\lambda x[\neg y_1(x)] \to \text{is not a } \text{N}'/y_1 \qquad \text{Det}/\lambda p\lambda q[\forall x(p(x) \to \neg q(x))] \to \texttt{no}$$
$$\text{NP}/y_1 \to \text{PropN}/y_1$$
$$\text{NP}/y_1(y_2) \to \text{Det}/y_1 \; \text{N}'/y_2 \qquad \text{N}/\text{cynic} \to \texttt{cynic}$$
$$\text{N}'/y_1 \to \text{N}/y_1. \qquad \text{N}/\text{philosopher} \to \texttt{philosopher}$$
$$\cdots$$

$$\text{PropN}/\lambda p[p(\text{socrates})] \to \texttt{Socrates}$$
$$\text{PropN}/\lambda p[p(\text{diogenes})] \to \texttt{Diogenes}$$
$$\cdots$$

Figure 2.5   Semantically annotated CFG generating the language of the syllogistic.

The framework of CFGs (and indeed the other grammar frameworks mentioned above) can be modi ed to yield such logical forms. Approaches vary, but one popular technique is to associate with each vocabulary item an expression of the simply typed λ-calculus (STLC) representing its meaning, and to associate with each production a prescription for combining the meanings of the items in its right-hand side. In the following explanation, we assume basic familiarity with STLC; for an in-depth account, the reader is referred to Hindley and Seldin (1986, Chapter 13). A production in such a grammar has the form

$$A/\xi \to B_1/y_1 \ldots B_m/y_m$$

where $y_1, \ldots, y_m$ are distinct variables, and ξ is an STLC-expression whose free variables are con ned to $y_1, \ldots, y_n$. Such a production functions exactly as in an ordinary CFG, except that the meaning of the phrase A is computed by substituting the (already computed) meanings of the $B_1, \ldots, B_m$ for all occurrences of the corresponding variables $y_1, \ldots, y_m$ in ξ, and then β-reducing. This approach is, more or less, that championed by Montague (1974) (see Chapter 15, Section 2.1). For an accessible modern treatment, including a relatively non-technical explanation of the relevant aspects of higher-order logic, see Blackburn & Bos (2005).

Consider, for example, the productions shown in Figure 2.5. The underlying CFG evidently recognizes the sentence 'Every cynic is a philosopher,' via the parse-tree shown in Figure 2.6. By computing the semantic values of each node in that tree, as shown, the (expected) rst-order translation

$$\forall x(\text{cynic}(x) \wedge \to \text{philosopher}(x))$$

is eventually generated. In fact, the grammar of Figure 2.5 recognizes the set of English sentences having the forms

$$\left\{ \left\{ \begin{array}{c} \text{Every} \\ \text{Some} \\ \text{No} \\ S \end{array} \right\} L \right\} \left\{ \begin{array}{c} \text{is a} \\ \text{is not a} \end{array} \right\} M,$$

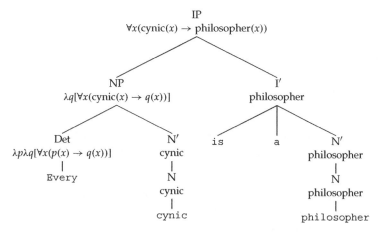

Figure 2.6   Meaning derivation in a semantically annotated CFG.

where S is a proper noun, and L and M are common nouns, yielding, in each case, the expected translation into rst-order logic. The question now arises: what is the computational complexity of recovering logical forms in this way?

The answer depends on how, exactly, logical forms are allowed to be represented. If the underlying grammar G is a CFG, then the CYK or Earley algorithms can again be modi ed to produce, in polynomial time, a compact representation of all meanings which G assigns to a given string σ, just as for parse-trees. However, these representations will not be β-reduced. That is, in order to produce ordinary logical translations such as (9), we need to compute the normal forms for the expressions which our parser yields. That these normal forms can be computed follows at once from the normalization theorem for STLC, though the complexity of the relevant function is high (Statman 1979):

THEOREM 23. *The problem of deciding whether one expression in STLC is the normal form of another has non-elementary complexity.*

In practice, however, the normalization of semantic representations produced by realistic semantically annotated CFGs is never a problem.

4   Determining Logical Relationships between Sentences

Computing anything is of little use if nothing is then done with the results. And while the uses to which humans put computed meanings may perhaps forever remain lost in the mists of psycholinguistics, complexity theory does have something to say about the more de nite subject of determining *logical* relationships between sentences in natural language. That is the topic of this nal section.

That sentences in natural language exhibit interesting logical relationships was recognized in antiquity. For example, the argument

(10)
Every logician is a philosopher
Some stoic is a logician
No dentist is a philosopher
——————————————
Some stoic is not a dentist

is evidently valid: every possible situation in which the premises are true is one in which the conclusion is true. Likewise valid, but less evidently so, is the argument

(11)
Every skeptic recommends every skeptic to every cynic
No skeptic recommends any stoic who hates any cynic
    to any philosopher
Diogenes is a cynic whom every skeptic hates
Every cynic is a philosopher
——————————————
No stoic is a skeptic

Observe that argument (11) uses a wider variety of grammatical constructions than argument (10), speci cally: transitive and ditransitive verbs, as well as relative clauses. The question therefore arises as to how the dif culty of determining logical relationships between sentences in naturally delineated fragments of natural languages depends on the grammatical resources included in those fragments. Are ditransitive verbs really harder than transitive verbs? Passives harder than actives? How much extra effort is required to deal with relative clauses (either subject relatives or object relatives)? Is 'donkey-anaphora' more computationally intensive than other forms of bound-variable anaphora? And so on.

Consider the grammar of Figure 2.5, which, as we saw in Section 3, yields the language of the traditional syllogistic. In particular, this grammar recognizes all the sentences in argument (10), and translates that argument to the   rst-order sequent

$$\forall x(\text{logician}(x) \rightarrow \text{philosopher}(x))$$
$$\exists x(\text{stoic}(x) \land \text{logician}(x))$$
$$\forall x(\text{dentist}(x) \rightarrow \neg\text{philosopher}(x))$$
$$\overline{\exists x(\text{stoic}(x) \land \neg\text{dentist}(x))}$$

Since the primary form-determining element in this fragment of English is the copula, we refer to it as *Cop*. With translations into   rst-order logic at our disposal, we can now formally characterize a notion of validity in this fragment. Speci cally, we take an argument in the fragment Cop to be *valid* just in case the   rst-order sequent into which it is translated is valid according to the semantics of   rst-order logic. Likewise, we take a set of sentences in Cop to be *satisfiable* just in case the set of formulas to which they are translated is satis able according to the semantics of   rst-order logic.

$$I'/y_1 \to VP/y_1$$
$$I'/y_1 \to NegP/y_1$$
$$NegP/\lambda x[\neg y_1(x)] \to Neg\ VP/y_1$$
$$VP/y_1(y_2) \to TV/y_1\ NP/y_2$$
$$Neg \to \texttt{does not}$$

$$TV/\lambda s\lambda x[s(\lambda y[\mathrm{admire}(x,y)])]$$
$$\to \texttt{admires}$$
$$TV/\lambda s\lambda x[s(\lambda y[\mathrm{despise}(x,y)])]$$
$$\to \texttt{despises}$$
$$\dots$$

Figure 2.7 Productions for extending the syllogistic with transitive verbs.

Thus, the fragment Cop is more than a mere set of strings (the grammatical sentences): it is a set of strings together with associated logical concepts of validity and satis ability. In particular, we may pose the satis ability problem for Cop: given a set E of sentences in Cop, determine whether E is satis able. Furthermore, since every sentence in Cop is logically equivalent to the negation of some other, satis - ability and validity are dual notions, in the familiar sense: an argument is valid just in case its premises together with the negation of its conclusion are unsatis able. Hence, the complexity of the validity problem for Cop can be read off immediately from the complexity of the satis ability problem.

It is routine to show that determining the satis ability of a collection of sentences in the fragment Cop is essentially the same as the problem of determining the satis ability of a collection of propositional clauses each of which contains at most two literals. Recalling Theorem 8, we have:

THEOREM 24. *The problem of determining the satisfiability of a set of sentences in Cop is NLOGSPACE-complete.*

It follows of course that the problem of determining the validity of an argument in Cop is also NLOGSPACE-complete, by Theorem 4. This con rms our subjective impression that this problem is nearly trivial.

What happens if we expand the fragment Cop? Let us de ne the fragment *Cop+TV* to be the set of sentences recognized by the productions of Figure 2.5 together with those of Figure 2.7. (We have simpli ed the treatment by ignoring verb in ections and negative-polarity determiners; these simpli cations are not computationally signi cant.) It is easy to see that this fragment contains the following sentence, and translates it to the indicated rst-order formula.

(12) Every stoic hates every sceptic
$$\forall x(\mathrm{stoic}(x) \to \forall y(\mathrm{sceptic}(y) \to \mathrm{hate}(x,y)))$$

We need to address the issue of scope ambiguities in the context of Cop+TV. There are two possibilities here: either we can resolve these ambiguities by at, taking subjects always to outscope objects; or we can augment the language with some form of marking to indicate quanti er scope. For simplicity, we choose the former course (though the latter would lead to essentially the same complexity results). Similarly, let *Cop+TV+DTV* be the fragment which extends Cop with both transitive and ditransitive verbs. (Writing the required productions is completely routine.) Thus, Cop+TV+DTV contains the following sentence, and translates it to the indicated rst-order formula.

(13) No stoic recommends every sceptic to some cynic
$\forall x(stoic(x) \rightarrow \neg\forall y(sceptic(y) \rightarrow \exists z(cynic(z) \wedge recommend(x,y,z))))$

Again, we take subjects to outscope direct objects, and direct objects to outscope indirect objects.

Is inference in these larger fragments more complex? The following two results (substantially) answer this question.

THEOREM 25. *The problem of determining the satisfiability of a set of sentences in Cop+TV is NLOGSPACE-complete.*

THEOREM 26. *The problem of determining the satisfiability of a set of sentences in Cop+TV+DTV is in PTIME.*

The proofs of these theorems are more elaborate than for Cop; we refer the reader to Pratt-Hartmann and Moss (2009) and Pratt-Hartmann and Third (2006) respectively.

Returning to the fragment Cop, what happens if we now add relative clauses? Thus, for example, we have the valid argument

> Every philosopher who is not a stoic is an Epicurean
> No Epicurean is a beekeeper
> No stoic is a beekeeper
> _____
> No philosopher is a beekeeper

It is straightforward to write a semantically annotated context-free grammar accepting such sentences, and generating the obvious semantics. Let us call the resulting fragment of English Cop+Rel (see Pratt-Hartmann 2004 for a formal definition). The rst-order formulas into which Cop+Rel sentences are translated all have one variable – that is to say, they lie within the one-variable fragment of rst-order logic. The satis ability problem for this fragment is essentially the same as that for clauses of the propositional calculus. Thus, from Theorem 6:

THEOREM 27. *The problem of determining the satisfiability of a set of sentences in Cop+Rel is NPTIME-complete.*

On the other hand, the fragment Cop+Rel+TV+DTV recognizes all the sentences in argument (11), and translates them into the rst-order sequent

$\forall x(sceptic(x) \rightarrow \forall y(sceptic(y) \rightarrow \forall z(cynic(z) \rightarrow recommend(x,y,z))))$
$\forall x(sceptic(x) \rightarrow \neg\exists y(stoic(y) \wedge \exists z(cynic(w) \wedge hate(y,w))\wedge$
$\qquad\qquad\qquad\qquad \exists z(philosopher(z) \wedge recommend(x,y,z))))$
$cynic(diogenes) \wedge \forall x(sceptic(x) \rightarrow hate(x,diogenes))$
$\forall x(cynic(x) \rightarrow philosopher(x))$
$\underline{}$
$\forall x(stoic(x) \rightarrow \neg sceptic(x))$

Again, we have the question: does adding transitive and ditransitive verbs to Cop+Rel lead to an increase in complexity? This time, the answer is yes.

THEOREM 28. *The problem of determining the satisfiability of a set of sentences in Cop+Rel+TV is EXPTIME-complete.*

THEOREM 29. *The problem of determining the satisfiability of a set of sentences in Cop+Rel+TV+DTV is NEXPTIME-complete.*

Theorem 29 con rms our subjective impression that determining the validity of argument (11) is harder than determining the validity of argument (10). For proofs of the above theorems, see Pratt-Hartmann (2004) and Pratt-Hartmann and Third (2006).

A remark is in order at this point to correct a false impression that the foregoing discussion may have created. As we have observed, the complexity of determining entailments within a fragment of a natural language evidently depends on the constructions made available by the syntax of that fragment. However, it also depends, of course, on the presence in the lexicon of words with a 'logical' character. Consider, for example, the effect of expanding the fragments Cop and Cop+TV with *numerical* determiners, yielding sentences such as

(14)   At least 13 artists are beekeepers

in the former case, and

(15)   At most 5 carpenters admire at most 4 dentists

in the latter. Calling the resulting fragments Cop+Num and Cop+TV+Num, we obtain the following results (Pratt-Hartmann 2008):

THEOREM 30. *The problem of determining the satisfiability of a set of sentences in Cop+Num is NPTIME-complete; the problem of determining the satisfiability of a set of sentences in Cop+TV+Num is NEXPTIME-complete.*

Thus, the complexity-theoretic impact of such numerical expressions is dramatic.

Finally, we consider the complexity-theoretic consequences of adding bound-variable anaphora to our fragments. Consider the sentences

No artist admires any beekeeper who does not admire himself
No artist admires any beekeeper who does not admire him

It is routine to add grammar rules to Cop+Rel+TV producing the conventional translations into rst-order logic:

$$\forall x (\text{artist}(x) \to \forall y (\text{beekeeper}(y) \land \neg\text{admire}(y, y) \to \neg\text{admire}(x, y)))$$
$$\forall x (\text{artist}(x) \to \forall y (\text{beekeeper}(y) \land \neg\text{admire}(y, x) \to \neg\text{admire}(x, y)))$$

For such anaphoric fragments, two further issues regarding the rst-order translations arise. First, we assume the (standard) universal interpretation of 'donkey-sentences'

Every farmer who owns a donkey beats it
$$\forall x \forall y (\text{farmer}(x) \wedge \text{donkey}(y) \wedge \text{own}(x,y) \rightarrow \text{beat}(x,y))$$

Second, we must decide how to treat anaphoric ambiguities. The sentence

(16)   Every sceptic who admires a cynic despises every stoic who hates him

has two interpretations:

(17) $\forall x(\text{sceptic}(x) \wedge \exists y(\text{cynic}(y) \wedge \text{admire}(x,y)) \rightarrow$
$$\forall z(\text{stoic}(z) \wedge \text{hate}(z,x) \rightarrow \text{despise}(x,z)))$$

(18) $\forall x \forall y(\text{sceptic}(x) \wedge \text{cynic}(y) \wedge \text{admire}(x,y) \rightarrow$
$$\forall z(\text{stoic}(z) \wedge \text{hate}(z,y) \rightarrow \text{despise}(x,z)))$$

according as the pronoun 'him' takes as antecedent the NP headed by 'sceptic' or the NP headed by 'cynic'. (The NP headed by 'stoic' is not available as a pronoun antecedent here.)

Note that, in the (standard) phrase-structure tree for this sentence, the NP headed by 'sceptic' is closer to the pronoun than is the NP headed by 'cynic'. This observation suggests making the arti cial stipulation that *pronouns must take their closest allowed antecedents*. Here, *closest* means 'closest measured along edges of the phrase-structure' and *allowed* means 'allowed by the principles of binding theory.' (We ignore case and gender agreement.) Thus, under this stipulation, sentence (16) has only the reading (17). Let the resulting fragment of English, with the stipulation of closest available pronomial antecedents, be called Cop+Rel+TV+RA ('RA' for *restricted anaphora*).

Formula (17) can be equivalently written

$\forall x(\text{sceptic}(x) \wedge \exists y(\text{cynic}(y) \wedge \text{admire}(x,y)) \rightarrow$
$$\forall y(\text{stoic}(y) \wedge \text{hate}(y,x) \rightarrow \text{despise}(x,y)))$$

with the variable z replaced by y. The resulting formula has only two variables. Indeed, it can be shown that every sentence of Cop+Rel+TV+RA translates into a formula in the two-variable fragment of rst-order logic. The satis ability problem for this fragment is known to be NEXPTIME-complete (see, e.g., Börger et al., 1997, Chapter 8). Moreover, Cop+Rel+TV+RA can easily be shown to encode a NEXPTIME-hard problem. Hence, we have:

THEOREM 31. *The problem of determining the satisfiability of a set of sentences in Cop+Rel+TV+RA is NEXPTIME-complete.*

We mention in passing that the reduction of NEXPTIME-hard problems to satis a-bility for sets of Cop+Rel+TV+RA sentences does not require the use of sentences featuring donkey-anaphora. However awkward such sentences may be for the smooth running of formal semantics, they do not lead to more complex inferential problems.

The restriction that pronouns take their closest possible antecedents is essential to the complexity bound of Theorem 31. As an alternative treatment of anaphoric ambiguity, we might augment the sentences of Cop+Rel+TV+RA with indices indicating antecedents in the normal way. Thus, for example, the sentence

Every sceptic$_1$ who admires a cynic$_2$ despises every stoic$_3$ who hates him$_2$

would have (18) as its only reading. Let the resulting fragment be denoted by Cop+Rel+TV+GA ('GA' for *general anaphora*). It is possible to show:

THEOREM 32. *The problem of determining the satisfiability of a set of sentences in Cop+Rel+TV+GA is not decidable.*

It seems clear that many more results of the kind outlined in this section await discovery.

See also: Chapter 1, FORMAL LANGUAGE THEORY, Chapter 4, THEORY OF PARSING, and Chapter 15, COMPUTATIONAL SEMANTICS.

3 Statistical Language Modeling

CIPRIAN CHELBA

Many practical applications such as automatic speech recognition, statistical machine translation, and spelling correction resort to variants of the well-established source-channel model for producing the correct string of words W given an input speech signal, sentence in foreign language, or typed text with possible mistakes, respectively. A basic component of such systems is a statistical language model which estimates the prior probability values for strings of words W.

1 Introduction to Statistical Language Modeling

A statistical language model estimates the prior probability values $P(W)$ for strings of words W in a vocabulary V whose size is in the tens, or hundreds of thousands. Typically the string W is broken into sentences, or other segments such as utterances in automatic speech recognition, which are assumed to be conditionally independent. For the rest of this chapter, we will assume that W is such a segment, or sentence.

Estimating full-sentence language models is computationally hard if one seeks a properly normalized probability model[1] over strings of words of nite length in V^*. A simple and suf cient way to ensure proper normalization of the model is to decompose the sentence probability according to the chain rule and make sure that the end-of-sentence symbol </s> is predicted with non-zero probability in any context. With $W = w_1, w_2, \ldots, w_n$ we get:

$$(1) \quad P(W) = \prod_{i=1}^{n} P(w_i|w_1, w_2, \ldots, w_{i-1})$$

Since the parameter space of $P(w_k|w_1, w_2, \ldots, w_{k-1})$ is too large, the language model is forced to put the context $W_{k-1} = w_1, w_2, \ldots, w_{k-1}$ into an equivalence class determined by a function $\Phi(W_{k-1})$. As a result,

The Handbook of Computational Linguistics and Natural Language Processing, First Edition.
Edited by Alexander Clark, Chris Fox and Shalom Lappin.
© 2013 Blackwell Publishing Ltd except for editorial material and organization
© 2013 Alexander Clark, Chris Fox, and Shalom Lappin. Published 2013 by Blackwell Publishing Ltd.

(2) $P(W) \cong \prod_{k=1}^{n} P(w_k | \Phi(W_{k-1}))$

The word strings encountered in a practical application are of nite length. The probability distribution $P(W)$ should assign probability 0.0 to strings of words of in nite length, and thus sum up to 1.0 over the set of strings of nite length – the support of $P(W)$. From a modeling point of view in a practical situation, the text gets broken into sentences, and the language model needs to predict the distinguished end-of-sentence symbol `</s>`. It can be easily shown that if the language model is smooth, i.e., $P(w_k | \Phi(W_{k-1})) > \epsilon > 0, \forall w_k, W_{k-1}$, then we also have $P(\texttt{</s>}|\Phi(W_{k-1})) > \epsilon > 0, \forall W_{k-1}$ which in turn ensures that the model assigns probability 1.0 to the set of word sequences of nite length.

Research in language modeling consists of nding appropriate equivalence classi ers Φ and methods to estimate $P(w_k | \Phi(W_{k-1}))$.

The most successful paradigm in language modeling uses the $(n-1)$-gram equivalence classi cation, that is, de nes

$$\Phi(W_{k-1}) \doteq w_{k-n+1}, w_{k-n+2}, \ldots, w_{k-1}$$

Once the form $\Phi(W_{k-1})$ is speci ed, only the problem of estimating $P(w_k | \Phi(W_{k-1}))$ from training data remains.

In most cases, $n = 3$, which leads to a trigram language model. The latter has been shown to be surprisingly powerful and, essentially, all attempts to improve on it in the last 30 years have failed. The one interesting enhancement, facilitated by maximum entropy estimation methodology, has been the use of triggers (Rosenfeld 1994) or of singular value decomposition (Bellegarda 1997) (either of which dynamically identify the topic of discourse) in combination with n-gram models. Other widespread choices are class-based language models, which further restrict the equivalence class of the context to $\Phi(W_{k-1})$ to use explicit equivalence classes on words, $[w]$; one can also predict the next word using its class: $P(w_k | [W_{k-1}]) = P([w_k] | [W_{k-1}]) \cdot P(w_k | [w_k])$, if the class membership $[w]$ is a function of w – a case referred to as hard clustering; if the class membership is ambiguous – soft clustering – one needs to sum over all possible class assignments for both the context and predicted words.

1.1 Measures of language model quality

1.1.1 Perplexity A statistical language model can be evaluated by how well it predicts a string of symbols W_t – commonly referred to as test data – generated by the source to be modeled.

Assume we compare two models M_1 and M_2 using the same vocabulary[2] $\mathcal{V}$. They assign probability $P_{M_1}(W_t)$ and $P_{M_2}(W_t)$, respectively, to the sample test string W_t. The test string has been neither used nor seen at the estimation step of either model and it was generated by the same source that we are trying to model. 'Naturally,' we consider M_1 to be a better model than M_2 if $P_{M_1}(W_t) > P_{M_2}(W_t)$.

A commonly used quality measure for a given model M is related to the entropy of the underlying source and was introduced under the name of perplexity (PPL) (Jelinek 1997):

$$(3) \quad PPL(M) = exp\left(-\frac{1}{N}\sum_{k=1}^{N}\ln[P_M(w_k|W_{k-1})]\right)$$

To give intuitive meaning to perplexity, it represents the number of guesses the model needs to make in order to ascertain the identity of the next word, when running over the test word string from left to right. It can be easily shown that the perplexity of a language model that uses the uniform probability distribution over words in the vocabulary V equals the size of the vocabulary; a good language model should of course have lower perplexity, and thus the vocabulary size is an upper bound on the perplexity of a given language model.

Very likely, not all words in the test string W_t are part of the language model vocabulary. It is common practice to map all words that are out-of-vocabulary to a distinguished unknown word symbol, and report the out-of-vocabulary (OOV) rate on test data – the rate at which one encounters OOV words in the test string W_t – as yet another language model performance metric besides perplexity. Usually the unknown word is assumed to be part of the language model vocabulary – open vocabulary language models – and its occurrences are counted in the language model perplexity calculated in equation (3). A situation far less common in practice is that of closed vocabulary language models where all words in the test data will always be part of the vocabulary V.

1.1.2   Task-specific measures   In many practical applications the language model is used as part of a larger statistical system, and the metrics for evaluating such systems are dictated by the problem at hand. Typical applications that use language models include, but are not restricted to: speech recognition, machine translation, spelling correction, case restoration (true-casing), spam   ltering, and other text classi   cation applications.

Although the language model performance in such a system is still reasonably correlated with perplexity, this correlation is not always strong. A particular class of systems is that using the source-channel paradigm, e.g., speech recognition or machine translation: given an input sequence F of continuous or discrete valued symbols, one wishes to determine the most likely word sequence W that would give rise to it:

$$(4) \quad \arg\max_{W} P(W|F) = \arg\max_{W} P(W) \cdot P(F|W)$$

For such situations the discriminative power of the language model relative to the channel model $P(F|W)$ is what matters most, rather than performance in isolation on correct text, as measured by perplexity.

An intuitive explanation is that, during the search for the maximum scoring word sequence in equation (4), the decoder examines a large set of word sequences, each being accompanied by the channel model score $P(F|W)$. Depending on the channel model quality, the language model may be asked the probability of n-grams that are rarely seen on correct text, and yet they may receive a reasonably high language model probability under the maximum likelihood estimate, instead of a strong negative vote of con dence.

Recent work demonstrates that signi cant performance gains can be obtained by training the language model in this way (Collins 2000). For the particular case of speech recognition, Chelba (2006) proposes an alternative to perplexity named acoustic-sensitive perplexity as an objective function for evaluating language models used in a source-channel setup.

1.2 Smoothing

Since the language model is meant to assign non-zero probability to unseen strings of words (or, equivalently, ensure that the cross-entropy of the model over an arbitrary test string is not in nite), a desirable property is that:

(5) $P(w_k|\Phi(W_{k-1})) > \epsilon > 0, \forall w_k, W_{k-1}$

This is also known as the smoothing requirement.

A large body of work has accumulated over the years on various smoothing methods for n-gram language models that ensure this to be true. The two most widespread smoothing techniques are probably Kneser–Ney (1995) and Katz (1987). Goodman (2001) is an excellent overview that is highly recommended to any practitioner of language modeling.

A simple smoothing method for discrete probability models due to Jelinek and Mercer (1980) is recursive linear interpolation among relative frequency estimates of different orders $f_k(\cdot), k = 0 \ldots n$ using a recursive mixing scheme (see Figure 3.1).

Let $\mathcal{U}$ be the vocabulary in which the predicted random variable u (not necessarily a word) takes values.

$P_n(u|z_1, \ldots, z_n) =$

$\lambda(z_1, \ldots, z_n) \cdot P_{n-1}(u|z_1, \ldots, z_{n-1}) + (1 - \lambda(z_1, \ldots, z_n)) \cdot f_n(u|z_1, \ldots, z_n),$

$P_{-1}(u) = uniform(\mathcal{U})$

where:

- $z_1, \ldots, z_n$ is the context of order n when predicting u;

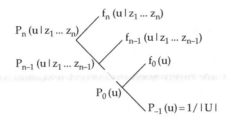

Figure 3.1   Recursive linear interpolation.

- $f_k(u|z_1,\ldots,z_k)$ is the order-k relative frequency estimate for the conditional probability $P(u|z_1,\ldots,z_k)$:

$$f_k(u|z_1,\ldots,z_k) = C(u,z_1,\ldots,z_k)/C(z_1,\ldots,z_k), \ k = 0\ldots n,$$

$$C(u,z_1,\ldots,z_k) = \sum_{z_{k+1}\in\mathcal{Z}_{k+1}} \cdots \sum_{z_n\in\mathcal{Z}_n} C(u,z_1,\ldots,z_k,z_{k+1}\ldots z_n),$$

$$C(z_1,\ldots,z_k) = \sum_{u\in\mathcal{U}} C(u,z_1,\ldots,z_k);$$

- $\lambda(z_1,\ldots,z_k) \in [0,1], \ k = 0\ldots n$ are the interpolation coefficients.

The $\lambda(z_1,\ldots,z_k)$ coefficients are grouped into equivalence classes – tied – based on the range into which the count $C(z_1,\ldots,z_k)$ falls; the count ranges for each equivalence class – also called buckets – are set such that a statistically suffi-cient number of events $(u|z_1,\ldots,z_k)$ fall in that range. The approach is a standard one (Jelinek & Mercer 1980). In order to determine the interpolation weights, we apply the deleted interpolation technique:

(1) split the training data in two sets – development and cross-validation respec-tively;
(2) get the relative frequency – maximum likelihood – estimates $f_k(u|z_1,\ldots,z_k), \ k = 0\ldots n$ from development data;
(3) employ the expectation-maximization (EM) algorithm (Dempster et al., 1977) for determining the maximum likelihood estimate from cross-validation data of the tied interpolation weights $\lambda(C(z_1,\ldots,z_k))$.

The cross-validation data cannot be the same as the development data; if this were the case, the maximum likelihood estimate for the interpolation weights would be $\lambda(C(z_1,\ldots,z_k)) = 0$, disallowing the mixing of different order relative frequency estimates and thus performing no smoothing at all.

It is a simple exercise to cast such a language model as a back-off n-gram model (Katz 1987).

As a final comment on LM smoothing, most of the techniques currently in use (Katz, Kneser–Ney, etc.) have been developed for tasks using relatively small

```
ARPA LM format with back-off rule for probability calculation:

p(wd3|wd1,wd2)=
    if(trigram exists)                 p_3(wd1,wd2,wd3)
    else if(bigram w1,w2 exists)  bo_wt_2(w1,w2)*p(wd3|wd2)
    else                               p(wd3|w2)
p(wd2|wd1)=
    if(bigram exists)                 p_2(wd1,wd2)
    else                               bo_wt_1(wd1)*p_1(wd2)

All probs and back-off weights (bo_wt) are given in log10 form.

Everything before the beginning of the data mark is a comment
Beginning of data mark: \data\ on a line by itself
End of data mark: \end\ on a line by itself
The data block is thus encoded as follows:

\data
ngram 1=nr              # number of unigrams
ngram 2=nr              # number of bigrams
ngram 3=nr              # number of trigrams

\1-grams:
p_1       wd         bo_wt_1

\2-grams:
p_2       wd1 wd2 bo_wt_2

\3-grams:
p_3       wd1 wd2 wd3

\end\
```

Figure 3.2   ARPA format for language model representation.

amounts of training data (1–100 million words). While the importance of LM smoothing cannot be overemphasized, the impact of a particular choice for the smoothing technique used in building a language model may become less important as large amounts of training data become available for a task of interest (Brants et al., 2007).

1.3 Language model representation in practice

A commonly accepted way of representing back-off n-gram models is the ARPA format described in Figure 3.2, which we consider to be self-explanatory.

In many practical situations, including automatic speech recognition, it is convenient to represent an n-gram language model as a nite state machine (FSM) that drives the decoding (search) process. An excellent starting point is the OpenFst toolkit (Allauzen et al., 2007).

In such a representation, the transitions are labeled with words in the language model vocabulary, and the costs on such arcs are the language model probabilities in an appropriate representation (usually as log-probabilities since that also has computational advantages in terms of the precision of oating point operations); the states in the FSM are the n-gram contexts of the LM. We note that, due to the smoothing constraint (see equation (5)), all $\mathcal{V}^{N-1}$ contexts of length $N-1$ would have to be represented, which is intractable for common vocabulary sizes of 100,000 words or more. A widespread approximation used for representing back-off language models as FSMs is to use as states only the contexts listed in the ARPA representation of the language model and to add back-off transitions whose cost is the back-off weight. This reduces the LM state space drastically, at a small cost in modeling accuracy – the LM representation is not exact, and non-deterministic.

As increasing amounts of training data become available, it becomes of particular interest to reduce the number of parameters, as well as ef ciently store language models. The number of n-grams in an LM can be reduced while having the least possible impact on model perplexity by using pruning techniques. They range from simple count cut-off pruning (discarding n-grams whose count in the training data is below a certain threshold) to the more sophisticated entropy-based pruning techniques (Seymore & Rosenfeld 1996; Stolcke 1998). The interaction between pruning and various smoothing techniques deserves a more careful study, in particular for more aggressive pruning regimes. One such example is the rapid deterioration of Kneser–Ney models with entropy pruning (Siivola et al., 2007).

The use of a trie for storing n-gram back-off language models is well established: the CMU (Rosenfeld 1995), SRILM (Stolcke 2002) toolkits, as well as others (Whittaker & Raj 2001; Hsu & Glass 2008) all rely on it in one form or another. Its re nement using array indexes instead of pointers for the trie representation is also an established idea – it was implemented in later versions of the CMU (Clarkson & Rosenfeld 1997) toolkit, as well as the more recent MITLM (Hsu & Glass 2008). The array sizes are known in advance and can be pre-allocated to avoid memory fragmentation.

The quantization of LogP/BoW values is also an established procedure for reducing the storage requirements. The work in Whittaker and Raj (2001) applies both techniques, and in addition makes the important connection between LM pruning and compression/quantization. By representing LogP/BoWs on a variable number of bits (codewords) at each n-gram order, quantizing recursively the differences between actual LogP value and quantized back-off estimate, and removing redundant n-grams using a similar criterion to Stolcke (1998) and Seymore and Rosenfeld (1996), the authors show that the LM performance on an ASR task can be preserved while dramatically reducing the memory footprint of the model.

More recent approaches (Harb et al., 2009) enhance the standard use of integer arrays to represent the trie by applying block compression techniques in order to reduce the storage requirements for both skeleton and payload. The compression methods used are lossless.

In a signi cant departure from traditional techniques, randomized encoding schemes (Talbot & Osborne 2007; Talbot & Brants 2008) achieve excellent compression performance by using a lossy representation of the model. These can store parameters in constant space per n-gram independent of either vocabulary size or n-gram order, but return an incorrect value for a 'random' subset of n-grams of tunable size: the more errors allowed, the more succinct the encoding. In the case of Talbot and Brants (2008), n-grams can also be looked up in constant time independent of the compression rate. On the other hand, these schemes cannot easily store a list of all future words for each n-gram context as required by certain applications, e.g., when representing the language model as an FSM.

We conclude our introduction to language modeling (in particular n-gram models) here. The rest of the chapter contains a presentation of the structured language model (Chelba & Jelinek 2000). This novel language modeling approach attempts to leverage n-gram modeling techniques in order to exploit the syntactic structure exhibited by natural language. Section 2 outlines the underlying probabilistic model and its estimation from training data annotated with syntactic parse-tree information. Section 3 details experiments in an automatic speech recognition setup, followed by Section 4 which presents re nements to the original formulation in an attempt to better capture the syntactic dependencies in language. Section 5 compares our approach to related ones, followed by conclusions suggesting research directions for language modeling, and the structured language model in particular.

2   Structured Language Model

As outlined in equation (2), a language model predicts the next word in a string of words based on an equivalence classi cation of the word pre x $\Phi(W_{k-1})$.

From a theoretical point of view, the nite-order Markov assumption on which the estimation of n-gram models rests is inadequate for modeling the dependencies in natural language. The main criticism is that such a model operates on the surface of the word string, and ignores the more complex dependencies exhibited in natural language syntax – best described using parse-trees. A more expressive formal language that is able to take into account such dependencies is the class of context-free grammars (CFGs).

The structured language model (SLM) we present addresses this problem by using a parser for classifying the word pre x hierarchically and proposing several possible equivalence classi cations $\Phi^l(W_{k-1}), l = 1 \ldots N$ for a given word pre x W_{k-1}, each accompanied by a probability $P(\Phi^l(W_{k-1})|W_{k-1})$.

We wish to emphasize that the encoding for a word sequence together with a parse-tree used by the SLM is different from that provided by a CFG. The excellent study in Abney et al. (1999) contrasts CFGs and the class of probabilistic push-down automata (to which the SLM belongs) from a learning, and power of expression, point of view.

The remaining part of the SLM presentation is structured as follows: the basic idea behind the hierarchical method for organizing the word pre x is outlined in the next section. One main constraint imposed on it by the incremental operation of the language model in a speech recognizer – see equation (1) – is that it has to proceed left to right through the word sequence.

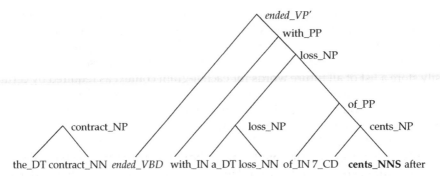

Figure 3.3   Partial parse.

Section 2.2 presents a model that assigns probability to each possible pair consisting of a word sequence and parse. This is then used to assign probability $P(\Phi^l(W_{k-1})|W_{k-1})$ to each equivalence classi cation of W_{k-1} considered by the model, and nally mix them to get a word-level probability $P(w_k|W_{k-1})$, as described in Section 2.4. A few shortcuts are introduced to make the computation feasible. Section 2.6 describes two successive stages of model parameters re-estimation. Finally, Section 2.7 presents experiments carried out on the UPenn Treebank corpus and compares the results of our approach to those obtained from the 3-gram model.

2.1   Basic idea and terminology

Consider predicting the word after in the sentence: the contract ended with a loss of 7 cents after trading as low as 9 cents. A 3-gram approach has to predict after from (7, cents) whereas it is intuitively clear that the strongest predictor would be (contract, ended) which is outside the reach of even 7-grams.

The linguistically correct partial parse of the word history when predicting after is shown in Figure 3.3; the word ENDED is called the headword of the constituent (ENDED ended (WITH with (...))) and ENDED is an exposed headword when predicting after – topmost headword in the largest constituent that contains it. A model that uses the two most recent exposed headwords would predict after from CONTRACT, ENDED, in agreement with our intuition. Another intuitive argument in favor of the headword prediction is the fact that the headword context is invariant to the removal of the (OF of (CENTS 7 cents)) constituent – yielding a correct sentence – whereas the trigram predictor is not invariant to this transformation.

Our working hypothesis is that syntactic structure lters out irrelevant words and points to the important ones – exposed headwords – thus providing an equivalence classi cation of the word pre x and enabling the use of long-distance information when predicting the next word.

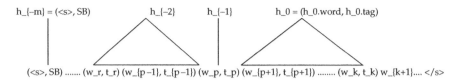

h_{-m} = (<s>, SB)   h_{-2}   h_{-1}   h_0 = (h_0.word, h_0.tag)

(<s>, SB) .... (w_r, t_r) (w_{p-1}, t_{p-1}) (w_p, t_p) (w_{p+1}, t_{p+1}) .... (w_k, t_k) w_{k+1}.... </s>

Figure 3.4 A word-and-parse k-pre x.

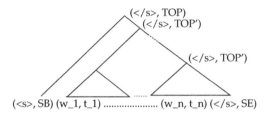

(</s>, TOP)
(</s>, TOP′)

(</s>, TOP′)

(<s>, SB) (w_1, t_1) .... (w_n, t_n) (</s>, SE)

Figure 3.5 Complete parse.

The SLM will attempt to build the syntactic structure incrementally while traversing the sentence left to right. It will assign a probability to every word sequence W and parse T – every possible POS tag assignment, binary branching parse, non-terminal label, and headword annotation for every constituent of T. The probability assignment is based on a simple encoding of the (W, T) pair that is described in the next section.

2.1.1 Word sequence and parse encoding Let W be a sentence of length n words to which we have prepended <s> and appended </s> so that $w_0 =$ <s> and $w_{n+1} =$ </s>. Let $W_k = w_0 \ldots w_k$ be the word k-pre x of the sentence and $W_k T_k$ the word-and-parse k-pre x. To stress this point, a word-and-parse k-pre x contains only those binary subtrees whose span is completely included in the word k-pre x, excluding $w_0 =$ <s>. Single words along with their POS tag can be regarded as root-only trees. Figure 3.4 shows a word-and-parse k-pre x; h_0...h_{-m} are the exposed heads, each head being a pair (head-word, non-terminal label), or (word, POS tag) in the case of a root-only tree. A complete parse – Figure 3.5 – is de ned to be any binary parse of the $(\text{<s>, SB}) (w_1, t_1) \ldots (w_n, t_n) (\text{</s>, SE})$[3] sequence with the restrictions that:

- (</s>, TOP) is the only allowed head;
- $(w_1, t_1) \ldots (w_n, t_n)$ (</s>, SE) forms a constituent headed by (</s>, TOP′).

Note that in a complete parse $(w_1, t_1) \ldots (w_n, t_n)$ *need not* form a constituent[4] but, for the parses where it does, there is no restriction on which of its words is the headword or what the non-terminal label is that accompanies the headword. To clarify this point, the constituents available at the time the end-of-sentence </s> is predicted are attached to </s> under the TOP′ non-terminal tag. For example, a valid SLM parse is one in which each word in the sentence is a separate constituent of span length one – corresponding to the regular n-gram model.

The model operates by means of three modules:

- WORD-PREDICTOR predicts the next word w_{k+1} given the word-and-parse k-pre x and then passes control to the TAGGER;
- TAGGER predicts the POS tag of the next word t_{k+1} given the word-and-parse k-pre x and the newly predicted word and then passes control to the CONSTRUCTOR;
- CONSTRUCTOR grows the already existing binary branching structure by repeatedly generating transitions from the set (unary, NTlabel), (adjoin-left, NTlabel), or (adjoin-right, NTlabel) until it passes control to the PREDICTOR by taking a null transition. NTlabel is the non-terminal label assigned to the newly built constituent and {left, right} speci es where the new headword is inherited from.[5]

The operations performed by the CONSTRUCTOR are illustrated in Figures 3.6–3.8 and they ensure that all possible binary branching parses with all possible headword and non-terminal label assignments for the $w_1 \ldots w_k$ word

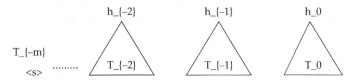

Figure 3.6   Before an adjoin operation.

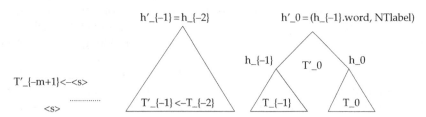

Figure 3.7   Result of adjoin-left under NTlabel.

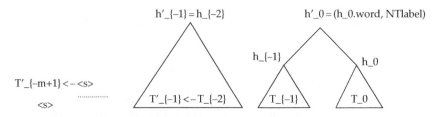

Figure 3.8   Result of adjoin-right under NTlabel.

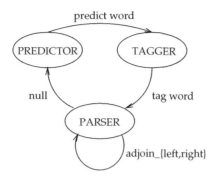

Figure 3.9 Language model operation as a nite state machine.

```
Transition t;            // a CONSTRUCTOR transition
predict (<s>, SB);
do {
  //WORD-PREDICTOR and TAGGER
  predict (next_word, POStag);
  //CONSTRUCTOR
  do {
    if (h_{-1}.word != <s>) {
      if (h_0.word == </s>) {
        t = (adjoin-right, TOP');
      } else {
        if (h_0.tag is in set of NTlabels)
          t = [(adjoin-{left,right}, NTlabel), null];
        else
          t = [(unary, NTlabel), (adjoin-{left,right}, NTlabel), null];
      }
    } else {
      if (h_0.tag is in set of NTlabels)
        t = null;
      else
        t = [(unary, NTlabel), null];
    }
  } while(t != null) //done CONSTRUCTOR
} while(!(h_0.word==</s> && h_{-1}.word==<s>))
t = (adjoin-right, TOP); //adjoin <s>_SB; DONE;
```

Figure 3.10 SLM operation.

sequence can be generated. The nite state machine in Figure 3.9 presents a simpli ed operation of the model. Algorithm (10) below formalizes the above description of the sequential generation of a sentence with a complete parse. The unary transition is allowed only when the most recent exposed head is a leaf of the tree – a regular word along with its POS tag – hence it can be taken at most once at a given position in the input word string. The second subtree in Figure 3.4 provides an example of the structure that results from a unary transition followed by a null transition.

It is easy to see that any given word sequence with a complete parse – see Figure 3.5 – and headword annotation is generated by a unique sequence of model actions.[6] Conversely, a generative model running according to algorithm (10) can only generate a complete parse.

2.2   *Probabilistic model*

The language model operation provides an encoding of a given word sequence along with a parse-tree (W, T) into a sequence of elementary model actions. In order to obtain a correct probability assignment $P(W, T)$ one has to simply assign proper conditional probabilities to each transition in the nite state machine that describes the model – see Figure 3.9.

The probability $P(W, T)$ of a word sequence W and a complete parse T can be calculated as:

$$P(W, T) = \prod_{k=1}^{n+1} \left[P(w_k | W_{k-1} T_{k-1}) \cdot P(t_k | W_{k-1} T_{k-1}, w_k) \cdot P\left(T_{k-1}^k \Big| W_{k-1} T_{k-1}, w_k, t_k \right) \right]$$

$$P\left(T_{k-1}^k | W_{k-1} T_{k-1} \right) = \prod_{i=1}^{N_k} P\left(p_i^k \Big| W_{k-1} T_{k-1}, w_k, t_k, p_1^k \ldots p_{i-1}^k \right)$$

where:

- $W_{k-1} T_{k-1}$ is the word-parse $(k-1)$-pre x;
- w_k is the word predicted by WORD-PREDICTOR;
- t_k is the tag assigned to w_k by the TAGGER;
- T_{k-1}^k is the parse structure attached to T_{k-1} that generates $T_k = T_{k-1} \parallel T_{k-1}^k$; we use $\parallel$ to denote this particular concatenation operation;
- $N_k - 1$ is the number of operations the CONSTRUCTOR executes at position k of the input string before passing control to the WORD-PREDICTOR (the N_k-th operation at position k is the `null` transition); N_k is a function of T;
- p_i^k denotes the i-th CONSTRUCTOR action carried out at position k in the word string: $p_i^k \in \{$ (adjoin-left, NTtag), (adjoin-right, NTtag)$\}, 1 \leq i < N_k, p_i^k = $ `null`$, i = N_k$.

Note that each $\left(W_{k-1} T_{k-1}, w_k, t_k, p_1^k \ldots p_{i-1}^k \right)$ de nes a valid word-parse k-pre x $W_k T_k$ at position k in the sentence, $i = 1 \ldots N_k$.

To ensure a proper probabilistic model over the set of complete parses for any sentence W, certain CONSTRUCTOR and WORD-PREDICTOR probabilities must be given speci c values:[7]

- $P($`null`$| W_k T_k) = 1$, if `h_{-1}.word` = `<s>` and `h_{0}` $\neq$ (`</s>`, `TOP'`) – that is, before predicting `</s>` – ensures that (`<s>`, `SB`) is adjoined in the last step of the parsing process;

- $P(\text{(adjoin-right, TOP)}|W_kT_k)=1,$ if   h_0 = (</s>, TOP') and h_{-1}.word = <s>
  $P(\text{(adjoin-right, TOP')}|W_kT_k)=1,$ if   h_0 = (</s>, TOP') and h_{-1}.word ≠ <s>
  both ensure that the parse generated by our model is consistent with the de nition of a complete parse;
- $\exists \epsilon > 0$ s.t. $\forall W_{k-1}T_{k-1}, P(w_k = </s>|W_{k-1}T_{k-1}) \geq \epsilon$ ensures that the model halts with probability 1, and thus is a proper probability model over strings of words of nite length; once the end of sentence symbol </s> is generated, the model wraps up (completes) the parse with probability 1. In practice smoothing (see equation (5)) makes sure this requirement is met.

2.2.1 Model component parameterization In order to be able to estimate the model components we need to make appropriate equivalence classi cations of the conditioning part for each component. The equivalence classi cation should identify the strong predictors in the context and allow reliable estimates from a treebank. Our choice relies heavily on exposed heads: the experiments in Chelba (1997) show that exposed heads are good predictors for the WORD-PREDICTOR component of the language model; Collins (1996) shows that they are useful for high accuracy parsing, making them the favorite choice for the CONSTRUCTOR model as well; our experiments showed that they are also useful in the TAGGER component model.[8]

(6) $P(w_k|W_{k-1}T_{k-1}) = P(w_k|[W_{k-1}T_{k-1}]) = P(w_k|h_0, h_{-1})$

(7) $P(t_k|w_k, W_{k-1}T_{k-1}) = P(t_k|w_k, [W_{k-1}T_{k-1}]) = P(t_k|w_k, h_0.tag, h_{-1}.tag)$

(8) $P\left(p_i^k|W_kT_k\right) = P\left(p_i^k|[W_kT_k]\right) = P\left(p_i^k|h_0, h_{-1}\right)$

The above equivalence classi cations are limited by the severe data sparseness problem faced by the 3-gram model and by no means do we believe that they cannot be improved upon, especially that used in CONSTRUCTOR model (8). Richer equivalence classi cations should use a probability estimation method that deals better with sparse data than the one presented in Section 2.2.2.

It is worth noting that the 3-gram model belongs to the parameter space of our model: if the binary branching structure developed by the parser were always right-branching – the null transition has probability 1 in the CONSTRUCTOR model – and we mapped the POS tag vocabulary to a single type, then our model would become equivalent to a trigram language model.

2.2.2 Modeling tool All model components – WORD-PREDICTOR, TAGGER, CONSTRUCTOR – are conditional probabilistic models of the type $P(u|z_1, z_2, \ldots, z_n)$ where $u, z_1, z_2, \ldots, z_n$ belong to a mixed set of words, POS tags, NTtags, and CONSTRUCTOR actions (u only). The smoothing technique of Jelinek and Mercer (1980) has been used for estimating all models.

2.3 *Pruning strategy*

Since the number of parses for a given word pre x W_k grows faster than exponen-tial[9] with k, $\Omega(2^k)$, the state space of our model is huge even for relatively short sentences. We thus have to prune most parses without discarding the most likely ones for a given pre x W_k. Our pruning strategy is a synchronous multi-stack search algorithm.

Each stack contains hypotheses – partial parses – that have been constructed by *the same number of PREDICTOR and the same number of CONSTRUCTOR opera-tions*. The hypotheses in each stack are ranked according to the $\ln(P(W_k, T_k))$ score, highest on top. The ordered set of stacks containing partial parses with the same number of PREDICTOR operations but different number of CONSTRUCTOR operations is referred to as a stack-vector.

The amount of search is controlled by two parameters:

- the maximum stack depth – the maximum number of hypotheses the stack can contain at any given time;
- log-probability threshold – the difference between the log-probability score of the topmost hypothesis and the bottommost hypothesis at any given state of the stack cannot be larger than a given threshold.

Figure 3.11 shows schematically the operations associated with the scanning of a new word w_{k+1}.[10] First, all hypotheses in a given stack-vector are expanded with the following word. Then, for each possible POStag the following word can take, we expand the hypotheses further. Due to the nite stack size, some are discarded. We then proceed with the CONSTRUCTOR expansion cycle, which takes place in two steps:

(1)   rst all hypotheses in a given stack are expanded with all possible CON-STRUCTOR actions excepting the null transition. The resulting hypotheses are sent to the immediately lower stack of the same stack-vector – same number of WORD-PREDICTOR operations and exactly one more CON-STRUCTOR move. Some are discarded due to nite stack size;

(2)   after completing the previous step, all resulting hypotheses are expanded with the null transition and sent into the next stack-vector. Pruning can still occur due to the log-probability threshold on each stack.

2.4 *Left-to-right perplexity*

To maintain a left-to-right operation of the language model, the probability assignment for the word at position $k + 1$ in the input sentence was made using:

$$(9)\quad P(w_{k+1}|W_k) = \sum_{T_k \in S_k} P(w_{k+1}|W_k T_k) \cdot \rho(W_k, T_k),$$

$$\rho(W_k, T_k) = P(W_k T_k) / \sum_{T_k \in S_k} P(W_k T_k)$$

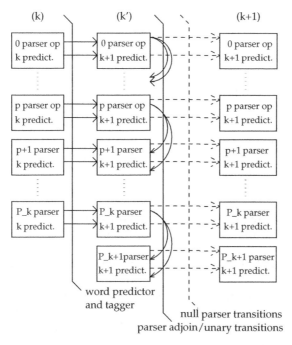

Figure 3.11 One search extension cycle.

where S_k is the set of all parses present in our stacks at the current stage k. This leads to the following formula for evaluating the perplexity:

$$(10) \quad \text{L2R-PPL} = exp\left(-1/N \sum_{i=1}^{N} \ln\left[P(w_i|W_{i-1})\right]\right)$$

2.5 *Separate left-to-right word predictor in the language model*

An important observation is that the next-word predictor probability $P(w_{k+1}|W_kT_k)$ in (9) *need not be the same* as the WORD-PREDICTOR probability (6) used to extract the structure T_k. Thus $P(w_{k+1}|W_kT_k)$ can be estimated separately. To be more speci c, we can in principle have a WORD-PREDICTOR model component that operates within the parser model whose role is to strictly extract syntactic structure and a second L2R-WORD-PREDICTOR model that is used only for the left to right probability assignment:

$$(11) \quad P_2(w_{k+1}|W_k) = \sum_{T_k \in S_k} P_{WP}(w_{k+1}|W_kT_k) \cdot \rho(W_k, T_k),$$

(12) $\rho(W_k, T_k) = P(W_k T_k) \Big/ \sum_{T_k \in S_k} P(W_k T_k)$

In this case the interpolation coef cient given by (12) uses the regular WORD-PREDICTOR model whereas the prediction of the next word for the purpose of word-level probability assignment is made using a separate model $P_{WP}(w_{k+1}|W_k T_k)$.

2.5.1 Initial parameters Each model component – WORD-PREDICTOR, TAGGER, CONSTRUCTOR – is initialized from a set of parsed sentences – a treebank – after the parses undergo headword percolation and binarization, as explained below.

Using the same notation as in the previous section, each binary parse-tree (W, T) with headword annotation is decomposed into its derivation $d(W, T)$. Separately for each m-th model component, we then:

- gather joint counts $C^{(m)}(u^{(m)}, \underline{z}^{(m)})$ from the derivations that make up the development data – about 90 percent of the training data;
- estimate the interpolation coef cients on joint counts gathered from cross-validation data – the remaining 10 percent of the training data – using the EM algorithm (Dempster et al., 1977). The buckets used for tying the interpolation weights are determined heuristically.

These are the initial parameters used with the re-estimation procedure described in the previous section.

2.5.1.1 Headword percolation In order to obtain training data for our model, we need to binarize the UPenn Treebank-style parse-trees and percolate headwords (Marcus et al., 1993). The procedure used was to rst percolate headwords using a context-free (CF) rule-based approach and then binarize the parses by again using a rule-based approach. Inherently a heuristic process, we were satis ed with the output of an enhanced version of the procedure described in Collins (1996).

The procedure rst decomposes a parse tree from the treebank into its phrase constituents, identi ed solely by the non-terminal/POS labels. Within each constituent we then identify the headword position and then, in a recursive third step, we ll in the headword position with the actual word percolated up from the leaves of the tree.

The headword percolation procedure is based on rules for identifying the headword position within each constituent. They are presented in Table 3.1.[11] Let $Z \rightarrow Y_1 \ldots Y_n$ be one of the context-free (CF) rules that make up a given parse. We identify the headword position as follows:

- identify in the rst column of the table the entry that corresponds to the Z non-terminal label;
- search $Y_1 \ldots Y_n$ from either left or right, as indicated in the second column of the entry, for the Y_i label that matches the regular expressions

Table 3.1   Headword percolation rules

TOP	right	_SE _SB
ADJP	right	<~QP|_JJ|_VBN|~ADJP|_$|_JJR>
		<^~PP|~S|~SBAR|_.|_,|_"|_"|_`|_'|_:|_LRB|_RRB>
ADVP	right	<_RBR|_RB|_TO|~ADVP>
		<^~PP|~S|~SBAR|_.|_,|_"|_"|_`|_'|_:|_LRB|_RRB>
CONJP	left	_RB <^_.|_,|_"|_"|_`|_'|_:|_LRB|_RRB>
FRAG	left	<^_.|_,|_"|_"|_`|_'|_:|_LRB|_RRB>
INTJ	left	<^_.|_,|_"|_"|_`|_'|_:|_LRB|_RRB>
LST	left	_LS <^_.|_,|_"|_"|_`|_'|_:|_LRB|_RRB>
NAC	right	<_NNP|_NNPS|~NP|_NN|_NNS|~NX|_CD|~QP|_VBG>
		<^_.|_,|_"|_"|_`|_'|_:|_LRB|_RRB>
NP	right	<_NNP|_NNPS|~NP|_NN|_NNS|~NX|_CD|~QP|_PRP|_VBG>
		<^_.|_,|_"|_"|_`|_'|_:|_LRB|_RRB>
NX	right	<_NNP|_NNPS|~NP|_NN|_NNS|~NX|_CD|~QP|_VBG>
		<^_.|_,|_"|_"|_`|_'|_:|_LRB|_RRB>
PP	left	_IN _TO _VBG _VBN ~PP
		<^_.|_,|_"|_"|_`|_'|_:|_LRB|_RRB>
PRN	left	~NP ~PP ~SBAR ~ADVP ~SINV ~S ~VP
		<^_.|_,|_"|_"|_`|_'|_:|_LRB|_RRB>
PRT	left	_RP <^_.|_,|_"|_"|_`|_'|_:|_LRB|_RRB>
QP	left	<_CD|~QP> <_NNP|_NNPS|~NP|_NN|_NNS|~NX> <_DT|_PDT>
		<_JJR|_JJ> <^_CC|_.|_,|_"|_"|_`|_'|_:|_LRB|_RRB>
RRC	left	~ADJP ~PP ~VP <^_.|_,|_"|_"|_`|_'|_:|_LRB|_RRB>
S	right	~VP <~SBAR|~SBARQ|~S|~SQ|~SINV>
		<^_.|_,|_"|_"|_`|_'|_:|_LRB|_RRB>
SBAR	right	<~S|~SBAR|~SBARQ|~SQ|~SINV>
		<^_.|_,|_"|_"|_`|_'|_:|_LRB|_RRB>
SBARQ	right	~SQ ~S ~SINV ~SBAR <^_.|_,|_"|_"|_`|_'|_:|_LRB|_RRB>
SINV	right	<~VP|_VBD|_VBN|_MD|_VBZ|_VB|_VBG|_VBP> ~S ~SINV
		<^_.|_,|_"|_"|_`|_'|_:|_LRB|_RRB>
SQ	left	<_VBD|_VBN|_MD|_VBZ|_VB|~VP|_VBG|_VBP>
		<^_.|_,|_"|_"|_`|_'|_:|_LRB|_RRB>
UCP	left	<^_.|_,|_"|_"|_`|_'|_:|_LRB|_RRB>
VP	left	<_VBD|_VBN|_MD|_VBZ|_VB|~VP|_VBG|_VBP>
		<^_.|_,|_"|_"|_`|_'|_:|_LRB|_RRB>
WHADJP	right	<^_.|_,|_"|_"|_`|_'|_:|_LRB|_RRB>
WHADVP	right	_WRB <^_.|_,|_"|_"|_`|_'|_:|_LRB|_RRB>
WHNP	right	_WP _WDT _JJ _WP$ ~WHNP
		<^_.|_,|_"|_"|_`|_'|_:|_LRB|_RRB>
WHPP	left	_IN <^_.|_,|_"|_"|_`|_'|_:|_LRB|_RRB>
X	right	<^_.|_,|_"|_"|_`|_'|_:|_LRB|_RRB>

listed in the entry; the rst matching Y_i is going to be the headword of the $(Z\ (Y_1 \ldots) \ldots (Y_n \ldots))$ constituent; the regular expressions listed in one entry are ranked in left-to-right order: rst we try to match the rst one, if unsuccessful we try the second one, and so on.

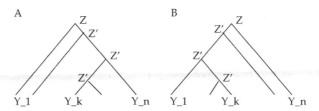

Figure 3.12   Binarization schemes.

A regular expression of the type <_CD|~QP> matches any of the constituents listed between angular parentheses. < ... > are used for constituent types which are desired as headwords, whereas <^ ... > are used for constituent types which are not acceptable as headwords. For example, the <^_.|_,|_''|_``|_'|_'|_:|_LRB|_RRB> regular expression will match any constituent that is *not* – list begins with <^ – among any of the elements in the list between <^ and >, in this case any constituent which is not a punctuation mark is eligible to be a headword. The terminal labels – POS tags – have _ prepended to them – as in _CD; the non-terminal labels have the ~ pre x – as in ~QP; | is merely a separator in the list.

2.5.1.2 Binarization   Once the position of the headword within a constituent is identi ed to be k, we binarize the constituent – equivalent with a CF production of the type $Z \to Y_1, \ldots Y_n$, where $Z, Y_1, \ldots Y_n$ are non-terminal labels or POS tags (only Y_i can be a POS tag) – as follows: a xed rule is used to decide which of the two binarization schemes in Figure 3.12 to apply depending only on the value of Z. The intermediate nodes created by the above binarization schemes receive the non-terminal label Z'.

The choice among the two schemes is made according to the list of rules presented in Table 3.2, based on the identity of the label on the left-hand side of a CF rewrite rule. Notice that whenever $k = 1$ or $k = n - a$ case which is very frequent – the two schemes presented above yield the same binary structure.

Another problem when binarizing the parse-trees is the presence of unary productions. Our model allows unary productions of the type $Z \to Y$ only, where Z is a non-terminal label and Y is a POStag. The unary productions $Z \to Y$ where both Z and Y are non-terminal labels were deleted from the treebank, only the Z constituent being retained: (Z (Y (.) (.))) becomes (Z (.) (.)).

Binarization brings the training data parse-trees to Chomsky normal form, and renders them suitable for the next stage of parameter estimation in our statistical model. Each tree is fed as input to the nite state machine that describes the model – see Figure 3.9. Each transition generates an n-gram event for one of the model components.

2.6 *Model parameter re-estimation*

As outlined in Section 2.4, the word-level probability assigned to a training/test set by our model is calculated using the proper word-level probability assignment

Table 3.2 Binarization rules

```
## first column : constituent label
## second column: binarization type : A or B
TOP       A
ADJP      B
ADVP      B
CONJP     A
FRAG      A
INTJ      A
LST       A
NAC       B
NP        B
NX        B
PP        A
PRN       A
PRT       A
QP        A
RRC       A
S         B
SBAR      B
SBARQ     B
SINV      B
SQ        A
UCP       A
VP        A
WHADJP    B
WHADVP    B
WHNP      B
WHPP      A
X         B
```

in equation (9). An alternative which leads to a de cient probability model is to sum over all the complete parses that survived the pruning strategy.

The estimation procedure of the SLM parameters takes place in two stages:

(1) the N-best training algorithm (see Section 2.6.1) is employed to increase the training data 'likelihood' calculated using the de cient sum-probability assignment. The initial parameters for this rst estimation stage are gathered from a treebank. The perplexity is still evaluated using the formula in equation (9);

(2) estimate a separate L2R-WORD-PREDICTOR model such that the likelihood of the training data according to the probability assignment in equation (11) is increased. The initial parameters for the L2R-WORD-PREDICTOR component are obtained by copying the WORD-PREDICTOR estimated at stage one.

As a nal step in re ning the model we have linearly interpolated the structured language model (9) with a trigram model.

Section 2.6.1 presents the basic idea behind the N-best training stage. Section 2.6.2 presents the training of a separate L2R-WORD-PREDICTOR model – the second re-estimation stage.

2.6.1 N-best EM re-estimation We would like to estimate the model component probabilities (6–8) such that the likelihood of the training data is increased. Since our problem is one of maximum likelihood estimation from incomplete data – the parse structure along with POS/NT tags and headword annotation for a given observed sentence is hidden – our approach makes use of the expectation-maximization algorithm (EM) (Dempster et al., 1977). Two speci c modi cations we make are:

- E-step: instead of scanning all the hidden events allowed – parses T – for a given observed one – sequence of words W – we restrict the algorithm to operate with N-best hidden events;[12] the N-best are determined using the search strategy described in Section 2.3. For a presentation of different modi cations to the EM, the reader is referred to Byrne et al. (1998).
- M-step: assuming that the count ranges and the corresponding interpolation values for each order are kept xed to their initial values – see Section 2.5.1 – the only parameters to be re-estimated using the EM algorithm are the maximal order counts $C^{(m)}(u, z_1, \ldots, z_n)$ for each model component. The interpolation scheme outlined in Section 2.2.2 is then used to obtain a smooth probability estimate for each model component.

The derivation of the re-estimation formulas, the initial parameter values and further comments and experiments on the rst model re-estimation stage are presented in Chelba and Jelinek (2000).

2.6.2 Second stage parameter re-estimation Once the model is trained according to the procedure described in the previous section, we proceed into a second stage of parameter re-estimation. In order to improve performance, we develop a model to be used strictly for word prediction – see (11) – different from the WORD-PREDICTOR model (6). We will call this new component the L2R-WORD-PREDICTOR.

In order to train this fourth model component, the key step is to recognize in (11) a hidden Markov model (HMM) with xed transition probabilities – although dependent on the position in the input sentence k – speci ed by the $\rho(W_k, T_k)$ values.

The E-step of the EM algorithm (Dempster et al., 1977) for gathering joint counts $C^{(m)}(y^{(m)}, \underline{x}^{(m)})$, L2R-WORD-PREDICTOR-MODEL, is the standard one whereas the M-step uses the same count smoothing technique as that described in Section 2.6.1. The second re-estimation step operates directly on the $\mathcal{L}^{L2R}(\mathcal{C}, P_\theta)$ likelihood.

The second re-estimation pass is seeded with the WORD-PREDICTOR model joint counts $C^{(m)}(y^{(m)}, \underline{x}^{(m)})$ resulting from the rst parameter re-estimation pass (see Section 2.6.1).

2.7 UPenn Treebank perplexity results

During the original development of the SLM we chose to work on the UPenn Treebank corpus (Marcus et al., 1993) – a subset of the *WSJ* (*Wall Street Journal*) corpus. This is a well-known corpus and the existence of a manual treebank makes it ideal for our experiments.

Unless speci ed otherwise in a speci c section, the vocabulary sizes were:

(1) word – also WORD-PREDICTOR operation – vocabulary: 10,000, open – all words outside the vocabulary are mapped to the <unk> token;
(2) POStag – also TAGGER operation – vocabulary: 40,000, closed;
(3) non-terminal tag vocabulary: 52,000, closed;
(4) CONSTRUCTOR operation vocabulary: 107,000, closed.

The training data was split into:

(1) *development* set (929,564 words (sections 00–20));
(2) *cross-validation* set (73,760 words (sections 21–2));
(3) *test* set (82,430 words (sections 23–4).

The *development* and *cross-validation* sets were used strictly for initializing the model parameters as described in Section 2.5.1 and then with the re-estimation techniques described in Sections 2.6.1 and 2.6.2.

The parameters controlling the search – see Section 2.3 – were set to: maximum-stack-depth = 10 and LnP-threshold = 6.91.

As explained in Section 2.6.1, the rst stage of model parameter re-estimation re-evaluates the maximal order counts for each model component.

Each iteration involves parsing the entire training data which is a time-consuming process – about 60 hours of Sun Sparc Ultra-2 CPU-time. Table 3.3 shows the results of the re-estimation iterations; E0-3 denote iterations of the re-estimation procedure described in Section 2.6.1; L2R0-5 denote iterations of the re-estimation procedure described in Section 2.6.2. A deleted interpolation trigram model derived from the same training data had perplexity 167.14 on the same test data.

Simple linear interpolation between our model and the trigram model:

$$Q(w_{k+1}/W_k) = \lambda \cdot P(w_{k+1}/w_{k-1}, w_k) + (1 - \lambda) \cdot P(w_{k+1}/W_k)$$

yielded a further improvement in PPL, as shown in Table 3.4. The interpolation weight was estimated on check data to be $\lambda = 0.36$. An overall relative reduction of 11 percent over the trigram model has been achieved.

Table 3.3   Parameter re-estimation results

Iteration number	DEV set L2R-PPL	TEST set L2R-PPL
E0	24.70	167.47
E1	22.34	160.76
E2	21.69	158.97
E3	21.26	158.28
L2R0 (=E3)	21.26	158.28
L2R5	17.44	153.76

Table 3.4   Interpolation with trigram results

Iteration number	TEST set PPL		
	$\lambda = 0.0$	$\lambda = 0.36$	$\lambda = 1.0$
E0	167.47	152.25	167.14
E3	158.28	148.90	167.14
L2R0 (=E3)	158.28	148.90	167.14
L2R5	153.76	147.70	167.14

2.7.1   Maximum depth factorization of the model   The word-level probability assignment used by the SLM can be thought of as a model factored over different maximum reach depths. Let $D(T_k)$ be the depth in the word pre x W_k at which the headword $h_{-1}.word$ can be found:

$$(13) \quad P(w_{k+1}|W_k) = \sum_{d=0}^{d=k} P(d|W_k) \cdot P(w_{k+1}|W_k, d),$$

where:

$$P(d|W_k) = \sum_{T_k \in S_k} \rho(W_k, T_k) \cdot \delta(D(T_k), d)$$

$$P(w_{k+1}|W_k, d) = \sum_{T_k \in S_k} P(T_k|W_k, d) \cdot P(w_{k+1}|W_k, T_k)$$

$$P(T_k|W_k, d) = \rho(W_k, T_k) \cdot \delta(D(T_k), d)/P(d|W_k)$$

We can interpret equation (13) as a linear interpolation of models that reach back to different depths in the word pre x W_k. The expected value of $D(T_k)$ shows how

Table 3.5 Maximum depth evolution
during training

Iteration number	Expected depth E[D]
E0	3.35
E1	3.46
E2	3.45

far the SLM reaches in the word pre x:

$$(14)\quad E_{SLM}[D] = 1/N \sum_{k=0}^{k=N} \sum_{d=0}^{d=k} d \cdot P(d|W_k)$$

For the 3-gram model we have $E_{3-gram}[D]=2$. We evaluated the expected depth of the SLM using the formula in equation (14). The results are presented in Table 3.5.

It can be seen that the memory of the SLM is considerably higher than that of the 3-gram model – whose depth is 2.

Figure 3.13 shows[13] the distribution $P(d|W_k)$, averaged over all positions k in the test string:

$$P(d|W) = 1/N \sum_{k=1}^{N} P(d|W_k)$$

It can be seen that the SLM makes a prediction which reaches farther than the 3-gram model in about 40 percent of cases, on the average.

2.7.1.1 Non-causal 'Perplexity' Attempting to calculate the conditional perplexity by assigning to a whole sentence the probability:

$$(15)\quad P(W|T^*) = \prod_{k=0}^{n} P\left(w_{k+1} | W_k T_k^*\right),$$

where $T^* = argmax_T P(W,T)$ – the search for T^* being carried out according to our pruning strategy – is not valid because it is not causal: when predicting w_{k+1} we would be using T^* which was determined by looking at the entire sentence. In order to have a valid perplexity calculation we would need to factor in the uncertainty of guessing the pre x of the nal best parse T_k^* *before predicting* w_{k+1}, based solely on the word pre x W_k.

However, the perplexity value calculated using (15) is an indication of the lower bound for the achievable perplexity of our model; for the above search parameters and E0 model statistics this bound was 98, corresponding to a relative reduction of 40 percent over the perplexity of the 3-gram model. For comparison, the value

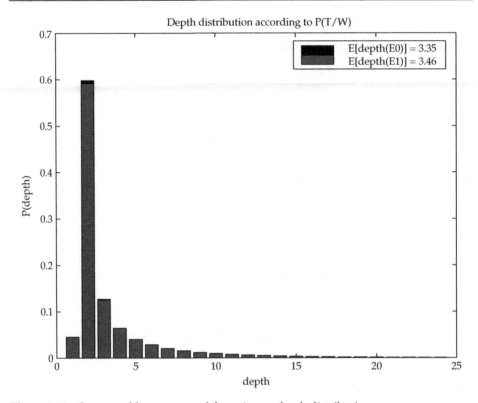

Figure 3.13   Structured language model maximum depth distribution.

when conditioning on the manual parses in the UPenn Treebank – which was used to get the E0 statistics – was 115. This shows that the parses found by our model are better predictors – under the exposed heads parameterization – than those in the treebank.

This suggests that a better parameterization in the SLM – one that reduces the entropy $H(\rho(T_k|W_k))$ of guessing the '*good*' parse given the word pre x – would lead to a better model. Indeed, as we already pointed out, the trigram model is a particular case of our model for which the parse is always right-branching and we have no POS/NT tag information, leading to $H(\rho(T_k|W_k)) = 0$ and a standard 3-gram WORD-PREDICTOR. The 3-gram model is thus an extreme case of the structured language model: one for which the '*hidden*' structure is a *function of the word prefix*. Our result shows that better models can be obtained by allowing richer '*hidden*' structure – parses – and that a promising direction of research is to nd the best compromise between the predictive power of the WORD-PREDICTOR – measured by $H(w_{k+1}|T_k, W_k))$ – and the ease of guessing the most desirable hidden structure $T_k|W_k$ – measured by $H(\rho(T_k|W_k))$ – on which the WORD-PREDICTOR operation is based. The re-estimation procedure we presented is one such method.

3 Speech Recognition Lattice Rescoring Using the Structured Language Model

The SLM was developed primarily for use in speech recognition. A simple way to evaluate a complex language model in such applications is a two-pass recognition approach:

- a computationally cheap decoding step is run as the rst pass;
- a set of hypotheses is retained as an intermediate result;
- a more sophisticated recognizer is run over these in a second pass – usually referred to as the rescoring pass.

The search space in the second pass is much more restricted compared to the rst pass so we can afford to use better – usually also computationally more intensive – acoustic and/or language models.

The two most popular two-pass strategies differ mainly in the number of intermediate hypotheses saved after the rst pass and the form in which they are stored.

In the so-called N-best rescoring method,[14] a list of complete hypotheses along with acoustic/language model scores are retained and then rescored using more complex acoustic/language models.

Due to the limited number of hypotheses in the N-best list, the second pass recognizer might be too constrained by the rst pass so a more comprehensive list of hypotheses is often needed. The alternative preferred to N-best list rescoring is lattice rescoring (Aubert et al., 1994). The intermediate format in which the hypotheses are stored is a directed acyclic graph in which the nodes are a subset of the language model states in the composite hidden Markov model and the arcs are labeled with words. Typically, the rst pass acoustic/language model scores associated with each arc – or link – in the lattice are saved and the nodes contain time alignment information.

Compared to *N*-best lists, lattices typically offer a higher density of paths for a given graph size (measured in number of arcs/nodes). For both cases one can calculate the *'oracle'* word error rate (WER): the word error rate along the hypothesis with the minimum number of errors. The oracle WER decreases with the number of hypotheses saved; thinking of it as an *'achievable'* WER is misleading, since there may not exist an AM/LM in the class of models used that can actually select the word sequence attaining it.

Of course, a set of N-best hypotheses can be assembled as a lattice, the difference between the two being just in the number of different hypotheses – with different time alignments – stored in the lattice. One reason which makes the N-best rescoring framework attractive is the possibility to use *'whole sentence'* language models: models that are able to assign a score only to complete sentences due to the fact that they do not operate in a left-to-right fashion. The drawbacks are that the number of hypotheses explored is too small and their quality re ects the models used in the rst pass. To clarify the latter assertion, assume that the second pass language model is dramatically different from the one used in the rst pass and that if we extracted the N-best list using the second (better) language model, different kinds of errors, speci c to this language model, would be observed. In that case, simple rescoring of the N-best list generated using the weaker language model may prevent the stronger language model from showing its merits.

It is thus desirable to have as complete a sample as possible of the possible word hypotheses – not biased towards a given model – and one of a manageable size. This is what makes lattice rescoring the chosen method in our case.

There are several reasons that make A^* appealing for lattice decoding using the SLM:

- the lattice can be conceptually structured as a pre x tree of hypotheses – the time alignment is taken into consideration when comparing two-word pre xes;
- the algorithm operates with whole pre xes x, making it ideal for incorporating language models whose memory is the entire utterance pre x;
- a reasonably good overestimate $h(y|x)$ and an ef cient way to calculate $h_L(x)$ are readily available using the n-gram language model.

We have applied the SLM for rescoring lattices on both *Wall Street Journal* (*WSJ*) and Switchboard (SWB). The word error rate reduction over a state-of-the-art 3-gram model was:

- 1% absolute (10.6% to 9.6%, 9% relative) on *WSJ*;
- 1% absolute (41.3% to 40.3%, 2% relative) on SWB.

We have also evaluated the perplexity reduction relative to a standard deleted interpolation 3-gram *trained under the same conditions as the SLM*. We have achieved a relative reduction in PPL of 15 percent and 5 percent on *WSJ* and SWB respectively.

4   Richer Syntactic Dependencies

The statistical parsing community have used various ways of enriching the dependency structure underlying the parameterization of the probabilistic model used for scoring a given parse-tree (Collins 1999; Charniak 2000). Recently, such models (Charniak 2001; Roark 2001a) have been shown to outperform the SLM in terms of both PPL and WER on the UPenn Treebank and *WSJ* corpora respectively. In Chelba (2001), a simple way of enriching the probabilistic dependencies in the CONSTRUCTOR component of the SLM also showed better PPL and WER performance; the simple modi cation to the training procedure brought the WER performance of the SLM to the same level with the best reported in Roark (2001a).

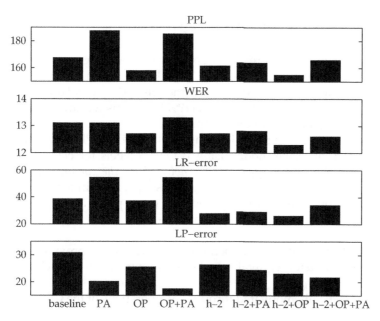

Figure 3.14   Comparison of PPL, WER, labeled recall/precision error.

The work reported in Xu et al. (2002) presents three simple ways of enriching the syntactic dependency structure in the SLM, extending on the work in Chelba (2001). The results show that indeed a good parser (as measured by LP/LR) is helpful in reducing the PPL and WER. Another remarkable fact is that a language model exploiting elementary syntactic dependencies obviates the need for a 3-gram model in N-best rescoring.

In particular, the best-performing enriching scheme achieved a 0.4 percent absolute WER reduction over the performance of the standard SLM. Overall, the enriched SLM achieves 10 percent relative reduction in WER over the 3-gram model baseline result.

The enriched SLM outperformed the 3-gram used to generate the lattices and N-best lists, without interpolating it with the 3-gram model. Although the N-best lists are already highly restricted by the 3-gram model during the rst recognition pass, this fact still shows the potential of a good grammar-based language model, especially when the SLM was trained on 20 million words of *WSJ*, while the lattice 3-gram model was trained on 45 million words of *WSJ* text. Our results are not indicative of the performance of SLM as a rst pass language model.

It is very interesting that labeled recall and language model performance (WER/PPL) are well correlated. Figure 3.14 compares PPL, WER ($\lambda = 0.0$ at training iteration 0), and labeled precision/recall error (100-LP/LR) for all models. Overall, the labeled recall is well correlated with the WER and PPL values. We believe that these results show that improvements in parser accuracy are expected to lead to improvements in WER.

5 Comparison with Other Approaches

The SLM shares many features with both class-based language models (Brown et al., 1992) and skip n-gram language models (Rosenfeld 1994); an interesting approach combining class-based language models and different order skip-bigram models is presented in Saul and Pereira (1997). It seems worthwhile to make two comments relating the SLM to these approaches.

The smoothing involving NT/POS tags in the WORD-PREDICTOR is similar to a class-based language model using NT/POS labels for classes. We depart, however, from the usual approach by *not making the conditional independence assumption* $P(w_{k+1}|w_k, \text{class}(w_k)) = P(w_{k+1}|\text{class}(w_k))$. Also, in our model, the '*class assignment*' – through the heads exposed by a given parse T_k for the word pre x W_k and its '*weight*' $\rho(W_k, T_k)$, see equation (9) – is:

- highly context-sensitive – it depends on the entire word pre x W_k;
- is randomized – a few equivalence classes are extracted from each context, each weighted by $\rho(W_k, T_k)$;
- and is syntactically motivated through the operations of the CONSTRUCTOR.

We also found the POS/NT labels in the PREDICTOR equivalence classi cation to be useful for better word prediction.

Recalling the depth factorization of the model in equation (13), our model can be viewed as a skip n-gram where the probability of a skip $P(d_0, d_1|W_k) - d_0, d_1$ are the depths at which the two most recent exposed headwords h_0, h_1 can be found, similar to $P(d|W_k)$ – is highly context-sensitive. Note that the hierarchical scheme for organizing the word pre x allows for contexts that do not necessarily consist of adjacent words, as in regular skip n-gram models.

6 Conclusion

Among the directions which we consider worth exploring in the future for improving the structured language model, there are:

- automatic induction of the SLM initial parameter values;
- study of other binarization schemes, in particular left-corner ones promise to be extremely suitable to the SLM operation;
- better integration of the 3-gram model and the SLM;
- better parameterization of the model components;
- study of the interaction between SLM and other language modeling techniques such as cache and trigger or topic language models.

In the broader scope, a couple of important and promising directions in statistical language modeling are:

- language model adaptation: how to leverage data sources that may not be fully matched to a scenario of interest;   nding relevant data to be used in an adaptation setup (Berger & Miller 1998) is of course equally important;
- discriminative training for language models – n-gram or more general ones – used in a source-channel paradigm.

Of particular interest is a direction worth highlighting separately: scalability. Scaling to very large training data sets and language models, along the lines of Brants et al. (2007), is a signi cant disruption as far as modeling techniques are concerned. Many techniques developed on small to medium data sets (10– 100 million words) may lose their edge, while others prove valuable by being more effective learners. Computational issues aside, the rate at which a given model improves when presented with increasing amounts of relevant training data becomes a critical aspect in such a data-rich regime. Despite its simplistic treatment of natural language, the n-gram model is extremely successful in practice, not least because of its ability to easily make use of large amounts of data. Techniques that attempt to model language better need to balance modeling power with simplicity in order to scale well with increasing amounts of data.

Finally, it is worth putting in perspective the fact that in a source-channel approach (see equation (4)), the language model is *nothing more than a prior guess* on the word sequence W, which completely disregards the input signal F. As such, its ability to reduce the conditional entropy $H(W|F)$ is expected to be limited, especially when the channel model is poor and provides limited information about the W string that gave rise to the signal F. An intuitive explanation is that the language model is our best guess for what the user might say or type at the input of an automatic speech recognition or statistical machine translation system respectively, *before* the input speech, or sentence F, is revealed!

From this point of view, it is unrealistic to expect a large impact on performance coming from the language model alone; it can do so to the extent that it complements the channel model well. Speculatively comparing the impact of similar-size language models across different applications (ASR, SMT, spelling correction) and similar tasks seems to support this view. The SMT noisy channel constrains the choice of output words much more than the ASR one: the latter starts from a pressure wave instead of a sentence in foreign language. As such, the sensitivity of SMT accuracy to LM performance is generally higher than in ASR. The same relationship seems to hold when comparing similar LMs used in spelling correction and SMT, the former being a more constrained noisy channel.

ACKNOWLEDGMENT

Parts of this chapter appeared in *Computer Speech & Language* 14(4):283–332, October 2000, and are used with the permission of Elsevier Limited.

NOTES

1   We note that in some practical systems the constraint on using a properly normalized language model is sidestepped at a gain in modeling power and simplicity.

2   Language models estimated on different vocabularies cannot be directly compared using perplexity, since they model completely different probability distributions.

3   SB/SE is a distinguished POS tag for sentence begin and end respectively.

4   The set of complete parses is a superset of the parses in the UPenn Treebank which insist that $(w_1, t_1) \ldots (w_n, t_n)$ forms a constituent.

5   Obviously, the headword origin after a unary transition is fully determined.

6   This will prove very useful in initializing our model parameters from a treebank – see Section 2.5.1.

7   The set of constraints on the probability values of different model components is consistent with algorithm 10.

8   Since the word to be tagged is in itself a very strong predictor for the POS tag, we limit the equivalence classi cation of the TAGGER model to include only the NTlabels of the two most recent exposed heads.

9   Thanks to Bob Carpenter, Lucent Technologies Bell Labs, for pointing out this inaccuracy in our paper (Chelba & Jelinek 1998).

10 P_k is the maximum number of adjoin operations for a k-length word pre x; since the tree is binary we have $P_k = k - 1$.

11 The origin of this table of rules is not clear, they are attributed to Magerman and Black.

12 For a better understanding, this procedure can be thought of as analogous to a compromise between the forward-backward and Viterbi re-estimation for hidden Markov models.

13 The non-zero value of $P(1|W)$ is due to the fact that the prediction of the rst word in a sentence is based on context of length 1 – sentence begin – in both SLM and 3-gram models.

14 The value of N is typically 100–1,000.

4 Theory of Parsing

MARK-JAN NEDERHOF
AND GIORGIO SATTA

1 Introduction

In the context of natural language processing, the term *parsing* refers to the process of automatically analyzing a given sentence, viewed as a sequence of words, in order to determine its possible underlying syntactic structures.

Parsing requires a mathematical model of the syntax of the language of interest. In this chapter, these mathematical models are assumed to be formal grammars. A *formal grammar* consists of a collection of rules that specify how elements of the language, e.g., words, may be combined to form sentences, and how sentences are structured. Rules may be concerned with purely syntactic information, such as grammatical functions, subject–verb agreement, word ordering, etc., but some models may also incorporate issues such as lexical semantics.

There is a wide range of grammatical formalisms, which depend on various syntactic theories, and the structures that result from parsing, or *parses*, may differ substantially between one such formalism and another. Many formalisms specify the syntactic analysis of a sentence in terms of a *phrase structure*, which is an ordered, labeled tree that expresses hierarchical relations among certain groupings of words called *phrases*. An alternative representation is *dependency structure*, which indicates binary grammatical relations between words in a sentence.

In contrast to these 'deep' representations, there are also 'shallow' representations of syntactic structures, where the maximum depth is severely restricted. Such representations are typically obtained using nite state techniques.

The main importance of parse structures lies in the grammatical information they convey to modules that implement semantic, pragmatic, and discourse processing, which are crucial in applications such as text summarization, question answering, and machine translation. Parsing can therefore be seen as a central part in typical natural language processing systems, and the accuracy of the parses can have much impact on the success of an application as a whole.

In this chapter we do not further discuss the interaction between parsing and the other types of linguistic processing mentioned above, nor do we discuss the

The Handbook of Computational Linguistics and Natural Language Processing, First Edition.
Edited by Alexander Clark, Chris Fox and Shalom Lappin.
© 2013 Blackwell Publishing Ltd except for editorial material and organization
© 2013 Alexander Clark, Chris Fox, and Shalom Lappin. Published 2013 by Blackwell Publishing Ltd.

criteria for the possible choices of grammatical formalisms and parse structures. Instead, we cast the parsing problem into an abstract framework, and analyze mathematical and computational aspects of parsing algorithms.

Parsing is related to *recognition*, which is the process of determining whether an input sentence is in a chosen language or, equivalently, whether some underlying syntactic structure can be assigned to a given sentence. Many of the algorithms that we will discuss in this chapter are recognition algorithms, but since they can be straightforwardly extended to perform parsing, we will sometimes blur the distinction between parsing and recognition.

The set of parses that a natural language grammar allows for a given input sentence is typically very large. This is because formal grammars often fail to capture subtle properties of the structure, meaning, and use of language, and consequently allow many parses that humans would not nd plausible. Signi cant practical dif culties in computing and storing the parses can be avoided by computing isolated fragments of these and storing them in a table. The advantage of this is that one such fragment may be shared among many different parses. This is called *tabular parsing*.

Many tabular parsing methods are capable of computing and storing exponentially many parses using only polynomial time and space. Tabular parsing, invented in the eld of computer science in the period roughly between 1965 and 1975, also became known later in the eld of computational linguistics as *chart parsing*. Tabular parsing is a form of dynamic programming, a standard paradigm in the design of computer algorithms.

In natural language systems, parsing is commonly one stage of processing among several others. The effectiveness of the stages that follow parsing generally relies on having obtained a small set of preferred parses, ideally only one, from among the full set of parses. This process is called *syntactic disambiguation*.

One common approach is to augment each grammar rule with some kind of numeric value, or *weight*. During parsing these values are combined to give values for entire parses, and the optimal value (which might be the minimum or the maximum, depending on the nature of the values) then determines the preferred parse.

One special case of this is *probabilistic parsing*, which relies on the assignment of probabilities to grammar rules. The probability of a parse is de ned as the product of the probabilities of the rules out of which it is constructed. Disambiguation is achieved by selecting the parse with the highest probability. The success of probabilistic parsing, and weighted parsing in general, is due to their exibility and scalability, in contrast to approaches to syntactic disambiguation that rely on much deeper knowledge of language.

The structure of this chapter is as follows. In Section 2 we look at simple recognition algorithms for context-free grammars. We then consider the parsing problem for context-free grammars in Section 3, and its probabilistic extension in Section 4. Section 5 explores the parsing problem for context-free grammars that have been augmented with lexical information. The related subject of dependency parsing is discussed in Section 6. Parsing of tree adjoining grammars, a formalism generatively more powerful than context-free grammars, is discussed in Section 7. In Section 8 we show how parsing algorithms can be exploited in syntax-based machine translation.

2   Context-Free Grammars and Recognition

In this section we consider two algorithms that perform context-free recognition. The input consists of a **context-free grammar** $G = (\Sigma, N, S, R)$ and a string $w = a_1 a_2 \cdots a_n$. Here Σ and N are two disjoint sets of terminal and non-terminal symbols respectively, $S \in N$ is the start symbol, and R is the set of rules of the grammar. The output is a Boolean value, depending on whether w is in the language generated by G.

Both algorithms are tabular, and run in polynomial time, both in the size of the input grammar and in the length of the input string. Furthermore, they are among the best-known and most widely used recognition algorithms in natural language processing, often in an extended form as parsing algorithms, as will be explained in the next section.

The older of the two algorithms is called the Cocke–Kasami–Younger algorithm, or *CKY algorithm* for short, after the three authors by whom it was independently discovered. The algorithm implements a pure bottom-up strategy, which means it starts by recognizing non-terminal occurrences near the leaves of parse-trees, and works upwards from there.

The CKY algorithm requires the grammar to be in *Chomsky normal form* (CNF), that is, each rule must have one of the following two forms:

$A \rightarrow B\ C$, where $B, C \in N$;
$A \rightarrow a$, where $a \in \Sigma$.

Any CFG, provided it does not derive the empty string, can be cast into CNF by a transformation that preserves the language. To accommodate for the empty string, some de nitions of CNF include $S \rightarrow \varepsilon$ as an allowable rule, provided that S does not occur in the right-hand side of any rule. To keep the presentation simple, however, we will further ignore rules of the form $S \rightarrow \varepsilon$.

We let $\mathcal{T}$ denote the table of the CKY algorithm. The elements stored in the table, which we will refer to as *items*, have the form $[i, A, j]$, where $A \in N$ and $0 \le i < j \le n$, and n is the length of the input string $w = a_1 \cdots a_n$. The numbers i and j are best thought of as *input positions*: the position 0 precedes a_1, each position i with $1 \le i \le n - 1$ separates the symbol occurrences a_{i-1} and a_i in w, and n is the position following a_n.

If an item $[i, A, j]$ is added to the table, this signi es that the substring $a_{i+1} \cdots a_j$ of w can be derived from non-terminal A, or formally $A \Rightarrow^+ a_{i+1} \cdots a_j$. This can be seen as a partial recognition result, and the main goal of the algorithm is to add item $[0, S, n]$ to the table. This item is found at the end of the process if and only if the input string is correct.

```
1: Function CKY(G, w) {w = a₁ ··· aₙ; R the rules of G}
2:   T ← ∅;
3:   for all j from 1 up to n do
4:      for all rules A → aⱼ in R do
5:         add [j − 1, A, j] to T;
6:      for all i from j − 2 down to 0 do
7:         for all k from i + 1 up to j − 1 do
8:            for all rules A → B C in R do
9:               if [i, B, k] and [k, C, j] are both in T then
10:                  add [i, A, j] to T;
11: if [0, S, n] is in T then
12:    return true;
13: else
14:    return false;
```

Figure 4.1   The CKY recognition algorithm.

	1	2	3	4
0	A	S, A	S, A	S, A
1		A	A	A
2			S	S
3				S

Figure 4.2   Table T obtained by the CKY algorithm.

The algorithm is presented in Figure 4.1. The table is initially empty (line 2). For each input position j, the algorithm considers substrings ending in j, and nds the non-terminals from which the substrings can be derived. First, substrings a_j of length 1 are considered. The Chomsky normal form implies that any parse of such a substring consists of a single rule occurrence of the form $A → a_j$. This justi es lines 4 and 5.

Then, substrings $a_{i+1} \cdots a_j$ of length greater than 1 are considered ($j > i + 1$). The CNF implies that if such a substring can be derived from A, then there is a rule $A → B\ C$, for some B and C, from which $a_{i+1} \cdots a_k$ and $a_{k+1} \cdots a_j$ can be derived respectively, for some choice of k, where $i < k < j$. This is the basis for lines 6 through 10.

As an example, consider the CFG with $\Sigma = \{a, b\}$, $N = \{S, A\}$, and with rules $S → S\ S, S → A\ A, S → b, A → A\ S, A → A\ A$, and $A → a$, and consider the input string $w = aabb$. The table T produced by the CKY algorithm is given in Figure 4.2, represented as an upper triangular matrix. Each cell at row i and column j contains all the non-terminals B such that $[i, B, j]$ is in T. This means that the main diagonal represents derivations of substrings of length 1, the next diagonal corresponds to substrings of length 2, etc. In the example, the string w is recognized since the start symbol S is found in the cell in the upper right corner.

An alternative way of describing a tabular algorithm is by means of a *deduction system*, where we have logical, declarative expressions in place of procedural ones. This is exempli ed for CKY recognition in Figure 4.3. A deduction system contains a set of inference rules, each consisting of a list of *antecedents*, which stand for items that we have already added to T, and, below a horizontal line, the *consequent*,

$$\frac{}{[j-1,A,j]}\{A \to a_j \quad \text{(a)}\}$$

$$\frac{[i,B,k]}{[k,C,j]}\{A \to B\,C \quad \text{(b)}\}$$

Figure 4.3   The CKY recognition algorithm, expressed as a deduction system.

which stands for an item that we derive from the antecedents and that is added to $\mathcal{T}$ unless it is already present. To the right of the horizontal line, we may also write a number of *side conditions*, which indicate when rules may be applied, on the basis of the given grammar.

One difference between pseudo-code as in Figure 4.1 and deduction systems as in Figure 4.3 is that the latter does not specify the exact order of the steps. Let us consider the upper triangular matrix in Figure 4.2. The contents of a cell depend, directly or indirectly, on cells that are (1) on the same row or a row further down, and (2) on the same column or a column further to the left. These dependencies between cells are consistent with an algorithm that computes the columns from left to right, and within each column computes the rows from bottom to top. This is realized in Figure 4.1. Another algorithm could for example compute the rows from bottom to top, and within each row compute the columns from left to right. The deduction system allows both strategies, as well as several others.

The time complexity of a recognition algorithm is commonly determined by the number of steps, but not by their relative order. A deduction system can therefore allow a simpler and more abstract description of an algorithm, while the computational properties remain identical to those of a speci cation of the same algorithm in pseudo-code.

In the case of the CKY algorithm, the complexity is dominated by the inference rule in Figure 4.3(b). As this inference rule involves one grammar rule and three input positions, the number of corresponding steps is $\mathcal{O}(|R|\,n^3) = \mathcal{O}(|\mathcal{G}|\,n^3)$, and this is also the total time complexity of the CKY algorithm. The number of items of the form $[i, A, j]$ is $\mathcal{O}(|N|\,n^2) = \mathcal{O}(|\mathcal{G}|\,n^2)$, and this is also the space complexity.

When considering the size of the grammar in the above analysis, one should remember that transformation to CNF is needed before the CKY algorithm can be applied, and such transformations may increase the size by a square function. The second algorithm we consider, called *Earley's algorithm*, circumvents this problem by allowing the input grammar to be an arbitrary context-free grammar. To simplify the presentation, however, we will assume that there is only one rule in R of the form $S \to \alpha$. (If this does not hold, it suf ces to add a new start symbol $S^\dagger$ and a rule $S^\dagger \to S$.)

The items for Earley's algorithm are of the form $[i, A \to \alpha \bullet \beta, j]$, where $A \to \alpha\beta$ is a rule from R. The components $A \to \alpha \bullet \beta$ are often called *dotted rules*. Intuitively, the dot separates the grammar symbols that have already been found to derive some portion of the input string (between positions i and j) from those grammar symbols that are still to be processed. Whereas CKY parsing only used combinations of i and j such that $i < j$, Earley's algorithm relaxes this constraint to $i \leq j$. The added case $i = j$ is particularly relevant if α is the empty string, but

```
 1: Function EARLEY(G, w) {w = a₁ ··· aₙ; R the rules of G}
 2:   T ← A ← {[0, S → • σ, 0]};
 3:   for all j from 0 to n do
 4:       for all items [i, A → α • aα', j − 1] in T do
 5:           if a = aⱼ then
 6:               add [i, A → αa • α', j] to T and to A;
 7:       while A ≠ ∅ do
 8:           remove some [k, A → α • α', j] from A;
 9:           if α' = Bβ then
10:               for all rules B → γ in R do
11:                   if item [j, B → • γ, j] is not in T then
12:                       add [j, B → • γ, j] to T and to A;
13:               for all items [j, B → γ • , j] in T do
14:                   if item [k, A → αB • β, j] is not in T then
15:                       add [k, A → αB • β, j] to T and to A;
16:           if α' = ε then
17:               for all items [i, B → β • Aγ, k] in T do
18:                   if item [i, B → βA • γ, j] is not in T then
19:                       add [i, B → βA • γ, j] to T and to A;
20:   if [0, S → σ • , n] is in T then
21:       return true;
22:   else
23:       return false;
```

Figure 4.4　The Earley recognition algorithm.

it may also occur if α merely *derives* the empty string by epsilon rules. (By *epsilon rule*, we mean a rule with an empty right-hand side.)

In addition, an item of the form $[i, A \to \alpha \bullet \beta, j]$ is only added to the table T if an occurrence of $A \to \alpha\beta$ starting at position i is consistent with the input preceding position i. More precisely, $[i, A \to \alpha \bullet \beta, j]$ is eventually added to T if and only if:

(1)　$S \Rightarrow^* a_1 \cdots a_i A\gamma$, for some γ, and
(2)　$\alpha \Rightarrow^* a_{i+1} \cdots a_j$.

The second condition mirrors the condition for items in the CKY algorithm, whereas the ﬁrst condition introduces a type of left-to-right directionality, in such a way that no rule occurrence can be considered unless it ﬁts in a parse-tree that is consistent with the input to the left of the position currently considered.

Earley's algorithm is presented as pseudo-code in Figure 4.4. Next to the familiar table T, there is another set A, in which items are stored that still need to be processed. We call this set the *agenda*. We ensure that items are never added to the agenda more than once, so that the parsing process is guaranteed to terminate.

Initially, in line 2, the agenda is made to contain a single item, with dotted rule $S \to \bullet \sigma$. This is sometimes called the *initializer step*. The intuition is that it starts the investigation whether the input can be derived from S, under the assumption we made earlier that $S \to \sigma$ is the only rule with left-hand side S. The dot is at the beginning of the right-hand side as no grammar symbols have been matched against the input yet.

$$\frac{}{[0, S \to \bullet\, \sigma, 0]} \text{ (a)}$$

$$\frac{[i, A \to \alpha \bullet a\beta, j-1]}{[i, A \to \alpha a \bullet \beta, j]}\{a = a_j \text{ (c)}$$

$$\frac{[i, A \to \alpha \bullet B\beta, j]}{[j, B \to \bullet\, \gamma, j]}\{B \to \gamma \text{ (b)}$$

$$\frac{\begin{array}{c}[i, A \to \alpha \bullet B\beta, k]\\ [k, B \to \gamma \bullet, j]\end{array}}{[i, A \to \alpha B \bullet \beta, j]} \text{ (d)}$$

Figure 4.5 Deduction system for Earley's algorithm.

Lines 4 to 6 are called the *scanner step*, as the processed part of the right-hand side is extended by matching one terminal symbol against a symbol from the input string. Lines 10 to 12 are called the *predictor step*, as they predict an occurrence of a rule starting at position j. The *completer step* consists of lines 13 to 15 and of lines 17 to 19. Both code fragments do essentially the same, namely combining two items associated with two consecutive substrings into a third item associated with the joint substring. One or the other code fragment is used depending on whether the rst or the second of these items is found rst. Lines 13 to 15 are in fact only necessary if there are epsilon rules; otherwise γ in line 13 cannot derive the empty string and therefore the item on that line cannot exist.

In the formulation as deduction system, in Figure 4.5, the completer step is expressed more succinctly, as inference rule (d). The initializer step appears as rule (a), the predictor step as rule (b), and the scanner step as rule (c).

The step that dominates the running time is clearly the completer step, as that involves three input positions and two rules, making the time complexity $\mathcal{O}(|\mathcal{G}|^2 n^3)$, which can be improved to $\mathcal{O}(|\mathcal{G}| n^3)$ with a small trick that we will not discuss here. The space complexity is $\mathcal{O}(|\mathcal{G}| n^2)$.

Let us consider the CFG consisting of the rules $S \to E$, $E \to E - E$, and $E \to a$, and consider the input string $w = a - a - a$. The table produced by Earley's algorithm can be represented as an upper triangular matrix, as illustrated in Figure 4.6. Each cell at row i and column j contains all the dotted rules $A \to \alpha \bullet \beta$ such that $[i, A \to \alpha \bullet \beta, j]$ is in $\mathcal{T}$.

This matrix is similar to the one in Figure 4.2, which was constructed by the CKY algorithm. One difference is that there is now an extra diagonal, which contains items that correspond to the empty string. Items resulting from the predictor step will end up in cells in this diagonal.

Observe that $[0, E \to E - E \bullet, 5]$ can be derived from $[0, E \to E- \bullet E, 4]$ and $[4, E \to a \bullet, 5]$ or from $[0, E \to E- \bullet E, 2]$ and $[2, E \to E - E \bullet, 5]$. This indicates that w is ambiguous.

3 Context-Free Parsing

In this section we look at the computation of parse-trees, and consider how recognition algorithms can be extended to become parsing algorithms. Since the number of parse-trees can be exponential in the length of the input string, and

	0	1	2	3	4	5
0	$S \to \bullet\, E$ $E \to \bullet\, E - E$ $E \to \bullet\, a$	$E \to a\, \bullet$ $S \to E\, \bullet$ $E \to E\, \bullet\, {-}E$	$E \to E{-}\, \bullet\, E$	$E \to E - E\, \bullet$ $S \to E\, \bullet$ $E \to E\, \bullet\, {-}E$	$E \to E{-}\, \bullet\, E$	$E \to E - E\, \bullet$ $S \to E\, \bullet$ $E \to E\, \bullet\, {-}E$
1						
2			$E \to \bullet\, E - E$ $E \to \bullet\, a$	$E \to a\, \bullet$ $E \to E\, \bullet\, {-}E$	$E \to E{-}\, \bullet\, E$	$E \to E - E\, \bullet$ $E \to E\, \bullet\, {-}E$
3						
4					$E \to \bullet\, E - E$ $E \to \bullet\, a$	$E \to a\, \bullet$ $E \to E\, \bullet\, {-}E$
5						

Figure 4.6   Table $\mathcal{T}$ obtained by Earley's algorithm.

even in nite when $\mathcal{G}$ is cyclic, one rst needs to nd a way to compactly represent the set of all parse-trees.

Let us assume a CFG $\mathcal{G} = (\Sigma, N, S, R)$ and an input string $w = a_1 \cdots a_n$ over Σ. A representation of all parse-trees of w is called a *parse forest* and is itself a CFG $\mathcal{G}_w$. The alphabet of $\mathcal{G}_w$ is the same as that of $\mathcal{G}$, and the non-terminals of $\mathcal{G}_w$ have the form (j, X, i), where $X \in N \cup \Sigma$ and $0 \leq j \leq i \leq n$. The start symbol of $\mathcal{G}_w$ is $(0, S, n)$.

If w is in the language generated by $\mathcal{G}$, then the rules of $\mathcal{G}_w$ should ideally be the rules $(i - 1, a_i, i) \to a_i$ $(1 \leq i \leq n)$ plus the rules $(i_0, A, i_m) \to (i_0, X_1, i_1) \cdots (i_{m-1}, X_m, i_m)$ such that:

(1) $(A \to X_1 \cdots X_m) \in R$,
(2) $S \Rightarrow^* a_1 \cdots a_{i_0} A a_{i_m+1} \cdots a_n$, and
(3) $X_j \Rightarrow^* a_{i_{j-1}+1} \cdots a_{i_j}$ for $1 \leq j \leq m$.

In words, there are two kinds of rules in $\mathcal{G}_w$. The rst, of the form $(i - 1, a_i, i) \to a_i$, is little more than a notational convenience. It attaches appropriate input positions to occurrences of terminals in the input. The second kind, of the form $(i_0, A, i_m) \to (i_0, X_1, i_1) \cdots (i_{m-1}, X_m, i_m)$, is obtained by taking a rule from $\mathcal{G}$ and annotating it with input positions that project the members of the right-hand side onto consecutive substrings of the input. Constraint (2) above guarantees that the rule occurrence thus speci ed is part of at least one complete parse-tree, which spans the entire input string and has label S at the root.

In intermediate stages of parsing, however, constraint (2) and sometimes also constraint (3) may be violated, which means that $\mathcal{G}_w$ contains *useless rules*, that is, rules that either do not derive any string, or that cannot be reached from the start symbol. Useless rules can be removed from a CFG by a process called *reduction*, which has a running time that is linear in the size of the grammar.

$(0, a, 1) \rightarrow a$

$(1, a, 2) \rightarrow a$

$(2, b, 3) \rightarrow b$

$(3, b, 4) \rightarrow b$

$(0, A, 1) \rightarrow (0, a, 1)$

$(1, A, 2) \rightarrow (1, a, 2)$

$(2, S, 3) \rightarrow (2, b, 3)$

$(3, S, 4) \rightarrow (3, b, 4)$

$(0, S, 2) \rightarrow (0, A, 1) \ (1, A, 2)$

$(0, A, 2) \rightarrow (0, A, 1) \ (1, A, 2)$ †

$(1, A, 3) \rightarrow (1, A, 2) \ (2, S, 3)$

$(2, S, 4) \rightarrow (2, S, 3) \ (3, S, 4)$

$(0, S, 3) \rightarrow (0, A, 1) \ (1, A, 3)$

$(0, S, 3) \rightarrow (0, S, 2) \ (2, S, 3)$

$(0, A, 3) \rightarrow (0, A, 1) \ (1, A, 3)$ †

$(0, A, 3) \rightarrow (0, A, 2) \ (2, S, 3)$ †

$(1, A, 4) \rightarrow (1, A, 2) \ (2, S, 4)$

$(1, A, 4) \rightarrow (1, A, 3) \ (3, S, 4)$

$(0, S, 4) \rightarrow (0, A, 1) \ (1, A, 4)$

$(0, S, 4) \rightarrow (0, S, 2) \ (2, S, 4)$

$(0, S, 4) \rightarrow (0, S, 3) \ (3, S, 4)$

$(0, A, 4) \rightarrow (0, A, 1) \ (1, A, 4)$ †

$(0, A, 4) \rightarrow (0, A, 2) \ (2, S, 4)$ †

$(0, A, 4) \rightarrow (0, A, 3) \ (3, S, 4)$ †

Figure 4.7 Parse forest associated with table T from Figure 4.2.

If the input string w is not in the language generated by G, then reduction of G_w removes all rules, including those of the form $(i - 1, a_i, i) \rightarrow a_i$, and thereby G_w generates the empty language. If the string is in the language, then G_w generates the singleton language $\{w\}$. Furthermore, the parse-trees of G_w are isomorphic to those parse-trees of G that derive w.

Many recognition algorithms can be easily extended to become parsing algorithms. For the CKY algorithm, this involves adding a rule of the form $(i, A, j) \rightarrow (i, B, k) \ (k, C, j)$ to G_w each time an item $[i, A, j]$ is found, based on the existence in the table of items $[i, B, k]$ and $[k, C, j]$ and a rule $A \rightarrow BC$. In the resulting parse forest, constraint (3) is always satis ed, but constraint (2) may be violated, and a top-down traversal may be needed to remove rules that are not reachable from $(0, S, n)$.

Let us return to the grammar from Section 2 with rules $S \rightarrow SS$, $S \rightarrow AA$, $S \rightarrow b$, $A \rightarrow AS$, $A \rightarrow AA$, $A \rightarrow a$, and input $w = aabb$. We have seen the table in Figure 4.2 that is produced by CKY recognition. The corresponding parse forest is given in Figure 4.7. Rules that are subsequently eliminated by reduction are marked by †.

As the CKY algorithm assumes the input grammar G is in CNF, the size of G_w is dominated by the number of rules of the form $(i, A, j) \rightarrow (i, B, k) \ (k, C, j)$, which is $\mathcal{O}(|G| n^3)$. From the resulting parse forest G_w, an individual parse-tree can be extracted in time proportional to the size of the parse-tree itself, which is $\mathcal{O}(n)$. In contrast, the table T can be stored with only $\mathcal{O}(|G| n^2)$ space, but extracting an individual parse-tree directly from T requires running time $\mathcal{O}(n^2)$.

For general CFGs, CKY parsing is not applicable, but we can extend Earley's algorithm to produce parse forests, as a side-effect of recognition. The size of a parse forest is then $|G_w| = \mathcal{O}(|G| n^{p+1})$, where p is the length of the longest right-hand side of a rule in G, which is considerably bigger than if the input grammar were in CNF.

For this reason, practical systems often store the set of parse-trees using a mod i ed form of parse forests, with rules having no more than two members in the right-hand side. The main differences with Chomsky normal form are that unary rules and epsilon rules are allowed. For such parse forests, extraction of an individual parse-tree is more involved, but can still be done in linear time in the size of that parse-tree.

4   Probabilistic Parsing

Many parsing algorithms can be extended to compute probabilities of strings or of parses, which we refer to as *probabilistic parsing*. One application is to identify the most likely parse of an input sentence, as a form of disambiguation. To simplify the presentation, we will here consider a form of disambiguation that is strictly separated from the parsing process. More precisely, we assume that a parse forest is constructed as rst step, for example by CKY parsing or Earley's algorithm. Subsequently, the parse forest is analyzed to identify the parse-tree with the highest probability. The presentation is further simpli ed by showing only how to compute that highest probability, rather than the parse-tree itself.

In order to assign probabilities to parse-trees, we de ne a *probabilistic context-free grammar* (PCFG) to be of the form $\mathcal{G} = (\Sigma, N, S, R, p)$, where (Σ, N, S, R) is a CFG and p is a mapping from rules in R to real numbers between 0 and 1. We say a PCFG is *proper* if for every non-terminal A:

$$\sum_{A \to \alpha} p(A \to \alpha) = 1$$

In other words, properness means that for each A, p de nes a probability distribution over the rules with left-hand side A.

Let us de ne the probability of an occurrence of a rule in a parse-tree as the probability of that rule, as speci ed by p. The probability of a parse-tree is then de ned as the product of the probabilities of the rule occurrences out of which it is constructed. We say that a PCFG is *consistent* if the sum of probabilities of all allowable parse-trees is 1. Many proper PCFGs that arise in practice are also consistent, but consistency is not guaranteed by properness.

Given a probabilistic CFG $\mathcal{G}$ and a string w, a parse forest $\mathcal{G}_w$ is constructed much as in the previous section. One difference in the present section is that $\mathcal{G}_w$ is itself also a probabilistic CFG. A rule of $\mathcal{G}_w$ of the form $(i-1, a_i, i) \to a_i$ is assigned the probability 1, and a rule of the form $(i_0, A, i_m) \to (i_0, X_1, i_1) \cdots (i_{m-1}, X_m, i_m)$ is assigned the probability $p(A \to X_1 \cdots X_m)$, where p is the probability assignment of the input grammar $\mathcal{G}$. The parse forest $\mathcal{G}_w$ is in general neither proper nor consistent, even when $\mathcal{G}$ is proper and consistent.

Consider for example the PCFG $\mathcal{G}$ with the following rules, with probabilities between brackets:

$$S \to A \quad (0.7)$$
$$S \to A S \quad (0.3)$$
$$A \to a \quad (0.8)$$
$$A \to A A \quad (0.2)$$

```
1: Function KNUTH(𝒢)
2:   ℰ ← Σ
3:   repeat
4:     ℱ ← {A | A ∉ ℰ ∧ ∃A → X₁ ⋯ Xₘ[X₁, …, Xₘ ∈ ℰ]}
5:     if ℱ = ∅ then
6:       return 'failure'
7:     for all A ∈ ℱ do
8:       q(A) ←        max           p(π) · pₘₐₓ(X₁) · … · pₘₐₓ(Xₘ)
                 π=(A→X₁⋯Xₘ):
                 X₁,…,Xₘ∈ℰ
9:     choose A ∈ ℱ such that q(A) is maximal
10:    pₘₐₓ(A) ← q(A)
11:    ℰ ← ℰ ∪ {A}
12:  until S ∈ ℰ
13:  return pₘₐₓ(S)
```

Figure 4.8   Knuth's generalization of Dijkstra's algorithm, applied to nding the most probable parse in a probabilistic context-free grammar $\mathcal{G}$.

With input $w = aa$, $\mathcal{G}_w$ is the following PCFG:

$$(0, S, 2) \rightarrow (0, A, 2) \qquad\qquad (0.7)$$
$$(0, S, 2) \rightarrow (0, A, 1)\,(1, S, 2) \quad (0.3)$$
$$(0, A, 2) \rightarrow (0, A, 1)\,(1, A, 2) \quad (0.2)$$
$$(1, S, 2) \rightarrow (1, A, 2) \qquad\qquad (0.7)$$
$$(0, A, 1) \rightarrow (0, a, 1) \qquad\qquad (0.8)$$
$$(1, A, 2) \rightarrow (1, a, 2) \qquad\qquad (0.8)$$
$$(0, a, 1) \rightarrow a \qquad\qquad\qquad\quad (1)$$
$$(1, a, 2) \rightarrow a \qquad\qquad\qquad\quad (1)$$

The two parse-trees in $\mathcal{G}_w$ have probabilities $0.7 * 0.2 * 0.8 * 0.8 = 0.0896$ and $0.3 * 0.8 * 0.7 * 0.8 = 0.1344$ respectively. Disambiguation could therefore opt for the second of these parses.

We have already observed in the previous section that parses of w have roughly the same structures as parses in $\mathcal{G}_w$. Because the probabilities of corresponding parses are identical as well, we can reduce the problem of nding the most likely parse of w with grammar $\mathcal{G}$ to the problem of nding the most likely parse in grammar $\mathcal{G}_w$.

Let us therefore consider an arbitrary PCFG $\mathcal{G}$, which may, but need not, be a parse forest produced by CKY parsing or a comparable parsing algorithm. One way of nding the most likely parse in $\mathcal{G}$ is the algorithm in Figure 4.8, which is due to Knuth. It generalizes Dijkstra's algorithm to compute the shortest path in a weighted graph. Knuth's algorithm nds the probability $p_{max}(A)$ of the most probable subparse with root labeled A. The value $p_{max}(S)$, where S is the start symbol, then gives us the probability of the most probable parse.

The set $\mathcal{E}$ contains all grammar symbols X for which $p_{max}(X)$ has already been established. At the beginning, this is just the set of terminals, assuming $p_{max}(a) = 1$ for all $a \in \Sigma$.

At each iteration, the set $\mathcal{F}$ contains non-terminals A such that a subparse with root labeled A exists consisting of a rule $A \rightarrow X_1 \cdots X_m$, and subparses with roots labeled $X_1, \ldots, X_m$ matching the values of $p_{max}(X_1), \ldots, p_{max}(X_m)$ found earlier. From these candidates, the non-terminal A for which such a subparse has the highest probability is then added to $\mathcal{E}$. The process ends normally when $p_{max}(S)$ is found. If there are no parses at all in the grammar, which may happen if the grammar is not reduced, then the algorithm returns a 'failure' value.

The number of iterations of Knuth's algorithm is linear in the number of non-terminals. Values of the form $p(\pi) \cdot p_{max}(X_1) \cdot \ldots \cdot p_{max}(X_m)$ need to be computed only once for each rule. The set $\mathcal{F}$ can be reused between two subsequent iterations, with minor modifications. The choice of A in line 9 relies on the arrangement of the elements in $\mathcal{F}$ in a priority queue according to the values of q. It follows that the running time is $\mathcal{O}(|\mathcal{G}| + |N| \log(|N|))$, where the factor $\log(|N|)$ corresponds to the running time of operations of the priority queue containing up to $|N|$ elements.

In the example above, the first two values of p_{max} that are found are $p_{max}((0, a, 1)) = 1$ and $p_{max}((1, a, 2)) = 1$. As the values are identical, they can be found in any order. Similarly, the next two values, $p_{max}((0, A, 1)) = 0.8$ and $p_{max}((1, A, 2)) = 0.8$, can be found in either order. Then, $p_{max}((1, S, 2)) = 0.7 * p_{max}((1, A, 2)) = 0.56$ and $p_{max}((0, A, 2)) = 0.2 * p_{max}((0, A, 1)) * p_{max}((1, A, 2)) = 0.128$ are found, and, lastly, $p_{max}((0, S, 2))$ is found as the maximum of $0.7 * p_{max}((0, A, 2)) = 0.0896$ and $0.3 * p_{max}((0, A, 1)) * p_{max}((1, S, 2)) = 0.1344$, which is 0.1344, as we have seen before.

If the input grammar is in Chomsky normal form, values of the form $p_{max}((i, A, j))$ can be computed in a fixed order, in such a way that all $p_{max}((i, B, k))$ and $p_{max}((k, C, j))$ are computed before any value $p_{max}((i, A, j))$. This is achieved by a probabilistic extension of CKY recognition. It is also regarded as an extension to CFGs of Viterbi's algorithm for probabilistic finite state models.

The probabilistic CKY algorithm is given by Figure 4.9. It is instructive to compare this to CKY recognition as presented in Figure 4.1. Instead of adding elements $[i, A, j]$ to $\mathcal{T}$, the probabilistic algorithm assigns non-zero values to $p_{max}([i, A, j])$. The two algorithms have the same time complexity. Finding the most likely parse based on values of p_{max} also has the same time complexity as the extraction of a parse-tree from $\mathcal{T}$.

5   Lexicalized Context-Free Grammars

A central issue in modeling the syntax of natural language is the sensitivity of syntactic structures to the choice of terminal symbols, also called *lexical elements*. Consider the difference between the following two sentences:

(1)   our *company* is training workers
(2)   our *problem* is training workers

In the first case, 'training workers' should be parsed as verb phrase with 'is' as auxiliary verb. In the second case, 'training workers' is used nominally as argument of

```
1: Function CKY(G, w) {w = a₁ ⋯ aₙ; R the rules of G}
2:   for all j from 1 up to n do
3:      for all non-terminals A do
4:         if there is a rule A → aⱼ then
5:            p_max([j − 1, A, j]) ← p(A → aⱼ);
6:         else
7:            p_max([j − 1, A, j]) ← 0;
8:      for all i from j − 2 down to 0 do
9:         for all non-terminals A do
10:           p_max([i, A, j]) ← 0;
11:           for all k from i + 1 up to j − 1 do
12:              for all rules A → B C in R do
13:                 p_max([i, A, j]) ←
14:                                max(p_max([i, A, j]),
                                         p(A → B C) · p_max([i, B, k]) · p_max([k, C, j]));
15: return p_max([0, S, n]);
```

Figure 4.9 The probabilistic CKY algorithm.

'is,' which requires a different parse. Traditional CFGs with non-terminals for basic categories such as noun, verb, noun phrase, etc., lack the means to distinguish between lexical elements, needed to disambiguate sentences such as the above.

A common solution is to incorporate a lexical element as a so-called *head* in each non-terminal of the CFG. These heads play an important role in the syntactic and semantic content of the derived string. In this section we consider a model called bilexical context-free grammar. This model is used extensively in natural language parsing. It allows us to write rules of the form S[training] → NP[company] VP[training], which expresses that a noun phrase whose main element is 'company' can combine with a verb phrase whose main element is 'training.' One might, however, want to exclude a rule of the form S[training] → NP[problem] VP[training] as, typically, a problem cannot be the subject of training. Alternatively, in *probabilistic* bilexical context-free grammars, which are discussed further at the end of this section, such a rule may be given a very low probability.

Formally, a *bilexical context-free grammar* (2-LCFG) is a CFG with non-terminal symbols of the form $A[a]$, where a is a terminal symbol and A is a symbol drawn from a set of so-called *delexicalized non-terminals*, which we denote as V_D. Every rule in a 2-LCFG has one of the following forms:

$A[a] → B[b] C[a]$,
$A[a] → B[a] C[c]$,
$A[a] → B[a]$,
$A[a] → a$.

Note that the terminal symbol associated with the left-hand side non-terminal is always inherited from the right-hand side.

We assume the existence of a dummy terminal \$ to the right of each sentence and nowhere else. A dummy delexicalized non-terminal represented by the same

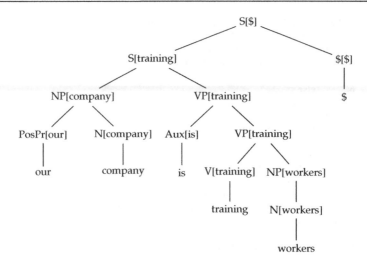

Figure 4.10   A parse of 'our company is training workers,' assuming a bilexical context-free grammar.

symbol allows terminal $ to be derived by $[$] $\rightarrow$ $. The start symbol of a 2-LCFG is $S[\$]$ and there are rules expanding it to $S[a]$ $\$[\$]$, where a can be, for example, the main verb of a sentence. Figure 4.10 presents a possible parse-tree.

A 2-LCFG can have $\Theta|V_D|^3 \cdot |\Sigma|^2$ binary rules, where Σ denotes the set of terminals. Whereas V_D is typically small, the set Σ can be very large. When parsing with a 2-LCFG, it is therefore preferable to restrict the grammar to those rules that contain lexical elements occurring in the input sentence w. With general context-free parsing as discussed in Section 3, the time complexity would then be $\mathcal{O}(|V_D|^3 \cdot |w|^5)$, under the reasonable assumption that $|w| < |\Sigma|$. Note that this is two factors of $|w|$ worse than the time complexity of unlexicalized parsing.

A recognition algorithm that was speci cally designed for lexicalized grammars reduces the time complexity by one factor of $|w|$. It is presented by Figure 4.11. It uses several types of items, the rst of the form $[i, A, h, j]$. This encodes that the lexicalized non-terminal $A[a_h]$ can derive the substring $a_{i+1} \cdots a_j$ of w. It is comparable to an item $[i, A[a_h], j]$ that we would have in the case of the CKY algorithm. In some steps of the algorithm below, it is convenient to ignore either the index i or the index j from $[i, A, h, j]$, by replacing one or the other by a hyphen.

There are also items of the form $[B, h, A, j, k]$. Such an item indicates that $[-, B, h, j]$ and $[j, C, h', k]$ were derived, for some C and h' such that $A[a_h] \rightarrow B[a_h]$ $C[a_{h'}]$ is a rule. This represents an intermediate step in establishing $[i, A, h, k]$, as illustrated in Figure 4.12. The reduction of the time complexity comes from the possibility to temporarily ignore the left boundary i of the substring derived from the left child $B[a_h]$.

$$\frac{}{[h-1,A,h,h]}\;\left\{\begin{array}{l}A[a_h]\to a_h\\ 1\le h\le n+1\end{array}\right. \quad (a)$$

$$\frac{[i,A,h,j]}{[i,A,h,-]}\quad (e)$$

$$\frac{[i,B,h,j]}{[i,A,h,j]}\;\{A[a_h]\to B[a_h]\}\quad (b)$$

$$\frac{[i,A,h,j]}{[-,A,h,j]}\quad (f)$$

$$\frac{\begin{array}{c}[-,B,h,j]\\ [j,C,h',k]\end{array}}{[B,h,A,j,k]}\;\{A[a_h]\to B[a_h]\,C[a_{h'}]\}\quad (c)$$

$$\frac{\begin{array}{c}[i,B,h,j]\\ [B,h,A,j,k]\end{array}}{[i,A,h,k]}\quad (g)$$

$$\frac{\begin{array}{c}[i,B,h',j]\\ [j,C,h,-]\end{array}}{[i,j,A,C,h]}\;\{A[a_h]\to B[a_{h'}]\,C[a_h]\}\quad (d)$$

$$\frac{\begin{array}{c}[j,C,h,k]\\ [i,j,A,C,h]\end{array}}{[i,A,h,k]}\quad (h)$$

Figure 4.11   Deduction system for recognition with a 2-LCFG. We assume $w=a_1\cdots a_n,\;a_{n+1}=\$$.

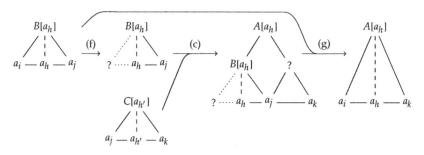

Figure 4.12   Illustration of the use of inference rules (f), (c), and (g) of bilexical recognition.

Items of the form $[i,j,A,C,h]$ have a symmetrical meaning, that is, they indicate that $[i,B,h',j]$ and $[j,C,h,-]$ were derived, for some B and h' such that $A[a_h]\to B[a_{h'}]\,C[a_h]$ is a rule.

Each of the inference rules involves no more than four input positions and three delexicalized non-terminals. This corresponds to $\mathcal{O}(|V_D|^3\cdot|w|^4)$ applications of each inference rule, which is also the total time complexity of the algorithm.

The above recognition algorithm can be extended to parsing, and especially probabilistic parsing with bilexical grammars. This requires only minor modi - cations. In practice, explicit representation of a probabilistic 2-LCFG as a set of lexicalized rules would require a prohibitive amount of storage and, furthermore, obtaining accurate probabilities for each of the rules is very hard.

Therefore, lexicalized rules are often produced on-the- y during parsing of the input string, and their probabilities are then computed as the product of proba-bilities of a number of features that together determine the rule. For example, the probability of $A[b]\to B[b]\,C[c]$ can be expressed as the probability of B given A and b, times the probability of C as second member in the right-hand side, given

A, *b*, and *B*, times the probability of *c* given *A*, *b*, *B*, and *C* as second member. The last probability can be approximated as, for example, the probability of *c* given *b* and *C*.

6 Dependency Grammars

Dependency grammars are a formalism for the syntactic representation of natural language based on dependencies between pairs of words. This formalism has a long tradition in descriptive linguistics. From a computational perspective, dependency grammars have also proved to be a simple yet exible formalism, which can be applied to several natural language processing tasks.

A dependency grammar represents syntactic structures by means of dependency trees. A *dependency tree* for a sentence *w* is a directed tree whose nodes are all the words of *w*. Each arc of the tree represents a single syntactic dependency directed from a word to its modi er, and is labeled with the speci c syntactic function that is encoded, e.g., SBJ for subject and NMOD for modi er of a noun. Figure 4.13 presents an example of a dependency tree. An arti cial token representing the root of the dependency tree is appended to the sentence as the right-most word, similarly to what we have done for 2-LCFGs.

A dependency tree is called *projective* if its edges can be drawn in the plane above the words of the sentence, without any edges crossing each other. Figure 4.13 is an example of a projective tree. In a *non-projective* dependency tree, this property is violated, as illustrated by Figure 4.14. Non-projectivity is typically needed to handle long-distance dependencies and exible word order.

In this section we mainly focus on dependency grammars that derive projective dependency trees and that are augmented with probabilities. Dependency grammars deriving projective trees can be enriched with probabilities in several ways. We consider here one of the simplest models, called *edge-factored*, which assigns a probability to each modi er word conditioned on the headword, and which assumes that decisions are independent, within the global constraint that the resulting structure must be a projective tree. To simplify the presentation, we also ignore dependency labels.

More formally, a *probabilistic projective dependency grammar* (PPDG) is a tuple $\mathcal{G} = (\Sigma, p)$, where Σ is a nite alphabet and p is a function with two arguments as explained below, taking real values in the interval $[0, 1]$. The notation includes special symbols $\mathcal{L}$, $\mathcal{R}$, \$, and $\bot$ not in Σ. The symbols $\mathcal{L}$ and $\mathcal{R}$ represent left and right direction respectively for a dependency relation, \$ represents the root symbol, and $\bot$ indicates halting of the generation process. Function p is de ned over the terms:

$$p(\$ \to a, \mathcal{L}), \quad a \in \Sigma$$
$$p(a \to b, D), \quad a, b \in \Sigma, \; D \in \{\mathcal{L}, \mathcal{R}\}$$
$$p(a \to \bot, D), \quad a \in \Sigma, \; D \in \{\mathcal{L}, \mathcal{R}\}$$

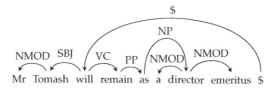

Figure 4.13   A projective dependency tree.

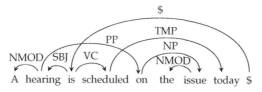

Figure 4.14   A non-projective dependency tree.

The root $ takes a unique dependent from Σ, always to its left. The probability that such a dependent is word a is $p(\$ \to a, \mathcal{L})$. The probability of generating a dependency between headword a and modifier word b at its left, conditioned upon a, is $p(a \to b, \mathcal{L})$, and the probability of stopping the generation of left dependents of a is $p(a \to \perp, \mathcal{L})$. Probabilities $p(a \to b, \mathcal{R})$ and $p(a \to \perp, \mathcal{R})$ have a symmetrical meaning with respect to the generation of dependents at the right direction.

The following normalization conditions must be satisfied by p:

$$\sum_{a \in \Sigma} p(\$ \to a, \mathcal{L}) = 1$$

and for every $a \in \Sigma$ and $D \in \{\mathcal{L}, \mathcal{R}\}$:

$$p(a \to \perp, D) + \sum_{b \in \Sigma} p(a \to b, D) = 1$$

For a dependency tree t, we define $p(t)$ as the product of the probabilities of all the involved dependencies, including the stop events. For a sentence w, we define $p(w)$ as the sum of all $p(t)$, with t a dependency tree of w. It is not difficult to see that a PPDG induces a probability distribution over projective dependency trees and over the generated strings.

There is a natural mapping from the class of PPDGs to the probabilistic 2-LCFGs from Section 5. This mapping preserves the probabilities of trees, modulo straightforward restructuring operations. Let $\mathcal{G} = (\Sigma, p)$ be some PPDG. We construct a probabilistic 2-LCFG $\mathcal{G}' = (\Sigma \cup \{\$\}, N, R, S[\$], p')$ with

$$N = \{A[a] \mid A \in \{\mathcal{H}_1, \mathcal{H}_2\},\ a \in \Sigma\} \cup \{S[\$], \$[\$]\}$$

and with R including all of the following rules with associated probabilities:[1]

$$S[\$] \to \mathcal{H}_1[a]\,\$[\$] \qquad\qquad p'(\cdot) = p(\$ \to a)$$
$$\mathcal{H}_1[a] \to \mathcal{H}_1[b]\,\mathcal{H}_1[a] \qquad p'(\cdot) = p(a \to b, \mathcal{L})$$
$$\mathcal{H}_1[a] \to \mathcal{H}_2[a] \qquad\qquad p'(\cdot) = p(a \to \perp, \mathcal{L})$$
$$\mathcal{H}_2[a] \to \mathcal{H}_2[a]\,\mathcal{H}_1[b] \qquad p'(\cdot) = p(a \to b, \mathcal{R})$$
$$\mathcal{H}_2[a] \to a \qquad\qquad\quad p'(\cdot) = p(a \to \perp, \mathcal{R})$$
$$\$[\$] \to \$ \qquad\qquad\qquad p'(\cdot) = 1$$

It is not dif cult to see that $\mathcal{G}'$ satis es the usual properness conditions de ned for PCFGs.

The above mapping allows us to reuse all of the algorithms developed for (probabilistic) CFGs, in order to do parsing for a PPDG, transferring the resulting parses back to projective dependency trees. For example, the recognition algorithm for 2-LCFGs from Section 5 would provide a $\mathcal{O}(|\mathcal{G}|\,n^4)$ time recognition algorithm for (probabilistic) PDGs.

In what follows, we derive a more ef cient recognition algorithm, running in time $\mathcal{O}(|\mathcal{G}|\,n^3)$. The improvement is obtained by specializing the recognition algorithm for 2-LCFGs to the speci c grammars resulting from the above mapping. Since this is a recognition algorithm, we focus on the underlying 2-LCFG, disregarding the probabilities attached to the rules.

The algorithm is based on the following idea. We observe that in $\mathcal{G}'$ there are no structural dependencies between the left and the right arguments (complements or modi ers) of any headword a. The sequences of the left arguments and the sequences of the right arguments can therefore be processed independently, and joined only when this is computationally convenient. We call left (right) *split* any partial parse consisting of a head and some of its left (right, respectively) arguments.

To simplify the presentation of the algorithm, we ignore the recognition of the rules $S[\$] \to \mathcal{H}_1[a]\,\$[\$]$, and $\$[\$] \to \$$, which is straightforward. We use items of the form $[h - 1, \mathcal{R}, j]$ to represent a right split with headword a_h, with zero or more right arguments extending up to position $j \geq h$. Similarly, an item $[i, \mathcal{L}, h]$ represents a left split with $i \leq h - 1$. An item $[h - 1, \mathcal{R}, h')$ represents a headword a_h with zero or more right arguments, followed at the right by the left split of one of its right arguments with headword $a_{h'}$, $h' > h$. Items of the form $(h' - 1, \mathcal{L}, h]$, with $h' < h$, have a symmetric interpretation.

The algorithm is given in Figure 4.15 by means of a deduction system. Inference rules (a) and (d) initialize a right and left split respectively, consisting of a single headword. Rule (b) extends a right split with headword a_h to the right, by means of a left split with headword $a_{h'}$, provided a constituent headed in $a_{h'}$ is a valid right argument for a constituent headed in a_h. As already discussed, the right arguments of the headword $a_{h'}$ can be ignored at this point.

Inference rule (e) completes the process started by (b), by attaching the missing right arguments of the headword $a_{h'}$. Inference rules (c) and (f) have a symmetrical interpretation.

The time complexity of the algorithm is determined by the maximum number of input positions in inference rules. This is 3, and the running time is therefore

$$\frac{}{[h-1,\mathcal{R},h]}\begin{cases}\mathcal{H}_2[a_h]\to a_h,\\1\le h\le n\end{cases}\text{(a)}\qquad\frac{}{[h-1,\mathcal{L},h]}\begin{cases}\mathcal{H}_1[a_h]\to\mathcal{H}_2[a_h],\\1\le h\le n\end{cases}\text{(d)}$$

$$\frac{[h-1,\mathcal{R},i]\quad[i,\mathcal{L},h']}{[h-1,\mathcal{R},h')}\{\mathcal{H}_2[a_h]\to\mathcal{H}_2[a_h]\,\mathcal{H}_1[a_{h'}]\}\text{ (b)}\qquad\frac{[h-1,\mathcal{R},h')\quad[h'-1,\mathcal{R},j]}{[h-1,\mathcal{R},j]}\text{ (e)}$$

$$\frac{[j,\mathcal{L},h]\quad[h'-1,\mathcal{R},j]}{(h'-1,\mathcal{L},h]}\{\mathcal{H}_1[a_h]\to\mathcal{H}_1[a_{h'}]\,\mathcal{H}_1[a_h]\}\text{ (c)}\qquad\frac{(h'-1,\mathcal{L},h]\quad[i,\mathcal{L},h']}{[i,\mathcal{L},h]}\text{ (f)}$$

Figure 4.15   Deduction system for recognition with PDGs. We assume $w = a_1 \cdots a_n$, and disregard the recognition of $a_{n+1} = \$$.

$\mathcal{O}(n^3)$. By looking at the maximum number of instantiations of the four types of items, we can conclude that the space complexity is $\mathcal{O}(n^2)$. These complexity results are independent of the size of the input grammar. For this reason, dependency parsing is sometimes called 'grammarless.'

Several algorithms for non-projective parsing have been proposed in the literature, often based on local relaxation of non-projectivity. Allowing arbitrary crossing of branches, however, amounts to treating the input as a multiset of words, and the resulting dependency structures as unordered trees. The parsing problem can then be reduced to the problem of nding the optimal spanning tree of a weighted graph. This graph has one vertex for each word in the input sentence, and one edge with appropriate weight for each allowable dependency between a corresponding pair of words. A standard method is applied for nding the directed spanning tree in the graph having the highest weight. This corresponds to the dependency tree with the highest probability.

Common algorithms to nd spanning trees in directed graphs make use of greedy approaches, and run in time $\mathcal{O}(m\log(n))$ for general graphs with m arcs and n vertices, and in time $\mathcal{O}(n^2)$ for dense graphs. In the case of dependency grammars, the graph is usually dense, and therefore non-projective dependency parsing can be done in quadratic time in the length of the input, whereas projective dependency parsing has a cubic time complexity. However, if the model is enriched with certain kinds of contextual information, then non-projective dependency parsing becomes NP-hard.

7   Tree Adjoining Grammars

For modeling the syntax of natural language, several grammatical formalisms have been investigated that fall beyond the generative power of context-free grammars. Of particular linguistic relevance is the class of tree adjoining grammars, which is a mildly context-sensitive formalism.

A *tree adjoining grammar* (TAG) is a tuple $\mathcal{G} = (\Sigma, N, S, \mathcal{I}, \mathcal{A})$, where Σ and N are nite, disjoint sets of terminal and non-terminal symbols respectively, $S \in N$ is the start symbol, and $\mathcal{I}$ and $\mathcal{A}$ are nite sets of *elementary* trees, called *initial* and

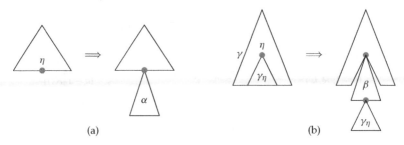

Figure 4.16   Substitution (a) and adjunction (b) in a tree adjoining grammar.

auxiliary trees respectively. In an elementary tree, internal nodes are labeled by symbols in N, and leaf nodes are labeled by symbols in $N \cup \Sigma \cup \{\varepsilon\}$. In addition, each auxiliary tree has a special leaf node, called *foot* node, having the same non-terminal label as its root node.

In a TAG, the notion of derivation is based on two operations involving tree composition, de ned in what follows. A substitution node η in an elementary tree (or a derivation thereof, see below) is a leaf node labeled by a non-terminal symbol and annotated with a set $Subst(\eta)$ of initial trees with root labeled by the same symbol as η. The *substitution* operation takes an initial tree $\alpha \in Subst(\eta)$ and replaces η with a copy of α, as illustrated in Figure 4.16(a).

An internal node η in an elementary tree γ (or a derivation thereof) is associated with a set $Adj(\eta)$ of auxiliary trees with root (and foot node) labeled by the same symbol as η. Let γ_η denote the complete subtree of γ rooted in η. The *adjunction* operation takes an auxiliary tree $\beta \in Adj(\eta)$ and produces a new tree speci ed as follows:

(1) γ_η is excised from γ;
(2)   a copy of β replaces γ_η in γ, with the root of β replacing the excised node η;
(3) γ_η is attached to the resulting tree, with the foot node of β replacing η in γ_η.

This is illustrated in Figure 4.16(b).

In a TAG, a *derivation* is the process of recursive composition of elementary trees using the substitution and the adjunction operations. The resulting trees are called *derived* trees. The language generated by a TAG is the set of strings that are yields of derived trees with S as root label and terminal symbols as labels of the leaf nodes.

We will now discuss a bottom-up tabular recognition algorithm for TAGs. To simplify the presentation, we assume that all elementary trees are binary, and that no leaf node is labeled by the empty string ε. The input string has the form $w = a_1 \cdots a_n, n \geq 1$ and $a_i \in \Sigma$ for each i with $1 \leq i \leq n$.

The algorithm uses items of the form $[\eta_X, i, j, f_1, f_2]$, denoting a complete sub-tree of an elementary tree, with possible substitutions and adjunctions. Here η is the root of the subtree, spanning the substring $a_{i+1} \cdots a_j$ of w, and the foot of the subtree spans the substring $a_{f_1+1} \cdots a_{f_2}$. We let $f_1 = f_2 = -$ if there is no foot node in the subtree. Symbol $X \in \{\bot, \top\}$ records whether adjunction at η has already

$$\frac{}{[\eta_\perp, i-1, i, -, -]} \left\{ \begin{array}{l} \eta \text{ labeled} \\ \text{by } a_i \end{array} \right. \quad (a)$$

$$\frac{}{[\eta_\perp^\beta, i, j, i, j]} \left\{ \begin{array}{l} \eta^\beta \text{ foot} \\ \text{of } \beta \in \mathcal{A}, \\ i < j \end{array} \right. \quad (b)$$

$$\frac{[\eta_\top', i, k, -, -]}{[\eta_\top'', k, j, f_1, f_2]} \left\{ \begin{array}{l} \eta', \eta'' \\ \text{children of } \eta \end{array} \right. \quad (c1)$$

$$\frac{[\eta_\top', i, k, f_1, f_2]}{[\eta_\top'', k, j, -, -]} \left\{ \begin{array}{l} \eta', \eta'' \\ \text{children of } \eta \end{array} \right. \quad (c2)$$

$$\frac{[\eta_\top', i, k, -, -]}{[\eta_\top'', k, j, -, -]} \left\{ \begin{array}{l} \eta', \eta'' \\ \text{children of } \eta \end{array} \right. \quad (c3)$$

$$\frac{[\eta_\top^\alpha, i, j, -, -]}{[\eta_\top, i, j, -, -]} \left\{ \begin{array}{l} \alpha \in Subst(\eta), \\ \eta^\alpha \text{ root of } \alpha \end{array} \right. \quad (d)$$

$$\frac{[\eta_\perp, i, j, f_1, f_2]}{[\eta_\top, i, j, f_1, f_2]} \quad (e)$$

$$\frac{[\eta_\top^\beta, i, j, f_1, f_2]}{[\eta_\top, i, j, f_1', f_2']} \left\{ \begin{array}{l} \beta \in Adj(\eta), \\ \eta^\beta \text{ root of } \beta \end{array} \right. \quad (f)$$

Figure 4.17 The TAG bottom-up recognition algorithm, expressed as a deduction system.

been checked ($X = \top$) or not ($X = \perp$). This is done to avoid multiple adjunction at a single node, which is forbidden in traditional TAGs.

The algorithm is presented by Figure 4.17. Rules (a) and (b) initialize the parsing table with items representing leaf nodes that are labeled with a terminal symbol, and leaf nodes that are foot nodes, respectively. In the latter case, we have to blindly guess the span over the input string, because at this point no lexical elements have been scanned to restrict allowable derivations.

Rules (c1), (c2), and (c3) combine items for two sibling nodes η' and η'' into a new item for their parent node η. Note that the spans of the two antecedent items must be adjacent within w. The three rules differ in whether η' or η'' dominates a foot node, or whether none of them does.

Rule (d) deals with the substitution at node η of an initial tree $\alpha \in Subst(\eta)$. Rule (e) deals with the case that no adjunction is performed at an internal node η. This is done simply by recording that adjunction has already been checked, through symbol $\top$, and leaving the rest of the item unchanged. If η does not dominate a foot node, then f_1 and f_2 are both $-$.

Finally, rule (f) processes adjunction of auxiliary tree $\beta \in Adj(\eta)$ at η. This step involves an antecedent representing a subtree rooted at node η, along with an antecedent representing a completely parsed auxiliary tree $\beta \in Adj(\eta)$. Note that the span of β must wrap around the span of node η. Again, f_1' and f_2' may both be $-$.

We de ne the size of a TAG $\mathcal{G}$, written $|\mathcal{G}|$, as the total number of nodes in all the trees in the set $\mathcal{I} \cup \mathcal{A}$. It is not dif cult to see that inference rule (f) dominates the time complexity of the algorithm. The maximum number of instantiations of that rule is $\mathcal{O}(|\mathcal{G}|^2 |w|^6)$, which is therefore the running time of the algorithm. With a small trick, this can be reduced to $\mathcal{O}(|\mathcal{G}| |w|^6)$. The space complexity is $\mathcal{O}(|\mathcal{G}| |w|^4)$.

8   Translation

Automatic translation between natural languages is one of the most challenging applications in NLP. State-of-the-art approaches to this task are based on syntactic models, usually enriched with statistical parameters. In this section we consider one such model, called *synchronous context-free grammar* (SCFG).

A SCFG consists of *synchronous rules*, each obtained by pairing two CFG rules with the same left-hand side. The right-hand sides of such a pair of rules must consist of identical multisets of non-terminals, possibly ordered differently, and possibly combined with different terminal symbols. Furthermore, there is an explicit bijection that pairs occurrences of identical non-terminals in the two right-hand sides.

As an example, the synchronous rule $\langle \text{VP} \rightarrow \text{VB}^{\boxed{1}}\, \text{PP}^{\boxed{2}},\ \text{VP} \rightarrow \text{PP}^{\boxed{2}}\, \text{VB}^{\boxed{1}}\, \text{ga}\rangle$ states that an English verb phrase composed of the two constituents VB ('verb in base form') and PP ('prepositional phrase') can be translated into Japanese by swapping the order of the translations of these constituents and by inserting the word 'ga' at the right. Note the use of integers within boxes as superscripts to indicate a bijection between non-terminal occurrences in the two context-free rules.

A SCFG can derive pairs of sentences as follows. Starting with the pair of non-terminals $\langle S^{\boxed{1}},\ S^{\boxed{1}}\rangle$, synchronous rules are applied to rewrite pairs of non-terminals that have the same index. At the application of a rule, the indices in the newly added non-terminals are consistently renamed, in order to avoid clashes with indices introduced at previous rewriting steps. The process stops when all non-terminals have been rewritten.

As an example, consider the SCFG based on the following synchronous rules:

$$s_1 : \langle S \rightarrow A^{\boxed{1}}C^{\boxed{2}},\ S \rightarrow A^{\boxed{1}}C^{\boxed{2}}\rangle \qquad s_5 : \langle A \rightarrow a_1,\ A \rightarrow a_2\rangle$$
$$s_2 : \langle C \rightarrow B^{\boxed{1}}S^{\boxed{2}},\ C \rightarrow B^{\boxed{1}}S^{\boxed{2}}\rangle \qquad s_6 : \langle A \rightarrow a_1,\ A \rightarrow \varepsilon\rangle$$
$$s_3 : \langle C \rightarrow B^{\boxed{1}}S^{\boxed{2}},\ C \rightarrow S^{\boxed{2}}B^{\boxed{1}}\rangle \qquad s_7 : \langle B \rightarrow b_1,\ B \rightarrow b_2\rangle$$
$$s_4 : \langle C \rightarrow B^{\boxed{1}},\ \qquad C \rightarrow B^{\boxed{1}}\ \rangle$$

An example derivation of the string pair $\langle a_1 b_1 a_1 b_1,\ a_2 b_2 b_2\rangle$ by the above SCFG is:

$$\langle S^{\boxed{1}},\ S^{\boxed{1}}\rangle \Rightarrow^{s_1} \langle A^{\boxed{2}}C^{\boxed{3}},\ A^{\boxed{2}}C^{\boxed{3}}\rangle$$
$$\Rightarrow^{s_3} \langle A^{\boxed{2}}B^{\boxed{4}}S^{\boxed{5}},\ A^{\boxed{2}}S^{\boxed{5}}B^{\boxed{4}}\rangle$$
$$\Rightarrow^{s_1} \langle A^{\boxed{2}}B^{\boxed{4}}A^{\boxed{6}}C^{\boxed{7}},\ A^{\boxed{2}}A^{\boxed{6}}C^{\boxed{7}}B^{\boxed{4}}\rangle$$
$$\Rightarrow^{s_4} \langle A^{\boxed{2}}B^{\boxed{4}}A^{\boxed{6}}B^{\boxed{8}},\ A^{\boxed{2}}A^{\boxed{6}}B^{\boxed{8}}B^{\boxed{4}}\rangle$$
$$\Rightarrow^{s_5} \langle a_1 B^{\boxed{4}}A^{\boxed{6}}B^{\boxed{8}},\ a_2 A^{\boxed{6}}B^{\boxed{8}}B^{\boxed{4}}\rangle$$
$$\Rightarrow^{s_7} \langle a_1 b_1 A^{\boxed{6}}B^{\boxed{8}},\ a_2 A^{\boxed{6}}B^{\boxed{8}}b_2\rangle$$
$$\Rightarrow^{s_6} \langle a_1 b_1 a_1 B^{\boxed{8}},\ a_2 B^{\boxed{8}}b_2\rangle$$
$$\Rightarrow^{s_7} \langle a_1 b_1 a_1 b_1,\ a_2 b_2 b_2\rangle$$

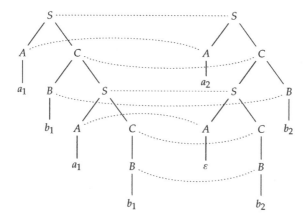

Figure 4.18   A pair of trees associated with a derivation in a SCFG. The dotted lines link pairs of non-terminal occurrences that had the same index during the rewriting process.

In the same way as a derivation in a CFG can be associated with a parse-tree, a derivation in a SCFG can be associated with a pair of parse-trees. These trees are obtained one from the other by reordering of internal sibling nodes, and relabeling, insertion, and deletion of leaf nodes, as illustrated in Figure 4.18. We will refer to the two trees in a pair as the input tree and the output tree.

Given a SCFG $\mathcal{G}$ and a string $w = a_1 \cdots a_n$, the expression $w \circ \mathcal{G}$ denotes the set of all pairs of parse-trees associated with derivations in $\mathcal{G}$ whose input tree has yield w. Note that all the strings that are translations of w under $\mathcal{G}$ can be easily produced if we can enumerate the elements of $w \circ \mathcal{G}$.

The set $w \circ \mathcal{G}$ can have size exponential in $|w|$, and the number of possible translations of w under $\mathcal{G}$ can likewise be exponential. (There may even be an in nite number of translations if there are synchronous rules whose left components are epsilon rules or unit rules.) In Section 3 we discussed a compact representation of a large set of parse-trees, in the form of a CFG. We will extend this to a construction of a SCFG $\mathcal{G}'$ that represents $w \circ \mathcal{G}$ in a compact way. This is referred to as *left composition*.

We assume, without loss of generality, that synchronous rules from $\mathcal{G}$ are either of the form $\langle A \rightarrow \alpha, \ A \rightarrow \alpha' \rangle$, where α and α' are non-empty strings of indexed non-terminals, or of the form $\langle A \rightarrow x, \ A \rightarrow y \rangle$, where x and y can each be a terminal symbol or the empty string. In the former case, we let a permutation π denote the bijective relation that pairs the non-terminal occurrences in α and α', and write a synchronous rule as:

$$\langle A \rightarrow B_1^{\boxed{1}} \cdots B_m^{\boxed{m}}, \ A \rightarrow B_{\pi(1)}^{\boxed{\pi(1)}} \cdots B_{\pi(m)}^{\boxed{\pi(m)}} \rangle$$

The non-terminals of $\mathcal{G}'$ have the form $[i, A, j]$, where i and j are input positions within w, and A is a non-terminal from $\mathcal{G}$. The algorithm for the left composition is given in Figure 4.19. It may introduce many synchronous rules that are useless.

1: **Function** LEFTCOMPOSITION$(w, \mathcal{G})$ $\{w = a_1 \cdots a_n\}$
2: $\mathcal{G}' \leftarrow$ SCFG with start non-terminal $[0, S, n]$ and empty set of synchronous rules
3: **for all** $\langle A \rightarrow B_1^{\boxed{1}} \cdots B_m^{\boxed{m}}, A \rightarrow B_{\pi(1)}^{\boxed{\pi(1)}} \cdots B_{\pi(m)}^{\boxed{\pi(m)}} \rangle$ from $\mathcal{G}$ **do**
4:     **for all** $i_0, \ldots, i_m$ $(0 \leq i_0 \leq \ldots \leq i_m \leq n)$ **do**
5:         add to $\mathcal{G}'$ the synchronous rule $\langle [i_0, A, i_m] \rightarrow [i_0, B_1, i_1]^{\boxed{1}} \cdots [i_{m-1}, B_m, i_m]^{\boxed{m}},$
        $[i_0, A, i_m] \rightarrow [i_{\pi(1)-1}, B_{\pi(1)}, i_{\pi(1)}]^{\boxed{\pi(1)}} \cdots [i_{\pi(m)-1}, B_{\pi(m)}, i_{\pi(m)}]^{\boxed{\pi(m)}} \rangle$
6: **for all** i $(1 \leq i \leq n)$ and $\langle A \rightarrow a_i, A \rightarrow y \rangle$ from $\mathcal{G}$ **do**
7:     add to $\mathcal{G}'$ the synchronous rule $\langle [i-1, A, i] \rightarrow a_i, [i-1, A, i] \rightarrow y \rangle$
8: **for all** i $(0 \leq i \leq n)$ and $\langle A \rightarrow \varepsilon, A \rightarrow y \rangle$ from $\mathcal{G}$ **do**
9:     add to $\mathcal{G}'$ the synchronous rule $\langle [i, A, i] \rightarrow \varepsilon, [i, A, i] \rightarrow y \rangle$
10: **return** $\mathcal{G}'$

Figure 4.19   An algorithm for the left composition of a sentence w and a SCFG $\mathcal{G}$.

Techniques to eliminate useless rules from $\mathcal{G}'$ are very similar to well-known techniques to eliminate useless rules from CFGs.

If we remove the left components from synchronous rules of $\mathcal{G}'$, then we obtain a CFG $\mathcal{G}''$ that generates parse-trees for all possible translations of w under $\mathcal{G}$. These parse-trees differ from the output trees in $w \circ \mathcal{G}$ only in the labels of internal nodes. In the former case these are of the form $[i, A, j]$ where in the latter they are A.

With the SCFG from the running example, $w = a_1 b_1 a_1 b_1$ can be translated into the ve strings $a_2 b_2 a_2 b_2$, $a_2 a_2 b_2 b_2$, $a_2 b_2 b_2$, $b_2 a_2 b_2$, and $b_2 b_2$. There are eight pairs of trees in $w \circ \mathcal{G}$, as there are three derivations with output $a_2 b_2 b_2$, and two derivations with output $b_2 b_2$. After applying left composition and reduction of the grammar, we obtain the following set of synchronous rules:

$$\langle [0, S, 4] \rightarrow [0, A, 1]^{\boxed{1}} [1, C, 4]^{\boxed{2}}, [0, S, 4] \rightarrow [0, A, 1]^{\boxed{1}} [1, C, 4]^{\boxed{2}} \rangle,$$
$$\langle [1, C, 4] \rightarrow [1, B, 2]^{\boxed{1}} [2, S, 4]^{\boxed{2}}, [1, C, 4] \rightarrow [1, B, 2]^{\boxed{1}} [2, S, 4]^{\boxed{2}} \rangle,$$
$$\langle [1, C, 4] \rightarrow [1, B, 2]^{\boxed{1}} [2, S, 4]^{\boxed{2}}, [1, C, 4] \rightarrow [2, S, 4]^{\boxed{2}} [1, B, 2]^{\boxed{1}} \rangle,$$
$$\langle [2, S, 4] \rightarrow [2, A, 3]^{\boxed{1}} [3, C, 4]^{\boxed{2}}, [2, S, 4] \rightarrow [2, A, 3]^{\boxed{1}} [3, C, 4]^{\boxed{2}} \rangle,$$
$$\langle [3, C, 4] \rightarrow [3, B, 4]^{\boxed{1}}, \qquad\qquad [3, C, 4] \rightarrow [3, B, 4]^{\boxed{1}} \qquad\qquad \rangle,$$

$$\langle [0, A, 1] \rightarrow a_1, [0, A, 1] \rightarrow a_2 \rangle,$$
$$\langle [0, A, 1] \rightarrow a_1, [0, A, 1] \rightarrow \varepsilon \rangle,$$
$$\langle [1, B, 2] \rightarrow b_1, [1, B, 2] \rightarrow b_2 \rangle,$$
$$\langle [2, A, 3] \rightarrow a_1, [2, A, 3] \rightarrow a_2 \rangle,$$
$$\langle [2, A, 3] \rightarrow a_1, [2, A, 3] \rightarrow \varepsilon \rangle,$$
$$\langle [3, B, 4] \rightarrow b_1, [3, B, 4] \rightarrow b_2 \rangle.$$

The size of a SCFG $\mathcal{G}$, written as $|\mathcal{G}|$, is de ned as the sum of the number of non-terminal and terminal occurrences in its synchronous rules. Let r be the length of the longest right-hand side of a context-free rule that is the input or output component of a synchronous rule. The time complexity and space complexity of left composition are both $\mathcal{O}(|\mathcal{G}| \cdot n^{r+1})$, where n is the length of the input string. In many practical applications, it is possible to factorize synchronous rules in such a way that the parameter r is reduced to a small integer. In the general case, however, a SCFG cannot be cast into an equivalent form with r bounded by a constant. This implies exponential behavior for our algorithm in the worst case.

9 Further Reading

For chart parsing, we refer to Thompson and Ritchie (1984). Transformation of CFGs to Chomsky normal form is discussed by Harrison (1978). Reduction of a CFG can be carried out in linear time in the size of the grammar, as shown in Sippu and Soisalon-Soininen (1988). For deduction systems in the context of parsing, see Shieber et al. (1995).

Earley's algorithm and some variants are due to Earley (1970); Aho and Ullman (1972); Graham and Harrison (1976); Graham et al. (1980). A more complex parsing strategy that is sometimes used for natural language processing is tabular LR parsing, also called generalized LR parsing in Tomita (1986). Its presentation requires the additional de nition of push-down automaton, which was not discussed in this chapter, but see for instance Nederhof and Satta (2004).

The parse forest representation is originally due to Bar-Hillel et al. (1964), with states of a nite automaton in place of positions in an input string. Parse forests have also been discussed by Tomita (1986). Construction of parse forests using push-down transducers is discussed by Billot and Lang (1989). Similar ideas were proposed for tree adjoining grammars by Lang (1994).

The problem of nding the most probable parse in a PCFG is discussed by Knuth (1977), who proposes a generalization of the algorithm by Dijkstra (1959). The probabilistic CKY algorithm is described by Jelinek et al. (1992) and is similar to Viterbi (1967).

The 2-LCFG formalism is an abstraction of several head-driven grammar models that have been used in statistical parsing; see for instance Collins (2003) and references therein. Our 2-LCFG recognition algorithm was originally presented by Eisner and Satta (1999).

The PPDGs de ned in this chapter are a simpli cation of a model discussed by Klein and Manning (2004). Our reduction from PPDGs to 2-LCFGs is related to one of the lexicalized CFG models proposed by Collins (2003). The PPDG recognition algorithm we have presented is related to a method originally discussed by Eisner (2000). The reduction from non-projective dependency parsing to the problem of spanning trees was rst proposed by McDonald et al. (2005a). The discussed hardness results for non-projective parsing are taken from McDonald and Satta (2007). See Koo et al. (2007) for further algorithms related to probabilistic parsing of non-projective dependency models.

A good introduction to TAGs can be found in Joshi and Schabes (1997). The discussed recognition algorithm is due to Vijay-Shanker and Joshi (1985).

SCFGs are a syntactic variant of the syntax-directed translation schemata of Aho and Ullman (1972). See the same publication for the discussed negative result on the factorization of synchronous rules.

NOTE

1 Symbol $\rightarrow$ indicating the dependencies of $\mathcal{G}$ is now overloaded by the same symbol indicating the rules in $\mathcal{G}'$. The intended interpretation will always be clear from the context.

Part II   Current Methods

5 Maximum Entropy Models

ROBERT MALOUF

1 Introduction

Maximum entropy (MaxEnt) models, variously known as log-linear, Gibbs, exponential, and multinomial logit models, provide a general-purpose machine learning technique for classi cation and prediction which has been successfully applied to elds as diverse as computer vision and econometrics. In natural language processing, recent years have seen MaxEnt techniques used for sentence boundary detection, part-of-speech tagging, parse selection and ambiguity resolution, machine translation, and stochastic attribute value grammars, to name just a few applications (Berger et al., 1996; Abney 1997; Ratnaparkhi 1998; Johnson et al., 1999; Foster 2000). Beyond these purely practical applications, statistical modeling techniques also offer a powerful set of tools for analyzing natural language data. A good statistical model can both clarify what the patterns are in a complex, possibly noisy, set of observations and at the same time shed light on the underlying processes that lead to those patterns (Breiman 2001b; McCullagh 2002).

The fundamental problem for stochastic data analysis is model selection. How do we choose a model out of a given hypothesis space which best ts our observations? In all but the most trivial cases, our hypothesis space will provide an in nite range of possible models. This is a general problem: how do we pick a probability distribution given possibly incomplete information?

More technically, suppose we have a random variable X, which can take on values $x_1, \ldots, x_n$. How do we choose a model, or an assignment of probabilities to outcomes? Any distribution we choose must satisfy this constraint:

$$\sum_i P(x_i) = 1$$

In addition, we presumably have some information about the real-world phenomenon that we are attempting to model, and we would like our probability distribution to re ect that knowledge.

The Handbook of Computational Linguistics and Natural Language Processing, First Edition.
Edited by Alexander Clark, Chris Fox and Shalom Lappin.
© 2013 Blackwell Publishing Ltd except for editorial material and organization
© 2013 Alexander Clark, Chris Fox, and Shalom Lappin. Published 2013 by Blackwell Publishing Ltd.

The *principle of insufficient reason* (variously attributed to Bernoulli, Laplace, Bayes, etc.) provides one model selection criterion: in the absence of any reason to believe that one outcome is more likely than another, we must assume that all outcomes are equally likely. More speci cally, if all we know about a random variable X is that it has n possible outcomes, then each outcome should be assigned the probability $\frac{1}{n}$.

But what if we are not in a position of 'insuf cient reason,' and we have a strong suspicion that not all outcomes are equally likely? Suppose that we have recorded the outcome of a very large number of ips of a coin, and from that we can see that heads came up much more often than tails. A uniform distribution is still a possible model for this coin. After all, in any nite sample, we will probably not get exactly as many heads as tails. However, if there are many more heads than tails, intuitively it seems like some non-uniform distribution would be a better model.

For this situation, Jaynes (1957) proposed an alternative to the principle of insuf cient reason – the *maximum entropy principle*: the least informative probability distribution maximizes the entropy H subject to known constraints. Here Jaynes is proposing to use Shannon's information entropy H as a measure of our ignorance about the value of X:

$$H(X) = -\sum_i P(x_i) \log P(x_i)$$

By choosing the distribution which maximizes the entropy, we are choosing the distribution with the least informational content. In other words, our probability estimates should re ect what we know and what we do not know: in general, ignorance is preferable to error.

Observations of the real world, in the form of training data, impose a set of constraints on our models. In most cases, however, the constraints underdetermine the model: many models will be consistent with the observed facts yet lead to very different conclusions. The MaxEnt principle gives us a general way of selecting a model out of the in nite range of possible models. MaxEnt models diverge from a uniform distribution only enough to respect the constraints. In the case where there are no known constraints beyond the number of possible outcomes, the distribution which maximizes the entropy is simply the uniform distribution. Given other kinds of empirical constraints, the MaxEnt principle leads to a wide variety of distributions (Kapur 1993; Jaynes 2003). In this chapter, we will consider distributions which are derived from the MaxEnt principle which are particularly useful for computational linguistics and natural language processing.

If the goal is to minimize the information content of the model, it is still reasonable to ask why one would want to maximize this particular measure of information content. Both Shannon and Jaynes show that other measures of information content either are equivalent to the information entropy H or lead to inconsistencies. Jaynes (1986) also offers another rationale for choosing the distribution that maximizes the information entropy while still satisfying the constraints created by the testable information. Suppose that, rather than constructing the model ourselves, we can leave model construction to an impartial third party – say, research assistants, or in Jaynes' example, monkeys. We give our assistants n balls, each worth $\delta = 1/n$ of the available probability mass, and have them randomly throw them into bins representing the m possible outcomes.

After all the balls have been distributed, we can count the balls in each bin, and assign a probability to each outcome. If outcome i received n_i balls, then we say its probability is

$$p_i = n_i \delta = \frac{n_i}{n}$$

If the resulting distribution ts the constraints, then we are done. We have found a distribution which ts the testable information but is otherwise free of bias or a priori assumptions. If it does not t the constraints, though, we retrieve the balls for our assistants and try again.

For a method like this to give good results even as a thought experiment, n needs to be much larger than m, and we might need a lot of attempts before we get a distribution that ts the constraints. Instead of actually carrying out this procedure, we can nd the most likely distribution of balls into bins given some simple assumptions.

The probability of any particular assignment of n balls into m bins $n_1 \ldots n_m$ is given by the multinomial distribution:

$$P(n_1, \ldots, n_m) = \binom{n}{n_1, \ldots, n_m} m^{-n} = \frac{n!}{n_1! \cdots n_m!} m^{-n}$$

Since n and m are xed, the most likely assignment is one that maximizes:

$$W = \frac{n!}{n_1! \cdots n_m!}$$

Equivalently, we could maximize a monotonic increasing function of W, for example, $\frac{1}{n} \log W$:

$$\frac{1}{n} \log W = \frac{1}{n} \log \frac{n!}{n_1! \cdots n_m!}$$

$$= \frac{1}{n} \log \frac{n!}{np_1! \cdots np_m!}$$

$$= \frac{1}{n} \left(\log n! - \sum_i \log np_i! \right)$$

Now we can bring in Stirling's approximation ($\log n! \approx n \log n - n$) to get:

$$\frac{1}{n} \log W = \frac{1}{n}(n \log n - n - \sum_i (np_i \log np_i - np_i)$$

$$= - \sum_i p_i \log p_i$$

Thus, the distribution which our research assistants are most likely to achieve by throwing balls into bins is the one which maximizes the information entropy of the resulting distribution. So, by maximizing the entropy, we are constructing a model which imposes the least structure on the problem beyond what is enforced by the choice of constraints.

2   Maximum Entropy and Exponential Distributions

The MaxEnt principle provides a general strategy for choosing distributions given certain testable pieces of information, but does not in itself lead to any speci c distribution. The particular parametric form for a 'maximum entropy' distribution will depend on the nature of the testable information we have about the situation. As we have seen, in the simple case where all we know is the number of possible outcomes, the uniform distribution is the one which maximizes the entropy. In most situations, however, we will have some additional useful information about the problem we are trying to model.

For many problems in computational linguistics, the testable information consists of event counts derived from a training corpus. In a large annotated sample of text, we can, for example, count how many times the word *respect* is tagged as a noun, or how many times the token *Mr.* ends a sentence. By itself, the raw count is dif cult to interpret, since it is in large part determined by the size of the corpus, which in turn is generally determined by external non-linguistic factors. But we can take the observed count as an estimate of the expected count given a corpus of a particular size.

More speci cally, we can divide the training corpus into observational units or *events* (words, sentences, etc.), each of which can be described by d-dimensional real-valued *feature vector* function f. For a part-of-speech tagging application, the events might be word/tag pairs, and one feature might be the indicator function:

$$f_m(w, t) = \begin{cases} 1 & \text{if } w \text{ is 'respect' and } t \text{ is NOUN} \\ 0 & \text{otherwise} \end{cases}$$

In the context of a probabilistic context-free parser, an event might be a tree, and one feature would be the number of times a particular rule was applied in the derivation of the tree.

In any case, the collected feature vectors constitute the testable information for the problem. For each possible event type x in the space of possible event types X, we can estimate the expected value of the feature vector:

$$\hat{E}[f] = \sum_{x \in X} \hat{p}(x) f(x)$$

from the observed probability of x in the training data. Our goal now is to construct a model distribution p which satis es the constraints imposed by the empirical distribution $\hat{p}$, in the sense that:

(1) $E[f] = \hat{E}[f]$

Additionally, our model p must be a proper probability distribution:

(2) $\sum_{x \in X} p(x) = 1$

In general, this problem is ill posed: a wide range of models will t the constraints in (1) and (2). In accordance with the principle of maximum entropy, we need to nd among these the distribution which maximizes the entropy $H(p)$.

This is a *constrained optimization* problem – maximize a function given a set of constraints – which can be solved using the method of Lagrange multipliers. First, we restate the constraints:

$$0 = \sum_i \sum_x p(x) f_i(x) - \hat{E}[f_i]$$

$$0 = \sum_x p(x) - 1$$

Next, we introduce the Lagrangian function:

$$\mathcal{L}(p, \lambda, \gamma) = - \sum_x p(x) \log p(x) - \sum_i \lambda_i \left(\sum_x p(x) f_i(x) - \hat{E}[f_i] \right) - \gamma \left(\sum_x p(x) - 1 \right)$$

The new variables, one $-\lambda_i$ for each feature in the testable information plus $-\gamma$ for the requirement that p be a proper probability distribution, are the Lagrange multipliers corresponding to the constraints. Since both the objective function and the constraints are convex, the maximum of $\mathcal{L}$ corresponds to a solution to the constrained problem posed above. We can now solve this unconstrained optimization problem by nding the p where the gradient of $\mathcal{L}$ is zero:

$$\nabla \mathcal{L}(p, \lambda, \gamma) = 0$$

We start with the partial derivative of $\mathcal{L}$ with respect to p for some particular event type x:

$$0 = \frac{\partial}{\partial p}\mathcal{L}(p, \lambda, \gamma)$$

$$= -(1 + \log p(x)) + \sum_i \lambda_i f_i(x) + \gamma$$

Solving for $p(x)$, we get:

$$p(x) = \exp(\gamma - 1)\exp\left(\sum_i \lambda_i f_i(x)\right)$$

We know that any solution p must satisfy the constraint in (2), so:

$$\sum_x p(x) = 1$$

$$\sum_x \exp(\gamma - 1)\exp\left(\sum_i \lambda_i f_i(x)\right) = 1$$

$$\exp(\gamma - 1) = \left(\sum_x \exp\left(\sum_i \lambda_i f_i(x)\right)\right)^{-1}$$

Finally, substituting in $p(x)$, we get the parametric form of the MaxEnt distribution given known expected values:

$$(3) \quad p(x) = \frac{\exp\left(\lambda^T f(x)\right)}{\sum_{y \in X} \exp\left(\lambda^T f(y)\right)}$$

where λ is a d-dimensional parameter vector and $\lambda^T f(x)$ is the inner product of the parameter vector and a feature vector.

3   Parameter Estimation

Given the general model form in (3), a set of event types, a feature function over events, and empirical expected values derived from a training corpus, the next step in constructing a MaxEnt distribution is to nd values for the parameters λ_i such that:

$$\sum_x p(x) f_i(x) = \hat{E}[f_i(x)]$$

Unfortunately, while parameter estimation for MaxEnt models is conceptually straightforward, in practice MaxEnt models for typical natural language tasks are very large. Estimation of such large models is not only expensive, but also, due to sparsely distributed features, sensitive to round-off errors. Thus, highly ef cient, accurate, scalable methods are required for estimating the parameters of practical models.

One theoretical complication which makes models of this form dif cult to apply to problems in natural language processing is that the events space X is often very large or even in nite, making the denominator in (3) impossible to compute. One modi cation we can make to avoid this problem is to consider conditional probability distributions instead (Berger et al., 1996; Chi 1998; Johnson et al., 1999). Suppose now that in addition to the event space X and the feature function f, we have also a set of contexts W and a function Y which partitions the members of X. In our PCFG example, W might be the set of possible strings of words, and $Y(w)$ the set of trees whose yield is $w \in W$. Computing the conditional probability $p(x|w)$ of an event x in context w as

$$(4) \quad p(x|w) = \frac{\exp\left(\lambda^T f(x)\right)}{\sum_{y \in Y(w)} \exp\left(\lambda^T f(y)\right)}$$

now involves evaluating a more much tractable sum in the denominator.

Given the parametric form of a MaxEnt model in (4),   tting a MaxEnt model to a collection of training data entails   nding values for the parameter vector λ which minimize the Kullback–Leibler divergence between the model p_λ and the empirical distribution $\hat{p}$:

$$D(\hat{p}||p_\lambda) = \sum_{w,x} \hat{p}(x,w) \log \frac{\hat{p}(x|w)}{p_\lambda(x|w)}$$

or, equivalently, which maximize the *log-likelihood*:

$$(5) \quad L(\lambda) = \sum_{w,x} \hat{p}(w,x) \log p_\lambda(x|w)$$

Again, we are faced with   nding the maximum of a concave function, and we proceed in the same way as we did in the previous section. The gradient of the log-likelihood function, or the vector of its   rst derivatives with respect to the parameter, λ, is:

$$G(\lambda) = \frac{\partial L(\lambda)}{\partial \lambda_i}$$

$$= \sum_{x,y} \hat{p}(x,y) f(y) - \sum_{x,y} \hat{p}(x) p_\lambda(y|x) f(y)$$

or, simply:

$$(6) \quad G(\lambda) = \hat{E}[f] - E_{p_\lambda}[f]$$

Since the likelihood function (5) is concave over the parameter space, it has a global maximum where the gradient is zero (when $\hat{E}[f] = E_{p_\lambda}[f]$). Unfortunately, simply setting $G(\lambda) = 0$ and solving for λ does not yield a closed form solution, so we proceed iteratively, following this general schema:

ESTIMATE $(\hat{p})$
1   $\lambda^0 \leftarrow 0$
2   $k \leftarrow 0$
3   **repeat**
4   compute $p^{(k)}$ from $\lambda^{(k)}$
5   compute update $\delta^{(k)}$
6           $\lambda^{(k+1)} \leftarrow \lambda^{(k)} + \delta^{(k)}$
7           $k \leftarrow k + 1$
8   **until** converged
9   **return** $\lambda^{(k)}$

At each step, we adjust an estimate of the parameters $\lambda^{(k)}$ to a new estimate $\lambda^{(k+1)}$ based on the divergence between the estimated probability distribution $p^{(k)}$ and the empirical distribution $\hat{p}$. We continue until successive improvements fail to yield a suf ciently large decrease in the divergence. Since the function that is being maximized is convex, this algorithm will converge to a unique solution.

While all parameter estimation algorithms we will consider take the same general form, the method for computing the updates $\delta^{(k)}$ at each search step differs substantially. This difference can have a dramatic impact on the number of updates required to reach convergence.

3.1   Iterative scaling

One widely used method for iteratively re ning the model parameters is *generalized iterative scaling* (GIS), due to Darroch and Ratcliff (1972). An extension of iterative proportional tting (Deming & Stephan 1940), GIS scales the probability distribution $p^{(k)}$ by a factor proportional to the ratio of $\hat{E}[f]$ to $E_{p^{(k)}}[f]$, with the restriction that $\sum_j f_j(x) = C$ for some constant c and for each event x in the training data (a condition which can be easily satis ed by the addition of a 'correction' feature). We can adapt GIS to estimate the model parameters λ rather than the model probabilities p, yielding the update rule:

$$\delta^{(k)} = \log\left(\frac{\hat{E}[f]}{E_{p^{(k)}}[f]}\right)^{\frac{1}{c}}$$

GIS has the advantage of being very simple, both conceptually and in terms of its implementation. However, in Malouf's (2002) comparison, GIS performed quite poorly. A key limitation of GIS is that the step size, and thus the rate of convergence, depends on the constant C: the larger the value of C, the smaller the step size. In case not all rows of the training data sum to a constant, the addition of a correction feature effectively slows convergence to match the most dif cult case. Both Goodman (2002) and Curran and Clark (2003) consider variations on traditional GIS which avoid this problem, leading to methods which converge more quickly.

In an earlier move to improve on the slow convergence of GIS and the need for a correction feature, Della Pietra et al. (1997) propose an *improved iterative scaling* (IIS) algorithm, whose update rule is the solution to the equation:

$$\hat{E}[f] = \sum_{w,x} \hat{p}(w) p^{(k)}(x|w) f(x) \exp(M(x) \delta^{(k)})$$

where $M(x)$ is the sum of the feature values for an event x in the training data. This is a polynomial in $\exp(\delta^{(k)})$, and the solution can be found straightforwardly using, for example, the Newton–Raphson method.

3.2 First-order methods

Iterative scaling algorithms have a long tradition in statistics and are still widely used for analysis of contingency tables. Their primary strength is that on each iteration they only require computation of the expected values $E_{p^{(k)}}$. They do not depend on evaluation of the gradient of the log-likelihood function, which, depending on the distribution, could be prohibitively expensive or simply impossible. In the case of MaxEnt models, however, the vector of expected values required by iterative scaling essentially *is* the gradient G. Thus, it makes sense to consider methods which use the gradient directly.

The most obvious way of making explicit use of the gradient is by *Cauchy's method*, or the method of *steepest ascent* (Zhu et al., 1997). The gradient of a function is a vector which points in the direction in which the function's value increases most rapidly. Since our goal is to maximize the log-likelihood function, a natural strategy is to shift our current estimate of the parameters in the direction of the gradient via the update rule:

$$\delta^{(k)} = \alpha^{(k)} G(\lambda^{(k)})$$

where the step size $\alpha^{(k)}$ is chosen to maximize $L(\lambda^{(k)} + \delta^{(k)})$. Finding the optimal step size is itself an optimization problem, though only in one dimension and, in practice, only an approximate solution is required to guarantee global convergence.

Since the log-likelihood function is concave, the method of steepest ascent is guaranteed to nd the global maximum. However, while the steps taken on each iteration are in a very narrow sense locally optimal, the global convergence rate of steepest ascent is very poor. Each new search direction is orthogonal (or, if an approximate line search is used, nearly so) to the previous direction, leading to a characteristic 'zig-zag' ascent with convergence slowing as the maximum is approached.

One way of looking at the problem with steepest ascent is that it considers the same search directions many times. We would prefer an algorithm which considered each possible search direction only once, in each iteration taking a step of exactly the right length in a direction orthogonal to all previous search directions. This intuition underlies *conjugate gradient* methods which choose a search direction which is a linear combination of the steepest ascent direction and the previous search direction. The step size is selected by an approximate line search, as in the steepest ascent method. Several non-linear conjugate gradient methods, such as the *Fletcher–Reeves* and the *Polak–Ribière positive* algorithms, have been proposed. While theoretically equivalent, they use slightly different update rules and thus show different numeric properties.

3.3   Second-order methods

Another way of looking at the problem with steepest ascent is that, while it takes into account the gradient of the log-likelihood function, it fails to take into account its curvature, or the gradient of the gradient. The usefulness of the curvature is made clear if we consider a second-order Taylor series approximation of $L(\lambda + \delta)$:

(7) $L(\lambda + \delta) \approx L(\lambda) + \delta^T G(\lambda) + \frac{1}{2}\delta^T H(\lambda)\delta$

where H is *Hessian matrix* of the log-likelihood function, the $d \times d$ matrix of its second partial derivatives with respect to λ. If we set the derivative of (7) to zero and solve for δ, we get the update rule for *Newton's method*:

(8) $\delta^{(k)} = H^{-1}(\lambda^{(k)})G(\lambda^{(k)})$

Newton's method converges very quickly (for quadratic objective functions, in one step), but it requires the computation of the inverse of the Hessian matrix on each iteration.

While the log-likelihood function for ME models in (5) is twice differentiable, for large-scale problems the evaluation of the Hessian matrix is computationally impractical, and Newton's method is not competitive with iterative scaling or rst-order methods. *Variable metric* or *quasi-Newton* methods avoid explicit evaluation of the Hessian by building up an approximation of it using successive evaluations of the gradient. That is, we replace $H^{-1}(\lambda^{(k)})$ in (8) with a local approximation of the inverse Hessian $B^{(k)}$:

$\delta^{(k)} = B^{(k)}G(\lambda^{(k)})$

with $B^{(k)}$ a symmatric, positive de nite matrix which satis es the equation:

$B^{(k)}y^{(k)} = \delta^{(k-1)}$

where $y^{(k)} = G(\lambda^{(k)}) - G(\lambda^{(k-1)})$.

Variable metric methods also show excellent convergence properties and can be much more efficient than using true Newton updates, but, for large-scale problems with hundreds of thousands of parameters, even storing the approximate Hessian is prohibitively expensive. For such cases, we can apply *limited memory variable metric* methods, which implicitly approximate the Hessian matrix in the vicinity of the current estimate of $\lambda^{(k)}$ using the previous m values of $y^{(k)}$ and $\delta^{(k)}$. Since in practical applications values of m between 3 and 10 suffice, this can offer a substantial saving in storage requirements over variable metric methods, while still giving favorable convergence properties (for algorithmic details and theoretical analysis of first- and second-order methods, see, e.g., Nocedal & Wright 1999).

3.4 *Comparing parameter estimation methods*

The performance of optimization algorithms is highly dependent on the specific properties of the problem to be solved. Worst-case analysis typically does not reflect the actual behavior on actual problems. Therefore, in order to evaluate the performance of the optimization techniques sketched in previous sections when applied to the problem of parameter estimation, we need to compare the performance of actual implementations on realistic data sets (Dolan & Moré 2002).

Minka (2001) offers a comparison of iterative scaling with other algorithms for parameter estimation in logistic regression, a problem similar to the one considered here, but it is difficult to transfer Minka's results to MaxEnt models. First, he evaluates the algorithms with randomly generated training data. However, the performance and accuracy of optimization algorithms can be sensitive to the specific numerical properties of the function being optimized; results based on random data may or may not carry over to more realistic problems. Second, Minka measures performance in terms of the number of floating point operations required to achieve a particular precision. But large-scale sparse problems are typically memory bandwidth bound, not CPU bound. Therefore, the number of floating point operations is not a very good indicator of the total time required to find a solution. And the test problems Minka considers are relatively small (100–500 dimensions). As we have seen, though, algorithms which perform well for small- and medium-scale problems may not always be applicable to problems with many thousands of dimensions.

To address these issues, Malouf (2002) undertook an empirical evaluation of several parameter estimation algorithms. This implementation (now available as the Toolkit for Advanced Discriminative Modeling),[1] was based on PETSc (the Portable, Extensible Toolkit for Scientific Computation), a software library designed to ease development of programs which solve large systems of partial differential equations (Balay et al., 2002). PETSc offers data structures and routines for parallel and sequential storage, manipulation, and visualization of very large sparse matrices.

For any of the estimation techniques, the most expensive operation is computing the probability distribution p and the expectations $E_p[f]$ for each iteration. In order to make use of the facilities provided by PETSc, we can store the training data as a (sparse) matrix F, with rows corresponding to events and columns to features. Then, given a parameter vector λ, the unnormalized probabilities $\dot{p}_\lambda$ are the matrix–vector product:

$$\dot{p}_\lambda = \exp F\lambda$$

and the feature expectations are the transposed matrix–vector product:

$$e_{p_\lambda}[f] = F^T p_\lambda$$

By expressing these computations as matrix–vector operations, we can take advantage of the high-performance sparse matrix primitives of PETSc. In addition, there are many possible optimizations which can be applied for particular classes of MaxEnt models (Lafferty & Suhm 1996; Wu & Khudanpur 2000; Lafferty et al., 2001) to speed up normalization of the probability distribution p. These improvements take advantage of a model's structure to simplify the evaluation of the denominator in (4). For general data sets and feature functions, such optimizations are unlikely to give any improvement. However, when these optimizations are appropriate, they will give a proportional speed-up to all of the algorithms. Thus, the use of such optimizations is independent of the choice of parameter estimation method.

In Malouf's (2002) evaluation experiments, iterative scaling methods performed relatively poorly, while Benson and Moré's (2001) limited memory variable metric algorithm as implemented in TAO (Benson et al., 2007) consistently performed the best, both in speed of convergence and in the accuracy of the nal model. These results have been further supported by evaluations based on different types of realistic data sets (e.g., Sha & Pereira 2003). In comparing GIS and IIS, while IIS converges in fewer steps than GIS it takes substantially more time, as the additional bookkeeping overhead required by IIS more than cancels any improvements in speed offered by accelerated convergence for unstructured problems.

In addition, the agreement between the estimated model and real held-out data was more or less the same for all of the algorithms for most of the data sets. Some degree of variability is to be expected, since all of the data sets considered in the evaluation were badly underdetermined and ill-conditioned. With a very large number of very rare features, the accumulation of numerical errors becomes important and many (apparently) different parameter settings will yield essentially the same likelihood. Which of these models the algorithm ultimately converges to will be determined by the particular sequence of arithmetic operations, and differences in test accuracy between these models is generally well below the threshold of statistical signi cance.

In a few cases, however, the prediction accuracy differs more substantially. For some problems, GIS showed a small advantage over the other methods. More dramatically, both iterative scaling methods performed very poorly on the one very sparse data set. In this case, many features were nearly 'pseudo-minimal' in the sense of Johnson et al. (1999). That is, for many features f_i, event types x for which $f_i(x) \neq 0$ are not observed in the training data. For these features, $\hat{E}[f_i] =$ and λ_i receives values approaching $-\infty$. Smoothing the reference probabilities or applying model regularization (see the next section) would likely improve the results for all of the methods and reduce the observed differences. However, this does suggest that gradient-based methods are robust to certain problems with the training data.

4   Regularization

The procedures described in the previous section nd a parameter vector λ which minimizes the KL divergence between the model and the training data. In other words, we nd the model which maximizes the likelihood of the training data. Maximum likelihood estimation of model parameters from natural language training data is well known to run into problems. Natural language data is notorious for being noisy and incomplete, with many event types occurring only once and many more possible event types (by chance) failing to occur at all. Just as maximum likelihood estimation causes problems for simple n-gram models, it often leads to overtraining effects and poor model performance in MaxEnt models as well.

In addition to the well-known problems with maximum likelihood estimation in general, the particular form of MaxEnt models makes them especially susceptible to sparse data problems. For a maximum likelihood bigram model, say, any sentence which contains a bigram which did not occur in the training data will be assigned a probability of 0 (clearly an undesirable result). For sentences which contain only attested bigrams, however, the model will still perform well. For a MaxEnt model, on the other hand, the only way an event type x can be assigned a probability of 0 (or 1) is if one or more of the parameters λ_i for the features f_i such that $f_i(x) > 0$ has the value $-\infty$ (or ∞). Given the iterative algorithm used to estimate MaxEnt models, no feature will ever be assigned a non- nite weight. Instead, the magnitude of the weights will become larger and larger on each iteration, leading to poor numerical accuracy for all the weights in the model.

Therefore, addressing sparse data problems is at least as important for MaxEnt models as it is for other model classes. And, in fact, the same methods developed for use with n-gram models (e.g., Chen & Goodman 1996) can be applied directly to smoothing the empirical expectations $\hat{E}[f]$. However, a more widely used approach to smoothing MaxEnt models that is more in keeping with the MaxEnt principle's Bayesian roots is to incorporate a prior distribution over parameter values into the estimation procedure. That is, we replace the maximum likelihood estimation of the previous section, which nds λ such that:

$$\lambda^{\mathrm{MLE}} = \underset{\lambda}{\operatorname{argmax}} \, p(x|w; \lambda)$$

with a maximum a posteriori estimate:

$$\lambda^{MAP} = \underset{\lambda}{\text{argmax}}\, q(x|w; \lambda)\, p(\lambda)$$

The prior $p(\lambda)$ is the probability of a particular parameter vector, independent from any evidence derived from the training data – in effect, the maximum likelihood estimates assumes a uniform $p(\lambda)$.

Building on an idea they attribute to Lafferty, Chen and Rosenfeld (1999) explore using a Gaussian prior distribution with a mean of 0 and a variance of σ for $p(\lambda)$. In the previous section, we found the parameter vector which maximized the log-likeliood (5). To nd the parameters which maximize the posterior probability, we can maximize the penalized log-likelihood:

$$(9)\quad L'(\lambda) = L(\lambda) + \sum_i \log \frac{1}{\sqrt{2\pi\sigma^2}} \exp\left(\frac{-\lambda_i}{2\sigma^2}\right)$$

$$= L(\lambda) - \sum_i \frac{\lambda_i^2}{2\sigma^2} + C$$

and the gradient G in (6) becomes:

$$G'(\lambda) = G(\lambda) - \sum_i \frac{\lambda_i}{\sigma_i^2}$$

Like L, L' is a concave function and can be maximized using the same methods. The hyperparameter σ controls the in uence of the prior in the nal estimate, with smaller values of σ leading to more aggressive smoothing. While it is possible to set different values of σ_i for each feature i, in practice a single value is typically used, with its value selected by cross-validation.

As Chen and Rosenfeld (1999) point out, using a Gaussian prior has much the same effect as discounting feature counts. At the solution, the constraints (1) are not met exactly. Instead, we nd λ such that:

$$E_\lambda[f_i] = \hat{E}[f_i] - \frac{\lambda_i}{\sigma_i^2}$$

Effectively reducing the observed count for feature i by λ_i/σ_i^2, the observed expectation is discounted by λ_i/σ_i^2, an amount that increases logarithmically with the observed frequency.

While the Gaussian prior is justi ed on Bayesian grounds and Chen and Rosenfeld (1999) explore its similarity to n-gram smoothing methods, it is also worth noting the similarity between the penalized log-likelihood (9) and the loss function minimized by support vector machines (SVMs), a non-parameteric machine learning method based on statistical learning theory (Vapnik 1996). As

Hastie et al. (2001) observe, both MaxEnt models and SVMs involve maximizing a penalized loss function. In the case of MaxEnt models, the loss function is the log-likelihood (5), while for classical SVMs the loss function is the 'hinge loss,' an upper bound on the error rate of the model on the training data. In both cases, the penalty is the same: the sum of the squares of the model parameters. For SVMs, however, the quadratic penalty is not introduced as a prior. For SVMs, the penalty term is used to control the *representational capacity* of the learner. By controlling the capacity of the model, we can avoid overtraining, the tendency for complex models to simply memorize accidental properties of noisy training data and miss the larger generalizations. The *structural risk minimization* principle, a key part of Vapnik's statistical learning theory, shows how model complexity can be balanced against the model's   t to the training data in order to maximize the model's expected accuracy on new, unseen data. This provides an alternative explanation as to why a Gaussian prior is as successful as it is for such a wide range of applications.

More recently, researchers have begun exploring the use of alternative regularization terms in the penalized likelihood. One that has received a fair amount of attention is the exponential prior over parameter values (Tibshirani 1996; Goodman 2004; Kazama & Tsujii 2005). This leads to the following penalized likelihood:

(10) $L'(\lambda) = L(\lambda) - \sum_i \alpha_i |\lambda_i|$

While the penalized likelihood in (9) tends to give models with parameter values close to zero, the likelihood in (10) yields models with many parameters exactly equal to zero. Since these parameters will have no effect in the   nal model, the corresponding features can be ignored, and the resulting sparse models can be applied much more ef ciently than standard MaxEnt models. Unfortunately, (10) does not have a smooth gradient and so the model parameters cannot be found using standard ef cient optimization techniques. However, a number of specialized algorithms have been proposed for estimating these models (Riezler & Vasserman 2004; Andrew & Gao 2007; Schmidt et al., 2007).

5   Model Applications

Maximum entropy models of the form (3) or (4) can be applied to any task in natural language processing which requires one to assign a probability to an event which can be described by a feature vector.

5.1   *Classification*

Berger et al. (1996), early proponents of MaxEnt models in NLP, consider two case studies in the use of MaxEnt models in statistical machine translation systems. One of these is a good example of a *classification* problem, a type of task which is frequently encountered in NLP and for which MaxEnt models are well suited. In this problem, Berger et al. are concerned with translations of French noun phrases of the form NOUN *de* NOUN into English. In some cases a word-for-word translation is best (e.g., *conflit d'intérêts* → *conflict of interest*), but in other cases translation as a compound noun is preferable (e.g., *taux d'intérêt* → *interest rate*). Berger et al. approach this as a classi cation problem: for each French NOUN *de* NOUN source phrase, we assign the label no-interchange if a direct translation is best and the label interchange if a compound noun translation is best. The training data consists of a collection of French noun phrase types, with their labels. The feature vector is made up of indicator functions which pick out conjunctions of a word and a class. For example, one feature might be:

$$
f(x,y) = \begin{cases} 1 & \text{if } x\text{'s left member is } \textit{système} \text{ and } y \text{ is interchange} \\ 0 & \text{otherwise} \end{cases}
$$

This feature will be 'active' for events like *système de surveillance* and *système de quota*, noun phrases whose left member is *système* and which are best translated as compound nouns. This feature will be inactive for noun phrases whose left member is not *système* and/or which should not be translated as a compound. Other features might depend on the right member or both members of the French noun phrases.

After training, each feature f_i will be associated with a weight λ_i. Given a novel noun phrase type x, the class $\hat{y}$ predicted by the model is the one which maximizes the conditional probability $p(y|x)$:

$$
\hat{y} = \underset{y}{\operatorname{argmax}}\, p(y|x)
$$

$$
= \underset{y}{\operatorname{argmax}}\, \frac{\sum_i \lambda_i f_i(x,y)}{\sum_i \lambda_i f_i(x, \text{interchange}) + \sum_i \lambda_i f_i(x, \text{no-interchange})}
$$

$$
= \underset{y}{\operatorname{argmax}}\, \sum_i \lambda_i f_i(x,y)
$$

In the experiments reported by Berger et al., the model assigned $p(\text{interchange}|x) \approx 0$ for noun phrases like *chambre de commerce* ('chamber of commerce') and $p(\text{interchange}|x) \approx 1$ for noun phrases like *saison d'hiver* ('winter season'). Many noun phrases like *coût de transport* ('transport cost, cost of transport'), which can be translated either way, received model probabilities $p(\text{interchange}|x) \approx p(\text{no-interchange}|x)$. Overall, the model chose the right translation for 80.4 percent of the noun phrases in a test sample, compared to 70.2 percent accuracy for a simple model which translated all noun phrases directly.

This same basic strategy can be applied to any classi cation problem. The system builder needs to de ne a set of *feature templates* which pick out properties of the events to be classi ed. The model features then will be conjunctions of feature templates and classes. In the noun phrase translation example, the feature templates looked at the rst word, the second word, and both words in the French noun phrases. For a problem like text classi cation, the feature templates may be based on a bag-of-words model. Nigam et al. (1999) propose a MaxEnt version of a naïve Bayes text classi er which uses features of the type:

(11) $f_w(d,c) = \begin{cases} \frac{N(d,w)}{N(d)} & \text{if } d\text{'s class is } c \\ 0 & \text{otherwise} \end{cases}$

where $N(d, w)$ is the number of times word w occurs in document d, and $N(d)$ is the total number of words in d. Nigam et al. report that their MaxEnt model outperforms a standard naïve Bayes classi er on the majority of test samples. Others (e.g., Kazama & Tsujii 2005) have explored using features values that combine the term frequency as in (11) with inverse document frequency, with broadly similar results.

5.2 Sequence models

MaxEnt models are also widely used for sequence labeling tasks, such as part-of-speech tagging and named entity recognition (Ratnaparkhi 1998; Borthwick 1999; McCallum et al., 2000). In the simplest sequence labeling models, the tag probabilities depend only on the current word:

$$P(t_1 \ldots t_n | w_1 \ldots w_n) = \prod_{i=1,n} P(t_i | w_i)$$

The effect of this is that each word in the test data will be assigned the tag which occurred most frequently with that word in the training data. Such a model does maximize the entropy given the constraints, but the constraints are too simple to capture very much of the linguistic reality of what we are trying to model. A more useful approach is suggested by a simple hidden Markov model (DeRose 1988; Charniak 1993), in which the tag probabilities depend on the current word and the previous tag. Suppose we assume that the word/tag probabilities and the tag sequence probabilities are independent, or:

(12) $P(w_i | t_i, t_{i-1}) = P(w_i | t_i) P(t_i | t_{i-1})$

Then by Bayes's theorem and the Markov property, we have:

$$P(t_1 \ldots t_n | w_1 \ldots w_n) = \frac{P(w_1 \ldots w_n | t_1 \ldots t_n) P(t_1 \ldots t_n)}{P(w_1 \ldots w_n)}$$

$$= \frac{\prod_{i=1,n} P(w_i | t_i) P(t_i | t_{i-1})}{P(w_1 \ldots w_n)}$$

Since the probability of the word sequence $P(w_1 \ldots w_n)$ is the same for all candidate tag sequences, the optimal sequence of tags satis es:

(13) $S = \underset{t_1 \ldots t_n}{\mathrm{argmax}} \prod_{i=1,n} P(w_i|t_i)P(t_i|t_{i-1})$

The probabilities $P(w_i|t_i)$ and $P(t_i|t_{i-1})$ can easily be estimated from training data. Using (13) to calculate the probability of a candidate tag sequence, the optimal sequence of tags can be found ef ciently using dynamic programming (Viterbi 1967).

   While this kind of HMM is simple and easy to construct and apply, it has its limitations. For one, (13) depends on the independence assumption in (12). One can avoid this by using a conditional MaxEnt model to estimate tag probabilities. In such a model, the optimal tag sequence satis es:

$$S = \underset{t_1 \ldots t_n}{\mathrm{argmax}} \prod_{i=1,n} P(t_i|w_i, t_{i-1})$$

where

(14) $P(t_i|w_i, t_{i-1}) = \dfrac{\exp\left(\sum_j \lambda_j f_j(t_{i-1}, w_i, t_i)\right)}{\sum_{\tau \in T} \exp\left(\sum_j \lambda_j f_j(t_{i-1}, w_i, \tau)\right)}$

   The indicator functions f_j ' re' for particular combinations of contexts and tags. For instance, in the context of a named entity recognition system, one such function might indicate the occurrence of the word *Javier* with the tag B-PER:

(15) $f(t_{i-1}, w_i, t_i) = \begin{cases} 1 & \text{if } w_i = \text{Javier \& } t_i = \text{B-PER} \\ 0 & \text{otherwise} \end{cases}$

and another might indicate the tag sequence O B-PER:

(16) $f(t_{i-1}, w_i, t_i) = \begin{cases} 1 & \text{if } t_{i-1} = \text{O \& } t_i = \text{B-PER} \\ 0 & \text{otherwise} \end{cases}$

Each indicator f_j function also has an associated weight λ_j, which is chosen so that the probabilities (14) minimize the relative entropy between the empirical distribution $\tilde{P}$ (derived from the training data) and the model probabilities P, or, equivalently, which maximize the likelihood of the training data. Unlike the parameters of an HMM, there is no closed form expression for estimating the parameters of a MaxEnt model from the training data. However, the iterative methods described in the previous section can be used to ef ciently estimate the model's parameters.

Using indicator functions of the type in (15) and (16), the model encodes exactly the same information as the HMM in (13), but with much weaker independence assumptions. This means we can add information to the model from partially redundant and overlapping sources. Features that have been explored for use in MaxEnt tagging models include capitalization features, which indicate whether the current word is capitalized, all upper case, all lower case, mixed case, or non-alphanumeric, and whether or not the word is the first word in the sentence. We can also add additional context sensitivity, so that the tag probabilities depend on the previous word, as well as the previous tag and the current word.

One potential problem with MaxEnt Markov models is what Lafferty et al. (2001) call the *label bias problem*: all probability going into one state in the model is passed on to successors and, in general, states with fewer outgoing transitions will be preferred to those with more. Lafferty et al. (2001) propose the use of conditional random fields to eliminate this source of error by assigning a probability to an entire labeled sequence in one step:

$$p(t_1 \ldots t_n | w_1 \ldots w_n) = \frac{1}{Z(w_1 \ldots w_n)} \exp \sum_i \lambda_i f_i(w_1 \ldots w_n, t_1 \ldots t_n)$$

The challenge in applying conditional random fields is to compute the partition function $Z(w_1 \ldots w_n)$, as in general there will be a very large number of possible tag sequences for a given word sequence. However, if our features are like those from typical HMM taggers, we can use a variant of the forward–backward algorithm to compute feature expectations during training.

5.3   Parsing models

As is the case for simple models like naïve Bayes text classifiers and hidden Markov models for tagging, we can easily construct a MaxEnt version of probabilistic context-free grammars (PCFGs). In a standard PCFG, we assume that the probability of a tree t is the product of the individual rule probabilities:

(17) $p(t) = \prod_i p(r_i(t))$

This depends crucially on the assumption that rule probabilities are independent. This assumption does not generally hold in the case of context-free grammars and, as Abney (1997) shows, is systematically violated by attribute value grammar rules.

Fortunately, the model in (17) can be straightforwardly recast as a MaxEnt model, with rules as features:

(18) $p(t) = \dfrac{\exp \sum_i \lambda_i r_i(t)}{\sum_{t'} \exp \sum_i \lambda_i r_i(t')}$

This version removes the independence assumptions of (17), allowing it to be applied in a wider range of situations (Abney 1997; Johnson et al., 1999; Riezler et al., 2002; Malouf & van Noord 2004; Clark & Curran 2007b). However, a potential drawback of MaxEnt models is that even the conditional version of equation (18) requires access to all parses of a given corpus sentence to compute the denominator. As the number of parses for a sentence grows exponentially with the length of the sentence, this model is dif cult to use in practice.

Two classes of solutions to this problem have been proposed. On the one hand, Geman and Johnson (2002) and Miyao and Tsujii (2002) present approaches where training data consists of parse (or feature) forests rather than sets of independent parses. If we enforce a strong locality condition on features, the denominator in (18) can be computed ef ciently by dynamic programming. Geman and Johnson (2002) suggest that it is always possible to localize arbitrary features in an attribute value grammar. However, for some classes of features used in practical systems, this localization would dramatically complicate the grammar and have severe impacts on parsing ef ciency. Another type of solution which does not depend on feature locality is offered in Osborne (2000). Osborne shows that it suf ces to provide training instances from an 'informative sample' of $Y(w)$. The feature weights chosen by maximizing (18) depend only on the expected values of the features in the training data. So any subsample of the parses in the training data which yields unbiased estimates of the feature expectations should result in as accurate a model as the complete set of parses. The vast majority of possible parses have a very small probability and do not contribute much to the sum in the denominator, so a relatively small sample can yield a fairly good estimate of the normalizing factor in (18).

A remaining issue is how the model, once it has been learned from the training data, can be applied ef ciently. In the approaches of Geman and Johnson (2002) and Miyao and Tsujii (2002) features are localized, and therefore an ef -cient dynamic programming algorithm can be used to extract the best parse from a parse forest. Malouf and van Noord (2004) present a beam-search generalization of such an algorithm, and they show that the algorithm can be used ef ciently to recover the best parse even in the presence of non-local features.

6   Prospects

MaxEnt models provide a general technique for constructing models given limited information integrated from multiple potentially overlapping sources. While MaxEnt models have been successfully used in many applications, they have recently fallen out of favor for classi cation problems and have been replaced by non-parameteric methods like the support vector machine. However, active research on MaxEnt models continues on at least two fronts.

As alluded to in section 4 above, MaxEnt models and SVMs share many important properties. Both incorporate information from training data via sets of constraints on feature functions, and both depend on minimization of a penalized loss function. So, while these two model classes have very different theoretical origins, in actual practice their application is not as different as one might expect.

This has led to the development of hybrid methods which incorporate aspects of both MaxEnt and SVM estimation in model construction (Sears 2007). For example, Smith et al. (2007) explores alternative loss functions for MaxEnt models, and Lafferty et al. (2004) and Zhu and Hastie (2005) consider the use of kernel functions to allow MaxEnt models to capture non-linear decision boundaries.

Another area in which active development of MaxEnt models continues is for applications in which non-parametric methods are not appropriate. For example, state-of-the-art machine translation systems based on noisy channel models combine probabilities estimated using several different models. Unlike classi ca-tion systems, in which the identity of an assigned label is more important than the estimate of its probability, Bayesian and noisy channel models depend on accurate estimation of complete probability distributions. Systems which replace components of the noisy channel model with MaxEnt distributions have shown considerable promise (Och & Ney 2001; Varea et al., 2002).

NOTE

1   http://tadm.sourceforge.net

6 Memory-Based Learning

WALTER DAELEMANS AND ANTAL VAN DEN BOSCH

1 Introduction

Most natural language processing (NLP) tasks require the translation of one level of representation to another. For example, in text to speech systems, it is necessary to have a component that translates the spelling representation of words to a corresponding phonetic representation; in part-of-speech (POS) tagging, the words of a sentence are translated into their contextually appropriate POS tags. Some tasks in NLP involve segmentation: identifying the syllable boundaries in a word or the syntactic phrases in a sentence are examples of such *chunking* tasks. Other tasks, such as document categorization and word-sense disambiguation require a choice between a limited number of possibilities.

What all these types of NLP tasks have in common is that they can be formulated as a *classification task*, and are therefore appropriate problems for discriminative supervised machine learning methods. With some effort, even tasks like coreference resolution and machine translation can be cast as a classi cation problem. In this chapter, we will see an assortment of examples of NLP problems formulated as classi cation-based learning.

Classi cation-based learning starts from a set of instances (examples) consisting each of a set of input features (a feature vector) and an output class. For example, for the NLP task of predicting the pronunciation of a word, given a number of words with their phonetic transcription as training material, we could create an instance for each letter, as in Table 6.1. One of the input features is the letter to be transcribed (here indicated as the focus feature) and other features would be the spelling symbols before and after the focus; in this case a context of three such symbols to the left and to the right are used to make a total of seven predictive features. The output class is the phoneme corresponding with the focus letter in that context. Data like this can be used as training material to construct a *classifier* that is subsequently used to classify feature vectors belonging to new words, not part of the training data. In this way, the classi er generalizes from the original training data, which is the purpose of machine learning.

The Handbook of Computational Linguistics and Natural Language Processing, First Edition.
Edited by Alexander Clark, Chris Fox and Shalom Lappin.
© 2013 Blackwell Publishing Ltd except for editorial material and organization
© 2013 Alexander Clark, Chris Fox, and Shalom Lappin. Published 2013 by Blackwell Publishing Ltd.

Table 6.1 Examples generated for the letter–phoneme conversion task, from the word–phonemization pair *booking*–[bukIN], aligned as [b-ukI-N]

Instance number	Left context	Focus letter	Right context	Classification
1	_ _ _	b	o o k	b
2	_ _ b	o	o k i	–
3	_ b o	o	k i n	u
4	b o o	k	i n g	k
5	o o k	i	n g _	I
6	o k i	n	g _ _	–
7	k i n	g	_ _ _	N

Memory-based learning (MBL) is one of the techniques that has been proposed to learn these NLP classi cation problems. Many other techniques for supervised classi cation-based learning exist. See Chapter 5, MAXIMUM ENTROPY MODELS, Chapter 7, DECISION TREES, Chapter 9, ARTIFICIAL NEURAL NETWORKS. In this chapter, we will show how MBL differs from these approaches.

MBL has as its de ning characteristic that it stores in memory all available instances of a task, and that it extrapolates from the most similar instances in memory to solve problems for which no solution is present in memory. What the most similar instances (the *nearest neighbors*) are is de ned by an adaptive *similarity metric*. The general principle is well known in arti cial intelligence and cognitive psychology, and can be found under different labels (case-based reasoning, exemplar-based models, *k*-NN, instance-based learning, memory-based reasoning, etc.). The approach has been used in application areas ranging from vision and speech via expert systems to robotics and models of human categorization.

In the remainder of this chapter, we introduce an operationalization of MBL, implemented in the open source software package TiMBL in Section 2. Applications in computational linguistics and computational psycholinguistics are discussed in Sections 3 and 4 respectively. We then move to a discussion of the strengths and limitations of the approach in Section 5, and show how Fambl, a variant of MBL based on careful abstraction, discussed in Section 6, can strike a balance between abstraction and memory.

2   Memory-Based Language Processing

MBL, and its application to NLP, which we will call memory-based language processing (MBLP) here, is based on the idea that learning and processing are two sides of the same coin. Learning is the storage of examples in memory, and processing is similarity-based reasoning with these stored examples. The approach is inspired by work in pre-Chomskyan linguistics, categorization psychology, and statistical pattern recognition. The main claim is that, contrary to majority belief since Chomsky, generalization (going beyond the data) can also be achieved without formulating abstract representations such as rules. Abstract representations such as rules, decision trees, statistical models, and trained arti cial neural networks forget about the data itself, and only keep the abstraction. Such *eager learning* approaches are usually contrasted with table lookup, a method that obviously cannot generalize. However, by adding similarity-based reasoning to table lookup, *lazy learning* approaches such as MBL are capable of going beyond the training data as well, and on top of that keep all the data available. This is arguably a useful property for NLP tasks: in such tasks, low-frequency or atypical examples are often not noise to be abstracted from in models, but on the contrary an essential part of the model. In the remainder of this section, we will describe a particular instantiation of memory-based approaches, MBLP, that we have found to work well for language processing problems and for which we make available open source software (TiMBL). The approach is a combination and extension of ideas from instance-based learning (Aha et al., 1991) and memory-based reasoning (Stan ll & Waltz 1986), and a direct descendent of the k-NN algorithm (Fix & Hodges 1951; Cover & Hart 1967).

2.1   *MBLP: an operationalization of MBL*

An MBLP system has two components: a *learning component* which is memory-based, and a *performance component* which is similarity-based. The learning component is memory-based as it involves storing examples in memory without abstraction, selection, or restructuring. In the performance component of an MBLP system the stored examples are used as a basis for mapping input to output; input instances are classi ed by assigning them an output label. During classi-cation, a previously unseen test instance is presented to the system. The class of this instance is determined on the basis of an extrapolation from the most similar example(s) in memory. There are different ways in which this approach can be operationalized. The goal of this section is to provide a clear de nition of the operationalizations we have found to work well for NLP tasks. TiMBL is an open source software package implementing all algorithms and metrics discussed here.[1]

First, a visual example serves to illustrate the basic concepts of memory-based or k-nearest neighbor classi cation. The left part of Figure 6.1 displays part of a two-dimensional Euclidean space with three examples labeled black (i.e., they are examples of the class 'black'), and three examples labeled white. Each example's two coordinates are its two numeric feature values. An example occupies a piece of the space, a Voronoi tile, in which it is the closest example. The so-called Voronoi tesselation depicted in the left part of Figure 6.1 is essentially a map of the decision boundaries of the 1-nearest neighbor classi cation rule: the tile on which a new instance is positioned determines the single nearest neighbor, and the subsequent classi cation step simply copies the class label of that nearest neighbor (here, black or white) to the new instance.

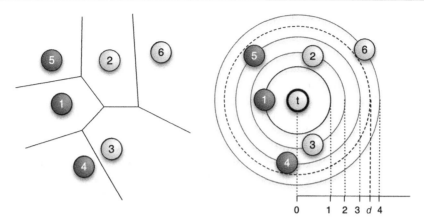

Figure 6.1   An example 2D space with six examples labeled white or black. Left: the Voronoi tesselation of the space. Right: around a new test item *t*, nearest neighbors are found at four different distances; some examples are equidistant. The parameter *k* can regulate the number of either nearest neighbors or distances. Alternatively, a distance *d* can specify the circle (Parzen window) within which nearest neighbors are sought.

Rather than pre-computing the Voronoi tesselation, which is restricted to be used for single nearest-neighbor classi cation, the common mode of operation of the more generic *k*-nearest neighbor classi er is to perform a search for the nearest examples around each new instance *t* to base a classi cation on. The key parameter *k* determines the number of examples within an expanding circle (or hyperball) around the new instance. This can either be the actual number of examples found while extending outwards, or the number of distance rings on which equidistant examples are found. In Figure 6.1, the six visible examples are found at four different distances. Alternatively, a distance *d* can be speci ed as the xed size of the hyperball or Parzen window (Parzen 1962) in which nearest neighbors are sought. Using Parzen windows implies ignoring the local example density; a Parzen window may contain no examples or all examples. In contrast, the *k*-nearest neighbor approach in its most basic form ignores the actual distance at which the *k*-nearest neighbors are found, and adapts the hyperball to the local example density around the new instance. In the remainder of this chapter we adopt the *k*-nearest neighbor approach, and show how the distance of the target to different neighbors can be factored into the classi cation.

As a side note, the *k*-nearest neighbor classi er has some strong formal consistency results. With $k = 1$, the classi cation rule is guaranteed to yield an error rate no worse than twice the Bayes error rate (the minimum achievable error rate given the distribution of the data) as the amount of data approaches in nity (Cover & Hart 1967). Another useful property of the classi er is its insensitivity to the number of classes; this number is a factor neither in learning (storage) nor in classi cation.

Abstracting over the particular type of feature spaces (such as Euclidean space in the example of Figure 6.1), the similarity between a new instance X and all examples Y in memory is computed using a *similarity metric* (that actually measures distance) $\Delta(X, Y)$. Classi cation works by assigning the most frequent class within the k most similar example(s) as the class of a new test instance.

The most basic metric that works for instances with symbolic features such as many data sets in language and speech processing is the *overlap metric* given in equations (1) and (2), where $\Delta(X, Y)$ is the distance between instances X and Y, represented by n features, and δ is the distance per feature. The distance between two patterns is simply the sum of the differences between the features. In the case of symbolic feature values, the distance is 0 with an exact match, and 1 with a mismatch. The k-NN algorithm with this metric is called IB1 in Aha et al. (1991).

$$(1) \quad \Delta(X, Y) = \sum_{i=1}^{n} \delta(x_i, y_i)$$

where:

$$(2) \quad \delta(x_i, y_i) = \begin{cases} |\frac{x_i - y_i}{max_i - min_i}| & \text{if numeric, otherwise} \\ 0 & \text{if } x_i = y_i \\ 1 & \text{if } x_i \neq y_i \end{cases}$$

Our de nition of this basic algorithm is slightly different from the IB1 algorithm originally proposed by Aha et al. (1991). The main difference is that in our version the value of k refers to k-nearest distances rather than k-nearest examples. As illustrated in the right-hand side of Figure 6.1, several examples in memory can be equally similar to a new instance. Instead of choosing one at random, all examples at the same distance are added to the nearest-neighbor set.

The distance metric in equation (2) simply counts the number of (mis)matching feature values in two instances being compared. In the absence of information about feature relevance, this is a reasonable choice. Otherwise, we can use domain knowledge to weight or select different features. We can also compute statistics about the relevance of features by looking at which features are good predictors of the class labels, using feature weighting methods such as information gain.

Information gain (IG) weighting looks at each feature in isolation, and estimates how much information it contributes to our knowledge of the correct class label. The information gain estimate of feature i is measured by computing the difference in uncertainty (i.e., entropy) between the situations without and with knowledge of the value of that feature (the formula is given in equation (3)), where C is the set of class labels, V_i is the set of values for feature i, and $H(C) = -\sum_{c \in C} P(c) \log_2 P(c)$ is the entropy of the class labels. IG is used in decision tree learning (Chapter 7, DECISION TREES) as an ordering criterion.

$$(3) \quad w_i = H(C) - \sum_{v \in V_i} P(v) \times H(C|v)$$

The probabilities are estimated from relative frequencies in the training set. For numeric features, an intermediate step needs to be taken to apply the symbol-based computation of IG. All real values of a numeric feature are temporarily discretized into a number of intervals. Instances are ranked on their real value, and then spread evenly over the intervals; each interval contains the same number of instances (this is necessary to avoid empty intervals in the case of skewed distributions of values). Instances in each of these intervals are then used in the IG computation as all having the same unordered, symbolic value per group. Note that this discretization is only temporary; it is not used in the computation of the distance metric.

The IG weight of a feature is a probability-weighted average of the informativeness of the different values of the feature. This makes the values with low frequency but high informativity invisible. Such values disappear in the average. At the same time, this also makes the IG weight robust to estimation problems in sparse data. Each parameter (weight) is estimated on the whole data set.

A well-known problem with IG is that it tends to overestimate the relevance of features with large numbers of values, MBLP therefore also includes the *gain ratio* normalization and several alternative feature-relevance weighting methods (chi-squared, shared variance, special metrics for binary features, etc.).

The choice of representation for instances in MBLP is the key factor determining the accuracy of the approach. The feature values and classes in NLP tasks are often represented by symbolic labels. The metrics that have been described so far, i.e., (weighted) overlap, are limited to either a match or a mismatch between feature values. This means that all values of a feature are seen as equally dissimilar to each other. However, we would like to express that some feature-*value* pairs are more or less similar than other pairs. For instance, we would like vowels to be more similar to each other than to consonants in problems where features are letters or phonemes, nouns more similar to other nouns than to verbs in problems where features are words, etc. As with feature weights, domain knowledge can be used to create a feature system expressing these similarities, e.g., by splitting or collapsing features. But again, an automatic technique might be better in modeling these statistical relations.

For such a purpose a metric was de ned by Stan ll and Waltz (1986) and further re ned by Cost and Salzberg (1993). It is called the (modi ed) value difference metric (MVDM; equation (4)), a method to determine the similarity of the values of a feature by looking at co-occurrence of values with target classes. For the distance between two values v_1, v_2 of a feature, we compute the difference of the conditional distribution of the classes $C_{1 \dots n}$ for these values.

(4) $\quad \delta(v_1, v_2) = \sum_{i=1}^{n} |P(C_i|v_1) - P(C_i|v_2)|$

MVDM differs considerably from overlap-based metrics in its composition of the nearest-neighbor sets. Overlap causes an abundance of ties in nearest-neighbor position. For example, if the nearest neighbor is at a distance of one mismatch

from the test instance, then the nearest-neighbor set will contain the entire partition of the training set that contains *any* value for the mismatching feature. With
the MVDM metric, however, either the nearest-neighbor set will contain patterns which have the value with the lowest $\delta(v_1, v_2)$ in the mismatching position,
or MVDM will select a totally different nearest neighbor which has less exactly
matching features, but a smaller distance in the mismatching features (Zavrel &
Daelemans 1997).

MBLP also contains different metrics for extrapolation from nearest neighbors
(linear or exponential distance-based decay) and for computing exemplar similarity with weighted examples. Such weights could be based on frequency of
instances, or on their goodness or typicality according to some criterion. MBLP
is not a new algorithm, rather, it is a set of algorithm parameterizations selected
and optimized for use with language processing data. We will not go into further details of MBLP here. However, we will return to the crucial discussion about
generalization and abstraction in lazy and eager learning methods in Section 6.
First we provide an overview of application areas of MBLP.

3   NLP Applications

As explained in Section 1, MBL shares its generic applicability to classi cation
tasks with any other machine learning classi er. Hence, when an NLP task is
framed as a classi cation task, memory-based learning can be applied to it. In
the past decade, memory-based learning has indeed been applied across a wide
range of NLP tasks. Before we turn to the limitations of memory-based learning in
Section 5, we provide an overview of types of NLP tasks in which memory-based
learning has been successful in this and the next section.

3.1   *Morpho-phonology*

Tasks at the phonological and morphological levels are often framed as sliding-
window tasks over sequences of letters or phonemes, where the task is framed
as a mapping of one symbol set to another (letters to phonemes), or a mapping
from an unsegmented string to a segmented string (words to morphological analyses). In case of segmentation tasks such as syllabi cation, the output symbol set
typically consists of a 'null' value that signi es that no boundary occurs at the
focus input symbol, and one or more positive values marking that some type of
boundary does occur at the focus letter. Example morpho-phonological tasks to
which memory-based learning has been applied are hyphenation and syllabi cation (Daelemans & van den Bosch 1992); grapheme-to-phoneme conversion (van
den Bosch & Daelemans 1993; Daelemans & van den Bosch 1996); and morphological analysis (van den Bosch & Daelemans 1999; de Pauw et al., 2004). Although
these examples are applied mostly to Germanic languages (English, Dutch, and
German), applications to other languages with more complicated writing systems or morphologies, or with limited resources, have also been presented: for

example, letter–phoneme conversion in Scottish Gaelic (Wolters & van den Bosch 1997), morphological analysis of Arabic (Marsi et al., 2006), or diacritic restoration in languages with a diacritic-rich writing system (Mihalcea 2002; de Pauw et al., 2007).

Most of these studies report the important advantage of the memory-based approach to faithfully reproduce all training data; essentially, the method can be seen as a compressed lexicon that also generalizes to unseen words if needed. As an average training lexicon typically covers unseen text at about 95 percent (i.e., 5 percent of the words in a new text are not in the lexicon), the key goal of the memory-based learner is to process the 5 percent unknown words as accurately as possible. In the reported studies, most attention is indeed paid to evaluating the classi ers' generalization performance on unseen words, often at the word level. Actual percentages are intrinsically linked to the task, the language, and the amount of training data, and can typically only be assessed properly in the context of a higher-level task, such as comparative human judgments of the understandability of a speech synthesizer with and without the module under evaluation.

3.2 Syntacto-semantics

In the mid-1990s, memory-based learning was among the early set of machine learning classi ers to be applied to tasks in shallow parsing and lexical semantics: part-of-speech tagging (Daelemans et al., 1996; Zavrel & Daelemans 1999; van Halteren et al., 2001) and PP-attachment (Zavrel et al., 1997), mostly on English benchmark tasks. Also, early developments of shallow parsing modules using memory-based learning contributed to the development of the eld of shallow parsing: subcategorization (Buchholz 1998); phrase chunking (Veenstra 1998; Tjong Kim Sang & Veenstra 1999); and the integration of memory-based modules for shallow parsing (Daelemans et al., 1999a; Buchholz et al., 1999; Yeh 2000a). More recently, memory-based learning has been integrated as a classi er engine in more complicated dependency parsing systems (Nivre et al., 2004; Sagae & Lavie 2005; Canisius et al., 2006).

Memory-based learning has been applied succesfully to lexical semantics, in particular to word-sense disambiguation (Stevenson & Wilks 1999; Kokkinakis 2000; Veenstra et al., 2000; Hoste et al., 2002; Mihalcea 2002; Decadt et al., 2004), but also in other lexical semantic tasks such as determining noun countability (Baldwin & Bond 2003), animacy (Orasan & Evans 2001), and semantic relations within noun compounds (Kim & Baldwin 2006; Nastase et al., 2006).

3.3 Text analysis

Extending the simple sliding-window approach that proved to be useful in phrase chunking, memory-based learning has also been used for named entity recognition (Buchholz & van den Bosch 2000; de Meulder & Daelemans 2003;

Hendrickx & van den Bosch 2003; Sporleder et al., 2006; Leveling & Hartrumpf 2007), and domain-dependent information extraction (Zavrel et al., 2000; Zavrel & Daelemans 2003; Ahn 2006).

Many NLP tasks beyond the sentence level tend not to be phrased (or phrasable) in simple sliding-window representations. Some tasks require more complicated structures, such as pairs of phrases in their context bearing some relation to be classi ed, as in anaphora and coreference resolution (Mitkov et al., 2002; Preiss 2002a; Hoste 2005), while other tasks appear to be best solved using vector space or bag-of-words representations, to which memory-based learning is also amenable, such as text classi cation (Spitters 2000), question classi cation (Cumbreras et al., 2006; Dridan & Baldwin 2007), or spam ltering (Androutsopoulos et al., 2000).

3.4   *Dialogue and discourse*

In the eld of discourse and dialogue modeling, memory-based learning has been used for shallow semantic analysis of speech-recognised utterances (Gustafson et al., 1999; van den Bosch et al., 2001; Lendvai et al., 2002; 2003a; Lendvai & Geertzen 2007), in dis uency detection in transcribed spontaneous speech (Lendvai et al., 2003b), and in classifying ellipsis in dialogue (Fernández et al., 2004). In most of these studies, the task is framed as a classi cation task into a limited number of labels (usually, some dialogue-act labeling scheme), while the input can be a mix of bag-of-word features, dialogue history features (e.g., previous dialogue acts), and acoustic features of recognized speech in the context of spoken dialogue systems. As memory-based learning handles numeric features as easily as symbolic features, it is unproblematic to mix these heterogeneous feature sets in a single classi er.

3.5   *Generation, language modeling, and translation*

While the general scope of natural language generation, language modeling, and translation comprises full sequences, memory-based learning has been applied to word or phrase-level subtasks within these more general problem elds. For instance, in natural language generation, memory-based learning has been applied particularly to morpho-syntactic generation subtasks: in ection generation, such as diminutive formation (Daelemans et al., 1998), article generation (Minnen et al., 2000), or determining the order of multiple prenominal adjectives (Malouf 2000).

Language modeling has mostly been the domain of stochastic n-gram models, but as Zavrel & Daelemans (1997) have already shown, there is an equivalence relation between back-off smoothing in n-gram models and memory-based classi-
cation. Essentially, language modeling in n-gram models can be phrased as the classi cation task of predicting the next word given a context of previous words. Indeed, memory-based language models can be developed that perform this task (van den Bosch 2006a). As a specialization of these generic language models,

memory-based confusable-speci c disambiguators can be trained to determine which of a confusable set of words (e.g., *to*, *too*, and *two*) is appropriate in a certain context. An accurate confusable disambiguator can be useful as a spelling correcting module in a proo ng environment.

In machine translation, memory-based learning bears a close relation to example-based machine translation (EBMT). A rst EBMT implementation using memory-based learning is described in van den Bosch et al. (2007b). Analogous to memory-based language modeling, memory-based translation maps a local context of words (a part of a source-language sentence) to a target word or *n*-gram of words (part of the corresponding target sentence), where the target word or center of the target *n*-gram is aligned to the source word according to an externally computed word alignment.

We have not tried to be exhaustive in this section. There are other implementations of *k*-nearest neighbor classi cation apart from TiMBL that have been used in NLP, and alternative memory-based algorithms have been proposed for speci c tasks. As a good example, Bob Damper and colleagues have developed a psycholinguistic proposal for modeling pronunciation (Pronunciation by Analogy) into a state-of-the-art grapheme-to-phoneme conversion approach (Damper & Eastmond 1997). Other researchers have argued for richer analogy processes in memory-based approaches than the basic overlap metric and its extensions that are used in the research described in this section (Pirrelli & Yvon 1999; Lepage & Denoual 2005a; Yvon & Stroppa 2007). This work is also relevant when memory-based approaches are intended as models of human language acquisition and processing as in the work we turn to next.

4 Exemplar-Based Computational Psycholinguistics

From the time Chomsky substituted the vague notions of analogy and induction existing in linguistics in his time (for instance in the work of de Saussure, Bloom- eld, and Harris) by a better formalized notion of rule-based grammars, most mainstream linguistic theories, even the functionally and cognitively inspired ones, have assumed rules to be the only or main means to describe any aspect of language. Also in computational modeling of human language processing and human language acquisition, mental rule application and acquisition has been the standard approach. See Chapter 17, COMPUTATIONAL PSYCHOLINGUISTICS. A good example is the dual mechanism model advocated by Pinker (1999) and others for in ectional morphology. In such a model, a mental rule governing the regular cases in in ectional morphology is complemented by an associative memory explaining subregularities and exceptions. In contrast, single mechanism models (mostly based on neural network approaches following Rumelhart & McClelland 1986) model regular and exceptional language behavior in a single model. See Chapter 9, ARTIFICIAL NEURAL NETWORKS.

MBLP can be considered an operationalisation of the pre-Chomskyan analogical approach to language, and as a predictive model for human language acquisition and processing that is an alternative to both rule-based and neural network approaches. The main advantage from a theoretical point of view is that no ontological distinction has to be made between regular and exceptional cases, and that the gradedness of language learning and processing is an emergent phenomenon of the way the model works. The approach is also incremental, in that the addition of new experience immediately affects processing without any need of recomputation of knowledge structures. Conceptually, to model language acquisition and processing, memorized experiences of previous language use are searched looking for instances similar to a new item, and a decision is extrapolated for the new item from these nearest neighbors. Language acquisition is simply the incremental storage of experience.

The analogical modeling (AM) approach of Skousen (1989; 1992; 2002) is an early alternative example of a computational operationalization of analogy in a memory-based context and its application in modeling language. It is memory-based in that all available training data (experience) is used in extrapolating to the solution for a new input. As it searches combinatorial combinations of input features, it is exponential in the number of features, which makes the approach impractical for problems with many features. The approach has been applied to different problems in language processing, mainly in the phonology and morphology domains. Although algorithmically very different from and more costly than MBLP (which is linear in the number of features), empirical comparisons have never shown important accuracy or output differences between AM and MBLP (Eddington 2002a; Daelemans 2002; Krott et al., 2002).

In ectional morphology has proven a useful and interesting testing ground for models of language acquisition and processing because of the relative simplicity of the processes (compared to syntax), the availability of lexical databases, and the ample psycholinguistic experimental data in the form of accounts of acquisition, adult processing experiments, production tasks on pseudo-words, etc. This makes possible controlled comparisons between different computational models. Problems like English past-tense formation, German and Dutch plural formation, etc., have therefore become important benchmark problems. Memory-based psycholinguistic models of in ectional morphology have been provided for the English past tense by Keuleers (2008), for Dutch plural formation by Keuleers et al. (2007); and Keuleers and Daelemans (2007); for Spanish diminutive formation by Eddington (2002c), and for Dutch and German linking phenomena in compounds by Krott et al. (2001; 2007). See Hay and Baayen (2005) for an overview of the state of the art in modeling morphology and the role of memory-based models in current theory formation. In phonology, memory-based models have been proposed and matched to psycholinguistic empirical data for such tasks as nal devoicing in Dutch (Ernestus 2006), Italian conjugation (Eddington 2002b), stress assignment in Dutch (Daelemans et al., 1994), Spanish (Eddington 2004), and English compounds (Plag et al., 2007), etc.

Much less work has attempted to develop memory-based models of syntactic processing. Data-oriented parsing (DOP) (Scha et al., 1999; Bod 2006b) is one in uential algorithm where parsing is seen as similarity-based lookup and reconstruction of memorized fragments of previously analyzed sentences, kept in memory. It has led to experiments modeling priming effects in syntactic processing (Snider 2007). See Hay and Bresnan (2006) for additional empirical work in exemplar-based syntax. In addition to work based on traditional parsing approaches rooted in phrase-based or dependency-based grammar theory, the memory-based shallow parsing research described in the previous section also makes possible psycholinguistic studies (e.g., on attachment preferences).

As for our overview of memory-based approaches in computational linguistics, we have not tried to be exhaustive here, but rather to point to interesting studies and starting points in the literature illustrating the power of memory-based models as models of language acquisition and use.

5   Generalization and Abstraction

As discussed in Section 3, the memory-based learning approach is functionally similar to other supervised discriminative machine learning methods capable of learning classi cation tasks. It is hard, if not fundamentally impossible, to say in general that one discriminative machine learning algorithm is better than the other (Wolpert 2002). Yet certain advantages of memory-based learning in learning NLP tasks have been noted in the literature. First, we expand in some detail the tenet that "forgetting exceptions is harmful in language learning" (Daelemans et al., 1999b); then, we review a few algorithmic advantages of memory-based learning.

"Forgetting" training examples is a common trait of many machine learning algorithms; the identity of training examples is lost while, in exchange, each training example in uences to a small extent the construction of an abstract model composed of probabilities or rules. In machine learning, learning is often equated with abstraction; in turn, abstraction is often equated with the capacity to generalize to new cases. A key realization is that memory-based learning is able to generalize, yet does not abstract from the data. In two studies, memory-based learning was contrasted against abstracting learners, namely decision tree learners and rule learners (Daelemans et al., 1999b; Daelemans & van den Bosch 2005), resulting in the consistent observation that the abstracting learners do not outperform the memory-based learners on any of a wide selection of NLP tasks. In a second series of experiments, Daelemans and van den Bosch show that selected removal of training examples from the memory of a memory-based classi er, guided by criteria that supposedly express the utility of an individual example in classi cation, does not produce better generalization performance, although, with some tasks, up to 40 percent of the examples can be removed from memory without damaging performance signi cantly (Daelemans & van den Bosch 2005). A safe conclusion from these studies is that when high accuracy is more important than optimal memory usage or speed, it is best to never forget training examples.

In practical terms, the k-nearest neighbor classi er has a number of advantages that make memory-based learning the method of choice in certain particular situations, compared to other rival discriminative supervised machine learning algorithms:

(1)   the basic version of the k-NN classi er that uses the overlap metric is insensitive to the number of class labels, in terms of ef ciency both in training and in classi cation. This makes memory-based learning suited for classi cation tasks with very large numbers of classes, such as word prediction or machine translation;

(2)   memory-based learning is able to reproduce the classi cation of training data awlessly, as long as there are no identical training instances in memory with different class labels. This advantage, an important component of the "forgetting exceptions is harmful" tenet, is especially useful in NLP tasks in which much of the training data can be expected to recur in new data, such as in word pronunciation, where a typical lexicon used for training will already contain the pronunciation of approximately 95 percent of all words in a new text;

(3)   memory-based learning allows for incremental learning at no cost, or with little cost if the similarity function uses weighting functions; this is practical in situations in which training examples become available over time, and the classi er needs to be retrained preferably with the availability of each new training example, e.g., in active learning (Thompson et al., 1999). Also, the algorithm is equally easily *decremental*, allowing for fast leave-one-out testing, a powerful evaluation scheme (Weiss & Kulikowski 1991);

(4)   as mentioned earlier, it has been shown that the 1-nearest neighbor classi er has an attractive error upper bound: as the amount of data approaches in n-ity, it is guaranteed to yield an error rate no worse than twice the Bayes error rate (the minimum achievable error rate given the distribution of the data) (Cover & Hart 1967).

The main disadvantage of memory-based learning, compared to most rival approaches, is its slow classi cation speed. Its worst-case complexity of classi cation is $O(nf)$, where n is the number of memorized examples, and f is the number of features; each new example needs to be compared against all of the memorized examples, each time involving a comparison of all f features. Implementing k-nearest neighbor classi cation in a trie (Knuth 1973) can under the proper conditions, namely highly differing feature weights, or by dropping the guarantee of nding the exact nearest neighbors (Daelemans et al., 1997b), reduce classi cation time to $O(f)$.

Another disadvantage of the memory-based learning approach that it shares with other discriminative classi ers is that its strength is in classi cation tasks with relatively low dimensionality in the class space. In the larger context of NLP tasks with structured output speci cations, such as parsing or machine translation, it is widely recognized that discriminative classi cation alone is not enough to perform these global tasks, as the class spaces that would cover entire sequences, or large subsequences, would be too high-dimensional, thus too sparse to allow for suf cient amounts of examples per class. Even memory-based learning, with its insensitivity towards the number of classes, suffers directly from such sparseness. Currently, the generally adopted solution is to combine discriminitive classi ers with an inference method that searches for an optimal global solution.

6 Generalizing Examples

To alleviate the computational inef ciency of the classi cation process in memory-based learning, part of the early work in k-NN classi cation focused on *editing* methods, i.e., methods for the removal of certain examples in memory that are estimated to be useless or even harmful to classi cation. Yet bad estimates may lead to the removal of useful examples, thus to loss of generalization performance. While keeping full memory may be a safe guideline to avoid any eventual harmful effect of editing, in the interest of speed of classi cation it is still interesting and tempting to explore other means to reduce the need for memory, provided that performance is not harmed. In this section we explore methods that attempt to abstract over memorized examples in a different and more careful manner, namely by merging examples into generalized examples, using various types of merging operations.

We start, in subsection 6.1, with an overview of existing methods for generalizing examples in memory-based learning. Subsequently, in subsection 6.2, we present Fambl, a memory-based learning algorithm variant that merges similar same-class nearest-neighbor examples into 'families.' In subsection 6.3 we compare Fambl to pure memory-based learning on a range of NLP tasks.

6.1 Careful abstraction in memory-based learning

Paths in decision trees can be seen as generalized examples. In IGTREE (Daelemans et al., 1997b) and C4.5 (Quinlan 1993) this generalization is performed up to the point where no actual example is left in memory; all is converted to nodes and arcs. Counter to this decision tree compression, approaches exist that start with storing individual examples in memory, and carefully merge some of these examples to become a single, more general example, only when there is some evidence that this operation is not harmful to generalization performance. Although overall memory is compressed, the memory still contains individual items on which the same k-nearest neighbor classi cation can be performed. The abstraction occurring in this approach is that after a merge, the merged examples incorporated in the new generalized example are deleted individually, and cannot be reconstructed. Example approaches to merging examples are NGE (Salzberg 1991) and its batch variant BNGE (Wettschereck & Dietterich 1995), and RISE (Domingos 1996). We provide brief discussions of two of these algorithms: NGE and RISE.

NGE (Salzberg 1991), an acronym for *Nested Generalized Exemplars*, is an incremental learning theory for merging instances (or exemplars, as Salzberg prefers to refer to examples stored in memory) into *hyper-rectangles*, a geometrically

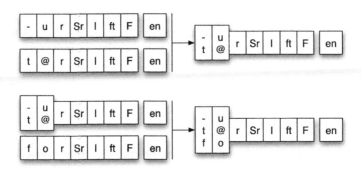

Figure 6.2   Two examples of the generation of a new hyper-rectangle in NGE: from a new example and an individual exemplar (top) and from a new example and the hyper-rectangle from the top example (bottom).

motivated term for merged exemplars. NGE adds examples to memory in an incremental fashion (at the onset of learning, the memory is seeded with a small number of randomly picked examples). Every time a new example is presented, it is matched with all exemplars in memory, which can be individual or merged exemplars (hyper-rectangles). When it is classi ed correctly by its nearest neighbor (an individual exemplar or the smallest matching hyper-rectangle), the new example is merged with it, yielding a new, more general hyper-rectangle.

Figure 6.2 illustrates two mergings of examples of a morphological task (German plural) with exemplars. On the top of Figure 6.2, the example *-urSrIftF* (from the female-gender word *Urschrift*), labeled with class *en* (representing the plural form *Urschriften*), is merged with the example *t@rSrIftF* (from the female-gender word *Unterschrift*), also of class *en*, to form the generalized exemplar displayed on the right-hand side. On the rst two features, a disjunction is formed of, respectively, the values *-* and *t*, and *u* and *@*. This means that the generalized example matches on any other example that has value *-* or value *t* on the rst feature, and any other example that has value *u* or value *@* on the second feature. The lower part of Figure 6.2 displays a subsequent merge of the newly generalized example with another same-class example, *forSrIftF* (the female-gender word *Forschrift*), which leads to a further generalization of the rst two features.

In nested generalized examples, abstraction occurs because it is not possible to retrieve the individual examples nested in the generalized example; new generalization occurs because the generalized example not only matches fully with its nested examples, but would also match perfectly with potential examples with feature-value combinations that were not present in the nested examples; the generalized example in Figure 6.2 would also match *torSrIft*, *f@rSrIft*, *furSrIft*, *-orSrIft*. These examples do not necessarily match existing German words, but they might – and arguably they would be labeled with the correct plural in ection class.

RISE (*Rule Induction from a Set of Exemplars*) (Domingos 1995; 1996) is a multi-strategy learning method that combines memory-based learning with rule

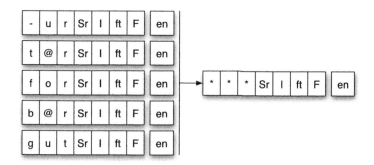

Figure 6.3   An example of an induced rule in RISE, displayed on the right, with the set of examples that it covers (and from which it was generated) on the left.

induction (Michalski 1983; Clark & Niblett 1989; Clark & Boswell 1991). As in NGE, the basic method is that of a memory-based learner and classi er, only operating on a more general type of example. RISE learns a memory lled with *rules* which are all derived from individual examples. Some rules are example-speci c, and other rules are generalized over sets of examples.

RISE inherits parts of the rule induction method of CN2 (Clark & Niblett 1989; Clark & Boswell 1991). CN2 is an incremental rule-induction algorithm that attempts to nd the 'best' rule governing a certain amount of examples in the example base that are not yet covered by a rule. 'Goodness' of a rule is estimated by computing its apparent accuracy, i.e., class prediction strength (Cost & Salzberg 1993) with Laplace correction (Niblett 1987; Clark & Boswell 1991).

RISE induces rules in a careful manner, operating in cycles. At the onset of learning, all examples are converted to example-speci c rules. During a cycle, for each rule a search is made for the nearest example not already covered by it that has the same class. If such an example is found, rule and example are merged into a more general rule. Instead of disjunctions of values, RISE generalizes by inserting wild-card symbols (that match with any other value) on positions with differing values. At each cycle, the goodness of the rule set on the original training material (the individual examples) is monitored. RISE halts when this accuracy measure does not improve (which may already be the case in the rst cycle, yielding a plain memory-based learning algorithm).

Figure 6.3 illustrates the merging of individual examples into a rule. The rule contains seven normally valued conditions, and two wild cards, '*'. The rule now matches on every female-gender example ending in *SrIft* (*Schrift*). When processing new examples, RISE classi es them by searching for the best-matching rule.

6.2   Fambl: merging example families

Fambl, for *FAMily-Based Learning*, is a variant of MBL that constitutes an alternative approach to careful abstraction over examples. The core idea of Fambl, in the spirit of NGE and RISE, is to transform an example base into a set of *example family expressions*. An example family expression is a hyper-rectangle, but the procedure for merging examples differs from that in NGE or in RISE. First, we outline the ideas and assumptions underlying Fambl. We then give a procedural description of the learning algorithm.

Classi cation of an example in memory-based learning involves a search for the nearest neighbors of that example. The value of k in k-NN determines how many of these neighbors are used for extrapolating their (majority) classi cation to the new example. A xed k ignores (smoothes) the fact that an example is often surrounded in example space by a number of examples of the same class that is actually larger or smaller than k. We refer to such a variable-sized set of same-class nearest neighbors as an example's *family*. The extreme cases are on the one hand examples that have a nearest neighbor of a different class, i.e., they have no family members and are a family on their own, and on the other hand examples that have as nearest neighbors all other examples of the same class.

Thus, families represent same-class clusters in example space, and the number and sizes of families in a data set re ect the *disjunctivity* of the data set: the degree of scatteredness of classes into clusters. In real-world data sets, the situation is generally somewhere between the extremes of total disjunctivity (one example per cluster) and no disjunctivity (one cluster per class). Many types of language data appear to be quite disjunct (Daelemans et al., 1999b). In highly disjunct data, classes are scattered among many small clusters, which means that examples have few nearest neighbors of the same class on average.

Figure 6.4 illustrates how Fambl determines the family of an example in a simple two-dimensional example space. All nearest neighbors of a randomly picked

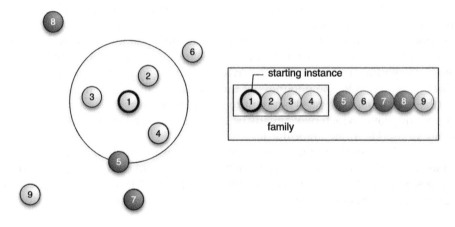

Figure 6.4   An example of a family in a two-dimensional example space (left). The family, at the inside of the circle, spans the focus example (marked with number 1) and the three nearest neighbors labeled with the same class (indicated by their color). When ranked in the order of distance (right), the family boundary is put immediately before the rst example of a different class, the gray example with number 5.

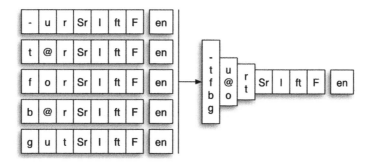

Figure 6.5 An example of family creation in Fambl. Five German plural examples (left) are merged into a family expression (right).

starting example (marked by the black dot) are searched and ranked in the order of their distance to the starting example. Although there are ve examples of the same class in the example space, the family of the starting example contains only three examples, since its fourth-nearest example is of a different class.

Families are converted in Fambl to *family expressions*, which are hyper-rectangles, by merging all examples belonging to that family simultaneously. Figure 6.5 illustrates the creation of a family expression from an example family. In contrast with NGE,

- family expressions are created in one non-incremental operation on the entire example base, rather than by step-wise nesting of each individual family member;
- a family is abstracted only once and is not merged later on with other examples or family expressions;
- families cannot contain 'holes,' i.e., examples with different classes, since the de nition of family is such that family abstraction halts as soon as the nearest neighbor with a different class is met in the local neighborhood.

The general mode of operation of Fambl is that it randomly picks examples from an example base one by one from the set of examples that are not already part of a family. For each newly picked example, Fambl determines its family, generates a family expression from this set of examples, and then marks all involved examples as belonging to a family (so that they will not be picked as a starting point or member of another family). Fambl continues determining families until all examples are marked as belonging to a family.

Families essentially re ect the locally optimal k surrounding the example around which the family is created. The locally optimal k is a notion that is also used in locally weighted learning methods (Vapnik & Bottou 1993; Wettschereck & Dietterich 1994; Wettschereck 1994; Atkeson et al., 1997); however, these methods do not abstract from the learning material. In this sense, Fambl can be seen as a local abstractor.

Procedure FAMBL FAMILY-EXTRACTION:
Input: A training set TS of examples $I_{1 \dots n}$, each example being labeled with a family-membership
   ag set to *FALSE*
Output: A family set FS of family expressions $F_{1 \dots m}$, $m \leq n$
$i = f = 0$
1   Randomize the ordering of examples in TS
2   While not all family-membership   ags are *TRUE*, Do
   • While the family-membership   ag of I_i is *TRUE* Do increase i
   • Compute NS, a ranked set of nearest neighbors to I_i with the same class as I_i, among all
      examples with family-membership   ag *FALSE*. Nearest-neighbor examples of a different
      class with family-membership   ag *TRUE* are still used for marking the boundaries of the
      family
   • Set the membership   ags of I_i and all remaining examples in NS to *TRUE*
   • Merge I_i and all examples in NS into the family expression F_f and store this expression along
      with a count of the number of examples merged in it
   • $f = f + 1$

Figure 6.6   Pseudo-code of the family extraction procedure in Fambl.

The Fambl algorithm converts any training set of labeled examples to a set of family expressions, following the procedure given in Figure 6.6. After learning, the original example base is discarded, and further classi cation is based only on the set of family expressions yielded by the family-extraction phase. Classi cation in Fambl works analogously to classi cation in pure memory-based learning (with the same similarity and weighting metrics as we used so far with MBL): a match is made between a new test example and all stored family expressions. When a family expression contains a disjunction of values for a certain feature, a match is counted when one of the disjunctive values matches the value at that feature in the new example. How the match is counted exactly depends on the similarity metric. With the overlap metric, the feature weight of the matching feature is counted, while with the MVDM metric the smallest MVDM distance among the disjuncted feature values is also incorporated in the count.

6.3   *Experiments with Fambl*

We performed experiments with Fambl on four language processing tasks. We rst introduce these four tasks, ranging from morpho-phonological tasks to semanto-syntactic tasks, varying in scope (word level and sentence level) and basic type of example encoding (non-windowing and windowing). We brie y describe the four tasks here and provide some basic data set speci cations in Table 6.2. At the same time, we also provide results for standard MBLP for comparison.

(1)   GPLURAL, the formation of the plural form of German nouns. The task is to classify a noun as mapping to one out of eight classes, representing the noun's plural formation. We collected 25,753 German nouns from the German part of

the CELEX-2 lexical database.[2] We removed from this data set cases without plurality marking, cases with Latin plural in -a, and a miscellaneous class of foreign plurals. From the remaining 25,168 cases, we extracted or computed for each word the plural suf x, the gender feature, and the syllable structure of the last two syllables of the word in terms of onsets, nuclei, and codas expressed using a phonetic segmental alphabet. We use a 50–50 percent split in 12,584 training examples and 12,584 test instances. Generalization performance is measured in accuracy, namely the percentage of correctly classi ed test instances.

(2) DIMIN, Dutch diminutive formation, uses a similar scheme to the one used in the GPLURAL task to represent a word as a single example. The task and data were introduced by Daelemans et al. (1997a). A noun, or more speci cally its phonemic transcription, is represented by its last three syllables, which are each represented by four features: (1) whether the syllable is stressed (binary), (2) the onset, (3) the nucleus, and (4) the coda. The class label represents the identity of the diminutive in ection, which is one out of ve (-je, -tje, -etje, -pje, or -kje). For example, the diminutive form of the Dutch noun *beker* (cup) is *bekertje* (small cup). Its phonemic representation is *['bek@r]*. The resulting example is _ _ _ _ + b e _ – k @ r tje. The data are extracted from the CELEX-2 lexical database (Baayen et al., 1993). The training set contains 2,999 labeled examples of nouns; the test set contains 950 instances. Again, generalization performance is measured in accuracy, namely the percentage of correctly classi ed test instances.

(3) PP, prepositional-phrase attachment, is the classical benchmark data set introduced by Ratnaparkhi et al. (1994). The data set is derived from the *Wall Street Journal* Penn Treebank (Marcus et al., 1993). All sentences containing the pattern 'VP NP PP' with a single NP in the PP were converted to four-feature examples, where each feature contains the headword of one of the four constituents, yielding a 'V N1 P N2' pattern such as '*each pizza with Eleni*,' or '*eat pizza with pineapple*.' Each example is labeled by a class denoting whether the PP is attached to the verb or to the N1 noun in the treebank parse. We use the original training set of 20,800 examples, and the test set of 3,097 instances. Noun attachment occurs slightly more frequently than verb attachment; 52 percent of the training examples and 59 percent of the test examples are noun attachment cases. Generalization performance is measured in terms of accuracy (the percentage of correctly classi ed test instances).

(4) CHUNK is the task of splitting sentences into non-overlapping syntactic phrases or constituents, e.g., to analyze the sentence '*He reckons the current account deficit will narrow to only $ 1.8 billion in September*.' as

> [He]$_{NP}$ [reckons]$_{VP}$ [the current account deficit]$_{NP}$ [will narrow]$_{VP}$ [to]$_{PP}$ [only $ 1.8 billion]$_{NP}$ [in]$_{PP}$ [September]$_{NP}$.

The data set, extracted from the *WSJ* Penn Treebank through a attened, intermediary representation of the trees (Tjong Kim Sang & Buchholz 2000), contains 211,727 training examples and 47,377 test instances. The examples represent seven-word windows of words and their respective part-of-speech tags computed by the Brill tagger (Brill 1992) (which is trained on a disjoint part of the *WSJ* Penn Treebank), and each example is labeled with a class using the IOB type of segmentation coding as introduced by Ramshaw & Marcus (1995). Generalization performance is measured by the F-score on correctly identi ed and labeled constituents in test data, using the evaluation method originally used in the 'shared task' subevent of the CoNLL-2000 conference (Tjong Kim Sang & Buchholz 2000) in which this particular training and test set were used.

As a rst experiment, we varied both the normal k parameter (which sets the number of equidistant neighbors in the nearest neighbor set used in k-NN classi cation), and the Fambl-speci c parameter that sets the maximum k distances in the family extraction stage, which we will refer to as K. The two parameters are obviously related – the K can be seen as a pre-processing step that 'pre-compiles' the k for the k-NN classi er. The k-nearest neighbor classi er that operates on the set of family expressions can be set to 1, hypothetically, since the complete example space is pre-partitioned in many small regions of various sizes (with maximally K different distances) that each represent a locally appropriate k.

If the empirical results would indeed show that k can be set to 1 safely when K is set at an appropriately large value, then Fambl could be seen as a means to factor the important k parameter out of MBL. We performed comparative experiments with normal MBL and Fambl on the four benchmark tasks, in which we varied both the k parameter in MBL, and the K parameter in Fambl while keeping $k = 1$. Both k and K were varied in the pseudo-exponential series $[0, 1, \ldots, 9, 10, 15, \ldots, 45, 50, 60, \ldots, 90, 100]$. The results of the experiments are illustrated in Figure 6.7.

A very large value of K means that Fambl incorporates virtually any same-class nearest neighbor at any furthest distance in creating a family, as long as there are no different-class nearest neighbors in between. It would be preferable to be able to x K at a very high value without generalization performance loss, since this would effectively factor out not only the k parameter, but also the K parameter. This situation is represented in the graph displaying the results of GPLURAL (top left corner of Figure 6.7). While a larger k in IB1 leads to a steady decline in generalization accuracy on test data of the GPLURAL task, Fambl's accuracy remains very much at the same level regardless of the value of K. The results with the other three tasks also show a remarkably steady generalization accuracy (or F-score, with CHUNK) of Fambl, with increasing K, but in all three cases Fambl's score is not higher than IB1's. Especially with the DIMIN and PP tasks, matching on families rather than on examples leads to less accurate classi cations at wide ranges of K.

While it retains a similar performance to MBL, Fambl also attains a certain level of compression. This can be measured in at least two ways. First, in Figure 6.8 the amount of compression (in terms of percentages) is displayed of the number

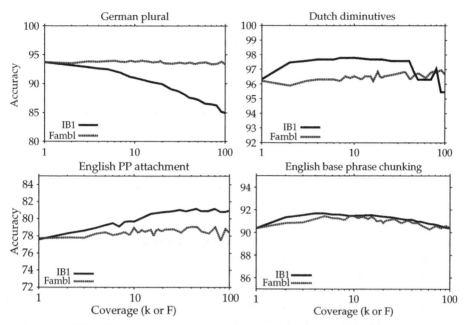

Figure 6.7 Generalization accuracies (in terms of percentage of correctly classi ed test instances) and F-scores, where appropriate, of MBL with increasing k parameter, and Fambl with $k = 1$ and increasing K parameter.

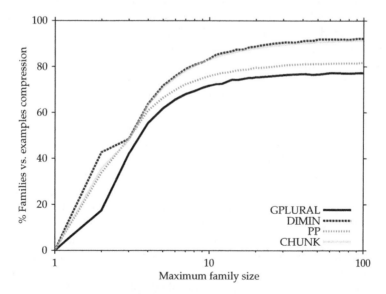

Figure 6.8 Compression rates (percentages) of families as opposed to the original number of examples, produced by Fambl at different maximal family sizes (represented by the x-axis, displayed at a log scale).

Table 6.2   Number of extracted families at a maximum family size of 100, the average number of family members, and
the raw memory compression, for four tasks

Task	Number of families	Av. number of members	Memory compression (%)
GPLURAL	1,749	7.2	62.0
DIMIN	233	12.9	73.4
PP	3,613	5.8	23.4
CHUNK	17,984	11.8	51.9

of families versus the original number of examples, with increasing values of K,
for four of our tasks. As Figure 6.8 shows, the compression rates converge for
all four tasks at similar and very high levels; from 77 percent for GPLURAL to
92 percent for DIMIN. Apparently, setting K at a large enough value ensures that
at that point even the largest families are identi ed; typically there will be 100
different distances or less in any found family.

Some more detailed statistics on family extraction are listed in Table 6.2,
measured for four tasks at the $K = 100$ mark. The actual number of families varies
widely among the tasks, but this correlates with the number of training examples.
The average number of members lies at about the same order of magnitude for
the four tasks – between 6 and 13. The table also shows the raw memory compression when compared with a straightforward storage of the   at example base. In
the straightforward implementation of Fambl, storing a family with one example
uses more memory than storing one example because of the bookkeeping information associated with storing possible disjunctions at each feature. The net gains
of the high compression rates displayed in Figure 6.8 are still positive: from 23
percent to 73 percent compression. This is, however, dependent on the particular
implementation.

Two example families, one for the PP and the other for the CHUNK task, are
displayed in Table 6.3. The   rst example family, labeled with the Verb attachment
class, represents the *attributed . . . to . . .* pattern, but also includes the example *bring
focus to opportunities*, which is apparently the closest neighbor to the other four
examples having the same class. The second family represents cases of the beginning of a noun phrase starting with *most of*. The context left of *most of* deviates
totally between the four examples making up the family, while the right context
represents a noun phrase beginning with *the* or *his*. This family would also perfectly match sentence fragments inside the family hyper-rectangle, such as *because
computers do most of the top*, or *he still makes most of the 50*, and many more recom-
binations. Analogously, the PP family example displayed in Table 6.3 would also
perfectly match *attributed decline to increases, bring focus to demand*, etc.

Overall, the comparison between Fambl and MBL shows that Fambl does not
pro t from the relatively large generalizing capacity of family expressions that

Table 6.3 Two example families (represented by their members) extracted from the PP and CHUNK data sets respectively. The part-of-speech tags in the CHUNK example family are left out for legibility. The bold words in the CHUNK example are the focus words in the windows

Task	Example family	Class
PP	*attributed gains to demand* *attributed improvement to demand* *attributed performance to increases* *attributed decline to demand* *bring focus to opportunities*	Verb attachment
NP	*because computers do* **most** *of the work* *demand rights to* **most** *of the 50* *he still makes* **most** *of his furs* *screens, said* **most** *of the top*	B-NP

in principle would allow some unseen examples to attain a higher score in the similarity function. Apart from the question of whether this relative re-ranking of examples would have any effect on classi cation, it is obvious that many examples covered by family expressions are unlikely to occur — consider, for example, *because computers do most of his furs*.

We conclude that Fambl has two main merits. First, Fambl can compress an example base down to a smaller set of family expressions (or a generalizing hyperrectangle), attaining various compression rates in the same ballpark as attained by editing methods, but with a steady generalization accuracy that is very close to IB1's. Second, Fambl almost factors out the k parameter. Fairly constant performance was observed while keeping $k = 1$ and varying K, the maximal number of family members, across a wide range of values. To sum up, Fambl is a successful local k pre-compiler.

In this section, we discussed the fundamental eager–lazy dimension in machine learning from the point of view of lazy learning approaches such as MBL. We argued that it makes sense to keep all training data available (including 'exceptional' cases) in learning language tasks because they may be good models to extrapolate from. At the same time, while being the cheapest possible learning approach, it is also an inherently expensive strategy during classi cation. There are several ways in which this problem can be alleviated: by using fast approximations of MBL such as IGTREE (Daelemans et al., 1997b; Daelemans & van den Bosch 2005), special optimized algorithms (Liu et al., 2003), or even use of special hardware (Yeh et al., 2007). In this section, we showed that an alternative way to approach this problem is to develop algorithms for weak, bottom-up generalization from the original instance space, making possible an ef ciency increase while keeping generalization accuracy at the same levels as with normal MBL.

7   Further Reading

General introductions to memory-based learning (lazy learning, *k*-nearest neighbor classi cation, instance-based learning) and its relation to other strands of machine learning can be found in (Mitchell 1997). Key historic publications on *k*-nearest neighbor classi cation are Fix and Hodges (1951), Cover and Hart (1967), Dudani (1976), Dasarathy (1991). The eld of machine learning adopted and adapted the *k*-nearest neighbor algorithm under different names, such as memory-based reasoning (Stan ll & Waltz 1986), instance-based learning (Aha et al., 1991), and locally weighted learning (Atkeson et al., 1997). An important development in these latter publications has been the introduction of similarity functions for non-numeric features (Aha et al., 1991; Cost & Salzberg 1993), which enabled the application to be used in symbolic language tasks. Stan ll (1987) and Weijters (1991) both showed that the neural network approach to grapheme–phoneme conversion of Sejnowski and Rosenberg (1987) could be emulated and improved by using a *k*-nearest neighbor classi er. From the beginning of the 1990s onwards, memory-based learning has been applied to virtually all areas of natural language processing. Daelemans and van den Bosch (2005) is a book-length treatise on memory-based language processing.

Sections 3 and 4 already pointed to studies using MBL and alternative memory-based approaches in various areas of computational linguistics and computational psycholinguistics. More references can be found in the regularly updated reference guide to the TiMBL software (Daelemans et al., 2007).

Relations to statistical language processing, in particular the interesting equivalence relations with back-off smoothing in probabilistic classi ers, are discussed in Zavrel and Daelemans (1997). Relations between classi cation-based word prediction and statistical language modeling are identi ed in van den Bosch (2005; 2006b).

In machine translation, *k*-nearest neighbor classi cation bears a close relation with example-based machine translation (EBMT). A rst EBMT-implementation using TiMBL is described in van den Bosch et al. (2007b).

The rst dissertation-length study devoted to the approach is van den Bosch (1997), in which the approach is compared to alternative learning methods for NLP tasks related to English word pronunciation (stress assignment, syllabi -cation, morphological analysis, alignment, grapheme-to-phoneme conversion). TiMBL is also central in the PhD theses of Buchholz (2002), Lendvai (2004), Hendrickx (2005), and Hoste (2005). In 1999 a special issue of the *Journal for Experimental and Theoretical Artificial Intelligence* (Vol. 11.3), was devoted to memory-based language processing. In this special issue, the approach was related also to exemplar-based work in the data-oriented parsing (DOP) framework (Scha et al., 1999) and analogy-based reasoning in NLP research (Pirrelli & Yvon 1999).

ACKNOWLEDGMENT

Parts of this chapter are based on Daelemans and van den Bosch (2005), *Memory-Based Language Processing*. Cambridge: Cambridge University Press. Reprinted with permission.

NOTES

1   The software, reference guide, and instructions on how to install it can be down-loaded from http://ilk.uvt.nl/timbl
2   Available from the Linguistic Data Consortium (www.ldc.upenn.edu/).

7 Decision Trees

HELMUT SCHMID

1 NLP and Classification

Many natural language processing (NLP) tasks require the annotation of linguistic entities with class labels: A part-of-speech tagger, for instance, assigns a part of speech to each word. Word-sense disambiguation chooses the correct reading of a word from a set of possible readings, and anaphora resolution decides whether two nominal expressions are coreferent or not.

Decision trees are one of the techniques for solving classi cation problems of this kind. Figure 7.1 shows a simple decision tree for the disambiguation of periods ('.'), which is a subtask of word segmentation. A period is in English either a full stop marking the end of the sentence (*'He snored.'*), or part of an abbreviation (*'Mrs. Jones'*), or both at the same time (*'This was proposed by Mr. Smith et al.'*). Correspondingly, the decision tree in Figure 7.1 assigns periods to one of the three classes *part of a token*, *punctuation*, or *both*.

A decision tree is applied as follows: We start at the top node and nd the answer to the test question of this node. Depending on the test result, we branch to the *'yes'* or *'no'* subnode and repeat this process until a terminal node is reached, whose label is returned as the result class. In order to disambiguate the period in the question *'You like London, Mr. Klipstein?'* with the decision tree shown in Figure 7.1, we rst check whether the period is followed by whitespace, which is the case. We follow the *'yes'* link, examine the preceding word, and nd that it is a known abbreviation. Finally, we check whether the following word is a capital-ized word which would normally be written in lowercase (such as *'The'*). This is not the case. We conclude that the period is part of a token, and not a punctuation mark.

Decision trees are easy to create (with one of the many available tools), to understand, and to apply, and they are quite accurate, but they are, of course, not the only classi cation method applied in NLP. Other important methods are maximum entropy models (see Chapter 5 of this book) memory-based learn-ing (see Chapter 6 of this book), neural networks (see Chapter 9 of this book),

The Handbook of Computational Linguistics and Natural Language Processing, First Edition.
Edited by Alexander Clark, Chris Fox and Shalom Lappin.
© 2013 Blackwell Publishing Ltd except for editorial material and organization
© 2013 Alexander Clark, Chris Fox, and Shalom Lappin. Published 2013 by Blackwell Publishing Ltd.

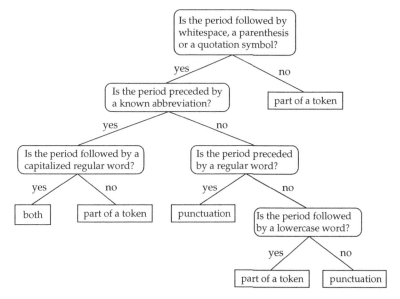

Figure 7.1   A simple decision tree for period disambiguation.

support vector machines (Joachims 2001), and transformation-based learning (Brill 1992).

The remainder of this chapter is organized as follows. Section 2 describes how decision trees are induced from training data. Section 3 presents NLP applications of decision trees. Section 4 discusses the advantages and disadvantages of decision trees, and lists available software packages. Section 5 concludes this chapter with suggestions for further reading.

2   Induction of Decision Trees

Decision trees are learned from training data. Each data item consists of a set of features describing an object and the class of the object. Table 7.1 shows a toy example with seven data items.

Decision trees are recursively built beginning with the topmost node by (1) computing the best test for the current node according to some *splitting criterion*, (2) creating a subnode for each possible outcome of the test, and (3) recursively expanding each subnode in the same way until a given *stopping criterion* is satis-

ed. Usually, the decision tree is afterwards simpli ed (*pruned*) in order to avoid over tting of the training data (see Section 2.4 below.)

The test of the topmost node divides the training data into two subsets. One subset contains the elements which pass the test, the other contains the elements which fail the test. During the induction of the tree, the two subsets are passed on to the *'yes'* and *'no'* subnodes respectively. The feature tests of the subnodes

Table 7.1 Training data consisting of seven objects which are characterized by the features 'size,' 'color,' and 'shape.' The rst four items belong to class '+,' the others to class '−.'

Size	Color	Shape	Class
medium	blue	circle	+
small	red	square	+
large	green	trapezoid	+
large	green	square	+
small	red	triangle	−
large	red	triangle	−
large	red	trapezoid	−

further subdivide the data subsets, and so on. The majority class of the data which reaches a terminal node becomes the result class of that node.

2.1   *The splitting criterion*

The best test for a node is selected according to the *splitting criterion*. A frequently used splitting criterion is the *information gain*. It is the difference between the *entropy* of the data set at the current node and the entropy in the two subsets induced by the test. The entropy of a data set measures to which degree the data is scattered over several classes. If a data set is *pure*, i.e., if all elements belong to the same class, the entropy is 0. If half of the data belongs to class A and half of the data to class B, the entropy is 1. The entropy is de ned by the formula

(1) $H(p) = -\sum_c p(c) \log_2 p(c)$

where $p(c)$ is the relative frequency (= empirical probability) of class c in the data set, i.e., the frequency of class c divided by the size of the data set.

The information gain is de ned as follows:

(2) $G = H(p) - w_1 H(p_1) - w_2 H(p_2)$

where $p(c)$ is the relative frequency of class c in the current data set, $p_1(c)$ and $p_2(c)$ are the relative frequencies of class c in the two subsets, and w_1 and w_2 are the proportions of data in the rst and second subset.

Consider the data in Table 7.1. The relative frequency of class '+' is 4/7 in this sample, and the relative frequency of class '−' is 3/7. The entropy at the top node is therefore:

(3) $-\left(\frac{4}{7} \log_2 \frac{4}{7} + \frac{3}{7} \log_2 \frac{3}{7}\right) \approx 0.985$

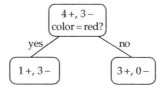

Figure 7.2   State of the decision tree after the expansion of the root node. Each box shows the number of objects of each class in the corresponding data subset and the feature test (if available).

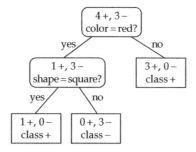

Figure 7.3   Decision tree learned from the example data. The number of objects of each class in the respective subset of the training data is given for each node.

Now we compute the information gain of the feature test *'color=red?'* The data subset with the test result *'yes'* contains the four red training objects, three of class '+' and one of class '−.' The entropy in this subset is:

$$(4) \quad -\left(\frac{1}{4}\log_2\frac{1}{4} + \frac{3}{4}\log_2\frac{3}{4}\right) \approx 0.811$$

The entropy in the other subset with non-red objects is 0 because all the green and blue objects belong to the class '+.' The information gain of the test *'color=red?'* is therefore:

$$(5) \quad 0.985 - 4/7 \times 0.811 - 3/7 \times 0 = 0.521$$

The information gain of any other test is lower. Thus the most informative test for the top node is *'color=red?'* Figure 7.2 shows the state of the decision tree after the top node was expanded.

The three non-red objects in the data subset of the right subnode all belong to the class '+.' Hence we can stop here and create a terminal node with the class '+.' The data subset of the left subnode with four red elements still contains objects of both classes. We compute the best test for this subset which is the test *'shape=square?'* It divides the data into two pure subsets. After creating a terminal node for each outcome of the test, the induction of the decision tree is nished. Figure 7.3 shows the result.

	red	green	blue
square	+	+	
circle			+
triangle	–		
trapezoid	–	+	

	red	green	blue
square	+	+	
circle			+
triangle	–		
trapezoid	–	+	

	red	green	blue
square	+	+	
circle			+
triangle	–		
trapezoid	–	+	

Figure 7.4   Partitions of the two-dimensional feature subspace spanned by the features *'color'* and *'shape.'* The leftmost partition is induced by the decision tree of Figure 7.3.

This decision tree divides the feature space into three regions. Each region corresponds to one leaf node of the decision tree and contains training objects of only one class. The rst table of Figure 7.4 shows this partition for the two-dimensional space spanned by the features *'color'* and *'shape.'* Objects in regions which are enclosed by bold lines are assigned to the class '+,' the others to the class '–.' The second table shows another partition which results in the same classi cation. It corresponds to a decision tree which examines the *'shape'* feature prior to the *'color'* feature. The partition of the last table de nes a different classi cation because objects with the feature combination *'red'* and *'circle'* are assigned to the class '+' rather than '–.' This partition is induced by a decision tree with four test nodes. This example shows that the classi cation problem is in general underdetermined and that several solutions exist.

The larger the number of terminal nodes of a decision tree, the smaller the average number of data items reaching a terminal node. And the smaller the number of data items at a node, the less reliable the classi cation at that node because the in uence of incidental properties of the training data increases. A decision tree learning algorithm should therefore choose the simplest (i.e., smallest) decision tree which accurately describes the training data.

The number of possible decision trees for a given data set is usually too large to compare all of them against each other in order to nd the simplest tree. This is the reason why most decision tree learning algorithms apply the *'greedy'*[1] search strategy based on the information gain (or a similar criterion) which was described in this section. It quickly nds a decision tree whose size is close – but not necessarily equal – to the optimum.

Another popular splitting criterion uses the *Gini index* which measures the impurity of a data set. It is the sum of products of all pairs of class probabilities.

$$(6) \quad Gini(p) = \sum_{c \neq c'} p(c)p(c') = \sum_{c} p(c)(1 - p(c)) = 1 - \sum_{c} p(c)^2$$

The Gini index reaches its maximum when all class frequencies are equal. It is zero if all data elements belong to the same class. The splitting criterion based on the Gini index selects the test for which the sum of the weighted Gini indices of the data subsets is minimal. For binary splits, the following expression is to be minimized:

(7) $w_1 Gini(p_1) + w_2 Gini(p_2)$

where w_1 and w_2 are the proportions of data in the two subsets.

2.2   *Stopping criterion*

The recursive expansion of the decision tree is stopped if either the data subset is pure or if all data items have the same feature representation. The latter case occurs when the data contains objects with identical feature values, but different classes. When such contradictory class assignments exist, there is no decision tree which correctly classi es all the training data.

Sometimes these stopping criteria are augmented by other criteria which may terminate the induction process earlier, such as:

(1)   the size of the data set being below a certain threshold;
(2)   the value of the splitting criterion for the best test being below a threshold.

2.3   *Feature tests*

Until now, we only considered feature tests which check whether some feature has a certain value or not, such as *'color=red?'* If the feature values are numeric – and in particular if they are real-valued – such equality tests often produce highly unbalanced data partitions with a very large subset and a very small subset. Tests which compare the feature value with some threshold (such as *'height > 1.75m?'*) create more balanced splits and are better suited for numeric features.

Many decision tree learning algorithms also allow *multi-valued* tests such as *'color=?'* with the possible outcomes *'red,'* *'green,'* and *'blue.'* The information gain criterion is not a good measure for the comparison of multi-valued tests because it strongly prefers tests with a large number of different outcomes, and creates decision trees which are overly complex and fragment the training data unnecessarily.

Why are tests with many outcomes preferred? The information gain of a binary-valued test is limited to 1. This is the information gain obtained when a data set with 50 percent positive and 50 percent negative examples is split into two pure subsets. A test with four possible outcomes is able to separate objects from four different classes. The maximal information gain is here $-4\left(\frac{1}{4} \log_2 \frac{1}{4}\right) = 2$. To give an extreme example, assume that some test assigns each data item to a separate subset. The information gain criterion will always select this test because it reduces the entropy to 0. The resulting classi er, however, will perform poorly because it fails to generalize to new data with unseen values of the test feature.

The information gain of a multi-valued test whose outcome t has the probability $p(t)$ could approach but never exceed the entropy of the test split

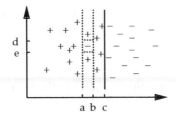

Figure 7.5 Data with overlapping classes and the class boundaries found by a decision tree.

$-\sum_t p(t) \log_2 p(t)$. By dividing the information gain with this test entropy, we get the *gain ratio* criterion proposed by Quinlan (1986) which penalizes multi-valued tests with many possible outcomes. Other splitting criteria for multi-valued tests were introduced, e.g., in Breiman et al. (1984) and in Mántaras (1991). A good splitting criterion tends to create smaller decision trees, but the effect on the classi cation accuracy is usually small. Therefore the choice of the splitting criterion is not so important if only the accuracy counts.

2.4   Pruning

Decision trees which are grown to their maximal size as described above tend to *overfit* the training data. Over tting occurs when the classi cation of the decision tree depends on accidental properties of the training data. Over tting is a problem because it leads to errors on new data. In order to avoid over tting, most decision tree learning algorithms add another step which simpli es the decision tree with *pruning*. Pruning identi es irrelevant feature tests and replaces the corresponding non-terminal nodes with terminal nodes.

Consider Figure 7.5 which shows a data sample with two classes and two real-valued features. A decision tree which is trained on this data rst splits the two-dimensional feature space along the solid line. Then it adds four more boundaries (dotted lines) in order to isolate the negative training item from the surrounding positive items. The resulting decision tree is shown in the left side of Figure 7.6. If the negative item within the cloud of positive items is just a random outlier, the classi cation performance of the full decision tree on new data will be worse than the performance of the simpler tree shown on the right side in Figure 7.6. Thus the left tree should be pruned back to the tree on the right side.

Many different pruning methods have been proposed. *Critical-value pruning* (CVP) (Mingers 1987) prunes at a node if the score of the splitting criterion (information gain, gain ratio, or other) is below a given threshold. The pruning proceeds bottom-up, and it only considers nodes whose subnodes are terminal nodes or pruned nodes. Let us take the decision tree in Figure 7.7 as an example. With a threshold of 4, CVP replaces the whole subtree headed by node N2 with a terminal node. With a threshold of 3, only N4 is pruned because N2 dominates the unpruned node N5 whose score exceeds the threshold.

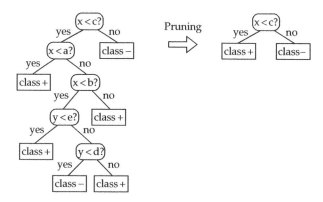

Figure 7.6   Decision tree induced from the data in Figure 7.5 before and after pruning.

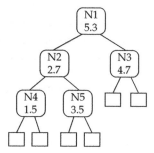

Figure 7.7   Decision tree with node numbers and information gain scores.

The size of the pruned tree depends on the threshold. Higher thresholds lead to smaller trees. In order to determine the optimal threshold, the decision tree is pruned with different thresholds. The pruned trees are evaluated on test data by computing the classi cation *accuracy*, which is the proportion of correctly clas- si ed test items. The tree with the highest accuracy is selected. It is important that the data used for this evaluation is fresh data which was not used to induce the tree. Otherwise, the tree will not be pruned because the full tree achieves the highest accuracy on the training data. If only a xed amount of training data is available for tree induction and pruning, part of the data has to be set aside for pruning before the tree is induced.

The *reduced error pruning* (REP) method invented by Quinlan (1987) also requires separate data for pruning, which is here directly used to decide which nodes to prune. A node is pruned if the number of errors on the pruning data is not increased by the pruning, i.e., if the total classi catioln error of the subnodes is at least as high as the classi cation error of the node after pruning. Again, nodes are only pruned if all non-terminal subnodes have been pruned before.

Figure 7.8 shows a decision tree in which each node is annotated with the respective number of classi cation errors on the pruning data. Node N4 is pruned

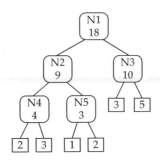

Figure 7.8   Decision tree with classi cation error counts.

because the number of errors at the subnodes (2+3 errors) is higher than the number of errors at N4 (4 errors). Similarly, N5 is pruned since the number of errors is unchanged (1+2 vs. 3). Pruning at N2 or N3 would increase the number of errors. N1 is not considered for pruning because of its unpruned non-terminal subnodes.

   Breiman et al. (1984) developed another important pruning strategy called *cost-complexity pruning* (CCP) which attempts to nd a balance between the complexity of the decision tree and the number of classi cation errors on the training data. CCP computes the pruned tree T which minimizes the expression

(8) $R_\alpha(T) = R(T) + \alpha|T|$

where $R(T)$ is the number of training items which are incorrectly classi ed by T, $|T|$ is the number of terminal nodes in T, and α is a balancing factor.

   For a given factor α, there is a unique pruned subtree that minimizes the cost-complexity measure $R_\alpha(T)$. Furthermore, for $\alpha_1 > \alpha_2$, the optimally pruned subtree corresponding to α_1 is a subtree of the one corresponding to α_2. By steadily increasing the complexity parameter, a nite sequence of pruned subtrees is generated. The best pruned tree from this sequence is selected by evaluating the accuracy of the different trees on separate test data and choosing the one with the smallest classi cation error.

2.5   *Bagging, boosting, and random forests*

Decision tree induction is often *unstable* in the sense that a small change in the training data leads to a rather large change in the resulting decision tree, and its performance. Such classi ers are also said to have a *high variance*. Instability is undesirable because the classi cation accuracy depends on accidental properties of the data, and is therefore often suboptimal. Pruning increases the stability of decision-tree induction and partially solves the problem. Further improvements are possible with the three methods presented next.

2.5.1   Bagging   Breiman (1996) proposed a method (called *bagging*) which combines a set of decision trees in order to obtain a more reliable classi er. The individual trees are induced from *bootstrap samples* of the original training set. A bootstrap sample has the same size as the original data set, and is created by drawing a random sample with replacement from the original set. The classi cations of the different trees are combined by choosing the most frequently predicted class.

Assume that the training data is the set {a,b,c,c,d}. Possible bootstrap samples obtained from this set are {a,a,b,c,d} and {a,c,c,c,d}, for instance.

Bagged decision trees are less likely to re ect accidental properties of the training data. Bagging therefore often increases the accuracy of decision trees if the induction of a single tree is unstable. On the other hand, bagging can also slightly degrade the performance if the tree induction is stable.

2.5.2 Boosting   Freund and Schapire (1995) also create multiple classi ers with bootstrap sampling, and combine their votes, but they use different sampling and voting methods. The bootstrap sampling method of bagging selects each data element with the same probability, whereas boosting chooses data elements which are hard to classify with a higher probability, thereby focusing the learning algorithm on the dif cult cases. The *weight* of a data element is proportional to the probability that the sampling algorithm chooses this element.

The induction of boosted decision trees starts with an initial decision tree which is induced from the original data set (without resampling). The data weights are initialized to $1/N$ (where N is the size of the training data). The training data is then reclassi ed with the decision tree, and the weight of misclassi ed elements is increased. Now a random bootstrap sample is drawn, a new decision tree is induced from this sample, and the votes of the two decision trees are combined. The algorithm continues until a prede ned number of trees (e.g., 50) has been generated. In each step i, a decision tree t_i is induced, the data is reclassi ed, an update factor β_i is computed, the weights are adjusted, and a new bootstrap sample is drawn. The update factor is given by $\beta_i = (1 - \epsilon)/\epsilon$, where ϵ is the sum of the weights of the misclassi ed data. The weights of the misclassi ed elements are multiplied by this factor. All weights are renormalized (i.e., divided by the sum of weights) in order to obtain a probability distribution for sampling.

Assume that the training data contains 10 elements and that the initial decision tree induced from this data correctly classi es eight elements, and gets two elements wrong. The total weight of the misclassi ed elements is 0.2 (because the initial weight of each element is 0.1). β_1 is therefore $0.8/0.2 = 4.0$. After the renormalization, the weight of the correctly classi ed elements is $1/16 = 0.0625$ and the weight of the misclassi ed elements is $4/16 = 0.25$.

The boosting algorithm combines the different decision trees by weighting the vote of each tree t_i with the factor $\log \beta_i$ and returning the majority vote.

2.5.3 Random forests   The *random forest* method (Breiman 2001a) is very similar to bagging. The only difference is that the feature set from which the best test (according to the splitting criterion) is chosen is restricted to a small random subset of the available features. Surprisingly, this modi cation often improves the

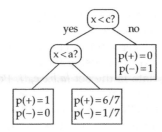

Figure 7.9   Probabilistic decision tree induced from the data in Figure 7.5.

classi cation performance considerably. A possible explanation is that the boot-strap samples of the bagging method are often very similar and the decision trees are therefore highly correlated. The restriction on the feature selection enforces more diversity in the decision trees. Random forests have a similar performance as boosted decision trees, but the training is more ef cient because only a subset of the features is considered at each node. Furthermore, the induction of the different trees can be performed in parallel. This is not possible with boosting where each new tree depends on the previous trees.

No decision tree variant consistently outperforms the others. Which method is best depends on the problem and the training data. The same holds for classi cation methods in general.

2.6 *Decision trees for probability estimation*

The result class which is assigned to a terminal node of a decision tree is the most probable class in the data subset of this node, but not necessarily the only possible class. The higher the fraction of items from other classes in the data set, the higher the probability of a classi cation error at that node. In order to provide some infor-mation about the reliability of the decisions, it is useful to store the probability of the different classes together with the result class. The (empirical) probability is estimated by dividing the frequency of the class by the size of the data subset. Figure 7.9 shows an example.

Decision trees which are extended in this way can also be used to estimate the conditional probabilities of the different classes given the feature representation of an object. Figure 7.9 shows a decision tree which returns, for an arbitrary object from the feature space displayed in Figure 7.5, the estimated probability that it belongs to class '+' or '−.'

Provost and Domingos (2003) observed that frequently used tree induction algo-rithms such as CART (Breiman et al., 1984) or C4.5 (Quinlan 1993) often perform poorly when they are used to estimate probabilities. They attributed this to the following factors:

(1) Pruning eliminates nodes which are relevant for probability estimation, but have no effect on the classi cation accuracy. (The second split in Figure 7.5 is

a good example. It is probably irrelevant for the classi cation performance, but might provide better probability estimates because it distinguishes the borderline region between a and c from the rest.)

(2) The data subsets at the leaf nodes are often too small to obtain reliable probability estimates, in particular for infrequent classes.

(3) Because decision trees divide the feature space into disjoint regions, the probability estimates are constant within a region and jump at the boundaries. A smoother distribution is often desirable.

Provost and Domingos modi ed the widely used C4.5 tree induction algorithm in order to obtain better probability estimates. They turned off pruning, and they smoothed the probability estimates with the 'Laplace correction' (see, e.g., Manning & Schütze 1999). The Laplace correction is a very simple smoothing technique which adds 1 to each frequency count and computes the probability estimates from the modi ed counts.

Liang et al. (2006a) evaluated Provost and Domingos' method and observed that the probability estimates were better than those of the competing methods. They also noted that bagging did not increase the accuracy of the probability estimates. Bagging was superior, however, when only the ranking[2] was evaluated. It seems that bagging increases the accuracy of the probability estimates relative to each other, but decreases the match with the actual probabilities by attening the probability distributions.

The Laplace correction used by Provost and Domingos is too simple a smoothing method. Ferri et al. (2003) proposed a better method where the probability distribution of each node is recursively smoothed with the distribution of the parent node, similar to the back-off smoothing strategies applied in language modeling (see Chapter 3 of this book).

3 NLP Applications

Decision trees have been applied to a wide range of NLP problems including grapheme-to-phoneme conversion (Black et al., 1998a; Suontausta & Hakkinenen 2000; Kienappel & Kneser 2001), part-of-speech tagging (Black et al., 1992; Schmid 1994; Màrquez & Padró 1997; Schmid & Laws 2008), tokenization (Palmer & Hearst 1997), parsing (Magerman 1994; Haruno et al., 1998), language modeling (Bahl et al., 1989; Xu & Jelinek 2006), classi cation of unknown proper names (Béchet et al., 2000), phrase-break prediction (Kim & Lee 2000; Sun & Applebaum 2001), coreference resolution (McCarthy & Lehnert 1995), and spam detection (Rios & Zha 2004).

Many of these methods directly apply decision trees as classi ers. Others (Bahl et al., 1989; Black et al., 1992; Schmid 1994; Haruno et al., 1998; Màrquez 1999; Béchet et al., 2000; Sun & Applebaum 2001; Xu & Jelinek 2006; Schmid & Laws

2008) use the decision trees to estimate the conditional probabilities of a statistical model. The next two sections describe a typical representative of each class.

3.1 Grapheme-to-phone conversion with decision trees

General-purpose speech synthesizers need a component which predicts the pronunciation of unknown words from their orthographic form. Such a grapheme-to-phone converter may be implemented with manually written rules. A better approach, however, is to learn the conversion rules from data.

Such a data-driven system is described in Black et al. (1998a). It uses decision trees to map each letter of an unknown word to zero, one, or two phones. The phone sequences are concatenated to obtain the pronunciation of the word. The decision trees are trained on data from a pronunciation dictionary. The dictionary data is initially pre-processed by semi-automatically aligning the letters and phones of each word as exempli ed here:

```
d  e  p  a  r  t m  e  n  t
D ih p  aa r  t  m ah n  t
```

Black et al. create a separate decision tree for each letter which predicts its pronunciation based on the surrounding letters. The training data for the decision tree of a given letter is extracted from the aligned dictionary data by nding all occurrences of that letter and taking the three preceding and three following letters as features and the phone sequence aligned with the target letter as the class. For the conversion of the letter 'a' of the word *'department,'* for instance, the letters 'd,''e,''p,' and 'r,''t,''m' are used as context. The non-terminal nodes of the decision trees are decorated with questions such as 'l_{-2}='e'?' (or more verbosely: '*Is the letter two positions to the left of the target letter the letter 'b'?'*). The terminal nodes of the decision trees are labeled with the resulting phone sequence (such as *'aa'*).

This grapheme-to-phone converter was successfully applied in the Festival speech synthesizer (Black et al., 1998b).

3.2 Using decision trees to estimate the contextual probabilities of a POS tagger

The application presented next is a part-of-speech (POS) tagger which uses decision trees to obtain more reliable estimates of conditional probabilities, instead of directly classifying the data as in the previous example. Before explaining how the decision trees are used here, I will brie y summarize what POS tagging is, how POS tagging with hidden Markov models works, and why the probability parameters need to be smoothed. Then I will explain how decision trees help to obtain better probability estimates.

3.2.1 Part-of-speech tagging   A part-of-speech (POS) tagger assigns a POS label to each word of an input text. The tagger rst obtains the set of possible POS tags

for each word from a lexicon and then disambiguates between them based on the word context. Here is an example sentence from the Penn Treebank corpus (Marcus et al., 1993) with the possible POS tags[3] of each word. The correct tags are underlined.

Put	NN <u>VB</u> VBD VBN
down	IN JJ NN <u>RB</u> RP
that	<u>DT</u> IN RB WDT
phone	<u>NN</u> VB VBP

3.2.2 Hidden Markov models   A hidden Markov model tagger (Manning & Schütze 1999) computes the POS tag sequence $t_1, t_2, \ldots, t_n$ whose joint probability with the input word sequence $w_1, w_2, \ldots, w_n$ is maximal. In a hidden Markov model (HMM), the joint probability is decomposed into a product of the *contextual probabilities* $p(t_i|t_{i-2}t_{i-1})$ – such as $p(\text{NN}|\text{IN,DT})$ – and the *lexical probabilities* $p(w_i|t_i)$ – such as $p(\text{phone}|\text{NN})$ – of all input words w_i:

$$(9)\quad p(w_1, t_1, w_2, t_2, \ldots, w_n, t_n) = \prod_{i=1}^{n} \underbrace{p(t_i|t_{i-2}t_{i-1})}_{\text{contextual prob.}} \underbrace{p(w_i|t_i)}_{\text{lexical prob.}}$$

3.2.3 Parameter estimation   The lexical and contextual probabilities of the HMM are estimated from training data. The larger the number of different POS tags is, and the more preceding POS tags a POS tag depends on, the more dif cult it is to estimate the contextual probabilities because many possible combinations of POS tags do not appear in the training data (sparse data problem).

The German Tiger treebank (Brants et al., 2002) contains about 700 different POS tags encoding information about number, gender, case, and other morpho-syntactic features. A simple trigram POS tagger needs to estimate 343 million parameters from about 900,000 tokens contained in the Tiger treebank.

The POS tagger described in Schmid & Laws (2008) approaches this sparse data problem as follows:

(1)   The POS tags t_i (e.g., 'ART.Def.Nom.Sg.Neut') are split into feature vectors $t_{i,1}, \ldots, t_{i,K}$, and the contextual probability $p(t_i|t_{i-k}, \ldots, t_{i-1})$ is replaced by the product

$$(10)\quad \prod_{l=1}^{K} p(\underline{t_{i,l}}|t_{i-k}, \ldots, t_{i-1}, t_{i,1}, \ldots, t_{i,l-1})$$

(2)   The conditioning contexts are simpli ed by choosing the most informative context features for the prediction of the new feature.

The probability $p(\text{ADJA.Pos.Nom.Sg.Neut}|\text{ART.Def.Nom.Sg.Neut}, \text{PART.Zu})$, for instance, is replaced by the product

p(ADJA | ART.Def.Nom.Sg.Neut, PART.Zu)
× p(Pos | ART.Def.Nom.Sg.Neut, PART.Zu, ADJA)
× p(Nom | ART.Def.Nom.Sg.Neut, PART.Zu, ADJA.Pos)
× p(Sg | ART.Def.Nom.Sg.Neut, PART.Zu, ADJA.Pos.Nom)
× p(Neut | ART.Def.Nom.Sg.Neut, PART.Zu, ADJA.Pos.Nom.Sg)

and then simpli ed to

p(ADJA | ART, PART.Zu)
× p(Pos | ART, PART, ADJA)
× p(Nom | ART.Nom, PART, ADJA)
× p(Sg | ART.Sg, PART, ADJA)
× p(Neut | ART.Neut, PART, ADJA)

These parameters can be reliably estimated from the treebank, and they capture all the information needed for disambiguation.

3.2.4 Estimation of contextual probabilities with decision trees   How are the relevant context attributes determined? The tagger has to nd those combinations of context attributes which provide most information about the predicted attribute. This is exactly what a decision tree learning algorithm does.

The tagger described in Schmid & Laws (2008) therefore uses decision trees to estimate the conditional probabilities of the predicted attributes given the context attributes. One option would be to create one decision tree for each feature (e.g., *'Gender'*) which provides probability estimates for the probabilities of all feature values (*'Masc,' 'Fem,' 'Neut'*).

Schmid & Laws instead create a separate decision tree for each feature value (such as *'Masc'*). Figure 7.10 shows an example tree. The advantage of this approach is that each decision tree is more focused, and that the training data is not fragmented by splits needed to discriminate between the other possible feature values. A drawback is that the probabilities of *'Masc,' 'Fem,'* and *'Neut'* usually do

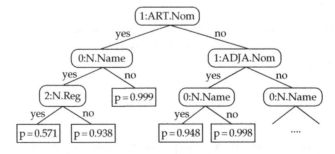

Figure 7.10   Part of a probabilistic decision tree for the nominative case of nouns. The test *'1:ART.Nom'* checks if the preceding word (position 1) is a nominative article. All features are word-class dependent: the case features of nouns and adjectives for example are considered as different features.

not exactly sum to 1 because the three decision trees use different tests and therefore produce different splits of the training data from which the probabilities are estimated. In order to obtain a well-de ned probability distribution, the probability of *'Masc,'* for instance, is renormalized by a division with the total probability of *'Masc,' 'Fem,'* and *'Neut.'*

The tagger uses binary tests as shown in Figure 7.10 and applies pre-pruning with the critical-value pruning strategy, i.e., the recursive expansion of the decision tree stops if the information gain of the best test is below a given threshold. The probabilities at the terminal nodes of the decision trees are recursively smoothed with the parent node probabilities.

The new parameter estimation technique for the contextual probabilities was integrated into an HMM POS tagger. In an evaluation (Schmid & Laws 2008) on two treebanks with very ne-grained tagsets – the German Tiger treebank and the Czech Academic corpus (Hladká et al., 2007) – this tagger outperformed state-of-the-art taggers.

4 Advantages and Disadvantages of Decision Trees

Decision trees are a fast classi cation method in terms of both training time and processing time. They are easy to interpret and require no parameter tweaking to obtain good results. Furthermore, they work with large data sets, large numbers of features, and mixtures of nominal and numeric features.

For many classi cation problems, the performance of simple decision trees is not state-of-the-art, but boosted trees and random forests are reported to be competitive with advanced methods such as support vector machines (Rios & Zha 2004; Bruce et al., 2007; Coussement & Var den Poel 2008), although there are also contradictory results (Statnikov & Aliferis 2007).

An advantage of decision trees is also the availability of mature software packages. The most widely used tools are probably C4.5 (Quinlan 1993), and CART (Breiman et al., 1984). Wagon is a reimplementation of CART which is part of the free Edinburgh Speech Tools Library (available at www.cstr.ed.ac.uk/projects/speech_tools). DTREG (www.dtreg.com) is a commercial software for boosted trees. A Fortran implementation of random forests is available from Leo Breiman's homepage at the University of Berkeley (www.stat.berkeley.edu/users/breiman). There are also open source implementations of decision trees in the IND package available from the NASA, in the WEKA collection of machine learning algorithms (http://sourceforge .net/projects/weka), and in the CRAN archive of the R project (http://cran.r-project.org).

5 Further Reading

The books written by Quinlan (1993) and Breiman et al. (1984) are good starting points to learn more about decision trees. Breiman et al. (1984) also discuss the application of decision trees to regression problems which is not covered in this chapter. The book by Manning and Schütze (1999) includes a section on decision trees from the perspective of statistical NLP. The website[4] of the AAAI organization includes a collection of pointers to online literature on decision trees. Further literature on more speci c topics can be found via the references in the respective sections.

NOTES

1   A greedy search strategy makes locally optimal decisions which may be suboptimal in a broader global context.
2   A and B are ranked correctly if the one with the higher probability according to the decision tree is in fact more likely.
3   The meaning of the tags is as follows: NN=regular noun, DT=determiner, IN=preposition, JJ=adjective, RB=adverb, RP=particle, VB=base verb, VBP= nite verb, VBN=past participle, WDT=relative pronoun.
4   www.aaai.org/aitopics/pmwiki/pmwiki.php/AITopics/DecisionTrees

8 Unsupervised Learning and Grammar Induction

ALEXANDER CLARK
AND SHALOM LAPPIN

In this chapter we consider unsupervised learning from two perspectives. First, we brie y look at its advantages and disadvantages as an engineering technique applied to large corpora in natural language processing. While supervised learning generally achieves greater accuracy with less data, unsupervised learning offers signi cant savings in the intensive labor required for annotating text. Second, we discuss the possible relevance of unsupervised learning to debates on the cognitive basis of human language acquisition. In this context we explore the implications of recent work on grammar induction for poverty of stimulus arguments that purport to motivate a strong bias model of language learning, commonly formulated as a theory of universal grammar (UG). We examine the second issue both as a problem in computational learning theory, and with reference to empirical work on unsupervised machine learning (ML) of syntactic structure. We compare two models of learning theory and the place of unsupervised learning within each of them. Looking at recent work on part-of-speech tagging and the recognition of syntactic structure, we see how far unsupervised ML methods have come in acquiring different kinds of grammatical knowledge from raw text.

1 Overview

1.1 Machine learning in natural language processing and computational linguistics

The machine learning methods presented in this handbook have been applied to a wide variety of problems in natural language processing. These range from speech recognition (Chapter 12) through morphological analysis (Chapter 14) and syntactic parsing (Chapter 4), to the complex text and discourse understanding applications dealt with in Part IV. ML has produced increasingly successful systems for handling a large domain of natural language engineering tasks. When evaluating different types of ML there are a variety of technological issues that

The Handbook of Computational Linguistics and Natural Language Processing, First Edition.
Edited by Alexander Clark, Chris Fox and Shalom Lappin.
© 2013 Blackwell Publishing Ltd except for editorial material and organization
© 2013 Alexander Clark, Chris Fox, and Shalom Lappin. Published 2013 by Blackwell Publishing Ltd.

arise, some of which we will consider in the context of the distinction between supervised and unsupervised learning procedures.

From an engineering perspective, the main issue to be addressed when comparing the relative merits of supervised vs. unsupervised learning, for a particular task, is the degree of accuracy that each method achieves in proportion to the cost of resources that it requires. As we will see, characterizing an optimal balance between accuracy and cost is not always straightforward. It is necessary to consider a variety of factors in calculating both of the values that determine this balance.

It is also interesting to consider if ML has implications for some of the scienti c questions that animate linguistics and cognitive science. Speci cally, it is worth asking if the success of ML methods in solving language engineering problems illuminates the sorts of learning processes that humans could, in principle, employ in acquiring knowledge of their language. Clearly the fact that an ML procedure is able to ef ciently acquire important elements of human grammatical knowledge from corpora does not, in itself, show that human learning operates according to this procedure. However, to the extent that grammar induction through domain-general learning methods succeeds on the basis of evidence of the kind available to children, we achieve insight into the computational credibility of such methods as models of language acquisition.

1.2   *Grammar induction as a machine learning problem*

A machine learning system implements a learning algorithm whose output is a function from a domain of input samples to a range of output values. We divide a corpus of examples into a training and a test set. The learning algorithm is spec-i ed in conjunction with a model of the phenomenon to be learned. This model de nes the space of possible hypotheses that the algorithm can generate from the input data. When the values of the model's parameters are determined through training of the algorithm on the test set, an element of the hypothesis space is selected. In the case of grammar induction the algorithm learns from the training data to construct a parser that assigns descriptions of syntactic structure to input strings from the test data. It provides a learning procedure for acquiring a grammar that parses new strings in the corpus.

If we have a gold standard of correct parses in a corpus, then it is possible to compute the percentage of correct parses that the algorithm produces when tested on an unseen subpart of this corpus. A more common procedure for scoring an ML algorithm on a test set is to evaluate its performance for *recall* and *precision*.[1]

The recall of a parsing algorithm $\mathcal{A}$ is the percentage of brackets of the test set that it correctly identi es, where these brackets specify the constituent tree structure of each sentence in the set. $\mathcal{A}$'s *precision* is the percentage of the brackets that it returns which correspond to those in the gold standard. A uni ed score for $\mathcal{A}$, known as an *F-score*, can be computed as an average of its recall and its precision.

The choice of parameters and their possible values de nes a bias for the language model by imposing prior constraints on the set of learnable hypotheses. All learning requires some sort of bias to restrict the set of possible hypotheses for the phenomenon to be learned. This bias can express strong assumptions about the nature of the domain of learning. Alternatively, it can de ne comparatively weak domain-speci c constraints, with learning driven primarily by domain-general procedures and conditions.

One way of formalizing a learning bias is as a *prior* probability distribution on the elements of the hypothesis space that favors some hypotheses as more likely than others. The paradigm of Bayesian learning in cognitive science implements this approach.[2] The simplicity and compactness measure that Perfors et al. (2006) use is an example of a very general prior. We can describe this measure as follows.

Let D be data, and H a hypothesis. *Maximum likelihood* chooses the H which makes the D most likely (the maximum probability value of D given H):

(1) $\arg\max_H (P(D|H))$

Posterior probability is proportional to the prior probability times the likelihood.

(2) $P(H|D) \propto P(H)P(D|H)$

The maximum a posteriori approach chooses the H which maximizes the posterior probability:

(3) $\arg\max_H (P(H)P(D|H))$

The bias of the model is explicitly represented in the prior $P(H)$. Perfors et al. (2006) de ne this prior to give higher values to grammars whose rule sets are of smaller cardinality, and whose rules are formulated with fewer non-terminal symbols.

1.3 Supervised learning

When the samples of the training set are annotated with the classi cations and structures that the learning algorithm is intended to produce as output for the test set, then learning is described as *supervised*. Grammar induction that is supervised involves training an ML system on a corpus annotated with the parse structures that correspond to a gold standard of correct parse descriptions. The learning algorithm infers a function for assigning appropriate parse output to input sentences on the basis of a training set of sentence argument-parse value pairs.

As an example of supervised grammar induction, consider the learning of a *probabilistic context-free grammar* (PCFG).[3] Such a grammar conditions the probability of a child sequence on that of the parent non-terminal. Each of its context-free grammar (CFG) rules $N \rightarrow X_1 \ldots X_n$ expands a non-terminal N into a sequence $X_1 \ldots X_n$ of non-terminal and terminal symbols, and the rule is assigned a probability value. The grammar provides conditional probabilities of the form $P(X_1 \ldots X_n | N)$ for each non-terminal N and sequence $X_1 \ldots X_n$ of items from the set of non-terminals and the vocabulary of terminals in the grammar. It also speci es a probability distribution over the label of the root of the tree $P_s(N)$. For a PCFG G, the conditional probabilities $P(X_1 \ldots X_n | N)$ correspond to probabilistic parameters that govern the expansion of a node in a parse-tree according to a corresponding context-free rule $N \rightarrow X_1 \ldots X_n$ in G.

The probabilistic parameter values of a PCFG can be learned from a parse annotated training corpus by computing the frequency of CFG rules instantiated in the corpus, in accordance with a *maximum likelihood estimation* (MLE) condition.

$$(4) \quad \frac{c(A \rightarrow \beta_1 \ldots \beta_k)}{c(A \rightarrow \gamma)}$$

where c(R) = the number of occurrences of a rule R in the annotated corpus.

In practice, MLE does not perform as well as more sophisticated estimation methods based on distribution-free techniques (see Collins 2004).

It is possible to signi cantly improve the performance of a PCFG by adding additional bias to the language model that it de nes. Collins (1999) constructs a *lexicalized probabilistic context-free grammar* (LPCFG) in which the probabilities of the CFG rules are conditioned on lexical heads of the phrases that non-terminal symbols represent. In Collins' LPCFG non-terminals are replaced by non-terminal/head pairs. The probability distributions of the model are of the form $P_s(N/h)$ and $P(X_1/h_1 \cdots H/h \cdots X_n/h_n \mid N/h)$ (where H is the category of the head of the phrase that expands N) . Collins' LPCFG achieves an F-measure performance of approximately 88 percent. Charniak and Johnson (2005) present an LPCFG with an F-score of approximately 91 percent.

Rather than encoding a particular categorical bias into his language model by excluding certain context-free rules, Collins allows all such rules. He incorporates bias by adjusting the prior distribution of probabilities over all lexicalized CFG rules. The model imposes the requirements that (1) sentences have hierarchical constituent structure, (2) constituents have heads that select for their siblings, and (3) this selection is determined by the headwords of the siblings.

The bias that Collins, and Charniak and Johnson, specify for their respective LPCFGs does not express the complex syntactic parameters that have been proposed as elements of a strong bias view of universal grammar (UG). So, for example, these models do not contain a parameter for head-complement directionality. However, they still learn the correct generalizations concerning head-complement order. The bias of a statistical parsing model has implications for the theory of UG. It expresses the prior constraints on the hypothesis space required for a particular learning procedure to achieve effective grammar induction from the input data that the corpus supplies.

1.4   Unsupervised learning

In unsupervised learning we do not annotate the training corpus with the structures or properties that the learning algorithm is intended to produce as its output values. Rather, the algorithm is provided with the data alone, and must learn some interesting structure through identifying distributional patterns and clustering properties of more basic features in the training data. In a machine learning sense, the most basic task of unsupervised learning is density estimation, which in NLP generally involves language modeling (see Chapter 3 of this book, STATISTICAL LANGUAGE MODELLING).

In the case of grammar induction, we are interested in recovering phrases and hierarchical constituent structure, which could be used for language modeling, machine translation, or other NLP tasks.

We will also brie y consider semi-supervised learning (see Abney 2008). This approach recognizes that in reality there will only be limited amounts of annotated data, and yet such data can be extremely useful when combined with much larger amounts of unannotated data.

2   Computational Learning Theory

One way of gaining insight into the problem of unsupervised learning is through theoretical analysis. While supervised learning has been the subject of detailed theoretical investigation that has yielded the design of ef cient classi cation algorithms (Vapnik 1998), unsupervised learning of language offers a different kind of challenge. The initial formulations of the problem, most notably by Gold (1967), suggested that it is fundamentally intractable. Subsequent accounts within the PAC (probably approximately correct) learning framework (Valiant 1984; Kearns & Vazirani 1994) appeared to con rm this conclusion. As a result, while there have been numerous attempts over the years to learn grammars from raw data, very few have been informed by theoretical learning models. Instead, these efforts have relied primarily on heuristics. The very earliest attempts at unsupervised grammar induction (Lamb 1961) lacked any theoretical underpinnings, and most current work in this area continues to pursue a non-theoretical, heuristic approach.

In our view, the theoretical problems have been misunderstood, and, in some cases, not properly formulated. Learnability results depend on quite subtle details of the formalisms. Small changes in the modeling assumptions can produce radically different results. In this section, we will review some of the competing theoretical models for unsupervised learning of natural languages, and draw conclusions that depart substantially from the received wisdom of the eld. Our goal is to use formal methods to illuminate the nature of learning through realistic assumptions. If the model trivializes the learning problem so that anything is learnable, then it is vacuous. Conversely, if it rules out ef cient learning where we know that learning takes place, then it is clearly misguided.

As we have noted, the eld of grammatical inference owes its origins to Gold (1967). In his paper Gold presents a number of different learning paradigms. We limit ourselves to the one in which the learner must acquire a language class only from positive data. As has been pointed out before, this model suffers from a number of serious shortcomings.[4] On one hand, it fails to place restrictions on the learner that are necessary to achieve rapid learning within the available resources of time and computation. On the other hand, it imposes excessively stringent limitations on learning by requiring that languages be acquired under far more dif cult circumstances than those which children have to deal with.

We will discuss one of these problems brie y to give a sense of what is involved. In the Gold paradigm the learner is provided with an in nite sequence of examples. His/her model requires the learner to produce correct grammaticality judgments after making only a nite number of errors. The learner must do this for every possible presentation of the language. A presentation is characterized so that every string in the language (every grammatical sentence) appears at least once in the data, and no ungrammatical sentences are included. These are the minimum requirements for a presentation to fully exhibit a particular language (rather than others). But on re ection this paradigm makes absurd demands on human learning. The learner is obliged to acquire a language on every presentation, even when the sequence of data samples are chosen by an in nitely powerful adversary, with knowledge of the internal structure of the learner, who is designing the presentation in order to make learning maximally dif cult. This situation does not correspond to the one in which children normally acquire their language. They are generally exposed to helpfully organized sequences of sentences from supportive adults interested in facilitating learning. It is instructive to work through the proof of Gold's most celebrated result, that no supra- nite language class is identi able in the limit, to see the crucial role that unconstrained presentations of data play in this proof.[5]

Conversely, because sample presentations are not restricted, Gold cannot constrain either the speed or the complexity of the learning process (although subsequent researchers have tried to add constraints to control these properties, such as Pitt (1989) and de la Higuera (1997)).

In the Gold model, there are two important positive results. The rst is that the class of all nite languages is learnable. The second is that any nite class of languages is learnable. The rst class is in nite, but its members are all nite. The second is nite, but one or more of its elements can be in nite. Both of these results use fairly trivial learning algorithms.

To learn the class of all nite languages the learner uses rote learning. He/she does not need to generalize at all, but can simply memorize the examples that have been seen. At each point, the learner returns the maximally conservative hypothesis that the language he/she is learning consists of only those sentences that he/she has already seen. It is easy to see that this very simple process of enumeration allows for only a nite number of errors, where the number of errors is bounded by the size of the language.

To learn a nite class of languages from a presentation, the learner proceeds as follows. The learner has access to a hypothesis space of all the languages in the class, where these languages are arranged in a superset hierarchy. The smallest language appears at the lowest point of the hierarchy and the largest at the top. As we noted, every data presentation consists of the strings of a language containing at least one appearance of each string. When a learner encounters a sentence in a presentation, he/she deletes from the hypothesis hierarchy any language that does not contain that sentence. He/she returns the rst language (hence the smallest) that is compatible with the strings of the presentation. It is easy to see that, as the presentation approaches the limit, the learner will return the correct language for the data.

Gold proves a negative result to the effect that no supra- nite language class can be learned in the limit from positive data samples presented arbitrarily from a corpus. However, he also demonstrates that with negative as well as positive evidence the class of primitive recursive languages can be learned in the limit. This class includes the set of context-sensitive languages as a proper subset. In this Gold learning paradigm negative evidence is provided by an informant who acts as a decision procedure, telling the learner for each data sample presented whether it is in the language to be learned, or in its complement set.

The view of learnability for language classes that is associated with Gold's theorems has provided one of the motivations for the principles and parameters (P&P) view of UG.[6] If the relevant formal results concerning grammar induction are those just cited and we assume that children do not have access to negative evidence, then, given that they do generalize, one might conclude that they can only effectively acquire their grammar if there is a nite number of possible human languages. This would seem to follow from Gold's learnability results, and the assumptions that (1) natural languages are in nite, and (2) children do not have access to negative evidence. The assertion that the class of natural languages is nite follows from the P&P claim that UG contains a nite set of parameters, with a nite set of values, ideally binary (Chomsky 1981). While both advocates and critics of linguistic nativism have, for the most part, agreed in the past that negative data does not play a signi cant role in language acquisition, this issue has become increasingly controversial in recent years.[7]

In fact the assumption that effective learning requires a nite hypothesis space of possible grammars is incorrect. There are many positive results even within the Gold paradigm which establish that in nite classes of in nite languages are learnable with some non-trivial algorithms (Angluin & Laird 1988; Clark & Eyraud 2007).

It is important to keep in mind that, because the Gold paradigm does not accurately re ect the situation of the child learner, any conclusions we draw from it are not likely to be reliable. Rather than trying to repair it by adding various constraints on presentations and polynomial bounds on the amount of possible computation, generating samples by a xed distribution, etc., we take a different approach. We will construct a model based on the actual facts of language learning, rather than rst starting with a model and then trying to force it onto the facts. We shall end up with a model that resembles that of Valiant (1984), but which departs from it in several key respects.

We start with some standard assumptions. The objects being learned are languages, which will normally be in finite objects, and these will be represented by finite systems. These systems can be thought of as grammars, though they might be encoded in another kind of formalism. The learner is provided with some information about the language. In the most basic case this will be examples of sentences in the language, though other sources of information may be considered. We assume that the learner is provided with the information one piece at a time, in a sequence of steps, and that at each step the learner either selects a hypothesis in the form of a representation of the language, or he/she abstains in the early phases of the algorithm. We say that the learner has successfully learned the language if, as the amount of data increases, the hypothesis converges (in a sense to be made precise) to the correct language.

This very rough outline provides a framework within which we can construct particular models of learning, through specifying precisely details like the classes of representations and languages, the sorts of information that the learner is provided with, the definition of convergence, and additional constraints one might want to place on the learner. Obviously, in order to achieve computational tractability we will need to make certain simplifying assumptions. In some cases, these assumptions will make learning more difficult, while in others they may make it easier. It is important to monitor these assumptions closely when interpreting the formal properties of each model. We need to emphasize that learning does, of course, occur in the real world. Therefore, if our model predicts that learning is impossible, it is clearly wrong.

We now proceed to develop this framework by making appropriate choices for the components that we have indicated. The first and most critical one to consider is the class of languages (or representations of them). This class corresponds to the set of possible grammars from which the child must select the grammar of his/her language. We know that it must include all of the attested natural languages, and presumably all languages that differ from them only through lexical changes, and other minor differences. The key questions are the following. How much larger can this class be while remaining effectively learnable? What are the defining properties of this class that determine its learnability?

We assume for the moment that the learner is provided only with positive examples. There are three possibilities to consider. First, the samples are provided by an adversary, as in Gold's model. Second, the samples are presented randomly. Under standard assumptions we can say that they are generated independently and identically from some fixed distribution. Third, the samples are produced helpfully, by a teacher trying to assist the learner (Goldman & Mathias 1996). While this last possibility may seem the most plausible, it is difficult to formalize in a way that does not trivialize the learning problem. Therefore, we will choose the random option as a reasonable model.

We observe that the child learns rapidly, in the sense that languages are complex objects, yet the amount of data which the child requires is only in the range of tens of millions of words. Hence we require the learner to learn in a time that is polynomially bounded in the size of the representation being learned, and we constrain the learner to be efficient, in that the computation it requires is bounded also by a polynomial function for the amount of data it sees.[8]

As for convergence, in the real world we generally do not see exact identification of a correct hypothesis: indeed we cannot directly observe the hypotheses. Instead we find that disagreements on grammaticality judgments are infrequent among members of a speech community. Generational differences do, of course, emerge as languages change. As a convergence criterion we can require that the probability of disagreement between the learner and the adult grammar tend to zero as it sees more data, and this must happen rapidly.

These conditions naturally yield a version of the PAC learning paradigm. In this framework a hypothesis (such as a grammar) is learned to within a range of error, represented by a constant ϵ, and a range of probability, expressed by a constant δ, in relation to the size of a data sample. An algorithm A PAC-learns a class of representations for languages $\mathcal{R}$, if and only if,

(1) there is a polynomial q, such that
  (a) for every $R \in \mathcal{R}$, which defines a language L
  (b) every probability distribution D on the samples of the data, and
  (c) every $\epsilon, \delta > 0$,
(2) whenever A sees a number of examples greater than $q(1/\epsilon, 1/\delta, |R|)$,
  (a) it returns a hypothesis H such that,
  (b) with probability greater than $1 - \delta$,
  (c) the error of the hypothesis $P_D((H - L) \cup (L - H)) < \epsilon$, and
(3) A runs in polynomial time in the total size of the examples seen.

These conditions require that learning be rapid for any language, that complex languages take more time than simple ones, but that the growth in time for learning in proportion to complexity of the language be slow.

Note that for a realistic model it is important to incorporate this dependency of learning time on language complexity, as removing it leads to the absurd conclusion that a rote learner cannot acquire finite languages. Thus for the class of finite grammars, where the representation is just a list of the grammatical sentences, it is unrealistic to expect the learner to be able to learn any list, no matter how long, in a fixed amount of time. A rote learner can learn lists of a restricted size within a reasonable time, but will require more time to learn longer lists. Thus it is reasonable, and standard in the machine learning literature, to allow the number of samples, as expressed by the polynomial q, to depend on the size of the representation $|R|$.

A standard PAC-model is distribution free, which entails that learning is equally rapid for all possible probability distributions on the data. From a mathematical perspective, this assumption is very convenient, and it forms the basis for the VC (Vapnik–Chervonenkis) theory of learnability (Vapnik 1998). However, it is unrealistic. The samples to which a child is exposed are generated by people in his/her environment who speak the language he/she is acquiring. The distributions of samples in the *primary linguistic data* (PLD) are not selected to make learning difcult, but rather to help it proceed.[9] Clearly, the distribution of the samples must depend on the language being learned: French children hear different sentences from English ones.

Many researchers (Li & Vitányi 1991) have noted that the distribution free assumption of the classical PAC framework is harsh, but yields powerful techniques. This approach may be mathematically desirable, and it might provide improvements over other estimation methods (Collins 2004). However, if we require learnability for any distribution, we nd that learning becomes intractably hard. By contrast, if we restrict the class of distributions in some way, for example to simple distributions (Li & Vitányi 1991; Denis 2001) or to distributions generated by the stochastic variations of the representations, such as probabilistic deterministic nite state automata (PDFA) or PCFGs, then we nd that ef cient learning is possible (Clark & Thollard 2004; Clark 2006).

Additional problems for learnability derive from the computational complexity of the learning problem. Learning statistical models of the kinds standardly employed in current NLP work is hard. So, for example Abe and Warmuth (1992) show that training a hidden Markov model (HMM) is computationally hard under common assumptions.[10] On standard cryptographic methods, computationally hard problems can be embedded in the learning of even simple acyclic deterministic automata (Kearns & Valiant 1989; Kearns et al., 1994). The natural conclusion is that the child would not be able to learn such classes. Indeed the sorts of languages that these problems give rise to bear no relation to natural languages, as they involve computing parity functions, or multiplying large integers together. From a formal point of view this means that uniform learning over the entire class of languages is not possible.

However, Ron et al. (1998) suggest a useful strategy for dealing with these difculties. A class of languages can be strati ed by a parameter that separates it into subclasses according to how hard each one is to learn. The speci c parameter for Ron is a distinguishability condition. Similar approaches can be applied to the learnability of context-free grammars (Clark 2006).

2.1   *Summary*

What insight can we gain from these formal results and considerations? Unsupervised learning of languages is dif cult but possible. This is a favorable outcome, as it implies that the study of learnability can offer us useful guidance in dealing with both engineering and cognitive issues in grammar induction.

Under the best possible theoretical analysis, we can see that negative results rule out uniform learning from positive data of the full classes of regular languages and context-free languages, but that regular languages, represented by deterministic nite state automata, and some subclasses of context-free languages, may be learnable when the distributions of examples are benignly speci ed. Both of these representations are based on observable properties of languages. The non-terminals or states are identi ed with distributional properties of the substrings of the languages. In the case of the regular languages, these are the residual languages (Clark & Thollard 2004), and with context-free languages these are the congruence classes (Clark 2006). Conversely it seems that representations based on deep hidden structures, such as trees, especially trees with many empty nodes, where the structure is not directly detectable from the surface utterance, may be hard to learn.

We might also be able to obtain positive results for a class of languages that is very restricted or even nite, although the languages in this class may themselves be in nite. But even here we may encounter problems. Finiteness in itself does not ensure ef cient computation. For example, the negative results in Kearns et al. (1994) are based on nite sets of nite languages. Despite the fact that they are nite, they are unlearnable, because the problem of identifying the correct hypothesis is too hard. Even though these families of languages are speci ed by a small number of binary valued parameters, the parameters are very tightly entwined in the computation of a parity function. This causes the class to be not ef ciently learnable.

From a theoretical point of view, the interesting question is whether these results rule out domain-general learning approaches, and necessitate a very restricted class of languages. The answer seems to be that they do not. They clearly point to different language classes from those in the Chomsky hierarchy. The classes that we use in our learning analyses do not necessarily correspond to normal families of languages, and certainly not to the Chomsky classes, such as context-free grammars. They might include, for example, some regular languages, some context-free languages, and some context-sensitive languages, but they may not cover all the members of these classes. It is also important not to confuse the hypothesis class of the learner with the class of languages that may be learnable. As Poggio et al. (2004: 422) say:

> Thus, for example, it may be possible that the language learning algorithm may be easy to describe mathematically while the class of possible natural language grammars may be dif cult to describe.

The hypothesis class could be very much larger than the class of languages for which it is guaranteed to learn. So, for example, the learner in Clark (2006) represents its hypotheses as context-free languages. All of these hypotheses lie within the (smaller) class of non-terminally separated (NTS) languages. The proof given there establishes that it will learn a PAC-learnable class of unambiguous languages under some plausible assumptions about the data sample distributions. But if the samples are generated adversarially (as in one of Gold's paradigms), then the learner is only guaranteed to acquire the still smaller class of substitutable languages (Clark & Eyraud 2007). The algorithm, however, remains unchanged.

These are rather different conclusions from other recent analyses. For example, Nowak et al. (2002) and Niyogi (2006) claim that the PAC-analysis rules out learning without speci c restrictions. This is largely because their approach does not allow the size of the language representation to depend on the amount of data that the learner can have, as discussed above in Section 1.1.

Our theoretical understanding of learning is changing rapidly. Modifying Chomsky's terminology somewhat, we can say that linguistic representations may achieve varying levels of adequacy. Observational adequacy is the requirement that the representations are suf ciently powerful to express the distinction between grammatical and ungrammatical sentences. Explanatory adequacy imposes the additional requirement that the representations can be learned from the available data.

We have not yet achieved explanatory adequacy. The most descriptively adequate frameworks use very powerful systems of representation, such as tree adjoining grammar (TAG) (Joshi 1987) or head driven phrase structure grammar (HPSG) (Pollard & Sag 1994), while the grammars developed to date that can be ef ciently learned are not powerful enough to cover the full complexity of natural language syntax. Whether there are observationally adequate grammars that can be learned using unsupervised learning from raw corpora remains very much an open question. Our theoretical analysis points in general towards shallower linguistic representations, regardless of whether these are conceived of in terms of parameters of a language model, formal grammars, or a more situated account of learning, which leverages extralinguistic context to a far greater extent than considered here.

3   Empirical Learning

We now turn to empirical work on unsupervised learning, where ML algorithms are applied to naturally occurring natural language corpora. We will look in detail at two NLP tasks. One is the unsupervised learning of word classes, and the other is unsupervised induction of syntactic parsing.

First, we will brie y take up the problem of evaluation, which is particularly problematic in the case of unsupervised learning.[11] Three methodologies have been used. The rst is naïve. It involves having observers evaluate an algorithm's output on the basis of their intuitions concerning the property or structure that the procedure is designed to identify. This approach may offer some insight into the strengths and weaknesses of the method, but it is both subjective and imprecise.

A second evaluation technique measures the correspondence between the results that the algorithm generates and those of a gold standard for the corpus. So, for example, when evaluating induced word classes one can compare the word classes that an ML procedure generates for a corpus with the traditional lexical categories that are assigned to the corpus by a reliable part-of-speech (POS) tagger that uses these categories. This comparison can be done using standard information theoretic criteria. For example the conditional entropy of the gold standard tags with respect to the induced tags will tell you how much of the information in the gold standard tags remains unaccounted for by the induced tags. If this number is very low or zero, then the gold standard tags are predictable from the induced tags.

Table 8.1 Comparison of different tag sets on IPSM data. Conditional entropy of row given column. Blanks (–) are where the two sets have different tokenization due to differing treatment of the possessive clitic

Tag set	n H	Brown	ICE	LLC	LOB	Parts	POW	Sec	UPenn
Brown	3.16	0.00	–	0.34	0.22	1.10	0.99	0.32	–
ICE	3.38	–	0.00	–	–	–	–	–	0.84
LLC	3.34	0.52	–	0.00	0.44	1.30	1.00	0.45	–
LOB	3.24	0.31	–	0.35	0.00	1.20	1.00	0.24	–
Parts	2.46	0.41	–	0.40	0.41	0.00	0.75	0.38	–
POW	2.72	0.55	–	0.42	0.46	1.00	0.00	0.43	–
Sec	3.24	0.40	–	0.35	0.24	1.20	0.95	0.00	–
Upenn	2.92	–	0.38	–	–	–	–	–	0.00

This comparison yields objective numerical evaluation, but the gold standard in linguistic annotation often incorporates theoretical assumptions that may not be well motivated. Alternative annotations of the text may be possible. The gold standard might simply re ect the prestige of the organization that produced the annotation, the theoretical framework it employs, the amount of data annotated, the availability of the corpus, or other factors irrelevant to a sound evaluation standard.

In part-of-speech annotations of English, for example, there are signi cant differences between various tag sets. Using data provided by the AMALGAM (Automatic Mapping Among Lexico-Grammatical Annotation Models) project (Atwell et al., 1995), which provided text annotated with eight different tag sets, we measured the conditional entropy of each tag set with respect to the others. Table 8.1 shows the results. We see that the conditional entropy here varies up to 1.3 for these equally valid, manually constructed tag sets,[12] and it is zero, as one would expect, down the leading diagonal. By comparing these competing gold standards against each other, we observe the range of possible outcomes that we might expect.

In unsupervised parsing this approach involves using a treebank and measuring derived trees against gold standard trees: an evaluation approach rst employed by van Zaanen (2000).

The third and nal evaluation technique is to invoke some objective and theoretically neutral evaluation strategy. For example, one can compute the predictive power of a derived language model for word class induction (Ney et al., 1994). This is usually de ned in terms of perplexity, which measures the ability of the model to predict the next word in a string or corpus.[13] This evaluation metric has two advantages. First, it directly measures a useful property of the model. Such models can be used in speech recognition, and models with lower (better) perplexity will perform with a lower error rate. Second, the metric does not depend on linguistic annotations, which as we have noted, are not uncontroversial. It relies solely on raw, naturally occurring data.

Alternatively, we could consider performance in an end-to-end problem in which the results of one procedure are taken as input for a second application. The output of the latter provide an indirect measure for the success of the former. Bod (2007a) does this when he uses the trees of his unsupervised parser to support a machine translation system. However, it is not clear how well this approach captures the linguistic accuracy of the rst algorithm.

3.1 Learning word classes

One of the earliest NLP problems to which unsupervised learning was successfully applied is the induction of parts of speech. The words in every language can be divided into lexical categories that partially correspond to traditional parts of speech. Nearly all lexical resources use some xed categories of this type, as do syntactically annotated corpora. While for many purposes manual tagging of text is adequate, it is frequently desirable, for reasons of ef ciency, to extract lexical classes from corpora automatically. Moreover, from a cognitive perspective it is important to determine the extent to which purely distributional algorithms can learn these categories, as they provide the basis for post-lexical syntactic analysis.

Corresponding to engineering and to cognitive concerns we nd two strands of research. The cognitive science approach is most notably represented by Nick Chater and his co-workers (Finch et al., 1995; Redington et al., 1998). The engineering direction focuses on statistical language modeling, where lexical categories are invoked to smooth n-gram models by specifying conditional probabilities for strings in terms of word classes rather than individual lexical items. The basic methods of this approach are studied in detail by Ney et al. (1994), Martin et al. (1998), and Brown et al. (1992).

We assume a vocabulary of words $V = \{W_1, \ldots\}$. Our task is to learn a deterministic clustering, which we can represent as a class membership function g from V into the set of class labels $\{1, \ldots, n\}$. The clustering can be used to de ne a number of simple statistical models. The objective function we try to maximise will be the likelihood of some model, understood as the probability of the data with respect to that model. The simplest candidate is the class-bigram model, though this approach can be extended to class-trigram models. Suppose we have a corpus $w_1, \ldots, w_N$ of length N. We can assume an additional sentence boundary token. Then the class-bigram model de nes the probability of the next word given the history as

$$(5) \quad P\left(w_i \left| w_1^{i-1}\right.\right) = P(w_i|g(w_i))P(g(w_{i-1})|g(w_{i-2}))$$

It is not computationally feasible to search through all of the exponentially many possible partitions of the vocabulary to nd the one with the highest likelihood value. Therefore we need a search algorithm that will give us a local optimum. The standard techniques (Ney et al., 1994; Martin et al., 1998) use an exchange algorithm similar to the k-means algorithm for clustering. This procedure (1) iteratively improves the likelihood of a given clustering by moving each word from its current cluster to the cluster that will give the maximum increase in likelihood, or (2) leaves it in its original cluster if no improvement can be found. There are a number of different ways in which an initial clustering can be chosen. It has been found that the initialization method has little effect on the nal quality of the clusters, but it can have a marked effect on the speed of convergence for the algo- rithm. A more important variation for our purposes is how rare words are treated. Martin et al. (1998) leave all words with a frequency of less than 5 in a particular class, from which they may not be moved.

These techniques, using purely distributional evidence, work remarkably well for frequent words. However, as Rosenfeld (2000b: 1313–14) points out, in lan- guage modeling the most important task is to cluster the infrequent words. We have suf ciently reliable information about the statistical properties of the fre- quent words that they do not need to be smoothed with the clusters, and so it is the *infrequent* words that are most in need of smoothing.[14] But it is these words that are most dif cult to cluster.

Distributional data is of course not the only information relevant to identify- ing the syntactic category of a word class. Words are not atoms, but sequences of letters or phonemes, and this information can be used by a learning algo- rithm. Moreover, words have relative frequency, and infrequent words will exhibit different frequency patterns from frequent words. Pronouns, for example, tend to be very frequent.

Consider a trivial case of the rst type from written language. If we encounter an unknown word, say £212,000, then merely looking at the sequence of characters that compose it may well be suf cient to allow us to reliably estimate its part of speech. Less trivially, suf xes like *-ing* or *-ly* on an English word are a strong clue as to its lexical category.

Clark (2003) presents a method for determining how frequency and morpho- logical information can be incorporated into this approach, and tests the method on a number of different languages from different families. He uses texts pre- pared for the MULTEXT-East project (Erjavec & Ide 1998), which consists of data (George Orwell's novel *1984*) in seven languages: the original English together with Romanian, Czech, Slovene, Bulgarian, Estonian, and Hungarian.

Table 8.2 from Clark (2003) shows the results of the cross-linguistic evaluation of this data (to get a sense of how to interpret the values in this table it is worth consulting Table 8.1 again).

This method was also evaluated by comparing the perplexity of a class-based language model derived from these classes.

3.2   *Unsupervised parsing*

Initial experiments with unsupervised grammar induction (like those described in Carroll & Charniak 1992) were not particularly encouraging. Far more promis- ing results have been achieved in work over the past decade. Klein and Manning (2002) propose a method that learns constituent structure from POS tagged input by unsupervised techniques. It assigns probability values to all subsequences of

Table 8.2 Cross-linguistic evaluation: 64 clusters, left all words, right $f \leq 5$. We compare the baseline with algorithms using purely distributional (D) evidence, supplemented with morphological (M) and frequency (F) information

	Base	D0	D5	D+M	D+F	D+M+F	Base	D0	D+M	D+F	D+M+F
$H(G\|C)$			*All words*						$f \leq 5$		
English	1.52	0.98	0.95	1.00	0.97	**0.94**	2.33	1.53	1.20	1.51	**1.16**
Bulgarian	2.12	1.69	1.55	1.56	1.63	**1.53**	3.67	2.86	**2.48**	2.86	2.57
Czech	2.93	2.64	2.27	2.35	2.60	2.31	4.55	3.87	3.22	3.88	3.31
Estonian	2.44	2.31	**1.88**	2.12	2.29	2.09	4.01	3.42	**3.14**	3.42	**3.14**
Hungarian	2.16	2.04	1.76	1.80	2.01	**1.70**	4.07	3.46	**3.06**	3.40	3.18
Romanian	2.26	1.74	1.53	1.57	1.61	**1.49**	3.66	2.52	**2.20**	2.63	2.22
Slovene	2.60	2.28	**2.01**	2.08	2.21	2.07	4.59	3.72	**3.25**	3.73	3.55

tagged elements in an input string, construed as possible constituents in a tree. The model that this method employs imposes the constraint of binary branching on all non-terminal elements of a parse-tree. Klein and Manning invoke an *expectation maximization* (EM) algorithm to select the most likely parse for a sentence. Their method identi es (unlabeled) constituents through the distributional co-occurrence of POS sequences in the same contexts. The model partially characterizes phrase structure by the condition that sister phrases do not have (non-empty) intersections. Binary branching and the non-overlap requirement are biases of the model.

Evaluated against Penn Treebank parses (Marcus 1993) as the gold standard, this unsupervised parse procedure achieves an F-measure of 71 percent on *Wall Street Journal* (*WSJ*) test data. This score is achieved despite a serious limitation imposed by the gold standard. The Penn Treebank allows for non-binary branching for many constituents. A binary branching parse algorithm of the sort that Klein and Manning employ can only achieve a maximum F-score of 87 percent against this standard. As it turns out, many of the algorithm's binary constituent analyses that are excluded by the gold standard are, in fact, linguistically defensible parses. So, for example, while the treebank analyzes noun phrases as having at structure, the iterated binary branching constituent structure that the Klein–Manning procedure assigns to NPs is well motivated on syntactic grounds.

The Klein–Manning parser is, in fact, constructed by semi-supervised, rather than fully unsupervised, learning. The input to the learning algorithm is a corpus annotated with the POS tagging of the Penn Treebank. If POS annotation is, in turn, provided by a tagger that uses unsupervised learning, then the entire parsing procedure can be construed as a sequenced process of unsupervised grammar induction.[15]

Klein and Manning (2002) report an experiment in which their parser achieves an F-score of 63.2 percent on *WSJ* text annotated by an unsupervised POS tagger. They observe that this tagger is not particularly reliable. Other unsupervised taggers, like the one presented in Clark (2003), produce good results that might well allow the Klein–Manning unsupervised constituency parser to perform at a level comparable to that which it achieves with Penn Treebank tags.

Klein and Manning (2004) present an unsupervised learning procedure for acquiring lexicalized head-dependency grammars. It assigns probabilities to possible dependency relations in a sentence S by estimating the likelihood that each word in S is a head for particular sequences of words to its left and to its right, taken as its syntactic arguments or adjuncts. The probabilities for these alternative dependency relations are computed on the basis of the context in which each head occurs. The context consists of the words (word classes) that are immediately adjacent to it on either side. The dependency structure model associated with the learning algorithm requires binary branching as a condition on dependency relations. The procedure achieves an F-measure of 52.1 percent on Penn Treebank test data.

Klein and Manning (2004) combine their dependency and constituent structure grammar induction systems into an integrated model that produces better results than either of its component parsers. The composite model computes the score for a tree as the product of the dependency and constituency structure grammars. This procedure employs both constituent clustering and head dependency relations to predict binary constituent parse structure. It achieves an F-score of 77.6 percent with Penn Treebank POS tagging, and an F-score of 72.9 percent with Schütze's (1995) unsupervised tagger.

Bod (2006a; 2007a; 2007b) proposes an alternative system for unsupervised parsing, which he refers to as *unsupervised data-oriented parsing* (U-DOP). U-DOP generates all possible binary branching subtrees for a sentence S. The preferred parse for S is the one which can be obtained through the smallest number of substitutions of subtrees into nodes in larger trees. In cases where more than one derivation satis es this condition, the derivation using subtrees with the highest frequency in previously parsed text is selected. Bod (2006a) reports an F-score of 82.9 percent when U-DOP is combined with a maximum likelihood estimator and applied to the *WSJ* corpus on which Klein and Manning tested their parsers.

While U-DOP improves on the accuracy and coverage of Klein and Manning's (2004) combined unsupervised dependency-constituency model, it generates a very large number of subtrees for each parse that it produces. Bod (2007a) describes a procedure for greatly reducing this number by converting a U-DOP model into a type of PCFG. The resulting parser produces far fewer possible subtrees for each sentence, but at the cost of performance. It yields a reported F-score of 77.9 percent on the *WSJ* test corpus (Bod 2007a).

An important advantage that U-DOP has over simple PCFGs is its capacity to represent discontinuous syntactic structures, like subject–auxiliary inversion in questions, and complex determiners such as *more . . . than . . .*, as complete constructions.[16] U-DOP incorporates binary branching tree recursion as the main bias of its model. It can parse structures not previously encountered, either through the equivalent of PCFG rules, or by identifying structural analogies between possible tree constructions for a current input and those assigned to previously parsed strings in a test set.

ADIOS is another recent unsupervised algorithm for grammar induction (Solan et al., 2005). It is interesting not so much for the algorithmic properties that it exempli es (these are largely taken from other models, although they are combined in a novel way), but for the extensive and original method of evaluation to which it is subjected. Solan et al. (2005) use a number of different techniques to demonstrate the robustness of ADIOS. These include a language modeling task, and application of the algorithm to test children's reading comprehension.

3.3   Accuracy vs. cost in supervised, unsupervised, and semi-supervised learning

In general supervised learning algorithms achieve greater accuracy than unsupervised procedures. So LPCFG parsers trained on *WSJ* corpora annotated with constituent structure information in the Penn Treebank obtain F-measures of 88 percent to 91 percent (Collins 1999; Charniak and Johnson 2005), while ef cient unsupervised parsers currently score in the mid to high 70s (Klein & Manning 2004; Bod 2007a). However, hand annotating corpora for training supervised algorithms adds a signi cant cost that must be weighed against the accuracy that these procedures provide. To the extent that unsupervised algorithms do not incur these costs, they offer an important advantage, if they can sustain an acceptable level of performance in the applications for which they are designed.

Banko and Brill (2001) use a method of semi-supervised learning that combines some of the bene ts of both systems. They train 10 distinct classi ers for a word disambiguation problem on an annotated test set. They then run all the classi ers on an unannotated corpus and select the instances for which there is full agreement among them. This automatically annotated data is added to the original hand annotated corpus for a new cycle of training, and the process is iterated with additional unannotated corpora. In the experiments they describe how accuracy is improved through unsupervised extensions of a supervised base corpus up to a certain phase in the learning cycles, after which it begins to decline. They suggest that this effect may be due to the learning process reaching a point at which the bene ts that additional data contribute are outweighed by the distortion of sample bias imported with the new samples, which causes over tting of the data.

Bank and Brill's approach can be generalized to grammar induction and parsing. This would involve training several supervised parsing systems on an initial parsed corpus and then optimizing these procedures through iterated parsing of text containing only POS tagging. The tagging can be done automatically using a reliable tagger.

There are, in fact, good engineering reasons for investing more research effort in the development of robust unsupervised and semi-supervised learning procedures. Very large quantities of raw natural language text are now available online and easily accessible. While supervised grammar induction has achieved a high level of accuracy, generating the necessary training corpora is an expensive and time-consuming process. The use of unsupervised and semi-supervised learning algorithms reduces much of this expense. The amount of data that hand annotated training sets provide is very limited in comparison to the corpora of unannotated text currently available at little or no cost. As the accuracy and coverage of unsupervised systems improves, they become increasingly attractive alternatives to supervised methods. It is reasonable, then, to expect a greater focus on the development of these systems in future NLP work.

4   Unsupervised Grammar Induction and Human Language Acquisition

The promising results of recent work on unsupervised procedures for grammar induction raise interesting questions for long-standing debates over the cognitive basis for human language acquisition. Theoretical linguistics has been dominated for the past 50 years by a strong version of linguistic nativism.[17] On this view, a set of rich, domain-speci c biases provide the basis for language acquisition. These biases are formulated as the constraints of a universal grammar, which constitutes a biologically determined, task-speci c language faculty.

The main consideration offered in support of this notion of a language faculty is the *argument from the poverty of the stimulus* (APS). According to the APS the amount and quality of the primary linguistic data available to children acquiring their rst language is not suf cient to account for the grammar that expresses adult linguistic competence if acquisition of the adult grammar is mediated primarily by domain-general procedures of induction, such as those applied in machine learning. A classic instance of the APS is the use of subject–auxiliary inversion to claim that language learners have an innate bias towards learning grammatical rules formulated in terms of a hierarchical phrase structure representation of sentences.[18]

(6) a. Is the student who is in the garden hungry?
     b. *Is the student who in the garden is hungry?

The rule of auxiliary inversion requires that (something like) the following structures be assigned to (6a), (6b), respectively.

(7) a. $[_{S'} is_2 [_S [_{NP}$ the $[_{N'}$ student $[_{RC}$ who $[_{VP} is_1$ in the garden$]]]] [_{VP} [_V e_2]$ hungry$]]]$
     b. $[_{S'} is_1 [_S [_{NP}$ the $[_{N'}$ student $[_{RC}$ who $[_{VP} e_1$ in the garden$]]]] [_{VP} [_V is_2]$ hungry$]]]$

Advocates of the APS maintain that the data to which children are exposed does not provide an adequate basis for inferring a structure-dependent rule of subject–auxiliary inversion unless the children come to the task of language acquisition already equipped with a mechanism for organizing strings of words into phrasal constituents of the sort that facilitate the formulation of this rule.

The APS has recently been subject to strong challenges.[19] Both sides of this debate have tended to focus on the availability of evidence for grammar induction through data-driven methods. However, it is not possible to decide how much, and what sort of, data is required for effective language acquisition independently of a clearly specied theory of learning. This question is meaningful and interesting only when considered in relation to a particular learning theory or class of such theories. Linguistic nativists have generally argued for the paucity of data without specifying a strong bias model that will generate the class of grammars which they posit, given the set of linguistic samples which they assume as evidence. Similarly, some critics of the APS have insisted that the child has access to sufcient linguistic data to produce the grammar of his/her rst language without indicating how learning is achieved.

To the extent that machine learning algorithms can acquire accurate and theoretically viable grammars of languages from corpora through unsupervised methods, employing weak rather than strong learning biases, they undermine the APS as an argument for strong linguistic nativism.[20] Specically, they show that it is possible to implement a learning algorithm that can effectively acquire a significant element of human linguistic knowledge relying primarily on generalized information theoretic techniques for classifying data, with comparatively weak domain-specic constraints on the set of possible grammars in its hypothesis space. As we have observed, unsupervised grammar induction has recently yielded encouraging results for parsing *WSJ* text according to the gold standard given by the Penn Treebank. Moreover, Bod (2006a, 2007a), and Clark and Eyraud (2006) present systems that learn subject–auxiliary inversion rules ef - ciently without being exposed to sample sentences like (6a) or its full declarative counterpart.

(8)   The student who is in the garden is hungry.

However, most of these unsupervised grammar-induction procedures incorporate learning biases that restrict their hypothesis spaces to constituent structure grammars of some kind.[21] An advocate of the APS can claim that these biases are precisely the sort of conditions that the argument is intended to motivate as necessary learning priors for language acquisition.

In fact it is possible to argue that a preference for hierarchical constituent structure is not, in itself, an irreducible bias on a language model. It can be derived from a more basic and general learning prior. As we have seen, Perfors et al. (2006) dene a very general prior for smaller grammars with fewer rules and fewer non-terminal symbols. It does not specify a bias towards constituent structure. They apply their Bayesian posterior probability measure, given in (3) ($\arg\max_H(P(H)P(D|H))$), to a hypothesis space of three types of grammar, which they evaluate on a subset of CHILDES (MacWhinney 1995), a corpus of child directed discourse.

The three types of grammar that Perfors et al. (2006) consider are:

(1)   a at grammar that generates strings directly from S without intermediate non-terminal symbols;

(2)   a probabilistic regular grammar (PRG); and
(3)   a probabilistic context-free grammar (PCFG).

They compute the posterior probability of each grammar for the CHILDES sentences. The PCFG receives a higher posterior probability value and covers signi -cantly more sentence types in the corpus than either the PRG or the at grammar. The grammar with maximum a posteriori probability makes the correct generalization. This result suggests that it may be possible to decide among radically distinct types of grammars on the basis of a Bayesian model with relatively weak learning priors, when using a corpus that accurately re ects the linguistic data that children are exposed to in the course of rst language acquisition. The prior that Perfors et al. (2006) invoke does not impose a constituent structure bias, but a general preference for smaller, more compact hypotheses.

While the success of weak bias unsupervised ML procedures in grammar induction (and related tasks) vitiates the APS case for strong domain-speci c learning priors as necessary conditions for language acquisition, it does not tell us anything about the actual cognitive mechanisms that humans employ in acquiring their rst language. Even discounting the APS, a strong nativist view of UG could, in principle, turn out to be correct on the basis of the psychological and biological facts of language acquisition.

Is there, then, any psycholinguistic evidence showing that ML methods play a signi cant role in human language learning? In fact there is. Saffran et al. (1996) report a set of experiments in which eight-month-old infants learn to identify word boundaries in continuous syllable sequences on the basis of a two-minute exposure to training data. The words are nonsense terms constructed out of three-syllable sequences. The transitional probabilities between syllables within a word are maximal (set at 1), while those between syllables crossing word boundaries are low (generally around 0.33). The transitional probability of a syllable pair XY (X followed by Y) is computed as the conditional probability $P(Y|X)$ according to its Bayesian MLE condition (where $c(\alpha)$ is the frequency count for the sequence α).

(9) $P(Y|X) = \dfrac{c(XY)}{c(X)}$

The infants were able to distinguish familiar words heard in the training samples from novel non-words on the basis of very limited exposure to a word set. Saffran et al. (1996) conclude that they employed the difference in transitional probabilities between word internal syllable sequences and word external pairs in order to infer word boundaries.[22]

Thompson and Newport (2007) extend this experimental approach to investigate the learning of phrasal boundaries and constituent structure. They describe a series of experiments in which English-speaking adults are exposed to training sets of samples from simple arti cial languages with six word classes, each containing three words (the word number of some classes is modi ed for one of the experiments). Phrases consist of word pairs where each element of the pair comes from a distinct word class. The training sets contain a canonical phrasal pattern of word class sequences, and variations on these patterns involving:

(1) the presence of repeated phrases,
(2) optional constituents,
(3) permutations of phrases (moved constituents), and
(4) variation in the lexical size of two of the four phrase types.

Each of the three conditions in (1)–(3) introduces a signi cant difference in intra-phrasal vs. inter-phrasal transitional probabilities between word classes. The former are set at 1, while the latter are lower. For each of these four conditions a control group is exposed to a training set in which the conditions do not apply to discrete phrases, but are formulated only for word classes. As a result, there is no substantial difference in the transitional probabilities that hold between different word class pairs in the control language.

After training, both the experimental and the control groups were tested on their ability to identify well-formed sentential and phrasal patterns in the language. Thompson and Newport (2007) found that for conditions (1)–(3) the experimental group outperformed the control group in learning both sentence and phrasal structure. When all four conditions were combined in a single language, the difference between intra-phrasal and inter-phrasal transitions substantially increased. In an experiment with variants of this language type in which the two groups were exposed to a comparatively small set of canonical sentence patterns (5 percent of the training set), the experimental subjects achieved far greater success than the control subjects in learning both sentence and phrasal patterns.

These results indicate that transitional probabilities can provide an important cue for identifying constituent structure from word sequences. While the experiments provide data only on syntax learning by adults, when taken together with Saffran et al.'s (1996) research on infant identi cation of word boundaries, they strongly suggest that Bayesian inference of the kind employed by ML methods in NLP plays a signi cant role in human language acquisition at a variety of levels of morphological and syntactic structure.

This work also gives credence to a bootstrapping view of language learning on which information theoretic methods yield an initial classi cation of linguistic entities that can then be used to construct successive levels of representation. Each previous cycle of learning provides a set of structural constraints on the entities out of which the next stage is developed by the same kinds of Bayesian inference. If this view is sustained by further research, then the weak bias model of language learning proposed in Lappin (2005), Lappin and Shieber (2007), and Clark (2004) will achieve psychological as well as computational credibility. Clearly much additional work remains to be done in clarifying these issues before any such model can be endorsed with any con dence as an account of human language acquisition. It does, however, provide a serious alternative to the strong nativist approach that has dominated linguistics and cognitive science for the past ve decades, generally without a learning theory to motivate it.

5   Conclusion

Unsupervised learning is a rich and varied area of research. It includes different motivations, techniques, and methods of evaluation. In this chapter we have surveyed the eld and provided an overview of what we regard as the most signi cant theoretical and engineering developments.

It is important to recognize that while the application of these techniques to practical problems in NLP is still at an early stage, unsupervised learning is almost certain to expand as an area of interest and activity.

It is also plausible to hope that, as we make progress in understanding the capacities and limits of unsupervised methods, we will achieve deeper insight into how much and what kinds of linguistic knowledge can be acquired by domain-general learning algorithms operating on raw linguistic data. Such insight is of direct signi cance to work in theoretical linguistics and the study of human cognition.

NOTES

1   See, Chapter 18 of this book, INFORMATION EXTRACTION, Section 3.4, and Jurafsky and Martin (2009: 455) for discussions of recall, precision, and weighted F-measures.

2   See Manning and Schütze (1999) for a discussion of Bayesian inference and the role of Bayesian reasoning about probability in statistical NLP.

3   See Chapter 13 of this book, STATISTICAL PARSING, Manning and Schütze (1999), and Jurafsky and Martin (2009) for accounts of probabilistic context-free grammars and lexicalized probabilistic context-free grammars as language models for supervised grammar induction.

4   See Lappin and Shieber (2007) and Clark (2001a, chapter 4) for discussions of some of the problematic assumptions in Gold's *identification in the limit* learning paradigm.

5   A supra- nite class includes all nite languages and at least one in nite language.

6   See, for example Crain and Thornton (1998) for arguments to the effect that, because the class of natural languages is unlearnable from positive evidence only, a rich innate UG must be posited to explain human language acquisition.

7   See, for example, Saxton (1997) and Chouinard and Clark (2003) for psycholinguistic research supporting the widespread availability and effectiveness of negative evidence in child grammar induction. See also Clark and Lappin (2009) for a proposal on how indirect negative evidence can be stochastically modeled within a PAC framework.

8   See Chapter 2, COMPUTATIONAL COMPLEXITY, for the relevant notions of complexity and ef ciency of computation.

9   Questions have been raised about the extent to which this helps the child (Gleitman et al., 2001).

10   The Baum–Welch algorithm (also known as the forward–backward algorithm) used to estimate the parameter values for such models only nds a local optimum. See Manning and Schütze (1999) for discussion of this procedure.

11   See Chapter 11, EVALUATION OF NLP SYSTEMS, and Chapter 10, LINGUISTIC ANNO-TATION, for discussions of this and related issues in connection with a variety of NLP tasks.

12   The texts were tagged automatically, which might introduce some variability.

13   See Chelba, STATISTICAL LANGUAGE MODELING, and Manning and Schütze (1999), Section 2.2 for discussions of perplexity and entropy.

14   See Chapter 3, STATISTICAL LANGUAGE MODELING, and Pereira (2000) on the application of smoothing techniques for statistical modeling, originally introduced by Good (1953), in NLP.

15   Actually, an unsupervised POS tagger will also rely on morphological analysis of the words in a corpus. This can be provided by an unsupervised morphological analyzer. See Goldsmith (2001), Chapter 14 of this book, SEGMENTATION AND MORPHOLOGY, and Schone and Jurafsky (2001) for alternative systems of unsupervised morphological analysis.

16   See Clark and Eyraud (2006) for a simple unsupervised distributional algorithm that learns a PCFG which correctly handles subject–auxiliary inversion.

17   See, *inter alia*, Chomsky (1965; 1971; 1981; 1986; 1995; 2000; 2005), and Pinker (1989; 1996).

18   See Chomsky (1971); Crain and Nakayama (1987); Crain (1991); Berwick and Chomsky (2009) for versions of this argument, and Clark and Lappin (2010) for critical discussion of it.

19   Pullum and Scholz (2002) and their critics conduct a lively debate on the APS in Volume 19 (2002) of *The Linguistic Review*. Scholz and Pullum (2006) offer an updated version of some of their criticisms of the APS.

20   For detailed discussion of the relevance of work in machine learning and computational learning theory to APS-based claims for linguistic nativism see Lappin (2005); Lappin and Shieber (2007); Clark (2004); and Clark and Lappin (2010).

21   This is not the case for the algorithm proposed in Clark and Eyraud (2006), which uses a simple criterion of distributional congruence to identify equivalence classes of words and phrases.

22   Yang (2004) disputes this conclusion. He reports a word identi cation experiment on a subset of the CHILDES corpus using transitional syllable probabilities. The results of the experiment indicate poor recall and precision for this procedure. As he observes, this is due to the fact that 85 percent of the words in his test set are monosyllabic. Therefore there is no signi cant distinction between intra-word and inter-word transitional probabilities for most of the terms in this corpus. Yang claims that his experiment shows that transitional probability is not an adequate cue for word boundary identi cation in realistic data of the sort that children receive. In fact, this claim is seriously undermotivated. Child directed speech of the kind that appears in CHILDES does not exhaust the linguistic samples to which children are exposed in their normal environments. They generally have access to the full range of multi-syllabic utterances of normal adult speech, even when it is not directed to them. There is no reason to exclude this additional data from the range of evidence that children can make use of when computing transitional probabilities for syllable pairs. It is not unreasonable to hypothesize that, when one takes account of the full range of evidence available to child language learners, a signi cant correlation between transitional probability patterns and word boundaries in real language data will prove robust.

9 Artificial Neural Networks

JAMES B. HENDERSON

1 Introduction

Artificial neural networks (ANNs) have been used in a variety of ways in the study of language. In this chapter we will focus on work in NLP within the framework of statistical modeling.[1] For statistical modeling, the most useful ANN architecture is the multi-layered perceptron (MLP). MLPs can be used for probability estimation and feature induction, and have been extended for modeling both sequential and structured data. Their most successful applications in NLP have been language modeling and parsing. MLPs have also been inspirational for much current research in machine learning methods, and can be reinterpreted in terms of approximations to latent variable models.

In this chapter we will first cover background material, and then discuss contemporary research. The emphasis will be on the usefulness of ANNs as an engineering tool, but theoretical motivations and context will be given wherever possible. ANNs have the advantages of being robust in training and testing, of being fast in testing, and of requiring little prior knowledge of the domain. ANNs are also interesting because they discover compact feature-based representations specific to the task they are trained on.

2 Background

The term 'artificial neural network,' or often just 'neural network,' refers to a variety of computational models which share certain properties inspired by the networks of neurons found in the brain. They consist of a distributed network of simple processing units, and usually they are designed to be trained from data. These were some of the earliest machine learning methods in artificial intelligence (AI), and they have been influential in many aspects of machine learning research. Within AI, most research on ANNs has lost any pretence of being neurologically motivated, and today is mostly of engineering interest. It is mostly its usefulness for engineering solutions which has interested research in NLP.

The Handbook of Computational Linguistics and Natural Language Processing, First Edition.
Edited by Alexander Clark, Chris Fox and Shalom Lappin.
© 2013 Blackwell Publishing Ltd except for editorial material and organization
© 2013 Alexander Clark, Chris Fox, and Shalom Lappin. Published 2013 by Blackwell Publishing Ltd.

Another property typically associated with ANNs is the unsupervised induction of representations during learning. Some of the processing units in the ANN have no prede ned meaning; they acquire their meaning during training. In some cases, these units are the output of the ANN, as for example for the unsupervised clustering of self-organizing maps (Kohonen 1984). In other cases, these units form an intermediate representation in between the input and the output of the ANN. Such units are called 'hidden units,' and are similar to latent variables, as we will discuss in Section 3.3. By far the most popular form of ANN has been the multi-layered perceptron (MLP), and its recurrent variants. MLPs are used for function approximation, categorization, and sequence modeling.

2.1   *Multi-layered perceptrons*

Multi-layered perceptrons (MLPs) (Rumelhart et al., 1986) were developed as an answer to the criticism that the perceptron algorithm could only learn a very limited class of problems (Minsky & Papert 1969). The perceptron algorithm learns to discriminate between output classes based on a linear combination of its input features. This linearity means that a perceptron can only solve linearly separable problems, where a line (or more generally a hyperplane) can be drawn in input space which separates the output classes. A simple example of a problem which is not linearly separable is the XOR function, since no line can separate the zero cases ($\langle 0,0 \rangle$, $\langle 1,1 \rangle$) from the one cases ($\langle 0,1 \rangle$, $\langle 1,0 \rangle$).

MLPs address this limitation by having multiple layers of units, where the middle layers have processing units whose outputs are a continuous non-linear function of their inputs. These middle layers, called hidden layers, allow an MLP to map the input space into a new space of features where the output classes are linearly separable. In fact, the non-linearity of the hidden units means that MLPs can approximate any arbitrary function (Hornik et al., 1989). Also, because the hidden unit functions are continuous, there is a simple learning algorithm for MLPs, called backpropagation (Rumelhart et al., 1986). In this section we discuss the MLP architecture and learning methods in more detail.

2.1.1   The MLP architecture   An MLP is illustrated in Figure 9.1. The nodes of the graph are the processing units, and the edges are weighted links. The units are organized into input units, output units, and hidden units. Given a vector of input values x placed on the input units, the MLP will compute a vector of output values y on its output units. In the process it will iteratively compute values for each layer of hidden units. MLPs are *feed-forward* networks, which means that there can be no loops in the directed graph of links, so this iterative computation can be done in a single pass from the inputs to the outputs.

A unit j computes its output value, called its activation, as a function of the weights w_{ji} on links from units i to unit j and the activations z_i of these units i. Usually this computation is some function of the weighted sum $w_{j0} + \sum_i z_i w_{ji}$ of

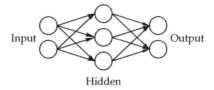

Figure 9.1   A multi-layered perceptron.

j's inputs z_i, where w_{j0} is the bias of j and w_{ji} is 0 if no such link exists. For the hidden units, the output of each unit z_j is often a normalized log-linear function of its weighted inputs, called a sigmoid function:

$$(1) \quad z_j = \frac{1}{1 + \exp\left(-\left(w_{j0} + \sum_i z_i w_{ji}\right)\right)}$$

This non-linear function ranges from 0 to 1.[2]

For the output units y_j, we can approximate a continuous function by simply using the weighted sum $w_{j0} + \sum_i z_i w_{ji}$, or we can do binary classi cation by thresholding this sum. Multi-class classi cation can be done using one output unit per class, and choosing the maximum weighted sum. But most often in NLP we are interested in a probability distribution over classes. For two classes, we can use the sigmoid function (as in logistic regression), and for more than two classes we can use a normalized exponential function. These will be discussed in more detail below when we discuss probability estimation.

The computation performed by a single layer of an MLP should be familiar to anyone familiar with logistic regression or maximum entropy models. The main interest of MLPs (and neural networks in general) is in their layers of hidden units between their inputs and outputs. There are several ways of interpreting hidden layers, but the most intuitive for our purposes is interpreting them as computing a new set of continuous-valued features from their input features. These vectors of features are often called distributed representations, to contrast them with the atomic symbols used in many other AI methods. As discussed above, the original motivation for this computation was to map into a new feature space where the problem could be solved with a (log-)linear model. Although this motivation has since been largely superseded by kernel methods, MLPs still have the advantage that their space of mappings is very general and ef cient, whereas kernels need to be chosen speci c to a problem to balance power against speed. A second motivation is to map a large number of features into a relatively small number of features (in contrast to the explosion of features with kernel methods). This compression provides both greater ef ciency and a form of smoothing across sparse feature spaces. As we will see in Section 2.2, this compression can be repeated iteratively to allow unbounded inputs to be compressed into nite feature vectors.

2.1.2   Learning in MLPs   The rst learning algorithm developed for MLPs was the backpropagation algorithm (Rumelhart et al., 1986). Backpropagation is a simple gradient descent algorithm; the algorithm starts with a random set of weights, and at each step changes the weights a little bit in the direction which will maximally reduce the error (discussed below). Calculating the direction for this update step requires computing the   rst derivative of the error with respect to every weight for a given datapoint, and then summing over datapoints in the training set. Computing this derivative can be easily done in MLPs by iteratively computing the derivative of the error for each layer, starting from the outputs and proceeding backward towards the inputs. As with computing outputs, computing these derivatives can be done in a single pass through the network. This process of propagating the error derivatives back through the network gives rise to the name 'backpropagation.'

There are now many other learning algorithms for MLPs, one of the most popular being conjugate gradient descent. These generally require more complex computations at each step, but converge in many fewer steps. However, due to its simplicity and applicability to many types of ANNs, we will focus on techniques for backpropagation.

While the non-linearity of MLP units gives MLPs the power to approximate any arbitrary function (Hornik et al., 1989), this non-linearity also makes learning much more dif cult. In particular, a fundamental dif culty of learning in MLPs is that pure gradient descent algorithms will only   nd a locally optimal set of weights. If we view an MLP's error as a function of its weights (called the 'error surface'), this function can have many positions where moving in any direction results in an increase in error, called local minima. When gradient descent reaches the bottom of a local minimum it will get trapped, thereby preventing it from   nding the global minimum. Usually we do not care about   nding the exact best set of weights, as long as we   nd a model that is reasonably close to the best, but it is still generally necessary to apply some technique to avoid local minima.

Two common techniques for avoiding local minima are multiple random initializations and stochastic gradient descent. Just by running our learning algorithm multiple times with different random initializations, we can get a sample of the minima and take the best one. This sample also gives us an idea about the extent to which local minima are a problem. Stochastic gradient descent adds randomness directly to each update step, so that the weights sometimes move uphill on the error surface. This allows the weights to 'jump' out of shallow local minima, but is not enough to jump out of the good deep minima. One simple and very common way to implement stochastic gradient descent is to perform updates after each datapoint in the training set (called on-line learning). Pure gradient descent learning requires summing the updates over the whole training set (called batch learning) before changing any weights. By changing weights after each datapoint, the total change is essentially the same as the summed updates, but individual changes vary randomly around that total.

In addition to on-line learning, several techniques have been developed for training MLPs which have proved important to their success. One is momentum, which computes the next update as a weighted average between the current datapoint's update and the previous update:

$$\Delta_{ji}^t = m\Delta_{ji}^{t-1} + (1-m)\delta_{ji}^t$$

where Δ_{ji}^t is the update actually performed for step t, m is the momentum weight, and δ_{ji}^t is the gradient descent update computed on datapoint t. This results in an update which is an exponentially decaying average over the gradient descent updates from the most recent datapoints. Momentum in effect makes on-line learning less random and more like batch learning, meaning that the stochastic gradient descent is less stochastic. This speeds up learning, at the risk of being more susceptible to local minima. By adjusting the momentum m, we can adjust this trade-off.

A second parameter which we can adjust is the learning rate. Weights are updated proportionately to a learning rate η:

$$w_{ji}^t = w_{ji}^{t-1} + \eta\Delta_{ji}^t$$

To guarantee that gradient descent will converge, η needs to be arbitrarily small, but to speed up learning η needs to be suf ciently large. Thus the learning rate is set at a high level early in training and reduced as training proceeds.

Neural networks are very powerful models, so it is important to prevent them from tailoring their weights so precisely to the training data that they do not generalize to the testing data, called 'over tting.' In particular, the larger the MLP's weights become, the more the MLP is able to over t the training data. Over tting is avoided through regularization. Two common forms of regularization for MLPs are weight decay and early stopping.

Weight decay penalizes large weights by subtracting a proportion ρ of each weight from itself:

$$w_{ji}^t = (1-\rho)w_{ji}^{t-1} + \eta\Delta_{ji}^t$$

This is equivalent to a Gaussian prior over weights. It is not applied to the bias weights, since we do not want to assume that unit outputs tend to be near 0.5. As with the learning rate, typically training starts with ρ at a high value and ρ is reduced during training.

Early stopping involves holding out a development set from the training set, and periodically evaluating the MLP on this development set. We stop training when performance on this development set goes down, and we use the best-performing set of weights as our nal model. As with weight decay, by stopping training before performance on the training set reaches its maximum, we prevent weights from growing too large.

2.1.3 Probability estimation Statistical approaches to NLP often require models which produce proper probability estimates. MLPs can be trained to produce probability estimates by choosing appropriate functions for the output and the error. If we use a normalized exponential output function and cross-entropy error

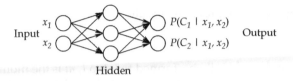

Figure 9.2   Category probabilities estimated by an MLP.

function, then after training, the MLP will output an estimate of the probability distribution over output categories (Bishop 1995).

The normalized exponential output function (often called 'softmax') takes the exponential function of the weighted sum of each category's inputs, and normalizes across categories:

$$(2) \quad y_j = \frac{\exp(w_{j0} + \sum_i z_i w_{ji})}{\sum_{j'} \exp(w_{j'0} + \sum_i z_i w_{j'i})}$$

where z_i is the activation of unit i, w_{ji} is the weight of the link from unit i to unit j, w_{j0} is the bias, and j' ranges over the set of alternative categories including j. The normalization ensures that this function ful ls the formal requirements for a probability distribution over the alternative output categories. When there are only two categories, it is equivalent to use the sigmoid function given in equation (1), where one category has probability estimate y_j and the other $1 - y_j$.

The cross-entropy error function is the negative log probability assigned to the correct category, summed over the training data:

$$(3) \quad error = - \sum_k \log \left(y^k_{target^k} \right)$$

where $y^k_{target^k}$ is the output for datapoint k for the correct category $target^k$.

Training tries to nd the weights which minimize the cross-entropy error function given the normalized exponential output function. Given enough data, the global minimum will be at weights which give us the true probability distribution $P(y^k|x^k)$ over output categories given the input x^k (Bishop 1995).[3] Since our training data is always limited, we cannot expect the model to compute the true probability distribution, but this property ensures that we can consider the outputs as estimates of the true probability.

2.2   Recurrent MLPs

Multi-layered perceptrons compute a function from a xed-length vector of input values to a xed-length vector of output values. This is often insuf cient for NLP tasks, because inputs and outputs are sequences which can be arbitrarily long, such as the words in a sentence. For such problems we can use *recurrent MLPs*. They are called 'recurrent' because their graph of links includes links which loop

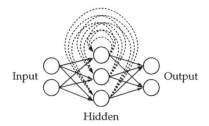

Input   Output

Hidden

Figure 9.3 A recurrent MLP, speci cally a simple recurrent network.

back towards the input, as illustrated by the dotted arrows in Figure 9.3. However, these recurrent links do not represent loops in the ow of information through the network, but instead are interpreted as connecting one position t in the sequence to the subsequent position $t + 1$ in the sequence.

With this de nition of the recurrent links, for any given sequence we can redraw the recurrent MLP as a feed-forward MLP by making a copy of the network for each position t in the sequence, and connecting each pair of adjacent copies t and $t + 1$ with the recurrent links (Rumelhart et al., 1986). Thus the weighted input for a unit j in the copy for position $t + 1$ is $w_{j0} + \sum_i z_i^{t+1} w_{ji} + \sum_i z_i^t w'_{ji}$, where z_i^t is the activation of the copy of unit i at position t, the w_{ji} are the normal link weights and the w'_{ji} are the recurrent link weights. This 'unfolding' can be done for any nite sequence length, so we can apply such a model to arbitrarily long sequences. The weights w_{ji} and w'_{ji} of links in each of the copies is the same as in the original recurrent network, which ensures that the regularities learned by the network generalize across positions t in the sequence. On the other hand, when we compute the activations of the units in the unfolded network, these activations z_i^t may differ across positions t in the sequence, allowing different inputs, hidden values, and outputs for each position.

As mentioned in section 2.1.1, hidden layers can be used to compress their input features into a smaller number of hidden features. With recurrent connections between hidden layers, a recurrent network can compute a compressed representation which itself includes information from previous compressed representations. By performing this compression repeatedly, at each step adding new input features, a recurrent network can compress an unbounded sequence into a nite vector of hidden features. This compression is trained to preserve the information about the sequence history which will be needed for future outputs. However, there is a strong bias in this training towards discovering correlations between inputs and outputs which are close together in the chain of connected hidden layers. If information must be passed through many hidden layers to reach an output with which it is correlated, then learning is unlikely to discover this correlation. For this reason, the pattern of interconnection between hidden layers has a big impact on the inductive bias of learning.

One simple and effective recurrent MLP architecture which uses unbounded compression is simple recurrent networks (SRNs) (Elman 1991), illustrated in Figures 9.3 and 9.4. SRNs use a single hidden layer at each position in a sequence,

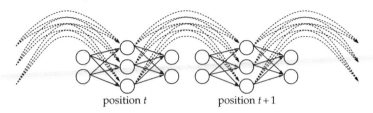

position *t*   position *t* + 1

Figure 9.4   A recurrent MLP unfolded over the sequence.

which has links from that position's input units and from the previous position's hidden units. It is appropriate for modeling sequences where correlations tend to be local in the sequence, because of the inductive bias discussed above.

Many natural language phenomena are best modeled with structures which are more complicated than sequences, such as constituency trees, dependency graphs, or predicate–argument structures. While such structures can be   attened into a sequential derivation, attempts to apply SRNs directly to these derivation sequences have not successfully scaled up beyond small parse-trees (Ho & Chan 1999). This is because correlations are local in the structure, not in the deriva- tion sequence, so a sequential pattern of interconnection imposes an inappropriate inductive bias. Also, the same link weights are applied between any two deriva- tion steps, while the structural relationship between two adjacent decisions can change radically depending on the preceding derivation.

One neural network architecture which has been proposed for such structured classi cation problems is recursive neural networks (RNNs) (Frasconi et al., 1998). RNNs can be applied to any directed acyclic graph, such as a tree. With this approach, a copy of the network is made for each node of the graph, and recur- rent connections are placed between any two copies which have an edge in the graph. This architecture is a direct instantiation of the idea that the pattern of interconnection between hidden layers should re ect locality in the structure being modeled. However, such a simple and direct interpretation of the structure does not always achieve good empirical performance, as was found when it was applied to constituency parsing (Costa et al., 2001).

Another recurrent MLP architecture which has been successfully applied to structure processing is simple synchrony networks (SSNs) (Lane & Henderson 2001; Henderson 2003). SSNs model structures through their derivation sequence (as with SRNs), but the pattern of interconnection between hidden layers is de ned in terms of the structure (as with RNNs), not just the sequence. An exam- ple of such a pattern of interconnection is given in Figure 9.6. Several architectures were originally proposed involving hidden layers assigned to both sentence posi- tions and derivation steps (Lane & Henderson 2001), but recent work has only used the simplest form of SSN architecture, which only has one hidden layer for each derivation step. This architecture is illustrated in Figure 9.5. A given deriva- tion step's hidden layer is linked to hidden layers from previous steps based on the partial structure which has been constructed at that derivation step. A set of

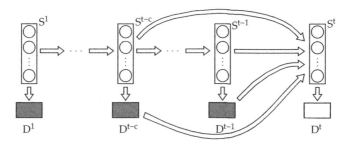

Figure 9.5 The SSN architecture, unfolded over a derivation sequence, with derivation decisions D^t and hidden layers S^t. Connections which are local in the derived structure can be arbitrarily long in the derivation sequence.

structural relationships are de ned which re ect how the designer expects decisions about different nodes in the structure to be correlated, and link weights are learned for each of these relationships. Whenever one of these relationships holds between the current decision and a previous one, their hidden layers are connected with the associated link weights. This architecture allows the system designer to tailor the inductive bias of the model to the appropriate notion of structural locality for the speci c task. SSNs have achieved competitive results in several natural language parsing tasks, as will be discussed more in Section 3.2.

3 Contemporary Research

In recent years, arti cial neural networks have often been viewed as a good engineering tool. They have achieved impressive empirical performance in a number of applications. Of particular note is their success in discovering useful features of words and joint models of multiple tasks. Experience from these successes continues to inspire research in other machine learning methods, such as kernel methods and latent variable models.

3.1 *Language modeling*

One of the main challenges in many NLP applications is the very large number of words that occur in any given language. Typically in NLP each different word (or at least each different lemma) is treated as a distinct atomic category, making it dif cult to generalize from one word to another. A good example of this problem occurs in language modeling, where n-gram models are standard. Neural networks have been used to exploit similarities between words by training feature-based representations of them.

Language modeling is the task of predicting the probabilities of sentences for a given language. The probability of a sentence $P(s_1, \ldots, s_m)$ can be decomposed into a sequence of probabilities $\prod_t P(s_t | s_1, \ldots, s_{t-1})$ for individual words s_t given the words preceding it. Typically these individual probabilities are estimated from a window of $n - 1$ previous words $P(s_t | s_{t-n+1}, \ldots, s_{t-1})$, using smoothed counts of n-grams of words. But n-gram counts become unreliable with large n, because the number of possible n-grams grows with the number of distinct words to the power of n.

3.1.1   Neural network language models   The application of neural networks to language modeling has been successful at improving accuracy over n-gram models by exploiting similarities between words, and thereby estimating reliable statistics even for large n-grams. Bengio et al. (2003) proposed a model consisting of two parts, one which models the similarities between words and one which models the individual probabilities $P(s_t | s_{t-n+1}, \ldots, s_{t-1})$. The latter component is an MLP for estimating probabilities over multiple classes, as discussed in Section 2.1.3. The input to this MLP is the concatenation of $n - 1$ feature vectors, one for each preceding word $s_{t-n+1}, \ldots, s_{t-1}$. These word features are computed with the rst component of the model.

The rst component of the model maps a word s_k to a vector of continuous valued features $C(s_k)$. The vector $C(s_k)$ is not dependent on the position of the word, so a given word is input to the MLP component as the same word features regardless of its relative position. This makes $C(s_k)$ a kind of lexicon. We want the feature vectors in this lexicon to re ect the similarities between words by having similar words share features. In addition, different pairs of words can be similar in different ways, as re ected in which features they share.

The word features $C(s_k)$ and the MLP estimating $P(s_t | s_{t-n+1}, \ldots, s_{t-1})$ are trained jointly to optimize the probability estimate. This results in word features $C(s_k)$ which are trained to re ect exactly the word similarities which are needed by the probability estimation model. For this reason, they work better than nding similarities based on some independent criteria (such as latent semantic indexing, Deerwester et al., 1990), or trying to specify them by hand.

In empirical comparisons, Bengio et al. (2003) found that their neural network model performed signi cantly better than state-of-the-art n-gram models. Further improvement could be achieved by mixing these two models, indicating that these two types of model do well on different parts of the data. Also, as the size of the word window n was increased, the neural network continued to improve with larger n while the n-gram models had stopped improving. This indicates that the representation of word similarity $C(s_k)$ succeeded in overcoming the unreliable statistics of large n-grams.

The main disadvantage Bengio et al. (2003) found was that training times for the neural network language model were very computationally demanding, requiring sophisticated methods for speeding up and parallelizing the computations. Schwenk and Gauvain (2005) succeeded in scaling this model up to even larger data sets (600 million words), and demonstrated an improvement in speech recognition using it.

3.1.2   Neural syntactic language models   One alternative to n-gram language models is to use a syntactic parse to select which previous words are conditioned on when predicting the next word, called a structured language model (Chelba & Jelinek 2000) (SLM, discussed in more detail in Chapter 3). Since the parse cannot be determined unambiguously, such models sum over a selected set of the most probable parses to compute the probability of the word sequence. To improve the accuracy of the language model, while keeping the parsing models simple enough to make parsing ef cient, some SLM models include a separate component which re-estimates the language model probabilities after the best parses have been found.

Emami and Jelinek (2005) investigated combining the advantages of SLMs with the techniques developed for the neural network language models of Bengio et al. (2003). They found signi cant improvements over their baseline SLM by using neural networks. In particular, the largest gain came from replacing the re-estimation component with a neural network. Also replacing the parsing components of the SLM model with neural networks achieved slightly better results, but at substantial computational cost.

3.2 *Parsing*

Natural language parsing (see Chapters 4 and 13) is an important challenge for any machine learning method, both because of the complexity of its structured outputs and because of its signi cance for linguistic and cognitive theories. Neural network parsing models have been amongst the best natural language parsers since Henderson (2003). There are neural network-based models for constituency parsing, dependency parsing, and semantic role parsing.

3.2.1 Constituency parsing The most common benchmark task for natural language parsing is training and testing on the *Wall Street Journal* portion of the Penn Treebank (*WSJ*). This is a corpus of sentences labeled with constituency trees. The standard performance measure is the harmonic mean of precision and recall on labeled constituents, called F-measure.

The only neural network architecture to achieve competitive results on the *WSJ* corpus has been simple synchrony networks. Henderson (2003) exploited SSNs' ability to encode structurally de ned inductive biases to train an SSN to be a statistical model of binarized left-corner derivations of the trees, and achieved 89.5 percent F-measure on the *WSJ* test set. The model includes enough types of interconnection between hidden layers so that any information in the history of the derivation could in theory be passed through a sequence of hidden layers to reach the current derivation decision, so the model imposes no hard independence assumptions. However, decisions about structurally local nodes in the tree are closer together in this ow of information, so correlations tend to be learned for these decisions. An example of the pattern of interconnections between hidden layers is given in Figure 9.6. Experiments where these hidden–hidden connections are replaced with hand-crafted features (non-terminal labels) indicate that the ability to pass information between hidden layers was the main reason for the good empirical performance of this model. The lack of improvement when head

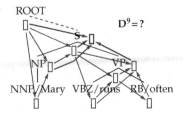

Figure 9.6   An SSN unfolded over a constituency structure.

identi cation was added to the model suggests that the SSN was able to discover the need to identify heads from the distributions in the data without heads being labeled.

As is often the case with neural network models, one of the challenges in designing a successful SSN parser was ef ciency. The choice of binarized left-corner derivations in Henderson (2003) was made because it allowed near-deterministic incremental parsing. This allowed the space of possible parses to be explored using a beam search through the space of possible derivations. The search could be pruned to a small number of candidates after each time the derivations reached a word.

The statistical model estimated by the SSN in Henderson (2003) is generative, meaning that it estimates the joint probability of both the output constituency tree and the input sentence. This means that the SSN tries to learn to accurately predict the words of the sentence, even though we know what those words are before we start parsing. This prediction is important to the model, because it manifests correlations between words and decisions which are made prior to that word in the derivation. If there is a decision in a given candidate derivation which is incompatible with a word to be predicted subsequently, then the model should give that word prediction a very small probability, thereby penalizing the whole derivation. In this way, derivations with compatible previous decisions will be given higher probabilities than those with incompatible previous decisions. Henderson (2004) proposed a method for training the SSN model of Henderson (2003) which maintained this ability to discriminate between compatible and incompatible previous parses, while removing the requirement to learn to accurately predict words which do not discriminate. The SSN was trained to optimize an approximation to the conditional probability of the constituency tree given the sentence. By itself, this discriminatively trained SSN parsing model performed slightly better than the generative SSN model. When the discriminatively trained SSN was used to re-rank candidate parses selected by the generative SSN, there was a substantial improvement, achieving state-of-the-art accuracies (90.1 percent F-measure on the *WSJ* test set) and relatively fast parsing times.

3.2.2   Dependency parsing   Dependency structures encode syntactic structure with labeled directed arcs (dependencies) between the headwords of constituents. Titov and Henderson (2007b) applied SSNs to this task for 10 different languages, achieving the best result for a single-model system in the CoNLL 2007 shared task (Nivre et al., 2007). The approach taken was the same as that taken in Henderson (2003). The SSN is trained to estimate the probabilities for a generative model of dependency structure derivations. Ef ciency is ensured by using derivations that allow near-deterministic parsing, in particular a version of the MALT parser derivations (Nivre et al., 2004). A set of hidden-to-hidden interconnections are de ned which bias towards learning structurally local correlations, and do not impose any hard independence assumptions. The learning of hidden vectors proved to be particularly robust across languages, because it did not suffer from the lack of expertise on particular languages, as would have been the case with methods which require hand-coded feature engineering. Also, the ability to use a very small beam in searching the space of MALT-style derivations means that the parser is rather fast.[4]

3.2.3 Functional and semantic role parsing As exempli ed in Bengio et al. (2003), work on neural networks has often found that sharing hidden representations for multiple related purposes can help the model generalize. This idea has been applied in several neural network models of parsing, where hidden layers are trained jointly for both syntactic parsing and parsing some form of semantic representation. The SSN architecture has been successfully trained on the combinations of constituency parsing with functional parsing (Merlo & Musillo 2005), constituency parsing with semantic role labeling (Musillo & Merlo 2006), and dependency parsing with semantic role labeling (Henderson et al., 2008b; Gesmundo et al., 2009).

Although it has generally been ignored in work on parsing, the Penn Treebank corpus (Marcus et al., 1993) includes extensions to some non-terminal labels which re ect the syntactic or semantic function of the constituents, such as NP-SBJ for *subject* noun phrases or PP-TMP for *temporal* prepositional phrases. Merlo and Musillo (2005) propose a parser which recovers this extended annotation by extending the SSN syntactic parser of Henderson (2003). By jointly training on both the syntactic annotation and the extended functional annotation, they achieve good accuracies on function parsing and a small (but non-signi cant) increase in performance on syntactic parsing.

Musillo and Merlo (2006) applied the same approach to jointly parse syntactic constituency structures and the semantic role labeling in PropBank (Palmer et al., 2005). Again, they modi ed the SSN parser of Henderson (2003) by extending syntactic constituent labels with semantic role labels. However, this approach does not directly encode the structural relationships between the constituents labeled with semantic roles and their predicates in the sentence, which limits the extent to which an appropriate structural domain of locality can be de ned. Empirical results showed no signi cant change in syntactic parsing performance, and good performance on the joint task, although not as good as the state of the art.

Henderson et al. (2008b) solve the problem of recovering both syntactic structure and semantic structure using a synchronous parsing approach. In this work, both syntax and semantics are annotated as dependency structures, consisting of labeled arcs between the headwords of constituents. Two different derivations are de ned, one for the syntactic dependency structure and one for the semantic role dependency structure. Both these derivations process the sentence incrementally from left to right. A joint model of the two structures is de ned by synchronizing these two derivations at each word, alternating between the two derivations each time they reach the prediction of a word.

Henderson et al. (2008b) use an SSN to estimate the probabilities for this joint model of syntactic and semantic structure. Hidden states are divided into two types, those used for making syntactic derivation decisions and those used for making semantic derivation decisions. This division re ects the large differences in the generalizations which need to be learned for the two structures. Interconnections are de ned both between hidden states of the same type and between hidden states of different types. The between-derivation interconnections allow the two derivations to condition their decisions on each other, thereby re ecting the fact that the two structures are highly correlated. Empirical results for this joint model demonstrated good accuracy, amongst the best group of systems on the CoNLL 2008 and 2009 shared tasks (Surdeanu et al., 2008; Hajic et al., 2009). When the two derivations are modeled separately, without the interconnections between syntactic and semantic hidden states, there is a very large drop in accuracy, indicating that joint modeling is crucial to this model's success.

3.2.4 Semantic role tagging   Semantic role labeling is de ned as the task of labeling semantic relationships between predicates and the syntactic constituents which are their arguments. Finding candidate syntactic constituents (or their dependency counterparts) for a predicate's argument roles requires a more complex processing architecture than is necessary for sequence labeling tasks, such as language modeling or part-of-speech tagging. However, not all applications require this form of semantic representation, so it is interesting to consider alternative tasks based on SRL. Collobert and Weston (2007) propose a task where, for each predicate, all the words in a constituent are tagged with the semantic role assigned to that constituent. Words which are not part of any constituent with a semantic role are given the *null* tag. We will call this task semantic role tagging (SRT). Accuracy is measured as the percentage of words tagged correctly, without trying to map these tags back to constituents.[5]

Collobert and Weston (2007) solve this sequence labeling problem by applying an MLP at each individual position of the sentence. The MLP is trained to estimate the probability of each semantic role tag for that word, given a window of words in the sentence. The novel aspect of this model is the way the inputs to the MLP are calculated. This calculation is a linear combination of two sets of parameters: features of each word in the window, and a weight matrix for the distances between this word and the target word and the predicate word. As with the language model of Bengio et al. (2003), the same word features are used wherever the word appears. These features, the distance parameters, and the MLP probability estimator are all trained jointly to optimize the SRT task. This relatively simple model performs well. It outperformed a state-of-the-art SRL system, when the SRL system was evaluated on the SRT task. How well the neural network SRT system would work if it were somehow evaluated on the SRL task is not clear.

A subsequent version of this neural network SRT system (Collobert and Weston 2008) also achieved impressive accuracies on the SRT task. It used a slightly more complicated neural network architecture, which was designed to allow joint learning of a large number of tasks (part-of-speech tagging, chunking, named entity tagging, semantic role tagging, language modeling, and identifying synonyms). As in the previous model, a lexicon of word feature vectors plays a central role in this architecture. These word features are trained jointly across all the tasks. Because only this lexicon is shared, there is no requirement that all the tasks be annotated on the same data set, thereby allowing each task to be trained on whatever data is available for that task. Collobert and Weston (2008) demonstrate that training jointly with other tasks helps nd word features which generalize well for SRT. The largest gain in SRT accuracy is from training the word features in a language model on a large amount of unlabeled data.

3.3 *Theoretical advances*

Neural networks were one of the earliest machine learning methods, and they have had a large in uence on recent advances in machine learning. For example, maximum entropy models can be thought of as single-layer neural networks, without any hidden layers. Also, much of the theory behind support vector machines is related to the theory behind categorization with neural networks. More importantly, latent variables in graphical models have an obvious resemblance to the hidden vectors of neural networks.

One way to understand the relationship between the hidden vectors of neural networks and the latent variables of graphical models has recently been formalized by Titov and Henderson (2007a). They show that MLPs can be interpreted as an approximation to a Bayesian network with the same graphical structure and with normalized exponential potential functions. In particular, they propose a form of Bayesian network called incremental sigmoid belief networks (ISBNs), which can be approximated by SSNs. Titov and Henderson (2007a) show that a more accurate alternative approximation performs better as a model of natural language parsing, but this alternative is much slower, so in many cases it is better to use an SSN. This was the reason SSNs were used in Titov & Henderson (2007b) and Henderson et al. (2008b), despite the discussion being cast in terms of ISBNs. This latent-variable interpretation of MLP models should allow a more theoretically driven advancement of neural network architectures, while maintaining the attractive engineering properties which have resulted in the wide range of empirical successes they have achieved.

4 Further Reading

Due to our focus on statistical modeling, we have not discussed self-organizing maps (SOMs) (Kohonen 1984). SOMs are a clustering method which discovers a multi-dimensional grid of related clusters. Using a two-dimensional grid, they have been applied to visualizing and browsing very large collections of text documents (Kohonen et al., 2000). The SOM learns to place related documents close together on the grid, resulting in a two-dimensional display of the range of topics in the text collection.

The early neurological motivations behind arti cial neural networks have led to many claims about the cognitive plausibility, or lack thereof, of various models. This perspective often goes by the name of connectionism, and contrasts with the non-statistical rule-based symbolic systems that were popular in AI at the time when MLPs were being popularized. Many of the original motivations for these arguments (experience-based, soft constraints, graceful degradation, etc.) are now subsumed by all statistical models. Chapter 17, COMPUTATIONAL PSYCHOLIN-GUISTICS, discusses several connectionist models and their use in psycholinguistic modeling.

The more extreme variants of connectionism, called the 'subsymbolic' approach, eschew any use of system-internal symbols (St. John & McClelland 1992; Miikkulainen 1993), and typically do not consider any architecture to be connectionist if it is more powerful than a recurrent MLP for sequence processing (as in Ho & Chan 1999). This perspective has been criticized on the grounds that such an architecture is not suf ciently powerful to account for the generalizations which exist in natural language (Fodor & McLaughlin 1990). The adequacy of such architectures has been investigated empirically in Lawrence et al. (2000), achieving very limited levels of generalization. A second, looser interpretation of connectionism allows for more powerful computational architectures, but preserves the distributed nature of computation (Henderson 1994; Stevenson 1994; Henderson & Lane 1998). These are sometimes referred to as hybrid connectionist-symbolic approaches. The cognitive plausibility of more powerful neural network architectures can be justi ed by theories of neurological mechanisms to solve the variable binding problem (Shastri & Ajjanagadde 1993; Henderson 2001).

NOTES

1 Note that we consider cognitive models to be outside the scope of this chapter, and connectionist models will only be surveyed brie y due to their poor empirical performance. See Chapter 17, COMPUTATIONAL PSYCHOLINGUISTICS, for discussion of these topics.

2 Often MLPs use the tanh function instead of the sigmoid function. This is just the sigmoid function rescaled so it ranges from −1 to 1. It makes no theoretical difference, but seems to work better in practice.

3 For this to be exactly true, we need to assume that the true probability distribution has an appropriate form, but this is a weak assumption when we have suf cient hidden units. See Bishop (1995) for details.

4 Much of Titov and Henderson (2007b) and Henderson et al. (2008b) (discussed below) describes their models in terms of a latent variable model, incremental sigmoid belief

networks, discussed in Section 3.3. However, the approximation to ISBNs which they use is an SSN, so the actual model tested is an SSN.

5   Collobert and Weston (2007) refer to this new task also as semantic role labeling, but this is inaccurate given the very different nature of the task. In particular, the evaluation measure they use gives equal weight to identifying the *null* tag, which forms the majority of tags for their task. It is therefore not surprising that models trained to optimize SRL do not perform as well on SRT as models trained to optimize SRT.

10 Linguistic Annotation

MARTHA PALMER
AND NIANWEN XUE

1 Introduction

The recent availability of linguistically annotated electronic text has revolutionized the elds of natural language processing and machine translation. The
creation of the Penn Treebank (Marcus et al., 1993) and the word-sense annotated
Semcor (Miller 1995; Fellbaum et al., 1998) showed how even limited amounts of
annotated data can result in major improvements in complex natural language
understanding systems. These and other annotated corpora have led to the training of stochastic natural language processing components which have resulted
in high-level improvements for parsing and word-sense disambiguation (WSD),
similar to the improvements for part-of-speech tagging attributed to the annotation of the Brown corpus and, more recently, the British National Corpus (BNC)
(Burnard 2000b). These successes have encouraged the development of an increasingly wide variety of corpora with richer and more diverse annotation. These
include the Automatic Content Extraction (ACE) annotations (named entity tags,
nominal entity tags, coreference, semantic relations and events); semantic annotations, such as more coarse-grained sense tags (Palmer et al., 2007); semantic role
labels as in PropBank (Palmer et al., 2005), NomBank (Meyers et al., 2004), and
FrameNet (Baker et al., 1998); and pragmatic annotations, such as coreference
(Poesio & Vieira 1998; Poesio 2004), temporal relations as in TimeBank
(Pustejovsky et al., 2003; 2005), the Opinion corpus (Wiebe et al., 2005), and the
Penn Discourse Treebank (Miltsakaki et al., 2004b), to name just a few.

The depth of representation that NLP systems currently aspire to is in fact
de ned by the availability of corresponding linguistic annotations. For machine
learning systems to be trained to produce transformations that add substantially
new information to textual input, they have to rst be exposed to similar information in context. In most cases these systems do an admirable job of automatically
reproducing the same types of annotation, assuming the annotation has been
carried out consistently. The higher the inter-annotator agreement, and the greater
the consistency and coherence of the original annotation, the higher the probability

The Handbook of Computational Linguistics and Natural Language Processing, First Edition.
Edited by Alexander Clark, Chris Fox and Shalom Lappin.
© 2013 Blackwell Publishing Ltd except for editorial material and organization
© 2013 Alexander Clark, Chris Fox, and Shalom Lappin. Published 2013 by Blackwell Publishing Ltd.

of acceptable performance of the trained systems. Not surprisingly, there is now an insatiable demand for more and more annotated data: the same types of annotations for different genres and different languages; newer, richer annotations for the original languages; parallel annotations of parallel corpora; the merging of annotations that were rst done independently; and new formatting for preexisting annotations that makes them easier to merge. For today's NLP systems, the annotation de nes the task, and increasingly rich annotations are the key to more sophisticated systems. Clearly annotation work needs to become much more widely distributed to cope with this need. The eld requires a better understanding of reliable annotation processes for several different types of linguistic annotation that can be readily ported.

It is tempting to assume that recent advances in semi-supervised and unsupervised machine learning (see Chapter 8) may eventually obviate the need for linguistic annotation, but this is not likely. Even unsupervised systems rely on manually annotated data for evaluation purposes. The ready portability of these systems to other genres and languages will simply increase the clamor for additional annotation, albeit in smaller amounts than would be necessary for supervised approaches. Meanwhile, applications that are aiming at the highest possible accuracy levels continue to rely on supervised machine learning.

In this chapter we rst present details of several different speci c annotation projects and then review the basic elements that must be considered to achieve consistent annotation, which are generally applicable to different types of annotation. These include:

- target phenomena de nition;
- corpus selection;
- annotation ef ciency and consistency;
- annotation infrastructure;
- annotation evaluation;
- the use of machine learning for pre-processing and sampling.

2 Review of Selected Annotation Schemes

Covering every individual annotation scheme in every language is beyond the scope of this chapter. In this section we review a representative set of widely used resources that range from syntactic annotation to pragmatic annotation, including:

Syntactic structure, e.g., treebanking Associating a manual syntactic parse (a complicated structure) with every sentence in a corpus consisting of a set of documents. Whether the target structure is dependency structure or phrase structure, this is an unusually dif cult type of annotation that requires in-depth training of annotators. A pre-processing step that involves tokenization, end-of-sentence detection and part-of-speech tagging is usually involved. Because of the labor-intensive nature of treebanking, it is usually done with single annotation – one person looks at each sentence.

Independent semantic classification, e.g., sense tagging   Based on a pre-existing sense inventory or set of semantic classes, every instance of a speci c lemma (a word form corresponding to a unique lexical entry) in a corpus is manually tagged with its relevant sense, or class. This usually involves the same pre-processing as treebanking, including part-of-speech tagging, and is typically done as double-blind annotation (two independent taggers) with adjudication of discrepancies. It requires only minimal training.

Semantic relation labeling, e.g., semantic role labeling   This is a more complex task, since it involves identifying a target relation and one or more participants in that relation. Semantic role labeling often begins with a corpus of parsed sentences, and the arguments associated with distinct subcategorization frames of verbs are given consistent label names according to a prede ned lexical resource of frame descriptions. This is also typically done as double-blind annotation, and can be applied to predicative nouns as well as verbs, or to other types of relations, such as discourse relations and temporal relations. Training must include familiarizing the annotators with the parses, if provided, and the relation descriptions.

Discourse relations   Since they typically involve relations between sentences or sentence fragments, discourse relations can be viewed as an additional type of semantic relation. For example, the Penn Discourse Treebank (PDTB), funded by NSF, is based on the idea that discourse connectives such as *and, but, then, while,* ... can be thought of as predicates with associated argument structures (Miltsakaki et al., 2004a).

Temporal relations   Our nal example of semantic relations consists of temporal relations, such as those found in TimeBank. Given a corpus where both nominal and verbal events and their participants have been identi ed, relations between the events, such as temporal and subordinating relations, are identi ed and labeled using a prede ned set of relationship types.

Coreference tagging   References to entities in a document are identi ed as mentions, and mentions of the same entity are linked as being coreferent, or members of a coreference set. These can include pronouns, nominal entities, named entities, elided arguments, and events. Techniques for annotating and evaluating entire sets of coreferences are signi cantly more complex than techniques for straightforward class-labeling or relation-labeling tasks.

Opinion tagging   The annotation of opinions, evaluations, emotions, sentiments, and other private states in text is collectively described as opinion tagging or sentiment tagging. At its simplest this could be seen as a type of semantic classi cation task, but since the tagging typically includes   lling in several different feature values rather than simply assigning class labels, it is discussed separately.

These different types of annotation are all described in more detail below.

2.1   *Syntactic structure, e.g., treebanking*

The dramatic improvement in natural language parsing achieved during the last two decades or so has been generally attributed to the emergence of statistical and machine learning approaches (Collins 1999; Charniak 2000). However, statistical and machine learning methods are only possible with the availability of large-scale treebanks, corpora of hand crafted syntactic trees. The Penn Treebank (PTB) (Marcus et al., 1993) played a special role in providing a shared data set on which competing parsing approaches are trained and tested. In our view, there are two main factors that contributed to the success of the Penn Treebank. The   rst one has to do with its size. Although not the   rst syntactically annotated corpus, the Penn Treebank is the   rst one that covers over two million words of text. Statistical approaches to natural language parsing require large quantities of training data to get reliable statistics for the large number of grammatical and lexical phenomena in a language, and this is provided by the Penn Treebank. The one-million-word *Wall Street Journal* subcorpus of the PTB is the most frequently used data set even though *Wall Street Journal* articles are not particularly representative of the English language. The other factor for the PTB's success is its pragmatic approach. Many key annotation decisions are driven by engineering desiderata rather than purely by linguistic considerations. This often means that theoretically important linguistic distinctions that are hard to make are left unspeci ed for the sake of annotation consistency. For example, the argument/adjunct distinction has been a key building block for theoretical linguistics, but is avoided in the Penn Treebank. In hindsight, this decision cuts both ways. On the one hand, it simpli es the annotation task and has led to more consistent annotation. On the other hand, it leaves out key information that has to be recovered later in the semantic layer of annotation. For example, the argument/adjunct distinction had to be made at least super cially in the development of the PropBank (Palmer et al., 2005), which adds a layer of predicate–argument annotation to the Penn Treebank.

2.1.1   Phrase-structure treebanks   The success of the Penn Treebank inspired the development of treebanks in other languages. At Penn, the Chinese (Xue et al., 2005), Korean (Han et al., 2002) and Arabic (Maamouri & Bies, forthcoming) treebanks have all been developed using a similar annotation scheme. This annotation scheme is characterized by labeled phrase structures, supplemented by functional tags that represent grammatical relations such as subject (-SBJ), temporal (-TMP) and locational modi ers (-LOC), as well as empty categories and co-indices that link empty categories to their explicit coreferents, a hallmark of generative grammar. Empty categories and co-indices are used to represent left-displacement, but they are by no means the only way to represent movement phenomena. The

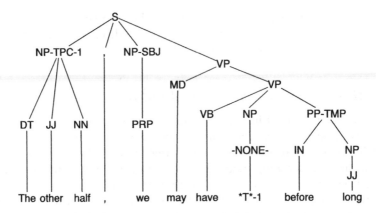

Figure 10.1   An example PTB tree.

different aspects of the representation scheme are illustrated in Figure 10.1: *The other half* is an NP with the functional tag -TPC, indicating it is an NP playing the role of a topic, a grammatical position in English syntax. This topic originates in the object position of the verb *have* and then moves to the sentence-initial position. This information is represented by the empty category *T* in the object position co-indexed with the topic in the sentence-initial position. The empty category and co-indexation mechanism localize the arguments for a predicate and thus make it easier to extract the predicate–argument structure. *The other half* is made adjacent to the verb *have* by positing an empty category *T* that is co-indexed with it. Although *head* is a prominent notion in generative grammar, it is not explicitly represented in the Penn Treebank. However, the notion of head is implicitly built into the structural con guration of a phrase and in principle can be identi ed via a nite set of rules de ned for each syntactic category. For example, the verb *have* is assumed to be the head of the VP *have *T*-1 before long* by virtue of being the rst verb in this VP. This set of rules is generally referred to as a head table and is widely referenced in statistical parsing literature (Xia & Palmer 2001). In practice, due to annotation errors and underspeci ed annotation, the head cannot always be reliably identi ed. Therefore, in some phrase-structure annotation schemes, the head is explicitly marked to avoid such pitfalls when extracting the head. For example, the Tiger corpus for German (Brants et al., 2002) explicitly marks the head of a phrase.

2.1.2   Dependency treebanks   The Prague Dependency Treebank (Hajic 1998) represents a radically different annotation scheme in the functional generative description framework, following the Prague dependency tradition. At the core of this annotation scheme is the dependency relation between a head and its dependent. While in a phrase-structure representation the explicit markup of the head is optional, identifying the head is essential in a dependency structure. The dependency relation between a head and its dependent is the building block of the dependency structure of a sentence. A dependency structure representation of the

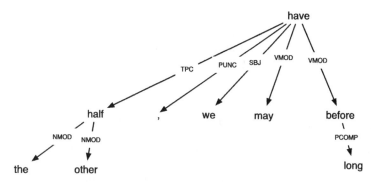

Figure 10.2 A labeled dependency structure.

same sentence as in Figure 10.1 is provided in Figure 10.2. While in a PTB-style phrase structure the dependency between the verb *have* and the topic *the other half* is mediated via a co-indexation mechanism, in the dependency structure this relation is represented directly. Another key difference is that, while the syntactic categories of constituents in a phrase-structure tree represent the distributional properties of the constituents, e.g., noun phrases generally occur in subject and object positions, etc., the focus of a dependency representation is on the relation between a head and its dependent. Therefore, while the nodes in a dependency tree are labeled by the head, which is not particularly informative other than saying the parent is the head and the child is the dependent, the edges are often labeled with dependency relations such as subject and object. For example, there is a SBJ relation between *have* and *we*, and a TPC relation between *have* and *the other half*. As Xia & Palmer (2001) showed, since there are no phrasal labels in a dependency representation and, more importantly, the subject and complement are all attached to the head at the same level, it is generally not possible to automatically convert a dependency tree such as the one in Figure 10.2 to the PTB-style phrase-structure representation. On the other hand, assuming that the head can be reliably identi ed, it is possible to automatically derive this dependency-structure representation from a phrase-structure representation. However, since there is no limit to the possible labels for dependency relations, it might be possible to label dependency relations in such a way that a phrase-structure representation can be reconstructed.

There is a growing realization that both dependency- and phrase-structure treebanks are needed. In fact, both tree adjoining grammar (TAG) and lexical functional grammar (LFG) provide in a sense a combination of phrase-structure and dependency-structure representations, with the LFG c-structure (constituent structure) corresponding to the phrase-structure layer and the LFG f-structure (functional structure) corresponding to the dependency-structure layer. With TAG the derivation tree is the constituent structure and the derived tree is closer to the dependency structure. Although there are no manually annotated large-scale LFG style or TAG-style treebanks that we are aware of, there have been efforts to convert the phrase-structure annotation of the Penn Treebank into both TAG structures (Xia et al., 2001) and LFG f-structures (Cahill et al., 2002), and this has provided training data for successful statistical TAG and LFG parsers. There is a recent initiative funded by NSF to build a Hindi/Urdu dependency treebank that has rich enough annotation that it can be readily converted to a phrase structure treebank (Bhatt et al., 2009).

2.2   *Semantic classification, e.g., sense tagging*

Sense tagging is essentially a semantic classi cation task. Given a set of prede ned semantic labels for a distinct lexical item, one or more labels are associated with each occurrence of that item in a sentential context in a corpus. For instance, the *call* lemma in (1) is tagged with the OntoNotes (see Section 2.8) Sense 1, corresponding to **communicate orally, usually in a loud, distinct tone**.

(1)   *"You people here think this is Russian music," she said with disdain, and* **called** *over to the waitress: "Could you turn it off?"*

In contrast, (2) is tagged with Sense 5, to **label with a name or quality**.

(2)   *"A spokesman for the state, however,* **calls** *the idea 'not effective or cost efficient.' "*

The traditional assumption is that the labels correspond to sense entries from a pre-existing sense inventory, such as a dictionary, and annotators apply these labels after reading the sentence containing the lemma.

There are other closely related tasks such as nominal entity tagging which are also basically semantic classi cation tasks but with different notions of where the class labels come from. Nominal entity tagging, as de ned by the Automatic Content Extraction (ACE) project (Strassel et al., 2008), is focused primarily on nouns and consists of choosing a semantic category from a prede ned category list (PERson, ORGanization, GeoPoliticalEntity, LOCation, FACility, SUBstance, VEHicle, WEApon)[1] for each occurrence of the noun in context in a corpus. Several nouns, especially proper nouns such as *the White House*, can have multiple tags, such as PER, GPE, or LOC. In these cases, determining which tag is appropriate, given a speci c sentence as the context, amounts to the equivalent of a sense-tagging task. An important difference is that for nominal entity tagging there is one set of sense tags for all nouns, rather than a unique set of sense tags for each lexical item. However, the entity type tags can easily be mapped to standard dictionary sense entries, which for nouns in particular are often separated according to semantic category. For instance, in the following example the de nition of *regulator* has two senses, one of which can be mapped to the SUBstance category and the other of which can be mapped to the ORGanization or PERson category. If a corpus containing this word had already been annotated with nominal entity categories, then those category labels for *regulator* could be deterministically mapped to either Sense 1 or Sense 2, providing a sense-tagged corpus.

regulator

1: a device to control the rate of some activity,
e.g., chemical or mechanical – SUBSTANCE

2: an of cial with responsibility to supervise some
domain of social activity – ORG, PER

2.2.1 Choosing the sense inventory Clearly the most important decision in creating sense-tagged corpora (or nominal entity tagged corpora) is the choice of the sense inventory (or label set) that will be used. For classic sense-tagging tasks this is a computational lexicon or a machine readable dictionary that partitions the meaning of each word into numbered senses, allowing the word plus a number to uniquely refer to an entry. An ideal sense inventory should make clear and consistent sense distinctions for each word. Unfortunately, sense inventories for a language can be discouragingly diverse, with signi cant differences with respect to entries for polysemous words, and different levels of granularity of the sense distinctions. Corpora tagged with two different English sense inventories will not provide coherent training data unless a comprehensive mapping can be provided between every entry, and the mappings are often not one-to-one (Palmer et al., 2007).

The sense-tagged data itself can be framed as either lexical sample data or as an all-words corpus. In the all-words corpus, all words (or all content words) in a running text or discourse are tagged. While super cially similar to part-of-speech tagging,[2] all-words tagging via a sense inventory is signi cantly different in that a different set of sense tags is required for each lemma. If public distribution is desired, this severely limits the choice of possible sense inventories, because it requires access to a publicly available, wide-coverage dictionary that is preferably also free or at least low-cost. For a lexical sample corpus, a sample of words is carefully selected from the lexicon, along with a number of corpus instances of each word to be tagged. Unlike all-words tagging, dictionary entries are required only for these selected words, so given a small enough sample of words, there could be more exibility in dictionary choice.

The methodology for manual annotation depends on the type of tagging. Words can be annotated more quickly and consistently if all instances of a word (type) are tagged at once (targeted tagging), instead of tagging all words sequentially as they appear in the text. The advantages of targeted tagging make lexical sample tagging easier to implement than all-words tagging. The largest all-words corpus, SemCor, based on the Brown corpus (Francis & Kucera 1982), is tagged with WordNet senses (Miller 1995). Created by George Miller and his team at Princeton University, WordNet (Miller et al., 1990b; Miller & Fellbaum 1991; Fellbaum et al., 1998) is a large electronic database organized as a semantic network built on paradigmatic relations including synonymy, hyponymy, antonymy, and entailment. WordNet has become the most widely used lexical database today for NLP research, and its approach has now been ported to several other languages, such as several European languages in EuroWordNet (Vossen 1998) and in BalkaNet (Stamou et al., 2002), as well a Japanese (Bond et al., 2008) and a Chinese Word-Net (Xu et al., 2008). WordNet lists the different senses for each English open-class word (nouns, verbs, adjectives, and adverbs). Sense tagging is typically done as double-blind annotation by two linguistically or lexicographically trained anno-tators, with a third tagger adjudicating between inter-annotator differences to create a gold standard. Because of issues that have been raised about low ITA rates due to ne-grained sense distinctions in English WordNet, and correspond-ing unacceptably low system performance, manual groupings of WordNet senses are now being used for tagging in a large DARPA-funded project (see Section 2.8).

2.3   Semantic relation labeling, e.g., semantic role labeling

A closely related but distinct semantic annotation task involves identifying within a single sentence a relation and its arguments, and then labeling the arguments. The classic example is a verb where the labels of the verb arguments, once they have been identi ed, correspond to *semantic role labels*. The semantic role labels are intended to indicate a speci c semantic relation between a verb and its argument that holds consistently even when the argument is in different syntactic positions. This description covers several current semantic role labeling tasks, in which the semantic roles can come variously from PropBank (Palmer et al., 2005), FrameNet (Baker et al., 1998), VerbNet (Kipper et al., 2006), or the Prague tecto-grammatical formalism (Hajic et al., 2000). It can also be extended to similar semantic roles that are introduced by other parts of speech, such as nominal or adjectival elements. A major difference between sense tagging and semantic role labeling is the inter-dependence between the semantic role labels. If the Agent, or Arg0, of a verb has already been labeled, that changes the available choices for the remaining argu-ments. This interdependence of labels is also the case for discourse relations and temporal relations; however, given the distinctive nature of these annotation tasks, they will be dealt with in separate sections. ACE relations, which are also similar, are discussed at the end of this section.

2.3.1   The Proposition Bank   The Proposition Bank, originally funded by ACE (DOD), focuses on the argument structure of verbs, and provides a corpus annotated with semantic roles, including participants traditionally viewed as arguments and adjuncts. Correctly identifying the semantic roles of the sentence constituents, or *Who did what to whom, and when, where and how?* is a crucial part of interpreting text and, in addition to forming a component of the information extraction problem, can serve as an intermediate step in machine translation, automatic summarization, or question answering.

At the beginning of the PropBank project, the decision was made to associate the semantic role labels directly with nodes in the Penn Treebank phrase-structure parses. The boundaries of the constituents corresponding to the nodes were already de ned, so the annotators did not have to add that task to their duties, simplifying their cognitive load. The PTB also had indicated empty arguments, so these could easily be given semantic role labels as well, making the annotation more complete. Finally, the assumption was that the syntax and semantics would be highly correlated, with the semantic roles occurring within the domain of locality of the predicating element. Therefore having access to the syntactic structure should help in simplifying and focusing the task for the annotators. In contrast, FrameNet (see below) annotation did not initially begin with pre-parsed sentences, and this was found to lower agreement among the annotators, primarily because of different constituent boundary decisions. Another feasible method is to annotate dependency structure parses directly with semantic role labels, and the Hindi/Urdu Treebank project will explore this approach in depth. One of the questions to be addressed is the issue of empty arguments; if empty arguments have not been inserted by the dependency annotation, should they be added at the PropBank level? Since the goal of this project is to eventually convert the dependency structure + PropBank annotation automatically into a phrase-structure treebank, having the empty arguments in place could simplify the conversion process (Bhatt et al., 2009).

The one-million word Penn Treebank II *Wall Street Journal* corpus has been successfully annotated with semantic argument structures for verbs and is now available via the Penn Linguistic Data Consortium as PropBank I (Palmer et al., 2005). More speci cally, PropBank annotation involves three tasks: argument labeling, annotation of modi ers, and creating coreference chains for empty arguments. The rst goal is to provide consistent argument labels across different syntactic realizations of the same verb, as in

(3)   a)   "[ARG0 John] [REL broke] [ARG1 the window]"
      b)   "[ARG1 The window] [REL broke]."

The Arg1 or PATIENT in (3a) is the same window that is annotated as the Arg1 in (3b), even though it is the syntactic subject in one sentence and the syntactic object in the other. As this example shows, semantic arguments are tagged with numbered argument labels, such as Arg0, Arg1, Arg2, where these labels are de ned on a verb-by-verb basis. The second task of the PropBank annotation involves assigning functional tags to all modi ers of the verb, such as MNR (manner), LOC (locative), TMP (temporal), DIS (discourse connectives), PRP (purpose) or DIR (direction), and others, as in (4).

(4)   "[ARG0 John] [REL broke] [ARG1 the window] [ARGM:TMP yesterday]."

Finally, PropBank annotation involves nding antecedents for empty arguments of the verbs, as in (5).

(5)   *"You people here think this is Russian music," she **said** [*T*-1] with disdain, and called over to the waitress: "Could you turn it off?"*

The object of the verb *say* in this example, *You people here think this is Russian music* is represented as an empty category [*T*-1] in the treebank. In PropBank, all empty categories that could be coreferred with an NP within the same sentence are linked in coreference chains. So the [*T*-1] is linked to *You people here think this is Russian music*. The primary goal of PropBank is to supply consistent, simple, general-purpose labeling of semantic roles for a large quantity of coherent text that can provide training data for supervised machine learning algorithms, in the same way the Penn Treebank has supported the training of statistical syntactic parsers. PropBank also provides a lexicon which lists, for each broad meaning of each annotated verb, its *Frameset*, i.e., the possible arguments in the predicate and their labels and all possible syntactic realizations. PropBank's focus is verbs, so NomBank, an annotation of nominalizations and other noun predicates using PropBank style Framesets, was done at NYU, also funded by ACE (Meyers et al., 2004).

2.3.2   FrameNet   FrameNet consists of collections of semantic frames, lexical units that evoke these frames, and annotation reports that demonstrate uses of lexical units. Each semantic frame speci es a set of frame elements, or arguments. Semantic frames are related to one another via a set of possible relations such as **is-a** and **uses**. Frame elements are classi ed in terms of how central they are to a particular frame, distinguishing three levels: core, peripheral, and extra-thematic. FrameNet is designed to group lexical items based on frame semantics, and sets of verbs with similar syntactic behavior may appear in multiple frames, while a single FrameNet frame may contain sets of verbs with related senses but different subcategorization properties. FrameNet places a primary emphasis on providing rich, idiosyncratic descriptions of semantic properties of lexical units in context, and making explicit subtle differences in meaning. As such it could provide an important foundation for reasoning about context-dependent semantic represen-tations. However, the large number of frame elements and the current sparse-ness of available annotations for each one has been an impediment to machine learning.

2.3.3   VerbNet   VerbNet is midway between PropBank and FrameNet in terms of lexical speci city, and is closer to PropBank in its close ties to syntactic struc-ture. It consists of hierarchically arranged verb classes, inspired by and extended from classes of Levin (1993). Each class and subclass is characterized by its set of verbs, by a list of the arguments of those verbs, and by syntactic and seman-tic information about the verbs. The argument list consists of thematic roles (23 in total) and possible selectional restrictions on the arguments expressed using binary predicates. Additional semantic predicates describe the participants dur-ing various stages of the event described by the syntactic frame, and provide class-speci c interpretations of the thematic roles. VerbNet now covers over 6,000 senses for 5,319 lexemes. A primary emphasis for VerbNet is the coherent syntactic and semantic characterization of the classes, which will facilitate the acquisition of new class members based on observable syntactic and semantic behavior.

2.3.4 SemLink Although PropBank, FrameNet, and VerbNet have all been created independently, with differing goals, they are surprisingly compatible in their shared focus on labeling verb arguments. PropBank uses very generic labels such as Arg0, as in (6).

(6) *"[ARG0 President Bush] has [REL approved] [ARG1 duty-free treatment for imports of certain types of watches]."*

In addition to providing several alternative syntactic frames and a set of semantic predicates, VerbNet marks the PropBank Arg0 in this sentence as an Agent, and the Arg1 as a Theme. FrameNet labels them as Grantor and Action respectively, and puts them in the Grant_Permission class. The additional semantic richness provided by VerbNet and FrameNet does not contradict PropBank, but can be seen as complementary. These resources can also be seen as complementary with WordNet, in that they provide explicit descriptions of participants and ties to syntactic structure that WordNet does not provide. The PropBank labels, being the most generic, will cover the widest number of WordNet senses for a particular word. A verb in a VerbNet class will also usually correspond to several WordNet senses, which are explicitly marked. FrameNet provides the nest sense granularity of these resources, and speci c FrameNet frames are more likely to map onto individual WordNet senses. There are signi cant differences in the coverage of lexemes and the structuring of data in each of these resources, which could be used to bootstrap coverage extensions for each one. The simple labels provided by PropBank are more amenable to machine learning, and have resulted in the training of successful automatic semantic role labeling systems. A semi-automatic mapping from PropBank to VerbNet has been produced (and hand corrected) which has been used to successfully train systems that can produce either PropBank or VerbNet semantic role labels (Yi et al., 2007). Altogether, 3,465 types have been mapped, comprising over 80 percent of the tokens in the PropBank. In parallel a type-to-type mapping table from VerbNet class(es) to FrameNet frame(s) has been created, as well as a mapping from role label to frame element. This will facilitate the generation of FrameNet representations for every VerbNet version of a PropBank instance that has an entry in the table.

2.3.5 ACE relations This style of annotation also bears a close resemblance to the ACE relation task, which is aimed at detecting within a sentence a particular type of relation and its arguments (LDC 2008). There is a shift in focus with ACE, however, from a lexically oriented, linguistically motivated task, such as semantic role labeling, to a more pragmatic, relation-type task. The relation types include: PHYSICALly located, as in LOCATED or NEAR (see (7)); PART-WHOLE, which could be a GEOGRAPHICAL PART-WHOLE relation, such as Colorado being PART of the United States, or SUBSIDIARY, as in Umbria being a SUBSIDIARY or PART of JD Powers; PERSONAL-SOCIAL, as in BUSINESS (co-workers), FAMILY (siblings), or LASTING-PERSONAL (life-long neighbors);

ORG-AFFILIATION, which includes EMPLOYMENT, OWNERSHIP, FOUNDER, etc.; AGENT-ARTIFACT, and others. For example, there is a *PHYSICALly Located* relation between 'Barack Obama' and 'Germany' in (7). An important distinction is that the same ACE relation type could be introduced by a verb, a noun or a preposition, so the annotators need to focus more on semantic content and less on syntactic structure.

(7)   "**Barack Obama** *traveled to* **Germany** *to give a speech at Buchenwald.*"

2.4   TimeBank

TimeBank (Pustejovsky et al., 2003) is a corpus annotated with temporal information based on TimeML (Pustejovsky et al., 2005), a general-purpose temporal markup language that has been adopted as an ISO (International Organization for Standardization) semantic annotation standard (ISO/TC 37/SC 4/WG 2, 2007). The basic elements of the TimeML are events, time expressions, and signals, as well as temporal relations between these temporal entities. For example, in (8), *glossed, warnings, strikes, do,* and *harm* would all be identi ed as anchors of events in the TimeBank annotation; *Thursday* would be marked up as a temporal expression; and *on* would be marked as a signal for the temporal relation between the glossing-over event and the temporal expression *Thursday.* Temporal relations also hold between events. For example, the *strike* event would precede the *harm* event, which would in turn be annotated as identical to the *do* event.

(8)   "*President Clinton, meantime,* **glossed** *over stern* **warnings** *from Moscow* **on Thursday** *that US air* **strikes** *against Iraq could* **do** *serious* **harm** *to relations with the Kremlin.*"

TimeML adopts a broad de nition of event. *Event* for TimeBank is a cover term for situations that *happen* or *occur.* Events can be punctual or last for a period of time. The TimeBank events also include *states* or *circumstances* in which something obtains or holds true. However, TimeBank does not mark up all states in a document. It only annotates states that are relevant to temporal interpretation, for example, states that are identi ably changed during the document time (9a), or states (9b) that are directly related to a temporal expression. States that persistently hold true are excluded from annotation. Syntactically, events can be realized as verbs, nominalizations, adjectives, predicative clauses, or prepositional phrases.

(9)   a)   "*All 75* **on board** *the Aeroflot Airbus died.*"
      b)   "*They* **lived** *in U.N.-run refugee camps for 2 1/2 years.*"

A time expression belongs to one of four types: Date, Time, Duration or Set. A Date describes a calendar time, and examples are *Friday, October 1, 1999, yesterday, last week.* Time refers to a time of day, even if it is inde nite, e.g., *ten minutes from three, five to eight, late last night.* Durations are assigned to explicit durations such as *2 months,* and *48 hours.* Finally, a Set describes a set of times, e.g., *twice a week* or *every two days*. Time expressions are also annotated with a normalized value. For example, *twelve o'clock midnight* would be normalized to **T24:00**.

A signal is a textual element that makes explicit the temporal relation between a temporal expression and an event, or between a temporal expression and a temporal expression, or between an event and an event. Signals are generally temporal prepositions such as *on, in, at, from, to,* or temporal conjunctions such as *before, after, while, when,* as well as special characters like '-' and '/' that indicate ranges of time.

Events, time expressions, and signals are temporal entities that are linked by temporal relations to form an overall temporal interpretation of a text. The main temporal relations are represented by Temporal Links (TLINKs), which represent the temporal relation between events, betwen times, or between an event and a time. The TLINK annotation is illustrated in (10), where there is a BEFORE relation between the events anchored by *invited* and *come*, which means the inviting event happens before the coming event.

(10)   *"Fidel Castro* **invited** *John Paul to* <u>come</u> *for a reason."*

Subordination Links (SLINKs) are another type of temporal link, and they are used to represent modal, factive, counter-factive, evidential, and negative evidential relations, as well as conditional relations that usually hold between a main event and a subordinate event. For example, in (11), an SLINK can be established between the events anchored by *adopt* and *ensure*.

(11)   *"The Environmental commission must* **adopt** *regulations to* <u>ensure</u> *people are not exposed to radioactive waste."*

A third and nal type of link is the Aspectual Link (ALINK), which represents the relationship between an aspectual event and its argument event. The relation that an ALINK represents can be one of ve types: Initiates, Culminates, Terminates, Continues, or Reinitiates. The example in (12) represents an Initiates relation between the events anchored by *began* and *trading*.

(12)   *"The stock* **began** <u>trading</u> *this summer at $14 apiece."*

Achieving consistency in the TimeBank annotation has proven to be very dif cult, with temporal ordering of events being the most challenging part of the annotation. It is neither feasible nor necessary to temporally order each pair of events in a document, but without some clear guidance, different annotators tend to choose different pairs of events to annotate, leading to poor inter-annotator agreement. In practical temporal annotation, some form of temporal inference mechanism has to be implemented (Verhagen 2005) so that the temporal ordering of some pairs of events can be automatically inferred. The ne-grained nature of some temporal relations also makes it dif cult to separate one relation from another.

2.5 Discourse relation annotation

Treebank and PropBank annotations are all focused on getting linguistic information from within the sentence. More recently, there have been efforts to annotate
linguistic structures beyond the sentence level. These new efforts make the structure of a whole text their target of annotation. In this subsection we discuss two
such projects, the RST Corpus and the Penn Discourse Treebank project, which
have taken very different approaches to discourse-structure annotation.

2.5.1 RST Corpus The RST Corpus (Carlson et al., 2003) consists of 385 articles
from the Penn Treebank, representing over 176K words of text. The RST Corpus is
hierarchically annotated in the framework of Rhetorical Structure Theory (Mann
and Thompson 1988). In rhetorical structure theory, the discourse structure of a
text is represented as a tree, and the leaves of the tree are text fragments that represent the minimal units of discourse, called *elementary discourse units* or EDUs.
Each node in the discourse tree is characterized by a *rhetorical relation* that holds
between two or more adjacent nodes, and corresponds to contiguous spans of text.
The rhetorical relation between the children of a node is characterized by *nuclearity*, with the nucleus being the essential unit of information, while a satellite
indicates a supporting or background unit of information.

The annotation of the RST Corpus starts off by identifying the elementary discourse units, or EDUs, which are building blocks of a discourse tree. The EDUs
roughly correspond to clauses, although not all clauses are EDUs. For example,
a subordinate clause that is an adjunct to the main clause is usually an EDU, but
clauses that are subjects, objects, or complements of a main clause are not usually
EDUs.

The discourse relations between child discourse units of a node in the discourse
tree can be either mononuclear or multinuclear, based on the relative salience of
the discourse units. A mononuclear relation is between two discourse units where
one is the nucleus and another is the satellite. The nucleus represents the more
salient or essential information while the satellite indicates supporting and background information. A multinuclear relation is between two or more discourse
units that are of equal importance and thus are all nuclei. This in a way paral-
lels the endocentric and exocentric structures at the sentence level. A total of 53
mononuclear and 25 multinuclear relations are used to annotate the RST Corpus;
these 78 relations fall into 16 broad classes. These discourse relations are identi ed
empirically, based on evidence from the corpus. 'Elaboration' is an example of a
mononuclear discourse relation, while 'list' is a multinuclear discourse relation.
For the complete set of discourse relations tagged in the RST, the reader is referred
to the discourse tagging manual of the RST Corpus.

2.5.2 The Penn Discourse Treebank While the RST annotation of discourse
relations is organized around EDUs, the building blocks of the Penn Discourse
Treebank (Miltsakaki et al., 2004) are discourse connectives and their arguments. The annotation framework of the Penn Discourse Treebank is based on

a theoretical framework developed in Webber and Joshi (1998), where discourse connectives are considered to be predicates that take abstract objects such as events, states, and propositions as their arguments. The Penn Discourse Treebank annotates both *explicit* and *implicit* discourse connectives and their arguments. Explicit discourse connectives include subordinating conjunctions and coordinating conjunctions, as well as discourse adverbials. While in most cases the arguments of discourse connectives are local and adjacent to the discourse connective, they do not have to be. Webber et al. (Webber & Joshi 1998) considers subordinating and coordinating conjunctions to be *structural* in the sense that their arguments are local to the discourse connective, while discourse adverbials are considered to be *anaphorical*, because their rst arguments can be long-distance.

Where explicit discourse connectives are absent, implicit discourse connectives are inserted between paragraph-internal sentence pairs, as illustrated in (13). In some cases, it may not be possible to insert a discourse connective because the discourse relation is expressed with a non-discourse connective element, or because discourse coherence is achieved by an entity chain, or simply because there is no relation of any kind.

(13)   *"Motorola is fighting back against junk mail. [ARG1 So much of the stuff poured into its Austin, Texas, offices that its mail rooms there simply stopped delivering it]. Implicit=so [ARG2 Now, thousands of mailers, catalogs and sales pitches go straight into the trash]."*

The lexically grounded approach of the Penn Discourse Treebank opens the door for the possibility that one discourse connective might be a lexical realization of multiple discourse relations. The Penn Discourse Treebank addresses this by specifying an inventory of discourse relations that serve as senses of the discourse connectives. In a way, this inventory is similar to the set of discourse relations adopted by the RST, while the actual discourse relations posited might be different. Like the RST Corpus, the discourse relations are hierarchically organized. The top level has four major semantic classes: TEMPORAL, CONTINGENCY, COMPARISON, and EXPANSION. For each class, a second level of *type* is de ned, and then for each type, there may be a third level of *subtype* de ned. There are 16 types and 23 subtypes. Some types do not have subtypes. The reader is referred to the PDTB annotation manual for details.

2.5.3 A comparison of the two approaches   The RST Corpus and the Penn Discourse Treebank represent very different approaches to the annotation of discourse relations. The most fundamental difference is that the RST Corpus is committed to building a discourse tree representation for the entire text. The leaves of the tree are elementary discourse units or EDUs, which are non-overlapping spans of text. Discourse units built on the EDUs are also non-overlapping spans of text, and discourse relations are always local in the sense that they only hold between adjacent discourse units. The Penn Discourse Treebank, on the other hand, is not committed to a tree representation of the entire text. The building blocks are discourse connectives, which are treated as predicates, the arguments of which are identi ed for each discourse connective instance in a text, whether they are explicit or implicit. Although the text spans that are identi ed as arguments of a discourse connective never overlap, there is no guarantee that arguments of different connectives do not overlap. In fact, Lee et al. (2006) show that there is a variety of possible patterns of dependencies between pairs of discourse relations, including nested, crossed, and other non-tree-like con gurations. Part of the reason for this complex structure is due to the anaphoric discourse relations for discourse adverbials, whose arguments are not necessarily local, as discussed above.

Another reason why there exist complex dependencies in the Penn Discourse Treebank is the way *attribution* is annotated. PDTB adopts the strict view that discourse relations are between abstract objects such as events, states, and propositions. Since attributions are relations between an agent and a proposition, the attribution annotation is treated as a separate layer of annotation. Depending on the context, the attribution may be included as part of an argument in some cases but excluded in others – (14) is an example. The higher verb 'He said' is included as an argument of ALTHOUGH, but excluded as an argument of ALSO. There is only a partial overlap between the arguments for these two discourse connectives. If the attribution is excluded from the discourse processing, then the discourse relation for ALTHOUGH would be properly contained as an argument for ALSO. RST, on the other hand, includes attribution as one type of discourse relation, not distinguished from other discourse relations. The RST Corpus also does not consider ALSO as a trigger for a discourse relation. Discourse connectives are used as cues to identify EDUs and determine their discourse relations, but they have no formal role in the RST annotation scheme.

(14)   *"He (Mr. Meek) said the evidence pointed to wrongdoing by Mr. Keating 'and others,' ALTHOUGH he didn't allege any specific violation. Richard Newsom, a California state official who last year examined Lincoln's parent, American Continental Corp., said he ALSO saw evidence that crimes had been committed."*

A nal difference between the RST annotation and the PDTB annotation is that PDTB only considers discourse relations between clauses, while RST also considers discourse relations between subclause relations. For example, EDUs in the RST Corpus can be phrases. A discourse relation can be between the head NP and its postmodi ers.

Measuring annotation consistency for discourse annotation can be very complicated. Carlson et al. (2003) report inter-annotator agreement on four levels of the RST Corpus: elementary discourse units, hierarchical spans, hierarchical nuclearity, and hierarchical relation assignments. The agreement is the highest for the identi cation of EDUs (0.97 kappa) and the lowest in discourse relation assignment (0.75 kappa), which is not unexpected. Miltsakaki et al. (2004a) reported inter-annotator agreement on the Penn Discourse Treebank using two different measures. The rst measure is more lenient and is calculated on a per-argument basis. That is, if two annotators assign the same argument label to the same spans of text, it is counted as a match, regardless of whether the other argument of the same discourse connective is a match or not. By this measure, the average agreement score is 90.2 percent. The second measure is more stringent and is calculated on a per-discourse relation basis. That is, two annotators have to agree on both arguments of a discourse connective in order for that to be counted as a match. By this measure the agreement is 82.8 percent. Although the consistency measures are not comparable between the two discourse annotation projects, it appears that both projects have achieved reasonably consistent scores, indicating the viability of these annotation schemes (see Section 3.5).

2.6 Coreference

References to entities in a document are identi ed as mentions, and mentions of the same entity are linked as being coreferences, or members of a coreference set. These can include pronouns, nominal entities, named entities, elided arguments, and events. For example, *Barack Hussein Obama II* and *he* in (15) corefer. Researchers at Essex (UK) were responsible for the coreference markup scheme developed in MATE (Poesio et al., 1999; Poesio 2004), partially implemented in the annotation tool MMAX and now proposed as an ISO standard. They have also been responsible for the creation of two small, but commonly used, anaphorically annotated corpora: the Vieira/Poesio subset of the Penn Treebank (Poesio & Vieira 1998), and the GNOME corpus (Poesio 2004). Their work also includes extended guidelines (Mengel et al., 2000), and annotation of Italian. Parallel coreference annotation efforts funded rst by ACE and more recently by DARPA GALE (see Section 2.8) have resulted in similar guidelines, best exempli ed by BBN's recent efforts to annotate named entities, common nouns and pronouns consistently (Pradhan et al., 2007c). These two approaches provide a suitable springboard for an attempt at achieving a community consensus on coreference.

(15) "**Barack Hussein Obama II** *is the 44th and current President of the United States.* **He** *is the first African American to hold the office.*"

Techniques for annotating and evaluating entire sets of coreferences are signi - cantly more complex than techniques for straightforward class-labeling tasks.

2.7 Opinion annotation

The Pittsburgh Opinion annotation project (Wiebe et al., 2005) funded by IARPA, focuses on the annotation of opinions, evaluations, emotions, sentiments, and other private states in text. A ne-grained annotation scheme has been developed for annotating text at the word and phrase levels. For every expression of a private state, a private state frame is de ned that identi es whose private state it is, what the private state is about, and various properties involving intensity, signi cance, and type of attitude. For example, in (16) a private state frame is anchored by *fear*.

The source of the private state is attributed to *the US*, and the attitude type of the private state is **negative**. The intensity of the private state is **medium**. A corpus of over 15,000 sentences has been annotated according to the scheme. The corpus is freely available at: nrrc.mitre.org/NRRC/publications.htm.

(16)   *"The US fears a spill-over."*

There are several applications for corpora annotated with rich information about opinions. Government, commercial, and political information analysts are all interested in developing tools that can automatically track attitudes and feelings in the news and in online forums. They would also be interested in tools that would support information extraction systems trying to distinguish between factual and non-factual information as well as question answering systems that could present multiple answers to non-factual questions based on opinions derived from different sources. In addition there is an interest in multi-document summarization systems, which would summarize differing opinions and perspectives.

2.8   *Multi-layered annotation projects*

The annotation resources we have described so far in this section are mostly one-dimensional tasks that focus on a single language processing goal. Treebanks are used to develop syntactic parsers and propbanks are used to train semantic role labelers. A recent trend in linguistic annotation is aimed at building multi-layered linguistic resources, fueled by the realization in the natural language processing community that there is great value in annotating the same linguistic source with multiple levels of linguistic information. A major advantage of having a multi-layered linguistic resource is that information encoded in one layer of representation can be used to infer that of another. For example, the role of syntactic parsing in semantic role labeling, a form of semantic parsing, is well documented (Gildea & Palmer 2002; Punyakanok et al., 2005). It is perhaps not a coincidence that many semantic annotation projects are built on top of syntactic annotation projects, as discussed in Section 2.3. For example, PropBank (Palmer et al., 2005) is built on top of the Penn Treebank (Marcus et al., 1993). The Salsa Project (Burchardt et al., 2006), a semantic annotation project for German, is built on top of the Tiger treebank (Brants et al., 2002), a syntactically annotated corpus. The Prague Dependency Treebank has a syntactic (the *analytical layer*) and semantic (the *tectogrammatical layer*) annotation layer. Perhaps the most ambitious multi-layered annotation project is OntoNotes (Pradhan et al., 2007a), funded through GALE, a large-scale DARPA program focused on automatic machine translation and summarization of Arabic and Chinese speech and text. OntoNotes is a ve-year, multi-site collaboration between BBN Technologies, the Information Sciences Institute of the University of Southern California, the University of Colorado, the University of Pennsylvania, and Brandeis University. The goal of the OntoNotes project is to provide linguistic data annotated with

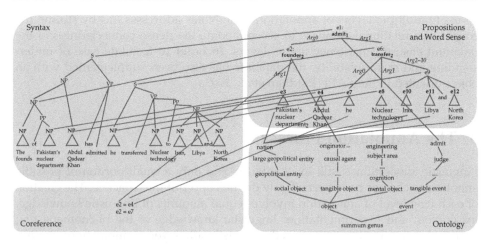

Figure 10.3   OntoNotes: a model for multi-layer annotation.

a skeletal representation of the literal meaning of sentences including syntactic parse, predicate–argument structure, coreference, and word senses linked to an ontology, allowing a new generation of language understanding technologies to be developed with new functional capabilities. The OntoNotes annotation covers multiple genres (newswire, broadcast news, broadcast conversation, and weblogs) in multiple languages (English, Chinese, and Arabic). The guiding principle has been to nd a 'sweet spot' in the space of inter-tagger agreement, productivity, and depth of representation. Figure 10.3 illustrates the inter-connection between the different layers of linguistic annotation in OntoNotes.

Many new challenges come with multi-layered annotation, particularly for annotation models like OntoNotes. Since the different layers of annotation are performed in different sites following different guidelines, incompatibilities can arise; (17) is an example with the same sentence annotated with both syntactic parses and semantic roles. By assigning different semantic roles to *a letter* (Arg1) and *for Mary* (Arg2), the PropBank annotator makes the implicit judgment that *for Mary* is an argument to the verb *wrote* and should be attached to this verb instead of the noun phrase *a letter*, a judgment that is different from the treebank annotation where the PP *for Mary* is treated as a modi er of *a letter*. In order to achieve coherent annotation, these incompatibilities need to be reconciled. Babko-Malaya et al. (2006) describe the many inconsistencies between syntactic parses and predicate–argument structure annotation that need to be resolved under the OntoNotes annotation effort.

(17)   a)   "(S (NP She)(VP wrote (NP (NP a letter)(PP for Mary))))"
     b)   "[Arg0 She] wrote [Arg1 a letter] [Arg2 for Mary]"

A linguistic source with multiple linguistic annotation also accentuates the data access problem. The most effective use of such a resource requires simultaneous access to multiple layers of annotation. OntoNotes addresses this by storing the corpus as a relational database to accommodate the dense connectedness of the data and ensure consistency across layers. In order to facilitate ease of understanding and manipulability, the database has also been supplemented with an object-oriented Python API (Pradhan et al., 2007a).

3 The Annotation Process

Linguistic annotation is still in its infancy, and only a small portion of possible annotation schemes have been clearly de ned and put into practice. The creation of each new level of annotation involves equal amounts of linguistic knowledge, inspiration, and experimentation: linguistic knowledge of the phenomena that need to be identi ed and described as a justi able layer of annotation; inspiration as to achievable levels of granularity and precision; and experimentation to determine the gaps and weaknesses in the guidelines. For any particular scheme a nite list of allowable annotations must be speci ed, with careful attention being paid to accounting for all possible contexts and to the cognitive load on the annotators. A clear understanding of linguistic phenomena does not necessarily translate directly into the development of annotated data that is suitable for training machine learning systems. The more precise the description of the linguistic phenomena, the greater the likelihood of a sparse data problem. Issues with respect to consistency, coherence, and clarity of the annotation scheme need to be well understood; a goal that can only be attained through trial implementations. From the perspective of the annotators, the ideal annotation scheme is clear and unambiguous in all circumstances and can be learned quickly by someone without an extensive linguistic background. This absolute goal may be unattainable, but efforts in its direction are rewarded by rapid, consistent annotation.

The development of an annotation scheme requires addressing at a minimum the following issues, each of which will be discussed in turn below:

- target phenomena de nition;
- corpus selection;
- annotation ef ciency and consistency;
- annotation infrastructure;
- annotation evaluation;
- the use of machine learning for pre-processing and sampling.

3.1 *The phenomena to be annotated*

The most important decision has to do with the phenomena to be annotated. Annotation can be an extremely expensive and labor-intensive process, so the rst question is: is it absolutely essential that this phenomena be manually annotated, or will automatic techniques be almost as good? Having decided that automatic techniques are insuf cient, there are several other questions that need to be addressed, such as: what is the scope of this annotation task, what other resources, including other annotation layers, might the annotators need access to, and what level of training will they require?

For example, with respect to de ning the scope of the task, given a coreference task, are bridging references and event references to be considered as well? Adding these types of coreference might make the annotation task more dif - cult for the annotators but, on the other hand, it might be impossible to de ne a coherent coreference task that does not include them.

With respect to other resources, given a semantic or pragmatic target area, the annotators might need access to prior syntactic or semantic annotation. For example, if a researcher is interested in relative clauses, is it possible to annotate a corpus for relative clauses in isolation without having to consider the overall syntactic structure of the sentence? If not, will it matter whether the syntactic analysis is phrase-structure based or dependency based? Alternatively, if the annotation task is sense tagging, which sense inventory will be the most appropriate lexical resource? How ne-grained do the senses need to be? If a parallel corpus is being annotated with sense tags, does a bilingual sense inventory need to be used?

As an example of determining necessary training, if a researcher is interested in providing syntactic analyses of sentences from biomedical texts, do all of the annotators need to become experts in biomedical terminology as well as in syntax?

The answers to any of these questions cannot be determined precisely without considering the task as a whole, the cognitive load on the annotators and the availability of appropriate corpora, resources, and tools. We will return to this topic at the end of this section, but for now will assume that a researcher starts with at least a general idea of the phenomena of interest in mind.

3.2   *Choosing a target corpus*

The criteria for corpus selection depend closely on the objectives for intended use. A large amount of data in a single genre, with as little variation in topic as possible, will yield the best possible performance when tested on similar data. If the characteristics of the test corpus are known in advance, then matching them as closely as possible in the training corpus is effective. However, a signi cant decrease in performance can be expected when testing on a disparate corpus. The same amount of data selected from a broader, more representative set of documents will yield lower initial performance but more robust results when tested on diverse data. The eld is only too familiar with the degradation in performance that occurs when parsers trained on the one-million-word *Wall Street Journal* Treebank are tested on different corpora. This was showcased in the 2005 CoNLL shared task for semantic role labeling (SRL) which included an evaluation on the Brown corpus, to "test the robustness of the presented systems" (Carreras & Màrquez 2005). The Charniak POS tagger degrades by 5 percent, and the Charniak parser F-score degrades by 8 percent, from 88.25 percent to

80.84 percent. For the 19 systems participating in the semantic role labeling evaluation, there was in general a 10 percent performance decrease from *WSJ* to Brown. The DARPA-GALE funded OntoNotes project (see Section 2.8) is speci - cally targeting 200,000 and 300,000 word selections of data from broadcast news, broadcast conversation (talk shows), newsgroups, and weblogs for treebanking, propbanking, sense tagging, and coreference annotation. The assumption is that a more balanced, more representative training corpus will improve the portability of systems trained on the data. For systems that are intended to be broad coverage, portability issues are of paramount importance.

3.2.1   Isolated sentences   Alternatively, broader coverage can be achieved by augmenting a target corpus with a hand selected set of constructions. Standard evaluation against a treebank simply selects a 10 percent or smaller chunk of the data for evaluation purposes. This has the bene t of testing against naturally occurring sentences, but there is no control over which types of phenomena, such as wh-movement, gapping, reduced relative clauses, etc., are covered. Unfortu- nately, a particular corpus may provide few instances of rare phenomena, and therefore this type of testing may not adequately cover performance on these types of constructions, especially if the initial corpus is small. If necessary a set of selected instances of rare constructions that are poorly represented in the training and test corpus can be prepared and added to the treebank corpora. Sentence (18) is an example of a statement that has a participial modi er, sometimes also called a reduced relative, that is in the passive voice and coincides with an in nitival con- struction. This may not occur frequently, but a few more similar examples should provide a statistical parser with suf cient training material to correctly analyze it when it does occur.

(18)   *"The student, found to be failing several subjects, was still promoted to the next grade."*

Another technique, given a large enough original target corpus, would be to carefully select a subset for annotation that ensures coverage of particular phenomena. A good illustration of hand selection/construction of instances of particular phenomena are the Test Suites for English pioneered by Stephen Oepen and Dan Flickinger (Oepen & Flickinger 1998; Oepen et al., 2002). The following examples illustrate the types of phenomena with marked word order for which a parser might require additional examples.[3]

- Heavy NP-shift: *"We saw on Tuesday a most amazing film."*
- Relative clause extraposition: *"Someone walked in whom I hadn't met."*
- Locative inversion: *"In the corner stood an antique coatrack."*

The dif culty of corpus selection is exacerbated when primarily lexical phe- nomena are under consideration. Discourse oriented annotation tasks such as coreference or discourse connectives require coherent chunks of text. Unfortu- nately, even a one-million-word corpus of coherent articles such as the *WSJ* treebank will not contain suf cient numbers of representative instances of most verbs to be suitable as a training corpus for semantic role labeling or sense tagging. Over half the verbs in WordNet are not present at all, and for those that are present, two thirds (2,167 out of 3,100) occur less than 10 times. Accurate automatic performance on these verbs can only be achieved by augmenting the *WSJ* corpus with additional instances. Yet annotating an additional 10 million words is clearly not feasible, and would also involve extremely tedious, unnecessary annotation of the 700 verbs that constitute 80 percent of the token coverage, and already have suf cient instances. The only solution is to once again augment the original target corpus with selected instances from other sources, with the knowledge that the lack of coherence in the augmentation will render it of little use to discourse annotation tasks.

Similar in spirit to the subset selection approach mentioned above, the OntoNotes sense-tagging group at Colorado is currently experimenting with both active learning and language modeling as techniques for nding more examples of rare senses to provide a more even distribution of the training data for a particular lemma (Dligach & Palmer 2009). The arithmetic sense of *add* is perhaps the most familiar one, but it actually occurs quite infrequently. The **say** sense, as in *"And I miss you, too." he added mendaciously* occurs more frequently by far. However, in certain domains it would be critical to correctly detect the arithmetic sense, and a few carefully selected additional training examples can signi cantly improve performance for this type of lemma.

3.2.2 Parallel corpora Perhaps the greatest challenge to corpus selection involves parallel corpora. Parallel treebanks and PropBanks are of increasing interest to syntax- and semantics-based statistical machine translation efforts, especially for evaluation purposes.[4] However, the ideal parallel corpus is almost impossible to nd. It should be equally uent with respect to both the source and the target languages, yet at the same time provide a translation that is as literal as possible and where each individual sentence can be aligned with a corresponding translated sentence, criteria that are at best at odds with each other. Parliamentary proceedings, such as the Hansards (the of cial records of the Canadian Parliament), the documents available through Europa (the European Union online), and radio shows that are simultaneously broadcast in multiple languages, such as FBIS, offer the most promising sources and are treasured by the community. Indeed, the availability of the Hansards sparked a major transformation in machine translation. These are kept by law in both French and English, and may be legally reproduced and distributed as long as "it is accurately reproduced and that it does not offend the dignity of the House of Commons or one of its Members." The researchers at IBM were thus provided with a large parallel French/English corpus of closely aligned, literal translations that proved ideal for statistical word alignment techniques (Brown et al., 1990). The astonishingly accurate translations their system was able to produce revolutionized the machine translation eld, and their approach is the basis for increasingly accurate statistical machine translation of Chinese and Arabic to English (funded by DARPA-GALE).

3.3　*Annotation efficiency and consistency*

When considering which phenomena are to be annotated, it is crucial to think through the decision making process the annotators will be faced with, and whether the task is best done as a single step or with multiple passes. If it is to be done in multiple passes, then the boundaries between the different layers of annotation need to be clearly de ned. Sometimes the most time-intensive step in the annotation process is comprehending the sentence or phrase to be annotated. There is always a trade-off between de ning simple, modular annotation steps with coherent decision spaces and multiplying the number of times a sentence has to be comprehended. The success of the annotation process will depend almost entirely on how constrained the choices are and on how clear and comprehensive the guidelines are. It is also important to consider the ef cacy of the resulting annotations with respect to training machine learning systems. Although it is no absolute guarantee, human accuracy at the task provides an encouraging indication of at least potential system accuracy. Poor human performance almost certainly presages poor system performance.

3.3.1　Annotation errors　A primary goal in achieving ef cient, consistent annotation is reducing unnecessary annotation errors. Apart from expected errors caused by carelessness or fatigue, which can usually be caught through double annotation, other annotation disagreements are almost entirely a direct result of confusion about the guidelines. The annotator may not have read the guidelines thoroughly enough, but more often the guidelines are themselves vague or ambiguous with respect to particular phenomena. It is also sometimes the case that the instances in the data are also vague and/or ambiguous, and open to multiple interpretations. It is important to give the annotators an escape hatch when they do not have a clear intuition about an appropriate label, so that they do not spend too much time agonizing.

3.3.2　Alternative guideline styles　Each different type of annotation requires a stable, language-independent methodology based on guidelines and widely accessible tools. The guidelines need to explicate the details of each individual annotation type as well as interactions between the different types of annotation. For instance, the guidelines for the Proposition Bank outline a process that begins with creating a Frameset for each individual verb in the corpus to be annotated. The Framesets provide invaluable additional direction for the annotation of the individual verbs over and above the general annotation guidelines. The Nom-Bank annotation in turn begins by referencing the verb Framesets for associated nominalizations whenever possible. The same approach has been used successfully for the Chinese PropBank/NomBank. In contrast, the guidelines for the treebank constitute over 300 pages of detailed syntactic description which have to be thoroughly analyzed and memorized before a treebanker can be considered to be fully trained.

Syntactic parsing, or treebanking, is undoubtedly one of the most demanding annotation tasks. Every single possible syntactic phenomenon has to be accounted for in the guidelines, with examples and explanations, and clearly distinguished from other, similar phenomena that it could be confused with, such as subject-control and object-control verbs, raising verbs, etc. The general rule of thumb is that the treebanking guidelines should not be nalized until at least 100,000 words have been successfully treebanked, which can easily take a year. It takes six months to fully train a treebanker, and there are no shortcuts. For phrase-structure treebanking, starting with a solid grounding in generative grammar helps, but since the guidelines make many departures from an exact theoretical interpretation, the treebanker also has to be exible and open minded, and not adhere too rigidly to theoretical generative grammar. However, given highly motivated annotators with a thorough understanding of syntax and the ability to pay close attention to detail, inter-annotator agreement rates of 95 percent and above have been achieved for English, Chinese, and Korean treebanking.

OntoNotes verb sense tagging, on the other hand, requires a very short training period of approximately 20 to 30 hours, which can take as little as two weeks. The guidelines amount to only 11 pages, 4 of which are very detailed instructions for logging onto unix and running the annotation tool. Sense taggers only need to know enough syntax to distinguish certain parts of speech, such as a main verb as opposed to a verbal past participle used as a modi er, or to recognize the difference between verb arguments that are noun phrases rather than sentential complements. One of the reasons for this brevity is that all of the information for distinguishing between the different senses of a verb has to be made explicit in the entry for that verb in the sense inventory. Each verb is different, and there are no overarching general principles for disambiguation that apply equally to all verbs. The sense inventory itself is the most critical component of the sense-tagging guidelines.

3.3.3 The annotation process As an illustration of the contrast between treebanking and sense tagging, treebanking is done on coherent text, sentence by sentence. Having the entire discourse context in mind can be helpful to the treebanker faced with referring pronouns and ambiguous attachment choices. On the other hand, sense tagging is most effectively done using a lexical sample approach, where all of the sentences from the target corpus containing the lemma to be tagged are extracted and displayed to the tagger in a single task. While tagging these instances the tagger only has to have the single lemma and its senses in mind, and does not have to stop and become familiar with several new entries for every sentence to be tagged.[5] This approach also facilitates the tagger making consistent choices for that lemma. Even so, if the lemma has too many senses, the cognitive load on the tagger is simply too high. All of the senses cannot be kept in mind, and the tagger has to repeatedly read through the sense entry looking for an appropriate sense label for each instance. This slows down the process and leads to inconsistencies, since the relevant sense might easily be missed. A useful number to keep in mind is Miller's 7, plus or minus 2. Taggers can manage up to 9 or 10 senses, or even in some cases as many as 12. More than that leads to inconsistency and delay. For the GALE OntoNotes annotation, senses for verb particle constructions for highly polysemous verbs (often accounting for close to half the instances) were split off from the entry for the main verb, and the instances for the verb were tagged in two passes. The rst pass allowed for selecting one of 10 to 12 entries for the verb or an additional entry for *multi-word expressions including verb particle constructions (MWE)*. The instances given the MWE tag were tagged in a second pass using a separate entry which split the verb particle constructions as well as idioms and metaphors into several senses. Overall, OntoNotes sense tagging has an ITA of 89 percent and is three to four times as fast as WordNet sense tagging.

3.3.4   Determining tagging candidates   Determining what constitutes an item to be tagged is just as important as knowing the set of possible labels. In treebank-ing the span is the entire sentence, so there is no room for confusion. For sense tagging, it is a single lexical item (or a multi-word expression based on a spe-ci c item) which has been predetermined and appears highlighted in the sentence. However, the choice of tagging candidates is not always so clear cut. For the ACE event tagging, the annotators had to select from a sentence the string of words that corresponded to each event participant, a major source of inter-annotator disagree-ment. For the initial TimeML annotation, the annotators could pick and choose which events in a paragraph were supposed to have temporal relations, again, a major source of disagreement. A major simplifying assumption for the PropBank annotation was the decision to base it on the existing treebank parses. The *events* corresponded to clausal verbs, and the event participants that received semantic role labels were all arguments of the verb. The annotators simply had to choose a node in the tree that corresponded to a verb argument and assign a label to it; the span of the node was already predetermined.

3.3.5   The necessity of pilots   Finally, no matter how much thought has gone into de ning the guidelines and constraining annotator choices, a pilot annotation phase is still essential. Annotators may not interpret the guidelines as intended, the data may present much more variance than was predicted, there could be (and almost certainly are) bugs in the annotation tools. Guidelines should never be nalized until they have been thoroughly tested on a substantial representative data set with several annotators. Any annotation proposal should include time for a pilot test, revision of the guidelines, and then another pilot test with additional revisions. The goal of guidelines development is to de ne a clear, unambiguous task which can be decided by rapid application of human intuition. If annotation agreement is lower than expected, it is much more likely the fault of the guidelines or the task de nition than the fault of the annotators.

3.4   Annotation infrastructure and tools

Because linguistic annotation is generally considered to be a 'data' project, anno-tation infrastructure and tools, which involve programming support, are an often overlooked area. It is not uncommon for a linguistic annotation project to have insuf cient funds to hire programmers to provide necessary programming support. This results in annotators having to make do with suboptimal annotation tools. Poor tools have a negative impact on both the quality and the quantity of the annotated data. This section will outline the infrastructure and tool needs before, during, and after annotation. For any large-scale, production-level annotation project, having the proper annotation infrastructure in place at the beginning, as well as equipping the annotator with user-friendly annotation tools, is essential for the success of the project.

3.4.1   Task assignment   For the infrastructure of large-scale annotation projects, before human annotation can take place, it is essential to think through two key issues: annotator management and data ow. Large-scale annotation projects cannot be done by one person and typically involve multiple annotators. Having a clear idea of who can access what data is crucial. For sense tagging and Prop-Banking, where the standard practice is to perform double-blind annotation where two (and only two) annotators are asked to annotate the same data, it is virtually impossible to ask the annotators themselves to keep track of which data they should or should not annotate. Sense taggers and propbankers are typically part-time annotators, and they tend to work on an annotation project for variable lengths of time. It is often a luxury to have the same two annotators nish annotating the same data during the lifetime of the project. As a result, it is necessary to build into the annotation infrastructure a mechanism to distribute annotation assignments to annotators so that the annotator can simply take the next available assignment and get on with it. Such a mechanism ensures that a given chunk of data is always double annotated if that is the goal and that an annotator does not accidentally re-annotate data that already has double annotations or skip data that needs annotations; mistakes that inevitably happen if the annotators are left to their own devices.

3.4.2   Data flow management   In addition to annotator management, it is also important to build into the infrastructure functionalities for data ow management. Annotation is expensive and time-intensive, and it is frustrating to lose annotated data. Annotators are usually linguistic experts who are familiar with the linguistic phenomena they are asked to annotate, but are not necessarily savvy computer users who could be expected to maintain data security. It is necessary to think through how the annotated data should be saved periodically while the annotator is annotating. It is also good practice to maintain version control of the annotated data using a version control facility such as CVS or SVN. Automatic version control systems allows multiple copies of data to be checked in, keeping track of any differences in the most recently checked in versions and of who checked them in and when.[6]

3.4.3   User-friendly annotation tools   After an annotation task is set up and the annotator starts tagging, the annotation tool becomes central to the annotation process. The quality of the annotation tool can have a great impact on annotation ef ciency and consistency. Although it seems counterintuitive, since mouse-based annotation tools have a shorter learning curve and are often preferred by novel annotators, veteran annotators generally prefer keyboard-based annotation interfaces, since they are faster and are less likely to result in issues such as tendonitis and carpal tunnel syndrome. Long hours spent at annotation have emphasized the ergonomic advantages and greater annotation ef ciency of the keyboard. The annotation interface used for the syntactic annotation of the Chinese Treebank is an Emacs-based tool that makes heavy use of keyboard strokes and uses very few mouse clicks. Quite a few mouse-based treebanking tools such as WordFreak and Tred have subsequently been built, and LDC now uses one for English, but the Emacs-based tool is still the preferred treebanking tool for many veteran treebankers, including Chinese and Korean treebankers. It is important to give annotators a choice of keyboard strokes versus mouse clicks.

Annotation tools also have a role in maintaining annotation consistency. If designed properly, an annotation tool can prevent an annotator from entering a label that is not in the tagset associated with the task, or from accidentally deleting or changing the source data, which is usually forbidden. Maintainability, customizability, and portability are also important considerations when designing an annotation tool. An annotation tool is often still used long after its original developers have moved on, so someone else needs to maintain it. It is thus advisable that the tool be well documented and written in a widely used programming language. Multi-lingual annotation is increasingly gaining in popularity, so portability to other natural languages is also an important consideration when choosing a programming language.

3.4.4 Postprocessing The annotation process does not stop when the human annotator nishes manual annotation. The output of the annotation tool is often not in the nal format that the annotation data users expect for processing. Also, for quality-control purposes, there is often a data validation process after the human annotation is done. For syntactic parsing, this validation can check if the parse is in a valid format, for example, if the left and right brackets match up and if the syntactic labels in the annotated data are all legitimate labels. For sense tagging, the validation process can check if the sense numbers correspond to the sense inventory entry choices. Certain predictable annotation errors can also be automatically detected and corrected. Just as there is user-friendly software, there is also user-friendly data. Not all users of linguistically annotated data are well versed in the linguistic concepts and their linguistic justi cations as encoded in the annotations, and some will lose interest if the representation is too complicated for them to understand. Putting the annotations in an easily understood format can maximize the usability of the data that has taken so much effort to produce.

3.5 *Annotation evaluation*

There are two main aspects to evaluating the annotation itself. One has to do with extrinsic measures of the annotation validity and consistency. The other focuses on the agreement between the annotators (ITA), which, since common wisdom treats human annotator agreement gures as an upper bound for system performance, is of central importance (see Chapter 11, EVALUATION OF NLP SYSTEMS, for a more detailed discussion).

The question then arises as to what to do with annotator disagreements. Are they just mistakes on the part of one annotator that need to be corrected via an adjudication mechanism? This is in fact often the case, but disagreements can also indicate especially vague or ambiguous linguistic phenomena which might need special handling. The OntoNotes sense-tagging project uses ITA as a measure of the clarity of the sense inventory. If ITA is below 90 percent the lexicographers are asked to re-examine the groupings of the WordNet senses for that lemma. They cannot examine the actual tagged instances, but they can look at a confusion matrix that shows which senses the annotators disagree on. The confusion matrix sometimes reveals a striking mix-up between two particular senses, pointing the lexicographer exactly to the senses that need clari cation. On the other hand, even after a new lexicographer has examined the confusion matrix and the groupings carefully, it may not be at all clear what could or should be changed. Even when all disagreements have been adjudicated to produce the gold standard data, system builders often want information about which lemmas, or senses, have been especially dif cult to tag, and the original anno-tator disagreements can be a useful source of this type of information. Evaluation techniques can be weighted to penalize systems less for missing the more dif cult cases.

The most straightforward measurement of ITA is simple percentage agreement, and this is also the gure that correlates the most highly with system performance (Chen & Palmer 2009). However, it has often been pointed out that there is a large discrepancy between 90 percent ITA when a lemma has a most frequent sense baseline of 85 percent, and 90 percent ITA when the most frequent sense base-line is 60 percent. Chance agreement, and therefore expected agreement, would be much higher with the former than with the latter. The kappa, k, coef cient of agreement can take this into account, and is generally considered as provid-ing a more accurate assessment of how much value the annotation is actually adding. The basic technique subtracts expected agreement, E, from observed agreement, A, and then divides it by 1 minus the expected agreement, as given below.

$$k = \frac{A - E}{1 - E}$$

There are several subtleties in how the expected agreement can be calculated, depending on whether or not there are more than two annotators, what the expected distribution of choices would be, and whether or not annotator bias needs to be taken into account. Artstein and Poesio do an excellent job of sur-veying the state of the art with respect to these various options (Artstein & Poesio 2008). In general a kappa score of 0.8 or higher is considered desirable.

An equally important consideration in measuring ITA is to decide exactly what is being taken into consideration. If treebankers are being evaluated, a simple Parseval score (Black et al., 1991) which matches the sequences of words that have been bracketed together is usually deemed suf cient. This technique produces precision (of the total number of bracketed constituents produced by an annotator, what percentage are correct) and recall (what percentage of the correct possible bracketed constituents did the annotator produce) gures as well as the number of crossing brackets. The F-score is a weighted harmonic mean of precision and recall. These scores may or may not take the labels of those bracketed phrases into account. For the Chinese Treebank, based on a randomly selected 20 percent portion of the corpus, the F-score for the average ITA is 93.8 percent. After discrepancies between the annotators are reconciled and a gold standard produced, annotator gold-standard comparisons, or accuracy comparisons, can be made. For the Chinese Treebank, the F-score for average accuracy was 96.7 percent.

However, many researchers feel the need for parsing evaluations that are more stringent than Parseval (Carroll et al., 2002, 2003; Hajic et al., 2009), which would translate into more detailed annotator comparisons as well.

With respect to sense tagging, the determination of ITA is from one perspective more straightforward. Senseval (Palmer et al., 2001) and Semeval (Pradhan et al., 2007b) evaluations typically provide pointers to the words to be tagged, so recall is always 100 percent and there is no need to calculate an F-score. Precision is therefore equivalent to accuracy. However, as discussed in Chapter 11, EVALUATION OF NLP SYSTEMS, if hierarchical sense entries are provided, the correctness of an answer tag may be weighted depending on its closeness to the correct tag in the hierarchy, making things more complex. In the same way, annotator agreements and disagreements on sense tags can be weighted based on the relatedness of the sense tags chosen.

Coreference annotation presents yet another set of challenges, since coreferences typically consist of sets of mentions. The question is how to score two coreference sets which are almost, but not quite, identical. Artstein and Poesio (2008) offer useful insights on this issue.

3.6 Pre-processing

There are several questions to be addressed when considering pre-processing:

- What types of pre-processing might facilitate the annotation, and can this be done automatically?
- Does the corpus need to be stripped of headers and extraneous markup? Will they need to be replaced later?
- Is there a pre-existing automatic annotation tool that can be applied without imposing undue bias?

There is considerable evidence that the productivity of manual annotation can be sped up by pre-processing the data with suf ciently accurate automatic taggers (Chiou et al., 2001). This method has been particularly successful with treebanking, where automatic parsers are rst run and then the output is hand corrected. Note that this is only useful if the automatic parsers already have high accuracy. Poor parsers simply slow down the process, and the treebankers would prefer to start from scratch.[7] However, in spite of demonstrated productivity gains from automatic pre-processing, current annotation practices frequently fail to take advantage of this approach, possibly because of the dif culty of integrating these systems into new annotation tasks.

Even more bene t could be derived from using sophisticated machine learning techniques to aid in the selection of instances to be tagged, in order to maximize their utility and minimize the total annotation effort. For simple classi cation tasks like word-sense disambiguation, there are accepted practices which utilize automatic WSD systems, such as active learning techniques (Chen et al., 2006a). However, for more complex annotations such as syntactic structure, pinpointing novel or unfamiliar items in the data remains a more challenging problem (Hwa 2004). Fundamental research is needed to develop informed sampling techniques for complex annotation that can be integrated into the annotation effort.

4 Conclusion

This chapter has brie y surveyed several speci c annotation layers and reviewed general principles for developing annotation projects. Annotation schemes are likely to be as varied as natural languages, and there are a host of reasons for choosing one annotation tool or evaluation technique over another. However, the principles stated by Krippendorf (2004) for a content analysis annotation scheme are equally applicable to linguistic annotation schemes for natural language processing systems:

- it must employ an exhaustively formulated, clear, and usable coding scheme together with step-by-step instructions on how to use it;
- it must use clearly speci ed criteria concerning the choice of coders (so that others may use such criteria to reproduce the data);
- it must ensure that the coders that generate the data used to measure reproducibility work independently of each other. (See Chapter 11, EVALUATION OF NLP SYSTEMS)

We all long for the day when unsupervised and semi-supervised techniques will automatically induce the grammars and sense clusters that drive our natural language processing systems. It may be the case that the more effectively and coherently we annotate the linguistic layers that we currently understand, the sooner that day will come.

ACKNOWLEDGMENT

The authors would like to express their gratitude to Stephanie Strassel, Randi Tangee, Christiane Fellbaum and Eduard Hovy, whose contributions as co-authors with Martha Palmer for the MINDS report on "Historical development and future directions in data resource development" informed this article in many ways.

NOTES

1 The ACE guidelines include complex subtypes for each of these categories and multitudinous examples.
2 Named entity (or nominal entity) tagging is very similar to part-of-speech tagging, in that one set of tags is used for all entities.
3 Dan Flickinger provided these examples during an oral presentation at an invitation-only treebank workshop held in conjunction with NAACL07, http://faculty.washington.edu/fxia/treebank/workshop07/formalisms/hpsg.pdf
4 The OntoNotes group, at the insistent request of the BBN, IBM, and SRI teams, is currently treebanking and PropBanking all of the evaluation data from the rst three years of the program.
5 This bene t has to be weighed against how many times the sentence will be read. If all the content words are to be tagged, and if several of them are polysemous (not likely), the sentence may be re-read several times.
6 See www.nongnu.org/cvs/ for CVS and http://en.wikipedia.org/wiki/Subversion_(software) for SVN.
7 This is similar to the dismay with which human translators face the task of hand correcting the output of machine translation systems.

11   Evaluation of NLP Systems

PHILIP RESNIK AND JIMMY LIN

1   Introduction

As the engineering branch of computational linguistics, natural language processing is concerned with the creation of artifacts that accomplish tasks. The operative
question in evaluating an NLP algorithm or system is therefore the extent to which
it produces the results for which it was designed. Because NLP encompasses an
enormous range of different tasks, each with its own particular criteria for assessing results, a single chapter on evaluation cannot hope to be comprehensive. In
this chapter, therefore, we have selected a number of basic issues, laying out some
fundamental principles of NLP evaluation, describing several of the most common evaluation paradigms, and illustrating how the principles and paradigms
apply in the context of two speci c tasks, word-sense disambiguation and question answering. For a comprehensive treatment, we refer the reader to Galliers and
Jones (1995).[1]

It must be noted that the design or application of an NLP system is sometimes connected with a broader scienti c agenda; for example, cognitive modeling
of human language acquisition or processing. In those cases, the value of a
system resides partly in the attributes of the theory it instantiates, such as con-
ciseness, coverage of observed data, and the ability to make falsi able predictions.
Although several chapters in this volume touch on scienti c as well as practical
goals (e.g., the chapters on computational morphology, unsupervised grammar
acquisition, and computational semantics), such scienti c criteria have fallen out
of mainstream computational linguistics almost entirely in recent years in favor of
a focus on practical applications, and we will not consider them further here.

In addition, like other types of computer software, NLP systems inherit a wide
range of evaluation concerns, criteria, and measures from the discipline of software quality evaluation. When assessing any software product, for example, it is
typical to consider such issues as cost, support, ef ciency, reliability, scalability,
interoperability, security, and so forth. Many relevant issues are covered by the

The Handbook of Computational Linguistics and Natural Language Processing, First Edition.
Edited by Alexander Clark, Chris Fox and Shalom Lappin.
© 2013 Blackwell Publishing Ltd except for editorial material and organization
© 2013 Alexander Clark, Chris Fox, and Shalom Lappin. Published 2013 by Blackwell Publishing Ltd.

ISO 9126 standard for software product evaluation (ISO 1991), and speci c extensions to that standard have been created speci cally for the purpose of evaluating
language technology (EAGLES 1996).

To introduce some of the ideas we will be looking at in greater detail below,
consider evaluation in the context of a 'semantic' search engine that utilizes NLP
components.[2] For purposes of illustration, suppose that the search engine matches
users' questions with facts that appear in documents, and that the underlying
method involves a component that analyzes sentences to produce normalized
subject–relation–object dependency tuples. The use of normalized dependency
tuples has the potential to allow more speci c concept-level matches; for example,
the question *When was the light bulb patented by Edison?*, can match *Thomas Edison's
patent of the electric light bulb* via the tuple [Thomas Edison, patented, bulbs].[3]

How might the quality of dependency tuple analysis be evaluated? One time-
tested approach that deserves mention would be to skip formal evaluation of this
component altogether, and instead perform a *demonstration* of the search engine
for the project's investors or other target audience. Well-designed demos are often
simple to execute, easy to understand, and surprisingly powerful in making a
compelling case for a system's value. However, demos can also be quite misleading because they rarely exercise the full range of a system's capabilities and can be
carefully orchestrated to hide known aws.

Another approach would be to perform a standard *intrinsic* evaluation of the
dependency extraction component. In a case like this, one would typically create a test set that contains a sample of test sentences for input, along with the
ground truth, i.e., an 'answer key' in the form of tuples that the system is expected
to create for each test sentence. The design of the evaluation would quantify the
system's agreement with the ground truth, much as a teacher counts up the agreements and disagreements between a student's multiple-choice test answers and
the answer key. In this case, each test sentence has a *set* of tuples that together
comprise the correct answer, and the goal is to produce all and only the tuples
in that set. In settings like this, one would usually calculate *recall*, measuring the
extent to which *all* the tuples were produced, *precision*, capturing the extent to
which *only* correct tuples are included in the output, and *F-measure*, a score that
combines recall and precision into a single gure of merit (see Section 3.2). One
might compare the F-measure for the current tuples analyzer against an earlier
version (a *formative* evaluation, measuring progress and informing new development) or against competing techniques (a *summative* evaluation, concerned with
the outcome of development).

The intrinsic evaluation helps to assess the quality of the tuples analyzer, but
how do we know that improvements in the analyzer actually make a difference
in the overall quality of the system (that is, better search results)? One answer is
to perform an *extrinsic* evaluation, which measures the quality of the analyzer by
looking at its impact on the effectiveness of the search engine. In this case, we
would create a test set not for the analyzer, but for *the search engine as a whole*. The
test items in this case would therefore be user questions, and the ground truth
for each question would be the answers that should be produced by the system.

Precision, recall, and F-measure could be used again here, but this time they would be used to quantify the extent to which the *search engine* produces all and only the correct answers to the test questions. Crucially, the quality of the dependency tuple analyzer is measured only indirectly, by evaluating the whole system with and without it, or by swapping out this analyzer and substituting another. To put this another way, the extrinsic evaluation treats the analyzer as an *enabling technology*, whose value is not intrinsic but rather resides in its contribution to a larger application (Resnik 2006).

Even an extrinsic evaluation may still be too far removed from quality in the real world, however. One way to address this would be to conduct a laboratory test involving real users employing the search engine to perform a standardized task, e.g., nding the answers to a set of test questions. This is, in effect, a variation on the extrinsic evaluation in which the 'system as a whole' actually includes not only the search engine but the user as well, and the setup makes it possible not only to measure the quality of the answers produced, but also to look at factors such as time taken and user satisfaction.

Ultimately, however, laboratory experimentation cannot completely predict how a technology will fare in a real-world environment with real users performing real tasks. For this, a system must be deployed, and observations made *in situ* of the system, the users, and their interaction. Learning how the technology does in the real world comes at the cost of experimental controls and replicability, but for many pieces of real-world technology, the nal test is not the laboratory measures, but the usefulness of the tools, the satisfaction of users, and their willingness to come back and use that technology again.

2 Fundamental Concepts

2.1 *Automatic and manual evaluations*

Perhaps the most basic dichotomy in evaluation is that between automatic and manual evaluation. Often, the most straightforward way to evaluate an NLP algorithm or system is to recruit human subjects and ask them to assess system output along some predetermined criteria. In many cases, this is the best approach for nding out whether a system is actually useful and whether users are pleased with the system – a criterion that goes beyond whether or not the system meets predetermined requirements or speci cations. Note that manual evaluations are the norm in many elds, for example, user studies in human–computer interaction.

Unfortunately, manual evaluations have two signi cant limitations: they often generate inconsistent results and they are slow. Human beings are notoriously inconsistent in their judgments about what is 'good' (both across multiple subjects and sometimes with themselves), and even with the adoption of standard best practices in study design (e.g., counterbalanced presentation of experimental conditions, calibration for learning effects and environmental settings, etc.), it is dif cult to control for unanticipated factors. In addition, manual evaluations are time-consuming and laborious. In addition to time for the actual experiment, human subjects must be recruited, scheduled, and trained. To arrive at statistically signi cant ndings, dozens of subjects are often necessary. All of these factors conspire to make well-designed manual evaluations a large investment of resources.

Modern NLP has evolved into an empirical, evaluation-driven discipline, which means that researchers have little patience for long turnaround between successive experiments. Thus, automatic evaluation methods are favored today by most. The development of evaluation algorithms that mimic the behavior of human assessors is an important sub eld in NLP, and such research can be readily found in the pages of conference proceedings and journal articles in the eld. However, recognizing that manual evaluations remain valuable, it is common practice to periodically conduct studies that establish a correlation between results of automatic and manual evaluations. If such a correlation is demonstrated, then researchers have a degree of con dence that improvements according to automatic evaluations will translate into *meaningful* improvements for users.

2.2   *Formative and summative evaluations*

The distinction between formative and summative evaluations is best summed up with a quote: "When the cook tastes the soup, that's formative; when the customer tastes the soup, that's summative."[4] Formative evaluations typically occur during the development of NLP systems – their primary purpose is to inform the designer as to whether progress is being made towards the intended goals. As such, formative evaluations tend to be lightweight (so as to support rapid evaluation) and iterative (so that feedback can be subsequently incorporated to improve the system). In contrast, summative evaluations are typically conducted once a system is complete (or has reached a major milestone in its development): they are intended to assess whether intended goals of the system have been achieved.

In NLP research, there is a tendency for formative evaluations to be automatic, so that they can provide rapid feedback in the development process. In contrast, summative evaluations often involve human judges, in order to assess the usefulness of the system as a whole for users.

2.3   *Intrinsic and extrinsic evaluations*

Intrinsic and extrinsic evaluations form another contrast that is often invoked in discussions of evaluation methodologies. In an intrinsic evaluation, system output is directly evaluated in terms of a set of norms or prede ned criteria about the desired functionality of the system itself. In an extrinsic evaluation, system output is assessed in its impact on a task external to the system itself. Evaluation of document summarization systems serves to illustrate this distinction. In an intrinsic evaluation, we would ask questions such as the following about system-generated summaries: How uently does the summary read? Does the summary contain coverage of key ideas? On the other hand, extrinsic evaluations consider tasks in which a document summarization system may be useful – for example, as a component of a search engine that summarizes results and presents short snippets to help users decide whether or not a document is relevant (i.e., worth reading). In the context of this particular task, we might ask: How accurately can a user make such relevance judgments, compared to having access to the entire document? How much more quickly can such judgments be made with summaries?[5]

In NLP research, at least, there is an af nity between intrinsic, formative, and automatic evaluations on the one hand, and extrinsic, summative, and manual evaluations on the other. The characteristics of these different approaches naturally explain these associations. Since extrinsic evaluations must be couched within the context of a user task, it is dif cult to avoid having human subjects. It is usually easier to develop automatic techniques for intrinsic evaluations since only the system output needs to be considered.

2.4   *Component and end-to-end evaluations*

Most NLP systems today are not monolithic entities, but rather consist of distinct components, often arranged in a processing pipeline. For example, identi cation of semantic role (e.g., agent, patient, theme) depends on syntactic parsing, which in turn depends on part-of-speech tagging, which in turn depends on tokenization. We could choose to evaluate each component individually, or instead consider multiple components at once. For example, when evaluating the accuracy of a syntactic parser that requires part-of-speech tags as input, one could assess the quality of the parse-trees based on the output of a real tagger that may contain errors (an end-to-end evaluation), or based on 'gold standard' part-of-speech tags supplied by a human (a component evaluation).[6]

Both component and end-to-end evaluations are useful, but for different purposes. Obviously, end-to-end evaluations provide a more meaningful quanti ca-tion of system effectiveness under real-world circumstances. However, measuring system characteristics under ideal circumstances may also be useful, since it isolates the system from errors in other components. With component evaluations, it is possible to arti cially manipulate input and observe the impact on system effectiveness. For example, in evaluating a syntactic parser one could start with gold standard part-of-speech tags and then arti cially degrade tagging accuracy in a controlled manner. Doing so would allow a researcher to understand the input–output characteristics of the component, i.e., sensitivity of the parser to tagging errors.

In most cases, it is desirable to conduct both component and end-to-end evaluation of NLP systems since components often interact in non-obvious ways. For some systems, the effects of errors are multiplicative: that is, since each component depends on the previous, errors propagate down a processing pipeline, so that the nal output may be quite poor despite high effectiveness for each of the components (consider the pipeline for identifying semantic roles described above).

For other systems, the overall effectiveness is much higher than one would expect given individual component-level effectiveness – these represent cases where the components are able to compensate for poor quality. One example of this is in cross-language information retrieval (CLIR), where the user issues a query in one language to retrieve documents in another language. Abstractly, one can think of CLIR systems as having a translation component and a search component. In even the most sophisticated systems, the translation component is little better than word-for-word translation – the quality of which is quite poor by human standards. Yet CLIR systems are about as effective as monolingual IR systems – since the inherent redundancy in documents and queries (i.e., the presence of multiple words referring to the same concepts) compensates for the poor translation quality.

2.5   *Inter-annotator agreement and upper bounds*

In many NLP evaluation settings – particularly intrinsic, component-level evaluations – the task being evaluated is to 'annotate' (tag, label) text. For example, part-of-speech taggers assign grammatical category tags to words, named entity extractors assign category labels (e.g., PERSON, ORGANIZATION) to phrases, and parsers can be viewed as assigning constituent labels like NP or VP to spans of text within a sentence. It is common practice in such cases to compare the performance of multiple *human* annotators, for two reasons. First, if human beings cannot reach substantial agreement about what annotations are correct, it is likely either that the task is too dif cult or that it is poorly de ned. Second, it is generally agreed that human inter-annotator agreement de nes the upper limit on our ability to measure automated performance; Gale et al. (1992: 249) observe that "our ability to measure performance is largely limited by our ability [to] obtain reliable judgments from human informants." As a well-known case in point, the WordNet lexical database includes sense tags that are notoriously ne-grained, e.g., distinguishing verb sense *chill* (make cool or cooler) from *chill* (lose heat) because the former involves *causing* a change and the latter *undergoing* a change in temperature (Palmer et al., 2007). Could we really expect any word-sense disambiguation algorithm to achieve 95 percent agreement with human-selected WordNet sense tags, for example, if the human taggers themselves can only agree 75 percent of the time when doing the task (Snyder & Palmer 2004)? For this reason, human agreement is generally viewed as the *upper bound* on automatic performance in annotation tasks.[7]

One way to measure agreement between two annotators is simply to measure their observed agreement on a sample of annotated items. This, however, may not constitute an accurate re ection of the true dif culty or upper bound on the task, because, for any given task, some agreements may occur according to chance. Consider a simple example: if the annotation task were to sense-tag instances of the word *bank* as either RIVERBANK or FINANCIALBANK, and two annotators make their choices independently by ipping a coin, they could be expected to agree 50 percent of the time. Therefore, in order to establish the validity of a coding scheme, as well as de ne upper bounds for the annotation task, it is now common practice to compute a measure of *chance corrected* agreement

(Artstein & Poesio 2008). Correction for chance is captured by measures that generally take the form

$$(1) \quad \frac{A_0 - A_e}{1 - A_e}$$

where A_0 is the observed agreement (total agreements divided by total number of items), and A_e is an estimate of chance agreement varying according to the speci c measure. Cohen's kappa is in widespread use for this purpose, but Artstein and Poesio (2008) provide a thorough discussion of its limitations and of alternative measures, as well as in-depth consideration of detailed issues, including, e.g., measuring agreement among three or more annotators, weighting some disagreements more heavily than others, and the interpretation of agreement coef cient values.

2.6 *Partitioning of data used in evaluations*

Within most NLP settings, system development and evaluation involves partitioning the available data into the following disjoint subsets:

- **Training data.** This term most often refers to a data set where input items are paired with the desired outputs, often as the result of manual annotation (cf. Section 2.5). It usually refers to the input for supervised learning algorithms, but it can refer more broadly to any data used in the process of developing the system's capabilities prior to its evaluation or use.[8]
- **Development (dev) data.** Some systems include parameters whose settings in uence their performance. For example, a tagger might choose its output based on a weighted vote $\sum \lambda_i p_i (\text{input})$, where each p_i is a different method of prediction and the λ_i are weights for the different methods. Rather than choosing weights or parameters arbitrarily, it is common to hold out some subset of the training data as a *development set*. A search for good values for λ_i is conducted, either in an ad hoc manual fashion or using an optimization technique such as expectation-maximization. In either case, performance on the development data measures the 'goodness' of the parameter choices.
- **Development-test (devtest) data.** Typically one or more data sets are also held out for use in formative evaluation (Section 2.2) as the system is developed. A devtest set is just a test set that is being used during the cycle of system development and improvement.
- **Test data.** This term describes the data that will be used to evaluate the system's performance after development has taken place, i.e., at the point of a summative evaluation.[9]

It is typical to reserve as much data as possible for training and development. For example, one might split the available data into 70, 20, and 10 percent for training, held-out (i.e., dev and devtest), and test data respectively.

Disjointness of the subsets is crucial, because a fundamental principle in NLP evaluation is that the technology being evaluated *cannot be informed by the test data*. In its purest form, this means that test data should remain entirely untouched and unseen by the researcher or developer until system development is frozen just prior to evaluation. The reasoning behind this stricture is simply that evaluations are intended to help predict a system's performance on future unseen data, i.e., to generalize. In machine learning, the error rate when testing on the training data is referred to as the *resubstitution error rate*, and it is regarded as a severe underestimate of the true error rate, as a result of over tting. Performance on the training data can be a useful reality check, of course, since something is probably wrong if it is not quite good. But it cannot be relied upon to predict future performance.

Moreover, it should be noted that evaluations can be overly optimistic even when test data are kept properly disjoint from data used in system development. For example, it is typical to assume that systems will be evaluated (or run) on the same kind of data that were used during system development, e.g., language that is similar in genre and topic. It is widely recognized, however, that system performance will suffer when this assumption is not met (e.g., Escudero et al., 2000; Gildea, 2001).

It is also worth noting that there are, in fact, some uses of the test data that are generally regarded as valid. The following are some examples:

- For research on machine translation systems, using the test set to automatically lter the phrase table, so that it contains only entries that are relevant for the given test set. This is a common way to reduce the size of the model so that it ts in memory (Lopez 2008a). Note that this affects the ef ciency of a system, but does not fundamentally alter its behavior.
- Using the test set automatically for model adaptation (e.g., Kim & Khudanpur 2003).
- Performing error analysis prior to moving on to a fresh test set – i.e., the current test set becomes devtest data.
- Looking just at performance numbers on test data, without examining the system's output. For example, parsing researchers test over and over again using Section 23 of the *Wall Street Journal* in the Penn TreeBank, and MT researchers test repeatedly on test sets from the NIST machine translation evaluation exercises.

2.7   Cross validation

Employing a single partition of the available data is common, but it does present two potential problems. First, regardless of whether the evaluation results are good or bad, one has to wonder whether the results re ect a particularly fortuitous (or infortuitous) selection of test data. More precisely, a single split provides only a point estimator for whatever measure or measures are used for evaluation, as opposed to an interval estimate such as a 95 percent con dence interval. Second, as a practical matter, even a 70 percent allocation may not produce a large enough training set for automatic learning methods if only a small quantity of annotated data is available.

Within NLP, the most common solution to these problems is *k-fold cross-validation*. Instead of creating a single split, the full set of available data is partitioned into *k* pieces, or folds, $\{f_1 \ldots f_k\}$.[10] Then evaluation is conducted as follows:

> for *i* from 1 to *k*
> > Let TEST $= f_i$ be the test set
> > Let TRAIN $= \cup_{j \neq i} \{f_j\}$ be used as the training set
> > Compute m_i, the evaluation measure, by training on TRAIN and testing on TEST
> Compute statistics, e.g., the mean and standard deviation, over the $\{m_i\}$.

If held-out data is needed for parameter tuning, TRAIN is subdivided into training and dev data.

K-fold cross-validation ensures that every item in the full data set gets used for both training and testing, while at the same time also ensuring that no item is used simultaneously for both purposes. Therefore it addresses the concern that the evaluation results only re ect a particularly good or particularly bad choice of test set. Indeed, addressing the second concern, the set $\{m_1 \ldots m_k\}$ can be used to compute not only the mean, as a scalar gure of merit, but also the standard deviation, enabling the computation of con dence intervals and tests of statistical signi cance when alternative algorithms or systems are compared. Finally, although values of *k* are typically between 4 and 10 – e.g., training uses from 75 percent to 90 percent of the available data – it is possible to use data even more ef ciently by employing a larger number of folds. At the extreme, one can set *k* equal to the number of items *N* in the full data set, so that each fold involves $N - 1$ items used for training and one item for testing. This form of cross-validation is known as *leave-one-out*, and is similar to the jackknife estimate (Efron & Gong 1983).

2.8 Summarizing and comparing performance

All quantitative evaluation paradigms make use of at least one *figure of merit*, sometimes referred to as an *evaluation measure* or *evaluation metric*, to summarize performance on a relevant property of interest. Some of the most important paradigms, and their associated evaluation measures, are discussed in Section 3.

Table 11.1 shows the typical structure for reporting results in NLP evaluations. The rst column of the table identi es the 'conditions,' i.e., variant approaches taken to the task. A single evaluation measure might be reported (e.g., accuracy, Section 3.1). Or there might be columns for multiple measures, often trading off against each other, with some single metric representing their combination (e.g., recall, precision, and F-measure, Section 3.2).

Turning to the rows, a results table almost always includes at least one *baseline* condition. The role of a baseline is similar to the control condition in an experiment studying the effectiveness of a new drug: in order for the study to successfully

Table 11.1   Structure of a typical summary of evaluation results

Condition	Measure 1	Measure 2	Combined Measure
Baseline 1	M_1^{B1}	M_2^{B1}	M_c^{B1}
Baseline 2	M_1^{B2}	M_2^{B2}	M_c^{B2}
Variation 1	M_1^{V1}	M_2^{V1}	M_c^{V1}
Variation 2	M_1^{V2}	M_2^{V2}	M_c^{V2}
Upper Bound	M_1^{U}	M_2^{U}	M_c^{U}

demonstrate that a drug is effective, patients taking the drug must show bene- ts over and above that experienced by patients taking a placebo. Similarly, the baseline condition in an NLP experiment de nes the performance that must be improved upon in order for the study to deliver a positive result. One category of baselines can be de ned independently of prior work in the literature; for example, choosing an answer at random, or always selecting an item's most frequent label in the training data, or applying something else that is equally obvious and simple.[11] Another kind of baseline is the effectiveness of some prior approach on the same data set. Generally the rst category can be viewed as a 'reality check': if you cannot beat one of these baselines, most likely something is fundamentally wrong in your approach, or the problem is poorly de ned (see Section 2.5).

The 'upper bound' for a task de nes the highest level of performance one could expect to attain in this experiment. Typically, upper bounds are de ned by human inter-annotator agreement (as discussed in Section 2.5). Sometimes, alternative upper bounds are de ned by allowing the system to use knowledge that it would not have access to in a fair evaluation setting. As an example, a machine translation system might be permitted to produce its 1000-best hypotheses for each input sentence, and the *oracle upper bound* would be de ned as the score of the hypothesis that performs best when compared against the reference translations. In practice, of course, an MT system cannot choose its single-best output by looking at correct translations of the input. But the oracle upper bound helps to quantify how much better the system could potentially get with better ranking of its hypotheses (Och et al., 2004).

When comparing system results against baselines, upper bounds, or across variations, it is important to recognize that not all differences between scores matter. One question to consider is whether or not an apparent difference is *statistically significant*; that is, if the difference is unlikely to have occurred as a result of chance variation. As a simple example, suppose we are selling a coin- ipping machine that will (we claim) make a fair coin more likely to land heads up. If we test the machine by performing an experiment with 10 ips, and the coin comes up heads 6 times instead of 5, should a potential buyer be convinced that our machine works as advertised, compared to typical, unassisted coin ips? Probably not: even with normal, 'unimproved' coin ipping, someone doing a large number of 10- ip experiments could be expected to get the same result, exactly

6 heads out of 10 flips, in fully 20 percent of those experiments, just by chance. So getting that particular result in this experiment could easily have happened even if the machine just flipped coins in the usual way. By convention, an experimental outcome is not usually considered 'statistically significant' unless the likelihood of its having occurred by chance is less than 5 percent, often written $p < .05$.[12]

Even if a difference in experimental conditions is statistically significant, however, it is essential to recognize that the result may not be large, important, or even meaningful. The 'significance' of an experimental improvement (in the ordinary sense of the word) is usually calibrated as a matter of folklore or common wisdom within a particular experimental community. In information retrieval, for example, a system might meet accepted criteria for a meaningful result by achieving a .05 absolute improvement in average 'precision at 10' (the precision computed using the ten most highly ranked hits in response to a query), with an improvement of .10 being considered substantial.[13] In machine translation, researchers might expect to see around a one-point improvement in BLEU score (Papineni et al., 2002) on one of the recent NIST evaluation data sets, with a gain of two points or more being considered substantial.[14]

However, the bottom line is that no hard-and-fast rule involving evaluation numbers or statistical significance can tell the full story when comparing alternative approaches to a problem. Ultimately, the potential value of a new contribution in NLP depends also on the relevance of the evaluation task, the representativeness of the data, the range of alternative approaches being compared, and a host of other more tangible and less tangible factors.

Finally, it is worth noting that sometimes the relative difference in performance metrics provides more insight than their absolute difference. On the combined measure, the *relative improvement* of Variation 1 over Baseline 1 in Table 11.1 is

$$(2) \quad \frac{M_c^{V1} - M_c^{B1}}{M_c^{B1}}$$

For example, improving accuracy from $M_c^{B1} = 35\%$ to $M_c^{V1} = 40\%$ is only a 5 percent improvement in absolute terms, but the relative improvement defined in (2) is more than 14 percent. To make the point more dramatically, if a system improves accuracy from 98 percent to 99 percent, this may seem like only a small accomplishment, only one percentage point. But the picture changes a great deal if the results are expressed in terms of error rate (100 percent − accuracy): the improved system cuts the number of errors in half, which can make a huge difference if the number of inputs is very large.

3 Evaluation Paradigms in Common Evaluation Settings

At the most basic level, NLP systems are designed to accomplish some task, which can be characterized by input–output characteristics. Thus, evaluation boils down to a conceptually simple question: for a set of inputs, to what extent does system output correspond to outputs that are *correct* or *desirable*? This question helps organize common paradigms in evaluation, discussed in this section. In some cases, there is a one-to-one correspondence between input and the correct output (e.g., part-of-speech tagging, word-sense disambiguation). In other cases, multiple outputs are desirable (e.g., information retrieval, parallel text alignment), the output takes the form of text (e.g., machine translation, document summarization), or the output contains complex structure (e.g., parsing). Finally, the output may involve values on a scale (e.g., language modeling, semantic similarity).

3.1   One output per input

The most straightforward evaluation paradigm in NLP is one in which each input produces a single output – a nominal value that can be considered a category or label (Stevens 1946) – and that output is compared against a single correct answer. This is analogous to multiple-choice tests, although for many NLP tasks the number of possible answers for any input can be quite large.

Classic word-sense disambiguation tasks fall into this category: each word, in its context, represents an input, and the possible outputs are de ned by an enumeration of sense labels. For example, suppose that the task involves deciding whether instances of the word *ash* are being used in the sense ASH$_1$, 'a tree of the olive family,' or in the sense ASH$_2$, 'the solid residue left when combustible material is burned' (Lesk 1986).[15]

To evaluate disambiguation performance in settings like this, one would run the system on inputs $\{a_1, \ldots, a_n\}$ (where each a_i is an instance of the word *ash* in context), producing single-best output label decisions $\{l_1, \ldots, l_n\}$ (where each $l_i \in \{\text{ASH}_1, \text{ASH}_2\}$), and then compare those decisions to 'ground truth' human-annotated sense labels $\{t_1, \ldots, t_n\}$ ($t_i \in \{\text{ASH}_1, \text{ASH}_2\}$). The primary gure of merit would be the percentage of agreement with the true labels, i.e., the *accuracy*:

$$(3) \quad A = \frac{\sum_{i=1..n} \text{agr}_i}{n} = \frac{\text{number correct}}{n}$$

where agr$_i$ is 1 if $l_i = t_i$ and 0 otherwise.[16] Sometimes the inverse of accuracy, or *error rate*, is reported instead: $1 - A$.

Sometimes a system is not required to produce any answer at all for some inputs; that is, l_i could remain unde ned. In some tasks, it might be preferable for the system to remain silent than to risk being wrong. In those cases, we can de ne d to be the number of de ned answers, and d replaces n in the denominator when accuracy is calculated. We then de ne *coverage* as d/n, in order to measure the extent to which answers were provided. By default, one can assume $d = n$, i.e., coverage is 100 percent, when accuracy is presented alone as the gure of merit. When $d < n$, accuracy and coverage can be traded off against each other – for example, a system can obtain high accuracy by providing an answer for an input only when it is very con dent, at the expense of coverage. This is quite similar to the trade-off between precision and recall discussed below in Section 3.2. Indeed, the

Table 11.2 Contingency table for a document retrieval task

	relevant	*¬relevant*
retrieved	r	n
¬retrieved	R	N

$$\text{Precision} = r/(r + n) = \frac{|\text{relevant} \cap \text{retrieved}|}{|\text{retrieved}|}$$

$$\text{Recall} = r/(r + R) = \frac{|\text{relevant} \cap \text{retrieved}|}{|\text{relevant}|}$$

terms 'precision' and 'recall' are sometimes used, in our view somewhat confusingly, to refer to accuracy and coverage in task settings where each input has only a single output.[17]

In a common variant of this paradigm, the desired output for each input is a sequence $y_1 \ldots y_k$. For example, in part-of-speech tagging, each input a_i would be a whole sentence, i.e., a sequence of tokens $x_1 \ldots x_k$, and the output label would be a sequence $y_1 \ldots y_k$ of grammatical category tags. When the output sequence stands in one-to-one correspondence with the input sequence, as in this example, it is most common simply to evaluate as if each input token comprises its own single-token labeling problem, even if that's not really how the output was produced. This is equivalent to concatenating all the output sequences to produce one long sequence of length n, and then computing A as de ned above.

When the output sequence can differ in length from the input sequence, the situation becomes a bit more complicated; we treat that case as a variant of structured output in Section 3.2.

3.2   *Multiple outputs per input*

For many NLP tasks, there is no single correct answer; multiple outputs are sought. Information (document) retrieval is perhaps the best illustration of this general evaluation paradigm. Given an information need expressed as a query (e.g., 'gardening in arid soil'), the task of the system is to return the set of documents that are relevant and, in most cases, there are multiple satisfactory documents. Formalizing the task abstractly in terms of set membership – a document is either retrieved by the system or it is not, and a document is either relevant to the information need or it is not – is an imperfect approximation of the real-world task, where documents may be relevant only to a greater or lesser extent, and systems may estimate degrees of con dence. But this abstraction makes it possible to de ne the quality of a system's set of retrieved documents in terms of two extremely useful and intuitive concepts: *precision* and *recall*. The contingency table in Table 11.2 illustrates how these are computed. Precision is the fraction of system output that is relevant, or $r/(r+n)$; recall is the fraction of relevant documents that is retrieved, or $r/(r + R)$.[18]

Notice that the numerator is the same in both cases: r counts the number of documents that were both relevant and retrieved by the system. For precision, we are interested in comparing that with the total number of documents retrieved by the system, hence $r + n$ in the denominator. If $n = 0$, i.e., no irrelevant documents were retrieved, then precision is perfect. For recall, we are interested in comparing r with the total number of documents that *should* have been retrieved, hence $r + R$ in the denominator. If $R = 0$, i.e., every relevant document was retrieved, then recall is perfect.

High precision is easy to obtain, at the expense of recall: just return the single document most likely to be relevant, or, more generally, do not return documents unless the system's con dence in their relevance is very high. This keeps n close to 0, but of course it also increases R, so recall suffers. Similarly, perfect recall is easy to achieve (just return all the documents in the collection, so $R = 0$), but at the expense of precision, since n is then likely to be large.

To balance the need for both precision and recall, F-measure (or F-score) is often reported:

$$(4) \quad F(\beta) = \frac{(\beta^2 + 1) \times P \times R}{\beta^2 \times P + R}$$

The F-measure computes a harmonic mean between precision and recall, where the relative emphasis on the two components is controlled by the β parameter (higher values of β place more emphasis on recall). The choice of β depends a lot on the task. For example, a person searching the web for gardening information does not want to slog through lots of irrelevant material, and does not require every single gardening article that is out there, so precision is a high priority. In contrast, a complex legal argument can be undermined by even a single court ruling overturning a previous precedent, so systems for legal research can be expected to place a heavy emphasis on recall.

F-measure is frequently used to compare different systems. In addition to combining two measures into a single gure of merit, F-measure has the attractive property of incurring a penalty in performance when precision and recall are very different from each other, thereby discouraging an emphasis on one at the expense of the other. Other common metrics in information retrieval (e.g., mean average precision, R-precision) derive from this set-based formalism, with the addition of other concepts such as document ranking. It is worth noting that all these metrics are intrinsic in nature, in that they do not measure how *useful* the retrieved documents are in a real-world task, e.g., writing a report, answering a complex question, making a decision, etc.

3.3   *Text output for each input*

Frequently in NLP, the task of the system is to produce text in response to the input. Machine translation is the most obvious example of the paradigm, since an output text in the target language is produced for the source-language input.

Text summarization is similar, producing an output text that condenses pertinent information from a set containing one or more input documents.

Evaluating text output introduces a difficult challenge: how do we account for the fact that the desired information can be expressed correctly in many different ways? Testing for exact equality is necessary when computing agreement in Section 3.1, or when computing the intersection |relevant∩retrieved| in Section 3.2, but string equality hardly seems appropriate as a way of evaluating whether or not two texts are saying the same thing. One solution to this problem is to rely on human judges to compare system outputs with correct answers (see Section 3.5), but that solution is extremely labor-intensive. It would generally be impractical, for example, to collect human judgments on a weekly basis in order to track progress during system development.

Most ways of dealing with this challenge involve two elements. First, texts being compared are broken down into units that *can* be compared via exact matching, e.g., word n-grams. Then a bag of n-grams from the system output can be compared with the n-grams present in the human 'gold standard' reference, quantifying the relationship using measures derived from precision and/or recall. In essence, the n-grams in gold standard references define the 'relevant' elements of the desired response to the input, and n-grams in the system output constitute what the system has 'retrieved.' This idea has been operationalized, for example, in the BLEU metric for machine translation (Papineni et al., 2002) and the ROUGE metric for text summarization (Lin & Hovy 2003), both of which are widely used in their respective communities, albeit not without some controversy.

A second useful strategy is to define multiple correct references for each input. For example, it is not uncommon in MT evaluations to provide anywhere from two to ten correct translations for each test input. The evaluation measure is then generalized to take into account correct or 'relevant' units from multiple valid outputs. For example, consider a system that produces the English sentence *my dog is always hungry*, with reference translations

my dog is hungry all the time
my pup is always famished

Using the BLEU metric, which focuses on precision, the system would get credit for having produced 'relevant' unigrams *my, dog, is, always,* and *hungry*; bigrams *my dog, dog is,* and *is always*; and the trigram *my dog is*. Notice that it is getting some credit for having conveyed both *always* and *hungry*, even though no single reference translation conveys the combined meaning *always hungry* using both of those words.

3.4   Structured outputs

The paradigm in Section 3.3 also provides a way of thinking about evaluation settings in which *structured* outputs are expected, whether or not multiple references are available. The basic idea is the same: to break the structured representations up into bags of smaller units and then compute precision and/or recall over those smaller units. Metrics like BLEU and ROUGE apply this concept to sequences (since sentences are sequences of tokens), which are broken up into bags of *n*-grams. But the idea is signi cantly more general; for example, the PARSEVAL measures (Abney et al., 1991) evaluate parsers by computing precision and recall over constituents.[19]

Another way to compare structured outputs, particularly sequences, is *edit distance* or its variants. For example, speech recognition researchers compute the *word error rate* between the system's output and the reference transcription:

$$(5) \quad \text{WER} = \frac{S + D + I}{n}$$

where S, D, and I are, respectively, the number of substitutions, deletions, and insertions in a minimum-cost edit transforming the system output into the reference. In machine translation, translation edit rate (TER) has gained currency. TER "measures the amount of editing that a human would have to perform to change a system output so it exactly matches a reference translation" (Snover et al., 2006: 223).[20]

3.5   *Output values on a scale*

Some tasks involve producing a value on a measurement scale, e.g., the traditional nominal, ordinal, interval, and ratio scales of Stevens (1946).[21] Producing values on nominal scales can be viewed simply as assigning a label or category to each input (one can only meaningfully ask about equality, but not relative ordering or magnitude). Comparisons of nominal outputs are addressed in Sections 3.1 and chance-corrected agreement is discussed in Section 2.5.

Ordinal scales capture a common situation in which desired outputs represent ratings, e.g., performing opinion analysis in order to assign a rating from one to ve stars given the text of a movie review. Output values are ordered with respect to each other, but the intervals on the scale are not necessarily comparable. One cannot assume that the 'distance' between a one-star and two-star review represents the same difference in quality as the distance between a four-star and a ve-star review – the number of stars merely tells you how the movies are ranked relative to each other. In these situations, it is common to compare a system's output ratings against human ratings by computing the Spearman rank order correlation coef cient, r_s (sometimes ρ), over the set $\{(o_i, t_i)\}$ of system outputs paired with human 'ground truth' ratings.

Interval scales are similar to ordinal measurements, with the additional assumption that differences between values constitute equivalent intervals. On the Celsius scale, for example, the difference in temperature between 1°C and 2°C is the same as the difference between 101°C and 102°C. Within NLP, comparisons of system scores against human ratings often assume this interpretation of the ratings scale is valid, and use the Pearson product–moment correlation (Pearson's r) over $\{(o_i, t_i)\}$

as a gure of merit. In machine translation, the validity of automatic evaluation metrics like BLEU (Papineni et al., 2002), TER (Snover et al., 2006), and METEOR (Banerjee & Lavie 2005) is sometimes supported by comparing automatic scores with human ratings of accuracy and uency, using Pearson's r. Similarly, automatic measures of semantic similarity are often evaluated via correlation with human similarity ratings, using pairs of words (e.g., *furnace, stove*) as the items for which similarity is being computed (Resnik 1999; Pedersen et al., 2007).

Ratio scales assume that there is meaning not only for sums and differences on the scale but also for products and ratios. Within NLP, the most common quantitative output on a ratio scale would be the assignment of probabilities to inputs, often in the context of language modeling. For example, when evaluating a trigram language model p_{tri}, the test set consists of a text $T = w_1 \ldots w_N$, and we measure either the cross entropy

$$(6) \quad H = -\frac{1}{N} \sum_{i=1}^{N} \log_2 p_{tri}(w_i|w_{i-2}w_{i-1})$$

or, more commonly, the perplexity, 2^H. Notice that whenever the model makes an accurate prediction in the test data, i.e., when the probability $p_{tri}(w_i|w_{i-2}w_{i-1})$ is high for an observed instance of w_i preceded by $w_{i-2}w_{i-1}$ in T, the contribution to H is small. Intuitively, perplexity is measuring the extent to which the model p_{tri} correctly reduces ambiguity, on average, when predicting the next word in T given its prior context. To put this another way, on average we are 'k-ways perplexed' about what the next word will be, with k ranging from 1 to the vocabulary size $|V|$.[22] In the worst case, the model might be no better than rolling a fair $|V|$-sided die, yielding perplexity $k = 2^{-\frac{1}{N}N \times \log \frac{1}{|V|}} = |V|$, meaning that the model provides no value at all in narrowing down the prediction of the next word. At the other extreme, a model that always predicts the next word perfectly (giving it a probability of 1 and therefore zero probability to all alternatives) would have a perplexity of $k = 2^0 = 1$.

Sometimes evaluation involves comparing output in the form of a probability distribution with ground truth that is also a distribution. In such cases, it is common to use Kullback–Leibler distance (also known as KL divergence or relative entropy) to compare the two distributions:

$$(7) \quad D(p||m) = \sum_{x \in \mathcal{X}} p(x) \log \frac{p(x)}{m(x)}$$

where p is the true probability distribution and m is the model being evaluated. Kullback–Leibler distance is zero when m is identical to p, and otherwise it is always positive. Its value can be interpreted as the cost, measured in bits of information, of encoding events in $\mathcal{X}$ using the imperfect model m rather than the truth p.[23]

4   Case Study: Evaluation of Word-Sense Disambiguation

Word-sense ambiguity is one of the earliest challenges singled out by researchers interested in automatically processing natural language. Some well-known early discussions of the problem include Weaver's (1949) memorandum on automatic translation, Bar-Hillel's (1960) argument that automatic high-quality translation requires comprehensive world knowledge in order to resolve lexical ambiguity, and Wilks's (1975) 'preference semantics' approach to semantic interpretation. *Word-sense disambiguation* (WSD) is conventionally regarded as the task of identifying which of a word's meanings (senses) is intended, given an observed use of the word and an enumerated list of its possible senses. In this section, we brie y review how approaches to WSD have been evaluated, with reference to the concepts we introduced earlier in the chapter. For informative general treatments of WSD, see Ide and Véronis (1998) and Agirre and Edmonds (2006), and for a more comprehensive discussion of recent WSD evaluation, see Palmer et al. (2006).

4.1   *Pre-Senseval WSD evaluation*

From the earliest days, assessing the quality of WSD algorithms has been primarily a matter of intrinsic evaluation, and "almost no attempts have been made to evaluate embedded WSD components" (Palmer et al., 2006: 76). Only very recently have extrinsic evaluations begun to provide some evidence for the value of WSD in end-user applications (Resnik 2006; Carpuat & Wu 2007). Until 1990 or so, discussions of the sense disambiguation task focused mainly on illustrative examples rather than comprehensive evaluation. The early 1990s saw the beginnings of more systematic and rigorous intrinsic evaluations, including more formal experimentation on small sets of ambiguous words (Yarowsky 1992; Leacock et al., 1993; Bruce & Wiebe 1994).[24]

Since word-sense disambiguation is typically de ned as selecting one sense among a number of possibilities, it is naturally regarded as a classi cation problem involving the labeling of words in context (Edmonds & Agirre 2008). Thus evaluation has required answering six main questions.[25]

How do you define the 'sense inventory,' i.e., the set of possible sense labels for a word? Early efforts involved a wide variety of answers to this question – for example, Roget's thesaurus, various paper dictionaries, and various machine readable dictionaries. By the mid-1990s, WordNet (Fellbaum 1998) had emerged as a standard, easily available lexical database for English, and WordNet's 'synonym sets' provided a widely used enumeration of senses for content words (nouns, verbs, adjectives, and adverbs).

How do you select input items?   Early experimentation focused on identifying a small set of 'interesting,' highly ambiguous words, e.g., *line* and *interest*, and collecting a sample of those words within their sentential contexts. Cowie et al. (1992) represent a notable exception, tackling the problem of disambiguating all the content words in a sentence simultaneously.

How do you obtain labels ('ground truth') for items in the data set? In early studies it was not uncommon for experimenters to label their own test sets, e.g., Yarowsky (1992); Leacock et al. (1993); Bruce and Wiebe (1994). Miller et al. (1993) and Ng and Lee (1996) introduced large-scale manual sense labeling of corpora using Word-Net, laying the groundwork for WSD approaches involving supervised learning techniques.

How do you compare system output against ground truth? In a setting where one correct label is assumed per input, the most natural gure of merit is accuracy, possibly accompanied by coverage if the system is permitted to abstain from labeling some inputs. Measures derived from cross-entropy (equation 6) can be used to give partial credit to systems that assign a probability distribution over senses (Resnik & Yarowsky 1999; Melamed & Resnik 2000).

What constitutes a lower bound on performance? An obvious but overly generous lower bound is chance, selecting randomly among a word's senses according to a uniform distribution. A more sensible lower bound is de ned by tagging each instance of a word with its most frequent sense.[26] It is also not uncommon to compare WSD algorithms against easily implemented dictionary-based techniques, e.g., Lesk (1986) or variants.

What constitutes an upper bound on performance? Word-sense disambiguation is a classic example of a task where human inter-annotator agreement, and particularly chance-corrected agreement, are used to de ne the limits on what can be expected from automated algorithms (Artstein & Poesio 2008).

4.2 Senseval

In April 1997, a workshop entitled "Tagging Text with Lexical Semantics: Why, What, and How?" was held in conjunction with the Conference on Applied Natural Language Processing (Palmer & Light 1999). At the time, there was a clear recognition that manually annotated corpora had revolutionized other areas of NLP, such as part-of-speech tagging and parsing, and that corpus-driven approaches had the potential to revolutionize automatic semantic analysis as well (Ng 1997). Kilgarriff (1998: 582) recalls that there was "a high degree of consensus that the eld needed evaluation," and several practical proposals by Resnik and Yarowsky (1997) kicked off a discussion that led to the creation of the Senseval evaluation exercises.

The Senseval-1 exercise involved 'lexical sample' tasks for English, French, and Italian (Kilgarriff 1998), essentially a community-wide version of evaluations previously conducted by individual researchers for words like *line* (Leacock et al.,

1993) and *interest* (Bruce & Wiebe 1994). As a community-wide gure of merit, Resnik and Yarowsky (1997) had suggested using cross-entropy rather than accuracy in order to accommodate systems with probabilistic output, thereby allowing a system A to obtain partial credit for word w_i even if the correct sense cs_i was not deemed most probable (cf. equation 6):

$$(8) \quad H = -\frac{1}{N} \sum_{i=1}^{N} \log_2 p_A(cs_i | w_i, \text{context}_i)$$

Senseval-1 adopted a variant of this suggestion proposed by Melamed and Resnik (2000), which accounted for ne- to coarse-grained distinctions in a sense hierarchy, and also permitted human annotators to specify a disjunction of correct answers in ground truth sense labelings.[27]

Following Senseval-1, other Senseval exercises continued for some time as the primary forum for evaluation of word-sense disambiguation. Senseval-2 dramatically expanded the scope of the exercise to include ten languages, using WordNet-based sense inventories. It also introduced 'all-words' tasks, requiring systems to assign a sense label to every content word within a document. Senseval-3 (Mihalcea & Edmonds 2004) continued lexical sample and all-words tasks, and added new semantic annotation tasks including semantic role labeling (Gildea & Jurafsky 2002), creation of logical forms, and sense disambiguation of the words in WordNet's de nitional glosses. More recently, Senseval has become Semeval, a series of evaluation exercises for semantic annotation involving a much larger and more diverse set of tasks (Agirre et al., 2009).

5   Case Study: Evaluation of Question Answering Systems

In response to a short query representing an information need, a search engine retrieves a list of 'hits,' or potentially relevant results. The user must then manually examine these results to nd the desired information. Given the amount of information available today on the web and in other electronic formats, typical queries retrieve thousands of hits. Question answering (QA) aims to improve on this potentially frustrating interaction model by developing technologies that can understand users' needs expressed in natural language and return only the relevant answers. From an algorithmic standpoint, question answering is interesting in that it combines term-level processing techniques (from information retrieval) with rich linguistic analysis. This section provides a case study on the evaluation of question answering systems.

The earliest question answering systems focused on fact-based questions that could be answered by named entities such as people, organizations, locations, dates, etc. A few examples of these so-called 'factoid' questions are shown below:

- What position did Satchel Paige play in professional baseball?
- What modern country is home to the ancient city of Babylon?

- Who was responsible for the killing of Duncan in *Macbeth*?
- What Spanish explorer discovered the Mississippi River?

For several years, the locus of question answering evaluation has resided at the Text Retrieval Conferences (TRECs).[28] TREC is a yearly evaluation forum, organized by the US National Institute of Standards and Technology (NIST), which brings together dozens of research groups from around the world to work on shared information retrieval tasks. Different 'tracks' at TREC focus on different problems, ranging from spam detection to biomedical text retrieval. Question answering occupied one such track from 1999 to 2007. During this time, the TREC QA tracks were recognized as the de facto benchmark for assessing question answering systems. These annual forums provide the infrastructure and support necessary to conduct large-scale evaluations on shared collections using common test sets, thereby providing a meaningful comparison between different systems. The TREC model has been duplicated and elaborated on by CLEF in Europe and NTCIR in Asia, both of which have introduced cross-language elements. This case study focuses specially on the TREC evaluations, recognizing, of course, that it merely represents one of many possible evaluation methodologies.

The TREC QA tracks occurred on an annual cycle. Several months in advance of the actual evaluation, the document collection to be used in the evaluation was made available to all participants, as well as results from previous years (to serve as training data). The actual evaluation occurred during the summer: participants were required to 'freeze' their systems (i.e., to conclude system development) before downloading the of cial test data. Results were due before a subsequent deadline (typically, about a week). System results were evaluated manually by a team of human assessors at NIST during the late summer or early fall. Each TREC cycle concluded with a workshop in November where all participants were invited to discuss their results and plan for next year.

One might think that evaluating answers to factoid questions would be straightforward, but even such a seemingly simple task has many hidden complexities. First is the issue of granularity: although the goal of a question answering system is to directly identify the answer, it might seem a bit odd if the system returned only the *exact answer* (i.e., a short phrase). Consider the question 'Who was the rst person to reach the South Pole?' A response of 'Roald Amundsen' might not be very helpful, since it provides the user with little context (Who was he? When was this feat accomplished? etc.). Giving the user a sentence such as 'Norwegian explorer Roald Amundsen was the rst person to reach the south pole, on December 14, 1911' would seem to be preferable – indeed, Lin et al. (2003a) present results from a user study that con rms this intuition.[29] In evaluating answers to factoid questions, what exactly should be assessed? Short phrases? Sentences? A case can certainly be made for evaluating answers 'in context,' but requiring exact answers makes the task more challenging and helps drive forward the state of the art. TREC eventually chose the route of requiring short, exact answers, accompanied by a document from which that answer was extracted.

Another issue is the notion of support: the document from which an answer derives should provide justi cation for the answer. Consider a sample question, 'What Spanish explorer discovered the Mississippi River?' An answer of 'Hernando de Soto,' extracted from a document that reads 'the sixteenth-century Spanish explorer Hernando de Soto, who discovered the Mississippi River …' would be considered correct. However, the same answer extract from a document that says 'In 1542, Spanish explorer Hernando de Soto died while searching for gold along the Mississippi River …' would be considered *unsupported*, since the passage does not actually answer the question. Of course, what counts as evidence varies from assessor to assessor.

Finally, for a number of questions there are simply differences in interpretation. A well-known example is the question 'Where is the Taj Mahal?' In addition to the famous structure in Agra, India, there is the Taj Mahal casino in Atlantic City, New Jersey. Whether or not the latter location was acceptable as an answer stirred quite a debate among both TREC assessors and participants. Such questions are actually not uncommon, especially since many noun phrases have ambiguous referents. This was resolved, somewhat arbitrarily, by instructing assessors to interpret such questions as always referring to the 'most famous' version of an entity.

Judging the correctness of system responses is the most dif cult and time-consuming aspect of TREC QA evaluations. Once the appropriate label has been assigned (e.g., *correct, inexact, unsupported, incorrect*), computing scores for system runs is relatively straightforward. The of cial metric varied from year to year, but the most basic method to quantify system effectiveness is through accuracy – of all the questions, how many were answered correctly.[30]

The summative nature of the TREC QA evaluations provides a fair, meaningful comparison across a large number of systems. Of cial results from TREC are viewed as authoritative, and the best systems are often used as yardsticks for assessing the state of the eld. There are, of course, downsides to the TREC question answering tracks. Organizing and administering each evaluation consumes a signi cant amount of resources and represents a signi cant investment from both NIST and the participants (in choosing to participate). The other obvious drawback of the TREC QA evaluations is the rigid yearly cycle.

To support formative evaluations for system development between each TREC event, researchers have developed regular expressions for answers that mimic the behavior of assessors, so that system output can be informally assessed without the need for human intervention.[31] The regular expressions were created by manually examining actual system outputs and assessors' judgments to capture correct answers for each question. However, these answer patterns were simultaneously too permissive and too restrictive. They were too restrictive in not being able to capture all variants of correct answers – it was very dif cult to predict a priori all variant forms of correct answers, e.g., different ways of writing numbers and dates. At the same time, the regular expressions were too permissive, in giving credit to system responses that happened to coincidentally contain words in the answer (without actually answering the question). Furthermore, the answer patterns did not address the problem of support: although it was possible to use the list of relevant documents from the manual assessment as a guide, the space of possible answer sources exceeded the number of documents that were assessed manually, making the automatic assessment of support problematic.

Despite inadequacies with using regular expression answer patterns, they were nevertheless useful for system development and for providing researchers with rapid experimental feedback – which is exactly the purpose of formative evaluation tools. The combination of annual summative evaluations at TREC and formative evaluations in between helped drive the state of the art in factoid question answering.

6 Summary

Evaluation plays a crucial role in the development of language technology. In this chapter, we have presented a set of fundamental evaluation concepts, descriptions of the most widely used evaluation paradigms, and two case studies drawing on the authors' experiences with evaluation of word-sense disambiguation and question answering systems.

NOTES

1 That book is a revised version of an earlier technical report (Galliers & Jones 1993). See also Palmer et al. (1990).

2 This illustration is modeled on the NLP-enabled Wikipedia search engine introduced by San Francisco-based Powerset in May 2008 (Auchard 2008). However, neither author of this chapter has any connection with Powerset, and our examples should not be relied on as an accurate depiction of its technology.

3 Notice that this example illustrates not only dependency tuple extraction but also one way to do normalization of dependency tuples. In particular, observe how a de - nite generic noun phrase *the . . . bulb* has been represented by a plural generic *bulbs*; cf. the semantic equivalence between *The dodo is extinct* and *Dodos are extinct* (McCawley 1993: 263ff). See Katz and Lin (2003) and references therein for additional discussion of search using dependency tuples.

4 This quote is attributed to "evaluation theorist Bob Stake" in Westat (2002: 8).

5 See Dorr et al. (2005) and references therein for actual studies along these lines.

6 This distinction is similar in some ways to *black-box* versus *glass-box* evaluation. The former is restricted to external measurements such as quality of output and speed, while the latter can take into account internal characteristics such as the quality of knowledge resources, as well as run-time internal workings of the system.

7 Note that it is conventionally assumed that the human annotators are working *independently*. In a post hoc review of one annotator's work, a second annotator is likely to give the rst annotator's choice the bene t of the doubt if there is a gray area, even though she might well have made a different choice when annotating independently. Chapter 10 in this volume, LINGUISTIC ANNOTATION, discusses in detail a wide variety of annotation projects, as well as general principles and processes for annotation.

8 Supervised learning, a paradigm that currently dominates NLP systems development, requires the availability of annotated training data. 'Unsupervised' systems do not require annotated training data, but they are nonetheless evaluated using annotated test data. Today NLP evaluation is rarely done in the absence of annotated test material, though at times clever tricks have been used to automatically create 'pseudo-annotated' test items without requiring an investment in actual annotation (e.g., Gale et al., 1992a).

9 Recall from Section 2.2 that a summative evaluation can take place after a system has been completely developed, or at some milestone in its development. In NLP research, such milestones typically occur a few days (or a few hours, or a few minutes) before a conference submission deadline.

10 Other forms of non-point estimation are also sometimes used, e.g., bootstrapping, which involves sampling with replacement rather than creating a partition (Efron & Gong 1983; Yeh 2000b; Krymolowski 2001).

11 Though see comments on the most frequent baseline in Section 4.

12 For a highly approachable introduction to statistical hypothesis testing, we recommend Gonick and Smith (1994).

13 According to Doug Oard (personal communication), Karen Sparck Jones advocated this threshold because it has a clear interpretation in terms of the user's experience. He comments: ".10 corresponds roughly to nding one more document near the top of the list, and 0.05 corresponds roughly to nding one more document near the top of the list about half the time. These are usually applied to MAP [mean average precision] in practice, where the correspondence is quite approximate to those moves, but in precision at 10 the correspondence is perfect."

14 In contrast to the IR example, it must be noted that these absolute gains have no direct interpretation in terms of improvements in the user experience.

15 See discussion of the Senseval 'lexical sample' paradigm in Section 4.

16 This notation, based on Artstein and Poesio (2008), makes it easy to generalize from simple agreement to chance-correct agreement as discussed in Section 2.5. Our A is equivalent to their observed inter-annotator agreement A_0 between annotators, where one annotator is the NLP system and the other is the ground truth.

17 For example, Palmer et al. (2006) de ne *precision, recall, accuracy,* and *coverage* in such a way that accuracy and recall are synonymous. Other closely related concepts include misses versus false alarms, sensitivity versus speci city, and Type I versus Type II errors.

18 The list of relevant documents forms an essential component of a *test collection,* a standard experimental tool in information retrieval research. Test collections are typically constructed through large-scale system evaluations, such as the Text Retrieval Conferences (TRECs) (for more details, see Harman 2005).

19 The original version of the metrics considered constituents to match in the gold standard and system-output parse-trees as long as they bracketed the same span of tokens, regardless of constituent label. Requiring the non-terminal symbols to also match is a straightforward and rather stricter variant. The PARSEVAL metrics also included a third measure, 'crossing brackets,' that penalizes irreconcilable differences between the system parse and the gold standard; for example, *(the (old men) and women)* can be reconciled with *(the ((old men) and women)),* since it is just missing one pair of brackets, but there is no way to reconcile it with *(the old (men and women)).*

20 Every necessary edit constitutes an error, and so the acronym TER is also sometimes expanded as 'translation error rate.' Snover et al. (2006) use 'edit,' but Mathew Snover et al. (2005) used 'error.'

21 The use of these data types is not without controversy (see, e.g., Velleman & Wilkinson 1993).
22 This nice connection between the formal de nition and the everyday idea of being perplexed is suggested in the Wikipedia page for *Perplexity*, June 2009.
23 Notice that in contrast to Kullback–Leibler distance, the computation of perplexity did not require knowing the 'true' distribution (for discussion, see Jurafsky & Martin 2009: 116ff.)
24 Yarowsky (1992: 458) observes that most previous authors had "reported their results in qualitative terms." He also cites a half dozen exceptions starting with Lesk (1986).
25 We have structured this discussion roughly following Palmer et al. (2006).
26 It must be noted that selecting the most frequent sense is best viewed as a supervised approach, and therefore an unfairly rigorous lower bound for unsupervised tech- niques, since accurately computing sense frequencies requires labeled training data. McCarthy et al. (2004) introduced an unsupervised method for nding predominant word senses in untagged text.
27 See Artstein and Poesio (2008) for an insightful analysis of this evaluation metric in the context of measuring inter-coder agreement.
28 Details about TREC can be found at http://trec.nist.gov/
29 Note that this nding illustrates potential differences between intrinsic and extrinsic evaluations.
30 See TREC QA tracks overview papers for details of different evaluation metrics that have been adopted.
31 For many years, Ken Litkowski headed up this effort.

Part III Domains of Application

12 Speech Recognition

STEVE RENALS AND THOMAS HAIN

1 Introduction

By *automatic speech recognition* we mean the process of speech-to-text transcription: the transformation of an acoustic signal into a sequence of words, without necessarily understanding the meaning or intent of what was spoken. Recognition without understanding is not always possible since some semantic context may be required, for instance, to disambiguate *Will the new display recognize speech?* from *Will the nudist play wreck a nice beach?* Automatic speech recognition corresponds to answering the question *who spoke what when?*;[1] in the general case this may involve transcribing the speech of two or more people taking part in a conversation, in which the speakers frequently talk at the same time. The solution to this task is often considered in two parts: *speaker diarization* (who spoke when?), and *speech-to-text transcription* (what did they say?). Of course, the speech signal contains much more information than just the words spoken and who said them. Speech acoustics also carries information about timing, intonation, and voice quality. These paralinguistic aspects convey information about the speaker's emotion and physiology, as well as sometimes disambiguating between different possible meanings. In this chapter, however, we shall focus on automatic speech-to-text transcription.

Speech-to-text transcription has a number of applications including the dictation of of ce documents, spoken dialogue systems for call centers, hands-free interfaces to computers, and the development of speech-to-speech translation systems. Each of these applications is typically more restricted than the general problem which requires the automatic transcription of naturally spoken continuous speech, by an unknown speaker in any environment. This is an extremely challenging task. There are several sources of variability which we cluster into four main areas: the *task domain*, *speaker characteristics*, *speaking style*, and the recognition *environment*. In many practical situations, the variability is restricted. For example, there may be a single, known speaker, or the speech to be recognized may be carefully dictated text rather than a spontaneous conversation, or the recording environment may be quiet and non-reverberant. In speech-to-text

The Handbook of Computational Linguistics and Natural Language Processing, First Edition.
Edited by Alexander Clark, Chris Fox and Shalom Lappin.
© 2013 Blackwell Publishing Ltd except for editorial material and organization
© 2013 Alexander Clark, Chris Fox, and Shalom Lappin. Published 2013 by Blackwell Publishing Ltd.

transcription a distinction is made between parts addressing acoustic variabil-ity (acoustic modeling), and parts addressing linguistic uncertainty (language modeling).

1.1.1 Task domain   Aspects of the speci c speech recognition task which affect the dif culty of the speech transcription process include the language and the size of the vocabulary to be recognized, and whether the speech comes from a limited domain. Different languages present different challenges for a speech recognizer. For example, agglutinative languages, such as Turkish and Finnish, have larger vocabularies than non-agglutinative languages (such as English) due to words formed from the concatenation of multiple morphemes. This has an effect on the lexical and language model. For English, a speech recognition sys-tem is considered to have a large vocabulary if it has the order of 10^4 word types in its vocabulary; a comparable system for a language such as Finnish, however, may have two orders of magnitude more word types. As another example, tonal languages, such as Chinese, use pitch movements to distinguish small sets of words, which has an effect on acoustic modeling.

The number of word types in the vocabulary of a speech recognizer gives an indication of the 'size' of the problem that may be misleading, however; perplex-ity[2] of the language model gives an indication of effective size. A spoken dialogue system concerned with stock prices, for instance, may have a relatively large vocabulary (due to the number of distinct words occurring in company names) but a small perplexity.

1.1.2 Speaker characteristics   Different speakers have differences in their speech production anatomy and physiology, speak at different rates, use differ-ent language, and produce speech acoustics with different degrees of intrinsic variability. Other differences in speaker characteristics arise from systematic vari-ations such as those arising from speaker age and accent. One way to deal with this variability is through the construction of *speaker-dependent* speech recogni-tion systems, but this demands a new system to be constructed for each speaker. *Speaker-independent* systems, on the other hand, are more   exible in that they are designed to recognize any speaker. In practice, a speaker-dependent speech recog-nition system will tend to make fewer errors than a speaker-independent system. Although speaker adaptation algorithms (Section 2.5) have made great progress over the past 15 years, it is still the case that the adaptability and robustness to different speakers exhibited by automatic speech recognition systems is very limited compared with human performance.

1.1.3 Style   In the early days of automatic speech recognition, systems solved the problem of where to locate word boundaries by requiring the speaker to leave pauses between words: the pioneering dictation product Dragon Dictate (Baker 1989) is a good example of a large-vocabulary *isolated word* system. However, this is an unnatural speaking style and most research in speech recognition is focused on *continuous* speech recognition, in which word boundary information is not easily available. The problem of continuous speech recognition thus involves segmentation into words, as well as labeling each word.

Until the mid-1990s most speech recognition research followed research in acoustic phonetics, using recordings of planned speech recorded in laboratory or quiet of ce conditions. However, it has become apparent that more natural styles of speech, as observed in spontaneous conversation, result in considerably more acoustic variability: this is re ected in the increased word error rates for *conversational* or *spontaneous* speech recognition compared with the recognition of dictation or other *planned* speech. A modern speech recognition system for the transcription of dictated newspaper text results in a typical word error rate of 5–10 percent; a state-of-the-art conversational speech recognition system will result in a word error rate of 10–30 percent when transcribing spontaneous conversations (Chen et al., 2006b; Hain et al., 2007).

1.1.4 Environment Finally the acoustic environment in which the speech is recorded, along with any transmission channel can have a signi cant impact on the accuracy of a speech recognizer. Outside of quiet of ces and laboratories, there are usually multiple acoustic sources including other talkers, environmental noise and electrical or mechanical devices. In many cases, it is a signi cant problem to separate the different acoustic signals found in an environment. In addition, the microphone on which the speech is recorded may be close to the talker (in the case of a headset or telephone), attached to a lapel, or situated on a wall or tabletop. Variations in transmission channel occur due to movements of the talker's head relative to the microphone and transmission across a telephone network or the internet. Probably the largest disparity between the accuracy of automatic speech recognition compared with human speech recognition occurs in situations with high additive noise, multiple acoustic sources, or reverberant environments.

1.2 Learning from data

The standard framework for speech recognition is statistical, developed in the 1970s and 1980s by Baker (1975), a team at IBM (Jelinek 1976; Bahl et al., 1983), and a team at AT&T (Levinson et al., 1983; Rabiner 1989). In this formulation the most probable sequence of words $\mathbf{W}^*$ must be identi ed given the recorded acoustics $\mathbf{X}$ and the model θ:

(1) $\quad \mathbf{W}^* = \arg\max_{\mathbf{W}} P(\mathbf{W} \mid \mathbf{X}, \theta)$

(2) $\qquad = \arg\max_{\mathbf{W}} \dfrac{p(\mathbf{X} \mid \mathbf{W}, \theta) P(\mathbf{W} \mid \theta)}{p(\mathbf{X} \mid \theta)}$

(3) $\qquad = \arg\max_{\mathbf{W}} p(\mathbf{X} \mid \mathbf{W}, \theta) P(\mathbf{W} \mid \theta)$

(4) $\qquad = \arg\max_{\mathbf{W}} \log p(\mathbf{X} \mid \mathbf{W}, \theta) + \log P(\mathbf{W} \mid \theta)$

Equation (1) speci es the most probable word sequence as the one with the highest posterior probability given the acoustics and the model. Equation (2) follows from (1) through the application of Bayes's theorem; since $p(X \mid \theta)$ is independent of the word sequence, we usually work with (3), or its log-domain version (4). P denotes a probability and p denotes a probability density function (pdf). In what follows, the dependence on the model θ (which is usually xed) is suppressed to avoid notational clutter.

Equations (3) or (4) may be regarded as splitting the problem into two components: *language modeling*, which is concerned with estimating the prior probability of a word sequence $P(W)$, and *acoustic modeling*, in which the likelihood of the acoustic data given the words, $p(X \mid W)$, is estimated. The parameters of both of these models are normally learned from large annotated corpora of data. Obtaining the optimal word sequence W^* is the *search* or *decoding* problem, discussed further in section 3.

The language model $P(W)$, which is discussed further in Chapter 3, STATISTICAL LANGUAGE MODELING, models a word sequence by providing a predictive probability distribution for the next word based on a history of previously observed words. Since this probability distribution does not depend on the acoustics, language models may be estimated from large textual corpora. Of course, the statistics of spoken word sequences are often rather different from the statistics of written text. The conventional n-gram language model, which approximates the history as the immediately preceding $n - 1$ words, has represented the state of the art for large-vocabulary speech recognition for 25 years. It has proven dif cult to improve over this simple model (Jelinek 1991; Rosenfeld, 2000). Attempts to do so have focused on improved models of word sequences (e.g., Bengio et al., 2003; Blitzer et al., 2005; Teh 2006; Huang & Renals 2007) or the incorporation of richer knowledge (e.g., Bilmes & Kirchhoff 2003; Emami & Jelinek 2005; Wallach 2006).

In this chapter we focus on acoustic modeling, and the development of systems for the recognition of conversational speech. In particular we focus on the trainable hidden Markov model/Gaussian mixture model (HMM/GMM) for acoustic modeling, the choice of modeling unit, and issues including adaptation, robustness, and discrimination. We also discuss the construction of a elded system for the automatic transcription of multiparty meetings.

1.3   Corpora and evaluation

The statistical framework for ASR is extremely powerful: it is scalable and ef - cient algorithms to estimate the model parameters from a corpus of speech data (transcribed at the word level) are available.

The availability of standard corpora, together with agreed evaluation protocols, has been very important in the development of the eld. The speci cation, collection, and release of the TIMIT corpus (Fisher et al., 1986) marked a signi cant point in the history of speech recognition research. This corpus, which has been widely used by speech recognition researchers for over two decades, contains utterances from 630 North American speakers, and is phonetically transcribed and time-aligned. The corpus de ned training and test sets, together with a commonly agreed evaluation metric (phone error rate – analogous to word error rate discussed below). This resulted in a training and evaluation protocol enabling the exact comparison of results between researchers.

Since the release of TIMIT, many speech corpora with corresponding evaluation protocols have been released. These include corpora of domain-speci c read speech (e.g., DARPA Resource Management), read aloud newspaper text (e.g., *Wall Street Journal*), domain-speci c human–computer dialogues (e.g., ATIS), broadcast news recordings (e.g., Hub4), conversational telephone speech (e.g., Switchboard), and recordings of multiparty meetings (e.g., AMI). Many of these corpora are available from the Linguistic Data Consortium (www.ldc.upenn.edu); the AMI corpus is available from http://corpus.amiproject.org. The careful recording, transcription, and release of speech corpora has been closely connected to a series of benchmark evaluations of automatic speech recognition systems, primarily led by the US National Institute of Standards and Technology (NIST). This cycle of data collection and system evaluation has given speech recognition research a solid objective grounding, and has resulted in consistent improvements in the accuracy of speech recognition systems (Deng & Huang 2004) – although Bourlard et al. (1996), among others, have argued that an overly strong focus on evaluation can lead to a reduction in innovation.

If the speech recognition problem is posed as the transformation of an acoustic signal to a single stream of words, then there is widespread agreement on word error rate (WER) as the appropriate evaluation measure. The sequence of words output by the speech recognizer is aligned to the reference transcription using dynamic programming. The accuracy of the speech recognizer may then be estimated as the string edit distance between the output and reference strings. If there are N words in the reference transcript, and alignment with the speech recognition output results in S substitutions, D deletions, and I insertions, the word error rate is de ned as:

(5) $\quad \text{WER} = 100 \cdot \dfrac{(S + D + I)}{N}\%$

(6) $\quad \text{Accuracy} = (100 - \text{WER})\%$

In the case of a high number of insertions, it is possible for the WER to be above 100 percent. Computation of WER is dependent on the automatic alignment between the reference and hypothesized sequence of words. As word timings are not used in the process this may lead to underestimates of true error rate in situations of considerable mismatch. In practice, the transition costs used in the dynamic programming algorithm to compute the alignment are standardized and embedded in standard software implementations such as the NIST sclite tool,[3] or the HResults tool in the HTK speech recognition toolkit.[4]

More generally, the desired output of a speech recognition system cannot always be expressed as a single sequence of words. Multiparty meetings, for instance, are characterised by multiple overlapping speakers. A measure of transcription quality for meetings might usefully include attributing each word to a meeting participant, as well as including of timing information, to take account of overlaps.

2   Acoustic Modeling

The statistical formulation of the speech recognition problem outlined in Section 1.2 provides the basic framework for all state-of-the-art systems. The acoustic model, which is used to estimate $p(X \mid W)$, may be interpreted as a generative model of a word sequence. Such a model must be decomposable into smaller units, since it is infeasible to estimate a separate model for each word sequence. Hidden Markov models (HMMs) (Baker 1975; Poritz 1988; Rabiner 1989; Jelinek 1998) have proven to be very well suited to this task.

HMMs are probabilistic nite state machines, which may be combined hierarchically to construct word sequence models out of smaller units. In large-vocabulary speech recognition systems, word sequence models are constructed from word models, which in turn are constructed from subword models (typically context-dependent phone models) using a pronunciation dictionary.

HMM acoustic models treat the speech signal as arising from a sequence of discrete phonemes, or 'beads-on-a-string' (Ostendorf 1999). Such a modeling approach does not (directly) take into account processes such as *coarticulation*, a phenomenon in which the place of articulation for one speech sound depends on a neighboring speech sound. For instance, consider the phoneme /n/ in the words *'ten'* and *'tenth.'* In *'ten,'* /n/ is dental, with the tongue coming into contact (or close to) the upper front teeth; in *'tenth,'* /n/ is alveolar, with the tongue farther back in the mouth (coming into contact with the alveolar ridge). Coarticulation gives rise to signi cant context-dependent variability. The use of context-dependent phone modeling (Section 2.3) aims to mitigate these effects, as does the development of richer acoustic models that take account of speech production knowledge (King et al., 2007).

2.1   *Acoustic features*

Speech recognition systems do not model speech directly at the waveform level; instead signal processing techniques are used to extract the *acoustic features* that are to be modeled by an HMM.[5] A good acoustic feature representation for speech recognition will be compact, without losing much signal information. In practice the acoustic feature representations used in speech recognition do not retain phase information, nor do they aim to retain information about the glottal source which (for many languages) is relatively independent of the linguistic message. Figure 12.1 shows a speech waveform and the corresponding *spectrogram*, a representation that shows the energy of the speech signal at different frequencies. Although a variety of representations are used in speech recognition, perhaps

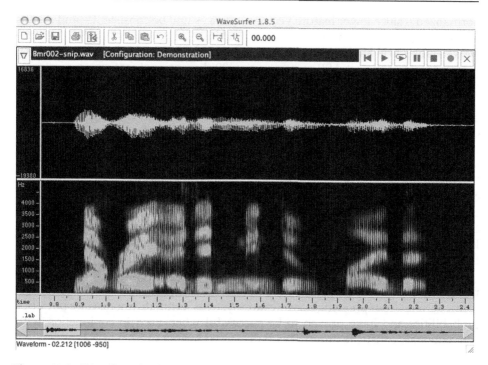

Figure 12.1 Waveform (top) and spectrogram (bottom) of conversational utterance *'no right I didn't mean to imply that.'*

the most widely used are Mel frequency cepstral coef cients (MFCCs) (Davis & Mermelstein 1980). MFCCs are based on the log spectral envelope of the speech signal, transformed to a non-linear frequency scale that roughly corresponds to that observed in the human auditory system. This representation is smoothed and orthogonalized by applying a discrete cosine transform, resulting in a cepstral representation. These acoustic feature vectors are typically computed every 10 ms, using a 25 ms Hamming window within the speech signal. Perceptual linear prediction (PLP) is a frequently used alternative acoustic feature analysis, which includes an auditory-inspired cube-root compression and uses an all-pole model to smooth the spectrum before the cepstral coef cients are computed (Hermansky 1990).

Speech recognition accuracy is substantially improved if the feature vectors are augmented with the rst and second temporal derivatives of the acoustic features (sometimes referred to as the deltas and delta-deltas), thus adding some information about the local temporal dynamics of the speech signal to the feature representation (Furui 1986). Adding such temporal information to the acoustic feature vector introduces a direct dependence between successive feature vectors, which is not usually taken account of in acoustic modeling; a mathematically correct treatment of these dependences has an impact on how the acoustic model is normalized – since fewer feature vector sequences will be consistent – and results in an approach that may be viewed as modeling an entire trajectory of feature vectors (Tokuda et al., 2003; Bridle 2004; Zhang & Renals 2006; Zen et al., 2007).

Many state-of-the-art ASR systems use a 39-dimensional feature vector, corresponding to twelve MFCCs (or PLP cepstral coef cients), plus energy, along with their rst and second derivatives. These acoustic feature representations have co-evolved with the basic acoustic models used in ASR: HMMs using multivariate Gaussian or Gaussian mixture output probability density functions, discussed in the next section. A particular advantage of cepstral representations compared with spectral representations is the decorrelation of cepstral coef cients, compared with the high correlations observed between neighboring spectral coef cients. Such decorrelations are very well matched with the distributional assumptions that underlie systems based on Gaussians with diagonal covariance matrices.[6] Furthermore, the compact smoothed representations obtained when using MFCC or PLP coef cients results in component multivariate Gaussians of lower dimension than would be obtained if spectral representations were used.

Hermansky et al. (2000) introduced a class of acoustic features that attempt to represent discriminant phonetic information directly. These so-called *tandem* features, derived from phonetic classi cation systems, estimate phone class posterior probabilities and have proven to be successful when used in conjunction with conventional acoustic features. This is discussed further in Section 5.2.

2.2   *HMM/GMM framework*

The statistical framework for ASR, introduced in Section 1.2, decomposes a speech recognizer into acoustic modeling and language components (equations 3 and 4). Conceptually, the process works by estimating the probability of a hypothesized sequence of words $\mathbf{W}$ given an acoustic utterance $\mathbf{X}$ using a language model to estimate $P(\mathbf{W})$ (see Chapter 3, STATISTICAL LANGUAGE MODELING) and an acoustic model to estimate $p(\mathbf{X}|\mathbf{W})$.

We can regard the machine that estimates $p(\mathbf{X}|\mathbf{W})$ as a *generative model*, in which the observed acoustic sequence is regarded as being generated by a model of the word sequence. Acoustic models in speech recognition are typically based on hidden Markov models. An HMM is a probabilistic nite state automaton, consisting of a set of states connected by transitions, in which the state sequence is hidden. Instead of observing the state sequence, a sequence of acoustic feature vectors is observed, generated from a pdf attached to each state. A hierarchical approach is used to construct HMMs of word sequences from simpler basic HMMs. The building blocks of an HMM-based speech recognition system are HMMs of 'subword units,' typically phones. A dictionary of pronunciations is used to build word models from subword models, and models of word sequences are constructed by concatenating word models. This approach, illustrated in Figure 12.2, enables information to be shared across word models: the number of distinct HMM states in a system is determined by the size of the set of subword units. In the simplest

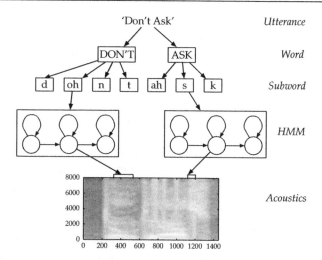

Figure 12.2 HMM-based hierarchical modeling of speech. An utterance model is constructed from a sequence of word models, which are each in turn constructed from subword models.

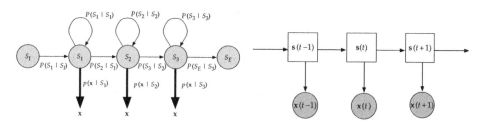

Figure 12.3 Representation of an HMM as a parameterized stochastic finite state automaton (left) and in terms of probabilistic dependences between variables (right).

case, an English speech recognition system might be constructed from a set of 40–60 base phone models with three states each. However, there is a lot of acoustic variability between different observed examples of the same phone. Much of this variability can be accounted for by the context in which a subword appears, and more detailed acoustic models can be achieved using context-dependent subwords, as discussed in Section 2.3. Between-word silence can be represented by special HMMs for silence and, since between-word silence is rare in continuous speech, adding a so-called 'skip' transition to make their existence optional.

An HMM is parameterized by an initial or prior distribution over the states q_i, $P(q_i)$, a state transition distribution $P(q_j \mid q_i)$, and an output pdf for each state $p(\mathbf{x} \mid q_i)$, where $\mathbf{x}$ is an acoustic feature vector. This is illustrated in Figure 12.3 (left) in terms of the model parameters, and in terms of the dependences between the state and acoustic variables in Figure 12.3 (right).

Each state has an output pdf de ning the relation between the state and the acoustic vectors. A simple form for the output pdf for state q_i is a d-dimensional Gaussian, parameterized by a mean vector μ_i and a covariance matrix Σ_i:

(7) $p(\mathbf{x}|q_i) = \mathcal{N}(\mathbf{x}; \mu_i, \Sigma_i) = \dfrac{1}{(2\pi)^{d/2}|\Sigma_i|^{1/2}} \exp\left(-\dfrac{1}{2}(\mathbf{x} - \mu_i)^T \Sigma_i^{-1}(\mathbf{x} - \mu_i)\right)$

For a typical acoustic vector comprising 12th-order MFCCs plus energy, with rst and second derivatives, $d = 39$.

Modeling speech using hidden Markov models makes two principal assumptions, illustrated in the graphical model shown in Figure 12.3 (left):

(1)   **Markov process.** The state sequence in an HMM is assumed to be a rst-order Markov process, in which the probability of the next state transition depends only on the current state: a history of previous states is not necessary.

(2)   **Observation independence.** All the information about the previously observed acoustic feature vectors is captured in the current state: the likelihood of generating an acoustic vector is conditionally independent of previous acoustic vectors given the current state.

These assumptions mean that the resultant acoustic models are computationally and mathematically tractable, with parameters that may be estimated from extremely large corpora. It has been frequently argued that these assumptions result in models that are unrealistic, and it is certainly true that a good deal of acoustic modeling research over the past two decades has aimed to address the limitations arising from these assumptions. However, the success of both HMM-based speech synthesis (Yamagishi et al., 2009) and HMM-based speech recognition is evidence that it is perhaps too facile to simply assert that HMMs are an unrealistic model of speech.

Acoustic modeling using HMMs has become the dominant approach due to the existence of recursive algorithms which enable some key computations to be carried out ef ciently. These algorithms arrive from the Markov and observation independence assumptions. To determine the overall likelihood of an observation sequence $\mathbf{X} = (\mathbf{x}_1, \ldots, \mathbf{x}_t, \ldots, \mathbf{x}_T)$ being generated by an HMM, it is necessary to sum over all possible state sequences $q_1 q_2 \ldots q_T$ that could result in the observation sequence X. Rather than enumerating each sequence, it is possible to compute the likelihood recursively, using the *forward algorithm*. The key to this algorithm is the computation of the forward probability $\alpha_t(q_j) = p(\mathbf{x}_1, \ldots, \mathbf{x}_t, q_t = q_j \mid \lambda)$, the probability of observing the observation sequence $\mathbf{x}_1 \ldots \mathbf{x}_t$ and being in state q_j at time t. The Markov assumption allows this to be computed recursively using a recursion of the form:

(8) $\alpha_t(q_j) = \displaystyle\sum_{i=1}^{N} \alpha_{t-1}(q_i) a_{ij} b_j(\mathbf{x}_t)$

This recursion is illustrated in Figure 12.4.

The decoding problem for HMMs involves nding the state sequence that is most likely to have generated an observation sequence. This may be solved using

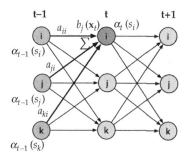

Figure 12.4   Forward recursion to estimate $\alpha_t(q_j) = p(\mathbf{x}_1, \ldots, \mathbf{x}_t, q_t = q_j \mid \lambda)$.

a dynamic programming algorithm, often referred to as *Viterbi decoding*, which has a very similar structure to the forward algorithm, with the exception that the summation at each time step is replaced by a max operation, since just the most probable state sequence is required. This is discussed further in Section 3.

By *training* we mean the estimation of the parameters of an HMM: the transition probabilities and the parameters of the output pdf (mean vector and covariance matrix in the case of a Gaussian). The most straightforward criterion to use for parameter estimation is maximum likelihood, in which the parameters are set so as to maximize the likelihood of the model generating the observed training data. Other training criteria may be used, such as maximum a posteriori (MAP) or Bayesian estimation of the posterior distribution, and discriminative training (Section 2.4). Maximum likelihood training can be approximated by considering the most probable state–time alignment, which may be obtained using the Viterbi algorithm. Given such an alignment, maximum likelihood parameter estimation is straightforward: the transition probabilities are estimated from relative frequencies, and the mean and covariance parameters from the sample estimates. However, this approach to parameter estimation considers only the most probable path, whereas the probability mass is in fact factored across all possible paths. Exact maximum likelihood estimation can be achieved using the *forward–backward* or *Baum–Welch* algorithm (Baum 1972), a specialization of the expectation-maximization (EM) algorithm (Dempster et al., 1977). Each step of this iterative algorithm consists of two parts. In the rst part (the E-step) a probabilistic state–time alignment is computed, assigning a *state occupation probability* to each state at each time, given the observed data. Then the M-step estimates the parameters by an average weighted by the state occupation probabilities. The EM algorithm can be shown to converge in a local maximum of the likelihood function. The key to the E-step lies in the estimation of the state occupation probability, $\gamma_t(q_j) = P(q_t = q_j \mid \mathbf{X}, \lambda)$, the probability of occupying state q_j at time t given the sequence of observations. The state occupation probabilities can also be computed recursively:

$$(9) \quad \gamma_t(q_j) = \frac{1}{\alpha_T(q_E)} \alpha_t(q_j) \beta_t(q_j)$$

where $\alpha_t(q_j)$ is the forward probability for state q_j at time t, $\beta_t(q_j) = p(\mathbf{x}_{t+1}, \mathbf{x}_{t+2}, \mathbf{x}_T \mid q_t = q_j, \lambda)$ is called the *backward* probability, and $\alpha_T(q_E)$ is a normalization factor (the forward probability for the end state q_E at the end of the observation sequence, time T). The backward probabilities are so called because they may be computed by a recursion that goes backwards in time.

The output pdfs are the most important part of this model, and restricting them to single Gaussians results in a signi cant limitation on modeling capability. In practice, Gaussian mixture model (GMMs) are used as output pdfs. A GMM is a weighted sum of Gaussians:

$$(10) \quad p(\mathbf{x}|q_i) = \sum_{k}^{K} c_{ik} \mathcal{N}(\mathbf{x}; \boldsymbol{\mu}_{ik}, \boldsymbol{\Sigma}_{ik})$$

where we have a mixture of K Gaussian components, with mixture weights c_{ik}. Training a GMM is analogous to HMM training: for HMMs the state is a hidden variable, for GMMs the mixture component is a hidden variable. Again the EM algorithm may be employed, with the E-step estimating the *component occupation probabilities*, and the M-step updating the means and covariances using a weighted average.

2.3 Subword modeling

As discussed in Section 2.2, and illustrated in Figure 12.2, there is no need to train individual HMMs for each sentence. Instead, the sentence HMMs can be constructed by concatenating *word* HMMs, which in turn may be constructed from *subword* HMMs. This is necessary as training of independent word models is not feasible for most applications: the *Oxford English Dictionary* contains more than 250,000 entries; for morphologically rich languages, such as Finnish or Turkish, there are many more possible words.[7] If we assume that at least 50 samples per word are necessary and take the usually observed average word duration of half a second, the amount of transcribed speech data for English would be approximately 1,700 hours. This calculation is an underestimate, however, as it does not take into account contextual effects, and assumes a uniform distribution over all words. Only very recently have such amounts of annotated data been available, and only for US English. Thus subword modeling seems an attractive alternative: for example the words of British English can be described using a set of about 45 phonemes.

It is possible to write the pronunciation of words in a language with a nite set of symbols, hence one can associate an HMM with each. In the TIMIT database a set of 39 phones is often used: the ARPABET, a phoneme set de ned for speech recognition in US English, identi es 40 distinct symbols. By using HMMs for individual phonemes, several important changes are made: a dictionary describing the transitions from words to phonemes has become necessary; the number of units has been drastically reduced; and the length of the units have become more

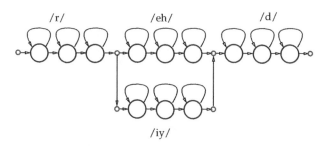

Figure 12.5   Hidden Markov models for phonemes can be concatenated to form models for words. Parallel paths indicate pronunciation variants.

similar. Although the TIMIT corpus was phonetically labeled, this is not a necessary requirement for using models for phonemes, as the phoneme sequence can be inferred from the word sequence using the dictionary and the sentence HMM is constructed by phoneme model concatenation. One issue arises in that the mapping from phonemes to words is not unique, e.g., the word 'read,' can be pronounced in two ways, /r iy d/ and /r eh d/. However, different pronunciations can be represented by using parallel paths in the sentence HMM (see Figure 12.5). Even more so, different weights can be given to these variants. Pronunciation modeling and/or lexical modeling (e.g., Strik & Cucchiarini 1999) usually focuses on how to best encode pronunciation variability.

Having fewer than 100 *small* HMMs does not allow to capture the large variability of speech, caused by individual variation in articulation and speaker differences (so called intra- and inter-speaker variability). In an attempt to deal with problems arising from acoustic phonetic context, such as coarticulation, many state-of-the-art systems are based on *context-dependent* phone models, often called *triphones*.

Triphone modeling has at its heart the idea of basic sounds that differ depending on their context. In particular, the context here is the immediate neighboring phonemes. Take for example the word '*sound*' and its ARPABET representation /s ow n d/. Instead of having a model for the phoneme /ow/ a model for /ow/ with left context /s/ and right context /n/ is constructed, typically written in the form [s-ow+n]. Taking a typical phoneme inventory size of 45 the number of such triphone models has now risen to 91,125 while retaining the trivial mapping from words to models. In order to avoid the same issues as with word models however, one, can start to declare some triphones as equivalent, e.g., /ow/ may sound very similar to any fricative appearing beforehand.

Most state-of-the-art speech recognition systems make use of clustered triphones or even phone models in a wider context (e.g., quin-/penta-phones, Woodland et al., 1995). A natural grouping approach would be knowledge-based (e.g., Hayamizu et al., 1988), but it has been repeatedly shown that automatic techniques give superior performance. As in many machine learning approaches clustering can operate bottom-up or top-down. The use of agglomerative clustering

(Hwang & Huang 1992) allows robust modeling but, if not all triphones have been observed in the training data, it is unclear how to represent words containing those triphones. Instead classi cation and regression trees (CARTs) were found to serve well in both cases (Bahl et al., 1991; Young et al., 1994). Here a binary decision tree is grown from a prede ned set of questions about the neighboring phonemes (e.g., if the left neighbor is a plosive). When growing the tree, at each point the one question yielding the highest gain in likelihood is chosen. Tree growing is abandoned if the gain in likelihood falls below a prede ned threshold. It is standard to cluster HMM states rather than whole models in this way and normally one decision tree per phoneme and per state position is derived. On average decision trees associated with vowels have greater depth than those associated with consonants.

Several weaknesses of the CART approach are known. For example, when clustering it is assumed that states are well represented by a single Gaussian density. Also, hard decisions are made on classes which are better represented as hidden variables (Hain 2001), and the dependency on neighboring phonemes is not the only property that in uences sounds. Alternatives include articulatory representations or factorization of graphical models (King et al., 2007).

In English the relationship between sounds and the written forms is looser than in other languages, for example German or Turkish. For these languages it was shown that using the graphemes directly for modeling can have good results (Killer et al., 2003), thus limiting the need for a manually crafted pronunciation lexicon. For tonal languages, questions on tonal context, including the current phoneme, can signi cantly improve performance (Cao et al., 2000).

2.4 Discriminative training

Learning of HMM parameters can be approached in fundamentally different ways. While generative learning tries to yield good estimates of the probability density of training samples, discriminative learning drives directly at nding those parameters that yield best classi cation performance. Within the generative family, maximum likelihood (ML) training is the most widely used scheme. The associated objective function is given by

$$\mathcal{F}_{\mathrm{ML}}\,(\theta) = \log p\,(\mathbf{X} \mid \theta)$$

which implies that the parameters θ are chosen to maximize the likelihood of the training data. As discussed in Section 2.2, ML training can be ef ciently carried out for HMMs, because the Baum–Welch algorithm enables the ef cient computation of the state/component occupation probabilities, supplies good asymptotic guarantees, and is relatively easy to code. Although the result of the algorithm is sensitive to the initialization of parameters, practical experience has shown that this is usually of little impact on error rates obtained.

Discriminative training is based on the idea that, given nite training data and a mismatch of the model being trained to the true model, it is better to focus on learning the boundaries between the classes. Discriminative approaches have become increasingly popular and several techniques have been developed over the past two decades. The most important criteria are maximum mutual information (MMI), minimum classi cation error (MCE), and minimum Bayes risk (MBR). All of these have in common that not only the correct, i.e., reference, sequence is used in training but also all incorrect word sequences. Since summation over all possible incorrect word sequences is not feasible for large-vocabulary speech recognition, the set of *competitors* is usually constrained to those that have significant probability mass compared with the correct sequence. This implies that the output of recognition of the complete training set must be generated, usually a computationally expensive process.

MCE training (Juang & Katagiri 1992) is based on the idea that model parameters only need correction if misrecognition occurs. The objective function to be maximized is based on the ratio between the likelihoods of the correct sequence and of the incorrect ones. The discriminant function is de ned as $d\,(\mathbf{X}|\boldsymbol{\theta}) = g\,(\mathbf{X}|\boldsymbol{\theta}) - \bar{g}\,(\mathbf{X}|\boldsymbol{\theta})$ where g denotes the log-likelihood of the correct sentence and $\bar{g}$ is the average likelihood of the competitors $\mathbf{W}_{\text{incorrect}}$:

$$\bar{g}\,(\mathbf{X}|\boldsymbol{\theta}) = \frac{1}{\eta} \log \left(\frac{1}{M-1} \sum_{\mathbf{W} \in \mathbf{W}_{\text{incorrect}}} \exp\left(\eta \log p\,(\mathbf{X}|\mathbf{W}, \boldsymbol{\theta})\right) \right)$$

Instead of using the above function directly the transition is smoothed with a sigmoid function, which serves as an approximation to a zero/one loss function (i.e., if the value of the discriminant function is larger or smaller than zero). The overall criterion function again is an average over all training samples of the smoothed discriminants. MCE training is mostly used for smaller vocabularies. Its main weakness is the inef cient use of training data since it only considers misrecognized examples. By allowing the smoothed functions to become a step function and the weight η to tend towards ∞ the criterion function can be shown to converge to the misclassi cation rate and hence has a clear relationship to MBR training (outlined below).

A recently more prominent alternative is MMI training. Although it was introduced at a similar time (discrete densities, Nadas et al., 1988; continuous, Normandin 1991) it was initially feasible only for small-vocabulary tasks or even discrete word recognition, partially because of the substantial computational cost incurred. The gains were substantial and the rst large-vocabulary implementation was reported by Valtchev et al. (1997) but the gains were modest in comparison. The MMI objective function is given by

$$(11) \quad \mathcal{F}_{MMI}\,(\boldsymbol{\theta}) = \mathcal{E} \left\{ \frac{p(\mathbf{X}|\mathbf{W}, \boldsymbol{\theta})}{p(\mathbf{X}|\boldsymbol{\theta})} \right\} = \mathcal{E} \left\{ \frac{p(\mathbf{X}|\mathbf{W}, \boldsymbol{\theta})}{\sum_{\mathbf{W}' \in \mathbf{W}_{\text{incorrect}}} p(\mathbf{X}|\mathbf{W}', \boldsymbol{\theta})^{\alpha} P(\mathbf{W}'|\boldsymbol{\theta})^{\beta}} \right\}$$

where $\mathcal{E}\{\cdot\}$ denotes the expectation. This is equivalent to the mutual information between word sequence $\mathbf{W}$ and acoustic features $\mathbf{X}$. Naturally the amount of information transferred is to be maximized. The criterion has an equivalent interpretation as a variant of conditional maximum likelihood (Nadas 1983). Optimization of the above criterion is mostly based on the extended Baum–Welch algorithm (Gopalakrishnan et al., 1989). In contrast to the standard Baum–Welch algorithm, a learning rate factor similar to gradient descent algorithms was introduced. The selection of the optimal learning rate is dif cult and was found to be best set such that the variances of the updated model parameters remain suf - ciently positive. Nevertheless, usually after only a few iterations, the algorithms tend to diverge.

Povey (2003) introduced two fundamental improvements that allowed not only to stabilize the algorithm, but also to improve performance on large-vocabulary tasks dramatically. Equation 11 shows two so far unexplained factors α and β. These factors allow to scale the contribution of the acoustic and language model components. Such scaling would be of no effect in ML training but equation 11 involves a sum. Scaling the language model scores is important in decoding (see Section 3) with the rationale that acoustic models underestimate the true likelihoods due to independence assumptions. The rationale in MMI training is identical, with even the same scale factor values being used (or the inverse to scale the acoustics down rather than the language model up). Secondly, smoothing of the update equation proved to be important. The ML estimate serves as a much more stable estimate and the addition of xed amounts of the MMI parameter updates was shown to greatly enhance the stability of the algorithm and thus improve performance. In Povey (2003), so-called I-smoothing adds a prede ned weight to the ML estimate in the update equations.

Both MCE and MMI training have interesting interpretations that are intuitive and t in well with ML training. However, in both cases one assumption is made that is in con ict with the decoding scheme, namely the use of likelihood to assess the correctness of a sentence. This correctness measure then drives the update of parameters. Speech recognizer output, however, is normally assessed with the word error metric which measures performance in the form of insertions, deletions, and substitutions of words (aka minimum edit or Levenshtein distance). For MCE and MMI the word error rate is of no concern, as long as the likelihood of an incorrect sentence is close to the correct, little change is made on the associated HMM parameters.

To alleviate this shortcoming, minimum Bayes risk training was introduced, initially in the form of so-called minimum phone error (MPE) training (Povey & Woodland 2002). Here explicit use is made of the Levenshtein string edit distance between the competing and reference utterances, $L(\mathbf{W}, \mathbf{W}_{ref})$. The criterion function is given by

$$\mathcal{F}_{MBR}(\boldsymbol{\theta}) = \sum_{\mathbf{W} \in \mathbf{W}} L(\mathbf{W}, \mathbf{W}_{ref}) P(\mathbf{W}|\mathbf{X}, \boldsymbol{\theta})$$

The posterior probability of the competing utterances is weighted by the amount of error in the target metric. Optimization of this criterion is more complicated because, as before, the above sum cannot be computed exactly. Whereas in the case of MMI the HMM properties allow reformation at state level, this becomes more complicated here. The error rate is associated with a whole sentence and the error value of a single word is not well de ned as the edit distance has no relation to time, i.e., only the errors of the token string are measured. In order to alleviate this problem two steps can be taken. First, a move to smaller units and, second, the measurement of local error led to the MPE criterion function

$$\mathcal{F}_{MPE}(\boldsymbol{\theta}) = \frac{\sum_{\mathbf{R}} P(\mathbf{X}|\mathbf{R}, \boldsymbol{\theta}) P(\mathbf{R}) A(\mathbf{R}, \mathbf{R}_{ref})}{\sum_{\mathbf{R}} P(\mathbf{X}|\mathbf{R}, \boldsymbol{\theta}) P(\mathbf{R})}$$

where **R** is a sequence of phonemes and $\mathbf{R}_{ref}$ is the sequence associated with the reference words, and $A(\cdot)$ denotes the count of raw phoneme errors. It can be shown that maximization of this function leads again to the extended Baum–Welch equations and updates similar to those obtained for MMI if the phoneme distance is replaced by a local estimate (Povey 2003) based on an approximation of frame overlap. Gibson (2008) provided a formal proof of local convergence.

Discriminative training allows signi cant gains in word error rate. On most large-vocabulary tasks, 10–20 percent relative improvement in word error rate is typically found in comparison to ML trained models which in most cases also serve as the starting point for training. The rate of improvement is rather dependent on model set size, and both MMI and MPE training allow much more compact models. Original work on large-scale MMI training postulated that gains increased with an increase in the amount of data (Woodland & Povey 2000), which is very different from the behavior observed for ML training. The computational cost of discriminative training is high and the complex solutions for optimization cause suboptimality in other areas such as speaker adaptation (see Section 2.5). Naturally discriminative training is sensitive to the quality of the reference labels.

2.5 *Speaker adaptation*

Speech signals vary substantially without signi cant changes in human percep-tion. A single person can vary the signal due to context, mood, or prosody. Despite the range of intra-speaker variations, listeners are easily capable of discerning dif-ferent speakers. The differences are manifold and include general speech behavior but also the physical characteristics of a person. The vocal tract shape, lungs, and vocal chords, etc., give a distinct characteristic to a person's voice. These character-istics are not as unique as ngerprints but suf cient to yield signi cant distinction in forensic applications. For the reminder of this section we focus on acoustic adaptation rather than adaptation to linguistic differences, as it is to date the far more common form of adaptation. Nevertheless, lexical and even language mod-els can be adapted to learn speaker-speci c characteristics (Strik & Cucchiarini 1999; Bellegarda 2004).

The natural variability of speech sounds themselves (aside from distortions introduced by the environment) is the main source of confusion and cause of errors. For the reasons outlined above it seems logical to separate physical variations from intentional ones. Hence the initial focus of speech recognition research was in the development of systems capable of dealing with a single speaker in order to achieve reasonable performance. In practice, these speaker-dependent (SD) systems are disadvantageous as large amounts of training data have to be collected and transcribed for each speaker, an approach only feasible for select applications.

The HMM-based framework was shown to cope with variability as long as it has been observed in the training data. This allowed the construction of so-called speaker independent (SI) model sets where the HMMs are simply trained on data from multiple speakers. Recognition of utterances from any speaker are then produced with the same models. While this approach is much more practical, the performance of an SI system is substantially inferior to that of an SD system trained on identical amounts of training data. Hence alternatives are required to bridge the gap. Human listeners are capable of adjusting to a new environment or speaker within a few words or sentences. Similarly for ASR, a few sentences can be used to adjust the models for recognition in order to yield better performance either in a second pass of recognition or for further sentences spoken by the target speaker.

Adaptation techniques can be classi ed in several ways: whether the acoustic models are changed or the extracted features or both (model or feature-based adaption); whether changes to the models are made prior to adaptation (adaptation or normalization); whether the labels used in adaptation can be assumed to be ground truth or with errors (supervised versus unsupervised adaptation). When the features alone are changed, the changes to speech recognition systems are normally small and hence such methods are often preferred. However, it turns out that in most cases changes to the features work best when changing the acoustic models at the same time, referred to as normalization. For most practical applications the ground truth is not known, in which case the adaptation technique must be able to cope with potentially high levels of word error rate. This has a particularly bad effect on discriminative adaptation techniques (Wang & Woodland 2002; Gibson & Hain 2007; Gibson 2008), however one effect usually alleviates that shortcoming: recognition errors are often phonetically similar to the correct word. The phoneme error rate is often lower than the word error rate (Mangu et al., 1999) and hence the correct models may still be chosen.

Since SD performance is assumed to be the best that can be obtained, an initial strategy is to rst cluster speaker-speci c models into distinct groups. Then the adaptation step would simply consist in nding the most likely group and using the associated model for decoding. Albeit capable of producing SD performance in the limit, it does not make good use of training data, as speaker cluster models are only trained on data of a subgroup and disregarded for the rest. A better approach is provided by the so-called eigenvoices method (Kuhn et al., 1998), where principal component analysis of the parameters of speaker cluster models (the means only are used in the original work) is carried out. Adaptation then is performed by constructing models by weighted combination of these principal components. The weights are found by maximum likelihood optimization on test data.

Another option to bridge the gap between SI and SD model performance is based on the estimation of a prior distribution over the model parameters. The speaker-independent models are used to provide the prior. Maximum a posteriori (MAP) adaptation (Gauvain & Lee 1994) describes the updates of Gaussian (SI) means by data observed in adaptation:

$$\hat{\mu} = \frac{\tau \mu_{\text{prior}} + \sum_{t=1}^{T} \gamma_t x_t}{\tau + \sum_{t=1}^{T} \gamma_t}$$

The new mean vector is changed from the old μ_{prior} with the average observation vector x_t which is weighted by the posterior probability that the vector has been produced by this Gaussian. The factor τ can be selected to re ect the speed of adaptation and, in practice, iterative application of the above rules shows the best performance (Hain et al., 2005a). While MAP adaptation can yield very good improvements it requires relatively large amounts of adaptation data to ensure that enough Gaussians have actually been observed and changed in the process. Discriminative versions of MAP exist to work with prior models that are already discriminatively trained (Povey et al., 2003).

A more knowledge-driven approach is to target the physical differences between speakers, in particular the vocal tract shape and size, with the latter being the most distinctive feature (e.g., male/female vocal tract sizes differ substantially due to the relative descent of the larynx in males during puberty – see Harries et al., 1998). The standard model of speech production is the source lter model (Fant 1960), with a vocal tract lter represented by linear prediction based on autocorrelation. Here the vocal tract is represented as an ideal acoustic tube with varying length. Change to the length of the tube can be interpreted as a simple shift of the magnitude spectrum with short lengths associated with a more compact spectrum (Cohen et al., 1995; Hain et al., 1999). Vocal tract length normalization (VTLN) implements the so-called warping of the frequency spectrum by shifting the Mel lter banks in MFCC or PLP feature extraction, subject to ensuring proper computation at boundaries (Hain et al., 1999). Furthermore, the optimal warp factor can be found by a search for the one factor that yields the highest likelihood given an HMM set (Hain et al., 1999). However, an SI model set would have been trained on speakers with different vocal tract lengths, increasing the variance of the distributions, an issue that can be avoided by prior training on normalized speaker data. Since the maximum likelihood estimation is used to nd the warp factors, models are trained iteratively, interleaving warp factor estimation and model training.

As outlined above, VTLN targets the length of the vocal tract only, allowing the estimation of a single parameter per speaker. This was shown to be equivalent to multiplying the vectors with a matrix of speci c structure (Claes et al., 1998). The idea of multiplication with a matrix without constraints leads to one of the most important techniques in speaker adaptation: maximum likelihood linear regression (MLLR) (Leggetter & Woodland 1995). Here the means are adjusted using a linear transform parameterised by a matrix **A** and a bias vector **b**.

$$\hat{\mu}_j = \mathbf{A}_{m(j)}\mu_j + \mathbf{b}_{n(j)}$$

The major difference with MAP adaptation is that the update of the mean of the jth component can use a matrix which is shared across many Gaussian distributions, selected by the index functions $m(j)$ and $n(j)$. These functions can be manually set or automatically found, similar to techniques used in triphone state clustering (see Section 2.3). The matrices can be found by maximizing the likelihood of test data using the transformed models. MLLR adaptation is very exible as the structure of the matrices and vectors can be arbitrarily chosen (e.g., using diagonal transforms only). Variance adaptation is equally possible (Gales & Woodland 1996) and joint optimization with a common transform leads to constrained MLLR, which can be implemented as a feature transform, thus again showing a connection with VTLN. As for VTLN, training on the normalized models also improves: speaker adaptive training can be implemented with constrained MLLR or normal MLLR (Anastasakos et al., 1996).

Speaker adaptation is a rich and extensive topic in automatic speech recognition and the space here is too small to give a full and in-depth account. Many valuable re nements have been made to the fundamental techniques above and some of the newer schemes have not been mentioned. The interested reader will nd a good review by Woodland (2001).

3 Search

Given an observed sequence of acoustic feature vectors **X**, and a set of HMMs, what is the most probable sequence of words $\hat{\mathbf{W}}$? This is referred to as the *search* or *decoding* problem, and involves performing the maximization of equations (1–4). Since words are composed of HMM state sequences, we may express this criterion by summing over all state sequences $\mathbf{Q} = q_1, q_2, \ldots, q_n$, noting that the acoustic observation sequence is conditionally independent of the word sequence given the HMM state sequence. If we wish to obtain only the most probable state sequence, then we employ the *Viterbi* criterion, by maximizing over $\mathcal{Q}_\mathbf{W}$, the set of all state sequences corresponding to word sequence **W**:

(12) $\hat{\mathbf{W}} = \arg\max_\mathbf{W} P(\mathbf{W}) \max_{\mathbf{Q} \in \mathcal{Q}_\mathbf{W}} P(\mathbf{Q} \mid \mathbf{W})P(\mathbf{X} \mid \mathbf{Q})$

Thus a decoding algorithm is required to determine $\hat{\mathbf{W}}$ using the above equation and the acoustic and language models.

Solving (12) by naïve exhaustive search of all possible state sequences is of course not feasible. Viterbi decoding (forward dynamic programming) exploits the

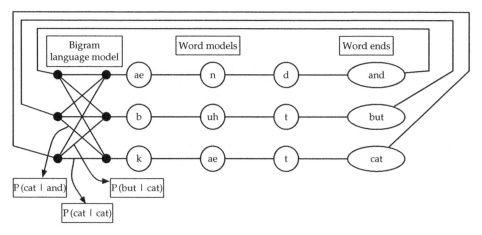

Figure 12.6 Connected word recognition with a bigram language model.

rst-order Markov assumption to solve the problem ef ciently. Given a state–time lattice, Viterbi decoding carries out a left-to-right time-synchronous processing. This is structurally similar to the forward recursion (Figure 12.4), except that the sum of probabilities of paths entering a state is replaced by a max operation. The Markov assumption is exploited by considering only the most probable path at each point in the state–time lattice: because the history is completely encapsulated by the current state, an extension to a lower probability path at a particular state–time location cannot become more probable than the same extension applied to the most probable path at that state–time location. Thus at each state–time point the single most probable path is retained, and the rest are discarded. The most probable path is the one at the end state at the nal time.

To recognize a word sequence, a composite HMM for each word is built (including multiple pronunciations, if necessary) and a global HMM is constructed (Figure 12.6). A bigram language model is easily incorporated; longer span models such as trigrams require a word history to be maintained. As mentioned in Section 2.4, the acoustic model log-likelihoods are often scaled by a factor $0 < \alpha < 1$, which takes into account the underestimate of the likelihood of an observation sequence arising from the conditional independence assumption.

Viterbi decoding is an ef cient, exact approach. However, an exact search is not usually possible for a large-vocabulary task since the absence of prede ned word boundaries means that any word in the vocabulary may start at each frame. Cross-word context-dependent triphone models and trigram language models add to the size of the search space and overall search complexity. Large-vocabulary decoding must make the problem size more manageable by reducing the size of the search space through pruning unlikely hypotheses, eliminating repeated computations, or simplifying the acoustic or language models. A commonly employed approach to shared computation, which does not include approximation, arises from structuring the lexicon as a pre x pronunciation tree (Gupta et al., 1988;

Bahl et al., 1993) in which common pronunciation pre xes are shared between word models; some extra bookkeeping is required to take account of context-dependent word models (Ravishankar 1996).

The most general approach to reducing the search space – and hence speeding up the decoding – is *beam search*. In beam search (Lowerre & Reddy 1980; Ney & Ortmanns 2000), unlikely search paths are pruned from the search, by removing modes in the time–state trellis whose path probability is more than a factor δ less probable then the best path, de ning a beam of width δ. Both the acoustic and language models contribute to pruning in this way. Naïvely, language models are applied at the end of a word, but it is possible to tighten the beam by applying a language model upper bound within the pronunciation tree. Applying beam search means that the decoding process is no longer exact, and hence increases in speed must be traded off against search errors – those errors that arise from incorrectly pruning a hypothesis that would go on to be the most probable. Some form of beam search is used in every large-vocabulary decoder.

Most modern large-vocabulary systems use a multi-pass search architecture (Austin et al., 1991), in which progressively more detailed acoustic and language models are employed – the AMI system, described in Section 4), is a good example of such a system. In multi-pass systems the search space is constrained by constructing word graphs (Ney & Ortmanns 2000) with less detailed models, which are then rescored by more detailed models. Such a system can also be used to combine differently trained models.

In the 1990s most approaches to large-vocabulary decoding constructed the search network dynamically. For a large-vocabulary system, with a trigram language model, constructing the complete network in a static manner seemed out of the question in terms of required memory resources. Several very ef - cient dynamic search space decoders were designed and implemented (Odell 1995). Although such decoders can be very resource ef cient, they result, for instance, in complex software with a tight interaction between the pruning algorithms and data structures. In contrast, searching a static network would offer the ability to decouple search network construction from decoding, and to enable algorithms to optimize the network to be deployed in advance. (Mohri et al., 2000; 2002) have developed an approach to ef cient static network construction based on weighted nite state transducer (WFST) theory. In this approach the components of the speech recognition system (acoustic models, pronunciations, language model) may be composed into a single decoding network, which is optimized using determinization and minimization procedures. This can result in a static network of manageable size, although the construction process may be memory-intensive. Such WFST approaches have now been used successfully in several systems. A number of freely available toolkits for WFST manipulation now exist.[8]

An alternative approach to large-vocabulary decoding is based on heuristic search: *stack decoding* (Jelinek 1969; Gopalakrishnan et al., 1995; Renals & Hochberg 1999). In stack decoding (which is essentially an A*-search), a 'stack' (priority queue) of partial hypotheses is constructed, with each hypothesis scored using on the probability of decoding to the current time point, plus an estimate of the remaining score. In this time-asynchronous approach to decoding, a best- rst approach is adopted. Since it does not rely on construction of a nite-state network it is well suited to long-span language models and acoustic models.

4 Case Study: The AMI System

Large-vocabulary speech recognition systems have been developed for a number of applications, using the basic acoustic modeling framework outlined in the previous sections. In the research community the most notable examples include read newspaper text, broadcast news, and conversational telephone speech. As discussed in Section 1, read or planned speech has less variability than conversational or spontaneous speech, and this is re ected in the much lower word error rates obtained by automatic speech recognition systems on planned speech tasks. For both planned and spontaneous speech, it has been found consistently that the accuracy of an HMM-based speech recognition system is heavily dependent on the training data. This dependence has two main characteristics. First, accuracy increases as the amount of training data increases (experience has shown the relationship to be logarithmic). Second, the availability of transcribed, in-domain acoustic data for training of acoustic and language models leads to signi cantly reduced errors. Word error rates can be halved compared with models that were trained on data recorded under different conditions, or from a different task domain.

In this section we consider the construction of a speech recognition system for multiparty meetings. Multiparty meetings, characterized by spontaneous, conversational speech, with speech from different talkers overlapping, form a challenging task for speech recognition. Since much of the work in this area has taken place in the context of the development of interactive environments, the data has been collected using both individual head-mounted microphones and multiple microphones placed on a meeting-room table (typically in some form of array con guration). Here we give a basic description of a system developed for the automatic transcription of meeting speech using head-mounted microphones; the system we outline was developed for the NIST Rich Transcription evaluation in 2006, and some of the nal system's complexity has been omitted for clarity.

The meetings domain forms an excellent platform for speech recognition research. Important research issues, necessary to the construction of an accurate system for meeting recognition, include segmentation into utterances by talker, robustness to noise and reverberation, algorithms to exploit multiple microphone recordings, multi-pass decoding strategies to enable the incorporation of more detailed acoustic and language models, and the use of system combination and cross-adaptation strategies to exploit system complementarity. The exploitation of system complementarity has proven to have a signi cant effect on word error rates. Speech recognition architectures may differ in terms of training data, features, or model topology, and these differences can result in systematically different errors. One can capitalize on such differences in two ways. First, unsupervised cross-adaptation enables the output of one part of the system to adapt another different part. This enables some of the adverse effects caused by unsupervised adaptation to be alleviated. Second, system combination allows the combination of the outputs of several stages of a system, for example by use of majority voting (Fiscus 1997).

Work on meeting transcription has in part been dominated by the fact that the amount of in-domain data is usually relatively small. As for any other spontaneous speech source, the cost of manual transcription is high (manual transcription of meeting data is about 25 times slower than real time). For the system described here, about 100 hours of acoustic training data from meetings were available, which is still modest. Hence most systems make use of adaptation of models from other domains. Stolcke et al. (2004) used a recognition system for conversational telephone speech as the starting point (others have reported that starting from broadcast news systems also works well, e.g., Schultz et al., 2004) and we have followed that strategy. Our experiments with language models for meeting data (Hain et al., 2005b) indicated that the vocabulary is similar to that used for broadcast news, with only a few additional out-of-vocabulary words. Later work has shown that meeting-speci c language models can give lower perplexity and word error rate, but the effect is small. Our systems have used a vocabulary of 50,000 words based on the contents of meeting transcriptions augmented with the most frequent words from broadcast news. Pronunciations were based on the UNISYN dictionary (Fitt 2000). The baseline language model for these experiments was a trigram built using the meeting transcripts, a substantial amount of broadcast news data, and most importantly data collected from the internet obtained by queries constructed from n-grams in the meeting transcripts (Bulyko et al., 2003; Wan & Hain 2006).

Figure 12.7 presents an overall schematic of the meeting transcription system. The initial three steps pre-process the raw recordings into segmented utterances suitable for processing by the recognizer. A least mean squares echo canceler (Messerschmitt et al., 1989) is applied to alleviate cross-talk in overlapped speech, followed by an automatic segmentation into speech utterances. The segmentation was performed on a per-channel basis and, in addition to using the standard speech recognition features (PLP features in this case), a number of other acoustic features were used including cross-channel normalized energy, signal kurtosis, mean cross-correlation, and maximum normalized cross-correlation (Wrigley et al., 2005; Dines et al., 2006). The segmentation is based on a multi-layered perceptron trained on 90 hours of meeting data. This exceptionally large amount of training data for a simple binary classi cation was necessary to yield good performance. The raw segment output is then smoothed in order to mirror the segmentation used in training of acoustic models.

The initial acoustic models were then trained using features obtained from a 12th-order MF-PLP feature analysis, plus energy. First and second temporal derivatives are estimated and appended to the feature vector, resulting in

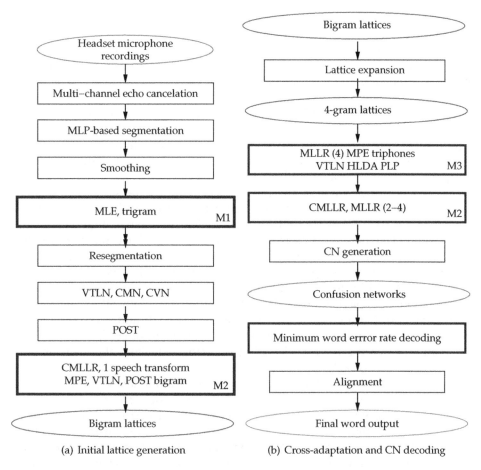

Figure 12.7 Block processing diagram showing the AMI 2006 system for meeting transcription (Hain et al., 2006). Square boxes denote processing steps, ellipses representations of the data. M1–M3 denote differently trained model sets.

39-dimensional feature vectors, which are then normalized on a per-channel basis to zero mean and unit variance (cepstral mean and variance normalization).

After these audio preparation stages, 39-dimensional MF-PLP feature vectors were extracted and cepstral mean and variance normalization (CMN/CVN) was performed on a per-channel basis. Then rst-pass transcripts are produced, using models trained on 100 hours of meeting data (M1) and a trigram language model. This initial transcript has several uses, including the provision of a rough transcript for estimation of VTLN warp factors, and to allow the data to be resegmented by realigning to the transcripts. This is possible because the acoustic models for recognition are more re ned than the models used for segmentation, but naturally segments can only get shorter. This is important as cepstral mean and variance normalization have a signi cant impact on word error rate and rely on the correct balance of silence in segments.

The next pass of decoding uses different features from those used previously. The standard PLP feature vector is augmented with phone-state posterior probabilities computed using multi-layered perceptrons (further details can be found in Section 5), and both components are normalized using VTLN. Acoustic models are now trained using the MPE criterion (Section 2.4) and further adapted using a single CMLLR transform (Section 2.5). As the system has more passes to follow, bigram lattices are produced at this stage in order to enable lattice rescoring using new acoustic and language models. If a faster system was required, decoding with a trigram as in the rst pass could have been chosen here.

The second part of the system, Figure 12.7(b), follows the strategy of using a constrained search space as represented in a lattice to quickly obtain improvements and apply models that could otherwise not be used. First a 4-gram language model (trained on the same data as used previously) is used to expand lattices and produce a new rst-best output. This is followed by decoding with two different acoustic model sets for the purpose of cross-adaptation. The rst acoustic model set uses standard PLP features only but models are trained by MAP adaptation from 300 hours of conversational data. After adaptation with MLLR, lattices are again produced that are rescored using the same models and features as in the second pass. Finally, lattices are compacted in the form of confusion networks and minimum word error rate decoding is performed. Final alignment is only performed to nd correct times for words.

Figure 12.8 shows results for all passes. If the initial automatic segmentation into utterances is replaced by a manual process, then the word error rate is decreased by 2–3 percent absolute. Considerable reductions of word error rates are achieved in each pass. Note that the rst pass error rate is almost twice the error rate of the nal pass, but the processes of adaptation and normalization in the second pass account for most of the gain. Even though the second pass uses the same acoustic models as the nal pass, cross-adaptation still brings an additional 2.4 percent absolute improvement in word error rate.

5   Current Topics

5.1   Robustness

The early commercial successes of speech recognition, for example dictation software, relied on the assumption that the speech to be recognized was spoken in a quiet, non-reverberant environment. However, most speech communication occurs in less constrained environments characterized by multiple acoustic sources, unknown room acoustics, overlapping talkers, and unknown microphones.

A rst approach to dealing with additive noise is by using multiple microphones to capture the speech. Microphone array beamforming uses delay-sum

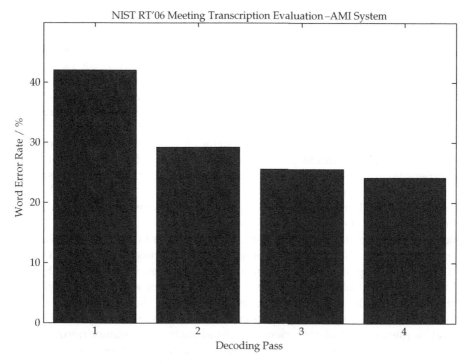

Figure 12.8   Word error rates (%) results in the NIST RT'06 evaluations of the AMI 2006 system on the evaluation test set, for the four decoding passes.

or lter-sum techniques to offer a gain in speci c directions, thus enabling competing acoustic sources to be separated based on location (Elko & Meyer 2008). These approaches have been used successfully in meeting transcription systems; using beamformed output of a microphone array will increase the word error rate by about 5 percent in the case of limited overlapping speech (Renals et al., 2008), and by up to 10 percent in more general situations.

Most work in robust speech recognition has focused on the development of models and algorithms for a single audio channel.[9] Increased additive noise will cause the word error rate of a speech recognizer trained in clean, noise-free conditions to increase rapidly. For the Aurora-2 task of continuously spoken digits with differing levels of arti cially added noise, the case of clean test data will result in word error rates of less than 0.5 percent using acoustic models trained on clean speech. A very low level of added noise (20 dB SNR – signal-to-noise ratio) results in 10 times more errors (5 percent word error rate) and equal amounts of noise and speech (0 dB SNR) results in a word error rate of about 85 percent (Droppo & Acero 2008). Thus the noise problem in speech recognition is signi cant indeed.

The reason for the dramatic drop in accuracy is related to acoustic mismatch; the noisy test data is no longer well matched to the models trained on clean speech.

If we knew that the noise would be of a particular type (say car noise) and at a particular level (say 10 dB SNR) then we could arti cially create well-matched training data and retrain a set of matched noisy models. However, it is rarely the case that the test noise conditions are known in such detail. In such cases multistyle training can be employed, in which the training data is duplicated and different types of noise added at different SNRs. This can be very effective: in the previous Aurora task, multistyle training decreases the 20 dB SNR word error rate from 5 percent to about 1 percent, and the 0 dB word error rate from 85 percent to 34 percent, while adding about 0.1 percent to the clean speech error rate (Droppo & Acero 2008). Multistyle training is thus very effective, but it is rather computationally expensive: it may be feasible for training a recognizer on digit strings (a task with an 11-word vocabulary); it is much less feasible for conversational speech recognition. Indeed, most of the techniques discussed in what follows have been developed largely on relatively small-vocabulary tasks.

Beyond the brute force approach of multistyle training, there are two main approaches to robustness: feature compensation and model compensation. The aim of feature compensation is to transform the observed noisy speech into a signal that is more closely matched to the clean speech on which the models were trained. It is usually of interest to develop techniques that work in the cepstral feature domain, since speech recognition feature vectors are usually based on PLP or Mel frequency cepstral coef cients. Cepstral mean and variance normalization (CMN/CVN) is a commonly applied technique which involves normalizing the feature vectors, on a component-by-component basis, to zero mean and unit variance. CMN can be interpreted in terms of making the features robust to linear ltering such as that arising from varying type or position of microphones, or characteristics of a telephone channel. For both the Aurora digits task and for large-vocabulary conversational telephone speech recognition, CMN and CVN can reduce word error rates by 2–3 percent absolute (Droppo & Acero 2008; Garau & Renals 2008).

More elaborate forms of feature normalization attempt to directly transform recorded noisy speech to speech that matches the trained models. One technique, designed primarily for stationary noise, is spectral subtraction, in which an estimate is made of the noise (in spectral domain), and subtracted from the noisy speech, to (theoretically) leave just clean speech (Lockwood & Boudy 1992). The subtraction process may be non-linear and dependent on the SNR estimate. This technique requires good segmentation of speech from non-speech in order to estimate the noise. If that is possible the technique works well in practice. The *ETSI Advanced Front End* for noisy speech recognition over cellular phones is based on CMN and spectral subtraction and can reduce errors from 9.9 percent to 6.8 percent on multistyle trained Aurora-2 systems (Macho et al., 2002).

Spectral subtraction may be regarded as a very simple noisy-to-clean mapping, that simply subtracts an estimate of the average noise. More sophisticated approaches are available, for example SPLICE, which is based on the estimation of a parameterized model of the joint density of the clean and noisy speech (Deng et al., 2000). A Gaussian mixture model is typically used, and stereo data containing parallel clean and noisy recordings of the same signal is required for training. Other approaches to feature compensation include missing feature models (Cooke et al., 2001) and uncertainty decoding (Droppo et al., 2002), in which areas of time-frequency space are attributed to speech or noise, and probabilistic enhancement approaches are used to reconstruct the clean speech.

It is also possible to use model-based compensation, in which the detailed acoustic models in the recognizer are used as the basis of the compensation scheme, as opposed to the previous approaches which construct speci c feature compensation models. In model-based compensation the clean speech models are combined with a noise model, resulting in a model of noisy speech. This is referred to as parallel model combination (Gales & Young 1996). There are two main technical challenges with parallel model combination. First, noise models that are more complex than a single state result in much greater complexity overall, due to the fact that the speech and noise models are combined as a product. Second, it is assumed that speech and noise are additive in the spectral domain. Since the models are constructed in the cepstral domain, it is necessary to transform the model parameters (Gaussian means and covariances) from the cepstral to the spectral domain. The noisy speech model statistics are then computed in the spectral domain, before transforming the parameters back to the cepstral domain.

5.2 Multiple knowledge sources

It is possible to obtain many different parameterizations of the speech signal and to use different acoustic model formulations. Often different representations and models result in different strengths and weaknesses, leading to systems which make complementary errors. It is possible that word error rates could be reduced if such systems are combined.

In feature combination approaches, multiple different feature vectors are computed at each frame, then combined. Although the most commonly employed acoustic parameterizations such as MFCCs and PLP cepstral coef cients result in low error rates, on average, it has been found that combining them with other representations of the speech signal can lower word error rates. For example, Garau and Renals (2008) combined MFCC and PLP features with features derived from the pitch-adaptive STRAIGHT spectral representation (Kawahara et al., 1999), and Schlueter et al. (2007) combined MFCC and PLP features with gammatone features derived from an auditory-inspired lterbank, each time demonstrating a reduction in word error rate.

The simplest way to combine multiple feature vectors is simply to concatenate them at each frame. This is far from optimal since it can increase the dimensionality quite substantially, as well as result in feature vectors with strong dependences between their elements. The latter effect can cause numerical problems when estimating covariance matrices. To avoid these problems, the feature vectors may be concatenated, then linearly transformed to both reduce dimensionality and decorrelate the components. Although principal component analysis is one way to accomplish this, it has been found that methods based on linear discriminant analysis (LDA) are preferable, since a different transform may be derived for each state. Hunt proposed the use of LDA to improve discrimination between syllables, and in later work used LDA to combine feature streams from an auditory model front end (Hunt & Lefebvre 1988). In LDA a linear transform is found that maximizes the between-class covariance, while minimizing the within-class covariance. LDA makes two assumptions: rst, all the classes follow a multivariate Gaussian distribution; second, they share the same within-class covariance matrix. Heteroscedatic LDA (Kumar & Andreou 1998) relaxes the second assumption and may be considered as a generalization of LDA.

As discussed further in Section 5.3, other feature representations have been explored, which have a less direct link to the acoustics. For example, considerable success has been achieved using so-called 'tandem' representations in which acoustic features such as MFCCs are combined with frame-wise estimates of phone posterior probabilities, computed using multi-layered perceptrons (MLPs). An advantage of this approach is that the MLP-based phone probability estimation can be obtained using a large amount of temporal context.

Other levels of combination are possible. Acoustic models may be combined using the combining probability estimates at the frame or at the segment level. Approaches such as ROVER (Fiscus 1997) enable system-level combination in which multiple transcriptions, each produced by a different system, may be combined using a dynamic programming search based on majority voting or on con dence scores. Such approaches have been used to great effect in recent large-scale research systems and are discussed further in Section 5.4.

5.3   *Richer sequence models*

One of the main weaknesses of HMM-based speech recognition is the assumption of conditional independence of speech samples, i.e.,

$$p(x_t|x_1 \ldots x_{t-1}, q_t) \equiv p(x_t|q_t)$$

where q_t denotes the current state and x_t denotes the acoustic vector at time t. The conditional independence assumption is incorrect, since it fails to re ect the strong constraints in the speed of movement of articulators, that adjacent frames have high correlation and changes in the spectrum are slow for most sound classes. Some interdependence is of course encoded in the state succession but transition probabilities only exist from one state to the next and are usually found to have a modest in uence on performance. This leads to considerable underestimation of true frame likelihoods and two approaches are commonly used to counteract that: the use of differentials (so-called delta features) in the feature vector to account for slope information; and scaling of the language model probabilities in decoding and also training to adjust for dynamic range differences. However, these changes are engineering solutions without a solid theoretical base and also account for part of the shortcoming.

There have been many attempts to address the issue and we cannot present all of those attempted over the years. However, recent interest in better temporal modeling of parameters has increased and considerable improvements have been obtained with some techniques. Sometimes results are dif cult to interpret because they include multiple changes to the systems and hence multiple interpretations of the realization are possible. In general all of the techniques are much more computationally elaborate and some are so complex that only rough approximations to the formulae make it possible to realize such structures. Even with modern large-scale computing resources proper implementations are not possible.

Segment models were introduced by Ostendorf and Roukos (1989) and interpreted as an extension to HMM-based modeling (Ostendorf et al., 1996). Instead of modeling single frames, multiple frames can be represented at the same time, for example by describing a moving mean of a Gaussian distribution. Similar to HMMs, one can represent states associated with segments that have variable length. The question on length of the segments and their proper representation is functional; form was (and still is) the topic of investigation, however the techniques have not found entry into large-scale systems, partially due to complexity reasons.

One of the issues pointed out by Tokuda et al. (2000) in the context of HMM-based speech synthesis is the incorrect use of Gaussians for differentials of the static features, noting that an implicit continuity constraint is missing. A formulation that adds this constraint to a standard HMM for recognition is given in Zen et al. (2007). In experiments, signi cant improvements in word error rates have been observed in some simple tasks, but these improvements have not been observed in more complex tasks (Zhang & Renals 2006).

A much simpler and very effective method has been introduced in the form of the so-called TRAPS features (Sharma et al., 2000), which have been implemented in several large-scale systems in many different applications and modi ed forms (e.g., the AMI system as presented in Section 4 uses so called LC/RC features as described in Schwarz et al., 2004). The basic idea is to convert long-term information into a single feature vector that is capable of extracting relevant information at the given time. Long-term information can cover up to half a second but most techniques make use of information compression by use of, e.g., a KLT transform on a frequency band basis. The compressed information is then ltered through a multi-layered perceptron that is trained to map features to phoneme state level posterior probabilities. This step is vital as it allows to construct a feature vector that is relevant to the current time without causing information diffusion. Such features can be combined with standard features but recent results seem to suggest that the potential loss in performance is small when they are used on their own. Substantial improvements are obtained on small- and large-scale tasks and gains are often complementary with other techniques.

This technique bears a strong relationship with another technique aimed at augmenting feature vectors. fMPE (Povey et al., 2005), or feature-based MPE training, tries to nd a matrix $\mathbf{M}$ such that a new feature vector $\mathbf{y}_t$ is more informative:

$$\mathbf{y}_t = \mathbf{x}_t + \mathbf{M}\mathbf{h}_t$$

This is achieved by providing additional information on neighboring frames to the current time in the form of a vector $\mathbf{h}_t$ but, instead of using the features directly, their projection into the model space is performed by using their likelihood for each Gaussian in the acoustic model set, thus providing a link to the models. The matrix is then trained using the MPE type criterion function. Substantial improvements are obtained but training of models and matrices is complex and the application of the matrix in decoding is costly. Hifny and Renals (2009) introduced a related discriminative method: augmented conditional random elds.

Much more advanced approaches try to model long-term dynamics in a more principled form using for example switching linear dynamical systems (Digalakis et al., 1993; Rosti & Gales 2003). Here the fundamental assumption necessary for Viterbi approximation, the assumption that the preceding model does not have an in uence on the current model, is normally not correct and hence search paths can not be merged. At this point, for many situations, only small-scale experiments are possible and even then substantial constraints have to be included.

5.4 Large scale

Since the 1990s there has been an intense interest in developing approaches to speech recognition that work well in natural situations. In particular there has been a signi cant focus on conversational telephone speech, broadcast news, and, more recently, multiparty meetings. Challenges for the recognition of conversational telephone speech include conversational style and the telephone channel. For broadcast news, the speech signals come from a variety of sources and are mixed with other sounds such as music or street noise. The meeting domain adds the challenge of far- eld recording and reverberation to conversational speech recognition. Much of this work has been performed in US English, since resources in other languages are usually much more sparse. Lately increased interest in Mandarin and Arabic, as well as 'international English,' has led to extensive resource generation in those languages. Work in different languages brings to the fore important aspects, such as larger vocabularies (over 500,000 words) due to different morphologies, different error metrics, such as character error rate, ambiguity in orthographic and spoken word, or additional sound classes such as Mandarin tones. Remarkably the basic structure in most systems remains identical and changes are mostly made to dictionaries or feature extraction.

The increasing amounts of data as well as the additional acoustic and speech complexity have substantial implications for system building. Segmentation and speaker clustering, optimal for speaker recognition or for playback, is normally not optimal for automatic speech recognition (Stolcke et al., 2004). Multiple microphone sources can affect the best strategies for acoustic modeling and adaptation. Automatic switching between microphones potentially causes substantial errors (Hain et al., 2008). Adapting models to the speaker and to the environment has proven to be extremely important, but the interaction between different model adaptations is complex. In particular, the order of application of techniques is important and may need changing depending on domain or data type.

Dependence on a domain and lack of generalizability are a major challenge. Techniques known to work on one domain do not necessarily work on another domain: this has been observed for VTLN (Kim et al., 2004), for instance. If the in-domain data is sparse, then improved accuracy can be obtained by adaptation from large corpora in related domains. This may require compensation techniques for mismatch between domains; an example of this is the approach of Kara at et al. (2007) to compensate for different audio bandwidths. Finally, the appropriate evaluation metric may be domain-speci c. Word error rate is not the only metric, and optimizing systems for speci c applications, such as machine translation (Gales et al., 2007), can lead to signi cant improvements.

The above illustrates that an almost limitless range of options for system building exists which can serve two fundamentally different purposes: to enhance system performance in one application by nding combinations of components that can enhance performance in another; or to nd the components that will yield the perfect result for a particular element of data. Only limited work has been carried out on the latter, but investigations on the AMI RT'07 system (Hain et al., 2007) show that the oracle combination of outputs of various stages of a system can yield 20 percent relative reduction in word error rate.

With the more widespread use of high-level system combination (Fiscus 1997; Evermann & Woodland 2000), recognition systems have become more complex. While attempts were made to describe generic all-purpose system architectures (Evermann & Woodland 2003), experience showed that the search for complementary systems may allow for much simpler structures (Schwartz et al., 2004) where in essence the output of one system is simply used to adapt another one and then the respective outputs are combined. Nevertheless systems that differ by such a margin are dif cult to construct. Hence more elaborate schemes, such as in the SRI-ICSI or AMI RT'07 systems (Stolcke et al., 2007; Hain et al., 2007), are developed. In these cases acoustic modeling, segmentation, and data representation is varied to yield complementarity.

The challenges for system development in the future are de ned in the list of requirements above. Since the complexity of systems is set to increase rather than decrease, a manual construction of system designs will always be suboptimal. In Hain et al. (2008) initial attempts are reported for automation of system design. However, at this point even the right form to describe the potential combinations ef ciently is unknown, let alone a multi-objective dynamic optimization scheme. To nd optimal systems, not only does an optimal combination and processing order have to be derived, but ideally the models and techniques are complementary and yield mutually additive gains. Approaches have been made to automate this process (e.g., Breslin & Gales 2006), but much more work is required, in particular in the context of different target metrics.

6 Conclusions

Automatic speech recognition was one of the rst areas in which the data-driven, machine learning, statistical modeling approach became standard. Since the 1990s, the basic approach has been developed in several important ways. Detailed models of speech may be constructed from training data, with the level of modeling detail speci ed by the data. Algorithms to adapt these detailed models to a speci c speaker have been developed, even when only a small amount of speaker-speci c data is available. Discriminative training methods, which optimize the word error rate directly, have been developed and used successfully. Because of these successful strategies speech recognition is available in commercial products in many forms. Public perception of speech recognition technology, however, ranges widely, from 'solved' to 'hopeless.' The reasons for the mixed acceptance lie in a number of major challenges for speech recognition that are still open today. First, speech recognition systems can only operate in a much more limited set of conditions, compared with people: additive noise, reverberation, and overlapping talkers pose major problems to current systems. Second, the integration of higher-level information is weak and often non-existent, although of obvious use to humans. Third, current models of speech recognition have a rather weak temporal model. The use of richer temporal models has had an inconsistent impact on the word error rate. Finally, systems lack generalizability: they are very dependent on matched training data. Moving a system from one domain to another, without training data resources for the new domain, will result in a greatly increased word error rate.

NOTES

1   This is sometimes referred to as speaker-attributed speech-to-text transcription.
2   An information theoretic measure of the expected number of words which may be expected to continue any word sequence; see Chapter 3, STATISTICAL LANGUAGE MODELING.
3   www.nist.gov/speech/tools
4   http://htk.eng.cam.ac.uk/
5   The autoregressive hidden lter model (Poritz 1982) is an intriguing alternative that performs modeling at the waveform level, and may be viewed as jointly optimizing signal processing and acoustic modeling. However, this approach relies on a linear prediction framework which is less powerful than the approaches employed in current systems.
6   Do not be misled, however; a mixture of diagonal covariance Gaussians is able to model correlations between feature dimensions. But it is a relatively weak way of modeling such correlations.
7   Note that derived forms are counted here as separate words whereas dictionaries such as the *Oxford English Dictionary* only list the base forms as independent entries.
8   WFST software: www.openfst.org/; http://people.csail.mit.edu/ilh/fst/; www.research. att.com/~fsmtools/fsm/
9   This is a general case, since microphone array beamforming will result in a single audio channel.

13   Statistical Parsing

STEPHEN CLARK

1   Introduction

Natural language parsing, in its most general form, is the process of assigning some structure to a natural language input. In this chapter we focus on the more speci c problem of taking a sentence as input and, using a prede ned grammar, assigning a syntactic structure to it. We will not be too speci c about the form of the syntactic structure, only that it need be some hierarchical representation of how the words in a sentence are related; this could be a phrase-structure tree or dependency graph, for example. We will use the general term *parse* to refer to such a representation.

This initial description of the problem raises a number of questions:

(1)   What is the grammar which de nes the set of legal syntactic structures for a sentence? How is that grammar obtained?
(2)   What is the algorithm for determining the set of legal parses for a sentence? What data structure is used to represent those parses?
(3)   What is the model for determining the plausibility of different parses for a sentence?
(4)   What is the algorithm, given the model and a set of possible parses, which nds the best parse (or the n-best parses)?

The rst three questions correspond roughly to the characterization of parsing in Steedman (2000) (although Steedman uses the term *oracle* for model). The additional fourth component is the *decoder*. If the possible parses can be ef ciently enumerated, then there is a trivial decoding algorithm: simply loop through each parse calculating its score, and return the highest-scoring one. However, as we shall see, the grammars used by statistical parsers are often wide-coverage, producing many parses for some sentences, far too many to enumerate. In this case, a more sophisticated representation of the possible parses, and decoding algorithm, is required.

The Handbook of Computational Linguistics and Natural Language Processing, First Edition.
Edited by Alexander Clark, Chris Fox and Shalom Lappin.
© 2013 Blackwell Publishing Ltd except for editorial material and organization
© 2013 Alexander Clark, Chris Fox, and Shalom Lappin. Published 2013 by Blackwell Publishing Ltd.

The examples in this chapter show that parsers do not always divide neatly into these four modules, and there can be considerable overlap between them. For example, many of the approaches to parsing the Penn Treebank (PTB), a standard parsing task, treat statistical parsing as essentially pattern recognition combined with search. Collins (1999), in a seminal work on parsing the PTB, characterizes the problem as follows:

(1) $T_{\text{best}} = \arg\max_{T} P(T, S)$

where T is a parse and S is a sentence. Here P is a joint probability distribution, often referred to as the *generative model*, over all possible (T, S) pairs.

The one aspect of this characterization that is clearly separated from the rest is the generative model: $P(T, S)$. However, there is considerable freedom in how to interpret the $\arg\max_{T}$, both in terms of the set of parses over which the $\arg\max$ is performed (not explicitly speci ed), and in how the search is carried out. Section 3 describes the Collins parser in more detail.

The motivation for statistical parsing arises mainly from question (3) in our original characterization. One of the surprising conclusions from early language processing research was that syntactic ambiguity is a serious problem for parsing (Church & Patil 1982). It is very dif cult to manually de ne a grammar whose rules determine a single parse for an arbitrary sentence, and statistical models provide a well-founded method for selecting between the alternative parses.

The ambiguity problem is especially severe for wide-coverage grammars, that is, grammars which cover a large proportion of the constructions found in naturally occurring text. Articles on parsing often give examples of ordinary-looking sentences which receive many hundreds or thousands of possible parses according to some grammar; however, with automatically extracted grammars, such as the CCG grammar described in Section 6, the problem is much more severe, with some newspaper sentences receiving many orders of magnitude more parses. The standard textbook examples of syntactic ambiguity, such as *see a man with a telescope*, are potentially misleading since the ambiguity in these examples is easily perceived; however, the majority of the ambiguity inherent in wide-coverage grammars is much more subtle, and it is the subtle ambiguities which lead to very large numbers of parses. In fact, we could not expect a statistical parsing model to resolve truly ambiguous cases such as the telescope example, since this would require a detailed representation of the context and sophisticated reasoning capabilities. Abney (1996) provides an illuminating discussion of this issue.

Further motivation for taking a statistical approach to parsing arises from the remaining questions in our original characterization. Even the grammar itself can be partly determined by the statistical parsing model. For example, Model 1 from Collins (1999) uses Markov processes to generate left and right sequences of verbal modi ers, where the Markov process is used to assign probabilities to particular sequences of non-terminals. The parser considers all possible combinations of non-terminals to be a legal sequence, and relies on the statistical model to rule out the unlikely ones.

Of course the grammar does not have to be so closely tied to the statistical model. In the parsers of Riezler et al. (2002) and Briscoe and Carroll (2006), the grammar is manually constructed and the statistical model is used for parse selection. But even with a manually constructed grammar, there is still a need for a statistical selection component if the grammar is to have wide enough coverage to be useful in language processing applications.

Finally, there are various ways in which the statistical model can interact with the parsing algorithm. Most statistical parsers use some form of heuristic search to manage the large search space, a standard example being probabilistic beam search. But there are also parsers in which the model and parsing algorithm interact more closely, in that the parsing model is used to guide the actions of the parser. This approach to statistical parsing is described in Section 5.

The focus in this chapter will be on supervised learning, in which we assume that training data for the parsing model, either in the form of gold standard parses or parser actions, is available in suf cient quantities to make supervised training feasible. Chapter 8 of this book, UNSUPERVISED LEARNING AND GRAMMAR INDUCTION, deals with the unsupervised case.

The majority of this chapter focuses on the various probability models for parsing, and how the parameters of the models are estimated. Note that *probability model* is being used here in a broad sense to include approaches such as the perceptron and support vector machines, even though these are often described as 'non-probabilistic.' There will also be some discussion of the parsing and decoding algorithms used (questions (2) and (4) in our original characterization).

The nal section describes work carried out with the grammar formalism combinatory categorial grammar (CCG). Here there has been much recent work on automatic grammar acquisition from the Penn Treebank and probability models for CCG, and this work provides a good example of robust, formalism-based statistical parsing.[1] This work also provides an example of statistical parsing with lexicalized grammars, which appear well suited to providing ef cient, robust, and wide-coverage parsers. In particular, the technique of *supertagging* (Bangalore & Joshi 1999) applied to CCG leads to a surprisingly ef cient formalism-based parser, and allows the estimation of large, complex parsing models.

There are many ways in which to describe the literature on statistical parsing: in terms of the representation used (e.g., phrase-structure vs. dependencies); in terms of the grammar formalism (e.g., LFG, HPSG, TAG, CCG); in terms of the parsing algorithm (e.g., bottom-up vs. top-down); or in terms of the parsing model (e.g., generative vs. discriminative). I have chosen the nal option for the majority of the chapter, since the literature has tended to focus on the statistical modeling problem, and the evolution of statistical parsers can be seen in terms of the move to more complex models (especially the shift from generative to discriminative models). I have also chosen to separate approaches which model the actions of the parser from models of the parses themselves. The large body of recent work on dependency parsing could also form a separate section by itself, but I have chosen to include examples of work on dependency parsing in the relevant sections.

2   History

Perhaps the rst attempt at statistical parsing was by Sampson (1986). Sampson's approach involved the use of manually parsed training material to obtain scores for local tree con gurations, which were combined to obtain a score for a complete parse-tree. The search to nd the highest-scoring parse was performed using a form of simulated annealing. Although the technical details of Sampson's work are perhaps less relevant now, given the advances in statistical modeling for parsing (and statistical NLP more generally), the idea of treating parsing as a machine learning problem, and recognizing the need for a method to combat the large search space, was farsighted and radical at the time.

The years following Sampson's attempt yielded some new approaches, for example Briscoe and Carroll's use of the Susanne treebank to model the moves made by a shift-reduce parser (Briscoe & Carroll 1993), and some theoretical papers on how to de ne stochastic versions of various grammar formalisms, for example stochastic tree adjoining grammar (Resnik 1992b). However, the event which led to the large interest in statistical parsing among the NLP community was the release of the Penn Treebank (Marcus et al., 1993). Magerman (1995) was among the rst to release parsing accuracies on the new treebank, and so began the parsing 'competition' which still continues today – the quest to obtain the highest scores on matching brackets using the Parseval metrics (Black et al., 1991). Magerman also introduced the idea of standard splits of the *Wall Street Journal* (*WSJ*) part of the PTB for training, development, and testing; sections 2–21 have typically been used for training, section 22 for development, and section 23 for testing.

The Magerman parser (named SPATTER) uses a *history-based* model, in which a parse is modeled as the sequence of decisions used to build it, with the probability of each decision conditioned on some limited aspect of the previous decisions (the history). SPATTER works in a bottom-up fashion, using decision trees to de ne a distribution over the possible moves available to the parser at each point in the parsing process. Examples of parser moves include assigning a POS tag to a word, or extending a node in a partially built tree by creating a parent–child arc. Magerman's approach extended work by the automatic speech recognition (ASR) group at IBM (Jelinek et al., 1994), and many of the techniques used by SPATTER, for example decision tree modeling, stack decoding for the search for the highest-scoring parse, and EM estimation for some of the model parameters, relate closely to the statistical techniques used to build ASR systems.

The accuracy scores achieved by SPATTER were 84.3 percent labeled precision and 84.0 percent labeled recall on the Parseval metrics, which compare the labeled nodes in the parse-tree returned by the parser with the labeled nodes in the gold standard PTB parse. These metrics have become the standard measure for evaluating PTB parsers, although there has been considerable debate regarding the suitability of these metrics in general for parser evaluation (Carroll et al., 1998). A year later Collins (1996) improved on Magerman's results, to 85.7 percent and

85.3 percent labeled precision and recall. At least as significant as the improved results was the simple nature of the Collins (1996) model, compared with SPATTER, showing that it is possible to obtain competitive results on the PTB parsing task with a simple model and parsing algorithm. Collins (1997) improved on these results further, with a theoretically more motivated approach based on a generative model. This approach to parsing is described in Section 3.

The impact of the PTB on statistical parsing has been immense, and has undoubtedly led to improvements in robust parsing technology. The downside of the PTB's domination is that there has been a focus on text from one particular genre, namely English newspaper text. In addition, PTB parsing is sometimes seen as 'standard parsing,' whereas the building of PTB style trees, although an interesting and useful task in itself, is a somewhat narrow view of natural language parsing. This situation is changing with the creation of treebanks based on particular grammatical frameworks, such as LFG, HPSG, TAG, and CCG, and with the creation of treebanks for domains other than newspaper text (Tateisi et al., 2005), and for languages other than English.

3   Generative Parsing Models

The years immediately following the introduction of the Penn Treebank saw a plethora of new parsing models; however, the most influential of these was the generative model of Collins (1997; 1999), and related work such as Eisner (1996), Goodman (1997), and Charniak (2000). This section describes the models of Collins (1997), although some of the innovations described may also be attributed to this related work. The work on generative parsing was particularly influential for the following reasons: it focused on the modeling of the parses themselves, rather than assigning scores to the moves made by the parser; it demonstrated the importance of sound probabilistic modeling; it produced impressive empirical results, at the time the best on the PTB; and it exploited a number of important ideas such as lexicalization.

Probabilistic parsing can be defined as finding the tree, T, with the highest conditional probability given the sentence, S:

(2) $T_{\text{best}} = \arg\max_{T} P(T|S)$

The move to generative models comes from recognizing that the maximization over the conditional probability can be written as a maximization over the joint, since $P(S)$ is constant for a given sentence:

(3) $T_{\text{best}} = \arg\max_{T} P(T|S)$

(4) $= \arg\max_{T} \dfrac{P(T,S)}{P(S)}$

(5) $= \arg\max_{T} P(T,S)$

The reason for using a joint model is that it is possible to de ne a *generative process* which generates the parse and sentence, and probabilities can be attached to the various parts of this process. Given certain independence assumptions, the probability of the complete parse and sentence can be de ned as the product of the probabilities of the parts. In addition, there exist simple and well-motivated methods for estimating the various probabilities. A probabilistic context-free grammar (PCFG) is the simplest example of this approach.[2]

The disadvantage of PCFGs is that they are essentially structural models of syntax, only incorporating lexical information in the form of emission probabilities at the leaves, where the words are generated from the pre-terminal nodes. One of the innovations of Collins (1997) and related work was the incorporation of *lexicalization*. Earlier work on PP-attachment ambiguities (Collins & Brooks 1995) had demonstrated the importance of lexical information for resolving some forms of syntactic ambiguity, and Collins (1997) extended this idea to complete parse-trees.

3.1   Collins – Models 1, 2, and 3

Collins (1997) introduced three generative parsing models, the second and third models building on the previous one by adding a level of linguistic sophistication. Model 1 is essentially a lexicalized PCFG, augmenting non-terminal nodes with lexical items, except that it uses Markov processes to generate the non-terminal nodes on the right-hand side of a rule. Model 2 extends Model 1 by making the complement/adjunct distinction and generating complements separately from modi ers. And Model 3 includes a probabilistic treatment of *Wh*-movement, based on the gap propagation analysis from GPSG (Gazdar et al., 1985). The following description of the Collins parser mirrors closely that given in Collins (1997).

For a PCFG, and a tree derived by n applications of context-free rewrite rules, $LHS_i \Rightarrow RHS_i$, $1 \leq i \leq n$, the joint probability of the tree, T, and sentence, S, is de ned as follows:

$$(6) \quad P(T, S) = \prod_{i=1}^{n} P(RHS_i | LHS_i)$$

The probability can be written in this way because of the following independence assumption: the probability of a non-terminal on the LHS of a rule expanding to a particular sequence of non-terminals on the right, is only dependent on the non-terminal on the left, and independent of any part of the tree outside of this rule application.

Model 1 extends the PCFG by making it lexicalized – associating with each non-terminal node a word and its POS tag. The word associated with a particular non-terminal is the linguistic head of the constituent corresponding to the non-terminal. Heads are found using a set of head- nding rules which, given a particular rule, deterministically return a head based on the sequence of non-terminals in the rule. Figure 13.1 gives an example lexicalized parse-tree from

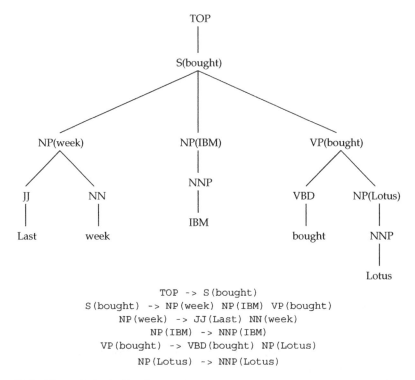

```
              TOP -> S(bought)
  S(bought) -> NP(week) NP(IBM) VP(bought)
     NP(week) -> JJ(Last) NN(week)
           NP(IBM) -> NNP(IBM)
    VP(bought) -> VBD(bought) NP(Lotus)
         NP(Lotus) -> NNP(Lotus)
```

Figure 13.1   Example lexicalized parse-tree.

Collins (1997) (with POS tags of headwords omitted on the non-terminal nodes), together with the rules it contains.

The use of lexicalization makes accurate estimation of the rule probabilities much harder. For a PCFG, the standard estimate for a conditional rule probability is simply the count of the number of times the LHS is seen expanded as the RHS, divided by the total number of times the LHS is seen in the training data. As well as being simple and intuitive, this estimate is theoretically well motivated: for a PCFG the relative frequency estimate is also the maximum likelihood estimate. However, lexicalization greatly expands the set of non-terminals, introducing a severe sparse data problem. For any given rule from a lexicalized PCFG, there are two possible problems: one, the LHS of a rule may not appear in the data – for example, if the head word associated with the LHS is unseen – leading to an unde-ned relative frequency estimate; and two, the LHS may appear in the data but never expand to the RHS, leading to a zero relative frequency estimate. Zeroes are especially problematic because they propogate through the product in (6) making the total probability of the parse equal to zero.

Collins's solution is to break up the generation of the rule into parts, and esti-mate the probability of each part separately. The RHS is generated from the head outwards, with rst-order Markov processes separately generating the modi ers

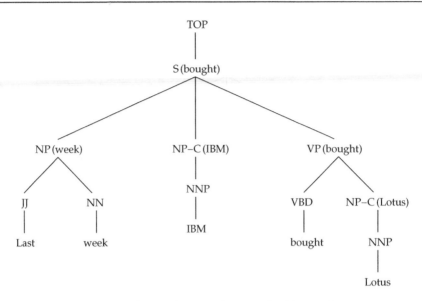

Figure 13.2   Example tree with complements distinguished from adjuncts.

to the left and right of the head. For reasons of space we omit the details here and refer readers to Collins (1999).

Model 2 incorporates an additional level of linguistic sophistication by making the complement/adjunct distinction and including the notion of subcategorization frame. In the tree in Figure 13.1, the only difference between *IBM* and *Last week* is that *IBM* occurs closer to the verb, even though *IBM* is a subject and *Last week* is a modi er. Clearly Model 1 is missing an important linguistic generalization. Collins solves this problem by adding a -C suf x to non-terminals which represent complements of verbs, including subjects (see Figure 13.2), and modifying the generative process to generate subcategorization frames as a separate step. Collins (1999: 173) contains some examples motivating the use of this distinction in the generative model.

The incorporation of subcategorization information in the generative model relies on the ability to distinguish between complements and adjuncts in the Penn Treebank. In fact this distinction is not made explicitly in the PTB, but complements can be identi ed fairly reliably using a set of heuristic rules based on some aspects of the annotation. For example, the PTB contains tags identifying some modifying expressions such as LOC for locative and TMP for temporal. Any constituent marked with TMP or LOC cannot serve as part of a subcategorization frame. Collins (1999: 174) describes the rules used to identify complements.

The nal model, Model 3, adds a further level of linguistic sophistication by accounting for wh-movement. The PTB contains a signi cant amount of information relating to 'movement,' such as extraction from a relative clause, in the form of traces in the tree. Figure 13.3 contains an example from Collins (1999),

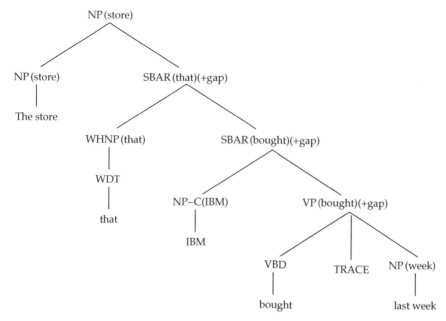

Figure 13.3   Example tree containing a trace and the gap feature.

together with the modi ed rules which encode the extraction. These modi ed
rules effectively encode the gap-propagation analysis from GPSG (Gazdar et al.,
1985), whereby a gap feature is added to the non-terminal nodes in the tree which
dominate the trace. The gap is 'discharged' at the NP node which represents the
extracted constituent.

Model 3 was found to offer little, if any, improvement over Model 2. However,
the attempt to directly model traces in the PTB was an important contribution,
since this information, which is crucial for obtaining predicate–argument structure, is largely ignored by most PTB parsers. There has been some work on
inserting traces into the output of a PTB parser, as a postprocessing phase (Johnson
2002; Levy & Manning 2004). Section 6 describes a CCG parser which incorporates
the trace information directly into the grammar and parsing process, without the
need for postprocessing.

3.2   *Parameter estimation*

The remaining issue with regard to the model is parameter estimation. Collins uses
a standard method to deal with sparse data, in which successively less speci c
contexts are used for maximum likelihood estimation, and the various estimates
combined in a weighted linear sum. For example, obtaining an accurate esti-
mate of $P(\text{VP}|\text{S},\text{VBD},\text{bought})$ – i.e., the probability of generating a VP node
given that the parent is S headed by bought with POS tag VBD – is dif cult if

bought occurs infrequently in the data. However, a relative frequency estimate of $P(\text{VP}\,|\,\text{S},\text{VBD})$ can also be used, and, since this conditioning event is a superset of the more speci c one, the estimate is likely to be more accurate. The various 'backed-off' estimates are then combined in the following way, where $\hat{P}$ denotes a relative frequency estimate of P:

$$\hat{P}(\text{VP}\,|\,\text{S},\text{VBD},\text{bought}) = \lambda_1 \hat{P}(\text{VP}\,|\,\text{S},\text{bought},\text{VBD})$$

$$+\,(1-\lambda_1)(\lambda_2 \hat{P}(\text{VP}\,|\,\text{S},\text{VBD})$$

$$+\,(1-\lambda_2)\hat{P}(\text{VP}\,|\,\text{S}))$$

$\lambda_1, \lambda_2, \lambda_3$ are smoothing parameters with values between 0 and 1, and the estimates are combined as above in order to produce a proper probability distribution. A similar technique is used for the other parameter types. A simple, but effective, method is used to set the values of the λ parameters, based on the frequency with which the context has been seen, and also the number of different outcomes that have been seen with a particular context. Again, readers are referred to Collins (1999) for the details.

3.3   *Parsing algorithm and search*

The parsing algorithm Collins uses is a bottom-up chart parsing algorithm. Note that the parsing algorithm is only indirectly related to the process used to de ne the generative model; this can be seen clearly in the fact that the generative model process is top-down, in that a PCFG starts with the root node and assigns probabilities to top-down applications of the rewrite rules, whereas the parsing algorithm is bottom-up. The model and parsing algorithm do interact, via the search process described below; however, the generative process was de ned primarily to facilitate the de nition of an accurate probability model for phrase-structure trees, with the interaction between parsing model and algorithm a secondary consideration.

The chart is a set of *edges*, where an edge is essentially a non-terminal label (augmented with head information) together with its span, i.e., the part of the sentence which the non-terminal dominates.[3] In the parser implementation an edge also contains additional information, such as pointers to the children which were combined to produce the edge, and the log-probability of the edge according to the model. The algorithm works by taking two existing edges and combining them to form a new edge. This combination is carried out in two ways: one in which the headword comes from the left edge, and one where it comes from the right. All possible combinations of contiguous edges in the chart are considered.

There are two strategies for making the parsing practical. First, dynamic programming is used to create a *packed chart*. The basic idea is that if two edges have the same label, the same headword (and POS), and the same span, then they are equivalent for the purposes of further parsing. The Viterbi algorithm exploits this equivalence by only considering the edge in an equivalence class with the highest probability, since any equivalent edge with a lower probability cannot be part of the highest-scoring parse. The complexity of this parsing algorithm is $O(n^5)$, where n is the length of the sentence.[4] This is too high for practical parsing, and so some form of heuristic search is required.

Collins uses a beam search in which low probability constituents are pruned from the chart. The obvious score to use for pruning is the *inside score* of a constituent, i.e., the conditional probability of the constituent's subtree, given its non-terminal label and headword. The problem with this measure is that it does not take into account the prior probability of seeing a constituent with a particular label and headword. A constituent can score highly according to this measure, and yet be unlikely in the larger context of a complete parse. Hence Collins also includes a prior probability factor in the score. Readers are referred to Collins (1999) for the details.

The beam simply discards all constituents in a chart cell (i.e., all constituents spanning the same part of the sentence) whose beam score is less than α times the maximum score for that cell, where α is a parameter which determines how agressive the pruning is. A typical value for α is 0.0001. Collins shows this beam search strategy to be highly effective, obtaining practical parsing speeds (roughly one sentence per second) but with little loss of accuracy due to the heuristic search.

The accuracies for Model 2 set the standard for the PTB parsing task: 87.5 percent labeled recall and 88.1 percent labeled precision on section 23, using the Parseval measures. Since then, parsing accuracies have increased to over 90 percent, but largely through incremental improvements due to improved modeling techniques and methods such as re-ranking (Charniak & Johnson 2005), rather than any signi cant conceptual leap in how to solve the PTB parsing problem.

4   Discriminative Parsing Models

One downside of the generative modeling approach is that the sentence is modeled, even though this is given and does not need to be inferred. Another disadvantage is the need for various independence assumptions to enable ef - cient estimation and decoding. This section describes conditional, or *discriminative*, models which do not model the sentence and do not make explicit independence assumptions in the way that generative models do; hence these models can be thought of as more direct solutions to the statistical parsing problem. Discriminative parsing models de ne the conditional probability of a parse, $P(T|S)$, directly, rather than indirectly via the joint distribution. The discriminative models we consider here are able to model complex dependencies between features; however, this exibility comes at a price, in that discriminative models typically require more complex training procedures for estimation.

The term *discriminative* derives from the idea that, during estimation, we would like the parsing model to directly compare the correct parse for each training sentence with the corresponding incorrect parses, and set the feature weights to 'discriminate against' the incorrect parses. There are many recent papers describing discriminative parsing models; examples include approaches based on support vector machines (Yamada & Matsumoto 2003), the linear perceptron (Collins & Roark 2004), and log-linear models (Riezler et al., 2002).

4.1   *Conditional log-linear models*

The approach we describe here is based on log-linear models (Riezler et al., 2002), also known as maximum entropy models (Ratnaparkhi 1998) and conditional random elds (Lafferty et al., 2001) in the NLP literature. We chose these models as an example because they possess the advantages of discriminative approaches – such as optimization of a discriminative criterion during estimation and some exibility in de ning features – but also some of the disadvantages, such as complex training procedures (at least compared to generative models). The presentation in this section is quite general; Section 6 has a concrete example of a log-linear model applied to wide-coverage CCG parsing.

The form of the probability model is as follows, where T is a parse and S is a sentence:

(7) $P(T|S) = \dfrac{e^{\sum_i \lambda_i f_i(T,S)}}{Z(S)}$

$Z(S)$ is a normalization factor ensuring a proper probability distribution: $Z(S) = \sum_{T_j \in \rho(S)} e^{\sum_i \lambda_i f_i(T_j,S)}$ where $\rho(S)$ is the set of possible parses for S. The features, f_i, are real-valued functions of (T, S) which identify particular aspects of a parse which might be useful for discriminating between good and bad parses. In early work on maximum entropy modeling, such as Ratnaparkhi (1998), features are indicator functions, taking the value 1 or 0, indicating whether a particular feature is present or absent in some context. For modeling complete parses, this idea is generalized to integer-valued functions which count the number of times some feature is present in a parse. In principle the features could be real-valued, although there has been little work on using real-valued features in log-linear parsing models (see Johnson & Riezler 2000 for one example).

The parse, T, can be any parse representation. Log-linear models have been applied in particular to constraint-based grammar formalisms, such as HPSG and LFG (Riezler et al., 2002; Malouf & van Noord 2004). The application of log-linear techniques to these grammars was argued for by Abney (1997), who showed that the complex dependencies encoded in feature structures in these grammars are dif cult to capture using generative models, and that previous attempts to do so had resulted in ill-motivated estimation techniques.

The form in (7) can be motivated in a number of ways. The presentation in Della Pietra et al. (1997) begins by choosing from a set of models which satisfy certain constraints – namely that the expected value of each feature according to the model is equal to the empirical expected value – and then selecting the single model from that set which is the most uniform, or has the *maximum entropy*. Johnson et al. (1999) start with the model form in (7), and set the values of the

weights by maximizing the conditional likelihood function. In fact, the two formulations result in identical models. See Chapter 5 of this book, MAXIMUM ENTROPY
MODELS, for more details.

Note that the probability in (7) applies to the whole parse, T, and not to individual parts, and that we have made no independence assumptions regarding the
features. In principle this allows great exibility in terms of the features that can be
de ned. In practice the parser developer is limited by two factors. First, there has
to be enough training data to obtain reliable estimates for the weights; features
which incorporate detailed or large parts of a parse-tree – for example features
encoding more than one lexical item – may appear infrequently, if at all, in the
training data. Second, the 'locality' of the features has a direct effect on the ef -
ciency of the model estimation and decoding. Section 6 has more discussion of
this issue.

From the perspective of maximum likelihood estimation, the maximum likelihood model, $\tilde{\Lambda}$, for a conditional parsing model is as follows:

$$(8) \quad \tilde{\Lambda} = \arg\max_{\Lambda} \prod_{i=1}^{m} P_{\Lambda}(T_i | S_i)$$

where $(T_1, S_1) \dots (T_m, S_m)$ is the training data consisting of gold standard parses
T_i for each sentence S_i. Note that the likelihood function is a *conditional* likelihood
function, consisting of the product of the conditional probabilities of the gold standard parses. Johnson et al. (1999) motivate the use of the conditional likelihood
(and use the term *pseudo-likelihood*).

In terms of maximizing the likelihood function in (8), a useful intuition is given
by Riezler et al. (2002): choosing weights to maximize the likelihood involves
putting as much mass as possible on the correct parse, relative to the incorrect
parses, for each sentence, whilst maintaining a conditional distribution for each
sentence in the training data. This intuition also ts well with the idea of choosing
weights which discriminate between the good and bad parses for each sentence.
Section 6 describes how the maximization can be performed in practice.

4.2 *Discriminative dependency parsing*

There is a large literature on data-driven dependency parsing, exempli ed by the
CoNLL shared tasks on this topic (Nivre et al., 2007), and this work provides some
notable examples of discriminative parsing models. This subsection begins with a
brief introduction to dependency parsing, and then focuses on the discriminative
models from McDonald et al. (2005b).

The advantages of dependency representations are that ef cient decoding algorithms exist, e.g., the $O(n^3)$ algorithm of Eisner (1996), and the representation
goes some way towards capturing the predicate–argument structure of a sentence,
making it useful for a variety of tasks such as question answering and syntax-
based statistical machine translation. Dependency representations are based on
linking words together in a dependency graph, where a link indicates that a

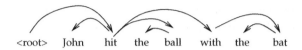

Figure 13.4 Example unlabeled dependency tree.

syntactic relation exists between the two words. The links can either be labeled – with syntactic relations such as *subject* and *object* and so on – or unlabeled. Figure 13.4 gives an example of an unlabeled dependency tree (taken from McDonald et al., 2005b). The direction of the link is away from the syntactic head.

Dependency formalisms have an established history in linguistics (Hudson 1984), and have been argued to be a more exible multi-lingual representation than phrase structure, applying to a wide variety of languages, as the CoNNL shared tasks demonstrate. Data-driven dependency parsers have also been shown to be accurate, with unlabeled dependency scores of over 90 percent on English newspaper text. However, whether dependency parsers for English could ever compete with their phrase-structure counterparts, which have access to a richer structure to perform disambiguation, is an open question. McDonald et al. (2005b) extracted dependencies from the phrase-structure output of the Collins parser, using head- nding rules, and found the Collins parser to be slightly more accurate (0.5 percent) at correctly assigning dependency links, even though the Collins parser was not trained for this particular task.

There have been two major approaches to data-driven dependency parsing: graph-based and transition-based. The transition-based approach uses a model of the parser moves made within a particular parsing architecture, e.g., shift-reduce, typically in conjunction with a greedy algorithm which makes a local decision at each point in the parsing process; this approach will be described in Section 5. The graph-based approach uses a model of the dependency structure itself, typically in conjuction with an exact inference algorithm.

A seminal paper in the graph-based approach is McDonald et al. (2005b), which uses a discriminative model to score dependency trees, together with an online, large margin-based algorithm for learning. Here we describe the perceptron learning algorithm, which is simpler conceptually, and which McDonald et al. (2005b) show to perform almost as well as the margin-based algorithm. The dependency model is a linear model which uses an edge-based factorization of the dependency graph. Let $\mathbf{x} = x_1 \ldots x_n$ be a sentence and $\mathbf{y}$ be a dependency tree for $\mathbf{x}$, then (i, j) denotes a dependency in $\mathbf{y}$ from word x_i to word x_j. The score for an edge is de ned as follows, where $\mathbf{f}$ is a feature representation of the edge and $\mathbf{w}$ is a corresponding weight vector:[5]

(9) $s(i, j) = \mathbf{w} \cdot \mathbf{f}(i, j)$

The score for a complete tree is simply the sum of the scores over the edges:

(10) $s(\mathbf{x}, \mathbf{y}) = \sum_{(i,j) \in \mathbf{y}} s(i, j) = \sum_{(i,j) \in \mathbf{y}} \mathbf{w} \cdot \mathbf{f}(i, j)$

Training data: $\mathcal{T} = \{(\mathbf{x}_t, \mathbf{y}_t)\}_{t=1}^{T}$

1. $\mathbf{w}_0 = 0;\ \mathbf{v} = 0;\ i = 0$
2. for $n : 1..N$
3.   for $t : 1..T$
4. $\mathbf{w}^{(i+1)} = $ update $\mathbf{w}^{(i)}$ according to instance $(\mathbf{x}_t, \mathbf{y}_t)$
5. $\mathbf{v} = \mathbf{v} + \mathbf{w}^{(i+1)}$
6. $i = i + 1$
7. $\mathbf{w} = \mathbf{v}/(N * T)$

Figure 13.5   Generic algorithm for online learning taken from McDonald et al. (2005b).

McDonald et al. (2005b) use the Eisner (1996) algorithm for decoding. This algorithm is based on the CKY chart parsing algorithm, creating a packed chart (or *forest*) and using the Viterbi algorithm to nd the highest scoring dependency tree, in a similar way to that described for the Collins parser in Section 3. The standard application of a packed chart and Viterbi to dependency parsing results in an $O(n^5)$ algorithm, where n is the sentence length, as for the Collins parser. However, Eisner (1996) noticed that if the left and right dependents of a word are parsed independently, and the de nition of equivalence for the packed chart is modi ed, then an $O(n^3)$ algorithm results. Appendix B of McDonald et al. (2005c) gives a detailed description and the intuition behind the new algorithm.

The $O(n^3)$ algorithm is especially useful for online learning, since this involves repeatedly parsing the training examples and updating the weight vector after each example (as opposed to *batch* learning in which the weights are updated all at once on each iteration). In fact, the repeated parsing of training examples is a bottleneck for discriminative approaches in general. The training algorithms for the log-linear models described in Section 4.1 calculate feature expectations on each iteration, which requires the alternative parses for each training sentence, as well as the correct parse, and so requires repeated parsing.[6] Thus it is only recently that discriminative models have been applied to the full PTB *constituent* parsing task (Carreras et al., 2008), following earlier attempts in which only short sentences were used for training and testing (Taskar et al., 2004); and even recent approaches to this task (Finkel et al., 2008) have restricted parser development to short sentences because of the expense of repeatedly parsing the training data with a constituency-based parser.

Online learning is conceptually very simple. Figure 13.5, taken from McDonald et al. (2005b), gives a generic algorithm for the online setting. $\mathbf{w}^{(i)}$ is the weight vector after the ith update, where an update occurs for every training instance, and N is the total number of passes through the data. In this description of the algorithm there is also an accumulated weight vector, $\mathbf{v}$, which is used to obtain the nal weight vector, $\mathbf{w}$, which is simply the average weight vector across all the updates. The reason for using averaging in this way is that it has been shown to be effective against over tting (Collins 2002).

$$\text{calculate } \mathbf{z}_i = \arg\max_{\mathbf{y} \in \text{GEN}(\mathbf{x}_{t(i)})} \mathbf{f}(\mathbf{x}_{t(i)}, \mathbf{y}) \cdot \mathbf{w}^{(i)}$$

$$\text{if } \mathbf{z}_i \neq \mathbf{y}_{t(i)}$$

$$\mathbf{w}^{(i+1)} = \mathbf{w}^{(i)} + \mathbf{f}(\mathbf{x}_{t(i)}, \mathbf{y}_{t(i)}) - \mathbf{f}(\mathbf{x}_{t(i)}, \mathbf{z}_i)$$

$$\text{else}$$

$$\mathbf{w}^{(i+1)} = \mathbf{w}^{(i)}$$

Figure 13.6   The perceptron update; $t(i)$ is the index of the training example corresponding to the ith update.

There are a number of ways of updating the weights after each training example. One simple, but effective, method is provided by the perceptron. Figure 13.6 gives the procedure for the ith update; $\mathbf{f}(\mathbf{x}, \mathbf{y})$, extending the notation introduced earlier, is the feature representation for the training example $(\mathbf{x}, \mathbf{y})$, that is, the sum of the feature vectors for each edge in $\mathbf{y}$: $\mathbf{f}(\mathbf{x}, \mathbf{y}) = \sum_{(i,j) \in \mathbf{y}} \mathbf{f}(i, j)$; and GEN($\mathbf{x}$), borrowing notation from Collins (2002), is the set of alternative analyses of $\mathbf{x}$, in our case dependency trees.

If the dependency tree returned by the parser, $\mathbf{z}_i$, is the same as the gold standard tree, $\mathbf{y}_{t(i)}$, then no update is performed; if the tree is different, then the weight vector is updated as shown: each feature which appears in the parser output, but not in the correct tree, has its weight reduced by one, and each feature which appears in the correct tree, but not in the parser output, has its weight increased by one. In this way the parser is effectively being encouraged to return the correct dependency tree for each training example, which also explains why the perceptron is prone to over tting, and the need for averaging parameters. Of course what we would like is for the resulting model to perform well on unseen data, not just the training data. Collins (2002) gives proofs showing that reducing errors on the training data, by using this update procedure, will lead to better parsing on unseen data.[7]

The remaining aspect of the model is the feature representation $\mathbf{f}(i, j)$ for each dependency. Note that dependency-parsing models are at a disadvantage compared to their phrase-structure counterparts, since the latter have access to phrase-structure as well as dependency structure when de ning the feature set. In fact, dependency graphs, if simply taken as unlabelled edges between words, are a highly impoverished representation for a statistical parsing model. McDonald et al. (2005b) solve this problem by making extensive use of POS tags, including the POS tags of words between dependents, and either side of dependents, as well as the POS of the dependents themselves; see McDonald et al. (2005b) for a detailed description of the feature set. The nal set contains almost 7 million features.

The standard split of the Penn Treebank was used by McDonald et al. (2005b) for the experiments: 2–21 for training, 22 for development, and 23 for testing; and a set of head- nding rules was used to extract the dependency structures. Since each word in the sentence has exactly one parent (assuming the existence of a root node at the root of the dependency tree), parsing performance can be measured in terms of accuracy: the percentage of words whose parent is correctly identi ed. No labels are assigned to the links by the parser, so this is unlabeled dependency accuracy.

The averaged perceptron model scored 90.6 percent on this evaluation, with the large margin-based method, MIRA, scoring 90.9 percent. Extracting dependencies from the output of the Collins phrase-structure parser gives an accuracy of 91.4 percent. However, the dependency parser is much faster, taking only ve minutes to parse the test set compared to 98 minutes for the Collins parser.[8]

Finally, the discussion so far has assumed that the dependency graph is *projective*, which, informally, means that the graph can be drawn so that no links in the graph cross. A dependency tree where each word has exactly one parent can be drawn in this way and so is projective. McDonald et al. (2005d) argue that projective trees are suf cient to analyze the majority of sentence types for English. However, for languages with more exible word order, non-projective dependencies are more frequent.

McDonald et al. (2005d) introduce a method for building non-projective dependency graphs, by formalizing the problem as nding the maximum spanning tree (MST) in a directed graph. The same edge-based factorization is used as described above for the projective case, and the same training algorithm. A standard algorithm for nding the MST exists (the Chu–Liu–Edmonds algorithm) for which there is an $O(n^2)$ implementation (so non-projective dependency parsing, perhaps surprisingly, can be performed more ef ciently than projective parsing). For reasons of space we do not go into the details of non-projective parsing here. McDonald et al. (2005d) give results for Czech and English, showing that, for Czech, there is a signi cant advantage in using the non-projective, rather than projective, parsing algorithm, resulting in an absolute increase of over 1 percent unlabeled parsing accuracy.

This section has focused on English, but there has been a large amount of work on dependency parsing for other languages. The CoNLL 2007 shared task (Nivre et al., 2007) performed an extensive evaluation, using a number of submitted systems, on Arabic, Basque, Catalan, Chinese, Czech, English, Greek, Hungarian, Italian, and Turkish. The accuracies were invariably higher for English than the other languages, but whether this is due to the dependency-parsing problem being harder for other languages; or due to smaller treebanks being available; or due to the multi-lingual application of inappropriate models which have been developed for English, is an open question.

5 Transition-Based Approaches

The approaches we have seen so far use models of parses to drive the statistical parsing process: probabilities are de ned over parses (or parts of parses) and these probabilities are used to guide the search for the most probable parse. Hence the probability model is somewhat divorced from the parsing algorithm: the algorithm builds subparses and the probability model is used to decide which parts are retained as hypotheses during the parsing process.

The strategy described above is a natural one considering that our aim is to nd the best parse, and that we usually do not care how the statistical parser nds that parse (as long as it does so ef ciently). However, there is an alternative strategy, which is to use a probability model to guide the moves made by the parsing algorithm. This is the approach taken by, among others, Briscoe and Carroll (2006), Ratnaparkhi (1999), and a number of recent papers in the dependency-parsing literature (Yamada & Matsumoto 2003; Nivre & Scholz 2004).

A strength of these approaches is that, since probabilities are being used to guide the parsing algorithm, extremely ef cient parsers can be built by following a greedy strategy of selecting the highest-scoring move at each decision point (or by selecting only a small number of high-scoring moves at each point). The disadvantage is that it is not always clear whether optimizing for parser moves leads to the selection of the most optimal parse (see Section 4 of Collins 1999 for a discussion of this issue).

We will use transition-based dependency parsing as an example, since the transition-based approach has been particularly successful for the dependency-parsing problem. However, there are a number of examples of constituent-based parsing which use this approach. Briscoe and Carroll (1993) were one of the earliest, using an LR-parser in conjunction with a manually de ned uni cation-based grammar and associating probabilities with the actions in the LR parse table. Briscoe and Carroll (2006) have recently extended the grammar and parser to handle WSJ text, arguing that the unlexicalized nature of the model makes it relatively easy to adapt the parser to new domains.

Magerman (1995) and Ratnaparkhi (1999) apply transition-based approaches to the PTB parsing task. Ratnaparkhi (1999) builds a parse-tree in three stages. Stage 1 uses a maximum entropy POS tagger to assign a POS tag to each word (Ratnaparkhi 1996). Stage 2 uses a maximum entropy tagger to assign chunk labels to each word, essentially grouping the words together into a at constituent structure. And nally the third stage uses maximum entropy models to link the chunks into a hierarchical parse-tree structure. The key point is that local probability models are used to assign a score to each action – whether it be assigning a POS tag to a word, for example, or linking two chunks – and the probability of a complete parse is de ned as the product of the probabilities of the actions used to build the parse. A beam search is used to search the space of possible actions, keeping some xed number of best-scoring hypotheses at each point in the parsing process, and extending the highest-scoring hypothesis at each point. This search procedure results in a parser that runs in linear time with respect to the sentence length.

The accuracies on the PTB for the Ratnaparkhi parser were competitive at the time, but not as high as those reported by Collins (1997). Lafferty et al. (2001) suggest that the model used by Ratnaparkhi – in which conditional probabilities for each action are multiplied to give a score for the complete parse – may suffer from the *label bias problem*. Put very simply, the use of local conditional probability distributions to make decisions at each point in the parsing process may lead to a choice which is not globally optimal; readers are referred to Lafferty et al. (2001) for the details.

5.1 Transition-based dependency parsing

Yamada and Matsumoto (2003) is a seminal paper on data-driven dependency parsing. Head- nding rules are used to convert phrase-structure trees from the Penn Treebank into dependency trees, giving trees where each word in the sentence (except the root) has exactly one parent. See Yamada and Matsumoto (2003) for an example phrase-structure tree and the corresponding dependency tree.

Dependency trees are built using a simple bottom-up shift-reduce parsing algorithm, operating from left to right along the sentence. There are three actions available to the parser: shift, left, and right. The state of the parser always has a pair of words acting as the 'focus' (using Yamada and Matsumoto's terminology). The shift action simply moves the focus one word to the right. The right action constructs a dependency relation between the two words in focus, where the word to the left becomes a child of the word to the right, and the child is taken out of focus. The left action works in the same way, but the word to the right becomes the child and moves out of focus. Again see Yamada and Matsumoto (2003) for an example of each action.

The parser uses a classi er to decide which of the three actions to take at any point in the parsing process, and uses a greedy method by selecting only the highest-scoring action at each point. Multiple passes over the input sentence are used to build a dependency tree. Yamada and Matsumoto apply a support vector machine to the classi cation problem, but in principle any classi er could be used. The feature set consists of a rich set of features describing the contexts of the words in focus, in terms of the subtrees already built, utilizing both words and POS tags.

Nivre and Scholz (2004) describe a similar approach, but use a shift-reduce parsing algorithm which is guaranteed to build a dependency tree in a single pass from left to right over the sentence. They also extend the dependency parsing problem by building trees with labeled edges, indicating the syntactic type of the dependency relation. Another difference is that Nivre and Scholz use a memory-based classi er rather than support vector machine. Nivre (2007) extends the transition-based approach to non-projective dependency parsing.

McDonald and Nivre (2007) show that the transition-based approach and graph-based approach result in remarkably similar performance across a range of languages, despite using different parsing algorithms and feature sets. They also show that the two approaches result in different errors, a fact exploited by Sagae and Lavie (2006), who use a parser recombination scheme to increase the accuracy over the individual parsers.

Finally, Zhang and Clark (2008) show that the transition-based approach does not have to be based on local greedy search, nor does the graph-based approach have to be based on exact global inference. They build a dependency parser based on beam search, utilizing both graph-based and transition-based features, and use a linear model trained with the generalized perceptron of Collins (2002). The innovation in this approach is to train a single model which utilizes features from both approaches, demonstrating accuracy gains over using each approach in isolation.

6　Statistical Parsing with CCG

The evolution of parsing models since the early Penn Treebank work has moved in two directions: towards more exible, discriminative parsing models; and towards more sophisticated grammar formalisms. The work described in this section represents both of these dimensions.

The attraction of using linguistic formalisms for parsing, such as lexical functional grammar (LFG), head driven phrase structure grammar (HPSG), tree adjoining grammar (TAG), and combinatory categorial grammar (CCG), is that these formalisms allow direct access to the underlying predicate–argument structure of a sentence (roughly who did what to whom), including long-range dependencies such as those inherent in coordination and extraction phenomena. Recovering such structure is arguably necessary for high performance on tasks such as question answering (QA), information extraction (IE), and machine translation (MT). I use 'arguably' here because, despite decades of research on automatic parsing, it is still the case that convincing evidence of the bene ts of parsing for NLP applications is lacking, especially for MT where phrase-based models currently provide the state of the art (although one of the most active areas of research in MT is currently syntax-based statistical MT).

Perhaps the best example of an application where parsing has been bene - cial is QA, where the use of a wide-coverage parser has now become standard (Harabagiu et al., 2001b). The recent development of formalism-based parsers which are also ef cient and robust, of which the CCG parser described in this chapter is a notable example, may lead to the increased adoption of parsers in NLP applications over the next few years, but this remains to be seen.

The CCG parser described here is representative of recent work in the area of robust, formalism-based parsing in a number of respects: it uses a formalism-speci c treebank derived from the Penn Treebank, both as a source for the grammar and as training data for the statistical models; it uses a discriminative parsing model de ned over complete parses, which is estimated using general numerical optimization techniques; it uses dynamic programming to allow both ef cient estimation and decoding; it uses a *supertagging* phase as a precursor to the parsing; and it uses gold standard resources annotated with grammatical relations for evaluation, including long-range dependencies. Other work which has some or all of these features includes Riezler et al. (2002), Sarkar and Joshi (2003), Cahill et al. (2004), and Miyao and Tsujii (2005).

The following description is taken largely from Clark and Curran (2007b). The section begins with a description of the grammar formalism and the resource used to build the parser, followed by a description of the parser model, and n- ishes with an explanation of how the modeling techniques are applied in practice. Note that there is nothing particularly 'CCG-speci c' about the application of log-linear models here, or the use of feature forests for estimation, but for expository purposes it is useful to have the modeling techniques grounded in a particular grammar formalism and parser.

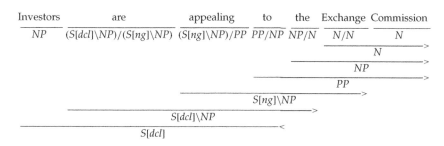

Figure 13.7 Example derivation using forward and backward application.

6.1 *Combinatory categorial grammar*

Combinatory categorial grammar (CCG) (Steedman 1996; 2000) is a type-driven lexicalized theory of grammar based on categorial grammar (Wood 1993). CCG lexical entries consist of a syntactic category, which de nes valency and directionality, and a semantic interpretation (not shown in the examples given here). Categories can be either basic or complex. Examples of basic categories are *S* (sentence), *N* (noun), *NP* (noun phrase), and *PP* (prepositional phrase). Complex categories are built recursively from basic categories, and indicate the type and directionality of arguments (using slashes), and the type of the result. For example, the following category for the transitive verb *bought* speci es its rst argument as a noun phrase to its right, its second argument as a noun phrase to its left, and its result as a sentence:

(11) bought := $(S \backslash NP)/NP$

Categories are combined in a derivation using *combinatory rules*. In the original categorial grammar (Bar-Hillel 1953), which is context-free, there are two rules of *functional application*:

(12) $X/Y \ Y \Rightarrow X$ (>)

(13) $Y \ X \backslash Y \Rightarrow X$ (<)

where X and Y denote categories (either basic or complex). The rst rule is *forward application* (>) and the second rule is *backward application* (<). Figure 13.7 gives an example derivation using these rules.[9]

CCG extends the original categorial grammar by introducing a number of additional combinatory rules. The rst is *forward composition*, which Steedman denotes by > **B** (since **B** is the symbol used by Curry to denote function composition in combinatory logic; Curry & Feys 1958):

(14) $X/Y \ Y/Z \Rightarrow_{\mathbf{B}} X/Z$ (> **B**)

the	agreement		which	the	fund	reached

```
  the    agreement              which              the    fund       reached
 ─────   ─────────      ──────────────────────    ─────   ────   ───────────────
 NP/N       N          (NP\NP)/(S[dcl]/NP)         NP/N     N     (S[dcl]\NP)/NP
 ──────────────>                                   ───────────────>
      NP                                                 NP
                                                   ──────────────>T
                                                     S/(S\NP)
                                                   ─────────────────────────────>B
                                                              S[dcl]/NP
                      ────────────────────────────────────────────────────>
                                        NP\NP
 ──────────────────────────────────────────────────────────────────────<
                                  NP
```

Figure 13.8   Example derivation using type-raising and forward composition.

Forward composition is often used in conjunction with *type-raising* (**T**), de ned according to the following two rule schemata:

(15) $X \Rightarrow_T T/(T\backslash X)$

(16) $X \Rightarrow_T T\backslash(T/X)$

T is a variable over categories, ranging over the result types of functional categories over X.

Figure 13.8 gives an example showing the combination of type-raising and composition. In this case type-raising takes a subject noun phrase (*the fund*) and turns it into a functor looking to the right for a verb phrase; *the fund* is then able to combine with *reached* using forward composition, giving *the fund reached* the category $S[dcl]/NP$ (a declarative sentence missing an object). It is exactly this type of constituent which the object relative pronoun category is looking for to its right: $(NP\backslash NP)/(S[dcl]/NP)$.

Further combinatory rules in the theory of CCG, and in the parser, include backward composition and backward crossed composition. There is also a coordination rule which conjoins categories of the same type, producing a further category of that type. Steedman (2000) motivates the need for the additional rules, and Clark and Curran (2007b) describe which rules are implemented in the parser.

The treebank used to develop the parser is CCGbank (Hockenmaier & Steedman 2002a; Hockenmaier 2003), a CCG version of the Penn Treebank (Marcus et al., 1993). The treebank performs two roles: it provides the lexical category set which makes up the grammar (plus some unary type-changing rules and punctuation rules used by the parser – see Clark and Curran (2007b) for the details), and it is used as training data for the statistical models. CCGbank was created by converting the phrase-structure trees in the Penn Treebank into CCG derivations. Hockenmaier (2003) gives a detailed description of the procedure used to create CCGbank. Figure 13.9 shows an example derivation for an (abbreviated) CCGbank sentence. The derivation has been inverted, so that it is represented as a binary tree.

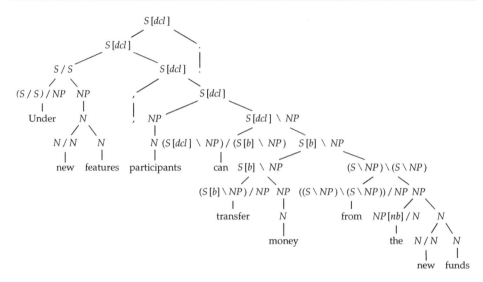

Figure 13.9 Example CCG derivation for the sentence *Under new features, participants can transfer money from the new funds.*

6.2 Log-linear parsing model for CCG

The log-linear modeling approach can be applied directly to CCG derivations, in the same way that it can be applied to any kind of linguistic structure. Thus there is nothing particularly CCG-speci c about the model, except that the features are de ned over CCG derivations. Clark and Curran (2003) give some motivation for applying log-linear models to CCG in particular, by arguing for the inclusion of long-range dependencies in the model; the seminal article of Abney (1997) contained a similar argument for constraint-based grammar formalisms.

According to the log-linear model, the probability of a derivation *d*, given a sentence, *S*, is de ned as follows:

$$(17) \quad P(d|S) = \frac{1}{Z_S} e^{\lambda . f(d)}$$

where $\lambda . f(d) = \sum_i \lambda_i f_i(d)$. The function f_i is the integer-valued frequency function of the *i*th feature; λ_i is the weight of the *i*th feature; and Z_S is a normalizing constant which ensures that $P(d|S)$ is a probability distribution:

$$(18) \quad Z_S = \sum_{d' \in \rho(S)} e^{\lambda . f(d')}$$

where $\rho(S)$ is the set of possible derivations for *S*. This is the same formalization as given in equation (7), but with a slightly different notation. The features used in the parser will be described later.

The training data consists of gold standard derivations from CCGbank. The discriminative estimation method follows Riezler et al. (2002) by maximizing the *conditional* log-likelihood of the model given the data, minus a Gaussian prior term to prevent over tting (Chen & Rosenfeld 1999; Johnson et al., 1999). Thus, given training sentences $S_1, \ldots, S_m$, and gold standard derivations, $d_1, \ldots, d_m$, the objective function for a model Λ is:

(19) $\quad L'(\Lambda) = L(\Lambda) - G(\Lambda)$

$$= \log \prod_{j=1}^{m} P_\Lambda(d_j|S_j) - \sum_{i=1}^{n} \frac{\lambda_i^2}{2\sigma^2}$$

The Gaussian prior simply implements the intuition that we do not expect the weights to get too high in absolute value, and prevents them doing so by penalizing any model whose second term in (19) becomes excessively large. The parameter σ is set empirically using held-out development data (by choosing the value which leads to the highest parsing accuracy on the held-out data).

Maximizing $L'(\Lambda)$ is a numerical optimization problem, for which there are a number of standard techniques available (Nocedal & Wright 1999). Early work in estimating log-linear models for NLP applications used iterative scaling methods (Della Pietra et al., 1997), although these were shown to be too slow for complex parsing and tagging models (Sha & Pereira 2003; Clark & Curran 2004). Malouf (2002) introduced general numerical optimization techniques to the NLP community and showed them to be signi cantly more ef cient than iterative scaling methods.

A useful function for optimizing $L'(\Lambda)$ is the *gradient*, i.e., the partial derivative with respect to each weight:

(20) $\quad \dfrac{\partial L'(\Lambda)}{\partial \lambda_i} = \sum_{j=1}^{m} f_i(d_j) - \sum_{j=1}^{m} \sum_{d \in \theta(S_j)} \dfrac{e^{\lambda.f(d)} f_i(d)}{\sum_{d \in \theta(S_j)} e^{\lambda.f(d)}} - \dfrac{\lambda_i}{\sigma^2}$

where d_j is the gold standard derivation for sentence S_j and $\theta(S_j)$ is the set of possible derivations for S_j. A useful intuition for understanding the optimization process is to think of the likelihood function as a surface (but in many dimensions), and the role of the optimization algorithm is to nd the 'top' of the surface, given some random starting point. Chapter 5, MAXIMUM ENTROPY MODELS, describes in detail how this optimization problem can be solved. The key point for this chapter is that any method for optimizing (19), including the iterative scaling algorithms, requires calculation of the gradient in (20).

Note that (20) is a difference in feature expectations (ignoring the third term resulting from the Gaussian prior). The rst term is simply the (unnormalized) empirical expectation for feature f_i, that is, the number of times the feature appears in the training data, and the second term is the model expectation for

f_i. Hence the estimation process can also be thought of in terms of the maximum entropy framework of Della Pietra et al. (1997), since setting the gradient in (20) to zero (required for maximizing $L'(\Lambda)$) yields the usual maximum entropy constraints, namely that the expected value of each feature is equal to its empirical value.

Crucially, calculation of the model expectations for each feature requires a sum over all derivations for each sentence in the training data; however, the number of derivations grows exponentially with the sentence length, and the number of derivations for a sentence, according to the automatically extracted CCG grammar, can be very large. The next section brie y explains how this calculation can be performed in practice.

6.3   *Efficient estimation*

Clark and Curran (2007b) adapt the *feature forest* method of Miyao and Tsujii (2002) to perform a sum over a potentially exponential number of CCG derivations, required for calculation of the feature expectations in (20). A key data structure for this approach is the *packed chart*, which can be seen as an instance of a feature forest and hence used to calculate the feature expectations.

A chart is an array which stores the constituents for each substring (or span) in the sentence, as was described for the Collins parser. A packed chart is based on the idea that, if there is more than one way of deriving a constituent of the same type with the same span, then only one of these chart entries needs to be considered for further parsing. Equivalent entries are grouped into equivalence classes, and, for an individual entry in a class, back pointers to the daughters indicate how that entry was created, so that any derivation can be recovered from the chart. The use of equivalence classes in this way allows a large set of derivations to be represented compactly.

Entries are equivalent when they have the same span, form the same structures in any subsequent parsing, and generate the same features in any subsequent parsing. For a CCG parse chart, any constituents with the same CCG category, the same span, and the same linguistic head are equivalent for the purposes of further parsing and the log-linear parsing model. Note that equivalence with regard to the parsing model is only guaranteed if the features in the model are suf - ciently *local*, in this case con ned to a single rule application.[10] In the models of Clark and Curran (2007b), features are de ned in terms of local rule instantiations, where a rule instantiation is the local tree arising from the application of a rule in the grammar.

A CCG packed chart is an instance of a feature forest (Miyao & Tsujii 2002) which can be used for ef cient calculation of the feature expectations. Representing a CCG packed chart as a feature forest is straightforward, but we refer readers to Clark and Curran (2007b) and Miyao and Tsujii (2002) for the technical details. Essentially, the packed chart representation enables the use of a dynamic programming algorithm to sum over all derivations containing a particular feature, which is required to calculate the feature's expectation.

Estimating the parsing model in practice consists of generating packed charts for each sentence in the training data, and then repeatedly calculating the values required by the estimation algorithm until convergence. Even though the packed charts are an ef cient representation of the derivation space, the charts for the complete training data (sections 2–21 of CCGbank) take up a considerable amount of memory. One solution is to only keep a small number of charts in memory at any one time, and to keep reading in the charts on each iteration. However, given that the estimation algorithms for log-linear models typically require hundreds of iterations to converge, this approach would be infeasibly slow.

The solution in Clark and Curran (2007b) is to keep all charts in memory by developing a parallel version of the L-BFGS training algorithm and running it on an 18-node Beowulf cluster. As well as solving the memory problem, another sig-ni cant advantage of parallelization is the reduction in estimation time: using 18 nodes allows the best-performing model to be estimated in less than three hours.

The log-linear modeling framework allows considerable exibility for repre-senting the parse space in terms of features. However, in order to use packed charts as feature forests for the estimation, the features are limited to those de ned over local rule instantiations. The features used in the parser constitute a fairly standard set for a statistical parsing model. There are features encoding local trees (two combining categories and the result category); features encoding word–lexical category pairs at the leaves of the derivation; features encoding the category at the root of the derivation; and features encoding word–word dependencies, some of these also with information regarding the distance between the depen-dents. Each feature type has variants with and without head information, with separate features encoding heads as lexical items and POS tags. Clark and Curran (2007b) describe the feature set in detail.

The best-performing model from Clark and Curran (2007b) had 475,537 features; converged in 610 iterations of the L-BFGS algorithm; required 22.5 GB of RAM, which was provided by the 18-node Beowulf cluster; and was trained in just over two hours.

6.4   *Parsing in practice*

Parsing with lexicalized grammar formalisms such as CCG is a two-stage pro-cess: rst, elementary syntactic structures – in CCG's case lexical categories – are assigned to each word in the sentence, and then the parser combines the structures together. Clark and Curran (2007b) use a supertagger (Bangalore & Joshi 1999) to perform step one. The supertagger uses log-linear models to de ne a distribution over the lexical category set for each local ve-word context containing the target word (Ratnaparkhi 1996). The features used in the models are the words and POS tags in the ve-word window, plus the two previously assigned lexical categories to the left. The conditional probability of a sequence of lexical categories, given a sentence, is then de ned as the product of the individual probabilities for each category. In order that the supertagger be accurate enough to serve as a front end to the parser, Clark and Curran (2007b) de ne a multi-tagger, in a fairly standard way, using the distribution over lexical categories for each word in the sentence to potentially assign more than one category to each word. The lexical category distributions for each word can be calculated ef ciently using the forward–backward algorithm.

The algorithm used to build the packed charts is the CKY chart parsing algorithm (Kasami 1965; Younger 1967) described in Steedman (2000). The CKY algorithm applies naturally to CCG since the grammar is binary. It builds the chart bottom-up, starting with constituents spanning a single word, incrementally increasing the span until the whole sentence is covered. The Viterbi algorithm is used to nd the most probable derivation from a packed chart.

There are a number of possible ways of evaluating the CCG parser. Hockenmaier and Steedman (2002b) argue against the use of the Parseval metrics applied to CCG derivations, since the binary-branching nature of CCG means that it is penalized more heavily according to these metrics than the atter PTB structures. Also, a primary motivation for CCG parsing is the recovery of long-range, as well as local, dependencies, making a dependency-based evaluation the natural choice.

Clark and Curran (2007b) perform two dependency-based evaluations. The rst uses the gold standard predicate–argument structures from CCGbank, including long-range dependencies, which are de ned in terms of the argument slots in CCG lexical categories. According to this evaluation, the best-performing model achieves an F-score of 85.5 percent on section 23, which rises to 87.6 percent if gold standard POS tags are fed to the supertagger and parser. There are two disadvantages to this evaluation: one, it is CCG-speci c, so the accuracies cannot be compared with the scores reported for parsers not based on CCGbank; and two, the accuracy gures are arguably in ated in that the CCG parser is being rewarded for reproducing any systematic biases or errors in the treebank, for example incorrect bracketing in complex noun phrases.[11]

Clark and Curran (2007b) attempt a formalism-independent evaluation by mapping the CCG dependencies to Briscoe and Carroll-style grammatical relations (GRs), and evaluating on DepBank, a 700-sentence subset of section 23 of the PTB which has been manually annotated with GRs. The mapping turned out to be surprisingly dif cult to perform, and evaluating the *gold standard* CCG dependencies from CCGbank against the GRs in DepBank (after applying the mapping) resulted in an F-score of only 84.8 percent. Thus the best that the CCG parser can be expected to achieve is 84.8 percent. Despite this relatively low upper bound, the CCG parser scored 81.1 percent on DepBank, almost ve percentage points higher than the RASP parser which it was compared against.

Finally, Clark and Curran (2007b) give parse times for the CCG parser, comparing against those reported for other parsers in the literature. The CCG parser is an order of magnitude faster than the Collins and Charniak parsers. The relatively low parse times are due primarily to the use of the supertagger, which is very effective in accurately limiting the search space. Parser ef ciency was the original motivation for supertagging when applied to LTAG parsing (Bangalore & Joshi 1999).

6.5 *Summary*

The CCG parsing work described here was perhaps the rst to develop a discriminative parsing model based on the Penn Treebank (or derivative of the PTB) using an automatically extracted grammar. The huge parse space resulting from the automatically extracted grammar was handled in two ways: one, through the use of a cluster and a parallelized estimation algorithm; and two, through the use of a supertagger as a parsing pre-processor. Similar techniques have recently been applied to the PTB parsing task. Finkel et al. (2008) use cluster recources to estimate a log-linear model, and Carreras et al. (2008) use a TAG-like grammar, together with a simpler pre-processing stage, to limit the parse space for discriminative estimation (although the pre-processing is a simpler *parsing* model, rather than a supertagger).

The CCG parser was perhaps also the rst to successfully use a supertagger in conjunction with an automatically extracted grammar. The supertagger not only makes discriminative estimation possible, but also results in a surprisingly fast formalism-based parser.

One of the motivations for using CCG is the ability to recover long-range dependencies. There has been little evaluation of parsers' ability in this regard; some examples include Clark et al. (2004) for the CCG parser, and Johnson (2002) for a postprocessor applied to PTB parsers. Steedman (2008) argues that the ability to handle long-range dependencies will become increasingly important, both as a way of improving basic language technology, and also to satisfy the increasing expectations of users of the technology.

7 Other Work

It is inevitable in a chapter such as this that many relevant pieces of work have been omitted. For the history section, Brill's work on transformation-based parsing was an early, in uential attempt at the PTB parsing task (Brill 1993).

For the generative parsing section, there is a large body of work on data-oriented parsing (DOP) (Bod 2003). DOP uses a highly exible representation in which any subtree appearing in the data can be used to compose trees for unseen sentences, motivated by the idea that important dependencies exist which cannot be captured by the usual head-based decomposition of a parse-tree. Much of the DOP parsing work is concerned with developing estimation and parsing algorithms to deal with the enormous search space which results from this representation. Collins and Duffy (2002) use a similarly exible representation, but within a kernel framework, showing how parsing models which use all subtrees of a parse-tree can be ef ciently estimated, even though the number of subtrees grows exponentially with the size of the tree.

Titov and Henderson (2007c) describe a PTB parsing model in which neural networks are used to estimate the parameters of a generative model. The innovation in this approach lies in their exible notion of history, in that the estimation process itself decides how much conditioning context is appropriate for each parameter. This work is described in more detail in Chapter 9 of this book, ARTIFICIAL NEURAL NETWORKS.

For the CCG parsing section, and formalism-based parsing more generally, Chiang (2000) developed a wide-coverage parser using an automatically extracted TAG grammar. Hockenmaier and Steedman (2002b) describe a generative CCG parsing model, applying the techniques from the PTB generative models to CCGbank. Miyao and Tsujii (2005), in tandem with the development of the CCG parser, have done similar work for automatically extracted HPSG grammars, in particular developing the theoretical framework for the discriminative estimation method used by the CCG parser (Miyao & Tsujii 2002), which also draws heavily on Riezler et al. (2002). Cahill et al. (2004) obtain competitive results on a GR evaluation by automatically extracting LFG representations from PTB parse-trees.

There has been some recent work on statistical parsing motivated by psycholinguistic considerations, for example Dubey and Keller (2003), with the parsing model and algorithm typically exhibiting some amount of incrementality. Roark (2001a) describes an incremental, top-down parser with the aim of de ning syntax-based language models for speech recognition, where incrementality is a useful feature as it allows the speech signal to be processed in real time.

Finally, this chapter has focused on the parsing of English. Whilst the majority of work on statistical parsing has been for English, of course there has been work for other languages, for example German (Dubey & Keller 2003), French (Arun & Keller 2005), Spanish (Cowan & Collins 2005), Czech (Collins et al., 1999), and Chinese (Wang et al., 2006). Section 4.2 referred to the CoNNL shared task in which a number of languages were investigated in the context of dependency parsing.

8 Conclusion

This chapter has discussed the signi cant advances that have taken place in wide-coverage parsing, through the adoption of statistical and data-driven methods. However, the publication of accuracy results of over 90 percent can give a misleading impression that parsing is close to being a solved problem. There are many areas in which there is large room for improvement in statistical parsing.

First, an overall accuracy gure hides that fact that there are many semantically important dependencies that are being recovered at accuracies much lower than 90 percent. In addition, an overall score is in ated by the fact that some frequent dependencies, such as determiner–noun and auxiliary–verb, can be recovered with very high accuracies. Dependency-based evaluation schemes are useful in this regard, since they allow accuracies to be presented for particular dependency types. For example, the Collins parser has an accuracy on PP modi cation dependencies of roughly 82 percent, and on coordination structures of roughly 62 percent (Collins 1999d: 193–4). PP-attachment and coordination have always been classic syntactic ambiguity problems, and remain so despite decades of work on the problem.

Second, the majority of work, or at least the most in uential work, in statistical parsing has been performed on the *WSJ* section of the Penn Treebank. It is well known that parsers trained on newspaper text can perform much worse in other domains (Gildea 2001). Given the demand for NLP tools in domains such as biomedical text, a key area for development in statistical parsing, and one in which there is a growing literature, is domain adaptation.

Third, the majority of the work in statistical parsing has been for English. It is an open question whether models developed for English can be applied to languages which have very different characteristics, such as complex morphology or free word order, or whether signi cantly different modeling techniques are required for these languages.

Fourth, the lack of data in domains other than newspaper text and languages other than English (and a handful of other languages which have treebanks) is a barrier to developing accurate parsing models outside of the *WSJ*. Currently there are two suggestions for how to solve this problem: one, through the use of clever ways of obtaining manually annotated data, such as active learning; and two, through the use of semi-supervised or unsupervised approaches. Self-training is a recent example of the latter approach (McClosky et al., 2006).

Finally, evaluation, which has gained importance across the whole of NLP, has taken an increasingly prominent role in parsing, because of the desire to compare parsers across linguistic frameworks. However, the development of an evaluation scheme which can be applied fairly to a number of parsers has proven surprisingly dif cult (Clark & Curran 2007a).

Despite the fact that parsing has been a central problem in NLP since its inception, and that many researchers believe that parsing is important for applications such as question answering and machine translation, it is still surprisingly dif - cult to nd compelling examples of language technology in which parsing plays a central role. The development of robust, wide-coverage, and ef cient parsers may change this state of affairs – a recent prominent example of parser-driven language technology is the search engine of Powerset, which uses an LFG parser (Riezler et al., 2002) – but whether parsers will become a standard component in future language technology remains to be seen.

NOTES

1   The term *formalism-based* is used in this chapter to denote parsing research based on speci c linguistic formalisms, such as TAG, LFG, HPSG, and CCG.
2   See Manning and Schütze (1999) for a textbook treatment of PCFGs.
3   Chapter 4 of this book, THEORY OF PARSING, contains a more detailed description of parsing algorithms.
4   Collins (1999) gives a more detailed analysis, considering the various constant factors related to the grammar and training data.

5   The rest of this chapter uses λ for the weight vector; here we use **w** to be consistent with McDonald et al. (2005b).

6   An alternative to repeated parsing, which is described in Section 6, is to create packed charts for each sentence only once, and either keep them in memory, if enough RAM is available, or store them on disk and read each one in individually.

7   This is a rough paraphrase of the theoretical result; readers should consult Collins (2002) for the details.

8   Fairly comparing parser speeds is dif cult, because of differences in implementation and so on; however, it is reasonable to assume in this case that some of the speedup is due to the more ef cient dependency-parsing decoder.

9   Figures 13.7, 13.8, and 13.9 originally appeared in Clark and Curran (2007b), and are used with the permission of the Association for Computational Linguistics.

10 Features could also incorporate any part of the *sentence*, since this is a conditional parsing model and the sentence is not being generated.

11 The   at structure of noun phrases in the PTB means that complex noun phrase structures in CCGbank are always right-branching, sometimes incorrectly so. See Vadas and Curran (2008) for work describing manual correction of complex noun phrases in the PTB and CCGbank, and the impact this has on the accuracy of the CCG parser.

14 Segmentation and Morphology

JOHN A. GOLDSMITH

1 Introduction

1.1 General remarks

The eld of morphology has as its domain the study of what a word is in natural languages. In practice, this has meant the study of four relatively autonomous aspects of natural language: (1) the identi cation of the lexicon of a language, (2) morphophonology, (3) morphosyntax, and (4) morphological decomposition, or the study of word-internal structure.

At rst blush, identifying the lexicon of a language – what the words are – may seem simple, especially in languages which are conventionally written with spaces between words, but, as we shall see below, the task is more complicated at more points than one would expect, and in some scienti c contexts we may be interested in knowing under what conditions the spaces that mark separation between words can be predicted. To explain what points (2) through (4) above cover, we introduce the notion of *morph* – a natural, but not entirely uncontroversial notion. If we consider the written English words *jump*, *jumps*, *jumped*, and *jumping*, we note that they all begin with the string *jump*, and three of them are formed by following *jump* by *s*, *ed*, or *ing*. When words can be decomposed directly into such pieces, and when the pieces recur in a functionally regular way, we call those pieces *morphs*. With the concept of *morph* in hand, we may consider the following de nitions:

- **Morphophonology**. It is often the case that two or more morphs are similar in form, play a nearly identical role in the language, and can each be analytically understood as the realization of a single abstract element – 'abstract' in the sense that it characterizes a particular grammatical function, and abstracts away from one or more changes in spelling or pronunciation. For example, the regular way in which nouns form a plural in English is with a suf xal -*s*, but words ending in *s*, *sh*, and *ch* form their plurals with a suf xal -*es*. Both -*s* and -*es* are thus morphs in English, and we may consider them as

The Handbook of Computational Linguistics and Natural Language Processing, First Edition.
Edited by Alexander Clark, Chris Fox and Shalom Lappin.
© 2013 Blackwell Publishing Ltd except for editorial material and organization
© 2013 Alexander Clark, Chris Fox, and Shalom Lappin. Published 2013 by Blackwell Publishing Ltd.

forming a class which we call a *morpheme*: the pair of morphs {*s*, *-es*}, whose grammatical function is to mark plural nouns. The principles that are involved in determining which morph is used as the correct realization of a morpheme in any given case is the responsibility of morphophonology. Morphophonology is the shared responsibility of the disciplines of phonology and morphology.

- **Morphosyntax**. Syntax is the domain of language analysis responsible for the analysis of sentence formation, given an account of the words of a language.[1] In the very simplest cases, the syntactic structure of well-formed sentences in a language can be described in terms of atomic and unanalyzed words, but grammar is never really that simple. In reality, the morphs that appear inside one word may also specify information about other words in the sentence – for example, the verbal suffix *-s* in *Sincerity frightens John* specifies that the subject of the verb is grammatically singular. Thus statements about syntax inevitably include some that peer into the internal structure of at least some words in a language, and in many languages this is the rule rather than the exception. Morphosyntax deals with the relationship between the morphemes found inside one word and the other words that surround it in the larger sentence; it is the shared responsibility of the disciplines of syntax and morphology.

- **Morphological decomposition**. While English has many words which contain only a single morpheme (e.g., *while*, *class*, *change*), it also has many words that are decomposable into morphs, with one or more suffixes (*help-ful*, *thought-less-ness*), one or more prefixes (*out-last*), or combinations (*un-help-ful*). But English is rather on the tame side as natural languages go; many languages regularly have several affixes in their nouns, adjectives, and, even more often, their verbs (e.g., Spanish *bon-it-a-s*, which consists of a root meaning 'good,' a diminutive suffix *-it*, a feminine suffix *-a*, and a plural suffix *-s*).

In the remainder of this introductory section, we will give a brief overview of the kinds of questions that have traditionally been the focus of the study of morphology in general linguistics. This will serve as background to the discussion of the following three questions which are specifically computational in character.

(1) Can we develop – and if so, how – a *language-independent* algorithm that takes as input a large sequence of symbols representing letters or phonemes and provides as output that same sequence with an indication of how the sequence is divided into words? This question puts into algorithmic form the question of how we divide a string of symbols into words.

(2) How can we develop a language-independent algorithm that takes as input a list of words and provides as output a segmentation of the words into morphemes, appropriately labeled as prefix, stem, or suffix – in sum, a basic morphology of the language that produced the word list?

(3) How can we implement our knowledge of morphology in computational systems in order to improve performance in natural language processing?

1.2   *Morphology*

Users of natural languages (which is to say, all of us) need no persuasion that words are naturally occurring units. We may quibble as to whether expressions like *of course* should be treated as one word or two, but there is no disagreement about the notion that sentences can be analytically broken down into component words. Linguists and others who think deeply about such questions as 'what is a *word*?' generally focus on the idea that there is evidence in each language from phonology, morphology, syntax, and semantics which points in the direction of a natural *chunk* corresponding to the traditional notion of word. From a phonological point of view, phenomena that occur inside a word are often quite distinct from phenomena that occur at word boundary – the conditions under which a *t* is a ap in American English differ considerably in this way, for example. In a similar way, we   nd that at the point in an utterance between two words, we can expand the utterance by adding material. For example, we can convince ourselves that *their* is a separate word, and not a pre x to the word *dream*, because we can say: *John and his wife will follow their – or at least his – dream next year*.

There are some dif cult intermediate cases which linguists call *clitics* – morphemes whose status as a full- edged word is dubious; the possessive suf- x *'s* in English is such a case, because although in many respects it seems like a suf x to the word that precedes it, it may nonetheless be syntactically and semantically associated with a preceding phrase, as in an example like *a friend of mine's first husband* (contrast this with *a friend of my first husband*).

In all languages, or virtually all, it is appropriate to analytically break words down into component pieces, called *morphs*, and then to bundle morphs back into the functional units we call morphemes; such an analysis is part of the functionality of a morphology, and is the central subject of this chapter (when a morpheme corresponds to only a single morph, as is often the case, we generally ignore the difference between a morph and a morpheme). In addition, we expect of a complete morphology that it will associate the appropriate set of morphosyntactic features with a word, to the extent that the word's morphological decomposition can serve as a basis of specifying those features. Thus *books* should be analyzed as *book* plus a suf x *-s*, and the suf x *-s* should be marked as indicating plurality for nouns in English.

Morphologies are motivated by four considerations: (1) the discovery of regularities and redundancies in the lexicon of a language (such as the pattern in *walk:walks:walking :: jump:jumps:jumping*); (2) the need to make explicit the relationship between grammatical features (such as nominal NUMBER or verbal TENSE) and the af xes whose function it is to express these features; (3) the need to predict the occurrences of words not found in a training corpus; and (4) the usefulness of breaking words into parts in order to achieve better models for statistical translation, information retrieval, and other tasks that are sensitive to the meaning of a text.

Thus morphological models offer a level of segmentation that is typically larger than the individual *letter*,[2] and smaller than the *word*. For example, the English word *unhelpful* can be analyzed as a single word, as a sequence of nine letters, or from a morphological point of view as a sequence of the prefix *un-*, the stem *help*, and the suffix *-ful*.

The distinction between *inflectional* morphology and *derivational* morphology is one drawn by most accounts of morphology, but it remains a controversial question for some as to whether a clear line can be drawn between the two. The intuition that lies behind the distinction is reasonable enough; to illustrate this, let us consider an example from English. We may wish to say that *jump, jumps,* and *jumped* are three words, but they are all different versions (in some sense) of a single verb stem. The verb stem (*jump*) is coherent in three ways: it has a recognizable phonological form (*jump*), it shares a coherent semantic content, and it is *inflected* in ways that it shares with many other stems: in particular, it takes a suffixal *-s* in the third person singular present tense, and an *-ed* in the past tense. In addition to the characteristics just mentioned, inflectional affixes also are usually *peripheral* – if they are suffixes, the inflectional suffixes are at the very end of the word, and if prefixes, at the very beginning, and while they contribute grammatical information to the word they contain, they do not shift the part of speech of their word. The suffixes *-s* and *-ed* are taken to be inflectional suffixes, and they differ from derivational suffixes such as *-ity* (as in *sanity*) or *-ness* (as in *goodness, truthiness*)[3] or *-ize* (as in *radicalize, winterize*). Derivational affixes more often than not play the role of indicating a change of part of speech, in the sense that *sane* is an adjective, and *san-ity* is a noun, just as *radicalize* and *winterize* are verbs, but contain within them stems of a different category (adjective and noun, respectively). In addition, the semantic relationship between pairs of words related by derivational affixes is often far less regular than that found between pairs of words related by inflectional affixes. Thus, while the relationship between *jump* and *jumped, walk* and *walked*, and so on, is semantically regular, the same cannot be said of the relationship between words such as *woman* and *womanize, author* and *authorize*, and *winter* and *winterize*.[4]

For all of these reasons, most accounts of morphology distinguish between the analysis of a word's inflectional morphology, which isolates a stem (an *inflectional stem*) from its inflectional affixes, and the word's derivational morphology, which further breaks the (inflectional) stem into component pieces. Thus *winterized* is analyzed into a stem *winterize* plus an inflectional suffix *-ed*, and the stem *winterize* is divided into a stem *winter* plus a derivational suffix *-ize*. The term *root* is often used to refer to a stem that cannot be morphologically decomposed. An inflectional stem is associated with a single lexical category, such as noun, verb, adjective, etc. Just as importantly, the inflectional stem is the item in a lexicon which can be (and usually is) associated with a particular meaning, one that is generally not strictly predictable from the meanings of its components.

It is not unusual to find situations in which (by what I have just said) we find two stems that are spelled and pronounced identically: *walk* is both a noun and a verb, for example. The term *conversion* is often used to refer to this situation, in which a stem is (so to speak) converted from one part of speech to another without any overt affixation, though such analysis generally assumes that one can determine which of the two (noun or verb, in this case) is the more fundamental category of the two, on a stem-by-stem basis.

In ectional stems can also be created by a process of compounding, as in *watch-dog* or *eyepatch*. Such compound stems may include in ectional af xes, though many languages impose rather severe restrictions on the in ectional morphology permitted inside a compound (this is distinct from the case in which in ectional af xes 'attach' to compounds, as in *watchdog-s*, and exceptions exist, such as *months-long*, which is quite different in meaning from *month-long*). In some languages, a compound is formed by concatenating two stems; in others, a short linking element appears between them. The linking element of Greek compounds, *-o-*, appears in many compounds borrowed into English, such as in *hipp-o-potamus*.

All of the broad generalizations that I have suggested to this point, like most such broad generalizations, only go so far, and there are always phenomena in a natural language which demand a more complex view. I will sketch here some of the ways in which complexities arise most often.

First of all, in in ectional systems, there are typically a set of anywhere from two to a dozen relatively independent grammatical features which may be relevant to a particular word class, such as noun or verb. For example, a verb may be speci- ed for the PERSON and NUMBER of its subject, of its object, and for its TENSE, and for other characteristics as well. Only rarely – indeed, vanishingly rarely – is each such feature realized separately as its own morph. In most cases, it is a small tuple of features that is linked to a particular af x, as in the case of the English verbal suf x *-s*, which marks third person & singular & present tense. On the other hand, it is often the case that a single af x is used to mark more than one tuple of features; in written French, the suf x *-is* marks the present-tense singular subject agreement marker for a certain class of verbs; for exam- ple, *finis* is either '(I) finish' or '(you (sg.)) finish,' in either the first or second person, but not in the third person (which is spelled *finit*).

For this reason, linguists often think of in ectional systems as being hyper- rectangles in a large space, where each dimension corresponds to a grammatical feature, and where the edge of a hyperrectangle is divided into intervals corre- sponding to the feature values that the feature may take on (that is, *person* is a feature, and it may take on the values first, second, or third; NUMBER is a feature, and it may take on the values singular and plural, in some languages). Each af x will be associated with one or, quite often, several small sub-hyper-rectangles in such a system.

The complexities do not stop there. It is often the case that there are two or more forms of the stem used, depending on which subpart of the in ectional hyper- rectangle we are interested in. An extreme case is that of the stem *went* in English, used as the stem in the past, when *go* is used otherwise. This case is a bit special, since the form of *go* and *went* is so different (when the stems are this different, linguists refer to this as *suppletion*), but it is often found that several related (but distinct) stems will be used for different parts of the system. In French, for exam- ple, the present tense stem for '*write*' is spelled '*écri-*' in the singular, but '*écriv-*' in the plural. This is often referred to as *stem alternation*.

In addition, a language may employ a whole arsenal of different inflectional hyper-rectangles, even within a single lexical category. The Romance languages are perfectly typical in having between three and six so-called 'verb classes,' which employ quite different sets of suffixal patterns for marking precisely the same set of grammatical features. It is the verb stem that decides which inflectional set will be used for its morphology (see Goldsmith & O'Brien 2006).

Finally, we must acknowledge that not all morphology is properly thought of as the concatenation of morphs. In English, and many of the other Indo-European languages, we find inflectional patterns on verbs which consist of sets of stems (these are called *strong verbs*) that differ primarily with regard to the vowel: the past of *stand* is *stood*, the past of *sing* is *sang*, and the past of *catch* is *caught*. We will focus on those aspects of morphology which are strictly concatenative – in which words can be analyzed as sequences of morphs – but we will return to the treatment of the more general case below as well.

1.3 Static and dynamic metaphors

Inflectional morphology is complex in most natural languages. It is common for nouns to be marked morphologically for NUMBER and CASE, and for verbs to be marked morphologically for TENSE, PERSON, NUMBER, MOOD (whether the verb is in the indicative or the subjunctive), and syntactic position (whether the verb is in a subordinate clause of the sentence or not), for example. In fact, the hallmark of inflectional morphology – how we recognize it when we see it – is the appearance of several features that are logically orthogonal to one another, all of which are relevant for the realization of all, or most, of the words in a given part of speech (noun, verb, adjective). To put that a bit more concretely: to know Latin morphology is to know that a given verb is specified for the features of person, number, tense, and mood. The verb *cantō* is in the first-person, singular, present-tense indicative form, and the same is true of a very large, and potentially unbounded, set of verbs ending in *-ō*.

Lying behind that very specific knowledge is the understanding that first person is a value of the feature PERSON, that singular is a value of the feature NUMBER, that present is a value of the feature TENSE, and that indicative is a value of the feature MOOD. There are some dependencies among these features: there are more tenses when the mood is indicative and fewer when it is subjunctive, but these dependencies are the exception rather than the rule among inflectional features. There is no logical ordering of the features, for the most part: there is no logical or grammatical reason for PERSON to precede NUMBER, or to follow it (there may well be linear ordering of the morphemes that realize these morphemes, though). For all of these reasons, inflectional systems can encode many different combinations of feature specifications – quite unlike what we find with derivational morphology.

Some regularities in the morphology of a language are best expressed in terms that refer only to these inflectional features: for example, while the feature TENSE in Spanish may take on four values in the indicative mood (present, future, aorist, and imperfective), it takes on only two values in the subjunctive mood (present and past); in German, the forms of the nominative and accusative are the same for all neuter nouns. On the other hand, other generalizations address characteristics of the phonological realization of these features as morphs: in Finnish nouns, plural NUMBER is marked (temporally, graphically) before CASE.

Much of contemporary linguistic theory is dominated in a curious way by the belief that there is a correct order in which various aspects of the representation of a word or sentence are *constructed*; derivational theories are the clearest example of this. Re ecting on this, Stump (2001) distinguishes between *incremental* approaches, in which the process of adding an af x also adds morphosyntactic features, and *realizational* approaches, in which the process of adding an af x has access to a representation in which morphosyntactic features are present (or *already* present, as a derivationalist would have it). However, it is frequently the case that the distinction between these two approaches vanishes in a computational implementation, either because the analysis is conceptually static rather than dynamic (that is, it places well-formedness conditions on representations rather than offering a step-by-step method of producing representations), or because the dynamic that the computational implementation embodies is a different one (for a detailed discussion of this point in the context of nite state transducers, see Roark & Sproat 2006, chapter 3).

All of the material presented in this section is the result of the work of generations of linguists re ecting on many languages. In the next two sections, we will consider how the problem of *learning* about words and morphological structure can be reconstructed as a computational question of learning.

2   Unsupervised Learning of Words

In this section, we will discuss the computational problem of discovering words from a large sequence of symbols that bear no explicit indication of where one word ends and the next begins. We will start by distinguishing two formulations of this problem: one relatively easy, and the other quite dif cult.

2.1   *The two problems of word segmentation*

Let us consider strings of symbols chosen from an alphabet Σ, which the reader may think of as the letters of a written language or the sounds of a spoken language. There are two broad families of ways in which we analyze the structure of strings of symbols. One uses probabilistic models, which tell us about the probabilities of selection of elements from Σ in the future, given the past, typically the very local, recent past. In such models, the structure that we impose lies in the departure of the system from a uniform distribution, and the probability of a symbol is typically conditioned by a small number of immediately preceding symbols. The other uses segmentation models, whose purpose is to allow for the restructuring of a string of elements from a ne-grained alphabet (such as Σ) to a coarser set $\mathcal{L}$ which we call a *lexicon*, and which should be thought of intuitively as a set of substrings generated from Σ, that is, as a subset of Σ^*. For now, we may simply think of the members of $\mathcal{L}$ as our *words*. We will focus primarily on the second family of models, those employing *chunking*, but I do not wish to even suggest that there is any sort of incompatibility between the two approaches, because there is not.

Each word $w \in \mathcal{L}$ is associated with an element of Σ^*, its *spell-out* – I write 'associated with' rather than 'is,' because w may be decorated with other information, including meaning, syntactic category, and so on; but for simplicity of exposition, we may assume that no two elements in a lexicon are associated with the same spell-out. $\mathcal{L}^*$ is any concatenation of words, and any member s of $\mathcal{L}^*$ has a natural way of being thought of as a member of Σ^*: any sequence of words is naturally thought of as a sequence of letters, too. So far, no delimiters, like space or other punctuation, have come into the picture.

We will always assume that each member of Σ is also a member of $\mathcal{L}$ (roughly speaking, each member of the alphabet is a word), and so we can be sure that any string in Σ^* corresponds to at least one member of $\mathcal{L}^*$, but in most cases that we care about, a string in Σ^* will correspond to more than one string in $\mathcal{L}^*$, which is just a way of saying that breaking a string into words is not trivial. Each member of $\mathcal{L}^*$ which corresponds to a given string of letters we call a *parse* of that string. The string *atone* has three natural non-trivial parses: *atone*, *at one*, and *a tone*, but it has others as well.

The *first* problem of word segmentation, then, is to nd a method to take a string that in fact consists of strings of words, but which is presented as a string of letters with no indication of where one word ends and the next begins, and then from this string to reconstruct where the word breaks are. It is easy to go from such a corpus C_1 in which words are separated by spaces to a corpus C_2 in which all spaces have been removed, but can we reconstruct C_1 from C_2 with no information beyond word frequency? Given a corpus C_1 which indicates word boundaries separating words, we can easily construct a lexicon L, and a new corpus C_2 in which the word boundaries have been eliminated. Can we nd a language-independent algorithm $\mathcal{S}_1(L, C_2)$ that can reconstruct C_1? Put another way, can we de ne a method (either foolproof or just very good) that is able to put spaces back into a text with no more than a knowledge of the lexicon of the language from which the text was drawn?

There is no guarantee that such an algorithm exists for a speci c language or for languages in general, nor is there a guarantee that, if it exists (for a language, or for languages), we can nd it. Two families of natural approaches exist: the greedy and the probabilistic. The greedy approach scans through the string S: at position i, it looks for the longest substring s^* in S beginning at point i that appears in the lexicon; it then decides that s^* appears there in S, and it then skips to position $i + |s^*|$ and repeats the operation. The probabilistic model assumes a Markov probabilistic model over $\mathcal{L}^*$ (typically a zero-order or rst-order Markov model), and nds the string in $\mathcal{L}^*$ with the highest probability among all such strings whose spell-out is S.

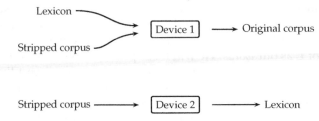

Figure 14.1 The two problems of word segmentation.

In general, we may wish to develop an algorithm that assigns a probability distribution over possible analyses, allowing for ranking of analyses: given a string *anicecream*, we may develop an algorithm that prefers *an ice cream* to *a nice cream* by assigning a higher probability to *an ice cream*. Linguists working on Chinese and Japanese have contributed signi cantly to improvements in our understanding of this problem (see, e.g., Sproat et al., 1996; Ando & Lee 2003; Teahan et al., 2000, and the series of Chinese word segmentation bakeoffs easily found on the internet).

The *second* problem of word segmentation is one large step harder than the rst: given a long string of symbols with no breaks indicated, can we infer what the words are? See Figure 14.1. This problem asks whether it is possible to nd a general algorithm S_2 which takes as input a corpus C_2, which was created by stripping boundaries from a corpus C_1, and which gives as output a lexicon $\mathcal{L}$ which will satisfy the conditions for the lexicon L needed for S_1, the solution to the rst problem.

Since, for any large corpus which has been stripped of its word boundaries, there are an astronomical number of different lexicons that are logically consistent with that stripped corpus, it should go without saying that if we can solve the second problem for naturally occurring corpora in real languages, we do not expect it to be extendable to just *any* randomly generable corpus: to put it another way, to the extent that we can solve this problem, it will be by inferring something about the nature of the device that generated the data in the rst place – something about the nature of human language, if it is natural language that we are exploring.

The problem of word segmentation may seem arti cial from the point of view of someone familiar with reading Western languages: it is the problem of locating the breaks between words in a corpus. In written English, as in many other written languages, the problem is trivial, since we effortlessly mark those breaks with white space. But the problem is not at all trivial in the case of a number of Asian languages, including Chinese and Japanese, where the white space convention is not followed, and the problem is not at all trivial from the point of view of continuous speech recognition, or that of the scienti c problem of understanding how infants, still incapable of reading, are able to infer the existence of words in the speech they hear around them.

Another computational perspective from which the problem of word breaking is interesting is this: to what extent do methods of analysis that have worked well in non-linguistic domains work well to solve this particular problem? This question is of general interest to the computer scientist, who is interested in a general way of regarding the range of problems for which an approach is suitable, and of considerable interest to the linguist, for the following reason. The most important contribution to linguistics of the work of Noam Chomsky since the mid-1950s has been his insistence that some aspects of the structure of natural language are unlearnable, or at the very least unlearned, and that therefore the speci cation of a human's knowledge of language *prior* to any exposure to linguistic data is a valid and an important task for linguistics. But knowledge of the lexicon of a given language, or the analysis of the words of the lexicon into morphemes, is a most unlikely candidate for any kind of innate knowledge. Few would seriously entertain the idea that our knowledge of the words of this book are matters of innate knowledge or linguistic theory; at best – and this is plausible – the linguist must attempt to shed light on the *process* by which the language learner infers the lexicon, given suf cient data. To say that the *ability* to derive the lexicon from the data is innate is something with which few would disagree, and to the extent that a careful study of what it takes to infer a lexicon or a morphology from data provides evidence of an effective statistically based method of language learning, such work sheds important light on quite general questions of linguistic theory.

The idea of segmenting a long string $S \in \Sigma^*$ into words is based on a simple intuition: that between two extreme analyses, there must be a happy medium that is optimal. The two extremes I refer to are the two 'trivial' ways to slice S into pieces: the rst is to not slice it at all, and to treat it as composed of exactly one piece, identical to the original S, while the second is to slice it into many, many pieces, each of which is one symbol in length. The rst is too coarse, and the second is too ne, for any long string that comes from natural languages (in fact, for most systems generating strings that are symbolic in any sense). The rst explains too much, in a sense, and over ts the data; the second explains too little. The challenge is to nd an intermediate level of chunking at which interesting structure emerges, and at which the average length of the chunks is greater than one, but not enormously greater than one. The goal is to nd the right intermediate level – and to understand what 'right' means in such a context. We will have succeeded when we can show that the string S is the concatenation of a sequence of members of a lexicon.

2.2 Trawling for chunks

There is a considerable literature on the task of discovering the words of an unlabeled stream of symbols, and we shall look at the basic ideas behind four major approaches.

2.2.1 Olivier The rst explicit computational model of word learning is found in Olivier (1968) (my description of this unpublished work is based primarily on

Kit (2000)). The algorithm begins with a division of the corpus, in some arbitrary fashion, into successive chapters which will be analyzed, one at a time and successively. Letting *i* be 1, we establish a 'provisional' lexicon from chapter *i*; it could be simply the lexicon consisting of all the individual letters of the alphabet that is used, and in some provisional fashion a probability distribution is established over the lexicon. Given that lexicon at pass *i*, we can relatively easily nd the division of the chapter into words that maximizes the probability of the string, on the assumption that the probability of a string is simply the product of the (unigram) probabilities of its words. This maximum likelihood parse provides us with a new set of *counts* of the items in the lexicon and, normalizing, we take these as forming a new probability distribution over the lexicon. We now modify the lexicon by adding and removing some of its members. If we nd that there is a sequence of two lexicon members that occurs more frequently than we would expect (by virtue of its frequency being greater than the product of the frequencies of its individual members), then we add that word to the lexicon. On the other hand, if a lexicon member occurs only once, we remove it from the lexicon. Having done this, we increment *i*, and reapply this process to the next chapter in the corpus.

This algorithm contains several elements that would be retained in later approaches to the problem but, in retrospect, we can see that its primary weakness is that it does not offer a principled answer to the question as to how large (i.e., how long) the words should be. It avoids the question in a sense by not reapplying recursively on a single text (chapter), but does not address the question head-on.

2.2.2   MK10   Another early lexicon-building approach was MK10, proposed by Wolff (1975; 1977). The initial state of the device is a lexicon consisting of all of the letters of the corpus. The iterative step is a continuous scanning through the text, parsing the text *C* at point *i* (as *i* goes from 1 to $|C|$) by nding the longest string *s* in the lexicon which matches the text from point *i* to point $i + |s - 1|$, and then proceeding from the next point, point $i + |s|$; when *i* reaches the end of the corpus, we begin the scan again. The algorithm keeps track of each *pair* of adjacent 'lexical items' that occur, and when the count of a particular pair exceeds a threshold (such as 10), the pair is added to the lexicon, all counts are reset to zero, and the process begins again. In sum, this is a greedy system that infers that any sequence which occurs at least 10 times is a single lexical item, or a part of a larger one.

Wolff's paper includes a brief discussion in which the relevance of his analysis is explicitly made to a number of important elements, including associationist psychology, the elimination of redundancy, natural selection, economy in storage and retrieval, induction, analysis by synthesis, probability matching, and the possibility of extending the algorithm to the discovery of lexical classes based on neighborhood-based distribution.

2.2.3   Sequitur   Craig Nevill-Manning, along with Ian Witten (see Nevill-Manning 1996; Nevill-Manning & Witten 1997) developed an intriguing non-probabilistic approach to the discovery of hierarchical structure, dubbed *Sequitur*.

They propose a style of analysis for a string S, employing context-free phrase-structure rules $\{R_i\}$ that are subject to two restrictions demanding a strong form of non-redundancy: (1) *no pair* of symbols S, T, in a given order, may appear twice in the set of rules, and (2) every rule must be used more than once. Violation of either principle gives rise immediately either to the creation of a new rule (if the rst is violated) or to the elimination of a rule (if the second is violated). Such sets of rules can be viewed as compressions of the original data which reveal redundancies in the data. An example will make clear how this is done.

Suppose the data is *thecatinthehatisnocat*. The algorithm will begin with a single rule expanding the root symbol S as the rst symbol, here t: $S \rightarrow t$. As we scan the next letter, we extend the rule to $S \rightarrow th$, and then to $S \rightarrow the$, and so on, eventually to $S \rightarrow thecatinth$. Now a violation of the rst principle has occurred, because *th* occurs twice, and the repair strategy invoked is the creating of a non-terminal symbol (we choose to label it 'A') which expands to the twice-used string: $A \rightarrow th$, which allows us to rewrite our top rule as $S \rightarrow AecatinA$, which no longer violates the principles. We continue scanning and extend the top rule now to: $S \rightarrow AecatinAe$, still maintaining the second rule, $A \rightarrow th$. Since *Ae* appears twice, we create a new rule, $B \rightarrow Ae$, and our top rule becomes: $S \rightarrow BcatinB$. But now rule A only appears once, in the rule expanding B, so we must dispense with it, and bulk up B so that it becomes: $B \rightarrow the$. We now see successful word recognition for the rst time. We continue three more iterations, till we have $S \rightarrow BcatinBhat$. Since *at* is repeated, we create a rule for it $C \rightarrow at$, and the top rule becomes $S \rightarrow BcCinBhC$. Scanning six more times, we arrive at $S \rightarrow BcCinBhCisnocC$, after the nal *at* is replaced by C. We then create a new rule $D \rightarrow cC$, leading to the top rule $S \rightarrow BDinBhCisnoD$. Here we stop, and we have the top-level parse corresponding to $the-cat-in-the-h-at-isno-cat$, with groups corresponding to *the* and to $c-at$. As this example illustrates, the very strict conditions set on the relationship between the rule set and the compression representation of the data lead to a powerful method of extracting local string regularities in the data.

Sequitur is an instance of what has come to be known as grammar-based compression (Kieffer & hui Yang 2000), whose goal is to develop a formal grammar that generates exactly one string: the text being compressed, and the grammar itself serves as a lossless compression of the text. That there should be a logical connection between an optimal compression of a string of symbols and the structure that inheres in the system that generated the string lies at the heart of the next perspective we discuss, minimum description length analysis.

2.2.4   MDL approaches   Some of the most interesting of the probabilistic approaches to word segmentation employ probabilistic models that are in uenced by Kolmogorov's notions of complexity, such as Rissanen's notion of minimum description length analysis.[5] These approaches provide explicit formulations of the idea mentioned above that word segmentation is a problem of nding a happy medium, somewhere between the two extremal analyses of a text string: one extreme in which the string is treated as a single, unanalyzed chunk, and the other in which it is treated as a concatenation of single symbols, each a 'chunk' separate from the previous one and the next one.

In a sense, the problem of discovering what the words of a text are means giving up any interest in what the speci c message is that is encoded there, at least for the time being. If that sounds paradoxical, just think about it: in asking what the words are in an utterance and nothing else, we care about the building blocks of the message, not the message itself. So a hypothesis about the correct segmentation of a text is, in part, a hypothesis about what information is in the *message* being encoded, and what information is part of the larger system being used to perform the encoding – which is to say, the language; it is a hypothesis about the factorization of linear information into system and message. If we say that the entire text (*A Tale of Two Cities*, by Charles Dickens, for example) is a single lexical item, then we have truly missed the generalization that the work actually shares a lexicon with any other text in English! If we say that the lexicon of the text is simply the 26 or so letters needed to write it out, then we have also missed the generalization that there are many often repeated strings of symbols, like *it*, *times*, and *Paris*.

The heart of the MDL approach is the realization that each of those two extremes results in an overloading of one of two encodings. The rst approach mentioned above, treating the text as a single lexical item, leads to the overloading of the lexicon; although it contains only one item, that single item is very, very long. The second approach leads to a single lexicon, with no more than a few dozen symbols in it, but specifying what makes *A Tale of Two Cities* different from any text which is not *A Tale of Two Cities* requires specifying every single successive letter in the text. That is simply too many speci cations: there are far better ways to *encode* the content of the text than by specifying each successive letter. The better ways are ones in which there is a lexicon with the real words of the language, and then a spelling out of the text by means of that lexicon. Because the average length of the words in the lexicon is much greater than one, the description of the text by specifying each *word*, one after the other, will take up much less space (or technically, far fewer bits of information) than specifying each letter, one after the other. The happy medium, then, is the analysis which minimizes the sum of these two complexities: the length of the lexicon and the length of the description of the text on the basis of that lexicon.

It turns out (though this is by no means obvious) that, if we make our lexicon probabilistic, it is easy to measure the number of bits it takes to describe a speci c text S, given a particular lexicon; that number is the negative base two logarithm of the probability of the text, as assigned by the lexicon (rounded up to the nearest integer); we write this $\lceil -log_2 pr(S) \rceil$. Probability plays a role here that is based entirely on *encoding*, and not on *randomness* (i.e., the presumption of the lack of structure) in the everyday sense. Making the lexicon probabilistic here means imposing the requirement that it assign a probability distribution over the words that comprise it, and that the probability of a word string S be the product of the probability of its component words (times a probability that the string is of the length that it actually happens to be). $\lceil -log_2 pr(S) \rceil$ speci es exactly how many bits it would take to encode that particular message, using the lexicon in question. This is not obvious, but it is true.

How do we measure the number of bits in the description of the lexicon? A reasonable rst approximation would be to calculate how much information it takes to specify a list of words, written in the usual way from an alphabet of a particular size. Ignoring a number of niceties, the length of a list of N words, each of length $|w_i|$, written in an alphabet consisting of m letters, is $log_2 N + \sum_{i=1}^{N} |w_i| log_2 m$, which is very close to the length of the lexicon (times a small constant), that is to say, the sum of the lengths of the words that make up the lexicon. This quantity, c_L, is naturally referred to as the complexity, or information content, of the lexicon. We will come back to this, and consider some alternatives which make the description shorter; what I have just mentioned is a simple baseline for length, a length that we know we can easily calculate. In a manner entirely parallel to what I alluded to in the preceding paragraph, there is a natural way to assign a well-formed probability to a lexicon as well, based on its complexity c_L: it is 2^{-c_L}.[6]

Minimum description length analysis proposes that, if we choose to analyze a string S into words (chunks that do not overlap, but cover the entire string), then the optimal analysis of S is by means of the lexicon L for which the sum of the two quantities we have just discussed forms a minimum: the rst quantity is $-log_2 pr(S)$ computed using given L, and the second quantity is c_L, which is the number of bits in the description of lexicon L.

We can now turn all of this discussion of description length into an algorithm for the discovery of the words of a corpus *if* we can nd a method for actually *finding* the lexicon that minimizes the combined description length.[7] A number of methods have been explored exploiting the observation that, as we build *up* a lexicon from small pieces (starting with the individual letters [Line 1]) to larger pieces, the only candidates we ever need to consider are pairs of items that occur next to each other somewhere in the string (and, most likely, a number of times in the string). In short, we batch process the text: we analyze the whole text several times [Line 2]. We begin with the 'trivial' lexicon consisting of just the letters of the alphabet, but we build the lexicon up rapidly by iteration. On each iteration, we nd the parse which maximizes the probability of the data, given the current hypothesized lexicon [Lines 3,4]. We consider as a tentative new candidate for the lexicon any pair of 'words' that occur next to each other in the string [Line 5]. We compute the description length of the entire string with and without the addition of the new lexical item, and we retain the candidate, and the new lexicon that it creates, if its retention leads to a reduction in the total description length [Line 8]. We set a reasonable stopping condition, such as having considered all adjacent pairs of words and nding none that satisfy the condition in Line 8.

MDL-based approaches work quite well in practice and, as a selling point, they have the advantage that they offer a principled answer to the question of how and why natural language should be broken up into chunks. Many variants on the approach sketched here can be explored. For example, we could explore the advantages of a lexicon that has some internal structure, allowing words to be speci ed in the lexicon as concatenation of two or more other lexical entries;

1: Start condition: $\mathcal{L} \Leftarrow \Sigma$
2: **repeat**
3:     $\pi^* \Leftarrow \arg\max_{\pi \in \{parses\ of\ D\}} pr(\pi)$, given $\mathcal{L}$
4:     Assign a probability distribution over $\mathcal{L}$ based on the counts of words in π^*
5:     Choose at random two adjacent words, $w_{i_k} w_{i_{k+1}}$
6:     $w^* \Leftarrow w_{i_k} \frown w_{i_{k+1}}$
7:     $\mathcal{L}^* \Leftarrow \mathcal{L} \cup w*$
8:     If DL(C,$\mathcal{L}^*$) < DL(C,$\mathcal{L}$), then $\mathcal{L} \Leftarrow \mathcal{L}^*$
9: **until** Stopping Condition is satis ed
10: **return** $\arg\max_{\pi \in \{parses\ of\ D\}} pr(\pi)$, given $\mathcal{L}$

Figure 14.2   Word discovery from an MDL point of view.

de Marcken's model permits this, thus encouraging the discovery of a lexicon whose entries are composed of something like morphs. We return to the general question shortly, in connection with the discovery of true linguistic morphology.

2.2.5 Hierarchical Bayesian models   In a series of recent papers, Goldwater, Johnson, and Grif ths (henceforth, GJG) have explored a different approach involving hierarchical Bayesian models, and they have applied this to the problem of inducing words, among other things (see Goldwater 2006; Goldwater et al., 2006; Johnson et al., 2006; Teh et al., 2006; Johnson 2008). Like MDL models, these grammars are non-parametric models, which is to say, in the study of different *sets* of data of the same *kind*, they consider models with different numbers of parameters – or to put it more crudely, the model complexity increases as we give the system more data. GJG describe the models by means of the process that generates them – where each model is a distribution, or a set of distributions over different bases – and what distinguishes this approach is that the history of choices made is cached, that is, made available to the process in a fashion that in uences its behavior at a given moment. The process leans towards reproducing decisions that it has often made in the past, based upon a scalar *concentration* parameter $\alpha > 0$. After having already generated n words, the probability that we generate a *novel* word from an internal base word-generating distribution is $\frac{\alpha}{\alpha+n}$, a value that diminishes rapidly as the process continues. Conversely, the probability of generating word w_k which has already occurred $[w_k]$ times is $\frac{[w_k]}{\alpha+[w_k]}$.

Such processes share with MDL models (though for quite different reasons) what sociologists call a *Matthew effect* (also called a *rich get richer* effect), whereby choices that have been selected over the past of the process are more likely to be selected in the future.

GJG use this process to model the generation of a lexicon, and Gibbs sampling to nd the appropriate lexicon parameters.[8] We describe the simplest of their models, the unigram model, here. As we have noted, the process has three parameters: a concentration parameter α; a nite lexicon, i.e., a nite set of elements of Σ^*, each of which is associated with a parameter corresponding to how often that word has been seen in the data at this point; and a base distribution Φ over Σ^* used eventually to create new words for the lexicon.

We thus have two abstract objects to consider in connection with any long unbroken string S: one is a string b of 1s (yes) and 0s (no), as to whether a word break occurs after the nth symbol of S; and the other is the nite lexicon (which is what we are trying to gure out, after all). Given S and a particular b, a speci c lexicon follows directly. The Gibbs sampling that is used provides a path from any initial set of assumptions about what b is (that is, any initial set of assumptions as to where the word breaks are) to essentially the same steady-state analysis of S into words. Here is how it does it, and it does not matter whether we begin with the assumption that there is a break between every symbol, between no symbols, or that breaks are initially assigned at random. We will iterate the following procedure until we reach equilibrium: we select an integer between 1 and $|S| - 1$, and calculate anew whether there *should* be a break there, i.e., we make a new decision as to whether b has a 0 or a 1 at position n, conditioned on the locations of the other breaks speci ed in b, which implicitly determines the words in the lexicon and their frequency. We do this by looking just at the righmost chunk to the left of position n and the leftmost chunk to the right of position n. For example, if the string is . . . *isawa* − *ca* − *t* − *inth* − *ewind* . . . (where the hyphen indicates a break, and no hyphen indicates no break), and we choose to sample the position between *ca* and *t*, then we calculate the probability of two different strings *cum* breaks: the one just indicated, and this one: . . . *isawa* − *cat* − *inth* − *ewind* . . . . If we assume words are generated independently of their neighbors (the unigram assumption), then we need simply compare the probability of *ca* − *t* and that of *cat*, and that decision will be made on the basis of the probability assigned by the process we have described. *That* probability, in turn, will not weigh heavily in favor of *cat* over *ca* and *t* early on, but if the corpus is in fact drawn from English, the counts of *cat* will begin to build up over those of *ca* and *t*, and the local decision made at position n will re ect the counts for all of the words that occur, given the analysis so far, in the string. GJG show that if we drop the unigram assumption about words, and assume essentially that the probability of each word is conditioned by the preceding word (more accurately, that the parameters of the Dirichlet process selecting a word are conditioned by the preceding word) and if we let the distribution Φ that proposes new words itself adapt to the language's phonotactics (which can be learned from the lexicon), then results are considerably improved.

2.3 Word boundary detectors

The very rst work on explicit development of boundary detectors was due to Zellig Harris, but his primary application of the notion was to morpheme detection, which we will return to shortly. Nonetheless, his ideas have inspired many subsequent workers, who have looked to see if there were local characteristics, detectable within a small window of ve or six letters, which would give a strong indication of where a word boundary falls in a text. We will look at one recent example, that of Cohen et al. (2002), which makes an effort to detect word boundaries both by nding likely boundary points and by nding likely word sequences. Cohen et al. (see also Cohen et al., 2007) let their hybrid model vote on the best spot to hypothesize a break to be, and so they call this a voting expert model. Their expert uses the log-frequency of a conjectured word chunk w as its measure of goodness as a word, and their measure of whether a point i is a good break point is what they call the boundary entropy, de ned roughly (but only roughly) as the entropy of the frequency distribution of individual letters that follow the hypothesized word that ends at point i. Thus, if a string *thusifastringisanalyzedat . . .* is analyzed at point 13 as containing the word *string* stretching from point 7 to point 13, then we compute the frequency of all of the letters that in fact follow the string *string* somewhere in the corpus. The greater the entropy of that multiset is, the likelier it is that the ending point of *string* is a word boundary (on the grounds that words are relatively poor as regards their ability to impose a decision on what letter should come next). This is the entropic version, employed by Hafer and Weiss (1974), of Harris's successor frequency notion, to which we return in the next section. Cohen et al. take into account phonological frequency effects by not using observed frequencies, but rather corresponding z-scores. For any sequence s of letters of length $|s|$ and frequency $f(s)$, they know both the average frequency $\mu(|s|)$ of distinct observed strings of length $|s|$ in the text, and the standard deviation from this mean of all of the strings of length $|s|$, so everywhere where one would expect to put a probability, they use a z-score instead (i.e., $\frac{freq(s)-\mu(|s|)}{\sigma}$): the measure of goodness of a chunk is the logarithm of that value, and the familiar notion of conditional entropy is modi ed to use this sort of z-score instead of a frequency.

The algorithm makes one pass over the string, shifting a window of limited size (the authors give an example of width 3, but in actual applications they use a window of 6, or more); at each stop of the window, the two measures (goodness of chunk, goodness of break point) each independently select the point within the window which maximizes their own measure, but looking only at the small substring within the window (and not, for example, what had been decided earlier on in the pass to segments 'to the left,' so to speak, except insofar as that information is implicit in the accrued voting). When the string has been scanned, a (non-linear) counting process decides how the votes which have been assigned to each point between the letters by the two measures should be transformed into hypotheses regarding word breaks.

2.4   *Successes and failures in word segmentation*

The largest part of the failures of all approaches to word segmentation are failures of level rather than failures of displacement: that is, failures are typically either of nding chunks that are too *large*, consisting of common pairs of words (*ofthe, NewYork*) or of not-so-common words composed of common pieces (*commit ment, artificial ly*), rather than errors like *c hunks*, though those certainly do appear as well. The most interesting result of all of the work in this area is this: there is no way to solve the word segmentation problem without also making major progress with the problem of automatic learning of morphology and syntax. Knowledge of the statistical properties of strings can be used to infer words only to the extent that the device that generated the strings in the rst place *used* knowledge of words, and only knowledge of words, to generate the string in the rst place; and, in actual fact, the systems that generate our natural language strings employ systems at several levels: it is not words, but *morphemes* that consist of relatively arbitrary sequences of letters, and words are the result of a system responsible for the linear placement of morphemes. In addition, there is a system responsible for the sequential placement of words – we call it *syntax* – and it too has a great impact on the statistics of letter placement. A system that tries to learn the structure of language on the basis of a model that is far poorer than the real structure of language will necessarily fail – we may be impressed by how well it does at rst, but failure is inevitable, unless and until we endow the learning algorithm with the freedom of thought to consider models that take into consideration the structure that indeed lies behind and within language. In the next section, we turn to the task of learning morphological structure.

3   Unsupervised Learning of Morphology

In this section, we will discuss the automatic learning of morphology. Most of the attention in this part of the literature has gone to the problem of segmentation, which is to say, the identi cation of the morphs and morphemes of a language, based entirely on naturalistic corpora. The identi cation and treatment of morphosyntactic features is an additional problem, which we shall touch on only in passing (though it is a real and important challenge). When we look at a sample of English, we certainly want to discover that *jumps* and *jumping* consist of a stem *jump* followed by the two suf xes *s* and *ing*, and a solution to the problem of identifying morphs gives us that information; but at the same time, we would like to know that -*s* marks the `third-person singular present` form of the verb. Such information goes well beyond the problem of segmentation, and brings us to the domain of morphosyntactic information, an area in which relatively little has been done in the domain of unsupervised learning of morphology.

3.1   *Zellig Harris*

All discussions of the problem of automatic segmentation aiming at discovering linguistically relevant units start with the work of Zellig Harris. In the mid 1950s, he noticed that one could de ne a function that, informally speaking, speci es how many alternative symbols may appear at any point in the string, given what has preceded. In light of both the method and the date, it is impossible not to sense an inspiration from Shannon's work, which had just appeared (Shannon & Weaver 1949). Harris himself published two papers addressing this approach

(1955; 1967), and returned to it brie y in other works till the end of his life (Harris 1991). At least as interesting for our purposes was the computational implementation of Harris's idea in Hafer and Weiss (1974). The presentation in this chapter relies primarily on Harris (1967) and Hafer and Weiss. We consider a family of Harrisian algorithms for segmenting words into morphemes, given a sample of words $W = \{w_i\}$ from a language, where each $w_i \in \Sigma^*$, for some alphabet Σ. We wish to associate a real value with the position that lies between each symbol in each word and, while we can imagine several slightly different ways to do this, the ways all attempt to capture the idea of measuring how many different ways the string to the left can be continued, in view of what we know about the entire set of words W. The core notion of *successorfrequency* is de ned as follows: The successor frequency $SF(p, W)$ of a string p in a set of words W is 0 if no words in W begin with p (i.e., there is no w in W which can be expressed as $p^\frown\alpha$ where $\alpha \in \Sigma^*$), and, more interestingly, it is equal to the number of distinct symbols $\{l_1, \ldots, l_k\}$ all of which can follow the pre x p in W: that is, our successor frequency is the size of the set $\{l_1, \ldots, l_k\}$ such that pl_i is a pre x of a word in W. A similar de nition can be constructed to de ne the predecessor frequency in a mirror-image fashion, specifying how many different letters can immediately precede any given word- nal substring.

Harris's intuition was that the successor frequency was high, or relatively high, at points in a string corresponding to morpheme boundaries, and the same is true for the predecessor frequency. But if the method works well in many cases, it fails in many others as well, due either to data sparsity or to other effects. One such effect arises when the set of suf xes to a given stem all sharing a common letter (for example, the words *construction* and *constructive* have a peak of successor frequency after *constructi*, and a peak of predecessor frequency after *construct*).

Hafer and Weiss (1974) tested 15 different interpretations of Harris's algorithm, and found a wide variety in precision and recall of the interpretations, ranging from 'completely unacceptable' when cuts were made at thresholds of successor frequency, to as high as 91 percent precision and recall of 61 percent; this was the result of making a morpheme cut when either of two conditions was met: (a) the word up to that point was also a free-standing word, and the predecessor frequency there was 5 or greater; or (b) the successor frequency at the point was greater than 1, and the predecessor frequency was greater than 16. One can see that some effort was expended to tune the parameters to suit the data.

3.2   Using description length

Anybody's list of words in a language, no matter how it is obtained, contains a great deal of redundancy, for all of the reasons that we discussed in the rst section of this paper: morphological roots appear with a variety of pre xes and suf xes, but that variety is limited to a relatively small number of patterns. The discovery of the morphological structure of a language is essentially the discovery of this

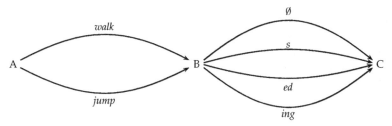

Figure 14.3 A signature for two verbs in English.

1: Start condition: $M \Leftarrow M_0(C)$
2: Some approaches: bootstrap operation B: $M \Leftarrow B(M_0(C))$
3: **repeat**
4:     $M' = F(M, M_0)$
5:     If condition $C(M, M')$ is satis ed, $M \Leftarrow M'$
6: **until** Stopping Condition

Figure 14.4 Morphology discovery as local descent.

kind of redundancy in the lexicon; removing the redundancy will both shorten the description of the lexicon and take us closer to an accurate characterization of the morphology. For example, if a language (in this case, English) contains a set of words *walk, walks, walked, walking, jump, jumps, jumped, jumping*, then rather than expressing all eight of the words separately, we can achieve greater simplicity by extracting the redundancy inherent in the data by identifying two stems, *walk* and *jump*, and four suf xes, Ø, *s*, *ed*, *ing*. See Figure 14.3.

But how do we turn that intuition into a computationally implemented approach? We employ a hill-climbing strategy, and focus on deciding what determines the shape of the landscape that we explore, and how to avoid discovering local maxima that are not global maxima.

We specify rst what the formal nature is of our morphology – typically, a nite state automaton (for a de nition of an FSA, see Section 4.3 of Chapter 1, FORMAL LANGUAGE THEORY, and Section 4.1 below). Given the nature of a morphology, it is always *possible* to treat a word as an unanalyzed morpheme, and an algorithm will generally begin by assuming that, in the initial state, the morphology treats all words of the corpus C as unanalyzable single morphemes (Step 1) (see Figure 14.4). We will call that state of a morphology $M_0(C)$. Some approaches take a one-time initial step of analysis (Step 2), with the aim of avoiding local optima that are not global optima. A loop is entered (Steps 3–5) during which hypotheses about morphological structure are entertained; any such hypothesis may either be dependent on what the current hypothesized morphology M is, or simply be based on information that is independent of the current M by using information that was already available in M_0, such as how often a string occurs in the corpus C (Step 4). A simplicity-based approach de nes some notion of simplicity – the function $C(\mathcal{M}, \mathcal{M}')$ in line 5 – to decide whether the modi ed morphology is preferable to the current hypothesis.

A method that employs minimum description length analysis,[9] such as Goldsmith (2001) and Goldsmith (2006), will use description length of the data as the condition in Step 5: a new morphology is preferred to the current one if the description length of the data is decreased with the new morphology, where the description length of the data is the sum of two quantities: (1) the inverse log probability of the data, and (2) the length of the morphology as measured in bits. How are these quantities calculated?

In order to calculate the probability of a word that the FST generates, we must associate a probability distribution with each set of edges that leaves a given state. Because a word, considered as a string of letters, typically is associated with only one path through the FST, it is easy to assign probabilities based on observed frequencies; we count the number of times each edge (n_i, n_j) is traversed when all of the data is traversed, and then assign the probability of going to node n_j, given that we are at node n_i, as $\frac{Count(n_i, n_j)}{\sum_k Count(n_i, n_k)}$, and the probability of any path through the FST (hence, of any word that it generates) is the product of the probabilities associated with each edge on the path. The number of bits required to encode such a word is, then, the negative log probability of the word, as just calculated.

How should we compute the length of a morphology in bits? In the discussion of MDL above concerning word segmentation, we saw one natural way to compute the length of a list of strings, and nothing would be simpler than to count the number of bits that were required in order to spell out the list of labels on each of the edges. The result would be $log_2 N + \sum_{i=1}^{N} |w_i| \, log_2 \, m$, where N is the total number of morphemes, m the number of symbols in the alphabet, and the set of labels is the set $\{w_i\}$.

In our discussion of MDL in connection with word discovery, we suggested that discovering the right lexicon is a matter of nding the right balance between a lexicon that was not overburdened and an encoding of the data that was not too intricate. Now we are saying something more: we are recognizing that we were not ambitious enough when we took it for granted that a lexicon was a list of words, because any lexicon that simply lists all its members is highly redundant in much the same way that a text in a particular language that is not analyzed into words is highly redundant. We therefore turn to the discovery of morphology as the means to reduce the redundancy in the lexicon.

This suggests a broader understanding of the cost of designing a particular morphology for a set of data: use information theory in order to make explicit what the cost of every single piece of the morphology is – which is to say, the morphology is a labeled, probabilistic FSA. It consists of a set of states $\{N\}$ (including a start state, and a set of nal, or accepting, states), a set of edges $E \subset N \times N$, a list of morphemes, and a label on each edge consisting of a pointer to an item on the morpheme list. The cost of the list of morphemes is calculated just as we discussed in Section 2.2.4, in the context of a lexicon of words. More interesting is the complexity, or cost, in bits associated with the FSA itself, which is the sum of the cost of each edge (n_i, n_j) and its associated label l_m. The cost of the edge is $-(\log pr_n(n_i) + \log pr_n(n_j))$, where $pr_n()$ is a probability distribution over nodes, or states, based on how often each node is traversed in parsing the data, as discussed four paragraphs above. The cost in bits of the pointer to an item on the morpheme list is equal to $-\log pr_\mu(m)$, where $pr_\mu()$ is a probability distribution over the items in the morpheme list, based on how many words in the corpus are generated by a path which includes an edge pointing to morpheme m.[10]

3.3 Work in the field

There has been considerable work in the area of automatic learning of morphology since the 1950s, and quite a bit of it since the mid-1990s. Subsequent to Zellig Harris's work mentioned earlier, there was work by Nikolaj Andreev (Andreev 1965; 1967, described in Cromm 1997) in the 1960s, and later by de Kock and Bossaert (1969; 1974). An interesting paper by Radhakrishnan (1978) in the text compression literature foreshadows some of the work that was yet to come. Several years later there was a series of papers by Klenk and others (Klenk & Langer 1989; Wothke & Schmidt 1992; Flenner 1995) which focused on discovery of local segment-based sequences which would be telltale indicators of morpheme boundaries. More recently, there has been a series of papers by Medina Urrea (2000; 2006) and Medina Urrea and Hlaváčová (2005). Approaches employing MDL have been discussed in van den Bosch et al. (1996), Kit and Wilks (1999), Goldsmith (2001; 2006), Baroni (2003), and Argamon et al. (2004). Important contributions have been made by Yarowsky and Wicentowski (2000), by Schone and Jurafsky (2001), and Creutz and colleagues (see Creutz & Lagus 2002; Creutz 2003; Creutz & Lagus 2004; 2005a; 2005b).

Clark (2001b; 2001c; 2002) explored the use of stochastic nite state automata in learning the concatenative suf xal morphology of English and Arabic, but also the more challenging case of strong verbs in English and broken plurals in Arabic, using expectation-maximization (Dempster et al., 1977c) to nd an optimal account, given the training data.[11] It is interesting to note that this work takes advantage of the active work in bioinformatics based on extensions of hidden Markov models, which itself came largely from the speech recognition community. Memory-based approaches such as van den Bosch and Daelemans (1999) (on Dutch) employ rich training data to infer morphological generalizations extending well past the training data.

Algorithms that learn morphology in a strictly unsupervised way are never certain about what pairs of words really are morphologically related; they can only make educated guesses, based in part on generalizations that they observe in the data. Some researchers have explored what morphological learners might be able to do if they were told what pairs of words were morphologically related, and the systems would have to induce the structure or principles by which they were related. This work is not strictly speaking unsupervised learning; the learner is helped along considerably by knowledge that pairs of words are indeed morphologically related.

Let us suppose, for purposes of discussion, that we have determined in some fashion that the pairs of words that we are given are largely distinguished by material on the right-hand side of the word: that is, that the system is largely suf xal. Then, given any pair of related words w_1 and w_2, where w_1 is not longer than w_2, then there are at most $|w_1 + 1|$ ways to account for the pairing, based solely on treating the relationship as based on morphs. Given the pair *jump/jumped*, there are ve generalizations we might consider, each specifying a pair of suf xes in that pair of words: $\emptyset/ed, p/ped, mp/mped, ump/umped$, and *jump/jumped*. As we consider a large set of pairs of words, it is not hard to see that the correct generalization will generally be the one which occurs most frequently among a large number of word pairs. This approach has the advantage that it can say something useful even about generalizations that involve a very small number of pairs (e.g., *say/said, pay/paid*); this is more dif cult for a purely unsupervised approach, because it is dif cult for a purely unsupervised approach to become aware that those pairs of words *should* be related, so to speak. An early effort along these lines was Zhang and Kim (1990). Research employing inductive logic programming to deal with this problem by automatically creating decisions lists or trees has included Mooney and Califf (1996) (on English strong verbs), Manandhar et al. (1998), Kazakov and Manandhar (1998) (an approach that also employs an algorithmic preference for simpler morphological analyses), Kazakov (2000) – which presents a very useful survey of work done in the 1990s on computational morphology – Erjavec and Džeroski (2004), which discusses the case of Slovene in some detail, and Shalonova and Flach (2007) (English and Russian). Baroni et al. (2002) took an interesting step of using mutual information between pairs of nearby words in a corpus as a crude measure of semantic relatedness. It had been noticed (Brown et al., 1992) that words that are semantically related have a higher probability than chance to occur within a window of 3 to 500 words of each other in a running text, and they explored the consequences for analyzing pairs of words (looking at English, and at German) that are both formally similar and with relatively large point-wise mutual information. This work therefore looks a lot like the work described in the preceding paragraph, but it resembles it in a rigorously unsupervised way.

4   Implementing Computational Morphologies

Sophisticated computational accounts of natural language morphology go back more than 40 years in the literature; we can still pro tably read early articles such as that by P. H. Matthews (1966).

There have been several excellent book-length studies of computational morphology in recent years, with considerable concern for actual, real-world implementation, notably by Beesley and Karttunen (2003) and Roark and Sproat

(2006), as well as Ritchie et al. (1992) and Sproat (1992). Current work in this area focuses to a very large extent on the use of finite state transducers as a means to carry out the functions of morphology. This work was stimulated by the work of Douglas Johnson (1972), Ronald Kaplan and Martin Kay (1981), Kimmo Koskenniemi (1983), and developed in a number of places by Lauri Karttunen and colleagues (1993). Beesley and Karttunen's recent book is especially detailed and lucid, and contains Xerox software that can be used by the reader.

A well-functioning computational morphology for a language can be vital for many practical applications. Spell-checking is a humble but honest function of many products appreciated by a wide range of end users, and in a language with a rich inflectional morphology, as we find in languages such as Finnish, Hungarian, Turkish, the Bantu languages, and many others, the total number of possible forms that a user might reasonably generate is far greater than the capacity of a computer to hold in its memory, unless the entire family of forms is compressed to a manageable size by virtue of the redundancies inherent in a computational morphology. It is typically the inflectional morphology which gives rise to the very large number of possible forms for nouns and verbs, and it is typically inflectional morphology which can most usefully be stripped off when one wishes to build a document-retrieval system based not on actual words, but on the most useful part of the words. Syntactic parsing in most languages requires a knowledge of the morphosyntactic features carried by each word, and that knowledge is generally understood as being wrapped up in the morphology (primarily the inflectional morphology) of the language.[12] A number of researchers have explored the effect on the quality of information and document retrieval that is produced by incorporating knowledge of inflectional and derivational morphology, including Harman (1991), Krovetz (2000), Hull (1996), Kraaij and Pohlmann (1996), Xu and Croft (1998), Goldsmith et al. (2001), Larkey (2002), and Savoy (2006).

Let us consider briefly how a practical system can be overwhelmed by the size of natural language word sets if morphology is not addressed in a systematic way. In Swahili, a typical Bantu language in this regard, a verb is composed of a sequence of morphemes. Without pretending to be exhaustive, we would include an optional prefix marking negation, a subject marker, a tense marker, an optional object marker, a verb root, a choice of zero or more derivational suffixes marking such functions as causative, benefactive, and reflexive, and ended by a vowel marking mood. Subject and object markers are chosen from a set of approximately 20 options, and tenses from a set of about 12. Thus each verb root is a part of perhaps 100,000 verbs. Similar considerations hold in many languages – in fact, almost certainly in the great majority of the world's languages.

4.1 Finite state transducers

A large part of the work on computational morphology has involved the use of finite state devices, including the development of computational tools and infrastructure. Finite state methods have been used to handle both the strictly morphological and morphotactic, on the one hand, and the morphophonology and graphotactics on the other. We have already encountered the way in which strictly morphological information can be implemented with a nite state automaton, as in Figure 14.3. By extending the notion of nite state automaton to that of nite state *transducer*, we can use much the same notions in order to not only generate the correct surface morphemes but also create a device that can map surface sequences of letters (or phones) to abstract morphosyntactic features such as NUMBER and TENSE.

Computational morphology has also applied the notion of nite state transducer (the precise details of which we return to shortly) to deal with the problem of accounting for regularities of various sorts concerning alternative ways of realizing morphemes. For example, both the English nominal suf x marking PLURAL and the English verbal suf x marking third person singular is normally realized as -*s*, but both are regularly realized as -*es* after a range of stems which end in -*s*, -*sh*, -*ch*, and -*z*.

We refer to these two aspects of the problem as *morphotactics* and *phonology* respectively. Two methods have been developed in considerable detail for the implementation of these two aspects within the context of nite state devices. One, often called 'two-level morphology,' is based on an architecture in which a set of constraints is expressed as nite state transducers that apply in parallel to an underlying and a surface representation. Informally speaking, each such transducer acts like a constraint on possible differences that are permitted between the underlying and the surface labels, and, as such, any paired underlying/surface string must satisfy all transducers. The other approach involves not a *parallel* set of nite state transducers, but rather a *cascaded* set of nite state transducers, which can be compiled into a single transducer. A lucid history of this work, with an account of the relationship between these approaches, can be found in Karttunen and Beesley (2005); a more technical, but accessible, account is given by Karttunen (1993).

The term 'two-level morphology,' due to Koskenniemi (1983), deserves some explanation: by its very name, it suggests that it is possible to deal with the complexities of natural language morphology (including morphophonology) without recourse to derivations or intermediate levels. That is, formal accounts which are in uenced by generative linguistics have tended uniformly to analyze language by breaking up phenomena into pieces that could be thought of as applying successively to generate an output from an input with several intermediate stages. It would take us too far a eld to go through an example in detail, but one could well imagine that the formation of the plural form of *shelf* could be broken up into successive stages: *shelf* → *shelf* + *s* → *shelv* + *s* → *shelves*. Here, we see the suf xation of the plural '*s*' happening (in some sense!) rst, followed by the change of *f* to *v*, followed in turn by the insertion of *e*. In contrast, nite state automata offer a way of dealing with the central phenomena of morphology without recourse to such a step-by-step derivation: hence the term 'two-level morphology,' which employs only two levels: one in which morphosyntactic features and lexical roots are speci ed, and one which matches the spelled (or pronounced) form of the word. We return to this in Section 4.2.

The notion of *finite state automaton* (often abbreviated as *FSA*) was rst presented in Kleene (1956), itself inspired by the work of McCulloch and Pitts (1943) some ten years earlier. An FSA is a kind of directed graph: a directed graph is by de nition a nite set of nodes $\mathcal{N}$, along with a set of edges E, where an edge is an ordered pair of nodes. *Nodes* in an FSA are often called *states*. For a directed graph to be an FSA, it must be endowed with three additional properties: it must have a distinguished node identi ed as its *start* state; it must have a set of one or more *stopping* (or *accepting*) states; and it must have a set of labels, $\mathcal{L}$, with each edge associated with exactly one label in $\mathcal{L}$. While $\mathcal{L}$ cannot in general be null, it may contain the null string as one of its members. In purely mathematical contexts, it is convenient to assume that each label is an atomic element, indivisible, but in the context of computational linguistics, we rather think of $\mathcal{L}$ as a subset of Σ^*, for some appropriately chosen Σ. In that way, the morphs of a given language (e.g., *jump, dog, ing*) will be members of $\mathcal{L}$, as will be descriptions of grammatical feature speci cations, such as `first person` or `past tense`.

When we explore an FSA, we are typically interested in the set of paths through the graph, and the strings associated with each such path – we say that a path *generates* the string. A path in a given FSA is de ned as a sequence of nodes selected from $\mathcal{N}$, in which the rst node in the sequence is the starting state of the FSA, the last node in the sequence is one of the stopping states of the FSA, and each pair of successive nodes (n_i, n_{i+1}) in the sequence corresponds to an edge e_j of the FSA. We associate a string S with a path p simply by concatenating all of the labels of the edges corresponding to the successive pairs of nodes comprising p. If we take a grammar of a language to be a formal device which identi es a set of grammatical strings of symbols, then an FSA is a grammar, because it can be used to identify the set of strings that correspond to all paths through it. Given a string S in $\mathcal{L}^*$, we can identify all paths through the FSA that generate S.

Finite state morphologies employ a generalization of the nite-state automaton called a nite state *transducer*, or *FST*, following work by Johnson (1972). An FST differs from an FSA in that an FST has two sets of labels (or in principle even more, though we restrict the discussion here to the more common case), one called *underlying* labels, $\mathcal{L}_\mathcal{U}$, and one called *surface* labels, $\mathcal{L}_S$, and each edge is associated with a *pair* of labels $(l_\mathcal{U}, l_S)$, the rst chosen from the underlying labels, and the second from the surface labels – it is traditional, however, to mark the pair not with parentheses, but with a simple colon between the two: $l_\mathcal{U} : l_S$. The FSA thus serves as a sort of translation system between $\mathcal{L}_\mathcal{U}^*$ and $\mathcal{L}_S^*$. In fact, an FST can be thought of as *two* (or even more) FSAs which share the same nodes, edges, starting states, and stopping states, but which differ with regard to the labels associated with each edge, and we only care about looking at pairs of identical paths through these two FSAs. The beauty of the notion of FST lies in the fact that it allows us to think about pairs of parallel paths through otherwise identical FSAs as if they were just a single path through a single directed graph. For this reason, we can say that FSAs are *bidirectional*, in the sense that they have no preference for the underlying

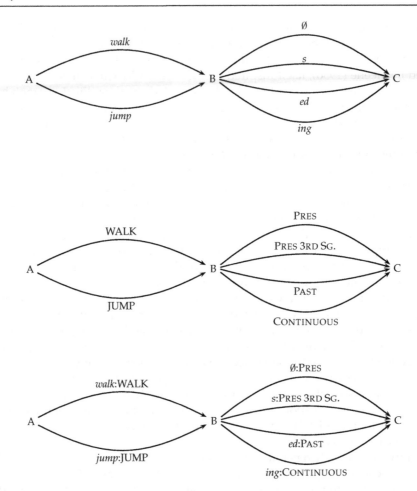

Figure 14.5   Building an FST from two FSAs.

labels or the surface labels: the same FST can translate a string from $\mathcal{L}_S^*$ to $\mathcal{L}_U^*$, and also from $\mathcal{L}_U^*$ to $\mathcal{L}_S^*$. If we construct an FST whose second set of labels is not underlying forms but rather category lables, then the same formalism gives us a parser: tracing the path of a string through the FST associates the string with a sequence of categories. Finite state automata are relatively simple to implement, and very rapid in their functioning once implemented. See Figure 14.5.

4.2 *Morphophonology*

Rare is the language which does not contain rules of its spelling system whose effect is to vary the spelling of a morpheme depending on the characteristics of the neighboring morphemes. English has many such cases: as we noted, some English words, like *wife* and *knife*, change their *f* to *v* in the plural; the plural suf x itself is sometimes -*s* and sometimes -*es*, depending on what precedes it. Since these patterns tend to recur within a given language, it is traditional to analyze this by saying that there is a single underlying label for the morpheme, but two or more surface labels that the transducer relates to the single underlying label.

Koskenniemi (1983) developed a system of notation widely used in nite state morphophonology to deal with this. The challenge of the task is to make explicit when any departure from simple identity is required, or permitted, between the underlying label u and the surface label s. Koskenniemi's idea was that for any given pairing like $f : v$, we can de ne a *context* that either permits or requires that correspondence, where by a *context* we mean a speci cation of the symbols that appear to the left and to the right, on both the underlying labels and the surface labels. For example, if every occurrence of underlying t corresponds to a surface s when and only when an i follows on *both* the underlying and surface labels, then we can specify this thus: $t : s \Leftrightarrow \_i : i$. If we wanted to express the generalization that when two vowels were adjacent on the string of underlying labels, only the second of them appears among the surface labels, then we would represent it this way: $V : \emptyset \Leftarrow \_V :$, where V is a cover symbol standing for any vowel. The $\Leftarrow$ is taken to mean that in the context described to the right of the arrow, any occurrence of the underlying label in the pair on the left *must* be realized as the surface label of the pair on the left (in this case, as the null symbol). If the arrow pointed to the right, as in $V : \emptyset \Rightarrow \_V :$, the rule would be saying that the correspondence of underlying V to surface $\emptyset$ can only occur when an underlying vowel follows.

In the case of *wife/wives*, we must account for the pair $(f : v)$. Since this same pairing is found in a good number of English words, an appealing way to formalize this is to specify that the morpheme underlying *wife* contains a special symbol, which we indicate with a capital F: *wiFe*. An underlying F corresponds to a surface v, when the plural suf x follows, or in all other cases to a surface f. If the underlying form of the plural form of *wife* is **wiFe+NounPlural**, then we can express this as: $F : v \Leftarrow e + NounPlural :$, and the associated surface label will be *wives*.

5 Conclusions

The computational study of morphology is of interest because of its importance in practical applications, both present and future, and because of its theoretical interest. We have seen that the words of a language are not simply a xed set of strings chosen from a language's inventory of letters, or phonemes; the vocabulary is in fact built out of a set of morphemes in ways that are potentially quite complex, and in ways that may give rise to complex modi cations of one or more morphemes in a word, each modi cation of each morpheme potentially sensitive to the choices of each of the other morphemes in the word.

While the number of distinct words in a language does not grow as rapidly with length as the number of sentences in a language does, it is nonetheless true that the size of the total lexicon of a language is vastly larger than the size of the set of morphemes used to generate those words. In order to ensure that a system handles the entire lexicon, it is both practically and theoretically necessary to generate the lexicon computationally in a way that re ects the true structure of the morphology of the language. In addition, the meaning and function of a word is in many respects decomposable into the meaning and function of its in ectional stem and in ectional af xes, and so morphological analysis is an important step in statistical and data-driven methods of machine translation, at least in languages with rich morphologies.

At the same time, the formal structure of the morphological grammar of a language may be quite a bit simpler than the syntactic grammar, and allow for greater success at this point in the task of automatically inferring the morphology from data with relatively little hand tagging of the data or contribution on the part of a human linguist. At present, the work on unsupervised learning in this area has focused on the problem of segmentation, but work is certain to procede in the direction of choosing the correct structure among alternative candidate FSAs, given a training corpus. Advances in this area will shed light on the more general problem of induction of regular languages, which in turn may be helpful in the goal of induction of more comprehensive grammars from natural language corpora.

ACKNOWLEDGMENT

I am endebted to many friends and colleagues, both for conversations on the topics discussed in this chapter and for comments on an earlier draft, including Carl de Marcken, Paul Cohen, Walter Daelemans, Tomaž Erjavec, Antonio Galves, Sharon Goldwater, Yu Hu, Mark Johnson, Chunyu Kit, Ursula Klenk, Kimmo Koskenniemi, Colin Sprague, Richard Sproat, Antal van den Bosch, J. G. Wolff, Aris Xanthos, and the editors of this volume; I hope that I have succeeded in correcting the errors they pointed out to me. Reader, bear in mind that all the ideas presented here have been simpli ed to improve comprehensibility. As always, if you are interested, read the original.

NOTES

1   See Chapter 4, THEORY OF PARSING, Chapter 8, UNSUPERVISED LEARNING AND GRAMMAR INDUCTION, and Chapter 13, STATISTICAL PARSING.
2   Since computational linguists have traditionally interested themselves more with written language than spoken language, I write here of *letters* rather than *phonemes*, but the reader who is interested in spoken language should substitute *phoneme* for *letter* in the text.
3   http://en.wikipedia.org/wiki/Truthiness

4 There are two suf xes -*ing* in English; the one that appears in sentences in the progres-
sive (*John is running*) is in ectional; the one that creates nominals is derivational (*No singing of songs will be tolerated*).

5 For general discussion of this approach, see Rissanen (2007), Li and Vitányi (1993). The rst general exploration of these ideas with application to linguistic questions was undertaken in Ellison (1994), and several developments along similar lines appeared in the early to mid-1990s, notably Rissanen and Ristad (1994), Cartwright and Brent (1994), Brent et al. (1995), Brent and Cartwright (1996), de Marcken (1996), Cairns et al. (1997), Brent (1999), and Kit and Wilks (1999), as well as Kit (2000). My discussion here presents a simpli ed version of the approach that is common to those accounts.

6 The reason for this is that the quantity c_L essentially counts the number of 0s and 1s that would be required to ef ciently express the lexicon in a purely binary format. If we also place the so-called *prefix property* condition on the encoding we use, which means that no such binary encoding may be identical to the beginning of another such encoding, then it is relatively straightforward to show that each such binary expression can be associated with a subinterval of [0,1], and that these subintervals do not overlap. The nal step of deriving a well-formed probability involves determining whether there are any subintervals of [0,1] which have not been put into correspondence with a lexicon, and dealing with the total length of such subintervals.

7 See pseudo-code in Figure 14.2.

8 On Gibbs sampling, see Mackay (2002), for example.

9 An open source project that implements such an approach can be found at http://linguistica.uchicago.edu

10 That is, if there are a total of V words in the corpus, and the number of occurrences of all of the morphemes in the corpus is M (and M, unlike V, depends on the morphology we assume), and if $K(m)$ is the number of words that contain the morpheme m (we make the realistic assumption that no word contains two instances of the same morpheme), then the cost of a pointer to m is equal to $pr_\mu(m) = log_2 \frac{M}{K(m)}$.

11 A number of studies have dealt with Arabic, such as Klenk (1994); see also van den Bosch et al. (2007a) and other chapters in that book.

12 Even for a language like English, in which the morphology is relatively simple, and one could in principle not do *too* badly in an effort to list all of the in ected forms of the known words of English, the fact remains that it is rarely feasible in practice to construct a list of all such words simply by data-scraping – that is, by nding the words in nature. To be sure that one had obtained all of the in ected forms of each stem, one would have to build a morphology to generate the forms, thereby bringing us back to the problem of building a morphology for the language.

15 Computational Semantics

CHRIS FOX

1 Introduction

In this chapter we will generally use 'semantics' to refer to a formal analysis of meaning, and 'computational' to refer to approaches that in principle support effective implementation, following Blackburn and Bos (2005).

There are many dif culties in interpreting natural language. These dif culties can be classi ed into speci c phenomena – such as scope ambiguity, anaphora, ellipsis and presuppositions. Historically, different phenomena have been explored within different frameworks, based upon different philosophical and methodological foundations. The nature of these frameworks, and how they are formulated, has an impact on whether a given analysis is computationally feasible. Thus the topic of computational semantics can be seen to be concerned with the analysis of semantic phenomena within computationally feasible frameworks.

Unfortunately, the range of phenomena and the number of frameworks that are of relevance to computational semantics are too vast and this chapter too short to be able to do the subject full justice in the space available. Instead, this contribution should be seen as offering merely a taste of some issues in computational semantics, focusing primarily on logic-based approaches. There are differing views on what counts as the canon of computational semantics, what aspects of semantics are deemed to be 'solved,' and which research questions are considered open and worthy of pursuit. For these reasons, the focus of the chapter will necessarily appear biased and unbalanced, re ecting the interests and prejudices of the author.

One factor that computational semantics requires over and above formal semantics is that we take seriously the notion of a semantic representation whose behavior can be expressed independently of any model-theoretic interpretation. This is because an effective implementation needs to be able to use and reason directly with this representation: an implementation cannot make a direct appeal to some abstract, external model in order to determine which inferences are valid.

The Handbook of Computational Linguistics and Natural Language Processing, First Edition.
Edited by Alexander Clark, Chris Fox and Shalom Lappin.
© 2013 Blackwell Publishing Ltd except for editorial material and organization
© 2013 Alexander Clark, Chris Fox, and Shalom Lappin. Published 2013 by Blackwell Publishing Ltd.

In a formal theory of semantics, the appropriate inferential behavior of the representation should be clearly and precisely formulated. Ideally, to ensure that the behavior corresponds with our intuitions, the relevant behaviors should be captured as transparently as possible.

For computational semantics, the entailments of the representation language should also be computationally feasible. The notions of *decidability* are relevant here (see Chapter 2 of this book, COMPUTATIONAL COMPLEXITY IN NATURAL LANGUAGE, Section 1.2). In a *decidable* system, we can determine what does and does not follow from an expression. In a *semi-decidable* system, we can only guarantee to compute things that follow from an expression. This is also called *recursive enumerability*. If something does not follow, then the decision procedure may never halt. In an *undecidable* system, we cannot even guarantee to be able to compute what follows from a statement.

If there is a choice, then typically a decidable formulation should be preferred to a semi-decidable one, which in turn should be preferred to an undecidable formulation. Even a logic that is not decidable in general might be decidable for those inferences that are of interest – as would be the case if the domain of discourse was nite, for example – but it might be better to adopt a formalism that captures this requirement by design or nature rather than contingently.

In addition to techniques based upon formal semantics, the remit of computational semantics may be taken to include corpus-based machine learning techniques applied to aspects of interpretation, such as word-sense disambiguation, and identi cation of entailments and semantic roles. Some such methods are touched upon (Section 5), although they are not the primary focus of this chapter.

1.1   *Outline*

This chapter is aimed at readers with some knowledge of syntactic theory (e.g., see Chapter 1 of this book, FORMAL LANGUAGE THEORY) and predicate logic. The primary focus here is on the formal and logical aspects of computational semantics, rather than on linguistic data, or statistical or corpus-based techniques. It is organized as follows. In Section 2 there is a basic introduction to formal semantics, including a discussion of compositionality, elementary types, model theory, and proof theory. In Section 3, the 'state of the art' treatment of the formal analysis of discourse and underspeci ed representations of quanti er scoping are outlined. In Section 4, some relatively open formal topics are sketched, covering type theory, intensionality, and the analysis of non-indicatives. This section also includes some discussion of the issue of power versus expressiveness of formal representation languages. This covers the idea of treating 'computability' as a constraint on formal semantic theories.

Due to limitations of space, it is unavoidable that many important semantic issues will not even be mentioned, including the full range of modalities, hypotheticals, the meaning of names, mass terms and plurals, and the formal analysis of topic and focus, and tense. It is also not possible to do full justice to the many relevant corpus-based techniques, but some of the latter are briefly summarized in Section 5, and are also discussed in Chapter 18, INFORMATION EXTRACTION, and Chapter 22, QUESTION ANSWERING.

2   Background

Given that our core characterization of computational semantics is founded on computationally tractable accounts of meaning that are rooted in formal semantics, it is appropriate to give an introductory account of what is usually meant by formal semantics.

Language is used to convey information. This can be directly, in terms of the literal 'content' of an expression, or indirectly, either through accommodating the presuppositions of an expression (van der Sandt 1992), or through some other forms of implicature (Grice 1975; 1981).[1]

We can use the following examples to illustrate the different kinds of information that can be conveyed.

(1)   a)   *'The sun is rising.'*
      b)   *'Pick the other one!'*
      c)   *'Can you pass the salt?'*

The literal content of the first sentence is the claim that the sun is rising. In the case of the second example, information is conveyed indirectly that there is more than one thing to pick, in addition to the more direct interpretation that something has to be picked. In the final case, we normally conclude that this is a request to pass the salt, not a mere inquiry about an ability.

Some of the more pragmatic notions of meaning may appeal to abilities outside the linguistic realm. In some contexts, the statement 'Wool is horrible when it is wet.' might actually be a request not to wear a particular garment. Such non-literal meaning may be described as being part of pragmatics (Kadmon 2001). The boundary between pragmatics and semantics is somewhat difficult to define (see Kamp 1979 for example). As a first approximation, one could claim that semantics is the meaning that can be deduced directly from an expression, with no extra-linguistic information, but ideally in a way that can accommodate any such information.

If we were to include in semantics that which has to be assumed in order to make any sense of what has been uttered, then that would include certain kinds of presuppositions. Indeed, there are claims that all semantic meaning may be characterized as some variety of accommodation (Kamp 2007). In this chapter we will explore the more 'traditional' view of semantics.

In the case of *computational* semantics, we are interested not just in abstract accounts of meaning, but also in their concrete formalization in ways that, at least in principle, are able to support implementation.

2.1   A standard approach

In general it is dif cult to reason directly in terms of sentences of natural language. There have been attempts to produce proof-theoretic accounts of sentential reasoning (for example, Zamansky et al., 2006; Francez & Dyckhoff 2007), but it is more usual to adopt a formal language, either a logic or some form of set theory, and then translate natural language expressions into that formal language. In the context of computational semantics, that means a precise description of an algorithmic translation rather than some intuitive reformulation of natural language.

Such translations usually appeal to a local principle of *compositionality*. This can be characterized by saying that the meaning of an expression is a function of the meaning of its parts. This idea is often attributed to Frege (although see Janssen 2001 for a different view).

In computational semantics there are two common approaches to specifying compositional functions. Essentially all that is required in most cases is some mechanism for combining the meaning of constituent expressions. This is typically achieved by substituting the meaning of one constituent into a place-holder contained in the meaning of the constituent with which it is being combined. Both uni cation (Moore 1989) and λ-calculus (Montague 1974; Blackburn & Bos 2005) can achieve this end. In the case of uni cation-based formalisms, syntactic expressions are typically in the form of feature-value structures, and the grammar gives rules of composition indicating how the features are to be uni ed (combined) and whether any additional constraints are to be imposed. Semantic interpretations can just be viewed as another feature, with variables that are also constrained by feature value constraints in the grammar and within the constituents.

When using the λ-calculus, the composition of semantic forms is expressed in a language that supports substitutions of arguments for variables in a term. Subject to some side conditions on variable names, an expression of the form $\lambda x.t$ when given an argument t' will be identical to t, but with all occurrences of x in t replaced by t'. To a rst approximation, $(\lambda y \ldots man'(y) \ldots)(John')$ will be identical to $\ldots man'(John') \ldots$.[2]

The choice of λ-calculus versus uni cation need not be exclusive, for example the instantiations of the arguments in a λ-calculus approach might itself be accomplished by way of uni cation. Also, uni cation-based formalisms might appeal to λ-calculus abstractions for certain phenomena. Indeed, the λ-calculus itself can be implemented within a uni cation-based framework (Pereira & Shieber 1987; Covington 1994; Blackburn & Bos 2005). Some have argued that λ-calculus expressions are complex in comparison with uni cation-based constraint formalisms (Moore 1989). This might be more a matter of taste: the uni cation approaches generally speaking adopt the machinery of constraint-based grammar formalisms, such as HPSG (Pollard & Sag 1994), whereas λ-calculus approaches adopt the machinery of higher-order logic (or similar formalisms) and categorial grammar (for example, Steedman 1993).

To be sure that we can translate every sentence covered by a grammar into a formal representation language, we need to associate each word with some semantic representation, and each rule with a piece of information that can be used to derive a representation for each possible category. Adopting the compositional approach entails that the meaning of a sentence then depends upon the meaning of its parts, as analyzed by the grammar.

In the case of the treatment proposed by Montague (1974), a categorial grammar (supplemented by transformational operations) was combined with higher-order intensional logic (see Sections 4.2 and 4.4) to produce the semantic analysis. Here we follow Blackburn and Bos (2005) and others in using a context-free grammar for the syntax, and a rst-order representation language combined with the λ-calculus for the semantic representations.[3]

With the grammar

(2) s $\longrightarrow$ np vp   det $\longrightarrow$ 'every'
     np $\longrightarrow$ det noun   n $\longrightarrow$ 'man'
     vp $\longrightarrow$ v   n $\longrightarrow$ 'woman'
     det $\longrightarrow$ 'a'   v $\longrightarrow$ 'laughed'

we can parse the following sentences.

(3) a) *'A man laughed.'*
     b) *'Every woman laughed.'*

In   rst-order predicate calculus, we want to give these sentences translations of the form:

(4) a) $\exists x(man'(x) \wedge laughed'(x))$
     b) $\forall x(woman'(x) \rightarrow laughed'(x))$

To this end, we can associate the words *'man,'* *'woman,'* and *'laughed'* with the predicates *man'*, *woman'*, and *laughed'* respectively. The determiners will have to contribute the following quanti ed expressions:

(5) a) $\exists x(\langle noun \rangle(x) \wedge \langle verb \rangle(x))$
     b) $\forall x(\langle noun \rangle(x) \rightarrow \langle verb \rangle(x))$

To perform compositional semantics we need some general way of composing the meanings of constituent categories (for example, the noun and the verb in this case) so that they ' ll' the correct 'slots' in the quanti ed expression. When we combine the determiner with the noun, we want the meaning of the noun to be substituted for $\langle noun \rangle$ to give the meanings of the noun phrases:

(6) a) $\exists x(man'(x) \wedge \langle verb \rangle(x)$
     b) $\forall x(woman'(x) \rightarrow \langle verb \rangle(x))$

When we subsequently combine a noun phrase with a verb phrase we want to substitute the meaning of the verb phrase (*laughed'* in this case) for $\langle verb \rangle$ in the meaning of the noun phrase. As mentioned above, this substitution could be performed if we could use some mechanism like uni cation, which is readily available in logic programming languages such as Prolog. Here we will use the λ-calculus. Typically, semantic annotations on the grammar will tell us which λ-calculus expressions to use at each stage, and the rules of the calculus will tell us how to produce the nal representation.

To perform compositional semantics with a context-free grammar, then for each rule in the grammar (and each word in the lexicon), we need to state how to compose the semantics of the category that is being de ned. This will be de ned in terms of the semantics of the constituent categories (those categories to the right of the arrow). We can use the notation: $[\![\langle category \rangle]\!]$ to indicate that we are referring to the semantics of $\langle category \rangle$.

(7)   An example of a grammar with semantic annotations

sentence	$\longrightarrow$ np vp	$[\![np]\!]([\![vp]\!])$
np	$\longrightarrow$ det noun	$[\![det]\!]([\![noun]\!])$
vp	$\longrightarrow$ verb	$[\![verb]\!]$
det	$\longrightarrow$ 'a'	$\lambda P.\lambda Q \exists x (P(x) \wedge Q(x))$
det	$\longrightarrow$ 'every'	$\lambda P.\lambda Q \forall x (P(x) \rightarrow Q(x))$
noun	$\longrightarrow$ 'man'	man'
noun	$\longrightarrow$ 'woman'	$woman'$
verb	$\longrightarrow$ 'laughed'	$laughed'$

In an attribute value grammar, we can represent such semantic annotations as one of the attributes of the categories (Johnson 1988).

The annotated grammar (7) is suf cient for the simple sentences of (3). The semantic annotations becomes more complicated if we consider more syntactic constructions such as transitive verbs, auxiliary verbs, adjectives, and adverbs. We would also need a richer semantic representation language if we were to take account of other aspects of meaning, such as tense, context-dependent meaning, knowledge, and belief.

To account for transitive verbs, we would need to add a rule of the form:

(8)   vp $\longrightarrow$ verb-trans np $[\![verb\text{-}trans]\!]([\![np]\!])$

together with transitive verbs in the lexicon, such as the following:

(9)   verb-trans $\longrightarrow$ 'loves' $\lambda R(\lambda y(R(\lambda x loves'(x,y))))$

We can then derive the semantics of some sentences with transitive verbs.

(10)   a)   'A man loves a woman.'
       b) $\exists x (man'(x) \wedge \exists y (woman'(y) \wedge loves'(x,y)))$

As it turns out, this is not always an appropriate representation for transitive verbs (Section 4.2).

There are cases of ambiguity in the semantic analysis that cannot be accounted for at other levels of analysis. A prime example is that of *quantifier scope ambiguity*. The sentence

(11)   'Every man loves a woman'

could have either of the following representations:

(12)   a) $\forall x(man'(x) \rightarrow \exists y(woman'(y) \wedge loves'(x,y)))$
       b) $\exists y(woman'(y) \wedge \forall x(man'(x) \rightarrow loves'(x,y)))$

The analysis given so far just produces the rst reading.

To a rst approximation, there can be as many interpretations as there are permutations of the orders of the quanti ers, or other scope-taking elements. A strictly compositional analysis will only nd one quanti er scoping. Extra machinery is required to obtain the additional readings, and to use the context to rule out inappropriate interpretations. There are other scoping ambiguities, some, such as prepositional attachment, have a syntactic characterization. We will look at solutions to the problem of quanti er scoping ambiguity in Section 3.2. Some proposals treat all of these ambiguities by way of *underspecification* (van Deemter 1996).

Another issue concerns the representation of anaphora and ellipsis. Additional work is required to resolve anaphora such as pronouns (Section 3.1). Indeed there are general questions about the most appropriate representation language and its features (Section 4). In the next section, we will say a few things about *types* in representational languages.

2.2   Basic types

When considering the representations of nouns, verbs, and sentences as properties, relations, and propositions respectively, we may have to pay attention to the nature of the permitted arguments. For example, we may have: properties of individuals; relationships between individuals; relationships between individuals and propositions (such as statements of belief and knowledge); and, in the case of certain modi ers, relations that take properties as arguments to give a new property of individuals. Depending upon the choice of permitted arguments, and how they are characterized, there can be an impact on the formal power of the underlying theory. This is of particular concern for a *computational* theory of meaning: if the theory is more powerful than rst-order logic, then some valid conclusions will not be derivable by computational means; such a logic is said to be *incomplete*,[4] which corresponds with the notion of *decidability* (Section 1, and Section 1.2 of Chapter 2, COMPUTATIONAL COMPLEXITY IN NATURAL LANGUAGE).

A critical reason for considering this issue arises if the λ-expressions used in the compositional interpretation of meaning are part of the representation language itself. There are good reasons for assuming that this is appropriate (see Section 4.2). Unfortunately, if we impose no constraints on how expressions may be combined, it is then possible to construct a logical paradox. Consider the property R of not being self-applicable. R can be de ned by (13).

(13) $R(p) =_{def} \neg p(p)$

If $R(p)$ is a proposition for a property p, then applying R to itself leads to a paradox.

(14) $R(R) \leftrightarrow \neg R(R)$

The conventional way of avoiding this problem is to ban self-application. The usual approach for expressing such constraints is to adopt a typed representation language. This allows us to implement well-formedness criteria for the language of representation by way of *typing constraints* that govern the well-formedness of expressions in the logic. Typically, the types are expressed as e for entity, t for a proposition, and $\langle a, b \rangle$ for an expression that takes an argument of type a and returns one of type b. The idea is that every well-formed expression has exacly one type. When interpreting this theory, it is usual to assume a set-theoretic model, where expressions of type $\langle e, t \rangle$, for example, are viewed as sets of elements e (the values for functions from entities to truth values). This gives rise to *simple type theory* (STT) (Church 1940). In such a system, it is in felicitous to use (13) to de ne a term R, as it is not possible to assign R exactly one type. Such terms are thus not permitted in the representation language, and the paradox of (14) does not arise.

Conventional *higher-order logic* (HOL) adopts simple type theory and allows quanti ers to range over expressions of any given type. The propositions of higher-order logic are expressions that have the type t. In effect, Montague's *intensional logic* (Montague 1974) is based on a variant of this type theory, except an additional (pseudo) type is added to account for intensionality (Section 4.2).

There is some further discussion of types in Section 4.1.

2.3 Model theory and proof theory

There are two ways in which traditional formal semantic accounts of indicatives have been characterized. First, we may be interested in evaluating the truth of indicatives (or at least their semantic representation) by evaluating their truth conditions with respect to the world (or, more precisely, some formal representation or model of a world). This can be described as *model-theoretic* semantics. Model-theoretic accounts are typically formulated in set theory. Set theory is a very powerful formalism that does not lend itself to computational implementation. In practice, the full power of set theory may not be exploited. Indeed, if the problem domain itself is nite in character, then an effective implementation should be possible regardless of the general computational properties of the formal framework (see Klein 2006 for example).[5]

On the second characterization of formal semantic accounts, the goal is to formalize some notion of inference or entailment for natural language. If one expression in natural language entails another, then we would like that relation to be captured by any formalization that purports to capture the meaning of natural language. This can be described as *proof-theoretic* semantics.[6] Such rules may lend themselves to fairly direct implementation (see for example van Eijck and Unger (2004); Ramsay (1995); Bos and Oka (2002), the last of which supplements theorem proving with model building).

Although a proof-theoretic approach may seem more appropriate for computational semantics, the practical feasibility of general theorem proving is open to question. Depending on the nature of the theory, the formalization may be undecidable. Even with a decidable or semi-decidable theory, there may be problems of computational complexity, especially given the levels of ambiguity that may be present (Monz and de Rijke 2001).[7]

These two different approaches may be considered, broadly speaking, to follow those of Tarski (interpretation) and Gentzen (proof) respectively (Tarski 1983; Gentzen 1969). With both the model-theoretic and the proof-theoretic approach, radically different assumptions may be made about the nature of the semantic framework, its ontology, the appropriate way of encoding information in the theory, and the underlying philosophical principles that are adopted. In practice, such choices may depend upon methodology, taste, and precedent rather than general, universal principles.

At an abstract level, the model-theoretic and proof-theoretic views of indicatives might not appear radically different from each other. Assuming our models of the world have some coherent notion of the relationships between the truth and falsity of various expressions that exactly mimics our understanding of language, then any entailment patterns in language can be captured by considering the patterns of truth for the interpretations of the sentences in all models. An indicative expression *A* entails *B* exactly when all those models in which *A* is interpreted as being true also interpret *B* as being true.

A key issue for computational semantics is the computational tractability of the semantic representation. We could have a representation of a set-theoretic model theory, although we might question whether in general that is computationally tractable. If possible, we would like to avoid representations that are so powerful that we cannot enumerate their theorems (let alone those for which we cannot even write down all the rules that govern their behavior). In general, set-theoretic interpretations are among those that are problematic when it comes to computational feasibility. An easier starting point is a relatively weak proof-theoretic representation, but with appropriate expressiveness for the phenomena in question.

2.4   Lexical semantics

The meaning of language is more than the ability to compose representations based on the form of sentences, and construct formal proofs. Other issues include the pragmatics of how language is used, and of course the meanings of words themselves (Pustejovsky 1995).

A lexicon may include lexical features that indicate salient information about the syntactic and semantic arguments of lexical items which are needed to obtain a formal semantic representation. But in general we may also be interested in the concept that is represented by a given word.

For natural language processing this may be dif cult to capture. But there may be some aspects of meaning that can be captured and represented. These include ontological classi cations of words, such *cause-of*, *agent*, and relationships between words. Such relationships might be semantic in character (such as hyponym and meronym relationships, etc.), or founded on co-location information, where a word is assumed to be related in meaning to other words that are used in a similar context, which might be described as 'distributional' lexical semantics. Many corpus-based techniques (Section 5) assume that at least some aspects of meaning are implicitly embodied in co-location data and, furthermore, that word classi cations can be learned (Chiu et al., 2007).

3   State of the Art

There are a range of analyses of natural language phenomena that may be said to constitute the state of the art of computational semantics. Here we pick two issues that have received a signi cant amount of attention over the years, namely the treatments of anaphora and of quanti er scoping. These are discussed in the sections on discourse (Section 3.1) and underspeci cation (Section 3.2). This is not to say that the analyses proposed are beyond question, or that all the relevant issues have been resolved, but there is certainly a relatively stable core of ideas and analyses that can be considered state of the art.

3.1   *Discourse*

Here 'discourse' is taken to refer to a sequence of sentences where each sentence is interpreted in the context of the preceding sentences. This context provides potential antecedents for anaphoric expressions such as inter-sentential pronouns, as in the very simple example given in (15), where the antecedent to which '*She*' refers is intended to be '*Mary.*'

(15)   '*Mary is a woman. She loves John.*'

The antecedent might be inferred but is not overtly mentioned in the text. The issue is how the discourse can be represented in a way that allows anaphoric relations to be represented in a manner that is sympathetic to concerns with quanti cation and scoping, and also captures intuitions about felicitous and infelicitous anaphoric reference.[8]

Montague's treatment of scope (Section 3.2) makes use of anaphora, but it cannot be generalized easily to other cases. One obvious solution would be to consider pronouns as variables, and de ne some mechanism for these variables to be bound appropriately by the quanti ers (nouns) to which they refer.

Given the sentence

(16)   *'Mary is a woman. She loves John'*

we can try to represent the pronoun *'She'* using a variable.

(17) $woman'(mary') \wedge loves'(x, john')$

Here, *'She'* is an anaphoric pronoun that needs to be resolved so that it is associated somehow with an appropriate *antecedent*. In this case, it would be legitimate to consider replacing the variable by *mary'*. Unfortunately, this solution does not generalize.

If we consider the sentences

(18)   a)   *'A man drank. He fell asleep'*
       b) $\exists x(man'(x) \wedge drank'(x)) \wedge fell\_asleep'(y)$

the pronoun, represented by y, cannot be resolved by just replacing it with a constant. Renaming y to be x also does not work, because it lies outside the syntactic scope of the existential quanti er, and so is not bound by it.[9]

Some particularly problematic examples are given by Geach (1972), including the following so-called 'donkey' examples:

(19)   a)   *'If a farmer owns a donkey, he beats it.'*
       b)   *'Every farmer who owns a donkey beats it.'*

The issue of concern here is that it is not clear that we have the correct analysis of quanti ers or conditionals. If pronouns are to be represented by variables, we need to ensure not only that they are bound correctly, but also that inde nites have universal force in the second example, which a naïve analysis would interpret incorrectly as something like

(20) $\exists x(farmer'(x) \wedge \exists y(donkey'(y) \wedge own'(x, y)) \rightarrow beat'(x, y))$

where both x and y in the consequent of (20) are outside the scope of the relevant quanti ers, and the sense of universality is not captured. These issues, among others, have led people to consider alternative ways of representing meaning, including *discourse representation theory* (DRT) (Kamp 1981; Kamp & Reyle 1993; and Section 3.1.1 below). In addition to putting emphasis on the representation itself, rather than focusing on the model theory, DRT also provided an algorithmic account of how to generate these representations from natural language input sentences. Both features are characteristic of computational semantics.

3.1.1   Discourse representation theory   Discourse representation theory (DRT) and related paradigms intend to capture the notions of discourse that are relevant for resolving anaphoric pronouns by reconsidering the representation of quanti ers and some of the other logical connectives (Kamp 1981; Kamp & Reyle 1993). The idea is to have a representation of the individuals that are introduced into a discourse, and allow them to be referred to in subsequent discourse where appropriate.

Using a *construction algorithm*, DRT systematically builds a representation of the individuals described in a discourse, and the properties and relationships that hold between them. The basic notion in DRT is that of a *discourse representation structure* (DRS), which has the following form:

(21)

$\langle referents \rangle$
$\langle conditions \rangle$

The top part of the box contains individuals described in the discourse. The bottom part contains conditions on those individuals. The conditions may include other DRSs.

Essentially, existentially quanti ed noun phrases introduce a new individual into the current DRS with appropriate conditions.

(22)   a)   *'A woman cried.'*

  b)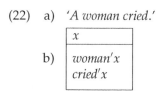

Universally quanti ed noun phrases introduce a conditional DRS as a condition of the DRS representing the current discourse.

(23)   a)   *'Every man laughed.'*

  b)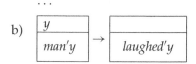

There are rules that govern from where a discourse referent may be referred to, and the construction algorithm indicates where analysis of subsequent discourse should appear in the DRS. Resolution of anaphora can be expressed as equations over discourse referents.

(24)   a)   *'Mary is a woman.'*

b)

$$
\begin{array}{|l|}
\hline
m \\
\hline
m = mary' \\
woman'(m) \\
\hline
\end{array}
$$

c) *'Mary is a woman. She loves John.'*

d)

$$
\begin{array}{|l|}
\hline
m, j, x \\
\hline
m = mary' \\
woman'(m) \\
j = john' \\
loves'(j, x) \\
x = m \\
\hline
\end{array}
$$

Here, the pronoun *'She'* is represented by x, and resolved by the condition $x = m$.

A typical 'donkey sentence' where the conditional is interpreted with universal force is exempli ed next.

(25)   a)   *'If a farmer owns a donkey, he beats it.'*

b)

$$
\begin{array}{|l|}
\hline
f, d \\
\hline
farmer'(f) \\
donkey'(d) \\
owns'(f, d) \\
\hline
\end{array}
\rightarrow
\begin{array}{|l|}
\hline
x, y \\
\hline
beats'(x, y) \\
x = f \\
y = d \\
\hline
\end{array}
$$

Accessibility of referents is de ned in such a way that the farmer and donkey (f, d) are not accessible from any subsequent discourse (at least, not as singular antecedents).

If DRT is combined with a notion of abstraction and application, then it is possible to produce a more conventional compositional presentation of the construction process (Blackburn & Bos 1999).

DRT has been exploited for more things than just pronominal anaphora. Examples include underspeci cation (for example, Asher 1993; Reyle 1993), presuppositions (van der Sandt 1988; 1992; Krahmer & Piwek 1999; Beaver 2002), and discourse relations (Asher & Lascarides 2003).

There are many issues that require a more sophisticated analysis, such as plural anaphora, as in

(26)   *'John$_i$ and Mary$_j$ went to Paris. They$_{i+j}$ met at the Eiffel tower.'*

conditional examples where universal quanti cation is not the most natural interpretation (Pelletier & Schubert 1989), as in

(27)   *'If you have a penny, put it in the box.'*

and examples where it is dif cult to see how the appropriate representation might be obtained (Heim 1990; Kadmon 1990), such as

(28)   *'Most farmers who own a donkey beat it.'*

where the most natural reading is that most donkey-owning farmers beat donkeys that they own, rather than the unnatural quanti cation over farmer–donkey pairs that would be obtained by an unmodi ed DRT-style analysis.

3.1.2   Dynamic accounts   There are many other approaches to dealing with pronominal anaphora. The accounts using *dynamic logic* effectively rede ne the meaning of quanti cation and conditionality (Groenendijk & Stokhof 1990a; 1991). The aim is to allow variables to be bound outside the syntactic scope of existential quanti ers and to give existentials a universal interpretation when appearing as the antecedent of a conditional. This is an example of where the need to deal with a particular phenomena leads to a re-appraisal of the formalism and techniques of conventional classical logic.

Syntactically, the net result is a logic that has the appearance of a classically quanti ed logic, but where examples such as (20) have the appropriate semantics by way of a modi ed interpretation of the logical operators and quanti ers.

DRT and logic are equivalent in their ability to analyze simple discourse with singular pronouns.

3.1.3   Type theoretic approaches   We nish this section on discourse by brie y mentioning some type-theoretic approaches. As Sundholm (1989) observed, there are certain aspects of constructive type theory that appear to capture the appropriate behavior for interpreting discourse involving singular anaphora. In particular, the dependent types that feature in constructive type theory can be used to capture contextual effects. This idea was developed by Ranta (1994) and Ahn and Kolb (1990).

There are alternative approaches that use types for dealing with discourse problems. For example, it is possible to exploit dependent types within a classical framework (Smith 1984; Turner 1992; Fox 2000). Perhaps a more radical approach is due to Lappin and Francez (1994) and Lappin (1989). Rather than characterizing the problem of resolving anaphora as one of nding an element with which to equate a pronoun, these proposals suggest that the problem can be construed as one of nding the appropriate *type* for the variable representing the pronoun. This idea is developed in Fox and Lappin (2005) in the context of *property theory with Curry typing* (PTCT).

Additional relevant information may also be found in Chapter 21, DIS-COURSE PROCESSING, and Chapter 16, COMPUTATIONAL MODELS OF DIALOGUE. We brie y mention constructive type theory and dependent types again in Section 4.1.4.

3.2   *Underspecification*

One problem for a compositional analysis is semantic ambiguity. This is typically exempli ed by the issue of quanti er scoping, but also arises with other scope-taking elements, such as modi er expressions, prepositional phrases, negation, and other logical operators, as well as anaphoric reference (Poesio & Reyle 2001). In the case of scoping, the issue is that a sentence with more than one scope-taking element is ambiguous in a way that is not usually evident in any syntactic analysis. For example, in an ambiguous sentence such as

(29)   *'Every student took a course'*

it is unclear whether there was one particular course taken by every student, or whether every student took at least one course, but not necessarily the same one in each case.

Montague (1974) offered an approach to the quanti er scoping problem that used additional rules which effectively reordered the quanti ers in the syntactic analysis, and hence changed the scope in the semantic representation. The current consensus is that it is better to have a systematic account that does not require changes to the syntactic analysis, and which provides an intermediate representation that is unspeci ed, or underspeci ed with respect to scope orderings, but which permits all appropriate scope orderings to be generated when required.

3.2.1   Cooper storage   The prime example of a system intended to allow the generation of scoped readings is Cooper storage (Cooper 1983). Although there are other proposals, they can be construed as variations and re nements of this proposal. Cooper storage builds semantic representations using a data structure known as a *store*. This can be thought of as providing an underspeci ed representation of the meaning of a sentence.

The store contains a 'core' representation (typically representing the main verb) together with the representations of the generalized quanti ers (typically representing the noun phrases). The argument positions in the core representation are associated with indices identifying which generalized quanti er (noun phrase) binds that position.

The approach can be illustrated by analyzing the following sentence using Cooper storage.

(30)   *'Every man loves a woman.'*

The stored representation will be something like[10]

(31) $\langle love'(z_6, z_7),$
  $(\lambda p(\forall x(man'(x) \rightarrow p(x))), 6),$
  $(\lambda p(\exists y(woman'(y) \wedge p(y))), 7)\rangle$

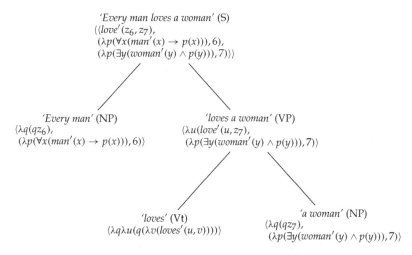

Figure 15.1 Derivation of semantic representation with storage.

The derivation of this is sketched in Figure 15.1.

Given an unscoped representation in the store, *retrieval* operations can be used to generate fully scoped representations. The generalized quanti ers can be applied to the core representation in any order, thus giving rise to the different quanti er scopings. The index is used to ensure that each generalized quanti er binds the correct argument position, so that the meaning of the sentence is not corrupted by the reordering of the quanti ers. Blackburn and Bos (2005: 108) give a worked example of this.

With our example, if we retrieve 6 ('*Every man*') rst, then the store is

(32) $\langle \lambda p(\forall x(man'(x) \rightarrow p(x)))(\lambda z_6(love'(z_6, z_7)),$
$(\lambda p(\exists y(woman'(y) \wedge p(y))), 7)\rangle$

Applying β-reduction gives us

(33) $\langle \forall x(man'(x) \rightarrow loves'(x, z_7)),$
$(\lambda p(\exists y(woman'(y) \wedge p(y))), 7)\rangle$

The second, and nal, retrieval operation gives us

(34) $\langle(\lambda p(\exists y(woman'(y) \wedge p(y)))(\lambda z_7 \forall x(man'(x) \rightarrow loves'(x, z_7))))\rangle$

which after β-reduction is

(35) $\langle \exists y(woman'(y) \wedge \forall x(man'(x) \rightarrow loves'(x, y)))\rangle$

Retrieving the items in the opposite order would give us the alternative scope reading for this example.[11]

In the account as given, there are some problems in handling relative clauses and complex noun phrases with prepositions. Such phrases can give rise to nested, or hierarchical, noun phrases. If the storage and retrieval operations are not sensitive to such structures, then ill-formed representations may be generated. Consider the following sentence:

(36)   *'Mary knows every owner of a pub.'*

We should not be able to retrieve the representation of *'a pub'* until we have retrieved the core part of the noun phrase *'every owner.'* The need for constraints on retrieval is addressed by *nested* or *Keller* storage, where nested stores are used to 'lock up' constituent parts of a noun phrase which can only be accessed once we have retrieved the core noun phrase that contains those parts (Keller 1988).

A comprehensive account of underspeci cation needs to handle scoping of negation, conjunction, modi cation, modalities, and propositional attitudes. Futhermore, we might consider approaches that allow *partially* speci ed representations that can accommodate incremental constraints on acceptable scopings, as in the following example (taken from Fox & Lappin, forthcoming):

(37)   a)   Speaker 1: *'Every student wrote a program for some professor.'*
       b)   Speaker 2: *'Yes, I know the professor. She taught the Haskell course.'*
       c)   Speaker 3: *'I saw the programs, and they were all list-sorting procedures.'*

We can assume the following:

(38)   a)   *'some professor'* in the rst sentence (37a) is the antecedent for both *'the professor'* and *'She'* in the second sentence (37b).
       b)   *'a program'* in the rst sentence (37a) is the antecedent for both *'the programs'* and *'they'* in the third sentence (37c).

The rst assumption (38a) gives *'some professor'* scope over *'every student'* in the rst sentence (37a). The second assumption (38a) leads to *'a program'* taking narrow scope with respect to *'every student'* in the rst sentence (37a). From this it can be seen that, as the discourse proceeds, (37b) and (37c) force on the rst sentence (37a) a fully resolved scope order, namely

(39)   *'some professor,' 'every student,' 'a program'*

Most treatments of quanti er scoping based on storage do not by themselves provide an ef cient analysis of such incremental constraints, nor do they necessarily support direct reasoning with such partially speci ed scopings.

3.2.2   Other treatments of scope ambiguity   Bos (1995), and Blackburn and Bos (1999) develop a constraint-based system for underspeci ed representation for rst-order logic that they refer to as *predicate logic unplugged* (PLU). This system is a generalization of the *hole semantics* approach to underspeci cation which Reyle (1993) rst developed within the framework of *underspecified discourse representation theory* (UDRT).

Minimal recursion semantics (Copestake et al., 2006) is an application of hole semantics within a typed feature structure grammar (HPSG). Normal dominance conditions (Koller et al., 2003) can be seen as a re nement and development of the central ideas of hole semantics.

Dalrymple et al. (1999) and Crouch and van Genabith (1999) suggest a theory in which representations of generalized quanti ers and core relations are expressed as premises in an underspeci ed semantic *glue language*. The premises are combined using the natural deduction rules of linear logic (Girard 1987) to yield a formula that represents the scope reading of a sentence.

Packed representations (Crouch 2005) 'compress' the scoped interpretations derived using glue language. Components of meaning shared by several readings are expressed as a single common clause. This uses an approach that is applied in chart parsing to construct a graph for non-redundant representation of the full set of possible syntactic structures for a parsed phrase.

Ebert (2005) gives a detailed discussion of the formal relationships between the various theories of underspeci cation with respect to their expressive power.

Van Eijck and Unger (2004) develop an approach to underspeci ed representations, in the functional programming language Haskell, which uses *relation reduction* and arbitrary arity relations. This is based on a proposal due to Keenan (1992). This work inspired a proposal by Fox and Lappin (2005) which represents underspeci ed representations in a data structure that can be formalized within the representation language PTCT itself. On this account, there is no appeal to meta-semantic machinery as such, and the full power of the representation language is used to express constraints governing the legitimate readings, including incremental constraints. This addresses the concerns of Ebert (2005) with regard to expressive completeness, although it still leaves outstanding the problem of dealing with the signi cant combinatorial complexity of computing the desired readings.

4 Research Issues

There are many open research questions in computational semantics. Some are concerned with how to analyze particular aspects of meaning, including phenomena that are not easily analyzed by way of a direct truth-conditional interpretation. Others are concerned with representations that provide the most appropriate machinery to express and reason with the meaning of natural language in a computationally tractable manner. Here there is only space to consider a small selection of such issues.

4.1 Type theory

Typically, the types used for natural language semantics are based on simple type theory (Section 2.2). But there are other kinds of types, and other ways of imposing typing constraints. Indeed, it is not entirely clear that simple type theory is the most appropriate type system for natural language semantics. Here we consider some other options.

4.1.1 Polymorphism   The simply typed higher order logic (Section 2.2) might be considered somewhat restrictive. One area in which it appears excessively rigid and inexpressive concerns certain type-general phenomena that are apparent in natural language, such as the apparent polymorphism of conjunction. The following examples illustrate that *'and'* can combine expressions of different categories.

(40) a) *'John and Mary saw Peter.'*
     b) *'John saw and heard Peter.'*
     c) *'The book was red and white.'*

However, the typing is not unconstrained: in each of these examples, the conjuncts and the conjunctive phrase itself are all of the same category. Partee and Rooth (1983) deal with this phenomena by introducing generalized quanti ca-tion that 'raises' the type of the basic conjunction and disjunction operators to t-ending types. An alternative is to adopt a more exible type system that permits polymorphic types of the form

(41) $\forall' X.T$

where $\forall'$ is a type quanti er that allows X in type T to range over all types.[12] As an example, an expression of the type $\forall' X.\langle X, t \rangle$ will form a proposition (type t) given an argument of any type. The type of a coordinating expression can then be given as

(42) $\forall' X.\langle X, \langle X, t \rangle \rangle$

This can also be used to capture other type-general phenomena – such as verbs like *'fun'* that can take nominal expressions, in nitives, and gerunds as arguments – without resorting to a universal type for example (Chierchia 1982).[13]

In addition to looking at ways in which the type system could be made more expressive to match the needs of natural language, as with polymorphic types, there may also be some merit in considering what *constraints* there are on the type system required for natural language.

4.1.2 First-order sorts   Rather than adopting a typed higher-order logic, an alternative approach to constraining the way in which entities of the theory may felicitously be combined is to have sortal predicates that classify terms as representing individuals, relations, and properties. Logical rules can then be given that express analogues of type inference rules.

For example, we might have predicates *entity'*, *property'*, *proposition'*, and a rule that says

(43) $(entity'(i) \wedge property'(p)) \rightarrow proposition'(p(i))$

Here the notion of *proposition'* and *property'* must be seen as distinct from those notions in the language in which these statements are being expressed.

Characterizing *properties* and *propositions* by way of sortal predicates means that properties and propositions are being treated as rst-order terms of the theory. We then need to nd some way of asserting that $p(i)$ is true. One option would be to introduce a predicate *holds'* (Kowalski & Sergot 1986; Miller & Shanahan 1999) that relates a *proposition'* to an event $(holds'(p(i), e))$, or situation (giving rise to a form of event calculus), or else introduce a truth predicate *true'*, as in *property theory* (see Turner 1992, for example). Care needs to be taken about what terms count as propositions in order to avoid paradoxes of the kind illustrated by (14).

Sortal constraints can mimic expressive types such as dependent types (Smith 1984; Turner 1992), which can provide a treatment for analyzing discourse anaphora (Sundholm 1989; Ranta 1994) (Section 3.1.3). There are alternative ways of mimicking higher-order type theory within a rst-order logic using Curry typing with polymorphic types without expressing types (Fox & Lappin 2005), as we shall see below.

4.1.3 Property theory with Curry typing It is possible to avoid some of the strictures of Church typing, by separating out the typing system from the λ-calculus presentation. That is, we can adopt the untyped λ-calculus, and then have typing rules that allow us to infer the types of the λ-expressions (Curry & Feys 1958). This is the approach adopted by *property theory with Curry typing* (PTCT) (Fox & Lappin 2005). This approach allows additional exibility in developing a type system that is focused on the speci c requirements of natural language semantics, including separation types (a form of subtype) and polymorphic types. This is formulated in an essentially rst-order language.

4.1.4 Constructive theories and dependent types Constructive type theory was mentioned before in relation to analyzing anaphora (Section 3.1.3). The constructive approach offers an alternative to classical logic. In constructive systems, propositions are only considered to be true if there is an appropriate proof or *witness*. Using the Curry–Howard isomorphism, propositions can then be viewed as types whose members are their proofs. Such logical systems are slightly weaker than corresponding classical formulations in that they do not support proof by contradiction.

As already noted, the intrinsically dynamic nature of the dependent types can be exploited in the analysis anaphoric phenomena, although such types are not exclusive to constructive theories.

There are other kinds of dependent types, including *record types*, which generalize the notion of dependency over a collection of type expressions. The use of such types has been proposed both for the analysis of discourse and as a language in which attribute value grammars can be formulated (Cooper & Ginzburg 2002; Cooper 2005).

4.2 *Intensionality*

We need to be able to represent sentences where the verb expresses a relationship involving not just individuals but also propositions and predicates, as in the following examples:

(44) a) *'John believes that every cat is furry.'*
      b) *'Mary likes red.'*

We also need to be able to distinguish between *de re* and *de dicto* interpretations of the arguments of some verbs. For example, in the sentences

(45) a) *'John seeks a football'*
      b) *'John seeks a unicorn'*

it is clear that in the rst example, John may be seeking a real entity that exists and is a football. This is a *de re* interpretation. In the latter case, he is seeking something that does not exist, but he can still be said to be *intending* to nd a unicorn. This is a *de dicto* interpretation. In the former case, with a *de re* interpretation we cannot be certain that John knows that he is seeking a football; he might know it by some other description, such as '*the object lying in the yard.'*

The conventional view is that this requires predicates that can take things other than individuals as their arguments.

A semantic interpretation along the following lines might seem appropriate:

(46) a) *'John believes that every cat is furry.'*
          $believe'(John', \exists x(cat'(x) \wedge furry'(x)))$
      b) *'Mary likes red.'*
          $likes'(Mary', red')$
      c) *'John seeks a football.'*
          (i) $\exists x(football'(x) \wedge seeks'(John', x))$ (*de re*)
          (ii) $seeks'(John', \lambda P \exists x(football'(x) \wedge P(x)))$ (*de dicto*)
      d) *'John seeks a unicorn.'*
          $seeks'(John', \lambda P \exists x(unicorn'(x) \wedge P(x)))$

The felicity of this approach depends in part upon the nature of propositions and predicates. If propositions are identi ed with truth values, then there are only two propositions. Further, any truth-conditionally equivalent propositions may be substituted for each other. This is a particular problem for mathematical truths which are necessarily true together but not identical. This gives some incorrect predictions about equivalence in the meaning of distinct sentences. Similarly, if predicates are just sets, then distinct predicates may be accidentally equated.

4.2.1   The Montagovian analysis   The classical approach to intensionality is attributed to Montague (1974), although it has its roots in earlier work (for example, Carnap 1947; Kripke 1963). In the representation, a *function*, or *operator* $^\cap$ is introduced that takes a single proposition or predicate as its argument. The result is an intensional expression that can appear as an argument to predicates that have an appropriate type. A second *function/operator* $^\cup$ can undo the operation of $^\cap$, so that $^{\cup\cap}p = p$.

For the so-called transparent verbs, such as *'find,'* *meaning postulates* can be introduced that allow the *de re* interpretation to be derived from the *de dicto* one.

Following Montague (1974) we can interpret this intensional theory using *possible worlds* semantics. Possible worlds are commonly used to model modality, such as *possibility*, and *necessity, permission*, and *obligation* for example (Carnap 1947; Kripke 1963; von Wright 1967). Propositions can be treated as sets of possible worlds, or (equivalently) functions from possible worlds to truth values. Properties can be modeled as functions from individuals to sets of possible worlds (propositions). Propositions that are true together in the current world may be distinguished from each other provided there are worlds in which their truth values differ.

If p is of type A, then $^\cap p$ will be of type $\langle s, A \rangle$. Following Gallin (1975), the type s can be thought of as corresponding to a possible world index. Types of the form $\langle s, A \rangle$ are then functions from world indices to expressions of type A.

4.2.2   Other approaches   Montague's possible-worlds approach is a dominant paradigm for analyzing the formal semantics of natural language, but it does have problems. The type system is inflexible and the notions of modality and intensionality are conflated. As a result, the analysis is not sufficiently fine-grained in its treatment of intensionality: for example, propositions that are necessarily true together cannot be distinguished from each other. Such propositions are exemplified by mathematical truths.

An alternative is to take what Montague writes as $^\cap p$ to be some kind of *representation* or *encoding* of p that does not conflate propositions merely because they are necessarily true (or false) together. We could take $^\cap p$ to be an individual (a term). The identity criteria for propositions would then be syntactic in nature, rather than truth conditional. Such prefixes $^\cap$ and $^\cup$ then serve as functions from propositions (and predicates) to terms, and terms to propositions (predicates). In practice, we may prefer that the default interpretation of p be a term rather than a truth-conditional proposition. This avoids conceptual problems in having a function $^\cap$ that increases the intensionality of its argument. Of course, some interpretation of these expressions is then required in order to find an appropriate model theory. This requires a relatively expressive language of terms.

There are potential risks with this strategy. If we are not careful about what can be represented as an individual (and hence appear as an argument to a predicate), then we may introduce paradoxes. Theories that take this approach (or variations of it) include *property theory* (Bealer 1982; Cocchiarella 1985; Turner 1992), property theory with Curry typing (PTCT) (Fox & Lappin 2005), and *situation theory*

(Barwise & Perry 1983; Barwise & Etchemendy 1990), the latter of which comes with a particular philosophical perspective on the nature of 'situated' meaning. Another alternative is to nd suitably intensional models for theories that are syntactically not far removed from Montague's IL (Thomason 1980; Gilmore 2001; Fox et al., 2002; Pollard, forthcoming), or use theory that combines different notions of intensionality (Tichý 1988; Materna et al., forthcoming). An alternative is to interpret our representation language using some form of intensional set theory (Jubien 1989).

4.3 Non-indicatives

So far we have only considered indicative sentences. Indeed this is the focus of perhaps the majority of work in computational semantics. But if we are interested in computing the meaning of language in general, then it is vital to consider non-indicatives.

As before, what follows is not intended to be a comprehensive survey of the work in the respective elds. We merely present a taste of some of the general methodological and practical issues that can arise in computational semantics. To this end, we brie y sample some proposals for the analysis of two signi cant non-indicative categories, namely questions and imperatives. The fundamental issue that lies behind all of these examples results from the fact that there are 'entailment' patterns which we might like to capture, but which are not overtly truth-conditional in nature: we do not usually think of questions or imperatives being 'true' or 'false.'

In the case of imperatives there is some debate about the appropriate nature of any entailment patterns, and even whether a logical approach is possible. In the case of questions, and their answers, it is generally accepted now that an appropriate notion which should be captured by 'entailments' between questions can be viewed in terms of answerhood criteria, although there is debate about how these are best expressed. The point of particular interest here lies in the dif culty of specifying what constitutes an answer in a computationally tractable fashion.

This is taken to illustrate the point that, in general, many of the core aspects of semantics, such as the truth of a proposition, answerhood for a question, etc., may not themselves be characterized completely within a computationally tractable theory. That is not to say this is a critical aw for the computational semantics programme, merely that some aspects of a computational theory in effect will include properties of implementations, rather than implementable properties.

4.3.1   Questions and answers   For questions and answers, we might consider the notion of *answerhood conditions* in place of *truth conditions*. Such an idea was proposed by Belnap (1982) among others. This requires consideration of what might constitute a legitimate answer to a question, and when an answer to one question is also an answer to another.

One in uential and comprehensive account of the semantics of questions is due to Groenendijk and Stokhof (1984; 1990b; 1997). In their model, a question partitions the set of all possible worlds, where each partition corresponds to a different possible answer. A yes/no question would give rise to two partitions, one corresponding to the underlying proposition being true, the other to it being false. A wh-question would give rise to a more complex set of partitions corresponding to the underlying property being applicable to different individuals. A true answer is then considered to be anything that provides the information needed for the questioner to determine in which partition the actual world lies. A partial, true answer would indicate a collection of partitions in which the actual world may lie. In general an answer (whether correct or not) will provide a means of 'eliminating' certain worlds, and hence certain possibilities, from consideration.

Due to the model-theoretic approach, Groenendijk and Stokhof's theory is not presented directly in terms of inference rules concerning the nature of answers and answerhood conditions; although it might provide a useful model, it does not necessarily lend itself to direct implementation. There is also the issue of combinatorial explosion when it comes to the evaluation of wh-questions. If the size of the domain is n, then checking the consistency of every field of a wh-question requires 2^n inferences (Bos & Gabsdil 2000).

One key question concerns the nature of the answerhood relationship itself, and in what way the rules governing answerhood may be implemented. We could try to build on the view advocated by Groenendijk and Stokhof and others, that yes/no questions are really questions of 'whether' something is true or false, and an answer to such a question allows you to determine that the proposition in question is true, or that it is false. We could seek to model this explicitly in terms of knowledge.

$$(47) \quad \frac{\text{'Know whether } p' \quad p \quad \text{True}}{\text{'Know that } p'} \quad \frac{\text{'Know whether } p' \quad \neg p \quad \text{True}}{\text{'Know that } \neg p'}$$

Alternatively, we might seek to express this internally as some state of 'knowledge' Γ.

(48) A proposition p answers a question q? in a context Γ if Γ and p together allow us to either infer q or infer $\neg q$ (and Γ by itself allows us to infer neither).[14]

However they are expressed, these are essentially constraints over reasoning systems involving answerhood, but in general they may not be directly expressible *within* the representation language itself, or any implementation of such a theory.

This issue is apparent even in other attempts to capture the notion of answerhood within a first-order framework. Bos and Gabsdil (2000) adopt answerhood conditions for wh-questions that are expressed in a first-order language. Essentially they translate wh-questions into a formula with domain D and body B. Putting to one side the DRT aspects of their notation, essentially wh-questions can then be given in the form $D?B$. An answer A is de ned as proper for the question if at least one of the following propositions is *consistent*, and at least one is *inconsistent*:

(49) a) $\forall x(Dx \rightarrow Bx) \wedge A$
      b) $\exists x(Dx \wedge Bx) \wedge A$
      c) $\exists x(Dx \wedge \neg Bx) \wedge A$
      d) $\neg\exists x(Dx \wedge Bx) \wedge A$

So if we had the question

(50) *'Who loves John?'*

this might be represented as something like

(51) *person'(x)?loves'(j',x)*

A proper answer is one that is consistent with at least one, but not all, of the following possibilities:

(52) a) *'Everybody loves John'*
      b) *'Somebody loves John'*
      c) *'Somebody does not love John'*
      d) *'Nobody loves John'*

This characterization loses some of the ne-grained distinctions that Groenendijk and Stokhof (1984; 1990b) make concerning answers and exhaustive answers, but reduces the number of permutations that have to be considered when determining whether A is a proper answer. Unfortunately it cannot avoid the fundamental problem that the property of answerhood for a given question is not necessarily tractable for arbitrary domains, and that it cannot be internalized into the representation language.

The extensional, model-theoretic interpretation of questions of Groenendijk and Stokhof (1984; 1990b; 1997) is not universally accepted. Ginzburg and Sag (2000) argue that it is incorrect to interpret questions by their exhaustive answerhood criteria. There may be contextual effects that change what constitutes an exhaustive answer, and different questions may have the same exhaustive answers. These arguments echo those concerned with propositions and truth conditions (Section 4.2); just as it can be argued that propositions are more than their truth conditions, perhaps questions are more than their answerhood conditions.

An alternative is to treat questions as something more basic, perhaps represented by propositions with abstracted variables. To do it justice, such an account needs to be formulated in a theory that does not automatically con ate any such propositional abstracts with 'mere' properties and relations. Ginzburg and Sag (2000) develop such an approach to questions and answers in the context of situation-theoretic semantics (Barwise & Perry 1983; Barwise & Etchemendy 1990). It should be possible to adapt the key aspects of this approach to other semantic frameworks.

4.3.2 Imperatives It seems appropriate to consider some kind of theory of entailment for imperatives that can determine when one imperative 'implies' another. As with propositional connectives, we may wish to consider notions of entailment between simple and complex imperatives, including conjoined imperatives, disjoined imperatives, and imperatives containing negation. Certainly it seems appealing to assume that there is a form of entailment relationship that can say something about the following pairs of examples.

(53) a) *'Go to work!'*
      b) *'Go to work and write a paper!'*
(54) a) *'Go to the beach or watch a film!'*
      b) *'Go to the beach!'*
(55) a) *'Eat the apple!'*
      b) *'Don't eat the apple!'*

The intuitions behind even these cases are not always straightforward. For example, in the case of disjunction there are two potential readings, the so-called free choice and weak readings (Kamp 1973). Imperatives may also combine with propositions.

(56) *'If you see John, say hello!'*

In such a case, we might want to 'infer' that there is an imperative to say hello in the event that John is seen (or possibly that the subject might want to avoid seeing John).

There are also the so-called pseudo-imperative constructions (Franke 2006) whose formal analysis appears non-trivial, as with the following examples.

(57) a) *'Have another drink and you will die!'*
      b) *'Have another drink and you will be happy!'*
      c) *'Have another drink or you will die!'*[15]

A fundamental question is what counts as a relevant notion of entailment for imperatives. There are similarities with questions, in that it does not seem appropriate to assign imperatives a direct truth-conditional interpretation. Unlike interrogatives, imperatives are not so easily embedded inside other expressions. Nor is there an overtly *linguistic* counterpart to an 'answer.' The question about what kinds of behavior should be modeled by a semantic analysis of imperatives revolves around notions of what are sometimes referred to as *satisfaction* and *validity* (Ross 1945). In the case of the former, there is a notion of an imperative being satisfied by some response, or behavior. Entailments may then be expressed in terms that describe which *other* imperatives are satisfied by such a response.

As elsewhere, different frameworks have been adopted and adapted to capture appropriate patterns of behavior associated with imperatives. Many accounts assume a possible-worlds perspective, with actions (or possible actions) that update the state of the world so that it satisfies some propositional analogue of the imperative. The question arises as to whether an imperative is satisfied by a propositional description of the desired state, or by a particular agent engaging in an appropriate action. Given the following imperative

(58)   *'Shut the window!'*

any natural utterance of this will typically be directed at an individual (or group of individuals), with the expectation that it is *that* individual who will cause the particular desired outcome, or that the particular individual engaging in the associated activity *is* the desired outcome, so that

(59)   *'John shuts the window'*

is a propositional description of the satisfaction criteria of (58). A more elaborate view might additionally contemplate a counter-factual element to satisfaction, so that John's shutting of the window only genuinely satisfies the imperative if John would not otherwise have shut the window.

Many accounts of imperatives (including those of Segerberg (1990), Lascarides and Asher (2004) and many others) have sought to avoid what has come to be known as *Ross's paradox*. This is the view expressed by Ross (1945) that it is not possible to formulate a logic of imperatives as it appears impossible to discern a coherent collection of inferences that encapsulate the notions of satisfaction and validity. That is, inferences cannot allow us to conclude both (a) which other imperatives are satisfied given that the imperative in the premise has been satisfied (satisfaction) and (b) that the requirement to comply with a particular command in the premise entails that we should comply with a command in the conclusion (validity). The example often cited in favor of this view concerns disjunction introduction. Consider the following two imperatives.

(60)   a)   *'Post the letter!'*
       b)   *'Post the letter or burn the letter!'*

To many, the most natural inference is from (60b) to (60a) (Kamp 1973). This corresponds to an inference concerning validity. However, if a logic of imperatives follows the usual rule of disjunction introduction, the inference should go the other way around. This can only correspond to an inference concerning satisfaction: if we have satisfied the requirement to post the letter, we would also have satisfied a requirement to post or burn the letter.

Even if both notions (satisfaction and validity) cannot be encapsulated by a single rule, that does not mean there can be no meaningful logics of satisfaction and validity. We might instead consider a logic of satisfaction independently of a logic of validity. The former might in many cases parallel inferences of indicative reasoning, whereas the latter may be more akin to a notion of *refinement* from computer science (Wirth 1971). This latter view may also correspond to a more pragmatic analysis of imperatives which characterizes the problem of 'what should be done' in terms of lists of obligations that need to be ful lled (Piwek 2000; Portner 2005).

4.4 Expressiveness, formal power, and computability

In computational semantics there is a tension. We want a theory that is computationally tractable but also suf ciently expressive to handle the natural language phenomena of interest. In many cases the most convenient way of obtaining expressiveness is by adopting a more powerful representation language. Yet more formal power is typically accompanied by computational intractability. In some cases, however, it is possible to nd a virtuous combination of appropriate expressiveness without an undesirable increase in formal power beyond what is computationally tractable.

The issue of computability arises in many guises. For example, theoremhood is, in general, intractable in higher-order formalisms. This is because such formalisms do not have a decidable proof theory: the theorems of higher-order theories are not recursively enumerable. This suggests that systems with the power of rst-order logic should be preferred to higher-order systems. There are other cases where a sacri ce in expressiveness may be appropriate. For example, in the case of arithmetic and quanti ers of number, we may prefer weaker, more tractable theories such as Presburger arithmetic (Presburger 1929) over the more usual Peano arithmetic. In general, these trade-offs in power may mean that certain pertinent notions are not expressible (such as the quanti er 'in nitely many' in the case of a genuinely rst-order theory, and the notion of multiplication in the case of Presburger arithmetic).

Related to this is the speci c problem of *impredicativity*. This can arise with type quanti cation – as used in (41) of Section 4.1.1. If we allow such type quanti cation to range over all types, including polymorphic types, then the evaluation of polymorphic types can be deeply problematic in a computational system (the evaluation of such a type requires us to quantify over the very type that we are attempting to evaluate). Fortunately it appears that natural language does not require such a powerful typing system; we can compromise by having the expressivity of polymorphic types, but restricted so that there is no problematic quanti cation over polymorphic types themselves. This is a case where it is possible to have a more *expressive* theory without increasing the *power* of the system beyond what is computationally tractable.

There are other notions that cannot be formalized within any computable theory besides impredicative types, such as the notion of truth, and answerhood conditions (Section 4.3.1). We may de ne constraints on how truth and answerhood should behave, but that does not mean the notions themselves are intrinsically amenable to de nition *within* a tractable theory. Here we might begin to see how notions relevant to computational semantics might not be directly expressed *by* an implementation, but they may be properties *of* such an implementation.

This suggests an alternative characterization of computational semantics, where the idea of computability itself is considered as a *constraint* on appropriate formalizations and models (Turner 2007). As a methodological constraint, this may be relevant even in the event that the behaviors being described by a formal theory are not directly relevant to any conceivable practical implementation. Rather, the claim might be made that a computable theory potentially has more explanatory power than a theory expressed in an intrinsically intractable framework.

Indeed, we can contemplate using the constraint of computability not just in the context of the formal representations of meaning, but also in the process of translating natural language into those representations. It is conventional only to require that the translation be compositional (Section 2.1). Unfortunately, it turns out that if there are no restrictions on the nature of the functions used to combine the meaning of the parts, then compositionality does not impose any effective restriction on the nature of the interpretation (Zadrozny 1994). In effect, compositionality is a constraint only on the form of the translation rules, and their coverage, not their function. That is, as usually de ned, compositionality is a restriction only on the general form of the semantic annotations, rather than necessarily being a restriction on the end result of that translation.

If we ignore the evaluation of the functions that are applied in a compositional translation, then the constraint of compositionality ensures that the translation process is recursive on the structure of the expression. For every syntactic constituency rule there should be a corresponding rule for determining the semantic representation to be associated with the head of the expression as a function of the semantic representation of its constituent parts. This guarantees that every syntactic analysis has a corresponding semantic interpretation.

Of course, the evaluation of the functions used in a compositional interpretation is important. If the functions themselves are meta-theoretic, and not part of the semantic theory as such, then they need to be applied to produce a well-formed representation. Even if they are part of the semantic theory, we may need to apply the functions in order to derive a representation in some 'normal form.' In either case, it would be appropriate to consider constraints on the nature of the functions themselves. At the very least, we would expect them to be computable.

5   Corpus-Based and Machine Learning Methods

Although the focus of this chapter, and indeed much work in computational semantics, has largely been on the application of techniques for computationally tractable semantic analysis based upon representations in formal logic, there are other computational approaches that involve less traditional forms of semantic analysis which do not rely upon strictly logical theories of meaning. These include approaches that exploit corpus-based techniques and machine learning. We will brie y survey a small sample of these techniques and their applications, and speculate on the role that a more formal analysis may play in their application, particularly in the case of textual entailment.

5.1 *Latent semantic analysis*

Latent semantic analysis (LSA) (Landauer et al., 1998; 2007) is a technique that aims to determine a 'conceptual' or 'semantic' space for words and the documents in which they occur. The number of 'concepts' used is invariably smaller than the number of different words in the documents. The idea is that words denoting similar concepts will be mapped on to similar vectors in this reduced space. The technique is able to determine when word meanings – and documents – are related, even when the words never occur in the same context and the documents have few words in common. Two words may be deemed to be conceptually related because the words that they appear with occur together in other documents. This allows us to compare and process words and documents in concept space.

The technique takes as input a word document matrix where each entry indicates the number of times a given word appears in a given document. It then uses *singular value decomposition* (SVD) (Golub & van Loan 1989) effectively to 'rotate' the word document space to a different set of dimensions. These dimensions (the 'latent space') are such that they give the axes of greatest variation for the original word document matrix. Dimension reduction can then be applied by pruning those dimensions with the smallest contribution. The dimensions that are left are considered to correspond to some notion of a 'concept.' In the matrix of reduced dimensionality, words which make a similar contribution are effectively merged together. The intuitive explanation is that different words will have similar vector representations in this reduced space if they denote a similar concept.

This technique has a number of applications (Landauer et al., 1998; 2007) including document indexing and search (*latent semantic indexing*, LSI) (Deerwester et al., 1990) and automatic essay marking (Landauer et al., 1998). It can also be used to cluster documents according to their conceptual similarity. In the case of LSI, the terms occurring in a query expression can also be mapped to the corresponding concepts, which are then used to retrieve the documents in which those concepts occur. This allows documents to be retrieved that do not necessarily contain the terms in question, but which do include terms that correspond to the same 'concepts.'

Terms that are combined by the dimension reduction into a single concept may be indicative of an underlying synonym, although the notion of a 'concept' here is a mathematical abstraction that need not correspond to any natural category.

It has been argued that the dimension reduction employed by LSA has certain problems including the fact that the reduced matrix can contain negative values, which is counterintuitive if the values are interpreted as counts of concept occurrences (Hofmann 2001; Quesada 2003). An alternative approach is *probabilistic latent semantic analysis* (PLSA), which employs a dimension reduction strategy that is claimed to have a more solid statistical foundation. In this technique, the number of concepts is decided, and words are   tted to those concepts using *expectation-maximization* (Hofmann 1999; 2001).

5.2   Extraction of semantic roles

Identi cation of semantic roles is useful for a range of problems, such as question answering (Narayanan & Harabagiu 2004; Sun et al., 2005; Kaisser 2006; Shen & Lapata 2007), dialogue systems (Liu 1995), and information extraction (Riloff 1993).

The notion of semantic role is connected with the notions of subcategorization and selection preferences, which may determine the syntactic function and 'thematic role' of an entity. (In some cases, coercion by way of metaphor or some other semantic relation may be needed to obtain a natural interpretation.) The syntactic role of a verb's complement can give an indication of the semantic role of nominal expressions, such as *agent, patient, theme*, etc. (Fillmore 1968; Dowty 1991). More speci c roles may also be de ned, as in Frame semantics (Fillmore 1976), and FrameNet languages (Baker et al., 1998). Resources such as PropBank (Palmer et al., 2005), provide a hand corrected body of predicate–argument annotations of the Penn Treebank.

There are machine learning methods (both supervised and unsupervised) for automatically determining semantic roles. Such methods can be used to learn to label constituents of a sentence with the semantic roles of a target frame (Gildea & Jurafsky 2002). One problem is that the correspondence between syntactic categories and semantic roles is not always direct or easy to predict. Machine learning techniques that have been applied to this problem include maximum entropy, rule-based, memory-based, and kernel methods.

For more on semantic role identi cation and tagging, see Chapter 9, ARTIFI-CIAL NEURAL NETWORKS, Chapter 10, LINGUISTIC ANNOTATION, and Chapter 18, INFORMATION EXTRACTION. More discussion on machine learning techniques is provided in Chapter 5, MAXIMUM ENTROPY MODELS, Chapter 6, MEMORY-BASED LEARNING, Chapter 7, DECISION TREES, Chapter 8, UNSUPERVISED LEARNING AND GRAMMAR INDUCTION, and Chapter 9, ARTIFICIAL NEURAL NETWORKS.

5.3   Word-sense disambiguation

Word-sense disambiguation (Ide & Véronis 1998) is a useful step when dealing with various essentially semantic issues, such as question answering and intelligent document retrieval. The objective is to be able to distinguish between various senses of a word. Machine learning techniques can be used in a variety of ways to achieve this. One common feature is to identify word senses from the different contexts in which a given word is used. For many tasks, a   ne discrimination between senses might not be required (Ide & Wilks 2006).

Knowledge-based approaches may use dictionaries and thesauri to provide examples of different word senses, and the other words associated with a given sense (Lesk 1986), as well as ontological relationships (Roberto Navigli 2005). In general such approaches may be limited by the quality and relevance of the information sources used.

Data-driven approaches seek to determine different senses of a word by identifying patterns, or clusters, of co-occurrences and contexts, both local and global (McCarthy et al., 2004). They may involve supervised or unsupervised learning. In the former case, sense-tagged corpora may be used to train a sense-disambiguation algorithm. In the latter case, clustering techniques may be used to identify different collocation contexts, which are assumed to correspond to different word senses. Various assumptions may be made to aid training. One such assumption is that, generally speaking, a word appearing more than once in a given document is likely to share the same word sense (Gale et al., 1992b).

Bilingual corpora may also be used to help identify the different senses of a word by identifying systematic differences in translation (Gale et al., 1992c; Kaji & Morimoto 2005).

Chapter 10, LINGUISTIC ANNOTATION, discusses word-sense disambiguation, and Chapter 11, EVALUATION OF NLP SYSTEMS, uses word-sense disambiguation as a case study.

5.4 Textual entailment

One of the purposes of a computationally feasible formal semantic analysis of language is to determine what is entailed by a given text. This is called *textual entailment*. It can be thought of as capturing relationships of the form $t \Rightarrow h$, where t is some natural language text, and h is some hypothesis, also expressed in natural language. Intuitively, the relevant notion of entailment is one where h would not follow without t; that is, h cannot be obtained from any of the background information that is being used to capture entailment relations. Textual entailment can be applied to the problems of information extraction, question answering (see Chapter 22, QUESTION ANSWERING), translation, summarization, and other NLP tasks (Glickman et al., 2005). In some cases, it is possible to capture a notion of textual entailment using statistical and probabilistic techniques, rather than a purely logic-based analysis of meaning. Indeed, the term 'textual entailment' is often used in a context that does not presuppose a rigorous, logic-based analysis of meaning.

The mechanisms for obtaining appropriate entailment patterns include hand coded rules, acquired knowledge, and machine learning (see Chapter 5, MAXIMUM ENTROPY MODELS, Chapter 6, MEMORY-BASED LEARNING, Chapter 7, DECISION TREES, Chapter 8, UNSUPERVISED LEARNING AND GRAMMAR INDUCTION, and Chapter 9, ARTIFICIAL NEURAL NETWORKS). For example, a range of machine learning techniques can be applied to nd approximations to human judgments concerning entailment patterns, or rules. Another possibility is to exploit patterns of words that indicate some intended inference or relation. For example, hyponyms and meronyms may be identi ed by discovering ontological relationships from corpora that are indicated by particular patterns (Hearst 1992; Berland & Charniak 1999). Various other semantic relationships may also be discovered, including causal relations (Girju 2003; Cole et al., 2006) and temporal ordering and other relationships between verb meanings (Chklovski & Pantel 2004). This may not be entirely robust. There may be problems to overcome with patterns that are overgeneral, negative polarity contexts, and anaphoric expressions (see Sanchez-Graillet et al., 2006; Sanchez-Graillet & Poesio 2007 for example).

The method may be made more robust if there is a notion of the semantic class of a word (Girju et al., 2006), although this requires additional work in identifying the relevant semantic classes (see Chapter 10, LINGUISTIC ANNOTATION and Chapter 18, INFORMATION EXTRACTION).

Such methods may help to identify particular kinds of entailments. There are, however, other more general corpus-based approaches to inference, some of which rely upon a traditional formal semantic analysis, where a semantic analysis of the documents in question is produced, along with the hypothesis that is to be checked. In general this requires a broad-coverage deep syntactic analysis, comprehensive semantic analysis, and a robust theorem prover. For some problem domains, such as question answering, it is possible that techniques based on pattern-matching of the semantic representations may be adequate (Ahn et al., 2005). Additional sources of information may have to be analyzed to determine relevant relationships between information in a given document (or document collection) and a hypothesis that is being tested, or a question that is being asked. In addition to nding evidence of such relationships from supplementary sources of information, there have been proposals to improve the robustness of theorem proving by allowing costed abductive assumptions (Raina et al., 2005) which allow some degree of exibility in unifying the terms that appear in a proof. Cost functions can be used to minimize the contribution of abductive reasoning that is permitted within a proof to avoid perverse results.

It is sometimes argued that contemporary formal techniques (which have been the focus of this chapter) are too fragile and incomplete to be used for such applications. Alternative approaches seek to represent knowledge, and capture textual entailments, using shallower, less abstract representations of the text. Such methods include hierarchical representations based upon description logics (de Salvo Braz et al., 2005). These seek to capture structural, relational, and other semantic properties. Other approaches use representations that are closer to the surface form of language, including lexically based parse-tree representations (Dagan et al., 2008a), perhaps augmented with annotations (for negation and modality, for example). A relevant work on this topic is Dagan et al. (2009). A comprehensive analysis of textual entailment almost certainly needs to address questions of resolving anaphora. But corpus-based methods have also been applied to this problem (Ge et al., 1998; Paul et al., 1999; Poesio & Alexandrov-Kabadjov 2004).

5.5 *Relationship to formal semantics*

We may wonder about the nature of the relationship between corpus-based methods and formal, logic-based approaches. The relevance of this issue is perhaps most obvious in the case of textual entailment, which aims to address one of the objectives of formal methods – that of capturing legitimate entailment relationships.

One question is whether it is realistic to assume that formal approaches will ever be able to model the full range of textual entailments, or whether entailments captured by corpus-based methods will ever be as trustworthy as logic-based inference. We offer no view on this matter here, but observe that some aspects of textual entailment may need to be informed by something resembling a formal analysis for us to know what counts as a legitimate or illegitimate entailment, and why – even if only to ensure an element of consistency, and con dence, in the conclusions drawn. Regardless of the underlying mechanism used for capturing textual entailment relationships, it seems appropriate to formalize normative rules concerning how a coherent notion of textual entailment should behave; that is, we should consider formulating a logic of textual entailment to characterize the properties that the relationship $t \Rightarrow h$ should support.

Another topic that may merit further exploration is a better understanding of the relationships, if any, between a logic-based conception of semantics, and the notion of semantics as used in work that builds on word and phrase co-occurrence data and its generalizations, such as LSA. At the time of writing, it appears there have been few if any attempts to reconcile these different views on the nature of natural language semantics.

6 Concluding Remarks

This chapter has presented some of the basic ideas behind computational semantics, with some sample topics and research questions. Some corpus-based techniques that embody a notion of semantics have been sketched, but the primary focus has been on logic-based approaches. One idea that arises in the presentation is not merely to think of computational semantics as describing theories of semantics that lend themselves to implementation, but to consider computability itself as a constraint on theories of meaning and semantic analysis. We can also distinguish between those aspects of a theory of meaning that lend themselves to direct implementation, and those that describe the properties of an implementation, without themselves necessarily being implementable.

NOTES

1   For criticisms of Grice, see for example Davis (1998).
2   This assumes that the y does not occur within the scope of another 'λy.'

3   In general there may be issues to resolve when combining a logic with a λ-calculus, which we put to one side at this point (see Section 2.2).

4   It is worth noting, however, that a rst-order *theory* (a theory de ned in a rst-order logic) may be incomplete, as Gödel demonstrated for rst-order arithmetic, for example.

5   See Section 4.4 for a little more discussion on the issue of power versus expressiveness.

6   Aristotelean syllogisms can be viewed as a form of proof-theoretic semantics, although one where the entailment patterns are captured directly in terms of natural language sentences.

7   Section 4 of Chapter 2, COMPUTATIONAL COMPLEXITY IN NATURAL LANGUAGE, considers the computational complexity of determining relationships between sentences.

8   We do not consider other issues concerning the analysis of discourse, such as topic and focus (Rooth 1993; Hajicová et al., 1998), or discourse segmentation. Note that there are non-logical, quantitative methods that have been applied to the latter problem (Hearst 1997).

9   In this case, we would want x to be evaluated in the same way as the other 'x's in the representation. This cannot happen if it is not bound by the same quanti er.

10 The precise values of the subscripts (in this case 6 and 7) and place-holder variable names (z_6, z_7) may vary.

11 Blackburn and Bos (2005: 108) provide more details of this approach.

12 We might restrict the quanti cation so that it only ranges over non-polymorphic types. See Section 4.4 and Fox and Lappin (2005).

13 An alternative approach would be to use *schematic* polymorphism (Pollard 2004).

14 This mirrors Groenendijk and Stokhof (1997, fact 4.3).

15 To be contrasted with '*Have another drink or you will be happy!*'

16 Computational Models of Dialogue

JONATHAN GINZBURG
AND RAQUEL FERNÁNDEZ

1 Introduction

Computational study of dialogue, the topic of this article, provides underpinnings for the design of dialogue systems and for models of human performance in conversational settings. Hence, among the central issues are ones pertaining to the information states of the agents participating in a conversation. Some of this information is *public* – available in principle to be grasped and manipulated by the conversational participants, while some of this information is, at the very least, not explicitly made public. The structure and makeup of participant information states – and the extent to which information in them is shared – are issues on which much of the account of dialogue we will present here rides. Linguistic phenomena will provide guidance towards the resolution of these issues: at this point in the state of the art, the challenge is to process 'real language' with all its fragments, dis uencies, and the like. Such utterances are highly context-dependent – to a far higher degree than is the situation with text processing. The participant information states will serve as context; being able to perform this role will, consequently, impose signi cant constraints on the information states.

One basic task for any theory of dialogue is to account for the coherence of a conversation – a given dialogue move can be coherently followed up by a wide variety of responses, but not by just any response. Coming up with such a theory of coherence presupposes a classi cation of the space of available moves. This raises a variety of interesting issues, a central one of which is: can this be done domain-independently? It is by now clear that domain dependence cannot be evaded – conversational coherence varies widely across domains. Nonetheless, as we will see, it also seems reasonably clear that there are aspects of coherence which can be explicated in a more or less domain-independent way. How to nd the proper balance is an important theme we will address at a number of points. After discussing a number of in uential taxonomies of dialogue moves, we will concentrate on characterizing in a theory-neutral way the fundamental properties

The Handbook of Computational Linguistics and Natural Language Processing, First Edition.
Edited by Alexander Clark, Chris Fox and Shalom Lappin.
© 2013 Blackwell Publishing Ltd except for editorial material and organization
© 2013 Alexander Clark, Chris Fox, and Shalom Lappin. Published 2013 by Blackwell Publishing Ltd.

of two of the commonest move types – queries and assertions. From this will emerge a series of benchmarks that theories of dialogue need to satisfy.

Meta-communicative interaction – interaction concerning the ongoing communicative process (e.g., acknowledgments of understanding and clari cation requests) – is a fundamental area for dialogue. It was long neglected in formal and computational linguistics, but has now become a much studied area, not least because utterances whose main function is meta-communicative are very frequent and play a crucial role in applications. As with queries and assertions, we will proceed initially in a theory-neutral way, gathering benchmarks along the way. Ultimately, one is after a theory which will explicate the coherence of meta-communicative utterances and allow them to be interpreted. This ties in with the nal phenomena we will characterize – the non-sentential fragments typical of conversation, many of which occur in meta-communicative utterances. We will address two types: the rst are sentential fragments – utterances like 'Bo.,' 'Bo?,' 'Why?,' 'Yes,' whose external syntax is non-sentential, but which express a complete message in context. The second are dis uencies – self-corrections, hesitations, and the like.

As we mentioned above, the computational study of dialogue provides formal underpinnings for the design of dialogue systems. The second part of this chapter is devoted to a survey of the most in uential paradigms in this area, which we informally evaluate in terms of the benchmarks that will have emerged in the rst part of the chapter. Dialogue systems are important because they constitute a highly promising technology. We will emphasize also the fact that they serve as a very useful testing ground for dialogue theories.

The third part of the chapter is devoted to sketching a theory of dialogue, known as KoS, in which meaning and interaction can be modeled. We will show how the lion's share of the benchmarks from the rst part of the article can be explicated in a uniform fashion within KoS. We formulate KoS in the framework of type theory with records (Cooper 2006). This is a framework that simultaneously allows sophisticated semantic modeling using λ-calculus style techniques, while also enabling rich structure to be encoded in a way that resembles typed feature structures. In contrast to typed feature structures, however, type theory with records provides as rst-class entities both types and tokens. This feature of the framework is of considerable importance for semantics, in particular with respect to modeling meta-communicative interaction.

The nal part of the article is devoted to offering pointers to other recent signi cant directions in research on dialogue, including work on machine learning, multiparty conversation, and multi-modal interaction.

2   The Challenges of Dialogue

A computational theory of dialogue needs to aspire to explicate how conversations start, proceed, and conclude. It should be able to underpin the participation of either a human or an arti cial agent in conversations like the following:

(1)   John: (1) Okay which one do you think it is?
              (2) Try F1 F1 again and we'll get
      Sarah: (3) Shift and F1?
      Sue: (4) It's, (5) no.
      John: (6) No, (7) just F1 F1.
      Sue: (8) It isn't that.
      John: (9) F1. (10) Right, (11) and that tells us
      Sue: (12) It's shift F7.

   (1) is, in fact, a rather humdrum conversation from the British National Corpus
(BNC) (Burnard 2000a) involving three people attempting to print a le some time
around 1990. Nonetheless, it exhibits features that radically distinguish it from a
text and even in several respects from the sort of arti cial travel agent or airline
booking system/user dialogue routinely described in AI/NLP papers on dialogue
in the 1980s and 1990s (e.g., Allen & Perrault 1980; Aust et al., 1995):

(1)   **Self-answering**: utterance (2) is a case of *self-answering*, unexpected on anal-
      ysis of queries as requests for information (following, e.g., Allen & Perrault
      1980).
(2)   **Multilogue**: the conversation involves more than two participants, the case
      handled by the vast majority of all analyses.
(3)   **Disagreement**: even in this essentially cooperative setting disagreement is
      rife.
(4)   **Partial comprehension**: Sarah's (3) is a clari cation request, indicating
      distinct states of semantic processing among participants.
(5)   **Incomplete utterances**: three of the utterances ((2), (4), (11)) are incomplete.
(6)   **Sentential fragments**: ve of the utterances ((3), (5), (6), (7), (9)) are not
      syntactically sentential, yet convey complete illocutionary messages.

   As with all tasks in NLP, one can perform dialogue processing at a variety
of levels, ranging from the very deep, designing agents that can participate in
real conversations, through medium, which could involve trying to perform
intentional analysis on a conversational participant's contribution, to shallow,
which could amount to producing a reasonable paraphrase of (1), for 'secretarial
purposes,' as in of ce assistants like CALO (Tur et al., 2010). Notice though that,
given the fact that form radically underspeci es content in dialogue, even producing such a periphrasis of (1), e.g., something along the lines of (2), involves
sophisticated resources – including techniques to resolve (a) the *move type* (or *illocutionary force*) of an utterance, which is rarely signaled explicitly, (b) the content of
sentential fragments (on which more below), and (c) the referents of anaphors:

(2)   John asked Sue which button did she think one needed to press. He sug-
      gested to try F1 F1 once again. Sarah wondered if he meant she should type

Shift and F1. Sue was a bit unsure but demurred and John indicated that he meant for her to type F1 F1. Sue disagreed with John that that was what needed doing. John suggested to try F1, which he thought might indicate something, and then Sue suggested it was shift F7.

Move type resolution: Which one do you think it is?↦ John asked Sarah and/or Sue which button did she think one needed to press.

Sentential fragment resolution + Move type resolution: Shift and F1? ↦ Sarah wondered if he meant she should type Shift and F1.

Anaphora resolution + Move type resolution: It isn't that. ↦ Sue disagreed with John that that was what needed doing.

2.1   Classifying and characterizing dialogue moves

2.1.1   Move classification   One important task for a theory of dialogue is to explicate the moves or acts that participants can make in a conversation. In so doing there is an inevitable tension between the domain-speci c and the domain-independent conversational possibilities. Some, following Wittgenstein (1953), would come close to denying the existence of domain-independent conversational possibilities (e.g., Allwood 1995; Rudnicky 2004), a position which is understandable for designers of dialogue systems. It is undeniable that knowing how to interact in an unfamiliar setting (shop, court, religious institution, academic lecture, informal meeting with people of different class/ethnic background) often requires considerable guidance. Nonetheless, an emotionally stable adult in an unfamiliar setting might initially miss a trick or even seven, but in many cases at least she is not completely oored and can navigate her way around, albeit with a certain number of stumbles. Moreover, she can acquire the necessary domain knowledge relatively easily, in contrast, for instance, to learning a new language. It thus seems a defensible strategy to try and isolate some domain-independent conversational possibilities (e.g., with respect to how questions are asked and responded to or how positive/negative feedback is provided), while acknowledging the possibility that any given domain might involve moves that are specialized in some way. Of course in addition to certain idiosyncrasies about moves, which by analogy with lexical idiosyncrasy need to be stipulated (e.g., the need to end each turn addressed to a judge in a British court with the word 'm'lud'), one also aspires to nd parameters by means of which one can characterize domain-speci c conversational possibilities (see Section 4.6).

Speech act theory (Searle 1969; Searle & Vanderveken 1985) emphasizes that there are hundreds of things one could do with words, not fewer than the number of illocutionary verbs that can be used performatively (e.g., 'I declare,' 'I name this ship,' etc.). Without dismissing the signi cance of performatives, the strategy in most recent taxonomies of the range of moves is far more empiricist, based on the classi cation of moves observed in corpora. One important empirical basis for such an explication are corpus studies of the range of moves found in conversation. The number of possible moves, based on grammatical cues such as sentence type or discourse particles, is reduced to between a dozen (as in the Map Task taxonomy (Carletta et al., 1996)[1] and about 20 in the DAMSL taxonomy (Core & Allen 1997). The main classes in these taxonomies are given, respectively, in (3a, 3b):[2,3]

(3) a. **Initiating moves**: instruct, explain, check, align, query-yn, query-w
          Response moves: acknowledge, reply-y, reply-n, reply-w, clarify (from Carletta et al., 1996)
     b. **Forward looking moves**: statement, in uencing-addressee-future-actions info-request, committing-speaker-future-action, conventional opening closing, explicit-performative, exclamation
          Backward looking moves: agreement (including accept, reject) under-standing (including signal understanding, signal non-understanding), answer

In line with our earlier remarks, such taxonomies can have no pretenses to the completeness aspired to by, e.g., POS taxonomies. Moreover, these taxonomies (and others proposed) have their own biases and different levels of grain, re ect-ing to some extent researcher biases. Nonetheless, these taxonomies enable coding of corpora at more or less reliable levels of inter-annotator agreement (Carletta 1996; Core & Allen 1997). We can draw certain conclusions from this:

- Initiating vs. response: one signi cant dimension distinguishing moves is whether they are initiating or responsive. Initiating moves require more domain-sensitive/agent-particular information for their characterization.
- Meta-communicative interaction: one of the features that distinguishes dia-logue from text is the pervasive presence in dialogue of moves that directly concern communication management, primarily acknowledgments of under-standing, clari cation requests (CRs), and self-corrections. In recent years much more detailed taxonomies of such moves have been provided, including Novick and Sutton (1994) and Muller and Prévot (2003) for acknowledgments, and Purver et al. (2001) and Rodriguez and Schlangen (2004) for CRs.

2.1.2 Move characterization: queries and assertions In general terms, a dia-logue theory should be able to offer answers to the questions in (4) about initiating moves, responsive moves, as well as taking a generation perspective:

(4) a. **Initiating move/Response space conditions**: what contextual condi-tions characterize initiating (responsive) moves? For a given such context, what are the possible moves?
     b. **Generation perspective**: given an agent A with a goal g in a context C, what can A say in C to ful ll g?

We now elaborate on these general tasks. The two main move types (or more precisely supertypes) are queries and assertions – they are also the commonest

means for interactions with dialogue systems. Hence, the move-related benchmarks we specify primarily concern their characterization. Many of these are
modeled on benchmarks formulated in Bohlin et al. (1999). The benchmarks are
loosely and atheoretically formulated, typically of the form 'Accommodate ...,'
this allows 'accommodate' to be understood in various ways, including from both
a generation and an interpretive perspective.

The minimal requirement for processing queries is the ability to recognize *simple*
answers:

(5) a. p is a simple answer to q iff p is an instantiation of q or a negation of
          such an instantiation.
     b.   For a polar question: $\{r \mid SimpleAns(r, p?)\} = \{p, \neg p\}$
     c.   For a unary wh-question: $\{r \mid SimpleAns(r, \lambda b.p(b))\} =$
          $\{p(a_1), \ldots, p(a_n), \neg p(a_1), \ldots, \neg p(a_n)\}$

(Q1) Query benchmark1: accommodate simple answers.

Simple answerhood covers a fair amount of ground. But it clearly underde-
termines the range of answers coherently concerning a given question that any
speaker of a given language can recognize, independently of domain knowledge and of the goals underlying an interaction, a notion dubbed 'aboutness' by
Ginzburg (1995). On the polar front, it leaves out the whole gamut of answers to
polar questions that are weaker than p or $\neg p$ such as conditional answers 'If r, then
p' (e.g., 6a) or weakly modalized answers 'probably/possibly/maybe/possibly
not p' (e.g., 6b). As far as wh-questions go, it leaves out quanti cational answers
(6c–g), as well as disjunctive answers. These missing classes of propositions are
pervasive in actual linguistic use. In some cases they constitute *goal fulfilling*
responses (e.g., (6a), (6c), (6d), (6e), (6g) below); the answer provided could very
well trigger a follow-up query (e.g., (7) below):

(6) a.   Christopher: Can I have some ice-cream then?
          Dorothy: You can do if there is any. (BNC, KBW)
     b.   Anon: Are you voting for Tory?
          Denise: I might. (BNC, KB?, slightly modi ed)
     c.   Dorothy: What did grandma have to catch?
          Christopher: A bus. (BNC, KBW, slightly modi ed)
     d.   Rhiannon: How much tape have you used up?
          Chris: About half of one side. (BNC, KB?)
     e.   Dorothy: What do you want on this?
          Andrew: I would like some yogurt please. (BNC, KBW, slightly modi-
          ed)
     f.   Elinor: Where are you going to hide it?
          Tim: Somewhere you can't have it. (BNC, KBW)
     g.   Christopher: Where is the box?
          Dorothy: Near the window. (BNC, KBW)

(7) a. Anon: Are you voting for Tory? Denise: I might.
        Anon: Well are you or aren't you?
     b. Dorothy: What did grandma have to catch? Christopher: A bus.
        Dorothy: Which bus?
     c. Elinor: Where are you going to hide it? Tim: Somewhere you can't
        have it.
        Elinor: But where?

This data leads to:

(Q2a) Query benchmark2a: accommodate non-resolving answers.

(Q2b) Query benchmark2b: accommodate follow-up queries to non-resolving answers.

Responses to queries can also contain more information than literally asked for, as exempli ed in (8):

(8) A: When is the train leaving? B2: 5:04, platform 12. (Based on an example due to Allen & Perrault 1980).

This 'excess information' should be utilized, leading to:

(Q3) Query benchmark3: accommodate 'overinformative' answers.

Answering a query with a query represents another signi cant class of possibilities. The commonest such cases are clari cation responses but, since these are triggered by essentially *any* move type, we discuss these below as part of a more general discussion of meta-communicative interaction (MCI). One class of query responses are queries that, intuitively, introduce an issue whose resolution is prior to the question asked:

(9) a. A: Who murdered Smith? B: Who was in town?
     b. A: Who is going to win the race? B: Who is going to participate?
     c. Carol: Right, what do you want for your dinner?
        Chris: What do you (pause) suggest? (BNC, KbJ)
     d. Chris: Where's mummy?
        Emma: What do you want her for? (BNC, KbJ)

(Q4) Query benchmark4: accommodate subquestions.

One nal class of responses, which are of some importance in applications, are 'irrelevant responses,' whose effect is to indicate lack of interest in the original query:

(10) a. A: Who is the homeowner? B: Who is the supervisor here?
      b. Rumpole: Do you think Prof Clayton killed your husband? Mercy
         Charles: Do you think you'll get him off? (Mortimer 1990: 100)
      c. A: Horrible talk by Rozzo. B: It's very hot here.

(Q5) Query benchmark5: accommodate topic changing, 'irrelevant' responses.

Moving on to assertions, the most obvious initial task concerns the potential effect their potential acceptance has on context.

(A1) Assertion benchmark1: if accepted, integrate propositional content with existing knowledge base.

One important feature of dialogue, a medium which involves distinct agents, is the possibility for disagreement:

(11) a.   A: I'm right, you're wrong. B: No, I'm right, you're wrong.
      b.   John: No, just F1 F1. Sue: It isn't that.

(A2) Assertion benchmark2: accommodate disagreement.

The nal two benchmarks are, in a sense, methodological. First, the same basic mechanism seems to regulate queries/assertions, across varying sizes of participant sets:

(12) a.   Monologue: self-answering (*A: Who should we invite? Perhaps Noam.*)
      b.   Dialogue: querier/responder (*A: Who should we invite? B: Perhaps Noam.*)
      c.   Multilogue: multiple discussants (*A: Who should we invite? B: Perhaps Noam. C: Martinu. D: Bedrich …*)

(SC) Scalability benchmark: ensure approach scales down to monologue and up to multilogue.

Second, as we mentioned at the outset, in moving from domain to domain, there are some aspects that are speci c to interacting in that domain and this cannot be avoided. However, we have claimed that human agents adapt well and with relatively little effort can reuse the interactional skills they bring with them from past experience. Hence:

(DA) Domain Adaptability benchmark: reuse interactional procedures from other domains, insofar as possible.

2.1.3 Move characterization: meta-communication As we saw earlier, a class of moves whose presence makes itself evident in taxonomies are meta-communicative moves. Such phenomena have been studied extensively by psycholinguists and conversational analysts in terms of notions such as *grounding*, *feedback* (in the sense of Clark 1996 and Allwood 1995 respectively) and *repair* (in the sense of Schegloff 1987). The main claim that originates with Clark and Schaefer (1989) is that any dialogue move m_1 made by A must be grounded (namely acknowledged as understood) by the other conversational participant B before it enters the common ground; failing this, clari cation interaction (henceforth *CRification*) must ensue. While this assumption about grounding is somewhat too strong, as Allwood argues, it provides a starting point, indicating the need to interleave the potential for grounding/CRi cation incrementally, the size of the increments being an important empirical issue. From a semantic theory, we might expect the ability to generate concrete predictions about forms/meanings of MCI utterances in context. More concretely, the adequacy of such a theory requires:

(GCR) Grounding/CRi cation conditions benchmark: the ability to characterize for any utterance type the update that emerges in the aftermath of successful grounding and the full range of possible CRs otherwise.

Let us make this benchmark more concrete, initially with respect to the content/context of grounding/CRi cation moves, later with respect to the realization of such moves. There are two main types of MC *interactions* – acknowledgments of understanding and clari cation requests (CRs).[4] A rough idea of the frequency of acknowledgments can be gleaned from the word counts for 'yeah' and 'mmh' in the demographic part of the BNC: 'yeah' occurs 58,810 times (rank: 10; 10–15 percent of turns), whereas 'mmh' occurs 21,907 times (rank: 30; 5 percent of turns). Clari cation requests (CRs) constitute approximately 4–5 percent of all utterances (see, e.g., Purver et al., 2001; Rodriguez & Schlangen 2004). Both acknowledgments and CRs, then, constitute central phenomena of interaction, even judged merely in terms of frequency.

An addressee can acknowledge a speaker's utterance, either once the utterance is completed, as in (13a, 13b), or concurrently with the utterance as in (13c). For conversations where the participants are visible to each other, gesture (head nodding, eye contact, etc.) also provides an option by means of which af rmative moves can be made (see Nakano et al., 2003).

(13) a. Tommy: So Dalmally I should safely say was my rst schooling. Even though I was about eight and a half. Anon 1: Mmh. Now your father was the the stocker at Tormore is that right? (BNC, K7D)
      b. Wizard: Then you want to go north on Speer Boulevard for one and one half miles to Alcott Street.
          User: Okay. I want to go right on Speer? (VNS Corpus, Novick & Sutton 1994)
      c. A: Move the train . . .
          B: Aha
          A: . . . from Avon . . .
          B: Right
          A: . . . to Danville (adapted from the Trains corpus)

From this we derive three benchmarks:

(Ack1) Completed Acknowledgments benchmark: accommodate completed acknowledgments.
(Ack2) Incremental Acknowledgments benchmark: accommodate continuation acknowledgments.
(Ack3) Multi-modal Acknowledgments benchmark: accommodate gestural acknowledgments.

Although, in principle, one can request clari cation concerning just about anything in a previous utterance, corpus studies of CRs in a general corpus (Purver et al., 2001), as well as task-oriented ones (Rodriguez & Schlangen 2004; Rieser & Moore 2005) indicate that there are four main categories of CRs:

- **Repetition**: CRs that request the previous utterance to be repeated:
  - (14) a. Tim (1): Could I have one of those (unclear)?

    Dorothy (2): Can you have what? (BNC, KW1)
    - b. s bust: Great memorial I think really isn't it?

      e bust: Beg pardon?

      s bust: Be a good appropriate memorial if we can afford it. (BNC, KM8)
- **Confirmation**: CRs that seek to con rm understanding of a prior utterance:
  - (15) a. Marsha: yeah that's it, this, she's got three rottweilers now and

    Sarah: three? (=Are you saying she's got THREE rottweilers now?)

    Marsha: yeah, one died so only got three now (BNC)
    - b. A: Is Georges here?

      B: You're asking if Georges Sand is here.
- **Intended content**: CRs that query the intended content of a prior utterance:
  - (16) a. Tim (5): Those pink things that af after we had our lunch.

    Dorothy (6): Pink things?

    Tim (7): Yeah. Er those things in that bottle.

    Dorothy (8): Oh **I know what you mean.** For your throat? (BNC)
    - b. A: Have a laugh and joke with Dick.

      B: Dick?

      A: Have a laugh and joke with Dick.

      B: Who's Dick?
- **Intention recognition**: CRs that query the goal underlying a prior utterance:
  - (17) a. X: You know what, the conference might be downtown Seattle. So I may have to call you back on that.

    PT: OK. Did you want me to wait for the hotel then? (Communicator corpus)
    - b. Norrine: When is the barbecue, the twentieth? (pause) Something of June.

      Chris: Thirtieth.

      Norrine: A Sunday.

      Chris: Sunday.

      Norrine: Mmh.

      Chris: Why? (= *Why do you ask when the barbecue is*)

      Norrine: Becau Because I forgot (pause) That was the day I was thinking of having a proper lunch party but I won't do it if you're going out. (BNC)

The ability to generate and understand such CRs requires correspondingly increasing complexity: from *repetition* (which can be done by very simple systems) to *intention recognition*, which requires a signi cantly complex processing architecture. Accordingly, we distinguish:

(CR1) Repetition CR benchmark: accommodate **repetition** CRs.
(CR2) Con rmation CR benchmark: accommodate **confirmation** CRs.
(CR3) Intended content CR benchmark: accommodate **intended content** CRs.
(CR4) Intention recognition CR benchmark: accommodate **intention recognition** CRs.

To conclude our discussion of MCI, let us note some higher-level benchmarks. The rst is a semantic *non-determinism*, given the fact that an utterance can give rise to distinct updates across participants (grounding in one, CRi cation in the other):

(SND) Semantic non-determinism benchmark: interpretation can lead to distinct updates across conversational participants.

MCI dictates the need for ne-grained utterance representations, given: the emergence of utterance-related presuppositions in the aftermath of grounding (18a, 18b); the hyperintensional nature of CRi cation conditions (18c, 18d) – 'lawyer' and 'attorney' are synonymous terms but give rise to distinct CRi cation conditions; and the existence of syntactic and phonological parallelism conditions on certain CR interpretations (18e, 18f):

(18) a. A: Banach was born in odz. B: It's interesting that the last word you uttered has a letter not on my keyboard.
      b. And even rain won't save you this time, Bruce, because you need to win one of the remaining matches. Sorry guys I mentioned 'win' there, you Poms might need to look that word up. (*The Guardian*, test match over by over coverage, August 25, 2005).
      c. Ariadne: Jo is a lawyer. Bora: A lawyer?/What do you mean a lawyer?/#What do you mean an advocate?/#What do you mean an attorney?
      d. Ariadne: Jo is an advocate. Bora: #What do you mean a lawyer?/An advocate?/What do you mean an advocate?/#What do you mean an attorney?
      e. A: Did Bo leave? B: Max? (cannot mean: intended content reading: **Who are you referring to?** or **Who do you mean?**)
      f. A: Did he adore the book? B: adore? / #adored?

Hence,

(FG) Fine-grained utterance representation benchmark: provide ne-grained utterance representation to accommodate syntactic and phonological parallelism conditions.

2.2 Fragment understanding

We distinguish between two classes of non-sentential utterances: sentential fragments and dis uencies.

2.2.1 Sentential fragments Sentential fragments (SFs) are intuitively complete utterances that lack a verbal (more generally predicative) constituent. SFs include 'short answers,' and reprise utterances used to acknowledge or request clari cation of prior utterances. Examples of these are provided in boldface in (19):

(19) A: Wasn't he refused the chair in Oxford?
  B: **Who?**
  A: **Skeat**. Wasn't he refused
  B: That's Meak.
  A: **Oh Meak, yes.** (London-Lund S.1.9, p. 245)

Estimates of the frequency of SFs are somewhat variable, depending on the classi cational criteria applied. De Weijer (2001) provides gures of 40 percent, 31 percent, and 30 percent, respectively, for the percentage of *one-word utterances* in the speech exchanged between adults and infant, adult and toddler, and among adults in a single Dutch speaking family consisting of two adults, one toddler and one baby across two months. Fernández (2006) cites a gure of 9 percent for the percentage of utterances lacking a verbal predicate, based on random sampling from (by and large) adult speech in the BNC, a gure that is replicated in other corpus studies she surveys.

There exist a number of recent corpus studies whose taxonomies achieve high coverage. These include Fernández and Ginzburg (2002) and Schlangen (2003). The taxonomy of Fernández and Ginzburg (2002) and the distribution it uncovers for the BNC is illustrated in Table 1.

The task of identifying the right SF class can be successfully learned using supervised machine learning techniques (Schlangen 2005; Fernández et al., 2007). Resolving SF content in context is a more challenging task. Of course the most general benchmark is to achieve comprehensive coverage, relative to a taxonomy such as the above. We can offer some partial benchmarks (as in (SF2) and (SF3)), motivated primarily by frequency: basic answers are crucial in interaction, as re ected in their majoritarian status, similarly with acknowledgments. The reprise fragment benchmark is more challenging: such fragments constitute a very high proportion of CRs, but are frequently ambiguous between uses that have a *confirmation* content and ones that have an *intended* content (see, e.g., (15a) and (16b) above):

(SF1) Sentential fragment benchmark1: achieve SF wide coverage.
(SF2) Basic answer resolution benchmark: accommodate short answers, af rma-
    tive answers, and rejection.

Table 16.1 NSUs in a subcorpus of the BNC

Sentential fragment classes	Example	Total
Plain acknowledgment	*A: ... B: mmh*	599
Short answer	*A: Who left? B: Bo*	188
Affirmative answer	*A: Did Bo leave? B: Yes*	105
Repeated acknowledgment	*A: Did Bo leave? B: Bo, hmm.*	86
Reprise fragment	*A: Did Bo leave? B: Bo?*	79
Rejection	*A: Did Bo leave? B: No.*	49
Factive modifier	*A: Bo left. B: Great!*	27
Repeated affirmative answer	*A: Did Bo leave? B: Bo, yes.*	26
Helpful rejection	*A: Did Bo leave? B: No, Max.*	24
Sluice	*A: Someone left. B: Who?*	24
Check question	*A: Bo isn't here. Okay?*	22
Filler	*A: Did Bo ... B: leave?*	18
Bare modifier phrase	*A: Max left. B: Yesterday.*	15
Propositional modifier	*A: Did Bo leave? B: Maybe.*	11
Conjunction + fragment	*A: Bo left. B: And Max.*	10
Total data set		**1,283**

(SF3) Reprise fragment resolution benchmark: accommodate reprise fragments, and recognize the potential for ambiguity they exhibit.

SFs are often adjacent to their source. But not always, as illustrated starkly by our initial motivating example (1), repeated here as (10), in which short answers (7) and (9) refer back to the query (1). Data from the BNC (Ginzburg & Fernández 2005) suggests that this is primarily a feature of short answers in multilogue, though not uncommon in two-person dialogue:

(20) John: (1) Okay which one do you think it is?
              (2) Try F1 F1 again and we'll get
      Sarah: (3) Shift and F1?
      Sue: (4) It's, (5) no.
      John: (6) No, (7) just F1 F1.
      Sue: (8) It isn't that.
      John: (9) F1. (10) Right, (11) and that tells us
      Sue: (12) It's shift F7.

(SF4) Distance benchmark: accommodate long-distance short answers.

The final benchmark for SFs concerns their appearance as initiating moves (i.e., without a prior linguistic antecedent or segment initially). These seem to require a rather stereotypical interactional setting (buying tickets at a train station, querying for directions in a taxi, etc.). Although such uses do not seem to have been recorded in recent corpus studies, they are clearly not marginal and should be accommodated:

(21)   Buying a train ticket:
   a.   Client: A return to Newcastle please. (=I want a return ... , please give me a return ..., ...)
   b.   Driver to passenger in a taxi: Where to?

(SF5) Initiating genre-sensitive SF benchmark: accommodate genre-sensitive initiating SFs.

2.2.2 Disfluencies Dis uencies are common in conversation: in the Trains corpus, for instance, 23 percent of speaker turns contain at least one repair, and 54 percent of turns with at least 10 words contain a repair (Heeman and Allen 1999). In this area there has been important early work by psycholinguists, most notably Levelt (see e.g., Levelt 1983), much recent work by speech researchers (e.g., Shriberg 1994) and corpus-based taxonomies (e.g., Besser & Alexandersson 2007).

In terms of bare functionality, it is clear that a fundamental benchmark is the ability to be unfazed by dis uencies. In other words, to be able to recognize a dis-uency and to effect the appropriate 'repair,' resulting in a 'cleaned up' utterance, as exempli ed in (22):

(22)   I was *one of the*, I was responsible for all the planning and engineering. $\mapsto$ I was responsible for all the planning and engineering

(D1) Dis uency benchmark1: Recognize and repair dis uencies.

Such an approach using machine learning techniques is demonstrated by Heeman and Allen (1999: 534), who suggest: "We propose that these tasks [including detecting and correcting speech repairs] can be done using local context and early in the processing stream."

Recently, evidence from psycholinguistics has begun emerging that self-corrected material has a long-term processing effect (Brennan & Schober 2001; Lau & Ferreira 2005), hence is not being 'edited away.' It can also bring about linguistic effects in whose interpretation it plays a signi cant role, for instance anaphora, as in (23a) from Heeman and Allen (1999). In fact, dis uencies yield information: (23a) entails (23b) and defeasibly (23c), which in certain settings (e.g., legal), given suf cient data, can be useful. Moreover, incorporating them in systems' output can improve naturalness (e.g., when speech processing is slow) and improve the user's empathy with the system. Given this, we formulate our second dis uency benchmark:

(23) a.   Andy: Peter was, well he was   red.
      b.   Andy was unsure about what he should say, after uttering 'was.'
      c.   Andy was unsure about how to describe what happened to Peter.

(D2) Dis uency benchmark2: explicate dis uency meaning without eliminating dis uencies from context.

3 Approaches to Dialogue System Design

Before presenting a formal framework that is able to account for the various dialogue phenomena described earlier, in this section we brie y describe several important approaches to the design of dialogue systems and evaluate them informally with respect to the benchmarks we have introduced in the previous section. We end with a short description of the information state approach to dialogue management, closest in spirit to the theory of interaction that we will present in Section 4.

3.1 Basic architecture of dialogue systems

Besides their commercial potential, dialogue systems are also an asset for the dialogue theorist since designing a conversational agent that can communicate naturally with a human can help in the evaluation of theories of dialogue. Of course, for practical reasons researchers do not usually create systems that can talk just about anything. Instead they design systems that are competent only in particular domains and can handle particular tasks – they are task-oriented, domain-dependent conversational systems. This is especially true of commercial systems, which tend to be simpler and less advanced than research prototypes. Applications that involve information retrieval tasks are very common, especially those related to travel planning and management. Other common applications are educational tutoring systems, device management (of in-car or in-home devices), and collaborative problem solving.

To a large extent, the complexity of a system will depend on its application. Most spoken dialogue systems, however, contain the following components: an automatic speech recognizer (ASR) that captures the user's input and converts it to a sequence of words; a natural language understanding (NLU) component that produces a meaningful representation of the input utterance; a dialogue manager (DM) that controls the dialogue ow by integrating the user contributions and deciding what to say next; a source of domain and task knowledge (KB); a natural language generation (NLG) component that chooses the words to express the response together with their prosody; and a text-to-speech (TTS) synthesis engine that outputs a spoken form of the response. Figure 16.1 shows the basic architecture of a spoken dialogue system. Similar diagrams and much more detailed explanations of the different components can be found in, e.g., McTear (2004); Delgado and Araki (2005); Jurafsky and Martin (2009).

The DM component is often considered the core of a dialogue system. It receives a representation of the input utterance from the NLU module, keeps track of some sort of dialogue state, interfaces with the external knowledge sources, and decides

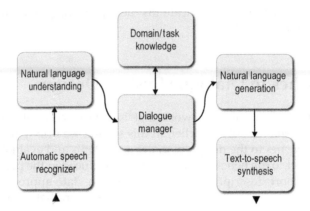

Figure 16.1   Basic components of a spoken dialogue system.

what should be passed to the NLG module. In the remainder of this section, we discuss three main types of dialogue management architectures: nite state DMs, frame-based DMs, and inference-based DMs. We   nish with a sketch of the information state update approach to dialogue management.

3.2   *Paradigmatic approaches to dialogue management*

3.2.1   Finite state dialogue management   The simplest dialogue managers represent the structure of the dialogue as a   nite state transition network. Figure 16.2 shows a basic   nite state DM for a ticket booking application. We can see that the states in the network are atomic and correspond to system contributions, while the transitions between states correspond to system actions dependent on the user responses. The set of possible paths along the graph represents the set of legal dialogues.

Finite state DM architectures give rise to conversational agents that fully control the dialogue. The system has the initiative at all times: it utters a series of prompts in a predetermined order, interpreting anything the user says as a direct response to the latest prompt. Any (part of a) user utterance that cannot be interpreted as directly addressing the latest prompt is either ignored or misrecognized. Restricting what the user can say to the latest prompt is often seen as an *advantage* of   nite state architectures by the dialogue system's engineer, as this allows one to simplify the ASR and NLU components of the system. Indeed,   nite state systems tend to use extremely simple understanding components, often limited to language models associated with particular dialogue states and tuned to recognize typical responses to a given prompt (such as city names or dates).

There are a few toolkits that allow fast development of   nite state systems, such as the Nuance Dialog Builder or the CSLU toolkit (McTear 1998). For a general overview of FSM-based systems see McTear (2004).

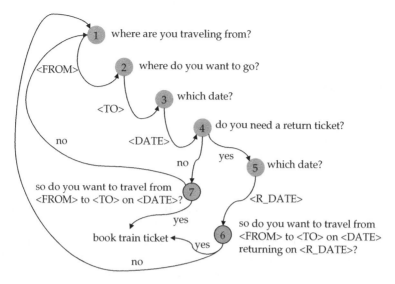

where are you traveling from?

where do you want to go?

which date?

do you need a return ticket?

which date?

<R_DATE>

so do you want to travel from
<FROM> to <TO> on <DATE>
returning on <R_DATE>?

so do you want to travel from
<FROM> to <TO> on <DATE>?

book train ticket

Figure 16.2   Finite state machine for a simple ticket booking application.

slot	value	prompt
ORIGIN	unknown	From which city are you leaving?
DESTINATION	unknown	Where are you traveling to?
DATE	unknown	When do you want to travel?

Figure 16.3   A simple frame.

3.2.2   Frame-based dialogue management   Frame-based DM offers some advantages over nite state systems. Although the system's prompts and the range of user contributions that can be handled still need to be determined at design time, frame-based DM allows for more exibility at the level of the dialogue ow. In frame-based DM, the dialogue states that the system keeps track of – so-called *frames* – have a richer internal structure than the atomic nodes of nite state transition networks. A frame typically consists of a series of slots, values and prompts, as exempli ed in Figure 16.3, where each slot corresponds to some bit of information the system needs to get from the user. Again, frame-based systems are especially well-suited for information tasks, where the system needs to nd out some information from the user in order to execute some task (such as booking a ticket or retrieving some information from a database).

In nite state DM the system's contributions are determined by the transition function of the FS network. In contrast, a frame-based dialogue manager includes a control algorithm that determines what to say next given the contents of the frame. The control algorithm keeps track of the slots lled so far and makes sure that lled slots are not revisited. The slots in the frame can be lled in any order

BOOK(*S, U, T*)
Constraints: *System*(*S*) ∧ *User*(*U*) ∧ *Ticket*(*T*)
Goal: *Booked*(*S, U, T*)
Preconditions: *Knows*(*S, Origin*(*T*)) ∧ *Knows*(*S, Dest*(*T*)) ∧ ...
Effects: *Booked*(*S, U, T*)
INFO_REQUEST(*A, B, P*)
Constraints: *Speaker*(*A*) ∧ *Addressee*(*B*) ∧ *Prop*(*P*)
Goal: *Know*(*A, P*)
Preconditions: ¬*Know*(*A, P*) ∧ *Desire*(*A, Know*(*A, P*)) ∧ *Believe*(*A, Know*(*B, P*)) ∧ ...
Effects: *Believe*(*B, Desires*(*A, Know*(*A, P*)))

Figure 16.4   Goal-oriented action schema.

and a single user's response can ll in more than one slot. The control algorithm speci es which frame con gurations need to be true for a particular prompt to be relevant. This speci cation can be as general as selecting the rst prompt in the frame which has an unknown value, or more speci c in the form of conditions such as 'If ORIGIN is filled and DESTINATION is unknown, utter DESTINATION prompt, else utter ORIGIN prompt.'

Thus, although the range of possible contributions is xed in advance, in contrast to FS systems, the dialogue ow is not completely predetermined at design time but driven by interaction. This increased exibility in turn requires more complex language models that can deal with multi-slot lling responses.

For a description of some systems that use a frame-based architecture see Aust et al. (1995), Constantinides et al. (1998), or Seneff and Polifroni (2000).

3.2.3   Inference-based dialogue management   Inference-based DM differs substantially from DM based on frames or nite state networks. In this approach, which combines planning techniques used in AI with ideas from speech act theory (Austin 1962; Searle 1969), dialogue management is considered a planning task driven forward by a *rational agent* (the dialogue system), whose behavior is determined by inference mechanisms. The approach, developed at the University of Toronto by Perrault and his collaborators (Cohen & Perrault 1979; Allen & Perrault 1980), models rational agents in terms of beliefs, desires, and intentions (BDI). The latter are formalized as predicates or modal operators in some version of rst-order (modal) logic. Agents are also equipped with a set of general rationality axioms and a set of plans and goals, plus a component for automatic plan-based reasoning such as a theorem prover.

Dialogue moves are seen as instances of goal-oriented rational actions, all of which are formalized as plans for goal achievement. A common way of formalizing plans is by means of action schemata. These can take different forms, but minimally distinguish between the preconditions required for an action to take place and its effects. Figure 16.4 shows a couple of examples of possible plans to book a ight and to request some information.

Dialogue managers based on the BDI model of rational agents typically keep track of a repository of shared beliefs or *common ground*, the goal motivating the current dialogue contribution, and information on the status of problem solving (e.g., on whether the preconditions of the current plan are met and its goal has been achieved). Deciding what the system should say next consists in advancing a step in the current plan. For instance, a system that is following a plan to book a ight for the user may decide to utter an INFO_REQUEST move with the goal of satisfying some preconditions of the booking plan, such as knowing the origin and the destination of the trip.

As mentioned earlier, plans are complemented by a set of general rationality axioms. These typically include cooperative axioms stating that agents adopt the intentions of their interlocutors (as long as they do not contradict their own). Also note that, as exempli ed by the Effects of the INFO_REQUEST action scheme in Figure 16.4, interpreting an utterance amounts to infering the plan-based intentions of the speaker.

Inference-based systems are intended for advanced tasks such as collaborative problem solving. This requires NLU components that are fairly sophisticated since the range of possible user utterances is much less constrained than in purely informational tasks. The TRAINS/TRIPS integrated dialogue system (Allen et al., 1995; Ferguson & Allen 1998) is one of the most in uential systems implementing this approach, but see also Sadek and de Mori (1998). The last chapter of Allen (1995) provides a good overview of inference-based DM.

3.3 *Comparison of dialogue management approaches*

In this section we look at how well standard versions of nite state-based, frame-based, and inference-based approaches to dialogue management can deal with the benchmarks introduced in Section 2. A summary is shown in Table 16.2.

3.3.1 Query and assertion benchmarks As we mentioned earlier, queries and assertions are the commonest move types in interaction with dialogue systems. All DM approaches we have seen can accommodate direct simple answers to queries and hence meet benchmark Q1. However, accounting for the other query benchmarks is more problematic. The ability to satisfy benchmarks Q2a and Q2b (accommodation of non-resolving answers and follow-up queries to them) in part depends on the sophistication of the NLU and KB components: to interpret a contribution as a non-resolving answer, the system needs to be able to reason over some sort of ontology with subtyping (in order to gure out, e.g., that 'Germany' may count as an answer to a destination prompt but is probably not speci c enough). This capability is standard in inference-based systems, while it is very unlikely to be present in a pure nite-state system, since the main advantage of this approach is the simpli cation of components by restricting possible user input. Assuming the capability to recognizing non-resolving answers was available, in a nite-state DM sub-queries to such answers could in principle be integrated as additional states. In a frame-based DM, non-resolving answers could be integrated by including a non-resolving value type that would trigger follow-up queries relative to each kind of slot. Within the plan-based approach of inference-based DM, an answer is considered 'resolving' if it full lls the relevant goals in the plan that motivated the question. Goals that are not fully satis ed motivate follow-up queries (*U: I need to travel some time in August. S: And what day in August did you want to travel?*).

Accommodating overinformative answers (benchmark Q3) poses practical problems for nite state systems. They could in principle be integrated as additional states (e.g., an extra state for answers that include information about both the destination and the origin, another one for those that include destination and date, and so forth), but only as long as they can be predicted at design time. Note, however, that even if they could be predicted, including them into the nite state network would easily lead to an explosion of the number of states, which would produce a rather cumbersome structure. Frame-based DMs are better equipped to deal with overinformative answers since multiple slots can be lled in by a single user response. Thus, if the overinformative answer contains information that directly addresses existing slots, this can be utilized to drive the task forward. In inference-based systems, overinformative answers are seen as a product of domain plan recognition: they are treated as cooperative responses that help achieve the recognized plan of the interlocutor by providing information that is required to achieve the current goal (e.g., the exchange *U: When is the train leaving? S: At 5:04, platform 12* can be explained by the ability of the system to recognize the user's plan to take the train).

Benchmarks Q4 and Q5 (accommodation of subqueries and accommodation of topic-changing responses) are highly problematic for nite state and frame-based DMs. Subqueries can be handled only to the extent that they can be predicted in advance and, as with Q3, this could lead to tractability problems. There are no means for these structured approaches to interpret an irrelevant response as a change of topic. An inference-based system would do slightly better. Regarding subqueries, it would only be able to accommodate those that are goal related (such as *U: How much is a ticket to Hamburg? S: When do you want to travel?*). A response that does not match any step in the current plan could potentially be interpreted as topic changing. However, the system would not be able to distinguish this kind of 'irrelevance' from situations where the mismatch requires clari cation.

We move now to the assertion benchmarks A1 and A2 (integration of propositional content and accommodation of disagreement respectively). None of them is satis ed by nite state systems. Benchmark A1 is not satis ed because in a nite state architecture states do not have any internal structure and therefore there is no propositional or contextual update beyond the information that emanates from the current position in the graph. This also rules out the possibility of accounting for disagreement since there is no propositional content which the agent can disagree about. Frame-based DMs make use of some limited form of contextual update since the control algorithm keeps track of the slots lled so far, but their simple architecture cannot accommodate disagreements. Certainly, inference-based systems satisfy A1 (one of the effects of asserting a propostion P is that P becomes common knowledge or common belief). As for A2, they can accommodate con icting beliefs and hence some form of diagreement. However, accounting for disagreement in the sense of non-cooperativity is more problematic since the BDI model is basically designed for cooperative tasks without con icting goals.

The nal two benchmarks within this section deal with scalability to monologue and multilogue (SC) and domain adaptability (DA). None of the approaches we have discussed satis es SC – they are all designed for two-agent dialogue. Finite state and frame-based DMs are strongly domain-dependent (except perhaps in their meta-communicative behavior, which we discuss below). In contrast, the BDI model underlying inference-based DMs aims to be a domain-independent theory of rational action. Although it is unclear to what extent procedures employed in actual inference-based systems can effectively be reused, in principle general rationality axioms should be valid across domains.

3.3.2 Meta-communication benchmarks Given the high number of recognition problems that dialogue systems face due to the poor performance of ASRs, meta-communicative interaction plays an important role in such implemented systems. Finite state and frame-based architectures usually take a generative perspective, where meta-communicative behavior comes from the system. This is not surprising since these approaches are highly system-initiating in design. Inference-based systems, on the other hand, have also addressed the problem of interpreting meta-communicative utterances.

The meta-communicative potential of nite state and frame-based systems in rather similar. What in nite state systems can be achieved by multiplying the number of states and transitions, in frame-based systems can be implemented by adding extra types of slot values and increasing the complexity of the control algorithm. Finite state systems usually include states to handle situations when there is no input or no recognition, as well as when there is a need to con rm information provided by the user (as in states 7 and 8 of the transition network in Figure 16.2). Acknowledgments of completed contributions (benchmark A1) can similarly be integrated as additional states. In a frame-based architecture, slot values (such as no-match) and/or con dence scores associated with lled values can be used to decide whether a contribution can be acknowledged or whether there is need to ask for repetition or con rmation. Thus, at least from a generation perspective, nite state and frame-based DMs meet benchmarks A1, CR1 (repetition CRs), and CR2 (con rmation CRs). However, more complex types of CRs such as those that query the intended content or the intention of a prior utterance (benchmarks CR3 and CR4) cannot be accommodated by these systems.

Satisfying benchmark A2 (accommodation of continuation acknowledgments) would require an incremental architecture not present in any of the systems we have discussed, where transitions to a different state are triggered by full utterances or moves. Gestural acknowledgments (benchmark A3) could in principle be integrated provided that the system is able to process multi-modal input and that the gestural acknowledgments acknowledge complete contributions.

Traditionally, inference-based DM has not been too concerned with meta-communication, focusing instead on plan recognition and cooperativity at the task domain. Simple grounding and clari cation behavior such as acknowledgments and repetition/con rmation CRs can in principle be accommodated in a way akin to the strategies we have already discussed (e.g., by using con dence scores or evaluating the output of the NLU component, which is more sophisticated in these systems). To account for other kinds of clari cation subdialogues, a hierarchical plan structure that incorporates discourse plans – or *metaplans* in the terminology of Litman and Allen (1984) – has been proposed. The idea is that metaplans are performed to obtain knowledge necessary to perform task plans and are inferred when an utterance cannot be interpreted as a step in the current domain plan. For instance, in the dialogue *S: At 5:04, platform 12. U: Where is it?*, the system would interpret the user's question as a metaplan to nd additional information to perform the task plan (presumably taking a train). Thus, in this approach CRs that go beyond asking for repetition or con rmation are only possible inasmuch as they are ultimately related to task plans.

The last two benchmarks related to meta-communication are SND (possibility of different updates across participants, or *semantic non-determinism*) and FG (ne-grained representations). The latter is not satis ed by any of the DM approaches we have considered: dialogue managers across the board get as input some sort of semantic representation. Operating on syntactic and phonological representations would be extremely complicated, if at all possible, in nite state or frame-based architectures. Inference-based systems could in principle include rich utterance representations (by using a parser that generates the desired output), but it is unclear how a plan-based approach would deal with them. SND is not satis ed either, at least explicitly. To some extent, any state that leads to a repetition CR implicitly assumes that there is an asymmetry between the user-intended utterance and the system's interpretation of it (or lack thereof). But this is not explicitly modeled.

3.3.3   Fragment understanding benchmarks   We now turn to the last set of benchmarks, which are related to fragment understanding. Since these benchmarks are directly concerned with how meaning is assigned to fragmentary utterances, they are more tightly linked to the NL modules than the move-related benchmarks (although, as we shall see in Section 4, their resolution requires a fair amount of interaction between the linguistic modules and the dialogue manager, which is the module that represents context).

While dialogue systems do not achieve comprehensive coverage of the corpus-based taxonomies of sentential fragments we mentioned in Section 2.2 (as required by benchmark SF1), they are typically able to accommodate basic fragmentary answers (benchmark SF2). For instance, a state-dependent language model can process short answers, af rmative answers and rejections, which, as long as they are direct simple answers, could be correctly interpreted by a nite state DM. We have seen examples of this in Figure 16.2. Similar techniques can be used in frame-based systems where, as mentioned earlier, language models tend to be more complex given the possibility of multi-slot lling.

Genre-sensitive initiating SFs (benchmark SF5) cannot be accommodated by a nite-state DM since the system has the initiative at all times. They can, however, be processed by frame-based systems, where the frame can be seen as encoding the relevant genre. For instance, if a user starts a dialogue with the utterance *To Hamburg, on Tuesday*, a frame-based DM for the travel domain with an appropriate language model could ll in the destination and date slots. However, long-distance short answers (benchmark SF4) cannot easily be accommodated by nite state or frame-based DMs.

In inference-based systems the interpretation of basic types of fragments (both responsive and initiating) is achieved by inferring the domain-dependent goals of the speaker (see e.g., Carberry 1990). However, it is not at all clear how long-distance short answers could be accommodated in this approach.

Given our discussion of the meta-communication benchmarks above, reprise fragments (benchmark SF3) cannot be successfully accommodated by any of the considered DM approaches.

Finally, we come to the dis uency benchmarks. The ability to recognize and repair dis uencies (benchmark D1) depends on the ASR/NLU components of a system. For instance, statistical language models tend to be rather robust for dis-uencies. A robust parser can then be applied to their output to extract the relevant information (relative to the latest system prompt, to any slot in a frame, or to the current domain plan). This sort of setting is more common in frame- and inference-based systems than in nite state ones, but in theory these processing components could be combined with any kind of dialogue manager. In contrast, D2 (accommodation of dis uency meaning without elimination of dis uencies from context) is a much more challenging benchmark that is not met by current systems.

Table 16.2 summarizes the comparison of the three approaches to dialogue management we have reviewed with respect to the benchmarks introduced in Section 2. For each dialogue management approach (nite state, frames, and inference-based), the symbol ✓ indicates that the approach sa s es the benchmark in the corresponding row; ~ that the benchmark could be met with some caveats, as explained in the text above; and — that the benchmark is not met by a standard version of the approach.

3.4 *The information state update framework*

To conclude this section, we shall brie y introduce the main ideas of the information state update (ISU) framework. The approach was developed during the European TRINDI project (TRINDI Consortium 2000) as a general framework to implement different kinds of dialogue management models. According to Traum and Larsson (2003), the components of an ISU model are the following:

- a formal representation of the information state (IS) and its components;
- a set of dialogue moves that trigger IS updates;

Table 16.2   Comparison of dialogue management approaches

Benchmarks	FSMs	Frames	Inference
Query and assertion			
Q1 simple answers	✓	✓	✓
Q2a non-resolving answers	~	✓	✓
Q2b follow-up queries	~	✓	✓
Q3 overinformative answers	~	✓	✓
Q4 subquestions	—	—	~
Q5 topic changing	—	—	—
A1 propositional content update	—	~	✓
A2 disagreement	—	—	~
SC scalability	—	—	—
DA domain adaptability	—	—	~
Meta-communication			
Ack1 completed acknowledgments	✓	✓	✓
Ack2 continuation acknowledgments	—	—	—
Ack3 gestural acknowledgments	~	~	~
CR1 repetition CRs	✓	✓	✓
CR2 con rmation CRs	✓	✓	✓
CR3 intended content CRs	—	—	—
CR4 intention recognition CRs	—	—	~
SND distinct updates	—	—	—
FG ne-grained representations	—	—	—
Fragments			
SF1 wide coverage of SFs	—	—	—
SF2 basic answer resolution	✓	✓	✓
SF3 reprise fragment resolution	—	—	—
SF4 long-distance short answers	—	—	—
SF5 genre-sensitive initiating SFs	—	✓	✓
D1 recognize and repair dis uencies	✓	✓	✓
D2 keep dis uencies in context	—	—	—

- a set of update and selection rules that govern how moves change the IS and how changes license future moves;
- an update strategy for deciding which rules to apply when.

Regardless of the particular model implemented within the framework, what makes the ISU approach attractive is the declarative way in which dialogue states and transitions between states are formulated. In fact, the approach can be seen as an extension of the frame-based architecture, where states can have a much more complex structure than slot-value frames and the procedural rules of the control algorithm are formulated as more general and declarative update and selection rules.

There are some toolkits to implement ISU-based dialogue managers and system architectures, most notably the TrindiKit (Larsson & Traum 2000) and DIPPER (Bos et al., 2003).[5] GODIS (Larsson et al., 2000) and EDIS (Matheson et al., 2000) are some of the systems implemented using this framework. In the next section we present a theory of dialogue interaction which is ISU-based in spirit.

4 Interaction and Meaning

In this section we sketch a comprehensive theory of interaction and meaning, indicating how it can be used to ful ll the various benchmarks we speci ed in earlier sections. This theory is based on the framework KoS (Ginzburg 1994; 1996; Larsson 2002; Ginzburg & Cooper 2004; Fernández 2006; Purver 2006; Ginzburg 2010). The latter reference contains a detailed exposition of the theory sketched below. Other comprehensive accounts of a theory of dialogue include work in the PTT framework[6] (e.g., Poesio & Traum 1997; 1998; Matheson et al., 2000; Poesio & Rieser 2009) and work within segmented discourse representation theory (SDRT) (e.g., Asher & Lascarides 2003; 2008).

In abstract terms, the model we present here revolves around the information states dialogue participants possess and how these get modi ed as a consequence of utterances and related interactions. Our exposition proceeds in a number of stages. First, we explicate the proposed structure of information states. We then illustrate how illocutionary interaction can be analyzed – the updates on the information states will be triggered entirely by dialogue *moves*. We then consider domain speci city and how it can be incorporated into this picture – this will involve a minor re nement of the information states. Our nal re nement will involve the integration of illocutionary and meta-communicative interaction: this will have two main consequences. Updates will be triggered by utterances – data structures involving parallel representation of phonological, syntactic, semantic, and contextual information – and the information states will be re ned slightly to take into account the potential for partial understanding.

Before we enter into all this, however, we introduce brie y the logical formalism in which KoS is formulated, type theory with records.

4.1 Type theory with records: the basics

As the underlying logical framework, we use type theory with records (TTR) (Cooper 2006), a model-theoretic descendant of Martin–Löf type theory (Ranta 1994). This provides a formalism with which to build a semantic ontology, and to write conversational and grammar rules. After introducing TTR, we will explain why we use TTR rather than typed feature structure-based formalisms (see Chapter 15, COMPUTATIONAL SEMANTICS, and, e.g., Carpenter 1992; Penn

2000), whose notation is quite similar and which have been used in much work in computational linguistics.

The most fundamental notion of TTR is the typing *judgment a : T* classifying an object *a* as being of type *T*. A record is a partially ordered set of elds of the form (24) – each assignment to a eld constituting a component of the tuple. Crucially, each successive eld can depend on the values of the preceding elds:

(24) a. $$\begin{bmatrix} l_i = k_i \\ l_{i+1} = k_{i+1} \dots \\ l_{i+j} = k_{i+j} \end{bmatrix}$$

   b. $$\begin{bmatrix} x = a \\ y = b \\ prf = p \end{bmatrix}$$

A record type is simply a partially ordered set of the form (25), where again each successive type can depend on its predecessor types within the record:

(25) $$\begin{bmatrix} l_i : T_i \\ l_{i+1} : T_{i+1} \dots \\ l_{i+j} : T_{i+j} \end{bmatrix}$$

Cooper (2006) proposes that situations and events be modeled as records. Situation and event types are then directly accommodated as record types. The type of a situation with a woman riding a bicycle would then be the one in (26a). A record of this type (a *witness* for this type) would be as in (26b), where the required corresponding typing judgments are given in (26c):

(26) a. $$\begin{bmatrix} x: \text{IND} \\ c1: \text{woman}(x) \\ y: \text{IND} \\ c2: \text{bicycle}(y) \\ time : \text{TIME} \\ loc:\text{LOC} \\ c3: \text{ride}(x,y,time,loc) \end{bmatrix}$$ b. $$\begin{bmatrix} \dots \\ x = a \\ c1 = p1 \\ y = b \\ c2 = p2 \\ time = t0 \\ loc = l0 \\ c3 = p3 \\ \dots \end{bmatrix}$$

   c. $a : \text{IND}; p1 : \text{woman}(a); b : \text{IND}; p2 : \text{bicycle}(b); t0 : \text{TIME}; l0 : \text{LOC}; p3 : \text{ride}(a,b,t0,l0)$

TTR offers a straightforward way for us to model propositions and questions using records, record types, and functions. A proposition is a record of the form in

(27a). The type of propositions is the record type (27b) and truth can be de ned as in (27c):

(27) a. $\begin{bmatrix} \text{sit} = r_0 \\ \text{sit-type} = T_0 \end{bmatrix}$

b. $\begin{bmatrix} \text{sit : Record} \\ \text{sit-type : RecType} \end{bmatrix}$

c. A proposition $\begin{bmatrix} \text{sit} = r_0 \\ \text{sit-type} = T_0 \end{bmatrix}$ is true iff $r_0 : T_0$

A question can be identi ed as a propositional abstract, which in TTR amounts to being a function from records into propositions:

(28) a. who ran

b. TTR representation $- (r : \begin{bmatrix} x : \text{Ind} \\ \text{rest} : \text{person(x)} \end{bmatrix}) \begin{bmatrix} \text{sit} = r_1 \\ \text{sit-type} = \begin{bmatrix} c : \text{run(r.x)} \end{bmatrix} \end{bmatrix}$

That is, a function that maps records $r : T_{who} = \begin{bmatrix} x : \text{Ind} \\ \text{rest} : \text{person(x)} \end{bmatrix}$ into

propositions of the form $\begin{bmatrix} \text{sit} = r_1 \\ \text{sit-type} = \begin{bmatrix} c : \text{run(r.x)} \end{bmatrix} \end{bmatrix}$

To explain the motivation for adopting TTR over a typed feature structure-based approach, we illustrate the difference in the respective treatment of utterance representation. In TTR, utterance events, like other events, are a kind of record, whereas lexical entries and phrasal rules are explicated as record types. One could, for instance, posit the sound/syntax/meaning constraint in (29a) as a rule of English. For a speech event $se0$, (29b), to be classi ed as being of this type, the requirements in (29c) will need to be met:[7]

(29) a. $\begin{bmatrix} \text{PHON : who did jo leave} \\ \text{CAT} = \text{V[+ n] : syncat} \\ \text{C-PARAMS} : \begin{bmatrix} \text{s0: SIT} \\ \text{t0: TIME} \\ \text{j: IND} \\ \text{c3: Named(j,jo)} \end{bmatrix} \\ \text{cont} = (r : \begin{bmatrix} x : \text{Ind} \\ \text{rest} : \text{person(x)} \end{bmatrix}) \begin{bmatrix} \text{sit} = \text{s0} \\ \text{sit-type} = \text{Leave(j,r.x,t0)} \end{bmatrix} : \text{Questn} \end{bmatrix}$

b.
$$
\begin{bmatrix}
\text{PHON} = \text{hu di jow live} \\
\text{CAT} = \text{V}[+\ n] \\
\text{C-PARAMS} = \begin{bmatrix} s0 = sit0 \\ t0 = time0 \\ j = j0 \\ c3 = c30 \end{bmatrix} \\
\text{cont} = (r : \begin{bmatrix} x : \text{Ind} \\ rest : person(x) \end{bmatrix}) \begin{bmatrix} sit = s0 \\ sit\text{-}type = Leave(j,r.x,t0) \end{bmatrix}
\end{bmatrix}
$$

c.   hu di jow liv : who did jo leave;
sit0 : SIT, time0 : TIME, j0 : IND, c30 : Named(j0,jo)
$$
cont0 = (r : \begin{bmatrix} x : \text{Ind} \\ rest : person(x) \end{bmatrix}) \begin{bmatrix} sit = sit0 \\ sit\text{-}type = Leave(j0,time0) \end{bmatrix} : \text{Questn}
$$

Speci cally: a witness for the type (29a) includes a phonetic token, contextual parameters – a situation, a time, an individual named Jo – and the question entity $(r : \begin{bmatrix} x : \text{Ind} \\ rest : person(x) \end{bmatrix}) \begin{bmatrix} sit = sit0 \\ sit\text{-}type = Leave(j0,r.x,time0) \end{bmatrix}$, a function from records into propositions. Thus, the fact that C-PARAMS represents the type of entities needed to instantiate a meaning is a direct consequence of what it means to be a witness of this type. In addition, the values of the CONT eld *are* already the semantic entities. Hence, to take one example, the function in (30a) is of the type in (30b), which is a supertype of the type in (30c). This latter is the type of a question such as (30d). These type assignments enable us to explain the fact that (30c) is intuitively a sub-question of (30a) and to de ne various notions of answerhood (see, e.g., Ginzburg 2005):

(30)   a. $r : T_{who} \mapsto \begin{bmatrix} sit & = r_1 \\ sit\text{-}type = c: leave(r.x,t) \end{bmatrix}$

b. $(T_{who} (= \begin{bmatrix} x & : \text{Ind} \\ rest : person(x) \end{bmatrix}) \to \text{Prop})$

c. $r : T_0 = [\ ]$
$\mapsto \begin{bmatrix} sit & = r_1 \\ sit\text{-}type = c: leave(j,t) \end{bmatrix}$

d. $(T_0 \to \text{Prop})$

This explanatory state of affairs contrasts with an account of such examples in a typed feature structure-based approach (e.g., Ginzburg & Sag 2000), given in (31). This AVM *looks* very much like the type (29a), but the appearance in this case is deceiving.

(31)
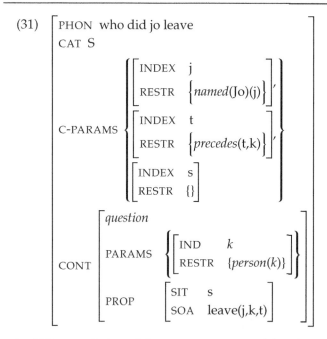

In (31) CONT is *intended* as representation of the abstract in (32):

(32) $\lambda x_{person(x)}leave(j, x, t)$

But, as Penn (2000: 63) puts it (in discussing a related set of issues):

> At this point, feature structures are not being used as a formal device to represent knowledge, but as a formal device to represent data structures that encode formal devices to represent knowledge.

Similarly, C-PARAMS is *intended* as a representation of the contextual parameters that need to be instantiated, but there is no explicit way of modeling this.

This latter point can be ampli ed. As we discussed in Section 2.1, the interaction over grounding of a speaker A's utterance *u* addressed to B typically leads to two outcomes: either B acknowledges u (directly, gesturally, or implicitly) and then responds to the content of *u*, or, alternatively, B utters a clari cation question about some unclear aspect of *u*. As we will see in Section 4.7, this interaction can be explicated as an attempt to nd a type T_u that uniquely classi es *u*. This involves *inter alia* recognizing the words used and instantiating the contextual parameters speci ed in T_u. CRi cation involves utilizing a partially instantiated content and posing a question constructed from *u* and T_u. TTR enables a theory of such interaction to be developed:

- **Simultaneous availability of utterance types and tokens**: in TTR both utterance tokens (records) and signs (record types) become available simultaneously in a natural way.

- **Partially instantiated contents**: a partial witness for C-PARAMS eld T_u.c-params is a record r_0 that is extendible to r_1 such that $r_1 : T_u$.c-params. This is exempli ed in (33b), where r_0 lacks elds for $j, c3$ from (33a):

(33) a. T_u.c-params $= \begin{bmatrix} \text{s0: SIT} \\ \text{t0: TIME} \\ \text{j: IND} \\ \text{c3: Named(j,jo)} \end{bmatrix}$

  b. $r_0 = \begin{bmatrix} \text{PHON} = \text{di jo liv} \\ \text{CAT} = V[+ \ n] \\ \\ \text{C-PARAMS} = \begin{bmatrix} \text{s0} = \text{sit0} \\ \text{t0} = \text{time0} \end{bmatrix} \end{bmatrix}$

  c. $r_0 = \begin{bmatrix} \text{PHON} = \text{di jo liv} \\ \text{CAT} = V[+ \ n] \\ \\ \text{C-PARAMS} = \begin{bmatrix} \text{s0} = \text{sit0} \\ \text{t0} = \text{time0} \\ \text{j} = \text{j0} \\ \text{c3} = \text{c30} \end{bmatrix} \end{bmatrix}$

- **Constructing clarification questions on the fly**: a crucial ingredient in this modeling is the ability to build functions from utterance tokens and utterance types into types of contexts, characterized in terms of various semantic objects such as propositions and questions. This is straightforward in TTR given the fact that it enables direct use of λ-calculus tools.

In contrast to these tools, all of which are intrinsic to TTR, typed feature structure-based formalisms can only simulate functions, abstraction, and assignments. Nor do they have types and tokens simultaneously as rst-class citizens.

4.2 *Information states*

We analyze conversations as collections of dynamically changing, coupled information states, one per conversational participant. The type of such information states is given in (34a). We leave the structure of the private part unanalyzed here (for details on this, see Larsson 2002). The dialogue gameboard (DGB) represents information that arises from publicized interactions. Its structure (or rather a preliminary version suitable for analyzing illocutionary interaction) is given in (34b):

(34) a. TotalInformationState TIS $=$
$\begin{bmatrix} \text{dialoguegameboard : DGB} \\ \text{private : Private} \end{bmatrix}$

b. DGB (initial de nition)

$$\begin{bmatrix} \text{spkr : Ind} \\ \text{addr : Ind} \\ \text{c-utt : addressing(spkr,addr)} \\ \text{Facts : Set(Prop)} \\ \text{Moves : list(IllocProp)} \\ \text{QUD : poset(Question)} \end{bmatrix}$$

- The spkr/hearer roles serve to keep track of turn ownership.
- FACTS represents the shared knowledge conversational participants utilize during a conversation. More operationally, this amounts to information that a conversational participant can use embedded under presuppositional operators.
- Moves: from within FACTS it is useful to single out LatestMove, a distinguished fact that characterizes the content of the most recent move made. The main motivation is to segregate from the entire repository of presuppositions information on the basis of which coherent reactions could be computed. As we see below (e.g., when discussing greeting interaction), keeping track of more than just the latest move can be useful.
- **QUD**: questions that constitute a 'live issue.' That is, questions that have been *introduced for discussion* at a given point in the conversation and whose discussion has not yet been *concluded*. There are additional, indirect ways for questions to get added into QUD, the most prominent of which is during meta-communicative interaction (see Section 4.7). Being maximal in QUD (MaxQUD) corresponds to being the current 'discourse topic,' and this is a key component of our account.

4.3 Illocutionary interaction

To get started, we abstract away from the communicative process, assuming perfect communication. The basic units of change are mappings between dialogue gameboards that specify how one gameboard con guration can be modi ed into another on the basis of dialogue moves. We call a mapping between DGB types a *conversational rule*. The types specifying its domain and its range we dub, respectively, the *preconditions* and the *effects*, both of which are supertypes of DGB. Notationally a conversational rule will be speci ed as in (35):

(35) $\begin{bmatrix} \text{pre(conds) : RType} \\ \text{effects : RType} \end{bmatrix}$

4.4 Move coherence

To illustrate how illocutionary interaction can be speci ed, we consider the example of greetings and partings. An initiating greeting typically occurs dialogue initially. The primary *contextual* effect of such a greeting is simply to provide the addressee with the possibility of reciprocating with a counter-greeting, though of course it has other *expressive* effects (indication of non-hostility, etc.). The conversational rule associated with greeting is given in (36a). The preconditions state that both Moves and QUD need to be empty, though obviously this does not apply to FACTS. The sole DGB effect a greeting has – remember we are abstracting away from utterance processing for the moment – is to update MOVES with its content. In the sequel we adopt a more economical notation: the preconditions can be written as $DGB \wedge PreCondSpec$, where $PreCondSpec$ is a type that includes information speci c to the preconditions of this interaction type. The effects can be written as $DGB \wedge PreCondSpec' \wedge ChangePreconSpec$, where $ChangePreconSpec$ represents those aspects of the preconditions that have changed. We notate conversational rules simply as (36b), and the rule for greeting as (36c):

(36) a.
$$\left[\text{pre} : \begin{bmatrix} \text{spkr: Ind} \\ \text{addr: Ind} \\ \text{moves} = \text{elist} : \text{list(IllocProp)} \\ \text{qud} = \text{eset} : \text{poset(Question)} \\ \text{facts} = \text{commonground1} : \text{Prop} \end{bmatrix} \right.$$
$$\left. \text{effects} : \begin{bmatrix} \text{spkr} = \text{pre.spkr} : \text{Ind} \\ \text{addr} = \text{pre.addr} : \text{Ind} \\ \text{LatestMove} = \text{Greet(spkr,addr)} : \text{IllocProp} \\ \text{qud} = \text{pre.qud} : \text{list(Question)} \\ \text{facts} = \text{pre.facts} : \text{Prop} \end{bmatrix} \right]$$

b.
$$\begin{bmatrix} \text{pre} : \text{PreCondSpec} \\ \text{effects} : \text{ChangePreconSpec} \end{bmatrix}$$

c.
$$\left[\text{pre} : \begin{bmatrix} \text{moves} = \text{elist} : \text{list(IllocProp)} \\ \text{qud} = \text{elist} : \text{list(Question)} \end{bmatrix} \right.$$
$$\left. \text{effects} : \begin{bmatrix} \text{LatestMove} = \text{Greet(spkr,addr)} : \text{IllocProp} \end{bmatrix} \right]$$

A counter-greeting involves turn change and grounds the original greeting; we capture this potential by the rule in (37):

(37)
$$\left[\text{pre} : \begin{bmatrix} \text{LatestMove} = \text{Greet(spkr,addr)} : \text{IllocProp} \\ \text{qud} = \text{elist} : \text{list(Question)} \end{bmatrix} \right.$$
$$\left. \text{effects} : \begin{bmatrix} \text{spkr} = \text{pre.addr} : \text{Ind} \\ \text{addr} = \text{pre.spkr} : \text{Ind} \\ \text{LatestMove} = \text{CtrGreet(spkr,addr)} : \text{IllocProp} \end{bmatrix} \right]$$

Parting can be speci ed in almost analogous terms, with the difference that only QUD needs to be empty – all raised issues have been resolved for current purposes – and that there exists a presupposition that a certain amount of interaction has taken place (see Ginzburg 2010 for details).

4.5 *Querying and assertion*

The basic protocol for two-person querying and assertion that we assume is in (38):

(38)

	querying	assertion
	LatestMove $=$ Ask(A,q)	LatestMove $=$ Assert(A,p)
	A: push q onto QUD; release turn	A: push p? onto QUD; release turn
	B: push q onto QUD; take turn make q-speci c utterance; take turn	B: push p? onto QUD; take turn Option 1: Discuss p? Option 2: Accept p
		LatestMove $=$ Accept(B,p)
		B: increment FACTS with p; pop p? from QUD
		A: increment FACTS with p; pop p? from QUD

q-speci c utterance: an utterance whose content is either a proposition p **about** MaxQUD (*partial answer*) or a question q_1 on which MaxQUD **depends** (*subquestion*).[8]

Two aspects of this protocol are not query-speci c:

(1) The protocol is like the one we have seen for greeting – a two-person turn exchange protocol (2-PTEP).

(2) The speci cation `make q-specific utterance` is an instance of a general constraint that characterizes the contextual background of reactive queries and assertions.

This latter speci cation can be formulated as in (39): the rule states that if q is QUD-maximal, then either participant may make a q-speci c move. Whereas the preconditions simply state that q is QUD-maximal, the preconditions underspecify who has the turn and require that the latest move – the rst element on the MOVES list – stand in the *Qspecific* relation to q:

(39)   QSpec:

$$
\left[
\begin{array}{ll}
\text{preconds} & : \left[\, \text{qud} = \langle q, Q \rangle : \text{poset(Question)} \,\right] \\[2ex]
\text{effects} & :
\begin{bmatrix}
\text{spkr} : \text{Ind} \\
\text{c1} : \text{spkr} = \text{preconds.spkr} \lor \text{preconds.addr} \\
\text{addr} : \text{Ind} \\
\text{c2}: \text{member(addr,}\{\text{preconds.spkr,preconds.addr}\}) \\
\land\ \text{addr} \neq \text{spkr} \\
\text{r} : \text{AbSemObj} \\
\text{R} : \text{IllocRel} \\
\text{Moves} = \langle R(\text{spkr,addr,r}) \rangle \oplus m : \text{list(IllocProp)} \\
\text{c1} : \text{Qspec}\ \ c(\text{r,preconds.qud.q})
\end{bmatrix}
\end{array}
\right]
$$

The only query-speci c aspect of the query protocol in (38) is the need to increment QUD with q as a consequence of q being posed:

(40)   Ask QUD-incrementation:

$$
\left[
\begin{array}{ll}
\text{pre} : & \left[
\begin{array}{l}
q : \text{Question} \\
\text{LatestMove} = \text{Ask(spkr,addr,q)} : \text{IllocProp}
\end{array}
\right] \\[3ex]
\text{effects} : & \left[\, \text{qud} = [q, \text{pre.qud}] : \text{list(Question)} \,\right]
\end{array}
\right]
$$

What are the components of the assertion protocol? Not speci c to assertion is the fact that it is a 2-PTEP; similarly, the discussion option is simply an instance of QSpec. This leaves two novel components: QUD incrementation with $p?$, which can be speci ed like (40) *mutatis mutandis*, and acceptance. Acceptance is a some-what more involved matter because a lot of the action is not directly perceptible. The labor can be divided here in two: rst, we have the action brought about by an acceptance utterance (e.g., 'mmh,' 'I see'). The background for an acceptance by B is an assertion by A and the effect is to modify LatestMove:

(41)   Accept move:

$$
\left[
\begin{array}{ll}
\text{pre} = &
\begin{bmatrix}
p : \text{Prop} \\
\text{LatestMove} = \text{Assert(spkr,addr,p)} : \text{IllocProp} \\
\text{qud} = [p?, \ldots] : \text{list(Question)}
\end{bmatrix} \\[4ex]
\text{effects} = &
\begin{bmatrix}
\text{spkr} = \text{pre.addr} : \text{Ind} \\
\text{addr} = \text{pre.spkr} : \text{Ind} \\
\text{LatestMove} = \text{Accept(pre.addr,spkr,p)} : \text{IllocProp}
\end{bmatrix}
\end{array}
\right]
$$

The second component of acceptance is the incrementation of FACTS by p. This is not quite as straightforward as it might seem: when FACTS gets incremented, we also need to ensure that p? gets downdated from QUD – only non-resolved questions can be in QUD (resolved questions have a use as 'rhetorical questions,' see Ginzburg 2010). In order to ensure that this is the case, we need to check, for each element of QUD, that it is not resolved by the new value of FACTS. Hence, accepting p involves both an update of FACTS and a downdate of QUD enforced via the function NonResolve – minimally just removing p?, but possibly removing other questions as well:

(42) Fact update/QUD downdate:

$$
\begin{bmatrix}
\text{preconds}: \begin{bmatrix} p : \text{Prop} \\ \text{LatestMove} = \text{Accept(spkr,addr,p)} \\ \text{qud} = [p?, \text{preconds.qud}] : \text{poset(Question)} \end{bmatrix} \\[4mm]
\text{effects} \quad : \begin{bmatrix} \text{facts} = \text{preconds.facts} \cup \{p\} : \text{Set(Prop)} \\ \text{qud} = \text{NonResolve(preconds.qud,facts)} : \text{poset(Question)} \end{bmatrix}
\end{bmatrix}
$$

With this in hand, we can exemplify the framework sketched so far with the example in (43):[9]

(43) A(1): Hi
B(2): Hi
A(3): Who's coming tomorrow?
B(4): Several colleagues of mine (are coming).
A(5): I see.
B(6): Mike (is coming) too.

Utt.	DGB update (conditions)	Rule
initial	MOVES $= \langle\rangle$ QUD $= \langle\rangle$ FACTS $=$ cg1	
1	LatestMove $:=$ Greet(A,B)	greeting
2	LatestMove $:=$ CounterGreet(B,A)	counter-greeting
3	LatestMove $:=$ Ask(A,B,q0) QUD $:= \langle q0 \rangle$	Free speech Ask QUD-incrementation
4	LatestMove $:=$ Assert(B,A,p1) (About(p1,q0)) QUD $:= \langle p1?, q0 \rangle$	QSpec Assert QUD-incrementation
5	LatestMove $:=$ Accept(A,B,p1) QUD $:= \langle q0 \rangle$ FACTS $:=$ cg1 $\wedge$ p1	Accept Fact update/QUD downdate
6	LatestMove $:=$ Assert(B,A,p2) (About(p2,q0)) QUD $:= \langle p2?, q0 \rangle$	QSpec Assert QUD-incrementation

We are also now in a position to explain how many of the earlier benchmarks can be met: accommodating *non-resolving answers, follow-up queries to non-resolving answers, sub-questions,* and *disagreement* are all fairly immediate consequences of QSpec: the rst three follow given that the QUD-maximality of *q* allows a *q-specific* utterance to be made, disagreement is accommodated since asserting *p* makes *p*? QUD-maximal, and *p*?-speci c utterances include disagreements. Two other benchmarks can be met due to the mechanism of fact update above: Assertion benchmark1: if accepted, integrate propositional content with existing knowledge base is a direct consequence. Accommodating 'overinformative' answers also follows, to a rst approximation, given that semantic information does not get 'wasted.' Full attention to 'overinformativity' is a long story involving implicature and private parts of information states (on which more below).

We can also say something about the Scaling Up benchmark. Self-answering is directly accommodated by QSpec given that it licenses MaxQUD-speci c utterances regardless of who the speaker of LatestMove is. Another consequence of QSpec is the possibility of posing two successive questions by a single speaker, where the second question in uences the rst; the second query becomes QUD maximal.

(44) a. Ann: What are your shifts next week? Can you remember offhand? James: Yes. I'm early Monday and Tuesday (pause) and Wednesday (pause) a day off Thursday (pause) Friday (pause) late (BNC, KC2 4968-4971)

b. Ann: Anyway, talking of over the road, where is she? Is she home? Betty: No. She's in the Cottage. (BNC, KC2 5121-5124)

QSpec also allows for successive assertions p_1, p_2, where p_2 is about p_1?. When the later assertion p_2 is accepted, the issue associated with the earlier assertion p_1 will be downdated iff FACTS (including p_2) resolves p_1?; this is an implicit mechanism for accepting p_1.

Not all successive queries and successive assertions can be dealt with in this way, and some require postulation of additional conversational rules in order to accommodate further rhetorical relations (for more discussion on this see in particular Asher & Lascarides 2003; Prévot 2003).

4.6 Domain specificity

(DA) Reuse interactional procedures across domains, insofar as possible.

So far we have discussed queries and assertions that arise *reactively.* Conventions regulating the *initiating* of such moves, conversation initially and periodically during extended interactions, are less domain-independent, far more dependent on the activity conversationalists are enagaged in, and on politeness, prior acquaintance between conversationalists, etc. The basic intuition one can pursue is that a move can be made if it *relates to the current activity*.[10] In some cases the activity is very clearly de ned and tightly constrains what can be said. In other cases the activity is far less restrictive on what can be said:

(45) a. **Buying a train ticket**: c wants a train ticket: c needs to indicate where to, when leaving, if return, when returning, which class; s needs to indicate how much needs to be paid
   b. **Buying in a boulangerie**: c needs to indicate what baked goods are desired; b needs to indicate how much needs to be paid
   c. **Buying goods in a minimarket stationed in a petrol station**: c needs to show what she bought; s needs to check if c bought petrol and to tell c how much needs to be paid.
   d. **Chatting among friends**:   rst: how are conversational participants and their near ones?
   e. **Buying in a boulangerie from a long-standing acquaintance**: combination of (b) and (d).

Trying to operationalize activity relevance presupposes that we can classify conversations into various *genres*, a term we use following Bakhtin (1986) to denote a particular type of interactional domain. There are at present remarkably few such taxonomies (though see Allwood 1999 for an informal one) and we will not attempt to offer one here. However, we can indicate how to classify a conversation into a genre. One way is by providing a description of an information state of a conversational participant who has *successfully* completed such a conversation. Final states of a conversation will then be records of type T for T a subtype of DGB_{fin}; here questions no (longer) under discussion (QNUD) denotes a list of issues characteristic of the genre which will have been resolved in interaction:

$$(46) \quad DGB_{fin} = \begin{bmatrix} \text{Facts : Prop} \\ \text{QNUD} = \text{list : list(question)} \\ \text{Moves : list(IllocProp)} \end{bmatrix}$$

In (47) we exemplify two genres, informally speci ed in (54):

(47) a. CasualChat:
$$\begin{bmatrix} \text{A : Ind} \\ \text{B : Ind} \\ \text{t: TimeInterval} \\ \text{c1 : Speak(A,t)} \vee \text{Speak(B,t)} \\ \text{facts : Set(Prop)} \\ \text{qnud : list(question)} \\ \text{c2:} \left\{ \lambda P.P(A), \lambda P.P(B) \right\} \subset \text{qnud} \\ \text{moves : list(IllocProp)} \end{bmatrix}$$

b.   BakeryChat:

$$
\begin{bmatrix}
\text{A : Ind} \\
\text{B : Ind} \\
\text{t: TimeInterval} \\
\text{c1 : Speak(A,t)} \vee \text{Speak(B,t)} \\
\text{facts : Set(Prop)} \\
\text{qnud : list(question)} \\
\text{c2} : \left\{ \begin{array}{l} \lambda P.P(A), \lambda P.P(B), \lambda x.\text{InShopBuy(A,x)}, \\ \lambda x.\text{Pay(A,x)} \end{array} \right\} \subset \text{qnud} \\
\text{moves : list(IllocProp)}
\end{bmatrix}
$$

We can then offer the following de nition of *activity relevance*: one can make an initiating move m0 if one believes that the current conversation updated with m0 is of a certain genre G0. Making move *m0* given what has happened so far (represented in *dgb0*) can be *anticipated* to conclude as nal state *dgb1* which is a conversation of type G0:

(48)   m0 is relevant to G0 in dgb0 for A iff there exists dgb1 such that *dgb0* ⊏ *dgb1*, and such that dgb1 : G0

4.7 *Meta-communicative interaction*

A theory of MCI needs to meet the high-level benchmarks we formu-lated earlier, speci cally those concerning `Semantic non-determinism` and `Fine-grained utterance representation`. KoS is already equipped to address the rst challenge due to the fact that each conversational participant is associated with a distinct DGB – concrete exempli cation of this is offered towards the end of this section. Therefore there is no single *context* in conversation but rather *coupled and potentially mismatched* dialogue gameboards. Only one modi - cation is required to the structure of the DGB, the postulation of a eld **Pending**, whose members are ungrounded utterances. For reasons we discuss shortly the type of **Pending** (and concomitantly that of **Moves**) is a list of *locutionary propo-sitions*, propositions consisting of an utterance record and a (grammatical) type which classi es it. This leads to a new de nition of DGB type:

(49)   DGB =
$$
\begin{bmatrix}
\text{spkr : Ind} \\
\text{addr : Ind} \\
\text{c-utt : addressing(spkr,addr)} \\
\text{Facts : Set(Prop)} \\
\text{Pending : list(LocProp)} \\
\text{Moves : list(LocProp)} \\
\text{QUD : poset(Question)}
\end{bmatrix}
$$

In the immediate aftermath of a speech event u, **Pending** gets updated with a record of the form $\begin{bmatrix} \text{sit} = u \\ \text{sit-type} = T_u \end{bmatrix}$ (of type *locutionary proposition* (LocProp)). Here T_u is a grammatical type for classifying u that emerges during the process of parsing u. In the most general case it should be thought of as a *chart* (Cooper, forthcoming), but in the cases we consider here it can be identi ed with a *sign* in the sense of head driven phrase structure grammar (HPSG). The relationship between u and T_u – describable in terms of the proposition $p_u = \begin{bmatrix} \text{sit} = u \\ \text{sit-type} = T_u \end{bmatrix}$ – can be utilized in providing an analysis of grounding/CRi cation conditions:[11]

(50) a. Grounding: p_u is true: the utterance type fully classi es the utterance token.
   b. CRi cation: T_u is weak (e.g., incomplete word recognition); u is incompletely speci ed (e.g., incomplete contextual resolution).

Postulating that Pending be of type LocProp allows us to meet the `Fine-grained utterance representation` benchmark: T_u provides the ne grain and the information needed to capture syntactic/phonological paral-lelism; u is necessary to instantiate the contextual parameters of T_u, as well as to provide the sub-utterance tokens that gure in CRs (on the latter see the discus-sion concerning example (68)).[12] We can also formulate the following utterance processing protocol, which interleaves illocutionary and meta-communicative interaction:

(51) **Utterance processing protocol**
   For an agent A with IS I: if a locutionary proposition $p_u = \begin{bmatrix} \text{sit} = u \\ \text{sit-type} = T_u \end{bmatrix}$

   is maximal in Pending:
   (a) if p_u is true, try to integrate p_u in A.DGB using a Moves update rule;
   (b) otherwise: try to accommodate p_u as a CR to LatestMove;
   (c) if (a) and (b) fail, seek a witness for T_u by asking a CR: introduce a clari cation issue derivable from p_u as the maximal element of QUD; use this context to formulate a clari cation request.

A full theory of MCI involves a compositional analysis of (a somewhat more sophisticated version of) this protocol using update rules entirely akin to those used for illocutionary interaction in Section 4.3. We concentrate here on elucidating how a CR gets asked and which are the available CRs. Given that any subutter-ance of a given utterance is potentially clari able, one prerequisite at the level of utterance representation is the accessibility of all subutterances. We achieve this by positing that the eld C-PARAMS of a given utterance type is a record type specifying two kinds of witnesses: (a) subutterance tokens, characterized in terms of their morpho-syntactic properties, and (b) referents, speci ed in terms

of their semantic contribution. Repetition and meaning-oriented CRs are specied by means of a particular class of conversational rules – clari cation context
update rules (CCURs). Each CCUR speci es an accommodated MaxQUD built up
from a subutterance u1 of the target utterance *MaxPending*. Common to all CCURs
is a license to follow up *MaxPending* with an utterance which is *co-propositional*
with MaxQUD.[13] In the current context co-propositionality amounts to: either a
CR which differs from MaxQUD at most in terms of its domain, or a correction –
a proposition that instantiates MaxQUD.

To make this concrete, we consider one speci c CCUR `Parameter`
`identification`, used to specify *intended content* CRs. (52) indicates that given
u0, a subutterance token of MaxPending, one may accommodate as MaxQUD
the issue 'What did spkr mean by u0.' Concomitantly, the next move must be
co-propositional with this issue:

(52)   Parameter identi cation:
$$
\left[
\begin{array}{l}
\text{preconds} : \left[
\begin{array}{l}
\text{Spkr : Ind} \\
\text{MaxPending : LocProp} \\
\text{u0} \in \text{MaxPending.sit.constits}
\end{array}
\right] \\
\text{effects} : \left[
\begin{array}{l}
\text{MaxQUD} = \text{What did spkr mean by u0? : Question} \\
\text{LatestMove : LocProp} \\
\text{c1: CoProp(LatestMove.cont,MaxQUD)}
\end{array}
\right]
\end{array}
\right]
$$

(52)   underpins CRs such as (53b, 53c) as follow-ups to (53a):

(53)   a.   A: Is Bo here?
       b.   B: Who do you mean 'Bo'?
       c.   B: Bo? (= Who is 'Bo'?)

We can also deal with corrections, as in (54). B's corrective utterance is
co-propositional with $\lambda x \text{Mean}(A,u0,x)$, and hence allowed by the speci cation:

(54)   B: You mean Jo.

In Figure 16.5 we provide an illustration of our account of the `semantic`
`non-determinism` benchmark: the same input leads to distinct outputs on the
'public level' of information states. In this case this arises due to differential ability
to anchor the contextual parameters. The utterance u0 has three subutterances, u1,
u2, u3, given in Figure 16.5 with their approximate pronunciations. A can ground
her own utterance since she knows the values of the contextual parameters, which
we assume here for simplicity include the speaker and the referent of the subutterance 'Bo.' This means that the locutionary proposition associated with u0 – the
proposition whose situational value is a record that arises by unioning u0 with the
witnesses for the contextual parameters and whose type is given in Figure 16.5 – is

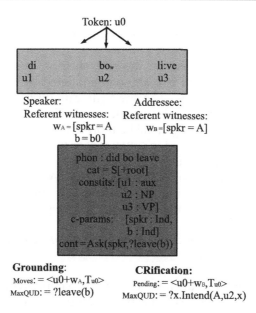

Figure 16.5   A single utterance gives rise to distinct updates of the DGB for distinct participants.

true. This enables the 'canonical' illocutionary update to be performed: the issue 'whether b left' becomes the maximal element of QUD. In contrast, let us assume that B lacks a witness for the referent of 'Bo.' As a result, the locutionary proposition associated with u0 which B can construct is not true. Given this, B uses the CCUR parameter identification to build a context appropriate for a clari cation request: B increments QUD with the issue λxMean(A,u2,x), and the locutionary proposition associated with u0 which B has constructed remains in Pending.

To conclude our discussion of the basics of MCI, we consider brie y relevance CRs and topic changing, 'irrelevant responses' (the latter our benchmark Q5). The basic trigger for both is the condition in (55), where the content of an utterance stands in the 'Irrelevant' relation to a DGB:

(55)   Irrelevant(u.cont,dgb)

Irrelevant(p,dgb0) here relates an illocutionary proposition p, the content of the 'irrelevant' move, to a DGB dgb0 just in case there is no update rule U such that U(dgb0).LatestMove.cont = p. For instance, given what we have said here, an irrel-evant follow-up to an utterance u which expresses a query q is an utterance which is neither q-speci c nor a clari cation request triggered by u:

(56)   a.   LatestMove = u; u.content = Ask(A,q),
         b. p is not q-speci c

    c. p is not co-propositional with any question q0 that satis es q0 =
CCUR1.qud(u) for some CCUR CCUR1

The potential for CRs concerning the relevance of an utterance is already,
with one potentially signi cant caveat, accommodated by the rule `parameter`
`identification` we saw above. The one signi cant difference of relevance CRs
is that the trigger is typically the irrelevance of a *fully instantiated utterance*. The
answer to such a CR will not in general be represented in the DGB, in contrast to
other CRs, where it could be found in C-PARAMS or PHON of the responder.

This means that we need to offer an alternative de nition for the Mean predicate
to the one appropriate for semantically oriented CRs. What we would need would
be a de nition along the following lines – identifying the speaker meaning with
the maximal element of the agenda of the utterance's speaker:

(57) Given u.sit.cont : IllocProp, Mean(A,u,c) iff u.c-param.spkr = A and
A.private.maxagenda = c

As for irrelevance implicatures, we can offer a 'short-circuited' version of the
Gricean account – irrelevance is a means of non-grounding the previous utterance, itself an instance of a more general process of ignoring commonly perceived
events. The short-circuited version takes the form of the update rule in (58) – given
that MaxPending is *irrelevant* to the DGB, one can make MaxPending into Latest-
Move while updating Facts with the fact that the speaker of MaxPending does not
wish to discuss MaxQUD:

(58)
$$
\left[
\begin{array}{l}
preconds : \left[\begin{array}{l} \text{dgb} : \text{DGB} \\ \text{c: IrRelevant(maxpending}^{content}\text{,dgb)} \end{array}\right] \\[2em]
effects : \left[\begin{array}{l} \text{LatestMove} = \text{pre.pending} : \text{LocProp} \\ \text{Facts} = \text{pre.Facts} \cup \\ \left\{\neg \text{WishDiscuss(pre.spkr,pre.maxqud)}\right\} \end{array}\right]
\end{array}
\right]
$$

Note that this does not make the *unwillingness to discuss* be the *content*
of the offending utterance; it is merely an inference. Still this inference will
allow MAXQUD to be downdated, via a slightly re ned version of `fact`
`update/question downdate` – if information is accepted indicating negative
resolution of ?WishDiscuss(q), then q may be downdated from QUD.

4.8 Disfluencies

The setup for meta-communicative *inter*action described in the previous section
extends straightforwardly to yield an account of *self-correction*, and other dis u-
encies. The sole, but signi cantly consequential, modi cation such an account
presupposes is to the structure of Pending. This now needs to incorporate also

utterances that are *in progress* and, hence, incompletely speci ed semantically and phonologically. This, in turn, requires the use of types that characterize utterances word by word (or minimally constituent by constituent), as, e.g., in combinatory categorial grammar (Steedman 2000), type logical grammar (Morrill 2000), dynamic syntax (Kempson et al., 2000), PTT (Poesio & Traum 1997), or by abstraction from a 'standard' grammar (as one could implement in HPSG$_{TTR}$, that version of HPSG whose logical underpinning is TTR). A variety of issues arise, in consequence, issues that are still very much open, including monotonicity in processing, and the nature of incremental denotations. Fortunately the account of dis uencies can be formulated without making commitments on these issues.

Incrementalizing Pending has the independent consequence of enabling us to account for the Incremental Acknowledgments benchmark (inspired by examples such as 13c) (Ack2). We can formulate a lexical entry for '*mmh*,' which enables a speaker to acknowledge the current addressee's most recently ungrounded utterance, regardless of whether it is complete (in which case its content would be an IllocProp) or not:

(59)
$$
\begin{bmatrix}
\text{PHON} : \langle \text{ mmh } \rangle \\
\text{CAT} = interjection : \text{syncat} \\
\text{c-params} : \begin{bmatrix} \text{spkr} : \text{IND} \\ \text{addr} : \text{IND} \\ \text{MaxPending} : \text{LocProp} \\ \text{c2} : \text{address(addr,spkr,MaxPending)} \end{bmatrix} \\
\text{CONT} = \text{Understand(spkr,addr,MaxPending)} : \text{IllocProp}
\end{bmatrix}
$$

The basic intuition behind this account of dis uencies is an analogy to CRi - cation: in the latter a CR provides the potential for an answer, which allows the original poser of the CR to x his utterance. For self-corrections, *editing phrases* (EditPs) (long silences, discourse particles like 'No . . .,' 'um,' etc.) correspond to CRs, whereas the *alternation*, that subutterance with the correcting material, corresponds to an answer to a CR. There are two remaining steps: rst provide for the coherence of the EditP. This is simple to do: all we need to say is that an EditP can be interpolated at any point where Pending is non-empty. Finally, take as input a state where the LatestMove is an EditP and specify as output a new state in which the MaxQUD is *What did spkr mean to utter at u0?* and where the new utterance has to be an instantiation of MaxQUD (propositional or polar question):[14]

(60) Utterance identi cation:
Input:
$$
\begin{bmatrix}
\text{Spkr} : \text{Ind} \\
\text{MaxPending} : \text{LocProp} \\
\text{LatestMove} = \text{EditP(Spkr,MaxPending)} : \text{IllocProp} \\
\text{u0} \in \text{MaxPending.sit.constits}
\end{bmatrix}
$$

Output: $\begin{bmatrix} \text{MaxQUD} = \text{What did spkr mean to say at u0? : Question} \\ \text{LatestMove : LocProp} \\ \text{c2 : InstPropQ(LatestMove.cont,MaxQUD)} \end{bmatrix}$

The same mechanism that updates the DGB after a CR and effects an update of information concerning a given utterance applies here. It ensures that the alteration of the original sub-utterance replaces or reinforces the repaired subutterance in PENDING. At the same time, the presupposition concerning the latter's taking place will remain in FACTS. We thereby meet

(61)   D2: Explicate dis uency meaning without eliminating dis uencies from context.

4.9 *Sentential fragments*

The approach we pursue here to sentential fragments is constructional, i.e., from a grammatical point of view we treat such constructions as *sui generis*, not as underlyingly canonical sentences, as is common in generative linguistics. The fundamental argument for this strategy is the existence of a wide array of mismatches between the syntactic and semantic properties of sentential fragments and putative sentential correlates (for extensive argumentation, see Ginzburg & Sag 2000; Schlangen 2003; Fernández 2006; Ginzburg 2010). (62) exempli es this claim – (62a) shows the distinct distribution of a direct sluice and of its putative canonical correlate; (62b) shows a similar datum for a short answer and its putative canonical correlate; nally (62c) illustrates that elliptical exclamatives cannot be embedded, in contrast to sentential exclamatives:

(62)   a.   A: Somebody stood outside the room. B: Who? / #Who the hell? / Who the hell stood outside the room?
   b.   Who stood outside the room? Not Bo. / #Not Bo stood outside the room.
   c.   A: What a shot! / *It's amazing what a shot. / It's amazing what a shot she made.

The existence of parallelism between source and NSU on various dimensions necessitates positing one additional contextual parameter, namely an antecedent subutterance (of the utterance which is MaxQUD). Intuitively, this parameter provides a partial speci cation of the focal (sub)utterance, and hence it is dubbed the *focus establishing constituent* (FEC): Varying roles are played by the FEC: in some cases it is crucial for semantic composition, while in others it plays a disambiguating role via morpho-syntactic or phonological parallelism.

Given that their lifetimes are as a rule identical, we can pair QUDs and FECs as part of contextual speci cation. Concretely this amounts to changing the type of QUD from *list(Questn)* to *list(Info-struc)*, where Info-Struc is the following type:

(63) Info-struc $= \begin{bmatrix} q : \text{Questn} \\ \text{fec} : \text{set(LocProp)} \end{bmatrix}$

It also means that FECs get introduced by (minor modi cations of) rules we have seen above for incrementing and downdating QUD, namely Ask-QUD incrementation and the CCURs.

With this in hand, we turn to illustrating KoS's approach to sentential fragment grammar and meaning.[15] Sentential fragments are essentially akin to indexicals ('I': speaker, 'you': addr, 'here': speech loc., ...) but, whereas the latter resolve to concrete elements of the utterance context, sentential fragment resolution is based on reference to DGB elements:[16]

4.9.1 Yes Its informal meaning is simply – MaxQUD's proposition. (64) includes a rudimentary lexical entry for this word which formalizes this intuition:

(64) $\begin{bmatrix} \text{phon} : \text{yes} \\ \text{cat} = \text{adv} : \text{syncat} \\ \text{max-qud} : \text{PolarQuestn} \\ \text{cont} = \text{max-qud}(\parallel): \text{Prop} \end{bmatrix}$

4.9.2 Short answers This construction can be described in the following terms: the content arises by function application of MaxQUD to the fragment's content; syntactically the fragment must bear an identical syntactic category to the FEC. (65) represents this construction in HPSG$_{TTR}$:

(65) *decl-frag-cl* $= \begin{bmatrix} \text{cat} = \text{V}[+ \text{ n}] : \text{syncat} \\ \text{hd-dtr} : \begin{bmatrix} \text{cat} = \text{max-qud.fec.cat} : \text{Syncat} \end{bmatrix} \\ \wedge \text{ sign} \\ \text{max-qud} : \text{WhQuestn} \\ \text{cont} = \text{max-qud(hd-dtr.cont)} : \text{Prop} \end{bmatrix}$

Given that the meaning of short answers is directly tied to MaxQUD, we can ful ll the `distance benchmark`: accommodate `long-distance short answers`: such answers are predicted to be possible insofar as the corresponding issue is still in QUD. Since QUD consists of elements of type *info-struc*, we can also capture the long-distance syntactic parallelism short answers exhibit.

We turn nally to two sentential fragments used in MCI, the *confirmation* and *intended content* readings of reprise fragments (RF).

4.9.3 Reprise fragments: confirmation reading   Assume the utterance to be
clari ed is (66a). B uses the CCUR parameter identification to build a
context as in (66b):

(66) a.   A: Did Bo leave?
      b. $\text{MaxQUD} = \lambda x \text{Mean}(A,u2,x)$; $\text{FEC} = $ A's utterance 'Bo'

Given this, the analysis of the construction is illustrated in (67): the construction *decl-frag-cl* builds the proposition Mean(A,u2,b); the construction *polarization*
builds a polar question from this:

(67)

$$
\begin{array}{c}
S \\
\left[\begin{array}{l} polarization \\ \text{cont} = \text{?hd-dtr.cont} = \text{?Mean}(A,u2,b) : \text{Questn} \end{array}\right] \\
\mid \\
S \\
\left[\begin{array}{l} decl\text{-}frag\text{-}cl \\ \text{maxqud} = \left[\begin{array}{l} q = \lambda x\, \text{Mean}(A,u2,x) : \text{Questn} \\ \text{fec} = \text{p2} : \text{LocProp} \end{array}\right] : \text{InfoStruc} \\ \text{hd-dtr} : \left[\begin{array}{l} \text{cont} : \left[x : \text{Ind}\right] \\ \text{cat} = \text{fec.cat} : \text{syncat} \end{array}\right] \\ \text{cont} = \text{maxqud.q(hd-dtr.cont.x)} \end{array}\right] \\
\mid \\
\text{NP} \\
\left[\text{BO}\right]
\end{array}
$$

4.9.4 Reprise fragments: intended content reading   Intended content readings
of RFs involve a complex mix of a *prima facie* non-transparent semantics and
phonological parallelism. Independently of intended content readings, we need
to capture the utterance anaphoricity of 'quotative' utterances such as (68):

(68) a.   A: Bo is coming. B: Who do you mean 'Bo'?
      b.   D: I have a Geordie accident. J: 'accident' that's funny.

We assume the existence of a grammatical constraint allowing reference to a
subutterance under phonological parallelism. (69) exempli es one way of formulating such a constraint: the PHON value is type identical with the PHON value of
an utterance identi ed with the focus establishing constituent, whereas the content is stipulated to be the utterance event associated with the focus establishing
constituent:[17]

(69) *utt-anaph-ph*

$$\begin{bmatrix} \text{tune} = \text{max-qud.fec.sit-type.phon : Type} \\ \text{phon : } \textit{tune} \\ \text{cat : syncat} \\ \text{max-qud : info-struc} \\ \text{cont} = \text{max-qud.fec.sit : Rec} \end{bmatrix}$$

With this in hand, we turn back to consider the issue of how *intended content* RFs arise grammatically. It is worth emphasizing that there is no way to bring about the desired content using *decl-frag-cl*, the short-answer/reprise sluice phrasal type we have been appealing to above, regardless of whether we analyze the NP fragment as denoting its standard conventional content or alternatively as denoting an anaphoric element to the phonologically identical to-be-clari ed subutterance. This is a prototypical instance of appeal to constructional meaning – a complex content that cannot be plausibly constructed using 'standard combinatorial operations' (function application, uni cation etc.) from its constituents. Thus, one way of accommodating *intended content* RF is to posit a new phrasal type, *qud-anaph-int-cl*. This will encapsulate the two idiosyncratic facets of such utterances, namely the MaxQUD/content identity and the HD-DTR being an *utt-anaph-ph*:

(70) *qud-anaph-int-cl* = $\begin{bmatrix} \text{max-qud : InfoStruc} \\ \text{cont} = \text{max-qud.q : Questn} \\ \text{hd-dtr : } \textit{utt-anaph-ph} \end{bmatrix}$

Given this, we can offer the following analysis of (71):

(71) a. A: Is Georges here? B: Georges?
      b. B lacks referent for 'Georges'; uses parameter identification to update MaxQUD accordingly:

$$\begin{bmatrix} \text{spkr} = \text{B} \\ \text{addr} = \text{A} \\ \text{pending} = \left\langle \begin{bmatrix} \text{sit} = \text{w0}' \\ \text{sit-type} = \text{IGH} \end{bmatrix} \right\rangle \\ \text{maxqud} = \begin{bmatrix} \text{q} = \lambda x \text{ Mean(A,p2,x) : Question} \\ \text{fec} = \text{p2 : LocProp} \end{bmatrix} : \text{InfoStruc} \end{bmatrix}$$

Using *qud-anaph-int-cl* yields:

(72)

$$
S
$$

$$
\begin{bmatrix}
\textit{qud-anaph-int-cl} \\
\text{maxqud} = \begin{bmatrix} \text{q} = \lambda x \ \text{Mean}(A,p2,x) : \text{Question} \\ \text{fec} = p2 : \text{LocProp} \end{bmatrix} : \text{InfoStruc} \\
\text{cont} = \text{maxqud.q}
\end{bmatrix}
$$

$$
S
$$

$$
\begin{bmatrix}
\textit{utt-anaph-ph} \\
\text{bu} = \text{max-qud.fec.sit-type.phon} : \text{Type} \\
\text{phon} : \text{bu}
\end{bmatrix}
$$

$$
\text{BO}
$$

5   Extensions

In this chapter we have surveyed some core phenomena that theories of dialogue need to tackle. We also sketched a uni ed treatment of these phenomena. For reasons of space we could not enter into discussion of various other highly signi cant aspects of dialogue. Here we point to some recent work that has tackled these aspects.

5.1   *Automatic learning of dialogue management*

Recent advances have been made in the application of machine learning (ML) techniques to dialogue management. One of the most common methods used in this line of research is reinforcement learning (Sutton & Barto 1998). In this approach, the conversational skills of a spoken dialogue system are modeled as a Markov decision process (MDP) (Levin & Pieraccini, 1997; Levin et al., 1998). The model consists of a nite set of states S, a nite set of actions A, a transition function $T(s',a,s)$ that speci es the probability of transitioning to state s' from state s after performing action a, and a reward function $R(s',a,s)$ that assigns a reward value to each transition. Given this model, the dialogue manager can be seen as a learning agent that learns an *optimal policy* $\pi : S \mapsto A$, that is, a mapping from states to actions that maximizes the overall reward (which is a function, usually a weighted sum, of all reward values obtained).

The use of ML techniques is attractive because it offers the possibility to develop data-driven approaches to dialogue management that bypass the need to hand craft the rules governing the behavior of a system. Instead of following hand crafted dialogue strategies (in the form of update or inference rules, or as states and transitions in a manually designed nite state graph), in a reinforcement learning (RL) framework the system learns interactively from the rewards it receives.

However, appealing as this may be, there are several drawbacks associated with this approach (see, e.g., Paek & Chickering 2005; Paek & Pieraccini 2008). One of them is that, like most ML methods, dialogue managers based on reinforcement techniques require large amounts of data for training. Collecting and annotating the dialogue corpora required to train the algorithms requires large amounts of time and effort. A related issue, crucial in RL approaches, concerns the modeling of the state space S. Again, like all ML approaches, RL faces the problem of selecting the appropriate features for training, i.e., deciding what state variables should be included in the model. This task is for the most part performed manually. Once an initial set of variables has been chosen, the set can be re ned with automatic feature selection methods, but the initial candidate variables are selected by hand. Finally, another important parameter that needs to be set and adjusted is the reward function, which directly affects the adopted policy and hence the behavior of the system. Although there is some research that explores methods to try to infer R from data (e.g., Ng & Russell 2000; Walker & Shannon 2000), the typical practice is to specify R manually, sometimes taking into account parameters linked to the task at hand or to user satisfaction (Singh et al., 1999; 2002).

In principle, dialogue management policies learned with RL methods can make use of complex sets of variables encoding rich information (such as the dialogue history, lled and con rmed slots, or information about the interlocutor). However, this can easily lead to an explosion of the state space that may be intractable for learning (Sutton & Barto 1998). Thus, in practice, researchers developing dialogue systems have concentrated on learning limited policies, such as for example con rmation strategies (Singh et al., 2002). Recent work attempts to address the problem of large state spaces to provide more general policies (see e.g., Rieser & Lemon, 2008; Henderson et al., 2008a).

Models can also take into account uncertain information such as the user's intentions and beliefs. This information is not directly observable by the system but in principle can be inferred from observable variables such as the user's utterance. This can be modeled as a partially observable MDP (POMDP) (Zhang et al., 2001; Young 2006; Williams & Young 2007). In a POMDP the uncertainty about the current state is represented as a probability distribution over S or a belief state. The reward function thus computes the expected reward over belief states, while a dialogue policy becomes a mapping from n-dimensional belief states to actions (see Kaelbling et al., 1995; 1996 for further details).

5.2 *Multiparty dialogue*

Our discussion has focused almost exclusively on two-person conversations, as has the lion's share of dialogue systems developed so far. However, the general case is *multiparty dialogue* (also known as *multilogue*). A number of multiparty dialogue systems have been developed at the Institute for Creative Technology, including the Mission Rehearsal Exercise project (Swartout et al., 2006), a virtual reality-based training system. Traum (2004) considers some of the basic issues relating multiparty and two-person dialogue; based on NSU data, Ginzburg and Fernández (2005) propose some benchmarks that two-person dialogue theories aspiring to scale up to multiparty need to ful ll and offer general scaling-up transformations applicable to two-person protocols. Kronlid (2008) re nes these transformations, while offering a detailed implementation of a turn-taking algorithm.

5.3 Multi-modal dialogue

Although spoken language is the basis for communication, other modalities such as gesture often play central roles in dialogue. There is an increasing amount of research dedicated to multi-modal communication and to the implementation of systems that can handle some form of multi-modal interaction. The simplest multi-modal systems combine speech with other multi-modal input and output such as the display of graphics or the recognition of pointing gestures such as mouse clicks. As discussed in the seminal paper by Nigay and Coutaz (1993), the key questions faced by these systems are how information coming from different modalities can be integrated into a single message (e.g., to disambiguate a refer-ring expression by means of a gesture) and how different modalities can be fused in generating multi-modal output. Delgado and Araki (2005) offer a good survey of multi-modal interfaces.

A parallel line of research focuses on developing animated characters or embod-ied conversational agents (Cassell et al., 2000). These are virtual characters that aim at communicating with humans using speech as well as natural facial expressions, hand gestures, and body posture.

6   Conclusions

Dialogue is one of the central disciplines of language sciences – languages are rst encountered, learned, and used in interaction and this has been the case for millenia. And yet the lion's share of both formal grammar and psycholinguistic work does not presuppose an interactive setting. Dialogue is a ourishing area in NLP and CL, though primarily in the context of developing dialogue systems.

In this chapter we have sought to develop an approach to dialogue that combines theoretical and systems perspectives. To do so, we grounded our discussion empirically in two dozen benchmarks, benchmarks concerning the treatment of querying and assertion, domain adaptability and scalability, meta-communication, and the treatment of fragments. We have used these benchmarks to informally evaluate several in uential current approaches to the development of dialogue managers for dialogue systems. We then sketched the theory KoS, for-mulated in the framework of type theory with records, which, with one or two exceptions, ful lls all the benchmarks. KoS involves formulating a rich theory of information states and showing how these get modi ed in interaction. One of the important features of this theory is that it allows for an interleaving of locutionary (e.g., grounding, clari cation, and self-correction) and illocutionary (e.g., querying and assertion) interaction.

KoS provides an existence proof of a theory of dialogue that can satisfy various benchmarks concerning dialogue coherence, while underpinning fairly sophisticated linguistic analysis. As we note in the text, this combination also characterizes a number of other recently developed dialogue frameworks such as PTT and SDRT. It is important to emphasize, nonetheless, that formal/computational work in dialogue is still at a fairly *early* stage. As we noted in Section 5, a comprehensive theory of dialogue needs to accommodate the multi-modal nature of interaction and the fact that two-person dialogue is a particular instance of multiparty dialogue, with the attendant complexity of turn allocation and split attention.

We believe, furthermore, that one of the important areas of development for work in dialogue is embracing both ontogenetic and phylogenetic perspectives. A phylogenetic or evolutionary perspective on language is gaining signi cant interest among language scientists and is, moreover, rooted in interaction among a community of agents. Nonetheless, such work has, to date, not made much contact with computational work on dialogue. But this is clearly only a matter of time. As discussed in Section 5, there is already a ourishing body of work on learning in dialogue, using various machine learning techniques. Such work is signi cant for practical reasons, not least because it has the promise of allowing domain speci city to be incorporated in a systematic and large-scale way. It is signi cant also because it should provide us with a theory of language learning that captures the fact that interaction between child and caregiver is a vital component in the emergence of linguistic competence. Indeed, taking interaction seriously, as pointed out in Chapter 8, UNSUPERVISED LEARNING AND GRAMMAR INDUCTION, could plausibly simplify the task of language learning signi cantly. An important challenge for future work is fusing machine language techniques with symbolic ones to achieve the robustness of the former with the linguistic sophistication of the latter.

A dialogical perspective is also, as yet, generally lacking from work on complexity and formal language theory (though see Fernández and Endriss (2007) for an example of how the latter can inform work on dialogue). But for all the reasons we have discussed above, there is nothing intrinsic in these lacunae, and one can con dently expect these to be lled in the coming decade.

ACKNOWLEDGMENT

We would like to thank the editors for their very useful comments. Portions of this paper were presented in our course on computational models of dialogue at the 2008 ESSLLI summer school in Hamburg; we would like to thank the participants there for their feedback. Parts of this paper were written while the second author was a research fellow at the Center for the Study of Language and Information, Stanford University. The work of the second author has been partially supported by a Dutch NWO Veni project (grant number 275-80-002).

NOTES

1   This taxonomy, inspired in part by earlier work by Sinclair and Coulthard (1975), in fact involves classi cation at a number of levels: the move level, the game level, and the transaction level.

2   Annotation in DAMSL involves multiple levels, including levels that concern intelligibility/completion, semantic content, *forward looking function* – how the current utterance affects the discourse and its participants, and *backward looking function* – how the current utterance relates to the previous discourse.

3   Some of the move types in DAMSL are actually supertypes, whose subtypes we have listed in parentheses in (3).

4   By far the commonest type of what one might call meta-communicative *intra*actions are *self-corrections*, often referred to under the rubric of *disfluencies*, on which more below.

5   See www.ling.gu.se/projekt/trindi/trindikit/ and www.ltg.ed.ac.uk/dipper/ for up-to-date information on the toolkits.

6   PTT is not an acronym, but has some relation to the initials of its progenitors.

7   A convention we employ here to distinguish phonological tokens and types is to refer to the latter with English words and the former with a mock representation of their pronunciation.

8   For answerhood and dependence plug your favorite semantics of questions (e.g., Groenendijk and Stokhof 1997; Ginzburg & Sag 2000).

9   Utterance (43(3)) is an *initiating* query. Any theory requires some means, typically one that makes reference to the domain in which the interaction takes place of licensing such queries. Here we appeal to the rule Free speech. This rule, from Ginzburg (2010), is a domain-independent principle that licenses the choice of *any* query or assertion assuming QUD is empty. We discuss how to re ne this with a principle that is domain-speci c in Section 4.6.

10 The approach sketched here is inspired by work in Larsson (2002), work implemented in the GODIS system.

11 A particularly detailed theory of grounding has been developed in the PTT framework, e.g., Poesio and Traum (1997); Poesio and Rieser (2009).

12 This argumentation carries over to identifying the type of LatestMove as LocProp – this information is required to enable A to integrate a CR posed by B concerning A's latest utterance. Data pointing towards the preservation of non-semantic structure in the longer term comes from alignment phenomena (Garrod & Pickering 2004). However, the extent to which this is the case or only content is preserved in context long term is very much an open question.

13 Two utterances u_0 and u_1 are *co-propositional* iff the questions q_0 and q_1 they contribute to QUD are co-propositional.

   (1)   qud-contrib(m0.cont) is m0.cont if m0.cont : Question
   (2)   qud-contrib(m0.cont) is ?m0.cont if m0.cont : Prop

   q_0 and q_1 are co-propositional if there exists a record r such that $q_0(r) = q_1(r)$. This means that, modulo their domain, the questions involve similar answers. For instance 'Whether Bo left,' 'Who left,' and 'Which student left' (assuming Bo is a student) are all co-propositional.

14 Some evidence towards the reality of the MaxQUD postulated in this CCUR is provided by examples such as the following attested example: "Hmm. Lots of people are

texting in and getting involved on 606, and, er, what's the word? Backtracking, that's it" (from a BBC webcast of a football match, November 12, 2008).

15 See Schlangen (2003) for an alternative approach to NSUs within SDRT.

16 We have space here only to discuss a small number of cases. In particular, direct sluicing, the most complex non-MCI sentential fragment, would require discussion of our treatment of quanti cation. For detailed treatments see Fernández (2006) and Ginzburg (2010).

17 (69) makes one simplifying assumption: identifying the PHON value of the focus establishing constituent with that of the utterance anaphoric phrase. In practice this should only be the segmental phonological value.

17 Computational Psycholinguistics

MATTHEW W. CROCKER

1 Introduction

Computational psycholinguistics is concerned with the development of computational models of the cognitive mechanisms and representations that underlie language processing in the mind/brain. As a consequence, computational psycholinguistics shares many of the goals of natural language processing research, including the development of algorithms that can recover the intended meaning of a sentence or utterance on the basis of its spoken or textual realization. Additionally, however, computational psycholinguistics seeks to do this in a manner that re ects how people process language.

Natural language is fundamentally a product of those cognitive processes that are co-ordinated to support human linguistic communication and interaction. The study of language therefore involves a range of disciplines, including linguistics, philosophy, cognitive psychology, anthropology, and arti cial intelligence. Computational psycholinguistics, perhaps more than any other area, epitomizes interdisciplinary linguistic inquiry: the ultimate goal of the enterprise is to implement models which re ect the means by which linguistic information is stored in, and utilized by, the mind and brain. But beyond modeling of the representations, architectures, and mechanisms that underlie linguistic communication, computational psycholinguistics is increasingly concerned with developing *explanatory* accounts, which shed light on why the human language faculty is the way it is. As such, models of human language processing must ultimately seek to be connected with accounts of language evolution and language acquisition.

This chapter presents some of the historically enduring ndings from research in computational psycholinguistics, as well as a state-of-the-art overview of current models and their underlying differences and similarities. While computational models of human language processing have been developed to account for various levels of language processing – from spoken word recognition and lexical access through to sentence production and interpretation – this chapter will place primary emphasis on models of syntactic processing. It will not be surprising that

The Handbook of Computational Linguistics and Natural Language Processing, First Edition.
Edited by Alexander Clark, Chris Fox and Shalom Lappin.
© 2013 Blackwell Publishing Ltd except for editorial material and organization
© 2013 Alexander Clark, Chris Fox, and Shalom Lappin. Published 2013 by Blackwell Publishing Ltd.

many accounts of human syntactic processing are heavily informed by computational linguistics, speci cally natural language parsing. A traditional approach
has been to try to identify parsing algorithms which exhibit the range of observed
human language processing behaviors, including incremental processing, local
and global ambiguity resolution, and parsing complexity (both time and space;
see Chapter 2, COMPUTATIONAL COMPLEXITY IN NATURAL LANGUAGE, and
Chapter 4, THEORY OF PARSING). Such symbolic approaches have the advantage of
being well understood computationally, transparent with respect to their linguistic basis, and scalable. An alternative approach has been to develop models using
neurally inspired connectionist networks (see Chapter 9, ARTIFICIAL NEURAL NET-
WORKS), which are able to learn from suf cient exposure to language, are robust,
and degrade gracefully (Elman 1990; Plunkett & Marchman 1996). Purely connectionist approaches often use distributed, rather than symbolic, representations,
making it dif cult to understand precisely what kinds of representations such
networks develop. Furthermore, they are typically relatively small-scale models, and it has proven dif cult to scale their coverage. Some cognitive models
of language are in fact best viewed as hybrids, exploiting a mixture of symbolic
representations, and connectionist-like computational mechanisms. Most recently,
probabilistic approaches have dominated, providing a transparent linguistic basis
on the one hand, with an experience-based mechanism on the other.

   Before considering the range of approaches, it is important to understand precisely the goals of computational psycholinguistics, and the kinds of data that
inform the development of models. Furthermore, while many ideas and algorithms have their roots in computational linguistics, we begin by identifying
where these two endeavors diverge, and why.

2   Computational Models of Human Language Processing

While psycholinguistic theories have traditionally been stated only informally,
the development of computational models is increasingly recognized as essential. Speci cally, computational models entail the explicit formalization of theories,
and also enable prediction of behavior. Implemented models are especially important, not only because human language processing is highly complex, involving
interaction of diverse linguistic and non-linguistic constraints, but also because it
is inherently a dynamic process: people are known to understand, and produce,
language incrementally as they read or hear a sentence unfold. This entails that the
recovery of meaning happens in real time, with the interpretation being in uenced
by a range of linguistic, non-linguistic, and contextual sources of information, on
the one hand, and also shaping our expectations of what will come next, on the
other.

   How is computational psycholinguistics different from computational linguistics? In fact, early conceptions of natural language processing explicitly

approached language as a cognitive process (Winograd 1983). Ultimately, however, research is shaped by the speci c goals of a particular research community. To understand this more clearly, it can be helpful to distinguish accounts of linguistic *competence* and *performance*. Broadly speaking, a theory of linguistic competence is concerned with characterizing what it means to 'know' language, including the kinds of syntactic and semantic rules and representations provided by a linguistic theory. A theory of performance, in contrast, characterizes the means by which such knowledge is used *on-line* to recover the meaning for a given sentence, as exempli ed by a psychologically plausible parsing algorithm.

Consider, for example, one of the classic examples from psycholinguistics, known as the main verb/reduced-relative clause ambiguity (Bever 1970):

(1)   *The horse raced past the barn fell.*

For many readers, this sentence seems ungrammatical. The confusion arises because the verb *raced* is initially interpreted as the main verb, leading the parser '*up the garden path*' (Frazier 1979). Only when the true main verb *fell* is reached can the reader potentially determine that *raced past the barn* should actually have been interpreted as a reduced-relative clause (as in *The horse which was raced past the barn fell*). In this relatively extreme example of a *garden-path* sentence, many readers are unable to recover the correct meaning at all, despite the sentence being perfectly grammatical (cf. *The patient sent the flowers was pleased* which is rather easier, but has the same structure). Thus our linguistic competence offers no explanation for this phenomena, rather it seems necessary to appeal to *how* people recover the meaning, resolving ambiguity as they encounter the sentence incrementally.

Computational linguistics and psycholinguistics have traditionally shared assumptions regarding linguistic competence; both are concerned with developing algorithms which recover a linguistically adequate representation of a sentence as de ned by current syntactic and semantic theories. At the level of performance, however, computational linguistics is rarely concerned with issues such as incremental sentence processing and the resolution of *local* ambiguities which are resolved by the end of the sentence. There is rather a greater interest in optimizing the computational properties of parsing algorithms, such as their time and space complexity. Computational psycholinguistics, in contrast, places particular emphasis on the incremental processing behavior of the parser.

As computational linguistics has increasingly shifted its focus towards application domains, the demands of these applications has further divided the computational linguistics and computational psycholinguistics communities. The acknowledged dif culty of computationally solving the *natural language understanding problem*, which in turn relies on a solution to the *artificial intelligence problem*,[1] has led to an increased focus in computational linguistics on developing less linguistically ambitious technologies which are scalable and able to provide useful technologies for particular subproblems. Robust methods for part-of-speech tagging, named entity recognition, and shallow parsing (see Chapter 5,

MAXIMUM ENTROPY MODELS), for example, can contribute to applications ranging from spam- ltering and document classi cation to information extraction, question answering, and machine translation (see Chapter 18, INFORMATION EXTRACTION, Chapter 22, QUESTION ANSWERING, and Chapter 19, MACHINE TRANSLATION). For the most part, however, the methods used to perform these tasks have no cognitive basis.

While the research goals of computational linguistics and computational psycholinguistics have diverged since the 1970s, there continues to exist a signi cant overlap in some of the methods that are exploited. An interesting result of the shift towards wide coverage and robust language processing has been a tremendous emphasis on statistical language processing, and machine learning. As we will see, many of the same underlying methods play a central role in cognitive models as well, with particular overlap coming from research on statistical language modeling (see Chapter 3, STATISTICAL LANGUAGE MODELING).

2.1 Theories and models

In developing accounts of human language processing, as with any other cognitive process, it is valuable to distinguish the expression of the theory from a given model which implements the theory. Theories typically relate to a particular aspect of language processing – such as lexical access, parsing, or production – and as such provide incomplete characterizations of language processing in general. Furthermore, theories often provide a relatively high-level characterization of a process, leaving open details about what speci c algorithms might be used to realize the theory. Marr (1982), in fact, identi es three levels at which cognitive processes may be described: (1) the *computational* level, which de nes *what* is computed, (2) the *algorithmic* level, which speci es *how* computation takes place, and (3) the *implementation* level, which states how the algorithms are actually realized in the neural assemblies and substrates of the brain. In the case of language processing, which is a relatively high-level cognitive function, there have been very few accounts at the third level: we simply have insuf cient understanding about how language is processed and represented at the neural level.

There are several reasons for why a distinction of these levels is important. One reason for wishing to state theories at a relatively high level is to emphasize the general properties of the system being described, and ideally some justi cation of why it is the way it is. Additionally, it is often the case that the relevant empirical data available may not permit a more detailed characterization. That is to say, in building a speci c model (at the algorithmic level) of a given theory (stated at the computational level), we are often required to specify details of processing which are underdetermined by the empirical data. While resolving those details is essential to building computational models that function, we may not wish to ascribe any psychological reality to all aspects of the model. In the event that there is some new piece of empirical evidence which the model incorrectly accounts for, such a distinction is critical: it may be a consequence of the original theory, either falsifying it or entailing some revision to it, or it may simply be a result of some (possibly purely pragmatically based) decision made in implementing the model, such that only a change at the algorithmic or implementation level, and not the computational level, is needed.

Theories of human language processing can be broadly characterized by the extent to which they assume that the mechanisms underlying language processing are *restricted* or *unrestricted* (Pickering et al., 2000a). Restricted accounts begin with the assumption that cognitive processes are resource bound, and that observed processing dif culties in human language processing are a consequence of utilizing or exceeding these resource bounds. In order to explain a number of experimentally observed behaviors, a range of restrictions have been identi ed which may play a role in characterizing the architecture and mechanisms of the human language processor.

> **Working Memory**: the language processor has limited capacity for storing linguistic representations, and these may be exceeded during the processing of certain grammatical structures, such as center-embeddings: '*The mouse [that the cat [that the dog chased] bit] died,*' in which three noun phrases must be maintained in memory before they can be integrated with their respective verbs (Miller & Isard 1964; Bever 1970; Gibson 1991).
>
> **Serial Processing**: while there may be many structures that can be associated with a sentence during incremental processing, the human parser only pursues one structure, rather than several or all of them, so as to minimize space complexity. This predicts that, if the sentence is disambiguated as having an alternative structure, some form of *reanalysis* will be necessary and cause processing dif culty (Frazier 1979).
>
> **Modularity**: Cognitive processes underlying sentence processing are simpli ed by restricting their representational and informational domains. This enables on-line syntactic processes to operate independently of more general, complex, and time-consuming cognitive processes such as pragmatics, world knowledge and inference (Fodor 1983).

Unrestricted accounts, in contrast, typically assume that the processing is not fundamentally constrained, and that people are able to bring diverse informational constraints (i.e., interactive rather than modular) to bear on deciding among possible structures and interpretations (i.e., parallel rather than serial). Such accounts do not deny that cognitive resources are ultimately limited, but do tacitly assume that the architectures and mechanisms for language processing are not fundamentally shaped by the goal of conserving such resources. Most current models are best viewed as lying somewhere between the two extremes.

2.2 *Experimental data*

As noted above, models of human language processing seek to model not only linguistic competence – the ability to relate a sentence or utterance with its intended meaning – but also human linguistic performance. Language processing is best viewed as a dynamic process, in which both the linguistic input and associated processing mechanisms unfold over time. Evidence concerning *how* people process language can be obtained using a variety of methods. An important aspect of all controlled psycholinguistic experiments, however, is a clear experimental design. Experiments are designed to test a specific hypothesis about language processing, usually as predicted by a particular theoretical proposal or model. As an example, let's consider the matter of serial, incremental processing: the claim that each word is attached into a single connected partial syntactic representation as the sentence is read. This claim makes the prediction that any local ambiguity will be resolved immediately and if that decision later turns out to be wrong, then some processing difficulty will ensue. Consider the following sentences:

(2) a. *The athlete* [VP *realized* [NP *her potential*]]
     b. *The athlete* [VP *realized* [S [NP *her potential*] [VP *might make her famous*]]]
     c. *The athlete* [VP *realized* [S [NP *her exercises*] [VP *might make her famous*]]]

In sentences (2a) and (2b), a local ambiguity occurs when we encounter the word 'her,' following the verb 'realized.' While the word 'her' certainly begins a noun phrase (NP), that NP can be either the direct object of the verb, as in the sentence (2a), or the subject of an embedded sentence, as in (2b). To investigate whether or not people immediately consider the direct object reading, Pickering et al. (2000b) compared processing of this ambiguity, manipulating only whether the NP following the verb was a plausible direct object. They argued that if people favor building the direct object reading, this will influence processing complexity in two ways. First, in (2b), they will attach the NP 'her potential' as the direct object, and then be surprised when they encounter the following VP, which forces them to reanalyze the object NP as the subject of the embedded clause. For (2c), they should also attempt the direct object attachment, but be surprised because it is implausible, and then assume it begins an embedded clause. In an eye-tracking study, they found evidence supporting exactly this prediction. Namely, in (2c) people spent longer reading the NP ('her exercises') following the verb, than they did reading the NP ('her potential') in (2b), suggesting they built a direct object structure only to realize it is implausible. In (2b), however, people spent longer reading the *disambiguating* region (the embedded VP) than in (2c), suggesting they had committed to the (plausible) direct object reading, and then needed to revise that analysis.

Since many different factors are known to influence reading times, most psycholinguistic experiments use a design like the one just described above, in which the *difference* in reading times for similar sentences (or regions of the sentence) are compared, and where only the factor which is of interest is varied between the sentences. One simple method which has been used effectively to investigate incremental reading processes is the *self-paced reading* (SPR) paradigm. Using this method, the sentence is presented one word at a time, and the participant must press a key to see the next word. The latency between key presses can then be averaged across both participants and a range of linguistic stimuli to obtain average reading times, which can then be analyzed to determine if there are statistically signi cant differences in reading times resulting from the experimental manipulation. Another more sophisticated method, eye tracking, provides an especially rich, real-time window into language processing, with the added advantage of not requiring any additional (possibly unnatural) task. Current eye-tracking technology enables the precise spatial and temporal recording of eye movements (saccades) and xations as people read a sentence which is displayed in its entirety on a display. Since people often look back to earlier points in the sentence while reading, several reading-time *measures* can be computed, such as *first pass* (the amount of time spent in a region before the eye moves out of the region), or *total time* (all the time spent reading a region, including looking back at it, etc.) (Rayner 1998).

When relating a theory or model of language processing to empirical data, it is important to be clear about the exact nature of the relationship that is being assumed, via a *linking hypothesis*. In the example described above, we implicitly assumed that it was the *surprise* – of either an implausible interpretation, or a subsequent cue that reparsing would be required – that would lead to increased reading time. But there are many characteristics of a computational model that one might argue would be re ected in empirically observable processing complexity. As we will see below, everything from the frequency of the word which is being processed, to the memory load associated with processing completely unambiguous sentences, can be observed in reading times. This is one reason why carefully controlled experiments are so essential, as are clear linking hypotheses that can be used to relate a processing model to some empirical measure.

Reading times offer a robust and well-understood *behavioral* method for establishing processing dif culty during sentence comprehension. More recently, however, neuroscienti c methods have become increasingly important for informing the development of psycholinguistic theories. This is particularly true of *event-related potentials* (ERPs), which can be observed using electroencephalography (EEG) methods. ERPs re ect brain activity, as measured by electrodes positioned on the scalp, in response to a speci c stimulus. Numerous ERP studies have demonstrated the incrementality of language comprehension as revealed by the on-line detection of semantic (e.g., Kutas & Hillyard 1980; 1983; van Petten & Kutas 1990) and syntactic (e.g., Osterhout & Holcomb 1992; 1993; Matzke et al., 2002) violations, indexed broadly by so-called N400 and P600 de ections in scalp activation respectively. However, while there are several theoretical processing accounts which are derived from such data (Friederici 2002; Bornkessel & Schlesewsky 2006), relatively few have led to the development of computational models (but see Crocker et al., 2010). For this reason, we will focus here primarily on models based on behavioral ndings.

Finally, the *visual world paradigm*, in which participants' eye movements to visually displayed objects are monitored as participants listen to an unfolding utterance, has revealed that people automatically map the unfolding linguistic input onto the objects in their visual environment in real time (Tanenhaus et al.,

1995). Using this method, Allopenna et al. (1998) demonstrated not only that increased inspections of visually present objects often occur within 200 ms of their mention, but also that such utterance-mediated fixations even reveal sublexical processing of the unfolding speech stream. Perhaps of even greater theoretical interest are the findings of Tanenhaus et al. (1995), revealing on-line interaction of visual and linguistic information for sentences such as '*Put the apple on the towel in the box.*' Not only did listeners rapidly fixate the mentioned objects, but their gaze also suggested the influence of the visual referential context in resolving the structural ambiguity in this sentence (namely, whether *towel* is a modifier of, or the destination for, the *apple*). In fact, this paradigm has also shown that comprehension is not just incremental, but often highly *predictive*: Altmann and Kamide (1999) demonstrated that listeners exploit the selectional restrictions of verbs like *eat*, as revealed by anticipatory looks to edible objects in the scene (before those objects have been referred to) (see also Federmeier (2007) for related findings from event-related potential studies).

3   Symbolic Models

Evidence that people understand language incrementally is perhaps one of the most ubiquitous findings in experimental research on human sentence processing. The importance of this finding for computational models is that it places a strong constraint on candidate parsing mechanisms. Not all early computational accounts adhered to the incrementality constraint, however. The *Parsifal* model (Marcus 1980), for example, proposed a deterministic model of human parsing to account for the observation that people are generally able to understand language in real time. Parsifal was essentially a bottom-up LR parser, which exploited up to three look-ahead symbols (which could be complex phrases, not just words) to decide upon the next parsing action with certainty. This look-ahead mechanism enabled the parser to avoid making incorrect decisions for most sentences, and Marcus argued that those sentences where the parser failed were precisely those cases where people also had substantial difficulty.

There are, however, several criticisms that can be leveled at Parsifal. Not only is the parser highly non-incremental, with the capacity to leave large amounts of the input on the stack, it also offers only a binary account of processing difficulty: easy versus impossible. Experimental research has shown, however, that some kinds of erroneous parsing decisions are much easier to recover from than others (for a direct comparison of two such cases, see Sturt et al., 1999). The *licensing-structure* parser (Abney 1989) responded to these criticisms by adapting a shift-reduce parsing architecture of Pereira (1985) to operate more incrementally. Since lookahead must be excluded in order to maintain incrementality, the parser often faces non-determinism during processing. For these cases, Abney proposes several preference strategies which are intended to reflect parsing principles motivated by human behavior such as *right association* (Kimball 1973) (attach incoming material low on the right frontier of the current parse) and *theta attachment* (Pritchett 1992) (attach constituents so as to maximize thematic role assignment, see Section 3.1). Abney additionally addressed the issue of *backtracking*, in case parsing fails and an alternative parse needs to be found. The licensing-structure parser, however, is still not strictly incremental, with some parse operations delaying the attachment of words and constituents. A further criticism, which applies to the accounts proposed by Marcus, Abney, and Pritchett, is their strong reliance on verb information to determine the parser's actions. While this approach works reasonably for languages like English, it is problematic for explaining parsing of verb- nal languages like Japanese, Turkish, and many others.

Resnik (1992a) reconsiders the role of space, or memory, utilization as a criteria for selecting psychologically plausible parsing algorithms. As noted above, embedding structures reveal an interesting property of human sentence processing, illustrated by Resnik's following examples (brackets indicate emdedded constituents):

(3) a. [[[*John's*] *brother's*] *cat*] *despises rats* EASY
     b. *This is* [*the dog that chased* [*the cat that bit* [*the rat that ate the cheese*]]] EASY
     c. [*The rat* [*that the cat* [*that the dog chased*] *bit*] *ate the cheese*] HARD

While people typically nd left-embeddings (3a) and right-embeddings (3b) relatively unproblematic, center-embeddings (3c) are often judged as dif cult, if not completely ungrammatical (though one can quite clearly demonstrate that they violate no rules of grammar). Building on previous work by Abney and Johnson (1991) and Johnson-Laird (1983), Resnik (1992a) demonstrates that neither strictly top-down (LL) nor bottom-up (LR) parsers can explain this observation. Top-down parsing predicts only right-embeddings to be easy, while bottom-up predicts only left-embeddings to be easy. Further, Resnik demonstrates that the standard version of a left-corner (LC) parser, which combines top-down and bottom-up parsing, is no different than the bottom-up parser with regard to stack complexity. However, an *arc-eager* variant of the LC parser – in which nodes that are predicted bottom-up can be immediately *composed* with nodes that are predicted top-down – models the human performance correctly: left- and right-embeddings have constant complexity, while center-embedding complexity increases linearly with the number of embeddings. A further advantage of the arc-eager LC parser is that it is incremental for all but a few sentence structures (for more detailed discussion of parsing mechanisms, see Crocker 1999).

3.1 Ambiguity resolution

A central element of any model of sentence processing concerns how it deals with lexical and syntactic ambiguity: how do we decide which representation to assign to the current input? The assumption of incremental processing further entails that decisions regarding which structure to pursue must be made as each word is processed. One simple solution to this issue is to propose a parallel model of processing, in which all possible syntactic analyses are pursued simultaneously during processing. Such a solution has traditionally been discarded for two reasons. First, for a large-scale grammar and lexicon, hundreds of analyses may be possible at any point during parsing – indeed, for grammars with left-recursion, there may in fact be an unbounded number of parses possible – and would arguably exceed cognitively plausible memory limitations. One solution to this is to assume *bounded* parallelism, in which only a limited subset of parses is considered. Second, even if one assumes parsing is (possibly bounded) parallel, there is strong evidence that only one interpretation is consciously considered, otherwise we would never expect to observe the kind of garden-path sentence discussed in Section 2. Thus, regardless of whether incremental processing is serial or parallel, any model requires an account of which parse is to be preferred.

There have been many proposals to explain such ambiguity preferences in the psycholinguistic literature. Frazier (1979), building on previous work by Kimball (1973), proposed the following two general principles:

Minimal attachment (MA): Attach incoming material into the phrase marker being constructed using the fewest nodes consistent with the well-formedness rules of the language.

Late closure (LC): When possible, attach incoming material into the clause or phrase currently being parsed.

Recall example (2) above. When the noun phrase '*her potential*' is encountered, it can be attached directly either as the object of '*realized*' (2a), or as the subject of the embedded clause (2b). The latter structure, however, requires an additional node in the parse-tree, namely an S node intervening between the verb and the noun phrase. Thus MA correctly predicts the human preference to interpret the noun phrase as a direct object, until syntactic or semantic information disambiguates to the contrary.

While these parsing principles dominated sentence processing for some time, they have been criticized on several grounds. First, as noted by Abney (1989) and Pritchett (1992), MA is highly sensitive to the precise syntactic analysis assigned by the grammar. The adoption of binary branching structures in many modern syntactic theories means that MA fails to differentiate between a number of ambiguities (including the one in Figure 17.2, discussed below). In response to this, several theories proposed a shift away from MA towards what Pritchett (1992) dubbed *theta attachment* (see also Abney 1989; Crocker 1996 for related proposals). Theta attachment states that the parser should attempt to maximally satisfy verb argument relations whenever possible, and thus prioritize the parsing of phrases into such argument positions, where they will receive a semantic, or *thematic*, role from the verb (Fillmore 1968). Returning to sentence (2a), theta attachment asserts that attaching the noun phrase '*her potential ...*' as a direct object is preferred because not only is the verb able to assign a thematic role (THEME) to the noun phrase, but the noun phrase also receives a thematic role at that point in processing. If the noun phrase were attached as the embedded subject, as in (2b), it would temporarily have no role assigned to it (until the embedded predicate '*might make . . .*' is processed). Thus the latter option is dispreferred.

The above approaches are typically associated with modular processing accounts (Fodor 1983), since they emphasize the role of purely syntactic decision strategies for parsing and disambiguation. Serial parsing is also assumed, namely that the human language processor only constructs one parse – backtracking or reanalyzing the sentence if that parse turns out to be incorrect. For these reasons, such models of processing are typically viewed as *restricted* accounts, since they fundamentally assume a processing architecture which is limited by the kinds of information it has access to (i.e., syntactic), and the memory resources available for parsing.

While there is a considerable body of experimental evidence supporting the importance of such syntactic strategies, there is also evidence suggesting that people are nonetheless able to draw upon a large repertoire of relevant constraints in resolving ambiguity, such as speci c lexical biases, and semantic plausibility (Gibson & Pearlmutter 1998). The general claim of such *interactive constraint-based* approaches is that parsing is not a serial process in uenced solely by syntactic strategies, but rather that '*multiple alternatives are at least partially available, and that ambiguity resolution is accomplished by the use of correlated constraints from other domains*' (Trueswell & Tanenhaus 1994). While one might envisage such a model in symbolic terms, they typically rely on the use of probabilistic constraints, and are better viewed as *hybrid* models, which we will we discuss in Section 6.

3.2   Working memory

The above discussion of the left-corner parser might lead one to believe that center-embeddings are the only unambiguous syntactic structures which cause processing dif culty. Gibson (1991), however, argues that processing complexity arising from working memory demands can also explain ambiguity resolution preferences. Building on Pritchett's *theta attachment* strategy (1992), Gibson attributes a *cost* to the parser's need to maintain thematic role assignments and role llers in memory. He argues that such a working-memory metric can be used not only to explain increased processing complexity for structures with locally high memory demands, but also to rank candidate parsers in the face of local ambiguity. That is, the parser will generally prefer interpretations which have lower cost with respect to unful lled role relations, thus predicting disambiguation behavior in a manner similar to Pritchett (1992). Gibson's *dependency locality theory* (1998) re nes this approach further, by taking into account the distance between role assigners and role recipients (see also Gibson 2003 for an overview). Lewis et al. (2006) propose an account of parsing which draws on a number of general observations concerning the dynamics of memory retrieval that have been established across cognitive domains. These principles have also been implemented within the general cognitive architecture ACT-R (Anderson et al., 2004), enabling Lewis and colleagues to provide an independently motivated proposal regarding the role of working memory in sentence processing.

4   Probabilistic Models

The symbolic accounts outlined above offer insight into both how hierarchical sentence structure and meaning are recovered incrementally, and when processing of such sentences may be dif cult as a consequence of either working memory limitations or the need to reanalyze the sentence if the parser has followed a garden path. A variety of empirical results, however, suggest that such symbolic, modular, and serial processing mechanisms may not scale suf ciently to account for human linguistic performance in general (Crocker 2005). First, serial backtracking parsers are known to be extremely inef cient as grammars are scaled up to provide realistic linguistic coverage. In addition, such models accord no role to linguistic experience despite a wealth of experimental ndings indicating that frequency information plays a central role in determining the preferred part of speech, meaning, and subcategorization frame for a given word. Finally, while cognitive resources like working memory undoubtedly constrain language processing, and provide an index of certain kinds of processing complexity, it has been argued that people are in general able to understand most language effectively and without conscious effort. Indeed, one of the most challenging tasks facing computational psycholinguistics is to explain how people are able to deal with the complexity and pervasive ambiguity of natural language so accurately and in real time: what Crocker (2005) dubs *the performance paradox*.

Probabilistic approaches offer a natural means to address the above issues. Not only do they provide a means to develop *experience-based* models, which can exploit the kinds of frequency information that people have been shown to use, but probabilistic methods have also proven extremely successful for developing wide-coverage models of language processing (see Chapter 3, STATISTICAL LANGUAGE MODELING, Chapter 4, THEORY OF PARSING, and Chapter 13, STATISTICAL PARSING). Perhaps more fundamentally, probabilistic methods invite us to view language processing less in terms of the dif culties people exhibit on some kinds of constructions, and instead emphasize the remarkable performance that people exhibit in understanding language in general. Chater et al. (1998) explicitly argue that human language processing may be fruitfully viewed as a *rational* process, in Anderson's sense of the term (1990). If one views language understanding as a rational cognitive process one can begin by rst identifying the *goal* of that process – e.g., to nd the correct interpretation of a sentence – and then reason about the function that best achieves that goal and accounts for observed behavior. One obvious rational analysis of parsing is to assume that the parser chooses operations so as to maximize the likelihood of nding the intended global interpretation of the sentence, taking into account known cognitive and environmental limitations. Given the overwhelming evidence that people process language incrementally, we can plausibly de ne the function that is implemented by the human language processor as follows:

(4) $\hat{t}_i = \underset{t_i}{\mathrm{argmax}}\ P_i(t_i|w_{1...i}, K), \forall t_i \in T_i$

This states that, as each word w_i is processed, the preferred analysis of the sentence-initial substring $w_1 \ldots w_i$, $\hat{t}_i$, corresponds to the analysis t_i – in the set of possible analyses T_i that span the sentence up to and including w_i – that has the highest likelihood given the words of the sentence, and our general knowledge K.[2] Crucially, this equation provides only a high-level characterization of how people process language, namely at Marr's *computational level*, which we will refer to as the *likelihood hypothesis*. It leaves aside many crucial issues concerning *how* the analyses are constructed and their probabilities estimated. In principle, the likelihood of a particular analysis of a sentence might re ect not only our accumulated linguistic experience as it relates to the current input, but also the current context and our general knowledge K. But just as statistical language processing techniques have vastly simpli ed the kind of information used to condition the probabilities, it may be reasonable to assume that people similarly approximate probabilities, at least during initial processing of the input. In the following sections we review several proposals that can be viewed as instances of the likelihood hypothesis.

4.1   *Lexical processing*

Much of the ambiguity that occurs in syntactic processing in fact derives from ambiguity at the lexical level (MacDonald et al., 1994). Furthermore, it is precisely at the lexical level that frequency effects have been most robustly observed: high-frequency words are processed more quickly than low-frequency ones (Grosjean 1980); words are preferentially understood as having their most likely part of speech (Trueswell 1996; Crocker & Corley 2002); verb subcategorization preferences rapidly in uence parsing decisions (Ford et al., 1982; Garnsey et al., 1997; Trueswell et al., 1993); and semantically ambiguous words are preferably associated with their more frequent sense (Duffy et al., 1988). These ndings all suggest that a likelihood-based resolution of lexical ambiguity will substantially reduce parsing ambiguity, and assist in guiding the parser towards the most likely parse in a manner that re ects human behavior.

Based on this rationale, Corley and Crocker (2000) propose a broad-coverage model of lexical category disambiguation as a means for substantially constraining the preferred syntactic analysis. Their approach uses a bigram model to incrementally determine the most probable assignment of part-of-speech tags, $\hat{t}_0 \ldots \hat{t}_i$, for the (sub)string of input words $w_0 \ldots w_i$, as follows:

(5) $\hat{t}_0 \ldots \hat{t}_i = \underset{t_0 \ldots t_i}{\mathrm{argmax}}\ P(t_0 \ldots t_i, w_0 \ldots w_i) \approx \prod_{j=1}^{i} P(w_j|t_j)P(t_j|t_{j-1})$

The bigram model results in the use of both the unigram likelihood of word w_j given a possible part of speech t_j, $P(w_j|t_j)$, as well as the context as captured by the immediately preceding part-of-speech tag $P(t_j|t_{j-1})$. The likelihood for a particular sequence of parts of speech, ranging from w_0 to w_i, is the product of this value as computed for each word in the string. In order to ef ciently determine the most likely part-of-speech sequence as the sentence is processed, the Viterbi algorithm is used (Viterbi 1967).

(6)   a.   *The warehouse prices are cheaper than the rest.*
      b.   *The warehouse makes are cheaper than the rest.*

This model capitalizes on the insight that many syntactic ambiguities have a lexical basis, as in (6). These sentences are ambiguous between a reading in which *'prices'* (6a) or *'makes'* (6b) serves as either the main verb or part of a compound noun. Once trained on a large corpus, the model predicts the most likely part of speech for *'prices,'* correctly accounting for the fact that people preferentially interpret *'prices'* as a noun, but *'makes'* as verb (Frazier & Rayner 1987; MacDonald 1993). In the latter case, a dif cultly in processing is observed once the sentence disambiguates *'makes'* as a noun (Crocker & Corley 2002). The model similarly accounts for the nding that categorially ambiguous words like *'that'* are resolved by their preceding context: in sentence-initial position, *'that'* is more likely to be a determiner, while post-verbally, it is more likely to be a complementizer (Juliano & Tanenhaus 1993).

Interestingly, the use of the Viterbi algorithm to determine the most likely sequence incrementally predicts that reanalysis may occur when the most probable part-of-speech sequence at a given point requires revising a preceding part of speech assigment. This behavior in the model nds support from a study by MacDonald (1994) showing that reduced-relative clause constructions, like those illustrated in (7) were rendered easier to process when the word following the ambiguous verb (simple past vs. participle) made the participle reading more likely.

(7)   a.   *The sleek greyhound admired at the track won four trophies.*
      b.   *The sleek greyhound raced at the track won four trophies.*

Since *'admired'* (7a) is transitive, the fact that is it not followed by a noun phrase is a clear cue that its part of speech should be past participle, and parse inside the relative clause. For *'raced'* (7b), however, which is preferentially intransitive, the preposition *'at'* provides no such cue for rapid reanalysis, resulting in a garden path when the main verb *'won'* is reached.

Importantly, however, the model not only accounts for a range of disambiguation preferences rooted in lexical category ambiguity, it also offers an explanation for why, in general, people are highly accurate in resolving such ambiguities. It is also worthwhile to distinguish between various aspects of this account in terms of Marr's three levels. Equation (5) provides the *computational* theory, the likelihood

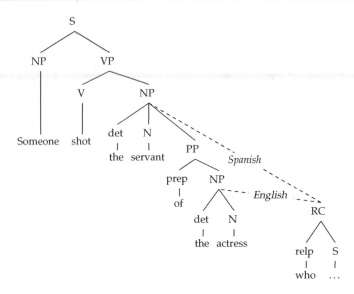

Figure 17.1   Relative clause attachment ambiguity.

function de ning the goal of the process, and its *algorithmic* instantiation in terms of the bigram model and the Viterbi algorithm. This highlights the point that one might change the algorithmic level – e.g., by using a trigram model, should there be empirical evidence to support this – without in any way changing the computational theory. The *implementation* level is not provided, since this would entail a characterization of how the bigram model is processed in the brain and how probabilities are estimated over the course of our linguistic experience (which we simply approximate using corpus frequencies).

4.2   Syntactic processing

While lexical disambiguation is an important part of sentence processing, and goes a considerable way towards resolving many structural ambiguities, Corley and Crocker's model (2000) is clearly not a full model of syntactic processing. Indeed, Mitchell et al. (1995) have taken the stronger view that the human parser not only makes use of lexical frequencies, but also keeps track of *structural* frequencies. Evidence from relative clause attachment ambiguity (see Figure 17.1) has been taken to support an experience-based treatment of structural disambiguation. Such constructions are interesting because they do not hinge on lexical preferences. When reading sentences containing the ambiguity in Figure 17.1, English comprehenders appear to follow Frazier's late closure strategy, demonstrating a preference for low attachment (where *'the actress'* is modi ed by the RC *'who…'*). Spanish readers, in contrast, when presented with equivalent Spanish sentences, prefer high attachment (where the RC concerns *'the servant'*) (Cuetos & Mitchell 1988).

This nding provided evidence against the universality of Frazier's late closure strategy (Section 3.1), leading Mitchell et al. (1995) to propose the *tuning hypothesis*, which asserts that the human parser deals with ambiguity by initially selecting the syntactic analysis that has worked most frequently in the past (Brysbaert & Mitchell 1996). Later experiments further tested the hypothesis, examining school children's preferences before and after a period of two weeks in which exposure to high or low examples was increased. The ndings con rmed that even this brief period of variation in *experience* in uenced the attachment preferences as predicted (Cuetos et al., 1996).

Models of human syntactic processing have increasingly exploited probabilistic grammar formalisms, such as probabilistic context-free grammars (PCFGs) to provide a uniform probabilistic treatment of lexical and syntactic processing and disambiguation (for PCFGs, see Manning & Schütze 1999, as well as Chapter 4, THEORY OF PARSING, and Chapter 13, STATISTICAL PARSING). PCFGs augment standard context-free grammars by annotating grammar rules with rule probabilities. A rule probability expresses the likelihood of the left-hand side of the rule expanding to its right-hand side. As an example, consider the rule VP → V NP in Figure 17.2(a). This rule says that a verb phrase expands to a verb followed by a noun phrase with a probability of 0.7. In a PCFG, the probabilities of all rules with the same left-hand side must sum to one:

(8) $\forall i \sum_{j} P(N^i \rightarrow \zeta^j) = 1$

where $P(N^i \rightarrow \zeta^j)$ is the probability of a rule with the left-hand side N^i and the right-hand side ζ^j. For example, in Figure 17.2(a) the two rules VP → V NP and VP → VP PP share the same left-hand side (VP), so their probabilities sum to one. The probability of a parse-tree generated by a PCFG is computed as the product of the rule probabilities:

(9) $P(t) = \prod_{(N \rightarrow \zeta) \in R} P(N \rightarrow \zeta)$

where R is the set of all rules applied in generating the parse-tree t. While rule probabilities are in theory derived during the course of a person's linguistic experience, most models rely on standard techniques for estimating probabilities such as *maximum likelihood estimation* – a *supervised* learning algorithm which calculates the probability of a rule based on the number of times it occurs in a parsed training corpus. An alternate, *unsupervised* method is the expectation-maximization (EM) algorithm (Baum 1972; see also Chapter 12, SPEECH RECOGNITION), which uses an unparsed training corpus to estimate a set of rule probabilities that makes the sentences in the corpus maximally likely (see also Chapter 8, UNSUPERVISED LEARNING AND GRAMMAR INDUCTION).

Just as lexical frequency may determine the ease with which words are retrieved from the lexicon, and the preferred morphological, syntactic, and semantic interpretations we associate with them, Jurafsky (1996) argues that the probability of a

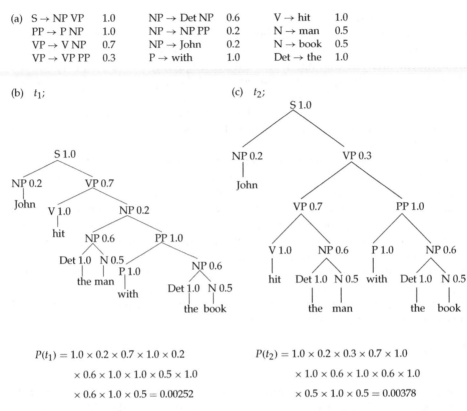

Figure 17.2   An example for the parse-trees generated by a probabilistic-context free grammar (PCFG) (adapted from Crocker & Keller 2006). (a) The rules of a simple PCFG with associated rule application probabilities. The two parse-trees, (b) and (c), generated by the PCFG in (a) for the sentence '*John hit the man with the book*,' with the respective parse probabilities, $P(t_1)$ and $P(t_2)$, calculated below.

grammar rule corresponds to how easily that rule can be accessed by the human sentence processor during parsing. The consequence of this claim is that structures with greater overall probability should be easier to construct, and therefore preferred in cases of ambiguity. The PCFG in Figure 17.2(a) generates two parses for the the sentence '*John hit the man with the book*.' The rst parse t_1 attaches the prepositional phrase '*with the book*' to the noun phrase (low attachment) with a total probability of 0.00252 (see Figure 17.2(b)). The alternative parse t_2, with the prepositional phrase attached to the verb phrase (high attachment) is assigned a probability of 0.00378 (see Figure 17.2(c)). Under the assumption that the probability of a parse determines processing ease, the grammar will predict that t_2 (high attachment) will be generally preferred to t_1, as it has a higher probability.

In applying PCFGs to the problem of human sentence processing, Jurafsky (1996) makes two important observations. First he assumes that parsing, and the computation of parse probabilities, takes place incrementally. The consequence is

Table 17.1 Conditional probability of a verb frame given a particular verb, as estimated using the Penn Treebank

Verb	Frame	P(Frame | Verb)
discuss	<NP PP>	0.24
	<NP>	0.76
keep	<NP PP>	0.81
	<NP>	0.19

that the parse faces a local ambiguity as soon as it hears the fragment *'John hit the man with ...'* and must decide which of the two possible structures is to be preferred. This entails that the parser is able to compute pre x probabilities for sentence-initial substrings, as the basis for comparing alternative (partial) parses (Stolcke 1995). For the example in Figure 17.2, it should be clear that the preference for t_2 would be predicted even before the   nal NP is processed, since the probability of that NP is the same for both structures.

The second major contribution of Jurafsky's approach (1996) is the proposal to combine structural probabilities generated by a probabilistic context-free grammar with probabilistic preferences of individual lexical items, using Bayes's rule. The model therefore integrates lexical and syntactic probabilities within a single mathematically founded probabilistic framework. As an example consider the sentences in (10), which have a similar syntactic ambiguity to that outlined in Figure 17.2.

(10) a. *'The women discuss the dogs on the beach.'*
      b. *'The women keep the dogs on the beach.'*

The intuition when one reads these sentences is that low attachment of the PP *'on the beach'* to the NP *'the dogs'* is preferred for (10a), while high attachment to the verb is preferred for (10b). A standard PCFG model, however, will always prefer one of these (in our example PCFG, high attachment). Following Ford et al. (1982), Jurafsky argues that we must also take into account the speci c subcategorization preferences of the verb (Table 17.1), in addition to the structural probabilities of the PCFG.

Jurafsky's model computes the probabilities of these two readings based on two sources of information: the overall structural probability of the high-attachment reading and the low-attachment reading, and the lexical probability of the verb occurring with a <NP PP> or a <NP> frame. The structural probability of a reading is independent of the particular verb involved; the frame probability, however, varies with the verb. This predicts that in some cases lexical probabilities can override the general structural probabilities derived from the PCFG. If we combine the frame probabilities from Table 17.1 with the parse probabilities determined with the PCFG in Figure 17.2, we can see that high-attachment preference is maintained for *'keep,'* but low attachment becomes more likely for *'discuss.'*

Strictly speaking, Jurafsky's model does not aim to recover the single most likely parse during processing, as suggested in equation (4). Rather he argues for a bounded parallel model, which pursues the most probable parses and prunes those parses whose probability is less than $\frac{1}{5}$ the probability of the most likely parse. Strong garden paths are predicted if the ultimately correct syntactic analysis is one which has been pruned during parsing.

4.3   *Wide-coverage models*

Jurafsky (1996) outlines how his framework can be used to explain a variety of ambiguity phenomena, including cases like (6) and (7) discussed above. However, it might be criticized for its limited coverage, i.e., for the fact that it uses only a small lexicon and grammar, manually designed to account for a handful of example sentences. Given that broad-coverage parsers are available that compute a syntactic structure for arbitrary corpus sentences, it is important that we demand more substantial coverage from our psycholinguistic models to ensure they are not *overfitting* to a small number of garden-path phenomena.

Crocker and Brants (2000) present the rst attempt at developing a truly wide-coverage model, based on the incremental probabilistic parsing proposals of Jurafsky (1996). Their approach combines the wide-coverage psycholinguistic bigram model of Corley and Crocker (2000) with the ef cient statistical parsing methods of Brants (1999). The resulting *incremental cascaded Markov model* has broad coverage, relatively good parse accuracy in general, while also accounting for a range of experimental ndings concerning lexical category and syntactic ambiguities. For practical reasons, Crocker and Brants (2000) do not include detailed subcategorization preferences for verbs, but rather limit this to transitivity, which is encoded as part of a each verb's part of speech. Adopting a parallel parsing approach not unlike that of Jurafsky, Crocker and Brants (2000) also argue that *re-ranking* of parses, not just pruning of the correct parse, is a predictor of human parsing complexity.

This research demonstrates that, when such models are trained on large corpora, they are indeed able to account for human disambiguation behavior such as that discussed by Jurafsky (1996). In related work, Brants and Crocker (2000) also demonstrate that broad-coverage probabilistic models maintain high overall accuracy even under strict memory and incremental processing restrictions. This is important to support the claim that rational models maintain their *near optimality* even when subject to such cognitively motivated constraints.

4.4   *Information-theoretic models*

The probabilistic parsing proposals of Jurafsky (1996) and Crocker and Brants (2000) provide relatively coarse-grained predictions concerning human processing dif culty, based on whether or not the ultimately correct parse was assigned a relatively low probability (or pruned entirely), and must be re-ranked (or even reparsed). Drawing on concepts developed in the statistical language modeling literature (see Chapter 3, STATISTICAL LANGUAGE MODELING), Hale (2001) proposes a more general linking hypothesis between incremental probabilistic processing and processing complexity. Speci cally, Hale suggests that the cognitive effort associated with processing the next word, w_i, of a sentence will be proportional to its *surprisal*. Surprisal is measured as the negative log-probability of a word, such that surprising (unlikely) words contribute greater information than words that are likely, or expected, given the pre x of the sentence, $w_1 \ldots w_{i-1}$.

(11) *Effort* $\propto -\log P(w_i|w_1 \ldots w_{i-1}, \text{Context}) \approx -\log \dfrac{P(T_i)}{P(T_{i-1})}$

The notion of information, here, derives from *information theory* (Shannon 1948), where highly likely or predictable words are viewed as providing little information, while unexpected words provide more. While, in principle, all our knowledge about the words $w_1 \ldots w_{i-1}$, linguistics constraints, and non-linguistic *context* will determine the probability of w_i, Hale assumes the probability can be reasonably approximated by a PCFG. Speci cally, he proposes that the probability of a given (sub)string $w_1 \ldots w_i$ is T_i, which is the sum of all possible parses t_i for the pre x string (equation 11). Thought of in this way, surprisal at word w_i will be proportional to the summed probability of all parses which are *disconfirmed* by the transition from word w_{i-1} to word w_i.

Hale's theory (2001) thus assumes full parallelism, and can be thought of as associating cognitive processing effort with the sum of *all* disambiguation that is done during parsing. This contrasts with standard accounts in which it is only discon rmation of the *preferred* interpretation which is assumed to cause processing dif culty. While the assumption of full parallelism raises some concerns regarding cognitive plausibility, Hale's model is able to account for a range of garden-path phenomena as well as processing complexity in unambiguous constructions, such as the dispreferred status of object versus subject relative clauses. In recent work, Levy (2008) re nes and extends Hale's approach (2001) in several respects, improving the mathematical properties of the *surprisal theory* while also extending the empirical coverage of the general approach. Hale (2003) proposes another variant on this approach, the *entropy reduction hypothesis*, in which cognitive effort is linked to a slightly different measure, namely the reduction in uncertainty about the rest of the sentence.

4.5 *Probabilistic semantics*

One major limitation of cognitive models of sentence processing is their emphasis on syntactic aspects of processing. This was arguably justi ed to some extent during the 1980s, when modular theories of language, and cognition in general, prevailed. Since then, however, a wealth of empirical results have shown that semantics and plausibility do not only in uence our nal interpretation of

a sentence, but that such information rapidly informs on-line incremental comprehension. In the case of the probabilistic parsing models discussed above,
probabilities are conditioned purely on syntactic and limited lexical frequencies.
For primarily practical reasons, a range of independence assumptions are made.
Our PCFG above, for example, will assign exactly the same probability to the sentences 'John hit the man with the book' and 'John hit the book with the man,' since
exactly the same rules of grammar are used in deriving the possible parse-trees.
Yet clearly the latter is semantically implausible, regardless of how it is parsed,
and therefore should be assigned a lower probability.

In experimental psycholinguistics, the on-line in uence of semantic plausibility
has been investigated by varying the argument of a particular verb–argument–
relation triple, often called *thematic fit*. McRae et al. (1998) investigated the
in uence of thematic t information on the processing of the main clause/reduced-
relative clause(MC/RR) ambiguity as illustrated in the sentences below.

(12)   a.   *'The pirate terrorized by his captors was freed quickly.'*
       b.   *'The victim terrorized by his captors was freed quickly.'*

During incremental processing of sentences like (12a), the pre x *'The pirate terrorized . . .'* is ambiguous between the more frequent main clause continuation (e.g.,
as in *'The pirate terrorized the Seven Seas'*) and a less frequent reduced-relative continuation as shown in (12a), where *'terrorized'* heads a relative clause that modi es
'pirate.' The subsequent *by*-phrase provides strong evidence for the reduced-
relative reading, signaling the absence of a direct object which would otherwise
be required if *'terrorized'* were in simple past tense, and suggests it is more likely a
past participle. Finally the main verb region *'was freed'* completely disambiguates
the sentence.

Evidence from reading-time experiments has shown that readers initially have
a strong preference for the main clause interpretation over the reduced relative,
but that this preference can be modulated by other factors (e.g., Rayner et al.,
1983; Crain & Steedman 1985; Trueswell 1996). McRae et al. (1998), in particular, showed that good thematic t of the rst NP as an object of the verb in the case
of *victim* in (12b) allowed readers to partially overcome the main clause preference and more easily adopt the dispreferred reduced-relative interpretation, which
makes the rst NP the object of the verb (as opposed to the main clause reading,
where it is a subject). Reading-time effects, both on the ambiguous verb and in
the disambiguating region, suggest that the thematic t of the rst NP and the
verb rapidly in uences the human sentence processor's preference for the two
candidate structures.

Narayanan and Jurafsky (1998) outline how Bayesian belief networks can be
used to combine a variety of lexical, syntactic, and semantic constraints. The
central idea is that we can construct a belief network which integrates multiple
probabilistic sources of evidence, including: structural probabilities determined
by the PCFG; subcategorization preferences as motivated by Jurafsky (1996); verb
tense probabilities; thematic t preferences; and so on. The central problem with

this framework is that, while extremely powerful and exible, there is at present no general method for parsing and constructing such Bayesian belief networks automatically. Rather, the networks must be constructed by hand for each possible structure to be modeled. We therefore leave aside a detailed discussion of this approach, while emphasizing that it may provide a valuable framework for modeling speci c kinds of probabilistic constraints (for a detailed discussion, see Jurafsky 2003).

In recent work, Pado et al. (2009) extend standard probabilistic grammar-based accounts of syntactic processing with a model of human thematic plausibility. The model is able to account for syntactic *and* semantic effects in human sentence processing, while retaining the main advantages of probabilistic grammar-based models, namely their ability naturally to account for frequency effects and their wide coverage of syntactic phenomena and unseen input.

The probabilistic formulation of the semantic model equates the plausibility of a verb–argument–role triple with the probability of that thematic role co-occurring with the verb–argument pair – e.g., *terrorized-victim-*AGENT. The semantic model (equation 13) estimates the plausibility of a verb–role–argument triple as the joint probability of ve variables. These are, apart from the identity of the verb v, argument a and thematic role r, the verb's sense s, and the grammatical function gf of the argument. The verb's sense is relevant because it determines the set of applicable thematic roles, while the grammatical function linking verb and argument (e.g., *syntactic subject* or *syntactic object*) carries information about the thematic role intended by the speaker.

(13) $Plausibility_{v,r,a} = P(v,s,gf,r,a)$

This type of *generative model* can predict the most likely instantiation for missing input or output values, allowing it to naturally solve its dual task of identifying the correct role that links a given verb and argument, and making a plausibility prediction for the triple. It predicts the preferred thematic role for a verb–argument pair, $\hat{r}_{v,a}$, by generating the most probable instantiation for the role, as shown in equation (14).

(14) $\hat{r}_{v,a} = \underset{r}{argmax}\ P(v,s,gf,r,a)$

The semantic model is to a large extent derived automatically from training data: clusters of semantically similar noun and verbs are used to reduce the number of *unseen* triples in the semantically annotated FrameNet corpus (Fillmore et al., 2003). The advantage of this approach is that it eliminates the need to obtain plausibility estimates experimentally (McRae et al., 1998).

In addition to demonstrating that the semantic model reliably predicts a range of plausibility judgment data, Pado et al. (2009) integrate the model into a broad-coverage sentence processing architecture. The so-called SynSem-Integration model, shown in Figure 17.3, combines a probabilistic parser, in the tradition of Jurafsky (1996) and Crocker and Brants (2000), with the semantic model described

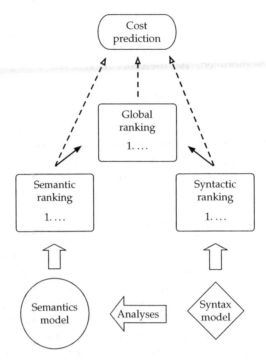

Figure 17.3   The architecture of the SynSem-Integration model, from Pado et al. (2009).

above. The syntax model, based on Roark's top-down probabilistic parser (2001b), incrementally computes all possible analyses of the input and their probabilities. The semantic model evaluates the resulting structures with respect to the plausibility of the verb–argument pairs they contain. Both models simultaneously rank the candidate structures: the syntax model ranks them by parse probability, and the semantic model by the plausibility of the verb–argument relations contained in the structures. The two rankings are interpolated into a *global* ranking to predict the structure preferred by people. Dif culty is predicted with respect to the global ranking and the two local rankings, via two cost functions: *conflict cost* quanti es the processing dif culty incurred in situations where the input yields con icting evidence for which analysis to prefer, while *revision cost* accounts for the processing dif culty caused by abandoning a preferred interpretation of the input and replacing it with another.

The integration of plausibility into a probabilistic sentence processing architecture enables Pado et al. (2009) to model the ndings of eight reading-time studies, covering four ambiguity phenomena, including the NP/S ambiguity (2), PP attachment (10), and reduced-relative clauses (12), discussed earlier. Crucially, each of the modeled studies revealed the on-line in uence of plausibility on disambiguation during human parsing. While previous models have accounted for some of these ndings with *hand crafted* models for speci c ambiguities (McRae et al., 1998; Narayanan & Jurafsky 1998; Tanenhaus et al., 2000), the SynSem-Integration model offers a wide-coverage model, trained on syntactically and semantically annotated corpora, avoiding the need to specify the set of relevant constraints and their probabilities by hand for each new phenomenon to be modeled.

5   Connectionist Models of Sentence Processing

Connectionist networks, also called *artificial neural networks* (see Chapter 9, ARTI-FICIAL NEURAL NETWORKS), offer an alternative computational paradigm with which to model cognitive development and processing. While there is a tremendous variety of network architectures, most derive their inspiration from an abstraction of how the brain works: massively interconnected simple processing units (often called neurons) that operate in parallel. These units are usually grouped into *layers*, that themselves are an abstraction of the functional organization of the brain. Connectionist models of human sentence processing are attractive in that they inherit the experience-based behavior of probabilistic models, as a direct consequence of their ability to learn. Connectionist systems are typically trained through the adjustment of connection strengths in response to repeated exposure to relevant examples, thereby providing an integrated account of how both acquisition and subsequent processing are determined by the linguistic environment.

Connectionist models have been successfully applied to various aspects of human lexical processing, and crucially emphasize the importance of experience, speci cally word frequency, for both learning and subsequent processing (Plunkett & Marchman 1996; Christiansen & Chater 1999a; 2001). Recent research, however, has also seen the emergence of sentence-level connectionist models which place similar emphasis on distributional information.

5.1   *Simple recurrent networks*

Simple recurrent networks (SRNs) provide an elegant architecture for learning distributional regularities that occur in sequential inputs (Elman 1990). SRNs process patterns (vectors) rather than symbolic representations. SRNs process sentences one word at a time, with each new input word represented in the *input layer* and interpreted in the context of the sentence processed so far – represented by the *context layer*, which is simply a copy of the *hidden layer* from the previous time-step (see Figure 17.4). The input layer and context layer are integrated and compressed into the hidden layer, enabling the network to incrementally develop a distributed representation of an unfolding sentence. Layers, in turn, may be partitioned into *assemblies* that are dedicated to speci c functional tasks. The *output layer* contains patterns that the SRN has been trained to compute by providing targets for each output assembly. The target output may be some desired syntactic or semantic

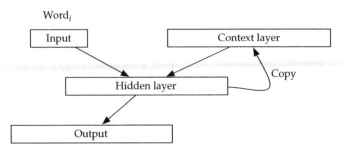

Figure 17.4   A simple recurrent network.

representation, but often SRNs are simply trained to predict the next word of the
input, much like a probabilistic language model (see Chapter 3, STATISTICAL LAN-
GUAGE MODELING). Each unit in the network receives a weighted sum of the input
units feeding into it, and outputs a value according to an activation function that
generally is non-linear in order to bound the output value in an interval such as
[0,1], such as the *logistic function*, $\sigma(x) = (1 + e^{-x})^{-1}$.

SRNs are trained by providing an input sequence and a set of targets into
which the network should transform the input sequence. The standard training
algorithm is *backpropagation*, an optimization technique that uses error signals
derived from the difference between the network's output and target to update
the network weights to more closely approximate the targets on the next round
of updates (Rumelhart et al., 1986). The weights between units could themselves
grow without bound during training, but an input vector **x** transformed by the
matrix of weights **W** to produce an output vector **y** that has been passed through
the activation function σ ensures **y** remains bounded. In sum, for each pair of layers connected by a weight matrix, the output vector can be calculated simply as
$\mathbf{y} = \sigma(\mathbf{Wx})$.

One of the strengths of SRNs is that they can be trained on unannotated linguistic data, using the so-called *prediction task*: the network is presented with sentences,
one word at a time, and is trained to output the *next* word in the sentence. To do
this successfully, the network must learn those probabilistic and structural properties of the input language that constrain what the next word can be. The key
insight of SRNs is the use of the context layer, which provides an exact copy of
the hidden unit layer from the previous time-step. This allows the network to
combine information about its state at the previous time-step with the current
input word when predicting what words can follow. SRNs have been successfully
trained on simpli ed, English-like languages based on grammars which enforce
a range of linguistic constraints such as verb frame, agreement, and embedding
(Elman 1991). To learn these languages, the network must not only learn simple
adjacencies, like the fact that *'the'* can be followed by *'boy,'* but not *'ate,'* but also
long-distance dependencies. Consider the following sentence-initial fragment:

(15)   *'The boy that the dog chased ___.'*

In predicting what word will follow *chased*, the network has to learn that, although *chased* is a transitive verb, it cannot be followed by a noun phrase in this context, because of the relative clause construction. Rather it must be followed by the main verb of the sentence, which must further be singular since *the boy* is a singular subject. Interestingly, however, SRNs do exhibit limitations which appear to correspond well with those exhibited by people, namely in the processing of center-embedding constructions, as discussed in Section 3 (Christiansen & Chater 1999b; MacDonald & Christiansen 2002).

As noted, SRNs provide a model of incremental sentence processing, in which the network is presented with a sentence, word by word, and at each point attempts to predict which words will follow. Not only are SRNs able to learn complex distributional constraints with considerable success, they do so in a manner which re ects the relative frequencies of the training corpus. When the SRN is presented with the initial words of some sentence, $w_1 \ldots w_i$, it activates outputs corresponding exactly to those words which could come next. Furthermore, the *degree* of activation of the next word w_{i+1} corresponds closely to the conditional probability, as would be computed by a statistical language model as shown in equation (16) (see Section 4 above, and Chapter 3, STATISTICAL LANGUAGE MODELING).

$$(16) \quad P(w_{i+1}|w_1 \ldots w_i) = \frac{f(w_1 \ldots w_{i+1})}{f(w_1 \ldots w_i)}$$

Here, $f(w_1 \ldots w_{i+1})$ and $f(w_1 \ldots w_i)$ are the training corpus frequencies for the word sequences $w_1 \ldots w_{i+1}$ and $w_1 \ldots w_i$ respectively. The SRN thus predicts not only which words can follow, but also the likelihood of each of those words, based on the conditional probabilities of those words in the training corpus.

One fundamental criticism of SRNs, however, is that there is only indirect evidence that syntactic structure is truly being acquired, at least in the conventional sense. Indeed, it has been argued that, although the language used to train the SRN was generated by a context-free grammar, the network may only be learning a weaker, probabilistic nite state approximation in (16), rather than the true hierarchical structure of the language (Steedman 1999). The lack of any explicit symbolic syntactic representation in SRNs also makes it dif cult to model empirical evidence concerning the processing of syntactic ambiguity, since such ambiguity is predicated on the notion that two or more distinct hypotheses about the structure of the sentence must be distinguished during processing. The visitation set gravitation model of Tabor et al. (1997), however, shows how reading times can be derived from a post hoc analysis of a trained SRN. This analysis yields a landscape of *attractors* – points in multi-dimensional space that are derived from the hidden unit activations, and which correspond to particular sentence structures. By observing how long it takes a particular hidden unit state (representing a word along with its left-context) to *gravitate* into an attractor (possibly representing a kind of semantic integration), Tabor et al. obtain a measure of the work a comprehender does integrating a word into a developing analysis.

Recursive neural networks (RNNs; Costa et al., 2003) can be seen as addressing Steedman's criticism (1999) by developing an explicit model of structure disambiguation processes. RNNs are trained on a complete hierarchical representation of a syntactic tree, which is encoded in a multi-layer feed-forward network in which the inputs represent the daughters and the output is the mother of a branch in the tree. The network is trained by exposing it recursively, from the leaves of the tree, to each branch of the tree until the root node is reached. The encoding of the root node thus represents an encoding of the entire tree. This enables training of the network using a parsed corpus (the Penn Treebank; Marcus et al., 1993), in which the network learns to make incremental parsing decisions, as in the relative clause attachment ambiguity shown in Figure 17.1. Just as the SRN estimates the conditional probability of the next word given the words seen so far, the RNN estimates the conditional probability of each possible attachment for the current word, given the tree that has been built up to that point. The model therefore resembles a probabilistic parser, with the exception that RNNs are crucially able to learn *global* structural preferences (Sturt et al., 2003), which standard PCFG models are not. RNNs can be seen as an implementation of the *tuning hypothesis* of Mitchell et al. (1995) (Section 4.2), in that they are trained solely on syntactic structure, and not speci c lexical items. One clear limitation of this approach, however, is that it does not account for lexical preferences or other kinds of non-structural biases (but see Costa et al., 2005 for discussion of some enhancements to this approach).

One recent SRN-based model has also sought to model aspects of visually situated language understanding, as revealed by the *visual worlds* experiments (see end of Section 2.2). Mayberry et al. (2009) build on the theoretical proposal of Knoeferle and Crocker (2007), claiming that utterance-mediated attention in the visual context is not only driven by incremental and anticipatory linguistic processing, but crucially that it is this modulation of visual attention that underpins the rapid in uence of the relevant visual context on comprehension – which they dub the *coordinated interplay account* (CIA). Mayberry et al's CIANet (2009) is based on a simple recurrent network (SRN; Elman 1990) that produces a case-role interpretation of the input utterance. To allow visual input, CIANet incorporates an additional input representation of a scene as (optional) visual context for the input utterance. Scenes contain two events, only one of which is relevant to the input utterance, where each of the two scene events has three constituents (*agent*, *action*, and *patient*) that are propagated to the SRN's hidden layer through shared weights (representing a common post-visual-processing pathway).

In line with the language-mediated visual attention mechanisms of the CIA, the unfolding linguistic input to CIANet modulates the activation of the relevant scene event based on the unfolding interpretation that is represented in the hidden layer. A gating vector implements the attentional mechanism in CIANet, and is multiplied element-wise with the corresponding units in each of the three lexical representations (agent, action, and patient) of one event (see Figure 17.5). Each unit of the gate is subtracted from 1.0 to derive a vector-complement that then modulates the second event. This means that more attention to one event in the model entails less attention to another. In this way, as the sentence is processed – possibly referring to the characters or actions in one of the scene events – the relevant

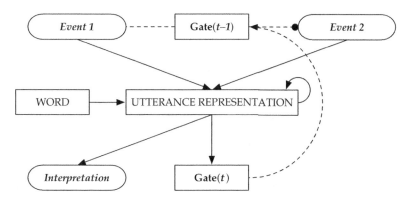

Figure 17.5   CIANet: a network featuring scene–language interaction with a basic attentional gating mechanism to select relevant events in a scene with respect to an unfolding utterance.

event is activated by the gating vector, causing it to have a greater in uence on the unfolding interpretation. The resulting network was shown to model the on-line in uence of scene events on comprehension (Knoeferle et al., 2005, Experiment 1), and the relative priority of depicted events versus stereotypical knowledge (Knoeferle & Crocker 2006, Experiment 2), with the gating vector providing a qualitative model of experimentally observed visual attention behavior. While the linguistic coverage of this model is currently limited to simple sentence structures, it is currently the only cognitive model of visually situated comprehension, and associated gaze behavior (but see Roy & Mukherjee 2005 for a psycholinguistically inspired account of how visual processing can in uence speech understanding).

6   Hybrid Models

Within computational psycholinguistics, hybrid models can broadly be seen as identifying that class of architectures that combine explicit symbolic representa-tions of linguistic structure and constraints with the use of connectionist inspired constraint satisfaction and competitive activation techniques. Typically the goal of such approaches is to combine the transparent use of symbolic linguistic rep-resentations, which are absent in pure connectionist architectures, with the kinds of distributed, competitive, and graded processing mechanisms that are absent in purely symbolic approaches. One early example is Stevenson's CAPERS model (1994), in which each word projects its phrasal structure as it is encountered, and initially all possible connections with the left-context are considered. Each possi-ble attachment is assigned an activation, based on the extent to which it satis es or violates lexical and syntactic constraints. Each node in the structure also has a limited amount of activation it can assign to its connections, such that as some connections gain in strength, activation is taken away from others. The parser *iterates* until it stabilizes on a single, well-formed syntactic parse as each word is

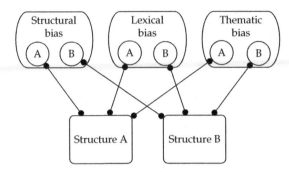

Figure 17.6   The competitive integration model (Spivey-Knowlton & Sedivy 1995).

input. Vosse and Kempen (2000) propose a related model of parsing, based on a lexicalized grammar, in which possible *unification links* between words are graded and compete via lateral inhibition (see also Tabor & Hutchins's SOPARSE (2004) for a related model, and more general discussion of this approach). The resulting model accounts for not only a range of standard parsing phenomena, but also the behavior found in some aphasic speakers.

As mentioned at the end of Section 3.1, constraint-based models of sentence disambiguation (MacDonald et al., 1994; Tanenhaus et al., 2000) deny that syntactic processes have any distinct modular status with the human language processor, rather assuming that all relevant constraints are integrated during processing. Such constraint-based accounts exploit the symbolic representations of linguistic constraints in combination with the use of competition-based constraint-satisfaction techniques (MacDonald et al., 1994). The *competitive integration model* (Spivey-Knowlton & Sedivy 1995; Spivey & Tanenhaus 1998), for example, emphasizes the interaction of various heterogeneous linguistic constraints in resolving syntactic ambiguity, each with its own bias (see Figure 17.6), to be combined in deciding between several structural interpretations. For example, one might identify a general structural bias (as proposed by the tuning hypothesis, Section 4.2), a lexical verb frame bias, and perhaps a thematic bias (e.g., the plausibility of either structure). McRae et al. (1998) proposed that the bias be established using experience-based measures: either corpus frequencies (e.g., for the structural and lexical constraint), or completions norms (e.g., for the thematic constraint). Once the relevant linguistic constraints are stipulated, the model allows two kinds of parameters to be set (Tanenhaus et al., 2000): (1) the *weight* of each constraint, e.g., structural, lexical, and thematic, must be determined, and (2) for each constraint, its *bias* towards Structure A versus Structure B must be established.

Once the parameters for the model have been determined, reading times are modeled by observing the time it takes the model to settle on a preferred structure as the different constraints compete. Informally, activation is propagated from each constraint to a particular structural candidate in accordance with the constraints bias. The activation of a given structure is then computed as the weighted sum of the activations from each constraint. This activation is then propagated back to the constraints, and another iteration is performed. Once the activation for a particular structure exceeds a speci c threshold value, the system begins processing the next word. The number of iterations required for processing each word is then directly linked to the reading times observed during self-paced reading. McRae et al. (1998) demonstrate how the model can be used successfully to predict reading times for reduced-relative clauses, as a function of their semantic plausibility, as in example (12), above.

One shortcoming of this approach, however, is that the model separates the mechanism which builds interpretations from the mechanism which chooses the interpretation. While independent modeling of the constraint reconciliation mechanisms might simply be viewed as *abstracting away* from the underlying structure building processes, the approach implies that structure building itself does not contribute to processing complexity, since the constraint integration mechanisms alone determine reading times. Furthermore, it has been standard practice to construct a separate model for each syntactic disambiguation phenomenon, each with different (possibly overlapping) constraints, and different constraint weights (Tanenhaus et al., 2000). This, combined with the already substantial number of degrees of freedom, clearly reduces the predictive capacity and falsi ability of such models. Further empirical challenges to such constraint satisfaction models have also been made (Frazier 1995; Binder et al., 2001; but see also Green & Mitchell 2006).

7 Concluding Remarks

The challenges of natural language understanding are daunting. Language is inherently complex – drawing on different levels of linguistic competence, as well as world and contextual knowledge – while also being highly ambiguous. That people are nonetheless able to comprehend language accurately and in real time is a remarkable feat that is unmatched by any arti cial system. Computational psycholinguistics is concerned with modeling how people achieve such performance, and seeks to develop implemented models of the architectures, mechanisms, and representations involved. The approaches are diverse, ranging from purely symbolic accounts to neurally inspired connectionist approaches, with hybrid and probabilistic models occupying the landscape in between. For reasons of space, we have focused our attention here on models of sentence processing, leaving aside models of lexical access (McClelland & Elman 1986; Norris 1999; Norris et al., 2000). Equally, we have not addressed the topic of language acquisition, which is concerned with how our linguistic knowledge emerges as a consequence of linguistic experience. While the goals of acquisition and processing models differ with respect to the kinds of empirical data they attempt to explain, ultimately it is essential that models of adult sentence comprehension be the plausible end result of the acquisition process. The increasing dominance of experience-based models of language processing, whether connectionist or probabilistic, holds promise for a uniform and possibly even integrated account of language acquisition and adult performance (Chater & Manning 2006). Indeed, language learning drove the early development of connectionist models of lexical and syntactic acquisition (Rumelhart & McClelland 1987; Elman 1990) which now gure prominently in computational psycholinguistics (Tabor et al., 1997; Christiansen & Chater 1999b; 2001; Mayberry et al., 2009). Probabilistic, especially Bayesian, approaches have also been applied to problems of learning argument structure (Alishahi & Stevenson 2008), syntax (Clark 2001a), and semantics (Niyogi 2002). Not surprisingly, however, many models of acquisition emphasize the role of visual scene information (see also Siskind 1996). Knoeferle and Crocker (2006) argue that this may explain the priority of visual context in adult sentence processing – as modeled by the CIANet architecture (Mayberry et al., 2009) – further demonstrating the kind of synergy that may be possible between acquisition and processing theories in future.

Virtually all modern accounts of sentence understanding share the assumption that language processing is highly incremental, with each encountered word being immediately integrated into an interpretation of what has been read or heard so far. Even this assumption, however, has been recently challenged by experimental ndings suggesting that comprehension processes may build interpretations which make sense *locally*, even when they are ungrammatical with respect to the entire preceding context (Tabor & Hutchins 2004). Nonetheless, incrementality is almost certainly the rule, even if there are occasional exceptions. Indeed, there is an increasing emphasis on the role of *predictive* mechanisms in parsing, to explain the wealth of experimental ndings that people not only process language incrementally, but in fact actively generate hypotheses about the words they expect to follow. Much in the way that statistical language models assign probabilities to the words that may come next, both probabilistic (Hale 2001; 2003; Levy 2008) and connectionist (Elman 1990; 1991; Mayberry et al., 2009; Crocker et al., 2010) psycholinguistic models potentially offer natural explanations of predictive behavior in people.

There remain some issues which truly distinguish competing theories. For example whether or not people actively consider multiple interpretations in the face of ambiguity, or adopt a single one, backtracking to some alternative when necessary. Similarly, the degree of modularity is often viewed as a de ning characteristic. While it has proven challenging to decide de nitively among these positions empirically, there is increasing consensus that language comprehension mechanisms must support the rapid and adaptive integration of virtually all relevant information – linguistic and world knowledge, as well as discourse and visual context – as re ected by incremental and predictive comprehension behavior (for an overview of relevant empirical ndings, see Crocker et al., 2010).

Finally, some models that appear quite different super cially may simply be offering accounts of processing at different levels of abstraction. Connectionist and probabilistic approaches most often share the idea that language understanding is an optimized process which yields, for example, the most likely interpretation for some input based on prior experience. Thus SRNs make very similar behavioral predictions to probabilistic language models based on *n*-grams or PCFGs. Typically, however, connectionist models intend to provide and account for the algorithmic or even implementation level in Marr's terms (recall Section 2.1), while probabilistic approaches may be construed as theories at the higher, *computational*, level. That is, while connectionist learning and distributed representations are postulated to have some degree of biological plausibility, the parsing and training mechanisms of probabilistic models typically are not. Hybrid architectures occupy a middle ground, combining explicitly stipulated symbolic representations with connectionist-inspired processing mechanisms.

The emergence of experience-based approaches represents a major milestone for computational psycholinguistics, resulting in models that offer broader coverage (Crocker & Brants 2000) and rational behavior (Chater et al., 1998; Crocker 2005), while also explaining a wide range of experimentally observed frequency effects (Jurafsky 2003). As can be seen from the models discussed in this article, however, there is a tendency to isolate language processing from other cognitive processes such as perception and action. As such, computational models are lagging behind emerging theories of situated and embodied language processing, which emphasize the interplay and overlap of language, perception and action (Barsalou 1999; Fischer & Zwaan 2008; Spivey & Richardson 2009). The CIANet model (Mayberry et al. 2009) is one attempt to model visually situated comprehension, thereby also connecting with situated language learning models, but computational psycholinguistics still lags behind current experimental results and theoretical claims concerning the integration of language with other cognitive systems. Future developments in this direction will likely connect with models of language acquisition, and ultimately contribute to a better understanding of the origins of the human capacity for language.

NOTES

1 The essence of this argument is that understanding language ultimately requires full intelligence – requiring both extensive world knowledge and reasoning abilities – which remain out of reach in the general case (Shapiro 1992).

2 I deliberately use the term *analyses* to abstract away from what particular linguistic representation – lexical, syntactic, semantic, etc. – we might be interested in.

18 Information Extraction

RALPH GRISHMAN

1 Introduction

Information extraction (IE) is the process of identifying and classifying instances of some sort in text, based on some semantic criterion. This de nition covers a wide range of tasks, including:

- **name extraction:** identifying the names in a text and classifying them as people, organizations, locations, etc.;
- **entity extraction:** identifying all phrases which refer to objects of speci c semantic classes, and linking phrases which refer to the same object;
- **relation extraction:** identifying pairs of entities in a speci c semantic relation;
- **event extraction:** identifying instances of events of a particular type, and the arguments of each event.

In this chapter we shall consider each of these types of extraction tasks and methods for addressing them.

Information extraction systems began as large collections of handwritten rules, which required considerable skill and time to develop. Since the mid-1990s, there has been a gradual transition to corpus-trained methods – initially supervised methods, more recently minimally supervised or even unsupervised methods. We shall trace this development for each of the types of extraction.

In contrast to semantic analysis (see Chapter 15, COMPUTATIONAL SEMANTICS), where the goal is to capture and formalize as much of the meaning as possible, the goal here is to only capture selected types of relations, types of events, and other semantic distinctions which are speci ed in advance. By limiting the task, we intend to make the task tractable: to identify information which we know how to extract (to some degree of accuracy).

We will concentrate on methods which apply to 'free text,' which appears with minimal markup, such as news reports, business reports, and scienti c and technical articles. Procedures have been developed for extraction from text with much more markup ('semi-structured text'), as is typical for web pages;

The Handbook of Computational Linguistics and Natural Language Processing, First Edition.
Edited by Alexander Clark, Chris Fox and Shalom Lappin.
© 2013 Blackwell Publishing Ltd except for editorial material and organization
© 2013 Alexander Clark, Chris Fox, and Shalom Lappin. Published 2013 by Blackwell Publishing Ltd.

these procedures, generally called 'wrappers,' rely heavily on the markup and the regularity of web page layout (that pages on the same site will mark up similar items in similar ways).

Information extraction systems are developed for a particular domain and incorporate the semantic structures of that domain. Much of the work on IE has been in the general news domain, and we shall draw our examples from that domain. However, there has been substantial work in other domains which have large quantities of text, repeated entities and events of the same type, and where there is a need to distill the information to a structured database form. Medical records and the biomedical literature, in particular, have received considerable attention.

2   Historical Background

The ideas of information extraction can be traced back to the proposals of Zellig Harris in the 1950s to identify the main semantic structures of scienti c sublanguages and then to automatically extract these structures from text (Harris 1958). This led to the work of Naomi Sager on extraction from scienti c papers and later from medical records (Sager et al., 1987). By the 1980s a number of groups were developing small systems for extracting different types of events from news and military texts.

To introduce some systematic evaluation to the eld of information extraction, the US Navy organized the Message Understanding Conferences (MUCs), with the rst one in 1987. Eventually seven MUCs were held, with the last in 1998.[1] Because IE covers such a broad range of possible tasks, the course of research and development in IE was heavily in uenced by these conferences, and the tasks they de ned. The rst MUCs essentially involved event extraction. MUC-6 (Grishman & Sundheim 1996) recognized that name and entity extraction were essential prerequisites for event extraction, and so introduced them as separate evaluations termed 'named entity' and 'template element'; MUC-7 added a relation extraction task called 'template relation.'

The ACE (Automatic Content Extraction) workshops followed MUC, starting in 2000, as evaluation forums for IE.[2] The ACE tasks have grown over the years to include entity, relation, and event extraction. Other innovations included multilingual extraction (MUC was primarily monolingual, though MUC-5 included Japanese) and multiple genres (including broadcast transcripts and weblogs).

This chapter will generally follow the ACE task organization, though we shall start with name extraction, which has been the most intensively studied and applied IE task.

3   Name Extraction

Most types of text are replete with names. Consequently, being able to identify these names, and determine whether they are the names of people, organizations, locations, or other entities is an essential   rst step in extracting information from a text.

When extracted, this information is typically represented in XML markup:

```
Mr <name type="person">Harry Hoople</name> was named CEO of
<name type="organization">Harry's Hogs</name> of
<name type="location">San Francisco</name>.
```

This task and notation were introduced as part of the MUC-6 evaluation.[3]

For news stories, these three types are fairly standard, but there are much richer type inventories, including type hierarchies with up to 200 name types (Sekine & Nobata 2004). Other domains will of course involve other name types; genomics texts, for example, involve gene and protein names. For a recent survey of the task and approaches, see Nadeau and Sekine (2007).

3.1   Hand coded rules

The   rst systems for performing named entity extraction were based on hand constructed rules. These rules consisted of regular expressions which, when they matched the text, caused a portion of the matched text to be tagged as a named entity. For example,

```
(capitalized-token)+ "Inc." → organization
```

(where the '+' indicates one or more instances) or

```
"Mr" [capitalized-token? initial? capitalized-token] → person
```

(where the '?' indicates optionality). In the latter case, the tokens in square brackets (excluding 'Mr') are taken as the person's name. Some person names can be recognized from common   rst names:

```
common-first-name initial? capitalized-token → person
```

Such common   rst names can be obtained from census data. These patterns can be complemented by lists of well-known people, companies, and locations, available from Wikipedia[4] and lists of major corporations.

The accuracy of recognition can typically be improved by several percent through the use of a *cache*: a list of names in the document which have already been identi ed and classi ed. Many names will appear more than once in a document. One instance may be in a context which allows the name to be classi ed, while another instance is in an uninformative context; by making two passes and identifying instances of the same name, we can classify both instances correctly. For example, in

Prescott Adams announced the appointment of a new vice president for sales. Mr Adams explained ...

the tagger may initially be uncertain whether '*Prescott Adams*' is the name of a rm or person. However, once it encounters '*Mr Adams*' it can tag '*Prescott Adams*' as a person with considerable con dence. Such a cache can even be extended to an entire collection of documents (Borthwick 1999).

Such hand coded rules are hard to beat if developed with a large test collection for assessing each rule revision, but require considerable skill and effort.

3.2 *Supervised learning*

Hand tagging a corpus with NE (named entity) information, using a small set of name classes, is a relatively straightforward and intuitive task. Consequently, there has been considerable work on training NE taggers from an NE-annotated corpus.

NE tagging involves identifying the extent and type of each name in the text. This can be reformulated as a task of assigning a tag to each token by using *BIO tags*. The rst token of a person name is tagged B-PERSON; subsequent tokens are tagged I-PERSON. Similarly, organization names are tagged with B-ORG and I-ORG; location names are tagged with B-LOCATION and I-LOCATION. Tokens which are not part of a name are assigned the tag O. For example,

Mr	O
Harry	B-PERSON
Hoople	I-PERSON
was	O
named	O
CEO	O
of	O
Harry's	B-ORG
Hogs	I-ORG
of	O
San	B-LOCATION
Francisco	I-LOCATION
.	O

Assigning a tag to each token in a sequence is termed a *sequence tagging task*. Several other natural language processing tasks can be formulated as sequence tagging tasks, including part-of-speech tagging and chunking. A number of different types of models have been developed and applied to these tasks; some of these are discussed in Chapter 5, MAXIMUM ENTROPY MODELS.

One of the earliest corpus-trained NE tagging systems was Nymble (Bikel et al., 1997), an HMM (hidden Markov model). Nymble used a simple state space, with a single state for each name type plus an 'other' (no name) state; context information (for example, that '*Mr*' precedes a person name) was captured by using bigram- and unigram-conditioned probabilities and several levels of smoothing. Alternatively, context information can be captured by using multiple states for each name type.

HMMs were followed by maximum entropy models (including MEMMs – maximum entropy Markov models), which provided greater flexibility in incorporating specialized features (such as particular lists of names or patterns of tokens) into the model (Borthwick et al., 1998).

Since then a wide range of other sequence models have been applied to NE tagging, including conditional random fields and models based on support vector machines (Tjong Kim Sang & de Meulder 2003).

3.3 Weakly supervised learners

If one instance of a token sequence is a name of a given type, other instances of the same sequence are likely to represent a name of the same type. We can take advantage of this property to create a 'bootstrapping' name tagger which is given only a small 'seed' set of names (or name contexts).

Suppose we start with a few indicative name contexts; for example, that '*Mr*' or '*Mrs*' is followed by a person name, and that a name ending in '*Inc.*' or '*Corp.*,' for example, is an organization name. We take a large, untagged corpus and tag all instances of names matching one of these patterns. Next, we tag all other instances of the same names. Then we examine the set of newly tagged names to see whether there are any contexts (besides those in the seed) which are consistently associated with names of a particular type. If so, we add them to the seed contexts and repeat the process.

An early description of this process was given in Strzalkowski and Wang (1996). Collins and Singer (1999) characterized this as an example of co-training and described several co-training procedures. Such bootstrapping is most effective if the name classes come close to exhaustively covering the set of names; if necessary, additional classes can be introduced to improve performance (Lin et al., 2003b).

These basic methods have been extended to the acquisition of hundreds or thousands of classes using web-scale corpora (Etzioni et al., 2005). To avoid the need for creating seed sets for each class, one can use patterns of the type introduced by Hearst (1992): looking for '*X such as Y*' will find class names '*X*' and their instances '*Y*'. For example, it would find '*British publishers*' paired with '*Blackwell*,' '*Macmillan*,' etc. These instances Y can then be used as a seed for finding additional patterns and names. This enables the completely unsupervised creation of large labeled name classes, just by starting from the name of the class (Paşca & van Durme 2008).

3.4 Evaluation

NE performance is measured in terms of recall, precision, and F-measure, by comparison with a hand tagged key (see Chapter 11, EVALUATION OF NLP SYSTEMS).

$$recall = \frac{\text{number of correct tags}}{\text{number of tags in key}}$$

$$precision = \frac{\text{number of correct tags}}{\text{number of tags in system response}}$$

$$F = \frac{2}{1/recall + 1/precision}$$

The MUC scorer gave partial credit to names which were properly identi ed but incorrectly classi ed. This produced somewhat higher scores than the CoNLL scorer, which only credited names which were correctly classi ed.

While percentage recall, precision, and F-scores for the best systems on news data are typically in the high 80s or low 90s, scores of corpus-trained systems are very dependent on the nature and similarity of the training and test corpora. Differences in genre, topic, or even time period between training and test (Mota & Grishman 2008) can lead to signi cant fall-off in performance. This must be kept in mind when acquiring a tagger trained on one type of corpus and applying it to quite different text.

The examples shown here are for mixed-case English text. Statistical taggers have also been applied to monocase text, as might be produced by speech-to-text systems, with performance degradations of a few percent on perfect transcripts. NE taggers have by now been applied to dozens of languages. The general strategies described above are broadly applicable, although special measures or features may be required for a particular language. In particular, for languages where names are in ected, it may be necessary to do morphological analysis prior to or as part of name tagging, so that in ected names will be recognized even if the in ected form does not appear in the training data.

4   Entity Extraction

Names are referring expressions – they refer to 'entities,' mostly things in the real world. A natural extension of name tagging is nding all referring expressions – names, nominal phrases (those headed by common nouns), and pronouns – and identifying those which refer to the same entity.

Such an 'entity extraction' task was introduced as part of the ACE evaluations, extending the 'template element' task in MUC-6 and 7. It involves:

- identifying and classifying all phrases which refer to entities of speci ed semantic types; this includes names, noun phrases, and pronouns. These are referred to as *entity mentions*;
- linking together all entity mentions which refer to the same entity.

Identifying the noun phrases is a standard task of syntactic analysis. For each noun phrase, we determine its *extent* and its syntactic *head*. For example, in the sentence 'The famous linguist from Limerick loved linguini,' the rst noun phrase has extent 'The famous linguist from Limerick' and head 'linguist.' Extents may be nested; thus this rst noun phrase contains a second noun phrase with extent and head 'Limerick.'

For noun phrases headed by a name, the semantic type of the phrase is the type of the name, as determined by name extraction. For noun phrases headed by a noun, the semantic type of the phrase is determined primarily by the sense (meaning) of the head of the phrase. For monosemous nouns (those with a single sense), a system need only look up a table mapping the noun sense to a semantic type. For polysemous nouns (those with multiple senses), context must be used to differentiate a *'power plant'* from a *'potted plant'* or a *'range of mountains'* from a *'range of options.'* There is an extensive literature on this task of *word-sense disambiguation*: using the words in the immediate context to identify the probable sense (and hence semantic type).

Linking together the entity mentions to form an entity is a problem of anaphora resolution, which is discussed in detail in Chapter 21, DISCOURSE PROCESSING.

5 Relation Extraction

In the context of information extraction, a *relation* represents some relationship between two entities; a *relation mention* is an expression of this relationship, and involves two entity mentions. Examples of relationships include

- location (permanent or temporary):
  Omaha-based Berkshire Hathaway
  Fred Smith, now living in Paris
- citizenship or origin (between a person and a country):
  New Zeland-born Rachel Hunter
  the famous Greek philosophers
- af liation (between a person and an organization):
  the president of Ford
- and family relationships:
  Fred's brother

Both relations and events are predications involving multiple entities; relations, being binary, are somewhat simpler to recognize.

Note that in some cases the same word (such as *'president'* or *'brother'*) expresses the relationship and serves as one of the arguments of the relationship. Thus, in the last example, both *'Fred'* and *'brother'* are classi ed (by entity extraction) as entity mentions of type *person*.[5] Relation extraction then, based on the word *'brother,'* recognizes an instance of a relation mention.

Our nal goal, in extracting information from the document, is to identify relations between entities. This is achieved by combining the relation mentions with coreference information from entity extraction. For example, if we had the phrase *'Fred's brother, Harry,'* coreference analysis would establish *'brother'* and *'Harry'* as coreferential (i.e., as mentions of the same entity), so we could establish a familial relation between the entities with names *'Fred'* and *'Harry.'* Taking this a step further, in the sentence

Fred introduced us to his brother, Harry

we would identify a relation mention between *'his'* and *'brother,'* coreference between *'Fred'* and *'his'* (assuming there are no other plausible antecedents), and coreference between *'brother'* and *'Harry,'* and combine these to establish the relation between *'Fred'* and *'Harry.'*

Relations were introduced in MUC-7 as 'template relations' and were limited to three relationships: employee_of, product_of, and location_of. A larger set of relations was introduced as one of the ACE tasks in 2002.

5.1   *Hand coded rules and supervised methods*

As is evident from the above examples, most (though not all) relations are expressed at a relatively short range, within a single noun phrase or clause. This makes it feasible to create patterns by hand to capture many of these relations.

It also suggests an approach to creating a relation tagger; namely, train a classifier on all pairs of 'nearby' entity mentions, with the outcome being either a type of relation or 'no relation.' The trained classifier can then be applied to all pairs of nearby entity mentions in the document to be tagged.

The connection between the two entities can be characterized by the sequence of words between the two mentions, the sequence of chunks, or as a path in a tree – either a full parse-tree or a shallow parse. Finding the best characterization has been the topic of research on relation extraction over the past few years.

As we have noted, most relations occur at relatively short range within a single sentence. Accordingly, most examples can be classified based on the heads of the two mentions, their semantic class (person, organization, …) and the intervening words. However, because the intervening words may include irrelevant modifiers (*'president of the rapidly growing fast-food company'*) or arguments (*'Fred operated a hot-dog stand in Chicago'* → located-in(Fred, Chicago)), a classifier based on word sequences alone is not adequate. Such examples can be handled by using the path in the dependency tree between the entity mentions (Culotta & Sorensen 2004). For the last example, the dependency tree would be as in Figure 18.1, so the path in the tree connecting the nodes *'Fred'* and *'Chicago'* would be *'operated–in'* (i.e., would consist of the two nodes *'operated'* and *'in'* in sequence).

Less frequently, a wider context than the words (or the path in the dependency tree) between the mentions is required. For example, in *'Fred and Mary were married for 20 years,'* the only intervening word is *'and,'* but the predicate (*'were married'*) is needed to identify the relation (Zhou et al., 2007).

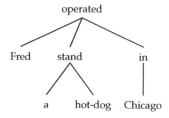

Figure 18.1 Example dependency tree.

Improved performance has been obtained by systems which combine evidence from several levels – words, chunks, and parses (Kambhatla 2004; Zhao & Grishman 2005). Using multiple levels of representation also reduces the impact of errors in syntactic analysis, a general problem for information extraction. In general, a 'deeper' representation (words → chunks → parses → regularized parses) is better at capturing the semantic relations of information extraction. However, deeper analyses are more likely to be incorrect analyses; chunking is more accurate than parsing. By combining evidence from multiple levels, we are able to gain some of the bene ts of each level.

When paths in parse or dependency trees are used for relation detection, they can be treated as atomic properties (only examples with identical paths are considered) or reduced to sets of features, such as the individual steps in the path, for feature-based classi ers such as maximum-entropy classi ers. However, nding an appropriate set of features to capture the notion of 'similar paths' may be dif cult. This similarity may be more directly captured in kernel-based classi ers such as support vector machines, by de ning a kernel over paths or trees (Zelenko et al., 2003; Culotta & Sorensen 2004) and combining multiple kernels (Zhao & Grishman 2005).

5.2   *Weakly supervised and unsupervised methods*

As for name extraction, the cost of manual annotation and the availability of large amounts of raw text data led to an interest in bootstrapping methods for relation extraction. The bootstrapping begins with a set of pairs of names which are examples of the relation of interest. For example, we might have a set of author–book pairs ([Herman Melville, Moby Dick], [J. R. R. Tolkien, The Hobbit], …). We look for all instances of these pairs in close proximity in a large corpus, and collect the sequences of intervening words (the patterns). We then look for other instances of these patterns. New pairs which appear in several of these patterns are added to the original set of pairs and the process repeats. This approach was introduced by Brin (1998) and extended by Agichtein and Gravano (2000).

As with supervised methods, these approaches vary in how the patterns are characterized, although the goal has been in general to use fast methods so that large amounts of text can be analyzed. Brin (1998) used xed word sequences;

Agichtein and Gravano (2000) used a weighted bag of words. More recently, Bunescu and Mooney (2007) used a subsequence kernel on the word sequences.

One crucial issue in such bootstrapping is ltering or ranking the patterns, since the patterns which are found may be very general and ambiguous. For example, one common pattern linking book and author is likely to be a comma (','), but a comma may of course have other signi cance. Agichtein and Gravano (2000) extracted company–headquarters location pairs, and relied on the fact that a company would (generally) have only one headquarters location; a pattern which extracted a company along with a location different from that previously extracted for the same company would be treated as a less reliable pattern. Bunescu and Mooney (2007) used a single bootstrapping step and provided explicit negative as well as positive examples.

Instead of a bootstrapping method which grows the set of linguistic patterns expressing a single relation, we can use a similar approach to group the patterns into clusters of like-meaning expressions, thereby identifying the dominant relation types in a corpus in a completely unsupervised fashion (Hasegawa et al., 2004). We de ne a similarity metric between patterns based on the number of overlapping argument pairs, and then use a clustering procedure based on this similarity to group the patterns.

Finally, we should note that these bootstrapping methods only apply to examples involving pairs of names. Applying them to cover relations involving nominals or pronouns would require some systematic extensions; these have not yet been explored.

6   Event Extraction

Event extraction was the   rst information extraction task to be studied. Given a speci cation of a type of event ('*terrorist attack*,' '*plane crash*,' '*hiring of a corporate executive*'), it involves identifying instances of this event and, for each instance, identifying its arguments and modi ers. In MUC terminology, the characterization of the event type was called a *scenario*, and the set of slots to be   lled (which sometimes included the effects of the central event) was called a *scenario template*.

One special case of event extraction arises when we know in advance that each document contains exactly one instance of an event, and the task is to   nd the arguments and modi ers. Examples include lecture announcements (where the objective is to extract the speaker, title, date, time, location of a talk), CVs (*curricula vitae*, where the goal is to extract speci ed biographical information), classi ed advertisements, etc. This task is often referred to as 'implicit relation extraction' (IRE). IRE is essentially a sequential modeling task (like name tagging), but with the constraint (in most cases) that there is only one instance of each   eld in a document. There is a considerable literature on IRE, as well as several standard test corpora. This section will focus, however, on the more general event task, where the number of events of a given type in a document is not known.

6.1   Hand coded rules

As in the case of other types of extraction, the earliest systems consisted of hand constructed 'patterns'. For events, the arguments to be identi ed may be names, but may also be general noun phrases. The constructs evoking events will typically be clauses and may include a variety of modi ers in addition to the central arguments, so some degree of syntactic analysis is required, at least suf cient to pull out the subject and object of relevant verbs; the patterns will be stated in terms of these syntactic relations. For example, the extraction patterns for executive succession (the hiring and ring of executives) might include a subject–verb–object structure such as:

```
NP(org) fire NP(person)
```

where NP(org) matches a noun phrase of semantic class organization (i.e., either the name of an organization or a pronoun or nominal referring to an organization), NP(person) matches a noun phrase of class person, and fire is an active verb group with head verb *'fire.'* Imposing semantic constraints on the subject and object allows us to distinguish this sense of *'fire'* from other usages, such as *'the policeman fired his gun.'*

An extraction task speci es a 'template' to be lled with the arguments of an event. For example, for executive succession it would include the organization, the person, the position, and the action (starting or ending the given position). The complete extraction rule would combine the pattern with a speci cation of how the template was to be lled:

```
NP(org)1 fire NP(person)2 →
event(org: 1, person: 2, position: -, action: end)
```

Similar rules would be included for noun phrases with their modi ers:

```
the retirement of NP(person)1 as NP(position)2 →
event(org: -, person: 1, position: 2, action: end)
```

A simple extraction system may ll the templates with the NP strings. In ACE terminology, it would generate *event mentions* containing references to entity mentions (and possibly other types of arguments, such as the *position* in the example above). This is not generally satisfactory, however, since it may yield template slots lled with uninformative strings such as *'she'* or *'the executive,'* even if these people have been named elsewhere in the document. As we did for relations, we need to couple entity and event extraction, that is, identify the NP as a mention of a particular entity, and put a reference to the entity in the template slot. In that way, if the entity was explicitly named elsewhere in the article, this information can be retrieved. It does mean, however, that coreference accuracy will be a critical factor in event extraction accuracy.

Since these patterns are based on syntactic relations (subject, object, noun modi er) it is natural to apply them to a parse generated by a full-sentence parser. As corpus-trained parsers (Chapter 13, STATISTICAL PARSING) have improved in accuracy this approach has been more widely adopted. However, extraction systems based on regular expressions, such as the FASTUS system (Appelt et al., 1993), have also proven to be effective. Such regular expressions must be able not only to match the required arguments but to skip over modi ers not relevant to the template, as in:

> *the unexpected retirement on Friday of John Smith, the well-known linguist, as executive vice president*

The regular expression patterns will be stated not in terms of general noun phrases but in terms of phrases of particular semantic types; this greatly reduces the attachment ambiguities compared to general syntactic pattern matching.

6.2 *Supervised systems*

A variety of approaches have been used to train event extractors from tagged data. Some of these build patterns similar in structure to those used in hand coded systems. For example, WHISK (Soderland 1999) develops a rule from each training instance, starting with a most general pattern and incrementally making the pattern more speci c. Each step is taken to optimize some balance of number of examples matched in the training set and number of incorrect matches. The pattern serves both to identify the event and to capture the event arguments.

An alternative approach uses standard classi ers, such as k-nearest neighbors or maximum entropy, which can incorporate a wide variety of features. Separate classi ers are built to identify the presence of an event and to determine whether a particular entity mention is an argument of that event (Ahn 2006b).

6.3 *Weakly supervised systems*

As with the other extraction tasks, there has been strong interest in moving towards minimally supervised methods in order to reduce the labor required to port a system to a new event type. The need is particularly great in the case of event extraction because of the large variety of possible tasks: while a handful of name types can account for the large majority of names in the news, these entities may be involved in dozens or hundreds of different types of events.

One approach was based on the distinction between relevant documents (documents which contained at least one instance of an event of interest) and irrelevant documents. Predicate–argument patterns which occurred much more often in relevant documents than in irrelevant documents are good candidates to be extraction patterns for the event. Riloff (1996) showed that the formula

$$score = \frac{\text{freq in relevant documents}}{\text{freq in all documents}} \times \log(\text{freq in relevant documents})$$

could be used to rank the patterns, producing a pattern set (at some score threshold) whose performance was fairly close to that of hand produced patterns.

This approach still requires manual judgments of document relevance for a substantial text collection. Yangarber et al. (2000) extended this to a bootstrapping approach in which the seed is a small set of extraction patterns. These patterns are used to retrieve some relevant documents and then the best new patterns are extracted using a variant of the Riloff metric (modi ed to capture the degree of con dence in the relevance). As in the case of bootstrapping for name extraction, performance can be improved by concurrent bootstrapping of multiple event types (Yangarber 2003). Sudo et al. (2003) used keywords as seeds, retrieving relevant documents with an information retrieval system. They showed the bene t of allowing arbitrary dependency subtrees to be used as patterns; while these are more dif cult to count ef ciently, they yield better extraction performance than more constrained patterns. Sekine and Oda (2007) demonstrated that this procedure, given a topic described by some keywords, could, within a minute, create an information extraction system for topic-related events and apply this system to construct tables of extracted information about such events.

One fundamental obstacle to the practical use of such 'on demand information extraction' is the ability to capture paraphrase relations between events. The Riloff metric can pick out predicates which are 'on topic,' but within that set cannot easily identify those with the same meaning. For example, in the executive succession scenario, it might nd 'hired,' 'selected,' and 'fired,' but not know that the rst two convey the same information. There has been some success, described above, in identifying paraphrases of relations involving named entities, based on common arguments. A similar approach can in principle be applied to nd event paraphrases, but the task is much more challenging because the argument structures for events can be much more variable (arguments can be pronominalized or omitted and appear only in the wider context). Paraphrase acquisition from corpora has become a major research topic of its own.

Event extraction, like relation extraction, can in principle be extended to unsupervised acquisition: to identify the most common types of events in a body of text, capture their argument structure, and group synonymous or near-synonymous events. This combines a number of challenges which are starting to be addressed in an integrated fashion (Shinyama & Sekine 2006). But much more will be required to meet the goal set forth by Z. Harris a half century ago ... to systematically learn the information structures of a sublanguage (Harris 1958).

7 Concluding Remarks

Most of the research and, in particular, nearly all of the evaluation of information extraction until now has involved single-document extraction. This simpli es evaluation; in addition, evaluation corpora are likely to be quite small and so will most likely have only one or a few documents mentioning a given entity or event.

In practice, however, what we often want from a system is a set of facts, which may have come from a single document or been gleaned from the combined evidence of multiple documents. In situations where a fact cannot be de nitively extracted from a single document (for example, because the predicted probability of an event is low but non-zero), it may be possible to retrieve related documents from which more de nitive information can be extracted (Ji & Grishman 2008). This will be increasingly important for web-based extraction, since information is typically encoded several times, with different forms of expression.

In this chapter we have presented a general progression from hand coded to supervised to weakly supervised systems for information extraction. Here too the redundancy of information provided by the web will be critical to improving the results of weakly supervised and unsupervised learning.

The web provides us with a very rich source of information – information which is, however, not easy to process because it is locked up in many linguistic forms. Information extraction, by structuring and standardizing the information representation, can be the key to unlocking this information for many applications.

NOTES

1 Proceedings of MUC-3 through 7 are available through the ACL Anthology web site, http://aclweb.org/anthology-new/
2 www.nist.gov/speech/tests/ace/
3 MUC-6 introduced the term 'named entities' (NE) for the task, and this name has persisted, but it should not be confused with the term 'entities' used in ACE for the task involving coreference.
4 www.wikipedia.org
5 Strictly speaking, the full extent of the second mention is 'Fred's brother.' For clarity, we shall refer to entity mentions by their head, in this case 'brother.'

Part IV   Applications

19   Machine Translation

ANDY WAY

This chapter has two main aims: (1) to present the state of the art in machine translation (MT), namely phrase-based statistical MT, together with the major competing paradigms used in MT research and development today; and (2) to provide an overview of the MT research carried out by my team at Dublin City University (DCU), characterized here in terms of 'hybrid MT.' In addition, we provide our views on the directions that MT research might take in the near future, and conclude the chapter with lists of further reading for the interested reader.

1   Introduction

There are many other overviews of machine translation (MT) available (e.g., Somers 2000; Hutchins 2003; Somers 2003a; Jurafsky & Martin 2009). In this chapter, we plan to inform the reader as to the state of the art in MT *now*, rather than giving a detailed history of the eld, much of which has been written before.

It is clear to all who are active in the area of MT today that the leading paradigm, especially in the research eld, is phrase-based statistical machine translation (PB-SMT) (Marcu & Wong 2002; Koehn et al., 2003). Until such papers appeared, SMT models of translation were based on the simple word alignment models of Brown et al. (1990; 1993). Now that SMT systems learn phrasal as well as lexical alignments, this has led to an unsurprising increase in translation quality compared to the IBM word-based models. In addition, it has become harder to describe the differences between statistical models of translation and example-based MT (EBMT), though the latter still accesses the corpus of source-to-target examples at run-time.[1]

When it comes to which commercial systems are available, however, the balance is tipped in completely the opposite direction, for the vast majority of such models are rule-based MT (RBMT) systems. Research systems such as Apertium (Armentano-Oller et al., 2006) are also prominent, and we give some attention to such models later in the chapter.

The Handbook of Computational Linguistics and Natural Language Processing, First Edition.
Edited by Alexander Clark, Chris Fox and Shalom Lappin.
© 2013 Blackwell Publishing Ltd except for editorial material and organization
© 2013 Alexander Clark, Chris Fox, and Shalom Lappin. Published 2013 by Blackwell Publishing Ltd.

The remainder of the chapter is organized as follows. In Section 2, we present a thorough overview of the leading paradigm in MT today, namely PB-SMT. We give an end-to-end description of all tasks involved, from pre-processing, to decoding, and thence to postprocessing and evaluation. In Section 3, we describe alternative approaches to this mainstream model, each of which has attracted a strong following. These include hierarchical and tree-based models of MT, EBMT, RBMT, and hybrid combinations of these approaches. In Section 4, we describe a number of MT applications, including online MT, undoubtedly *the* biggest growth area for MT in the last few years. In addition, we describe translation memories, spoken language translation, and MT for non-spoken languages. Section 5 then focuses on our own MT research and development at DCU, presented in the form of hybrid systems. In Section 6 we summarize the state of affairs in MT today, and provide our view on the directions that MT research might take in the next few years. Finally, we provide a list of further reading for the interested reader to follow up on any of the core sections.

2   The State of the Art: Phrase-Based Statistical MT

Phrase-based statistical machine translation (PB-SMT) (Marcu & Wong 2002; Koehn et al., 2003) is clearly the dominant paradigm in MT today. In this section, we take the reader through all the steps involved in developing a PB-SMT system, from gathering training resources, through pre-processing, run-time application, and postprocessing.

2.1   Pre-processing

Notwithstanding the particulars of the approach taken, the developer of any corpus-based system will be confronted with the following stages of development prior to running the system: corpus collection and clean-up, and system training (i.e., word and phrase alignment, and parameter tuning). We describe each of these steps in the following sections.

2.1.1   Data   A prerequisite for the training of a data-driven MT system is a parallel corpus of sentences and their translations aligned at sentence level. In the simplest case, the 'source' side of the bitext consists of the original sentences, and the 'target' side consists of the translations of those sentences. However, it is quite often the case that either some texts may have been translated from language A to language B and others the other way round, or more than two languages are involved and both parts were translated from one or several other languages (cf. Ozdowska and Way (2009) for an interesting investigation of the effect on translation quality of training SMT systems with such more or less appropriate sets of training data).

E1: Often, in the textile industry, businesses close their plant in Montreal to move to the Eastern townships.
F1: Dans le domaine du textile souvent, dans Montréal, on ferme et on va s'installer dans les Cantons de l'Est.

E2: There is no legislation to prevent them from doing so, for it is a matter of internal economy.
F2: Il n'y a aucune loi pour empêcher cela, c'est de la régie interne.

E3: That is serious.
F3: C'est grave.

Figure 19.1   A sentence-aligned corpus.

> **E1:** Hon. members opposite scoff at the freeze suggested by this party; to them it is laughable.
> **F1:** Les deputés d'en face se moquent du gel qu'a proposé notre parti.
> **F2:** Pour eux, c'est une mesure risible.

Figure 19.2   A non-exact alignment.

Of course, even in the simplest scenario above, the bitext can be used just as easily for translation from 'target' into the 'source' language; the system itself does not care. Given a text in language A, its translated counterpart version B and an SMT system translating from A to B, SMT training assumes A to be the source language and B to be the target language irrespective of the original translation direction or languages involved. Moreover, given that the parallel corpus is assumed to be aligned at sentence level, sentence alignment is usually performed automatically prior to training. Examples of 1:1 and 1:2 alignments from the Canadian Hansards[2] are given in Figures 19.1 and 19.2 (adapted from Arnold et al., 1994: 203).

Creating and promoting resources (corpora and tools) is now a well-established tradition in the area of NLP in general, and in SMT in particular. This is done through linguistic data centers such as the Linguistic Data Consortium (LDC)[3] or the Evaluations and Language resources Distribution Agency (ELDA),[4] which allow broad access to resources of various kinds (parallel and monolingual corpora, tokenizers, segmentation tools, aligners, etc.) for a wide range of languages, in some cases in return for a license. For example, the LDC provides data for two of the major MT evaluation shared tasks (cf. Section 2.5): NIST[5] and IWSLT.[6] On the other hand, some resources are also made freely available within MT-related projects such as EuroMatrix,[7] or certain MT shared tasks such as WMT.[8] WMT makes available to all participants a complete set of resources for the state of the art as well as advanced experiments in MT allowing for comparable results within a common framework.

SMT quality is strongly conditioned by the size of the training corpora, and further by the type and amount of resources used (linguistic tools, dictionaries, etc.). Systems are usually trained on several million words of data in order to achieve good translation quality. In this respect, the availability of corpora suitable for SMT mainly depends on two criteria: language pair, and domain (or genre) of texts. Large parallel corpora exist only for a limited number of language pairs.

The richest languages in terms of corpora are those in which international institutions or governments are required to produce translations. Texts coming from such organizations are amongst the largest and most widely used corpora in MT, especially for European languages; this is the case for the Europarl corpus (Koehn 2005),[9] the JRC-Acquis,[10] and Canadian Hansards as far as number of covered languages and size are concerned. Parallel and monolingual corpora of variable yet sufﬁcient size for MT also exist for languages of a particular political/economic interest such as Chinese, Arabic, or Indian languages in combination with English, mostly consisting of news agency material.

Although the number and/or size of available parallel corpora is increasing, the scope remains somewhat limited in terms of languages and domains covered. Apart from the languages mentioned above, recent MT-related shared tasks featured language pairs with less abundant resources such as Japanese-to-English,[11] English-to-Inuktitut,[12] or Romanian-to-English.[13] As these corpora mainly come from governments, international institutions, or news agencies, they are rather open/general in terms of domain, even for Europarl, which is often considered to be a 'sublanguage,' but is in fact extremely heterogeneous. By contrast, large specialized corpora suitable for MT remain rare.

2.1.2 Corpus clean-up, segmentation, and tokenization

Corpora are usually not created with MT in mind, and so a number of issues need to be borne in mind before using them 'as is' for MT training.

The ﬁrst thing to check is whether a special character encoding (e.g., UTF-8, the Unicode (Unicode Consortium 2006) attempt to encode characters from *all* languages, as opposed to those supported only in ASCII (American National Standards Institute 1986) is required for the translator output or by the linguistic tools used. In this case, if the encoding does not match that used in a particular corpus, an encoding conversion solves the problem (assuming the corpus is correctly encoded). Some characters reserved by the tools used must be protected. For example, the Moses decoder (Koehn et al., 2007) stumbles over vertical bars ('|') in the input. Filtering multiple and initial or ending white spaces makes the corpus cleaner and avoids processing errors at later stages.

The main issue of corpus pre-processing – *tokenization* – is the division of the sentences into tokens separated by a white space. In some languages (Latin script languages, Arabic, etc.) this division exists naturally in the form of words. In others, like Chinese or Japanese, word boundaries are not orthographically marked and the tokenization problem is distinct and more difﬁcult (it is often called 'segmentation'). When word boundaries are orthographically marked, the problem is reduced to determining when special signs such as punctuation marks should be considered as part of the word or not. This is the case, for example, in abbreviations or acronyms, but not when acting as a punctuation mark ('Mr. Obama was elected President of the U.S.A.'). Most tokenizers are based on machine learning approaches, or use dictionaries of abbreviations and acronyms, for example.

Because the execution time of the training algorithms used in MT grows very fast as the input increases, very long sentences are often removed from the corpora. Sentence pairs having a very different number of source and target tokens usually correspond to an incorrect source-to-target mapping and may also be ltered.

Finally, for some languages, special pre-processing is appropriate. Examples include the separation of clitics in Spanish, and pre xes and suf xes in Arabic, which allows for a reduction in data sparseness. Grouping compound words (such as the head verb and its particle with German compound verbs) can help to make source- and target-language word order more similar, which facilitates subsequent processing.

2.1.3 Word alignment Word alignment, which determines the translational correspondences at word level given a bilingual corpus such as those just described, is a fundamental component in all SMT variants. A set of high-quality word alignments is essential for phrase-based SMT systems since the phrase extraction normally relies on word alignment.

The most common approach to word alignment is *generative models*, which view the translation (or alignment) process as the generation of a sentence (or word) in one language from another. Here we assume the generation of a target-language sentence t_1^I from a source sentence s_1^J.[14] The transformation from source to target language in the generative model may include word insertion or deletion, word reordering ('distortion'), 1-to-n alignments ('fertility'), and so on (cf. the 'IBM models' of Brown et al., 1993). Depending on whether fertility is explicitly modeled or not, these generative models can be broadly classi ed into fertility-based versus non-fertility models.

The most widely used non-fertility models are HMM-based models. IBM model 1 and 2 are zero-order HMM models where a source position is rst selected for each position in the target sentence, and a target word is produced as the translation of the selected source word. In IBM model 1, the source position is selected uniformly, while in IBM model 2 the selection depends on the *target* position in question. The rst-order HMM model of Vogel et al. (1996) re nes the generative story by further assuming that the selection of a source position depends on the previously selected *source* position. In the context of SMT, the search for the best target translation t_1^I given a source sentence s_1^J is achieved in the *noisy channel model* by maximizing the conditional probability $P(t_1^I|s_1^J)$. Using a Bayesian transformation, this maximization criterion can be reformulated as in (1):

(1) $P\left(s_1^J \middle| t_1^I\right) P\left(t_1^I\right)$

where $P(s_1^J|t_1^I)$ is the *translation model* and $P(t_1^I)$ is the *language model*.

The alignment a_1^J, which describes the mapping from a source-word position j to a target position a_j, is introduced as a hidden variable in modeling the translation probability, as in (2):

(2) $P\left(s_1^J\middle|t_1^I\right) = \sum_{a_1^J} P\left(s_1^J, a_1^J\middle|t_1^I\right)$

where the *alignment model* $P(s_1^J, a_1^J|t_1^I)$ can be decomposed in different ways to model the transformation from the source to the target language. However, non-fertility models are generally considered to be relatively weak models, mainly because of the simplicity of the generation process.

Fertility-based alignment models, most notably IBM models 3 and 4, are much more complicated, as they introduce fertility into the alignment model. These models rst determine the source-word fertility, i.e., how many target words each source-word should generate, e.g., *not* ⟶ *ne … pas* would mean that *not* has a fertility of 2 (French words). For each source word, that many target words will be preferred as the translation of the source word. The model then arranges the hypothesized target words to produce a target string according to the *distortion models*. IBM model 3 utilizes a zero-order distortion model, i.e., each target position is chosen independently for the target words generated by each source word, whereas IBM model 4 utilizes a simpli ed rst-order dependence (i.e., a context of the neighboring previous word) in positioning the target words. However, both distortion models assign some probability to invalid target strings in order to achieve a more simpli ed approximation, resulting in the problem of 'de ciency,' which is resolved in IBM model 5.

The generative models described above consist of a large number of parameters which are normally estimated in an unsupervised manner (given that annotated data is dif cult to obtain) using the expectation-maximization (EM) algorithm (Dempster et al., 1977; cf. also Manning & Schütze 1999: 518f.) on a large bilingual corpus. There exist ef cient training and searching algorithms for HMM models; however, we are unaware of any ef cient algorithm for fertility-based IBM models. Consequently, such an approach can only be implemented by approximate hill-climbing methods, and parameter estimation can be very slow, memory-intensive and dif cult to parallelize. Given this, Deng and Byrne (2005) proposed an HMM-based word-to-phrase alignment model which explores the desirable features in IBM fertility-based models while keeping the parameter estimation step tractable. Furthermore, previous generative models have also faced the criticism that they make unreasonable assumptions about word alignment structure, i.e., the 1-to-*n* assumption, meaning that each target word can be aligned to zero or more source words, but not vice versa. Such an asymmetric alignment structure cannot capture the pervasive *m*-to-*n* alignments in real-world alignment tasks. Consequently, heuristics are needed to derive alignments from bidirectional word alignments in order to produce high-quality phrase pairs for phrase-based SMT (cf. Section 2.1.4) or translation rules for syntax-based SMT (cf. Section 3.1). Fraser and Marcu (2007a) attempted to address such a problem by proposing a new generative model capturing *m*-to-*n* alignment structures. In general, generative models have been shown to have powerful modeling capabilities and can produce high-quality alignments with successful application to various types of statistical (and other data-driven) MT systems. The most often used implementation of HMM models and IBM models 3, 4, and 5 is GIZA++[15] (Och 2003), and the MTTK[16] (Deng & Byrne 2006) implementation models HMM word-to-phrase alignments.

Discriminative word alignment models were developed with the speci c intention of overcoming the shortcomings faced by generative models. First, such models can incorporate various features encoded in the input data. Second, these models require only a relatively small amount of annotated word alignment data for training. Formally, an estimate $\hat{a}$ of the optimal ('arg max' in (3), i.e., the highest score) alignment a is searched for by maximizing a log-linear combination of a set of i features h_i, as in (3):

(3) $\hat{a} = \arg\max_{a} \sum_{i} \lambda_i h_i(s, a, t)$

The parameters (or 'weights') λ_i can be learned in a supervised manner using various machine learning techniques, including perceptron (Moore 2005), maximum entropy (Ittycheriah & Roukos 2005; Liu et al., 2005), support vector machines (Taskar et al., 2005; Cherry & Lin 2006), and conditional random elds (Blunsom & Cohn 2006). Despite having the exibility to incorporate various features, the need for a certain amount of annotated word alignment data is often put forward as a criticism of such approaches, given that the annotation of word alignments is a highly subjective task. Moreover, parameters optimized on manually annotated data are not necessarily optimal for MT tasks. Fraser and Marcu (2007b) showed that alignment error rate (AER) (Och & Ney 2000), the widely used metric to measure word alignment quality against manually annotated data, has a weak correlation with MT quality in terms of BLEU (Papineni et al., 2002) in a PB-SMT system. Therefore, some approaches have been proposed to optimize the parameters according to the MT task rather than on annotated data (Lambert et al., 2007). Some semi-supervised approaches have also been used to take advantage of both generative and discriminative approaches (Fraser & Marcu 2006; Wu et al., 2006). However, we have not yet seen a consistent discriminative word alignment model that can outperform generative models when used for SMT.

Another class of approaches to word alignment are *heuristics-based methods*, which obtain word alignment using similarity functions (Smadja et al., 1996; Ker & Chang 1997; Melamed 2000). Such approaches are extremely simple compared to both generative and discriminative models. However, the use of similarity functions can be somewhat arbitrary and the performance of such methods is inferior compared to the above-mentioned statistical approaches (Och & Ney 2003).

2.1.4   Phrase alignment and translation models
2.1.4.1 Motivation for phrase-based models Word-based SMT systems (e.g., Germann 2003) learn lexical translation models describing one-to-one mappings between a given language pair. However, words are not the best atomic units of

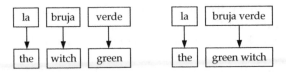

Figure 19.3   In the word-based translation on the left we see that the noun–adjective reordering into English is missed. On the right, the noun and adjective are translated as a single phrase and the correct ordering is modeled in the phrase-based translation.

translation because we can have one-to-many mappings between languages. Furthermore, by translating word for word, no contextual information is made use of during the translation process. To attempt to overcome some of these issues, sequences of words can be translated together. By using these sequences of words, so-called 'phrases' (but not in the linguistic, 'constituent' sense of the word; a 'phrase' in SMT is any sequence of length *n* of contiguous words, hence '*n*-grams'), it is possible to avoid many cases of translational ambiguity and better capture instances of local reordering. An example of this is illustrated in Figure 19.3.

The set of phrase pairs extracted from the bilingual parallel corpus constitutes the core translation model (*phrase table,* or *t(ranslation)-table*) of the phrase-based SMT system.

2.1.4.2   Learning phrase-based translation models   There are a number of ways to extract a phrase table from a parallel corpus. We will describe the most common method here and refer the reader to Section 7 for alternative approaches. To learn the phrase translation model we ﬁrst induce a word alignment between the sentence pairs in the parallel corpus, as described in Section 2.1.3. Then for each word-aligned sentence pair we extract the set of phrase pairs consistent with the word alignment.

A more formal deﬁnition of *consistency* is as follows: a phrase pair $(\tilde{s}|\tilde{t})$ is consistent with an alignment *A*, if all words $s_1, \ldots, s_n$ in $\tilde{s}$ that have alignment points in *A* have these with words $t_1, \ldots, t_n$ in $\tilde{t}$ and vice versa (Koehn 2010).

We then estimate a probability distribution over the set of phrase pairs where the probability of a phrase pair $P(\tilde{s}|\tilde{t})$ is its relative frequency in the entire set of phrase pairs:

(4) $$P(\tilde{s}|\tilde{t}) = \frac{count(\tilde{t}, \tilde{s})}{\sum_{\tilde{s}_i} count(\tilde{t}, \tilde{s}_i)}$$

This model is then included as a core factor in the log-linear model (cf. (3) and (10)).

2.1.4.3   Refined word alignments for phrase extraction   Both the quality and the quantity of the word alignments have a signiﬁcant effect on the extracted phrase translation model. One might think that the better the word alignments the better the subsequently extracted phrases should be, but many studies have shown that an expected correlation between an intrinsic improvement in word and phrase alignment quality (as measured by AER, or precision, recall, and F-score) and an increase in performance on the extrinsic MT task (as calculated by BLEU, say) is by no means guaranteed (Liang et al., 2006b; Ma et al., 2008). Vilar et al. (2006) show similar ndings by optimizing word alignment on BLEU, and reporting MT scores using F-score (i.e., the other way round, compared to Liang et al., 2006b; Ma et al., 2008). Zhang et al. (2008) and Ma et al. (2009) also show that the correlation is weak when the intrinsic quality is measured with F-score.

As mentioned in Section 2.1.3, word alignment is a directional task, so when we align a source sentence to a target sentence, each target word can be aligned to one source word at most. This is undesirable as it may be correct in many instances to have a target word map to multiple source words. In order to overcome this problem we carry out *symmetrization* of the word alignments.

This process involves running the word alignment in both directions: source to target and target to source. We can then merge the two sets of alignments by taking their union or the intersection. This process is illustrated in Figure 19.4. These alignments can be further re ned by 'growing' additional alignment points (Och & Ney 2003). For SMT a higher-recall word alignment is preferred as it leads to fewer spurious additions to the phrase translation model. For this reason, the union of the two sets of alignments along with additional re nements is generally preferred. For other precision-based tasks, however, this may not be the case, and the union of word alignments will be chosen instead.

2.2 Reordering models

Another important feature of phrase-based systems that we only mention brie y here is the *reordering model*. The problems posed by differences in the word order of languages naturally depends on the language pair at hand. For instance, between English and French, modeling short local movements (adjective–noun reordering, say) may suf ce. However, for English and German, where long-range movement of verbs is common, such a model would be inadequate.

Many state-of-the-art systems (e.g., Tillmann 2004; Koehn et al., 2007) employ lexicalized reordering models in which the reorderings are conditioned directly on the phrases (or 'blocks'). These models are learned synchronously with the phrase translation model. Each phrase pair in the lexicalized reordering model is assigned one of three orientations: monotone (m), swap (s), or discontinuous (d). The orientation is assigned based on the position of the phrase relative to other word alignments for the sentence pair. For example, in Figure 19.4, the phrase pair ⟨he,er⟩ has an alignment pointing to the top left, i.e., to the phrase pair ⟨that,dass⟩. Accordingly, this means that the orientation type of the phrase pair ⟨he,er⟩ is monotone, as the preceding English word aligns to the preceding German word. For an English-to-French phrase pair ⟨wine,vin⟩ in a translation *white wine ⟶ vin blanc*, there would be an alignment pointing to the top right, i.e., to the phrase pair ⟨white,blanc⟩. This indicates that there is evidence for a swap with the previous

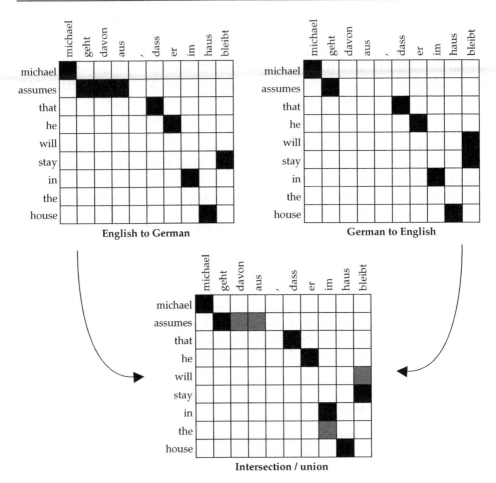

Figure 19.4   Merging source-to-target and target-to-source alignments (from Koehn 2010).

pair, indicating that by and large English adjective–noun sequences like *white wine* are mapped to noun–adjective sequences like *vin blanc* in French.

When a phrase pair is extracted for the translation model, its orientation for the reordering model is also extracted. A probability distribution p_o for the reordering model is then estimated based on the counts of how often speci c phrase pairs occur with each of the three orientation types using the maximum likelihood (ML) principle (Manning & Schütze 1999: 197), as in (5):

$$(5) \quad p_o(orientation|\tilde{f},\tilde{e}) = \frac{count(orientation|\tilde{e},\tilde{f})}{\sum_o count(o,\tilde{e},\tilde{f})}$$

where an *orientation* $\in \{m, s, d\}$ is predicted for each source-to-target phrase pair for all possible orientations o.

2.2.1 Language models In the noisy channel model of SMT (cf. (1)), $P(t)$ refers to the language model (LM), which is a probability distribution over target strings t that attempts to re ect the frequency with which each string t occurs as a sentence in text or speech. Especially in SMT, it can smooth and adjust the word orders to some extent by providing contextual information. In this section, we mainly focus on the n-gram LM which is used in most state-of-the-art SMT systems, as well as other data-driven models.

2.2.1.1 n-gram language model In an n-gram LM, the probability $P(t)$ of a string t is expressed as the product of the probabilities of the words or tokens in t, with each word probability conditioned on a number of previous words. That is, if $t = \{w_1, w_2, \ldots, w_l\}$ we have (6):

(6) $P(t) = P(w_1)P(w_2 \mid w_1)P(w_3 \mid w_1, w_2) \cdots P(w_l \mid w_1, \ldots, w_{l-1})$

In typical usage, given the string t, the LM estimation using the above chain rule and an order-3 (i.e., trigram) or higher-order Markov assumption leads to (7):

(7) $P(t) = \prod_{i=1}^{l} P\left(w_i \mid w_1^{i-1}\right) \approx \prod_{i=1}^{l} P\left(w_i \mid w_{i-n+1}^{i-1}\right)$

where w_i^j denotes the words $w_i, \ldots, w_j$.

Consider the case $n = 3$. To estimate the probabilities $P(w_i \mid w_{i-2}, w_{i-1})$ in (7), a simple ML algorithm, as in (9), can estimate the approximate probabilities from the training data:

(8) $P(w_i \mid w_{i-2}, w_{i-1}) = \dfrac{P(w_{i-2}, w_{i-1}, w_i)}{P(w_{i-2}, w_{i-1})}$

(9) $\qquad\qquad = \dfrac{count(w_{i-2}, w_{i-1}, w_i)}{(w_{i-2}, w_{i-1})}$

2.2.1.2 Language model smoothing Given the training data, it is easy to build an n-gram LM, because all we need to do is count the occurrences of the word n-gram events from the training data. However, the ML estimate does not perform well when the amount of training data is small or sparse compared to the size of the model being built. From the statistical point of view, if the training data cannot cover the test data (i.e., if a string α does not occur in the training data, but α occurs in the test data), then a problem arises that a zero probability is generated, which is clearly inaccurate as this probability should be larger than zero. Accordingly, we need to estimate or predict the probability of events which were not seen in the training data.

ML estimates are based on the observations from the training data so, according to (9), unseen word n-grams will obtain a zero probability. Furthermore, according to (7), the sentence t will also receive a zero probability because of the products, which indicates that the sentence is not possible at all. Therefore, every sentence which contains *n*-grams which do not occur in the training data will be deemed impossible. As we pointed out in Section 2.1.1, in practice, the amount of training data available is limited, so data sparseness is often a real issue. Thus if we are unable to estimate the unseen *n*-gram sequences and give them an appropriate probability, it will have a fatal in uence on many practical applications. Improving the model in (9) so that no word sequence receives zero probability is called *smoothing* (Jelinek 1977). This process involves techniques for adjusting the ML estimate to hopefully produce more accurate probabilities.

The basic idea of smoothing techniques is to reserve some small probability mass from the relative frequency estimates (cf. (9)) of the probabilities of seen events, and to redistribute this probability to unseen events. There are several smoothing techniques which work fairly well for SMT and other applications. The main differences relate to how much probability mass is subtracted out ('discounting') and how it is redistributed ('back-off'). The most popular method is Kneser–Ney smoothing (Kneser & Ney 1995).

2.3   Log-linear representation

As described in the previous sections, PB-SMT consists of three probabilistic components: a phrase translation model (TM), a reordering (distortion) model, and the language model (LM). Och and Ney (2002) represent these probabilistic components as a log-linear model interpolating a set of feature functions as in (10):

(10) $t^* = \arg\max_t \prod_{f \in F} H_f(s, t)^{\lambda_f}$

The set F is a nite set of features and λ_f are the interpolation weights over feature functions H_f of the aligned source-to-target sentence pairs s and t. The set of different features consists of the following:

(1)   an *n*-gram LM over target sequences;
(2)   a source-to-target t-table;
(3)   a target-to-source t-table (the reverse of the previous table);
(4)   lexical translation probabilities in both directions;
(5)   a phrase reordering model;
(6)   the standard word/phrase penalty which allows for control over the length of the target sentence.

2.3.1   Minimum error rate training   The parameters of each component of the log-linear model components are estimated independently. For example, the phrase translation probabilities are estimated from a bilingual corpus while the language model probabilities are estimated usually from a much larger monolingual corpus. The various components are interpolated in the log-linear framework by a set of parameters following the maximum entropy (MaxEnt) approach as shown in (10).

In the MaxEnt framework, each feature is associated with a weight. These weights can be estimated using iterative search methods to nd a single optimal solution under the MaxEnt principle, but this is a computationally expensive process. Therefore, Och (2003) proposed an approximation technique called minimum error rate training (MERT) to estimate the model parameters for a small number of features, discussed in Section 2.4. An error function that corresponds to the translation accuracy (Section 2.5) is de ned and MERT estimates the log-linear model parameters such that this error function is minimized using the n-best output of the MT system. MERT proceeds as follows:

(1) Initialize all parameters with random values.
(2) Produce the n-best translations using the current parameter set.
(3) Compute the error function using the reference translations.
(4) Optimize each parameter to minimize the error function while xing all other parameters.
(5) Iterate over all parameters.

MERT provides a simple and ef cient method to estimate the model parameters; however, it can only handle a small number of parameters, and when the number of parameters increases there is no guarantee that MERT will nd the most suitable combination (Chiang et al., 2008).

2.4 *Decoding*

At present, the state-of-the-art implementation of decoding for PB-SMT is a beam search decoder (Koehn et al., 2003). The decoder uses a log-linear model which is a MaxEnt (Jelinek 1977) direct translation model. The decoding process includes (1) the selection of translation options, (2) future cost estimation, (3) beam search, and (4) n-best list generation, all of which are explained in the following sections.

2.4.1 Translation options selection Given an input string of words and a phrase table, only a certain number of phrases in the table are related to the input string, so we just need to collect these related phrases before decoding. This not only lowers the amount of memory required, but also increases decoding speed. During the selection, typically the following information is stored:

(1) rst and last source word covered;
(2) corresponding target-phrase translation;
(3) phrase translation probability.

Given an input string of source words, all possible phrases with a limited span are found which are in accordance with the maximum length of the extracted

Maria	no	daba	una	bofetada	a	la	bruja	verde
Mary	not	give	a	slap	to	the	witch	green
	did not			a slap	by			green witch
	no			slap		to the		
	did not give					to		
						the		
				slap			the witch	

Figure 19.5   All possible source segmentations with all possible target translations (from Koehn 2004; reproduced with permission from Springer).

phrase table. Then, for each source phrase, the phrase table is searched and the matching target phrases stored.

2.4.2 Future cost estimation   In the decoding process, the target output sentence is generated left to right in the form of hypotheses which store the target phrase, translation cost and other related information. Each hypothesis is then stored in a stack which has the same source words covered. As shown in Figure 19.5, many possible segmentations for the source sentence along with many possible translations are available from the phrase table.

In order to reduce the search space (cf. Section 2.4.3 below), a breadth- rst beam search is used in decoding so that pruning is applied in a stack. In the pruning phase, not only the current translation cost but also the future cost is considered. The future cost is tied to the source words that have not yet been translated. Thus, we are looking for the cheapest cost (or the maximum probability) for the source words that are not yet covered. This future cost estimation should favor hypotheses that have already covered dif cult parts of the sentence and have only easy parts left, while discounting hypotheses that have covered the easy parts rst.[17]

For the translation options in Section 2.4.1, each source phrase $\tilde{s}_i^j$ has one or more target-phrase candidates $\tilde{t}$, so the maximum probability for a source phrase $\tilde{s}_i^j$ consisting of words i to j can be obtained by (11):

(11) $$P\left(\hat{t} \mid \tilde{s}_i^j\right) = arg\,max \sum_m \lambda_m \log(p_m(\tilde{t}, \tilde{s}))$$

where $p_m(\tilde{t}, \tilde{s})$ is a product of the bidirectional phrase probabilities, bidirectional lexicalized probabilities, phrase length penalty, and LM probability. Since we do not know the preceding target words for a translation operation, we approximate the LM cost by computing the LM score for the generated target words alone.

The future cost score for a source phrase can be ef ciently estimated a priori by dynamic programming (Koehn 2010), and simply looking up the score for this hypothesis in the cache. The lowest cost for any particular phrase will be the cheapest cost of a particular translation option, or the cheapest sum of costs from two smaller phrases that completely cover the phrase.

2.4.3   Beam search   Typical phrase-based decoders like Moses (Koehn et al., 2007) employ a beam search algorithm. Starting from the initial hypothesis where no source input words have yet been translated, source words are then expanded in a monotone or non-monotone manner, i.e., following the source-word/phrase order or not. New hypotheses can be generated from the expanded hypotheses with a phrasal translation that covers some of the source input words which have not yet been translated.

Each hypothesis is added into a beam stack as a new node, which is represented by:

(1)   a link back to the best previous state (needed for tracing the best translation of the sentence by backtracking through the search states);
(2)   the source words covered so far;
(3)   the last n-1 target words generated (if an n-gram-based LM is used);
(4)   the end of the last source phrase covered (needed for computing future distortion costs);
(5)   the most recently added target phrase;
(6)   the cost so far;
(7)   an estimate of the future cost;
(8)   feature functions (cf. Section 2.3);
(9)   additional arcs (needed for generating the n-best list).

The nal states in the search are hypotheses that cover all source words. Among these hypotheses, the one with the lowest cost (highest probability) is selected as the best translation. If we want to output an n-best list, we can generate the translations with a ranked cost during the backtracking process. The hypothesis expansion process in a beam search decoder is illustrated in Figure 19.6.

In Figure 19.6, each stack is marked by the covered source words during expansion. A newly created hypothesis will be placed in a new stack further down, e.g., the top phrase in stack 2 (comprising two words, *the man*, say) is linked to various hypotheses in stacks 3 (*goes*, i.e., three words are now covered), 4 (*does go*, four words), and 5 (*might be going*, ve words).

In order to improve decoding speed and to reduce the search space, pruning techniques (such as recombining hypotheses, or histogram pruning; Koehn 2010) are employed to optimize the search by discarding hypotheses that cannot be part of the path to the best translation (i.e., they have a low score).

2.4.4   *n*-best list generation   After the expansion process, the nal translation can be generated by backtracking. Generally, we just need one translation with

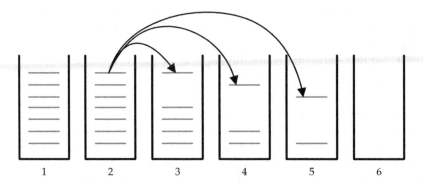

Figure 19.6 Hypothesis expansion via stack decoding (from Koehn 2004; reproduced with permission from Springer).

the maximum highest probability as the nal output, but in some cases such as MERT (Och 2003; cf. Section 2.3.1) or re-ranking (cf. Section 2.6), the *n*-best list will be needed. In typical approaches to phrase-based decoding, the A* algorithm is used to generate *n*-best lists (Koehn 2010).

2.5 MT evaluation

The constant development of MT systems using test sets of hundreds or thousands of sentences has meant that automatic MT evaluation metrics have become indispensable for quickly and cost-effectively rating candidate translations, and by extension the MT engines themselves. Some of the more widely used metrics include:

- BLEU (Papineni et al., 2002): a precision-based metric that compares a system's translation output against reference translations by summing over the 4-grams, trigrams, bigrams, and unigram matches found, divided by the sum of those found in the reference translation set. It produces a score for the output translation of between 0 and 1. A higher score indicates a more accurate translation.
- **Sentence error rate (SER):** computes the percentage of incorrect full sentence matches by comparing the system's candidate translations against the reference translations. With all error rates, a lower percentage score indicates better candidate translations.
- **Word error rate (WER)** (Levenshtein 1966): computes the distance between the reference and candidate translations based on the number of insertions, substitutions, and deletions in the words of the candidate translations divided by the number of correct reference words.
- **Position-independent word error rate (PER)** (Tillmann et al., 1997): computes the same distance as the WER but without taking word order into account.

- METEOR (Banerjee & Lavie 2005): performs two stages of comparative matching for candidate and reference translations: (1) exact matching of unigrams, and (2) stemmed matching, where remaining unmatched words are decomposed into stems using the Porter stemmer and subsequently form matches. Stem matching and synonym matching are based on WordNet models (Miller et al., 1990). Scores are obtained by calculating the sum of n-gram matches.
- **General text matcher (GTM)** (Turian et al., 2003): bases its evaluations on accuracy measures such as recall, precision, and F-score.
- **Dependency-based evaluation** (Owczarzak et al., 2007b): employs lexical functional grammar (LFG) (Kaplan & Bresnan 1982; Bresnan 2001) dependency triples using paraphrases derived from the test set through word/phrase alignment with BLEU and NIST (Doddington 2002). It evaluates translations on a structural rather than string level and allows for lexical variance.

Automatic evaluation metrics are designed to assess linear text output, requiring the provision of at least one 'gold standard' version of the testing data as a reference for comparison. The majority, including BLEU, are string-based matching algorithms that do not take syntactic or lexical variation into account and penalize any divergence from the reference sentence(s). This can mean that candidate sentences which translate the source sentence both uently and accurately, but have different lexical or syntactic choices to the reference sentence(s), may be given a low score. More recent developments, such as dependency-based evaluation, do allow for variance in lexical items (such as paraphrasing or synonyms), increasing the likelihood of a candidate sentence getting a good score.

While automatic evaluation best facilitates MT in terms of speed, human evaluation is often used as well. A panel of human evaluators with native knowledge of the target language can be asked to assess the output translations based on a prescribed set of criteria noting scales of delity and intelligibility, such as those outlined by Pierce et al. (1966).

In summary, both methodologies have their advantages, depending on whether the aim is speed of evaluation or a broader assessment of intelligibility and delity.

2.6 Re-ranking

SMT decoders may not nd the best translation from the large number of candidate translation hypotheses. Re-ranking MT output is performed by obtaining the n-best translation candidates for each sentence using a baseline translation system. The candidates are re-ranked using features extracted from these n-best candidates to obtain a better translation than the one proposed by the decoder.

Generally, SMT re-rankers train a discriminative model that can use features from the proposed n-best candidates to discriminate between the different translation candidates.

Och et al. (2004) used a large number of POS tags and syntactic features for re-ranking the n-best output of the baseline system using the log-linear model. Shen and Joshi (2005) used the best features from Och et al. (2004) to train a perceptron classi er for re-ranking the *n*-best list of candidate translations. Unlike these last two approaches, Yamada and Muslea (2006) trained the re-ranker on the entire corpus, not only on the test set.

In general, the improvements provided by re-ranking the SMT output are modest due to the fact that the number of translation candidate variations, even with a very large *n*-best list, is not enough to guarantee that a better translation will be obtained.

3 Other Approaches to MT

3.1 *Hierarchical models*

In contrast to Koehn et al. (2003), who demonstrated that using syntax to constrain their phrase-based system actually harmed its quality, a number of researchers have, to different degrees, reported improvements when grammatical information is incorporated into their models of translation. We focus in the next few sections on perhaps the most popular alternative to the pure phrase-based approach, namely the hierarchical phrase-based model proposed by Chiang (2005).

3.1.1 Model In general, given a source sentence *s*, a *synchronous CFG*[18] will have many source-side derivations that yield (i.e., produce the sentence) *s*, and therefore many possible translations *t* on the target side. In hierarchical phrase-based MT, the model over derivations *D* (of the form $X \rightarrow \langle \gamma, \alpha \rangle$, with X a non-terminal, γ strings of terminals, and α strings of non-terminals) is also de ned as a log-linear model, as in (12):

$$(12) \quad P(D) \propto \prod_i \phi_i(D)^{\lambda_i}$$

where ϕ_i are features de ned on derivations and λ_i are feature weights. In Chiang (2005), typical features used are $P(\gamma \mid \alpha)$, $P(\alpha \mid \gamma)$, lexical weights $P_w(\gamma \mid \alpha)$ and $P_w(\alpha \mid \gamma)$ (derived via word alignments), and a phrase penalty $\exp(1)$, where the system can learn preferences for longer or shorter derivations (cf. the phrase penalty in PB-SMT of Koehn et al. (2003) in Section 2.3).

For hierarchical phrase-based decoding, the integration of the LM is quite differ-ent compared to phrase-based decoding (cf. Section 3.1.3), so the LM is regarded as a special feature $P_{LM}(t)$ in the log-linear model, while the remainder of the features are de ned as products of functions on the rules used in the derivation, as in (13):

$$(13) \quad \phi_i(D) = \prod_{(X \rightarrow \langle \gamma, \alpha \rangle) \in D} \phi_i(X \rightarrow \langle \gamma, \alpha \rangle)$$

By merging (12) and (13), we end up with (14) as the model:

$$(14) \quad P(D) \propto P_{LM}(t)^{\lambda_{LM}} \times \prod_{i \neq LM} \prod_{(X \to \langle \gamma, \alpha \rangle) \in D} \phi_i(X \to \langle \gamma, \alpha \rangle)$$

That is, the weight of D is the product of the weights of the rules used in translation $(X \to \langle \gamma, \alpha \rangle) \in D)$, the language model $P_{LM}(t)^{\lambda_{LM}}$, and any other functions ϕ_i such as the phrase penalty.

As Chiang (2005) notes, it is perhaps more convenient from a notational point of view to factor out the LM and word penalty probability models, although it is cleaner (and ensures polynomial-time complexity in decoding) to integrate them into the rule weights, in order to maintain the whole model as a weighted synchronous CFG.

3.1.2 Features   The basic features used in a hierarchical phrase-based system are analogous to the default feature set of Pharaoh (Koehn 2004; cf. Section 2.3). The rules extracted from the training bitext have the following features:

(1) $P(\gamma \mid \alpha)$ and $P(\alpha \mid \gamma)$, the bidirectional phrase/rule probabilities which are estimated by counting the frequency of rules;
(2) the lexical weights $P_w(\gamma \mid \alpha)$ and $P_w(\alpha \mid \gamma)$, which estimate how well the words in α translate the words in γ (Koehn et al., 2003);
(3) a penalty $\exp^{-1}$ for hierarchical rules, similar to the phrase penalty of Koehn (2003), which allows the model to learn a preference for longer or shorter derivations;
(4) $\exp^{-1}$ for the 'glue rule,' so that the model can learn a preference for hierarchical phrases over serial combination of phrases;
(5) $\exp^{-1}$ for each of the four types of rules (numbers, dates, names, bylines);
(6) a word penalty $\exp^{-count(T(\alpha))}$, where $count(T)$ is a count of terminals in the target sentence t.

3.1.3 Decoding   The decoder is a CKY parser (Younger 1967) with beam search together with a postprocessor for mapping source derivations to target derivations. The parsing process starts with the axioms, and proceeds by applying inference rules to prove more items until a goal is proven. We refer the interested reader to Chiang (2007) for more details.

3.1.3.1 Incorporating the language model   For hierarchical phrase-based MT, incorporating the LM is a challenging problem. Chiang proposed three solutions: rst, using the above-mentioned parser to obtain an n-best list of translations and rescoring it with the LM; second, incorporating the LM directly into the grammar in a construction reminiscent of intersection of a CFG with a nite-state automaton; third, a hybrid method called *cube pruning*. In his experiments, the third method proved to be the most practical one which is a compromise and balances speed and accuracy. Again, we invite the reader to consult the primary sources for more on these possible solutions.

3.2   Tree-based models

Recently in the MT community many researchers have come to the realization that, in order to build good quality MT systems, new translation models need to be developed that are capable of handling complex source language syntactic and semantic representations, as well as their correspondences in the target language. This has led to the emergence of several models that employ syntactically parsed data to varying extents. In this section we will outline the most prominent developments.

3.2.1   Tree-to-string models   Yamada and Knight (2001) present a tree-to-string model that adheres largely to the standard noisy channel model of MT; the target-language sentence is produced after applying certain operations to the source-language sentence. Its main difference to the standard PB-SMT models is that it uses parsed data on the source-language side. The operations that this model encodes are the following:

- **reorder**: where the children of a node in the source-side parse-tree may be reordered arbitrarily;
- **insert**: where a target-language word may be inserted at any position in the source-side tree; and
- **translate**: where the surface string of the source-side tree is translated word for word to obtain the target-language sentence. The tree structure is discarded after the translate operation.

The parameters of this model are the channel operations that can be performed and their probabilities for all available contexts. The values for these parameters are estimated automatically using the EM algorithm (Dempster et al., 1977). Due to the vast number of possible contexts, the computation of all possible combinations of parameters is very expensive. Nevertheless, Yamada and Knight (2001) present an ef cient algorithm that estimates the probabilities in polynomial time. Evaluation results are presented on automatic word alignments in which improvements in alignment average score are seen over a baseline IBM model 5 system.

3.2.2   Unsupervised tree-to-tree models   Nesson et al. (2006) strive to develop an expressive and exible formalism for MT that at the same time allows for ef cient parsing. Thus they introduce probabilistic synchronous tree-insertion grammar, which is an unsupervised tree-to-tree translation model.

The basis for their formalism lies with tree insertion grammars (TIGs) (Schabes & Waters 1995). TIGs are a computationally attractive alternative to tree adjoining grammars (TAGs) (Joshi 1985) while continuing to use the same operations of sub-stitution and adjunction. The main difference lies in additional restrictions on the form of elementary trees that TIG imposes. The restrictions limit the formalism to context-free expressivity and $O(n^3)$ parsability (Chapter 2, COMPUTATIONAL COMPLEXITY IN NATURAL LANGUAGE).

Synchronous TIG (STIG) extends the TIG formalism by using elementary struc-tures consisting of pairs of TIG trees with links between particular nodes in those trees. Derivation for STIG proceeds as for TIG with the requirement that all opera-tions have to be paired. A STIG can express lexically based dependencies and can generally be parsed in $O(n^6)$ time (Chapter 2, COMPUTATIONAL COMPLEXITY IN NATURAL LANGUAGE).

Translation is performed using slightly modi ed inference rules that account for not having the target sentence during parsing. Having produced the possible derivation trees in this way it is trivial to generate the target-language sentences.

The full model presented in Nesson et al. (2006) learns a probability for every combination of tree pairs in the training corpus. Thus, in a corpus with high word co-occurrence the number of free parameters will be of the order of $O(n)^4$, where n is the size of the largest monolingual vocabulary (Chapter 2, COMPUTA-TIONAL COMPLEXITY IN NATURAL LANGUAGE). This slows the model and may lead to over tting of the training data. Therefore the authors propose to pre-process the word co-occurence data to eliminate word pairs that are unlikely to encode true relationships. This introduces another possible problem, however, where too many word pairs could be pruned, thus rendering the model unable to parse some training sentence pairs.

By evaluating the model on a translation task, Nesson et al. (2006) show an improvement in BLEU and uency scores over Pharaoh (Koehn 2004) and GIZA++ (Och 2003) systems trained on the same data, while achieving compa-rable adequacy scores.

3.2.3 Supervised tree-to-tree models Data-oriented translation (DOT) is a hybrid model of translation which combines examples, linguistic information and a statistical translation model. The DOT model is speci ed in terms of (1) the type of representation expected in the example base; (2) how fragments are to be extracted from these representations; (3) how extracted fragments are to be recom-bined when analyzing and translating input sentences; and (4) how the resulting translations are to be ranked.

Tree-DOT (Hearne 2005; Hearne & Way 2006; cf. also Section 5.2.4) was designed to utilize parallel treebanks, i.e., bilingual corpora annotated with syn-tactic structures for both the source and the target side and with links between corresponding constituents in corresponding sentence pairs. From such a paral-lel treebank, linked subtree pairs can be extracted with associated probabilities. These subtree pairs can be used to analyze source-side sentences and construct compositionally corresponding target-side translations. An example is given in Figure 19.7.

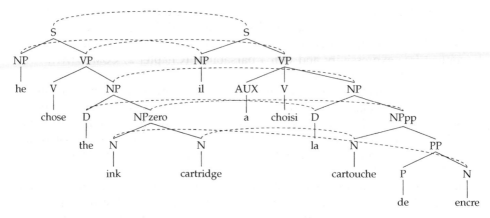

Figure 19.7   An aligned tree pair in DOT for the sentence pair: *he chose the ink cartridge,*
il a choisi la cartouche d'encre.

Tree-DOT standardly uses phrase-structure trees as training data. Links
between the constituents of two trees represent semantic/translational equivalence between these constituents. The translational equivalence relation is re exive, symmetric, and transitive. For training, from all tree pairs in a parallel
treebank a bag of all possible linked subtree pairs is created, where linked
subtree pairs occur exactly as often as they can be identi ed in the parallel
treebank. These subtree pairs can be composed together to produce analyses of
complete sentence pairs.

For translation, the source-language sentence is analyzed, whereby all possible
derivations for the sentence are generated using linked subtree pairs. The correspondences in the subtree pair fragments can be used to generate target-language
translations.

3.2.4   Supervised tree-to-tree and tree-to-string model   Hanneman et al. (2008)
present a general framework for the development of search-based syntax-driven
machine translation systems: Stat-XFER. This framework uses a declarative formalism for symbolic transfer grammars which consist of syncronous context-free
rules that can additionally be augmented by uni cation-style feature constraints.
These transfer rules specify the correspondences between phrase structures in the
source and target languages.

The transfer formalism was designed considering the fact that the rules have to
be simple enough so that they can be learned automatically, but also expressive
enough to allow for manually crafted rule additions and changes. The rules incorporate the following components (Hanneman et al. (2008) use 'x-side' to refer to
the source language, and 'y-side' for the target language):

- **Type information**: identi es the type of transfer rule and generally corresponds to a syntactic constituent type. The formalism allows for the x- and
  y-side type information to be different.

- **POS/constituent information**: represents a linear sequence of components that constitute an instance of the rule type. These correspond logically to the right-hand sides of CFG rules for the x- and y-sides.
- **Alignments**: explicitly describe how the set of source-language components in a rule align and transfer to the set of target-language components. The formalism allows for both no and many-to-many alignments.
- x-**side constraints**: apply to the source language and determine at run-time whether a transfer rule applies to a given sentence.
- y-**side constraints**: apply to the target language and guide the generation of the target-language sentence.
- xy-**constraints**: provide information about the feature values that transfer from the source to the target language.

The transfer engine uses lexical transfer rules from a bilingual lexicon, while the higher-level structural rules can be either manually developed or automatically acquired. This engine fully integrates parsing, transfer, and generation in a bottom-up 'parse-and-transfer' algorithm that is essentially an extended chart parser (Kaplan 1973; Kay 1973). Parsing is performed using the source grammar, where x-side constraints are applied. Then the transfer rules are used to generate the target language side, constrained by the target grammar (where y-side and xy constraints are enforced). See Chapter 4, THEORY OF PARSING, for more information on parsing.

3.3   Example-based machine translation

Especially since the introduction of PB-SMT (Marcu & Wong 2002; Koehn et al., 2003), there has been a strong convergence between the leading corpus-based approaches to MT. As we stated in Way and Gough (2005a), before PB-SMT was introduced, describing the differences used to be easy, as since its inception (Nagao 1984) EBMT has sought to translate new texts by means of a range of subsentential data – both phrasal and lexical – stored in the system's memory. Until quite recently, by contrast, SMT models of translation were based on the simple word alignment models of Brown et al. (1993). Now that SMT systems learn phrasal as well as lexical alignments, this has led to an unsurprising increase in translation quality compared to the IBM word-based models (Brown et al., 1993; cf. Section 2.1.3 above).

A very wide array of techniques are used in EBMT today (cf. Carl & Way 2003). Nonetheless, it is widely accepted that there are three main stages in translating with an example-based model, namely:

- **matching**: searching for fragments of the source text in the reference corpus;
- **alignment**: identifying the corresponding translation fragments;
- **recombination**: composing these translation fragments into the appropriate target text.

Just like PB-SMT, EBMT is a dynamic, fully automatic translation process. All three of the above stages depend very heavily on the nature of the training examples in the system's database. The initial *matching* process uses a distance-based metric to compare the input string against examples from the source side of the reference corpus. In EBMT, the 'classical' similarity measure is the use of a thesaurus to compute word similarity on the basis of meaning or usage (Nagao 1984; Sato & Nagao 1990; Sumita et al., 1990; Furuse & Iida 1992; Nomiyama 1992; Matsumoto & Kitamura 2005). Other approaches calculate similarity based on the relative length and content of strings (Way & Gough 2003). 'Similar' examples are searched for, and a cost is calculated taking into account deletions, insertions, and substitutions, e.g., a missing comma would be penalized less than a missing adjective.[19]

Probably the biggest divergence in approach among different types of EBMT systems can be seen in the second *alignment* (or *adaptation*) phase, which again depends largely on the nature of the examples used in the EBMT system. A rich diversity of models can be seen, for example:

(1)   pure string-pairs with no additional information (e.g., Nagao 1984; Somers et al., 1994; Lepage & Denoual 2005);
(2)   annotated constituency tree (from context-free phrase-structure grammars; Chomsky 1957) pairs (e.g., Hearne 2005; Hearne & Way 2006, cf. Sections 3.2.3 and 5.2.4);
(3)   dependency tree pairs (e.g., Watanabe 1992; Menezes & Richardson 2003);
(4)   LFG f-structure pairs (e.g., Way 2003);
(5)   tree-to-string systems (e.g., Langlais & Gotti 2006; Liu et al., 2006);
(6)   generalized examples (e.g., Brown 1999; Cicekli & Güvenir 2003; Way & Gough 2003).

Particularly in relation to generalized examples, EBMT has successfully integrated translation templates into its models, in a similar manner to rule-based approaches. It is fair to state that the use of generalized templates has not caught on anywhere near as much in PB-SMT as it has in EBMT, despite the well-received 'alignment template' approach in PB-SMT (Och & Ney 2004), which mirrors quite closely the method of generalization most widely used in EBMT.

While the third *recombination* stage also differs according to the nature of the examples used in the appropriate EBMT model, it is broadly similar to the *decoding* stage in SMT (cf. Germann 2003 for word-based models, and Koehn 2004; Koehn et al., 2007 for phrase-based approaches, cf. Section 2.4). Indeed, many systems which are called 'example-based' currently use Moses as their decoder, and more and more the term 'recombination' is being replaced by the PB-SMT term 'decoding.'

3.4 Rule-based machine translation

As mentioned in the introduction, the leading paradigm in published MT research is PB-SMT; however, most available commercial systems are rule-based MT

(RBMT) systems. The main reason why RBMT systems are still being developed is that the vast bilingual and monolingual training corpora needed to build PB-SMT systems are not available for all language pairs. Furthermore, the translation errors produced by RBMT systems tend to have a more repetitive nature than those of a PB-SMT system,[20] which may render RBMT systems more predictable and easier for human translators to post-edit.

It may be useful to offer a contrast between RBMT and corpus-based systems such as PB-SMT and EBMT. RBMT systems are deductive: they use rules, dictionaries, etc., explicitly coded in a computer-readable form by experts using knowledge *deduced* or derived from their linguistic knowledge. This process may involve *elicitation*, that is, making explicit the implicit knowledge of translators and linguists. In contrast, PB-SMT and EBMT systems are *inductive*; they use information *inferred* from sentence-aligned parallel texts.

However, this deductive RBMT knowledge is somewhat hidden in commercial products. As we said earlier, commercial MT is overwhelmingly dominated by the rule-based paradigm. Most commercial MT companies tend to withhold information about the inner workings of their products, to avoid compromising their competitiveness in a license-based closed-software business model; therefore, papers describing real RBMT systems are somewhat scarce (cf. Section 7 for some examples). However, a moderate effort of *reverse engineering* (Forcada 2001) using carefully prepared test sets may be easily used to reveal the strategies and rules used by these systems, with 'incorrect' translations playing an important role in the extraction of this information.

While it may take some effort to see what 'rules' might be underpinning existing commercial systems, it is important to note that not all RBMT systems are closed. For example, the Logos system has been released as free/open source software as 'OpenLogos,'[21] and there is also very active development around a free/open source MT platform called Apertium (Armentano-Oller et al., 2006),[22] mainly by private companies.

Despite such shifts, it remains the case that these open source systems use technologies that have been around for decades: Apertium uses a classical partial syntactic-transfer architecture (also known as a 'transformer' architecture; Arnold et al., 1994, chapter 4). The indirect strategy used by Logos is harder to characterize in terms of a standard architecture (Scott 2003).

With respect to closed source systems, one of the leaders is the Barcelona-based Translendium,[23] which may be seen as a modern version of Siemens-Nixdorf's full syntactic-transfer METAL system (White 1985). Systems such as Softissimo's Reverso[24] use a partial syntactic-transfer strategy, able to translate correctly *The senior expert's large desk* or *The computer expert's desk* but failing to translate a slightly more complex phrase such as *The senior computer expert's large desk* because of lack of a suitable pattern to detect and translate it, revealing the application of shorter patterns.

RBMT systems (of the transformer and transfer kind) were designed in the 1970s and 1980s to run on mainframe computers. They were then ported to become slow desktop applications for personal computers in the 1990s, and subsequently they have been run on high-performance web-based systems without changes in their basic design. The commercial nature of these products and the apparent lack of innovation may explain why it is hard to nd papers describing new developments in RBMT, as compared to those in corpus-based MT.

3.5 *Hybrid methods*

While we feel it is appropriate here to feature systems which espouse to exhibit some degree of hybridity, we should perhaps begin with a word of caution:

> Much current research in MT is neither based purely on linguistic knowledge nor on statistics, but includes some degree of hybridization. At AMTA 2004 and MT Summit 2005 just about all commercial MT developers also claimed to have hybrid systems. But is this mostly a good way to allow painting oneself into whatever paradigm that current 'fashion' suggests one should be? (Cavalli-Sforza & Lavie 2006)

Accordingly, we make a distinction in what follows between serial system combination (or 'multi-engine MT') and truly integrated systems. In what follows, we assume that only the latter qualify for the label 'hybrid.' Nonetheless, ROVER-like system combinations (Fiscus 1997) are increasingly to be seen, especially in large-scale open MT evaluations, and we feature some examples below. In Section 5, we discuss the contributions of our own work in the context of hybridity in translation, so the interested reader should also look there for comparisons with the work cited in the current section.

3.5.1 Multi-engine MT The term 'multi-engine machine translation' (MEMT) was rst introduced by Frederking and Nirenburg (1994) in their Pangloss system. Broadly speaking, MEMT systems try to select the best output from a number of MT hypotheses generated by different systems, while leaving the individual hypotheses intact.

Alegria et al. (2008) report a hierarchical strategy to select the best output from three MT engines for Spanish-to-Basque translation. First they apply EBMT (if it covers the input), then SMT (if the con dence score is higher than a given threshold), and then RBMT. The best results were obtained by the combination of EBMT and SMT.

Mellebeek et al. (2006) report a technique in which they recursively decompose the input sentence into smaller chunks and produce a consensus translation by combining the best chunk translations, selected through majority voting, a trigram LM score, and a con dence score assigned to each MT engine. This is a quite different approach to all the other methods presented here, which operate on the MT outputs for complete sentences.

Van Zaanen and Somers (2005) report a language-independent 'plug-and-play' MEMT system that constructs a consensus translation from the outputs of off-the-shelf MT systems, relying solely on a simple edit-distance-based alignment of the translation hypotheses, with no training required.

The work of Paul et al. (2005a; 2005b) presents a multi-engine hybrid approach to MT, making use of statistical models to generate the best possible output from various MT systems. When using an SMT model to select the best output from multiple initial hypotheses produced by a number of SMT and EBMT systems, Paul et al. (2005a) found that a PB-SMT system modeled on HMMs provided the best results.

3.5.2 Integrated systems Rosti et al. (2007) look at sentence-, phrase-, and word-level system combinations exploiting information from n-best lists, system scores, and target-to-source phrase alignments. Accordingly, it could be described as either MEMT or integrated, but we choose to discuss it here rather than in the previous section.

Chen et al. (2007) describe an architecture that allows combining SMT with one or more RBMT systems in a multi-engine setup. It uses a variant of standard SMT technology to align translations from RBMT systems with the source text and incorporates phrases extracted from these alignments into the phrase table of the SMT system. In related work, Eisele et al. (2008) report on two hybrid architectures combining RBMT with SMT. In the rst architecture, several existing RBMT engines are used in a multi-engine setup to enrich the lexical resources (phrase table) available to the SMT decoder, which combines the best expressions proposed by different engines. The modi ed phrase table combines statistically extracted phrase pairs with phrase pairs generated by linguistic rules. The second architecture uses lexical entries found using a combination of SMT technology together with shallow linguistic processing and manual validation, to extend the lexicon of the RBMT engine.

Seneff et al. (2006) exploit techniques to combine an interlingual MT system with phrase-based statistical methods, for translation from Chinese into English.

Bangalore et al. (2001) also use insights from post-editing to compute a consensus translation via majority voting from several translation hypotheses encoded in a confusion network. However, since edit-distance only focuses on insertions, deletions, and substitutions, the model is unable to handle translation hypotheses with signi cantly different word orders. Jayaraman and Lavie (2005) try to overcome this problem by allowing non-monotone alignments of words in different translation hypotheses for the same sentence. They use a basic edit-distance (Levenshtein 1966) that ignores case and which uses a stemmer to increase the number of matches.

Matusov et al. (2006) compute the consensus translation by voting on a confusion network (Mangu et al., 2000; Hakkani-Tür & Riccardi 2003) constructed from pair-wise word alignments of the multiple hypotheses to explicitly capture word reordering.

4 MT Applications

Advances in MT have meant that translation quality is now good enough to facilitate the needs of the general public with online MT systems (Section 4.1), assist human translators through the development of translation memory systems

(Section 4.2), and help address speci c problems such as intercultural communication (Section 4.4). It can also be combined with other NLP technologies (Section 4.3).

4.1   Online MT systems

Consistent development of MT technology and the increasing need for translation at great speed with little cost has fueled the proliferation of online MT systems such as Systran,[25] Google Translate,[26] Babel sh,[27] and Windows Live Translator.[28] These systems predominantly offer their services free of charge as part of a web-based platform. They provide real-time translation to the general public through web-based platforms that allow users to type sentences, paragraphs of text, or URLs for almost instantaneous translation into their chosen language. Although online MT systems may not be the best choice for highly accurate, large-scale, domain-speci c translation, they adequately serve the small-scale, open-domain translation needs of the general public – as can be seen by the millions of hits per day that such sites receive – where the need for *gisting* (i.e., access to the basic information contained in the document) is greater than a perfect translation.

4.2   Translation memory tools

Translation memories (Garcia 2007; Biçici & Dymetman 2008) comprise bilingual corpora of previously translated phrases usually within a particular domain. Translation memory tools are used to assist human translators and, as well as the memories themselves, they contain glossary and terminology management components, alignment technology, pre-translate functions, etc. Input phrases, or phrases selected using a computer-assisted translation tool, are compared against the corpus, and a set of relevant target-language sentences are produced for the translator to select appropriate parts from each to combine together to produce the output translation (cf. Section 3.3 for a comparison with EBMT).

4.3   Spoken language translation

As MT technology has developed, the range of use scenarios has increased particularly with respect to combining approaches with other NLP technologies. Coupling MT and speech technology, for example, particularly facilitates communication when text input is not convenient or where literacy skills impede such usage. For instance, the 'Phraselator'[29] used by the US military is a handheld speech-to-speech translation system that aids communication where one party does not speak English, without the need for an interpreter or literacy skills. Such technology also bypasses the need for both parties to be able to operate the device, which may speed up the language exchange in time-critical situations. A further example of this is the role of MT in healthcare for patients with limited

English (Somers 2007). MT combined with speech recognition and synthesis can play an important role in safety-critical situations such as doctor–patient communication where patients are vulnerable, and may have little English or few literacy skills.

4.4 *Sign languages*

MT can also be a valuable tool to bridge the cross-modal communication gap between spoken and signed languages. Although research in this area is still relatively novel compared to mainstream spoken language MT, it has gained ground over the decade of its development with work in both rule-based (e.g., Veale et al., 1998) and more recently data-driven approaches (Morrissey et al., 2007). Where language barriers exist, person-to-person communication usually requires one or the other party to break from using their native language, something which may not be possible for either party in the context of deaf–hearing communication. In this context MT can act as a useful substitute, and help maintain con dentiality in situations such as doctor–patient scenarios which are currently compromised by the use of teletype phones and human interpreters.

5 Machine Translation at DCU

The MT group[30] at DCU initially carried out research on EBMT (Carl & Way 2003), and especially marker-based approaches (Way & Gough 2003; Gough & Way 2004; Gough 2005; Way & Gough 2005a). However, in the intervening period, we have worked on a very wide range of other areas of MT research and development, including:

(1)   syntax-driven statistical machine translation (Hassan et al., 2006; 2007b; 2008; van den Bosch et al., 2007b; Stroppa et al., 2007; Haque et al., 2009);
(2)   hybrid statistical and example-based machine translation (Way & Gough 2005a; Groves & Way 2005a; 2005b; Groves 2007);
(3)   tree-based machine translation (Hearne & Way 2003; Hearne 2005; Hearne & Way 2006);
(4)   word alignment (Ma et al., 2007a; 2007b; 2008; 2009);
(5)   subsentential alignment for machine translation (Tinsley et al., 2007a; 2007b; Hearne et al., 2008; Zhechev & Way 2008);
(6)   improvement of rule-based machine translation (Mellebeek et al., 2006);
(7)   evaluation in machine translation (Owczarzak et al., 2007a; 2007b; He & Way 2009);
(8)   controlled language and machine translation (Way & Gough 2004; 2005b);
(9)   human factors in machine translation (Morrissey et al., 2007).

We will outline some of this work in the following sections.

5.1   *Hybridity on the source side*

5.1.1   Adding source-language context into PB-SMT   The DCU MATREX system (Stroppa & Way 2006; Hassan et al., 2007a; Tinsley et al., 2008) uses Moses (Koehn et al., 2007) as a backbone. In a different strand of work, a novel (albeit uncompetitive) decoder based on a memory-based classi er smoothed with a trigram LM is presented in van den Bosch et al. (2007b). Contrast this with the work of Carpuat and Wu (2007), who use a pre-existing word-sense disambiguation tool to demonstrate improvements over an SMT baseline. Later work (Stroppa et al., 2007) improves on the method of van den Bosch et al. (2007b) by integrating a memory-based classi er as a kind of 'pre-decoder.' It is demonstrated that a PB-SMT system using Moses improves signi cantly when context-informed features from the source language are used. We are able to (1) introduce context-informed features *directly* in the original log-linear framework (cf. (10) above), and (2) still bene t from the existing training and optimization procedures of standard PB-SMT.

Essentially, we use two sets of context-informed features: word-based features and class-based features. As far as the former are concerned, we can use a feature that includes the direct left- (s_{b_k-1}) and right-context (s_{j_k+1}) words of a given source phrase $\tilde{s}_k = s_{b_k} \dots s_{j_k}$ derived from a particular sentence pair s_1^K (consisting of words $1 \dots K$), as in (15):

$$(15) \quad h_m\left(s_1^J, t_1^I, s_1^K\right) = \sum_{k=1}^{K} \tilde{h}_m(\tilde{s}_k, s_{b_k-1}, s_{j_k+1}, \tilde{t}_k, s_k)$$

Here, the context is a window of size 3 (focus phrase + left-context word + right-context word), centered on the source phrase $\tilde{s}_k$. As in (10), $\tilde{h}_m$ are the weights of the various features. Larger contexts may also be considered, so more generally, we have (16):

$$(16) \quad h_m\left(s_1^J, t_1^I, s_1^K\right) = \sum_{k=1}^{K} \tilde{h}_m(\tilde{s}_k, CI(\tilde{s}_k), \tilde{t}_k, s_k)$$

where $CI(\tilde{s}_k)$ denotes some contextual information (neighboring words, phrases, part-of-speech (POS) tags, etc.) about $\tilde{s}_k$.

In addition to the context words themselves, it is possible to exploit several knowledge sources characterizing the context. For example, we can consider the POS of the focus phrase and of the context words. In our model, the POS of a multi-word focus phrase is the concatenation of the POS tags of the words composing that phrase. Here, the context for a window of size 3 looks as in (17):

$$(17) \quad CI(\tilde{s}_k) = \langle POS(\tilde{s}_k), POS(s_{b_k-1}), POS(s_{j_k+1}) \rangle$$

We can, of course, combine the class-based and the word-based information together if it leads to further improvements.

Essentially, the source context (words and/or POS tag sequences) suggest target-language sequences for incorporation into the log-linear PB-SMT model. When testing on the Italian-to-English and Chinese-to-English IWSLT 06 data (Stroppa et al., 2007), we found a consistent improvement for all metrics, for each type of contextual information: words only, POS only, and (for one of the language pairs) words+POS. Compared to the baseline PB-SMT system, the signi cance of the improvements depended on the metric. Interestingly, the words+POS combination leads to a slight improvement for Italian-to-English, but not for Chinese-to-English (due to the poor quality of the Chinese POS tagging).

This work is extended in Haque et al. (2009) to include supertags (cf. Section 5.3.1 below) as an additional, bene cial source-language contextual feature.

5.2 Hybridity in the translation phase

5.2.1 Comparing EBMT and word-based SMT Rather surprisingly, until our work in Way and Gough (2005a), there had been *no* published comparative research between the respective merits of SMT and EBMT, largely due to (1) the relative unavailability of EBMT systems; (2) the lack of participation of EBMT researchers in competitive evaluations; and (3) the clear dominance of SMT.

In Way and Gough (2005a), on a 203,000 sentence pair translation memory from *Sun Microsystems*, and on a 4,000 test set (average sentence length 13.1 words for English, 15.2 words for French) taken from the same collection, our EBMT system in Gough and Way (2004) outperformed a baseline word-based SMT system (Giza++ (Och 2003), CMU-Cambridge statistical toolkit (Clarkson & Rosenfeld 1997), ISI ReWrite Decoder (Germann et al., 2001; Germann 2003) for French to English and especially English to French, according to BLEU (Papineni et al., 2002).

5.2.2 Combining EBMT and PB-SMT chunks However, as PB-SMT had already been developed in Marcu and Wong (2002), it was clear that, despite being of interest, the research in Way and Gough (2005a) was not an entirely fair comparison. Accordingly, in a range of papers, we conducted a variety of experiments to compare EBMT and PB-SMT, including:

(1) comparing EBMT and PB-SMT on *Sun Microsystems* translation memory data (Groves & Way 2005a; 2005b);
(2) combining EBMT and PB-SMT chunks (Groves & Way 2005a; 2005b);
(3) changing domain to Europarl (322,000 sentences) (Groves & Way 2005a; 2005b);
(4) different language pairs (Spanish to English) and more data (958,000 sentences) (Armstrong et al., 2006);
(5) quite different language pairs (Basque to English, 273,000 sentences) (Stroppa et al., 2006).

On the *Sun Microsystems* translation memory, our EBMT system outperformed the PB-SMT system. However, one interesting nding was that the PB-SMT system, seeded in the usual way with Giza data (cf. Section 2.1.4), outperforms a PB-SMT system built with EBMT data. We also built a 'semi-hybrid' system consisting of EBMT phrases and Giza++ words, as well as a 'fully hybrid' system comprising Giza++ words and phrases and EBMT words and phrases.

Using the *Sun Microsystems* translation memory, we observed that the 'semi-hybrid' system (with a total of 430,000 entries in the t-table) performed signi - cantly better than the same system seeded with EBMT data (403,000 entries) alone. This showed us that the Giza++ word lexicon was much better than the EBMT system's, and henceforth we abandoned our EBMT word-level lexicon. Using *all* (i.e., Giza++ words and phrases and EBMT words and phrases) data (2.05 million entries) improves the PB-SMT system, i.e., EBMT data improves the PB-SMT system, and for French to English, the fully hybrid 'example-based PB-SMT' system improves over the EBMT system, i.e., combining chunks from both systems improves over both the SMT and EBMT baselines.

On the *Europarl* data (Koehn 2005), we observed, unsurprisingly, that doubling training data (78,000, 156,000, 322,000) improves both EBMT and PB-SMT systems. This time, however, the PB-SMT system signi cantly outperforms our EBMT system. We put this down to the relative homogeneity (i.e., consistency of domain) of the *Sun Microsystems* translation memory compared to the heterogeneity of Europarl. Adding the Giza++ word lexicon improves the EBMT system a little, and the hybrid 'statistical EBMT' system seeded with all PB-SMT and EBMT data improves over the EBMT baseline. Adding the EBMT data to the hybrid 'example-based PB-SMT' system beats the baseline PB-SMT system, even when trained using only half the amount of data (156,000 vs. 322,000) for French to English. For English to French, the hybrid PB-SMT system using 78,000 sentences of training data has almost the same performance as the baseline PB-SMT system trained on four times as much data (322,000).

On other language pairs and corpora, we found that adding EBMT chunks to a baseline Pharaoh system (Koehn 2004) adds four BLEU points for Spanish to English (Armstrong et al., 2006) trained on nearly 1 million sentences of Europarl data. Furthermore, we showed that adding EBMT chunks to a baseline Pharaoh system adds   ve BLEU points for Basque to English (Stroppa et al., 2006).

5.2.3 Adding statistical language models to EBMT Groves and Way (2005a; 2005b) showed that adding a statistical LM to their EBMT helps improve translation performance. However, unlike in PB-SMT, we did not integrate the target LM (cf. Section 2.2.1) *directly* into the EBMT system, but rather used it only for EBMT re-ranking (cf. Section 2.6). Adding the target LM improves both the baseline and the hybrid 'statistical EBMT' systems (10 percent and 6–7 percent relative improvement in BLEU respectively).

5.2.4 Tree-based translation We have already described in Section 3.2.3 the basic system architecture of our DOT tree-to-tree MT system. One might be able to claim with some conviction that tree-to-tree translation (e.g., Hearne 2005;

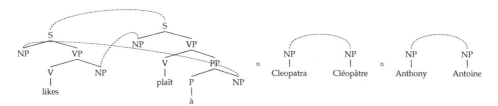

Figure 19.8   Composition in tree-DOT.

Hearne & Way 2006) *is* hybrid MT, seeing as the DOT model includes examples (trees, in tree-DOT), source and target syntax (in the trees), rules (how the trees relate), and statistics (in the probability model) (see Figure 19.7).

There are two fragmentation operations in DOT which allow smaller, more general aligned tree pairs to be extracted from larger aligned tree pairs. The *root* operation selects a linked node pair to be root nodes and deletes all except these nodes, the subtrees they dominate, and the links between them. The *frontier* operation selects a set of linked node pairs to be frontier nodes and deletes the subtrees they dominate.

The tree-DOT composition operation (∘) requires that tree fragments be composed at the leftmost site on the fragment's source side, and at the target site *linked to* the leftmost source site. This ensures that each derivation is unique, and that translational equivalences encoded in the example base are respected (Way 2003). An example derivation is given in Figure 19.8.

The probability model in DOT is a sum-of-products model, consisting of the probability of a fragment $< s_x, t_x >$ (comprising a source fragment s_x and its translation t_x), the probability of a derivation D_x, the probability of a parse $< S_x, T_x >$, and the probability of a source-to-target sentence pair s, t. Combined together, we derive the probability model in (18):

$$(18) \quad \sum_{<S_x,T_x> \text{ yields } s,t} \sum_{D_x \text{ yields } <S_x,T_x>} \prod_{<s_x,t_x> \,\in\, D_x} \frac{|<s_x,t_x>|}{\sum_{root(s)=root(s_x)\wedge root(t)=root(t_x)} |<s,t>|}$$

As for disambiguation strategies, in Hearne and Way (2006) we compared a range of different techniques, including:

- **most probable translation** (MPT): the *most probable sequence of target terminals* given the input string;
- **most probable parse** (MPP): the sequence of target terminals read from the *most probable bilingual representation* for the input string;
- **most probable derivation** (MPD): the sequence of target terminals read from the *most probable derivation of a bilingual representation* for the input string;
- **shortest derivation** (SDER): the sequence of target terminals read from the *shortest derivation of a bilingual representation* for the input string.

Table 19.1   Number of fragments for English-to-French and French-to-English HomeCentre experiments

	link depth=1	depth≤2	depth≤3	depth≤4
English to French:	6,140	29,081	148,165	1,956,786
French to English:	6,197	29,355	150,460	2,012,632

The first two of these were computed using *Monte Carlo Sampling* (Bod 1998), while the latter two were calculated using the *Viterbi* algorithm (Viterbi 1967).

Using the English-to-French section of the HomeCentre corpus, we split 810 parsed, subsententially aligned translation pairs into 12 training/test sets, six for English to French, and six for French to English. The splits were randomly produced such that all test words occurred in the training set, i.e., there were no OOV items.

One problematic issue with DOT models is grammar size. For our experiments, the grammar sizes are given in Table 19.1 (using the notion of 'link depth' from Hearne & Way 2003).

The full results for English to French and French to English in terms of exact match, BLEU, and F-score, averaged over the splits, are given in Hearne and Way (2006). In sum, the DOP hypothesis (Bod 1998) is confirmed for both language directions, i.e., as fragment depth increases, accuracy increases. For English to French, for all metrics and depths bar MPP at link depth 2, either MPD or SDER is preferred. Interestingly, MPT does not achieve highest accuracy at any depth for any metric and, overall, the highest performance is at link depth 4 using MPD or SDER. For French to English, except for the BLEU score at link depth 3, the MPT scores best for both BLEU and F-score, whereas for exact match there are no significant trends to report.

As might be expected, execution time increases as link depth increases. However, the extra time required is spent building the translation space rather than disambiguating, and we note that translating from French takes longer because the average sentence length is longer. For English to French, we see that SDER = MPD < MPP < MPT, while for French to English, MPT < SDER = MPD < MPP. Interestingly, ranking with Monte Carlo sampling does not take longer than ranking with the Viterbi algorithm for this data set.

One of the major remaining issues for us is scaling DOT to training sizes of at least two orders of magnitude larger than those used to date. Data acquisition has been a problem, which resulted in our building an automatic subtree aligner, described in Tinsley et al. (2007b). See also Galron et al. (2009) for a novel method of rescoring the DOT fragments with the evaluation metrics (see Section 2.5 above) used to measure the performance with the MT end task in mind.

5.2.5 Augmenting PB-SMT with subtree pairs   Once we had developed our automatic subtree aligner (Tinsley et al., 2007b), we incorporated subtree alignments into PB-SMT systems (Tinsley et al., 2007a; Hearne et al., 2008). The motivation for this work was the observation that most state-of-the-art MT systems (1) are not syntax-aware, (2) use models which are based on *n*-grams, and (3) incorporate only a limited amount of linguistic information.

Parallel treebanks are not widely used in MT, if at all. However, we believe that the data encoded within parallel treebanks could be useful in MT.[31] In order to con rm this view, we built large parallel treebanks automatically, using off-the-shelf parsers and our subtree aligner, and then used these parallel treebanks to train a range of PB-SMT systems.

In Tinsley et al. (2007a), we used two data sets for two different language pairs. For English to German we used a small subset of Europarl data (Koehn 2005), with a 9,000:1,000 sentence split for training and testing. The monolingual parsers used were Bikel (2002) for English, and BitPar (Schmid 2004) for German (trained on the Tiger treebank). For English to Spanish we used a 4,500:500 sentence split of Europarl data for training and testing. The parser of Bikel (2002) was again used for English, with a version of the same parser adapted by Chrupa a and van Genabith (2006) (trained on the Cast3LB treebank; Civit & Martí 2004) used for Spanish.

There were three main ndings: (1) the parallel treebank word and phrase pairs improve translation quality when combined with traditional corpus-based extraction; (2) the parallel treebank word pairs are better for translation than those given by traditional word alignment; but also (3) that the parallel treebank phrase pairs are too few in number to be used alone for translation.

Nonetheless, just like the work of Groves and Way (2005a; 2005b), this strand of work clearly demonstrates that restricting word and phrase extraction to one particular method will lead to suboptimal performance.

In Hearne et al. (2008), the authors demonstrate that the subtree aligner of Tinsley et al. (2007b) can also be used to extract word and phrase pairs from dependency parses. In brief, the authors demonstrate that while both constituency- and dependency-based sets of alignments improved a baseline PB-SMT system, the combination caused system performance to deteriorate. Working out precisely why this is the case is the subject of ongoing work.

5.3   Hybridity on the target side

5.3.1   Incorporating supertags into PB-SMT   In Hassan et al. (2006; 2007b; 2008), we have shown that supertags (both CCG and LTAG) improve the performance of a state-of-the-art PB-SMT system on large data sets: for Arabic to English, on the NIST'05 data,[32] and for German to English, on the ACL 2007 MT Workshop shared task (WMT 2007) (Callison-Burch et al., 2007).

Our approach can be described with respect to the noisy channel model (cf. (1)) as well as the log-linear model (cf. (3)). The noisy channel formulation would extend equation (1) as in (19):

$$\arg\max_{t} \sum_{ST} P(s \mid t, ST) P_{ST}(t, ST) \approx$$

$$\arg\max_{t,ST} P(s \mid t, ST) P_{ST}(t, ST) \approx$$

(19) $\arg\max\limits_{\sigma,t,ST} P(\phi_s \mid \phi_{t,ST}) P(O_s \mid O_t)^{\lambda_o} P_{ST}(t, ST)$

where $P(\phi_s \mid \phi_{t,ST})$ is the translation model containing supertags on the target side, $P(O_s \mid O_t)^{\lambda_o}$ is the distortion model, and $P_{ST}(t, ST)$ is the target-language model containing supertags. ST is the supertag sequence for the target string t. We use σ to indicate a segmentation into supertagged phrase pairs, just as in the baseline model.

We can also formalize our approach in terms of the log-linear model, as in (20):

(20) $t^* = \arg\max\limits_{t,\sigma,ST} \prod\limits_{f \in F'} H_f(s, t, \sigma, ST)^{\lambda_f}$

Our model interpolates (log-linearly) a novel set of *supertagged features f* with the features of the baseline model F'. These include $H_{lm.st}(s, t, \sigma, ST) = P(ST)$, a Markov supertagging language model (hence *lm*) over sequences of supertags (hence *st*), as in (21):

(21) $P(ST) = \prod\limits_{i=1}^{n} p\left(st_i \left| st_{i-4}^{i-1}\right.\right)$

We also use two weight functions $H_{\phi.st}(s, t, \sigma, ST) = P(\phi_s \mid \phi_{t,ST})$ and its reverse $H_{r\phi.st}(s, t, \sigma, ST) = P(\phi_{t,ST} \mid \phi_s)$. The supertagged phrase translation probability is approximated in the usual (i.e., bidirectional) way:

(22) $P(\phi_s \mid \phi_{t,ST}) \approx \prod\limits_{\langle s_i, t_i ST_i\rangle \in (\phi_s \times \phi_{t,ST})} p(s_i \mid t_i, ST_i)$

(23) $P(\phi_{t,ST} \mid \phi_s) \approx \prod\limits_{\langle s_i, t_i ST_i\rangle \in (\phi_s \times \phi_{t,ST})} p(t_i, ST_i \mid s_i)$

In both (22) and (23), $\langle s_i, t_i, ST_i\rangle$ is a supertagged phrase pair consisting of the phrases $\langle s_i, t_i\rangle$ where t_i is supertagged with ST_i. As usual, the parameters $p(s \mid t, ST)$ and $p(t, ST \mid s)$ are estimated with the relative frequency in the multiset of all supertagged phrase pairs extracted from the parallel corpus, as in (24):

$$P(s \mid t, ST) = \frac{count(s, t, ST)}{\sum_s count(s, t, ST)}$$

(24) $P(t, ST \mid s) = \dfrac{count(s, t, ST)}{\sum_{t,ST} count(s, t, ST)}$

Finally, we employ two more feature functions ($x.\phi.st$ and $x.r\phi.st$) capturing the statistics $p(s_i \mid ST_i)$ and $P(ST_i \mid s_i)$, which in effect smooth the feature functions $\phi.st$ and $r\phi.st$.

In sum, incorporating supertags into PB-SMT demonstrates clearly that lexical syntax helps, for a number of reasons: (1) supertags t seamlessly with PB-SMT as they are lexical, linguistically rich and can be used in ef cient HMMs; (2) supertags do not admit (much) redundant ambiguity into the phrase translation tables; (3) the huge amount of baseline PB-SMT phrases are constrained using *bona fide* syntactic constraints; (4) more informed decisions regarding the best candidate can be taken; and (5) there is no need for full parsing or treebanking.

If the reader needs any further persuasion that adding lexical syntax really helps, our Arabic-to-English system (Hassan et al., 2007a) was ranked rst at IWSLT-07 (Fordyce 2007) according to human judges.

5.4 What works?

Given all the above, it might be useful to summarize what we have found to work well in practice.

As far as incorporating hybridity into EBMT is concerned, adding Giza++ lexical and phrasal chunks, and using target LMs for re-ranking have proven very effective.

Regarding the incorporation of hybridity into PB-SMT, adding EBMT lexical and phrasal chunks improves translation quality, and reduces the t-table size for the hybrid system while continuing to compare favorably with much larger baseline PB-SMT systems. This may be important for language pairs with scarce resources, as well as situations where systems with a much smaller footprint are required. In addition, factoring in parallel treebank word and phrase pairs improves translation quality, as does incorporating supertags into the target LMs and the target side of the TM. Finally, adding source-language features directly into the log-linear model improves translation quality quite considerably.

5.5 Future research directions

Much of the above research is work in progress, and the intention is to continue to improve on the steps taken so far. Some of the issues to be tackled include:

(1)   combining the content-word generalized templates (*CMU,* in (25)) of Brown (1999) with our own marker-based generalized templates (*DCU,* in (26)):

(25)   *CMU : Flights from* <PLACE> *to* <PLACE>

(26)   *DCU : Flights* <PREP> *New York* <PREP> *Denver*

(2)   incorporating a target LM *directly* into our EBMT system;
(3)   combining all source, target, and translational improvements in *one* system.

In the context of the Centre for Next Generation Localisation (CNGL),[33] there are a number of open research avenues, including many of the issues raised here.

However, other work packages address the development of probabilistic transfer engines, the tuning of MT systems to text type and genre, the development of general alignment models capable of inducing subsentential alignments for any type of annotated data, the incorporation of controlled language guidelines into the range of MT systems being developed in our team, and the development of intelligent engines for speech-to-speech translation. We continue to extend the range of language pairs that our systems can cope with (cf. English to Hindi; Srivastava et al., 2008), as well as participate in large-scale MT evaluation competitions.

6 Concluding Remarks and Future Directions

For a number of reasons, it can be said with some conviction that the eld of MT currently nds itself in a quite good state of health:

(1)   there is evidence of increased levels of funding (especially in the US, Europe, and Asia);
(2)   MT is being used more widely than ever before;
(3)   more free and open source tools are available to MT developers;
(4)   large-scale MT evaluation competitions are attracting more and more systems, for an ever widening array of language pairs.

There exists, therefore, a real opportunity for our community to drive forward MT research and development to demonstrate clearly that good quality output can be achieved, which is useful to a wide array of potential users, both in industry and in the wider public.

Failure to do so may result in a return to the post-ALPAC report[34] (Pierce et al., 1966) state of affairs where funding is cut – especially given the current economic environment – in favor of more fundamental requirements. Despite the wide variety of tools and techniques featured in this chapter, it remains the case that most MT research and development today is rather monolithic in the approaches taken, largely due to the availability of tools for PB-SMT. When it comes to purchasing MT systems, customers do not know what to buy. While MT evaluation metrics such as BLEU are well understood by the research community, they do not provide any insight to potential users as to the effectiveness of such solutions, and bear little relation to the translation memory notion of 'fuzzy match score' widely used in industry. When BLEU appeared in 2002, it was clear that it was more than capable of informing developers whether their systems had improved incrementally. Now, however, research systems have overtaken the ability of the available MT evaluation metrics to discern the quality of the output translations. Accordingly, better MT evaluation metrics are needed, not just for MT developers, but also for potential users of our systems.

As well as improvements in MT evaluation, it is widely agreed that more linguistic knowledge can indeed play a role in improving today's statistical systems, in all phases of the process. Syntax *is* of use in PB-SMT in the source, translation, and target phases, as has been acknowledged for some time in RBMT and EBMT. Furthermore, it is recognized in the tree-to-string and string-to-tree models that having structure on one side helps, and in the near future we can expect to see large-scale, robust systems with trees on both sides.

While there has clearly been a movement away from RBMT to statistical methods, now the pendulum is swinging back (slowly) in the opposite direction. We predict that, just like in the old rule-based times, the community will move further up the 'Vauquois Pyramid' (Vauquois 1968) and avail itself of more diverse sources of linguistic information; while syntax is useful, a new ceiling will be approached where further improvements will only be brought about by the use of *semantic* knowledge. As a nal remark, note that this is not at all contrary to the original IBM models (Brown et al., 1993), a fact that most of the MT community seems to have overlooked, if not forgotten entirely.

7 Further Reading

For *sentential alignment* (cf. Section 2.1.1), consult Brown et al. (1991); Gale and Church (1993) for length-based algorithms (words and characters, respectively) and Kay and Röscheisen (1993) for a dictionary-based solution using 'anchors.'

The primary sources on *word alignment* (cf. Section 2.1.3) are Brown et al. (1993) and Och (2003). For improvements to IBM model 1, consult Moore (2004), and Toutanova et al. (2002); Lopez and Resnik (2005); Liang et al. (2006b) for extensions to the rst-order HMM models. Other approaches include inversion transduction grammar (Wu 1997), which performs synchronous parsing on bilingual sentence pairs to establish translational correspondences, and the tree-to-string alignment model of Yamada and Knight (2001), which aligns a source tree to a target string. For an approach which bootstraps word alignments via optimizing word segmentations, consult Ma et al. (2007b). With respect to investigations into the effect of balancing precision and recall on MT performance, Mariño et al. (2006) observed that an alignment with higher recall improved the performance of an *n*-gram-based SMT system, while Ayan and Dorr (2006) observed that higher precision alignments are more useful in phrase-based SMT systems, although this nding is not con rmed by Fraser and Marcu (2007b).

Regarding other methods of *phrase extraction* (cf. Section 2.1.4), Marcu and Wong (2002) describe a joint phrase model by which phrase pairs are estimated directly from the parallel corpus using the expectation-maximization (EM) algorithm (Dempster et al., 1977). Other proposed methods can be found in Tillmann and Xia (2003), Ortiz-Martínez et al. (2005), and Zhang and Vogel (2005), amongst others.

As for *reordering* (cf. Section 2.2), the method of Galley and Manning (2008) differs from those of Tillmann (2004) and Koehn et al. (2007) by estimating sequences of orientations directly from data, and by dynamically updating the segmentation of the source and target sentences with hierarchical phrases.

With respect to *language modeling* (cf. Section 2.2.1), the main sources are Jelinek (1977) and Kneser and Ney (1995), with more details to be found in Chen and Goodman (1998), especially for 'modi ed' Kneser–Ney smoothing, and Kim et al. (2001), on lowering the perplexity of the structured language model of Chelba and Jelinek (2000).

As far as *minimum error rate training* (MERT) is concerned (cf. Section 2.3.1), two novel papers which will bene t the reader are those of Moore and Quirk (2008), where trade-offs in terms of decoding and MERT time are considered, and Chiang et al. (2008), where alternative models are given in which a much larger number of features can be integrated.

For *decoding* (cf. Section 2.4), the reader is directed towards the primary sources, namely Koehn (2004) and Koehn et al. (2007).

With respect to *re-ranking* (cf. Section 2.6), useful sources include Och et al. (2004), Shen and Joshi (2005) (who use the best subset of features tested by Och et al. (2004)), and Yamada and Muslea (2006), who train their re-ranker on the whole training corpus, as opposed to just re-ranking on the test set.

If interested in *MT evaluation* (cf. Section 2.5), consult the primary sources given in Section 2.5. A nice recent paper which we recommend is that of Hwa and Albrecht (2008).

For two quite different overview papers on *statistical MT* (SMT), we recommend Way (2009a) for a critique of the paradigm, and Hearne and Way (2009), which explains *phrase-based SMT* (PB-SMT) for the non-expert.

The primary sources on *hierarchical phrase-based models* (cf. Section 3.1) are Chiang (2005; 2007). Huang and Chiang (2005) provides a valuable explanation of *cube pruning* (cf. Section 3.1.3).

For good summaries of *example-based MT* (EBMT) (cf. Section 3.3), we encourage the reader to consult Somers (1999; 2003b) and Way (2009b). The monograph by Carl and Way (2003) provides a representative sample of the myriad array of techniques used in EBMT.

Some examples of current research in *rule-based MT* (RBMT) (cf. Section 3.4) include Probst et al. (2002) and Lavie et al. (2004) on knowledge elicitation for under-resourced languages. Font-Llitjós et al. (2007) address the issue of rule re nement, while Zhu and Wang (2005) investigate the relationship between the number of rules and the performance of RBMT systems. Menezes and Richardson (2003); Caseli et al. (2006); Sánchez-Martínez and Forcada (2007) all focus on automatically obtaining some of the resources required for RBMT.

Good papers on *hybrid models* (cf. Section 3.5) include those of Tidhar and Küssner (2000); Callison-Burch and Flournoy (2001); Akiba et al. (2002). For a novel view on hybridity in MT, we encourage the reader to consult Wu (2005), where a 3-D space of hybrid models of translation is presented. Systems are categorized according to the extent to which they may be described as statistical vs. logical, example-based vs. schema-based, and compositional vs. lexical. Another novel paper is that of Simard et al. (2007), who present a combination of MT systems based on a post-editing strategy, in which the PB-SMT system Portage corrects the output of the Systran RBMT system.

Two good papers on *translation memory* (cf. Section 4.2) are those of Planas and Furuse (2003) and Garcia (2007), while the papers of Vogel and Ney (2000) and Marcu (2001) demonstrate how translation memories can be automatically extracted. Carl and Hansen (1999) show how translation memories can be integrated with EBMT. A nice recent paper that shows how PB-SMT can upgrade translation memory *fuzzy matches* to classes that require less post-editing is that of Biçici and Dymetman (2008).

A recent paper on *spoken language translation* (cf. Section 4.3) emanating from the TC-STAR project is that of Fügen et al. (2007). One notable nding in TC-STAR was that today's leading PB-SMT systems are robust in the face of errors coming from the automatic speech recognition phase.

As regards our own work described in Section 5, the primary sources listed will provide the reader with further information on any of the topics of interest.

ACKNOWLEDGMENT

Thanks to Jinhua Du, Hany Hassan, Patrik Lambert, Yanjun Ma, Sara Morrissey, Sudip Naskar, Sylwia Ozdowska, John Tinsley, and Ventsislav Zhechev, for their considerable help in putting this chapter together. Special thanks are due to Mikel Forcada and Felipe Sánchez-Martínez for helping with the section on RBMT. The work described in this chapter is partially funded by a number of Science Foundation Ireland (http://www.s .ie) awards, namely: Principal Investigator Award 05/IN/1732, Basic Research Award 05/RF/CMS064, and CSET Award 07/CE/I1142.

NOTES

1 Note, however, that Lopez (2008b) describes an SMT system which uses pattern matching to avoid the problem of computing infeasibly large statistical models. His approach directly accesses the training corpus at run-time, but his model is by any measure an EBMT system, despite the steps taken to avoid the term.
2 www.isi.edu/natural-language/download/hansard/index.html
3 www.ldc.upenn.edu/
4 www.elda.org/
5 National Institute of Standards and Technology: www.nist.gov/speech/tests/mt/
6 International Workshop on Spoken Language Translation. For the 2008 edition see http://mastarpj.nict.go.jp/IWSLT2008/
7 www.euromatrix.net/
8 Workshop on Statistical Machine Translation. For the 2009 edition see www.statmt.org/ wmt09/
9 www.iccs.inf.ed.ac.uk/~pkoehn/publications/europarl/
10 http://langtech.jrc.it/JRC-Acquis.html
11 http://iwslt07.itc.it/

12   www.cse.unt.edu/~rada/wpt05/

13   www.cse.unt.edu/~rada/wpt/

14   Newcomers to the eld may be somewhat confused at differences between the notation used in this chapter and some of the primary sources noted here and in Section 7. It is much more common to use f_1^J (to be read as 'foreign') to indicate the source sentence, and e_1^J ('English') to represent the target sentence, At rst sight, the use of such terms might be upsetting for non-English speakers, and betray to an extent the Anglocentric nature of our eld, given that most translation in MT *is* into English. Instead, it might be more fruitful perhaps to think of them as simple mnemonics for the terms in the various equations used to describe (especially) statistical MT systems; cf. (1) and (3) below. In any case, here and in the rest of this chapter, we will stick to the less widely used (yet less emotive) terms *s* and *t* to indicate source and target respectively.

15   www.fjoch.com/GIZA++.html

16   http://mi.eng.cam.ac.uk/~wjb31/distrib/mttkv1/

17   The 'ease' or 'dif culty' associated with translating certain parts of a sentence is usually expressed in terms of weighted log-probabilities which take into account (at least) language model, translation model, and reordering costs. As you might expect, common words are 'easier' to translate in this model than less frequent words, despite these being among the 'hardest' words to get right for humans.

18   Originally known as 'syntax-directed transduction grammars' (Lewis & Stearns 1968) or 'syntax-directed translation schemata (Aho & Ullman 1969), 'inversion transduction grammars' (Wu 1997) are a special case of synchronous CFGs, while a more recent terminological introduction is '2-multitext grammars' (Melamed 2003).

19   Although it is not described until Section 4.2, a quick comparison between EBMT and translation memory is apposite here. Although the latter is a translation tool as opposed to an MT system per se, the initial *matching* process is extremely similar in nature in both approaches. Where the examples in the EBMT system consist of (unannotated) text pairs, the matching process is identical. In translation memory systems such as *Trados* (www.trados.com), 'fuzzy' (i.e., non-exact) matches have an associated measure of similarity which can be put to good use by the translator in honing the search for higher precision (imposing a high threshold of fuzziness) or recall (lowering the threshold). Note that the second and third EBMT phases do not form part of any translation memory system; rather, the end user (usually a quali ed translator) selects the appropriate parts of each fuzzy match for manual combination into the appropriate target-language sentence.

20   This can be easily demonstrated by trying some simple examples through Google Translate. For instance, the December 4, 2008 Spanish-to-English version gave the translation of the sentence *Me los regaló tu hermanastro* (lit. 'To-me them gave-as-a-present your half-brother,' i.e., 'Your half-brother gave them to me as a present') as *I gave you the half-brother*, while *Me los regaló tu madre* is translated as *Your mother gave me*, and *Me los regaló tu hermano* is translated as *I am your brother the gift*; note that the three Spanish sentences only differ with respect to the noun acting as subject (*hermanastro, madre, hermano*).

21   http://logos-os.dfki.de/

22   www.apertium.org

23   www.translendium.com

24   www.reverso.net

25   www.systran.co.uk

26 http://translate.google.com
27 http://babel sh.yahoo.com
28 www.windowslivetranslator.com
29 www.voxtec.com/phraselator
30 www.nclt.dcu.ie/mt/
31 Consult Zhechev and Way (2008) for how our subtree aligner can be used to auto-matically generate parallel treebanks, for any language for which constituency- or dependency-based parsers exist.
32 www.nist.gov/speech/tests/mt/
33 www.cngl.ie. The CNGL is a large ve-year project funded by the Irish Government involving four academic and nine industrial partners.
34 www.nap.edu/books/ARC000005/html

20 Natural Language Generation

EHUD REITER

Natural language generation (NLG) systems generate texts in English and other human languages. Although they are based on many of the same linguistic and algorithmic insights that underlie other kinds of natural language processing systems, they are not simply natural language understanding systems run 'in reverse.'

In this chapter, I will brie y review NLG. In Sections 1–4, I summarize the basic concepts of NLG, and try to highlight issues which are important to building NLG systems and also potentially interesting to linguists and psycholinguists. Then, in Section 5, I discuss some contemporary research in NLG, in areas which are of personal interest to me and which I believe should be of interest to other researchers in the language community. The research topics discussed are by no means exhaustive – they are just a sample of what the NLG research community is working on. I conclude (Section 6) with a brief summary of resources (software, corpora, information) for researchers who wish to work in NLG.

1 High-Level Perspective: Making Choices about Language

From a high-level perspective, perhaps the biggest difference between NLG and other types of NLP is the central role of choice making. NLG systems have to make numerous choices about their output texts, ranging from high-level choices about appropriate content to low-level choices about the use of pronouns. Although choice making of course also occurs in other NLP tasks (for example machine translation systems have to decide which target-language word to use when translating a source-language word), choice making is arguably more central to NLG than to most other areas of NLP.

Sometimes NLG choices can be made on the basis of linguistic correctness, as in the following example of a pronominalization choice:

The Handbook of Computational Linguistics and Natural Language Processing, First Edition.
Edited by Alexander Clark, Chris Fox and Shalom Lappin.
© 2013 Blackwell Publishing Ltd except for editorial material and organization
© 2013 Alexander Clark, Chris Fox, and Shalom Lappin. Published 2013 by Blackwell Publishing Ltd.

(1)   a)   * *'Mary read about Mary.'*
      b)   *'Mary read about herself.'*

In this case the NLG system can use binding theory (Büring 2005) to determine that a re exive pronoun must be used in this context, and hence decide to generate (1b).

However, in other cases, such as the example below, both choices lead to linguistically correct texts:

(2)   a)   *'I bought an apple. I ate it.'*
      b)   *'I bought an apple. I ate the apple.'*

Since both choices lead to valid texts, the NLG system must decide between them using other criteria. Often such decisions are made based on readability factors, which in turn are based on psycholinguistic models of language comprehension; in the above example such models might suggest that (2a) will be read faster, and hence should be generated. Decisions may also be in uenced by genre constraints; for example, pronoun usage may be discouraged in safety-critical texts such as operation manuals for nuclear power plants, so in such genres (2b) should be generated. Genre models are typically based on corpus analysis or explicit genre writing guides. In some cases decisions are also in uenced by the linguistic abilities and preferences of the reader of the text; for example an NLG system may choose (2b) if its reader is not uent in English.

NLG is thus largely the study of choice making, including analyses of individual choices; architectures and systems that can be used to make sets of choices; and methodologies for creating and evaluating new choice making rules and systems. Analyses of individual choices are often based on linguistic and/or psycholinguistic research; analyses of choice making architectures and systems often build on arti cial intelligence techniques; and methodologies for creating and evaluating rules draw on both AI and (psycho)linguistics.

2   Two NLG Systems: SumTime and SkillSum

In order to illustrate choice making and other aspects of NLG, it is useful to examine some real NLG systems. In this section we look at SumTime, which generates weather forecasts, and SkillSum, which generates feedback reports on educational assessments.

2.1   *SumTime: Weather Forecasts*

One popular application of NLG is generating textual weather forecasts from numerical weather prediction data. NLG systems such as FOG (Goldberg et al., 1994), MultiMeteo (Coch 1998), SumTime (Reiter et al., 2005), and RoadSafe (Turner et al., 2008) take as their input a large set of numbers which predict temperature, precipitation, wind speed, and so forth at various points and times.

Table 20.1 Numerical wind forecast for September 19, 2000

Time	Wind Dir.	Wind Speed
06:00	SE	11
09:00	SSE	13
12:00	SSE	14
15:00	SSE	15
18:00	SE	18
21:00	SE	23
00:00	SE	28

Corpus (human) text:
SSE 10–15 INCREASING 15–20 BY EVENING AND 25–30 LATER.

SumTime text:
SE 9–14 veering SSE 13–18 by mid-afternoon, then increasing SE 26–31 by midnight.

Figure 20.1 Human and corpus wind descriptions for September 19, 2000.

These numbers are produced by a supercomputer running a numerical weather simulation, and modi ed by human forecasters based on their knowledge of local meteorological conditions. From this input data, the systems produce weather forecast texts (sometimes in multiple languages) which are sent to forecast users (usually after being checked and post-edited by the human forecasters) (Sripada et al., 2004). Table 20.1 shows a simple extract from one of SumTime's data sets, showing 24 hours of predicted wind speed and direction for an offshore oil rig in the North Sea. Figure 20.1 shows the text produced by SumTime from this data, and also the corpus text for this data (that is, a text written by a human forecaster, which was actually sent to users on the oil rig).

In order to generate the output text shown in Figure 20.1 from the input data shown in Table 20.1, SumTime needs to make many kinds of choices.

- **Choices about document content and structure**: SumTime must decide what information to communicate in the text, and also how the document is structured around this information. This is called *document planning*. In this example, SumTime has decided to communicate information about the wind at the beginning and end of the period, and also at one point in the middle, 15:00 ('*by mid-afternoon*'). The human forecaster has similarly chosen to describe the wind at the beginning and end, and at one intermediate point but has chosen a different intermediate point – 18:00 instead of 15:00.

One of these sentences has a word which is wrong.
Click on it.

- He was walking to the canteen when he slipped on a wet oor.
- I was walking to the canteen when I slipped on a wet oor.
- They was walking to the canteen when they slipped on a wet oor.

Figure 20.2   An example literacy screener question (SkillSum input).

Thank you for doing this.
You got 19 questions right. <u>Click here for more information.</u>
Your skills seem to be OK for your Health and Social Care course.
You got all except 3 of the reading questions right. But you made 5
    mistakes on the questions about writing.
Perhaps you would like to take a course to help you with your English.
A course might help you to practise your reading skills, because you
    said you do not read much.
<u>Click here for Key Skills at XXX College.</u>

Figure 20.3   Example text produced by SkillSum.

- **Choices about linguistic structures**: SumTime must decide which linguistic structures (words, syntax, sentences) should be used to communicate the desired information. This is called *microplanning*. An example of word choice is communicating the time 00:00; in the above example the human forecaster has referred to this time using the phrase *'later,'* while SumTime has used the phrase *'by midnight.'*
- **Choices about word order and forms**: SumTime must decide which forms of words to use, and which order words will appear in, based on the above decisions. This is called *realization*. An example of word-form choice is that both the human forecaster and SumTime use the present participle (*'+ing'*) form of verbs; this is based on the genre conventions of this type of weather forecast.

2.2   *Example NLG system: SkillSum*

SumTime generates short summaries of numerical data for specialist users (workers in the offshore oil industry). Our second example system, SkillSum (Williams & Reiter 2008), generates summaries of performance on an educational assessment (of basic numeracy and literacy skills). Its users are students at further education (community) colleges who are enrolled in a course which requires certain levels of basic skills. The input to SkillSum is some background information about the user, plus his or her responses to a set of multiple-choice questions which test basic literacy or numeracy; an example is shown in Figure 20.2. The output of SkillSum is a short text summarizing the user's performance on the test; an example is shown in Figure 20.3.

Although SkillSum's input data and output text are very different from
SumTime's, it must make the same kind of choices. SkillSum's document planner
must decide what information to give; for example, how much detail to go into
about the user's mistakes. SkillSum's microplanner must decide how to linguistically express this information; for example, whether to say *'You got 19 questions
right'* or *'You got 19 questions correct.'* SkillSum's realizer must make low-level
word-form and ordering choices, such as using *'questions'* instead of *'question'* in
the above sentence.

2.3   *Other NLG applications*

Many other applications of NLG have been explored, including:

- Summarizing other kinds of data, including medical data (Portet et al., 2007),
  engineering data (Yu et al., 2007), nancial data (Kukich 1983), and sports data
  (Robin & McKeown 1996). The input to these systems, like SumTime, is usually
  a combination of numeric data and event records (Reiter 2007).
- Generating initial drafts of documents, such as instruction manuals (Paris et al.,
  1995), legal documents (Sheremetyeva et al., 1996), clinical documents (Hüske-
  Kraus 2003), and business letters (Coch 1996). The input to these systems is
  usually a knowledge base which describes the content of the document; sometimes the NLG system is integrated with the knowledge-base authoring tool
  (Power et al., 1998).
- Generating explanations of reasoning in AI systems, including expert systems
  (Lacave & Diez 2004), Bayesian reasoners (Lacave & Diez 2002), and theorem
  provers (Fiedler 2005). The input to these systems is usually a trace of the
  reasoning used by the AI reasoning system.
- Generating texts that are intended to persuade or motivate users (Reiter et al.,
  2003a), make users less anxious (Cawsey et al., 2000), or entertain users
  (Binstead & Ritchie 1997). The input to these systems is quite varied, but
  usually includes a user model of the reader.
- Supporting users with disabilities; for example letting blind users examine
  graphs (Ferres et al., 2006), and helping non-speaking users create stories about
  what they have done (Reiter et al., 2009).

Despite these efforts, NLG has not been widely used in real-world applications.
A number of NLG systems have been used in a limited way; for example Sum-
Time was used for a few years by the Aberdeen of ce of a weather forecasting
company to generate draft forecasts which human forecasters post-edited (Sripada
et al., 2004), and indeed an evaluation showed that forecast users preferred some
of SumTime's (unedited) forecasts to forecasts written by human meteorologists
(Reiter et al., 2005). However, to the best of my knowledge, no NLG system has
entered long-term widespread use, in the sense of being used by many organizations for many years. In this regard NLG has been less successful than other areas
of NLP such as speech recognition, dialogue systems, machine translation, and

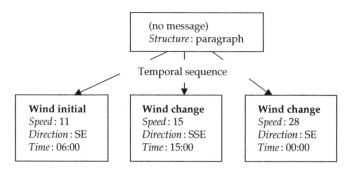

Figure 20.4 Example SumTime document plan.

grammar checking; and also less successful than simple text-generation systems based on ll-in-the-blank templates or mail-merge. My personal belief is that one of the keys to making NLG technology more practically useful on real applications is a better understanding of the research issues which I discuss at the end of this chapter; for example SumTime would probably have been used much more if it had been embedded into an interactive multi-modal meteorological information system (Section 5.3).

3   NLG Choices and Tasks

NLG is often divided into the three stages of document planning, microplanning, and realization. In this section we discuss each of these stages, and brie y summarize the types of choices each stage must make. For more information about the stages, including algorithms and representations, see Reiter and Dale (2000).

3.1   *Document planner*

The document planner decides what information to communicate in the text (*content determination*), and how this information should be organized (*document structuring*).

From a software perspective, the input to the document planner is the input to the entire NLG system; for example numerical weather prediction data in SumTime, and responses to the test questions in SkillSum. The output of the document planner is typically a tree of *messages*. Messages are chunks of information (extracted from the input data), which can be linguistically expressed as a clause or phrase; they are sometimes represented as instances in an AI knowledge-base system such as Protégé.[1] The edges of the tree are often used to represent rhetorical relations between messages. Nodes of the tree can also be annotated to represent document structures (Power et al., 2003) such as paragraphs.

An example of a simple SumTime document plan is shown in Figure 20.4; this is for the SumTime text shown in Figure 20.1. The tree consists of a root node which does not contain a message, but does establish that this text is a 'paragraph' document structure. This node has three children, which are in a temporal sequence relation. Each child communicates a single message about the wind. The rst child is a **wind initial** message, which communicates the initial state of the wind; the remaining children are **wind change** messages, which communicate a change in the wind. Each of these messages has the parameters *speed*, *direction*, and *time*. Although SumTime does not use Protégé, these messages could easily be represented in a Protégé ontology (and we would use this representation if we were reimplementing SumTime today).

As this example suggests, the heart of document planning in SumTime is selecting a small number of wind changes to mention, from the input data (Table 20.1). In this case SumTime has chosen to mention the wind changes at 15:00 and 00:00, it assumes the user can interpolate between these points if necessary. This process is guided by a limit to interpolation error, which is based on expert advice from meteorologists as to how much interpolation error is acceptable to end users, considering the tasks that they typically perform using the weather forecasts. Document structure is very simple in SumTime: the messages are always linked by a temporal sequence relation as in the example of Figure 20.4.

As can be seen in this example, document planning typically involves reasoning about the data and how it will be used. Explicit linguistic reasoning may play a role in deciding on document structure (how messages are organized into a tree), but often has a fairly minor role in deciding on document content (which messages are in the tree).

The reasoning performed by document planning can be more complex than SumTime's use of maximum allowable interpolation error. For example, the STOP system (Reiter et al., 2003a), which generated smoking-cessation letters based on the responses to a smoking questionnaire, largely based its document planning on a psychological model of what information should be given to smokers, based on their attitudes towards and beliefs about smoking cessation (Prochaska & diClemente 1992).

Unfortunately, it is dif cult to generalize about document planning; for example, the algorithms used by SumTime to decide what information is most appropriate for a weather forecast reader on an offshore oil rig are completely different from the algorithms used by STOP to decide what smoking-cessation information would be most effective for a particular user. In very general terms, the goal of document planning is to identify the information that is useful to the user, and structure it into a coherent document, and it has proven dif cult to create a general model of how this should be done.

In the early 1990s Hovy (1993) and other researchers tried to formalize document planning as an AI planning problem based on formal models of rhetorical relations, such as rhetorical structure theory (RST) (Mann & Thompson 1988). However, this approach did not work well in practice. One major problem was that RST-like models of the semantics of relations are too vague to be used in document planners, and also (because they attempt to be general) do not capture important genre-speci c aspects of document structure. For example, weather forecasts for offshore oil rigs describe each aspect of the weather (wind, temperature, precipitation, etc.) separately, and describe events about the same aspect (e.g., wind) in strict temporal order. This structure cannot be derived from theories of optimal rhetorical presentation; it is a convention which has arisen in this genre and (for better or for worse) must be adhered to.

An alternative approach to document planning is to try to imitate what human writers do, without explicitly modeling or reasoning about what content would be best for the user. This is typically done by analyzing corpora of human-authored texts and/or explicitly conducting knowledge acquisition sessions with human writers (Reiter et al., 2003b); this approach was used in developing the Skill-Sum document planner (Williams & Reiter 2005), for example. Recently there has been interest in trying to automate this process using machine learning techniques (Barzilay & Lapata 2005a).

Perhaps the biggest problem with this approach is data sparsity and incompleteness. This kind of analysis usually requires a data-text corpus, which contains the input data (e.g., the data shown in Table 20.1) as well as the human-written texts (e.g., the texts shown in Figure 20.1). Unfortunately, most existing data-text corpora are either too small to provide good coverage of the different cases, and/or do not include all of the data used by the human writers. For example, the SkillSum corpus contained just 16 texts, and Barzilay and Lapata only had corresponding input data for one third of the sentences in their corpus.

Because of these problems, document planners cannot (at the time of writing) be based purely on corpus analysis. Human developers must extrapolate rules to cover gaps in the corpus, based on their domain knowledge and feedback from domain experts and pilot experiments (Williams & Reiter 2005). There is undoubtedly considerable scope for improving the process of creating document planners in this fashion, by improving corpus-analysis and gap- lling methodologies.

3.2 *Microplanning*

The microplanner decides how information is linguistically expressed in the generated text. This process requires many choices to be made, including the following:

- **lexical choice**: choosing which content words should be used to express domain concepts and data;
- **reference**: choosing referring expressions to identify domain entities;
- **syntactic choice**: choosing syntactic structures in generated sentences;
- **aggregation**: choosing how many messages should be expressed in each sentence.

The input to the microplanner is the document plan, which is created by the document planner. The output of the microplanner is a *text specification*; essentially this is a tree whose internal nodes specify document structure (for example, paragraphs), and whose leaf nodes specify deep syntactic structures of sentences.

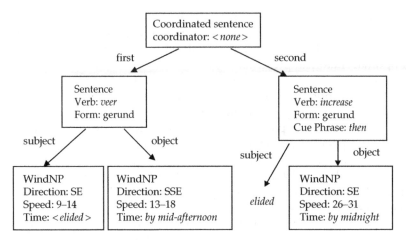

Figure 20.5   Example SumTime deep syntactic structure.

The latter specify content words, coreference, syntactic relationships, and sentence boundaries. The exact form of the deep syntactic structure varies considerably depending on the system's realizer and the grammatical theory (if any) that the realizer is based on.

An example of a deep syntactic structure is shown in Figure 20.5; this is for the document plan shown in Figure 20.4. We do not show the text speci cation for this example, it would simply contain a root node indicating document structure (very similar to the root node of the document plan shown in Figure 20.4), and a leaf node containing the abstract syntactic structure shown in Figure 20.5.

The deep syntactic structure shown in Figure 20.5 is based on intuitive ideas such as subject and noun phrase, but is customized for the speci c genre used in weather forecasts. Thus for example the SumTime realizer accepts a 'syntactic' structure called WindNP which communicates wind speed, direction, and time; this seemed more sensible than trying to force the realizer to use standard noun phrase structures which do not really t the sublanguage (genre) used in weather forecasts.

In any case, Figure 20.5 illustrates many of the choices that the SumTime microplanner must make. An example of lexical choice is choosing the verb *'veer'* to communicate the change between the wind at 06:00 and the wind at 15:00; this involves deciding which aspect of the change to focus on (in this case the focus is on the change in wind direction), and then choosing the verb based on what occurred in this aspect (in this case *'veer'* as the wind direction changed clockwise). Other lexical choice examples include choosing *'by mid-afternoon'* to communicate the time 15:00, and *'13–18'* to communicate the speed 15. The latter choice could be regarded as a content (document planner) choice instead of a lexical (microplanner) choice, the distinction between the two is not always clear cut.

No referring decisions are needed to generate SumTime texts, including the one shown in Figure 20.5. An example of a referential choice in the SkillSum text shown in Figure 20.3 is *'your Health and Social Care course.'* Other potential ways of referring to this entity include *'your course'* and *'your Health and Social Care course at Aberdeen College'*; the referential choice is choosing which of these referring expressions to use in the generated text.

An example of a syntactic choice in the Figure 20.5 SumTime text is using the gerund form of the verbs (for example, *'veering'* instead of *'veers'*). Another example is the decision to elide (omit) the time phrase from the first WindNP.

An example of an aggregation choice is the decision to express the content in a single sentence. An alternative would have been to use two sentences, for example *'SE 9–14 veering SSE 13–18 by mid-afternoon. Increasing SE 26–31 by midnight.'*

Microplanning choices in SumTime, as in many NLG systems, are made with different levels of sophistication. Some choices are forced by the sublanguage (Grishman & Kittredge 1986); for example SumTime always uses the gerund forms of verbs in wind descriptions, because this is how such texts are conventionally written. Some choices require little computation but are based on substantial linguistic analyses and/or psycholinguistic data. For example lexical choice in SumTime is done using fixed concept-to-word mappings (a trivial computational mechanism), but these mappings are based on an extensive linguistic analysis of word usage in corpus texts and also feedback from users about their word choice preferences. And some choices require non-trivial algorithms (whose design is informed by (psycho)linguistic data); this is the case for aggregation and ellipsis decisions in SumTime.

Perhaps the best studied microplanning choices are referential ones; see Reiter and Dale (2000) for more details on these and other microplanning decisions. In particular a considerable amount of work has been done on the generation of definite noun phrases to identify visible or otherwise salient physical objects (such as *'the red book'*); indeed there has even been a shared task evaluation in this area (Belz & Gatt 2007).

One interesting observation from the work on reference, which has since been observed in other areas of NLG, is that the language produced by human speakers and writers is not necessarily ideal for human listeners and readers (Oberlander 1998). This means that algorithms that generate high-quality referring expressions cannot just be based on corpus analysis and other studies of human language production – they must also be based on studies (often psycholinguistic ones) of human language comprehension.

This raises the more general question of what the goals of microplanning choices are. Is the goal to produce texts that are similar to those produced by human writers (under what metric?); texts that are appropriate for human readers (under what criteria?); or texts that satisfy some other criteria (for example, minimizing legal liability)? Of course, such questions could be asked about all aspects of NLG, but they seem especially prominent in microplanning.

Lexical choice (choosing content words which communicate the information in messages) is extremely important for producing high-quality texts, but is less well understood than referential choices. In principle, it would be nice to base lexical choice algorithms on linguistic theories of lexical semantics (Cruse 1986), but in fact such theories have not proven very useful in NLG. This is because they focus on the relationship between semantic primitives (usually in rst-order logic) and words, but very few NLG systems have semantic primitives as their input. The NLG community needs a better understanding of how to map the input data that NLG systems actually get (sensor readings, databases, etc.) on to words (Roy & Reiter 2005), and how this mapping is affected by contextual factors. Such contextual factors include alignment (Brennan & Clark 1996) and other dialogue issues, individual differences between readers' language (idiolect) (Reiter & Sripada 2002), and the desirability or otherwise of varying word choice. These issues are further discussed in Section 5.2. In some cases we also need to consider affective issues (Section 5.4) such as the emotional impact on users of particular word choices; for example, SkillSum needs to use words which not only are understandable and convey the correct meaning, but also are not perceived by the reader as patronizing or disheartening.

A similar situation applies to aggregation choices, that is deciding when and how to combine multiple messages into one sentence. Again aggregation is very important for achieving high-quality texts, but it is not well understood. While many papers have been published on aggregation, there is still considerable uncertainty about when and how to aggregate messages in speci c contexts. This is partially because the amount and type of aggregation performed is very dependent on the domain and genre. There are also major differences in the amount of aggregation preferred by different readers, and in the aggregation choices made by different writers.

The nal microplanning task we discuss here is high-level syntactic choices, such as whether a sentence should be active or passive, and which tense should be used. In principle many such choices could be based on linguistic theories. For example, centering theory could be used to guide information structure choices such as passivization, and a Reichenbach model could be used to make choices about tenses. In practice such theories often need considerable further elaboration before they are precise enough to be useful in NLG systems (Poesio et al., 2004).

In summary, microplanning requires an NLG system to make decisions about the best way to linguistically express information. With the partial exception of referring expressions, there is little in the way of general theories for guiding NLG microplanners today, instead systems tend to rely on empirical analysis of how language is used in a particular domain and genre. If linguists can help develop a better theoretical underpinning for microplanning tasks, this would be very helpful to the NLG community.

3.3   Realization

The realizer generates an actual text (surface form), based on the information selected by the document planning module and the linguistic choices made by the microplanner. For example, the SumTime realizer generates the text shown in Figure 20.1 from a syntactic structure such as the one shown in Figure 20.5.

Realization is perhaps the best understood aspect of NLG, and indeed many software packages have been developed to carry out this task (which is not true of document planning or microplanning). Most of these packages combine an engine based on a particular grammatical formalism, and one or more grammars based on this engine. These systems include KPML, which is based on systemic functional grammar (Bateman 1997); FUF/SURGE, which is based on functional uni cation grammar (Elhadad & Robin 1997); RealPro, which is based on meaning-text theory (Lavoie & Rambow 1997); and OpenCCG, which is based on categorial grammar (White et al., 2007). There are also some atheoretical packages which provide less linguistic functionality but allow linguistic constructs to be integrated with templates, such as TG2 (Busemann & Horacek 1998) and Simplenlg (Reiter 2007); van Deemter et al. (2005) discuss in general terms how templates of different levels of sophistication can be used by an NLG system. Morphological generators have also been created, such as Morphg (Minnen et al., 2001).

Some realizers support *overgeneration and selection*. In this mode, the realizer generates several possible surface forms, and uses a separate mechanism to select one of these. The most common selection mechanism is *n*-gram language models which are derived from corpora (these are described in Chapter 3, STATISTICAL LANGUAGE MODELING). OpenCCG, for example, supports this architecture. In principle, an overgenerate-and-select architecture should allow the grammar writing task to be simpli ed, because subtle constraints such as adjective ordering can be implicit in the language model – they do not need to be explicitly programmed. Also this architecture should make it easier to adapt systems to different genres, because genre linguistic preferences can be implicit in the language model, and do not need to be explicitly coded.

On the other hand, from a practical engineering perspective, it is not clear how to perform testing, quality assurance, and maintenance on systems which are based on language models which are automatically built from corpus texts. For example, if we look at adjective ordering, explicitly encoding adjective ordering rules is a lot of work, but once this is done the rules can be tested and checked, and also modi ed if users want a different ordering. Implicitly deriving adjective ordering rules from a language model is much less work, but it is harder to test such systems to ensure that they do not produce inappropriate texts in some cases, and more dif cult to modify such systems if users request a different ordering.

One pragmatic solution to this problem, which in fact is supported by systems such as OpenCCG, is to combine a symbolic grammar which handles important linguistic decisions which must be correct and which users may wish changed, with a language model which takes care of less important decisions. If it subsequently turns out that a decision made by the language model is more important than initially expected and/or is the subject of user change requests, the symbolic grammar can be expanded to incorporate this decision.

As can be seen from the above discussion, the state of the art in realization is suf ciently advanced (compared to other aspects of NLG) that we can seriously consider software engineering issues such as quality assurance, maintenance, ease of software integration, and documentation quality. Indeed these factors often play a larger role than theoretical factors (such as underlying linguistic theories) when system builders are deciding which realizer to use in their software.

3.4   Other comments

As many people have pointed out (for instance, Mellish et al., 2006), the boundaries between the above stages are not precise. For example, in the above architecture I have said that paragraph boundaries are decided upon in document planning, while sentence boundaries are decided upon in microplanning; but one could also argue that these decisions should be made together, not in different modules. Similarly I have said that the microplanner makes linguistic choices and the realizer implements them; but of course the realizer probably needs to make some choices (especially low-level ones) as well. So the above architecture should be thought of as a starting point; real systems could and should modify it to suit their needs.

The above discussion should also make clear that there are considerable differences in how well different NLG tasks are understood. Our understanding of realization is relatively good, and indeed a number of software packages are available for this task. Our understanding of microplanning is patchy: reasonable in some places (for example, generating de nite noun phrases to refer to objects), limited in some places (such as aggregation), and poor in others (such as affective issues in lexical choice). Our understanding of document planning is perhaps weakest of all; current document planners are mostly based on empirical work in a domain with very limited contribution from theoretical models.

4   NLG Evaluation

An important issue in NLG, as in other aspects of NLP, is how to evaluate systems. See Chapter 11, EVALUATION OF NLP SYSTEMS, for a general introduction to the evaluation of natural language processing systems, including terminology, underlying concepts, and common techniques.

In very general terms, one can evaluate how well individual choices are made in NLG; how well NLG modules work; and/or how well complete NLG systems work. Evaluations can also try to determine how effective generated texts are for human readers (reader-based evaluation), or how successfully generated texts match texts produced by human writers (writer-based evaluation). The type of evaluation depends of course on its purpose. For example, if the purpose is to enable a user to decide whether to use an NLG system, then a reader-based system evaluation is most appropriate. On the hand, if the purpose of the evaluation is to test the cognitive plausibility of a model of reference generation, then a writer-based module evaluation would be most appropriate.

Probably the most prominent kinds of evaluation in NLG are reader-based system evaluations, so I will focus on these in the rest of this section. In very general terms, there are three ways of trying to determine how effective an NLG system is at achieving its communicative goal. The most direct approach is an *extrinsic evaluation* which directly measures whether the system achieves its goal. Such evaluations almost always involve human subjects, and generally tend to be relatively expensive and time-consuming. A cheaper alternative is a *non-task-based human evaluation*, where human subjects are asked to read generated texts, and rate, post-edit, or comment on them. A   nal (and more controversial) alternative is a *metric-based corpus evaluation*; this involves using metrics such as BLEU and ROUGE (these are discussed in Chapter 11, EVALUATION OF NLP SYSTEMS) to measure how similar generated texts are to corpus texts (in other words, we perform a writer-based evaluation in the hope that its results are good predictors of reader-based evaluation).

4.1   *Extrinsic evaluations*

The most trusted system evaluations are extrinsic ones that directly measure the system's effectiveness at achieving its communicative goal; this is especially true of evaluations which are intended to convince people outside the NLP community, such as doctors, teachers, and mariners. For example, the STOP system was evaluated in a clinical trial with 2,000 smokers (Reiter et al., 2003a). All of the smokers   lled out our smoking questionnaire. One third of them received STOP letters, one third received a control non-tailored letter, and one third just received a thank you letter. We contacted them six months after the letters had been sent, and found out how many in each group had managed to stop smoking.

SkillSum was also evaluated extrinsically (Williams & Reiter 2008). We recruited 230 people who were about to start a course at a UK further education college, and asked them to complete the SkillSum literacy and numeracy assessment. The students were again divided into three groups of roughly equal size; two of the groups received variants of SkillSum texts, while the third received a control text (essentially the text produced by the existing software). We asked students to judge whether their skills were suf   cient for the course they were signed up for, both before and after they took the assessment and read the texts, and computed how many students in each of the groups increased the accuracy of their self-assessment of their skills.

Both of these evaluations were expensive and time-consuming. The STOP evaluation took 20 months (including planning and data analysis) and cost UK£75,000. The SkillSum evaluation was not separately costed, but required roughly 8 months to carry out (including planning and data analysis) and cost on the order of UK£25,000.

4.2   *Non-task-based human evaluations*

Extrinsic evaluations may be appropriate as   nal evaluations of systems with sizable development budgets and timescales, but they may not be realistic for smaller projects and indeed for pilot studies (intended to detect problems and improve systems) in large projects. In such contexts we need evaluation techniques which are quicker and cheaper.

In NLG, such evaluations are usually done using experiments with human subjects, most commonly asking subjects to rate texts on ordinal scales (often Likert scales) or to compare texts; subjects are also usually asked to comment on problems in texts and how to improve them.

For example, the SumTime system was evaluated (Reiter et al., 2005) by generating three alternative texts from data sources: one produced by SUMTIME, one written by humans (professional meteorologists), and one produced by a modi ed version of SumTime which essentially extracted document plans from the human texts but microplanned and realized these using SumTime. Subjects were shown the texts (without knowing their origin), and asked comprehension questions about the texts; they were also shown different variants of the texts and asked which variant they thought was most accurate, which was easiest to read, and which was overall the best. In another exercise, several systems with SumTime-like functionality were evaluated by having the systems generate alternative forecasts from the same data set, and then asking human subjects to rate the generated texts (Reiter & Belz 2009).

There are a number of other activities we can ask subjects to perform, in addition to rating texts. One is to ask them to edit generated texts and see what changes they make; such an exercise was in fact carried out with SumTime texts (Sripada et al., 2005). Post-editing seems less useful for quantitative comparisons, because there are very large differences in the amount of post-editing which different people perform, and hence a lot of noise in the quantitative data. But it is very useful for qualitative analyses of problems and potential improvements, because the post-edit data tells developers what speci c parts of the texts subjects did not like, and how they thought the texts should be improved.

We can also time subjects and see how long it takes them to read texts; this was done in SkillSum, for example, since one of the goals of the project was to generate texts which low-skilled readers could easily read. Simply asking people to silently read a text and press a button when nished is problematic, because some subjects may read in depth while others just skim. It is better to ask subjects to read a text for a concrete purpose, such as answering comprehension questions; another possibility (for low-skill readers in particular) is to ask subjects to read texts aloud. Experiments of both of these types were done in SkillSum (Williams & Reiter 2008).

Last but not least, we can ask subjects to simply read texts and qualitatively comment on them. This can be useful especially in the initial stages of a project; this probably works best with subjects who are articulate and have some idea of the project's goals.

4.3   *Metric-based corpus evaluations*

As discussed in Chapter 11, EVALUATION OF NLP SYSTEMS, some elds of NLP routinely use automatic metrics such as BLEU and ROUGE to evaluate output texts; these metrics work by comparing the output of the system to human-written reference texts. Such metrics are occasionally used in NLG as well, but in a much more limited way than in machine translation and document summarization. This is largely because of doubts as to how well such metrics correlate with (predict) the results of human evaluations.

Reiter and Belz (2009), who worked in the SumTime domain, empirically evaluated how well BLEU and ROUGE scores correlated with human ratings of weather-forecast texts generated by a number of systems. They found that, while BLEU and ROUGE ratings did not correlate with human evaluations of the content quality of generated texts, some variants of BLEU did correlate with human ratings of the linguistic quality of generated texts, provided that the generated texts were produced by systems built with similar technology (BLEU ratings do not correlate well with human ratings of texts produced by systems built with different technologies; Belz & Kow 2009). They conclude that BLEU could be used, with caution, in formative evaluations, but should not be used in summative evaluations (this terminology is explained in Chapter 11, EVALUATION OF NLP SYSTEMS).

Other studies have been more negative. For example, Gatt et al. (2009) evaluated systems that generated referring expressions using extrinsic task-based measures (whether human subjects were able to successfully identify the reference target, and how long it took subjects to do this); non-task-based human ratings, and several automatic metrics (BLEU, ROUGE, and string edit distance). They found that none of the automatic metrics they looked at had a signi cant correlation with the extrinsic task-performance measures; the human ratings, in contrast, were reasonably well correlated with the results of the extrinsic evaluation.

All of the above studies looked at existing automatic metrics, which were developed for other areas of NLP such as machine translation. Perhaps metrics can be developed speci cally for NLG, which do a better job of evaluating NLG systems; this is one of the research challenges for the NLG community.

5   Some NLG Research Topics

In this section I discuss some (by no means all!) current research themes in NLG.

5.1   *Statistical approaches to NLG*

Statistical corpus-based techniques are very common in other areas of NLP (as is clear from the other chapters in this handbook), and many researchers are investigating how to use such techniques in NLG.

Perhaps the earliest use of statistical corpus-based techniques in NLG was realizers which overgenerated and then used a language model to select between the options (Langkilde & Knight 1998). As mentioned in Section 3.3, this approach is attractive because it reduces the amount of knowledge that must be explicitly encoded in a grammar, although it can raise quality assurance and maintenance concerns.

The overgeneration approach can be used with other selection mechanisms in addition to *n*-gram models. For example, Walker et al. (2007) have created a microplanner based on the overgenerate-and-select approach. The selection is based on ranking rules which are learned from a corpus of example texts which have been ranked by humans. As Walker et al. point out, one advantage of this approach is that it enables the microplanner to adapt to speci c genres and even individual differences, if appropriate training data is available; this is very important since dealing with such differences is one of the main challenges in microplanning.

Another statistical approach to NLG is to build statistical models of speci c choices that NLG systems must make. Rambow and colleagues have written a number of papers about individual choices, including VP ellipsis (Hardt & Rambow 2001) and lexical choice between near-synonyms (Bangalore & Rambow 2000).

Belz has tried to create a statistical model of the entire microplanning and realization process. Her pCRU framework (Belz 2008) models the generation process as a series of context-free rules. Corpus data is used to create a probabilistic model of the likelihood of each of these rules being used. Given an input data set, the pCRU system then repeatedly invokes the most likely rule, until an output data text is produced; the system also has a Viterbi mode which maximizes the likelihood of all decisions needed to generate a text (the Viterbi algorithm is discussed in Chapter 12, SPEECH RECOGNITION).

The above researchers have tried to create statistical models which can be incorporated into current NLG systems; such models need to be reliable and have good coverage in the target domain. Perhaps for this reason, these researchers have tended to focus on either relatively well-understood choices (such as realization) and/or on domains with relatively simple language (such as weather forecasts). Barzilay and Lapata have taken the different approach of trying to build stand-alone statistical models (i.e., models that are not part of an NLG system) of poorly understood choices such as content selection (Barzilay & Lapata 2005a) and aggregation (Barzilay & Lapata 2006), in linguistically complex texts (sports stories in newspapers). It is not clear if Barzilay and Lapata's models are comprehensive and reliable enough to be used in real systems, but they show how statistical techniques might be used to solve some of the hardest problems in NLG.

Relatively little evaluation has been conducted on how well statistical NLG approaches work when incorporated into complete NLG applications of the kind discussed in this chapter; this is perhaps one reason why the uptake of statistical techniques in the NLG community has been slower than in other NLP communities. One exception is Belz (2008), who created pCRU systems in the SumTime domain, and showed that human evaluators regarded pCRU texts to be similar in quality to human-written weather forecasts.

5.2 NLG inputs: connecting language to the world

Of course statistical techniques are an important research focus in almost all areas of NLP. Two research questions which are more specic to NLG concern the inputs and outputs of an NLG system. In this section we will look at some research issues involving inputs; in the next section we will look at some research issues involving outputs.

As mentioned previously, it is rare for the input to an NLG system to be the sort of formal semantic representation which is described in Chapter 15, COMPU-TATIONAL SEMANTICS. Usually the input to the system is some combination of databases, knowledge bases, sensor data, event logs, outputs of other systems, and human-authored texts – in other words, the kind of data that computer systems typically store and manipulate. Hence the NLG system must be able to either work with such input data itself, or interface with an external data analysis system. This raises a number of interesting technological, scientic, and even philosophical questions. In this section I will briey discuss three of the research issues involved in generating texts which are based on non-linguistic input data; see Roy and Reiter (2005) for a description of some of the numerous other challenges involved in connecting an NLP system to real-world input data.

5.2.1 Language and the world: what do words mean? There is a tradition in linguistics, including computational linguistics, of treating language as a 'stand-alone' symbolic system and de-emphasizing how language relates to the non-linguistic world. But of course language evolved to enable humans to communicate about their world (social, intellectual, and physical), not as an isolated symbolic system. In particular, linguistic symbols (that is, words) should have relationship to the non-linguistic world shared by the computer system and its human users.

The problem of mapping data to words is a difcult one, which has received surprisingly little attention in the linguistic community. Lexical semanticists have examined how logical forms are mapped into words, but this is only part of the problem. Using an example from Roy and Reiter (2005), if an NLG system is trying to describe the visual appearance of an object based on camera data, it is not particularly helpful to know that the predicate $Red(X)$ maps to the adjective 'red.' What the system really needs to know is what pixel values from the camera can be described as 'red,' and how this is inuenced by context (lighting conditions, other objects in the scene, user's background, and object being described). The system also may need to know when an object which incorporates many colors can still be described as 'red' (for example, an apple whose skin is mostly red but has a brown stalk and some greenish areas on its skin). Last but not least, the NLG system may want to know if 'red' means more than just color; for example, if an apple is visually on the borderline between being 'red' and 'green,' perhaps the decision as to which term to use should depend on how ripe it is, since 'green apple' suggests an apple which is not ripe as well as an apple which is visually green.

Some of these issues were empirically investigated in the SumTime project, especially for choosing phrases to describe time, and choosing verbs to communicate increases and decreases (Reiter et al., 2005). The analysis was performed by aligning the input data (numerical weather predictions) with the corpus texts, and then trying to learn how corpus authors choose words, using both machine learning techniques and manual analysis. The main nding of this investigation was that there were large individual differences in how different forecasters mapped data to words. For example, some forecasters used *'by evening'* to mean roughly 6pm, while others used *'by evening'* to mean midnight. An example involving a verb is that one forecaster said he used the verb *'easing'* (instead of *'decreasing'*) to communicate a decrease in wind speed when the absolute wind speed was low; another said he used *'easing'* when the absolute wind speed was high.

There were also differences between the forecast authors and the forecast readers. For example, the forecast authors all used *'later'* to mean near the end of a forecast period, but some forecast users interpreted *'later'* to mean after a period of at least 12 hours. A few of the forecast readers (but none of the authors) also thought that time terms should depend on season (because they were linked to sunrise and sunset) and/or on country (because they were linked to cultural expectations about when people woke up, ate, and went to sleep).

Thus, SumTime showed that there were large differences in how different individuals mapped data to words in the weather domain (and in fact psychologists and linguists have observed such differences in many other domains; Reiter and Sripada 2002). In other words, this aspect of language is not standardized across a linguistic community in the same way that syntax and spelling are. Such problems may be overcome in human language use by lexical alignment mechanisms (Brennan & Clark 1996); these help human participants in a dialogue agree on word usage. However, we do not understand alignment well enough to let a computer NLP system align with a human, and in any case most NLG systems do not participate in dialogues with their users.

5.2.2 Data analysis for linguistic communication   A data-to-text system typically must include data analysis and reasoning modules as well as linguistic modules (Reiter 2007). Another interesting research issue is how these modules are affected by the need to generate textual summaries. In other words, how do linguistic constraints and requirements affect the non-linguistic parts of a data-to-text system?

Sripada et al. (2003) addressed this issue, and in particular hypothesized that such data analysis modules are affected by the Gricean maxims (Grice 1975). For example, the Gricean maxim of quality says that utterances should be truthful. One popular data analysis technique is linear segmentation, which involves tting a straight line to a set of datapoints. For data analysis purposes, this is often done by nding the line which best ts the data points, even if the end points of such a line are not real datapoints. Sripada et al. argue (largely on the basis of linguistic work such as corpus analysis) that if such line segments are explicitly mentioned in generated texts, it is better to use line segments anchored on real datapoints, as this is more truthful.

Sripada et al.'s hypothesis is an interesting one, and more research is needed to investigate to what degree Gricean maxims do indeed affect data analysis and interpretation in systems that produce textual output. If this turns out to be the case, it would be a very interesting example of how a linguistic theory (Gricean maxims) affects what seems to be a non-linguistic task (data interpretation).

5.2.3 Integrating linguistic and non-linguistic knowledge   Another important research topic is representations and models that include both linguistic and non-linguistic information. This is not straightforward because a vision system, a knowledge-based reasoner, and an NLP system (for example) may represent very different kinds of information. For example, an NLP system may need to know that *rain* can be communicated using a verb which takes a dummy subject; a knowledge-based meteorological reasoner may need to know that *rain* is a type of precipitation; and a vision system may need to know that *rain* consists of many small semi-spherical objects falling from the sky. It is unclear to what degree it makes sense to try to integrate these types of knowledge into a single representation, and to what degree it is better to keep them distinct. Intuitively it seems that there should be some information which is shared by the different reasoners; for example, *rain* is similar to *snow* from a linguistic perspective (both can appear as verbs with dummy subjects, or as nouns), a knowledge perspective (both are kinds of precipitation), and a visual perspective (both consist of many small objects falling from the sky). But we do not know how to design knowledge representations which capture such commonalities while still effectively representing the information needed by the different kinds of reasoners.

Even without integrated representation in the above sense, systems can still use models and algorithms which utilize both linguistic and non-linguistic data. For example, Kelleher et al. (2005) used both linguistic and visual data in a referring-expression generation task. They computed the visual salience of objects in a visual scene, and used this information, together with a conventional linguistic discourse model, to generate referring expressions to objects in the scene.

5.3 NLG outputs, the role of language in human–computer interaction

From a system perspective, an NLG module is usually part of a larger system whose goal is to inform, assist, motivate, persuade, and/or entertain a user. The larger system may be interactive, include graphical as well as textual outputs, and be sensitive to the user's disabilities, background, and tasks. This raises a number of interesting research questions, ranging from basic questions about the effectiveness of language vs. graphics as a communication tool, to more applied questions such as what sort of language is most appropriate for blind people using a screen reader. Collectively these can be considered as questions about the appropriate role of generated language in human–computer interaction (HCI). As with the language-and-world issues mentioned in the previous section, these issues have not received much attention in the linguistic community.

5.3.1 Text and graphics Perhaps the most studied of these issues is text and graphics. In the 1990s there were many publications about 'media choice,' that is the problem of deciding whether a particular bit of information should be presented linguistically or graphically. For example, Feiner and McKeown (1990) suggested, in the context of generating instruction manuals, that physical location should be communicated graphically, and conditional information should be communicated linguistically. Bernsen (1995) proposed an abstract theory which guided the choice of text vs. graphics. Other researchers pointed out that there were many similarities between text and graphics, and in particular many linguistic phenomena, such as conversational implicature (Marks & Reiter 1990), rhetorical structure theory (André & Rist 1994), and sublanguages (Reiter 1995), applied to graphics as well as text.

Of course, what most users really want is not text-only or graphics-only documents, but rather integrated documents that combine text and graphics. More recent research has focused on integrating text and graphics, primarily in the context of embodied conversational agents (ECA), that is animated characters which move, gesture, and talk. I will not discuss ECAs here as they typically communicate using speech instead of written language, but the interested reader can nd out more about recent NLG-related ECA research by looking at proceedings of the Multimodal Output Generation (MOG) workshop (for example, Theune et al., 2007 and van der Sluis et al., 2008). Bateman and his colleagues (Bateman et al., 2001) have looked at integrating text and graphics in written documents, taking into consideration layout issues.

One of the dif culties in this research area is evaluation. Users like graphics, even if they are not actually useful and effective (Law et al., 2005). Hence evaluations of multi-modal systems which are based on user ratings or preferences may not be good predictors of task effectiveness. In this area even more than other areas of NLG, we need careful task-effectiveness studies to evaluate systems, and indeed to provide the basis for good theories of media choice and integration.

One common observation about text and graphics is that the choice depends on user characteristics. Most obviously, graphics are probably not appropriate for a visually impaired user, and speech is not appropriate for a hearing-impaired user. Less obviously but perhaps more importantly, the choice may depend on the expertise of the user. In particular, as many visualization experts have pointed out (Tufte 1983), it is easy to mislead people with graphics, intentionally or unintentionally; viewers need some experience using graphs in order to be able to interpret them correctly. Of course language can also mislead people, but almost all users have decades of experience in using language, whereas relatively few people have this much experience using visualizations.

5.3.2 Interaction Another aspect of the 'HCI of NLG' is interaction. One of the most impressive aspects of current visualization systems is their interactivity; users do not just see a static graph, they can interact with the system and request close-ups, choose to have different information presented, etc. In contrast, most current NLG systems generate static texts which cannot be interacted with; indeed better interactivity is one of the most common requests I receive from potential users of NLG systems. Of course dialogue systems (see Chapter 16, COMPUTA-TIONAL MODELS OF DIALOGUE) allow interaction, but the current state of the art in dialogue technology makes it dif cult to build systems with which the user can reliably interact.

An alternative is to allow the user to interact with an NLG system via mouse clicks and/or keyboard commands, as indeed users interact with visualization systems. One way of structuring this interactivity is via 'dynamic hypertext.' Such NLG systems generate texts which include hyperlinks, and some of these hyperlinks invoke the NLG system to generate different texts. The ILEX system (O'Donnell et al., 2001), for example, generated descriptions of museum items, which had hyperlinks to related items. Clicking on one of these links would invoke ILEX to generate a description of the related item; this description could include references and comparisons to the original description.

Other interaction models are also possible. For example, IGRAPH (Ferres et al., 2006), which helps blind users browse statistical data sets, uses a keyboard interface with keys which allow users to browse forward and backward in the data set, and to get higher-level summaries or lower-level details. This interface is similar to a screen reader, which of course is what most blind users are used to.

Most work on NLG interaction attempts to adapt existing types of interfaces, such as hypertext and screen readers. But perhaps what NLG really needs is new types of interfaces. One interesting idea is WYSIWYM (Power et al., 1998), which uses NLG to help users construct knowledge bases and queries; the user constructs these entities by manipulating a feedback text, which is generated from the actual knowledge base entity or query being authored. Another innovative authoring interface is used in STANDUP (Ritchie et al., 2006), which allows children with learning dif culties to create jokes. STANDUP uses an interface which presents the process of creating a joke as a bus journey, with stops such as 'Word Shop.' Hopefully we will see more experimentation with novel interfaces to NLG systems in the future.

5.3.3 User modeling As should be clear by now, there are major differences between individual users of NLG systems, in terms of the type of language they prefer, (dis)abilities, expertise, and task. In principle it would be nice to represent these differences in a user model, and take the user model into account during the generation process.

Zukerman and Litman (2001) summarize research on user modeling in NLG (and other aspects of NLP). In very broad terms, most research on user modeling for NLG has either explicitly asked users to classify themselves into one of a small number of categories (such as 'novice' and 'expert'), or tried to implicitly acquire user models based on how a user interacts with the NLG system. Neither of these approaches allows very detailed models of users to be created; and hence neither approach allows sophisticated in-depth tailoring of generated texts to the particulars of individual users.

However, the bene t of tailoring texts to shallow user models does not seem to be very high, at least in my experience. Detailed user models probably would allow much better texts to be generated, but we do not know how to acquire such models. Researchers have proposed ideas for acquisition of detailed models; for example perhaps it would be possible to create detailed models (at least of a user's linguistic expertise) via corpus analysis of texts that a user has written, or by asking users to rate a large number of texts and analyzing their ratings (Walker et al., 2007). However, to the best of my knowledge no one has yet tried to use these techniques to obtain a good empirical understanding of how language varies between individuals in a linguistic community. This is a pity, because such research could shed light on fundamental questions about language, as well as improve NLG technology.

5.4   Affective NLG: going beyond informing and helping users

Most research on NLG has assumed that the purpose of generated texts is to inform users and help them achieve a task. But of course language is used for many other purposes, including motivation, persuasion, stress reduction, social engagement, and entertainment. NLG systems which have such goals are called *affective* NLG systems (de Rosis & Grasso 2000).

5.4.1   Motivation and persuasion   Perhaps the best-studied affective NLG goals are motivation and persuasion. There is of course an extensive literature in psychology and marketing on the best way to motivate and persuade people; and also a rich literature in philosophy and logic in formal models of argumentation. Several NLG systems have attempted to use theories from these communities to persuade and/or motivate people.

For example, the STOP system (Reiter et al., 2003a), which produced tailored smoking-cessation letters, was based on a popular psychological model of how people can change addictive behaviors (Prochaska & diClemente 1992). Unfortunately, an evaluation of STOP showed that the system was not effective; recipients of STOP letters were no more likely to stop smoking than recipients of control non-personalized letters. This may be because STOP used fairly shallow user models, and effective tailoring requires detailed user models (as discussed in Section 5.3.3).

Another approach was taken by Carenini and Moore (2006), who based their system on argumentation and decision theory. Their GEA system generated real-estate descriptions of houses, and tried to make these descriptions more effective (in terms of persuading potential buyers to seriously consider a house) by tailoring the description based on a quantitative model of the buyer's preferences.

GEA was tested in an arti cial context (with subjects who were pretending to be house buyers, not real house buyers), with mixed but overall encouraging results.

More recently, Guerini et al. (2007) developed a sophisticated system which attempted to persuade people to visit a museum. Guerini's system was based on an embodied conversational agent, so his system could display facial expressions and use appropriate tones of voice. His system also had rich user models, which included information about cognitive state (beliefs, desires, and intentions), emotional state, and social relationships. Unfortunately Guerini's system has only been evaluated in small pilot evaluations (which did not see a signi cant effect), so its effectiveness is unclear.

All of the above-mentioned systems relied heavily on user models; it may be that the quality of the user model is one of the main limiting factors in the performance of persuasive NLG systems. As mentioned in Section 5.3.3, acquiring good information about users is a major challenge in itself.

5.4.2   Improving emotional state   Another communicative goal is to make people feel better; a particular goal of interest is to reduce stress. We know that stress is often inversely correlated with sense of control; someone who feels they have no control over a situation is likely to feel more stressed than someone who feels that they are at least partially in control. Furthermore we know that, in medical contexts in particular, people are likely to feel more in control if they know more; patients of course are entitled to make decisions about their own health care, but they can only effectively make decisions if they understand their situation. Also, understanding one's medical situation can reduce uncertainty, and reduced uncertainty can reduce stress.

For these reasons, it seems plausible that a system which informs patients about their medical condition could reduce their stress about their medical condition; such a system would be very useful in many medical contexts. This hypothesis was investigated by Cawsey et al. (2000), who built several systems which tried to increase patients' understanding of their medical record, using a browsing dynamic hypertext interface. An evaluation showed that patients liked the system, but unfortunately there was no signi cant reduction in stress among patients who used the system.

A new area of research is using NLG to promote social interaction, for example by helping friends and relatives provide support to parents of sick babies (Moncur & Reiter 2007), and by helping people with communication disabilities engage in social conversations (Reiter et al., 2009).

5.4.3   Entertainment   Last but not least, some NLG systems generate texts that are intended to entertain readers. For example Binstead and Ritchie (1997) developed a computer system which generated puns, and Ritchie et al. (2006) adapted this technology to help humans (children with learning dif culties) create puns. These systems combined theories of what makes a good pun with databases which hold the necessary information about word pronunciation, meaning, etc.

There has also been considerable research on computer systems which generate stories. This includes both research on the content and structure of computer-generated stories (Perez y Perez & Sharples 2004) (much of this is carried out in the computational creativity community), and research on appropriate language for stories (Callaway & Lester 2002). Much of this research is presented at conferences which involve the computer-gaming community, such as Interactive Digital Storytelling (Spierling & Szilas 2008).

6 NLG Resources

I conclude this chapter with a short survey of practical resources which might be of interest to people who want to get involved in NLG research. One good general source of NLG resources is the NLG portal of the Association for Computational Linguistics wiki.[2]

Probably the most commonly requested resource is NLG software. There are a number of realizers (Section 3.3) which are freely available on the web. These realizers vary greatly in linguistic sophistication and ease of use, with the simplest realizers (in linguistic terms) generally being the easiest to use. They also vary in practical aspects such as documentation and programming language.

Unfortunately there are currently no software resources for microplanning and document planning which have been successfully used outside the groups which created them. Hopefully this situation will improve in the near future.

Data resources can also be very useful. Quite a few researchers have made resources available on the web, but few of these have actually been used by other people at the time of writing. Exceptions include the SumTime corpus,[3] which contains numerical weather predictions and human-written forecasts based on these predictions; and the TUNA corpus,[4] which contains scene descriptions and referring expressions produced by human subjects from these scene descriptions.

Turning to information resources, such as textbooks and web sites, contemporary NLP textbooks unfortunately say little about NLG. There is one specialist NLG textbook, Reiter and Dale (2000), but it does not present developments since 2000. Bateman and Zock maintain a useful web page which lists NLG systems, including links to homepages and key references.[5] Other than that, the main source of information is conference proceedings, especially the International NLG Conference and the European NLG workshop; proceedings of many of these are available from the ACL Anthology.[6]

NOTES

1 http://protege.stanford.edu
2 http://aclweb.org/aclwiki
3 www.csd.abdn.ac.uk/research/sumtime/
4 www.csd.abdn.ac.uk/research/tuna/corpus/
5 http://www.nlg-wiki.org/systems/
6 www.aclweb.org/anthology/

21 Discourse Processing

RUSLAN MITKOV

This chapter discusses concepts related to the computational processing of discourse, and theories and methods related to or employed in this task. Section 1 introduces basic notions of discourse and Section 2 illustrates discourse structure through examples from different genres. Section 2 also covers topic segmentation and outlines major works such as Hearst's *TextTiling* approach to text segmentation.

Section 3 examines theories and formalisms which deal with the computational treatment of coherence relations. Hobbs's coherence theory and rhetorical structural theory (RST) as popular theories of organizing text in terms of coherence relations are introduced. Another popular theory which models local coherence, namely centering theory, is discussed in greater detail.

Section 4 covers anaphora, which make a vital contribution to the cohesion of discourse and whose interpretation is crucial for discourse understanding. A considerable part of this section is dedicated to the computational processing of anaphora. The process of anaphora resolution with its distinct stages is covered and major algorithms for anaphora resolution are outlined.

Section 5 discusses the role of discourse processing in NLP applications and nally Section 6 points to references for further reading.

1 Discourse: Basic Notions and Terminology

Natural language texts do not normally consist of isolated pieces of text or sentences but of sentences which form a uni ed whole and which make up what we call discourse. According to the Longman dictionary,[1] *discourse* is (1) a serious speech or piece of writing on a particular subject, (2) serious conversation or discussion between people, or (3) the language used in particular types of speech or writing. What Longman presumably mean by 'serious' (but do not explicitly say) is that the text produced is not a random collection of symbols or words, but (a) *related* and (b) *meaningful* sentences which have a particular communicative goal.

The Handbook of Computational Linguistics and Natural Language Processing, First Edition.
Edited by Alexander Clark, Chris Fox and Shalom Lappin.
© 2013 Blackwell Publishing Ltd except for editorial material and organization
© 2013 Alexander Clark, Chris Fox, and Shalom Lappin. Published 2013 by Blackwell Publishing Ltd.

The reference to 'related' and 'meaningful' sentences has to do with the fact that discourse is expected to be both *cohesive* and *coherent*.

Discourse typically manifests *cohesion*, which is about the way textual units are linked together. Cohesion occurs where the interpretation of some element in the discourse is dependent on that of another and involves the use of abbreviated or alternative linguistic forms which can be recognized and understood by the hearer or the reader, and which refer to or replace previously mentioned items in the spoken or written text.

Consider the following extract from Jane Austen's *Pride and Prejudice* (Austen 1995: 23):

(1)   *Elizabeth* looked archly, and turned away. *Her* resistance had not injured her with the gentleman.

Although it is not stated explicitly, it is normal to assume that the second sentence is *related* to the rst one and that *her* refers to *Elizabeth*. It is this reference which ensures the cohesion between the two sentences. If the text is changed by replacing *her* with *his* in the second sentence or the whole second sentence is replaced with *This chapter is about discourse processing*, cohesion does not occur any more: the interpretation of the second sentence in both cases no longer depends on the rst sentence. In the above example it is the use of the pronoun *her* (see also the section on *anaphora* below) that secures cohesion, but *lexical cohesion* is also possible through simple repetition of words, synonyms, or hypernyms.[2]

Whereas cohesion in texts is more about linking sentences or, more generally, textual units through cohesive devices such as anaphors and lexical repetitions, discourse is also expected to manifest *coherence*, which is about it *making sense*. More speci cally coherence has to do with the meaning relations between two units and how two or more units combine to produce the overall meaning of a speci c discourse.

(2)   George passed his exam. He scored the highest possible mark.
(3)   George passed the exam. He enjoyed red wine.

Whereas example (2) makes perfect sense in that the second sentence elaborates on the fact the George excelled in his exam, example (3) sounds a bit odd and somehow lacks overall meaning: most readers may even nd the two sentences in (3) unrelated. Leaving aside the hypothetical possibility/explanation that, because George has passed his exam and he likes red wine, he is likely to treat himself to a nice bottle of Rioja red wine, readers would nd (3) hardly coherent as opposed to (2) where the second sentence is in a meaningful relation to the rst one in that it elaborates on the fact presented in the rst sentence.

Discourse could take the form of a *monologue* where a writer or speaker is the author of the text.[3] A particular form of discourse is the *dialogue* (see Chapter 16, COMPUTATIONAL MODELS OF DIALOGUE, for more on dialogue), where there is an interaction or conversation,[4] usually between two participants. Another form of discourse is the *multiparty discourse* which usually takes place at meetings.

2   Discourse Structure

Discourse structure is a type of structure used to "refer to the structure of some postulated unit higher than the sentence, for example the paragraph or some larger entity such as episode or topic unit" (Halliday & Hasan 1976: 10). It is safe to say that every genre has its own discourse structure (Halliday & Hasan 1976).[5] In fact, under normal circumstances texts are organized logically and follow a speci c structure of discourse topics. The stereotypical sequence of discourse topics is characteristic of certain documents and genres and accounts for the way texts are organized and segmented by topics.

2.1   Text organization

As an illustration of how a speci c discourse is organized, consider the following entry[6] from *The Hamlyn Pocket Dictionary of Wines* which was written for the explicit discourse goal of de ning Flagey-Echezeaux (Paterson 1980: 2).

(4)   Flagey-Echezeaux (*France*). Important red wine township in the Cote de Nuits with two front-ranking vineyards, Echezeaux and Grands Echezeaux. The rst produces a ne rich, round wine and the second, which is not a single vineyard but a group, is also capable of producing ne wine but, like other divided properties, the quality of its wine is variable. The lesser wines of Flagey-Echezeaux are entitled to the appellation Vosne-Romanee.

The author does not randomly order the sentences in the text, but rather plans an overall organizational framework within which the individual sentences are produced. In the case of the above example, the framework chosen is typical of de nitions. Here, the author rst identi es Flagey-Echezeaux by describing its superordinate ('important red wine township in the Cote de Nuits'), and then introduces two of its constituents (Echezeaux and Grands Echezeaux). Next, a description about each of the vineyards is provided in turn and nally the author presents additional information about Flagey-Echezeaux in the last sentence. The way the above discourse is organized can be explained in terms of *rhetorical predicates*, where these are the means by which a writer or speaker can describe information and organize the text. In this particular example the rst sentence corresponds to the rhetorical predicate *identification* ('important red wine township in the Cote de Nuits'), followed by *constituency* ('with two front-ranking vineyards'). Building on Grimes's (1975) and Williams's (1893) predicates, McKeown observes typical patterns of rhetorical predicates referred to as *schemata* which she uses to analyze text and then to apply these as text organization strategies in natural language generation (for more on natural language generation, see Chapter 20, NATURAL LANGUAGE GENERATION). McKeown's schemata include *attributive* schema, *identification* schema, and *constituency* schema. Each schema consists of a stereotypical sequence of rhetorical predicates with the *identification* schema featuring a possible sequence of the following predicates: *identification, attributive, amplification*, and *particular illustration*. For details, see McKeown (1985).

It is widely accepted that scienti c papers and their abstracts have a prede ned structure which can be exploited in NLP applications. In its simplest form, a scienti c paper can be considered to have a *problem–solution* structure (Hutchins 1977), but, in general, a more detailed organization can be identi ed in scienti c papers: *background information* about the domain tackled in the paper, *the problem* to be addressed in the paper, *the solution* to the problem, *evaluation* of the solution and *conclusion* (Swales 1990). These sections are normally referred to as *moves* or *rhetorical predicates*. Research in the structure of abstracts con rms that, by and large, these moves hold, but it is not unusual for abstracts to include only a subset of the moves (Salanger-Meyer 1990; Orasan 2001).

Another example of how text is organized are online medical patient information lea ets (Connor 2006). Such lea ets exhibit typical discourse structure in that different topics are not presented randomly but follow an established order. In line with Clerehan and Buchbinder (2006), Connor (2006) identi es the structure in terms of rhetorical moves or predicates. The lea ets rst provide background information on the medicine (rhetorical predicate *inform*), then give a summary on the use of the medicine (*describe*), provide dosage instructions (*instruct*), followed by an outline/explanation of the bene t of the medicine (*explain*). These lea ets next feature information on the side effects (realized by the rhetorical predicate *inform*), and then proceed with information about monitoring (*suggest*), constraints on patient behavior (*inform, warn*), storage instructions (*instruct*), and the description of circumstances when medical advice is necessary. Finally disclaimers for online contents are displayed.

2.2   *Text segmentation algorithm*

The examples above illustrate how discourse can be organized and segmented on the basis of different topics. For many practical NLP implementations the automatic segmentation of text according to the topics covered is crucial. Among the different algorithms which have been developed to address this task, the *TextTiling* (Hearst 1994; 1997b) approach is perhaps the best known. Hearst's algorithm does not attempt to capture any hierarchical relations and dependencies that hold between topic segments (discourse units) as rhetorical structure theory does.[7] Instead, it splits documents into a linear sequence of multi-paragraph segments, each of which focuses upon a distinct subtopic within the main topic of the discourse. Its name derives from the fact that the goal of *TextTiling* is to partition texts into contiguous, non-overlapping subtopic segments, broadly resembling tiles, that are assumed to occur within the scope of one or more overarching main topics, which span the length of the text.

Under this approach, the structure of a document is treated as a sequence of subtopical discussions that occur in the context of one or more main topic discussions. This conception is illustrated in Hearst (1997) by the example of a 21-paragraph science news article called 'Stargazers', whose main topic is the existence of life on earth and other planets. Its contents can be described as consisting of nine subtopic discussions, presented below. In the example, the numbers indicate paragraphs within the document so that paragraphs 1–3 present 'Intro – the search for life in space,' paragraphs 4–5 present 'The Moon's chemical composition,' etc.

1–3	Intro – the search for life in space
4–5	The Moon's chemical composition
6–8	How early Earth–Moon proximity shaped the Moon
9–12	How the Moon helped life evolve on Earth
13	Improbability of the Earth–Moon system
14–16	Binary/trinary star systems make life unlikely
17–18	The low probability of non-binary/trinary systems
19–20	Properties of Earth's Sun that facilitate life
21	Summary

The approach assumes that a particular set of lexical items is in use during the course of a given subtopic discussion and, when the subtopic changes, a signi - cant proportion of the vocabulary changes too. The method assumes three broad categories of lexical items to be found within a text:

(1) words that occur frequently throughout the text, which are often indicative of its main topic(s);
(2) words that are less frequent but more uniform in distribution, which do not provide much information about the divisions between discussions;
(3) groups of words that are 'clumped' together with high density in some parts of the text and low density in other parts. These groups of words are indicative of subtopic structure.

The problem of subtopic segmentation is thus the problem of determining where these clusters of words in the third category begin and end. Hearst presents a *block comparison* algorithm that addresses this task. Here, a block is de ned as a sequence of *n* contiguous sentences. Pairs of blocks are compared for their overall lexical similarity and the 'gap' between each pair of blocks is assigned the result-ing *lexical score*. The more words that the blocks have in common, the higher the score assigned to the gap between them. If a gap with a low lexical score is fol-lowed and preceded by gaps with high lexical scores, then the low-scoring gap is likely to indicate a shift in vocabulary that corresponds to a subtopic change. In its initial implementation, the blocks are represented by vectors and the lex-ical score is computed as the normalized inner product of the two vectors. The *TextTiling* system identi es subtopic shifts at gaps whose lexical score falls below some threshold. Evaluation of the *TextTiling* approach to subtopic segmentation revealed that performance levels were encouraging. When assessed on its ability to classify gaps between blocks as subtopic shifts, different con gurations of the system obtained F-scores ranging from 0.61 to 0.705, compared to human judges' reliability scores on the same data (F-score of 0.77). When computing F-score, true positives are gaps between blocks that both the *TextTiling* system and a human annotator agree to be either points of subtopic shift or gaps that simply happen to lie within a subtopic segment.

Since its original statement, several authors have experimented with different parameters of the original *TextTiling* algorithm described in Hearst (1994). Alternate methods for scoring the gaps between text blocks, including *vocabulary introductions* and *lexical chains*, were applied in Hearst (1997). Choi et al. (2001) successfully applied *latent semantic analysis* (LSA) in their variant of the *TextTiling* algorithm, achieving signi cantly improved performance levels from the system. Under this approach, the improvement is brought about by using LSA to replace each word used in the text blocks with appropriate groups of words that co-occur with them. The initial vectors are thus converted into matrices of vectors whose similarity is computed by taking the sum of the cosine scores between each of them. In this way, the approach can more accurately reduce the computed depth of gaps between blocks that contain non-matching but semantically related words.

Kozima (1993) describes a similar approach to discourse segmentation in which each block of text in a document is assigned a *lexical cohesion profile*, de ned as a record of the lexical cohesiveness (semantic similarity) of the words in the block. Low levels of lexical cohesiveness within a block imply that it spans discourse segments and contains a subtopic shift.

Numerous alternative approaches to discourse segmentation, based on different assumptions and methodologies, have been introduced since the inception of *TextTiling*. Crowe (1996) describes an approach in which references to events are identi ed in texts and each paragraph that mentions an event is then concatenated to form a representative discourse segment. Kan et al. (1998) implements an approach to discourse segmentation based on lexical chains combined with a weighting scheme established in a supervised training step. Paragraphs in the text are then assigned a weight with reference to the type of chain link occurring within them and their position with respect to other links. Paragraphs with a high aggregate weight are considered likely to represent the beginning of a new subtopic segment in the text. The authors report that this segmentation method outperforms the *TextTiling* algorithm. Utiyama and Isahara (2001) present a probabilistic method exploiting a graph search algorithm to nd the most likely topic segmentation of an input text.

Supervised approaches to discourse segmentation have been scarce due to a lack of available training data. Litman and Passoneau (1995) present one supervised approach exploiting a decision tree classi er in the context of transcribed dialogues. The method uses information about prosodic cues, cue phrases, and anaphora within blocks of text. System performance compared favorably with that of human annotators.

3   Discourse Coherence

In the previous section we discussed the issue of discourse structure. In fact the way that units are connected into meaningful relationships is another factor which contributes to the acceptability of the structure of a speci c discourse. In the next section we shall discuss theories for text coherence which have played an in uential part in different computational models of discourse and NLP applications.

3.1   *Hobbs's theory of coherence relations*

In Hobbs's model (1979), discourse structure comprises text units and *coherence relations* between them. Consider the following example, where the second sentence is an *elaboration* of the   rst one as it expands on the   rst without giving additional instructions:

(5)   Go down Washington Street. Just follow Washington Street three blocks to Adams Street.

Building on the work by Grimes (1975) and Halliday and Hasan (1976), Hobbs proposed a set of 12 coherence relations, including *cause, evaluation, background, parallel*, and *elaboration*. Hobbs's work goes beyond previous similar or related work in that he proposes an inference mechanism for reasoning about the coherence relations.

As an illustration, Hobbs (1979) considers the text below, where the two sentences are claimed to be in an elaboration relation by virtue of the second sentence elaborating on the   rst one.

(6)   John can open Bill's safe. He knows the combination.

Following the outlines in Hobbs (1979) and Lochbaum et al. (2000), the propositions expressed by the two sentences can be represented as follows:

can(John, open(Safe))
know(he, combination(Comb,y))

Here *John, Safe* and, *Comb* are literals and *he* and *y* are variables. Then, by employing domain axioms which express general facts about generating states of affairs and more speci c facts about the relation between safes and combinations, it is possible to reason from the   rst of these propositions to the following proposition:

know(John, cause(do(John, a), open(Safe)))
'John knows that his doing some action a opens the safe.'

Similarly, the following proposition can be pragmatically implied from the second proposition:

know(he, cause(dial(z, Comb, y), open(y)))
'He knows that z's dialing the combination of y causes it to open.'

The requirements of the *elaboration* relation will be satis ed by these two propositions if dialing the combination of the safe is recognized as a specialization of doing some action which will open the safe. The second statement thus elaborates on the rst by providing this additional property of how John can open the safe.

Hobbs's work differs from previous approaches not only because of the central role it assigns to reasoning, but also because it incorporates reference resolution as a by-product of reasoning about coherence. For example, to recognize that the *elaboration* relation held in the foregoing example, the variables *he* and *z* have to be identi ed with John and the variable *y* with the safe. Therefore the anaphor *he* in the second sentence was resolved to the antecedent *John* as part of the process of reasoning about coherence.

3.2   Rhetorical structure theory

Rhetorical structure theory (RST) is a model of text organization initially proposed by Mann and Thompson (1987) and later used by a number of NLP researchers (e.g., Marcu 1997; 2000; see section 5). In RST relations are de ned to hold between two non-overlapping spans or text units called the *nucleus* and the *satellite*. The nucleus is expected to be more central or topical to the author and can be interpreted independently. The satellite is less central and usually its interpretation is connected with the nucleus. Mann and Thompson de ne a set of 25 rhetorical relations. These relations include the *evidence* relation which applies to two text spans where the satellite provides evidence for the claim contained in the nucleus. Following the authors' convention, the arrow in Figure 21.1 represents the *evidence* relation by means of an asymmetric arrow.

In this example, the unit representing the second sentence is in an *evidence* relation with the unit representing the rst sentence and increases the reader's belief in the claim expressed in this unit.

In the *evidence* relation the satellite supports the nucleus, but does not contribute to it. This is different to the *circumstance* relation where the satellite sets a framework (e.g., temporal or spatial) within which the nucleus can be interpreted. Following Mann and Thompson (1987), consider the example:

(7)   Probably the most extreme case of Visitors Fever I have ever witnessed was a few summers ago when I visited the relatives in the Midwest.

In this example the satellite ('when I visited the relatives in the Midwest') provides a temporal framework for interpreting the nucleus (the preceding part of the sentence).

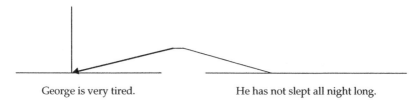

George is very tired.   He has not slept all night long.

Figure 21.1   Example of the RST relation evidence.

As another example of a relation, consider the following text:

(8)   The next LREC conference will take place in Marakesh, Morroco. I shall
      give you more details in due course, but now is a good time to reserve a
      hotel.

In this example, the units represented by the two clauses contained in the
second sentence are in a *justify* relation with the unit represented by the rst sentence. They tell readers why the writer believes he has the right to say unit one
('I shall give you more details in due course') without giving more details, and in
particular without providing the dates for the conference.
  In the original version of RST (Mann & Thompson 1987), relations are formally
de ned by a set of *constraints* on the nucleus (N) and satellite (S) which explain the
goals and beliefs of the writer (W) and reader (R), and by the *effect* on the reader.
By way of example, the *justify* relation is de ned as follows:

Relation name: Justify
Constraints on N: R might not believe N to a degree satisfactory to W
Constraints on S: R believes S or will nd it credible
Constraints on the
N+S combination: R's comprehending S increases R's belief of N
Effect: R's belief in N is increased

There are different sets of rhetorical relations in RST and variations of the theory.
By way of example, the RST TreeBank (Carlson et al., 2001) features 78 distinct
relations, grouped into 16 classes.

3.3   *Centering*

Centering is a theory about local discourse coherence and is based on the idea that
each *utterance* features a topically most prominent entity called the *center*. Centering
theory regards utterances[8] which continue the topic of preceding utterances as more
coherent than utterances which feature a topic shift (or ag up an impending shift).
  The main idea of centering theory (Grosz et al., 1983; 1995) is that certain entities mentioned in an utterance are more central than others and this imposes

constraints on the use of referring expressions and in particular on the use of pronouns. It is argued that the coherence of a discourse depends on the extent to
which the choice of the referring expressions conforms to the centering properties.
    As an illustration, consider the following examples:

(9)   **Discourse A**
        (a)   John works at Barclays Bank.
        (b)   He works with Lisa.
        (c)   John is going to marry Lisa.
        (d)   He is looking forward to the wedding.

      Discourse B
        (a)   John works at Barclays Bank.
        (b)   He works with Lisa.
        (c)   John is going to marry Lisa.
        (e)   She is looking forward to the wedding.

    Centering predicts that discourse B is less coherent than discourse A. In both
examples the discourse entity realized by John is the center in utterances (9b) and
(9c),[9] but whilst in (9d) the center remains the same, utterance (9e) shifts the center to the discourse entity realized by Lisa. The shift in center and the use of a
pronominal form to realize the new center contribute to making B less coherent
than A. In utterance (9d), unlike (9e), it is the center of utterances (9b) and (9c)
which has been pronominalized.
    Discourses consist of continuous discourse segments. A *discourse segment* D con-
sists of a sequence of utterances $U_1, U_2, \ldots, U_N$. Each utterance U in D is assigned
a set of potential next centers known as *forward looking centers* Cf (U, D)[10] which
correspond to the discourse entities evoked by the utterance. Each utterance (other
than the first) in a segment is assigned a single center defined in centering theory
as the *backward looking center*[11] Cb (U). The backward looking center Cb (U) is a
member of the set Cf (U) and is the discourse entity the utterance U is about. The
Cb entity connects the current utterance to the previous discourse: it focuses on an
entity that has already been introduced. A central claim of centering is that each
utterance has exactly one backward looking center.[12]
    The set of forward looking centers Cf (U) is partially ordered according to their
discourse salience. The highest-ranked element in Cf (U) is called *the preferred center* Cp (U) (Brennan et al., 1987). The preferred center in a current utterance U_N
(denoted as Cp (U_N)) is the most likely backward looking center of the following
utterance (denoted as Cb (U_{N+1})). Discourse entities in subject position are preferred over those in object position, which are preferred over discourse entities in
subordinate clauses or those performing other grammatical functions.[13]
    Grosz et al. (1995) define three types of transition relations across pairs of
utterances.

(1)   Center *continuation*: Cb $(U_{N+1}) =$ Cb (U_N), i.e., the backward looking cen-
        ter of the utterance U_{N+1} is the same as the backward looking center in the

utterance U_N and this entity is the preferred center of Cf (U_{N+1}). In this case Cb (U_{N+1}) is the most likely candidate for Cb (U_{N+2}).

(2) Center *retaining*: Cb (U_{N+1}) = Cb (U_N), but this entity is not the most highly ranked element in Cf (U_{N+1}). In this case, therefore, Cb (U_{N+1}) is not the preferred candidate for Cb(U_{N+2}) and, although it is retained as Cb in U_{N+1}, it is not likely to ll that role in U_{N+2}.

(3) Center *shifting*: Cb (U_{N+1}) ≠ Cb (U_N)

Brennan et al. (1987) distinguish between *smooth-shift* or *shifting-1* (if Cb(U_{N+1}) = Cp(U_{N+1})) and *rough-shift* or simply *shifting* (if Cb (U_{N+1}) ≠ Cp(U_{N+1})).

To exemplify the theory, here are two very simple discourses differing in their last sentences from Discourses A and B:

(9) **Discourse C**
    (a) John works at Barclays Bank.
    (b) He works with Lisa.
    (c) John is going to marry Lisa.
    (f) Lisa has known him for two years.

Discourse D
    (a) John works at Barclays Bank.
    (b) He works with Lisa.
    (c) John is going to marry Lisa.
    (g) She has known John for two years.

Sentence (9c) exhibits center continuation; the backward looking centers of (9b) and (9c) and the forward looking centers of sentences (9a), (9b), and (9c) are listed as follows:

(9) (a) John works at Barclays Bank.
    Cb unspeci ed[14]
    Cf = {John, Barclays Bank}

    (b) He works with Lisa.
    Cb = John
    Cf = {John, Lisa}

    (c) John is going to marry Lisa.
    Cb = John
    Cf = {John, Lisa}

In sentence (9f), we have center retaining:[15]

(9) (f) Lisa has known him for two years.
    Cb = John
    Cf = {Lisa, John}

Whereas in (g) we have a center shift.

> (g)   She has known John for two years.
>   Cb = Lisa
>   Cf = {Lisa, John}

In addition to the transitions outlined above, centering theory also includes two rules which state:

> **Rule 1**: If some element of Cf (U_N) is realized as a pronoun in U_{N+1}, then Cb (U_{N+1}) must also be realized as a pronoun.
> **Rule 2**: Transition states are ordered in terms of preference. The *continue* transition is preferred to the *retain* transition, which is preferred to the *shift* transition.[16]

Rule 1 stipulates that if there is only one pronoun in an utterance, then this pronoun should be the (backward looking) center. It is reasonable to assume that if the next sentence also contains a single pronoun, then the two pronouns corefer. The center is the most preferred discourse entity in the local context which is to be referred to by a pronoun.[17] The use of a pronoun to realize the backward looking center indicates that the speaker/writer is talking/writing about the same thing. Psycholinguistic research (Hudson-D'Zmura 1988; Gordon et al., 1993) and cross-linguistic research (Kameyama 1985; 1986; 1998; Di Eugenio 1990; Walker et al., 1994) have validated that Cb is preferentially realized by a pronoun (e.g., in English) or by equivalent forms such as zero pronouns in other languages (e.g., Japanese).

Rule 2 provides an underlying principle for coherence of discourse. Frequent shifts detract from local coherence, whereas continuation contributes to coherence. Maximally coherent segments are those which do not feature changes of center, concentrate on one main discourse entity (topic) only, and therefore require less processing effort.

Rule 2 is used as a preference in anaphora resolution (Brennan et al., 1987; Walker 1989). As an illustration, consider the following discourse:

> (9)   **Discourse E**
>   (h)   Although Jenny was in a hurry, she was glad to bump into Kate.
>   (i)   She told her some exciting news.

This discourse segment consists of the following utterances:

> U1 = Jenny was in a hurry
> U2 = she was glad to bump into Kate
> U3 = She told her some exciting news

The discourse entity 'Jenny' is both the backward looking center of the second utterance Cb (U_2) and the preferred center Cp (U_2) on the list of forward looking centers. Since continuation is preferred over retaining (Rule 2, see above), centering favors 'Jenny' as both Cb (U_3) and Cp (U_3), therefore predicting *she* as 'Jenny' and *her* as 'Kate' (the instantiations *she* = 'Kate' and *her* = 'Jenny' would have signaled retaining since in this case we would have had Cp (U_3) = 'Kate,' Cb (U_3) = 'Jenny').[18]

Centering has proved to be a powerful tool in accounting for local coherence and has been used successfully in anaphora resolution. However, as with every theory in linguistics, it has its limitations (see also Kehler 1997). For instance, the original centering model only accounts for local coherence of discourse. In an anaphora resolution context, when the candidates for the antecedent of an anaphor in the current utterance U_K have to be identi ed, centering proposes that the discourse entities in the immediately preceding utterance U_{K-1} be considered. Centering, however, does not offer a solution for resolving anaphors in U_K whose antecedents can be found only in U_{K-2} (or even further back in the discourse). To overcome this restriction, Hahn and Strube (1997) put forward an alternative centering model that extends the search space for antecedents.

Walker (1998) goes even further and argues that the restriction of centering to operate within a discourse segment should be abandoned in favor of a new model integrating centering into the global discourse structure. To this end it is proposed that a model of attentional state, the so-called *cache model*, be combined with the centering algorithm.

For more work on centering see the references in Section 6.

4   Anaphora Resolution

(1)   *Elizabeth* looked archly, and turned away. *Her* resistance had not injured her with the gentleman.

We saw in this example how the pronoun *her* serves as a link and ensures cohesion between the two sentences. Such words which point to previous items of discourse and contribute to its cohesion are referred to as *anaphors*. The understanding of a discourse usually involves the understanding of anaphors whose interpretation depends on either previous sentences or preceding words of the current sentence. The interpretation of anaphors (made possible by *anaphora resolution*, see Section 4.2) is of vital importance and has attracted considerable interest in the area of computational discourse.

4.1   *Anaphora: linguistic fundamentals*

We de ne *anaphora* as the linguistic phenomenon of pointing back to a previously mentioned item in the text. The word or phrase 'pointing back'[19] is called an *anaphor* and the entity to which it refers or for which it stands is its *antecedent*. When the anaphor refers to an antecedent and when both have the same referent in the real world, they are termed *coreferential*. Therefore *coreference* is the act of referring to the same referent in the real world.

Consider the following example from Huddleston (1984):

(10)   *The Queen* is not here yet but *she* is expected to arrive in the next half an hour.

In this example, the pronoun *she* is an anaphor, *the Queen* is its antecedent and *she* and *the Queen* are coreferential. Note that the antecedent is not the noun *Queen* but the noun phrase (NP) *the Queen*. The relation between the anaphor and the antecedent is not to be confused with that between the anaphor and its referent; in the example above the referent is *the Queen* as a person in the real world (e.g., Queen Elizabeth) whereas the antecedent is *the Queen* as a linguistic form.

A speci c anaphor and more than one of the preceding (or following) noun phrases may be coreferential, thus forming a *coreferential chain* of discourse entities which have the same referent. For instance in (11), *Sophia Loren, she, the actress*, and *her* are coreferential. Coreference partitions discourse into equivalence classes of coreferential chains and in (11) the following coreferential chains can be singled out: {Sophia Loren, she, the actress, her}, {Bono, the U2 singer}, {a thunderstorm}, and {a plane}.

(11)   *Sophia Loren* says *she* will always be grateful to Bono. *The actress* revealed that the U2 singer helped *her* calm down during a thunderstorm while traveling on a plane.

Note that not all varieties of anaphora have a referring function. Consider verb anaphora, for example.

(12)   When Manchester United swooped to lure Ron Atkinson away from the Albion, it was inevitable that his mid eld prodigy would *follow*, and in 1981 he *did*.

This sentence features the verb anaphor *did* which is a substitution for the antecedent *followed* but does not have a referring function and therefore we cannot speak of coreference between the two. Also, the anaphor and the antecedent may refer but may still not be coreferential, as in the case of identity-of-sense anaphora:[20]

(13)   The man who gave *his paycheck* to his wife was wiser than the man who gave *it* to his mistress (Karttunen 1969).

as opposed to identity-of-reference anaphora:

(14)   This man gave *his paycheck* to his wife in January; in fact, he gave *it* to her in person.

In (13) the anaphor *it* and the antecedent *his paycheck* are not coreferential whereas in (14) they are.

Bound anaphora is another example where the anaphor and the antecedent are not coreferential.

(15)   *Every speaker* had to present *his* paper.

Anaphora normally operates within a document (e.g., article, chapter, book), whereas coreference can be taken to work across documents. We have seen that there are varieties of anaphora that do not involve coreference. It is also possible to have coreferential items that are not anaphoric with *cross-document coreference* being an obvious example: two mentions of the same person in two different documents will be coreferential, but will not stand in an anaphoric relation.

The most widespread type of anaphora is *pronominal anaphora*. Pronominal anaphora can be exhibited by personal, possessive, or re exive pronouns ('A knee jerked between *Ralph*'s legs and *he* fell sideways busying *himself* with *his* pain as the   ght rolled over *him*') as well as by demonstrative pronouns ('*This* was more than he could cope with'). Relative pronouns are regarded as anaphoric too. First- and second-person singular and plural pronouns are usually used in a deictic manner[21] ('*I* would like *you* to show me the way to San Marino'), although their anaphoric function is not uncommon in reported speech or dialogues as demonstrated by the use of *I* in the last sentence of (16).

Lexical noun phrase anaphors take the form of de nite noun phrases also called *definite descriptions*, and *proper names*. Although pronouns, de nite descriptions, and proper names are all considered to be de nite expressions, proper names and de nite descriptions, unlike pronouns, can have a meaning independent of their antecedent. Furthermore, de nite descriptions do more than just refer. They convey some additional information as in (16) where the reader can learn more about *Roy Keane* through the de nite description *Alex Ferguson's No.1 player*.

(16)   *Roy Keane* has warned Manchester United he may snub their pay deal. *United's skipper* is even hinting that unless the future Old Trafford Package meets *his* demands, *he* could quit the club in June 2000. *Irishman Keane*, 27, still has 17 months to run on *his* current £23,000-a-week contract and wants to commit *himself* to United for life. *Alex Ferguson's No.1 player* con rmed: "If it's not the contract I want, I won't sign."

In this text, *Roy Keane* has been referred to by anaphoric pronouns (*he, his, himself, I*), but also by de nite descriptions (*United's skipper, Alex Ferguson's No. 1 player*) and a proper name modi ed by a common noun (*Irishman Keane*). On the other hand, *Manchester United* is referred to by the de nite description *the club* and by the proper name *United*.

Noun phrase anaphors may have the same head as their antecedents (*the chapter* and *this chapter*) but the relation between the referring expression and its antecedent may be that of synonymy (*a shop ... the store*), generalization/hypernym (*a boutique ... the shop*, also *Manchester United ... the club* as in (16)) or specialization/hyponym (*a shop ... the boutique*, also *their pay deal ... his current £23,000-a-week contract* as in (16)).[22] Proper names usually refer to antecedents which have the same head (*Manchester United ... United*) with exact repetitions not being uncommon.

According to the form of the anaphor, anaphora occurs as *verb anaphora* ('Stephanie *balked*, as *did* Mike') or *adverb anaphora* ('We shall go to *McDonalds* and meet you *there*'. *Zero anaphora*, which is typical of many languages such as Romance, Slavonic and oriental languages, is also exhibited. Consider the example in Spanish:

(17)   *Gloria* is very tired. (*She*) has been working all day long.
         Gloria está muy cansada. Ø Ha estado trabajando todo el día.

In the last example Ø stands for the omitted anaphor *she*.

Nominal anaphora arises when a *referring expression* – pronoun, de nite noun phrase, or proper name – has a non-pronominal noun phrase as antecedent. This most important and frequently occurring class of anaphora has been researched and covered extensively, and is well understood in the NLP literature. Broadly speaking, there are two types of nominal anaphora: *direct* and *indirect*. *Direct anaphora* links anaphors and antecedents by such relations as identity, synonymy, generalization, and specialization (see above). In contrast, *indirect anaphora* links anaphors and antecedents by relations such as part-of ('Although *the store* had only just opened, *the food hall* was busy and there were long queues at *the tills*') or set membership ('Only a day after heated denials that *the Spice Girls* were splitting up, *Melanie C* declared she had already left the group'). Resolution of indirect anaphora normally requires the use of domain or world knowledge. Indirect anaphora is also known as *associative* or *bridging* anaphora.[23] For more on the notions of anaphora and coreference, and on the different varieties of anaphora, see Hirst (1981) and Mitkov (2002).

4.2   *Anaphora resolution*

The process of determining the antecedent of an anaphor is called *anaphora resolution*. In anaphora resolution the system has to determine the antecedent of the anaphor. For identity-of-reference nominal anaphora, any preceding NP which is coreferential with the anaphor is considered as the correct antecedent. On the other hand, the objective of *coreference resolution* is to identify all coreferential chains. However, since the task of anaphora resolution is considered successful if any element of the anaphoric (coreferential) chain preceding the anaphor is identi ed, annotated corpora for automatic evaluation of anaphora systems require markup of anaphoric (coreferential) chains and not only anaphor-closest antecedent pairs.

The process of automatic resolution of anaphors consists of the following main stages: (1) identi cation of anaphors, (2) location of the candidates for antecedents, and (3) selection of the antecedent from the set of candidates on the basis of anaphora resolution factors.

4.2.1 Identification of anaphors In pronoun resolution, only the anaphoric pronouns have to be processed further, therefore non-anaphoric occurrences of the pronoun *it* as in (18) have to be recognized by the program.

(18)   It must be stated that Oskar behaved impeccably.

When a pronoun has no referential role, and it is not interpreted as a bound variable ('Every man loves his mother'), then it is termed pleonastic. Therefore, grammatical information as to whether a certain word is a third-person pronoun would not be suf cient: each occurrence of *it* has to be checked in order to nd out rst if it is referential or not. Several algorithms for identi cation of pleonastic pronouns have been reported in the literature (Paice & Husk 1987; Lappin & Leass 1994; Evans 2000; 2001; Boyd et al., 2005).

The search for anaphoric noun phrases can be even more problematic. De nite noun phrases are potentially anaphoric, often referring back to preceding noun phrases, as *The Queen* does in (19):

(19)   *Queen Elizabeth* attended the ceremony. *The Queen* delivered a speech.

It is important to bear in mind that not every de nite noun phrase is necessarily anaphoric. Typical examples are de nite descriptions which describe a speci c, unique entity, or de nite descriptions used in a generic way. In (20) the NP *The Duchess of York* is not anaphoric and does not refer to *the Queen*.

(20)   The Queen attended the ceremony. The Duchess of York was there too.

As in the case of the automatic recognition of pleonastic pronouns, it is important for an anaphora resolution program to be able to identify those de nite descriptions that are not anaphoric. Methods for identi cation of non-anaphoric de nite descriptions have been developed by Bean and Riloff (1999), Vieira and Poesio (2000), and Muñoz (2001).

Finally, proper names are regarded as potentially anaphoric to preceding proper names that partially match in terms of rst or last names (e.g., John White ... John ... Mr White).

4.2.2 Location of the candidates for antecedents Once the anaphors have been detected, the program has to identify the possible candidates for their antecedents. The vast majority of systems only handle nominal anaphora, since processing anaphors whose antecedents are verb phrases, clauses, sentences, or sequences of sentences is a more complicated task. Typically in such systems all noun phrases (NPs) preceding an anaphor within a certain search scope are initially regarded as candidates for antecedents.

The search scope takes a different form depending on the *processing model* adopted and may vary in size depending on the *type of anaphor*. Since anaphoric relations often operate within/are limited to a discourse segment,[24] the search scope is often set to the *discourse segment* which contains the anaphor. Anaphora resolution systems which have no means of identifying the discourse segment boundaries usually set the search scope to the *current and N preceding* sentences, with N depending on the type of anaphor. For pronominal anaphors, the search scope is usually limited to the current and two or three preceding sentences. Definite noun phrases, however, can refer further back in the text and, for such anaphors, the search scope is normally larger. Approaches which search the current or the linearly preceding units to locate candidates for antecedents are referred to by Cristea et al. (2000) as *linear models* as opposed to the *hierarchical models* which consider candidates from the current or the hierarchically preceding discourse units such as the discourse-VT model based on veins theory (Cristea et al., 1998; also see Section 6). Cristea et al. (2000) show that, compared with linear models, the search scope of the discourse-VT model is smaller, which makes it computationally less expensive, and potentially more accurate in picking out the potential candidates. However, in fact, the automatic identi cation of veins cannot, at present, be performed with satisfactory accuracy and therefore this model is not yet suf ciently attractive for practical anaphora resolution systems.

4.2.3   The resolution algorithm: factors in anaphora resolution   Once the anaphors have been detected, the program will attempt to resolve them by selecting their antecedents from the identi ed sets of candidates. The resolution rules based on the different sources of knowledge and used in the resolution process (constituting the anaphora resolution algorithm), are usually referred to as *anaphora resolution factors*. These factors can be *constraints* which eliminate certain noun phrases from the set of possible candidates. The factors can also be *preferences* which favor certain candidates over others. Constraints are considered to be obligatory conditions that are imposed on the relation between the anaphor and its antecedent. Therefore, their strength lies in discounting candidates that do satisfy these conditions; unlike preferences, they do not propose any candidates. Typical constraints in anaphora resolution are gender and number agreement,[25] c-command constraints,[26] and selectional restrictions. Typical preferences are recency (the most recent candidate is more likely to be the antecedent), center preference in the sense of centering theory (the center of the previous clause is the most likely candidate for antecedent), or syntactic parallelism (candidates with the same syntactic function as the anaphor are the preferred antecedents). However, it should be made clear that it is not dif cult to nd examples which demonstrate that such preferences are not absolute factors since very often they are overriden by semantic or real-world constraints.[27] Approaches making use of syntactic constraints, such as Hobbs (1976, 1978) and Lappin and Leass (1994) or the knowledge-poor counterpart of the latter (Kennedy & Boguraev 1996), have been particularly successful and have received a great deal of attention, one of the reasons for this is that such constraints are good at ltering antecedent candidates at intra-sentential (within the sentence) level.

4.3   *Algorithms for anaphora resolution*

Anaphora resolution algorithms can be broadly classed into rule-based and machine learning (ML) approaches. Initially it was the rule-based approaches such as Hobbs's naïve algorithm (Hobbs 1976; 1978) and Lappin and Leass's (1994) resolution of anaphora procedure (henceforth RAP) which gained popularity (see below). In recent years there has been a considerable amount of work reported on machine learning (ML) approaches to pronoun (and, in general, to anaphora and coreference) resolution (Soon et al., 2001; Ng & Cardie 2002; Müller et al., 2002; Strube & Müller 2003). Ge et al.'s statistically enhanced implementation of Hobbs's algorithm has previously been reported to perform better than Hobbs's original algorithm itself (Ge et al., 1998), even outperforming Lappin and Leass's RAP (Preiss 2002c) and it is fair to say that ML approaches to anaphora resolution are/have been an important direction of research. However, the results from a number of studies (Barbu 2001; Preiss 2002a; Stuckardt 2002; 2004; 2005) suggest that ML algorithms for pronoun resolution do not necessarily perform better than traditional rule-based approaches.

In this section we shall brie y outline ve popular rule-based approaches: two approaches based on full parsing and three based on partial parsing. Historically, the approaches based on partial parsing (referred to as 'knowledge-poor approaches') were proposed in the 1990s and followed those applying to the output of full parsers. Most knowledge-poor algorithms share a similar pre-processing methodology. They do not rely on a parser to process the input and instead use POS taggers and NP extractors. Nor do any of the methods make use of semantic or real-world knowledge. The drive towards knowledge-poor and robust approaches was further motivated by the emergence of cheaper and more reliable corpus-based NLP tools such as POS taggers and shallow parsers, alongside the increasing availability of corpora and other NLP resources (e.g., ontologies). For a historical outline of anaphora resolution algorithms, see Mitkov (2002).

4.3.1   Approaches based on full parsing

4.3.1.1   Hobbs's naïve algorithm   Hobbs's (1976; 1978) naïve algorithm[28] operates on fully parsed sentences. The original approach assumes that the surface parse-trees represent the correct grammatical structure of the sentence with all adjunct phrases properly attached and that they feature 'syntactically recoverable omitted elements' such as elided verb phrases and other types of zero anaphors or zero antecedents. Hobbs also assumes that an NP node directly dominates an N-bar node, with the N-bar identifying a noun phrase without its determiner. Hobbs's algorithm traverses the surface parse-tree in a left-to-right and breadth- rst fashion, looking for a noun phrase of the correct gender and number. Parse-trees of previous sentences in the text are traversed in order of recency. Hobbs's algorithm was not implemented in its original form, but later implementations relied either on manually parsed corpora (Ge et al., 1998; Tetreault 1999) or a full parser (Dagan & Itai 1991; Lappin & Leass 1994; Baldwin 1997).

4.3.1.2 Lappin and Leass's RAP   Lappin and Leass's (1994) algorithm[29] termed resolution of anaphora procedure (RAP), operates on syntactic representations generated by McCord's slot grammar parser (McCord 1990; 1993). It relies on salience measures derived from syntactic structure as well as on a simple dynamic model of attentional state to select the antecedent of a pronoun from a list of NP candidates. RAP consists of the following components: an intrasentential syntactic lter, a morphological lter, a procedure for identifying pleonastic pronouns, an anaphor binding algorithm which handles re exive and reciprocal pronouns, a procedure for assigning values to several salience parameters for an NP, a procedure for identifying anaphorically linked NPs as an equivalence class, and a decision procedure for selecting the preferred candidate for antecedent. The algorithm does not employ semantic information or real-world knowledge in selecting from the candidates.

4.3.2   Approaches based on partial parsing

4.3.2.1 Mitkov's knowledge-poor approach   Mitkov's robust pronoun resolution approach[30] (Mitkov 1996; 1998) works from the output of a text processed by a part-of-speech tagger and an NP extractor, locates noun phrases which precede the anaphor within a distance of two sentences and checks for gender and number agreement. The resolution algorithm is based on a set of boosting and impeding indicators applied to each antecedent candidate. The boosting indicators assign a positive score to an NP, re ecting a likelihood that it is the antecedent of the current pronoun. In contrast, the impeding ones apply a negative score to an NP, re ecting a lack of con dence that it is the antecedent of the current pronoun. A score is calculated based on these indicators and the discourse referent with the highest aggregate value is selected as the antecedent.

4.3.2.2 Kennedy and Boguraev's approach   Kennedy and Boguraev (1996)[31] report on a modi ed version of Lappin and Leass's (1994) RAP which does not require full syntactic parsing but applies to the output of a part-of-speech tagger enriched with annotations of grammatical function. They use a phrasal grammar for identifying NP constituents and, similar to Lappin and Leass (1994), employ salience preferences to rank candidates for antecedents. The general idea is to construct coreference equivalence classes that have an associated value based on a set of ten factors. An attempt is then made to resolve every pronoun to one of the previously introduced discourse referents by taking into account the salience value of the class to which each possible antecedent belongs. It should be pointed out that Kennedy and Boguraev's approach is not a simple knowledge-poor adaptation of RAP. It is rather an extension, given that some of the factors used are unique.

4.3.2.3 Baldwin's CogNIAC   CogNIAC (Baldwin 1997)[32] makes use of limited knowledge and resources and its pre-processing includes sentence detection, part-of-speech tagging and recognition of base forms of noun phrases, as well as basic semantic category information such as gender and number (and, in one variant, partial parse-trees). The pronoun resolution algorithm employs a set of 'high-con dence' rules which are successively applied to the pronoun under consideration. The processing of a pronoun terminates after the application of the rst relevant rule. The original version of the algorithm is non-robust, a pronoun being resolved only if a speci c rule can be applied. The author also describes a robust extension of the algorithm, which employs two additional weak rules to be applied if no others are applicable.

4.3.3 Comparing pronoun resolution algorithms

Mitkov and Hallett (2007) compare the above ve algorithms using the evaluation workbench, an environment for comparative evaluation of rule-based anaphora resolution algorithms (Mitkov 2000; Barbu & Mitkov 2001). The evaluation was conducted on 2,597 anaphors from the three corpora, each one of them covering a different genre: technical manuals, newswire, and literary texts. The evaluation results show that, on the whole, Lappin and Leass's algorithm performed best (success rate 60.65 percent), followed closely by Hobbs's naïve algorithm (60.07 percent). Mitkov's approach was third and emerged as the best performing knowledge-poor algorithm (57.03 percent), followed by Kennedy and Boguraev's method (52.08 percent), both systems surpassing Baldwin's CogNIAC (37.66 percent).

These results con rm the results from previous studies (Mitkov et al., 2002) that fully automatic pronoun resolution is more dif cult than previous work had suggested. The results also depart signi cantly from the results reported in the authors' papers describing their algorithms. In fact, they are much lower than the original results reported. Mitkov and Hallett believe that the main reason for this is the fact that all algorithms implemented in the evaluation workbench operate in a fully automatic mode, whereas in their original form they relied on some form (to a lesser or higher degree) of post-editing of the output of their parsers, which of course favored the performance of the algorithm. As a result, some of the implemented algorithms could not bene t from speci c rules which required more accurate pre-processing, such as identi cation of pleonastic pronouns or identi cation of gender or animacy, identi cation of clauses within sentences, etc. Another important reason for the lower performance could have been the fact that the evaluation corpus of technical manuals used in their study was taken in its original format and as such featured texts that were frequently broken into non-narrative sections.

Mitkov and Hallett's results suggest that the best-performing pronoun resolution algorithms score slightly higher than 60 percent if they operate in a fully automatic mode. These results are comparable to those reported in a related independent study carried out by Preiss (2002b) which evaluates Lappin and Leass's algorithm with different parsers and which reports an average success rate of 61 percent when the pre-processing is done with Charniak's parser. In addition, different versions of Mitkov's algorithm were also evaluated on technical manuals in Mitkov et al. (2002) where the performance of the original, non-optimized version of this algorithm was comparable to the results reported in this paper.

5 Applications

5.1 *Text organization and discourse segmentation applications*

The way in which discourse is organized has been exploited in numerous NLP projects. As mentioned earlier, McKeown (1985) applies text organization strategies in the form of schemata of *rhetorical predicates* in *natural language generation*.

This explicit structure of scienti c papers in terms of moves (background information, problem, solution, evaluation, conclusion) was used by Teufel (1999) and Teufel and Moens (2002) to produce *summaries* automatically. Their work was based on the assumption that these moves can be identi ed not only in the full papers, but also in scienti c abstracts. The *automatic summarization* task is a two-stage procedure: identi cation of important sentences followed by recognition of moves also referred to as the *rhetorical roles* of the extracted sentences. For both stages, a Bayesian classi er inspired by the work described in Kupiec et al. (1995) is used. In order to classify sentences as worthy of inclusion in the summary and to identify their rhetorical roles, a set of low-level properties of sentences are extracted and used as features for the classi er. Examples of features include the presence of indicator phrases, the presence of indicator phrases which correspond to a particular rhetorical class, and sentence relative location. For training data, a corpus of 80 scienti c articles was annotated with information about the rhetorical category of each sentence. Teufel and Moens (2002) report an accuracy of 66 percent for the classi cation of sentences as being worth including in a summary. In addition, the classi er can identify the correct rhetorical role for 64 percent of the correctly extracted sentences.

Mitkov and Corpas (2008) employ the identi cation of *rhetorical predicates* to enhance the performance of a third generation *translation memory* system (Pekar & Mitkov 2007). This TM system attempts to match sentences (segments) not only in terms of syntax but also in terms of semantics. With semantic processing being far from perfect, if two sentences (segments) under consideration for a semantic match are also labeled with the same rhetorical predicate, the probability of their matching is increased.

The identi cation of subtopic segments within a text has been exploited in many different NLP applications, especially those concerned with processing long documents. These applications include high-level discourse planning in natural language generation, summarization of topic structure, visualization and the development of reading aids, information retrieval, and the ef cient navigation of documents.

In the area of information access, Tombaugh et al. (1987) found that a more ef -
cient way to read long texts on computer screens is to divide the screen into two
windows. The rst window displays information about the content of the overall
document and provides readers with visual cues about the locations of portions of
previously read text. This information can be presented as a ne-grained hyper-
linked table of contents that assists readers in their recall and ability to quickly
locate information that has already been read once. The second window of the
interface displays the segment of text associated with the hyperlink selected in the
 rst. Hearst (1997) notes that the effectiveness of such systems is improved when
they are capable of tokenizing long texts in terms of subtopic segments as opposed
to sentences or paragraphs.

Choi (2000) uses discourse segmentation to improve document navigation for
users who have visual impairment. Under his approach, telegraphic text compression methods are applied to sentences and topic segments in a text in order to
create an index of entries that are read to the visually impaired user. The user may
then select entries of interest to be read more fully.

Hearst (1997) also demonstrates that discourse segmentation could be useful in
presenting a *search engine*'s results to a user. In the implemented *TileBar* system,
returned documents are presented visually, in the form of bars in which different
subtopic segments are represented by 'tiles' color-coded according to their relevance to the input query. Clicking on a tile in the bar allows the user to access the
full document, with the browser initially displaying the discourse segment that
corresponds to the clicked tile.

Mooney et al. (1990) use linear discourse segmentation in the *generation* of
explanatory text. The authors argued that hierarchical structures of the kind
derived under approaches such as RST do not apply well to the generation of
extended explanations in which it is important to accurately obtain the high-
level structure of the hierarchy. They show that discourse segmentation is more
appropriate for high-level discourse planning in a natural language generation
system.

Discourse segmentation has also been used to facilitate automatic *text summarization*. It is useful when summarizing long documents to identify different
topic segments within the input text and then apply a summarization method to
each topic in turn, concatenating and returning those outputs in the nal summary. Barzilay and Elhadad (1997) used an approach to discourse segmentation to
produce a model of topic progression for a text for this purpose.

Harabagiu and Lacatusu (2005) employ ve different topic representation
approaches, including the *TextTiling* algorithm (Hearst 1997) to generate multi-
document summaries. Boguraev and Neff (2000) propose a summarization
methodology based on linear discourse segmentation. Topic shifts are detected in a
text and integrated into a linguistically aware summarizer which exploits salience
by picking different chains of cohesively connected segments. Angheluta et al.
(2002) use generic topical cues for identifying the thematic structure of a text to
extract summaries in the form of tables of contents. Following this work, Moens
(2008) also describes a system which segments a text into topics and subtopics

and which she uses for the *generation of tables of contents*. Each segment is characterized by important key terms which are extracted from it as well as by its start and end position in the text. A table of contents is built using the hierarchical and sequential relationships between topical segments identi ed in a text. The table of contents generator employs linguistic theories (deterministically and probabilistically modeled) related to the topic and comment of a sentence. It also utilizes patterns of thematic progression in text. The system is applied to English texts (news, web, and encyclopedic texts).

5.2 *Applications of discourse coherence theories*

Rhetorical structure theory (RST) was initially developed with text generation in mind (Mann & Thompson 1987) but later received considerable attention from a number of NLP researchers. RST was widely used in summarization, mainly due to Marcu's (1997; 2000) work.

The distinction between nuclei and satellites made in *rhetorical structure theory* was successfully employed to produce summaries automatically (Ono et al., 1994; Marcu 1997; Corston-Oliver 1998). The underlying idea of these methods is that a summary can be produced from the rhetorical structure tree by keeping only the nuclei and removing the satellites. According to RST, the understanding of nuclei does not depend on the satellites, and therefore the resulting summary is a coherent text. This method is dif cult to use because it is not trivial to determine the type of each span and the relations between them. In addition, the method also requires the organization of the spans into a tree structure.

Ono et al. (1994) determine relations between sentences or blocks of sentences in Japanese texts using linguistic clues such as connectives, anaphoric expressions, and idiomatic expressions. These relations are used to evaluate the importance of each sentence and to produce a summary. The method was evaluated on 30 editorial articles and 42 technical papers that were annotated with information which indicated the important sentences. The proposed method extracts 60 percent of the most important sentences from editorials and 74 percent from technical papers. The authors argue that their method is very useful because the generated abstract contains well-connected units rather than fragmentary sentences.

A formalized algorithm to build rhetorical structure (RS) trees was proposed by Marcu (1997). The algorithm operates in three stages. First, it determines the textual units and the discourse markers, and hypothesizes a set of relations between the units. On the basis of these elements, in the second step all the trees satisfying a set of constraints are built. The last step of the algorithm is to choose the best tree among the ones constructed in the previous step. A corpus analysis was used to identify the set of constraints and discourse markers used by the algorithm, as well as how the best tree should be built. Once the tree is constructed, it is possible to determine a partial order between the units of the text, which in turn can be used to produce summaries of the desired length. The approach was evaluated on ve texts, and comparison between the units annotated by human judges;

those selected by the program as important reported a recall of 52.77 percent and precision of 50 percent.

The algorithm proposed by Marcu can prove very slow in building the tree as it tries all the possible combinations of units. This problem is addressed by Corston-Oliver (1998), who proposes an algorithm to build RS trees which combines a backtracking algorithm with a greedy approach. In addition, the algorithm does not rely only on cue phrases, as is the case in most of the previous work, but instead it combines them with syntactic analysis and logical form. Even though Corston-Oliver's work is presented in the context of automatic summarization, the paper contains only a preliminary evaluation of the quality of the RST produced.

Rhetorical information is also used by Alonso i Alemany and Fuentes Fort (2003) to improve the performance of a *summarizer* based on lexical chains. Instead of building the RS tree of the source, and producing a summary based on the tree, rhetorical relations between textual units are used to further compress the text by removing the satellites of the selected sentences. In addition, the argumentative structure of the text is used to boost a lexical cohesion method. The advantage of this method is that it only requires the identi cation of the spans and the relations between them, and not the building of the whole tree.

Whereas the most popular application of *centering theory* has been in anaphora resolution algorithms (Brennan et al., 1987; Walker 1989; Tetreault 1999; 2001), it was also successfully used in automatic summarization to produce and evaluate summaries. Barzilay and Lapata (2005b) discuss how local coherence can be used in multi-document summarization by building an entity grid which captures the transitions between sentences. Orasan (2006) takes a similar approach to that used in text generation by Karamanis and Manurung (2002) and produces summaries which minimize the number of violations of the *continuity principle*.[33] Evaluation of the summaries produced reveals that the summaries are more informative than those produced using other methods, but not necessarily more coherent as initially assumed. The justi cation for this is that centering theory is a theory of local cohesion, so it cannot deal very well with sentences extracted from different parts of a document.

Hasler (2007) uses centering theory to evaluate summaries. Even though, in her case, the summaries are analyzed manually, the proposed method could be easily implemented with a view to conducting automatic analysis. The evaluation method assigns scores to summaries on the basis of a preferred ordering of transitions which occur between utterances within them. Pairs of summaries were compared by judges using the proposed method, and an agreement rate of 70 percent was observed.

Miltsakaki and Kukich (2004) apply centering theory to improve the task of *essay scoring*. They experiment with the *e-rater* essay scoring system and nd that the use of rough-shift transitions as a measure of local discourse coherence contributes to the task of essay evaluation. More speci cally, a metric based on rough-shift (see Section 3.3) improves the performance of e-rater signi cantly, in that it better approximates human scores and provides the option of giving additional instructional feedback to the student. A by-product of this project is the con rmation that the rough-shift transition, insuf ciently covered in the literature, reliably accounts for incoherence.

5.3 *Anaphora resolution applications*

Anaphora resolution has been extensively applied in NLP. The successful iden- ti cation of anaphoric or coreferential links is vital to a number of applications such as machine translation, automatic abstracting, dialogue systems, question answering, and information extraction.

The interpretation of anaphora is crucial for the successful operation of a *machine translation* system. In particular, it is essential to resolve anaphoric relations when translating into languages which mark the gender of pronouns. Unfortunately, the majority of MT systems developed do not adequately address the problems of identifying the antecedents of anaphors in the source language and producing the anaphoric 'equivalents' in the target language. As a consequence, only a limited number of MT systems have been successful in translating discourse, rather than isolated sentences. One reason for this situation is that, in addition to anaphora resolution itself being a very complicated task, translation adds a further dimen- sion to the problem in that the reference to a discourse entity encoded by a source language anaphor by the speaker (or writer) has not only to be identi ed by the hearer (translator or translation system), but also re-encoded in a different lan- guage. This complexity is partly due to gender discrepancies across languages, to number discrepancies of words denoting the same concept, to discrepancies in the gender inheritance of possessive pronouns, and discrepancies in target-language anaphor selection (Mitkov & Schmidt 1998).

Anaphora resolution in information extraction could be regarded as part of the coreference resolution task which takes the form of merging partial data objects about the same entities, entity relationships, and events described at different discourse positions. The importance of coreference resolution in *information extrac- tion* has led to the inclusion of the coreference resolution task in the Message Understanding Conferences (MUC-6 and MUC-7). This in turn gave considerable impetus to the development of coreference resolution algorithms and as a result several new systems emerged (Baldwin et al., 1995; Kameyama 1997; Gaizauskas & Humphreys 2000).

Researchers in *text summarization* are increasingly interested in anaphora res- olution since techniques for extracting important sentences are more accurate if anaphoric references of indicative concepts are taken into account as well. More generally, coreference and coreferential chains have been extensively exploited for abstracting purposes. Baldwin and Morton (1998) describe a query-sensitive doc- ument summarization technique which extracts sentences containing phrases that corefer with expressions in the query. Azzam et al. (1999) use coreferential chains to produce abstracts by selecting a 'best' chain to represent the main topic of a text. The output is simply the concatenation of sentences from the original docu- ment which contain one or more expressions occurring in the selected coreferential chain. Boguraev and Kennedy (1997) employ their anaphora resolution algorithm (Kennedy & Boguraev 1996) in what they call 'content characterization' of technical documents. Orasan (2006; 2009), Mitkov et al. (2007), and Kabadjov (2007) investigated the effect of anaphora resolution on text summarization. The results of these studies suggest that fully automatic anaphora resolution in spite of its low performance still has a bene cial, albeit limited, effect on text summarization. An interesting observation from these studies is that, once the success rate of anaphora resolution reaches levels closer to 80 percent, summarization is almost guaranteed to improve and that the performance of a summarizer also depends on how anaphoric knowledge is incorporated.

It should be noted that *cross-document coreference resolution* has emerged as an important trend due to its role in *cross-document summarization*. Bagga and Baldwin (1998) describe an approach to cross-document coreference resolution which extracts all sentences containing expressions coreferential with a speci c entity (e.g., *John Smith*) from each of several documents. In order to establish cross-document coreference and, in this particular application, decide whether the documents discuss the same entity (i.e., the same *John Smith*), the authors employ a vector space model to resolve ambiguities between people having the same name. Witte et al. (2005) identify both within-document and cross-document coreference chains in order to establish the most important entities within a document or across documents and produce a summary on the basis of one or several documents.

Coreference resolution has proven to be helpful in question answering (QA). Morton (1999) retrieves answers to queries by establishing coreference links between entities or events in the query and those in the documents.[34] The sentences in the searched documents are ranked according to the coreference relationships, and the highest-ranked sentences are displayed to the user. Anaphora resolution is employed for question answering in Harabagiu et al. (2001a). Watson et al. (2003) demonstrate experimentally that anaphora resolution is highly relevant to open domain QA. Recent experiments employing anaphora resolution in QA are reported in Negri and Koulekov (2007) and in Bouma et al. (2007).

Mitkov et al. (2007) also conducted a study to investigate the impact of anaphora resolution on *term extraction* and *text categorization*. As in the case of the results on summarization, fully automatic anaphora resolution with performance in the range of 50 percent has a positive, albeit limited, effect. Finally, Hendrickx et al. (2008) report similar impact of coreference resolution with regard to *information extraction*.

6 Further Reading

Kehler (1995) shows how the recognition of coherence relations affects the interpretation of a variety of linguistic phenomena including verb phrase ellipsis, gapping, tense, and pronominal reference. In later work, Kehler et al. (2008: 2) revisit Hobbs's theory which maintains that the mechanisms supporting pronoun interpretation are "driven predominantly by semantics, world knowledge, and inference, with particular attention drawn to how these are used to establish the coherence of a discourse." On the basis of three new experimental studies, the authors evaluate a coherence-driven analysis with respect to four previously proposed interpretation biases – grammatical role parallelism, thematic roles, implicit causality, and subjecthood – and argue that the coherence-driven analysis can explain the underlying source of the biases and predict in what contexts evidence for each will surface.

Radev (2000) introduces *cross-structure theory* (CST), which describes relationships between two or more sentences from different source documents related to the same topic. CST is related to *rhetorical structure theory* (RST) but takes into account the features of multi-document structure and does not have an underlying tree representation or make assumptions about writers' intentions. There are 18 domain-independent relations such as *identity, equivalence, subsumption, contradiction, overlap, fulfilment*, and *elaboration* between text spans. Radev argues that being aware of these relations during multi-document summarization could help to minimize redundancy or the inclusion of contradictions from different sources, and therefore improve the quality of the summary. Radev et al. (2003) developed the CSTBank, a corpus annotated for CST which could be useful for multi-document summarization as it provides a theoretical model for issues that arise when trying to summarize multiple texts.

Strube (1998) proposes an alternative framework to centering by replacing the backward looking center and the centering transitions with an ordered list of salient discourse entities (referred to as *S-list*). The S-list ranking gives preference to hearer-old over hearer-new discourse entities (Prince 1981) and can account for the difference in salience between de nite NPs (usually hearer-old) and inde nite NPs (usually hearer-new). In contrast to centering, Strube's model can also handle intra-sentential anaphora.

Kibble (2001) discusses a reformulation of the centering transitions. Instead of de ning a total preference ordering, the author argues that a partial ordering emerges from the interaction between 'cohesion' (maintaining the same center), 'salience' (realizing the center as subject), and Strube and Hahn's notion of 'cheapness' (realizing the anticipated center of a following utterance as subject).

A corpus-based study (Poesio et al., 2000; 2004) investigates the validity of the claim that each utterance has exactly one backward looking center (apart from the rst utterance in the discourse segment) and of the claim stating that, if any Cf (U_N) is pronominalized in U_{N+1}, then Cb (U_{N+1}) must also be pronominalized. It found that both these claims are subject to frequent violation. The authors experimented with different de nitions of utterances (Suri & McCoy 1994; Kameyama 1998) such as sentences or nite clauses, and also treating adjuncts as embedded utterances. They allowed a discourse entity to serve as a Cb of an utterance even if it was only indirectly referred to by a bridging reference. This led to fewer violations of the rst claim but to more violations of the second. The study concludes that texts can be coherent even if the above claims do not hold since coherence can be achieved by other means such as rhetorical relations.

Mitkov and Orasan (2004) report on another corpus-based study whose aim is to evaluate speci c conventions of centering theory and to establish whether they should be revisited. In particular, their study explores the relation between discourse coherence and several parameters such as the de nition of an utterance, the varieties of anaphora considered, the forms of the discourse entities, and the type of genre. The results obtained in this study point to a number of interesting observations which merit further investigation. Mitkov and Orasan nd that the centering theory considers a discourse more coherent in English, when possessive pronouns and zero pronouns are also counted as discourse units. In this case de ning the utterance as a coordinate clause would by and large result in better coherence than if only sentences were considered. In most cases counting indirect realizations yielded improved coherence. The study also found that the sample of newswire texts was more coherent than the sample of encyclopedic texts. Whereas the authors cautiously regard the study carried out and the results obtained as preliminary, they believe that they indicate the value of revisiting some of the current conventions in centering theory – e.g., reconsidering issues like the best de nition of an utterance or a discourse entity, and asking whether indirect realization should be counted as well.

Cristea et al. (1998) propose veins theory (VT) as a generalization of centering theory by extending the applicability of centering rules from local to global discourse. The authors de ne veins over discourse structure trees similar to the trees used in RST which delimit domains of referential accessibility for each unit in a discourse. Once identi ed, reference chains can be extended across segment boundaries, thus enabling the application of centering theory over the entire discourse.

Walker et al. (1998) is a good collection of papers on centering.

For a detailed account on *anaphora resolution*, the reader is referred to Mitkov (2002). For the latest research on anaphora resolution, see the proceedings of the recent Discourse Anaphora and Anaphor Resolution Colloquium (DAARC) conferences or the volumes based on these conferences (e.g., Branco 2007; Branco et al., 2005).

For work and publications on *dialogue*, see Chapter 16 of this book, COMPUTATIONAL MODELS OF DIALOGUE. Recently there has been growing interest in *multiparty dialogue* (e.g., Purver et al., 2006; 2007; Gupta et al., 2007; Ehlen et al., 2008; Hawes et al., 2008).

Of the *surveys* on the computational treatment of discourse, chapter 21 in Jurafsky and Martin (2009) is worth reading.

ACKNOWLEDGMENT

I am greatly indebted to Constantin Orasan, Gloria Corpas, Elena Lloret, Laura Pack-Hagan, Erin Phillips, and especially Richard Evans for their help, comments, and suggestions.

NOTES

1 www.ldoceonline.com/
2 Cohesion is exhibited at grammatical level through the use of anaphora, ellipsis, or substitution (*grammatical cohesion*), or at lexical level through the repetitions of words (*lexical cohesion*). As with many linguistic phenomena, grammatical cohesion and lexical cohesion cannot always be regarded as clear-cut distinctions and there are borderline cases (Halliday & Hasan 1976: 6).
3 Monologues are usually intended for a reader or readership (in the case of a writer) or hearer or audience (in the case of a speaker) but may not be intended for any readership or audience (as in the case of personal diaries). Monologues may have more than one author.
4 Dialogue usually involves freer interchange and turn taking.
5 This includes informal, spontaneous conversation which includes the principles of taking of turns. See Chapter 16, COMPUTATIONAL MODELS OF DIALOGUE, for more on dialogue.
6 This example was used for illustrative purposes in McKeown (1985).
7 Rhetorical structure theory (RST) (see Section 3.2 of this chapter) and other discourse theories such as discourse representation theory (Kamp & Reyle 1993) represent hierarchical structures and relations, and do not merely reﬂect linear sequences of topics.
8 In very broad terms, we can think of an utterance as a ﬁnite clause or a sentence (in fact, this is one of the various parameters that need to be deﬁned when employing centering).
9 Centering does not assign a center to the ﬁrst utterance of a discourse segment.
10 To simplify notation, I shall drop D which denotes the discourse segment of which the utterance is part.
11 The backward looking center is often referred to simply as the center. However, the qualiﬁcation 'backward looking' is in line with the requirement that the backward looking center of a current utterance establishes a link to the previous utterance and must be on its list of forward looking centers.
12 Apart from the initial utterance of a discourse segment.
13 This statement is valid for English and for a number of other languages.
14 According to Grosz et al. (1995), the ﬁrst utterance in a discourse segment is not assigned a center. It could be argued that there are cases where the most salient element is clearly identiﬁable even in the ﬁrst utterance (e.g., with cleft constructions).
15 Note that if there is one pronoun, it realizes the center (see below, rule 1).
16 As deﬁned by Brennan et al. (1987), smooth-shift is preferred to rough-shift.
17 Deleted as a zero pronoun in languages exhibiting extensive use of zero pronouns such as Japanese, Italian, Spanish, and Bulgarian.
18 Note that *she* and *her* in U_3 cannot be coreferential (see Section 4.1 for deﬁnition of coreferential).
19 The word (phrase) 'pointing back' is also called a *referring expression* if it has a referential function.
20 In identity-of-sense anaphora, the anaphor and the antecedent do not correspond to the same referent in the real world but to ones of a similar description.

21   Deictic expressions are those words whose interpretation is derived from speci c features of the utterance (e.g., who the speaker is, who the addressee is, where and when the utterance takes place), and not from previously introduced words, as is the case with anaphors.

22   It should be noted that these are only the basic relationships between the anaphoric de nite NP and the antecedent but not all possible relations.

23   Note that some authors consider synonymy, generalization, and specialization as examples of indirect anaphora.

24   Discourse segments are stretches of discourse in which the sentences are addressing the same topic (Allen 1995).

25   However, Barlow (1998) and Mitkov (2002) point out that there are a number of exceptions.

26   A node A c-commands a node B if and only if (1) A does not dominate B, (2) B does not dominate A, and (3) the rst branching node dominating A also dominates B (Haegeman 1994). Therefore, in a tree generated by the rules S → AB, A → E, B → CD, C → F, and D → G, A c-commands B, C, F, D, and G, B c-commands A and E, C c-commands D and G, and D c-commands C and F.

27   Mitkov (2002) explains that constraints and preferences usually work in combination towards the goal of identifying the antecedent. Applying a speci c constraint or preference alone may not result in the tracking down of the antecedent.

28   The original algorithm handles personal and possessive pronouns whose antecedents are NPs.

29   The original algorithm handles third-person pronouns, including re exives and reciprocals, whose antecedents are NPs.

30   The original algorithm handles third-person personal pronouns whose antecedents are NPs.

31   The original algorithm handles personal, re exive, and possessive third-person pronouns whose antecedents are NPs.

32   The original algorithm handles third-person personal pronouns whose antecedents are NPs.

33   The continuity principle is the most general of the four principles proposed in Kibble and Power (2000) to rede ne centering theory and requires that two consecutive utterances have at least one entity in common. The nal version of Kibble and Power (2000) does not use any name for this principle, but it is referred to as continuity principle in Karamanis and Manurung (2002).

34   The coreference relationships that Morton's system supports are identity, part–whole, and synonymy.

22 Question Answering

BONNIE WEBBER AND NICK WEBB

1 What is Question Answering?

Questions are asked and answered every day. Question answering (QA) technology aims to deliver the same facility online. It goes further than the more familiar search based on *keywords* (as in Google, Yahoo, and other search engines), in attempting to recognize what a question expresses and to respond with an actual answer. This simpli es things for users in two ways. First, questions do not often translate into a simple list of keywords. For example, the question

(1) Which countries did the pope visit in the 1960s?

does not simply translate to the keywords 'countries,' 'pope,' 'visit,' '1960s' because a search on those keywords will only nd documents (web pages) that contain the *words* 'countries' (or 'country,' if the search engine recognizes plurals), 'pope,' and '1960s,' and not words or phrases that denote particular countries (such as 'United Kingdom,' or the 'United States'), or the pope ('head of the Catholic church,' for example), or a date within the 10-year time span between '1960' and '1970.' A much more complex set of keywords is needed in order to get anywhere close to the intended result, and experience shows that people will not learn how to formulate and use such sets.

Second, QA takes responsibility for providing answers, rather than a searchable list of links to potentially relevant documents (web pages), highlighted by *snippets* of text that show how the query matched the documents. While this is not much of a burden when the answer appears in a snippet and further document access is unnecessary, QA technology aims to move this from being an accidental property of search to its focus.

In keyword search and in much work to date on QA technology, the information seeking process has been seen as a one-shot affair: the user asks a question, and the system provides a satisfactory response. However, early work on QA (Section 1.1) did not make this assumption, and newly targeted applications are hindered by it: while a user may try to formulate a question whose answer is the information

The Handbook of Computational Linguistics and Natural Language Processing, First Edition.
Edited by Alexander Clark, Chris Fox and Shalom Lappin.
© 2013 Blackwell Publishing Ltd except for editorial material and organization
© 2013 Alexander Clark, Chris Fox, and Shalom Lappin. Published 2013 by Blackwell Publishing Ltd.

they want, they will not know whether they have succeeded until something has been returned for examination. If what is returned is unsatisfactory or, while not the answer, is still of interest, a user needs to be able to ask further questions that are understood in the context of the previous ones. For these target applications, QA must be part of a collaborative search process (Section 3.3).

In the rest of this section, we give some historical background on QA systems (Section 1.1), on dialogue systems in which QA has played a signi cant role (Section 1.2), and on a particular QA task that has been a major driver of the eld over the past 8 years (Section 1.3). Section 2 describes the current state of the art in QA systems, organized around the de facto architecture of such systems. Section 3 discusses some current directions in which QA is moving, including the development of *interactive QA*. We close with some pointers to further reading.

1.1   Early question answering systems

Early QA systems were developed to enable users to ask interesting questions about well-structured data sets such as baseball statistics, personnel data, or chemical analyses of lunar rock and soil samples. (Simmons (1965) provides an early survey.) These early QA systems essentially attached a front end and a back end to a database system. The front end performed parsing and interpretation, mapping questions phrased in everyday terms onto a form that speci ed a *computation* to be carried out over the database – for example, the question

(2)   What is the average concentration of aluminum in high-alkali rocks?

would be mapped to a computation that identi es the high-alkali rocks in the database,   nds the aluminum concentration in each, and then computes an average over those values.

Given the potential complexity of such queries, differences between the system's and the user's underlying models of the data, as well as users' frequent lack of awareness of what information is actually in the database, early QA development focused on such issues as:

- mapping user questions to computable database queries;
- handling questions that could not be parsed or that could not be interpreted as a valid query;
- resolving syntactic and referential ambiguities detected in questions;
- handling differences in how user and system conceptualized the domain (e.g., user queries about the age of lunar rocks versus system data on potassium/ rubidium and uranium isotope ratios, as well as differences between what user and system believed to be true in the domain (Kaplan 1982; Mays et al., 1982; Pollack 1986; Webber 1986);
- identifying, in the case of distributed databases, what information needed to be imported from where, in order to answer the user's question (Hendrix et al., 1978).

User–system interactions designed to resolve ambiguities or reconcile mismatches between user and system beliefs about the domain showed that satisfying a user's information needs required the user to do more than just ask questions and the system to do more than just answer them. But systems were still viewed as question answerers, carrying out other types of interactions on an 'as needed' basis.

This rst foray into database QA was essentially abandoned in the late 1980s for two reasons – one technical, and one social. Technically, considerable effort was needed to guarantee an effective and reliable mapping between user questions and database queries. Not only did the correct mapping depend on the structure of the particular database, but many disparately phrased user questions needed to be mapped onto the same database query. Even worse, questions that differed only minimally needed to be mapped onto very different database queries. The only solution to these problems available at the time was more and more mapping rules that had to be written by hand by system experts. As a solution, this was neither scalable nor portable. The social problem involved the lack of a signi cant audience for the technology: ordinary people lacked access to large data sets, and managers whose companies maintained large data sets lacked suf cient interest in accessing the data themselves. Companies such as Symantic which developed state-of-the-art software for database QA (Hendrix 1986) ended up abandoning it.

With the advent of the web, this social problem disappeared, and machine learning techniques that have proved so useful in other areas of language technology are beginning to be applied to the problem of learning (complex) mappings between user questions and database queries (Mooney 2007; Zettlemoyer & Collins 2007). While it is still early days, this does mean that the growing number of databases containing rich and useful information may again be primed for access through natural language questions.

1.2   *Question answering in dialogue systems*

QA was also a feature of early systems whose main purpose in interacting with users in natural language was something other than answering their questions. In one of the earliest of such *dialogue systems*, SHRDLU (Winograd 1973), users could converse with an animated robot (with a visible arm) that could both act (in response to user requests) and re ect on its actions (in response to user questions). More generally, users could question SHRDLU about the state of its world (e.g., where objects were, what objects were where) or about its previous actions or its plans (e.g., why or when it performed some action), which SHRDLU could answer in terms of the history it maintained of its goals and actions.

Interactions with SHRDLU, and with another animated robot system called the Basic Agent (Vere & Bickmore 1990), were through typed text. Later systems supported limited speech interaction (Allen et al., 1996; Lemon et al., 2001; Eliasson 2007). Because these robots did not have any goals of their own, apart from those adopted in response to user requests/commands, and because no mechanism was provided for user–robot collaboration, the dialogic capability of these systems did not extend to asking questions of the user or to making requests themselves.

Other more recent dialogue systems, which take on other roles with respect to the user, also include QA capabilities in their repertoire. In *intelligent tutoring systems*, the system has goals in its role of tutor – e.g., assessing the student's knowledge, correcting the student's errors, and imparting information that the student is missing. Dialogues can thus involve the system introducing and describing a topic for tutoring, after which it might ask the student a question about some aspect of the problem, explain why the student's response is correct or incorrect, and/or remind the student of something already said previously during the interaction. Here, it is the student who answers questions or says he/she does not know, but it is still the system's job to determine if an answer is correct. Again, the earliest tutoring systems, like SOPHIE (Brown & Burton 1975), interacted through typed text, while later systems such as ITSPOKE (Litman & Forbes-Riley 2006) allow for spoken interaction.

The most industrially relevant role played by dialogue systems has been in information provision and user assistance, such as in helping users to plan travel (Goddeau et al., 1994), book ights (Seneff 2002), or nd an appropriate restaurant (Walker et al., 2004), or in routing user telephone calls (Chu-Carroll & Carpenter 1999) or handling directory inquiries (de Roeck et al., 2000). All such tasks involve the system getting suf cient information from the user to fully or partially instantiate some form (often called a *frame*) which the system can evaluate (just like a database query) and present the results to the user as a basis for further interaction. In such cases, the user's information needs may be anywhere from completely formed to vague. They may or may not be able to be satis ed given the underlying data, and queries may need to be reformulated on the basis of additional knowlege and relaxed constraints. Dialogues can thus involve the system asking the user questions related to values of frame elements; the user specifying such values (either precisely or vaguely); the system listing and/or describing the results (when too numerous to list); the user choosing some item from among the results or modifying or replacing some already speci ed values; and the system requesting con rmation of its understanding.

A key emerging element of dialogue approaches is their inherent generality – the potential for subdialogue structures independent of task or application (such as for error correction or clari cation) that will, in the future, allow them to be seamlessly integrated with QA systems (Section 3.3). For more detailed discussion of the issues and technology underlying dialogue systems, see Chapter 16, COMPUTATIONAL MODELS OF DIALOGUE.

1.3   *Question answering in TREC*

Returning to straight QA systems, the advent of the web has made increasing amounts of information accessible to people. To nd the bits of interest, people are using search methods pioneered in text retrieval (a eld revitalized by the web), but scaled up to nearly instant response to vast numbers of users. In this context, QA too has found a second life, with the idea that users would nd not just relevant documents (web content), but the particular information they are seeking.

This vision of QA differs signi cantly from QA over databases, where (as noted in Section 1.1) questions map onto *computations* carried out over a database of known structure. Instead, in what has been called *open domain question answering*, the answer to a question must be *found* and *extracted* rather than *computed*, as a natural extension to text retrieval. Advances in open domain QA have been accelerated by its adoption within the Text Retrieval Conference (TREC).

Initially, TREC QA focused on 'factoid' questions – questions of *who, what, where*, and, to some extent, *when*, that can be answered by a short word or phrase. From 1999 to 2007, TREC QA advanced on several fronts, to address increasingly large document collections, increasingly complex questions, and increasingly complex evaluation strategies. While the basic approach to factoid QA is now well understood, challenges remain. This basic approach and the current state of the art are described in Section 2, and some challenges that are now beginning to be addressed, in Section 3.

2   Current State of the Art in Open Domain QA

A basic QA system involves a cascade of processes that takes a user's question as input and responds in the end with an answer or rank-ordered list of top answer candidates, along with an indication of the source of the information (see Figure 22.1). This embodies the de facto paradigm for QA characterized by Paşca (2007) as:

- retrieve potentially relevant documents;
- extract potential answers (called here *answer candidates*);
- return top answer(s).

We discuss *question typing* in Section 2.1, *query construction* and *text retrieval* in Section 2.2, *text processing for answer candidates* (including weighting, ranking, and ltering candidates) in Section 2.3, and *answer rendering* in Section 3.3. Performance evaluation is brie y discussed in Sections 2.4 and 3.4, and at greater length in Chapter 11, EVALUATION OF NLP SYSTEMS.

2.1   *Question typing*

Questions generally undergo two initial processes to identify what type of information is being sought (*question typing*) and in what piece of text it is likely to be found (*query construction*). Although these processes can be carried out in parallel, *query construction* is so intimately tied up with *text retrieval*, that we will discuss them together in Section 2.2. *Question typing* aims to associate a label (QType) with

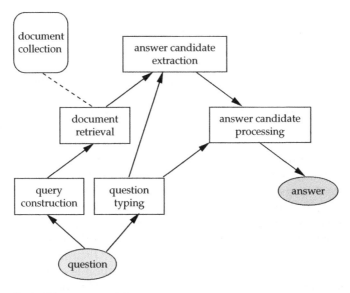

Figure 22.1   Basic QA system architecture.

a question, indicating the kind of information being sought – e.g., the meaning of an abbreviation (ABBREV) or of a word or phrase (DEFINITION), the name of the person who has or had some particular property or set of properties (PERSON), etc. For more on the location of speci c entities in text, see Section 3 on name extraction in Chapter 18, INFORMATION EXTRACTION. These labels provide testable semantic constraints on possible answer candidates. Labels assigned by *question typing* have also been used to support *text retrieval* through *predictive annotation* (Section 2.2), as well as to support the processing involved with identifying and ranking answer candidates. For example, a system that has done text retrieval on short passages may lter out ones that lack anything of the appropriate type as an answer candidate (Section 2.3).

While manually constructed rules have been used for *question typing* – for example,

- If the question starts with *Who* or *Whom*, QType is PERSON.
- If the question starts with *Where*, QType is LOCATION.

state-of-the art systems (Li & Roth 2006; Moschitti et al., 2007) use probabilistic classi ers, P(QType | Q), where the question Q is represented as a set of features. The features used have become more sophisticated over time, now extending to syntactic and semantic, as well as lexical features.

Using syntactic features alone, Li and Roth (2006) achieve state-of-the-art performance, using the SNoW classi er (Carlson et al., 1999) over the question types in the widely available TREC 10 and 11 question sets (Voorhees 2002; available from http://l2r.cs.uiuc.edu/~cogcomp/). This corpus of 1,000 manually annotated questions has both coarse-grain (i.e., ABBREVIATION, ENTITY, DESCRIPTION, HUMAN, LOCATION, NUMERIC) question types, and a further 50 re nements of those categories (so for example the coarse-grain category HUMAN can be represented by four ne-grain categories: GROUP, INDIVIDUAL, TITLE, and DESCRIPTION). For the coarse-grain question types, Li and Roth (2006) achieve 92.5 percent accuracy, and 85 percent on the ne grain. Using semantic information, including named entities and some manually extracted word class information, did not signi cantly improve classi cation accuracy over the coarse-grain question types, but boosted accuracy over the ne-grain categories to 89.3 percent.

Such accuracy gures disguise the fact that a question can often have more than one type of answer. For example, is *What is an SME?* an ABBREV question for which an appropriate strategy would involve patterns commonly used to relate abbreviations with their full-text forms, or is it a DESCRIPTION question, for which an appropriate strategy would involve patterns commonly used in de ning terms? A *who* question may be answered by a PERSON (*Who won the Masters tournament in 1985?*), or an ORGANIZATION (*Who won the Nobel Peace Prize in 1999?*), or a COUNTRY (*Who won the World Cup in 2006?*). When a question is asked, a system may know neither which kind of information the user is seeking nor what information the corpus contains. Allowing questions to have more than one possible type permits the system to rst see what kind of answers the corpus supports and, if more than one, provide the user with answers that cover the different alternatives. It is only because TREC has required systems to produce a single minimal answer to a question that work on QA has by and large ignored the possibilities of such helpful responses.

2.2   Query construction and text retrieval

In open domain QA, questions are always answered with respect to a corpus of texts. This can be as vast and diverse as the web or more specialized, such as the collection of biomedical abstracts in MedLine (www.ncbi.nlm.nih.gov/PubMed) or the collection of news articles in the AQUAINT corpus (Voorhees & Tice 2000). Because both the types of queries that one can construct and their success in retrieving text with good answer candidates re ect characteristics of the corpus and its access methods, it makes sense to discuss *query construction* and *text retrieval* together. More speci cally, the kind of query a system constructs depends on which of two forms of retrieval is used to nd text that might contain an answer to a user's question: *relevance-based retrieval* or *pattern-based retrieval*. These are discussed in the next subsections.

2.2.1   Relevance-based retrieval   In *relevance-based retrieval*, queries are interpreted as requests for texts *relevant to* a topic. Relevance may be assessed in terms of MATCHING a Boolean combination of terms or proximity to a weighted vector of terms or language model, just as in standard text retrieval (Manning et al., 2008). The problem, as already noted, is that QA demands answers, rather than the texts that contain them, and such answers are generally expressed very *locally* in a text. (With complex questions, the evidence supporting an answer may actually be distributed across one or even several texts. This is discussed in Section 3.2.) Although standard word-based indexing of texts supports very fast and ef cient retrieval, such indexing characterizes texts in terms of their gross lexical properties, not by local information. For example, a news article on the 1987 *Herald of Free Enterprise* ferry disaster may mention in passing 'It was the worst peacetime disaster involving a British ship since the *Titanic* sank in 1912.' While this sentence contains an answer to the question

(3)　When did the *Titanic* sink?

this local information might simply be noise with respect to more prominent lexical properties of the article, such that it might not be retrieved on a relevance-based search for '*Titanic*' and 'sink,' or it might not be ranked high enough for the answer candidate extraction process to ever get to it (Section 2.3). So, with respect to a given question, *text retrieval* using relevance-based methods is not guaranteed to return texts with a high likelihood of having an answer somewhere within them. And if text retrieval fails to return texts containing answers, any subsequent processing might as well not happen. Attempts to improve this situation are usually found under the rubric *information retrieval for question answering (IR4QA)*.

A simple and widely adopted solution to the locality problem in relevance-based retrieval is simply to break texts into a set of separate passages, each of which is separately indexed for text retrieval (*passage retrieval*), assuming that there is a better correlation between standard metrics of *relevance* and *answers* in short texts.

Other text retrieval techniques used instead of, or in addition to, segmentation into smaller passages involve extensions to what is indexed. In *predictive annotation* (Prager et al., 2000), texts are indexed not just by the position of each (non-stop) word in the text, but also by the position of each of 20 types of named entities (called here *QA-tokens*), each of which could answer a question of a given type. For example, predictive annotation of the sentence

(4)　Sri Lanka boasts the highest per capita income in South Asia.

would index the QA-token COUNTRY$ as occuring over the rst two words of the sentence, and the QA-token PLACE$ as occuring over the last two. (Techniques used here are similar to those used in information extraction, as discussed in Chapter 18, INFORMATION EXTRACTION.)

QA-tokens are used as well in *query construction*. When user questions are mapped to queries, not just keywords from the question are included in the query, but also an appropriate QA-token (or disjunction thereof) for the question type. For example, the *where* question

(5)　Where is the capital of Sri Lanka?

would be mapped to a query comprising the keywords 'capital,' 'Sri,' and 'Lanka,' along with a disjunct of the QA-tokens (PLACE$, COUNTRY$, STATE$, NAME$), all of which can potentially answer a *where* question. Such a query would cause to be retrieved any passage containing the sentence in (4), although, as Prager notes, it is important to discard the match between COUNTRY$ and the annotation of 'Sri Lanka' as COUNTRY$, in order to answer the question correctly. (Even where QA-tokens, or answer types, are not themselves indexed, they may still be used to lter out retrieved texts or passages that lack any instance of the QA-token/answer type.)

While *predictive annotation* reduces 'false positives' in text retrieval by demanding passages that contain candidate answers of particular types, they can also be reduced by indexing not just words and their positions but how the words are used. This is illustrated in the *Joost* system (Bouma et al., 2005), which indexes each word along various linguistic dimensions (e.g., part of speech, dependency relations, etc.), as well as indexing the type and span of each named entity. Using a genetic algorithm to optimize various weightings, Bouma and his colleagues found a 10 percent improvement in passage retrieval on a test set of 250 questions, measured by MRR (*mean reciprocal ranking*) over passages containing a correct answer. Moreover, Morton (2005) found that when third-person pronouns were resolved and indexed by the full NPs with which they corefer, the frequency of both 'false positives' and 'false negatives' could be reduced by narrowing the distance between potential answer candidates and terms from the question (all treated as full NPs through coreference resolution).[1]

In all this work, the basic idea is that the more frequently a system can rely on top-ranked passages to contain a correct answer, the fewer passages need to be examined in the next stage of processing. It should be remembered, however, that any ranking in text retrieval is a ranking on texts, not on the answers they may contain. A separate process of answer candidate ranking is carried out at a later stage (Section 2.3).

A survey of passage retrieval techniques for QA can be found in Tellex et al. (2003).

2.2.2   Pattern-based retrieval   The other type of text retrieval used in QA is *pattern-based retrieval*. This relies on the *quoted string* search capabilities of search engines, re ecting the assumption that, although natural language usually provides multiple ways to express the same information, it is expressed in the same or a similar way to the question somewhere in the corpus. Pattern-based retrieval also differs from relevance-based retrieval in taking the result of retrieval to be the *snippet* returned as evidence for the match (cf. Section 1) rather than a pointer to the text that contains it. Thus pattern-based retrieval does not derive any bene t from breaking texts into smaller passages, as does relevance-based retrieval, because it targets snippets rather than their source.

Pattern-based retrieval systems differ from one another in the kinds of string patterns they use in performing the match. The well-known AskMSR system

(Brill et al., 2002) used different sets of string patterns for different types of questions. For *where is* questions, for example, retrieval patterns were generated with 'is' in every possible position – e.g.

    (6)   Where is the Vale of Tears?
          is the Vale of Tears
          the is Vale of Tears
          the Vale is of Tears
          the Vale of is Tears
          the Vale of Tears is

Patterns usually re ect a direct relationship between questions and their answers. For example, since wh-questions in English (where, when, who, what, which, why) usually involve *fronting* the question phrase (and, in some cases, an auxiliary as well), as in:

    (7)   When was the telephone invented?
    (8)   In which American state is Iron Mountain located?
    (9)   What is the largest whale?

their answers are likely to be found non-fronted, directly to the right of the strings:

- *the telephone was invented in* <answer>
- *Iron Mountain is located in* <answer>
- *the largest whale is* <answer>

Other syntactic relationships predict other string patterns, such as:

- *invented the telephone in* <answer>
- *the telephone, invented in* <answer>
- *in* <answer> *the telephone was invented*
- *Iron Mountain, located in* <answer>
- <answer> *is the largest whale*
- <answer> *is the largest of the whales*

    As Lin (2007) notes, a quoted string search does not guarantee that the snippet returned from a search engine as evidence will actually contain a ller for the question phrase (i.e., an answer). There are several reasons for this. First, the answer material may be outside the boundaries of the snippet. Secondly, since search engines (as of this writing) ignore punctuation and case, a quoted string can also match over successive sentences and/or clauses (i.e., across nal punctuation), producing false positive matches that have to be ltered out later on, as in

    (10)   He was six when *the telephone was invented. In 1940,* he ...

which a search engine would nd as a match for the string *the telephone was invented in*.

More recently, researchers have shown how lexical resources such as WordNet (Miller et al., 1990) and FrameNet (Baker et al., 1998) can be used to construct additional string patterns that can be used in pattern-based retrieval (Kaisser & Webber 2007). Again, one must be aware that any ranking here is the search engine's ranking on the documents, not on any answer candidates contained in the snippets. The ranking of answer candidates themselves is discussed in Section 2.3, after answer candidate extraction.

2.3   *Processing answer candidates*

Once a set of passages or snippets has been retrieved, a system must determine what, if anything, in each separate passage or snippet might serve as an answer to the question (*answer candidate extraction*) and how good an answer it might be (*answer candidate evaluation*). The latter requires assessing the candidate and its textual context, possibly comparing it as well with the other, separately extracted candidates. Candidates are then ranked based on this assessment, with the top-scoring candidate (or top N scoring candidates) presented to the user. Techniques for these different aspects of answer candidate processing are described below.

Two kinds of patterns are used for extracting answer candidates from passages or snippets. They can be extracted directly, using *string patterns* that identify the contents of a particular bounded span as an answer candidate, or they can be extracted using *structured patterns*, from the output of parsing, semantic role labeling, and/or interpreting the passages or snippets.

String patterns are the simplest. They can be derived directly from the user's question (exactly as in pattern-based retrieval, Section 2.2.2), authored manually, or computed by bootstrapping from questions with known answers. To illustrate the latter, known [entity, location] pairs such as [Taj Mahal, Agra], [Grant's Tomb, New York City], etc., can be used to retrieve texts that suggest the following patterns for identifying the answer to location questions:

> <NAME> [is | are] located in <ANSWER>.
> <NAME> in <ANSWER>,
> <NAME> [lies | lie] on <ANSWER>.

In each case, the answer candidate is bounded on its left and right by an identi - able word or symbol. Such patterns can also be characterized by their reliability – how often they pick up a candidate of the right type, as opposed to a random string. Because patterns are so simple, they are rarely completely reliable, as in example 11, where 'the background' is identi ed as an answer candidate. Because parentheticals, adverbial modi ers, and adjuncts can occur so freely within a sentence, no set of patterns can reliably capture all desired answer candidates, as in example 12, where the adverbials 'all the way up' and 'all the way down' block the 'located in' pattern from matching.

> (11)   'Where are the Rocky Mountains?'
>   <NAME> in <ANSWER>

'Denver's new airport, topped with white berglass cones in imitation of the Rocky Mountains in **the background**, continues to lie empty.'

(12) 'Where are the Rocky Mountains?'
<NAME> [is | are] located in <ANSWER>.
'The Rocky Mountains are located all the way up to Alaska and all the way down to Mexico.'

To reduce false positives (as in example 11), answer candidates found by string patterns are commonly ltered by tests derived from the question type (Section 2.1). For example, for a *where* question, <ANSWER> must be classi able as a LOCATION. For a *who* question, it must be classi able as a PERSON, or in some cases, a PERSON or a COMPANY. Named entity recognition, often in conjunction with WordNet and/or Wikipedia categories, has been used in this ltering.

Answer candidate extraction rarely produces a single candidate answer, so one or more best candidates need to be selected and displayed to the questioner. To produce a ranking of such candidates so as to be able to select the best, their quality needs to be assessed. The simplest and most common method of doing so involves computing their frequency of occurrence within the set of answer candidates (Brill et al., 2002). To re ect true frequency, this requires recognizing answer candidates that should be treated as equivalent, such as 'Clinton,' 'Bill Clinton,' 'William Jefferson Clinton,' and 'ex-President Clinton,' rather than as distinct candidates. Online resources such as Wikipedia are useful in this regard.

A more complex method can be used when correct answers to questions occur only infrequently in the corpus. This method involves assessing the probability that an answer candidate is the correct answer to the question (Xu et al., 2002; Ko et al., 2007). Since lack of suf cient data prevents such probabilities from being computed precisely, they are approximated using such features as the ways in which the context of answer A_i matches question Q, whether A_i is correctly typed for the argument role that the question word plays in Q, whether A_i is supported as an answer by online resources such as gazetteers, WordNet, Wikipedia and/or the snippets returned from web search. Probabilities based on these approxima-tions have been shown to indeed increase the ranking of good answers, thereby improving system performance.

Result of answer candidate extraction and evaluation is a rank-ordered list of answer candidates, of which the top (or top N) is/are presented as the answer(s), with each supported by either a document ID or a speci c piece of text meant to serve as evidence. In the case of answer candidates that occur multiple times, each with different support, there has as yet been no attempt to assess the quality of that evidence – whether one piece of text might provide either stronger or clearer support for an answer.

2.4 Evaluating performance in QA

Factoid QA in TREC treats every question as having a single correct answer, although it may be described in different ways (e.g., a distance question with an answer given in miles or in kilometers, with a precise value or an approximate one, etc.). In early QA tracks, groups were allowed to return a list of ve possible answers for each question, in rank-order, so that a question could be scored by the *reciprocal rank* of the rst correct answer: if it ranks rst, it gets a score of 1; if it ranks second, it gets a score of 1/2; etc. If only the fth answer is correct, it gets a score of 1/5. Otherwise it scores a 0. Over a set of questions, then, a system could be assessed in terms of *mean reciprocal rank* (MRR) – i.e., the average of the reciprocal rank score of the question set. MRR is still often used to measure system performance, as it is more lenient than assessing only a single answer.

Although *recall* and *precision* are also used in assessing system performance, because they do not take account of the ranked position of answers and because only the top-ranked correct answer to a given question actually matters (not how many correct answers have been returned for the question), *coverage* and *answer redundancy* are sometimes used as alternatives to recall and precision for assessing retrieval in QA (Roberts & Gaizauskas 2004).

- *Coverage* is the proportion of the question set for which a correct answer can be found within the top *n* passages retrieved for each question.
- *Answer redundancy* is the average number, per question, of passages within the top *n* retrieved that contain a correct answer.

Coverage is preferable to *recall* because, since factoid questions are taken to have a single answer, it does not make sense to worry about *recall* (i.e., the proportion of documents containing that answer).

These metrics all assume that every question has a correct answer (or different descriptions of the correct answer), so at issue is where judgments of correctness come from. When evaluating QA systems, one must keep the document collection xed, so that differences in performance do not simply re ect differences in the corpus. Because it is expensive to nd all possible answers (or possible ways to phrase every answer) in a large corpus, a method called *pooling* was developed.

As used in large, multi-system QA evaluations, pooling involves collecting the rank-ordered results from all runs of all the participating systems; selecting N runs per system; taking the top X documents from each of those N runs and merging them into a judgment pool for that query, eliminating duplicates, and, nally, manually assessing correctness judgments on only these pooled answers. Importantly, pooling has been found not to be biased towards systems that contribute to the pool – that is, there is no performance bene t to be gained by participating in the pooling system. On the other hand, pooling makes it harder to assess new techniques which may produce answers that may be correct but do not occur in the pool formed from earlier results.

To allow for the development of such techniques, Lin and Katz (2006) attempted to nd all possible answers in the AQUAINT corpus for a subset of questions from TREC, while, more recently, Kaisser and Lowe (2008) have used the *Mechanical Turk* to create an even larger set of 8,107 [question, document id, answer, answer source sentence] tuples for the over 1,700 TREC questions from 2002 to 2006.

More discussion of evaluation methods used in QA can be found in Chapter 11,
EVALUATION OF NLP SYSTEMS.

3 Current Directions

QA technology is moving in several different directions, but here we will focus
on the three that we nd most important: (1) extending the relationship between
question and corpus; (2) broadening the range of questions that can be answered;
and (3) deepening the relationship between user and system. We brie y discuss
each in turn, and then follow with a brief discussion of the consequences for
evaluation.

3.1 *Extending the relation between question and corpus*

We have mentioned several times that open domain QA involves *finding* answers
in text, while database QA involves *computing* them, usually from an assortment of other, simpler facts. Section 2.2 showed that evidence that enabled an
answer to be located could take the form of words from the user's question, possibly augmented by the syntactic relations between them, or the form of lexical
and/or syntactic variations on the question that could be predicted from hand-
made resources such as WordNet and FrameNet or from patterns found through
text mining. As Kaisser and Webber (2007) showed, however, this is not enough:
while a corpus as large as the web might yield an answer phrased similarly to
a given question, especially if the answer is widely discussed, this is much less
likely with a less extensive corpus or a popular topic. The corpus may still be able
to serve as the source of an answer, but only through inference.

 Textual entailment captures the intuition that one piece of text – in this case, text
containing a correct answer to a given question – can be inferred from another. To
date, progress has been gauged by the PASCAL Recognising Textual Entailment
(RTE) Challenge (Bar-Haim et al., 2006; Dagan et al., 2008b).

 Formally, the textual entailment task is to determine, given some text, T, and
hypothesis, H, whether the meaning of H can be inferred from the meaning of T.
For QA, H would be derived from a question such as:

(13)   How many inhabitants does Slovenia have?

and T would be an answer passage such as:

 In other words, with its 2 million inhabitants, Slovenia has only 5.5 thousand
 professional soldiers.

Recognizing the value of RTE to QA, the RTE Challenge includes manually
annotated $T–H$ data for training and testing, based on question–answer passage pairs from TREC (http://trec.nist.gov) and CLEF QA (http://clef-qa.itc.it)

(see Chapter 10, LINGUISTIC ANNOTATION, for a discussion on annotating language resources). To create the *T–H* pairs, annotators extract from the answer passages answers of the correct type – but not necessarily the correct answer. The original question with the selected answer term included becomes *H*, and the answer passage becomes *T*. If, from example 13, annotators chose the answer '2 million inhabitants' from *T*, they could create a positive entailment pair, with 'Slovenia has 2 million inhabitants' as *H*. Alternatively, if they chose '5.5 thousand' from *T*, they could create a negative entailment pair with 'Slovenia has only 5.5 thousand inhabitants' as *H*.

The RTE challenge has tested systems on a 50–50 mix of positive and negative *T–H* pairs, where 50 percent would be the baseline accuracy. For the second RTE challenge, most systems obtained between 55 percent and 61 percent (Bar-Haim et al., 2006), where the majority of approaches drew on some combination of lexical overlap (often using WordNet; Miller et al., 1990), semantic role labeling, using FrameNet (Baker et al., 1998), and extensive use of background knowledge. The top-performing system was LCC's GROUNDHOG (Hickl et al., 2006), which achieved an accuracy of 75.4 percent. Around 10 percent of this score was obtained by expanding the training set of positive and negative entailment examples by following Burger and Ferro (2005), collecting around 100,000 positive examples consisting of the headline and   rst sentence of newswire texts. To create negative examples, they extracted pairs of sequential sentences that included mentions of the same named entity from a newswire corpus. Sample testing with human annotators determined that both of these example sets were accurate to the ninetieth percentile.

Although, intuitively, we might expect a deeper level of analysis to be required to achieve high accuracy in the RTE task, systems that have employed such analysis have so far failed to improve over the 60 percent baseline performance achieved by simple lexical matching, a technique already exploited in QA. Any future breakthrough in RTE is likely to be quickly and widely adopted in QA and elsewhere.

3.2   *Broadening the range of answerable questions*

We noted in Section 1.3 that open domain QA has primarily addressed *factoid* questions of *who, what, when, how many*, and *where* – in particular, ones that can be answered with a word or short phrase from the corpus. Little effort has gone into discovering systematic ways of answering *why* and *how* questions, which usually require longer answers. This may primarily have to do with the problem of evaluating such answers. And completely ignored are polar ('yes'/'no') questions such as

    (14)   Is pinotage another name for pinot noir?

    (15)   Is calcium citrate better absorbed and a more effective treatment for osteoporosis than calcium carbonate?

Scenario 1: The al-Qaida Terrorist Group
Your division chief has ordered a detailed report on the al-Qaida Terrorist Group due in three weeks. This report should present information regarding the most essential concerns, including who are the key gures involved with al-Qaida along with other organisations, countries, and members that are af liated, any trades that al-Qaida has made with organisations or countries, what facilities they possess, where they receive their nancial support, what capabilities they have (CBW program, other weapons, etc.) and how have they acquired them, what is their possible future activity, how their training program operates, who their new members are.

Figure 22.2   An ARDA scenario (from Small & Strzalkowski 2009).

because nding and presenting good evidence for an answer is more important than the answer itself and because the problem of assessing the quality of evidence has not really been addressed.

Nevertheless, there are now efforts to move beyond factoid QA in order to address questions that require information from more than a single source text or from multiple paragraphs within a text, possibly coupled with inference as above. These are called *complex questions*, the simplest form of which Bouma et al. (2005) have called 'which questions,' as in

(16)   Which ferry sank southeast of the island Utö?

Answering this requires combining evidence that some entity sank southeast of the island Utö with evidence that the entity is a ferry. Complex QA often requires additional knowledge to process (from the data, from a model of the world, or from the user), and is used to accumulate evidence to support a particular position or opinion. This moves QA signi cantly away from the text retrieval dominated paradigm of factoid QA. The US ARDA AQUAINT program has been a major driver in the development of systems to address complex questions, often in the context of an explicit task or *scenario*, such as in Figure 22.2.

Complex QA has been approached in different ways, two of which we describe here: (1) decomposing the problem into subproblems and then dealing with each one in turn; and (2) more complex document/passage indexing.

In question decomposition, a complex question is reduced to a set of subquestions, using linguistic and/or domain-speci c knowledge. The subquestions are meant to be ones that can be answered by existing factoid QA technology. For example, the START system (Katz 1997) syntactically decomposes the question

(17)   Who was the third Republican president?

into the sequence of questions Q1 (*Who were the Republican presidents?*), followed by Q2 (*Who is/was the third of them?*), where 'them' stands for the list of answers to Q1. Saquete et al. (2004) perform similar syntactic decomposition in answering temporal questions such as

(18)   Where did Bill Clinton study before going to Oxford University?

which gets split into the pair of questions Q1 (*Where did Bill Clinton study?*) and Q2 (*When did Bill Clinton go to Oxford University?*), with a constraint that the answer to Q1 fall in the period *before* the time associated with Q2.

The problem with syntactic decomposition is that it quickly becomes computationally expensive to generate and evaluate all syntactically legal decompositions of a complex question. For the question

(19)   What American companies have introduced a generic drug in a European country?

possible subquestions include *What companies have introduced a drug in a European country?*, *What American companies have introduced a generic drug?*, and so on. One really only wants to generate those which have answers in the corpus, and that is the goal of the second way of addressing complex questions – complex indexing.

In Section 2.2, we mentioned various ways in which text is indexed for QA – by words (or stems), by named entities, by part-of-speech tags, and by dependency relations. Even more complex indexing is used, either alone or with question decomposition, in the *parameterized annotations* used in START (Katz et al., 2005) and elsewhere, as a way of answering complex questions. Parameters take the form of domain-speci c templates with parameterized slots – such as the following, from Katz et al. (2005):

In <year>, <group type> <group name> carried out a <event type> in <country>, involving <agent type> <agent name>.

When used to index a passage, slots would be replaced by appropriate named entities. Berrios et al. (2002) use similar templates to index paragraphs in medical textbooks, in order to answer common clinical questions, including:

(20)   What is the <Pathophysiology/Etiology> of <Manifestation/Pathology>?
(21)   How can <Pharmacotherapy> be used to treat <Disease/Syndrome>?

Here the parameters are disjunctions of Uni ed Medical Language System (UMLS) categories (www.nlm.nih.gov/research/umls/) that can be lled by a term or phrase that belongs to any one of them.

Templates such as these function in a similar way to syntactic decomposition, in that they can collect lists of responses for each subquery, then perform constraint propagation to nd responses that satisfy all parts of the original query. However, these templates need to be built for each domain or data resource under consideration by the QA system – a signi cant overhead.

The LCC system (Lacatusu et al., 2005) achieves question decomposition in a similar way. Top-down decomposition is driven by syntactic information. Bottom-up decomposition is achieved by using predictive question–answer pairs (stored in a question–answer base, and referred to as QUABs) to expand the answer space. These QUABs are selected from a database of 10,000 question–answer pairs created of ine by human annotators. So for a question such as *What has been the impact of job outsourcing programs on India's relationship with the US?*, those QUABs which closely match the question, and are therefore adjudged to anticipate the user's information need, are presented to the user. Both methods of decomposition are powerful approaches, but require a high degree of manual knowledge construction – creating templates or the construction of question–answer pairs – in order to be effective. Some initial work has been undertaken to incorporate existing large-scale knowledge sources, such as CYC (Curtis et al., 2005), into the complex QA scenario, without yielding signi cant improvements in either domain-speci c or open domain QA, possibly due to the incompleteness of the information represented in these knowledge sources.

3.3 Relation between user and system

Open domain QA has basically assumed a single correct answer to every factoid question, very much a re ection of its origins in IR, which abstracts individual relevancy judgments away to those of an average user, to serve as a *gold standard*. But it should be clear that different correct answers will be appropriate for different users. The most obvious example of this comes in the degree of speci city desirable in answering *where is* questions, such as:

(22)   Where is the Verrazano-Narrows Bridge?
(23)   Where is the Three Gorges Dam?

where someone in North America might appreciate a speci c answer to the rst (e.g., New York City, or between Brooklyn and Staten Island) and a general answer to the second (e.g., China), while for someone in Asia, the reverse might be true (e.g., New York, and Western Hubei Province).

Addressing another aspect of tailoring responses to users, Quarteroni and Manandhar (2009) show how a user's age and assumed reading level can be used to choose the most appropriate among possible correct answers to a question. Alternatively, rather than trying to choose the most appropriate among possible correct answers, a different approach would be to offer all of them, allowing users to choose for themselves, as in the answer model for the question *Where is Glasgow?* given in Figure 22.3.

Dalmas and Webber (2007) show that a similar approach can be taken in presenting answers to ambiguous questions, such as the famous question *Where is the Taj Mahal?* (the tomb? the casino/hotel? the local Indian restaurant? etc.)

But the main way of enriching the relationship between user and QA system involves the use of interaction. In Section 1.2 we described early systems that could engage in dialogue in the process of providing answers to user questions. Such systems relied on complete descriptions of the target domain in order to choose the next dialogue move, and so could only work in conceptually simple domains

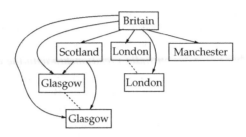

Figure 22.3   An answer model for the question: *Where is Glasgow?* (Dalmas & Webber 2007), showing both Scotland and Britain as possible answers. Here → conveys a part-of relation, and a dashed line, an equivalence relation.

such as travel planning (Goddeau et al., 1994; Seneff 2002), nding an appropri- ate restaurant (Walker et al., 2004), automated banking (Hardy et al., 2005), etc. In more complex applications, a complete description of the domain is unlikely, and systems must be able to ask questions of their own in order to work towards providing the user with the information he/she is after. On the other hand, as user questions become more complex, it becomes more dif cult to anticipate all possi- ble ways of answering them, and systems require dialogue to help guide them to what it is that the user wants. This is the issue that we focus on, under the rubric *interactive question answering* or *IQA*.

IQA can be seen as a process in which the user is a continual part of the informa- tion loop – as originator of the query, arbitrator over information relevance, and consumer of the nal product. This mode of operation is useful for both factoid and complex QA, but perhaps provides greatest bene t in those cases where the user's information need is still vague, or involves complex multifaceted concepts, or re ects misconceptions or opinions – all cases where the expected information content returned is complex, with a degree of variability not present in factoid QA. Interactive QA systems borrow from dialogue systems their interaction, their emphasis on completion of user task, their handling of incomplete or underspeci- ed (as well as overspeci ed) user input and the constraint and relaxation phases of the query process, while remaining focused on large or open domains, such as law, biomedicine, or international politics.

Rather than attempting to resolve complex question ambiguity independently of either the user or the context, both can be used to generate follow-up queries to the user that can serve as signi cant directional tools to guide the information seeking process. To achieve this requires an understanding of the context of the user's query and some knowledge about the domain of inquiry, or at least the domain as represented by results returned by the speci c query.

In the previous section, we described the use of predictive question–answer pairs (QUABs) to expand the range of answerable questions. They are also used in the interactive QA system FERRET (Harabagiu et al., 2005) to support interaction. When the user asks a question, those QUABs that relate to the query are offered to the user, as a way of expanding the search space. These QUABs can address not only subquestions decomposed from the original question, but also other information that may be tangentially related to the question. However, this data is often created manually, and thus is an expensive overhead. HITIQA (Small & Strzalkowski, 2009) exempli es an IQA system that does not rely on *a priori* knowledege of the domain. Rather, HITIQA creates just-in-time semantic representations of retrieved passages, using domain-independent 'frames', which are approximations of the underlying relationships between entities. While less precise or targeted than the parameterized annotations used in the START system (Katz et al., 2005) described in Section 3.2, they are suf cient for capturing the essence of a paragraph.

A similar framing process is applied to the questions posed to the system, creating a goal frame. This allows for systematic comparison between the analyst's question and the retrieved text passages and for selection of instantiated frames for answer passages. HITIQA uses interactive dialogue with the analyst to negotiate the scope of the answer, and experiments with several groups of analysts showed that users accept system suggestions regarding the current question scope as well as those that relate to other aspects of their task, thus speeding up their work. Dialogue is enabled through the frame-based representation of content and more speci cally through the mismatches between the goal frame and the data frames in the answer space. This is best illustrated through the example interaction taken from a live demonstration to the ARDA AQUAINT community in 2005 in Figure 22.4.

This interaction exploits the goal frame that was created for the question (Figure 22.5) and the frames built for each of the retrieved passages (Figures 22.6 and 22.7). The passages in Figures 22.6 and 22.7 are represented by one-con ict data frames in the analyst's answer space (i.e., where there is one con ict between the data frame and the question frame). The con icts on the relation attribute were, respectively: status vs. retirement and status vs. private accounts. These relations

---

Analyst: *"What is the status of the Social Security System?"*
[exact match answer passages are displayed]
HITIQA: *"Would you be interested in information on **retirement** relative to your question?"*
Analyst: *"Yes"*
HITIQA: *"Do you want to see information on **private accounts**?"*
Analyst: *"Yes"*
HITIQA: *"Thank you, Please view your answer"*
[final selection of passages are displayed]

Figure 22.4 Example interaction taken from a live demonstration to the ARDA AQUAINT community in 2005.

RELATIONS	status
ORGANIZATION	Social Security System

Figure 22.5 Goal frame for the question: *What is the status of the Social Security system?*

*Last week, the General Accounting Office, the auditing arm of Congress, issued a chilling report. Without badly needed reform, Social Security is rapidly headed for financial ruin. By 2017, when baby boomers are well into **retirement**, the program will start running annual deficits that will eventually bankrupt the system, the GAO warned.*

RELATION	retirement
ORGANIZATION	General Accounting Office, Social Security, Congress, GAO
DATE	2017

*Social Security is sound for today's seniors and for those nearing **retirement**, but it needs to be fixed for younger workers – our children and grandchildren. The goverment has made promises it cannot afford to pay for with the current pay-as-you-go system.*

RELATION	retirement
ORGANIZATION	Social Security

Figure 22.6   Two cluster seed passages and their corresponding frames relative to the retirement clari cation question.

*One reform approach, favored by Bush, would let workers divert some of the 12.4% they and their employers pay in Social Security taxes into **private accounts** in exchange for cuts in guaranteed Social Security benefits. In the short term, however, it would take $1 trillion out of the system, as taxes diverted to the **private accounts** wouldn't be available to pay benefits for current retirees.*

RELATION	private accounts
ORGANIZATION	Social Security, GAO
PERSON	Bush
NUMBER	12.4%, 1 trillion

*On Jan. 11, Bush kicked off his new campaign by telling a town hall meeting that younger workers should be able to take some of their payroll tax and "set it aside in the form of a personal savings account." Social Security only provides returns of about 2% a year after inflation, and **private accounts**, says the President, could top that easily if they were invested even partially in stocks.*

RELATION	private accounts
ORGANIZATION	Social Security, town hall
PERSON	Bush
NUMBER	2%
DATE	Jan. 11

Figure 22.7   Two cluster passages and their corresponding frames relative to the private accounts clari cation question.

were obtained from the passage's cluster relations: one cluster containing retirement (Figure 22.6) and the other cluster containing private accounts (Figure 22.7). From the system's viewpoint each of these clusters represents an alternative interpretation of the user's question about the status of Social Security, and so each is offered to the user through automatically generated clari cation questions. This data-driven approach allows the system to work effectively in any domain and with any text genre, without necessitating costly knowledge engineering.

3.4 *Evaluating extended QA capabilities*

As QA broadens and deepens to include the extensions described in this section, so evaluation methods need to develop so that we can continue to assess how well a method performs and/or how much better it is than the alternative(s).

In Section 2.4, we described some of the metrics used and the issues involved in evaluating system performance on factoid questions, where it is assumed that speci c *gold standard* answers can be identi ed and agreed upon prior to evaluation. (See also Chapter 11, EVALUATION OF NLP SYTEMS.) Here, for each way of extending QA from where it is today, one can consider whether existing evaluation methods suf ce or whether new ones are needed.

Extending the relation between question and corpus is a matter of *textual entailment* (Section 3.1), so methods used in assessing correctness in that task should apply here as well, provided that QA systems identify the minimal set of sentences within a document that entails the provided answer (rather than simply a pointer to the document).

For answering *why* and *how* questions, nugget methods (Dang & Lin 2007) should suf ce initially, though one might also want to assess temporal, causal, and/or subsumption relations that should be seen to hold between the nuggets. Evaluating performance on answering *polar questions* could also be taken to be a matter of textual entailment, where providing the minimal set of evidential sentences would again be crucial for evaluation, not least for user acceptance. For what Bouma et al. (2005) have called *which* questions, standard QA metrics should suf ce, though, as with textual entailment, systems should probably also identify the set of sentences (within a document or across multiple documents) that were used in computing the answer.

It is in the more complex relation between user and system that one nds a challenge for QA evaluation. But even here, there is a gradient. Quarteroni and Manandhar (2009) assess a QA system's ability to tailor answers to a user's age and reading level by asking outside assessors to provide judgments on the answers. For simple information needs, such as a list of the names of the N upcoming conferences on language technology, along with their locations and acceptance rates (Bertomeu et al., 2006) – i.e., the sort of information that one might be able to get from a database if such a database existed – evaluation metrics developed in dialogue system technology such as task completion, time to task completion, and user satisfaction (Walker et al., 2000) would probably be equally effective here. But unlike the setup where assessors are considered the nal consumers of answers, as they are in a gold standard model, here motivated users must become system assessors.

This is even more true as user information needs become more complex and users may not even know what information might be relevant. Here there has been an attempt to develop objective evaluation criteria – in the ciQA track at TREC (www.umiacs.umd.edu/~jimmylin/ciqa/), but see also iCLEF (Gonzalo & Oard 2004; Gonzalo et al., 2006, and ACLIA (Advanced Cross-lingual Information Access) track (http://aclia.lti.cs.cmu.edu/wiki/moin.cgi/Home) in NTCIR. We want to argue, however, that ciQA and its evaluation criteria do not re ect the true character of users attempting to solve complex information needs.

A key element in a successful evaluation paradigm is the de nition of the central concepts. Evaluation metrics have gained increased prominence in recent years, as they often in uence the research agenda. Unfortunately, ciQA's view of complex interactive QA re ects TREC's IR bias, and consequently fails to showcase the true potential of the interaction process. In particular, it assumes that the user's information need does not have to be expressed via natural language queries: it can be expressed in a template that represents the question in canonical form. Only additional context (the *narrative*) is provided in natural language. For example:

Template: What evidence is there for transport of <drugs> from <Bonaire> to <the United States>?
Narrative: *The analyst would like to know of efforts made to discourage narco traffickers from using Bonaire as a transit point for drugs to the United States. Specifically, the analyst would like to know of any efforts by local authorities as well as the international community.*

This narrative elaborates on the information need, providing context or a ner-grained statement of interest, or a focus on particular topical aspects. While this narrative could be used automatically by systems that adopt a question decomposition approach, or could be exploited by a motivated user, to drive an interaction around tangential issues surrounding the central concepts, ciQA evaluation has not been designed to discriminate between any attention being paid to the narrative or not.

This template approach seems similar to the use of such templates in some of the decomposition approaches discussed in Section 3.2, but with a fundamental difference. Whereas those approaches attempt to process large amounts of data into a form that has the potential to match a range of queries, here the templates are known *a priori*, greatly reducing the problem space. Within IR, when evaluation was xed on a known data set, and xed set of associated queries, performance increased over time, but again many approaches failed to scale when the data set increased, or substantially changed in form and content.

A second problem with ciQA with respect to showcasing the true potential of interaction is its limited de nition of the term. In particular, it allowed only a single interaction (2006) or single ve-minute period of interaction (2007). This single interaction or period of interaction re ects the mistaken view (deriving from an idealization adopted in IR) that interaction involves no more than re ning the original query to better re ect the available data. However, as Wizard-of-Oz experiments into the use of interaction in QA continue to show (cf. Bertomeu 2007), success and satisfaction can depend on support for a variety of different interchanges and answer strategies, including clari cation subdialogues, explanation subdialogues, responses that *overanswer* a question (providing more information and more kinds of information than the user actually requested), being unaware of their relevance when the question was originally asked.

Since it is clear that neither the type of interaction supported in ciQA nor its evaluation criteria (in terms of the 'information nuggets' contained in the system responses) are a fair representation of the capabilities of a true interactive system, it should be no surprise that the results of the rst ciQA event were largely negative; standard IR approaches performed as well as complex QA approaches. Of the 12 individual runs in 2006, only two scored higher than the manual baseline sentence retrieval system. Thus Kelly and Lin (2007) note that 'interaction doesn't appear to help much (at present),' although they acknowledge both that the evaluation design could be awed (in limiting interaction to a single turn, and limiting the time for that interaction), and that the types of interaction deployed (a variant of relevance feedback) are not appropriate for this kind of task. Indeed, Lin (2007) points to a truism that should be very revealing. Current IR paradigms maximize recall – by returning *more of the same*. Complex QA, in contrast, values novelty – what information the user has not seen, that may present another aspect of the scenario. Some systems, such as HITIQA (Small & Strzalkowski 2009), explicitly encode this assumption, remembering in the dialogue history both what users have seen, and what they have indicated they like, versus what does not interest them. This does not have to be explicit: interest can be gauged by a user copying information into a report, or dismissing a window after just a few seconds, for instance.

Perhaps a more useful indicator of evaluation is related work by Kelly et al. (2009), which addresses the issue of instability of traditional evaluation metrics in multi-user environments, and describes the use of questionnaires to evaluate a range of IQA systems, as a method of garnering effective user feedback about the systems themselves, and involving users in a subjective evaluation process. Key is the ability to discriminate between the resulting systems on the basis of several hypotheses, such as effort and ef ciency. However, the assumption here, re ecting a fact that the eld will have to face fairly soon, is that effective evaluation of complex interactive QA systems can only truly be achieved by subjective evaluations by motivated users. This is certainly more expensive, and less statistically clear cut than previous evaluation paradigms for QA, but may lead us to real discoveries of strategies for complex interactive question answering.

4 Further Reading

A survey of work on database QA can be found in Webber (1986), while the most comprehensive description of a database QA system remains Woods (1978). Prager (2007) provides the best introduction to open domain QA, while an incisive component-by-component performance analysis of an open domain QA system can be found in Moldovan et al. (2003). For collections of papers on open domain QA, the reader is referred to Maybury (2003) and Strzalkowski and Harabagiu (2006), and to special issues of the *Journal of Applied Logic* (on *Questions and Answers: Theoretical and Applied Perspectives* 5:1, March 2007) and of the *Journal of Natural Language Engineering* (cf. Webb & Webber 2009, a special issue on interactive question answering). Papers on QA appear regularly in conferences sponsored by the Association for Computational Linguistics (ACL) and by the Special Interest Group on Information Retrieval (SIGIR).

NOTE

1 Even when pronoun resolution is not used to support enhanced indexing, but only answer candidate extraction and/or evaluation, it has been shown to be of bene t and worth the cost (Vicedo & Ferrández 2000).

References

Abe, N., & M. K. Warmuth (1992), On the computational complexity of approximating distributions by probabilistic automata. *Machine Learning* 9:205–60.

Abney, S. (1989), A computational model of human parsing. *Journal of Psycholinguistic Research* 18:129–44.

Abney, S. (1996), Statistical methods and linguistics, in Judith L. Klavans & Philip Resnik (eds.), *The Balancing Act: Combining Symbolic and Statistical Approaches to Language*. Cambridge, MA: MIT Press, 2–26.

Abney, S. (1997), Stochastic attribute-value grammars. *Computational Linguistics* 23(4):597–618.

Abney, S. (2008), *Semisupervised Learning for Computational Linguistics*. Boca Raton, FL: Chapman and Hall.

Abney, S., & Mark Johnson (1991), Memory requirements and local ambiguities of parsing strategies. *Journal of Psycholinguistic Research* 20:233–50.

Abney, S., David McAllester, & Fernando Pereira (1999), Relating probabilistic grammars and automata. *Proceedings of ACL*, 541–9.

Abney, S., S. Flickenger, C. Gdaniec et al. (1991), Procedure for quantitatively comparing the syntactic coverage of English grammars. *HLT '91: Proceedings of the Workshop on Speech and Natural Language*, 306–11. http://dx.doi.org/10.3115/112405.112467

Agichtein, Eugene, & Luis Gravano (2000), Snowball: extracting relations from large plain-text collections. *DL '00: Proceedings of the 5th ACM Conference on Digital Libraries*, 85–94. http://doi.acm.org/10.1145/336597.336644

Agirre, Eneko, & Phil Edmonds (eds.) (2006), *Text, Speech and Language Technology*, vol. 33: *Word Sense Disambiguation: Algorithms and Applications*. Dordrecht: Springer.

Agirre, Eneko, Lluís Màrquez, & Richard Wicentowski (2009), Computational semantic analysis of language: SemEval-2007 and beyond. *Language Resources and Evaluation* 43(2):97–104.

Aha, D. W., D. Kibler, & M. Albert (1991), Instance-based learning algorithms. *Machine Learning* 6:37–66.

Ahn, David (2006), The stages of event extraction. *Proceedings of the Workshop on Annotating and Reasoning about Time and Events*, 1–8.

Ahn, Kisuh, Johan Bos, James R. Curran, Dave Kor, Malvina Nissim, & Bonnie Webber (2005), Question answering with QED at TREC-2005. *Proceedings of the 14th*

The Handbook of Computational Linguistics and Natural Language Processing, First Edition.
Edited by Alexander Clark, Chris Fox and Shalom Lappin.
© 2013 Blackwell Publishing Ltd except for editorial material and organization
© 2013 Alexander Clark, Chris Fox, and Shalom Lappin. Published 2013 by Blackwell Publishing Ltd.

Text Retrieval Conference (TREC 2005).
http://trec.nist.gov/pubs/trec14/papers/
uedinburgh-nissim.qa.pdf

Ahn, René M. C., & Hans-Peter Kolb (1990),
Discourse representation meets
constructive mathematics. *Papers from the
2nd Symposium on Logic and Language*,
105–24.

Aho, A., & J. D. Ullman (1969), Syntax
directed translations and the pushdown
assembler. *Journal of Computer and System
Sciences* 3:37–56.

Aho, A., & J. D. Ullman (1972), *The Theory of
Parsing, Translation and Compiling*, vol. 1:
Parsing. Englewood Cliffs, NJ:
Prentice-Hall.

Akiba, Yasuhiro, Taro Watanabe, & Eiichiro
Sumita (2002), Using language and
translation models to select the best
among outputs from multiple MT
systems. *Proceedings of the 19th
International Conference on Computational
Linguistics (COLING 2002)*, 1079–85.

Alegria, Iñaki, Arantza Casillas,
Arantza Díaz de Ilarraza et al. (2008),
Mixing approaches to MT for Basque:
selecting the best output from RBMT,
EBMT and SMT. *MATMT 2008: Mixing
Approaches to Machine Translation*,
27–34.

Alishahi, Afra, & Suzanne Stevenson
(2008), A computational model of early
argument structure acquisition. *Cognitive
Science* 32(5):789–834.

Allauzen, Cyril, Michael Riley, Johan
Schalkwyk, Wojciech Skut, & Mehryar
Mohri (2007), OpenFst: a general and
ef cient weighted nite-state transducer
library. *Proceedings of the 9th International
Conference on Implementation and
Application of Automata (CIAA 2007)*,
Lecture Notes in Computer Science
4783:11–23. www.openfst.org

Allen, James (1995), *Natural Language
Understanding*. Redwood City, CA:
Benjamin/Cummings.

Allen, James, & Ray Perrault (1980),
Analyzing intention in utterances.
Artificial Intelligence 15:143–78.

Allen, James, Bradford Miller, Eric Ringger,
& Tiresa Sikorski (1996), A robust system
for natural spoken dialogue. *Proceedings
of the 34th Annual Meeting of the
Association for Computational Linguistics*,
62–70.

Allen, James, Lenhart K. Schubert, George
Ferguson et al. (1995), The trains project:
a case study in building a conversational
planning agent. *Journal of Experimental
and Theoretical AI* 7:7–48.

Allopenna, Paul D., James S. Magnuson, &
Michael K. Tanenhaus (1998), Tracking
the time course of spoken word
recognition using eye-movements:
evidence for continuous mapping
models. *Journal of Memory and Language*
38:419–39.

Allwood, Jens (1995), An activity based
approach to pragmatics. *Gothenburg
Papers in Theoretical Linguistics* 76.
Reprinted in Harry Bunt & William Black
(eds.) (2000), *Abduction, Belief and Context
in Dialogue: Studies in Computational
Pragmatics*. Amsterdam: John Benjamins,
47–80.

Allwood, Jens (1999), The Swedish spoken
language corpus at Göteborg University.
*Proceedings of Fonetik 99, Gothenburg
Papers in Theoretical Linguistics* 81:5–9.

Alonso i Alemany, L., & M. Fuentes Fort
(2003), Integrating cohesion and
coherence for automatic summarization.
*Proceedings of the 11th Meeting of the
European Chapter of the Association for
Computational Linguistics*, 1–8.

Altmann, Gerry T. M., & Yuki Kamide
(1999), Incremental interpretation at
verbs: restricting the domain of
subsequent reference. *Cognition*
73:247–64.

American National Standards Institute
(1986), *ANSI X3.4-1986. American National
Standard for Information Systems – Coded
Character Sets – 7-bit American National
Standard Code for Information Interchange
(7-bit ASCII)*. New York: ANSI.

Anastasakos, T., J. McDonough,
R. Schwartz, & J. Makhoul (1996),

A compact model for speaker-adaptive training. *Proceedings of ICSLP '96*, 1137–40.

Anderson, John R. (1990), *The Adaptive Character of Thought*. Hillsdale, NJ. Lawrence Erlbaum Associates.

Anderson, John R., Daniel Bothell, Michael D. Byrne, Scott Douglass, Christian Lebiere, & Yulin Qin (2004), An integrated theory of the mind. *Psychological Review* 111:1036–60.

Ando, Rie Kubota, & Lillian Lee (2003), Mostly-unsupervised statistical segmentation of Japanese kanji sequences. *Journal of Natural Language Engineering* 9:127–49.

André, Elizabeth, & Thomas Rist (1994), Generating coherent presentations employing textual and visual material. *Artifical Intelligence Review* 9:147–65.

Andreev, Nikolaj D. (ed.) (1965), *Statistiko-kombinatornoe modelirovanie jazykov*. Moskow: Nauka.

Andreev, Nikolaj D. (1967), *Statistiko-kombinatorney metody v teoretičeskom i prikladnom jazykovedenii*. Leningrad.

Andrew, Galen, & Jianfeng Gao (2007), Scalable training of L^1-regularized log-linear models. *Proceedings of the 24th International Conference on Machine Learning*, 33–40.

Androutsopoulos, I., G. Paliouras, V. Karkaletsis, G. Sakkis, C. D. Spyropoulos, & P. Stamatopoulos (2000), Learning to lter spam e-mail: a comparison of a naive Bayesian and a memory-based approach. *Proceedings of the 'Machine Learning and Textual Information Access' Workshop of the 4th European Conference on Principles and Practice of Knowledge Discovery in Databases*, 1–13.

Angheluta, Roxana, Rik De Busser, & Marie Francine Moens (2002), The use of topic segmentation for automatic summarization. *Proceedings of the ACL-2002 Post-Conference Workshop on Automatic Summarization*, 66–70.

Angluin, D., & P. Laird (1988), Learning from noisy examples. *Machine Learning* 2(4):343–70.

Appelt, Douglas, Jerry Hobbs, John Bear, David Israel, & Mabry Tyson (1993), FASTUS: a nite-state processor for information extraction from real-world text. *Proceedings of IJCAI-93* 1172–8.

Argamon, Shlomo, Navot Akiva, Amihood Amir, & Oren Kapah (2004), Ef cient unsupervised recursive word segmentation using minimum description length. *Proceedings of the 20th International Conference on Computational Linguistics (COLING 2004)*, 22–9.

Armentano-Oller, Carmen, Rafael Carrasco, Antonio Corbí-Bellot et al. (2006), Open-source Portuguese–Spanish machine translation. *Computational Processing of the Portuguese Language, Proceedings of the 7th International Workshop on Computational Processing of Written and Spoken Portuguese, PROPOR 2006, Lecture Notes in Computer Science* 3960:50–9.

Armstrong, Stephen, Marian Flanagan, Yvette Graham et al. (2006), MaTrEx: machine translation using examples, *TC-STAR OpenLab on Speech Translation* (not numbered).

Arnold, Doug, Lorna Balkan, Lee Humphreys, Siety Meijer, & Louisa Sadler (1994), *Machine Translation: An Introductory Guide*. Oxford: Blackwell.

Artstein, Ron, & Massimo Poesio (2008), Inter-coder agreement for computational linguistics (survey article). *Computational Linguistics* 34(4):555–96.

Arun, Abhishek, & Frank Keller (2005), Lexicalization in crosslinguistic probabilistic parsing: the case of French. *Proceedings of the 43rd Annual Meeting of the Association for Computational Linguistics*, 306–13.

Asher, Nicholas (1993), *Reference to Abstract Objects in English: A Philosophical Semantics for Natural Language*

Metaphysics, Studies in Linguistics and Philosophy. Dordrecht: Kluwer.

Asher, Nicholas, & Alex Lascarides (2003), *Logics of Conversation.* Cambridge: Cambridge University Press.

Asher, Nicholas, & Alex Lascarides (2008), Commitments, beliefs and intentions in dialogue. *Proceedings of LonDial, the 12th Workshop on the Formal Semantics and Pragmatics of Dialogue,* 35–42.

Atkeson, C., A. Moore, & S. Schaal (1997), Locally weighted learning. *Artificial Intelligence Review* 11(1–5):11–73.

Atwell, E., J. Hughes, & C. Souter (1995), AMALGAM: Automatic Mapping Among Lexico-Grammatical Annotation Models. *Proceedings of SIGDAT-95, EACL-95, Dublin.*

Aubert, X., H. Ney, C. Dugast, & V. Steinbiss (1994), Large vocabulary continuous speech recognition of Wall Street Journal data. *ICASSP '94 Proceedings,* 129–32.

Auchard, Eric (2008), Web start-up unveils semantic Wikipedia search tool. *Reuters.* www.reuters.com/article/technology News/idUSL1244854220080512

Aust, H., M. Oerder, F. Seide, & V. Steinbiss (1995), The Philips automatic train timetable information system. *Speech Communication* 17(3–4):249–62.

Austen, Jane (1995), *Pride and Prejudice.* London: Penguin.

Austin, John L. (1962), *How to Do Things with Words.* Oxford: Clarendon Press.

Austin, S., R. Schwartz, & P. Placeway (1991), The forward-backward search algorithm. *Proceedings of IEEE ICASSP-91,* 697–700. http://dx.doi.org/10.1109/ ICASSP.1991.150435

Ayan, Necip Fazil, & Bonnie Dorr (2006), Going beyond AER: an extensive analysis of word alignments and their impact on MT. *Proceedings of the 21st International Conference on Computational Linguistics and 44th Annual Meeting of the Association for Computational Linguistics,* 9–16.

Azzam, S., K. Humphreys, & R. Gaizauskas (1999), Using coreference chains for text summarisation. *Proceedings of the ACL '99 Workshop on Coreference and its Applications,* 77–84.

Baayen, R. H., R. Piepenbrock, & H. van Rijn (1993), *The CELEX Lexical Data Base on CD-ROM.* Philadelphia, PA: Linguistic Data Consortium.

Babko-Malaya, Olga, Ann Bies, Ann Taylor et al. (2006), Issues in synchronizing the English treebank and propbank. *Proceedings of the Workshop on Frontiers in Linguistically Annotated Corpora 2006,* 70–7.

Bagga, A., & B. Baldwin (1998), Entity-based cross-document coreferencing using the vector space model. *Proceedings of the 18th International Conference on Computational Linguistics (COLING '98)/ACL '98 Conference,* 79–85.

Bahl, L. R., F. Jelinek, & R. Mercer (1983), A maximum likelihood approach to speech recognition. *IEEE Transactions on Pattern Analysis and Machine Intelligence* 5(2):179–90.

Bahl, Lalit R., Peter F. Brown, Peter V. de Souza, & Robert L. Mercer (1989), A tree-based statistical language model for natural language speech recognition. *IEEE Transactions on Acoustics, Speech, and Signal Processing* 37(7):1001–8.

Bahl, L. R., P. V. de Souza, P. S. Gopalakrishnan, D. Nahamoo, & M. A. Picheny (1991), Context dependent modeling of phones in continuous speech using decision trees. *Proceedings of DARPA Speech and Natural Language Processing Workshop,* 264–70.

Bahl, L. R., S. V. de Gennaro, P. S. Gopalakrishnan, & R. L. Mercer (1993), A fast approximate acoustic match for large vocabulary speech recognition. *IEEE Transactions on Speech and Audio Processing* 1(1):59–67.

Baker, Collin F., Charles J. Fillmore, & John B. Lowe (1998), The Berkeley FrameNet project. *Proceedings of the 18th International Conference on Computational Linguistics (COLING '98)/ACL '98 Conference,* 86–90.

Baker, J. (1975), The DRAGON system – an overview. *IEEE Transactions on Acoustics, Speech, and Signal Processing* 23(1):24–9.

Baker, J. (1989), DragonDictate – 30K: Natural language speech recognition with 30,000 words. *Proceedings of Eurospeech '89*, 161–3.

Bakhtin, M. M. (1986), *Speech Genres and Other Late Essays*. Austin, TX: University of Texas Press.

Balay, Satish, William D. Gropp, Lois Curfman McInnes, & Barry F. Smith (2002), PETSc users manual, Technical Report ANL-95/11–Revision 2.1.2, Argonne National Laboratory.

Baldwin, B. (1997), CogNIAC: high precision coreference with limited knowledge and linguistic resources. *Proceedings of Workshop on Operational Factors in Practical, Robust Anaphora Resolution for Unrestricted Texts*, 38–45.

Baldwin, B., & Thomas S. Morton (1998), Dynamic coreference-based summarization. *Proceedings of the 3rd Conference on Empirical Methods in Natural Language Processing (EMNLP-3)*, 1–6.

Baldwin, B., J. Reynar, M. Collins, et al. (1995), Description of the University of Pennsylvania system used for MUC-6. *Proceedings of the 6th Message Understanding Conference (MUC-6)*, 177–91.

Baldwin, T., & F. Bond (2003), A plethora of methods for learning English countability. *Proceedings of the 2003 Conference on Empirical Methods in Natural Language Processing*, 73–80.

Banerjee, Satanjeev, & Alon Lavie (2005), Meteor: an automatic metric for MT evaluation with improved correlation with human judgments. *Proceedings of the ACL Workshop on Intrinsic and Extrinsic Evaluation Measures for Machine Translation and/or Summarization*, 65–72.

Bangalore, Srinivas, & Aravind Joshi (1999), Supertagging: an approach to almost parsing. *Computational Linguistics* 25(2):237–65.

Bangalore, Srinivas, & Owen Rambow (2000), Corpus-based lexical choice in natural language generation. *Proceedings of the 38th Annual Meeting of the Association for Computational Linguistics (ACL-2000)*, 464–71.

Bangalore, Srinivas, German Bordel, & Giuseppe Riccardi (2001), Computing consensus translation from multiple machine translation systems. *Workshop on Automatic Speech Recognition and Understanding*, 351–4.

Banko, M., & E. Brill (2001), Scaling to very very large corpora for natural language disambiguation. *Proceedings of the 39th Annual Meeting of the Association of Computational Linguistics*, 26–33.

Bar-Haim, Roy, Ido Dagan, Bill Dolan et al. (2006), The second PASCAL recognising textual entailment challenge. *Proceedings of the Second PASCAL Challenges Workshop on Recognising Textual Entailment*.

Bar-Hillel, Y. (1953), A quasi-arithmetical notation for syntactic description. *Language* 29:47–58.

Bar-Hillel, Y. (1960), The present status of automatic translation of languages, in F. L. Alt (ed.), *Advances in Computers*, 1. New York: Academic Press, 91–163.

Bar-Hillel, Y., Y. M. Perles, & Eli Shamir (1961), On formal properties of simple phrase structure grammars. *Zeitschrift für Phonetik, Sprachwissenschaft und Kommunikationsforschung* 14:143–72.

Bar-Hillel, Y., M. Perles, & E. Shamir (1964), On formal properties of simple phrase structure grammars, in Y. Bar-Hillel (ed.), *Language and Information: Selected Essays on their Theory and Application*. Reading, MA: Addison-Wesley, 116–50.

Barbu, C. (2001), Automatic learning and resolution of anaphora. *Proceedings of the International Conference Recent Advances in Natural Language Processing, RANLP'01*, 22–7.

Barbu, Catalina, & Ruslan Mitkov (2001), Evaluation tool for rule-based anaphora resolution methods. *Proceedings of the*

39th Annual Meeting of the Association for Computational Linguistics, 34–41.

Barlow, Michael (1998), Feature mismatches and anaphora resolution. *Proceedings of DAARC2*, 34–41.

Baroni, M. (2003), Distribution-driven morpheme discovery: a computational/experimental study. *Yearbook of Morphology*, 213–48.

Baroni, M., J. Matiasek, & H. Trost (2002), Unsupervised discovery of morphologically related words based on orthographic and semantic similarity. *Proceedings of the Workshop on Morphological and Phonological Learning*, SIGPHON-ACL, 11–20.

Barsalou, L. W. (1999), Perceptual and symbol systems. *Behavioural and Brain Sciences* 22:577–609.

Barwise, Jon, & John Etchemendy (1990), Information, infons, and inference, in Robin Cooper, Kuniaki Mukai, & John Perry (eds.), *Situation Theory and Its Applications, I, CSLI Lecture Notes* 22. Stanford, CA: CSLI Publications, 33–78.

Barwise, Jon, & John Perry (1983), *Situations and Attitudes*. Cambridge, MA: MIT Press.

Barzilay, R., & M. Elhadad (1997), Using lexical chains for text summarization. *Proceedings of the ACL Workshop on Intelligent Scalable Text Summarization*, 10–17.

Barzilay, R., & Mirella Lapata (2005a), Collective content selection for concept-to-text generation. *Proceedings of the 2005 Conference on Empirical Methods in Natural Language Processing (EMNLP-2005)*, 331–8.

Barzilay, R., & Mirella Lapata (2005b), Modeling local coherence: an entity-based approach. *Proceedings of the 43rd Annual Meeting of the Association for Computational Linguistics (ACL '05)*, 141–8.

Barzilay, R., & Mirella Lapata (2006), Aggregation via set partitioning for natural language generation. *Proceedings of the Human-Language Technology Conference of the North American Chapter of the Association for Computational Linguistics*, 359–66.

Bateman, John (1997), Enabling technology for multilingual natural language generation: the KPML development environment. *Natural Language Engineering* 3:15–55.

Bateman, John, Thomas Kamps, Jorg Kleinz, & Klaus Reichenberger (2001), Towards constructive text, diagram, and layout generation for information presentation. *Computational Linguistics* 27:409–49.

Baum, Leonard E. (1972), An inequality and associated maximization technique in statistical estimation for probabilistic functions of Markov processes. *Inequalities* 3(1):1–8.

Bealer, G. (1982), *Quality and Concept*. Oxford: Clarendon Press.

Bean, David L., & Ellen Riloff (1999), Corpus-based identi cation of non-anaphoric noun phrases. *Proceedings of ACL '99*, 373–80.

Beaver, David I. (2002), Presupposition projection in DRT: a critical assessment, in David Beaver, Stefan Kaufmann, Brady Clark, & Luis Casillas (eds.), *Stanford Papers on Semantics*. Stanford, CA: CSLI Publications.

Béchet, Frédéric, Alexis Nasr, & Franck Genet (2000), Tagging unknown proper names using decision trees. *Proceedings of the 38th Annual Meeting of the ACL*, 77–84.

Beesley, Kenneth R., & Lauri Karttunen (2003), *Finite-State Morphology: Xerox Tools and Techniques*. Stanford, CA: CSLI Publications.

Bellegarda, J. R. (1997), A latent semantic analysis framework for large-span language modeling. *Proceedings of Eurospeech 97*, 1451–4.

Bellegarda, J. R. (2004), Statistical language model adaptation: review and perspectives. *Speech Communication* 42(1):93–108.

Belnap, Nuel D. (1982), Questions and answers in Montague grammar, in S. Peters & E. Saarinen (eds.), *Processes,*

Beliefs, and Questions. Dordrecht: D. Reidel, 165–98.

Belz, Anja (2008), Automatic generation of weather forecast texts using comprehensive probabilistic generation-space models. *Natural Language Engineering* 14:431–55.

Belz, Anja, & Albert Gatt (2007), The attribute selection for GRE challenge: overview and evaluation results. *Proceedings of Second Workshop on Using Corpora in NLG (UCNLG-2007)*, 75–83.

Belz, Anja, & Eric Kow (2009), System building cost vs. output quality in data-to-text generation. *Proceedings of the 12th European Workshop on Natural Language Generation (ENLG-2009)*, 16–24.

Bengio, Yoshua, Réjean Ducharme, Pascal Vincent, & Christian Janvin (2003), A neural probabilistic language model. *Journal of Machine Learning Research* 3:1137–55.

Benson, Steven, & Jorge J. Moré (2001), A limited memory variable metric method for bound constrained minimization, Preprint ANL/ACS-P909-0901, Argonne National Laboratory.

Benson, Steven, Manojkumar Krishnan, Lois Mcinnes, Jarek Nieplocha, & Jason Sarich (2007), Using the GA and TAO toolkits for solving large-scale optimization problems on parallel computers. *ACM Transactions on Mathematical Software (TOMS)* 33(2):11.

Berger, A., & R. Miller (1998), Just-in-time language modelling. *Proceedings of the International Conference on Acoustics, Speech and Signal Processing* 2:705–8.

Berger, A., Stephen Della Pietra, & Vincent Della Pietra (1996), A maximum entropy approach to natural language processing. *Computational Linguistics* 22(1):39–72.

Berland, Matthew, & Eugene Charniak (1999), Finding parts in very large corpora. *Proceedings of the ACL 1999*, 57–64.

Bernsen, Niels (1995), Why are analogue graphics and natural language both needed in HCI?, in F. Paternó (ed.),

Design, Specification and Verification of Interactive System. Heidelberg: Springer-Verlag, 235–51.

Berrios, Dan, Russell Cucina, & Lawrence Fagan (2002), Methods for semi-automated indexing for high precision information retrieval. *Journal of the American Medical Informatics Association* 9:637–52.

Bertomeu, Núria (2007), A memory and attention-based approach to fragment resolution and its application in a question answering system. PhD thesis, Universität des Saarlandes.

Bertomeu, Núria, Hans Uszkoreit, Anette Frank, Hans-Ulrich Krieger, & Brigitte Jörg (2006), Contextual phenomena and thematic relations in database QA dialogues: results from a Wizard-of-Oz experiment. *Proceedings of the HLT-NAACL 2006 Workshop on Interactive Question Answering*, 1–8.

Berwick, R. C., & Amy S. Weinberg (1984), *The Grammatical Basis of Linguistic Performance: Language Use and Acquisition*. Cambridge, MA: MIT Press.

Berwick, R. C., & Noam Chomsky (2009), 'Poverty of the stimulus' revisited: recent challenges reconsidered. *Proceedings of the 30th Annual Conference of the Cognitive Science Society*, 383.

Besser, Jana, & Jan Alexandersson (2007), A comprehensive dis uency model for multi-party interaction. *Proceedings of SigDial* 8:182–9.

Bever, Tom (1970), The cognitive basis for linguistic structures, in J. R. Hayes (ed.), *Cognition and the Development of Language*. New York: Wiley, 279–362.

Bhatt, Rajesh, Bhuvana Narasimhan, Martha Palmer, Owen Rambow, Dipti Sharma, & Fei Xia (2009), A multi-representational and multi-layered treebank for Hindi/Urdu. *Proceedings of the 3rd Linguistic Annotation Workshop, Held in Conjunction with ACL-2009*, 186–9.

Biçici, Ergun, & Marc Dymetman (2008), Dynamic translation memory: using statistical machine translation to improve translation memory fuzzy matches. *Computational Linguistics and Intelligent Text Processing, Lecture Notes in Computer Science* 4919:454–65.

Bikel, Daniel (2002), Design of a multi-lingual, parallel-processing statistical parsing engine. *Proceedings of HLT 2002, Second International Conference on Human-Language Technology Conference*, 178–82.

Bikel, Daniel, Scott Miller, Richard Schwartz, & Ralph Weischedel (1997), Nymble: a high-performance learning name- nder. *Proceedings of the Fifth Conference on Applied Natural Language Processing*, 194–201.

Billot, S., & B. Lang (1989), The structure of shared forests in ambiguous parsing. *27th Annual Meeting of the Association for Computational Linguistics, Proceedings of the Conference*, 143–51.

Bilmes, J. A., & K. Kirchhoff (2003), Factored language models and generalized parallel backoff. *Proceedings of HLT/NACCL*, 4–6.

Binder, Katherine S., Susan A. Duffy, & Keith Rayner (2001), The effects of thematic t and discourse context on syntactic ambiguity resolution. *Journal of Memory and Language* 44:297–324.

Binstead, Kim, & Graeme Ritchie (1997), Computational rules for pruning riddles. *Humor* 10:25–76.

Bishop, Christopher M. (1995), *Neural Networks for Pattern Recognition*. Oxford: Oxford University Press.

Black, Alan W., Kevin Lenzo, & Vincent Pagel (1998a), Issues in building general letter to sound rules. *Proceedings of the ESCA Synthesis Workshop*, 77–80.

Black, Alan W., Paul Taylor, & R. Caley (1998b), The Festival speech synthesis system. www.cstr.ed.ac.uk/projects/festival/

Black, E., S. Abney, D. Flickenger et al. (1991), A procedure for quantitatively comparing the syntactic coverage of English grammars. *HLT '91: Proceedings of the Workshop on Speech and Natural Language*, 306–11.

Black, E., Frederick Jelinek, John Lafferty, Robert Mercer, & Salim Roukos (1992), Decision tree models applied to the labeling of text with parts of speech. *Proceedings of the DARPA Speech and Natural Language Workshop*, 117–21.

Blackburn, Patrick, & Johan Bos (1999), Working with discourse representation theory: an advanced course in computational semantics. Draft book.

Blackburn, Patrick, & Johan Bos (2005), *Representation and Inference for Natural Language: A First Course in Computational Semantics*. Stanford, CA: CSLI Publications.

Blitzer, J., A. Globerson, & F. Pereira (2005), Distributed latent variable models of lexical co-occurrences. *Proceedings of the 10th International Workshop on Artificial Intelligence and Statistics*.

Blunsom, Phil, & Trevor Cohn (2006), Discriminative word alignment with conditional random elds. *Proceedings of the 21st International Conference on Computational Linguistics and 44th Annual Meeting of the Association for Computational Linguistics*, 65–72.

Bod, R. (1998), *Beyond Grammar: An Experience-Based Theory of Language*. Stanford, CA: CSLI Publications.

Bod, R. (2003), An ef cient implementation of a new DOP model. *Proceedings of the 10th Meeting of the EACL*, 19–26.

Bod, R. (2006a), An all-subtrees approach to unsupervised parsing. *Proceedings of ACL-COLING 2006*, 865–72.

Bod, R. (2006b), Exemplar-based syntax: how to get productivity from examples. *The Linguistic Review* 23(3):291–320.

Bod, R. (2007a), Is the end of supervised parsing in sight? *Proceedings of the 45th Annual Meeting of the Association of Computational Linguistics*, 400–7.

Bod, R. (2007b), A linguistic investigation into unsupervised DOP. *Proceedings of the*

Workshop on Cognitive Aspects of Computational Language Acquisition, 1–8.

Boguraev, B., & C. Kennedy (1997), Salience-based content characterisation of documents. *Proceedings of the ACL '97/EACL '97 Workshop on Intelligent Scalable Text Summarisation*, 3–9.

Boguraev, B., & Mary S. Neff (2000), Discourse segmentation in aid of document summarization. *HICSS '00: Proceedings of the 33rd Hawaii International Conference on System Sciences* 3:3004.

Bohlin, P., J. Bos, S. Larsson, I. Lewin, C. Matheson, & D. Milward (1999), Survey of existing interactive systems. *Deliverable D 1.3.*

Bond, Francis, Hitoshi Isahara, Kyoko Kanzaki, & Kiyotaka Uchimoto (2008), Bootstrapping a WordNet using multiple existing WordNets. *Proceedings of the 2008 Language Resources and Evaluation Conference*, 1619–24.

Börger, Egon, Erich Grädel, & Yuri Gurevich (1997), *The Classical Decision Problem, Perspectives in Mathematical Logic.* Berlin: Springer-Verlag.

Bornkessel, Ina, & Matthias Schlesewsky (2006), The extended argument dependency model: a neurocognitive approach to sentence comprehension across languages. *Psychological Review* 113:787–821.

Borthwick, Andrew (1999), A maximum entropy approach to named entity recognition. PhD thesis, New York University.

Borthwick, Andrew, John Sterling, Eugene Agichtein, & Ralph Grishman (1998), Exploiting diverse knowledge sources via maximum entropy in named entity recognition. *Proceedings of the 6th Workshop on Very Large Corpora*, 152–60.

Bos, Johan (1995), Predicate logic unplugged. *Proceedings of the 10th Amsterdam Colloquium*, 133–42.

Bos, Johan, & Malte Gabsdil (2000), First-order inference and the interpretation of questions and answers.

Fourth Workshop on the Semantics and Pragmatics of Dialogue, 43–50.

Bos, Johan, & Tetsush Oka (2002), An inference-based approach to dialogue system design. *Proceedings of the 19th COLING*, 113–19.

Bos, Johan, Ewan Klein, Oliver Lemon, & Tetsushi Oka (2003), DIPPER: description and formalisation of an information-state update dialogue system architecture. *Proceedings of the 4th SIGdial Workshop on Discourse and Dialogue*, 115–24.

Bouma, G., Ismail Fahmi, Jori Mur, Gertjan van Noord, Lonneke van der Plas, & Jörg Tiedemann (2005), Linguistic knowledge and QA. *Traitement Automatique des Langues (TAL)* 46(3):15–39.

Bouma, G., G. Kloosterman, J. Mur, G. van Noord, L. van der Plas, & J. Tiedemann (2007), Question answering with Joost at CLEF. *Proceedings of CLEF '2007*, 257–60.

Bourlard, H., H. Hermansky, & N. Morgan (1996), Towards increasing speech recognition error rates. *Speech Communication* 18(3):205–31.

Boyd, Adriane, Whitney Gegg-Harrison, & Donna Byron (2005), Identifying non-referential it: a machine learning approach incorporating linguistically motivated patterns. *Proceedings of the ACL Workshop on Feature Selection for Machine Learning in NLP*, 40–7.

Branco, A. (ed.) (2007), *Anaphora: Analysis, Algorithms, and Applications.* Dordrecht: Springer.

Branco, A., A. McEnery, & R. Mitkov (eds.) (2005), *Anaphora Processing: Linguistics, Cognitive and Computational Modelling.* Amsterdam: John Benjamin Publishers.

Brants, Sabine, Stefanie Dipper, Silvia Hansen, Wolfgang Lezius, & George Smith (2002), The TIGER treebank. *Proceedings of the Workshop on Treebanks and Linguistic Theories*, 24–41.

Brants, T. (1999), Cascaded Markov models. *9th Conference of the European Chapter of the Association for Computational Linguistics (EACL '99)*, 118–25.

Brants, T., & Matthew W. Crocker (2000), Probabilistic parsing and psychological plausibility, *Proceedings of the 18th International Conference on Computational Linguistics*, 111–17.

Brants, T., A. C. Popat, P. Xu, F. J. Och, & J. Dean (2007), Large language models in machine translation. *Proceedings of the 2007 Joint Conference on Empirical Methods in Natural Language Processing and Computational Natural Language Learning (EMNLP-CoNLL)*, 858–67.

Breiman, L. (1996), Bagging predictors. *Machine Learning* 24(2):123–40.

Breiman, L. (2001a), Random forests. *Machine Learning* 45(1):5–32.

Breiman, L. (2001b), Statistical modeling: the two cultures. *Statistical Science* 16:199–231.

Breiman, L., J. H. Friedman, R. A. Olshen, & C. J. Stone (1984), *Classification and Regression Trees*. Paci c Grove, CA: Wadsworth and Brooks.

Brennan, Susan E., & Herbert Clark (1996), Conceptual pacts and lexical choice in conversation. *Journal of Experimental Psychology: Learning, Memory, and Cognition* 22:1482–93.

Brennan, Susan E., Marilyn W. Friedman, & Carl J. Pollard (1987), A centering approach to pronouns. *Proceedings of the 25th Annual Meeting of the ACL*, 155–62.

Brennan, Susan E., & Michael F. Schober (2001), How listeners compensate for dis uencies in spontaneous speech. *Journal of Memory and Language* 44: 274–96.

Brent, Michael (1999), An ef cient, probabilistically sound algorithm for segmentation and word discovery. *Machine Learning* 34(1–3):71–105.

Brent, Michael R., & Timothy A. Cartwright (1996), Distributional regularity and phonotactics are useful for segmentation. *Cognition* 61:93–125.

Brent, Michael R., Sreerama K. Murthy, & Andrew Lundberg (1995), Discovering morphemic suf xes: a case study in MDL

induction. *Proceedings of the Fifth International Workshop on Artificial Intelligence and Statistics.*

Breslin, C., & M. J. F. Gales (2006), Generating complementary systems for speech recognition. *Proceedings of Interspeech '06*, 1541–4.

Bresnan, Joan (2001), *Lexical-Functional Syntax*. Oxford: Blackwell.

Bresnan, Joan, Ronald M. Kaplan, Stanley Peters, & Annie Zaenen (1982), Cross-serial dependencies in Dutch. *Linguistic Inquiry* 13(4):613–35.

Bridle, J. S. (2004), Towards better understanding of the model implied by the use of dynamic features in HMMs. *Eighth International Conference on Spoken Language Processing*, 725–8.

Brill, Eric (1992), A simple rule-based part of speech tagger. *Proceedings of the 3rd Conference on Applied Natural Language Processing*, 152–5.

Brill, Eric (1993), Transformation-based error-driven parsing. *Proceedings of the 3rd International Workshop on Parsing Technologies.*

Brill, Eric, Susan Dumais, & Michele Banko (2002), Analysis of the AskMSR question-answering system. *Proceedings, Conference on Empirical Methods in Natural Language Processing (EMNLP-2002)*, 257–64.

Brin, Sergey (1998), Extracting patterns and relations from the world-wide web. *Proceedings of the 1998 International Workshop on the Web and Databases at the 6th International Conference on Extending Database Technology, EDBT '98*, 172–83.

Briscoe, E., & John Carroll (1993), Generalised probabilistic LR parsing of natural language (corpora) with uni cation-based grammars. *Computational Linguistics* 19(1):25–9.

Briscoe, E., & John Carroll (2006), Evaluating the accuracy of an unlexicalized statistical parser on the PARC DepBank. *Proceedings of the Poster Session of the Joint Conference of the International Committee on Computational*

Linguistics and the Association for Computational Linguistics (COLING/ACL-06), 41–8.

Brown, John Seeley, & Richard Burton (1975), Multiple representations of knowledge for tutorial reasoning, in D. G. Bowbrow & A. Collins (eds.), *Representation and Understanding*. New York: Academic Press, 311–49.

Brown, Peter, John Cocke, Stephen Della Pietra et al. (1990), A statistical approach to machine translation. *Computational Linguistics* 16(2):79–85.

Brown, Peter, Jennifer Lai, & Robert Mercer (1991), Aligning sentences in parallel corpora. *29th Annual Meeting of the Association for Computational Linguistics*, 169–76.

Brown, Peter, Vincent J. Della Pietra, Peter V. de Souza, Jenifer C. Lai, & Robert Mercer (1992), Class-based n-gram models of natural language. *Computational Linguistics* 18:467–79.

Brown, Peter, Stephen Della Pietra, Vincent Della Pietra, & Robert Mercer (1993), The mathematics of statistical machine translation: parameter estimation. *Computational Linguistics* 19(2):263–311.

Brown, Ralf (1999), Adding linguistic knowledge to a lexical example-based translation system. *Proceedings of the 8th International Conference on Theoretical and Methodological Issues in Machine Translation*, 22–32.

Bruce, Craig L., James L. Melville, Stephen D. Pickett, & Jonathan D. Hirst (2007), Contemporary QSAR classi ers compared. *Journal of Chemical Information and Modeling* 47(1):219–27.

Bruce, Rebecca F., & Janyce Wiebe (1994), Word-sense disambiguation using decomposable models. *ACL*, 139–46.

Brysbaert, Marc, & Don C. Mitchell (1996), Modi er attachment in sentence parsing: evidence from Dutch. *Quarterly Journal of Experimental Psychology* 49A(3):664–95.

Buchholz, S. (1998), Distinguishing complements from adjuncts using

memory-based learning. *Proceedings of the ESSLLI-98 Workshop on Automated Acquisition of Syntax and Parsing*, 41–8.

Buchholz, S. (2002), Memory-based grammatical relation nding. PhD thesis, University of Tilburg.

Buchholz, S., & A. van den Bosch (2000), Integrating seed names and n-grams for a named entity list and classi er. *Proceedings of the 2nd International Conference on Language Resources and Evaluation*, 1215–21.

Buchholz, S., J. Veenstra, & W. Daelemans (1999), Cascaded grammatical relation assignment. *EMNLP-VLC '99, the Joint SIGDAT Conference on Empirical Methods in Natural Language Processing and Very Large Corpora*, 239–46.

Büchi, J. R. (1960), Weak second-order arithmetic and nite automata. *Zeitschrift für Mathematische Logik und Grundlagen der Mathematik* 6:66–92.

Bulyko, Iyer, Mari Ostendorf, & Andreas Stolcke (2003), Getting more mileage from web text sources for conversational speech language modeling using class-dependent mixtures. *Proceedings of the Human-Language Technology Conference 2003*, 7–9.

Bunescu, Razvan, & Raymond J. Mooney (2007), Learning to extract relations from the web using minimal supervision. *Proceedings of the 45th Annual Meeting of the Association of Computational Linguistics*, 576–83.

Burchardt, A., K. Erk, A. Frank, A. Kowalski, S. Pado, & M. Pinkal (2006), The SALSA Corpus: a German corpus resource for lexical semantics. *Proceedings of LREC 2006*, 969–74.

Burger, John, & Lisa Ferro (2005), Generating an entailment corpus from news headlines. *Proceedings of the ACL workshop on Empirical Modeling of Semantic Equivalence and Entailment*, 49–54.

Büring, Daniel (2005), *Binding Theory*. Cambridge: Cambridge University Press.

Burnard, L. (2000a), *Reference Guide for the British National Corpus (World Edition)*.

Oxford: Oxford University Computing Services.

Burnard, L. (2000b), User reference guide for the British National Corpus. Technical report, Oxford University Computing Services.

Busemann, Stephan, & Helmut Horacek (1998), A exible shallow approach to text generation. *Proceedings of the 9th International Workshop on Natural Language Generation (INLG-1998)*, 238–47.

Byrne, W., A. Gunawardana, & S. Khudanpur (1998), Information geometry and EM variants. Technical report CLSP Research Note 17, Department of Electical and Computer Engineering, The Johns Hopkins University.

Cahill, A., Mairad McCarthy, Josef Van Genabith, & Andy Way (2002), Automatic annotation of the Penn Treebank with LFG-structure information. *Proceedings of the LREC 2002 Workshop on Linguistic Knowledge Representation – Bootstrapping Annotated Language Data*, 8–15.

Cahill, A., M. Burke, R. O'Donovan, J. van Genabith, & A. Way (2004), Long-distance dependency resolution in automatically acquired wide-coverage PCFG-based LFG approximations. *Proceedings of the 42nd Meeting of the ACL*, 320–7.

Cairns, P., R. Shilcock, N. Chater, & J. Levy (1997), Bootstrapping word boundaries: a bottom-up corpus-based approach to speech segmentation. *Cognitive Psychology* 33:111–53.

Callaway, Charles, & James Lester (2002), Narrative prose generation. *Artificial Intelligence* 139:213–52.

Callison-Burch, Chris, & Raymond Flournoy (2001), A program for automatically selecting the best output from multiple machine translation engines. *MT Summit VIII: Machine Translation in the Information Age, Proceedings*, 63–6.

Callison-Burch, Chris, Cameron Fordyce, Philipp Koehn, Christof Monz, & Josh Schroeder (2007), (Meta-)evaluation of machine translation. *Proceedings of the 2nd Workshop on Statistical Machine Translation*, 136–58.

Canisius, S., T. Bogers, A. van den Bosch, J. Geertzen, & E. Tjong Kim Sang (2006), Dependency parsing by inference over high-recall dependency predictions. *Proceedings of the 10th Conference on Computational Natural Language Learning, CoNLL-X*, 176–80.

Cao, Yang, Yonggang Deng, Hong Zhang, Taiyi Huang, & Bo Xu ((2000), Decision tree based Mandarin tone model and its application to speech recognition. *Proceedings of the ICASSP'00*, 1759–62.

Carberry, Sandra (1990), *Plan Recognition in Natural Language Dialogue*. Cambridge, MA: MIT Press.

Carenini, Giuseppe, & Johanna D. Moore (2006), Generating and evaluating evaluative arguments. *Artificial Intelligence* 170:925–52.

Carl, Michael, & Andy Way (eds.) (2003), *Text, Speech and Language Technology*, vol. 21: *Recent Advances in Example-Based Machine Translation*. Dordrecht: Kluwer Academic Publishers.

Carl, Michael, & Silvia Hansen (1999), Linking translation memories with example-based machine translation. *MT Summit VII 'MT in the Great Translation Era'*, 617–24.

Carletta, Jean (1996), Assessing agreement on classi cation tasks: the kappa statistic. *Computational Linguistics* 2(22):249–55.

Carletta, Jean, Amy Isard, Stephen Isard, Jacqueline Kowtko, Gwyneth Doherty-Sneddon, & Anne Anderson (1996), Map Task coder's manual. HCRC Research Paper RP-82.

Carlson, A., C. Cumby, J. Rosen, & D. Roth (1999), The SNoW learning architecture. Technical report UIUCDCS-R-99-2101, UIUC Computer Science Department.

Carlson, L., D. Marcu, & M. E. Okurowski (2001), Building a discourse-tagged corpus in the framework of rhetorical structure theory. *Proceedings of SIG-DIAL*, 1–10.

Carlson, L., Daniel Marcu, & Mary Ellen Okurowski (2003), Building a discourse-tagged corpus in the framework of rhetorical structure theory, in Jan van Kuppevelt & Ronnie W. Smith (eds.), *Current and New Directions in Discourse and Dialogue*. Dordrecht: Kluwer Academic Publishers, 85–1.

Carnap, Rudolf (1947), *Meaning and Necessity*. Chicago: University of Chicago Press.

Carpenter, B. (1992), *The Logic of Typed Feature Structures: With Applications to Unification Grammars, Logic Programs, and Constraint Resolution*. Cambridge: Cambridge University Press.

Carpenter, B. (1997), *Type-Logical Semantics*. Cambridge, MA: MIT Press.

Carpuat, Marine, & Dekai Wu (2007), Improving statistical machine translation using word sense disambiguation. *Proceedings of the 2007 Joint Conference on Empirical Methods in Natural Language Processing and Computational Natural Language Learning (EMNLP-CoNLL)*, 61–72.

Carreras, Xavier, & Lluís Màrquez (2005), Introduction to the CoNLL-2005 shared task: semantic role labeling. *Proceedings of CoNLL-2005*, 152–64.

Carreras, Xavier, Michael Collins, & Terry Koo (2008), Dynamic programming and the perceptron for ef cient, feature-rich parsing. *Proceedings of the Twelfth Conference on Natural Language Learning (CoNLL-08)*, 9–16.

Carroll, G., & E. Charniak (1992), Two experiments on learning probabilistic dependency grammars from corpora. *Working Notes of the Workshop on Statistically-Based NLP Techniques*, 1–13.

Carroll, J., E. Briscoe, & Antonio San lippo (1998), Parser evaluation: a survey and a new proposal. *Proceedings of the 1st LREC Conference*, 447–54.

Carroll, J., A. Frank, D. Lin, D. Prescher, & H. Uszkoreit (eds.) (2002), *Proceedings of the Workshop 'Beyond PARSEVAL – Towards Improved Evaluation Measures for Parsing Systems' at the 3rd International Conference on Language Resources and Evaluation*. Las Palmas: LREC.

Carroll, J., G. Minnen, & E. Briscoe (2003), Parser evaluation: using a grammatical relation scheme, in A. Abeillé (ed.), *Treebanks: Building and Using Parsed Corpora*. Dordrecht: Kluwer, 299–316.

Cartwright, Timothy, & Michael Brent (1994), Segmenting speech without a lexicon: the roles of phonotactics and the speech source. *Proceedings of the First Meeting of the ACL Special Interest Group in Computational Phonology*, 83–91.

Caseli, Helena, Maria das Graças Nunes, & Mikel Forcada (2006), Automatic induction of bilingual resources from aligned parallel corpora: application to shallow-transfer machine translation. *Machine Translation* 20(4):227–45.

Cassell, Justine, Joseph Sullivan, Scott Prevost, & Elisabeth Churchill (eds.) (2000), *Embodied Conversational Agents*. Cambridge, MA: MIT Press.

Cavalli-Sforza, V., & A. Lavie (2006), Hybrid machine translation: why and how? www.mt-archive.info/AMTA-2006-Cavalli-Sforza-1.pdf

Cawsey, Alison, Ray Jones, & Janne Pearson (2000), The evaluation of a personalised health information system for patients with cancer. *User Modelling and User-Adapted Interaction* 10:47–72.

Charniak, Eugene (1993), *Statistical Language Learning*. Cambridge, MA: MIT Press.

Charniak, Eugene (2000), A maximum-entropy-inspired parser. *Proceedings of the 1st Meeting of NAACL*, 132–9.

Charniak, Eugene (2001), Immediate-head parsing for language models. *Proceedings of the 39th Annual Meeting and 10th*

Conference of the European Chapter of ACL, 116–23.

Charniak, Eugene, & Mark Johnson (2005), Coarse-to- ne n-best parsing and MaxEnt discriminative reranking. *Proceedings of the 43rd Annual Meeting of the Association for Computational Linguistics (ACL '05)*, 173–80.

Chater, Nick, & Christopher D. Manning (2006), Probabilistic models of language processing and acquisition. *Trends in Cognitive Science* 10(7):335–44.

Chater, Nick, Matthew W. Crocker, & Martin J. Pickering (1998), The rational analysis of inquiry: the case for parsing, in Nick Chater & M. Oaksford (eds.), *Rational Analysis of Cognition*. Oxford: Oxford University Press, 441–68.

Chelba, Ciprian (1997), A structured language model. *Proceedings of ACL-EACL*, 498–500, student section.

Chelba, Ciprian (2001), Portability of syntactic structure for language modeling. *Proceedings of ICASSP*, 544a–d.

Chelba, Ciprian (2006), Acoustic sensitive language model perplexity for automatic speech recognition. *Proceedings of Machine Learning Workshop*.

Chelba, Ciprian, & Frederick Jelinek (1998), Exploiting syntactic structure for language modeling. *Proceedings of COLING-ACL*, 225–31.

Chelba, Ciprian, & Frederick Jelinek (2000), Structured language modeling. *Computer Speech and Language* 14(4):283–332.

Chen, Jinying, & Martha Palmer (2009), Improving English verb sense disambiguation performance with linguistically motivated features and clear sense distinction boundaries. *Language Resources and Evaluation* 43:181–208.

Chen, Jinying, Andrew Schein, Lyle Ungar, & Martha Palmer (2006a), An empirical study of the behavior of active learning for word sense disambiguation. *HLT-NAACL 2006*, 120–7.

Chen, S. F., & Joshua Goodman (1996), An empirical study of smoothing techniques for language modeling. *ACL-96*, CMU-CS-99-108, 310–18.

Chen, S. F., & Joshua Goodman (1998), An empirical study of smoothing techniques for language modeling. Technical report TR-10-98, Harvard University.

Chen, S. F., & Ronald Rosenfeld (1999), A Gaussian prior for smoothing maximum entropy models. Technical report CMU-CS-99-108, Computer Science Department, Carnegie Mellon University.

Chen, S. F., B. Kingsbury, Lidia Mangu, D. Povey, G. Saon, H. Soltau, & G. Zweig (2006b), Advances in speech transcription at IBM under the DARPA EARS program. *IEEE Transactions on Audio, Speech and Language Processing* 14(5):1596–1608.

Chen, Yu, Andreas Eisele, Christian Federmann, Eva Hasler, Michael Jellinghaus, & Silke Theison (2007), Multi-engine machine translation with an open-source decoder for statistical machine translation. *ACL 2007: Proceedings of the Second Workshop on Statistical Machine Translation*, 193–6.

Cherry, Colin, & Dekang Lin (2006), Soft syntactic constraints for word alignment through discriminative training. *Proceedings of the 21st International Conference on Computational Linguistics and 44th Annual Meeting of the Association for Computational Linguistics*, 105–12.

Chi, Zhiyi (1998), *Probability models for complex systems*. PhD thesis, Brown University.

Chiang, David (2000), Statistical parsing with an automatically-extracted tree adjoining grammar. *Proceedings of the 38th Meeting of the ACL*, 456–63.

Chiang, David (2005), A hierarchical phrase-based model for statistical machine translation. *43rd Annual Meeting of the Association for Computational Linguistics (ACL '05)*, 263–70.

Chiang, David (2007), Hierarchical phrase-based translation. *Computational Linguistics* 33(2):201–28.

Chiang, David, Yuval Marton, & Philip Resnik (2008), Online large-margin training of syntactic and structural translation features. *Proceedings of the 2008 Conference on Empirical Methods in Natural Language Processing*, 224–33.

Chierchia, Gennaro (1982), Nominalisation and Montague grammar: a semantics without types for natural languages. *Linguistics and Philosophy* 5:303–54.

Chiou, Fu-Dong, David Chiang, & Martha Palmer (2001), Facilitating treebank annotating using a statistical parser. *Proceedings of the Human-Language Technology Conference (HLT-2001)*, 1–4.

Chiu, Andy, Pascal Poupart, & Chrysanne DiMarco (2007), Generating lexical analogies using dependency relations. *Proceedings of the International Conference on Empirical Methods in Natural Language Processing (EMNLP)*, 561–70.

Chklovski, Timothy, & Patrick Pantel (2004), VerbOcean: mining the web for ne-grained semantic verb relations. *Proceedings of Conference on Empirical Methods in Natural Language Processing (EMNLP-04)*, 33–40.

Choi, F. (2000), Linear text segmentation: approaches, advances and applications. *Proceedings of CLUK 3*.

Choi, F., P. Wiemer-Hastings, & J. Moore (2001), Latent semantic analysis for text segmentation. *Proceedings of EMNLP '01*, 109–17.

Chomsky, N. (1956), Three models for the description of language. *I. R. E. transactions on information theory, Proceedings of the symposium on information theory*, vol. IT-2, 113–23.

Chomsky, N. (1957), *Syntactic Structures*. The Hague: Mouton & Co.

Chomsky, N. (1959), On certain formal properties of grammars. *Information and Control* 2(2):137–67.

Chomsky, N. (1962), Context-free grammars and pushdown storage. Quarterly progress report 65, Research Laboratory of Electronics, MIT.

Chomsky, N. (1965), *Aspects of the Theory of Syntax*. Cambridge, MA: MIT Press.

Chomsky, N. (1971), *Problems of Knowledge and Freedom*. New York: Pantheon.

Chomsky, N. (1981), *Lectures on Government and Binding*. Dordrecht: Foris Publications.

Chomsky, N. (1986), *Knowledge of Language: Its Nature, Origin, and Use*. New York: Praeger.

Chomsky, N. (1995), *The Minimalist Program*. Cambridge, MA: MIT Press.

Chomsky, N. (2000), *New Horizons in the Study of Language and Mind*. Cambridge: Cambridge University Press.

Chomsky, N. (2005), Three factors in language design. *Linguistic Inquiry* 36:1–22.

Chomsky, N., & George A. Miller (1958), Finite state languages. *Information and Control* 1(2):91–112.

Chouinard, M., & E. Clark (2003), Adult reformulations of child errors as negative evidence. *Journal of Child Language* 30:637–69.

Christiansen, Morten H., & Nick Chater (1999a), Connectionist natural language processing: the state of the art. *Cognitive Science* 23:417–37.

Christiansen, Morten H., & Nick Chater (1999b), Toward a connectionist model of recursion in human linguistic performance. *Cognitive Science* 23(2):157–205.

Christiansen, Morten H., & Nick Chater (2001), Connectionist psycholinguistics: capturing the empirical data. *Trends in Cognitive Sciences* 5(2):82–8.

Chrupa a, Grzegorz, & Josef van Genabith (2006), Using machine-learning to assign function labels to parser output for Spanish. *44th Annual Meeting of the Association for Computational Linguistics (ACL'06)*, 136–43.

Chu-Carroll, Jennifer, & Bob Carpenter (1999), Vector-based natural language call routing. *Computational Linguistics* 25:361–88.

Church, Alonzo (1940), A formulation of the simple theory of types. *Journal of Symbolic Logic* 5:56–68.

Church, Kenneth, & Ramesh Patil (1982), Coping with syntactic ambiguity or how to put the block in the box on the table. *American Journal of Computational Linguistics* 8(3–4):139–49.

Cicekli, Ilyas, & Altay Güvenir (2003), Learning translation templates from bilingual translation examples, in Michael Carl & Andy Way (eds.), *Recent Advances in Example-Based Machine Translation*. Dordrecht: Kluwer Academic Publishers, 255–86.

Civit, Montserrat, & Maria Antònia Martí (2004), Building Cast3LB: a Spanish treebank. *Research on Language and Computation* 2(4):549–74.

Claes, Tom, Ioannis Dologlou, Louis ten Bosch, & Dirk Van Compernolle (1998), A novel feature transformation for vocal tract length normalization in automatic speech recognition. *IEEE Transactions on Speech and Audio Processing* 6(6):349–57.

Clark, A. (2001a), Unsupervised language acquisition: theory and practice. Unpublished thesis PhD, University of Sussex.

Clark, A. (2001b), Learning morphology with pair of hidden Markov models. *ACL (Companion Volume)*, 55–60.

Clark, A. (2001c), Partially supervised learning of morphology with stochastic transducers. *NLPRS*, 341–8.

Clark, A. (2002), Memory-based learning of morphology with stochastic transducers. *Proceedings of the 40th Annual Meeting of the Association for Computational Linguistics*, 513–20.

Clark, A. (2003), Combining distributional and morphological information for part of speech induction. *Proceedings of the 10th Annual Meeting of the European Association for Computational Linguistics (EACL)*, 59–66.

Clark, A. (2004), Grammatical inference and the argument from the poverty of the stimulus. *AAAI Spring Symposium on Interdisciplinary Approaches to Language Learning*.

Clark, A. (2006), PAC-learning unambiguous NTS languages. *Proceedings of the 8th International Colloquium on Grammatical Inference (ICGI)*, 59–71.

Clark, A., & Franck Thollard (2004), Partially distribution-free learning of regular languages from positive samples. *Proceedings of COLING*, 85–91.

Clark, A., & Rémi Eyraud (2006), Learning auxiliary fronting with grammatical inference. *Proceedings of the 10th Conference on Computational Language Learning (CoNLL-X)*, 125–32.

Clark, A., & Rémi Eyraud (2007), Polynomial identi cation in the limit of substitutable context-free languages. *Journal of Machine Learning Research* 8:1725–45.

Clark, A., & Shalom Lappin (2009), Another look at indirect negative evidence. *Proceedings of the EACL Workshop on Cognitive Aspects of Computational Language Acquisition*, 26–33.

Clark, A., & Shalom Lappin (2010), *Linguistic Nativism and the Poverty of the Stimulus*. Oxford: Wiley-Blackwell.

Clark, H. (1996), *Using Language*. Cambridge: Cambridge University Press.

Clark, H., & Edward Schaefer (1989), Contributing to discourse. *Arenas of Language Use*, 259–94.

Clark, P., & R. Boswell (1991), Rule induction with CN2: some recent improvements. *Proceedings of the 6th European Working Session on Learning*, 151–63.

Clark, P., & T. Niblett (1989), The CN2 rule induction algorithm. *Machine Learning* 3:261–84.

Clark, Stephen, & James R. Curran (2003), Log-linear models for wide-coverage CCG parsing. *Proceedings of the EMNLP Conference*, 97–104.

Clark, Stephen, & James R. Curran (2004), Parsing the WSJ using CCG and log-linear models. *Proceedings of the 42nd Meeting of the ACL*, 104–11.

Clark, Stephen, & James R. Curran (2007a), Formalism-independent parser evaluation with CCG and DepBank. *Proceedings of the 45th Meeting of the ACL*, 248–55.

Clark, Stephen, & James R. Curran (2007b), Wide-coverage ef cient statistical parsing with CCG and log-linear models. *Computational Linguistics* 33(4):493–552.

Clark, Stephen, Mark Steedman, & James R. Curran (2004), Object-extraction and question-parsing using CCG. *Proceedings of the EMNLP Conference*, 111–18.

Clarkson, Philip, & Roni Rosenfeld (1997), Statistical language modeling using the CMU-Cambridge toolkit. *Proceedings of ESCA Eurospeech 1997*, 2707–10.

Clerehan, R., & R. Buchbinder (2006), Towards a more valid account of functional test quality: the case of the patient information lea et. *Text and Talk* 26(10):39–68.

Cocchiarella, Nino (1985), Two lambda-extensions of the theory of homogeneous simple types as a second order logic. *Notre Dame Journal of Formal Logic* 26:377–407.

Coch, José (1996), Overview of AlethGen. *Proceedings of the 8th International Workshop on Natural-Language Generation (INLG-1996) (Demonstrations and Posters)*, 25–8.

Coch, José (1998), Interactive generation and knowledge administration in MultiMeteo. *Proceedings of the 9th International Workshop on Natural-Language Generation (INLG-1996)*, 300–3.

Cohen, J., T. Kamm, & A. Andreou (1995), Vocal tract normalization in speech recognition: compensating for systematic speaker variability. *Journal of the Acoustical Society of America*, 97:3246–7.

Cohen, Paul, Brent Heeringa, & Niall M. Adams (2002), An unsupervised algorithm for segmenting categorical timeseries into episodes. *Proceedings of the ESF Exploratory Workshop on Pattern Detection and Discovery*, 49–62.

Cohen, Paul, Niall Adams, & Brent Heeringa (2007), Voting experts: an unsupervised algorithm for segmenting sequences, *Intelligent Data Analysis* 11(6):607–25.

Cohen, Philip, & Ray Perrault (1979), Elements of a plan-based theory of speech acts. *Cognitive Science* 3:177–212.

Cole, Stephen V., Matthew D. Royal, Marco G. Valtorta, Michael N. Huhns, & John B. Bowles (2006), A lightweight tool for automatically extracting causal relationships from text. *SoutheastCon, 2006. Proceedings of the IEEE*, 125–9. http://dx.doi.org/10.1109/second.2006.1629336

Collins, M. (1996), A new statistical parser based on bigram lexical dependencies. *Proceedings of the 34th Meeting of the ACL*, 184–91.

Collins, M. (1997), Three generative, lexicalised models for statistical parsing. *Proceedings of the 35th Meeting of the ACL*, 16–23.

Collins, M. (1999), Head-driven statistical models for natural language parsing. PhD thesis, University of Pennsylvania.

Collins, M. (2000), Discriminative reranking for natural language parsing. *Proceedings of the 17th International Conference on Machine Learning*, 175–82.

Collins, M. (2002), Discriminative training methods for hidden Markov models: theory and experiments with perceptron algorithms. *Proceedings of EMNLP*, 1–8.

Collins, M. (2003), Head-driven statistical models for natural language parsing. *Computational Linguistics* 29(4):589–637.

Collins, M. (2004), Parameter estimation for statistical parsing models: theory and practice of distribution-free methods, in H. Bunt, J. Carrol, & G. Satta (eds.), *New Developments in Parsing Technology*. Dordrecht: Kluwer, 19–55.

Collins, M., & Brian Roark (2004), Incremental parsing with the perceptron algorithm. *Proceedings of the 42nd Meeting of the ACL*, 111–18.

Collins, M., & James Brooks (1995), Prepositional phrase attachment through a backed-off model. *Proceedings of the 3rd Workshop on Very Large Corpora*, 27–38.

Collins, M., & Nigel Duffy (2002), New ranking algorithms for parsing and tagging: kernels over discrete structures, and the voted perceptron. *Proceedings of the 40th Annual Meeting of the Association for Computational Linguistics (ACL-02)*, 263–70.

Collins, M., & Yoram Singer (1999), Unsupervised models for named entity classi cation. *Proceedings of the Joint SIGDAT Conference on Empirical Methods in Natural Language Processing and Very Large Corpora*, 100–10.

Collins, M., Jan Hajic, Lance Ramshaw, & Christoph Tillmann (1999), A statistical parser for Czech. *Proceedings of the 37th Meeting of the ACL*, 505–12.

Collobert, Ronan, & Jason Weston (2007), Fast semantic extraction using a novel neural network architecture. *Proceedings of the 45th Annual Meeting of the Association for Computational Linguistics*, 560–7.

Collobert, Ronan, & Jason Weston (2008), A uni ed architecture for natural language processing: deep neural networks with multitask learning. *Proceedings of the 25th International Conference (ICML 2008)*, 160–7.

Connor, Ulla (2006), Discourse structure and corpus linguistics. *The 7th Annual Conference of the American Association of Applied Corpus Linguistics*.

Constantinides, Paul, Scott Hansma, Chris Tchouand, & Alexander Rudnicky (1998), A schema based approach to dialog control. *Proceedings of the 5th International Conference on Spoken Language Processing*, 409–12.

Cook, S. A. (1971), The complexity of theorem-proving procedures. *Proceedings of the 3rd IEEE Symposium on the Theory of Computation*, 151–8.

Cooke, M., P. Green, L. Josifovski, & A. Vizinho (2001), Robust automatic speech recognition with missing and unreliable acoustic data. *Speech Communication* 34(3):267–85.

Cooper, Robin (1983), *Quantification and Syntactic Theory, Synthese Language Library*. Dordrecht: D. Reidel.

Cooper, Robin (2005), Records and record types in semantic theory. *Journal of Logic and Computation* 15(2):99–112. http://dx.doi.org/10.1093/logcom/exi004

Cooper, Robin (2006), Austinian truth in Martin-Löf type theory. *Research on Language and Computation* 3:333–62.

Cooper, Robin, & Jonathan Ginzburg (2002), Using dependent record types in clari cation ellipsis. *Proceedings of the 6th Workshop on the Semantics and Pragmatics of Dialogue (EDILOG)*, 45–52.

Cooper, Robin (forthcoming), Type theory and semantics in ux, in Ruth Kempson, Nicholas Asher, & Tim Fernando (eds.), *Handbook of the Philosophy of Science*, vol. 14: *Philosophy of Linguistics*. Amsterdam: Elsevier.

Copestake, Ann, Dan Flickinger, & Ivan A. Sag (2006), Minimal recursion semantics. *Research on Language and Computation* 3:281–332.

Core, Mark, & James Allen (1997), Coding dialogs with the DAMSL scheme. *Working notes of the AAAI Fall Symposium on Communicative Action in Humans and Machines*, 28–35.

Corley, Steffan, & Matthew Crocker (2000), The modular statistical hypothesis: exploring lexical category ambiguity, in Matthew Crocker, Martin J. Pickering, & Charles Clifton (eds.), *Architectures and Mechanisms for Language Processing*. Cambridge: Cambridge University Press, 135–60.

Corston-Oliver, Simon H. (1998), Beyond string matching and cue phrases: improving the ef ciency and coverage in discourse analysis. *AAAI Spring*

Symposium on Intelligent Text Summarisation, 9–15.

Cost, S., & S. Salzberg (1993), A weighted nearest neighbour algorithm for learning with symbolic features. *Machine Learning* 10:57–78.

Costa, Fabrizio, Vincenzo Lombardo, Paolo Frasconi, & Giovanni Soda (2001), Wide coverage incremental parsing by learning attachment preferences. *Lecture Notes in Computer Science* 2175: 297–307.

Costa, Fabrizio, Paolo Frasconi, Vincenzo Lombardo, & Giovanni Soda (2003), Towards incremental parsing of natural language using recursive neural networks. *Applied Intelligence* 19:9–25.

Costa, Fabrizio, Paolo Frasconi, Vincenzo Lombardo, & Giovanni Soda (2005), Ambiguity resolution analysis in incremental parsing of natural language. *IEEE Transactions on Neural Networks* 16:959–71.

Coussement, Kristof, & Dirk van den Poel (2008), Churn prediction in subscription services: an application of support vector machines while comparing two parameter-selection techniques. *Expert Systems with Applications* 34(1):313–27.

Cover, T. M., & P. E. Hart (1967), Nearest neighbor pattern classi cation. *Institute of Electrical and Electronics Engineers Transactions on Information Theory* 13:21–7.

Covington, Michael A. (1994), *Natural Language Processing for Prolog Programmers*. Englewood Cliffs, NJ: Prentice-Hall.

Cowan, Brooke, & Michael Collins (2005), Morphology and reranking for the statistical parsing of Spanish. *Proceedings of the HLT/EMNLP Conference*, 795–802.

Cowie, Jim, Joe Guthrie, & Louise Guthrie (1992), Lexical disambiguation using simulated annealing. *HLT '91: Proceedings of the Workshop on Speech and Natural Language*, 238–42. http://dx.doi.org/10.3115/1075527

Crain, S. (1991), Language acquisition in the absence of experience. *Behavioral and Brain Sciences* 14:597–650.

Crain, S., & M. Nakayama (1987), Structure dependence in grammar formation. *Language* 63:522–43.

Crain, S., & Mark Steedman (1985), On not being led up the garden path: the use of context by the psychological parser, in D. Dowty, L. Karttunnen, & A. Zwicky (eds.), *Natural Language Parsing*. Cambridge, MA: Cambridge University Press, 320–58.

Crain, S., & R. Thornton (1998), *Investigations in Universal Grammar: A Guide to Experiments in the Acquisition of Syntax and Semantics*. Cambridge, MA: MIT Press.

Creutz, Mathias (2003), Unsupervised segmentation of words using prior distributions of morph length and frequency. *Proceedings of the 41st Annual Meeting of the Association for Computational Linguistics*, 280–7.

Creutz, Mathias, & Krista Lagus (2002), Unsupervised discovery of morphemes. *Proceedings of the Workshop on Morphological and Phonological Learning of ACL-02*, 21–30.

Creutz, Mathias, & Krista Lagus (2004), Induction of a simple morphology for highly-in ecting languages. *Proceedings of 7th Meeting of the ACL Special Interest Group in Computational Phonology (SIGPHON)*, 43–51.

Creutz, Mathias, & Krista Lagus (2005a), Inducing the morphological lexicon of a natural language from unannotated text. *Proceedings of the International and Interdisciplinary Conference on Adaptive Knowledge Representation and Reasoning (AKRR'05)*, 106–13.

Creutz, Mathias, & Krista Lagus (2005b), Unsupervised morpheme segmentation and morphology induction from text corpora using Morfessor 1.0. Technical report 481, Helsinki University of Technology.

Cristea, D., N. Ide, & L. Lomary (1998), Veins theory: a model of global discourse cohesion and coherence. *Proceedings of the 36th Annual Meeting of the Association for*

Computational Linguistics and of the 18th International Conference on Computational Linguistics (COLING '98/ACL '98), 281–5.

Cristea, D., Nancy Ide, Daniel Marcu, & Valentin Tablan (2000), An empirical investigation of the relation between discourse structure and co-reference. *Proceedings of the 18th International Conference on Computational Linguistics (COLING2000)*, 208–14.

Crocker, Matthew W. (1996), *Computational Psycholinguistics: An Interdisciplinary Approach to the Study of Language.* Dordrecht: Kluwer.

Crocker, Matthew W. (1999), Mechanisms for sentence processing, in Simon Garrod & Martin J. Pickering (eds.), *Language Processing.* London: Psychology Press, 191–232.

Crocker, Matthew W. (2005), Rational models of comprehension: addressing the performance paradox, in Anne Cutler (ed.), *Twenty-First Century Psycholinguistics.* Hillsdale, NJ: Lawrence Erlbaum Associates, 363–80.

Crocker, Matthew W., & Frank Keller (2006), Probabilistic grammars as models of gradience in language processing, in G. Fanselow, C. Féry, R. Vogel, & M. Schlesewsky (eds.), *Gradience in Grammar: Generative Perspectives.* Oxford: Oxford University Press, 227–45.

Crocker, Matthew W., & Steffan Corley (2002), Modular architectures and statistical mechanisms: the case from lexical category disambiguation, in Suzanne Stevenson & Paola Merlo (eds.), *The Lexical Basis of Sentence Processing: Formal, Computational, and Experimental Issues.* Amsterdam: John Benjamins, 157–80.

Crocker, Matthew W., & Thorsten Brants (2000), Wide-coverage probabilistic sentence processing. *Journal of Psycholinguistic Research* 29(6):647–69.

Crocker, Matthew W., Pia Knoeferle, & Marshall Mayberry (2010), Situated sentence comprehension: the coordinated interplay account and a neurobehavioral

model. *Brain and Language* 112(3):189–201.

Cromm, Oliver (1997), Af xerkennung in Deutschen Wortformen. *LDV Forum* 14(2):4–13.

Crouch, Richard (2005), Packed rewriting for mapping semantics to KR. *Proceedings of the 6th International Workshop on Computational Semantics*, 103–14.

Crouch, Richard, & Josef van Genabith (1999), Context change, under-speci cation, and structure of glue language derivations, in M. Dalrymple (ed.), *Semantics and Syntax in Lexical Functional Grammar.* Cambridge, MA: MIT Press, 117–89.

Crowe, Jeremy (1996), Shallow techniques for the segmentation of news reports. *Proceedings of the Workshop Language Engineering for Document Analysis and Recognition LEDAR*, 78–85.

Cruse, D. (1986), *Lexical Semantics.* Cambridge: Cambridge University Press.

Cuetos, Fernando, & Don C. Mitchell (1988), Cross-linguistic differences in parsing: restrictions on the late closure strategy in Spanish. *Cognition* 30:73–105.

Cuetos, Fernando, Don C. Mitchell, & Martin M. B. Corley (1996), Parsing in different languages, in Manuel Carreiras, J. García-Albea, & N. Sabastián-Gallés (eds.), *Language Processing in Spanish.* Mahwah, NJ: Lawrence Erlbaum Associates, 145–89.

Culotta, Aron, & Jeffrey Sorensen (2004), Dependency tree kernels for relation extraction. *Proceedings of the 42nd Meeting of the Association for Computational Linguistics (ACL'04), Main Volume*, 423–9.

Cumbreras, M. A. García, L. A. Ureña López, & F. Martínez Santiago (2006), Bruja: question classi cation for Spanish. *Proceedings of the EACL 2006 Workshop on Multilingual Question Answering*, 39–44.

Curran, James R., & Stephen Clark (2003), Investigating GIS and smoothing for maximum entropy taggers. *Proceedings of the 10th Conference on European Chapter of* the Association for Computational Linguistics, 91–8.

Curry, Haskell B., & Robert Feys (1958), *Combinatory Logic, Studies in Logic.* Amsterdam: North Holland Publishing Co.

Curtis, J., G. Matthews, & D. Baxter (2005), On the effective use of CYC in a question answering system. *IJCAI Workshop on Knowledge and Reasoning for Answering Questions*, 61–70.

Daelemans, W. (2002), A comparison of analogical modeling to memory-based language processing, in R. Skousen, D. Lonsdale, & D. B. Parkinson (eds.), *Analogical Modeling*. Amsterdam: John Benjamins.

Daelemans, W., & A. van den Bosch (1992), Generalisation performance of back-propagation learning on a syllabi cation task. *Proceedings of TWLT3: Connectionism and Natural Language Processing*, 27–37.

Daelemans, W., & A. van den Bosch (1996), Language-independent data-oriented grapheme-to-phoneme conversion, in J. P. H. Van Santen, R. W. Sproat, J. P. Olive, & J. Hirschberg (eds.), *Progress in Speech Processing*. Berlin: Springer-Verlag, 77–89.

Daelemans, W., & A. van den Bosch (2005), *Memory-Based Language Processing.* Cambridge: Cambridge University Press.

Daelemans, W., S. Gillis, & G. Durieux (1994), The acquisition of stress: a data-oriented approach. *Computational Linguistics* 20(3):421–51.

Daelemans, W., J. Zavrel, P. Berck, & S. Gillis (1996), MBT: a memory-based part of speech tagger generator. *Proceedings of the 4th Workshop on Very Large Corpora*, ACL SIGDAT, 14–27.

Daelemans, W., P. Berck, & S. Gillis (1997a), Data mining as a method for linguistic analysis: Dutch diminutives. *Folia Linguistica* 31(1–2):57–75.

Daelemans, W., A. van den Bosch, & A. Weijters (1997b), IGTree: using trees for compression and classi cation in lazy learning algorithms. *Artificial Intelligence Review* 11:407–23.

Daelemans, W., J. Zavrel, K. van der Sloot, & A. van den Bosch (1998), TiMBL: Tilburg Memory Based Learner, version 1.0, reference manual. Technical report ILK 98-03, ILK Research Group, Tilburg University.

Daelemans, W., S. Buchholz, & J. Veenstra (1999a), Memory-based shallow parsing. *Proceedings of CoNLL*, 53–60.

Daelemans, W., A. van den Bosch, & J. Zavrel (1999b), Forgetting exceptions is harmful in language learning. *Machine Learning, Special issue on Natural Language Learning* 34:11–41.

Daelemans, W., J. Zavrel, K. van der Sloot, & A. van den Bosch (2007), TiMBL: Tilburg Memory Based Learner, version 6.1, reference guide. Technical report ILK 07-07, ILK Research Group, Tilburg University.

Dagan, Ido, & Alon Itai (1991), A statistical lter for resolving pronoun references, in Y. A. Feldman & A. Bruckstein (eds.), *Artificial Intelligence and Computer Vision.* Amsterdam: Elsevier, 125–35.

Dagan, Ido, Roy Bar-Haim, Idan Szpektor, Iddo Greental, & Eyal Shnarch (2008a), Natural language as the basis for meaning representation and inference. *CICLing, Lecture Notes in Computer Science* 4919:151–70.

Dagan, Ido, Oren Glickman, & Bernardo Magnini (2008b), The PASCAL Recognising Textual Entailment Challenge. *MLCW 2005, LNAI* 3944:177–90.

Dagan, Ido, Dan Roth, Fabio Zanzotto, & Graeme Hirst (eds.) (2009), *Recognizing Textual Entailment, Synthesis Lectures on Human-Language Technologies*, San Rafael, CA: Morgan and Claypool.

Dalmas, Tiphaine, & Bonnie Webber (2007), Answer comparison in automated question answering. *Journal of Applied Logic* 5(1):104–20.

Dalrymple, Mary, John Lamping, Fernando Pereira, & Vijay Saraswat (1999),

Quanti cation, anaphora, and intensionality, in M. Dalrymple (ed.), *Semantics and Syntax in Lexical Functional Grammar*. Cambridge, MA: MIT Press, 39–89.

Damper, R., & J. Eastmond (1997), Pronunciation by analogy: impact of implementational choices on performance. *Language and Speech* 40:1–23.

Dang, Hoa Trang, & Jimmy Lin (2007), Different structures for evaluating answers to complex questions: pyramids won't topple, and neither will human assessors. *Proceedings, 45th Annual Meeting of the Association for Computational Linguistics*, 768–75.

Dantsin, Evgeny, Thomas Eiter, Georg Gottlob, & Andrei Voronkov (2001), Complexity and expressive power of logic programming. *ACM Computing Surveys* 33(3):374–425.

Darroch, J., & D. Ratcliff (1972), Generalized iterative scaling for log-linear models. *Annals of Mathematical Statistics* 43:1470–80.

Dasarathy, B. V. (1991), *Nearest Neighbor (NN) Norms: NN Pattern Classification Techniques*. Los Alamitos, CA: IEEE Computer Society Press.

Davis, S., & P. Mermelstein (1980), Comparison of parametric representations for monosyllabic word recognition in continuously spoken sentences. *IEEE Transactions on Acoustics, Speech and Signal Processing* 28(4): 357–66.

Davis, Wayne A. (1998), *Implicature: Intention, Convention, and Principle in the Failure of Gricean Theory*. Cambridge: Cambridge University Press.

de Champeaux, Dennis (1986), About the Paterson-Wegman linear uni cation algorithm. *Journal of Computer and System Sciences* 32:79–90.

de Kock, J. & W. Bossaert (1969), Towards an automatic morphological segmentation. *International Conference on Computational Linguistics: COLING 1969*, 10.

de Kock, J., & W. Bossaert (1974), Estudios y Ensayos, vol. 202: *Introducción a la lingüística automática en las lenguas románicas*. Madrid: Gredos.

de la Higuera, C. (1997), Characteristic sets for polynomial grammatical inference. *Machine Learning* (27):125–38.

de Marcken, Carl (1996), Unsupervised language acquisition. PhD thesis, MIT.

de Meulder, F., & W. Daelemans (2003), Memory-based named entity recognition using unannotated data. *Proceedings of CoNLL-2003*, 208–11.

de Pauw, G., T. Laureys, W. Daelemans, & H. Van hamme (2004), A comparison of two different approaches to morphological analysis of Dutch. *Proceedings of the ACL 2004 Workshop on Current Themes in Computational Phonology and Morphology*, 62–9.

de Pauw, G., P. Waiganjo, & G.-M. de Schryver (2007), Automatic diacritic restoration for resource-scarce languages. *Proceedings of Text, Speech and Dialogue, 10th International Conference, Lecture Notes in Computer Science* 4629:170–9.

de Roeck, Anne, Udo Kruschwitz, Paul Scott, Sam Steel, Ray Turner, & Nick Webb (2000), The YPA – an assistant for classi ed directory enquiry. *Intelligent Systems and Soft Computing: Prospects, Tools and Applications, Lecture Notes in Artificial Intelligence (LNAI)* 1804:239–58.

de Rosis, Fiorella, & F. Grasso (2000), Affective natural language generation, in Ana Paiva (ed.), *Affective Interactions: Towards a New Generation of Computer Interfaces*. Heidelberg: Springer, 204–18.

de Salvo Braz, Rodrigo, Roxana Girju, Vasin Punyakanok, Dan Roth, & Mark Sammons (2005), Knowledge representation for semantic entailment and question-answering. *IJCAI-05 Workshop on Knowledge and Reasoning for Answering Questions*, 71–80.

de Weijer, Joost Van (2001), The importance of single-word utterances for early word recognition. *Proceedings of ELA 2001*.

Decadt, B., V. Hoste, W. Daelemans, & A. van den Bosch (2004), GAMBL, genetic algorithm optimization of memory-based WSD. *Proceedings of the 3rd International Workshop on the Evaluation of Systems for the Semantic Analysis of Text (Senseval-3)*, 108–12.

Deerwester, Scott, Susan Dumais, Thomas. K. Landauer, George W. Furnas, & Richard A. Harshma (1990), Indexing by latent semantic analysis. *Journal of the American Society for Information Science* 41(6):391–407.

Delgado, Ramon, & Masahiro Araki (2005), *Spoken, Multilingual And Multimodal Dialogue Systems*. Oxford: John Wiley.

Della Pietra, Stephen, Vincent Della Pietra, & John Lafferty (1997), Inducing features of random   elds. *IEEE Transactions Pattern Analysis and Machine Intelligence* 19(4):380–93.

Deming, W. E. & F. F. Stephan (1940), On a least squares adjustment of a sampled frequency table when the expected marginals are known. *Annals of Mathematical Statistics* 11:427–44.

Dempster, Arthur, Nan Laird, & Donald Rubin (1977), Maximum likelihood from incomplete data via the EM algorithm. *Journal of the Royal Statistical Society Series B* 39:1–38.

Deng, L., & X. D. Huang (2004), Challenges in adopting speech recognition. *Communications of the ACM* 47(1):69–75. http://doi.acm.org/10.1145/962081

Deng, L., A. Acero, M. Plumpe, & X. D. Huang (2000), Large-vocabulary speech recognition under adverse acoustic environments. *Proceedings of the ICSLP*, 806–9.

Deng, Yonggang, & William Byrne (2005), HMM word and phrase alignment for statistical machine translation. *Proceedings of Human-Language Technology Conference and Conference on Empirical Methods in Natural Language Processing*, 169–76.

Deng, Yonggang, & William Byrne (2006), MTTK: an alignment toolkit for statistical machine translation. *Proceedings of the Human-Language Technology Conference of the NAACL*, 265–8.

Denis, F. (2001), Learning regular languages from simple positive examples. *Machine Learning* 44(1–2):37–66.

DeRose, Steven J. (1988), Grammatical category disambiguation by statistical optimization. *Computational Linguistics* 14:31–9.

Di Eugenio, B. (1990), Centering theory and the Italian pronominal system. *Proceedings of the 13th International Conference on Computational Linguistics (COLING'90)*, 270–5.

Digalakis, V., J. R. Rohlicek, & M. Ostendorf (1993), ML estimation of a stochastic linear system with the EM algorithm and its application to speech recognition. *IEEE Transactions on Speech and Audio Processing* 1(4):431–42. http://dx.doi.org/10.1109/89.242489

Dijkstra, E. W. (1959), A note on two problems in connexion with graphs. *Numerische Mathematik* 1:269–71.

Dines, J., J. Vepa, & T. Hain (2006), The segmentation of multi-channel meeting recordings for automatic speech recognition. *Proceedings of Interspeech*, 1213–16.

Dligach, Dmitriy, & Martha Palmer (2009), Using language modeling to select useful annotation data. *Proceedings of the Student Research Workshop, Held in Conjunction with NAACL-HLT 2009*, 25–30.

Doddington, George (2002), Automatic evaluation of MT quality using n-gram co-occurrence statistics. *Proceedings of Human-Language Technology Conference 2002*, 138–45.

Dolan, Elizabeth D., & Jorge J. Moré (2002), Benchmarking optimization software with performance pro   les. *Mathematical Programming* 91:201–13.

Domingos, P. (1995), The RISE 2.0 system: a case study in multistrategy learning. Technical report 95-2, University of California at Irvine, Department of Information and Computer Science.

Domingos, P. (1996), Unifying instance-based and rule-based induction. *Machine Learning* 24:141–68.

Dorr, Bonnie J., Christof Monz, Stacy President, Richard Schwartz, & David Zajic (2005), A methodology for extrinsic evaluation of text summarization: does ROUGE correlate? *Proceedings of the ACL 2005 Workshop on Intrinsic and Extrinsic Evaluation Measures for MT and/or Summarization*, 1–8.

Dowty, David (1991), Thematic proto-roles and argument selection. *Language* 67(3):547–619.

Dridan, R., & T. Baldwin (2007), What to classify and how: experiments in question classi cation for Japanese. *Proceedings of the 10th Conference of the Pacific Association for Computational Linguistics*, 333–41.

Droppo, J., & A. Acero (2008), Environmental robustness, in Jacob Benesty, M. Mohan Sondhi, & Yiteng Huang (eds.), *Springer Handbook of Speech Processing*. Berlin: Springer, 653–79.

Droppo, J., A. Acero, & L. Deng (2002), Uncertainty decoding with SPLICE for noise robust speech recognition. *Proceedings IEEE ICASSP*, 57–60.

Dubey, Amit, & Frank Keller (2003), Probabilistic parsing for German using sisterhead dependencies. *Proceedings of the 41st Annual Meeting of the Association for Computational Linguistics*, 96–103.

Dudani, S. A. (1976), The distance-weighted k-nearest neighbor rule. *IEEE Transactions on Systems, Man, and Cybernetics*, vol. SMC-6, 325–7.

Duffy, Susan A., Robin K. Morris, & Keith Rayner (1988), Lexical ambiguity and xation times in reading. *Journal of Memory and Language* 27:429–46.

EAGLES (1996), Evaluation of natural language processing systems: nal report. Technical report EAGLES document EAG-EWG-PR.2. www.issco.unige.ch/projects/ewg96/ewg96.html

Earley, J. (1970), An ef cient context-free parsing algorithm. *Communications of the ACM* 13(2):94–102.

Ebert, Christian (2005), Formal investigation of underspeci ed representations. Unpublished PhD thesis, King's College London.

Eddington, D. (2002a), A comparison of two analogical models: Tilburg memory-based learner versus analogical modeling, in R. Skousen, D. Lonsdale, & D. B. Parkinson (eds.), *Analogical Modeling*. Amsterdam: John Benjamins, 141–55.

Eddington, D. (2002b), Dissociation in Italian conjugations: a single-route account. *Brain and Language* 81(1–3):291–302.

Eddington, D. (2002c), Spanish diminutive formation without rules or constraints. *Linguistics* 40(2):395–419.

Eddington, D. (2004), Issues in modeling language processing analogically. *Lingua* 114(7):849–71.

Edmonds, Philip, & Eneko Agirre (2008), Word sense disambiguation. *Scholarpedia* 3(7):4358.

Efron, Bradley, & Gail Gong (1983), A leisurely look at the bootstrap, the jackknife, and cross-validation. *The American Statistician* 37(1):36–48.

Ehlen, P., M. Purver, J. Niekrasz, S. Peters, & K. Lee (2008), Meeting adjourned: off-line learning interfaces for automatic meeting understanding. *Proceedings of the International Conference on Intelligent User Interfaces*, 276–84.

Eisele, Andreas, Christian Federmann, Hans Uszkoreit, et al. (2008), Hybrid machine translation architectures within and beyond the EuroMatrix project. *EAMT 2008: 12th annual conference of the European Association for Machine Translation*, 27–34.

Eisner, J. (1996), Three new probabilistic models for dependency parsing: an exploration. *Proceedings of the 16th COLING Conference*, 340–5.

Eisner, J. (2000), Bilexical grammars and their cubic-time parsing algorithms, in

H. Bunt & A. Nijholt (eds.), *Advances in Probabilistic and other Parsing Technologies*. Amsterdam: Kluwer Academic Publishers, 29–61.

Eisner, J., & G. Satta (1999), Ef cient parsing for bilexical context-free grammars and head automaton grammars. *37th Annual Meeting of the Association for Computational Linguistics, Proceedings of the Conference*, 457–64.

Elhadad, Michael, & Jacques Robin (1997), SURGE: a comprehensive plug-in syntactic realisation component for text generation. Technical report, Computer Science Department, Ben-Gurion University.

Eliasson, Karolina (2007), Case-based techniques used for dialogue understanding and planning in a human-robot dialogue system. *Proceedings of the International Joint Conference on Artificial Intelligence*, 1600–5.

Elko, G. W., & J. Meyer (2008), Microphone arrays, in Jacob Benesty, M. Mohan Sondhi, & Yiteng Huang (eds.), *Springer Handbook of Speech Processing*. Springer, Berlin: 1021–41.

Ellison, T. Mark (1994), The machine learning of phonological structure. PhD thesis, University of Western Australia.

Elman, Jeffrey L. (1990), Finding structure in time. *Cognition Science* 14(2):179–211.

Elman, Jeffrey L. (1991), Distributed representations, simple recurrent networks, and grammatical structure. *Machine Learning* 7:195–225.

Emami, Ahmad, & Frederick Jelinek (2005), A neural syntactic language model. *Machine Learning* 60(1–3):195–227.

Erjavec, Tomaž, & Nancy Ide (1998), The MULTEXT-East corpus. *First International Conference on Language Resources and Evaluation, LREC '98*, 971–4.

Erjavec, Tomaž, & Sašo Džeroski (2004), Machine learning of morphosyntactic structure: lemmatizing unknown Slovene words. *Applied Artificial Intelligence* 18:17–40.

Ernestus, M. (2006), Statistically gradient generalizations for contrastive phonological features. *The Linguistic Review* 23(3):217–33.

Escudero, Gerard, Lluis Marquez, & German Rigau (2000), A comparison between supervised learning algorithms for word sense disambiguation. *Proceedings of CoNLL-2000, ACL*, 31–6.

Etzioni, Oren, Michael Cafarella, Doug Downey et al. (2005), Unsupervised named-entity extraction from the web: an experimental study. *Artificial Intelligence* 165(1):91–134.

Evans, Richard (2000), A comparison of rule-based and machine learning methods for identifying non-nominal it. *Proceedings of Natural Language Processing – NLP2000*, 233–41.

Evans, Richard (2001), Applying machine learning toward an automatic classi cation of It. *Literary and Linguistic Computing* 16(1):45–57.

Evermann, G., & P. C. Woodland (2000), Posterior probability decoding, con dence estimation and system combination. *Proceedings of the Speech Transcription Workshop*, 27–30.

Evermann, G. & P. C. Woodland (2003), Design of fast LVCSR systems. *Proceedings of ASRU '03*, 7–12.

Fant, Gunnar (1960), *Acoustic Theory of Speech Production*. The Hague: Mouton.

Federmeier, Kara (2007), Thinking ahead: the role and roots of prediction in language comprehension. *Psychophysiology* 44:491–505.

Feiner, Steve, & Kathleen R. McKeown (1990), Coordinating text and graphics in explanation generation. *Proceedings of the 8th National Conference on Artificial Intelligence (AAAI-1990)*, 442–9.

Fellbaum, Christiane (ed.) (1998), *WordNet: An Electronic Lexical Database*. Cambridge, MA: MIT Press.

Fellbaum, Christiane, Joachim Grabowski, & Shari Landes (1998), Performance and con dence in a semantic annotation task, in Christiane Fellbaum (ed.), *WordNet: An Electronic Lexical Database*. Cambridge, MA: MIT Press, 217–37.

Ferguson, George, & James Allen (1998), Trips: an integrated intelligent problem-solving assistant. *Proceedings of the 15th National Conference on AI (AAAI-98)*, 26–30.

Fernández, R. (2006), Non-sentential utterances in dialogue: classi cation, resolution and use. PhD thesis, King's College London.

Fernández, R., & Jonathan Ginzburg (2002), Non-sentential utterances: a corpus study. *Traitement automatique des langues*, 43(2):13–42.

Fernández, R., & Ulle Endriss (2007), Abstract models for dialogue protocols. *Journal of Logic, Language and Information* 16(2):121–40.

Fernández, R., J. Ginzburg, & S. Lappin (2004), Classifying ellipsis in dialogue: a machine learning approach. *Proceedings of the 20th International Conference on Computational Linguistics, COLING 2004*, 240–6.

Fernández, R., Jonathan Ginzburg, & Shalom Lappin (2007), Classifying ellipsis in dialogue: a machine learning approach. *Computational Linguistics* 33(3):397–427.

Ferres, Leo, Avi Parush, Shelley Roberts, & Gitte Lindgaard (2006), Helping people with visual impairments gain access to graphical information through natural language: the iGraph system. *Proceedings of the 10th International Conference on Computers Helping People with Special Needs*, 1122–30.

Ferri, C., P. Flach, & J. Hernández-Orallo (2003), Improving the AUC of probabilistic estimators trees. *Proceedings of 14th European Conference on Machine Learning (ECML '03)*, 121–32.

Fiedler, Armin (2005), Natural language proof explanation, in Dieter Hutter & Werner Stephan (eds.), *Mechanizing Mathematical Reasoning*. Berlin: Springer-Verlag, 342–63.

Fillmore, C. J. (1968), The case for case, in Emmon Bach & Robert T. Harms (eds.), *Universals in Linguistic Theory*. New York: Holt, Reinhart and Winston, 1–88.

Fillmore, C. J. (1976), Frame semantics and the nature of language. *Annals of the New York Academy of Sciences: Conference on the Origin and Development of Language and Speech* 280:20–32.

Fillmore, C. J., Christopher Johnson, & Miriam Petruck (2003), Background to framenet, *International Journal of Lexicography* 16:235–250.

Finch, S., N. Chater, & M. Redington (1995), Acquiring syntactic information from distributional statistics, in Joseph P. Levy, Dimitrios Bairaktaris, John A. Bullinaria, & Paul Cairns (eds.), *Connectionist Models of Memory and Language*. London: UCL Press, 229–42.

Finkel, Jenny Rose, Alex Kleeman, & Christopher D. Manning (2008), Feature-based, conditional random eld parsing. *Proceedings of the 46th Meeting of the ACL*, 959–67.

Fischer, Martin H., & Rolf A. Zwaan (2008), Embodied language: a review of the role of the motor system in language comprehension. *Quarterly Journal of Experimental Psychology* 61(6): 825–50.

Fiscus, Jonathan (1997), A post-processing system to yield reduced word error rates: Recognizer Output Voting Error Reduction (ROVER). *Proceedings of IEEE Automatic Speech Recognition and Understanding Workshop (ASRU'1997)*, 347–54.

Fisher, W. M., G. R. Doddington, & K. M. Goudie-Marshall (1986), The DARPA speech recognition research database: speci cations and status. *Proceedings of DARPA Workshop on Speech Recognition*, 93–9.

Fitt, S. (2000), Documentation and user guide to UNISYN lexicon and post-lexical rules. Technical report, Centre for Speech Technology Research, Edinburgh.

Fix, E., & J. L. Hodges (1951), Disciminatory analysis – nonparametric discrimination; consistency properties. Technical report project 21-49-004, report no. 4, USAF School of Aviation Medicine.

Flenner, Gudrun (1995), Quantitative Morphsegmentierung im Spanischen auf phonologischer Basis. *Sprache und Datenverarbeitung* 19(2):3–79.

Fodor, Jerry A. (1983), *Modularity of mind.* Cambridge, MA: MIT Press.

Fodor, Jerry A., & B. McLaughlin (1990), Connectionism and the problem of systematicity: why Smolensky's solution doesn't work. *Cognition* 35: 183–204.

Font-Llitjós, Ariadna, Jaime Carbonell, & Alon Lavie (2007), Improving transfer-based MT systems with automatic re nements. *Proceedings of MT Summit XI*, 183–90.

Forcada, Mikel L. (2001), Learning machine translation strategies using commercial systems: discovering word reordering rules. *Machine Translation Review* 12:13–18.

Ford, Marilyn, Joan Bresnan, & Ronald Kaplan (1982), A competence-based theory of syntactic closure, in Joan Bresnan (ed.), *The Mental Representation of Grammatical Relations.* Cambridge, MA: MIT Press, 727–96.

Fordyce, Cameron (2007), Overview of the IWSLT07 evaluation campaign. *Proceedings of the International Workshop on Spoken Language Translation*, 1–12.

Foster, George (2000), A maximum entropy/minimum divergence translation model. *Proceedings of the 38th Annual Meeting of the Association for Computational Linguistics*, 45–52.

Fox, Chris (2000), *The Ontology of Language.* Stanford, CA: CSLI Publications.

Fox, Chris, & Shalom Lappin (2005), *Formal Foundations of Intensional Semantics.* Oxford: Blackwell.

Fox, Chris, & Shalom Lappin (forthcoming), Expressiveness and complexity in underspeci ed semantics, in Johan van Benthem,

Michael Moortgat, and Wojiech Buszkowski (eds.), *Linguistic Analysis 36*, special issue, *A Festschrift for Jim Lambek.*

Fox, Chris, Shalom Lappin, & Carl Pollard (2002), A higher-order, ne-grained logic for intensional semantics. *Proceedings of the 7th Symposium for Logic and Language*, 37–46.

Francez, Nissim, & Roy Dyckhoff (2007), Proof-theoretic semantics for natural language. *10th Meeting of the Association for Mathematical Language (MOL).*

Francis, W. Nelson, & Henry Kucera (1982), *Frequency Analysis of English Usage.* Boston, MA: Houghton Mif in.

Franke, Michael (2006), Pseudo-imperatives: a case study in the ascription of discourse relations. *28th Annual Meeting DGfS.*

Frasconi, P., M. Gori, & A. Sperduti (1998), A general framework for adaptive processing of data structures. *IEEE Transactions on Neural Networks* 9:768–86.

Fraser, Alexander, & Daniel Marcu (2006), Semi-supervised training for statistical word alignment. *Proceedings of the 21st International Conference on Computational Linguistics and 44th Annual Meeting of the Association for Computational Linguistics*, 769–76.

Fraser, Alexander, & Daniel Marcu (2007a), Getting the structure right for word alignment: LEAF. *Proceedings of the 2007 Joint Conference on Empirical Methods in Natural Language Processing and Computational Natural Language Learning (EMNLP-CoNLL)*, 51–60.

Fraser, Alexander, & Daniel Marcu (2007b), Measuring word alignment quality for statistical machine translation. *Computational Linguistics* 33(3):293–303.

Frazier, Lyn (1979), On comprehending sentences: syntactic parsing strategies. Unpublished PhD thesis, University of Connecticut.

Frazier, Lyn (1995), Constraint satisfaction as a theory of sentence processing. *Journal of Psycholinguistic Research* 24:437–68.

Frazier, Lyn, & Keith Rayner (1987), Resolution of syntactic category ambiguities: eye movements in parsing lexically ambiguous sentences. *Journal of Memory and Language* 26:505–26.

Frederking, Robert, & Sergei Nirenburg (1994), Three heads are better than one. *Proceedings of the 4th International Conference on Applied Natural Language Processing (ANLP4)*, 95–100.

Freund, Yoav, & Robert E. Schapire (1995), A decision-theoretic generalization of on-line learning and an application to boosting. *European Conference on Computational Learning Theory*, 23–37.

Friederici, Angela D. (2002), Towards a neural basis of auditory sentence processing. *Trends in Cognitive Science* 6(2):78–84.

Fügen, Christian, Alex Waibel, & Muntsin Kolss (2007), Simultaneous translation of lectures and speeches. *Machine Translation* 21(4):209–52.

Furui, S. (1986), Speaker-independent isolated word recognition using dynamic features of speech spectrum. *IEEE Transactions on Acoustics, Speech, and Signal Processing* 34(1):52–9.

Furuse, Osamu, & Hitoshi Iida (1992), An example-based method for transfer-driven machine translation. in *4th International Conference on Theoretical and Methodological Issues in Machine Translation: Empiricist vs. Rationalist Methods in MT, TMI-92*, 139–50.

Gaizauskas, Robert, & Kevin Humphreys (2000), Quantitative evaluation of coreference algorithms in an information extraction system, in Simon Botley & Antony Mark McEnery (eds.), *Corpus-Based and Computational Approaches to Discourse Anaphora*. Amsterdam: John Benjamins, 145–69.

Gale, William, & Ken Church (1993), A program for aligning sentences in bilingual corpora. *Computational Linguistics* 19(1):75–102.

Gale, William, Kenneth Ward Church, & David Yarowsky (1992a), Estimating upper and lower bounds on the performance of word-sense disambiguation programs. *Proceedings of the 30th Annual Meeting on Association for Computational Linguistics*, 249–256. http://dx.doi.org/10.3115/981967.981999

Gale, William A., Kenneth W. Church, & David Yarowsky (1992b), One sense per discourse. *Proceedings of the DARPA Speech and Natural Language Workshop*, 233–7.

Gale, William A., Kenneth W. Church, & David Yarowsky (1992c), Using bilingual materials to develop word sense disambiguation methods. *4th International Conference on Theoretical and Methodological Issues in Machine Translation*, 101–12.

Gales, M. J. F., & Phil C. Woodland (1996), Mean and variance adaptation within the MLLR framework. *Computer Speech & Language* 10:249–64.

Gales, M. J. F., & S. J. Young (1996), Robust continuous speech recognition using parallel model combination. *IEEE Transactions on Speech and Audio Processing* 4(5):352–9. http://dx.doi.org/10.1109/89.536929

Gales, M. J. F., X. Liu, R. Sinha et al. (2007), Speech recognition system combination for machine translation. *Proceedings of the IEEE International Conference on Acoustics, Speech, and Signal Processing*, 1277–80.

Galley, Michel, & Christopher D. Manning (2008), A simple and effective hierarchical phrase reordering model. *Proceedings of EMNLP 2008, Conference on Empirical Methods in Natural Language Processing*, 848–56.

Galliers, Julia Rose, & Karen Sparck Jones (1993), Evaluating natural language processing systems. Technical report 291, Computer Laboratory, University of Cambridge. http://citeseer.ist.psu.edu/galliers93evaluating.html

Galliers, Julia Rose, & Karen Sparck Jones (1995), *Evaluating Natural Language Processing Systems: An Analysis and Review*. New York: Springer.

Gallin, Daniel (1975), *Intensional and Higher-Order Modal Logic*. Amsterdam: North Holland Publishing Co.

Galron, Daniel, Sergio Penkale, & Andy Way (2009), Accuracy-based scoring for DOT: towards direct error minimization for data-oriented translation. *Proceedings of EMNLP 2009*, 371–80.

Garau, Giulia, & Steve Renals (2008), Combining spectral representations for large vocabulary continuous speech recognition. *IEEE Transactions on Audio, Speech and Language Processing* 16(3):508–18.

Garcia, Ignacio (2007), Power shifts in web-based translation memory. *Machine Translation* 21(1):55–68.

Garnsey, Susan M., Neal J. Pearlmutter, Elisabeth M. Myers, & Melanie A. Lotocky (1997), The contributions of verb bias and plausibility to the comprehension of temporarily ambiguous sentences. *Journal of Memory and Language* 37(1):58–93.

Garrod, Simon, & Martin J. Pickering (2004), Toward a mechanistic psychology of dialogue. *Behavioural and Brain Sciences* 27:169–90.

Gatt, Albert, Anja Belz, & Eric Kow (2009), The TUNA-REG challenge 2009: overview and evaluation results. *Proceedings of the 12th European Workshop on Natural Language Generation (ENLG-2009)*, 1174–82.

Gauvain, Jean-Luc, & Chin-Hui Lee (1994), Maximum a posteriori estimation for multivariate Gaussian mixture observations of Markov chains. *IEEE Transactions on Speech and Audio Processing* 2(2):291–8.

Gazdar, Gerald (1988), Applicability of indexed grammars to natural languages, in Uwe Reyle & Christian Rohrer (eds.), *Natural Language Parsing and Linguistic Theories*. Dordrecht: Reidel Publishing Company, 69–94.

Gazdar, Gerald. E., Ewan Klein, Geoffrey K. Pullum, & Ivan A. Sag (1985), *Generalized Phrase Structure Grammar*. Cambridge, MA: Harvard University Press.

Ge, Niyu, John Hale, & Eugene Charniak (1998), A statistical approach to anaphora resolution. *Proceedings of the 6th Workshop on Very Large Corpora, COLING-ACL '98*, 161–70.

Geach, Peter T. (1972), A program for syntax, in Donald Davidson & Gilbert Harman (eds.), *Semantics of Natural Language*. Dordrecht: D. Reidel, 483–97.

Geman, Stuart, & Mark Johnson (2002), Dynamic programming for parsing and estimation of stochastic uni cation-based grammars. *Proceedings of the 40th Annual Meeting of the ACL*, 279–86.

Gentzen, Gerhard (1969), *The Collected Papers of Gerhard Gentzen*. Amsterdam: North Holland Publishing Co.

Germann, Ulrich (2003), Greedy decoding for statistical machine translation in almost linear time. *HLT-NAACL: Human-Language Technology Conference of the North American Chapter of the Association for Computational Linguistics*, 72–9.

Germann, Ulrich, Michael Jahr, Kevin Knight, Daniel Marcu, & Kenji Yamada (2001), Fast decoding and optimal decoding for machine translation. *Association for Computational Linguistics, 39th Annual Meeting and 10th Conference of the European Chapter, Proceedings*, 228–35.

Gesmundo, Andrea, James Henderson, Paola Merlo, & Ivan Titov (2009), A latent variable model of synchronous syntactic-semantic parsing for multiple languages. *Proceedings of the 13th Conference on Computational Natural Language Learning (CoNLL 2009): Shared Task*, 37–42.

Gibson, Edward (1991), A computational theory of human linguistic processing: memory limitations and processing breakdown. PhD thesis, Carnegie Mellon University.

Gibson, Edward (1998), Linguistic complexity: locality of syntactic dependencies. *Cognition* 68:1–76.

Gibson, Edward (2003), Linguistic complexity in sentence comprehension, in Philipp Strazny (ed.), *The Encyclopedia of Cognitive Science*. New York: MacMillan, 240–1.

Gibson, Edward, & Neal J. Pearlmutter (1998), Constraints on sentence comprehension. *Trends in Cognitive Sciences* 2(7):262–8.

Gibson, Matthew (2008), Minimum Bayes risk acoustic model estimation and adaptation. PhD thesis, University of Sheffeld.

Gibson, Matthew, & Thomas Hain (2007), Temporal masking for unsupervised minimum Bayes risk speaker adaptation. in *Proceedings of Interspeech 2007*.

Gildea, Daniel (2001), Corpus variation and parser performance. *2001 Conference on Empirical Methods in Natural Language Processing (EMNLP)*, 167–202.

Gildea, Daniel, & Daniel Jurafsky (2002), Automatic labeling of semantic roles. *Computational Linguistics* 28(3):245–88.

Gildea, Daniel, & Martha Palmer (2002), The necessity of parsing for predicate argument recognition. *Proceedings of the 40th Meeting of the Association for Computational Linguistics*, 239–46.

Gilmore, Paul Carl (2001), An intensional type theory: motivation and cut-elimination. *Journal of Symbolic Logic* 66:383–400.

Ginzburg, Jonathan (1994), An update semantics for dialogue. *Proceedings of the 1st International Workshop on Computational Semantics*.

Ginzburg, Jonathan (1995), Resolving questions, i, *Linguistics and Philosophy* 18:459–527.

Ginzburg, Jonathan (1996), Interrogatives: questions, facts, and dialogue, in Shalom Lappin (ed.), *Handbook of Contemporary Semantic Theory*. Oxford: Blackwell, 359–423.

Ginzburg, Jonathan (2005), Abstraction and ontology: questions as propositional abstracts in constructive type theory. *Journal of Logic and Computation*, 113–30.

Ginzburg, Jonathan (2010), *The Interactive Stance: Meaning for Conversation*. Oxford: Oxford University Press.

Ginzburg, Jonathan, & Ivan A. Sag (2000), *Interrogative Investigations: The Form, Meaning and Use of English Interrogatives*, CSLI Lecture Notes 123. Stanford: CA: CSLI Publications.

Ginzburg, Jonathan, & Raquel Fernández (2005), Scaling up to multilogue: some benchmarks and principles. *Proceedings of the 43rd Meeting of the Association for Computational Linguistics*, 231–8.

Ginzburg, Jonathan, & Robin Cooper (2004), Clarifcation, ellipsis, and the nature of contextual updates. *Linguistics and Philosophy* 27(3):297–366.

Girard, Jean-Yves (1987), Linear logic. *Theoretical Computer Science* 50(1):1–102.

Girju, Roxana (2003), Automatic detection of causal relations for question answering. *Proceedings of the 41st Annual Meeting of the Association for Computational Linguistics (ACL 2003)*, 76–83.

Girju, Roxana, Adriana Badulescu, & Dan Moldovan (2006), Automatic discovery of part–whole relations. *Computational Linguistics* 32(1):83–136.

Gleitman, L. R., E. L. Newport, & H. Gleitman (2001), The current status of the motherese hypothesis. *Journal of Child Language* 1984:43–79.

Glickman, Oren, Ido Dagan, & Moshe Koppel (2005), A probabilistic classifcation approach for lexical textual entailment. *Twentieth National Conference on Artificial Intelligence (AAAI-05)*, 1050–5.

Goddeau, D., E. Brill, J. Glass et al. (1994), GALAXY: a human-language interface to on-line travel information. *Proceedings International Conference on Spoken Language Processing*, 707–10.

Gold, E. M. (1967), Language identifcation in the limit. *Information and control* 10(5):447–74.

Goldberg, Eli, Norbert Driedger, & Richard Kittredge (1994), Using natural-language processing to produce weather forecasts. *IEEE Expert* 9(2):45–53.

Goldman, S. A., & H. D. Mathias (1996), Teaching a smarter learner. *Journal of Computer and System Sciences* 52(2):255–67.

Goldsmith, John A. (2001), Unsupervised learning of the morphology of a natural language. *Computational Linguistics* 27(2):153–98.

Goldsmith, John A. (2006), An algorithm for the unsupervised learning of morphology. *Natural Language Engineering* 12(4):353–71.

Goldsmith, John A., & Jeremy O'Brien (2006), Learning in ectional classes. *Language Learning and Development* 2(4):219–50.

Goldsmith, John A., Derrick Higgins, & Svetlana Soglasnova (2001), Automatic language-speci c stemming in information retrieval. *Cross-Language Information Retrieval and Evaluation: Proceedings of the CLEF 2000 Workshop*, 273–83.

Goldwater, Sharon (2006), Nonparametric Bayesian models of lexical acquisition. PhD thesis, Brown University.

Goldwater, Sharon, Thomas L. Grif ths, & Mark Johnson (2006), Contextual dependencies in unsupervised word segmentation. *International Conference on Computational Linguistics and Association for Computational Linguistics (COLING/ACL)*, 673–80.

Golub, Gene H., & Charles F. van Loan (1989), *Matrix Computations*. Baltimore, MD: The Johns Hopkins University Press.

Gonick, Larry, & Woollcott Smith (1994), *The Cartoon Guide to Statistics*. New York: HarperResource.

Gonzalo, J., & Douglas Oard (2004), iCLEF 2004 track overview: interactive cross-language question answering. *CLEF-2004 Workshop*, 310–22.

Gonzalo, J., P. Clough, & A. Vallin (2006), Overview of the CLEF 2005 interactive track. *CLEF-2004 Workshop, Lecture Notes in Computer Science (LNCS)* 4022: 251–62.

Good, I. J. (1953), The population frequencies of species and the estimation of population parameters. *Biometrika* 40:237–64.

Goodman, Joshua (1997), Probabilistic feature grammars. *Proceedings of the International Workshop on Parsing Technologies*, 89–100.

Goodman, Joshua (2001), A bit of progress in language modeling, extended version. Technical report, Microsoft Research.

Goodman, Joshua (2002), Sequential generalized iterative scaling. *Proceedings of the 40th Annual Meeting of the Association for Computational Linguistics*, 9–16.

Goodman, Joshua (2004), Exponential priors for maximum entropy models. *Proceedings of the North American Chapter of the Association for Computational Linguistics*, 305–12.

Gopalakrishnan, P., D. Kanevsky, A. Nadas, & D. Nahamoo (1989), A generalization of the Baum algorithm to rational objective functions. *Proceedings ICASSP'89*, 631–4.

Gopalakrishnan, P., L. R. Bahl, & R. L. Mercer (1995), A tree search strategy for large-vocabulary continuous speech recognition. *Proceedings of the IEEE ICASSP-95*, 572–5.

Gordon, P., B. J. Grosz, & L. Gilliom (1993), Pronouns, names and the centering attention in discourse. *Cognitive Science* 17(3):311–47.

Gough, Nano (2005), Data-oriented models of parsing and translation. PhD thesis, Dublin City University.

Gough, Nano, & Andy Way (2004), Robust large-scale EBMT with marker-based segmentation. *Proceedings of the 10th International Conference on Theoretical and Methodological Issues in Machine Translation*, 95–104.

Graham, S. L., & M. A. Harrison (1976), Parsing of general context free languages. *Advances in Computers* 14:77–185.

Graham, S. L., M. A. Harrison, & W. L. Ruzzo (1980), An improved context-free recognizer. *ACM Transactions on Programming Languages and Systems* 2:415–62.

Green, Matthew J., & Don C. Mitchell (2006), Absence of real evidence against competition during syntactic ambiguity resolution. *Journal of Memory and Language* 55:1–17.

Grice, H. Paul (1975), Logic and conversation, in P. Cole & J. Morgan (eds.), *Syntax and Semantics, Vol 3: Speech Acts*. New York: Academic Press, 43–58.

Grice, H. Paul (1981), Presuppositions and conversational implicatures, in P. Cole (ed.), *Radical Pragmatics*. New York: Academic Press, 183–98, Reprinted in *Studies in the Ways of Words*, ed. H. P. Grice (1989). Cambridge, MA: Harvard University Press, 269–82.

Grimes, Joseph E. (1975), *The Thread of Discourse*. Seria Minor: Mouton.

Grishman, Ralph, & Beth Sundheim (1996), Message understanding conference-6: a brief history. *Proceedings of the 16th International Conference on Computational Linguistics*, 466–71.

Grishman, Ralph, & Richard Kittredge (eds.) (1986), *Analyzing Language in Restricted Domains: Sublanguage Description and Processing*. Hillsdale, NJ: Lawrence Erlbaum.

Groenendijk, J., & Martin Stokhof (1984), On the semantics of questions and the pragmantics of answers, in F. Landman & F. Veltman (eds.), *Varieties of Formal Semantics*. Dordrecht: Foris, 143–70.

Groenendijk, J., & M. Stokhof (1990a), Dynamic Montague grammar. *Papers from the Second Symposium on Logic and Language*, 3–48. Also available as ITLI Prepublication Series LP–90–02.

Groenendijk, J., & Martin Stokhof (1990b), Partitioning logical space. Annotated handout, Second European Summer School on Logic, Language and Information, Leuven.

Groenendijk, J., & M. Stokhof (1991), Dynamic predicate logic. *Linguistics and Philosophy* 14(1):39–100.

Groenendijk, J., & Martin Stokhof (1997), Questions, in Johan van Benthem & Alice ter Meulen (eds.), *Handbook of Logic and Language*. MIT Press, Cambridge, MA: 1055–124.

Grosjean, Francois (1980), Spoken word recognition processes and the gating paradigm. *Perception and Psychophysics* 28:267–83.

Grosz, B. J., A. Joshi, & S. Weinstein (1983), Providing a unified account of definite noun phrases in discourse. *Proceedings of the 21st Annual Meeting of the Association for Computational Linguistics (ACL'83)*, 44–50.

Grosz, B. J., Aravind K. Joshi, & Scott Weinstein (1995), Centering: a framework for modelling the local coherence of discourse. *Computational Linguistics* 21(2):203–25.

Groves, Declan (2007), Hybrid data-driven models of machine translation. PhD thesis, Dublin City University.

Groves, Declan, & Andy Way (2005a), Hybrid data-driven models of machine translation. *Machine Translation* 19(3–4):301–23.

Groves, Declan, & Andy Way (2005b), Hybrid example-based SMT: the best of both worlds? *Proceedings of the Workshop on Building and Using Parallel Texts: Data-Driven Machine Translation and Beyond, ACL 2005*, 183–90.

Guerini, Marco, Oliviero Stock, & Massimo Zancanaro (2007), A taxonomy of strategies for multimodal persuasive message generation. *Applied Artificial Intelligence* 21:99–136.

Gupta, S., J. Niekrasz, M. Purver, & D. Jurafsky (2007), Resolving 'You' in multiparty dialog. *Proceedings of the 8th SIGdial Workshop on Discourse and Dialogue*, 227–30.

Gupta, V., M. Lennig, & P. Mermelstein (1988), Fast search strategy in a large vocabulary speech recognizer. *Journal of the Acoustical Society of America* 84:2007–17.

Gustafson, J., N. Lindberg, & M. Lundeberg (1999), The August spoken dialogue system. *Proceedings of Eurospeech'99*.

Haegeman, L. (1994), *Introduction to Government and Binding Theory*. Oxford: Blackwell.

Hafer, M. A., & S. F. Weiss (1974), Word segmentation by letter successor varieties. *Information Storage and Retrieval* 10:371–85.

Hahn, Udo, & Michael Strube (1997), Centering in-the-large: computing referential discourse segments. *Proceedings of the 35th Annual Meeting of the Association for Computational Linguistics and of the 8th Conference of the European Chapter of the Association for Computational Linguistics*, 105–11.

Hain, T. (2001), Hidden model sequence models for automatic speech recognition. PhD thesis, University of Cambridge.

Hain, T., Phil C. Woodland, T. R. Niesler, & E. W. D. Whittaker (1999), The 1998 HTK system for transcription of conversational telephone speech. *Acoustics, Speech, and Signal Processing, ICASSP '99*, 57–60.

Hain, T., Lukas Burget, John Dines et al. (2005a), The development of the AMI system for the transcription of speech in meetings. *Machine Learning for Multimodal Interaction, Lecture Notes in Computer Science* 3869:344–56. http://dx.doi.org/10.1007/11677482_30

Hain, T., Giulia Garau, John Dines et al. (2005b), Transcription of conference room meetings: an investigation. *Proceedings of Interspeech'05*, 1661–4.

Hain, T., Lukas Burget, John Dines et al. (2006), The AMI meeting transcription system: progress and performance. *Machine Learning for Multimodal Interaction*, Lecture Notes in Computer Science 4299:419–31. http://dx.doi.org/10.1007/11965152

Hain, T., L. Burget, J. Dines et al. (2007), The AMI system for the transcription of speech in meetings, in *Proc. IEEE ICASSP–07*, 15–20.

Hain, T., Asmaa El Hannani, Stuart N. Wrigley, & Vincent Wan (2008), Automatic speech recognition for scientific purposes – WEBASR. *Interspeech 2008*, 504–7.

Hajic, Jan (1998), Building a syntactically annotated corpus: the Prague dependency treebank. *Issues of Valency and Meaning*, 106–32.

Hajic, Jan, Alena Böhmová, Eva Hajicová, & Barbora Vidová-Hladká (2000), The Prague dependency treebank: a three-level annotation scenario, in A. Abeillé (ed.), *Treebanks: Building and Using Parsed Corpora*. Amsterdam: Kluwer, 103–27.

Hajic, Jan, Massimiliano Ciaramita, Richard Johansson et al. (2009), The CoNLL-2009 shared task: syntactic and semantic dependencies in multiple languages. *Proceedings of the 13th Conference on Computational Natural Language Learning (CoNLL 2009): Shared Task*, 1–18.

Hajicová, Eva, Barbara Hall Partee, Petr Sgall, & Eric Sgall (1998), *Topic-focus articulation, tripartite structures, and semantic content*. Dordrecht: Kluwer.

Hakkani-Tür, Dilek, & Giuseppe Riccardi (2003), A general algorithm for word graph matrix decomposition. *Proceedings of the IEEE International Conference on Acoustics, Speech and Signal Processing (ICASSP)*, 596–9.

Hale, John (2001), A probabilistic Earley parser as a psycholinguistic model. *Proceedings of the 2nd Conference of the North American Chapter of the Association for Computational Linguistics*, 1–8.

Hale, John (2003), The information conveyed by words in sentences. *Journal of Psycholinguistic Research* 32(1):101–22.

Halliday, Michael A. K., & Ruqaiya Hasan (1976), *Cohesion in English, English Language Series*. London: Longman.

Han, Chunghye, Narae Han, Eonsuk Ko, & Martha Palmer (2002), Korean treebank: development and evaluation. *Proceedings of the 3rd International Conference on Language Resources and Evaluation (LREC2002)*, 1635–42.

Hanneman, Greg, Edmund Huber, Abhaya Agarwal et al. (2008), Statistical transfer systems for French–English and German–English machine translation. *Proceedings of the 3rd Workshop on Statistical Machine Translation at the 46th Meeting of the Association for Computational Linguistics (ACL-2008)*, 163–6.

Haque, Rejwanul, Sudip Naskar, Yanjun Ma, & Andy Way (2009), Using supertags as source language context in SMT. *Proceedings of EAMT-09, the 13th Annual Meeting of the European Association for Machine Translation*, 234–41.

Harabagiu, Sanda, & Finley Lacatusu (2005), Topic themes for multi-document summarization. *Proceedings of the 28th Annual International ACM SIGIR Conference on Research and Development in Information Retrieval*, 202–9.

Harabagiu, Sanda, D. Moldovan, M. Paşca et al. (2001a), Answering complex, list and context questions with LCC's question-answering server. *Proceedings of TREC-10*, 355–61.

Harabagiu, Sanda, Dan Moldovan, Marius Paşca et al. (2001b), The role of lexico-semantic feedback in open-domain textual question-answering. *Proceedings of the 39th Meeting of the ACL*, 274–81.

Harabagiu, Sanda, Andrew Hickl, John Lehmann, & Dan Moldovan (2005), Experiments with interactive question-answering. *Proceedings of the 43rd Annual Meeting of the Association for Computational Linguistics (ACL'05)*, 205–14.

Harb, B., C. Chelba, J. Dean, & S. Ghemawat (2009), Back-off language model compression. *Proceedings of Interspeech*.

Hardt, Daniel, & Owen Rambow (2001), Generation of VP-ellipsis: a corpus-based approach. *Proceedings of the 39th Meeting of the Association for Computational Linguistics (ACL-01)*, 282–9.

Hardy, Hilda, Alan Biermann, R. Bryce Inouye et al. (2005), The AMITIÉS System: data-driven techniques for automated dialogue. *Speech Communication* 48:354–73.

Harman, Donna (1991), How effective is suf xing. *Journal of the American Society for Information Science* 42:7–15.

Harman, Donna (2005), The TREC test collections, in Ellen M. Voorhees & Donna K. Harman (eds.), *TREC: Experiment and Evaluation in Information Retrieval*. Cambridge, MA: MIT Press, 21–52.

Harries, M., S. Hawkins, J. Hacking, & I. Hughes (1998), Changes in the male voice at puberty: vocal fold length and its relationship to the fundamental frequency of the voice. *The Journal of Laryngology and Otology* 112:451–4.

Harris, Zellig (1955), From phoneme to morpheme. *Language* 31:190–222.

Harris, Zellig (1958), Linguistic transformations for information retrieval. *Proceedings of the International Conference on Scientific Information*, 158.

Harris, Zellig (1967), Morpheme boundaries within words: report on a computer test. *Transformations and Discourse Analysis Papers* 73.

Harris, Zellig (1991), *A Theory of Language and Information: A Mathematical Approach*. Oxford: Clarendon Press.

Harrison, M. A. (1978), *Introduction to Formal Language Theory*. London: Addison-Wesley.

Haruno, Masahiko, Satoshi Shirai, & Yoshifumi Ooyama (1998), Using decision trees to construct a practical parser. *Proceedings of the 17th international conference on Computational linguistics*, 505–11. http://dx.doi.org/10.3115/980845.980930

Hasegawa, Takaaki, Satoshi Sekine, & Ralph Grishman (2004), Discovering relations among named entities from large corpora. *Proceedings of the 42nd Meeting of the Association for Computational Linguistics (ACL'04), Main Volume*, 415–22.

Hasler, L. (2007), From extracts to abstracts: human summary production operations for computer-aided summarisation. PhD thesis, University of Wolverhampton.

Hassan, Hany, Mary Hearne, Andy Way, & Khalil Sima'an (2006), Syntactic phrase-based statistical machine translation. *Proceedings of the IEEE 2006 Workshop on Spoken Language Translation*, 238–41.

Hassan, Hany, Yanjun Ma, & Andy Way (2007a), MATREX: the DCU machine translation system for IWSLT 2007. *Proceedings of the 4th International Workshop on Spoken Language Translation*, 69–75.

Hassan, Hany, Khalil Sima'an, & Andy Way (2007b), Supertagged phrase-based statistical machine translation. *Proceedings of the 45th Annual Meeting of the Association for Computational Linguistics*, 288–95.

Hassan, Hany, Khalil Sima'an, & Andy Way (2008), Syntactically lexicalized phrase-based SMT. *IEEE Transactions on Audio, Speech and Language Processing* 16(7):1260–73.

Hastie, Trevor, Robert Tibshirani, & Jerome Friedman (2001), *The Elements of Statistical Learning*. New York: Springer-Verlag.

Hawes, T., J. Lin, & P. Resnik (2008), Elements of a computational model for multiparty discourse: the turn-taking behavior of supreme court justices. Technical report LAMP-TR-147/ HCIL-2008-02, University of Maryland.

Hay, J., & J. Bresnan (2006), Spoken syntax: the phonetics of giving a hand in New Zealand English. *The Linguistic Review* 23(3):321–49.

Hay, J., & R. H. Baayen (2005), Shifting paradigms: gradient structure in morphology. *Trends in Cognitive Sciences* 9(7):342–8.

Hayamizu, S., K. Tanaka, & K. Ohta (1988), A large vocabulary word recognition system using rule-based network representation of acoustic characteristic variations. *Proceedings of ICASSP '88*, 211–14.

He, Yifan, & Andy Way (2009), Learning labelled dependencies in machine translation evaluation. *Proceedings of EAMT-09, the 13th Annual Meeting of the European Association for Machine Translation*, 44–51.

Hearne, Mary (2005), Example-based machine translation using the marker hypothesis. PhD thesis, Dublin City University.

Hearne, Mary, & Andy Way (2003), Seeing the wood for the trees: data-oriented translation. *Machine Translation Summit IX*, 165–72.

Hearne, Mary, & Andy Way (2006), Disambiguation strategies for data-oriented translation. *11th Annual Conference of the European Association for Machine Translation, Proceedings*, 59–68.

Hearne, Mary, & Andy Way (2009), On the role of translations in state-of-the-art statistical machine translation. *COMPASS*.

Hearne, Mary, Sylwia Ozdowska, & John Tinsley (2008), Comparing constituency and dependency representations for SMT phrase-extraction. *15ème Conférence sur le Traitement Automatique des Langues Naturelles (TALN '08)*.

Hearst, Marti A. (1992), Automatic acquisition of hyponyms from large text corpora. *Proceedings of the 14th International Conference on Computational Linguistics*, 539–45.

Hearst, Marti A. (1994), Multi-paragraph segmentation of expository text. *Proceedings of the 32nd Annual Meeting of the Association for Computational Linguistics*, 9–16.

Hearst, Marti A. (1997), Texttiling: segmenting text into multi-paragraph subtopic passages. *Computational Linguistics* 23(1):33–64.

Heeman, Peter A., & James F. Allen (1999), Speech repairs, intonational phrases and discourse markers: modeling speakers' utterances in spoken dialogue. *Computational Linguistics* 25(4):527–71.

Heim, Irene Roswitha (1990), E-type pronouns and donkey anaphora. *Linguistics and Philosophy* 13:137–77.

Henderson, James (1994), Connectionist syntactic parsing using temporal variable binding. *Journal of Psycholinguistic Research* 23(5):353–79.

Henderson, James (2001), Segmenting state into entities and its implication for learning, in Stefan Wermter, Jim Austin, & David Willshaw (eds.), *Emergent Neural Computational Architectures based on Neuroscience*. Heidelberg: Springer-Verlag, 227–36.

Henderson, James (2003), Inducing history representations for broad coverage statistical parsing. *Proceedings of the Joint Meeting of North American Chapter of the Association for Computational Linguistics and the Human-Language Technology Conference*, 103–10.

Henderson, James (2004), Discriminative training of a neural network statistical parser. *Proceedings of the 42nd Meeting of the Association for Computational Linguistics (ACL'04), Main Volume*, 95–102.

Henderson, James, & Peter Lane (1998), A connectionist architecture for learning to parse. *Proceedings of COLING-ACL*, 531–7.

Henderson, James, Oliver Lemon, & Kallirroi Georgila (2008a), Hybrid reinforcement / supervised learning of dialogue policies from xed datasets. *Computational Linguistics* 34(4):487–511.

Henderson, James, Paola Merlo, Gabriele Musillo, & Ivan Titov (2008b), A latent variable model of synchronous parsing for syntactic and semantic dependencies. *Proceedings of the CoNLL-2008 Shared Task*, 178–82.

Hendrickx, I. (2005), Local classi cation and global estimation: explorations of the k-nearest neighbor algorithm. PhD thesis, Tilburg University.

Hendrickx, I., & A. van den Bosch (2003), Memory-based one-step named-entity recognition: effects of seed list features, classi er stacking, and unannotated data. *Proceedings of CoNLL-2003*, 176–9.

Hendrickx, I., Gosse Bouma, Frederik Coppens et al. (2008), A coreference corpus and resolution system for Dutch.

Proceedings of the LREC'08 conference, 202–9.

Hendrix, Gary (1986), Bringing natural language processing to the microcomputer market. *Proceedings of the 24th Annual Meeting of the Association for Computational Linguistics*, 2.

Hendrix, Gary, Earl Sacerdoti, Daniel Sagalowicz, & Jonathan Slocum (1978), Developing a natural language interface to complex data. *ACM Transactions on Database Systems* 3:105–47.

Hermansky, H. (1990), Perceptual linear predictive (PLP) analysis of speech. *The Journal of the Acoustical Society of America* 87:1738. http://dx.doi.org/10.1121/1.399423

Hermansky, H., D. P. W. Ellis, & S. Sharma (2000), Tandem connectionist feature extraction for conventional HMM systems. *Proceedings of IEEE ICASSP '00* 3:1635–8.

Hickl, Andrew, John Williams, Jeremy Bensley, Kirk Roberts, Bryan Rink, & Ying Shi (2006), Recognizing textual entailment with LCC's groundhog system. *Proceedings of the 2nd PASCAL Challenges Workshop on Recognising Textual Entailment*, 80–5.

Hifny, Y., & S. Renals (2009), Speech recognition using augmented conditional random elds. *IEEE Transactions on Audio, Speech and Language Processing* 17(2):354–65.

Hindley, J. Roger, & Jonathan P. Seldin (1986), *Introduction to Combinators and λ-Calculus*. Cambridge: Cambidge University Press.

Hirst, G. (1981), *Anaphora in Natural Language Understanding*. Berlin: Springer-Verlag.

Hladká, Barbora Vidová, Jan Hajic, Jiří Hana, Jaroslava Hlavácová, Jiří Mírovský, & Jan Votrubec (2007), *Czech Academic Corpus 1.0 Guide*. Prague: Karolinum Press.

Ho, E. K. S., & L. W. Chan (1999), How to design a connectionist holistic parser. *Neural Computation* 11(8):1995–2016.

Hobbs, Jerry (1976), Pronoun resolution. Research report 76-1, City College, City University of New York.

Hobbs, Jerry (1978), Resolving pronoun references. *Lingua* 44:339–52.

Hobbs, Jerry (1979), Coherence and coreference. *Cognitive Science* (3):67–90.

Hockenmaier, Julia (2003), Data and models for statistical parsing with combinatory categorial grammar. PhD thesis, University of Edinburgh.

Hockenmaier, Julia, & Mark Steedman (2002a), Acquiring compact lexicalized grammars from a cleaner treebank. *Proceedings of the 3rd LREC Conference*, 1974–81.

Hockenmaier, Julia, & Mark Steedman (2002b), Generative models for statistical parsing with combinatory categorial grammar. *Proceedings of the 40th Meeting of the ACL*, 335–42.

Hofmann, Thomas (1999), Probabilistic latent semantic analysis. *Proceedings of Uncertainty in Artificial Intelligence, UAI'99*.

Hofmann, Thomas (2001), Unsupervised learning by probabilistic latent semantic analysis. *Machine Learning* 42(1–2):177–96.

Hopcroft, John E., & Jeffrey D. Ullman (eds.) (1979), *Introduction to Automata Theory, Languages and Computation*. Reading, MA: Addison-Wesley.

Hornik, K., M. Stinchcombe, & H. White (1989), Multilayer feedforward networks are universal approximators. *Neural Networks* 2:359–66.

Hoste, V. (2005), Optimization in machine learning of coreference resolution. PhD thesis, University of Antwerp.

Hoste, V., I. Hendrickx, W. Daelemans, & A. van den Bosch (2002), Parameter optimization for machine learning of word sense disambiguation. *Natural Language Engineering* 8(4):311–25.

Hovy, Eduard (1993), Automated discourse generation using discourse structure relations. *Artificial Intelligence* 63:341–85.

Hsu, B. J. P. & J. Glass (2008), Iterative language model estimation: ef cient data structure & algorithms. *Proceedings of Interspeech*, 841–4.

Huang, Liang, & David Chiang (2005), Better k-best parsing. *Proceedings of the 9th International Workshop on Parsing Technologies (IWPT)*, 53–64.

Huang, S., & S. Renals (2007), Hierarchical Pitman-Yor language models for ASR in meetings. *Proceedings of the IEEE Workshop on Automatic Speech Recognition and Understanding (ASRU '07)*, 124–9.

Huddleston, R. (1984), *Introduction to English Grammar*. Cambridge: Cambridge University Press.

Hudson, Richard (1984), *Word Grammar*. Oxford: Blackwell.

Hudson-D'Zmura, S. (1988), The structure of discourse and anaphor resolution: the discourse center and the roles of nouns and pronouns. PhD thesis, University of Rochester.

Hull, David A. (1996), Stemming algorithms: a case study for detailed evaluation. *Journal of the American Society for Information Science* 47: 70–84.

Hunt, M. J., & C. Lefebvre (1988), Speaker dependent and independent speech recognition experiments with an auditory model. *Proceedings of IEEE ICASSP*, 215–18.

Hüske-Kraus, Dirk (2003), Suregen 2: a shell system for the generation of clinical documents. *Proceedings of the 10th Conference of the European Chapter of the Association for Computational Linguistics (EACL-2003) (Research Notes and Demos)*, 215–18.

Hutchins, W. J. (1977), On the structure of scienti c texts. *UEA Papers in Linguistics* 5(3):18–39.

Hutchins, W. J. (2003), Machine translation: general overview, in Ruslan Mitkov (ed.), *The Oxford Handbook of Computational Linguistics*. Oxford: Oxford University Press, 501–11.

Hwa, Rebecca (2004), Sample selection for statistical parsing. *Computational Linguistics* 30(3):253–76.

Hwa, Rebecca, & Josh Albrecht (2008), Regression for machine translation evaluation at the sentence level. *Machine Translation* 22(1–2):1–27.

Hwang, Mei-Yuh, & Xuedong D. Huang (1992), Subphonetic modelling with Markov states – senone. *Proceedings of the International Conference on Acoustics, Speech, and Signal Processing (ICASSP) 1992*, 33–6.

Ide, Nancy, & Jean Véronis (1998), Word sense disambiguation: the state of the art. *Computational Linguistics* 24(1):2–40.

Ide, Nancy, & Yorick Wilks (2006), Making sense about sense, in Eneko Agirre & Philip Edmonds (eds.), *Word Sense Disambiguation: Algorithms and Applications*, 47–74.

Immerman, N. (1988), Nondeterministic space is closed under complement. *SIAM Journal on Computing* 17:935–8.

ISO (1991), International Standard ISO/IEC 9126. Information technology – Software product evaluation – Quality characteristics and guidelines for their use. International Organization for Standardization, International Electrotechnical Commission.

ISO/TC 37/SC 4/WG 2 (2007), Language Resource Management – Semantic Annotation Framework (SemAF) – Part 1: Time and events.

Ittycheriah, Abraham, & Salim Roukos (2005), A maximum entropy word aligner for Arabic–English machine translation. *Proceedings of Human-Language Technology Conference and Conference on Empirical Methods in Natural Language Processing*, 89–96.

Janssen, Theo M. V. (2001), Frege, contextuality and compositionality. *Journal of Logic, Language and Information* 10(1):115–36.

Jayaraman, Shyamsundar, & Alon Lavie (2005), Multi-engine machine translation guided by explicit word matching.

Proceedings of the 10th Conference of the European Association for Machine Translation (EAMT-05), 143–52.

Jaynes, E. T. (1957), Information theory and statistical mechanics. *Physical Review* 106:620–30.

Jaynes, E. T. (1986), Monkeys, kangaroos and *N*, in J. H. Justice (ed.), *Maximum-Entropy and Bayesian Methods in Applied Statistics*. Cambridge: Cambridge University Press, 26–58.

Jaynes, E. T. (2003), *Probability Theory: The Logic of Science*. Cambridge: Cambridge University Press.

Jelinek, F. (1969), Fast sequential decoding algorithm using a stack. *IBM Journal of Research and Development* 13(6):675.

Jelinek, F. (1976), Continuous speech recognition by statistical methods. *Proceedings of the IEEE* 64(4):532–56.

Jelinek, F. (1977), *Statistical Methods for Speech Recognition*. Cambridge, MA: MIT Press.

Jelinek, F. (1991), Up from trigrams! the struggle for improved language models. *Proceedings of Eurospeech* 3:1034–40.

Jelinek, F. (1997), *Information Extraction from Speech and Text*. Cambridge, MA: MIT Press.

Jelinek, F. (1998), *Statistical Methods for Speech Recognition*. Cambridge, MA: MIT Press.

Jelinek, F., & Robert Mercer (1980), Interpolated estimation of Markov source parameters from sparse data. *Pattern Recognition in Practice*, 381–97.

Jelinek, F., J. D. Lafferty, & R. L. Mercer (1992), Basic methods of probabilistic context free grammars, in P. Laface & R. De Mori (eds.), *Speech Recognition and Understanding – Recent Advances, Trends and Applications*. New York: Springer-Verlag, 345–60.

Jelinek, F., J. Lafferty, D. Magerman, R. Mercer, A. Ratnaparkhi, & S. Roukos (1994), Decision tree parsing using a hidden derivation model. *Proceedings of the 1994 Human-Language Technology Workshop*, 272–7.

Ji, Heng, & Ralph Grishman (2008), Re ning event extraction through cross-document inference. *Proceedings of ACL-08: HLT*, 254–62.

Joachims, Thorsten (2001), Learning to classify text using support vector machines. PhD thesis, Universität Dortmund.

Johnson, C. Douglas (1972), *Formal Aspects of Phonological Description*. The Hague: Mouton.

Johnson, Mark (1988), *Attribute-Value Logic and the Theory of Grammar*. Stanford, CA: CSLI Publications.

Johnson, Mark (2002), A simple pattern-matching algorithm for recovering empty nodes and their antecedents. *Proceedings of the 40th Meeting of the ACL*, 136–43.

Johnson, Mark (2008), Using adaptor grammars to identify synergies in the unsupervised acquisition of linguistic structure. *Proceedings of ACL-08: HLT*, 398–406.

Johnson, Mark, & Stefan Riezler (2000), Exploiting auxiliary distributions in stochastic uni cation-based grammars. *Proceedings of the 1st Meeting of the NAACL*, 154–61.

Johnson, Mark, Stuart Geman, Stephen Canon, Zhiyi Chi, & Stefan Riezler (1999), Estimators for stochastic 'uni cation-based' grammars. *Proceedings of the 37th Meeting of the ACL*, 535–41.

Johnson, Mark, Thomas L. Grif ths, & Sharon Goldwater (2006), Adaptor grammars: a framework for specifying compositional nonparametric Bayesian models, in Bernhard Schölkopf, John C. Platt, & Thomas Hoffman (eds.), *Advances in Neural Information Processing Systems*. Cambridge, MA: MIT Press, 641–8.

Johnson-Laird, Philip N. (1983), *Mental Models*. Cambridge, MA: Harvard University Press.

Jones, Neil D., & William T. Laaser (1977), Complete problems for deterministic polynomial time. *Theoretical Computer Science* 3(1):105–18.

Joshi, A. K. (1985), Tree adjoining grammars: how much context sensitivity is required to provide a reasonable structural description, in D. Dowty, I. Karttunen, & A. Zwicky (eds.), *Natural Language Parsing*. Cambridge: Cambridge University Press, 206–50.

Joshi, A. K. (1987), An introduction to tree adjoining grammars, in A. Manaster-Ramer (ed.), *Mathematics of Language*. Amsterdam: John Benjamins, 87–114.

Joshi, A. K. (2003), Tree-adjoining grammars, in Ruslan Mitkov (ed.), *The Oxford handbook of Computational Linguistics*. Oxford: Oxford University Press, 483–500.

Joshi, A. K. & Y. Schabes (1997), Tree-adjoining grammars, in G. Rozenberg & A. Salomaa (eds.), *Handbook of Formal Languages*, vol. 3: *Beyond Words*. Springer-Verlag, Berlin: 69–123.

Joshi, A. K., L. Levy, & M. Takahashi (1975), Tree adjunct grammars. *Journal of Computer and System Sciences*, 136–63.

Juang, B.-H., & S. Katagiri (1992), Discriminative learning for minimum error classi cation. *IEEE Transactions on Signal Processing* 40(12):3043–54.

Jubien, Michael (1989), On properties and property theory, in G. Chierchia, B. Partee, & R. Turner (eds.), *Properties, Types and Meaning*. Dordrecht: Kluwer, 159–75.

Juliano, Cornell, & Michael K. Tanenhaus (1993), Contingent frequency effects in syntactic ambiguity resolution. *15th Annual Conference of the Cognitive Science Society*, 593–603, 681–6.

Jurafsky, Daniel (1996), A probabilistic model of lexical and syntactic access and disambiguation. *Cognition Science* 20:137–94.

Jurafsky, Daniel (2003), Probabilistic modeling in psycholinguistics: linguistic comprehension and production, in

Rens Bod, Jennifer Hay, & Stefanie Jannedy (eds.), *Probabilistic Linguistics*. Cambridge, MA: MIT Press, 39–95.

Jurafsky, Daniel, & James Martin (2009), *Speech and Language Processing: An Introduction to Natural Language Processing, Computational Linguistics, and Speech Recognition*, 2nd edn, *Series in Artificial Intelligence*. Upper Saddle River, NJ: Prentice Hall.

Kabadjov, M. A. (2007), A comprehensive evaluation of anaphora resolution and discourse-new classi cation. PhD thesis, University of Essex.

Kadmon, Nirit (1990), Uniqueness. *Linguistics and Philosophy* 13:237–324.

Kadmon, Nirit (2001), *Formal Pragmatics: Semantics, Pragmatics, Presupposition, and Focus*. Oxford: Wiley-Blackwell.

Kaelbling, Leslie Pack, Michael L. Littman, & Anthony R. Cassandra (1995), Planning and acting in partially observable stochastic domains. *Artificial Intelligence* 101:99–134.

Kaelbling, Leslie Pack, Michael L. Littman, & Andrew W. Moore (1996), Reinforcement learning: a survey. *Journal of Artificial Intelligence Research* 4:237–85.

Kaisser, Michael (2006), Web question answering by exploiting wide-coverage lexical resources. *Proceedings of the 11th ESSLLI Student Session*, 203–13.

Kaisser, Michael, & Bonnie Webber (2007), Question answering based on semantic roles. *ACL 2007 Workshop on Deep Linguistic Processing*, 41–8.

Kaisser, Michael, & John Lowe (2008), A research collection of question–answer sentence pairs. *Proceedings of the Language Resources and Evaluation Conference (LREC)*.

Kaji, Hiroyuki, & Yasutsugu Morimoto (2005), Unsupervised word sense disambiguation using bilingual comparable corpora. *IEICE Transactions on Information and Systems*, vol. E88-D, 289–301.

Kambhatla, Nanda (2004), Combining lexical, syntactic, and semantic features with maximum entropy models for information extraction. *The Companion Volume to the Proceedings of 42nd Annual Meeting of the Association for Computational Linguistics*, 178–81.

Kameyama, M. (1985), Zero anaphora: the case of Japanese. PhD thesis, Stanford University.

Kameyama, M. (1986), A property-sharing constraint in centering. *Proceedings of the 24th Annual Meeting of the Association for Computational Linguistics (ACL '86)*, 200–6.

Kameyama, M. (1997), Recognizing referential links: an information extraction perspective. *Proceedings of the ACL '97/EACL '97 Workshop on Operational Factors in Practical, Robust Anaphora Resolution*, 46–53.

Kameyama, M. (1998), Intrasentential centering: a case study, in M. Walker, A. Joshi, & E. Prince (eds.), *Centering Theory in Discourse*. Oxford: Clarendon Press, 89–112.

Kamp, Hans (1973), Free choice permission. *Proceedings of the Aristotelian Society* 74:57–74.

Kamp, Hans (1979), Semantics versus pragmatics, in Franz Guenthner & Siegfried J. Schmidt (eds.), *Formal Semantics and Pragmatics for Natural Language, Synthese Language Library*. Dordrecht: D. Reidel, 255–87.

Kamp, Hans (1981), Theory of truth and semantic representation, in J. A. K. Groenendijk, T. M. V. Janssen, & M. B. J. Stokhof (eds.), *Formal Methods in the Study of Language, Mathematical Centre Tracts* 135. Amsterdam: Mathematisch Centrum, 277–322.

Kamp, Hans (2007), Discourse linking as (simultaneous) constraint solving. Henry Sweet lecture, talk at the LAGB.

Kamp, Hans, & Uwe Reyle (1993), *From Discourse to Logic: Introduction to Modeltheoretic Semantics of Natural Language, Formal Logic and Discourse Representation Theory, Studies in Linguistics and Philosophy* 42. Dordrecht: Kluwer.

Kan, Min-Yen, Judith L. Klavans, & Kathleen R. McKeown (1998), Linear segmentation and segment signi cance. *Proceedings of the 6th International Workshop of Very Large Corpora*, 197–205.

Kaplan, Jerrold (1982), Cooperative responses from a portable natural language database query system, in Michael Brady & Robert Berwick (eds.), *Computational Models of Discourse*. Cambridge MA: MIT Press, 167–208.

Kaplan, Ronald (1973), A general syntactic processor, in Randall Rustin (ed.), *Natural Language Processing*. New York: Algorithmics Press, 193–241.

Kaplan, Ronald, & Joan Bresnan (1982), Lexical-functional grammar: a formal system for grammatical representation, in J. Bresnan (ed.), *The Mental Representation of Grammatical Relations*. Cambridge, MA: MIT Press, 173–281.

Kaplan, Ronald, & Martin Kay (1981), Phonological rules and nite-state transducers. Linguistic Society of America *Meeting Handbook, 56th Annual Meeting*.

Kaplan, Ronald, & Martin Kay (1994), Regular models of phonological rule systems. *Computational Linguistics* 20(3):331–78.

Kapur, J. N. (1993), *Maximum-Entropy Models in Science and Engineering*. New Dehli: Wiley Eastern Ltd.

Kara at, Martin, Lukas Burget, Thomas Hain, & Jan Cernocky (2007), Application of CMLLR in narrow band wide band adapted systems. *Proceedings of the 8th International Conference INTERSPEECH 2007*, 4.

Karamanis, Nikiforos, & Hisar Maruli Manurung (2002), Stochastic text structuring using the principle of continuity. *Proceedings of International Natural Language Generation Conference*, 81–8.

Karttunen, Lauri (1969), *Pronouns and variables. CLS* 5: 108–16.

Karttunen, Lauri (1991), Finite-state constraints. *Proceedings of the International Conference on Current Issues in Computational Linguistics*.

Karttunen, Lauri (1993), Finite-state constraints, in John Goldsmith (ed.), *The Last Phonological Rule: Reflections on Constraints and Derivations*. Chicago: University of Chicago Press, 173–94.

Karttunen, Lauri, & Kenneth R. Beesley (2005), Twenty- ve years of nite-state morphology, in Antti Arppe, Lauri Carlson, Krister Lindén et al. (eds.), *Inquiries into Words, Constraints and Contexts: Festschrift for Kimmo Koskenniemi on his 60th Birthday*. Stanford, CA: CSLI Publications, 71–83.

Karttunen, Lauri, Jean-Pierre Chanod, Gregory Grefenstette, & Anne Schiller (1996), Regular expressions for language engineering. *Natural Language Engineering* 2(4):305–28.

Kasami, J. (1965), An ef cient recognition and syntax analysis algorithm for context-free languages. Technical report AFCRL-65-758, Air Force Cambridge Research Laboratory, Bedford, MA.

Katz, Boris (1997), Annotating the World Wide Web using natural language. *Proceedings of the 5th RIAO Conference on Computer Assisted Information Searching on the Internet (RIAO '97)*, 136–59.

Katz, Boris, & Jimmy Lin (2003), Selectively using relations to improve precision in question answering. *Proceedings of the EACL 2003 Workshop on Natural Language Processing for Question Answering*, 43–50.

Katz, Boris, Gary Borchardt, & Sue Felshin (2005), Syntactic and semantic decomposition strategies for question answering from multiple resources. *Proceedings of the AAAI 2005 Workshop on Inference for Textual Question Answering*, 35–41.

Katz, S. (1987), Estimation of probabilities from sparse data for the language model component of a speech recognizer. *IEEE Transactions on Acoustics, Speech and Signal Processing* 35:400–1.

Kawahara, Hideki, Ikuyo Masuda-Katsuse, & Alain de Cheveigné (1999),

Restructuring speech representations using a pitch-adaptive time-frequency smoothing and an instantaneous-frequency-based F0 extraction: possible role of a repetitive structure in sounds. *Speech Communication* 27(3–4):187–207. http://dx.doi.org/10.1016/S0167-6393(98)00085-5

Kay, Martin (1973), The MIND system, in Randall Rustin (ed.), *Natural Language Processing*. New York: Algorithmics Press, 155–88.

Kay, Martin, & M. Röscheisen (1993), Text-translation alignment. *Computational Linguistics* 19(1):121–42.

Kazakov, Dimitar (2000), Achievements and prospects of learning word morphology with inductive logic programming, in J. Cussens & S. Dzeroski (eds.), *Learning Language in Logic*. New York: Springer-Verlag, 89–109.

Kazakov, Dimitar, & Suresh Manandhar (1998), A hybrid approach to word segmentation. *Inductive Logic Programming: Proceedings of the 8th International Workshop (ILP-98)*, 125–34.

Kazama, Jun'ichi, & Jun'ichi Tsujii (2005), Maximum entropy models with inequality constraints: a case study on text categorization. *Machine Learning* 60:159–94.

Kearns, M. J., & Umesh V. Vazirani (1994), *An Introduction to Computational Learning Theory*. Cambridge, MA: MIT Press.

Kearns, M. J. & G. Valiant (1989), Cryptographic limitations on learning Boolean formulae and nite automata. *21st Annual ACM Symposium on Theory of Computation*, 433–44.

Kearns, M. J., Y. Mansour, D. Ron, R. Rubinfeld, R. E. Schapire, & L. Sellie (1994), On the learnability of discrete distributions. *Proceedings of the 25th Annual ACM Symposium on Theory of Computing*, 273–82.

Keenan, Edward (1992), Beyond the Fregean boundary. *Linguistics and Philosophy* 15:199–221.

Kehler, A. (1995), Interpreting cohesive forms in the context of discourse inference. PhD thesis, Harvard University.

Kehler, A. (1997), Current theories of centering and pronoun interpretation: a critical evaluation. *Computational Linguistics* 23(3):467–75.

Kehler, A., L. Kertz, H. Rohde, & J. L. Elman (2008), Coherence and coreference revisited. *Journal of Semantics* 25(1):1–44.

Kelleher, John, Fintan Costello, & Josef van Genabith (2005), Dynamically structuring, updating and interrelating representations of visual and linguistic discourse context. *Artificial Intelligence* 167:62–102.

Keller, William R. (1988), Nested Cooper storage: the proper treatment of quanti cation in ordinary noun phrases, in U. Reyle & C. Rohrer (eds.), *Natural Language Parsing and Linguistic Theories*. Dordrecht: Reidel.

Kelly, Diane, & Jimmy Lin (2007), Overview of the TREC 2006 ciQA task. *SIGIR Forum* 41(1):107–16.

Kelly, Diane, P. B. Kantor, E. L. Morse, J. Scholtz, & Y. Sun (2009), Questionnaires for eliciting evaluation data from users of interactive question answering systems. *Journal of Natural Language Engineering: Special Issue on Interactive Question Answering* 15(1):119–41.

Kempson, Ruth, Wilfried Meyer-Viol, & Dov Gabbay (2000), *Dynamic Syntax: The Flow of Language Understanding*. Oxford: Blackwell.

Kennedy, Christopher, & Branimir Boguraev (1996), Anaphora for everyone: pronominal anaphora resolution without a parser. in *Proceedings of the 16th International Conference on Computational Linguistics (COLING '96)*, 113–18.

Ker, Sue, & Jason Chang (1997), A class-based approach to word alignment. *Computational Linguistics* 23(2):313–43.

Keuleers, E. (2008), Memory-based learning of in ectional morphology. PhD thesis, University of Antwerp.

Keuleers, E., & Walter Daelemans (2007), Memory-based learning models of in ectional morphology: a methodological case study. *Lingue e linguaggio* (2):151–74.

Keuleers, E., D. Sandra, W. Daelemans, S. Gillis, G. Durieux, & E. Martens (2007), Dutch plural in ection: the exception that proves the analogy. *Cognitive Psychology* 54(4):283–318.

Kibble, Rodger (2001), A reformulation of rule 2 of centering theory. *Computational Linguistics* 27(4): 579–87.

Kibble, Rodger, & Richard Power (2000), An integrated framework for text planning and pronominalisation. *Proceedings of International Natural Language Generation Conference*, 77–84.

Kieffer, John C., & En hui Yang (2000), Grammar based codes: a new class of universal lossless source codes. *IEEE Transactions on Information Theory* 46:2000.

Kienappel, A. K., & R. Kneser (2001), Designing very compact decision trees for grapheme-to-phoneme transcription. *Proceedings of the Eurospeech Conference* 1911–14.

Kilgarriff, Adam (1998), Senseval: an exercise in evaluating word sense disambiguation programs. *Proceedings of LREC*, 581–8.

Killer, Mirjam, Sebastian Stuker, & Tanja Schultz (2003), Grapheme based speech recognition. *Proceedings of EUROSPEECH '93*, 3141–4.

Kim, Byeongchang, & Geunbae Lee (2000), Decision-tree based error correction for statistical phrase break prediction in Korean. *Proceedings of the 18th International Conference on Computational Linguistics (COLING 2000)*, 1051–5.

Kim, D. Y., S. Umesh, M. J. F. Gales, T. Hain, & P. C. Woodland (2004), Using VTLN for broadcast news transcription. *Proceedings of ICSLP '04*.

Kim, S. N., & T. Baldwin (2006), Interpreting semantic relations in noun compounds via verb semantics.

Proceedings of the COLING/ACL 2006 Main Conference Poster Sessions, 491–8.

Kim, Woosung, & Sanjeev Khudanpur (2003), Language model adaptation using cross-lingual information. *Eurospeech*, 3129–32.

Kim, Woosung, Sanjeev Khudanpur, & Jun Wu (2001), Smoothing issues in the structured language model. *Proceedings of EuroSpeech 2001*, 717–20.

Kimball, J. (1973), Seven principles of surface structure parsing in natural languages. *Cognition* 2:15–47.

King, S., J. Frankel, K. Livescu, E. McDermott, K. Richmond, & M. Wester (2007), Speech production knowledge in automatic speech recognition. *Journal of the Acoustical Society of America* 121(2):723–43.

Kipper, K., A. Korhonen, N. Bryant, & M. Palmer (2006), Extending VerbNet with Novel Verb Classes. *Proceedings of LREC*, 25–32.

Kit, Chunyu (2000), Unsupervised lexical learning as inductive inference. PhD thesis, University of Shef eld.

Kit, Chunyu, & Yorick Wilks (1999), Unsupervised learning of word boundary with description length gain. *Proceedings of the CoNLL99 ACL Workshop*, 1–6.

Kleene, S. C. (1956), Representation of events in nerve nets and nite automata, in Claude Shannon & John McCarthy (eds.), *Automata Studies*. Princeton, NJ: Princeton University Press, 3–4.

Klein, D., & C. Manning (2002), A generative constituent-context model for improved grammar induction. *Proceedings of the 40th Annual Meeting of the Association for Computational Linguistics*, 128–35.

Klein, D., & C. Manning (2004), Corpus-based induction of syntactic structure: models of dependency and constituency. *42nd Annual Meeting of the Association for Computational Linguistics, Proceedings of the Conference*, 478–85.

Klein, Ewan (2006), Computational semantics in the *Natural Language Toolkit*. *Proceedings of the 2006 Australasian Language Technology Workshop (ALTW2006)*, 26–33.

Klenk, Ursula (1994), Automatische morphologische Analyse arabischer Wortformen. *Beihefte der Zeitschrift für Dialektologie und Linguistik* 83:84–101.

Klenk, Ursula, & Hagen Langer (1989), Morphological segmentation without a lexicon. *Literary and Linguistic Computing* 4(4):247–53.

Kneser, Reinhard, & Hermann Ney (1995), Improved backing-off for m-gram language modeling. *Proceedings of the IEEE International Conference on Acoustics, Speech and Signal Processing*, 181–4.

Knoeferle, P., & M. W. Crocker (2006), The coordinated interplay of scene, utterance, and world knowledge: evidence from eye tracking. *Cognitive Science* 30:481–529.

Knoeferle, P., & M. W. Crocker (2007), The in uence of recent scene events on spoken comprehension: evidence from eye movements. *Journal of Memory and Language* 57:519–43.

Knoeferle, P., Matthew W. Crocker, Christoph Scheepers, & Martin J. Pickering (2005), The in uence of the immediate visual context on incremental thematic role-assignment. *Cognition* 95:95–127.

Knuth, D. E. (1973), *The Art of Computer Programming*, vol. 3: *Sorting and Searching*. Reading, MA: Addison-Wesley.

Knuth, D. E. (1977), A generalization of Dijkstra's algorithm. *Information Processing Letters* 6(1):1–5.

Ko, Jeongwoo, Luo Si, & Eric Nyberg (2007), A probabilistic framework for answer selection in question answering. *HLT-NAALL* 524–31.

Koehn, Philipp (2003), Noun phrase translation. PhD thesis, University of Southern California.

Koehn, Philipp (2004), Pharaoh: a beam search decoder for phrase-based statistical machine translation models.

Proceedings of the 6th Biennial Conference of the Association for Machine Translation in the Americas, 115–24.

Koehn, Philipp (2005), Europarl: a parallel corpus for statistical machine translation. *Machine Translation Summit X*, 79–86.

Koehn, Philipp (2010), *Statistical Machine Translation*. Cambridge: Cambridge University Press.

Koehn, Philipp, Franz Och, & Daniel Marcu (2003), Statistical phrase-based translation. *HLT-NAACL: Human-Language Technology Conference of the North American Chapter of the Association for Computational Linguistics*, 127–33.

Koehn, Philipp, Hieu Hoang, Alexandra Birch et al. (2007), Moses: open source toolkit for statistical machine translation. *Proceedings of the 45th Annual Meeting of the Association for Computational Linguistics Companion Volume Proceedings of the Demo and Poster Sessions*, 177–80.

Kohonen, T. (1984), *Self-Organization and Associative Memory*. Berlin: Springer-Verlag.

Kohonen, T., Samuel Kaski, Krista Lagus et al. (2000), Self organisation of a massive document collection. *IEEE Transactions on Neural Networks* 11(3):574–85.

Kokkinakis, D. (2000), PP-attachment disambiguation for Swedish: combining unsupervised and supervised training data. *Nordic Journal of Linguistics* 23(2):191–213.

Koller, Alexander, Joachim Niehren, & Stefan Thater (2003), Bridging the gap between underspeci ed formalisms: hole semantics as dominance constraints. *Proceedings of 11th EACL*, 195–202.

Koo, T., A. Globerson, X. Carreras, & M. Collins (2007), Structured prediction models via the matrix-tree theorem. *Proceedings of the 2007 Joint Conference on Empirical Methods in Natural Language Processing and Computational Natural Language Learning*, 141–50.

Koskenniemi, Kimmo (1983), Two-level morphology: a general computational model for word-form recognition and production. PhD thesis, University of Helsinki.

Kowalski, Robert, & Marek Jozef Sergot (1986), A logic-based calculus of events. *New Generation Computing* 4:67–95.

Kozen, Dexter C. (2006), *Theory of Computation*. London: Springer-Verlag.

Kozima, Hideki (1993), Text segmentation based on similarity between words. *Proceedings of the 31st Annual Meeting (Student Session) of the Association for Computational Linguistics*, 286–8.

Kraaij, Wessel, & Ren Ee Pohlmann (1996), Viewing stemming as recall enhancement. *Proceedings of the 19th Annual International ACM SIGIR Conference on Research and Development in Information Retrieval*, 40–8.

Krahmer, Emiel, & Paul Piwek (1999), Presupposition projection as proof construction, in H. Bunt & R. Muskens (eds.), *Computing Meanings: Current Issues in Computational Semantics, Studies in Linguistics and Philosophy Series*, Dordrecht: Kluwer Academic Publisher, 281–300.

Kripke, Saul (1963), Semantical considerations on modal logic. *Acta Philosophica Fennica* 16:83–9.

Krippendorf, Klaus (2004), *Content Analysis: An Introduction to Its Methodology*. Thousand Oaks, CA: Sage.

Kronlid, Fredrik (2008), Steps towards multi-party dialogue management. PhD thesis, Gothenburg University.

Krott, A., R. H. Baayen, & R. Schreuder (2001), Analogy in morphology: modeling the choice of linking morphemes in Dutch. *Linguistics* 39(1):51–93.

Krott, A., Robert Schreuder, & R. Harald Baayen (2002), Analogical hierarchy: exemplar-based modeling of linkers in Dutch noun–noun compounds, in R. Skousen, D. Lonsdale, & D.B. Parkinson (eds.), *Analogical Modeling*. Amsterdam: John Benjamins, 181–206.

Krott, A., R. Schreuder, R. H. Baayen, & W. U. Dressler (2007), Analogical effects on linking elements in German compound words. *Language and Cognitive Processes* 22(1):25–57.

Krovetz, Robert (2000), Viewing morphology as an inference process. *Artificial Intelligence* 118(1–2):277–94.

Krymolowski, Yuval (2001), Using the distribution of performance for studying statistical NLP systems and corpora. *Proceedings of the Workshop on Evaluation for Language and Dialogue Systems*, 1–8. http://dx.doi.org/10.3115/1118053.1118060

Kuhn, Roland, Patrick Nguyen, Jean-Claude Junqua et al. (1998), Eigenvoices for speaker adaptation. *ICSLP-1998*, 1771–4.

Kukich, Karen (1983), Design and implementation of a knowledge-based report generator. *Proceedings of 21st Annual Meeting of the Association for Computational Linguistics (ACL-1983)*, 145–50.

Kumar, N., & A. G. Andreou (1998), Heteroscedastic discriminant analysis and reduced rank HMMs for improved recognition. *Speech Communication* 26:283–97.

Kupiec, Julian, Jan Pederson, & Francine Chen (1995), A trainable document summarizer. *Proceedings of the 18th ACM/SIGIR Annual Conference on Research and Development in Information Retrieval*, 68–73.

Kutas, M., & S. A. Hillyard (1980), Reading senseless sentences: brain potentials re ect semantic incongruity. *Science* 207:203–5.

Kutas, M., & S. A. Hillyard (1983), Event-related brain potentials to grammatical errors and semantic anomalies. *Memory and Cognition* 11:539–50.

Lacatusu, Finley, Andrew Hickl, & Sanda Harabagiu (2005), The impact of question decomposition on the quality of answer summaries. *Proceedings of the 7th*

Language Resources and Evaluation Conference (LREC 2006).

Lacave, Carmen, & Francisco Diez (2002), A review of explanation methods for Bayesian networks. *The Knowledge Engineering Review* 17:107–27.

Lacave, Carmen, & Francisco Diez (2004), A review of explanation methods for heuristic expert systems. *The Knowledge Engineering Review* 19:133–46.

Lafferty, John, & Bernhard Suhm (1996), Cluster expansions and iterative scaling for maximum entropy language models, in K. Hanson & R. Silver (eds.), *Maximum Entropy and Bayesian Methods*. Dordrecht: Kluwer.

Lafferty, John, Andrew McCallum, & Fernando Pereira (2001), Conditional random elds: probabilistic models for segmenting and labeling sequence data. *Proceedings of the 18th International Conference on Machine Learning*, 282–9.

Lafferty, John, Xiaojin Zhu, & Yan Liu (2004), Kernel conditional random elds: representation and clique selection. *Machine Learning: Proceedings of the 21st International Conference (ICML)*, 504–11.

Lamb, Sydney M. (1961), On the mechanisation of syntactic analysis. *1961 Conference on Machine Translation of Languages and Applied Language Analysis, National Physical Laboratory Symposium* 13:674–85.

Lambek, Joachim (1958), The mathematics of sentence structure. *American Mathematical Monthly* 65(3):154–70.

Lambert, Patrik, Rafael Banchs, & Josep Crego (2007), Discriminative alignment training without annotated data for machine translation. *Human-Language Technologies 2007: The Conference of the North American Chapter of the Association for Computational Linguistics*, 85–8.

Landauer, Thomas, Peter W. Foltz, & Darrell Laham (1998), Introduction to latent semantic analysis. *Discourse Processes* 25:259–84.

Landauer, Thomas, Danielle S. McNamara, Simon Dennis, & Walter Kintsch (2007), *Handbook of Latent Semantic Analysis*. New York: Routledge.

Lane, Peter, & James Henderson (2001), Incremental syntactic parsing of natural language corpora with Simple Synchrony Networks. *IEEE Transactions on Knowledge and Data Engineering* 13(2):219–31.

Lang, B. (1994), Recognition can be harder than parsing. *Computational Intelligence* 10(4):486–94.

Langkilde, Irene, & Kevin Knight (1998), Generation that exploits corpus-based statistical knowledge. *Proceedings of 36th Annual Meeting of the Association for Computational Linguistics and 17th International Conference on Computational Linguistics (COLING-ACL 1998)*, 704–10.

Langlais, Philippe, & Fabrizio Gotti (2006), EBMT by tree-phrasing. *Machine Translation* 20(1):1–23.

Lappin, S. (1989), Donkey pronouns unbound. *Theoretical Linguistics* 15:263–86.

Lappin, S. (2005), Machine learning and the cognitive basis of natural language. *Proceedings of Computational Linguistics in the Netherlands 2004*, 1–11.

Lappin, S., & Herbert J. Leass (1994), An algorithm for pronominal anaphora resolution. *Computational Linguistics* 20(4):535–62.

Lappin, S., & Nissim Francez (1994), E-type pronouns, I-sums, and donkey anaphora. *Linguistics and Philosophy* 17:391–428.

Lappin, S., & S. M. Shieber (2007), Machine learning theory and practice as a source of insight into univeral grammar. *Journal of Linguistics* 43:393–427.

Larkey, Leah S. (2002), Improving stemming for Arabic information retrieval: light stemming and co-occurrence analysis. *SIGIR 2002*, 275–82.

Larsson, Staffan (2002), Issue based dialogue management. PhD thesis, Gothenburg University.

Larsson, Staffan, & David Traum (2000), Information state and dialogue management in the TRINDI dialogue move engine toolkit. *Natural Language Engineering* 6:323–40.

Larsson, Staffan, Peter Ljunglöf, Robin Cooper, Elisabet Engdahl, & Stina Ericsson (2000), GoDiS – an accommodating dialogue system. *Proceedings of ANLP/NAACL-2000 Workshop on Conversational Systems*, 7–10. www.ling.gu.se/publikationer/GPCL/00-1.ps

Lascarides, Alex, & Nicholas Asher (2004), Imperatives in dialogue, in Peter KÃijhnlein, Hans Rieser, & Henk Zeevat (eds.), *The Semantics and Pragmatics of Dialogue for the New Millenium*. Amsterdam: John Benjamins, 1–24.

Lau, Ellen F., & Fernanda Ferreira (2005), Lingering effects of dis uent material on comprehension of garden path sentences. *Language and Cognitive Processes* 20(5):633–66.

Lavie, Alon, Katharina Probst, Erik Peterson et al. (2004), A trainable transfer-based machine translation approach for languages with limited resources. *Proceedings of the 9th EAMT Workshop, Broadening Horizons of Machine Translation and its Applications*, 116–23.

Lavoie, Benoit, & Owen Rambow (1997), A fast and portable realizer for text generation. *Proceedings of the 5th Conference on Applied Natural-Language Processing (ANLP-1997)*, 265–8.

Law, Anna, Yvonne Freer, Jim Hunter, Robert Logie, Neil McIntosh, & John Quinn (2005), Generating textual summaries of graphical time series data to support medical decision making in the neonatal intensive care unit. *Journal of Clinical Monitoring and Computing* 19:183–94.

Lawrence, Steve, C. Lee Giles, & Sandiway Fong (2000), Natural language grammatical inference with recurrent neural networks. *IEEE Transactions on Knowledge and Data Engineering* 12(1):126–40.

LDC (2008), ACE English annotation guidelines for relations, version 6.2.

Leacock, Claudia, Geoffrey Towell, & Ellen Voorhees (1993), Corpus-based statistical sense resolution. *HLT '93: Proceedings of the Workshop on Human-Language Technology*, 260–265. http://dx.doi.org/10.3115/1075671.1075730

Lee, Alan, Rashmi Prasad, Aravind Joshi, Nikhil Dinesh, & Bonnie Webber (2006), Complexity of dependency in discourse: are dependencies in discourse more complex than in syntax? *Proceedings of the 5th International Workshop on Treebanks and Linguistic Theories*.

Leggetter, Chris J., & Philip C. Woodland (1995), Maximum likelihood linear regression for speaker adaptation of continuous density HMMs. *Computer Speech and Language* 9(2):171–86.

Lemon, Oliver, Anne Bracy, Alexander Gruenstein, & Stanley Peters (2001), The WITAS multi-modal dialogue system I. *Proceedings of EuroSpeech*, 1559–62.

Lendvai, P. (2004), Extracting information from spoken user input: a machine learning approach. PhD thesis, Tilburg University.

Lendvai, P., & J. Geertzen (2007), Token-based chunking of turn-internal dialogue act sequences. *Proceedings of the 8th SIGdial Workshop on Discourse and Dialogue*, 174–81.

Lendvai, P., A. van den Bosch, E. Krahmer, & M. Swerts (2002), Improving machine-learned detection of miscommunications in human-machine dialogues through informed data splitting. *Proceedings of the ESSLLI Workshop on Machine Learning Approaches in Computational Linguistics*, 1–15.

Lendvai, P., A. van den Bosch, & E. Krahmer (2003a), Machine learning for shallow interpretation of user utterances in spoken dialogue systems. *Proceedings of the EACL Workshop on Dialogue Systems: Interaction, Adaptation and Styles of Management*, 69–78.

Lendvai, P., A. van den Bosch, & E. Krahmer (2003b), Memory-based dis uency chunking. *Proceedings of*

Disfluency in Spontaneous Speech Workshop (DISS '03), 63–6.

Lepage, Yves, & Etienne Denoual (2005), Purest ever example-based machine translation: detailed presentation and assessment. *Machine Translation* 19(3–4):251–82.

Lesk, Michael (1986), Automatic sense disambiguation using machine readable dictionaries: how to tell a pine cone from an ice cream cone. *SIGDOC '86: Proceedings of the 5th Annual International Conference on Systems Documentation*, 24–6. http://doi.acm.org/10.1145/318723.318728

Leveling, J., & S. Hartrumpf (2007), On metonymy recognition for geographic IR. *Proceedings of GIR-2006, the 3rd Workshop on Geographical Information Retrieval.*

Levelt, Willem J. (1983), Monitoring and self-repair in speech, *Cognition* 14(4):41–104.

Levenshtein, Vladimir (1966), Binary codes capable of correcting deletions, insertions, and reversals. *Soviet Physics Doklady* 10:707–10.

Levin, E. (1993), *English Verbs and Alternations: A Preliminary Investigation*. Chicago: Chicago University Press.

Levin, E., & R. Pieraccini (1997), A stochastic model of computer–human interaction for learning dialogue strategies. *Proceedings of Eurospeech*, 1883–6.

Levin, E., R. Pieraccini, & W. Eckert (1998), Using Markov decision processes for learning dialogue strategies. *Proceedings of IEEE Transactions on Speech and Audio Processing*, 11–23.

Levinson, S. E., L. R. Rabiner, & M. M. Sondhi (1983), An introduction to the application of the theory of probabilistic functions of a Markov process to automatic speech recognition. *The Bell System Technical Journal* 62(4): 1035–74.

Levy, Roger (2008), Expectation-based syntactic comprehension. *Cognition* 106(3):1126–77.

Levy, Roger, & Christopher Manning (2004), Deep dependencies from context-free statistical parsers: correcting the surface dependency approximation. *Proceedings of the 42nd Meeting of the ACL*, 328–35.

Lewis, Philip, & Richard Stearns (1968), Syntax-directed transduction. *Journal of the ACM* 15:465–88.

Lewis, Philip, Richard Stearns, & Juris Hartmanis (1965), Memory bounds for recognition of context-free and context-sensitive languages. *Proceedings of the IEEE 6th Annual Symposium on Switching Circuit Theory and Logical Design*, 191–202.

Lewis, Richard L., Shravan Vasishth, & Julie A. Van Dyke (2006), Computational principles of working memory in sentence comprehension. *Trends in Cognitive Science* 10:447–54.

Li, M., & P Vitányi (1991), Learning simple concepts under simple distributions. *SIAM Journal on Computing* 20:911.

Li, M., & P Vitányi (1993), *An introduction to Kolmogorov Complexity and Its Applications*. New York: Springer-Verlag.

Li, Xin, & Dan Roth (2006), Learning question classi ers: the role of semantic information. *Natural Language Engineering* 12(3):229–49.

Liang, Han, Harry Zhang, & Yuhong Yan (2006a), Decision trees for probability estimation: an empirical study. *Proceedings of the 18th IEEE International Conference on Tools with Artificial Intelligence (ICTAI06)*, 756–64.

Liang, Percy, Ben Taskar, & Dan Klein (2006b), Alignment by agreement. *Proceedings of Human-Language Technology Conference and Conference on Empirical Methods in Natural Language Processing*, 104–11.

Libkin, Leonid (2004), *Elements of Finite Model Theory*. Berlin: Springer.

Lin, Chin-Yew, & Eduard Hovy (2003), Automatic evaluation of summaries using n-gram co-occurrence statistics. *Proceedings of the 2003 Human-Language*

Technology Conference of the North American Chapter of the Association for Computational Linguistics (HLT/NAACL 2003), 71–8.

Lin, Jimmy (2007), An exploration of the principles underlying redundancy-based factoid question answering. *ACM Transactions on Information Systems* 25(2):1–55.

Lin, Jimmy, & Boris Katz (2006), Building a reusable test collection for question answering. *Journal of the American Society for Information Science and Technology* 57(7):851–61.

Lin, Jimmy, Dennis Quan, Vineet Sinha, Karun Bakshi, David Huynh, Boris Katz, & David R. Karger (2003a), What makes a good answer? The role of context in question answering. *Proceedings of the 9th IFIP TC13 International Conference on Human–Computer Interaction (INTERACT 2003)*, 25–32.

Lin, Winston, Roman Yangarber, & Ralph Grishman (2003b), Bootstrapped learning of semantic classes from positive and negative examples. *Proceedings of the ICML-2003 Workshop on the Continuum from Labeled to Unlabeled Data*, 103–11.

Litman, Diane, & James Allen (1984), A plan recognition model for clari cation subdialogues. *Proceedings of the 10th Annual Meeting of the Association for Computational Linguistics*, 302–11.

Litman, Diane, & Kate Forbes-Riley (2006), Correlations betweeen dialogue acts and learning in spoken tutoring dialogues. *Natural Language Engineering* 12:161–76.

Litman, Diane, & Rebecca J. Passoneau (1995), Combining multiple knowledge sources for discourse segmentation. *Proceedings of the 33rd Annual Meeting of the Association for Computational Linguistics*, 108–15.

Liu, Bing (1995), Intelligent air travel and tourist information systems. *Proceedings of the 8th International Conference on Industrial and Engineering Applications of Artificial Intelligence and Expert Systems*, 603–10.

Liu, Ting, Andrew W. Moore, & Alexander Gray (2003), Ef cient exact k-nn and nonparametric classi cation in high dimensions. *Proceedings of Neural Information Processing Systems*, 15.

Liu, Yang, Qun Liu, & Shouxun Lin (2005), Log-linear models for word alignment. *Proceedings of the 43rd Annual Meeting of the Association for Computational Linguistics*, 459–66.

Liu, Zhanli, Haifeng Wang, & Hua Wu (2006), Example-based machine translation based on tree–string correspondence and statistical generation. *Machine Translation* 20(1):25–41.

Lochbaum, Karen, Barbara J. Grosz, & Candace Sidner (2000), Discourse structure and intention recognition, in R. Dale, H. Moisl, & H. Somer (eds.), *Handbook of Natural Language Processing*. New York: Marcel Dekker, 123–46.

Lockwood, P., & J. Boudy (1992), Experiments with a nonlinear spectral subtractor (NSS), hidden Markov models and the projection, for robust speech recognition in cars. *Speech Communication* 11(2–3):215–28. http://dx.doi.org/ 10.1016/0167-6393(92)90016-Z

Lopez, Adam (2008a), Statistical machine translation. *ACM Computing Surveys* 40(3), 1–49.

Lopez, Adam (2008b), Tera-scale translation models via pattern matching. *Proceedings of the 22nd International Conference on Computational Linguistics (Coling 2008)*, 505–12.

Lopez, Adam, & Philip Resnik (2005), Improved HMM alignment models for languages with scarce resources. *Proceedings of the ACL Workshop on Building and Using Parallel Texts*, 83–6.

Lowerre, B., & R. Reddy (1980), The Harpy speech understanding system, in W. A. Lea (ed.), *Trends in Speech Recognition*. Englewood Cliffs, NJ: Prentice-Hall, 340–60.

Ma, Yanjun, Nicolas Stroppa, & Andy Way (2007a), Alignment-guided chunking.

Proceedings of the 11th International Conference on Theoretical and Methodological Issues in Machine Translation, 114–21.

Ma, Yanjun, Nicolas Stroppa, & Andy Way (2007b), Bootstrapping word alignment via word packing. *Proceedings of the 45th Annual Meeting of the Association of Computational Linguistics*, 304–11.

Ma, Yanjun, Sylwia Ozdowska, Yanli Sun, & Andy Way (2008), Improving word alignment using syntactic dependencies. *Proceedings of the ACL-08: HLT Second Workshop on Syntax and Structure in Statistical Translation (SSST-2)*, 69–77.

Ma, Yanjun, Patrik Lambert, & Andy Way (2009), Tuning syntactically enhanced word alignment for statistical machine translation. *Proceedings of the 13th Annual Meeting of the European Association for Machine Translation (EAMT 2009)*, 250–7.

Maamouri, Mahamed, & Ann Bies (forthcoming), The Penn Arabic Treebank, in A. Farghaly & K. Megerdoomian (eds.), *Computational Approaches to Arabic Script-Based Languages: Current Implementation in NLP*. CSLI Stanford, CA: Publications.

MacDonald, Maryellen C. (1993), The interaction of lexical and syntactic ambiguity. *Journal of Memory and Language* 32:692–715.

MacDonald, Maryellen C. (1994), Probabilistic constraints and syntactic ambiguity resolution. *Language and Cognitive Processes* 9:157–201.

MacDonald, Maryellen C., & Morton H. Christiansen (2002), Reassessing working memory: a comment on Just & Carpenter (1992) and Waters & Caplan (1996). *Psychological Review* 109:35–54.

MacDonald, Maryellen C., Neal J. Pearlmutter, & Mark S. Seidenberg (1994), The lexical nature of syntactic ambiguity resolution. *Psychological Review* 101:676–703.

Macho, D., L. Mauuary, B. Noé, et al. (2002), Evaluation of a noise-robust DSR front-end on Aurora databases. *Proceedings of the ICSLP*, 17–21.

Mackay, David J. C. (2002), *Information Theory, Inference & Learning Algorithms*. Cambridge: Cambridge University Press.

MacWhinney, B. (1995), *The CHILDES Project: Tools for Analyzing Talk*, 2nd edn. Hillsdale, NJ: Lawrence Erlbaum.

Magerman, David (1994), Natural language processing as statistical pattern recognition. PhD thesis, Stanford University.

Magerman, David (1995), Statistical decision-tree models for parsing. *Proceedings of the 33rd Meeting of the ACL*, 276–83.

Malouf, R. (2000), The order of prenominal adjectives in natural language generation. *Proceedings of the 38th Annual Meeting of the Association for Computational Linguistics*, 85–92.

Malouf, R. (2002), A comparison of algorithms for maximum entropy parameter estimation. *Proceedings of the 6th Conference on Natural Language Learning (CoNLL-2002)*, 49–55.

Malouf, R. & Gertjan van Noord (2004), Wide coverage parsing with stochastic attribute value grammars. *IJCNLP-04 Workshop: Beyond Shallow Analyses – Formalisms and Statistical Modeling for Deep Analyses*.

Manandhar, Suresh, Sašo Džeroski, & Tomaž Erjavec (1998), Learning multilingual morphology with CLOG. *Lecture Notes in Computer Science* 1446:135–44.

Manaster-Ramer, Alexis (1987), Dutch as a formal language. *Linguistics and Philosophy* 10:221–46.

Mangu, L., E. Brill, & A. Stolcke (1999), Finding consensus among words: lattice-based word error minimization. *Proceedings of the European Conference on Speech Communication and Technology 1999 (Eurospeech99)*, 495–8.

Mangu, L., Eric Brill, & Andreas Stolcke (2000), Finding consensus in speech recognition: word error minimization and other applications of confusion networks. *Computer Speech and Language* 14(4):373–400.

Mann, William, & Sandra Thompson (1987), Rhetorical structure theory: a theory of text organization. Technical report RS-87-190, Information Sciences Institute.

Mann, William, & Sandra Thompson (1988), Rhetorical structure theory: towards a functional theory of text organisation. *Text* 3:243–81.

Manning, Christopher, & Hinrich Schütze (1999), *Foundations of Statistical Natural language processing*. Cambridge, MA: MIT Press.

Manning, Christopher, Prabhakar Raghavan, & Hinrich Schütze (2008), *Introduction to Information Retrieval*. Cambridge: Cambridge University Press.

Mántaras, R. López De (1991), A distance-based attribute selection measure for decision tree induction. *Machine Learning* 6(1):81–92.

Marcu, Daniel (1997), The rhetorical parsing, summarization and generation of natural language texts. PhD thesis, University of Toronto.

Marcu, Daniel (2000), *The Theory and Practice of Discourse Parsing and Summarisation*. Cambridge, MA: MIT Press.

Marcu, Daniel (2001), Towards a uni ed approach to memory- and statistical-based machine translation. *Association for Computational Linguistics, 39th Annual Meeting and 10th Conference of the European Chapter, Proceedings*, 378–85.

Marcu, Daniel, & William Wong (2002), A phrase-based, joint probability model for statistical machine translation. *Proceedings of the Conference on Empirical Methods in Natural Language Processing (EMNLP-02)*, 133–9.

Marcus, M. (1980), *A Theory of Syntactic Recognition for Natural Language*. Cambridge, MA: MIT Press.

Marcus, M. (1993), Building a large annotated corpus of English: the Penn Treebank. *Computational Linguistics* 19:313–30.

Marcus, M., B. Santorini, & M. Marcinkiewicz (1993), Building a large annotated corpus of English: the Penn Treebank. *Computational Linguistics* 19(2):313–30.

Mariño, José, Rafael Banchs, Josep Crego, Adrià de Gispert, Patrik Lambert, José Fonollosa, & Marta Costa-jussà (2006), N-gram-based machine translation. *Computational Linguistics* 32(4):527–49.

Marks, Joseph, & Ehud Reiter (1990), Avoiding unwanted conversational implicatures in text and graphics. *Proceedings of the 8th National Conference on Artificial Intelligence (AAAI-1990)*, 450–6.

Màrquez, Lluís (1999), POS tagging: a machine learning approach based on decision trees. PhD thesis, Universitat Politecnica de Catalunya.

Màrquez, Lluís, & Lluís Padró (1997), A exible POS tagger using an automatically acquired language model. *Proceedings of the 35th Annual Meeting of the ACL*, 238–45.

Marr, David (1982), *Vision*. San Francisco, CA: W. H. Freeman and Company.

Marsi, E., A. van den Bosch, & A. Soudi (2006), Memory-based morphological analysis generation and part-of-speech tagging of Arabic. *Proceedings of the ACL Workshop on Computational Approaches to Semitic Languages*, 1–8.

Martin, Sven, Jörg Liermann, & Hermann Ney (1998), Algorithms for bigram and trigram word clustering. *Speech Communication* 24:19–37.

Materna, Pavel, Marie Duzi, & Bjørn Jespersen (forthcoming), *Procedural Semantics for Hyperintensional Logic (Foundations and Applications of TIL)*. Berlin: Springer.

Matheson, Colin, Massimo Poesio, & David Traum (2000), Modeling grounding and discourse obligations using update rules. *Proceedings of the 1st Annual Meeting of the North American Chapter of the ACL*, 1–8.

Matsumoto, Yuji, & Mihoko Kitamura (2005), Acquisition of translation rules from parallel corpora, in R. Mitkov & N. Nicolov (eds.), *Recent Advances in Natural Language Processing: Selected Papers from the Conference*. Amsterdam: John Benjamins, 405–16.

Matthews, P. H. (1966), A procedure for morphological encoding. *Mechanical translation and Computational Linguistics* 9(1):15–21.

Matusov, Evgeny, Nicola Uef ng, & Hermann Ney (2006), Computing consensus translation from multiple machine translation systems using enhanced hypotheses alignment. *Proceedings of the 11th Conference of the European Chapter of the Association for Computational Linguistics*, 33–40.

Matzke, Mike, Heinke Mai, Wido Nager, Jascha Rüsseler, & Thomas Münte (2002), The costs of freedom: an ERP-study of non-canonical sentences. *Clinical Neuropsychology* 113:844–52.

Mayberry, Marty, Matthew W. Crocker, & P. Knoeferle (2009), Learning to attend: a connectionist model of the coordinated interplay of utterance, visual context, and world knowledge. *Cognitive Science* 33:449–96.

Maybury, Mark (ed.) (2003), *New Directions in Question Answering: Papers from the 2003 AAAI Symposium*. Stanford, CA: AAAI Press.

Mays, Eric, Aravind Joshi, & Bonnie Webber (1982), Taking the initiative in natural language data base interactions: monitoring as response. *Proceedings of the European Conference on Artificial Intelligence*, 255–6.

McCallum, Andrew, Dayne Freitag, & Fernando Pereira (2000), Maximum entropy Markov models for information extraction and segmentation. *Proceedings of the 17th International Conference on Machine Learning*, 591–8.

McCarthy, Diana, Rob Koeling, Julie Weeds, & John Carroll (2004), Finding predominant senses in untagged text.

Proceedings of the 42nd Annual Meeting of the Association for Computational Linguistics, 279–86.

McCarthy, J. F., & W. G. Lehnert (1995), Using decision trees for coreference resolution. *Processings of the International Joint Conference on Artificial Intelligence (IJCAI)*, 1050–5.

McCawley, James (1993), *Everything that Linguists Have Always Wanted to Know about Logic but Were Ashamed to Ask*. Chicago: University of Chicago Press.

McClelland, Jay L., & Jeffrey L. Elman (1986), The TRACE model of speech perception. *Cognitive Psychology* 18:1–86.

McClosky, David, Eugene Charniak, & Mark Johnson (2006), Effective self-training for parsing. *Proceedings of the Conference on Human-Language Technology and North American Chapter of the Association for Computational Linguistics (HLT-N AACL)*, 152–9.

McCord, M. (1990), Slot grammar: a system for simpler construction of practical natural language grammars, in R. Studer (ed.), *Natural Language and Logic: International Scientific Symposium, Lecture Notes in Computer Science*. Berlin: Springer-Verlag, 118–45.

McCord, M. (1993), Heuristics for broad-coverage natural language parsing. *Proceedings, APRA Human-Language Technology Workshop*, 82–8.

McCullagh, Peter (2002), What is a statistical model? *Annals of Statistics* 30:1225–1310.

McCulloch, Warren S., & Walter Pitts (1943), A logical calculus of ideas immanent in neural activity. *Bulletin of Mathematical Biophysics* 5:115–33.

McDonald, R., & G. Satta (2007), On the complexity of non-projective data-driven dependency parsing. *Proceedings of the 10th International Conference on Parsing Technologies*, 121–32.

McDonald, R., & Joakim Nivre (2007), Characterizing the errors of data-driven dependency parsing models. *Proceedings* of the 2007 Joint Conference on Empirical Methods in Natural Language Processing and Computational Natural Language Learning (EMNLP-CoNLL), 122–31.

McDonald, R., F. Pereira, K. Ribarov, & J. Hajic (2005a), Non-projective dependency parsing using spanning tree algorithms. *Human-Language Technology Conference and Conference on Empirical Methods in Natural Language Processing*, 523–30.

McDonald, R., Koby Crammer, & Fernando Pereira (2005b), Online large-margin training of dependency parsers. *Proceedings of the 43rd Meeting of the ACL*, 91–8.

McDonald, R., Koby Crammer, & Fernando Pereira (2005c), Spanning tree methods for discriminative training of dependency parsers. Technical report, University of Pennsylvania.

McDonald, R., Fernando Pereira, Kiril Ribarov, & Jan Hajic (2005d), Non-projective dependency parsing using spanning tree algorithms. *Proceedings of the HLT/EMNLP Conference*, 523–30.

McKeown, Kathleen R. (1985), *Text Generation: Using Discourse Strategies and Focus Constraints to Generate Natural Language, Studies in Natural Language Processing*. Cambridge: Cambridge University Press.

McRae, Ken, Michael J. Spivey-Knowlton, & Michael K. Tanenhaus (1998), Modeling the in uence of thematic t (and other constraints) in on-line sentence comprehension. *Journal of Memory and Language* 38:283–312.

McTear, Michael (1998), Modelling spoken dialogues with state transition diagrams: experiences with the CSLU toolkit. *Proceedings of the 5th International Conference on Spoken Language Processing*, 1223–6.

McTear, Michael (2004), *Spoken Dialogue Technology: Toward the Conversational User Interface*. London: Springer-Verlag.

Medina Urrea, Alfonso (2000), Automatic discovery of af xes by means of a corpus: a catalog of Spanish af xes. *Journal of Quantitative Linguistics* 7(2):97–114.

Medina Urrea, Alfonso (2006), Af x discovery by means of corpora: experiments for Spanish, Czech, Ralámuli and Chuj, in Alexander Mehler & Reinhard Köhler (eds.), *Aspects of Automatic Text Analysis: Festschrift in Honour of Burghard Rieger*. Berlin: Springer, 277–99.

Medina Urrea, Alfonso, & J. Hlavácová (2005), Automatic recognition of Czech derivational pre xes. *Proceedings of CICLing 2005, Lecture Notes in Computer Science* 3406:189–97.

Melamed, Dan (2000), Models of translational equivalence among words. *Computational Linguistics* 26(2):221–49.

Melamed, Dan (2003), Multitext grammars and synchronous parsers. *HLT-NAACL: Human-Language Technology Conference of the North American Chapter of the Association for Computational Linguistics*, 79–86.

Melamed, Dan, & Philip Resnik (2000), Evaluation of sense disambiguation given hierarchical tag sets. *Computers and the Humanities* 1–2.

Mellebeek, Bart, Karolina Owczarzak, Josef Van Genabith, & Andy Way (2006), Multi-engine machine translation by recursive sentence decomposition. *AMTA 2006, Proceedings of the 7th Conference of the Association for Machine Translation in the Americas, Visions for the Future of Machine Translation*, 110–18.

Mellish, Chris, Donia Scott, Lynn Cahill, Daniel Paiva, Roger Evans, & Mike Reape (2006), A reference architecture for natural language generation systems. *Natural Language Engineering* 12:1–34.

Menezes, Arul, & Steve Richardson (2003), A best- rst alignment algorithm for automatic extraction of transfer mappings from bilingual corpora, in Michael Carl & Andy Way (eds.), *Recent Advances in Example-Based Machine Translation*. Dordrecht: Kluwer Academic Publishers, 421–42.

Mengel, A., L. Dybkjaer, J. M. Garrido et al. (2000), MATE Dialogue Annotation Guidelines.

Merlo, Paola, & Gabriele Musillo (2005), Accurate function parsing. *Proceedings of Human-Language Technology Conference and Conference on Empirical Methods in Natural Language Processing*, 620–7.

Messerschmitt, D., D. Hedberg, C. Cole, A. Haoui, & P. Winship (1989), Digital voice echo canceller with a TMS32020. Application report SPRA129, Texas Instruments.

Meyers, A., R. Reeves, C. Macleod et al. (2004), The NomBank Project: an interim report. *Proceedings of the NAACL/HLT Workshop on Frontiers in Corpus Annotation*, 24–31.

Michalski, R. S. (1983), A theory and methodology of inductive learning. *Artificial Intelligence* 11:111–61.

Mihalcea, R. (2002), Instance-based learning with automatic feature selection applied to word sense disambiguation. *Proceedings of the 19th International Conference on Computational Linguistics (COLING 2002)*, 1–7.

Mihalcea, R., & Philip Edmonds (eds.) (2004), *Proceedings of Senseval-3: 3rd International Workshop on the Evaluation of Systems for the Semantic Analysis of Text.* www.senseval.org/senseval3/proceedings

Miikkulainen, Risto (1993), *Subsymbolic Natural Language Processing: An Integrated Model of Scripts, Lexicon, and Memory.* Cambridge, MA: MIT Press.

Miller, George A. (1995), WordNet: a lexical database for English. *Communications of the ACM* 38(11):39–41.

Miller, George A., & Christiane Fellbaum (1991), Semantic networks of English. *Cognition* 41:197–229.

Miller, George A., & Stephen Isard (1964), Free recall of self-embedded English sentences. *Information and Control* 7:292–303.

Miller, George A., Richard Beckwith, Christiane Fellbaum, Derek Gross, & Katherine Miller (1990), Introduction to

WordNet: an on-line lexical database. *International Journal of Lexicography* 3(4):235–44.

Miller, George A., Claudia Leacock, Randee Tengi, & Ross T. Bunker (1993), A semantic concordance. *HLT '93: Proceedings of the Workshop on Human-Language Technology*, 303–8. http://dx.doi.org/10.3115/1075671. 1075742

Miller, Philip (1999), *Strong Generative Capacity: The Semantics of Linguistic Formalism*, Stanford, CA: CSLI Publications.

Miller, Rob S., & Murray P. Shanahan (1999), The event-calculus in classical logic – alternative axiomatizations. *Electronic Transactions on Artificial Intelligence* 3(1):77–105.

Miltsakaki, E., & K. Kukich (2004), Evaluation of text coherence for electronic essay scoring systems. *Natural Language Engineering* 10(1):25–55.

Miltsakaki, E., R. Prasad, A. Joshi, & B. Webber (2004a), The Penn Discourse Treebank. *Proceedings of the NAACL/HLT Workshop on Frontiers in Corpus Annotation.*

Miltsakaki, Eleni, Rashmi Prasad, Aravind Joshi, & Bonnie Webber (2004b), The Penn Discourse TreeBank. *Proceedings of the Language Resources and Evaluation Conference.*

Mingers, John (1987), Expert systems – rule induction with statistical data. *Journal of the Operational Research Society* 38:39–47.

Minka, Thomas P. (2001), Algorithms for maximum-likelihood logistic regression. Statistics technical report 758, CMU.

Minnen, G., F. Bond, & A. Copestake (2000), Memory-based learning for article generation. *Proceedings of the 4th Conference on Computational Natural Language Learning and the Second Learning Language in Logic Workshop*, 43–8.

Minnen, G., John Carroll, & Darren Pearce (2001), Applied morphological processing of English. *Natural Language Engineering* 7:207–23.

Minsky, Marvin L., & Seymour A. Papert (1969), *Perceptrons: An Introduction to Computational Geometry*. Cambridge, MA: MIT Press.

Mitchell, Don C., Fernando Cuetos, Martin Corley, & Marc Brysbaert (1995), Exposure-based models of human parsing: evidence for the use of coarse-grained (nonlexical) statistical records. *Journal of Psycholinguistic Research* 24:469–88.

Mitchell, T. (1997), *Machine Learning*. New York: McGraw-Hill.

Mitkov, R. (1996), Pronoun resolution: the practical alternative. *Proceedings of the Discourse Anaphora and Anaphor Resolution Colloquium (DAARC)*.

Mitkov, R. (1998), Robust pronoun resolution with limited knowledge. *Proceedings of the 18th International Conference on Computational Linguistics (COLING '98/ACL '98)*, 869–75.

Mitkov, R. (2000), Towards more comprehensive evaluation in anaphora resolution. *Proceedings of the 2nd International Conference on Language Resources and Evaluation*, 1309–14.

Mitkov, R. (2002), *Anaphora resolution*. London: Longman.

Mitkov, R., & C. Hallett (2007), Comparing pronoun resolution algorithms. *Computational Intelligence* 23(2), 262–97.

Mitkov, R., & C. Orasan (2004), Discourse and coherence: revisiting speci c conventions of the centering theory. *Proceedings of the 5th Discourse Anaphora and Anaphor Resolution Colloquium (DAARC'2004)*, 109–14.

Mitkov, R., & G. Corpas (2008), Improving third generation translation memory systems through identi cation of rhetorical predicates. *Proceedings of LangTech'2008*.

Mitkov, R., & P. Schmidt (1998), On the complexity of pronominal anaphora resolution in machine translation, in C. Martín-Vide (ed.), *Mathematical and Computational Analysis of Natural Language*. Amsterdam: John Benjamins, 207–22.

Mitkov, R., R. Evans, & C. Orasan (2002), A new, fully automatic version of Mitkov's knowledge-poor pronoun resolution method. *Proceedings of the 3rd International Conference on Computational Linguistics and Intelligent Text Processing*, 168–86.

Mitkov, R., R. Evans, C. Orasan, L. A. Ha, & V. Pekar (2007), Anaphora resolution: to what extent does it help NLP applications? in A. Branco (ed.), *Anaphora: Analysis, Algorithms, and Applications*. Dordrecht: Springer, 179–90.

Miyao, Yusuke, & Jun'ichi Tsujii (2002), Maximum entropy estimation for feature forests. *Proceedings of Human-Language Technology Conference (HLT 2002)*, 292–7.

Miyao, Yusuke, & Jun'ichi Tsujii (2005), Probabilistic disambiguation models for wide-coverage HPSG parsing. *Proceedings of the 43rd meeting of the ACL*, 83–90.

Moens, M. F. (2008), Using patterns of thematic progression for building a table of contents of a text. *Journal of Natural Language Engineering* 14(2), 145–72.

Mohri, Mehryar, Fernando Pereira, & Michael Riley (2000), The design principles of a weighted nite-state transducer library. *Theoretical Computer Science* 231(1):17–32.

Mohri, Mehryar, Fernando Pereira, & Michael Riley (2002), Weighted nite-state transducers in speech recognition. *Computer Speech & Language* 16(1):69–88.

Moldovan, Dan, Marius Paşca, Sanda Harabagiu, & Mihai Surdeanu (2003), Performance issues and error analysis in an open-domain question answering system. *ACM Transactions on Information Systems* 21:133–54.

Moncur, Wendy, & Ehud Reiter (2007), How much to tell? Disseminating affective information across a social network. *Proceedings of 2nd International Workshop on Personalisation for e-Health*.

Montague, Richard (1974), The proper treatment of quanti cation in ordinary English, in R. Thomason (ed.), *Formal Philosophy*. New Haven, CT: Yale University Press, 247–70.

Monz, Christof, & Maarten de Rijke (2001), Deductions with meaning. *Logical Aspects of Computational Linguistics, Lecture Notes in Computer Science* 2014:1–10. http://dx.doi.org/10.1007/3-540-45738-0_1

Mooney, R. J. (2007), Learning for semantic parsing. *Proceedings, 8th International Conference on Computational Linguistics and Intelligent Text Processing*, 311–24.

Mooney, R. J., & Mary Elaine Califf (1996), Learning the past tense of English verbs using inductive logic programming, in S. Wermter, E. Riloff, & G. Scheler, *Connectionist, Statistical, and Symbolic Approaches to Learning for Natural Language Processing*. London: Springer-Verlag, 370–84.

Mooney, R. J., S. Carberry, & K. F. McCoy (1990), The generation of high-level structure for extended explanations. *Proceedings of the 13th International Conference on Computational Linguistics*, 276–81.

Moore, Robert (1989), Uni cation-based semantic interpretation. *Proceedings of the 27th Annual Meeting of the Association for Computational Linguistics*, 33–41. http://dx.doi.org/10.3115/981623.981628

Moore, Robert (2004), Improving IBM word alignment model 1. *42nd Meeting of the Association for Computational Linguistics (ACL'04), Main Volume*, 518–25.

Moore, Robert (2005), A discriminative framework for bilingual word alignment. *Proceedings of Human-Language Technology Conference and Conference on Empirical Methods in Natural Language Processing*, 81–8.

Moore, Robert, & Chris Quirk (2008), Random restarts in mimimum error rate training for statistical machine translation. *Coling 2008, the 22nd International Conference on Computational Linguistics, Proceedings*, 585–92.

Morrill, Glyn (2000), Incremental processing and acceptability. *Computational Linguistics* 26(3): 319–38.

Morrissey, Sara, Andy Way, Daniel Stein, Jan Bungeroth, & Hermann Ney (2007), Combining data-driven MT systems for improved sign language translation. *Proceedings of Machine Translation Summit XI*, 329–36.

Mortimer, John (1990), *Rumpole à la Carte*. London: Penguin.

Morton, T. (1999), Using coreference for question answering. *Proceedings of the ACL'99 Workshop on Coreference and its Applications*, 85–9.

Morton, T. (2005), Using semantic relations to improve information retrieval. PhD thesis, University of Pennsylvania.

Moschitti, Alessandro, Silvia Quarteroni, Roberto Basili, & Suresh Manandhar (2007), Exploiting syntactic and shallow semantic kernels for question/answer classi cation. *Proceedings, 45th Annual Meeting of the Association for Computational Linguistics*, 776–83.

Mota, Cristina, & Ralph Grishman (2008), Is this NE tagger getting old? *Proceedings of the 6th International Conference on Language Resources and Evaluation (LREC 2008)*, 1196–202.

Müller, C. S., S. Rapp, & M. Strube (2002), Applying co-training to reference resolution. *Proceedings of the 40th Annual Meeting of the Association for Computational Linguistics, ACL '2002*, 352–9.

Muller, P., & L. Prévot (2003), An empirical study of acknowledgement structures. *Proceedings of DiaBruck*, 3.

Muñoz, R. (2001), Tratamiento y resolución de las descripciones de nidas y su applicación en sistemas de extracción de información. PhD thesis, University of Alicante.

Musillo, Gabriele, & Paola Merlo (2006), Accurate parsing of the proposition bank. *Proceedings of the Human-Language*

Technology Conference of the NAACL, Companion Volume: Short Papers, 101–4.

Nadas, A. (1983), A decision-theoretic formulation of a training problem in speech recognition and a comparison of training by unconditional versus conditional maximum likelihood. *IEEE Transactions on Acoustics, Speech and Signal Processing* ASSP-31(4): 814–17.

Nadas, A., D. Nahamoo, & M. Picheny (1988), On a model-robust training algorithm for speech recognition. *IEEE Transactions on Acoustics, Speech and Signal Processing* 36:1432–6.

Nadeau, David, & Satoshi Sekine (2007), A survey of named entity recognition and classi cation. *Lingvisticae Investigationes* 30(1), 3–26.

Nagao, Makoto (1984), A framework of a mechanical translation between Japanese and English by analogy principle, in Alick Elithorn & Ranan Banerji (eds.), *Artificial and Human Intelligence*. Amsterdam: North Holland Publishing Co., 173–80.

Nakano, Yukiko, Gabe Reinstein, Tom Stocky, & Justine Cassell (2003), Towards a model of face-to-face grounding. *Proceedings of the 41st Annual Meeting of the Association for Computational Linguistics*, 553–61.

Narayanan, Srini, & Daniel Jurafsky (1998), Bayesian models of human sentencing processing. *Proceedings of the 20th Annual Conference of the Cognitive Science Society*, 752–7.

Narayanan, Srini, & Sanda Harabagiu (2004), Question answering based on semantic structures. *International Conference on Computational Linguistics (COLING 2004)*, 184–91.

Nastase, V., J. Sayyad-Shiarabad, M. Sokolova, & S. Szpakowicz (2006), Learning noun-modi er semantic relations with corpus-based and WordNet-based features. *Proceedings of the 21st National Conference on Artificial Intelligence and the 18th Innovative Applications of Artificial Intelligence Conference*, 781–6.

Nederhof, M.-J., & G. Satta (2004), Tabular parsing, in C. Martín-Vide, V. Mitrana, & G. Paun (eds.), *Formal Languages and Applications*. Amsterdam: Springer, 529–49.

Negri, M., & M. Koulekov (2007), Who are we talking about? Tracking the referent in a question answering series, in A. Branco (ed.), *Anaphora: Analysis, Algorithms and Applications*. Dordrecht: Springer, 167–78.

Nepomnyashchii, V. A. (1975), Spatial complexity of recognition of context-free languages. *Cybernetics and Systems Analysis* 11(5):736–41.

Nerode, Anil (1958), Linear automaton transformations. *Proceedings of the American Mathematical Society* 9:541–4.

Nesson, Rebecca, Stuart M. Shieber, & Alexander Rush (2006), Induction of probabilistic synchronous tree-insertion grammars for machine translation. *AMTA 2006, Proceedings of the 7th Conference of the Association for Machine Translation in the Americas, Visions for the Future of Machine Translation*, 128–37.

Nevill-Manning, Craig G. (1996), Inferring sequential structure. PhD thesis, University of Waikato.

Nevill-Manning, Craig G., & Ian H. Witten (1997), Identifying hierarchical structure in sequences: a linear-time algorithm. *Journal of Artificial Intelligence Research* 7(1):67–82.

Ney, H., & S. Ortmanns (2000), Progress in dynamic programming search for LVCSR. *Proceedings of the IEEE* 88(8):1224–40.

Ney, H., Ute Essen, & Reinhard Kneser (1994), On structuring probabilistic dependencies in stochastic language modelling. *Computer Speech and Language* 8:1–38.

Ng, A. Y., & S. Russell (2000), Algorithms for inverse reinforcement learning.

Proceedings of the 17th International
Conference on Machine Learning, 663–70.

Ng, Hwee Tou (1997), Getting serious about
word sense disambiguation. *Proceedings
of the ACL SIGLEX Workshop on Tagging
Text with Lexical Semantics: Why, What,
and How?* 1–7.

Ng, Hwee Tou, & Hian Beng Lee (1996),
Integrating multiple knowledge sources
to disambiguate word sense: an
exemplar-based approach, 40–7.

Ng, Vincent, & Claire Cardie (2002),
Improving machine learning approaches
to coreference resolution. *Proceedings of
the 40th Annual Meeting of the Association
for Computational Linguistics (ACL2002)*,
104–11.

Niblett, T. (1987), Constructing decision
trees in noisy domains. *Proceedings of the
2nd European Working Session on Learning*,
67–78.

Nigam, Kamal, John Lafferty, & Andrew
McCallum (1999), Using maximum
entropy for text classi cation. *Proceedings
of the IJCAI-99 Workshop on Machine
Learning for Information Filtering*, 61–7.

Nigay, Laurence, & Joëlle Coutaz (1993),
A design space for multimodal systems:
concurrent processing and data fusion.
*CHI '93: Proceedings of the INTERACT '93
and CHI '93 Conference on Human Factors
in Computing Systems*, 172–8. http://doi.
acm.org/10.1145/169059.169143

Nivre, J. (2007), Incremental non-projective
dependency parsing. *Proceedings of
Human-Language Technologies: The Annual
Conference of the North American Chapter of
the Association for Computational
Linguistics (NAACL-HLT)*, 396–403.

Nivre, J., & M. Scholz (2004), Deterministic
dependency parsing of English text.
Proceedings of COLING-04, 64–70.

Nivre, J., J. Hall, & J. Nilsson (2004),
Memory-based dependency parsing.
*Proceedings of the 8th Conference on
Computational Natural Language Learning
(CoNLL 2004)*, 49–56.

Nivre, J., J. Hall, S. Kübler et al. (2007), The
CoNLL 2007 shared task on dependency

parsing. *Conference on Empirical Methods
in Natural Language Processing and Natural
Language Learning*, 915–32.

Niyogi, P. (2006), *The Computational Nature
of Language Learning and Evolution*.
Cambridge, MA: MIT Press.

Niyogi, Sourabh (2002), Bayesian learning
at the syntax-semantics interface, in
*Proceedings of the 24th annual conference of
the Cognitive Science Society*,
(697–702).

Nocedal, Jorge & Stephen J. Wright (1999),
Numerical Optimization, Springer,
New York.

Nomiyama, Hiroshi (1992), Machine
translation by case generalization.
*Proceedings of the 15th [sic] International
Conference on Computational Linguistics,
COLING-92*, 714–20.

Normandin, Yves (1991), Hidden Markov
models, maximum mutual information
estimation and the speech recognition
problem. PhD thesis, McGill University.

Norris, Dennis (1999), Computational
psycholinguistics, in R. Wilson & F. Keil
(eds.), *MIT Encyclopedia of the Cognitive
Sciences*. Cambridge, MA: MIT Press,
168–9.

Norris, Dennis, James McQueen, & Anne
Cutler (2000), Merging information in
speech processing: feedback is never
necessary. *Behavioral and Brain Sciences*
23(3):299–370.

Novick, David, & Stephen Sutton (1994),
An empirical model of acknowledgment
for spoken-language systems. *Proceedings
of the 32nd Annual Meeting of the
Association for Computational Linguistics*,
96–101.

Nowak, M. A., N. L. Komarova, & P. Niyogi
(2002), Computational and evolutionary
aspects of language. *Nature* 417:611–17.

Oberlander, Jon (1998), Do the right
thing . . . but expect the unexpected.
Computational Linguistics 24:501–7.

Och, Franz (2003), Minimum error rate
training in statistical machine translation.
*41st Annual Meeting of the Association for
Computational Linguistics*, 160–7.

Och, Franz, & Hermann Ney (2000), A comparison of alignment models for statistical machine translation. *Coling 2000 in Europe: The 18th International Conference on Computational Linguistics, Proceedings*, 1086–90.

Och, Franz, & Hermann Ney (2001), Discriminative training and maximum entropy models for statistical machine translation. *Proceedings of the 40th Annual Meeting of the Association for Computational Linguistics*, 295–302.

Och, Franz, & Hermann Ney (2002), Discriminative training and maximum entropy models for statistical machine translation. *40th Annual Meeting of the Association for Computational Linguistics*, 295–302.

Och, Franz, & Hermann Ney (2003), A systematic comparison of various statistical alignment models. *Computational Linguistics* 29(1):19–51.

Och, Franz, & Hermann Ney (2004), The alignment template approach to statistical machine translation. *Computational Linguistics* 30(4):417–49.

Och, Franz, Dan Gildea, Sanjeev Khudanpur et al. (2004), A smorgasbord of features for statistical machine translation. *Proceedings Human-Language Technology and North American Association of Computational Linguistics (HLT-NAACL)*, 161–8.

Odell, Julian J. (1995), The use of context in large vocabulary speech recognition. PhD thesis, University of Cambridge.

O'Donnell, Mick, Chris Mellish, Jon Oberlander, & Alistair Knott (2001), ILEX: an architecture for a dynamic hypertext generation system. *Natural Language Engineering* 7:225–50.

Oepen, S., & Dan Flickinger (1998), Towards systematic grammar pro ling: test suite technology ten years after. *Journal of Computer Speech and Language* 12:411–35.

Oepen, S., K. Toutanova, S. M. Shieber, C. D. Manning, D. Flickinger, & T. Brants (2002), The LinGO Redwoods treebank: motivation and preliminary applications. *Proceedings of COLING'2002*, 1–5.

Oettinger, A. (1961), Automatic syntactic analysis and pushdown storage. *Proceedings of the 12th Symposium in Applied Mathematics*, 104–29.

Olivier, D. C. (1968), Stochastic grammars and language acquisition mechanisms. PhD thesis, Harvard University.

Ono, Kenji, Kakuo Sumita, & Seiji Miike (1994), Abstract generation based on rhetorical structure extraction. *Proceedings of the 15th International Conference on Computational Linguistics (COLING-94)*, 344–8.

Orasan, C. (2001), Patterns in scienti c abstracts. *Proceedings of Corpus Linguistics 2001 Conference*, 433–43.

Orasan, C. (2006), Comparative evaluation of modular automatic summarisation systems using CAST. PhD thesis, University of Wolverhampton.

Orasan, C. (2009), The in uence of pronominal anaphora resolution on term-based summarisation, in N. Nicolov, G. Angelova, & R. Mitkov (eds.), *Recent Advances in Natural Language Processing V*, vol. 309. Amsterdam: John Benjamins, 291–300.

Orasan, C., & R. Evans (2001), Learning to identify animate references. *Proceedings of the 5th Workshop on Computational Language Learning, CoNLL-2001*, 129–36.

Ortiz-Martínez, Daniel, Ismael Garcia-Varea, & Francisco Casacuberta (2005), Thot: a toolkit to train phrase-based models for statistical machine translation. *Proceedings of Machine Translation Summit X*, 141–8.

Osborne, Miles (2000), Estimation of stochastic attribute-value grammars using an informative sample. *Proceedings of the 18th International Conference on Computational Linguistics (COLING 2000)*, 586–92.

Ostendorf, M. (1999), Moving beyond the 'beads-on-a-string' model of speech. *Proceedings IEEE ASRU Workshop*, 79–84.

Ostendorf, M., & S. Roukos (1989), A stochastic segment model for phoneme-based continuous speech recognition. *IEEE Transactions Acoustics, Speech & Signal Processing* 32(12): 1857–69.

Ostendorf, M., V. Digalakis, & O. Kimball (1996), From HMMs to segment models. *IEEE Transactions on Speech & Audio Processing* 4(5):360–78.

Osterhout, Lee, & P. J. Holcomb (1992), Event-related brain potentials elicited by syntactic anomaly. *Journal of Memory and Language* 31:785–806.

Osterhout, Lee, & P. J. Holcomb (1993), Event-related potentials and syntactic anomaly: evidence of anomaly brain potentials. *Psychophysioloy* 30: 170–82.

Owczarzak, Karolina, Josef van Genabith, & Andy Way (2007a), Evaluating machine translation with LFG dependencies. *Machine Translation* 21(2):95–119.

Owczarzak, Karolina, Josef van Genabith, & Andy Way (2007b), Labelled dependencies in machine translation evaluation. *Proceedings of the 2nd Workshop on Statistical Machine Translation at the 45th Annual Meeting of the Association for Computational Linguistics (ACL-07)*, 104–11.

Ozdowska, Sylwia, & Andy Way (2009), Optimal bilingual data for French–English PB-SMT. *Proceedings of EAMT-09, the 13th Annual Meeting of the European Association for Machine Translation*, 96–103.

Pado, Ulrike, Matthew W. Crocker, & Frank Keller (2009), A probabilistic model of semantic plausibility in sentence processing. *Cognitive Science* 33:794–838.

Paek, T., & D. M. Chickering (2005), On the Markov assumption on spoken dialogue management. *Proceedings of the 6th SIGDIAL Workshop on Discourse and Dialogue*, 35–44.

Paek, T., & R. Pieraccini (2008), Automating spoken dialogue management design using machine learning: an industry perspective. *Speech Communication* 50:716–29.

Paice, Chris D., & G. D. Husk (1987), Towards the automatic recognition of anaphoric features in English text: the impersonal pronoun *it*. *Computer Speech and Language* 2:109–32.

Palmer, David D., & Marti A. Hearst (1997), Adaptive multilingual sentence boundary disambiguation. *Computational Linguistics* 23(2):241–69.

Palmer, Martha, & Marc Light (1999), ACL SIGLEX workshop on tagging text with lexical semantics: what, why, and how? *Natural Language Engineering* 5(2):i–iv.

Palmer, Martha, Tim Finin, & Sharon Walters (1990), Workshop on the evaluation of natural language processing systems. *Computational Linguistics* (3):175–81.

Palmer, Martha, Christiane Fellbaum, Scott Cotton, Lauren Delfs, & Hoa Trang Dang (2001), English tasks: all-words and verb lexical sample. *Proceedings of SENSEVAL-2: Second International Workshop on Evaluating Word Sense Disambiguation Systems*, 21–4.

Palmer, Martha, Daniel Gildea, & Paul Kingsbury (2005), The proposition bank: an annotated corpus of semantic roles. *Computational Linguistics* 31(1):71–106. http://dx.doi.org/10.1162/ 0891201053630264

Palmer, Martha, Hwee Tou Ng, & Hoa Trang Dang (2006), Evaluation of WSD systems, in Eneko Agirre & Phil Edmonds (eds.), *Word Sense Disambiguation: Algorithms and Applications, Text, Speech and Language Technology*, vol. 33. Amsterdam: Springer, 75–106.

Palmer, Martha, Hoa Trang Dang, & Christiane Fellbaum (2007), Making ne-grained and coarse-grained sense distinctions, both manually and automatically. *Natural Language Engineering* 13(2):137–63.

Papadimitriou, Christos H. (1994), *Computational Complexity*. Reading, MA: Addison-Wesley.

Papineni, Kishore, Salim Roukos, Todd Ward, & Wei-Jing Zhu (2002), BLEU: a method for automatic evaluation of machine translation. *Proceedings of the 40th Annual Meeting of the Association for Computational Linguistics (ACL 2002)*, 311–18.

Paris, Cecile, Keith Vander Linden, Marcus Fischer et al. (1995), A support tool for writing multilingual instructions. *Proceedings of the 14th International Joint Conference on Artificial Intelligence (IJCAI-1995)*, 1398–404.

Partee, Barbara, & Mats Rooth (1983), Generalised conjunction and type ambiguity, in R. Bäuerle, C. Schwartze, & A. von Stechow (eds.), *Meaning, Use and Interpretation of Language*. Berlin: Walter de Gruyter, 361–83.

Partee, Barbara, Alice ter Meulen, & Robert E. Wall (1990), *Mathematical Methods in Linguistics, Studies in Linguistics and Philosophy*. vol. 30 Dordrecht: Kluwer Academic Publishers.

Parzen, E. (1962), On the estimation of a probability density function and the mode. *Annals of Mathematical Statistics* 33:1065–76.

Paşca, Marius (2007), Lightweight web-based fact repositories for textual question answering. *CIKM '07: Proceedings, 16th ACM Conference on Information and Knowledge Management*, 87–96.

Paşca, Marius, & Benjamin van Durme (2008), Weakly-supervised acquisition of open-domain classes and class attributes from web documents and query logs. *Proceedings of ACL-08: HLT*, 19–27.

Paterson, J. (1980), *The Hamlyn Pocket Dictionary of Wines*. New York: Hamlyn.

Paterson, M. S., & M. N. Wegman (1978), Linear uni cation. *Journal of Computer and System Sciences* 16:158–67.

Paul, Michael, Kazuhide Yamamoto, & Eiichiro Sumita (1999), Corpus-based anaphora resolution towards antecedent preference. *Proceedings of 1999 ACL Workshop on Coreference and Its Applications*, 47–52.

Paul, Michael, Takao Doi, Youngsook Hwang, Kenji Imamura, Hideo Okuma, & Eiichiro Sumita (2005a), Nobody is perfect: ATR's hybrid approach to spoken language translation. *Proceedings of the International Workshop on Spoken Language Translation*, 55–62.

Paul, Michael, Eiichiro Sumita, & Seiichi Yamamoto (2005b), A machine learning approach to hypotheses selection of greedy decoding for SMT. *Proceedings of 2nd Workshop on Example-Based Machine Translation, MT Summit X*, 117–24.

Pedersen, Ted, Serguei V. S. Pakhomov, Siddharth Patwardhan, & Christopher G. Chute (2007), Measures of semantic similarity and relatedness in the biomedical domain. *Journal of Biomedical Informatics* 40(3):288–99. http://dx.doi.org/10.1016/j.jbi.2006.06.004

Pekar, V., & R. Mitkov (2007), New generation translation memory: content-sensitive matching. *Proceedings of the 40th Anniversary Congress of the Swiss Association of Translators, Terminologists and Interpreters*.

Pelletier, Francis Jeffry, & Lenhart K. Schubert (1989), Generically speaking, in G. Chierchia, B. H. Partee, & R. Turner (eds.), *Properties, Types, and Meaning*, vol. 2. Dordrecht: Kluwer, 193–268.

Penn, Gerald (2000), The algebraic structure of attributed type signatures. PhD thesis, Carnegie Mellon University.

Pentus, M. (1993), Lambek grammars are context free. *Proceedings, 8th Annual Symposium on Logic in Computer Science*, 429–33.

Pentus, M. (1994), Language completeness of the Lambek calculus. *Proceedings, 9th Annual Symposium on Logic in Computer Science*, 487–96.

Pentus, M. (1997), Product-free Lambek calculus and context-free grammars. *Journal of Symbolic Logic* 62(2):648–60.

Pentus, M. (2006), Lambek calculus is NP-complete. *Theoretical Computer Science* 357(1–3):186–201.

Pereira, F. (2000), Formal grammar and information theory: together again? *Philosophical Transactions of the Royal Society*, 1239–53.

Pereira, F. (1985), A new characterization of attachment preferences. *Natural Language Parsing – Psychological, Computational and Theoretical perspectives*, 307–19.

Pereira, F., & David H. D. Warren (1980), De nite clause grammars for language analysis – a survey of the formalism and a comparison with augmented transition networks. *Artificial Intelligence* 13(3):231–78.

Pereira, F., & Stuart M. Shieber (1987), *Prolog and Natural-Language Analysis*, *CSLI Lecture Notes Series* vol. 10. Stanford, CA: CSLI Publications. Italian translation: *Prolog e Analisi del Linguaggio Naturale*. Milan: Tecniche Nuove, 1992.

Perez y Perez, Rafael, & Mike Sharples (2004), Three computer-based models of storytelling: BRUTUS, MINSTREL, and MEXICA. *Knowledge-Based Systems* 17:15–29.

Perfors, Amy, Joshua B. Tenenbaum, & Terry Regier (2006), Poverty of the stimulus? A rational approach. *28th Annual Conference of the Cognitive Science Society*, 663–8.

Peters, P. Stanley, Jr., & R. W. Ritchie (1973), On the generative power of transformational grammars. *Information Sciences* 6:49–83.

Pickering, Martin J., Charles Clifton, & Matthew W. Crocker (2000a), Architectures and mechanisms in sentence comprehension, in Matthew W. Crocker, Martin J. Pickering, & Charles Clifton (eds.), *Architectures and Mechanisms for Language Processing*. Cambridge: Cambridge University Press, 1–28.

Pickering, Martin J., Matthew J. Traxler, & Matthew W. Crocker (2000b), Ambiguity resolution in sentence processing: evidence against frequency-based accounts. *Journal of Memory and Language* 43:447–75.

Pierce, John, John Carroll, Eric Hamp et al. (1966), Language and machines: computers in translation and linguistics. Technical report, Automatic Language Processing Committee, National Academy of Sciences, National Research Council, Washington, DC.

Pinker, S. (1989), *Learnability and Cognition*. Cambridge, MA: MIT Press.

Pinker, S. (1996), *Language Learnability and Language Development*, 2nd edn. Cambridge, MA: Harvard University Press.

Pinker, S. (1999), *Words and Rules: The Ingredients of Language*. New York: Basic Books.

Pirrelli, Vito, & François Yvon (1999), The hidden dimension: a paradigmatic view of data-driven NLP. *Journal of Experimental and Theoretical Artificial Intelligence* 11(3):391–408.

Pitt, L. (1989), Inductive inference, DFA's, and computational complexity. *Lecture Notes in Artificial Intelligence*, 8–14.

Piwek, Paul (2000), Imperatives, commitment and action: towards a constraint-based model. *LDV Forum: GLDV-Journal for Computational Linguistics and Language Technology, Special Issue on Communicating Agents* 17(1–2).

Plag, I., G. Kunter, & S. Lappe (2007), Testing hypotheses about compound stress assignment in English: a corpus-based investigation. *Corpus Linguistics and Linguistic Theory* 3(2):199–232.

Planas, Emmanuel, & Osamu Furuse (2003), Formalizing translation memory, in Michael Carl & Andy Way (eds.), *Recent Advances in Example-Based Machine Translation*. Dordrecht: Kluwer Academic Publishers, 157–88.

Plunkett, Kim, & Virginia A. Marchman (1996), Learning from a connectionist model of the acquisition of the English past tense. *Cognition* 61(3):299–308.

Poesio, Massimo (2004), Discourse annotation and semantic annotation in the GNOME corpus. *Proceedings of the ACL Workshop on Discourse Annotation*, 72–9.

Poesio, Massimo, & David Traum (1997), Conversational actions and discourse situations. *Computational Intelligence* 13:309–47.

Poesio, Massimo, & David Traum (1998), Towards an axiomatization of dialogue acts. *Proceedings of TwenDial 98, 13th Twente Workshop on Language Technology*, 207–21.

Poesio, Massimo, & Hannes Rieser (2009), (Prolegomena to a theory of) completions, continuations, and coordination in dialogue. University of Essex and Bielefeld University MS.

Poesio, Massimo, & Mijail Alexandrov-Kabadjov (2004), A general-purpose, off-the-shelf system for anaphora resolution. *Proceedings of LREC.*

Poesio, Massimo, & Renata Vieira (1998), A corpus-based investigation of de nite description use. *Computational Linguistics* 24(2):183–216.

Poesio, Massimo, & Uwe Reyle (2001), Underspeci cation in anaphoric reference. *Proceedings of the 4th International Workshop on Computational Semantics.*

Poesio, Massimo, Florence Bruneseaux, & Laurent Romary (1999), The MATE meta-scheme for coreference in dialogues in multiple languages. *Proceedings of the ACL Workshop on Standards for Discourse Tagging*, 65–74.

Poesio, Massimo, Hua Cheng, Renate Henschel, Janet Hitzeman, Rodger Kibble, & Rosemary Stevenson (2000), Specifying the parameters of centering theory: a corpus-based evaluation using text from application-oriented domains. *Proceedings of the 38th ACL*, 400–7.

Poesio, Massimo, Rosemary Stevenson, Barbara Di Eugenio, & Janet Hitzeman (2004), Centering: a parametric theory and its instantiation. *Computational Linguistics* 30(3):309–63.

Poggio, T., R. Rifkin, S. Mukherjee, & P. Niyogi (2004), General conditions for predictivity in learning theory. *Nature* 428:419–22.

Pollack, Martha (1986), Inferring domain plans in question-answering. PhD thesis, University of Pennsylvania.

Pollard, C. (1984), Generalized phrase structure grammars, head grammars and natural language. PhD thesis, Stanford University.

Pollard, C. (2004), Higher-order categorial grammar. *Proceedings of the International Conference on Categorial Grammars (CG2004)*. 340–61.

Pollard, C. (forthcoming), Hyperintensions. *Journal of Logic and Computation.*

Pollard, C., & I. A. Sag (1994), *Head-Driven Phrase Structure Grammar*. Stanford, CA: CSLI Publications.

Poritz, A. (1982), Linear predictive hidden Markov models and the speech signal. *Acoustics, Speech, and Signal Processing, IEEE International Conference on ICASSP '82*, 1291–4.

Poritz, A. (1988), Hidden Markov models: a guided tour. *Proceedings IEEE ICASSP-88*, 7–13.

Portet, François, Ehud Reiter, Jim Hunter, & Somayajulu Sripada (2007), Automatic generation of textual summaries from neonatal intensive care data. *Proceedings of the 11th Conference on Artificial Intelligence in Medicine (AIME 2007)*, 227–36.

Portner, Paul (2005), The semantics of imperatives within a theory of clause types. *Proceedings of Semantics and Linguistic Theory 14*. http:// semanticsarchive.net/Archive/ mJlZGQ4N/PortnerSALT04.pdf

Povey, D. (2003), Discriminative training for large vocabulary speech recognition. PhD thesis, University of Cambridge.

Povey, D., & P. C. Woodland (2002), Minimum phone error and i-smoothing for improved discriminative training. *Proceedings ICASSP '92*, 105–8.

Povey, D., M. J. F. Gales, D. Y. Kim, & P. C. Woodland (2003), MMI-MAP and MPE-MAP for acoustic model adaptation. *Proceedings of Eurospeech'03*, 1981–4.

Povey, D., B. Kingsbury, L. Mangu, G. Saon, H. Soltau, & G. Zweig (2005), fMPE: discriminatively trained features for speech recognition. *Proceedings of ICASSP'05*, 961–4.

Power, Richard, Donia Scott, & Roger Evans (1998), What you see is what you meant: direct knowledge editing with natural language feedback. *Proceedings of 13th European Conference on Artificial Intelligence (ECAI-1998)*, 677–81.

Power, Richard, Donia Scott, & Nadjet Bouayad-Agha (2003), Document structure. *Computational Linguistics* 29:211–60.

Pradhan, Sameer, Eduard Hovy, Mitch Marcus, Martha Palmer, Lance Ramshaw, & Ralph Weischedel (2007a), Ontonotes: a uni ed relational representation. *International Journal of Semantic Computing* 1(4):405–19.

Pradhan, Sameer, Edward Loper, Dmitriy Dligach, & Martha Palmer (2007b), SemEval Task-17: English lexical sample, SRL and all words. *Proceedings of the 4th International Workshop on Semantic Evaluations (SemEval-2007), Held in Conjunction with ACL-2007*, 87–92.

Pradhan, Sameer, Lance Ramshaw, Ralph Weischedel, Jessica MacBride, & Linnea Micciulla (2007c), Unrestricted coreference: identifying entities and events in OntoNotes . *Proceedings of the IEEE International Conference on Semantic Computing (ICSC)*, 446–53.

Prager, John (2007), *Open Domain Question Answering*. Boston: Now Publishers.

Prager, John, Eric Brown, Anni Coden, & Dragomir Radev (2000), Question answering by predictive annotation. *Proceedings, 23rd Annual International SIGIR Conference*, 184–91.

Pratt-Hartmann, Ian (2004), Fragments of language. *Journal of Logic, Language and Information* 13:207–23.

Pratt-Hartmann, Ian (2008), On the computational complexity of the numerically de nite syllogistic and related logics. *Bulletin of Symbolic Logic* 14(1):1–28.

Pratt-Hartmann, Ian, & Allan Third (2006), More fragments of language. *Notre Dame Journal of Formal Logic* 47(2):151–77.

Pratt-Hartmann, Ian, & Lawrence S. Moss (2009), Logics for the relational syllogistic. *Review of Symbolic Logic* 2(4):647–83.

Preiss, J. (2002a), Anaphora resolution with memory based learning. *Proceedings of the Annual Computational Linguistics UK conference (CLUK-5)*, 1–9.

Preiss, J. (2002b), Choosing a parser for anaphora resolution. *Proceedings of the Discourse Anaphora and Anaphora Resolution Colloquium (DAARC2002)*, 175–80.

Preiss, J. (2002c), A comparison of probabilistic and non-probabilistic anaphora resolution algorithms. *Proceedings of the Student Workshop at ACL '02*, 42–7.

Presburger, Mojzesz (1929), Über die Vollständigkeit eines gewissen Systems der Arithmetik ganzer Zahlen, in welchem die Addition als einzige Operation hervortritt. *Comptes Rendus du I Congrès de Mathématiciens des Pays Slaves, Warszawa*, 92–101.

Prévot, Laurent (2003), Structures sémantiques et pragmatiques pour la modélisation de la cohérence dans des dialogues nalisés. PhD thesis, Université Paul Sabatier, Toulouse.

Prince, E. (1981), Toward a taxonomy of given-new information, in E. Cole (ed.), *Radical Pragmatics*. New York: Academic Press, 223–55.

Pritchett, B. L. (1992), *Grammatical Competence and Parsing Performance*. Chicago: University of Chicago Press.

Probst, Katharina, Lori Levin, Erik Peterson, Alon Lavie, & Jaime Carbonell (2002), MT for minority languages using elicitation-based learning of syntactic transfer rules. *Machine Translation* 17(4):245–70.

Prochaska, James, & Carlo diClemente (1992), *Stages of Change in the Modification of Problem Behaviors*. Newbury Park, CA: Sage.

Provost, Foster, & Pedro Domingos (2003), Tree induction for probability-based ranking. *Machine Learning* 52(3):199–215.

Pullum, G., & B. Scholz (2002), Empirical assessment of stimulus poverty arguments. *The Linguistic Review* 19:9–50.

Pullum, G., & Gerald Gazdar (1982), Natural languages and context-free languages. *Linguistics and Philosophy* 4:471–504.

Punyakanok, Vasin, Dan Roth, & W. Yih (2005), The necessity of syntactic parsing for semantic role labeling. *Proceedings of IJCAI-2005*, 1124–9.

Purver, M. (2006), CLARIE: handling clari cation requests in a dialogue system, *Research on Language & Computation* 4(2):259–88.

Purver, M., Jonathan Ginzburg, & Patrick Healey (2001), On the means for clari cation in dialogue, in Jan van Kuppevelt & Ronnie Smith (eds.), *Current and New Directions in Discourse and Dialogue*. Dordrecht: Kluwer, 235–56.

Purver, M., P. Ehlen, & J. Niekrasz (2006), Detecting action items in multi-party meetings: annotation and initial experiments, in S. Renals, S. Bengio, & J. Fiscus (eds.), *Machine Learning for Multimodal Interaction, Lecture Notes in Computer Science* 4299. Amsterdam: Springer-Verlag, 200–11.

Purver, M., J. Dowding, J. Niekrasz, P. Ehlen, S. Noorbaloochi, & S. Peters (2007), Detecting and summarizing action items in multi-party dialogue. *Proceedings of the 8th SIGdial Workshop on Discourse and Dialogue*, 18–25.

Pustejovsky, James (1995), *The Generative Lexicon*. Cambridge, MA: MIT Press.

Pustejovsky, James, Patrick Hanks, Roser Sauri et al. (2003), The TimeBank Corpus. *Corpus Linguistics*, 647–56.

Pustejovsky, James, Bob Ingria, Roser Sauri et al. (2005), The speci cation language TimeML, in I. Mani, J. Pustejovsky, & R. Gaizauskas (eds.), *The Language of Time: A Reader*. Oxford: Oxford University Press, 545–58.

Quarteroni, Sylvia, & Suresh Manandhar (2009), Designing an interactive open-domain question answering system. *Journal of Natural Language Engineering: Special Issue on Interactive Question Answering* 15(1):73–95.

Quesada, Jose (2003), Latent problem solving analysis (LPSA): a computational theory of representation in complex, dynamic problem solving tasks. PhD thesis, University of Granada.

Quinlan, J. Ross (1986), Induction of decision trees. *Machine Learning* 1:81–106.

Quinlan, J. Ross (1987), Simplifying decision trees. *International Journal of Man–Machine Studies* 27(3):221–34.

Quinlan, J. Ross (1993), *C4.5: Programs for Machine Learning*. San Mateo, CA: Morgan Kaufmann.

Rabbin, Michael O., & Dana Scott (1959), Finite automata and their decision problems. *IBM Journal of Research and Development* 3(2):114–25.

Rabiner, L. R. (1989), A tutorial on hidden Markov models and selected applications in speech recognition. *Proceedings of the IEEE* 77(2):257–86.

Radev, D. (2000), A common theory of information fusion from multiple text sources, step one: cross-document structure. *Proceedings, 1st ACL SIGDIAL Workshop on Discourse and Dialogue*, 74–83.

Radev, D., J. Otterbacher, & Z. Zhang (2003), CSTBank: cross-document structure theory bank. http://clair. si.umich.edu/clair/CST Bank/

Radhakrishnan, T. (1978), Selection of pre x and post x word fragments for data compression. *Information Processing and Management* 14(2):97–106.

Raina, Rajat, Andrew Y. Ng, & Christopher Manning (2005), Robust textual inference via learning and abductive reasoning. *20th National Conference on Artificial Intelligence (AAAI-05)*, 1099–1105.

Ramsay, Allan (1995), Theorem proving for intensional logic. *Journal of Automated Reasoning* 14:237–55.

Ramshaw, L. A. & M. P. Marcus (1995), Text chunking using transformation-based learning. *Proceedings of the 3rd ACL/SIGDAT Workshop on Very Large Corpora*, 82–94.

Ranta, Aarne (1994), *Type Theoretic Grammar*. Oxford: Oxford University Press.

Ratnaparkhi, A. (1996), A maximum entropy part-of-speech tagger. *Proceedings of the EMNLP Conference*, 133–42.

Ratnaparkhi, A. (1998), Maximum entropy models for natural language ambiguity resolution. PhD thesis, University of Pennsylvania.

Ratnaparkhi, A. (1999), Learning to parse natural language with maximum entropy models. *Machine Learning* 34(1–3): 151–75.

Ratnaparkhi, A., J. Reynar, & S. Roukos (1994), A maximum entropy model for prepositional phrase attachment. *Workshop on Human-Language Technology*, 250–5.

Ravishankar, M. K. (1996), Ef cient algorithms for speech recognition. PhD thesis, Carnegie Mellon University.

Rayner, Keith (1998), Eye movements in reading and information processing: 20 years of research. *Psychological Bulletin* 124:372–422.

Rayner, Keith, Marcia Carlson, & Lyn Frazier (1983), The interaction of syntax and semantics during sentence processing: eye movements in the analysis of semantically biased sentences.

Journal of Verbal Learning and Verbal Behavior 22:358–74.

Redington, Martin, Nick Chater, & Steven Finch (1998), Distributional information: a powerful cue for acquiring syntactic categories. *Cognitive Science* 22(4):425–69.

Reiter, Ehud (1995), Sublanguages in text and graphics. *Proceedings of the 1st International Workshop on Intelligence and Multimodality in Multimedia Interfaces (IMMI-1995)*.

Reiter, Ehud (2007), An architecture for data-to-text systems. *Proceedings of the 11th European Workshop on Natural Language Generation (ENLG 2007)*, 97–104.

Reiter, Ehud, & Anja Belz (2009), An investigation into the validity of some metrics for automatically evaluating natural language generation systems. *Computational Linguistics*, 529–58.

Reiter, Ehud, & Robert Dale (2000), *Building Natural Language Generation Systems*. Cambridge: Cambridge University Press.

Reiter, Ehud, & Somayajulu Sripada (2002), Human variation and lexical choice. *Computational Linguistics* 28:545–53.

Reiter, Ehud, Roma Robertson, & Liesl Osman (2003a), Lessons from a failure: generating tailored smoking cessation letters. *Artificial Intelligence* 144:41–58.

Reiter, Ehud, Somayajulu Sripada, & Roma Robertson (2003b), Acquiring correct knowledge for natural language generation. *Journal of Artificial Intelligence Research* 18:491–516.

Reiter, Ehud, Somayajulu Sripada, Jim Hunter, & Jin Yu (2005), Choosing words in computer-generated weather forecasts. *Artificial Intelligence* 167:137–69.

Reiter, Ehud, Ross Turner, Norman Alm, Rolf Black, Martin Dempster, & Annalu Waller (2009), Using NLG to help language-impaired users tell stories and participate in social dialogues. *Proceedings of the 12th European Workshop on Natural Language Generation (ENLG-2009)*, 1–8.

Renals, S., & M. M. Hochberg (1999), Start-synchronous search for large vocabulary continuous speech recognition. *Speech and Audio Processing, IEEE Transactions* 7(5):542–53.

Renals, S., Thomas Hain, & Herve Bourlard (2008), Interpretation of multiparty meetings: the AMI and AMIDA projects. *IEEE Workshop on Hands-Free Speech Communication and Microphone Arrays, 2008, HSCMA 2008*, 115–18.

Resnik, Philip (1992a), Left-corner parsing and psychological plausibility. *Proceedings of the 14th International Conference on Computational Linguistics*, 191–7.

Resnik, Philip (1992b), Probabilistic tree-adjoining grammar as a framework for statistical natural language processing. *Proceedings of the 14th International Conference on Computational Linguistics*, 418–24.

Resnik, Philip (1999), Semantic similarity in a taxonomy: An information-based measure and its application to problems of ambiguity in natural language. *Journal of Artificial Intelligence Research (JAIR)* 11:95–130.

Resnik, Philip (2006), WSD in NLP applications, in Eneko Agirre & Phil Edmonds (eds.), *Word Sense Disambiguation: Algorithms and Applications*. Dordrecht: Springer, 299–338.

Resnik, Philip, & David Yarowsky (1997), A perspective on word sense disambiguation methods and their evaluation. *ACL SIGLEX Workshop on Tagging Text with Lexical Semantics: Why, What, and How?* 79–86.

Resnik, Philip, & David Yarowsky (1999), Distinguishing systems and distinguishing senses: new evaluation methods for word sense disambiguation. *Natural Language Engineering* 5(2):113–33.

Reyle, Uwe (1993), Dealing with ambiguities by underspeci cation: construction, representation and deduction. *Journal of Semantics* 10:123–79.

Rieser, Verena, & Joanna Moore (2005), Implications for generating clari cation

requests in task-oriented dialogues. *Proceedings of the 43rd Meeting of the Association for Computational Linguistics*, 239–46.

Rieser, Verena, & Oliver Lemon (2008), Learning effective multimodal dialogue strategies from Wizard-of-Oz data: bootstrapping and evaluation. *Proceedings of ACL*, 638–46.

Riezler, Stefan, & Alexander Vasserman (2004), Incremental feature selection and L_1 regularization for relaxed maximum-entropy modeling. *Proceedings of EMNLP'04*, 174–81.

Riezler, Stefan, Tracy H. King, Ronald M. Kaplan, Richard Crouch, John T. Maxwell, & Mark Johnson (2002), Parsing the Wall Street Journal using a lexical-functional grammar and discriminative estimation techniques. *Proceedings of the 40th Annual Meeting of the ACL*, 271–8.

Riloff, Ellen (1993), Automatically constructing a dictionary for information extraction tasks. *National Conference on Artificial Intelligence*, 811–16.

Riloff, Ellen (1996), Automatically generating extraction patterns from untagged text. *Proceedings of the 13th National Conference on Artificial Intelligence (AAAI-96)*, 1044–9.

Rios, Gordon, & Hongyuan Zha (2004), Exploring support vector machines and random forests for spam detection. *Proceedings of the Conference on Email and Anti-Spam (CEAS)*.

Rissanen, Jorma (2007), *Information and Complexity in Statistical Modeling*. Dordrecht: Springer.

Rissanen, Jorma, & Eric Sven Ristad (1994), Language acquisition in the MDL framework. *Language Computations, American Mathematical Society*, 149–66.

Ritchie, G. D., G. J. Russell, A. W. Black, & S. G. Pulman (1992), *Computational Morphology*. Cambridge, MA: MIT Press.

Ritchie, G. D., Rulu Manurang, Helen Pain, Annalu Waller, & Dave O'Mara (2006),

The STANDUP interactive riddle builder. *IEEE Intelligent Systems* 21:67–9.

Ritchie, R. W., & F. N. Springsteel (1972), Language recognition by marking automata. *Information and Control* 20(4):313–30.

Rizzi, Luigi (1990), *Relativized Minimality*. Cambridge, MA: MIT Press.

Roark, Brian (2001a), Probabilistic top-down parsing and language modeling. *Computational Linguistics* 27:249–76.

Roark, Brian (2001b), Robust probabilistic predictive syntactic processing: motivations, models, and applications. PhD thesis, Brown University.

Roark, Brian, & Richard Sproat (2006), *Computational Approaches to Morphology and Syntax*. Oxford: Oxford University Press.

Roberto Navigli, Paola Velardi (2005), Structural semantic interconnections: a knowledge-based approach to word sense disambiguation. *IEEE Transactions on Pattern Analysis and Machine Intelligence (PAMI)* 27(7):1–12.

Roberts, Ian, & Rob Gaizauskas (2004), Evaluating passage retrieval approaches for question answering. *Advances in Information Retrieval*, 72–84.

Robin, Jacques, & Kathleen R. McKeown (1996), Empirically designing and evaluating a new revision-based model for summary generation. *Artificial Intelligence* 85:135–79.

Roche, Emmanuel, & Yves Schabes (eds.) (1997a), *Finite-State Language Processing, Language, Speech and Communication*. Cambridge, MA: MIT Press.

Roche, Emmanuel, & Yves Schabes (1997b), Introduction, in Emmanuel Roche & Yves Schabes (eds.), *Finite-State Language Processing, Language, Speech and Communication*. Cambridge, MA: MIT Press, 1–65.

Rodriguez, Kepa, & David Schlangen (2004), Form, intonation and function of clari cation requests in German task-oriented spoken dialogues.

Proceedings of Catalog'04, the 8th Workshop on the Semantics and Pragmatics of Dialogue.

Rogers, James (2003), Syntactic structures as multi-dimensional trees. *Journal of Language and Computation* 1(3–4):265–305.

Ron, D., Y. Singer, & N. Tishby (1998), On the learnability and usage of acyclic probabilistic nite automata. *Journal of Computer and Systems Sciences* 56(2):133–52.

Rooth, Mats (1993), A theory of focus interpretation. *Natural Language Semantics* 1:75–116.

Rosenfeld, R. (1994), Adaptive statistical language modeling: a maximum entropy approach. PhD thesis, Carnegie Mellon University.

Rosenfeld, R. (1995), The CMU statistical language modeling toolkit and its use in the 1994 ARPA CSR evaluation. *Proceedings of the Spoken Language Systems Technology Workshop*, 47–50.

Rosenfeld, R. (2000), Two decades of statistical language modeling: where do we go from here? *Proceedings of the IEEE* 88(8):1270–8.

Ross, Alf (1945), Imperatives and logic. *Philosophy of Science* 11:30–46.

Rosti, A., & M. J. F. Gales (2003), Switching linear dynamical systems for speech recognition. Technical report CUED/F-INFENG/TR.461, University of Cambridge.

Rosti, A., Bing Xiang, Spyros Matsoukas, Richard Schwartz, Necip Fazil Ayan, & Bonnie Dorr (2007), Combining outputs from multiple machine translation systems. *Human-Language Technologies 2007: The Conference of the North American Chapter of the Association for Computational Linguistics*, 228–35.

Rounds, W. (1988), LFP: a logic for linguistic descriptions and an analysis of its complexity. *Computational Linguistics* 14(4):1–9.

Rounds, W., Alexis Manaster-Ramer, & Joyce Friedman (1987), Finding natural languages a home in formal language theory, in Alexis Manaster-Ramer (ed.), *Mathematics of Language*. Amsterdam: John Benjamins, 349–59.

Roy, Deb, & Ehud Reiter (2005), Connecting language to the world. *Artificial Intelligence* 167:1–12.

Roy, Deb, & Niloy Mukherjee (2005), Towards situated speech understanding: visual context priming of language models. *Computer Speech and Language* 19:227–48.

Rozenberg, Grzegorz, & Arto Salomaa (eds.) (1997), *Handbook of Formal Languages*. New York: Springer-Verlag.

Rudnicky, Alex (2004), Learning to talk by listening. Talk presented at Catalog '04, The 8th Workshop on the Semantics and Pragmatics of Dialogue, Universitat Pompeu Fabra, Barcelona, July 2004.

Rumelhart, D. E., & J. L. McClelland (1986), On learning the past tenses of English verbs, in J. L. McClelland & D. E. Rumelhart (eds.), *Parallel Distributed Processing: Explorations in the Microstructure of Cognition*, vol. 2: *Psychological and Biological Models*. Cambridge, MA: MIT Press, 216–71.

Rumelhart, D. E., & J. L. McClelland (1987), Learning the past tenses of English verbs: implicit rules or parallel distributed processing. *Mechanisms of Language Acquisition* 195–248.

Rumelhart, D. E., Geoffrey E. Hinton, & Ronald J. Williams (1986), Learning internal representations by error propagation, in David E. Rumelhart & James L. McClelland (eds.), *Parallel Distributed Processing: Explorations in the Microstructure of Cognition*, Vol. 1: *Foundations*. Cambridge, MA: MIT Press, 318–62.

Ruzzo, Walter L. (1979), On the complexity of general context-free language parsing and recognition. *Automata, Languages and Programming, 6th Colloquium, Lecture Notes in Computer Science* 71: 479–88.

Sadek, David, & Renato de Mori (1998), Dialogue systems, in R. de Mori (ed.),

Spoken Dialogues with Computers. London: Academic Press, 523–61.

Saffran, J., R. Aslin, & E. Newport (1996), Statistical learning by 8-month-old infants. *Science* 274:1926–8.

Sagae, K., & A. Lavie (2005), A classier-based parser with linear run-time complexity. *Proceedings of the 9th International Workshop on Parsing Technologies*, 125–32.

Sagae, K., & A. Lavie (2006), Parser combination by reparsing. *Proceedings of the Short Papers of the Conference on Human-Language Technology and North American Chapter of the Association for Computational Linguistics (HLT-NAACL)*, 129–32.

Sager, Naomi, Carol Friedman, Margaret Lyman, & members of the Linguistic String Project (1987), *Medical Language Processing: Computer Management of Narrative Data*. Reading, MA: Addison-Wesley.

Salanger-Meyer, F. (1990), Discoursal aws in medical English abstracts: a genre analysis per research- and text-type. *Text* 10(4):365–84.

Salzberg, S. (1991), A nearest hyperrectangle learning method. *Machine Learning* 6:277–309.

Sampson, Geoffrey (1986), A stochastic approach to parsing. *Proceedings of the 11th International Conference on Computational Linguistics*, 151–5.

Sanchez-Graillet, Olivia, & Massimo Poesio (2007), Negation of protein–protein interactions. *Bioinformatics* 23(13):424–32.

Sanchez-Graillet, Olivia, Massimo Poesio, Mijail A. Kabadjov, & Roman Tesar (2006), What kind of problems do protein interactions raise for anaphora resolution? – a preliminary analysis. *Proceedings of the 2nd International Symposium on Semantic Mining in Biomedicine (SMBM 2006)*, 9–12.

Sánchez-Martínez, Felipe, & Mikel Forcada (2007), Automatic induction of shallow-transfer rules for open-source machine translation. *Proceedings of the*

11th Conference on Theoretical and Methodological Issues in Machine Translation (TMI 2007), 181–90.

Saquete, Estela, P. Martinez-Barco, R. Muñoz, & J. L. Vicedo (2004), Splitting complex temporal questions for question-answering systems. *Proceedings, 42nd Annual Meeting of the Association for Computational Linguistics*, 567–74.

Sarkar, Anoop, & Aravind Joshi (2003), Tree-adjoining grammars and its application to statistical parsing, in Rens Bod, Remko Scha, & Khalil Sima'an (eds.), *Data-oriented parsing*. Standford, CA: CSLI Publications.

Sato, Satoshi, & Makoto Nagao (1990), Toward memory-based translation. *COLING-90, Papers Presented to the 13th International Conference on Computational Linguistics*, 247–52.

Satta, Giorgio (1994), Tree-adjoining grammar parsing and Boolean matrix multiplication. *Computational Linguistics* 20(2), 173–91.

Saul, Lawrence, & Fernando Pereira (1997), Aggregate and mixed-order Markov models for statistical language processing. *Proceedings of the 2nd Conference on Empirical Methods in Natural Language Processing*, 81–9.

Savitch, W. (1970), Relationship between nondeterministic and deterministic tape complexities. *Journal of Computer and System Sciences* 4:177–92.

Savitch, W., Emmon Bach, William Marsh, & Gila Safran-Naveh (eds.) (1987), *The Formal Complexity of Natural Language, Studies in Linguistics and Philosophy*, vol. 33 Dordrecht: D. Reidel.

Savoy, Jacques (2006), Light stemming approaches for the French, Portuguese, German and Hungarian languages. *SAC '06: Proceedings of the 2006 ACM Symposium on Applied Computing*, 1031–5. http://doi.acm.org/10.1145/1141277.1141523

Saxton, M. (1997), The contrast theory of negative input. *Journal of Child Language* 24(1):139–61.

Scha, Remko, Rens Bod, & Khalil Sima'an (1999), A memory-based model of syntactic analysis: data-oriented parsing. *Journal of Experimental and Theoretical Artificial Intelligence* 11:409–40.

Schabes, Yves (1994), Left-to-right parsing in lexicalized tree-adjoining grammars. *Computational Intelligence* 10(4):506–24.

Schabes, Yves, & Richard Waters (1995), Tree insertion grammar – a cubic-time, parsable formalism that lexicalizes context-free grammar without changing the trees produced. *Computational Linguistics* 21:479–513.

Schegloff, Emanuel (1987), Some sources of misunderstanding in talk-in-interaction. *Linguistics* 25:201–18.

Schlangen, David (2003), A coherence-based approach to the interpretation of non-sentential utterances in dialogue. PhD thesis, University of Edinburgh.

Schlangen, David (2005), Towards nding and xing fragments: using machine learning to identify non-sentential utterances and their antecedents in multi-party dialogue. *Proceedings of the 43rd Meeting of the Association for Computational Linguistics*, 247–54.

Schlueter, R., I. Bezrukov, H. Wagner, & H. Ney (2007), Gammatone features and feature combination for large vocabulary speech recognition. *Proceedings IEEE ICASSP*, 649–52.

Schmid, Helmut (1994), Probabilistic part-of-speech tagging using decision trees. *Proceedings of the International Conference on New Methods in Language Processing*, 44–9.

Schmid, Helmut (2004), Ef cient parsing of highly ambiguous context-free grammars with bit vectors. *Coling, 20th International Conference on Computational Linguistics, Proceedings*, 162–8.

Schmid, Helmut, & Florian Laws (2008), Estimation of conditional probabilities with decision trees and an application to ne-grained POS tagging. *Proceedings of the 22nd International Conference on*

Computational Linguistics (COLING 2008), 465–72.

Schmidt, Mark, Glenn Fung, & Romer Rosales (2007), Fast optimization methods for L1 regularization: a comparative study and two new approaches. *Lecture Notes in Computer Science* 4701:286–97.

Scholz, B., & G. Pullum (2006), Irrational nativist exuberance, in R. Stainton (ed.), *Debates in Cognitive Science*. Oxford: Blackwell, 59–80.

Schone, Patrick, & Daniel Jurafsky (2001), Knowledge-free induction of in ectional morphologies. *Proceedings of the 2nd Meeting of the North American Chapter of the Association for Computational Linguistics (NAACL-01)*, 1–9.

Schultz, Tanja, Qin Jin, Kornel Laskowski, Yue Pan, Florian Metze, & Christian Fügen (2004), Issues in meeting transcription – the ISL meeting transcription system. *Proceedings ICSLP '04*, 1709–12.

Schütze, H. (1995), Distributional part-of-speech tagging. *Proceedings of the European Chapter of the Association for Computational Linguistics (EACL 7)*, 141–8.

Schützenberger, Marcel Paul (1963), On context-free languages and pushdown automata. *Information and Control* 6(3):217–55.

Schwartz, R., T. Colthurst, N. Duta et al. (2004), Speech recognition in multiple languages and domains: the 2003 BBN/LIMSI EARS system. *Proceedings ICASSP'04*, 753–6.

Schwarz, P., P. Matìjka, & J. Cernocký (2004), Towards lower error rates in phoneme recognition. *Proceedings of 7th International Conference on Text, Speech and Dialogue*, 465–72.

Schwenk, Holger, & Jean-Luc Gauvain (2005), Training neural network language models on very large corpora. *Proceedings of the Conference on Human-Language Technology and Empirical Methods in Natural Language Processing (HLT-EMNLP 2005)*, 201–8.

Scott, Bernard (2003), The Logos model: an historical perspective. *Machine Translation* 18(1):1–72.

Searle, John (1969), *Speech Acts*. Cambridge: Cambridge University Press.

Searle, John, & Daniel Vanderveken (1985), *Foundations of Illocutionary Logic*. Cambridge: Cambridge University Press.

Sears, Timothy D. (2007), From MaxEnt to machine learning and back. *Proceedings of the 27th International Workshop on Bayesian Inference and Maximum Entropy Methods in Science and Engineering*, 117–24.

Segerberg, Krister (1990), Validity and satisfaction in imperative. *Notre Dame Journal of Formal Logic* 31(2):203–11.

Sejnowski, T. J., & C. S. Rosenberg (1987), Parallel networks that learn to pronounce English text. *Complex Systems* 1:145–68.

Sekine, Satoshi, & Akira Oda (2007), System demonstration of on-demand information extraction. *Proceedings of the 45th Annual Meeting of the Association for Computational Linguistics Companion Volume: Proceedings of the Demo and Poster Sessions*, 17–20.

Sekine, Satoshi, & Chikashi Nobata (2004), De nition, dictionary and tagger for extended named entities. *Proceedings of the 4th International Conference on Language Resources and Evaluation*, 1977–80.

Seneff, Stephanie (2002), Response planning and generation in the MERCURY ight reservation system. *Computer Speech and Language* 16:283–312.

Seneff, Stephanie, & Joseph Polifroni (2000), Dialogue management in the MERCURY ight reservation system. *Workshop On Conversational Systems*, 11–16.

Seneff, Stephanie, Chao Wang, & John Lee (2006), Combining linguistic and statistical methods for bi-directional English Chinese translation in the ight domain. in *AMTA 2006, Proceedings of the 7th Conference of the Association for Machine Translation in the Americas, Visions for the Future of Machine Translation*, 213–22.

Seymore, K., & R. Rosenfeld (1996), Scalable back-off language models. *Proceedings ICSLP*, 232–5.

Sha, Fei, & Fernando Pereira (2003), Shallow parsing with conditional random elds. *Proceedings of the HLT/NAACL Conference*, 213–20.

Shalonova, Ksenia, & Peter Flach (2007), Morphology learning using tree of aligned suf x rules. *Proceedings of the ICML-2007 Workshop on Challenges and Applications of Grammar Induction*.

Shannon, C. E. (1948), A mathematical theory of communication. *Bell System Technical Journal* 27:379–423, 623–56.

Shannon, C. E., & W. Weaver (1949), *The Mathematical Theory of Communication*. Urbana: University of Illinois Press.

Shapiro, Stuart C. (1992), Arti cial intelligence, in Stuart C. Shapiro (ed.), *The Encyclopedia of Artificial Intelligence*. New York: John Wiley & Sons, 54–7.

Sharma, S., D. Ellis, S. Kajarekar, P. Jain, & H. Hermansky (2000), Feature extraction using non-linear transformation for robust speech recognition on the Aurora database. *Proceedings ICASSP 2000*, 1117–20.

Shastri, Lokendra, & Venkat Ajjanagadde (1993), From simple associations to systematic reasoning: a connectionist representation of rules, variables, and dynamic bindings using temporal synchrony. *Behavioral and Brain Sciences* 16:417–51.

Shen, Dan, & Mirella Lapata (2007), Using semantic roles to improve question answering. *Proceedings of the 2007 Joint Conference on Empirical Methods in Natural Language Processing and Computational Natural Language Learning*, 12–21.

Shen, Libin, & Aravind Joshi (2005), Ranking and reranking with perceptron. *Machine Learning* 60(1–3):73–96.

Sheremetyeva, Svetlana, Sergei Nirenburg, & Irene Nirenburg (1996), Generating patent claims from interactive input. *Proceedings of the 8th International*

Workshop on Natural Language Generation (INLG '96), 61–70.

Shieber, S. M. (1985), Evidence against the context-freeness of natural language. *Linguistics and Philosophy* 8:333–43.

Shieber, S. M., Y. Schabes, & F. C. N. Pereira (1995), Principles and implementation of deductive parsing. *Journal of Logic Programming* 24:3–36.

Shinyama, Yusuke, & Satoshi Sekine (2006), Preemptive information extraction using unrestricted relation discovery. *Proceedings of the Human-Language Technology Conference of the NAACL, Main Conference*, 304–11.

Shriberg, Elizabeth E. (1994), Preliminaries to a theory of speech dis uencies. PhD thesis, University of California at Berkeley.

Siivola, V., T. Hirsimaki, & S. Virpioja (2007), On growing and pruning Kneser–Ney smoothed *n*-gram models. *IEEE Transactions on Audio, Speech, and Language Processing* 15(5):1617–24.

Simard, Michel, Nicola Uef ng, Pierre Isabelle, & Roland Kuhn (2007), Rule-based translation with statistical phrase-based post-editing. *ACL 2007: Proceedings of the 2nd Workshop on Statistical Machine Translation*, 203–6.

Simmons, R. F. (1965), Answering English questions by computer: a survey. *Communications of the ACM* 8(1):53–70.

Sinclair, J. M. H. & R. M. Coulthard (1975), *Towards an Analysis of Discourse: The English Used by Teachers and Pupils*. Oxford: Oxford University Press.

Singh, S., M. Kearns, D. Litman, & M. Walker (1999), Reinforcement learning for spoken dialogue systems. *Proceedings of NIPS '99*.

Singh, S., D. Litman, M. Kearns, & M. Walker (2002), Optimizing dialogue management with reinforcement learning: experiments with the Njfun system. *Journal of Artificial Intelligence Research* 16:105–33.

Sippu, S., & E. Soisalon-Soininen (1988), *Parsing Theory*, vol. 1: *Languages and*

Parsing, EATCS Monographs on Theoretical Computer Science, vol. 15. Dordrecht: Springer-Verlag.

Siskind, Jeffrey M. (1996), A computational study of cross-situational techniques for learning word-to-meaning mappings. *Cognition* 61(1–2):39–91.

Skousen, R. (1989), *Analogical modeling of language*. Dordrecht: Kluwer Academic Publishers.

Skousen, R. (1992), *Analogy and Structure*. Dordrecht: Kluwer Academic Publishers.

Skousen, R. (2002), An overview of analogical modeling, in R. Skousen, D. Lonsdale, & D. B. Parkinson (eds.), *Analogical Modeling: An Exemplar-Based Approach to Language*. Amsterdam: John Benjamins, 11–26.

Smadja, Frank, Kathleen R. McKeown, & Vasileios Hatzivassiloglou (1996), Translating collocations for bilingual lexicons: a statistical approach. *Computational Linguistics* 22(1):1–38.

Small, Sharon, & Tomek Strzalkowski (2009), HITIQA: High-Quality Intelligence through Interactive Question Answering. *Journal of Natural Language Engineering: Special Issue on Interactive Question Answering* 15(1):31–54.

Smith, Jan M. (1984), An interpretation of Martin-Löf's type theory in a type-free theory of propositions. *Journal of Symbolic Logic* 49:730–53.

Smith, Noah, John Lafferty, & Doug Vail (2007), Computationally ef cient M-estimation of log-linear structure models. *Proceedings of Conference of the Association for Computational Linguistics*, 752–9.

Snider, Neal (2007), Exemplars in syntax: evidence from priming in corpora. *Proceedings of the Workshop on Exemplar-Based Models of Language Acquisition and Use.*

Snover, Matthew, Bonnie Dorr, Richard Schwartz, John Makhoul, Linnea Micciula, & Ralph Weischedel (2005), A study of translation error rate with targeted human annotation. Technical report LAMP-TR-126, CS-TR-4755, UMIACS-TR-2005-58, University of Maryland, College Park and BBN Technologies.

Snover, Matthew, Bonnie Dorr, Richard Schwartz, Linnea Micciulla, & Ralph Weischedel (2006), A study of translation edit rate with targeted human annotation. *Proceedings of AMTA 2006*, 223–31.

Snyder, Benjamin, & Martha Palmer (2004), The English all-words task. *ACL 2004 Senseval-3 Workshop*, 41–3.

Soderland, Stephen (1999), Learning information extraction rules for semi-structured and free text. *Machine Learning* 34(1):233–72.

Solan, Zach, David Horn, Eytan Ruppin, & Shimon Edelman (2005), Unsupervised learning of natural languages. *Proceedings of the National Academy of Sciences* 102:11629–34.

Somers, Harold (1999), Review article: example-based machine translation. *Machine Translation* 14:113–57.

Somers, Harold (2000), Machine translation, in Robert Dale, Hermann Moisl, & Harold Somers (eds.), *A Handbook of Natural Language Processing*. New York: Marcel Dekker, 329–46.

Somers, Harold (2003a), Machine translation: latest developments, in Ruslan Mitkov (ed.), *The Oxford Handbook of Computational Linguistics*. Oxford: Oxford University Press, 512–28.

Somers, Harold (2003b), An overview of EBMT, in Michael Carl & Andy Way (eds.), *Recent Advances in Example-Based Machine Translation*. Dordrecht: Kluwer Academic Publishers, 3–57.

Somers, Harold (2007), Theoretical and methodological issues regarding the use of language technologies for patients with limited English pro ciency. *Proceedings of the 11th Conference on Theoretical and Methodological Issues in Machine Translation (TMI-07)*, 206–13.

Somers, Harold, Ian McLean, & Danny Jones (1994), Experiments in multilingual example-based generation. *CSNLP 1994: 3rd International Conference on the Cognitive Science of Natural Language Processing.*

Soon, Wee Meng, Hwee Tou Ng, & Daniel Chung Young Lim (2001), A machine learning approach to coreference resolution of noun phrases. *Computational Linguistics* 27(2):521–44.

Spierling, Ulrike, & Nicolas Szilas (eds.) (2008), *Interactive Storytelling: Proceedings of the 1st Joint International Conference on Interactive Digital Storytelling.* Dordrecht: Springer.

Spitters, M. (2000), Comparing feature sets for learning text categorization. *Proceedings of the 6th Conference on Content-Based Multimedia Access (RIAO 2002),* 1124–35.

Spivey, Michael J., & Daniel C. Richardson (2009), Language embedded in the environment, in P. Robbins & M. Aydede (eds.), *The Cambridge Handbook of Situated Cognition.* Cambridge: Cambridge University Press, 382–400.

Spivey, Michael J., & Michael K. Tanenhaus (1998), Syntactic ambiguity resolution in discourse: modeling the effects of referential context and lexical frequency. *Journal of Experimental Psychology: Learning, Memory, and Cognition* 24:1521–43.

Spivey-Knowlton, Michael J., & Julie Sedivy (1995), Resolving attachment ambiguities with multiple constraints. *Cognition* 55:227–67.

Sporleder, C., M. van Erp, T. Porcelijn, & A. van den Bosch (2006), Identifying named entities in text databases from the natural history domain. *Proceedings of the 5th International Conference on Language Resources and Evaluation, LREC-2006.*

Sproat, Richard (1992), *Morphology and Computation.* Cambridge, MA: MIT Press.

Sproat, Richard, Chilin Shih, William Gale, & Nancy Chang (1996), A stochastic nite-state word-segmentation algorithm for Chinese. *Computational Linguistics* 22:377–404.

Sripada, Somayajulu, Ehud Reiter, Jim Hunter, & Jin Yu (2003), Generating English summaries of time series data using the Gricean maxims. *Proceedings of 9th ACM SIGKDD International Conference on Knowledge Discovery and Data Mining (KDD-2003),* 187–96.

Sripada, Somayajulu, Ehud Reiter, Ian Davy, & Kristian Nilssen (2004), Lessons from deploying NLG technology for marine weather forecast text generation. *Proceedings of 3rd Prestigious Applications Intelligent Systems Conference (PAIS-2004),* 760–4.

Sripada, Somayajulu, Ehud Reiter, & Lezan Hawizy (2005), Evaluation of an NLG system using post-edit data: lessons learned. *Proceedings of the 10th European Workshop on Natural Language Generation (ENLG-2005),* 133–9.

Srivastava, Ankit, Rejwanul Haque, Sudip Naskar, & Andy Way (2008), MaTrEx: the DCU MT system for ICON 2008. *Proceedings of the NLP Tools Contest: Statistical Machine Translation (English to Hindi), 6th International Conference on Natural Language Processing.*

St. John, Mark, & James McClelland (1992), Parallel constraint satisfaction as a comprehension mechanism, in Ronan Reilly & Noel Sharkey (eds.), *Connectionist Approaches to Natural Language Processing.* Hove: Lawrence Erlbaum Associates, 97–136.

Stamou, S., K. O azer, K. Pala et al. (2002), BALKANET: a multilingual semantic network for the Balkan languages. *Proceedings of the International WordNet Conference,* 12–14.

Stan ll, C. (1987), Memory-based reasoning applied to English pronunciation. *Proceedings of the 6th National Conference on Artificial Intelligence,* 577–81.

Stan ll, C., & D. Waltz (1986), Toward memory-based reasoning. *Communications of the ACM* 29(12):1213–28.

Statman, Richard (1979), The typed λ-calculus is not elementary recursive. *Theoretical Computer Science* 9:73–81.

Statnikov, Alexander, & Constantin F. Aliferis (2007), Are random forests better than support vector machines for microarray-based cancer classi cation? *American Medical Informatics Association 2007 Proceedings*, 686–90.

Steedman, Mark (1993), Categorial grammar (tutorial overview). *Lingua* 90:221–58.

Steedman, Mark (1996), *Surface Structure and Interpretation*. Cambridge, MA: MIT Press.

Steedman, Mark (1999), Connectionist sentence processing in perspective. *Cognitive Science* 23:615–34.

Steedman, Mark (2000), *The Syntactic Process, Language, Speech and Communication*. Cambridge, MA: MIT Press.

Steedman, Mark (2008), On becoming a discipline. *Computational Linguistics* 34(1):137–44.

Stevens, S. S. (1946), On the theory of scales of measurement. *Science* 103(2684):677–80.

Stevenson, M., & Y. Wilks (1999), Combining weak knowledge sources for sense disambiguation. *Proceedings of the International Joint Conference on Artificial Intelligence*, 884–9.

Stevenson, Suzanne (1994), Competition and recency in a hybrid network model of syntactic disambiguation. *Journal of Psycholinguistic Research* 23(4):295–322.

Stockmeyer, L., & A. R. Meyer (1973), Word problems requiring exponential time: a preliminary report. *Proceedings of the 5th Annual ACM Symposium on Theory of Computing*, 1–9.

Stolcke, Andreas (1995), An ef cient probabilistic context-free parsing algorithm that computes pre x probabilities. *Computational Linguistics* 21(2):165–201.

Stolcke, Andreas (1998), Entropy-based pruning of back-off language models. *Proceedings of News Transcription and Understanding Workshop*, 270–4.

Stolcke, Andreas (2002), SRILM – an extensible language modeling toolkit. *Proceedings of the International Conference on Spoken Language Processing*, 901–4.

Stolcke, Andreas, C. Wooters, N. Mirghafori et al. (2004), Progress in meeting recognition: the ICSI-SRI-UW spring 2004 evaluation system. *Proceedings NIST RT04S Workshop.*

Stolcke, Andreas, Xavier Anguera, Ko Boakye et al. (2007), The SRI-ICSI spring 2007 meeting and lecture recognition system. *Lecture Notes in Computer Science* 4625:450–63.

Strassel, Stephanie, Mark Przybocki, Kay Peterson, Zhiyi Song, & Kazuaki Maeda (2008), Linguistic resources and evaluation techniques for evaluation of cross-document automatic content extraction. *Proceedings of the 6th International Conference on Language Resources and Evaluation (LREC 2008).*

Strik, H., & C. Cucchiarini (1999), Modelling pronunciation variation for ASR: a survey of the literature. *Speech Communication* 29:225–46.

Stroppa, Nicolas, & Andy Way (2006), MaTrEx: the DCU machine translation system for IWSLT 2006. *Proceedings of IWSLT 2006 Workshop*, 31–6.

Stroppa, Nicolas, Declan Groves, Andy Way, & Kepa Sarasola (2006), Example-based machine translation of the Basque language. *Proceedings of the 7th biennial conference of the Association for Machine Translation in the Americas*, 232–41.

Stroppa, Nicolas, Antal van den Bosch, & Andy Way (2007), Exploiting source similarity for SMT using context-informed features. *Proceedings of the 11th International Conference on Theoretical and Methodological Issues in Machine Translation*, 231–40.

Strube, M. (1998), Never look back: an alternative to centering. *Proceedings of the 17th International Conference on Computational Linguistics (COLING '98/ACL '98)*, 1251–1257.

Strube, M., & C. S. Müller (2003), A machine learning approach to pronoun resolution in spoken dialogue. *Proceedings of the 41st Annual Meeting of the Association for Computational Linguistics, ACL'2003*, 521–44.

Strzalkowski, Tomek, & Jin Wang (1996), A self-learning universal concept spotter. *Proceedings of the 16th International Conference on Computational Linguistics (COLING-96)*, 931–6.

Strzalkowski, Tomek, & Sanda Harabagiu (eds.) (2006), *Advances in Open Domain Question Answering*. Dordrecht: Springer.

Stuckardt, R. (2002), Machine-learning-based vs. manually designed approaches to anaphor resolution–the best of two worlds. *Proceedings of the Discourse Anaphora and Anaphora Resolution Colloquium, DAARC'4*, 211–16.

Stuckardt, R. (2004), Three algorithms for competence-oriented anaphor resolution. *Proceedings of the Discourse Anaphora and Anaphora Resolution Colloquium, DAARC'5*, 157–63.

Stuckardt, R. (2005), A machine learning approach to preference strategies for anaphor resolution, in A. Branco, A. McEnery, & R. Mitkov (eds.), *Anaphora Processing Linguistic, Cognitive and Computational Modeling*. Amsterdam: John Benjamins, 47–72.

Stump, Gregory T. (2001), *Inflectional Morphology: A Theory of Paradigm Structure, Cambridge Studies in Linguistics*, vol. 93. Cambridge: Cambridge University Press.

Sturt, Patrick, Martin J. Pickering, & Matthew W. Crocker (1999), Structural change and reanalysis dif culty in language comprehension: is reanalysis the last resort? *Journal of Memory and Language* 40(1):136–50.

Sturt, Patrick, Fabrizio Costa, Vincenzo Lombardo, & Paolo Frasconi (2003), Learning rst-pass structural attachment preferences using dynamic grammars and recursive neural networks. *Cognition* 88:133–69.

Sudo, Kiyoshi, Satoshi Sekine, & Ralph Grishman (2003), An improved extraction pattern representation model for automatic IE pattern acquisition. *Proceedings of the 41st Annual Meeting of the Association for Computational Linguistics (ACL '03)*, 224–31.

Sumita, Eiichiro, Hitoshi Iida, & Hideo Kohyama (1990), Translating with examples: a new approach to machine translation. *3rd International Conference on Theoretical and Methodological Issues in Machine Translation of Natural Language*, 203–21.

Sun, Renxu, Jing Jiang, Yee Fan Tan, Hang Cui, Tat-Seng Chua, & Min-Yen Kan (2005), Using syntactic and semantic relation analysis in question answering. *Proceedings of the 14th Text Retrieval Conference (TREC 2005)*.

Sun, Xuejing, & Ted H. Applebaum (2001), Intonational phrase break prediction using decision tree and n-gram model. *Proceedings of 7th European Conference on Speech Communication and Technology (Eurospeech)*, 537–40.

Sundholm, Göran (1989), Constructive generalized quanti ers. *Synthese* 79: 1–12.

Suontausta, J., & J. Hakkinenen (2000), Decision tree based text-to-phoneme mapping for speech recognition. *Proceedings of the International Conference on Spoken Language Processing (ICSLP)*, 831–4.

Surdeanu, Mihai, Richard Johansson, Adam Meyers, Lluís Màrquez, & Joakim Nivre (2008), The CoNLL-2008 shared task on joint parsing of syntactic and semantic dependencies. *Proceedings of the 12th Conference on Computational Natural Language Learning (CoNLL-2008)*, 159–77.

Suri, L., & K. McCoy (1994), RAFT/RAPR and centering: a comparison and discussion of problems related to preceding complex sentences. *Computational Linguistics* 20(2):301–17.

Sutton, Richard, & Andrew Barto (1998), *Reinforcement Learning*. Cambridge, MA: MIT Press.

Swales, John M. (1990), *Genre Analysis: English in Academic and Research Settings, The Cambridge Applied Linguistics Series*. Cambridge: Cambridge University Press.

Swartout, W., J. Gratch, R. Hill et al. (2006), Toward virtual humans. *AI Magazine* 27(2):96.

Tabor, Whitney, & Sean Hutchins (2004), Evidence for self-organized sentence processing: digging-in effects. *Journal of Experimental Psychology: Learning, Memory and Cognition* 30:431–50.

Tabor, Whitney, Cornell Juliano, & Michael K. Tanenhaus (1997), Parsing in a dynamical system: an attractor-based account of the interaction of lexical and structural constraints in sentence processing. *Language and Cognitive Processes* 12:211–71.

Talbot, David, & Miles Osborne (2007), Smoothed Bloom lter language models: Tera-scale LMs on the cheap. *Proceedings of the 2007 Joint Conference on Empirical Methods in Natural Language Processing and Computational Natural Language Learning (EMNLP-CoNLL)*, 468–76.

Talbot, David, & Thorsten Brants (2008), Randomized language models via perfect hash functions. *Proceedings of ACL-08: HLT*, 505–13.

Tanenhaus, Michael K., Michael J. Spivey-Knowlton, Kathleen M. Eberhard, & Julie C. Sedivy (1995), Integration of visual and linguistic information in spoken language comprehension. *Science* 268:1632–4.

Tanenhaus, Michael K., John C. Trueswell, & J. E. Hanna (2000), Modeling thematic and discourse context effects with a multiple constraints approach: implications for the architecture of the language comprehension system, in M. W. Crocker, Martin J. Pickering, & C. Clifton (eds.), *Architectures and Mechanism for Language Processing*.

Cambridge: Cambridge University Press, 90–118.

Tarski, Alfred (1983), *Logic, Semantics, Metamathematics*, 2nd edn. Indianapolis: Hackett.

Taskar, B., D. Klein, M. Collins, D. Koller, & C. Manning (2004), Max-margin parsing. *Proceedings of the EMNLP Conference*, 1–8.

Taskar, B., Simon Lacoste-Julien, & Dan Klein (2005), A discriminative matching approach to word alignment. *Proceedings of Human-Language Technology Conference and Conference on Empirical Methods in Natural Language Processing*, 73–80.

Tateisi, Yuka, Akane Yakushiji, Tomoko Ohta, & Jun'ichi Tsujii (2005), Syntax annotation for the GENIA corpus. *Proceedings of the Companion Volume of the 2nd International Joint Conference on Natural Language Processing (IJCNLP-05)*, 222–7.

Teahan, W. J., Rodger Mcnab T., Yingying Wen T., & Ian H. Witten (2000), A compression-based algorithm for Chinese word segmentation. *Computational Linguistics* 26:375–93.

Teh, Y. W. (2006), A hierarchical Bayesian language model based on Pitman–Yor processes. *Proceedings of the Annual Meeting of the ACL* 44, 985–92.

Teh, Y. W., M. I. Jordan, M. J. Beal, & D. M. Blei (2006), Hierarchical Dirichlet processes. *Journal of the American Statistical Association* 101(476):1566–81.

Tellex, Stefanie, Boris Katz, Jimmy Lin, Aaron Fernandes, & Gregory Marton (2003), Quantitative evaluation of passage retrieval algorithms for question answering. *Proceedings, 26th Annual SIGIR Conference*, 41–7.

Tetreault, J. (1999), Analysis of syntax-based pronoun resolution methods. *Proceedings of the 37th Annual Meeting of the Association for Computational Linguistics (ACL '99)*, 602–5.

Tetreault, J. (2001), A corpus-based evaluation of centering and pronoun resolution. *Computational Linguistics* 27(4), 507–20.

Teufel, Simone (1999), Argumentative zoning: information extraction from scienti c text. PhD thesis, University of Edinburgh.

Teufel, Simone, & Marc Moens (2002), Summarizing scienti c articles: experiments with relevance and rhetorical status. *Computational linguistics* 28(4):409–45.

Thatcher, J., & J. Wright (1968), Generalized nite automata theory with an application to a decision problem of second-order logic. *Mathematical systems theory* 2:57–81.

Theune, Mariet, Yulia Bachvarova, Elizabeth André, & Ielka van der Sluis (eds.) (2007), *Proceedings of the AISB Symposium on Multimodal Output Generation (MOG 2007)*. Twente: University of Twente.

Thomason, R. (1980), A model theory for propositional attitudes. *Linguistics and Philosophy* 4:47–70.

Thompson, C. A., M. E. Califf, & R. J. Mooney (1999), Active learning for natural language parsing and information extraction. *Proceedings of the 16th International Conference on Machine Learning*, 406–14.

Thompson, H., & G. Ritchie (1984), Implementing natural language parsers, in T. O'Shea & M. Eisenstadt (eds.), *Artificial Intelligence: Tools, Techniques, and Applications*. New York: Harper & Row, 245–300.

Thompson, S., & E. Newport (2007), Statistical learning of syntax: the role of transitional probability. *Language Learning and Development* 3:1–42.

Tibshirani, Robert (1996), Regression shrinkage and selection via the LASSO. *Journal of the Royal Statistical Society, Series B* 58:267–88.

Tichý, Pavel (1988), *The Foundations of Frege's Logic*. Berlin: De Gruyter.

Tidhar, Dan, & Uwe Küssner (2000), Learning to select a good translation. *Coling 2000 in Europe: The 18th International Conference on Computational Linguistics, Proceedings*, 843–9.

Tillmann, Christoph (2004), A unigram orientation model for statistical machine translation. *Proceedings Human-Language Technology and North American Association of Computational Linguistics (HLT-NAACL)*, 101–4.

Tillmann, Christoph, & Fei Xia (2003), A phrase-based unigram model for statistical machine translation. *Proceedings of the Joint Meeting of the Human-Language Technology Conference and the North American Chapter of the Association for Computational Linguistics (HLT-NAACL 2003)*, 106–8.

Tillmann, Christoph, Stephan Vogel, Hermann Ney, Hassan Sawaf, & Alex Zubiaga (1997), Accelerated DP-based search for statistical translation. *Proceedings of the 5th European Conference on Speech Communication and Technology (EuroSpeech '97)*, 2667–70.

Tinsley, John, Mary Hearne, & Andy Way (2007a), Exploiting parallel treebanks to improve phrase-based statistical machine translation. *Proceedings of the 6th International Workshop on Treebanks and Linguistic Theories (TLT-07)*, 175–87.

Tinsley, John, Venstislav Zhechev, Mary Hearne, & Andy Way (2007b), Robust language-pair independent sub-tree alignment. *Machine Translation Summit XI*, 467–74.

Tinsley, John, Yanjun Ma, Sylwia Ozdowska, & Andy Way (2008), MaTrEx: the DCU MT system for WMT 2008. *Proceedings of the 3rd Workshop on Statistical Machine Translation*, 171–4.

Titov, Ivan, & James Henderson (2007a), Constituent parsing with incremental sigmoid belief networks. *Proceedings of the 45th Annual Meeting of the Association for Computational Linguistics (ACL'07)*, 632–9.

Titov, Ivan, & James Henderson (2007b), Fast and robust multilingual dependency parsing with a generative latent variable model. *Proceedings of the Joint Conference on Empirical Methods in Natural Language*

Processing and Computational Natural Language Learning (EMNLP-CoNLL 2007), 947–51.

Titov, Ivan, & James Henderson (2007c), A latent variable model for generative dependency parsing. *Proceedings of the 10th International Workshop on Parsing Technologies*, 144–55.

Tjong Kim Sang, E., & Fien de Meulder (2003), Introduction to the CoNLL-2003 shared task: language-independent named entity recognition. *Proceedings of the 7th Conference on Natural Language Learning (CoNLL-2003)*, 142–7.

Tjong Kim Sang, E., & J. Veenstra (1999), Representing text chunks. *Proceedings of EACL'99*, 173–9.

Tjong Kim Sang, E., & S. Buchholz (2000), Introduction to the CoNLL-2000 shared task: chunking. *Proceedings of CoNLL-2000 and LLL-2000*, 127–32.

Tokuda, K., T. T. Yoshimura, K. T. Masuko, & T. Kitamura (2000), Speech parameter generation algorithms for HMM-based speech synthesis. *Proceedings ICASSP 2000*, 1315–18.

Tokuda, K., H. Zen, & T. Kitamura (2003), Trajectory modeling based on HMMs with the explicit relationship between static and dynamic features. *8th European Conference on Speech Communication and Technology*, 865–8.

Tombaugh, J., A. Lickorish, & P. Wright (1987), Multi-window displays for readers of lengthy texts. *International Journal of Man–Machine Studies* 26:597–615.

Tomita, M. (1986), *Efficient Parsing for Natural Language*. Amsterdam: Kluwer Academic Publishers.

Toutanova, Kristina, Tolga Ilhan, & Christopher Manning (2002), Extensions to HMM-based statistical word alignment models. *Proceedings of the 2002 Conference on Empirical Methods in Natural Language Processing*, 87–94.

Traum, D. (2004), Issues in multiparty dialogues. *Lecture Notes in Computer Science*, 201–11.

Traum, D., & Staffan Larsson (2003), The information state approach to dialogue management, in Jan van Kuppevelt & Ronnie Smith (eds.), *Current and New Directions in Discourse and Dialogue*. Amsterdam: Kluwer, 325–53.

TRINDI Consortium (2000), *The TRINDI Book*. Gothenburg: University of Gothenburg. www.ling.gu.se/projekt/trindi/book.ps

Trueswell, John C. (1996), The role of lexical frequency in syntactic ambiguity resolution. *Journal of Memory and Language* 35:566–85.

Trueswell, John C., & Michael K. Tanenhaus (1994), Toward a lexicalist framework for constraint-based syntactic ambiguity resolution, in Charles Clifton, Lyn Frazier, & Keith Rayner (eds.), *Perspectives in Sentence Processing*. Hillsdale, NJ: Lawrence Erlbaum, 155–79.

Trueswell, John C., Michael K. Tanenhaus, & C. Kello (1993), Verb-specic constraints in sentence processing: separating effects of lexical preference from garden-paths. *Journal of Experimental Psychology: Learning, Memory and Cognition* 19:528–53.

Tufte, Edward (1983), *The Visual Display of Quantitative Information*. Cheshire, CT: Graphics Press.

Tur, Gokhan, Andreas Stolcke, Lynn Voss et al. (2010), The CALO meeting assistant system. *IEEE Transactions on Audio, Speech and Language Processing*.

Turian, Joseph, Luke Shen, & Dan Melamed (2003), Evaluation of machine translation and its evaluation. *Machine Translation Summit IX*, 386–93.

Turing, Alan (1936–7), On computable numbers, with an application to the *Entscheidungsproblem*. *Proceedings of the London Mathematical Society (Series 2)* 42:230–65.

Turner, Raymond (1992), Properties, propositions and semantic theory, in M. Rosner & R. Johnson (eds.), *Computational Linguistics and Formal Semantics*, Cambridge: Cambridge

University Press, *Studies in Natural Language Processing*. 159–80.

Turner, Raymond (2007), Computable models. *Journal of Logic and Computation* 18(2):283–318.

Turner, Ross, Somayajulu Sripada, Ehud Reiter, & Ian Davy (2008), Using spatial reference frames to generate grounded textual summaries of georeferenced data. *Proceedings of the 5th International Conference on Natural Language Generation (INLG-2008)*, 16–24.

Unicode Consortium (2006), *The Unicode Standard, Version 5.0*. Boston, MA: Addison-Wesley Professional.

Utiyama, Masau, & Hitoshi Isahara (2001), A statistical model for domain-independent text segmentation. *Proceedings of the 39th Annual Meeting of the Association for Computational Linguistics*, 491–8.

Vadas, David, & James R. Curran (2008), Parsing noun phrase structure with CCG. *Proceedings of the 46th Meeting of the ACL*, 335–43.

Valiant, L. (1984), A theory of the learnable. *Communications of the ACM* 27(11):1134–42.

Valtchev, V., Julian J. Odell, Philip C. Woodland, & Steve J. Young (1997), MMIE training of large vocabulary recognition systems. *Speech Communication* 22:303–14.

van Deemter, Kees (1996), Towards a logic of ambiguous expressions, in Kees van Deemter & Stanley Peters (eds.), *Semantic Ambiguity and Underspecification*. Stanford, CA: CSLI Publications, 203–37.

van Deemter, Kees, Emiel Krahmer, & Marier Theune (2005), Real vs. template-based NLG: a false opposition? *Computational Linguistics* 31:15–23.

van den Bosch, A. (1997), Learning to pronounce written words: a study in inductive language learning. PhD thesis, Universiteit Maastricht.

van den Bosch, A. (2005), Memory-based understanding of user utterances in a spoken dialogue system: effects of feature selection and co-learning. *Workshop Proceedings of the 6th International Conference on Case-Based Reasoning*, 85–94.

van den Bosch, A. (2006a), Scalable classification-based word prediction and confusible correction. *Traitement Automatique des Langues* 46(2):39–63.

van den Bosch, A. (2006b), Spelling space: a computational test bed for phonological and morphological changes in Dutch spelling. *Written Language and Literacy* 9(1):25–44.

van den Bosch, A., & W. Daelemans (1993), Data-oriented methods for grapheme-to-phoneme conversion. *Proceedings of the 6th Conference of the EACL*, 45–53.

van den Bosch, A., & W. Daelemans (1999), Memory-based morphological analysis. *Proceedings of the 37th Annual Meeting of the ACL*, 285–92.

van den Bosch, A., Walter Daelemans, & T. Weijters (1996), Morphological analysis as classification: an inductive learning approach. *Proceedings of NEMLAP 1996*, 59–72.

van den Bosch, A., E. Krahmer, & M. Swerts (2001), Detecting problematic turns in human–machine interactions: rule-induction versus memory-based learning approaches. *Proceedings of the 39th Meeting of the Association for Computational Linguistics*, 499–506.

van den Bosch, A., E. Marsi, & A. Soudi (2007a), Memory-based morphological analysis and part-of-speech tagging of Arabic, in A. Soudi, G. Neumann, & Antal van den Bosch (eds.), *Arabic Computational Morphology: Knowledge-Based and Empirical Methods*. Dordrecht: Springer, 203–19.

van den Bosch, A., Nicolas Stroppa, & Andy Way (2007b), A memory-based classification approach to marker-based EBMT. *Proceedings of the METIS-II Workshop on New Approaches to Machine Translation*, 63–72.

van der Sandt, Rob A. (1988), *Context and Presupposition*. London: Croom Helm.

van der Sandt, Rob A. (1992), Presupposition projection as anaphora resolution. *Journal of Semantics* 9(4):333–77. http://dx.doi.org/10.1093/jos/9.4.333

van der Sluis, Ielka, Mariet Theune, Ehud Reiter, & Emiel Krahmer (eds.) (2008), *Proceedings of the Workshop on Multimodal Output Generation (MOG 2008)*. AISB.

van Eijck, Jan, & Christina Unger (2004), Computational semantics with functional programming.

van Halteren, H., J. Zavrel, & W. Daelemans (2001), Improving accuracy in word class tagging through combination of machine learning systems. *Computational Linguistics* 27(2):199–230.

van Petten, Cyma, & Marta Kutas (1990), Interactions between sentence context and word frequency in event-related brain potentials. *Memory and Cognition* 18:380–93.

van Zaanen, M. (2000), ABL: alignment-based learning. *Proceedings of COLING*, 961–7.

van Zaanen, M., & Harold Somers (2005), Democrat: deciding between multiple outputs created by automatic translation. *MT Summit X, The 10th Machine Translation Summit*, 173–80.

Vapnik, V. (1996), *The Nature of Statistical Learning Theory*. New York: Springer-Verlag.

Vapnik, V. (1998), *Statistical Learning Theory*. Oxford: John Wiley.

Vapnik, V., & L. Bottou (1993), Local algorithms for pattern recognition and dependencies estimation. *Neural Computation* 5(6):893–909.

Varea, Ismael García, Franz J. Och, Hermann Ney, & Francisco Casacuberta (2002), Improving alignment quality in statistical machine translation using context-dependent maximum entropy models. *Proceedings of the 19th International Conference on Computational Linguistics*, 1–7.

Vauquois, Bernard (1968), A survey of formal grammars and algorithms for recognition and transformation in machine translation. *IFIP Congress-68*, 254–60.

Veale, Tony, Alan Conway, & Brona Collins (1998), The challenges of cross-modal translation: English to sign language translation in the Zardoz system. *Machine Translation* 13(1):81–106.

Veenstra, J. (1998), Fast NP chunking using memory-based learning techniques. *Proceedings of BENELEARN '98*, 71–8.

Veenstra, J., A. van den Bosch, S. Buchholz, W. Daelemans, & J. Zavrel (2000), Memory-based word sense disambiguation. *Computers and the Humanities* 34(1–2):171–7.

Velleman, Paul F., & Leland Wilkinson (1993), Nominal, ordinal, interval, and ratio typologies are misleading. *The American Statistician* 47(1):65–72.

Vere, Steven, & Timothy Bickmore (1990), A basic agent. *Computational Intelligence* 6(1):41–60.

Verhagen, M. (2005), Temporal closure in an annotation environment. *Language Resources and Evaluation* 39(2):211–41.

Vicedo, José L., & Antonio Ferrández (2000), Importance of pronominal anaphora resolution in question answering systems. *Proceedings, 38th Annual Meeting, Association for Computational Linguistics*, 555–62.

Vieira, Renata, & Massimo Poesio (2000), An empirically based system for processing de nite descriptions. *Computational Linguistics* 26(4): 539–93.

Vijay-Shanker, K., & A. K. Joshi (1985), Some computational properties of tree adjoining grammars. *23rd Annual Meeting of the Association for Computational Linguistics, Proceedings of the Conference*, 82–93.

Vijay-Shanker, K., & David Weir (1993), Parsing some constrained grammar formalisms. *Computational Linguistics* 19(4):591–636.

Vijay-Shanker, K., & David Weir (1994), The equivalence of four extensions of context-free grammars. *Mathematical Systems Theory* 27:511–45.

Vilar, David, Maja Popovic, & Hermann Ney (2006), AER: Do we need to 'improve' our alignments? *Proceedings of the International Workshop on Spoken Language Translation*, 205–12.

Viterbi, A. J. (1967), Error bounds for convolutional codes and an asymptotically optimum decoding algorithm. *IEEE Transactions on Information Theory* 13(2):260–9.

Vogel, Stephan, & Hermann Ney (2000), Construction of a hierarchical translation memory. *Coling 2000 in Europe: The 18th International Conference on Computational Linguistics, Proceedings*, 1131–5.

Vogel, Stephan, Hermann Ney, & Christoph Tillmann (1996), HMM-based word alignment in statistical translation. *Proceedings of the 16th International Conference on Computational Linguistics*, 836–41.

von Wright, Georg Henrik (1967), Deontic logics. *American Philosophical Quarterly* 4:136–43.

Voorhees, E. (2002), Overview of the TREC-2002 question answering track. *Proceedings of the 11th Text Retrieval Conference*, 115–23.

Voorhees, E., & Dawn Tice (2000), Building a question answering test collection, *Proceedings, 23rd Annual International SIGIR Conference*, 200–7.

Vosse, Theo, & Gerard Kempen (2000), Syntactic structure assembly in human parsing: a computational model based on competitive inhibition and a lexicalist grammar. *Cognition* 75: 105–43.

Vossen, Piek (ed.) (1998), *EuroWordNet: A Multilingual Database with Lexical Semantic Networks*. Dordrecht: Kluwer Academic Publishers.

Walker, M. (1989), Evaluating discourse processing algorithms. *Proceedings of the 27th Annual Meeting of the ACL (ACL'97)*, 251–61.

Walker, M. (1998), Centering, anaphora resolution and discourse structure, in M. Walker, A. Joshi, & E. Prince (eds.), *Centering Theory in Discourse*. Oxford: Clarendon Press, 401–35.

Walker, M., & A. T. T. Shannon (2000), An application of reinforcement learning to dialogue strategy selection in a spoken dialogue system for email. *Journal of Artificial Intelligence Research* 12:387–416.

Walker, M., M. Iida, & S. Cote (1994), Japanese discourse and the process of centering. *Computational Linguistics* 20(2): 193–232.

Walker, M., Aravind K. Joshi, & Ellen Prince (eds.) (1998), *Centering Theory in Discourse*. Oxford: Oxford University Press.

Walker, M., Candace Kamm, & Diane Litman (2000), Towards developing general models of usability with PARADISE. *Natural Language Engineering* 6(3–4):363–77.

Walker, M., Steve Whittaker, & Amanda Stent (2004), Generation and evaluation of user tailored responses in dialogue. *Cognitive Science* 28:811–40.

Walker, M., Amanda Stent, François Mairesse, & Rashi Prasad (2007), Individual and domain adaptation in sentence planning for dialogue. *Journal of Artificial Intelligence Research* 30:413–56.

Wallach, H. M. (2006), Topic modeling: beyond bag-of-words. *Proceedings ICML2006*, 977–84.

Wan, Vincent, & Thomas Hain (2006), Strategies for language model web-data collection. *Proceedings ICASSP'06*, 1069–72.

Wang, L., & P. C. Woodland (2002), Discriminative adaptive training using the MPE criterion. *Proceedings ASRU*, 279–84.

Wang, Mengqiu, Kenji Sagae, & Teruko Mitamura (2006), A fast, accurate deterministic parser for Chinese. *Proceedings of the Joint Conference of the International Committee on Computational Linguistics and the Association for*

Computational Linguistics (COLING/ACL-06), 425–32.

Watanabe, Hideo (1992), A similarity-driven transfer system. *Proceedings of the 15th International Conference on Computational Linguistics, COLING-92,* 770–6.

Watson, R., J. Preiss, & E. Briscoe (2003), The contribution of domain-independent robust pronominal anaphora resolution to open-domain question-answering. *Proceedings of the International Symposium on Reference Resolution and its Application to Question-Answering and Summarisation,* 75–82.

Way, Andy (2003), Machine translation using LFG-DOP, in Rens Bod, Remko Scha, & K. Sima'an (eds.), *Data-Oriented Parsing.* Stanford, CA: CSLI Publications, 359–84.

Way, Andy (2009a), A critique of statistical machine translation. *Journal of Translation and Interpreting Studies: Special Issue on Evaluation of Translation Technology,* 17–41.

Way, Andy (2009b), Panning for EBMT gold, or 'remembering not to forget.' *Machine Translation* 23.

Way, Andy, & Nano Gough (2003), wEBMT: developing and validating an EBMT system using the World Wide Web. *Computational Linguistics* 29(3):421–57.

Way, Andy, & Nano Gough (2004), Example-based controlled translation. *Proceedings of the 9th EAMT Workshop, Broadening Horizons of Machine Translation and Its Applications,* 73–81.

Way, Andy, & Nano Gough (2005a), Comparing example-based and statistical machine translation. *Natural Language Engineering* 11(3):295–309.

Way, Andy, & Nano Gough (2005b), Controlled translation in an example-based environment. *Machine Translation* 19(1):1–36.

Weaver, Warren (1949), Translation, in William N. Locke & A. Donald Booth (eds.), *Machine Translation of Languages.* Oxford: John Wiley & Sons, 15–23.

Webb, Nick, & Bonnie Webber (2009), Interactive question-answering: introduction. *Special Issue of the Journal of Natural Language Engineering on Interactive Question-Answering* 15:1–8.

Webber, B. (1986), Questions, answers and responses, in Michael Brodie & John Mylopoulos (eds.), *On Knowledge Base Systems.* New York: Springer-Verlag, 365–401.

Webber, B., & A. Joshi (1998), Anchoring a lexicalized tree-adjoining grammar for discourse. *ACL/COLING Workshop on Discourse Relations and Discourse Markers,* 86–92.

Weijters, A. (1991), A simple look-up procedure superior to NETtalk? *Proceedings of the International Conference on Artificial Neural Networks – ICANN-91,* 1645–8.

Weiss, S. F., & C. Kulikowski (1991), *Computer Systems that Learn.* San Mateo, CA: Morgan Kaufmann.

Westat, Joyce Frechtling (2002), The 2002 user friendly handbook for project evaluation. Technical report NSF02057.

Wettschereck, D. (1994), A study of distance-based machine learning algorithms. PhD thesis, Oregon State University.

Wettschereck, D., & T. G. Dietterich (1994), Locally adaptive nearest neighbor algorithms, in J. D. Cowan et al. (ed.), *Advances in Neural Information Processing Systems* vol. 6. Palo Alto, CA: Morgan Kaufmann, 184–91.

Wettschereck, D., & T. G. Dietterich (1995), An experimental comparison of the nearest-neighbor and nearest-hyperrectangle algorithms. *Machine Learning* 19:1–25.

White, John (1985), Characteristics of the METAL machine translation system at production stage. *Proceedings of the Conference on Theoretical and Methodological Issues in Machine Translation of Natural Languages,* 359–69.

White, Michael, Rajakrishnan Rajkumar, & Scott Martin (2007), Towards broad coverage surface realization with CCG. *Proceedings of the 2007 Workshop on Using Corpora for NLG: Language Generation and Machine Translation*.

Whittaker, E., & B. Raj (2001), Quantization-based language model compression. Technical report TR-2001-41, Mitsubishi Electric Research Laboratories.

Wiebe, Janyce, Theresa Wilson, & Claire Cardie (2005), Annotating expressions of opinions and emotions in language. *Language Resources and Evaluations* 39(2–3):165–210.

Wilks, Yorick (1975), A preferential, pattern-seeking, semantics for natural language inference. *Artificial Intelligence* 8:75–97.

Williams, J. D., & S. J. Young (2007), Partially observable Markov decision processes for spoken dialog systems. *Computer Speech and Language* 21(2):231–422.

Williams, Sandra, & Ehud Reiter (2005), Deriving content selection rules from a corpus of non-naturally occurring documents for a novel NLG application. *Proceedings of Corpus Linguistics Workshop on Using Corpora for NLG*, 41–8.

Williams, Sandra, & Ehud Reiter (2008), Generating basic skills reports for low-skilled readers. *Natural Language Engineering* 14:495–535.

Williams, W. (1893), *Composition and Rhetoric*. Boston: Heath and Co.

Winograd, Terry (1973), A procedural model of language understanding, in Roger Schank & Ken Colby (eds.), *Computer Models of Thought and Language*. San Francisco: W. H. Freeman, 152–86. Reprinted in *Readings in Natural Language Processing*, ed. B. Grosz et al. (1986). Los Altos, CA: Morgan Kaufmann, 249–66.

Winograd, Terry (1983), *Language as a Cognitive Process*. Reading, MA: Addison Wesley.

Wirth, Niklaus (1971), Program development by stepwise re nement. *Communications of the ACM* 14(4):221–7.

Witte, Rene, Ralf Krestel, & Sabine Bergler (2005), Coreference-based summarization reloaded. *Proceedings of Document Understanding Workshop (DUC)*, 9–10.

Wittgenstein, Ludwig (1953), *Philosophical Investigations*. Oxford: Basil Blackwell, Citations from 2nd edn, 1988 reprint.

Wolff, J. G. (1975), An algorithm for the segmentation of an arti cial language analogue. *British Journal of Psychology* 66(1):79–90.

Wolff, J. G. (1977), The discovery of segments in natural language. *British Journal of Psychology* 68:97–106.

Wolpert, D. H. (2002), The supervised learning no-free-lunch theorems. *Proceedings of the 6th Online World Conference on Soft Computing in Industrial Applications*.

Wolters, M., & A. van den Bosch (1997), Automatic phonetic transcription of words based on sparse data. *Workshop Notes of the ECML/MLnet Familiarization Workshop on Empirical Learning of Natural Language Processing Tasks*, 61–70.

Wood, Mary McGee (1993), *Categorial Grammars*. London: Routledge.

Woodland, P. C. (2001), Speaker adaptation for continuous density HMMs: a review. *Proceedings ITRW Adaptation Methods for Speech Recognition*, 11–19.

Woodland, P. C., & D. Povey (2000), Large scale discriminative training for speech recognition. *Proceedings ASR2000 – Automatic Speech Recognition: Challenges for the New Millenium*, 7–16.

Woodland, P. C., C. J. Leggetter, J. J. Odell, V. Valtchev, & S. J. Young (1995), The development of the 1994 HTK large vocabulary speech recognition system. *ARPA: Spoken Language Systems Technology Workshop*, 73–6.

Woods, Williams (1978), Semantics and quanti cation in natural language question answering. *Advances in Computers*, 1–87.

Wothke, Klaus, & Rudolf Schmidt (1992), A morphological segmentation procedure for German. *Sprache und Datenverarbeitung* 16(1):15–28.

Wrigley, Stuart N., Guy J. Brown, Vincent Wan, & Steve Renals (2005), Speech and crosstalk detection in multichannel audio. *IEEE Transactions on Speech and Audio Processing* 13(1):84–91.

Wu, Dekai (1997), Stochastic inversion transduction grammars and bilingual parsing of parallel corpora. *Computational Linguistics* 23(3):377–403.

Wu, Dekai (2005), MT model space: statistical vs. compositional vs. example-based machine translation. *Machine Translation* 19(3–4):213–27.

Wu, Hua, Haifeng Wang, & Zhanyi Liu (2006), Boosting statistical word alignment using labeled and unlabeled data. *Proceedings of the 21st International Conference on Computational Linguistics and 44th Annual Meeting of the Association for Computational Linguistics*, 913–20.

Wu, Jun, & Sanjeev Khudanpur (2000), Efficient training methods for maximum entropy language modelling. *Proceedings of ICSLP2000*, 114–17.

Xia, Fei, & Martha Palmer (2001), Converting Dependency Structures to Phrase Structures. *1st International Conference on Human-Language Technology Research*, 61–5.

Xia, Fei, Martha Palmer, Chung-hye Han, & Aravind Joshi (2001), Automatically extracting and comparing lexicalized grammars for different languages. *Proceedings of the 17th International Joint Conference on Artificial Intelligence (IJCAI-2001)*, 1321–6.

Xu, Jinxi, & W. Bruce Croft (1998), Corpus-based stemming using co-occurrence of word variants. *ACM Transactions on Information Systems* 16:61–81.

Xu, Jinxi, Ana Licuanan, Jonathan May, Scott Miller, & Ralph Weischedel (2002), Trec2002 QA at BBN: answer selection and confidence estimation. *Proceedings, 11th Text Retrieval Conference (TREC 2002)*, 134–7.

Xu, Ming-Wei, Jia-Fei Hong, Shu-Kai Hsieh, & Chu-Ren Huang (2008), CWN-Viz: semantic relation visualization in Chinese WordNet. *Proceedings of the 4th Global WordNet Conference*, 506–19.

Xu, P., & Frederick Jelinek (2006), Random forests and the data sparseness problem in language modeling. *Computer Speech and Language* 21(1):105–52.

Xu, P., C. Chelba, & F. Jelinek (2002), A study on richer syntactic dependencies for structured language modeling. *Proceedings of ACL*, 191–8.

Xue, Nianwen, Fei Xia, Fu dong Chiou, & Martha Palmer (2005), The Penn Chinese TreeBank: phrase structure annotation of a large corpus. *Natural Language Engineering* 11(2):207–38.

Yamada, Hiroyasu, & Yuji Matsumoto (2003), Statistical dependency analysis with support vector machine. *Proceedings of the International Workshop on Parsing Technologies*, 195–206.

Yamada, Kenji, & Ion Muslea (2006), Re-ranking for large-scale statistical machine translation. *Proceedings of NIPS-06 Workshop on Machine Learning for Multilingual Information Access*.

Yamada, Kenji, & Kevin Knight (2001), A syntax-based statistical translation model. *Association for Computational Linguistics, 39th Annual Meeting and 10th Conference of the European Chapter, Proceedings*, 523–30.

Yamagishi, Junichi, Takashi Nose, Heiga Zen et al. (2009), Robust speaker-adaptive HMM-based text-to-speech synthesis. *IEEE Transactions on Audio, Speech and Language Processing*, 1208–30.

Yang, C. (2004), Universal grammar, statistics or both. *Trends in Cognitive Sciences* 8:451–6.

Yangarber, Roman (2003), Counter-training in discovery of semantic patterns.

Proceedings of the 41st Annual Meeting of the Association for Computational Linguistics (ACL'03), 343–50.

Yangarber, Roman, Ralph Grishman, Pasi Tapanainen, & Silja Huttunen (2000), Automatic acquisition of domain knowledge for information extraction. *Proceedings of the 18th International Conference on Computational Linguistics (COLING-2000)*, 940–6.

Yarowsky, D. (1992), Word-sense disambiguation using statistical models of Roget's categories trained on large corpora. *Proceedings of the 14th Conference on Computational Linguistics*, 454–60. http://dx.doi.org/10.3115/992133.992140

Yarowsky, D., & R. Wicentowski (2000), Minimally supervised morphological analysis by multimodal alignment. *Proceedings of the 38th Meeting of the Association for Computational Linguistics*, 207–16.

Yeh, A. (2000a), Comparing two trainable grammatical relations nders. *Proceedings of the 18th International Conference on Computational Linguistics*, 1146–50.

Yeh, A. (2000b), More accurate tests for the statistical signi cance of result differences. *Proceedings of the 18th Conference on Computational Linguistics*, 947–53, http://dx.doi.org/10.3115/992730.992783

Yeh, Y. J., H. Y. Li, W. J. Hwang, & C. Y. Fang (2007), FPGA implementation of kNN classi er based on wavelet transform and partial distance search. *Lecture Notes in Computer Science* 4522:512.

Yi, Szu-Ting, Edward Loper, & Martha Palmer (2007), Can semantic roles generalize across genres? *Proceedings of the Human-Language Technology Conferences/North American Chapter of the Association for Computational Linguistics Annual Meeting (HLT/NAACL-2007)*, 548–55.

Young, S. J. (2006), Using POMDPs for dialog management. *IEEE/ACL Workshop on Spoken Language Technology (SLT 2006)*.

Young, S. J., J. J. Odell, & P. C. Woodland (1994), Tree-based state tying for high accuracy acoustic modelling. *Proceedings of the Workshop on Human Language Technology 1994*, 307–12.

Younger, D. (1967), Recognition and parsing of context-free languages in time n^3. *Information and Control* 10(2): 189–208.

Yu, Jin, Ehud Reiter, Jim Hunter, & Chris Mellish (2007), Choosing the content of textual summaries of large time-series data sets. *Natural Language Engineering* 13:25–49.

Yu, Sheng (1997), Regular languages, in G. Rozenberg & A. Salomaa (eds.), *Handbook of Formal Languages*, vol. 1. Berlin: Springer, 41–110.

Yvon, F., & N. Stroppa (2007), Proportions in the lexicon (re) discovering paradigms. *Lingue e Linguaggio* (2):201–26.

Zadrozny, Wlodek (1994), From compositional to systematic semantics. *Linguistics and Philosophy* 17:329–42.

Zamansky, Anna, Nissim Francez, & Yoad Winter (2006), A 'natural logic' inference system using the Lambek calculus. *Journal of Logic Language and Information (JoLLI)* 15(3):273–95. http://dx.doi.org/10.1007/s10849-006-9018-x

Zavrel, J., & W. Daelemans (1997), Memory-based learning: using similarity for smoothing. *Proceedings of the 35th Annual Meeting of the Association for Computational Linguistics*, 436–43.

Zavrel, J., & W. Daelemans (1999), Recent advances in memory-based part-of-speech tagging. *VI Simposio Internacional de Comunicacion Social*, 590–7.

Zavrel, J., & W. Daelemans (2003), Feature-rich memory-based classi cation for shallow NLP and information extraction, in G. Nakhaeizadeh, J. Franke, & I. Renz (eds.), *Text Mining, Theoretical Aspects and Applications*. Heidelberg: Springer Physica-Verlag, 33–54.

Zavrel, J., W. Daelemans, & J. Veenstra (1997), Resolving PP attachment ambiguities with memory-based learning. *Proceedings of the Workshop on Computational Language Learning (CoNLL'97)*, 136–44.

Zavrel, J., P. Berck, & W. Lavrijssen (2000), Information extraction by text classi cation: corpus mining for features. *Proceedings of the Workshop Information Extraction Meets Corpus Linguistics.*

Zelenko, Dmitry, Chinatsu Aone, & Anthony Richardella (2003), Kernel methods for relation extraction. *Journal for Machine Learning Research* 3:1083–106.

Zen, Heiga, Keiichi Tokuda, & Tadashi Kitamura (2007), Reformulating the HMM as a trajectory model by imposing explicit relationships between static and dynamic feature vector sequences. *Computer Speech & Language* 21(1):153–73.

Zettlemoyer, Luke, & Michael Collins (2007), Online learning of relaxed CCG grammars for parsing to logical form. *Empirical Methods in Natural Language Processing (EMNLP)*, 678–87.

Zhang, Bo, Qingsheng Cai, Jianfeng Mao, & Baining Guo (2001), Planning and acting under uncertainty: a new model for spoken dialogue system. *Proceedings of the 17th Conference in Uncertainty in Artificial Intelligence*, 572–9.

Zhang, Byoung-Tak, & Yung-Taek Kim (1990), Morphological analysis and synthesis by automated discovery and acquisition of linguistic rules. *Proceedings of the 13th Conference on Computational Linguistics*, 431–6.

Zhang, Le, & Steve Renals (2006), Phone recognition analysis for trajectory HMM. *Proceedings of Interspeech '06.*

Zhang, Ruiqiang, Keiji Yasuda, & Eiichiro Sumita (2008), Improved statistical machine translation by multiple Chinese word segmentation. *Proceedings of the 3rd Workshop on Statistical Machine Translation*, 216–23.

Zhang, Ying, & Stephan Vogel (2005), An ef cient phrase-to-phrase alignment model for arbitrarily long phrase and large corpora. *Proceedings of the 10th Conference of the European Association for Machine Translation (EAMT-05)*, 294–301.

Zhang, Yue, & Stephen Clark (2008), A tale of two parsers: investigating and combining graph-based and transition-based dependency parsing using beam-search. *Proceedings of the 2008 Conference on Empirical Methods in Natural Language Processing (EMNLP-08)*, 562–71.

Zhao, Shubin, & Ralph Grishman (2005), Extracting relations with integrated information using kernel methods. *Proceedings of the 43rd Annual Meeting of the Association for Computational Linguistics (ACL'05)*, 419–26.

Zhechev, Ventsislav, & Andy Way (2008), Automatic generation of parallel treebanks. *Proceedings of the 22nd International Conference on Computational Linguistics (Coling 2008)*, 1105–12.

Zhou, GuoDong, Min Zhang, DongHong Ji, & QiaoMing Zhu (2007), Tree kernel-based relation extraction with context-sensitive structured parse tree information. *Proceedings of the 2007 Joint Conference on Empirical Methods in Natural Language Processing and Computational Natural Language Learning (EMNLP-CoNLL)*, 728–36.

Zhu, Jiang, & Haifeng Wang (2005), The effect of adding rules into the rule-based MT system. *MT Summit X, the 10th Machine Translation Summit*, 298–304.

Zhu, Jie, & Trevor Hastie (2005), Kernel logistic regression and the import vector machine. *Journal of Computational and Graphical Statistics* 14:185–205.

Zhu, Song Chun, Ying Nian We, & David Mumford (1997), Minimax entropy principle and its application to texture modeling. *Neural Computation* 9:1627–60.

Zukerman, Ingrid, & Diane Litman (2001), Natural language processing and user modeling: synergies and limitations. *User Modeling and User-Adapted Interaction* 11:129–58.

Author Index

The Handbook of Computational Linguistics and Natural Language Processing, First Edition.
Edited by Alexander Clark, Chris Fox and Shalom Lappin.
© 2013 Blackwell Publishing Ltd except for editorial material and organization
© 2013 Alexander Clark, Chris Fox, and Shalom Lappin. Published 2013 by Blackwell Publishing Ltd.

Subject Index

The Handbook of Computational Linguistics and Natural Language Processing, First Edition.
Edited by Alexander Clark, Chris Fox and Shalom Lappin.
© 2013 Blackwell Publishing Ltd except for editorial material and organization
© 2013 Alexander Clark, Chris Fox, and Shalom Lappin. Published 2013 by Blackwell Publishing Ltd.

Printed and bound by CPI Group (UK) Ltd, Croydon, CR0 4YY

10/04/2024

14481465-0005